BEHAVIORAL DEVELOPMENT

The Bielefeld Interdisciplinary Proj

BEHAVIORAL DEVELOPMENT

The Bielefeld Interdisciplinary Project

Edited by
KLAUS IMMELMANN, GEORGE W. BARLOW,
LEWIS PETRINOVICH,
and
MARY MAIN

CAMBRIDGE UNIVERSITY PRESS
Cambridge
London New York New Rochelle
Melbourne Sydney

Published by the Press Syndicate of the University of Cambridge
The Pitt Building, Trumpington Street, Cambridge CB2 1RP
32 East 57th Street, New York, NY 10022, USA
296 Beaconsfield Parade, Middle Park, Melbourne 3206, Australia

First published 1981

Printed in the United States of America

Library of Congress Cataloging in Publication Data
Main entry under title:
Behavioral development.
Includes bibliographical references and index.
1. Child psychology. 2. Developmental psychology.
3. Psychology, Comparative. I. Immelmann, Klaus.
II. Title: The Bielefeld interdisciplinary project.
BF721.B344 156'.5 80-29668
ISBN 0 521 24058 1 hard covers
ISBN 0 521 28410 4 paperback

CONTENTS

CONTRIBUTORS

Barlow, George W.
Department of Zoology, University of California, Berkeley, California, U.S.A.

Bateson, Patrick
Subdepartment of Animal Behaviour, Cambridge University, Cambridge, England

Bekoff, Anne
Department of Environmental, Population, and Organismic Biology, University of Colorado, Boulder, Colorado, U.S.A.

Bekoff, Marc
Department of Environmental, Population, and Organismic Biology, University of Colorado, Boulder, Colorado, U.S.A.

Bjerke, Tore
NLHT, Institute of Psychology, University of Trondheim, Trondheim, Norway

Byers, John A.
Department of Environmental, Population, and Organismic Biology, University of Colorado, Boulder, Colorado, U.S.A.

Cairns, Robert B.
Department of Psychology, University of North Carolina–Chapel Hill, Chapel Hill, North Carolina, U.S.A.

Collis, Glyn M.
Department of Psychology, University of Strathclyde, Glasgow, Scotland

Elsner, Norbert
Zoologisches Institut, Universität Göttingen, Göttingen, West Germany

Emde, Robert N.
University of Colorado, Medical Center, Denver, Colorado, U.S.A.

Fentress, John C.
Department of Psychology, Dalhousie University, Halifax, Nova Scotia, Canada

Gaensbauer, Theodore
University of Colorado, Medical Center, Denver, Colorado, U.S.A.

Golani, Ilan
Department of Zoology, University of Tel Aviv, Tel Aviv, Israel
Goude, Gunnar
Department of Psychology, University of Stockholm, Sweden
Grossmann, Karin
Fachbereich Psychologie und Pädagogik, Lehrstuhl für Psychologie IV, Universität Regensburg, Regensburg, West Germany
Grossmann, Klaus
Fachbereich Psychologie und Pädagogik, Lehrstuhl für Psychologie IV, Universität Regensburg, Regensburg, West Germany
Immelmann, Klaus
Fakultät für Biologie, Universität Bielefeld, Bielefeld, West Germany
Keeton, William T., deceased
Division of Neurobiology and Behavior, Cornell University, Ithaca, New York, U.S.A.
Kroodsma, Donald E.
Field Research Center for Ecology and Ethology, Rockefeller University, Millbrook, New York, U.S.A.
Leiderman, P. Herbert
Department of Psychiatry, Stanford University, Stanford, California, U.S.A.
Main, Mary
Department of Psychology, University of California, Berkeley, California, U.S.A.
Miller, David B.
Dorothea Dix Hospital, Raleigh, North Carolina, U.S.A.
Noakes, David L. G.
Department of Zoology, University of Guelph, Guelph, Ontario, Canada
Parke, Ross D.
Department of Psychology, University of Illinois–Urbana–Champaign, Champaign, Illinois, U.S.A.
Petrinovich, Lewis
Department of Psychology, University of California, Riverside, California, U.S.A.
Plomin, Robert
Institute for Behavioral Genetics, University of Colorado, Boulder, Colorado, U.S.A.
Sackett, Gene P.
Regional Primate Research Center, Seattle, Washington, U.S.A.
Sameroff, Arnold J.
College of Arts and Science, University of Rochester, Rochester, New York, U.S.A.
Studdert-Kennedy, Michael
Department of Communication, Arts, and Sciences, Queens College, City University of New York, Flushing, New York, U.S.A.

Suomi, Stephen J.
Department of Psychology, University of Wisconsin, Madison, Wisconsin, U.S.A.

Waters, Everett
Department of Psychology, State University of New York at Stonybrook, Stonybrook, New York, U.S.A.

Watson, John S.
Department of Psychology, University of California, Berkeley, California, U.S.A.

Wolff, Joachim R.
Institut für Histologie und Neuroanatomie, Universität Göttingen, Göttingen, West Germany

PREFACE

For two reasons, this book is unlike most collections of essays originating in conferences. First, all the chapters are new contributions. Second, they were formulated, written, and criticized while the authors were interacting with one another. Thus this is more than a compilation of independent papers. The volume has profited from the extensive exchanges that are only possible when the contributors live together. We owe the opportunity for this close involvement to the Bielefeld Center for Interdisciplinary Research, an institution so unique and central to the success of our project that its nature and role must be explained.

The Center for Interdisciplinary Research (ZiF) is a central research institute of the young University of Bielefeld in West Germany. It started its work in 1968, one year before the first departments of the University were opened. This temporal priority reflects the importance attached to interdisciplinary research by the University of Bielefeld from its founding. The Center initiates and conducts interdisciplinary research, supports the interdisciplinary projects initiated by outside scientists and institutions, and promotes joint interdisciplinary research projects involving scientists at the University of Bielefeld and at various institutions in Germany and abroad.

Two kinds of interdisciplinary meetings are sponsored by the Center: short-term conferences and workshops of two to eight days duration and long-term research programs that last up to ten months. The outside participants in the second category of meetings live in the Center in order to facilitate close cooperation with their Bielefeld colleagues for the solution of specific problems. The subjects and projects dealt with in both kinds of meetings encompass all areas of pure and applied arts and sciences.

The project on "Early Development in Animals and Man" was the first to involve biological and psychological scientists. Its origin was a joint seminar on behavior development in animals and man, organized by Klaus Grossmann, then at the Department of Psychology of the Bielefeld Teachers' College, and Klaus Immelmann, of the Department of Ethology, within the Faculty of Biology of the University of Bielefeld. During this seminar, which ran for two years, it became apparent that the areas of joint interest, both methodological and theoretical, were large and that a continuation and expansion of the interdisciplinary dialog would be profitable. The Board of Directors of the

Center expressed interest in arranging an interdisciplinary research group in the field of behavior sciences, and a formal proposal on behavior ontogeny by Klaus Grossmann and Klaus Immelmann was approved by the Advisory Board of the Center and the Academic Senate of the University of Bielefeld.

An international committee of psychologists and ethologists was invited by the ZiF to plan the project. It met in Bielefeld in July and December, 1976. The following scientists were members of the committee and attended one or both meetings:

G. W. Barlow (Berkeley, California)
H. von Bernuth (Bielefeld)
J. H. Crook (Bristol)
G. Gottlieb (Raleigh, North Carolina)
K. Grossmann (Bielefeld)
H. H. Hendrichs (Bielefeld)
K. Immelmann (Bielefeld)
G. Kestermann (Bielefeld)
A. Manning (Edinburgh)
H. Papousek (Munich)
A. Rasa (Marburg)
A. Sameroff (Rochester, New York)
S. Sjölander (Stockholm)

The planning committee discussed which fields of ethology, comparative psychology, human psychology, and related disciplines would offer promising possibilities for interdisciplinary dialog, and it prepared a list of representatives to be invited from the various fields. The committee discussed the organization of the meeting and compiled a provisional plan for the temporal course of discussions as well as a preliminary schedule of topics.

In the interest of having a wide interdisciplinary scope, people from many nations were invited: participants came from Australia, Britain, Canada, France, Israel, the Netherlands, Norway, Sweden, Switzerland, the United States, and the German Federal Republic. Continuity was assured through the creation of a core group, present throughout the project. Other participants joined only for the time span relevant to their specialty. A number of specialists from more distant fields – for example, game theory, genetics, neurophysiology, and ecology – were called in for short visits when the discussions made it clear that a specialist was needed to provide either further information or critical evaluation of speculations. Although the majority of the participants were representatives of either ethology or psychology, there were also representatives of such fields as linguistics, psychiatry, pediatrics, history, and mathematics.

A foundation was first laid through extensive and critical examination of basic concepts and theories. A special effort was made to come to grips with the nature–nurture controversy and to seek ways of resolving the conflict between essentially hereditarian and environmentalist approaches (e.g., by focusing interest on plasticity and constraints on learning instead of on the traditional division between innate and learned). Particularly fruitful topics were found in the recent work on phase specificity in development and in the problem of continuities versus discontinuities in the behavior of developing organisms.

The preliminary sessions led to a general examination of social organization, especially the organization of parent–young relationships. New developments in this field of animal behavior were compared to the results obtained from extensive research on human babies and mother–child relationships. To complete the picture, historical studies of the treatment of children, as well as anthropological data from different cultures, were included in the discussions. Aspects of clinical and therapeutic work were similarly addressed. A more direct approach to the principles of ontogenetic development was also traced through examination of the results from a variety of research programs dealing with such processes. Some useful principles were found when considering the ontogeny of such acoustical communication as bird song and language development in the human child, including the correlates found in brain physiology and anatomy.

During the project it became clear that the participating disciplines had evolved methods of study that could be applied profitably in other areas, and so it was decided that some time would be given to presentation and comparison of different methods of collecting and treating behavioral data. In this case, the profit was somewhat biased toward biology because of the greater amount of work done in many psychological areas and the resulting refinement of methods. Finally, perception and cognitive development were extensively treated in a number of presentations, including some of not-yet-published research on human ontogeny.

The project itself lasted from September 1, 1977, to May 31, 1978. It began immediately after the end of the XVth International Ethological Conference, which was held at the University of Bielefeld from August 23 to 31, 1977. The project consisted of three phases. The first was devoted to mutual exchange of information. In this two-month phase, all participants met almost daily for several hours, and representatives from the different disciplines gave state-of-the-art lectures on their specialties. Each presentation was followed by a plenary discussion of methods, results, and theoretical implications of the material that had been presented.

In the second phase, work in smaller discussion groups was interspersed with plenary sessions in which the groups concentrated on topics that had proven to be particularly profitable for interdisciplinary work. The results of such discussions were then reported in plenary meetings. Preliminary plans were also made for the publication of the results of the project.

In the final phase, it became necessary to add a number of plenary presentations and discussions, for people in the areas that had crystallized during the second phase often perceived the need for additional help from neighboring scientific disciplines. The last six weeks were spent in daily discussions, often full-day, in which now-completed manuscripts from the participants were criticized. For this purpose, a number of scientists from different disciplines were asked to come to Bielefeld to act as advisors and critics. The extensive treatment of each contribution assured that both psychological and ethological aspects were considered, with the specific objective of interdisciplinary exchange in mind.

From an organizational point of view, the large span of the project, both in time and in subject, made it necessary to give the participants continuous information, especially those who joined the project for shorter periods. Thus participants were asked not only to send relevant papers prior to their arrival but also to send a summary of the material to be presented and discussed. This material was then distributed to all participants. The session chair made a comprehensive summary of each discussion and presentation, and this summary was distributed among the participants and was also sent to those who had participated earlier or who were planning to participate. In this way, participants arriving later in the project were able to join the activities with a knowledge of preceding events and discussions. Because every presentation and discussion was tape recorded, further information was available for those who wanted to get an even more detailed picture when preparing their contributions.

The decision to publish a volume of "proceedings" drawing together the threads of the project was made by the plenary group, which also selected the four editors. Several meetings concerning the layout and contents of the book were held by the plenary group and by the editorial board before the end of the project. Subsequent meetings of the editorial board were held both in Bielefeld and Berkeley.

All prospective manuscripts were discussed intensively during the final six weeks of plenary sessions. In many if not most cases, these discussions resulted in rather substantial changes of the original papers and in a further broadening of their interdisciplinary scope. Written comments subsequently received by many authors from those project participants who could not attend the last series of seminars also led to further alterations and additions to the manuscripts. As a result, most of the contributions to this volume have been rewritten a number of times in order to reflect as closely as possible the scope of the project.

We would like to acknowledge the contributions of the following participants not listed as chapter authors: G. Ågren (Stockholm), R. Balda (Flagstaff, Arizona), J. Block (Berkeley, California), H. v. Bernuth (Bielefeld), G. M. Burghardt (Knoxville, Tennessee), S. Chevalier-Skolnikoff (San Francisco, California), J. H. Crook (Bristol), R. Dawkins (Oxford), V. Denenberg (Storrs, Connecticut), M. DeVries (Rochester, New York), A. Etienne (Genf, Switzerland), S. Glickman (Berkeley, California), S. Goldberg (Cambridge, Massachusetts), E. Goody (Cambridge), G. Gottlieb (Raleigh, North Carolina), M. M. Haith (Denver, Colorado), B. Hassenstein (Freiburg im Breisgau, West Germany), H. Hendricks (Bielefeld), A. Kalverboer (Groningen, Netherlands), G. Kestermann (Bielefeld), A. Lang (Bern), M. Lewis (Princeton, New Jersey), B. B. Lloyd (Brighton), J. Maynard-Smith (Falmer), W. Mason (Davis, California), G. McBride (St. Lucia, Australia), H. Papousek (Munich), E. Pröve (Bielefeld), A. Rasa (Marburg/Lahn, West Germany), J. S. Rosenblatt (Newark, New Jersey), S. Sjölander (Bielefeld), R. Sossinka (Bielefeld), E. Thoman (Storrs, Connecticut), D. Todt (Berlin), and J. M. Vidal (Rennes, France).

We would, on behalf of all participants in the project, also like to express our deep gratitude to the University of Bielefeld for its substantial financial support and for making the Center for Interdisciplinary Research, with all its facilities, available to the group for nine months. Warm thanks are extended to the staff of the Center who, during the course of the project and also in the preparatory phase, devoted a substantial part of their time and energy to our group and to all the major and minor problems and requests that arose almost every day. They contributed greatly to the success of the project.

Bielefeld, November 1980 K.I.
Berkeley, November 1980 G.W.B., L.P., and M.M.

GENERAL INTRODUCTION

KLAUS IMMELMANN, GEORGE W. BARLOW, LEWIS PETRINOVICH, and MARY MAIN

Nearly 30 years ago a debate started between the ethologists in Europe and the comparative psychologists in North America. Sometimes acrimonious but often stimulating, that argument drew considerable attention within science and in the public realm. The ethologists argued that attention should be devoted to the study of species-typical behavior in natural environments, whereas the comparative psychologists were more concerned with the detailed analysis of selected behaviors within the laboratory. As the two groups resolved their differences, one clear point of agreement emerged: Understanding development is pivotal to explaining behavior. One continues to hear that belief stated at conferences or noted in articles. In fact, there seems to be a growing endorsement for the study of behavioral development as the wave of the future, and this field of investigation may now be emerging.

The difficulty is that the field still lacks a coherent framework. There is no powerful supporting theory that generates productive hypotheses about the development of behavior. There is an active group of scientists conducting research on behavioral development. These scientists have, over the years, produced an ample literature and suggested various concepts and approaches, some founded in a theory of sorts, others springing from empirical analyses, and yet others arising from their several methodologies. They have not provided in one place anything resembling a comprehensive treatment of this diverse and hazily delimited field (but see Burghardt & Bekoff 1978). The Bielefeld Project reflects this perceived need (see Preface).

It soon became obvious in Bielefeld that a biology–psychology dichotomy was impractical. There are many kinds of developmental psychologists and more than a few types of biologists who do work relevant to the development of behavior. Those who study the development of human behavior are also found among the ranks of anthropologists, psychiatrists, physicians, linguists, and others. Investigators who journeyed to Bielefeld, then, constituted a spectrum of scientists ranging from embryologists through geneticists, field naturalists, experimentalists, child psychologists, and cross-cultural anthropologists, to name but a few specializations.

Despite this array, there persisted throughout the project a covert recognition of three weakly defined and somewhat overlapping categories of behavioral developmentalists. Participants naturally fell into these groups as issues arose and were debated, though some individuals happily straddled the three, and a few were not comfortable in any of them. We will call the areas *biology, comparative psychology,* and *developmental psychology.* The biologists were distinguishable by their abiding faith in the logic of natural selection. To most of them, behavior is but one aspect, albeit the most fascinating one, of an evolved system. (It proved difficult, but possible, to locate biologists who investigate behavioral development; that there are so few is an interesting and unexpected finding.)

The comparative psychologists concentrated on the processes controlling behavior, asking how behavior works. What further set them apart was that they often investigated those processes in tractable, convenient animals, employing tightly designed experiments. Although often interested in biological aspects of behavior, their main concern seemed to be the explication of mechanisms with sufficient generality to be relevant to human behavior. In this, their concern meshed well with that of the developmental psychologists.

A major problem with a project oriented in three directions is how to connect the pieces. An editor can only do so much – writers can be headstrong or even functionally deaf. Thus it is worth stressing that these chapters are more connected than they may appear to be. In the conventional symposium volume, the editor often cross-references the contributions by an appropriate insertion, such as "(see Chap. 18)." We do some of that. However, the reader may find much of the interdependence of the contributions hard to discern because of the way the chapters grew. To understand this, it is essential to read the Preface.

This project was conceived to bring together biology and human behavior. Though we discovered that it was necessary to make fine distinctions among participants, and though they clustered into roughly three categories, we now find it useful, in reflecting on the conceptual highlights, to return to that simple dichotomy between biology and psychology *sensu lato.* We are asking ourselves, really, about the flow of ideas between these two disciplines. It is our view that there has been more exchange than is generally appreciated. That is, not only was an interdisciplinary undertaking worthwhile, it has been foreshadowed.

THE SEARCH FOR UNIVERSALS

A central precept in comparative psychology is that there are common denominators underlying the behavior of all complex organisms. Important principles of behavior discovered in a rat ought to be found as well in fish and primates. This is virtually a truism, because importance is in proportion to generality. This is the well-known general-process view of behavior, which has been the driving force behind the extensive comparative studies of learning.

Unfortunately, truly general principles tend to be self-evident and thus not interesting. It takes no trained researcher to see that animals profit from their experiences by changing their behavior to maximize the good things in life and to minimize the bad ones. The difficulties start with the more explicit statements of general processes that are not so obvious and that promise progress in our understanding and control of behavior (see under "Environmentalism and learning," later in this introduction).

The general-process school made and argued for a number of assumptions about the process of learning: Effective reinforcement requires a short delay, or none, between stimulus and reward. For learning to occur, the organism must perform the response. The organism can learn equally well to associate any stimulus with any response so long as it can detect the stimulus and has the motor capacity to respond. All of these assumptions are now in question. Some might argue, less charitably, that the general-process position is in intellectual shambles. Certainly, the entire situation needs revision in light of the recent studies on taste aversion and constraints on learning (Garcia et al. 1973; Hinde & Stevenson-Hinde 1973).

Despite the erosion of the general-process assumptions, one could argue that its adherents stimulated research that has led to a sophisticated understanding of learning even if the processes are not general in the fullest sense. That may be true of the assumptions we mentioned, but it is not valid for another important assumption that was made: Although there are some changes in the general ability to learn with age, there are no specific differences that depend on age. That position discouraged the search for age-specific learning, for which there is now growing evidence from other sources (see Chaps. 10, 14, 19, 20). We are left, then, with a great deal of information about the processes involved in learning, but with a weak or nonexistent theory to organize it (see "Environmentalism and learning").

Perhaps the problem is inherent in the search for the quality of sameness in organisms whose diversity staggers the imagination. The biological ideas that permeated the Bielefeld Project suggested that instead we should seek an explanation for the diversity of behavior itself. The first step in such a search is to extract recurring themes that hint at an underlying pattern. The assumption is that organisms have evolved in response to selective pressures. Because no two species face the same situation, each has evolved a unique system for coping with its environment.

At this point, we need to digress to clear up two points that are potential sources of confusion. The first is the way we refer to biology. The second is the distinction between evolution and adaptation.,

It has become fashionable to use the term *biological* in psychology with one of two connotations. The first refers to an examination of the physiological substrates of behavior. The second refers to aspects of an animal's behavior that are species-typical, inherent, preprogrammed, maturational, unlearned, or simply unexplained in any other model. In short, in the first usage *biological* almost becomes a euphemism for *physiological* and in the second for *innate* or *instinctive*. We want to make it clear in this introductory chapter that our use of *biological* is different from either, and that it reflects the usage of the term during the project.

By *biological* we refer to behavior that has been shaped by natural selection and is therefore adaptive in the environment in which it evolved. This is not a genetically deterministic position because we allow for the interaction of genome, tissues, and environment in the development and functioning of the phenotype (see Clutton-Brock & Harvey 1979). This perception differs from the one common in the psychological literature in that it emphasizes the purposefulness of behavior in the context of an evolved adaptation. It is an overtly teleonomic position (Mayr 1974; Pittendrigh 1958).

Adaptation differs from evolution in that it includes a demonstrable situation for a given behavioral trait, or an ensemble of them, whereas evolution is a process. The belief in evolution is solidly grounded, but it relies on multiple, interlocking, consistent lines of evidence. For any form of behavior, say the nursing of pups by a mother rat, it is not possible to prove how the behavior evolved, though the evidence from broadly comparative studies suggests a probable line of descent. In contrast, the adaptiveness of suckling can be demonstrated by preventing pups from suckling and also by augmenting suckling. Just how behavior is adaptive often may not be obvious or easy to test. Some of the more fascinating studies in evolutionary biology today are directed toward tests of adaptiveness of complex social behavior. This is the kind of biological approach that stimulated lively discussions in Bielefeld. It is not an approach with which one becomes comfortable in a short time.

The biological approach becomes interesting when it becomes predictive; the mere statement that behavior is adaptive is no more interesting than the declaration that animals learn. Prediction becomes possible as more is learned about the nature of adaptation. Although each species is unique, adaptations often have much in common. Thus, schools of fish, flocks of birds, and herds of mammals represent similar solutions to living in the open, where it is difficult to hide from predators. Such aggregations may also operate as communication networks, transmitting information about unevenly distributed food or about migratory pathways. As a result, schools, flocks, and herds show remarkable similarities in internal organization and in the behavior of the individuals in them. Likewise, a careful examination of flocking behavior in closely related species of birds will usually reveal differences within a general pattern of similarity; these differences can be related to significant differences in ecology.

The essential point is that species and individuals can be enormously different systems, yet relatively deterministic in the context of a multidimensional environment that includes such things as physical surroundings, food, predators, mates, rivals, and offspring. In such a scheme, study of the development of behavior should be central to understanding how behavior is adaptive. That study, in turn, should enable us to reverse the logic, to suggest how behavior should develop in other species when enough is known about their ecology. Knowing the causal relations between ecology and behavior enables us to make increasingly better predictions of the behavior of species.

Thinking in this truly comparative sense expands one's horizons. For example, most of us accept internal fertilization and gestation as givens when reflecting on the development of human behavior; they seem both to drive and to constrain the system. In an evolutionary model, in contrast, this viviparity is regarded as an adaptation in itself that needs explaining. What is it, or was it, about the ecology and demography of mammals that led to retaining the embryo in a specialized chamber, the womb?

Among fishes, some species shed eggs into the water, whereas closely related forms retain the embryos; and among the shed eggs of different species, the embryos may hatch at radically different stages of development (Chap. 18). Among mammals, there are major differences in litter size and interbirth intervals. That some species produce large litters frequently whereas others, such as we, generally produce single, widely spaced young is an adaptive difference of major proportions that bears heavily on our understanding of differences in parent–offspring relationships. Several chapters in this book are concerned with profitable cross-species comparisons that include the human species. For example, Chapter 23 discusses sex differences in aggression in both human and nonhuman primates and the considerations of mechanisms are enriched by data from nonhuman primates. Chapter 28 takes up male involvement with infants across primate species, and there is some evidence for similarity in function. Chapter 24 considers coorientation to objects in the environment by animal conspecifics, although the author's own research is concerned with pointing in human mothers and babies.

There is thus a fundamental difference between the evolutionary biology and the general-process approaches. (In the foregoing we may have seemed to put them in opposition, but they are not.) The first approach looks for ultimate causes of behavior whereas the second seeks proximate causes (see Chap. 14). Briefly, *ultimate* refers to the survival value of the behavior in relation to the organism's environment. An ultimate explanation of why a bird sings deals with factors such as the likelihood of repelling a rival male, attracting a mate, or avoiding a predator. A proximate explanation centers on the mechanisms producing song, such as level of testosterone, neural organization, or the circumstances of song acquisition. Ultimate and proximate factors are sometimes referred to as the "why" and "how," respectively, of behavior and are thus complementary.

The adaptive, or teleonomic, perspective therefore gives meaning to the behavior; it suggests the end to which the behavior has evolved and thereby gives the researcher powerful clues about the design features of proximate mechanisms and when to expect them to be similar or different. It is not surprising, then, that rodents that often eat novel foods have the ability to associate taste with gastric upset that may follow hours later.

This seemingly obvious difference between proximate and ultimate causation occasionally proved troublesome in our seminars. Failure to make the distinction led to considerable confusion. This was nowhere more evident than during our sessions on the nature–nurture issue.

THE NATURE–NURTURE ISSUE

The nature–nurture issue is pervasive. One of the major stumbling blocks when discussing it, we found, was that biologists and psychologists habitually deal with behavior at different levels. An obvious example is speech, a species-specific trait. As such, an evolutionary biologist might see merit in treating the acquisition of speech as an adaptive, evolved trait and inquire into the ultimate factors that led to selection for speech. In contrast, a psychologist would concentrate on the proximate factors of speech acquisition with an eye toward the role of experience, practice, and the like.

In the speech example, the logical separation into proximate and ultimate factors is clear. However, when we investigated processes more closely, discussants tended to lose sight of the distinction or to confuse it. This is because at any level both ultimate and proximate explanations can be adduced. In learning a language, for instance, proposed mechanisms such as an inherent deep structure or the use of conditioning models can be dealt with in terms of adaptiveness or in terms of physiological mechanisms. Again, the alternatives are complementary rather than opposing ways of explaining behavior. To mix explanations, nonetheless, confuses the issue. Worse yet, it is easy to fall into the trap of equating ultimate with innate and proximate with environmentally controlled. Often that amounts to yielding to the temptation to resolve developmental problems conceptually into genetic and environmental components.

No matter how vigorously we agreed on the futility of a nature–nurture dichotomization, we still managed to speak past one another at times when discussing the essence of the developmental interaction of the genome and its environment. Perhaps the difficulty is fundamentally a matter of the way our minds function. We seem to think in discrete categories. Although interactive dynamics of genome and environment are now generally accepted, almost of necessity individuals divide the problem into genetic and environmental components. This is forgivable for experimental analysis, but it is disturbing as a mental habit.

We had a particularly stimulating period discussing the issue, reviewing and clarifying it. Afterward, we seldom found the need to lapse into a discussion of nature–nurture. Nonetheless, the discerning reader will recognize that many of the concepts delineated in this book relate to the perception that the causation of behavior rests in some set of environmental events, or conversely in some developmental program, presumably under genetic control.

We mention this point only to make clear how pervasive is the mental set of analytical thought: One part of the system is held constant while the other is varied. Investigators can become locked into one component or the other and consequently adhere to a one-sided conception of behavioral development. This does not seem to be a problem in the chapters that follow. But overstating the issue now creates a sensitivity to the more subtle manifestations of this conceptual dichotomy.

DESCRIPTIVE APPROACHES TO BEHAVIORAL DEVELOPMENT

As might be expected in an underdeveloped field, many of the concepts are merely descriptive (see Chap. 25). That description is involved is clear enough when the phenomena are overt. In the more interesting cases, however, there is an element, sometimes large, of inference about the phenomena described. Sometimes the inference is a hypothesis about emerging organization, so that it is not clear whether the organization exists outside the mind of the observer. Another inference relates to processes presumed to produce the observed development or to result from that development. For these reasons, the separation of concepts into those that merely describe and those that characterize processes is somewhat artificial.

Neural structure

It is accepted by all that behavior is a consequence of neural activity. The pattern of neural activity, in turn, depends on the architecture of the nervous system. The development of the nervous system is therefore fundamental to the development of behavior. Most would agree that the process to understand here is the way neurons connect with one another to form a functioning network. This has been demonstrated particularly clearly in studies of invertebrates (Chap. 17).

We only dimly understand the significance of *synaptogenesis* – how neural synapses are formed. It seems reasonable, however, to assume that the plasticity of behavior should somehow be proportionate to the degree of synaptogenesis. In fact, the greatest proliferation of connections seems to occur before the appropriate behavior is expressed (Chaps. 6, 7). In humans, neural proliferation and synaptogenesis in the brain continue long after birth (Chap. 7).

This structural approach is in the fine tradition of embryology. Morphological structures are followed from first appearance through morphogenesis to their definitive form. Periods of active development of structures, through their characteristic timing, give rise to a lengthy series of developmental stages. It is important to note, however, that stages are commonly named only for utilitarian purposes, so that we can consistently refer to a particular level of development for reasons of description or experimentation. In this usage, developmental time is more meaningful than real time; it is especially critical for work on cold-blooded organisms, whose rate of development is temperature-dependent. It is also important when making comparisons between species. A developmental stage need not refer to some period of major reorganization or to a time when several systems develop in synchrony, though often that is the case. The structural usage contrasts sharply to the usage of stages of development in the study of behavior. For example, in the work of Piaget, developmental stages refer to periods of major reorganization of behavior.

Except for instances of remarkable reorganization of morphology, as in tadpoles metamorphosing into frogs or caterpillars into butterflies, biologists tend to regard development as a process characterized by continuity of structures, with new ones emerging as the organism grows. For example, by marking cells in the undifferentiated blastula, it is possible to track the movements of cells and the distinctive cell lineages that arise from them. These lineages, in turn, give rise to particular tissues, and these to their particular organs. Working backward, embryologists are able to construct fate maps on the surface of the blastula that relate each region to its future involvement in the embryo (Chap. 8). These two features of embryogenesis, the tracking of development and the designating of stages, gave rise to two major descriptive approaches widely employed in the study of the development of behavior. The major departure is that the term *stage* carries a greater theoretical burden in the study of behavior.

Tracking ontogenetic progressions

Following and characterizing the development of behavior in young humans has a long and a rich history (Gesell 1954). Whether or not the course of development is predictable also has a history, one full of sharply differing interpretations.

Although the descriptive ontogenetic method originated in embryology, few ethologists have taken the trouble to describe the ontogeny of behavior among animals. Yet the approach has considerable promise in the area of developmental genetics of behavior (Chap. 8). It is also fundamental to understanding how behavior is organized, whether we deal with the behavioral systems of an individual or the interaction between individuals (Chaps. 8, 12, 13). Careful analysis of the progression of behavioral development is a necessary precursor to the question of stages in development.

Developmental stages

Whether or not there are stages in the development of behavior is a disputed issue in psychology (Ambrose 1976) closely connected to problems of conceptualization of structure. The concept of stage is a cornerstone of some descriptive systems, such as the treatment of child development by Gesell (1954) or Piaget's (1952) biologically influenced theory of cognitive development. Having said that, we might find it paradoxical that ethological analyses of behavioral ontogeny are relatively empirical and do not necessarily resolve into a progression of stages. However, as mentioned earlier, the biologist's relatively atheoretical approach to stages of development has historically been one of demarcating points in a developmental progression without great concern for whether clear steps emerge.

Continuity and discontinuity

Whether behavioral development exhibits continuity, discontinuity, or both has become a major argument in developmental psychology. A large portion of our first discussion period in Bielefeld was therefore devoted to this issue. Almost at once we found ourselves confused by an elusive conceptual framework, which derived from more than one meaning of *discontinuity*. After one session a participant commented that this term had been employed with at least four different meanings. Although at times it is useful not to have terms precisely defined, in this case lack of definition obviously confused the issue.

Chapter 1 is directed to the clarification of the discontinuity problem. Chapter 10 seeks to illustrate an example of discontinuity and its causation. We do not pretend to be so bold as to resolve the confusion in a few sentences. But it may help the reader if we state what we perceive as the distillate of our seminar discussions with regard to the meanings of *discontinuity*. (We presume that for the most part what we say about discontinuity refers in a complementary way to continuity.)

People use the notion of discontinuity basically in two ways. The first is descriptive: Development moves from periods of steady quantitative progression to periods of more perceptible qualitative change. Chapter 22 shows that human infants seem to experience periods of emotional reorganization at about 2 months and again at 7 to 9 months of age. With the advantage of experimentation, Chapter 10 goes further, illustrating how experience and age interact to produce the distinct shift in behavior that accompanies weaning in kittens.

Chapter 1 employs a linear model of development to make the authors' meaning clear. A discontinuity occurs when there is a sharp inflection in the curve. The critical issue thus is both a philosophical and an empirical one: How much change must occur? Philosophically, it is the old problem that all qualitative changes can be quantified. Empirically, it is a matter of deciding where a statistically significant change has taken place, an important question that is considered in detail in Chapter 4. Such a simple model, however, seldom satisfies the needs of an investigator who is tracking a complex constellation of behavioral traits, whether motor, perceptual, emotional, cognitive, or social, though the model may help to keep thinking straight. (Note here the convergence with behavioral development, which is seen as consisting of stages.)

The second and more provocative usage of *discontinuity* is the one that stresses independence from one point in development to another. At its simplest, and necessarily so, it is descriptive. Measures of behavior taken at one point do not correlate with the same measures, or measures presumably of the same behavior, later in development. Examples are lack of continuity between walking movements of neonates and walking in 1-year-olds, or precocial and adult sexuality. More controversial are studies of emotional or cognitive development, which some investigators claim are discontinuous whereas others argue for continuity.

At the process level there seemed to be little agreement. In apparent accord with Clarke and Clarke (1976), some participants appeared to resurrect an extreme environmentalist position: All that matters, at least for human infants, is the present situation. Even early experience is regarded as having little or no influence.

A contrary position is that the perceived reorganizations and discontinuities are biological in a maturational sense (Kagan 1979). Note that here, too, early experience is given no special weight in the organization or reorganization of behavior. Rather, the progressive changes observed in behavioral development are held to result from a reading out of a genetically preprogrammed sequence. It is important to distinguish both of these views from a third – phase-specific learning, the notion of phases in the life of an organism in which particular things are learned with special ease (see *"Phase specificity"*).

Neoteny

Evolutionary biologists have long been fascinated by neoteny, the slowing of development such that sexual maturity is achieved before the organism has completed development. It is an evolutionary concept that follows from the comparison of related species, and it and related concepts have been resurrected in an exciting book by Gould (1977). The key issue is the changing of rates of development of different systems within the same organism. The consequences of changing rates of development are considered in Chapters 1, 8, and 18.

Neoteny is but one type of change that occurs through the alteration of developmental rates. Students of behavior have been particularly attracted to this type of alteration because it has been suggested so often that humans are neotenic. The idea has been used to account for our advanced cognition with explicit reference to our lengthy, slow, presexual development, which is characterized by a prolonged period of cognitive plasticity (e.g., Mason 1979).

Biologists have recently returned to considerations of the role of development in the evolution of structural differences. Alberch et al. (1979) have presented a formal model representing ontogenetic changes in crucial characteristics of development. These parameters are time of onset of the process, how long it continues (time when it stops), and how quickly or slowly it develops. By increasing or decreasing each parameter, and by employing all parameters in combination, any type of change can be characterized quantitatively. The formal models also produce a simplified vocabulary. This is an obviously rich source of models to bring to comparative studies of the development of behavior.

PROCESSES IN BEHAVIORAL DEVELOPMENT

Here, as in the preceding section, it is not always possible to separate sharply concepts about developmental processes from those that are prescriptions for description. In any event, this section treats a number of concepts that seem pertinent to processes and that were recurring themes in the Bielefeld Project.

Epigenesis

The term *epigenesis* is usually associated with the name of Waddington, the British geneticist and embryologist. However, the essential idea goes back to embryology in the mid-nineteenth century even though the nature of the gene was still not known. The concept is simplicity itself: Development is a dynamic interaction between the genome and its environment. To expand on this would be to belabor the earlier parts of this chapter.

Genetics of behavioral development

A remarkable feature of the Bielefeld Project was the discovery of how little we actually know about the role of genes in the development of behavior. The field of behavior genetics is flourishing, but so far it has made only a small impression on development (see Chaps. 8, 9). That seems odd, because those studying behavioral development stress the epigenetic perspective. Yet they analyze almost exclusively the effect of the environment, with little regard for the genetic substrate of that development.

Canalization

Waddington (e.g., 1966) advocated a model of development called *canalization.* The course of development was likened to a ball rolling down the side of a mountain, the epigenetic landscape. The ball has choice points as it descends, the options being to go right or left down one depression or another in the landscape of the ever-deeper valley. If the ball rolls up the side of a hill, it encounters ever-stronger forces directing it back into the valley. Its course is thus canalized.

The interesting thing about Waddington's model is that canalization is produced by both the genome and the environment through an inseparable combined action that produces the landscape. Thus a given trait may develop so that it appears phenotypically the same in two individuals even if they have different alleles for that trait. Likewise, two individuals with the same alleles but experiencing different environmental conditions may be phenotypically the same. For behavior, Bateson (1976) has referred to this as *equifinality.*

There are three important things to note about Waddington's model. First, traits are referred to as being variously canalized. A weakly canalized trait is one in which the landscape has lower relief so that the ball may more easily surmount a ridge and thereby move along a different path. Second, canalization is sometimes cited as an alternative to genetic determinism, but actually it can be even more deterministic. Third, there is little evidence to support canalization, at least not in proportion to its acceptance.

Another point is this: Waddington (1961) was concerned with an evolutionary process he called *genetic assimilation.* Suppose that through experience an animal modifies its behavior in a way that improves its chances of surviving and reproducing. For example, it learns that the most nutritious prey are found under flat rocks. Obviously, selection will favor those individuals that so modify their behavior. Waddington assumed, with reason, that the modifiability and the ability to perform the behavior are heritable; some individuals are more predisposed to turn over flat rocks and/or to make the association with choice food. Such individuals will be energetically better prepared to reproduce, all else being equal. Gradually, through natural selection, control of this plasticity may shift to the genome. The concept of genetic assimilation is relevant to many misunderstandings about the control of behavioral development, especially when comparative studies are involved. Similar behaviors in different species, such as bird song, may require a particular type of stimulation to develop normally in one species but not in another.

Induction, facilitation, and maintenance

Induction, facilitation, and maintenance are particularly clear examples of concepts from embryology applied to the development of behavior. Gottlieb (1976) took the three terms from embryology and presented parallel definitions in the context of behavioral development, along with some examples. His review of his article during the Bielefeld Project led to a spirited discussion of the adequacy of the formulation. The concepts are deceptively direct and obvious at first glance, but their application can present difficulties.

Induction means that some event is a necessary signal or stimulant to the development of a trait; without it, development miscarries. *Facilitation* means that development can proceed in its absence. *Maintenance* is what keeps the trait viable once it has developed; without it, the trait may atrophy. The utility of this formulation is that it suggests a way to partition the various causal factors in development. Even though it proved difficult to differentiate rigorously among the three concepts, keeping them in mind seemed to reduce confusion when talking about the processes of development. That is, induction, facilitation, and maintenance are intuitively apparent in application even though not easily defined.

Environmentalism and learning

One of the dominant themes in American psychology has been an emphasis on environmentalism, particulary as it relates to development. This emphasis has led to a concentration on the effects of environmental influences almost to the exclusion of other factors as critical determinants of behavior. This view has been used widely to understand the nature of the behavior of humans and other animals and stems from the philosophical tradition of the British associationists (e.g., John Locke and James Mill). In its barest form, this tradition is based on the assumption that knowledge is the result of environmental experience; the hand of experience writes on the "clean slate" of the mind. To understand the behavior of organisms, then, it is necessary to know the experiences to which they have been exposed and the principles by which these experiences become organized. In this primitive view, all members of a given species are considered essentially the same, short of any inherited organic defect, and unique characteristics are due to unique experience.

J. B. Watson (e.g., 1913) expounded this view with great force and conviction. It was readily accepted by the egalitarian and pragmatic American academia, especially those concerned with the study of the development of behavior. The almost apocryphal story of conditioning the child Albert to fear all furry objects was one of the cornerstones of developmental behavior theory. (See Harris 1979 for an analysis and discussion of the history and transmittal of this finding.) American developmental psychology became identified with environmentalism and was stongly opposed to anything suggesting an innate component. (See Clarke & Clarke 1976 for a recent restatement of this general position.)

Thorndike (1898) developed the scientific rationale and provided the means to obtain objective data of the kind many psychologists accepted as scientific. His method was to use the problem box in which an animal, reared and maintained under standard conditions, could be exposed to controlled procedures and its responses used to obtain a standard reward noted.

Thorndike argued that there was a universal principle that provided the basis of all animal learning, and that principle was association. One should attempt to understand the laws by which simple associations are formed and can then be combined into more complex assemblages. The differences between species would be due to the number and complexity of basic associations that each species was capable of forming. (See Petrinovich 1973 for a more detailed examination of this tradition as compared to the Darwinian biological tradition.)

The elaboration of these views led to the learning theories of the 1940s, which provided the basis of much American developmental theory through the 1960s. The most influential of these learning theories was proposed by C. L. Hull (1943), who added a biological caveat that a response would be reinforced if it led to the reduction of a primary bodily need, or if it was associated with a stimulus that had frequently been linked to such a reduction. This nod in the direction of biology was almost entirely concerned with events at the proximate level.

Another influential learning psychologist of this period was B. F. Skinner (e.g., 1938), one of the most articulate latter-day behaviorists, who has argued that one should concentrate on the empirical relationships between responses and consequences. He extended his analysis of behavior contingencies to account for such things as the art and practice of teaching, psychotherapy, and the acquisition of language by children (Skinner 1953).

Beginning in the 1960s, the grand and global learning theories began to disintegrate. This disintegration seems to have been a symptom of what Lakatos (1970) has called a *degenerating research program.* As anomalies begin to appear, theory has to be changed continually to accommodate them without gaining any new empirical content. Rather than expanding to encompass new facts and to predict novel, hitherto unexpected ones, the theory requires ad hoc shifts as new data accrue.

With the disintegration of the general theories, a series of miniature models was developed, each to apply to a restricted problem area of research. These models were put forth with the implicit or explicit expectation that when each was fully developed within its own sphere, it might be extended to join with other models and thereby arrive at a general theory of behavior. What seems to have occurred is that the miniature models have remained miniature, although offering an admirable degree of precision for those working within the domain of concern.

Conceptions of learning have dominated psychologists' notions of developmental processes, just as they have dominated those of most areas of psychology. As mentioned above, Watson based many of his conceptions on loosely conducted developmental studies; later ideas, such as social learning theory, have been applied widely to understand the development of the child (e.g., Chap. 3).

Plasticity

The parallels between behavioral development and morphogenesis that have become apparent in the foregoing subsection by the application of concepts and terms from embryology are particularly distinct in two areas: early plasticity and phase specificity.

In most animals, early stages in development are characterized by a higher degree of plasticity than later stages. Developing cells and tissues have the capacity to differentiate in various directions and to participate in the formation of different tissues and organs. During the course of development, however, the developmental potentialities of target cells and tissues are increasingly restricted through the instructive role of different combinations of factors, the so-called organizers, which determine their developmental direction. This process is known as *induction* (which is the original embryological meaning of the term). Induction has been found to be a general and widespread phenomenon in morphogenesis. Once the process of differentiation has been completed, major alterations in the attributes of morphological structures are no longer possible.

This general principle can also be applied, within limits, to behavioral development. Again, there tends to be a larger amount of plasticity in younger than in older organisms. The two clearest examples are provided by play and vocalizations. In play behavior, which is generally restricted to young animals, many characters tend to show a higher degree of freedom and a greater amount of intraindividual variability than is found in the more stereotyped adult nonplay behavior. This refers not only to the structure and combination of behavior patterns but also to the occurrence of role reversals, breakdowns in dominance, or the combination of activities from a variety of contexts (Chap. 11).

The same trend is found in the development of vocalizations. The males of many species of passerine birds, for example, go through a period of low-intensity singing before developing their true functional song. Such subsong is characterized by a greater number and a more variable sequence of song elements and also usually by a greater range in frequency. During the change to functional song, some elements disappear and the sequence of the remaining ones becomes more stereotyped.

Such early plasticity in avian vocalizations shows remarkable parallels with the development of human speech, which changes from the babble of babies, with its greater variety in structure and sequence of sound elements, to the more formalized language of the adult. This change demonstrates how widespread is the phenomenon of early plasticity among organisms (Chaps. 20, 21; see also Chap. 2).

Phase specificity

Through transplantation experiments in embryological research, it soon became apparent that the instructive role of the organizers is not the same throughout early development. There are, rather, specific times when such influence is greatest and periods after which the process of induction is no longer possible. Such intervals in development have been called *critical periods* because of the detrimental effects on morphogenesis of experimentally withholding the inducing organizers until after the period has passed.

Readers familiar with the ethological literature will recall that *critical period* is the term that has been used, and sometimes still is, to characterize the privileged periods of early learning. The term was deliberately borrowed from embryology by Konrad Lorenz to point to the remarkable parallels between the phase-specific aspects of morphogenesis and the phenomenon of phase specificity of certain early learning processes that he called *imprinting*. (For various reasons, most authors now speak of *sensitive phases* for imprinting; see Chap. 14.)

Countless experimental investigations of imprinting that followed Lorenz's early observations have shown that phase specificity in early learning is a widespread phenomenon. It is not restricted to the following reaction of nidifugous (precocial) birds, for which it had first been described. Rather, it is found in a variety of animal species and in remarkably different (social and nonsocial) behavioral systems. The beginning and length of sensitive phases, as well as the impact they have on subsequent development (see Chap. 14), vary between species and behavioral systems. But the principle of privileged periods in certain areas of behavior development seems always the same.

The widespread occurrence of phase specificity leads to two points of general discussion that were also addressed during the Bielefeld Project. It contradicts the general-process view (see above), and it raises the question of possible parallels in early human development.

The general-process view is contradicted in two ways. First, the occurrence of sensitive phases demonstrates that the organism cannot learn equally well during its whole life span. On the contrary, there are phases during which learning capacities are increased remarkably, and such phases come to their close long before the general decrease of learning capacities during old age. Moreover, as mentioned, comparative studies have shown that sensitive phases may have different onsets and durations in different, sometimes even closely related, species. This means that there are species-specific – at least temporal – constraints on learning that again demonstrate the diversity of behavior between organisms.

The second point refers to the impact of imprinting research on developmental psychology. In ethology, it is commonly accepted that if a certain behavior characteristic is widespread, say among primates, mammals, or even vertebrates in general, there is at least a suspicion that it may also occur, as a phylogenetic vestige, in humans. Phase specificity is a clear example of one such widespread phenomenon in vertebrates. A certain degree of phase specificity has been found in humans, as in language development or in the early capacity for socialization. Here, the interdisciplinary dialogue between ethologists and developmental psychologists, resulting in increased interest in studies of early human development, may even have an impact within the applied sphere. We refer here to the interesting possibility that mother–baby contact shortly after delivery may have important consequences for the establishment of social relationships (see Chap. 16).

Attachment

Relatively early work on attachment (Bowlby 1969) suggested a possible analogy between the sensitive phase described by ethologists working with imprinting phenomena and the development of human infant–caregiver *attachments* (defined functionally as relationships designed to provide an infant with protection and security, and descriptively as relationships involving strong and specific proximity seeking on the part of the infant). The proposed analogy to imprinting was based on studies of human infants who had had insufficient opportunity for interaction with caregivers to allow the development of an attachment to any specific person. Clinical evidence suggested that when a child had no person to serve as an attachment figure during the first 3 years of life, he or she experienced grave difficulties in forming attachments to other persons thereafter.

Careful and controlled studies of children who have been deprived of such opportunities have yet to be carried out. The existence of a human sensitive phase for the formation of attachments, therefore, has yet to be disproven. The studies are almost impossible to conduct, because children found living under such conditions must humanely be immediately removed from them, and the actual experience of children believed to have already lived under such conditions is seldom known to researchers.

Work on human infant attachment has now moved into a new phase in which different kinds of infant–parent attachment relationships are being examined (see Chaps. 25, 26, 27). Careful studies of individual infant–caregiver relationships, that is, case studies, are necessary for this new phase of the study of attachment relationships. The question now addressed is not the effects of the absence of attachment formation during the early phase of life but rather the effects of having experienced different types of relationships with parents. Thus researchers are asking whether an adult personality will be affected by early experiences of rejection of proximity seeking by attachment figures.

Here again, the realities of research on humans, the impossibility of designing controlled life experiences, and the need for longitudinal case studies obtrude. To tie this work to questions of phase specificity, we would need controls that are both humanely and theoretically impossible to provide; we would, for example, have to look for the differential effects of rejecting proximity seeking at ages 3 and 30. Rather than being able to provide this tie to studies of phase specificity in nonhuman animals, developmental psychologists find themselves involved in debates (discussed above) about continuity and discontinuity in personality. The heart of these new debates is the impact of early parental influence (Kagan 1979) and the stability and coherence of human personality (Sroufe 1979).

RETROSPECTIVE

A retrospective on the Bielefeld Project is probably premature. But then it is always difficult to assess the effects of such an endeavor. It may have altered the paths of some participants while being little more than a detour on the highway for others. Time will tell.

We think, nonetheless, that we perceived some changes in the participants. The psychologists became involved with evolutionary theory, particularly as it relates to life-history strategies. The population biology concepts of r- and K-selection fascinated several of them and stimulated their thoughts (see Mason 1979 for an example of one such application), even though more sophisticated formulations are now replacing that concept in biology (Horn 1978). Another concept that promises some interesting twists in developmental psychology is that of the *evolutionarily stable strategy (ESS),* as articulated by Maynard Smith (1979); (see Chap. 5). The ESS spawned a subgroup at Bielefeld that continued to interact a year after the project ended. In short, we sensed a growing confidence and interest in evolutionary theory among the psychologists.

For their part, the biologists were struck by the power of studying individual differences, an approach more often seen in psychology. That is almost paradoxical because the theory of natural selection depends absolutely on individual differences. Biologists have also thought little about the way one analyzes development. However, those in Bielefeld became sensitive to methodological issues in developmental work (e.g., Wohlwill 1973), such as the merits of comparing cohorts of one age to those of another, as opposed to longitudinal studies of individual development.

We are convinced that we identified problems, contributed to the clarification of concepts and terms, and stimulated one another in new directions. The chapters that follow cannot pretend to convey the totality of the Bielefeld experience, but nonetheless they provide a rich sample.

REFERENCES

Alberch, P., S. J. Gould, G. F. Oster, & D. B. Wake. 1979. Size and shape in ontogeny and phylogeny. *Paleobiology* 5:296–317.

Ambrose, A. 1976. Methodological and conceptual problems in the comparison of developmental findings across species. *In:* M. von Cranach (ed.), *Methods of inference from animal to human behavior.* Aldine, Chicago, pp. 296–317.

Bateson, P. P. G. 1976. Rules and reciprocity in behavioural development. *In:* P. P. G. Bateson & R. A. Hinde (eds.), *Growing points in ethology.* Cambridge University Press, Cambridge, pp. 401–421.

Bowlby, J. 1969. *Attachment and loss,* vol. 1; *Attachment.* Basic Books, New York.

Burghardt, G. M., & M. Bekoff (eds.). 1978. *The development of behavior: comparative and evolutionary aspects.* Garland Press, New York.

Clarke, A. M., & A. D. B. Clarke. 1976. *Early experience: myth and evidence.* Free Press, New York.

Clutton-Brock, T. H., & P. H. Harvey. 1979. Comparison and adaptation. *Proceedings of the Royal Society, Series B* 205:547–565.

Garcia, J., J. C. Clarke, & W. G. Hankins. 1973. Natural responses to scheduled rewards. *In:* P. P. G. Bateson & P. H. Klopfer (eds.), *Perspectives in ethology.* Plenum Press, New York, pp. 1–41.

Gesell, A. L. 1954. The ontogenesis of infant behavior. *In:* L. Carmichael (ed.), *Manual of child psychology,* 2nd ed. Wiley, New York, pp. 335–373.

Gottlieb, G. 1976. Conceptions of prenatal development: behavioral embryology. *Psychological Review* 83:215–234.

Gould, S. J. 1977. *Ontogeny and phylogeny.* Harvard University Press, Cambridge, Massachusetts.

Harris, B. 1979. Whatever happened to Little Albert? *American Psychologist* 34:151–160.

Hinde, R. A., & J. Stevenson-Hinde (eds.). 1973. *Constraints on learning.* Academic Press, New York.

Horn, H. S. 1978. Optimal tactics of reproduction and life-history. *In:* J. R. Krebs & N. B. Davies (eds.), *Behavioural ecology: an evolutionary approach.* Sinauer, Sunderland, Massachusetts, pp. 411–429.

Hull, C. L. 1943. *Principles of behavior.* Appleton, New York.

Kagan, J. 1979. Family experience and the child's development. *American Psychologist* 34:886–891.

Lakatos, I. 1970. Falsification and the methodology of scientific research programmes. *In:* I. Lakatos & A. Musgrave (eds.), *Criticism and the growth of knowledge.* Cambridge University Press, Cambridge, pp. 91–196.

Mason, W. 1979. Ontogeny of social behavior. *In:* P. Marler & J. G. Vandenbergh (eds.), *Social behavior and communication: handbook of behavioral neurobiology,* vol. 3. Plenum, New York, pp. 1–28.

Maynard Smith, J. 1979. Game theory and the evolution of behaviour. *Proceedings of the Royal Society, Series B* 205(1161):475–488.

Mayr, E. 1974. Teleological and teleonomic: a new analysis. *Boston Studies in the Philosophy of Science* 14:91–117.

Petrinovich, L. 1973. Darwin and the representative expression of reality. *In:* P. Ekman (ed.), *Darwin and facial expression.* Academic Press, New York, pp. 223–256.

Piaget, J. 1952. *The origins of intelligence in children.* International Universities Press, New York.

Pittendrigh, C. 1958. Adaptation, natural selection, and behavior. *In:* A. Roe & G. G. Simpson (eds.), *Behavior and evolution.* Yale University Press, New Haven, pp. 390–416.

Skinner, B. F. 1938. *The behavior of organisms.* Appleton, New York.

1953. *Science and human behavior.* Crowell Collier–Macmillan, New York.

Sroufe, L. A. 1979. The coherence of the individual. *American Psychologist* 34:834–841.

Sroufe, L. A., & E. Waters. 1977. Attachment as an organizational construct. *Child Development* 48:1184–1199.

Thorndike, E. L. 1898. Animal intelligence: an experimental study of the associative processes in animals. *Psychological Review Monograph Supplement* (whole no. 8).

Waddington, C. H. 1961. Genetic assimilation. *Advances in Genetics* 12:257–293.

1966. *Principles of development and differentiation.* Macmillan, New York.

Watson, J. B. 1913. Psychology as the behaviorist views it. *Psychological Review* 20:158–177.

Wohlwill, J. F. 1973. *The study of behavioral development.* Academic Press, New York.

PART 1

THEORETICAL AND METHODOLOGICAL ISSUES

INTRODUCTION

LEWIS PETRINOVICH

This part of the book traces some broad conceptual issues that underlie many of the more specific portions of later chapters. All the authors represented here agree that investigations of the processes of development must be conducted in a manner that does not distort normal developmental influences. Some basic definitional questions are posed, and some suggestions for the conduct of longitudinal studies are offered. All these chapters attempt to deal both with analytic studies of behavioral processes and with evolutionary adaptations in behavior.

Chaper 1 deals with a conceptual issue that has troubled those studying developmental phenomena. The authors pose the question as follows: How can continuity and persistence be achieved in an organism's system that necessarily undergoes maturational, interactional, and cultural–social change? An attempt is made to outline a research model adapting Gottlieb's tripartite distinction of induction, facilitation, and maintenance to the understanding of developmental processes. The model is used to untangle the process variables involved in the development of behavioral systems during individual ontogeny. This untangling is considered to be a necessary correlate to the usual study of behavioral outcomes. The authors conclude that continuity is often found when the environment does not change in any important features and that discontinuity is likely to occur when important environmental factors are added to or subtracted from the developmental setting.

Chapter 2 is concerned with the concept of normality as it relates to the study of behavior in general and its ontogeny in particular. It stresses the importance of assuring that one's observations are representative of an organism's adjustments, that is, of the response modes studied, the characteristics of the stimuli employed, and the range of situations examined. This theme reflects the arguments in Chapter 4 that the study of behavior within a representative sampling of situations is of paramount importance in understanding organism-environment interactions.

Chapter 2 emphasizes the importance of the concept of plasticity in the organization of developmental processes, in much the same way that Chapters 20 and 21 do when they discuss concrete instances of the development of bird song and language, respectively. Chapter 2 argues for the importance of studying atypical plasticity in development in order to characterize the range of variability that organisms can exhibit. The study of such atypical influences may be useful in gaining an understanding of the limits of malleability, and might perhaps contribute to an appreciation of the behavioral preadaptations of importance in the adaptive modifications of a species.

We generally think of objects as being known for or categorized according to their physical characteristics. Chapter 3, however, argues that objects can be categorized according to their temporal relationship to our own behavior, especially when that relationship provides us with a *contingency experience* (footsteps following our own is given as the first example). The chapter argues that contingency experience with an object can directly affect behavior or development. It begins with examples from human infancy, presenting evidence that infants categorize objects as social if they are responsive to (contingent upon) the behavior of the infant. It next discusses the way that social reactions in rats, territorial defense reactions in the white-crowned sparrow, and the reproductive development of female ring doves are influenced by contingency experiences.

Chapter 4 addresses some of the methodological issues involved in the study of developmental processes. It develops a general methodological view of the proper conduct of scientific research, contrasts it to some prevailing views, and outlines the statistical procedures that can be used to implement the approach used. It then presents a case history based on the author's research on habituation in birds to illustrate how the general design principles can be incorporated in studies and to demonstrate their heuristic value. Finally, the research scheme is generalized for use in the individual case. This is important because there is widespread agreement that an adequate understanding of developmental processes must be based on the longitudinal study of individuals.

Chapter 4 argues that careful attention should be given to the study of the natural behavior of organisms within a representative sampling of environmental contexts. It describes a conceptual model originated by Egon Brunswik and develops Brunswik's conception of the lens model as an aid to the construction of an adequate theory of behavior.

Chapter 5 applies Brunswik's lens model to evolutionarily significant events. It describes the lens model and develops a probabilistic version (in contrast to the usual correlational one adopted in Chapter 4). This conceptual schema is elaborated within the context of Maynard Smith's idea of an evolutionarily stable strategy. The lens model is then used to conceptualize social contest situations in terms of different perceptual and cognitive substrategies. This chapter, then, relates evolutionary and ecological considerations to the psychological considerations of the lens model.

1

CONTINUITY IN BEHAVIORAL DEVELOPMENT: THEORETICAL AND EMPIRICAL ISSUES

GENE P. SACKETT, ARNOLD J. SAMEROFF, ROBERT B. CAIRNS, and STEPHEN J. SUOMI

The study of development poses a major paradox for students of behavior. The problem arises from the fact that change is an essential property of development. Virtually all features of the organism undergo modification during its life span. On the other hand, continuity over time seems essential for individual uniqueness, organization, and the maintenance of integrated patterns of behavior. The paradox is simply this: How can continuity and persistence be achieved in an organismic system that necessarily undergoes maturational, interactional, and cultural–social change?

This question brings us directly to the problem of continuity and discontinuity in development. Resolution of this problem will depend on a number of issues. These include clear definitions of exactly what is meant by a developmental continuity or discontinuity, identification of a research strategy that can yield results that arrive at conclusions about continuity consistent with these definitions, analysis of the types of measures and inferential methods that can be used to arrive at such conclusions, and examination of the longitudinal research designs that are required for studying developmental continuities.

DEVELOPMENTAL DISCONTINUITY DEFINED

Definitions of developmental continuities have frequently confounded two types of analysis. The first type relates to developmental functions, whereas the second refers to individual differences.

Wohlwill (1973) defines a *developmental function* as the frequency of a given behavior or set of behaviors across time. An age plot of height or intelligence would be an example of a developmental function. These developmental functions can be continuous or discontinuous. Typically height is thought to be a continuous function, whereas a Piagetian stage view of cognitive development would be seen as a discontinuous function (McCall 1977). The continuity in height is seen as a consequence of quantitative changes in a single underlying growth process. The discontinuity in cognitive development is seen as a consequence of qualitative changes in the way in which the world is known. Whereas changes in height are attributed to changes in a single process, changes in intelligence are attributed to a shift from one process to another.

The understanding of developmental function has frequently been confused with a focus on changes in individual rankings with age. Emmerich (1964) has argued that the question of stability or instability of individual differences is different from the question of continuity or discontinuity in function. Stability is usually assessed by correlating measures of a group of individuals at one age with another set of measures at a later age. If a high correlation is found, the usual conclusion is that a continuity has been demonstrated. Quite the contrary; stability of individual differences has little to do with continuity. McCall (1977) makes the simple point that because correlation coefficients are independent of the means of the two measures being correlated, the resulting coefficient is potentially independent of the status of the developmental function at the two ages.

Even more critically, the stability definition of continuity has frequently served to mask developmental functions. The typical intelligence test is designed to measure individual differences rather than developmental function. The intelligence quotient (IQ) score gives no indication of what an individual knows but only how he or she ranks among age peers. As a consequence, the use of typical intelligence tests tell us little about the development of intelligence.

For the purposes of this chapter, continuity and discontinuity will be used only in relation to developmental function and not in the sense of stability or instability of individual differences. However, even if we restrict the definition of discontinuity to qualitative changes in a developmental function, we are still faced with two potential definitions of discontinuity. On the one hand, continuity or discontinuity can be restricted to mean only that a qualitative change has or has not occurred. On the other hand, continuity or discontinuity can be used to refer to the relationship between the earlier process and the later one. In this latter sense, continuity would mean that the earlier process has a deterministic influence on the later one, whereas discontinuity would mean that the earlier process does not determine the later process. These formal definitions will be given content in what follows.

DEVELOPMENTAL FUNCTIONS AND THE CONTINUITY–DISCONTINUITY PROBLEM

Developmental questions concern the origins of behavioral functions and activities, and how they are maintained or transformed during the organism's life history. Neither traditional learning formulations nor classical behavior evolution concepts have been framed in these developmental terms – that is, in ways that permit an investigator to study simultaneously effects of changing structure and changing function over long periods of time. A significant step toward formulating a set of concepts appropriate for studying structure-function relationships in behavioral development has been made by Gottlieb (1976a, 1976b).

Gottlieb proposes that experience can serve three distinct roles in the development of a function or activity; namely, *induction, facilitation,* and *maintenance.* Experience can induce an activity or function into the individual's behavioral repertoire that would not appear except for that experience. Experience can facilitate the rate of development of an activity or function so that it appears earlier, or disappears more rapidly, than would be expected in a species-typical case. Experience can influence the maintenance of an activity or function such that its presence yields a species-typical course and its absence leads to arrest or actual deterioration. Our model for studying continuity in development is based on translating these three concepts into empirically testable propositions applied to concrete developmental problems. Our working definitions of these concepts can be stated as follows.

An *inducing* variable is any prior genetic, maturational, self-stimulated, or environmental event or sets of events necessary for the emergence of a response pattern. Induction thus refers to the process by which a response pattern initially appears in the behavioral repertoire.

A *facilitating* variable is an event necessary for quantitative variation in the rate of change of a response after its emergence. Examples include factors affecting thresholds, perceptual tuning of neural mechanisms, and increases in ability levels. However, for some behaviors such as neonatal reflexes, typical development involves response disappearance. In such cases, facilitation refers to factors influencing the rate of response decay and may overlap with maintaining variables.

A *maintaining* variable is an event necessary for keeping a developing behavioral system intact during periods of stability (plateaus in development) or at maturity. Maintaining events are those supporting the integrity of the system, preventing decay or degeneration, and/or preserving the possibility for later growth. In some processes, facilitation and maintenance may be affected by the same variables. In other processes, different factors may influence these functions. Furthermore, inducing variables may also be quite different from either facilitating or maintaining events.

To use these working definitions, it will be necessary to know about the normal course of development for the relevant activity or function. *Facilitation* and *maintenance* are relative terms, used with respect to some standard. At best, this standard will represent the species-typical course of development. With less generality, this standard could represent a normative course that is actually characteristic for a particular species developing under any set of well-defined environmental conditions. One major value of this research perspective is that it requires investigators to obtain information at the start of a study concerning normal development. This information will, at the least, include the appearance and sequential timing of key features of the referent activity or function.

Gottlieb (1976a, 1976b) has applied his three concepts with considerable success to the analysis of several sensory, perceptual, and motor functions. Bateson (1978) has proposed that these concepts can be extended to incorporate genetic as well as experiential events, with the role of genetic factors being described and studied in terms of their inducing, facilitating, and maintaining properties. One major task for the research model outlined in this chapter is to determine whether these concepts can be applied with success to more variable patterns of behavior, including diverse social and sexual activities. Thus, highly variable behavior may pose a major obstacle in applying this scheme beyond the relatively simple sensory and motor patterns studied by Gottlieb. Can social activity – from the expression of aggression to affiliation to fear – be viewed as following a species-typical or even normative course from conception to maturity in a way that is analogous to sensory systems? Maintenance implies attainment of an optimal endpoint, as well as a canalized developmental trajectory that can be kept intact, hastened, or retarded. However, what if there are many routes of development, and multiple endpoints are possible along these various routes? To the extent that patterns of social behavior are relative to the society and ecological context in which they develop, decisions about species-typical outcomes and rates of development may become blurred.

Discussion of the continuity problem has been largely theoretical, involving concepts about the antecedent conditions necessary for development of a behavioral system during the whole of its ontogeny. The term *continuity* has been used in at least three distinguishable ways. It can refer to (1) the continuous operation of a particular process across development, (2) the persistence of a particular behavior or physiological outcome across development, or (3) the cumulative nature of development in which earlier structures or functions are successively transformed or integrated into later structures or functions. Thus, a continuity position assumes that inducing, facilitating, and/or maintaining events operate sequentially in development, with later response patterns being causally dependent on these earlier events. The major problem for this view is to obtain direct empirical evidence identifying causal events affecting processes and outcomes that may be separated from these events by long periods of developmental time.

A discontinuity position assumes that the important factors influencing development are discrete, and that behavioral innovations can appear that have no important earlier antecedents. Response patterns appearing later in development may thus emerge from unique processes. Prior response patterns and their inducing, facilitating, or maintaining determinants are assumed to provide only the structural preconditions necessary, but not sufficient, for explaining the emergent function. The new process is assumed to have an organizational basis that did not exist before. The problem for this view is to show that, in fact, apparently emergent processes or behavioral outcomes cannot be predicted or explained from prior events. This is not simply the reverse of the continuity theorist's problem – that is, accepting as evidence for a discontinuity the failure to show that a particular prior event has a direct effect on current functioning. This approach, which is the typical one seen in the discontinuity literature, is akin to using failure to reject a null hypothesis as direct proof that an independent variable exerts no effect on an outcome measure. Rather, the discontinuity theorist must either identify and measure the factors responsible for an emergent function, provide details concerning the interrelationships that constitute a reorganized behavioral system, or develop a set of principles that can predict exactly when, and under what conditions, a particular set of earlier events will not exercise an influence upon later behavior.

Logically, continuities and discontinuities can coexist in the development of a particular behavior system. It is not necessary that a response pattern be completely determined by either a continuous progression of related events or a discrete series of independent steps. In normal development, one level of a process may depend on a discontinuity, whereas other levels of the same process may be maintained in a stable or continuous fashion. One way of viewing the actual study of developmental problems is in terms of discovering the continuity and discontinuity relationships that underlie behavioral ontogeny.

Organismic theorists such as Werner (1948) treat continuity as a function of the whole, whereas structure is the seat of discontinuity. For example, in embryological development, continuity is found in the separation of an organism as a discrete entity from its environment. Although there is a clear progression from zygote to embryo to fetus to newborn, the structure at each of these stages is qualitatively different. The functions of the organism can be viewed in the same light. There is continuity in many basic life functions, yet there is discontinuity in the structures that carry out these functions.

Consider respiration as a basic life function. In mammals, oxygenation of the fetus is accomplished through placental mechanisms. Air breathing after birth represents a complete discontinuity in process. The effects of oxygenation on many cells, tissues, and organs of the body remain the same as before the discontinuity, whereas effects of air breathing produce marked changes in the brain and in behavior (Sedlacek 1974). Thus, this key developmental milestone includes both discontinuities and continuities that are essential for maintaining the integrity of the whole organism.

HIERARCHICAL ORGANIZATION AND CONTINUITY

One major source of controversy in continuity–discontinuity arguments concerns hierarchical organization of behavior. For biologists viewing whole complex organisms, there are clear levels of organization of life in subordinate–superordinate relationships (e.g., Dawkins 1976). The organization of cells is qualitatively different from, and superordinate to, the organization of their constituent molecules. The organization of organs is qualitatively different from, and superordinate to, the organization of their constituent tissues. For psychologists, a hierarchical model of functioning is less evident and more controversial. A nonhierarchical view, such as that of a strict behaviorist, builds development from a continuous process of increasingly complex habits and associations. Discontinuities, in the sense of emergent processes and complete reorganization of basic functions, have no place in such a theory.

In hierarchical models (e.g., Werner 1948), higher, more complex levels of functioning arise from lower, less complex levels. If continuity holds when one level evolves out of another, the properties of the higher will be derived from those of the lower and there will be a consequent deterministic relationship between the two. If discontinuity holds, the higher may develop from simpler levels of organization, but their more complex functioning may be independent of many properties of the subordinate level. Such a discontinuity process has the very important implication that deviancies in behavior that may exist at simpler levels need not be translated into deviancies at more complex levels of organization. Waddington's (1966) ideas concerning self-righting tendencies in development are an expression of such a discontinuity concept. In contrast, there is the corollary position that a developing organism that behaved quite normally at earlier stages might display signs of deviancy as new levels of behavioral organization are achieved.

A general systems theory approach to development can explain how properties of lower levels need not affect the functioning of higher levels (Pattee 1973). A physiological example can illustrate this point. The heart is an organ composed of parts called *muscle tissues,* which are themselves composed of parts called *cells.* Many properties of cellular organization that are important to the structure and function of the muscle may be irrelevant to the function of the heart as a whole. To anthropomorphize, the heart is concerned only that the muscle does its job of contracting. Whether cell A is to the right or left of cell B is a property of muscle irrelevant to the primary heart function of pumping blood. Higher up in the system hierarchy, the body as a whole relates to the heart in terms of its pumping ability. Many heart properties influence this ability, but these are irrelevant to the rest of the body, which does not care how the job is done, as long as it gets done. If this were not so, heart surgeons might be put out of business.

Application of a general systems analysis to behavior requires a hierarchical theory of psychological development. Such a theory has been proposed by Piaget (1950). In the heart example, higher levels would collapse without the functioning of lower levels – no cells, no heart. Similarly in Piaget's theory, without the prior development and contemporary functioning of lower levels of cognition, the higher levels would neither be induced nor maintained. But, as in the heart example, although the parts that compose a more complex, higher-level organization may develop out of prior levels, the higher-level properties may be determined by their new interrelationships and not by the properties of subordinate prior levels.

Consider the following analysis from Piaget's theory. Babies are born with a number of sensory capacities. Through each modality the infant obtains a partial view of reality. This fragmented perspective is assumed to have two consequences. First, the visual properties of an object are not known by the infant to be related to the tactile or olfactory properties of that object. Second, infants are unable to separate the properties of the object from their own activity because the object is a visual stimulus only when looked at, and the baby cannot give it an existence independent of the looking activity. Throughout the first 2 years, the infant increasingly coordinates information from separate sensory modalities about individual objects. As these visual, tactile, and olfactory properties become coordinated, the infant achieves a new level of cognitive organization in which objects have an existence of their own even when not being observed or touched. The resulting property of object permanence still depends on the sensory features that characterized the prior level of cognitive organization. But objects now have a new property that is discontinous with their sensory properties, namely, an existence independent of the infant's sensory activity.

Any particular object has an infinite number of properties or relationships that differentiate it from other objects. The infant, however, needs to recognize and coordinate only a few of these properties to achieve an understanding of object permanence. Thus, in Piaget's theory of hierarchically organized cognitive structures, early deficits need not be transmitted from one level to another. This discontinuity is clear from data showing that infants with physical or perceptual disabilities still manage to attain object permanence. Children who are deaf, blind, or have missing limbs or cerebral palsy thus show both continuity and discontinuity in their mature functioning. Continuity is seen in the fact that they retain their specific physical handicaps. Discontinuity arises when despite these handicaps the person reaches a high level of adult cognitive functioning. This is possible because apparently only a small portion of functioning at subordinate levels is required for attaining complete functioning at a superordinate level.

In an approach such as this, the continuity–discontinuity issue takes on both theoretical and empirical substance. There may exist continuities within a given level of the organism: Cell A will always be to the left of cell B; blind infants will not see during any stages of their cognitive development. Yet these continuities within levels do not necessarily predict that deficits must occur at succeeding levels of development. The research problem for a view such as this involves (1) identifying the processes and functions that constitute each level in the hierarchy of organization and (2) specifying which aspects of subordinate prior organization and function, if any, are minimally required for achieving superordinate states.

DEVELOPMENTAL THEORY

Although problems of method, including abundant use of correlational procedures, deserve some of the blame for retarding our understanding of developmental continuities, research design and analytic technique are only part of the problem (e.g., Bateson 1978). Theoretical shortcomings, especially in relating developmental concepts to appropriate research strategies, are also a primary culprit. One major source of difficulty is the overly narrow conception of the role of experience in producing developmental changes and transitions.

Theories of behavioral development consist of principles for explaining the emergence, growth, innovation, replacement, or disappearance of response patterns in the repertoire of individuals. Developmental concepts thus concern the determinants of (1) when behaviors will appear and (2) how behaviors will change during ontogeny. Models of this process vary across a wide range of concepts and parameters. At one extreme, mechanistic models view development as an automatic, machinelike, process. At the opposite extreme, organismic models view development as a dynamic process in which change depends on complex interactions among genetic, internal, and external environmental factors. Reese and Overton (1970; Overton & Reese 1973) have contrasted the different methodologies and conclusions drawn from these disparate perspectives. They emphasize the importance for the scientist of being explicit about underlying models, because the model will influence both the selection and the interpretation of research problems. Our analysis of the continuity paradox employs an organismic view of development. Therefore, we will spend some effort explicating the nature and assumptions of organismic models.

AN ORGANISMIC VIEW OF ADAPTATION, MATURATION, AND EXPERIENCE

The essence of an organismic model is that each successive change during development results from a continuous interplay between organism and environment. Traditional ethologists (Tinbergen 1951; Lorenz 1965) spent great effort identifying species-specific patterns of behavior that were largely independent of experience. This relatively nativist orientation postulated that basic innate behavior patterns unfolded, with the effects of learning then added to these hereditary structures. In contrast, Schneirla (1966) argued that this approach overlooked major functions intervening between genes and behavior. He further argued that improved empirical methods would not resolve the problem unless accompanied by a redefinition of terms and a clarification of concepts. A reformulation would include genetic factors. However, it would exclude a nativist conception of maturation as the simple unfolding of gene-determined patterns because the organismic model assumes that no emerging system is independent of external factors.

The organismic model proposes that at each point in development the organism is sensitive to various inputs, is capable of various outputs, and has changing capacities for relating input and output to its internal structures. The biological metaphor of a living cell provides an apt analogy. Depending on the state of the genetic structure at a given time, the same extranuclear biochemicals will be incorporated into different structures or will not be incorporated at all. If incorporated, these biochemicals change the state of the genetic structure by turning various combinations of genes on or off. Such transactions between the genome and the rest of the cell that forms its effective environment are prototypical of all succeeding developmental processes. An almost literal translation of this model appears in Piaget's (1960) theory of cognitive development. The developmental process is defined as identical to adaptation – the organism's self-regulatory activity functioning to maintain equilibration between the organism and its environment.

Kuo (1976) arrived at a similar view after extensive investigation of the embryogenesis of behavior. He defined development as a set of gradual and complex changes arising from progressive biochemical, physiological, and physical events in which the patterns of each stage result from reorganization of patterns at earlier stages. This position contrasts to the conventional view that genetic and environmental factors are separate entities that have distinct functions in producing development.

Gottlieb (1976a) also questions the view of development as a unidirectional structure-to-function process in which genes produce new structures, which only then lead to new functions. His bidirectional model assumes that genes act in a reciprocal feedback relationship with structural maturation. Further, structure is itself in a reciprocal feedback relationship with function well before complete maturity of any behavioral system is achieved. Examples of such inseparable interactions are seen in Gottlieb's research showing that neural activity, sensory stimulation, and feedback from motor movement act together in inducing, facilitating, and maintaining both neuroembryological development and species-typical behavior.

The traditional model in which biological variables produce invariant material structures, whereas psychological variables produce plastic informational associations, seems inadequate from both sides. Investigators such as Schneirla, Kuo, and Gottlieb described the role that function and experience can play in physiological and anatomical development. Others such as Piaget and Seligman (1970) identified the constraints placed on behavioral plasticity by anatomical and physiological structures of the organism. This breakdown of conceptual barriers between biology and psychology opens the way for an empirical search for the actual reciprocal interactions between structure and function. The model that emerges suggests a continuity of process between biological and psychological functioning. The continuity resides in the organism's active engagement in adaptive transactions with its environment. Such transactions simultaneously determine both behavioral change and modification of existing structures. This holistic view of development emphasizes the fusion of age-related morphological, neurological, and biochemical changes with experiential–behavioral changes.

In order for empirical models to examine fully developmental functions, the role of experience must be carefully evaluated. However, experience can be defined only in terms of a given structure in a given environment. As a consequence, the careful description of environment is an essential adjunct to the definition of function, and it will be included in the empirical models to be proposed.

CONTINUITY AND IRREVERSIBILITY

An issue related closely to continuity is that of irreversibility of earlier effects on later behavior. The basic continuity position is assumed in concepts such as critical periods or less strict views that ascribe special importance to the effect of early experience on the emergence, facilitation, and maintenance of later behavior. Views such as Freudian theory predict relatively irreversible effects of early life experiences on the course of subsequent development. Until recently challenged by a number of writers (e.g., Cairns 1977; Clarke & Clarke 1977; Sameroff 1975) on empirical grounds, the preeminence of early experiences was an almost universal assumption among developmentalists. These challenges hinge on three types of evidence:

1 A number of studies assessed the development of abnormally behaving infants who grew up in deviant environments such as orphanages or parentally induced social isolation. Many of these individuals attained normal scores on standard psychological tests after living in more typical environmental circumstances later in life. Thus, the early experiences and consequent behaviors appear to be discontinuous with later development.
2 Correlations between IQ measures at different times during development generally fail to show even moderate positive values (e.g., McCall et al.

1977). This lack of stability in individual differences is also interpreted as a lack of continuity in development.

3 Research on the stability of early social attachments has shown flexibility in birds (Immelmann 1975), mammals (Cairns 1966), and nonhuman primates (Suomi 1977), again suggesting at least some degree of discontinuity between earlier events and later behavior.

Unfortunately, both critical period theorists and their antagonists have argued either for or against a theoretical view that sees normal development as a sequential string of causal events producing mature behavior. Given the interactive nature of genetic, environmental, and social factors in development, the form of this argument has been overly simplistic. Assuming even the most strict continuity position, it does not follow that development must be irreversibly deviant if a species-typical event is not experienced or if atypical events occur. Irreversible abnormalities should occur only if critical events are necessary to maintain the potential for developing a given behavior. If the physiological, anatomical, or behavioral structures required for inducing or maintaining a response pattern depend on the occurrence of particular events at critical maturational periods, then a continuity view predicts irreversible effects of the failure to experience these events. On the other hand, if such structures are intact even though current behavior is deviant, a continuity view would predict reversibility of the deviancy or induction of a normal response pattern at ages later than those typically found for a particular species.

Another important distinction that is not commonly made in irreversibility debates concerns the domains of behavior being considered. For example, there may be major differences in early experience effects on social, cognitive, and emotional spheres. Most discontinuity arguments are based on cognitive functioning (Clarke & Clarke 1977; McCall et al. 1977), whereas most continuity arguments are based on personality or emotionality variables (Block & Block 1973; Kagan & Moss 1963). These domain differences may be related to the hierarchy issue. In domains where hierarchies of behavior are proposed, as in cognition, discontinuity arguments are strong. In domains where such hierarchies are not often postulated, as in social and emotional development, continuity arguments are more common. In either case, the burden of proof should rest on appropriately collected data rather than on pure theory or the logic of an argument.

The center of the continuity and reversibility issues seems to lie in the depth of developmental analysis applied to the problems under study. Only a few investigators of human behavior have paid attention to the details of empirical evidence needed to conclude that a behavior is either dependent on or independent of prior events (e.g., Kagan 1978; Wohlwill 1973). In discussing empirical issues, Bateson (1978) describes at least six reasons why apparent discontinuities may relate more to testing and measurement problems than to continuity of the developmental process.

1 Reduced variability between individuals with increasing age can produce regression toward the mean and consequent lack of correlation over time.
2 Nonmonotonic developmental functions can reorder the rank among individuals depending on the particular point on the curve for a given

individual at the time of testing. This reordering also produces an apparent instability of individual differences.

3 Differential maturation rates can also produce reordering of ranks depending on the ages of the individuals tested. This reordering may suggest a discontinuity when in fact measurement scale problems have occurred.

4 Self-stabilization of developmental processes can place an individual back on a normal trajectory after some temporary disturbance or trauma. If measures before or after the disturbance are compared with ones taken during the abnormal period, data will appear to indicate a discontinuity that does not exist.

5 Lack of equivalence between behaviors measured at different maturational periods can result in little or no correlation over time. Rather than a discontinuity, this situation arises because of comparing "apples with oranges."

6 Introduction of new environmental events may alter the expression of an actually unchanged behavioral or physiological–anatomical process. Thus, an outcome measure of response may indicate a discontinuity, whereas a measure of an underlying process variable may be stable, indicating continuity.

Bateson's analysis suggests that a detailed study of development must focus on at least three general empirical dimensions. These include (1) the specific response patterns being measured at different ages, (2) the organismic and behavioral processes that underlie these response patterns, and (3) the environmental–social conditions forming the individual's developmental experiences. Few studies of specific issues relevant to the continuity or reversibility problem have included all three of these dimensions in their analyses. The discussion to follow aims at identifying some of the important empirical considerations involved in drawing conclusions about continuities, discontinuities, and irreversible effects of prior experience on later development.

TYPES OF DEVELOPMENTAL RELATIONSHIPS AND CRITERIA FOR THEIR ASSESSMENT

Table 1.1 presents a summary of assessment criteria and analytical indices that have been used to study three aspects of developmental relationships – processes, outcomes, and environmental effects. Bracketed material pertains to all types of relationships in that section of the table. Nonbracketed material refers only to the specific relationship in that row of the table. The specific characteristics of these relationships represent the data from which developmental continuities or discontinuities are inferred.

Process development

The most difficult aspect of behavioral development to define and study concerns the actual genetic, physiological, anatomical, and/or organizational mechanisms underlying the ontogeny of a particular response pattern. Such

Table 1.1. *Summary of types of developmental relationships, assessment criteria, and analytical indexes*

Type of relationship	Assessment criteria	Analytical indexes
Processes		
Age dependent	Process can be induced, facilitated, or maintained during only one phase of development	Inference from theory
Age independent	Process can be induced, facilitated, or maintained at many phases of development	Time series analysis in Conditions × Age longitudinal research design
Sequence dependent	Different processes emerge in a series of causal stages	Scaling the order of appearance and dropping out of traits or characteristics over time
Behavioral outcomes		
Within-individual stability of traits or characteristics	Measure of trait or characteristic is the same value over time	Absolute scores on experimental measures or standard tests
Between-individual stability of a developing behavior	Same rank position relative to a norm or reference group over time	Correlation or concordance coefficient
Environmental effects		
Optimal or specific stimulation is needed for induction, facilitation, and/or maintenance of a process or outcome	Process simulation	
Constancy of stimulation is needed for facilitation and/or maintenance of a process or outcome	Natural or manipulative experiments	Time series analysis in a Conditions × Age longitudinal research design
Changes in stimulation are needed for facilitation and/or maintenance of a process or outcome	Parametric studies	

mechanisms are termed *process* variables in this chapter. Very few of these mechanisms are known. Most are hypothesized from theory or inferred from relationships among outcome response measures. Thus, in theories of behavioral development most processes exist as unmeasured constructs.

Developmental processes can include internal psychological mechanisms such as learning or equilibration; biological functions such as gonadal secretions or dendritic growth; genes and their ontogenetic effects; and interactional environmental events such as social reciprocity or reactivity to social stimulation. To the extent that a process, once induced, continues to affect behavior throughout the course of development, the content and substance of an individual's activity as measured in outcomes are likely to undergo marked change. Hence, continuity of process under such conditions is associated with facilitation - predictable changes in observed behaviors. To illustrate, consider the continued secretion of the growth hormone somatotropin. This continuing event ensures predictable changes in the physical structure and behavioral properties of the individual. Cessation of this hormone, its discontinuity, then brings about a maintenance state of stability in those forms and structures whose changes were dependent upon its prior activity. As another example, consider the testicular hormones produced and secreted by male primate fetuses (Resko 1970). These hormones are responsible for the induction of many characteristics of sexual dimorphism even in the fetal stage. These hormones are almost identical to those produced at reproductive maturity (Reyes et al. 1974). Thus, the process of male hormone production - but not necessarily its effects on behavior - is continuous between two disparate phases of life even though the process does not apparently operate during an intervening maintenance period. Also, the adult process appears to be strictly determined by induction of the process during fetal life.

On the other hand, all processes that can influence development are not strictly biological or physiological. Social interaction processes such as those involved in social regulation are of equal importance for understanding stability or change in social behavior patterns. To the extent that social interchanges are regulated by experiencing the actions and reactions of others, events in the immediate social context will determine whether or not a given response pattern occurs. Complete stability of social behavior during development would thus require either an arrest of interchange processes or an unchanging social environment. Consider, for example, the transactions that occur between a human infant and its caregiver(s) during development. This process produces predictable changes in specific behavior patterns in much the same way that somatotropin produces predictable changes in physical structure. Thus, the organization of interchanges over time can be viewed as a behavioral process variable that can have the same degree of impact on induction, facilitation, or maintenance of response patterns as any fundamental biological process.

Process development is assessed by measuring the identity or relative similarity of earlier and later functioning of the mechanism in question. Three types of process development are identified in the top section of Table 1. 1. *Age dependence* is the basic critical or sensitive period concept. Such a process can be induced, facilitated, and/or maintained only if a set of necessary events are present at the right time. In the case of age-dependent induction, subsequent facilitation or maintenance of the process can occur only if the process was induced at the critical time. Other processes may be *age independent* for their induction, facilitation, and/or maintenance within a broad range of the life span. Such processes would develop in a species-typical fashion regardless of timing, as long as events necessary for induction, facilitation, and maintenance occurred. Alternatively, a process may be inducible at an atypical developmental period, but its facilitation and/or maintenance may then be quite deviant due to age dependence of these factors. For example, congenitally blind adults with restored vision do not develop all of the visual abilities of people sighted from birth.

Indices for measuring these two types of process development involve some form of time series analysis and usually require longitudinal data. Measures of a process variable are studied over a time, varying two or more conditions that are assumed to affect induction, facilitation, and/or maintenance of the process. This leads to a Conditions × Age research design. Statistical and methodological issues in such longitudinal studies have been discussed by Gottman (1973), King (1958), Solomon and Lessac (1968), and Schaie (1965). Unfortunately, a complete discussion of this topic is beyond the scope of this chapter.

It should be noted that when process variables are hypothetical, process development can only be inferred theoretically from outcome response measures. In such cases, which constitute the vast majority of information about development, it will not be possible actually to perform empirical studies of process variables – and as usual, continuity–discontinuity conclusions will be based on assumption rather than direct evidence.

A third type of process development, *sequence dependence*, involves mechanisms that are assumed to appear in a series of causal stages. Each stage is dependent on achieving the integration and organization of processes at the immediately preceding stage. However, the emergence and actual organization of processes at a later stage may be qualitatively different from that at the earlier stage. Generally, sequence theorists assume that continuity of the process occurs within a stage. In effect, stages are themselves defined as periods of time during which the individual's responses are stable and determined by the same process. Discontinuity, involving the emergence of a new process serving to organize or mediate response patterns, defines the appearance of a new stage. If there is a causal relationship between stages, the next step in the sequence can appear in an individual's behavioral repertoire only when the behaviors characteristic of the prior stage have been attained. This indicates that the prior process had been functioning. If a variety of responses can result from a hypothesized prior process, it will not be possible to test a theory such as this without having actual measures of the process variable. Continuity in this type of theory thus involves demonstrating that the series of process changes occurs in an invariant sequence, and that breaking this sequence would yield species-deviant development.

Alternatively, it seems possible that continuity may be provided, at least in part, by processes governing transitions from one stage to the next. As regards Piaget's (1960) theory, transition from one cognitive level to the next may depend on adequately paced environmental situations placing increasingly greater demands on the individual's cognitive adaptive organization. Sequentially dependent stages may occur because during evolution the social, ecological, and economic resources of the environment placed sequential demands on developing intellectual abilities. For example, in most young mammals the newborn faces few direct cognitive challenges. Development proceeds initially by self-stimulation and input within the caregiving situation. Maturation and motor development bring the infant in contact with a wider range of the environment. Reduced caregiving produces demands for greater independence of action. Eventually, the individual must generate most of its own resources and must operate in a wider social circle, including friendly and hostile contacts. Adapting to each change in this sequence may require increasingly more complex intellectual skills. Thus, the process causing transition between cognitive stages could be increased demands on adaptive behavior from changed social and environmental conditions. Such a process might operate at all sequentially dependent cognitive stages, thereby providing continuity to the overall course of cognitive development.

Analytical indices for measuring sequence dependency have included normative data on steps in solving problems scaled for difficulty of intellectual demands by theoretical considerations. Although some experiments have facilitated the speed of acquisition of known sequences, these are not relevant to the basic question of sequential causality. Stage assessment focuses on invariance in attaining patterns of problem solutions, not on age. Coombs and Smith (1973) offer an elegant scaling technique for measuring the order of appearance and dropping out of behavioral attributes during development. Their method can provide a relatively direct test of the degree of sequential invariance among normal and deviant individuals assessed under normative or deviant conditions. However, it seems unlikely that simply scaling invariance can identify actual causal processes unless the scaled behaviors are known to be important to facing the demands of an actual developmental environment. Charlesworth (1978) has begun to tackle this problem. He has designed systematic observational methods for assessing cognitive performance under natural free-behavior conditions. His methods deal with less arbitrary attributes of cognitive behavior than those generated from purely theoretical considerations. Therefore, they may appear to be more likely to illuminate actual development processes underlying intelligent behaving than the traditional test- and clinically oriented assessment techniques.

Genetic and prenatal processes

Genes and prenatal variables are obviously important parts of the total developmental process. Recent advances in embryology and animal obstetrics (e.g., Markert & Petters 1978) and in in vitro fertilization of human and nonhuman primate ova (e.g., Steptoe & Edwards 1978) offer an elegant potential experimental tool relevant to the experimental model proposed here. It is possible to study genetic versus prenatal influences directly by implanting fertilized ova from donor females having a genetic characteristic of interest into recipient females having other traits. This technique is essentially one of prenatal cross fostering. For example, females at high risk for abortion could receive fertilized ova transplants from females at low risk for abortion. We would have direct evidence for a genetic basis of abortion in the high-risk population if normal-term infants were produced. Coupled with artificial insemination, genetic effects can be separated both from effects surrounding conception and early embryonic development and from later prenatal factors. Genetic factors can, in principle, also be studied by performing microsurgery on four- or eight-cell embryos. When properly cleaved, these embryos can grow into exact identical twins who can then be transplanted to groups of females differing in characteristics of interest. Finally, it is possible to graft together cleaved mouse embryos from different individuals and produce viable neonates containing characteristics from more than two parents.

Outcome development

A second issue has to do with development of behavioral outcomes (Table 1.1, middle section). Outcome persistence has been a typical concern in many studies of development. Measurement of outcomes, with no assessment of underlying process variables, constitutes the majority of relevant data in the behavior development literature. Persistence or stability has been assessed in two basically different ways.

Within-individual stability is evaluated on an absolute basis, measuring whether a behavior has undergone transformation or change in some critical respect. Does a child solve an arithmetic problem more rapidly or skillfully at age 15 than at age 10? Is there a change in social preferences from the immediate posthatching period to maturity? Answering such questions depends on information about early and later performance of the same individual. Variation about the individual's mean performance is sufficient to determine whether or not there has been stability or persistence. Statistical assessment can be expressed in terms of variation from an initial test score or changes in mean values or proportions.

Some examples of within-individual stability are shown in Figure 1.1. Preference for one's own versus other species members is measured at different ages. In P_1 the choice for one's own species is high and constant. If the age at exposure 1 is prior to any contact with own-species members, we would have evidence that induction of this preference did not depend on postnatal experience. In P_2 the preference for one's own species occurs suddenly, in an all-or-none fashion. This suggests that the process inducing the preference may be discontinuous with prior events, and no facilitation is needed to maintain the behavior. In P_3 the preference gradually rises to a stable level. This suggests that there is outcome continuity in induction, facilitation, and maintenance of the behavior. It should be noted that these three different curves represent equal degrees of outcome stability once maintenance has been achieved.

Unfortunately, changes in absolute performance are the rule, not the exception, in behavioral development. Therefore, the majority of studies measuring outcome persistence have used a relative standard to judge stability. This standard is the performance of some reference group. The relative standing of an individual is expressed either in terms of that individual's rank order within the reference group or in terms of the individual's distance from the reference group mean measured in standard score units. However, such between-individual measures do not assess persistence of behavioral outcome. Rather, they assess persistence of the ranking or relative position within a group. Such ranking may remain stable over time even though the characteris-

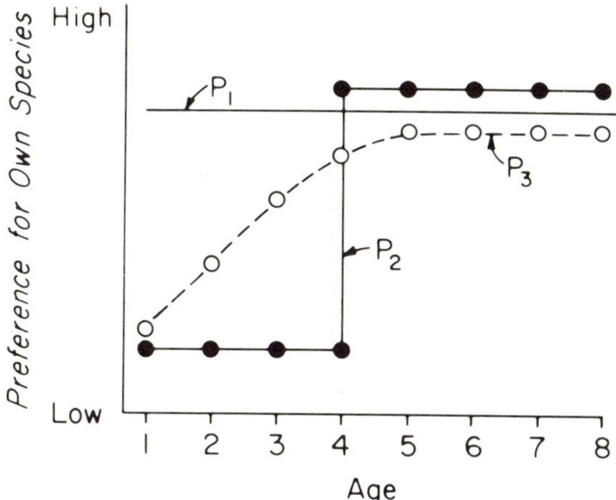

Figure 1.1. Hypothetical examples of three types of within-individual stability relationships: (P_1) a potentially unlearned preference; (P_2) an all-or-none induction function; (P_3) a function showing induction, facilitation, and maintenance of the outcome.

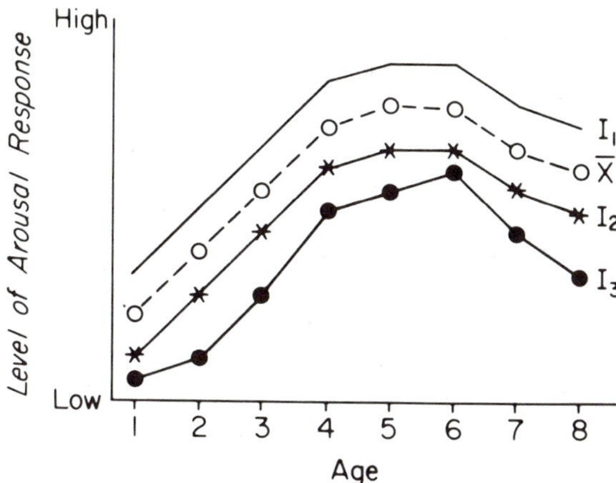

Figure 1.2. Hypothetical examples of between-individual stability relationships in which curves I_1, I_2, and I_3 maintain both their rank orders and their deviations from a mean value over age.

tic on which the ranking is based changes markedly. Statistics used to measure the degree of between-individual stability include correlation and concordance coefficients.

Figure 1. 2 presents curves illustrating between-individual stability. Level of arousal, indexed by a response such as latency to orient or startle magnitude to loud sounds, is measured over age. Although arousal increases and then decreases, the curve for each individual relative to either the mean values or values of the other individuals maintains the same rank position.

Failures to find within- or between-individual stabilities are often interpreted as discontinuity evidence; earlier outcomes or effects of earlier processes do not persist into later behavior. If this interpretation is true, two possible conclusions are that (1) the process underlying the current behavior is different from that influencing earlier development, or (2) earlier conditions have not altered the processes underlying the possibility for later facilitation of the behavioral outcome in question. However, as reviewed above (Bateson 1978), a number of methodological factors can produce apparent variability in outcome measures even when the underlying process or overall levels of the outcome are actually stable. In order to conclude that a discontinuity exists, such methodological factors must be controlled or systematically studied and eliminated as causes of the instability.

One major factor – change in environment – can also produce instability of within- and between-individual measures. This may happen because a particular environmental factor is essential to maintain either the process or the outcome. For example, suppose that motivation to engage in interactions with agemates depends on the availability of physical contact with them. Early in development physical contact is available, and outcome measures of visual and auditory interaction are at high levels. Subsequently, physical contact is denied, and the individual fails to exhibit interactions with agemates at a distance. The developmental curve would show a discontinuity. But this would result from the changed and inadequate stimulus situation rather than a change in the mediating process.

A hypothetical test of process–outcome continuity

Some of our ideas concerning process and outcome development are illustrated by hypothetical data shown in Figure 1.3. The experiment involves development of a response pattern and an underlying process assumed necessary for occurrence of the pattern. The left graph shows normative development of fear of novelty and adrenal steroid secretion. The normative relationship suggests that fear occurs only after a large rise in circulating steroids. Subsequent manipulative, natural, or clinical studies can test what happens if steroids never rise or the rise occurs at an atypical age.

The middle graph shows two possibilities if steroids fail to rise. Compared with the normative data, effect C suggests that fear is not dependent on steroid rise for either induction or facilitation. The apparent correlation seen in the normative data is spurious. Effect A′ suggests that fear does depend on steroid rise but offers no evidence concerning age dependence because the steroid rise never occurs.

In the right graph, steroids rise at an age later than normal. Effect B suggests that fear induction is dependent on steroid rise. However, there is no age dependency because fear develops normally, although steroid induction occurred at an abnormal age. Effect B identifies a time lag dependency between steroid induction and the amount of time that must pass before fear is induced.

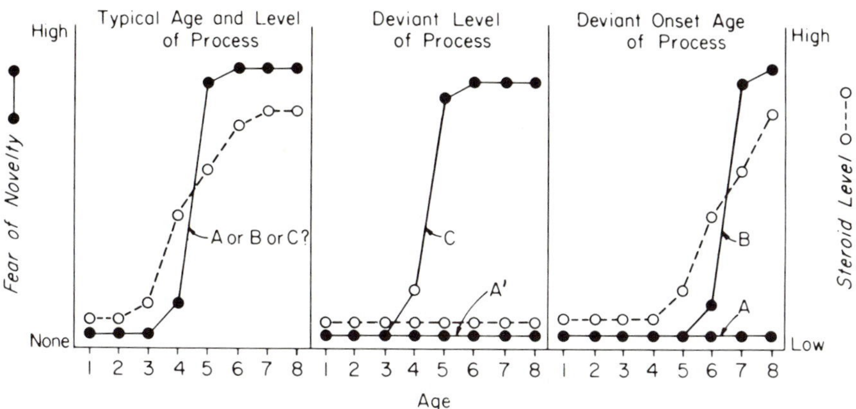

Figure 1.3. Identification of a potential process–outcome relationship (left curve), and experiments testing whether induction of adrenal steroids causes the consequent fear of novelty (see text for explanation).

Effect A suggests that fear is age-dependent; steroids must rise at a critical age for fear to occur at all. It is also possible for steroids to rise toward an intermediate value, then be maintained steadily or fall. If fear was induced and facilitated normally, we would have evidence that its induction but not its facilitation depended on continued steroid rise. If fear rose and then fell when steroids ceased to rise, we would have evidence for both induction and facilitation of fear dependent on steroids.

To show process continuity in the maintenance of this system, a continued dependence on steroids for obtaining fear in a novel situation must be demonstrated. If fear occurred at ages later than those shown in the absence of high steroid levels – affected perhaps by surgical or chemical adrenal treatment – we would have evidence for a discontinuity of process. Fear would have become autonomous of steroids, thus implying that a new process variable is responsible for maintaining fear.

It should be noted that this example illustrates one fact about studying developmental continuity. When the underlying process variable is purely hypothetical – inferred from outcome measures or simply assumed – it is not possible to test empirically any statements about continuity between behavioral outcomes and their inducing, facilitating, or maintaining processes.

Environmental context

It is, of course, a truism that specific behavioral outcomes are always a function of both genetic–maturational and environmental factors. In this chapter we have emphasized the view that these factors reciprocally and equally influence development. In this view, process–outcome relationships will often, or perhaps always, depend on environmental contexts during development and even after maturity is achieved.

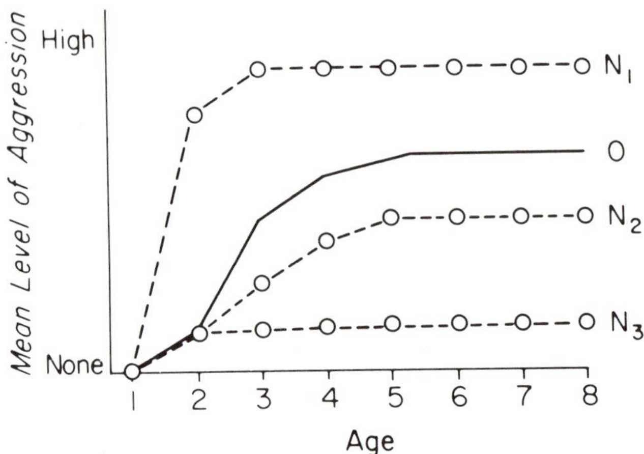

Figure 1.4. Hypothetical developmental functions when environments (N_1, N_2, N_3) deviate from an absolute or optimal environment (O) necessary to achieve species-typical development.

Sources of relevant environmental variables can range from precisely measured values of specific stimuli to multidimensional social experiences such as adequate mothering or the impact of society. In the following discussion it is assumed that (1) environmental variables relevant to development can be operationally defined and (2) at least two different qualitative or quantitative values of relevant variables can be studied empirically. Our most critical assumption is that (3) the developmental process or outcome can be studied in either a natural situation or some normative situation containing environmental factors known to be relevant for the species under study. However, it is not assumed that there is a single natural environment or that development can proceed in one, and only one, normal way. The concept of a *natural environment* is an important one for us. It has been discussed in this volume (Chap. 2), along with the concept of *normal development*.

As summarized in the bottom section of Table 1.1, environmental continuity can involve at least three aspects of experience. The first concerns specific input or input within an optimal range that may be necessary for induction, facilitation, and/or maintenance of a process or outcome. For example, herring gull chicks peck at the lower portion of the parent's beak, which elicits feeding by the parent. A red dot on the parent's beak is part of the stimulus configuration releasing this behavior. It could be that only dots of a specific size or color would work. Alternatively, any stimulus in an optimal range of size or color might stimulate the behavior. Thus, induction could depend on either a specific or a more general quality of the dot. Finally, facilitation and/or maintenance may depend on the same dot qualities or may be discontinuous with the inducing mechanism – released by any beak-shaped object that is perceived.

Figure 1.4 illustrates several possible outcomes under the specific or optimal stimulation situation. Aggression is measured by assessing the amount of threat plus physical attack behavior at different ages. Curve O shows the

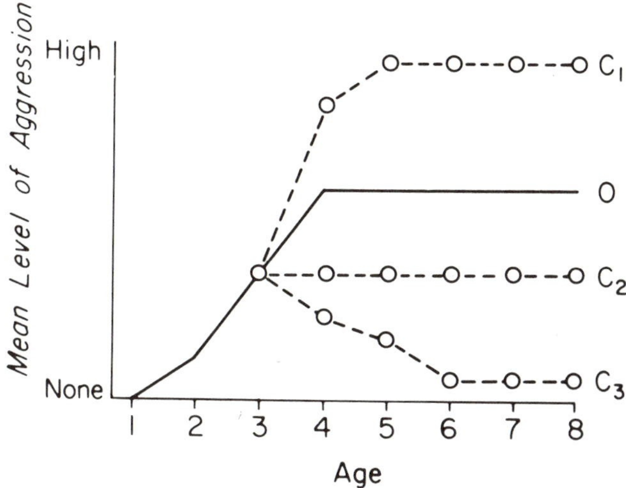

Figure 1.5. Hypothetical developmental functions when environments (C_1, C_2, C_3) deviate from a normal situation (O) that contains constant stimulation necessary to facilitate and maintain species-typical development.

normal course of aggression in what is known to be a typical developmental environment. For many primate species this might include a maternal caregiver, agemates, juveniles, adults of both sexes, and the opportunity to observe others acting aggressively.

The other curves represent developmental environments containing deviations at age 1 from the typical situation. N_1 might be total social isolation. When placed in the typical environment at ages 2 to 8, isolates showed rapid facilitation and maintained hyperaggression. Prior social experience was not necessary for aggression induction but was essential for rate of increase and maintenance level. Curve N_2 might represent an environment containing only mothers and agemates at age 1 year, followed by the normal situation. Aggression is induced but is facilitated at a lower rate and maintained at a lower level than normal. Curve N_3 might be for animals reared without agemate contact at age 1 year, then raised normally. Only a low level of aggression is induced, with no facilitation after age 2. To show long-term continuity effects, the atypical curves must remain outside the normal range even though the individuals involved are subjected to normal or other therapeutic conditions. Suppose that normal levels, indexing a discontinuity with earlier experience, were found following therapy. This would provide evidence that either (1) the facilitation and maintenance processes are not destroyed by inadequate early experiences or (2) other processes later in development can produce the same outcome as that found after species-typical early experience.

A second type of environmental continuity involves the need for stimulus constancy to facilitate or maintain a process or outcome once it has been induced. Figure 1.5 presents some examples of this idea, again illustrated by aggression.

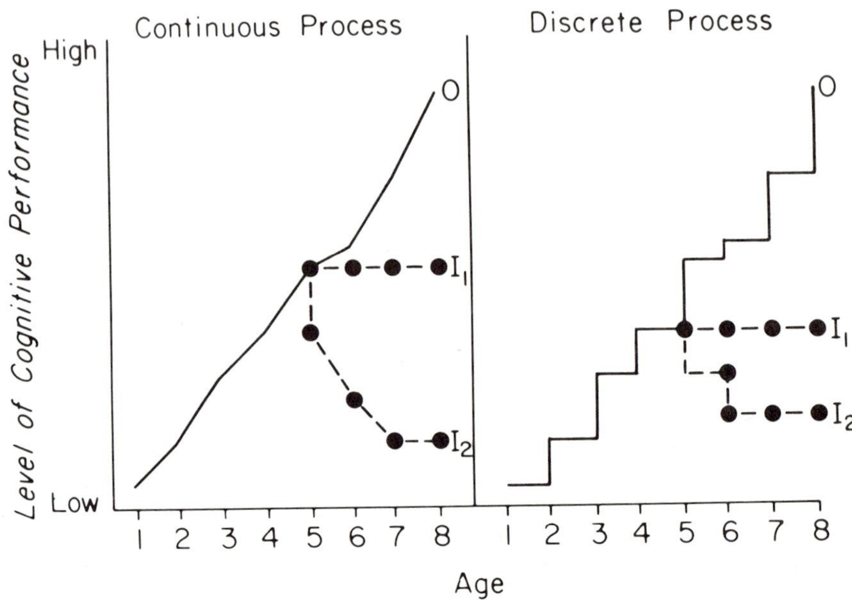

Figure 1.6. Hypothetical developmental functions (I_1, I_2) when environments do not contain optimal stimulus changes (O) representing paced demands for behavior change on the part of developing individuals.

Curve O represents the development of individuals who grow up in a species-typical environment. The other groups also live in the normal situation until age 3. In curve C_1 all adult males are removed from the social group. This results in an increased aggression rate and above-normal maintenance. In curve C_2 individuals are moved with their mothers to a new species-typical social group. Aggression fails to show further facilitation, being arrested at the level reached prior to moving. Curve C_3 might result from loss of the mother. This produces a decaying facilitation, with complete disappearance of aggression. In each of these atypical situations, the developmental function has depended on the continuity (constancy) of the social context in which later development occurred.

A third potential type of environmental influence involves unidirectional changes in stimulation – normal development depending on the occurrence of new (discontinuous) stimulus qualities or quantities. The developmental function would then be governed by the types of new input needed to support normal development. Figure 1.6 presents examples of this situation.

Suppose that the level of cognitive development is measured by presenting tasks of increasing difficulty at a number of ages. Outcome O is the normal developmental curve for a gradual process (left) or a discrete sequence dependency (right). It is assumed that in either case normal development depends on gradually paced environmental demands for new intellectual skills in order to cope with changing social and ecological conditions. At age 5 conditions are modified for individuals I_1 and I_2. This may involve experiencing situations that are (1) too complex – far beyond the individual's current ability level, (2) too simple – well below the current ability level, or (3) fixed and unchanging. Any of these situations define inadequate pacing of stimulation.

The I_1 outcome is arrested development at the level normal for age 5. This would be most likely if environmental demands became fixed or lowered below the individual's current ability level. The I_2 outcome reveals degeneration of performance. This might occur if demands became too great, thereby exceeding the individual's current ability level by a large amount. I_2 might also occur if physical trauma lowered the individual's ability level, making an otherwise normal increase in demands too great for the reduced ability level.

The criteria for assessing environmental context effects on developmental functions must be experimental. Simple normative data or demonstrations will not suffice. Environmental effects concern causal, not correlative, relationships among stimuli, responses, and underlying processes. Such experiments can be conducted under manipulative laboratory or field conditions, or data might be obtained from relevant natural events. Parametric research, varying a wide range of stimuli above and below normative levels, will be required for defining optimal stimulation and adequate pacing ranges. In general, these studies will focus on mean differences in developmental functions using time series analyses in a Conditions × Age longitudinal research design. If the problem can be phrased mathematically, computers could be used to simulate the effects of parametric manipulations. Selected simulation outcomes, especially ones that are nonobvious or counterintuitive, could then be tested empirically without actually conducting a complete parametric experiment (Bateson 1978).

A RESEARCH PLAN TO STUDY DEVELOPMENTAL CONTINUITY–DISCONTINUITY RELATIONSHIPS

Developmental information has ranged from simple normative curves of change in anatomy, physiology, or behavior over age to complex experiments factorially varying environmental variables over some range of the life span. Unfortunately, developmental curves may change as a result of variations in an almost infinite number of organismic and environmental factors. Normative curves can, at best, identify age correlations only between organismic and behavioral parameters. Typical manipulative psychological experiments tend to have limited generality because of the often arbitrary and/or artificial environments in which development is assessed. The validity of such studies is often in doubt because they lack any definable relationship to the environmental conditions yielding species-typical change in the specific behaviors or processes being measured.

We next turn to a research plan for studying developmental relationships offered as an alternative to classical psychological methods involving either simple age functions or complex factorial research designs. The purposes of this strategy are (1) to identify actual developmental relationships between process and outcome variables and (2) to assess the degree to which these

Table 1.2. *Potential empirical relationships between process and outcome induction and potential environmental effects on these induction relationships*

Process-outcome relationships	Environmental effects
I. Outcome induction age has a time-lagged dependency on age of process induction.	1. An early normal environment a. Is needed to obtain the normal induction age b. Has a critical period effect for induction c. Inhibits early induction
II. Induction of outcome depends on a critical age for process induction	2. A normal environment at the typical induction age a. Is needed to obtain the normal induction age b. Has a critical period effect for induction c. Has a critical consolidation time before induction can occur
III. Process is necessary for induction of outcome, but not sufficient to determine the exact outcome induction age	3. An atypical early environment a. Produces early induction b. Retards normal induction age
IV. Deviant age of process induction retards age of outcome induction	4. An atypical induction age environment retards the normal induction age
V. An unspecifiable dependency holds between process and outcome	5. Unspecifiable environmental effects
VI. Induction of outcome is not dependent on postulated process; spurious correlation in the normative data; another process determines the outcome	6. Induction does not depend on environment for occurrence; process-outcome continuity is completely independent of environment
VII. The outcome induction age is found deviant in the normative environment; indicates either poor definition of the normal situation, poor control over a replication environment, or measurement inadequacies	

relationships depend on environmental factors, using (3) a minimally complex methodology that has (4) biological validity and the possibility of some degree of generality.

Identifying process-outcome relationships

Our strategy is based on the assumption that it is possible to obtain reliable and valid normative data. To do this, it will be necessary to identify a normative environment or to simulate in a laboratory the features of such an environment known to be important for development of the system under study. For some research problems, this might be the natural environment in which the species to be studied evolved. For other problems, there may be no obvious current natural environment, as with domestic animals, humans, and many nonhuman primate species found in a wide range of ecological and social conditions. In these cases, it will be necessary to define an average expected environment for the population and behaviors of interest. Although this involves a degree of arbitrary choice, the procedure can be systematic and operational.

Suppose that the problem under study is the development of social attachment in humans. Theoretically the measures are expected to index the formation of social bonds between a developing infant and the persons in its environment. Questions of special interest may involve critical or sensitive periods, permanence or reversibility of bonds, unlearned biases, and interrelationships between social attachment and development of cognitive abilities.

The first research step will be to generate an ethogram of developing human infant social and cognitive behaviors. This will provide developmental functions for outcome and process variables known, or postulated, to be relevant for attachment behavior. This step might involve studying literature presenting developmental functions for a variety of environments. If literature is unavailable or insufficient, the ethogram will have to be made as part of the study. The subjects generating the ethogram must come from a population living in an environment known to contain the stimulus conditions necessary for attachment, even though those stimuli may be as yet unknown. At a minimum in the case of human infants, this is certain to be the presence of a mother. Regardless of the particulars of human evolution, it is certain that attachment will occur when babies have mothers. So, the minimal requirement for an average expected environment is that a biological mother or suitable substitute caregiver be present. Depending on the range of generality desired from the normative data, more stringent requirements might include a nuclear family, a particular socioeconomic class, or any other factors known to be present in situations that produce attachment behavior in infants.

Once the ethogram has been made for the well-defined average expected environment, the next step is theoretical. Utilizing prior theory and age-correlated process–outcome relationships from the ethogram, a developmental relationship is postulated between one or more specific processes and one or more specific behavioral outcomes from among those known to occur in the normative data. It makes no sense to study relationships among variables that do not exist in the normative environment or to postulate causal effects of processes that may be idiosyncratic or even nonexistent in nature. We can now experimentally test the postulated relationship.

Normative data generate functions like those in the top panel of Figure 1.7. Any of these four outcomes may be induced by the process variable. The left side of Table 1.2 identifies general relationships that might be found empirically between a process and its postulated outcome(s). (Roman numerals in Figure 1.7 refer to conclusions from the left side of Table 1.2.) Induction relationships must be studied prior to facilitation because facilitation cannot occur before an outcome has been induced.

The four normative outcomes in the top panel all suggest an as yet unspecifiable dependency between process and outcome. The first outcome (dot curve) occurs just prior to process induction and thus seems to indicate no dependency. However, an error in measuring the true process onset time could result in the initial outcome appearance being prior to that for the process. So, such cases might not be dropped from consideration as a possible dependency. Next, we manipulate the process experimentally in the normative situation or find naturally occurring variations in the normative environment.

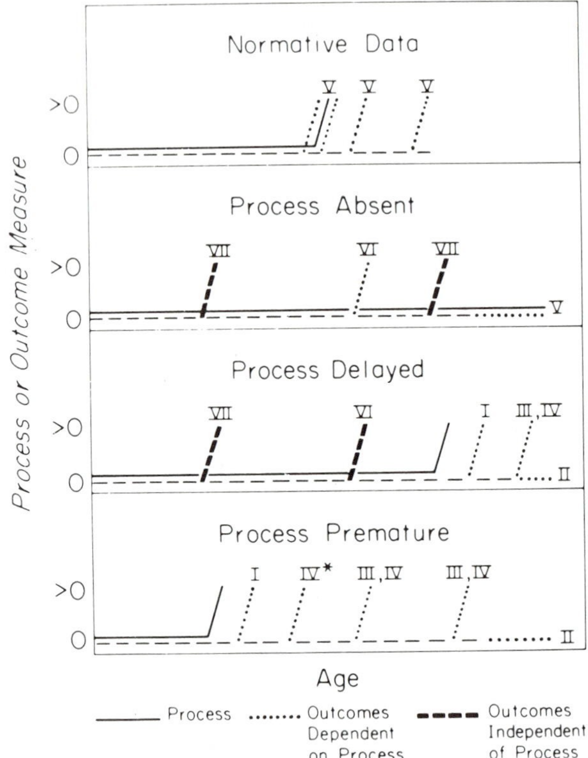

Figure 1.7. A minimal research design for determining causal process–outcome induction relationships. Normative correlative data (top panel) suggest a potential causal relationship between induction of a process and induction of a consequent behavioral outcome. Experiments eliminating the process (panel two from top), delaying process onset (panel three), and producing the process prematurely (bottom panel) are conducted. These yield conclusions about basic process–outcome dependence and about specific types of temporal relationships between process onset and outcome appearance.

First (Figure 1.7, panel 2), the process is removed. Any result other than an outcome induction failure (V) means that the outcome is not dependent on the process (VI) or that we have methodological problems (VII). These may include poor definition of the normative situation, poor control of the replication environment, or measurement unreliability. If result V is obtained, we conclude that outcome induction depends on the prior or concurrent induction of the process.

The second step is to delay the onset of the process. If the outcome occurs normally (VI), we have evidence that outcome induction does not depend on this process. If outcome induction is earlier than normal (VII), we have evidence of both independence and outcome methodological problems. If the process–outcome time lag is the same as in the normative data (I) but is displaced in age, we have evidence for a time-lag dependent relationship with no critical period. If the time lag from process to outcome induction is longer than usual, we may have evidence that retardation of process induction lengthens the time required for subsequent induction of the outcome (IV). Alternatively, process induction may be necessary to get the outcome but may not determine exactly when the outcome will be induced (III). If the outcome fails to occur at all (V), we have evidence that the process must be induced at a critical age for the outcome to appear.

For a complete analysis, we would test what happens if it is possible to induce the process prematurely (Figure 1.7, bottom panel). If we again obtain the normative time delay between process and outcome induction (I), we would have strong evidence for a time-lag dependency. If we again get a retarded time delay (IV), we would have strong evidence that any deviant process induction age produces a constant amount of retardation in time to induce the outcome. If the outcome is even later (III, IV) than in the delayed process condition, there are three possible conclusions. We could have evidence that premature process induction has a greater retardation effect than delayed process induction if result III had occurred in the delayed condition. Premature induction may cause retardation, but delayed induction does not if the result for the delayed condition was I. Or we could have outcome measurement problems. If the outcome is absent (II) and it was also absent in the delayed process condition, we would have strong evidence for a critical period effect of the process induction age.

Testing environmental effects on process–outcome induction

Once we have demonstrated that a process and an outcome are in fact dependent in the normative environment, we can proceed to questions about environmental effects. Table 1.3 gives the basic experimental design for testing environmental effects.

In this scheme, process and outcome induction ages are dependent variables. The independent variable(s) concerns whether the environment, before and during the normal induction age, is typical of or deviant from the normative environment in operationally defined ways. In a minimal experiment the four basic test conditions are (1) typical environment throughout; (2) deviant environment throughout; (3) typical environment early, then deviant environment during the normal induction time; and (4) deviant environment early, then typical environment during the normal induction time. Unless there is a reason to replicate the normative condition, prior normative data will already exist and only three conditions need to be tested.

A number of possible environmental effects are listed on the right side of Table 1.2. The cells in Table 1.3 identify the major implications from any set of actual results. Under conditions that adversely affect the process, we should find abnormal or absent outcome measures. It is also possible that a deviant environment will not alter the process itself but will alter its expression in the outcome being measured – so-called homeotypic discontinuity (Kagan 1978).

Referring to Table 1.3, if the normal situation is replicated (section 1) and process or outcome induction is premature, delayed, or absent, we can

Table 1.3. *Research design for assessing effects of environmental variation on process–outcome induction, and conclusions following from various results*

Environment	Effect on process and/or outcome induction[a]			
	Normal	Premature	Delayed	Absent
Typical before and during normal age for induction	Normative data	Methodological troubles (VII)		
Deviant before and during normal age for induction	6	1c, 3a	5	4
Typical before, deviant during normal induction age	Not 2a, 2b, 2c	Method problems (VII)	4	2b
Deviant before, typical during normal induction age	Not 1a, 1b, or 1c	1c, 3a	2c, 3b	1b

[a]The conclusions in the body of the table are identified with the material in Table 1.2.

conclude that either (1) our previous process–outcome research was faulty or (2) we have methodological problems in measurement or replication of the normative conditions. If the environment is deviant throughout the total period of study (section 2) and the process–outcome relationship is normal, we can conclude that this relationship is independent of the environmental factor studied (6).

If the environment is deviant throughout and the process or outcome appears prematurely, we have evidence for some type of early experience effect. An atypical early environment may produce early induction (3a), or the normal early environment may actually operate to inhibit early induction (1c). For example, monkeys raised in total social isolation during the second 6 months of life exhibit physical aggression at 12 months of age at intensities never seen in like-age socially raised animals. It could be that isolation at this age induces processes underlying aggression earlier than usual. Alternatively, social rearing may inhibit the rate of developing processes underlying aggression. These alternatives can be distinguished only by measuring the process variables underlying aggression.

With a continuously deviant environment, induction might be delayed beyond the normal age or be totally absent. In either case, the deviant environment will have affected induction. However, whether this is an early experience effect or due to deviant stimulation during the induction period is not clear from this result alone. We must then turn to other experimental manipulations.

In one of these further manipulations, the situation is typical early and then deviant during the normal induction age (section 3). If induction occurs normally, we have evidence that experience during induction is not essential for the process–outcome relationship. If induction is premature, even though the environment was typical during the early period, we again have methodological problems. If induction is delayed, we have evidence for a retardation effect of atypical stimulation during the induction period (4). If induction is absent, we can conclude that there is a critical period effect of normal stimulation during the induction period (2b).

In the final manipulation the environment is deviant early, then normal (bottom section). If induction is normal, we can conclude that the process–outcome relationship is independent of early experience. If induction is premature, we again have evidence that either deviant early experience produces early induction (3a) or that a normal early environment inhibits early induction (1c). If induction is delayed, either deviant early experience has retarded the normal induction age or the typical induction environment must be available for some time period actually to obtain induction (2c). The latter result would occur when a critical duration of exposure to the normal environment is required to consolidate effects. Consolidation may involve either inducing the process or allowing a performance factor to be manifest in the outcome measure. If induction does not occur with this manipulation, we would have evidence for a critical period effect of the early experience (1b).

It is, of course, possible to go beyond this minimal experiment, testing a variety of deviations from the normative situation. If one has confidence in the normative data, it should not be necessary to repeat that situation. By testing first for effects of a deviant condition throughout the period of interest, many potential determinants of this process–outcome relationship can be ruled out. The important difference between this and more conventional designs is that all comparisons are made with respect to known and well-defined standards for normal development. In this sense, each experiment is a single degree of freedom test involving a planned comparison of a treatment against a norm. The design can also be used to vary the exact age at which deviant stimulation is instituted or withdrawn. Varying the age will pinpoint more closely critical or sensitive periods that have been identified roughly by the minimal experimental design.

TESTING ENVIRONMENTAL EFFECTS ON PROCESS–OUTCOME FACILITATION AND MAINTENANCE

We now turn to that set of problems that constitute the majority of experiments in behavior development research – process–outcome relationships during facilitation and maintenance of a developmental function. Table 1.4 presents our efforts at identifying a minimal research plan for such studies.

There are four types of process–outcome relationships of interest during facilitation and maintenance of a developmental function. These are (1) complete process–outcome continuity, (2) discontinuity of outcome, (3) discontinuity of both process and outcome, and (4) discontinuity of process with normal outcome. The fourth possibility, if not due to methodological problems, is a situation of functional autonomy in which a new process takes

Table 1.4. *Research design for assessing the effects of environmental variation on process–outcome facilitation or maintenance relationships, and conclusions from potential experimental results*

Type of environmental variation		Experimental results	
Facilitation or maintenance	Preinduction	Continuity: normal process and outcome	Discontinuity: deviant outcome or process and outcome
Typical facilitation and maintenance	Typical	Normative data	Methodological problems
	Deviant	No effect of early environment	Effect of early environment
Deviant facilitation and maintenance	Typical	No effect of facilitation or maintenance environments	Effect of facilitation and/or maintenance environment
	Deviant	Complete environmental independence	Effect of early facilitation and/or maintenance environment
Typical facilitation, deviant maintenance	Typical	No effect of maintenance environment	Effect of maintenance environment
	Deviant	No effect of early or maintenance environment	Effect of early and/or maintenance environment
Deviant facilitation, typical or therapeutic maintenance	Typical	No effect of facilitation environment	Irreversible effect of facilitation environment
	Deviant	No effect of early or facilitation environment	Irreversible effect of early and/or facilitation environment

over from the one originally controlling the outcome behavior. Rather than being a bad result, this possibility simply underscores the organismic view that change is a complex phenomenon. The task now is to identify the new process and determine if its induction or facilitation depends on the prior occurrence of the original process. This task relates to the important, if not overriding, issue of equifinality of behavioral outcomes and self-stabilization of temporarily deviant developmental pathways. *Equifinality* refers to the idea that the same endpoint can be reached by a large number of different routes. *Self-stabilization* refers to the idea that development for each individual is canalized along a particular route to an endpoint that can tolerate a number of temporary perturbations from its main channel. These problems are complex ones beyond the scope of this chapter. However, they must be empirically solvable if an organismic approach is actually to explain the development of behavioral systems. The following research plan attempts to provide a practical experimental strategy for studying the way in which process, outcome, and environment do or do not interact in the development of particular behavioral systems. The design is the final sequential step in the experimental series of identifying actual process–outcome induction relationships, then determining the degree to which these relationships depend on environmental factors.

Variations from the normative environment are imposed either before the process-outcome induction ("Preinduction" column) or during the normal period for facilitation and/or maintenance ("Type of Environmental Variation"). Each deviant environment is studied with respect to the normative situation for deviant outcomes, processes, or both. If the process variable is affected but the outcome is not (situation not described in Table 1.4), a search for the new process variable associated with the still normal outcome will have to be made.

In the top section of Table 1.4, both facilitation and maintenance occur in the normative environment. In the upper row, the preinduction environment is also normal; this represents a replication of normative development. If normative development does not occur, there is strong evidence for methodological problems. In the lower row of this section, the preinduction environment is deviant. If normal facilitation and maintenance are found in both rows, we have evidence that the early environment did not affect later development. If a discontinuity occurs (deviant results in the row 2 experiment), we have evidence that the early environment is important for the course of later development.

In section 2 of Table 1.4, deviant facilitation and maintenance environments follow either typical or deviant preinduction environments. If discontinuities result, we have evidence for environmental effects but may not be able to localize accurately their developmental period to the early, facilitation, or maintenance environments. If the discontinuity occurs during facilitation and the preinduction environment was typical, then the environment during facilitation is important. If the discontinuity occurs during maintenance, the exact period for environmental effects is unclear. If all three developmental periods have a deviant environment yet continuity is still found, we have strong evidence that the process–outcome relationship is independent of the environmental factor under study. This result will allow us to stop the experiment, as we need to know nothing more about this source of environmental variation. If the first two studies (sections 1 and 2 of Table 1.4) have not clearly identified the existence and locus of an environmental effect or if we are concerned with long-term irreversibility issues, we turn to the bottom two sections of Table 1.4.

The experiments called for in section 3 study variations of the maintenance environment. The first row determines whether a deviant maintenance environment disrupts a normal developmental process. The second row can determine (1) that neither the early nor maintenance environment affects the process–outcome relationship or (2) that one or the other of these periods has effects. The exact interpretation depends on the result found when the early environment is deviant but the facilitation and maintenance environments are normal.

The experiments in section 4 study deviant facilitation environments in combination with normal or deviant early environments, and irreversibility of effects from these sources. To determine the precise locus of effects, it may be necessary to compare the results of deviant facilitation and early environment with those obtained when only the early environment is deviant (section 1, row 1). To study irreversibility (i.e., continuity) following a deviant effect, the normative environment or environments with attributes postulated to be therapeutic would be instituted during the maintenance period.

LONGITUDINAL EXPERIMENTATION

Our basic research model, its theoretical orientation, and various caveats concerning normative data collection have now been described. We stressed the fact that developmental research must, by its nature, involve longitudinal research designs. Continuity implies stability of process, outcome, and/or environment over some span of the lifetime. To study stability, measures must be obtained on different occasions. Given our research model, a complete developmental study must collect data at a minimum of four longitudinal time points: (1) before normal process induction, (2) during normal induction, (3) during normal facilitation, and (4) during normal maintenance. Developmental relationships will thus be thoroughly explored in proportion to the number of longitudinally sampled time points. Unfortunately, cost, effort, and contamination of the variables being studied by the measurement technique itself may increase as frequency of repeated sampling increases. These and other important issues involving longitudinal study are discussed by Wohlwill (1973). Another important source of information can be found in a number of papers by Schaie (e.g., 1965) and by Baltes (e.g., 1968). These should certainly be studied before attempting to utilize our proposed research model.

SUMMARY

In this chapter we have attempted to present both a theoretical and empirical perspective for studying changes in behavioral systems during individual ontogeny. From our perspective, understanding any developmental relationship requires an organismic approach that is focused on processes as well as outcomes. The organismic approach also requires an understanding of the environmental substrate for any functioning structure. This environment can range from internal and external events at the time of conception to the social conditions of the postnatal individual.

Unfortunately, correlation statistics measuring individual stability over time comprise most of our information concerning behavioral developmental relationships. High temporal correlation values, revealing stable individual differences, are assumed to reflect continuity in outcome and/or process. Lack of correlation is assumed to indicate a discontinuity in process or outcome. Environmental continuity is almost never assessed in this research. Rather than outcome or process discontinuity, low temporal correlations on measures such as IQ or personality traits may actually reflect the fact that the environment has changed. This change can either (1) actually alter the process or outcome in a fundamental way or (2) simply offer opportunities for new behavior patterns to occur without actually changing the process. Our view, untested to date as far as we can discover, is that continuity defined as stability will often be found when the environment does not change in any important features. Discontinuity, defined as instability, is likely to occur when important environmental factors are added to or subtracted from the developmental setting. The logic of our analysis, like the study of behavioral development itself, is complex. We offer this theory and research strategy as a beginning for studying causality in behavioral development. We know that the difficulties in identifying real as opposed to hypothetical process variables are many, and it is difficult actually to measure environments. However, we believe that such variables can and must be studied before significant progress can be made in understanding the fundamentals of behavioral development.

ACKNOWLEDGMENTS

The authors express their deepest thanks to the Center for Interdisciplinary Research for providing the unique opportunity to think about the issues dealt with in this chapter and the many other important developmental problems discussed during the tenure of the conference. We thank especially Dr. Klaus Immelmann for his leadership, warm hospitality, and personal friendship; Dr. Sverre Sjölander for his excellent humor, good sense, and organizational talent; and the administrative staff of the Center, who made our stay in Bielefeld trouble-free, enjoyable, and professionally worthwhile.

REFERENCES

Baltes, P. 1968. Longitudinal and cross-sectional sequences in the study of age and generation effects. *Human Development* 11:145–171.

Bateson, P. P. G. 1978. How does behavior develop? *In:* P. P. G. Bateson & P. Klopfer (eds.), *Perspectives in ethology,* vol. 3, Plenum Press, New York,

Block, J., & J. H. Block. 1973. *Ego development and the provenance of thought: a longitudinal study of ego and cognitive development in young children.* Progress report, National Institutes of Health, grant MH 16080.

Cairns, R. B. 1966. Development, maintenance, and extinction of social attachment behavior in sheep. *Journal of Comparative and Physiological Psychology* 66: 298–306.

1977. Beyond social attachment: the dynamics of interactional development. *In:* T. Alloway, P. Pliner, & L. Krames (eds.), *Attachment behavior.* Plenum Press, New York.

Charlesworth, W. R. 1978. Ethology: its relevance for observational studies of human adaptation. *In:* G. P. Sackett (ed.), *Observing behavior,* vol. 1, *Theory and applications in mental retardation.* University Park Press, Baltimore.

Clarke, A. M., & A. D. Clarke. 1977. *Early experience: myth and evidence.* Free Press, New York.

Coombs, C. H., & J. E. Smith. 1973. On the detection of structure in attitudes and developmental processes. *Psychological Review* 80:344–358.

Dawkins, R. 1976. Hierarchical organization: a candidate principle for ethology. *In:* P. P. G. Bateson & R. Hinde (eds.), *Growing points in ethology.* Cambridge University Press, Cambridge.

Emmerich, W. 1964. Continuity and stability in early social development. *Child Development* 35:311–332.

Gottlieb, G. 1976a. Conceptions of prenatal development: behavioral embryology. *Psychological Review* 83:215–234.

1976b. The roles of experience in the development of behavior and the nervous system. *In:* G. Gottlieb (ed.), *Neural and behavioral specificity.* Academic Press, New York.

Gottman, J. M. 1973. N-of-one and N-of-two research in psychotherapy. *Psychological Bulletin* 80:93–105.

Immelmann, K. 1975. The evolutionary significance of early experience. *In:* G. Baerends, C. Beer & A. Manning (eds.), *Function and evolution in behavior.* Clarendon Press, Oxford.

Kagan, J. 1978. Continuity and stages in human development. *In:* P. P. G. Bateson & P. K. Klopfer (eds.), *Perspective in ethology,* vol. 3, Plenum Press, New York.

Kagan, J., & H. A. Moss. 1963. Personality and social development: family and peer influences. *Review of Educational Research* 31:463–474.

King, J. A. 1958. Parameters relevant to determining the effects of early experience upon the adult behavior of animals. *Psychological Bulletin* 55:46–58.

Kuo, Z. Y. 1976. *The dynamics of behavior development.* Plenum Press, New York.

Lorenz, K. 1965. *Evolution and modification of behavior.* University of Chicago Press, Chicago.

Markert, C. L., & R. M. Petters. 1978. Manufactured hexaparental mice show that adults are derived from three embryonic cells. *Science* 202:56–59.

McCall, R. B. 1977. Challenges to a science of developmental psychology. *Child Development* 48:333–344.

McCall, R. B., D. H. Eichorn & P. S. Hogarth. 1977. Transitions in early mental development. *Monographs of the Society for Research in Child Development* 42:1–108.

Overton, W. F., & H. W. Reese. 1973. Models of development: methodological implications. *In:* J. R. Nesselroade & H. W. Reese (eds.), *Lifespan developmental psychology: methodological issues.* Academic Press, New York.

Pattee, H. H. 1973. *Hierarchy theory: the challenge of complex systems.* Braziller, New York.

Piaget, J. 1950. *The psychology of intelligence.* Harcourt, New York.

1960. *The child's conception of the world.* Littlefield-Adams, Paterson, New Jersey.

Reese, H. W., & W. F. Overton. 1970. Models of development and theories of development. *In:* L. R. Goulet & P. B. Baltes (eds.), *Life-span developmental psychology: research and theory.* Academic Press, New York.
Resko, J. A. 1970. Androgen secretion by the fetal and neonatal rhesus monkey. *Endocrinology* 87:680–687.
Reyes, J. A., R. S. Boroditsky, J. S. D. Winter & G. Faiman. 1974. Studies on human sexual development. 2. Fetal and maternal serum gonadotropin and sex steroid concentrations. *Journal of Clinical Endocrinology and Metabolism* 38:612–620.
Sameroff, A. J. 1975. Early influences on development: fact or fancy. *Merrill-Palmer Quarterly* 21:267–294.
Schaie, K. W. 1965. A general model for the study of developmental problems. *Psychological Bulletin* 64:92–107.
Schneirla, T. C. 1966. Aspects of stimulation and organization in approach/withdrawal processes underlying vertebrate behavioral development. *Advances in the Study of Behavior* 1:1–74.
Sedlacek, J. 1974. Developmental fetal and perinatal changes of cerebral cortex in guinea pigs. *Czech Journal of Physiology* 6:501–517.
Seligman, M. 1970. On the generality of the laws of learning. *Psychological Review* 77:406–418.
Solomon, R. L. & M. S. Lessac. 1968. A control group design for experimental studies of developmental processes. *Psychological Bulletin* 70:145–150.
Steptoe, P. C. & R. G. Edwards. 1978. Birth after the reimplantation of a human embryo. *Lancet* 2:366.
Suomi, S. J. 1977. Development of attachment and other social behaviors in rhesus monkeys. *In:* T. Alloway, P. Pliner & L. Krames (eds.), *Attachment behavior.* Plenum Press, New York.
Tinbergen, N. 1951. *The study of instinct.* Oxford University Press, London.
Waddington, C. H. 1966. Fields and gradients. *In:* M. Lock (ed.), *Major problems in developmental biology.* Academic Press, New York.
Werner, H. 1948. *Comparative psychology of mental development.* Follett, Chicago.
Wohlwill, J. 1973. *The study of behavioral development.* Academic Press, New York.

2

CONCEPTUAL STRATEGIES IN BEHAVIORAL DEVELOPMENT: NORMAL DEVELOPMENT AND PLASTICITY

DAVID B. MILLER

A persistent problem in the study of behavioral development is the extent to which data obtained via experimental manipulations elucidate the normal course of development in the species under scrutiny. Experimentation, in both laboratory and field, dictates that an organism be subjected to conditions that are quantitatively or qualitatively different from those it would usually encounter in the absence of such interference. Although relatively unobtrusive observations and descriptions of ongoing behaviors of organisms in a variety of naturalistic, species-typical contexts provide a necessary anchor for comparison with laboratory studies (Miller 1977a), a firm understanding of the causative and functional aspects of behavioral ontogeny necessitates an experimental approach whereby certain variables are held relatively constant while others are systematically varied.

Lehrman aptly explicates the importance of experimental interference in understanding normal development:

> I am not convinced that a biologist interested in understanding *development* is obligated to recoil from any treatment that disturbs . . . the living organism. Indeed, a very good case can be made for the proposition that it is precisely by interfering with normal development and noting in what way the resulting abnormalities develop that we gain the most illuminating insights into the normal processes of development.
> [Lehrman 1970:39]

In partial agreement with a criticism by Lorenz (1965) of certain experimental approaches to the study of behavior, Lehrman hastens to add that "experimental treatments cannot be selected at random; they must be chosen with some intuitive feeling for their relevance to the normal phenomenon, the development of which we wish to understand" (1970:39).

This concern was echoed by McCall (1977), who distinguished between "can" and "does" questions in experimental approaches to behavioral development. According to McCall, developmental psychology has preferred to ask the question, Under certain circumstances, can factor X produce behavior Y? (e.g., can infants learn a response by operant conditioning?). The question that has largely been neglected is, Under typical natural circumstances, does factor X produce behavior Y? (e.g., do infants learn by operant conditioning in conventional family environments?).

The distinction between, and potential interrelationship of, these "can" and "does" questions are central to the thesis of the present chapter. What I shall advocate is a conceptual framework for the practice of studying species-typical behavior under species-atypical conditions.

The extent of deviation associated with experimentation can limit the interpretation of the behavioral outcomes that are measured. As a safeguard against overgeneralizing the fruits of our experimental labors, it may be useful to consider the experimental study of behavioral development in the framework of two basic conceptual strategies. One strategy focuses on elucidating the course of normal behavioral development for a given species (i.e., what does the animal do?). The other strategy involves assessing a kind of plasticity by examining the extent to which behavioral development can be modified beyond (or assessed outside) the range of species-typical variability (i.e., what can the animal do?).

DEFINITIONS

Before explaining these two strategies and showing how they can be interrelated, several typically ambiguous terms should be defined in the hope of avoiding needless semantic controversy.

Normality

The concept of *normality* can best be defined in terms of a normative statistical approach incorporating ethological description within an ecological framework. Normality is a context-specific construct in the sense that what an animal will typically do depends on its physical surroundings (including social relationships) as well as on its internal state (e.g., hormonal factors, hunger level) and the species-typical neuroanatomical and neurophysiological mechanisms that constrain how it perceives and acts on its environment. Thus, an appreciation of normality as an ecologically valid construct involves tedious observation and description of behavior patterns and stimulus conditions across a wide range of contexts throughout the animal's life span (Bronfenbrenner 1977; Kuo 1976). Moreover, it is particularly important to avoid a purely anthropocentric approach to normative investigations (e.g., Dethier 1978). For example, numerous studies reveal that some nonhuman organisms respond to stimuli beyond the range of normal human sensitivity (e.g., infrasound, Yodlowski et al. 1977; ultrasound, Sales & Pye 1974; geomagnetism and other orientational cues, summarized by Emlen 1975 and Keeton 1974).

An important consideration defining normality is that there are two major classes of factors encompassed by normative description. One class consists of motor output, or species-typical behavior patterns. This class includes the range of modal action patterns (Barlow 1968, 1977) that an animal performs (e.g., display behavior, vocalizations) as well as reflexes and responses to normally occurring environmental stimuli (e.g., comfort movements, proximity-maintaining behavior, feeding). In addition to describing what an animal typically does, normative description must address a second class of factors pertaining to the actual environmental conditions under which the behaviors are emitted. This class includes not only a description of ecological factors (e.g., weather, types of physical objects comprising the biotope) but also a description of species-typical stimuli, including the particular aspects provided by other individuals (conspecifics as well as potential predators and prey) that may influence an organism's behavior. As I shall discuss later, knowledge and application of species-typical stimuli are at the crux of the problem of understanding the extent to which experimental manipulation elucidates normal behavioral development.

Taking the above factors into account, I propose a definition of *normality* by applying the term to stimuli that are usually or potentially encountered and behavioral acts that are usually emitted by an organism in specific contexts throughout development in its species-typical (i.e., unrestrained, self-selected) habitat. I use the term usually in a normative statistical sense to encompass what is modal for the species, as well as the range of variability about the mode (Barlow 1968, 1977).

The concept of normality thusly defined is not necessarily synonymous with nonexperientially influenced (i.e., strictly genetically determined) phenomena. Behaviors that are supposedly instinctive, species-typical, modal, and normal are very often the products of varying degrees of experience (Gottlieb 1976a; see "Plasticity").

Natural environment

In accord with the above definition of normality, the impetus for such developmental investigations is derived from behavioral adaptations occurring in the natural environment. However, the concept of natural environment is not always easy to characterize (see also Tunnell 1977). As I have discussed elsewhere (Miller 1977a), the term naturalistic does not have an absolute meaning but rather is descriptive of relative environmental conditions. These conditions can differ radically from one species to the next in the sense that the same physical environment that is natural for one species may be unnatural for another – a caveat dating back to von Uexküll's (1934) *Umwelt* concept. Thus, the natural environment must be defined with regard to the particular species under study. For the present purpose, I denote a natural environment as a habitat in which the species is usually found, one that is self-selected by the species and therefore relatively unrestrained and conducive for reproduction and rearing young.

One problem with this definition is that it would appear to complicate the study of behavioral development in domestic breeds, the natural environments of which are man-made, restrained, and not self-selected (though it should be recognized that certain wild species do select man-made environments, as, for example, in nest site selection by such bird species as chimney swifts and barn swallows). For investigators interested in studying the development of the behavior of domestic animals, I would advocate, if possible, first collecting naturalistic baseline data on the wild progenitor of the domestic breed (e.g., Collias & Collias 1967; Dewsbury 1975; Miller 1977a, 1978; Miller & Gottlieb 1978; Rood 1972); second, studying the behavior of the domestic breed in the habitat of the wild progenitor or in a seminatural habitat that closely approximates the natural habitat – a procedure often called *feralization* (e.g., Boice 1977; King 1956; Miller 1977c; McBride et al. 1969); and third, comparing behavioral development of domestic breeds in a species-typical habitat with the development of their behavior in the artificial environment. Because domestic animals are often fairly well adapted to (i.e., will reproduce and rear young within) their artificial environments, such an environment may be construed as normal for the breed (though not normal for the species). It is conceivable that some domestic animals may be so dependent on human care that they would not survive if returned to the species-typical environment. Because feralization may not always succeed, one should (whenever possible) collect data on the wild progenitor to assess the extent to which the intense artificial selection attendant to domestication may or may not have affected species-typical behavior patterns and/or perceptual capabilities.

A final complication with regard to the definition of *natural environment* concerns those particular species that occupy such a wide range of qualitatively different types of habitats that an attempt to define natural is bound to be meaningless. Such is the case, for example, with respect to certain primates (e.g., man and the rhesus monkey), rodents (e.g., the Norway rat), and birds (e.g., feral pigeons). In cases such as these, one has the option of either evaluating behavior in the environment most closely approximating that in which the species evolved (as opposed to those in which it is presently evolving due to man's alteration of habitats) or sampling behavior in the different conditions in which the animals are found contemporarily to assess the extent to which varying ecological demands influence behavioral development. It may be reasonable to expect that many features of behavioral development in a given species, such as parent–offspring interaction, may be fairly constant across a wide range of habitats frequented by the species, though this is not necessarily true with regard to certain species, as evinced by cross-cultural studies of humans (Leiderman et al. 1977). However, making such an assumption in the absence of data can be risky (see, for example, Curtin & Dolhinow 1978), and ultimately the presumed similarity of behavior across habitats requires observational validation. The particular approach one takes will depend upon the question one is asking.

Plasticity

Plasticity is synonymous with *modifiability* and refers to the extent to which a behavior can be changed with regard to a normative reference point. It is important to recognize that the concept of plasticity represents different forms of modifiability that vary along a continuum with respect to the extent to which a particular behavior pattern or perceptual capability lies within or beyond the range of species-typical variability.

At one end of the continuum, plasticity denotes the extent of adaptability occurring within the range of normal variability for the species. This kind of plasticity is absolutely consistent with the concept of normal development inasmuch as a certain degree of plasticity is essential for survival.

The other end of the continuum represents the kind of plasticity that I address throughout the present chapter. Such plasticity encompasses the extent to which behavior can be modified beyond or outside the range of normal variability for the species. Certain environmental contingencies can exert an inductive effect on species-typical behavioral development (Gottlieb 1976a), as well as on species-atypical development, by tapping into the range of behavioral potentials that an organism has but that typically do not occur in the absence of the particular experience. This form of plasticity, or *inductive malleability*, typically is manifest only in the realm of experimental manipulation, whereas the former kind of plasticity occurs contemporarily in nature as well as in the realm of experimentation.

Plasticity is a multidimensional concept. The particular continuum described above is only one of many possible ways of distinguishing different forms of plasticity. Other writers have discussed plasticity along other dimensions (e.g., evolutionary or phylogenetic, genetic, and histogenetic plasticity – de Beer 1958; morphological and physiological plasticity – Bradshaw 1965; structural–functional and social plasticity – Kuo 1976; general plasticity and special sensitivity – Callaway 1970, Mason 1979). The present formulation of plasticity is offered only to help clarify the theme of this chapter and should not be regarded as an inclusive representation of this highly dynamic concept.

MODES OF DEVELOPMENTAL ANALYSIS

Within the framework of the conceptual strategies posited in this chapter, naturalistic observation (to whatever extent possible) is an essential component in ultimately understanding the extent to which experimental manipulation elucidates normal aspects of behavioral development. The approach most characteristic of the ethological tradition has been to begin a particular study by observing and describing ongoing behavior in the field for the subsequent purposes of (1) generating hypotheses that are amenable to experimental validation and (2) providing baseline data with which to compare and evaluate data obtained via experimentation. However, one can also obtain normative baseline data after having engaged in experimentation for the purpose of validating the previously obtained experimental findings (Miller 1977a).

Once having charted the course of normal development of a particular behavior pattern vis-à-vis the observational–descriptive approach discussed above, one can proceed to identify experimentally the environmental factors that functionally contribute to the development of the behavior under scrutiny. There are five basic types of manipulations to which an organism can be subjected in the course of the experimental analysis of behavioral development (cf. Gottlieb 1977). The first type is *experiential attenuation*, in which the organism is for some specified period of time prevented from perceiving normally occurring, modality-specific stimuli and/or prevented from engaging in normally occurring motor activity. This type of manipulation is, in essence, the same as the deprivation experiment. I find the term experiential attenuation semantically more acceptable than deprivation or isolation because the latter terms often imply more than what is actually the case. Recent studies on intermodality experiential effects (see the brief overview by Tees 1976) as well as self-stimulation effects (e.g., Gottlieb 1971; Vidal 1975) offer compelling evidence that experience is considerably easier to attenuate than to eliminate.

The second type of manipulation, *experiential transposition*, involves rearranging normally occurring stimuli without directly attenuating any of the component elements. This technique, which has been relatively neglected, has been fruitfully applied to the study of bird migration and orientation. Perhaps the best example of this method comes from Emlen's (1969, 1970) studies of experiential influences on stellar orientation in indigo buntings. By attenuating their early experience of star patterns via indoor rearing, Emlen initially found that stars provide an important orientational cue for these nocturnal migrants. Birds reared indoors failed to orient correctly upon their first exposure to a night sky. Using a form of experiential transposition, Emlen proceeded to identify the particular aspect of the night sky that influences correct orientation. He reared birds under a planetarium sky that rotated about Betelgeuse rather than Polaris (the North Star) and found that these birds subsequently oriented as if they regarded Betelgeuse as the North Star. Thus, the presence of an axis of rotation of the night sky during development has a profound influence on stellar orientation in this species, as evinced by a combination of the methods of experiential attenuation and transposition.

The third type of experimental manipulation is *experiential enhancement*, in which the organism is subjected to more stimulation than it would normally encounter. Experiential enhancement involves administering more of the normally occurring stimulation than would usually be encountered, as, for example, by artificially incubating chicken eggs for varying periods of illumination and subsequently assessing the time of hatching. Such a manipulation tends to accelerate hatching time (Adam & Dimond 1971; Lauber & Shutze 1964). Enhancement can also involve stimuli that are different from those that would normally be encountered (although there are bound to be similarities along certain stimulus dimensions). For example, Capretta et al. (1975) found that rats come to accept novel flavors as a function of early exposure to a variety of different flavors that, in this particular experiment, were more or less species-atypical.

The fourth type of manipulation is *experiential substitution*, according to which normally occurring stimulation is denied and replaced by a different form of stimulation. This type of manipulation is best illustrated by the experimental study of imprinting, in which animals are exposed to maternal surrogates at an early age and their preferences for these surrogates are later assessed with regard to either filial attachment or sexual preference. The work of Harlow and his associates (e.g., Harlow et al. 1971) employing cloth surrogate mothers for rhesus monkey infants also illustrates this approach, as does the cross-fostering approach of Mason and Kenney (1974), who used dogs as rearing partners for rhesus infants. An interesting example of substitution in the realm of human development comes from the practice by some hospitals of simulating features of the intrauterine environment for preterm infants. Kramer and Pierpont (1976) found that preterm infants placed on rocking waterbeds and exposed to auditory stimuli (i.e., a woman's voice and a simulated heartbeat) exhibited better growth than did nonexposed controls.

The final type of manipulation is what Gottlieb (1977) refers to as *displacement* - a relatively specific technique involving a temporal shift of developmental events for the purpose of delineating sensitive phases in ontogeny (see Chap. 14). Another facet of the displacement procedure involves the rectification of deficits incurred via experiential attenuation by rehabilitative therapy at later ages. For example, McKay et al. (1978) reported that chronically undernourished children show improved cognitive ability as a function of nutritional, health, and educational treatments between 3.5 and 7 years of age and that the extent of subsequent improvement is positively correlated with the duration of the therapy within this period. Another example of this displacement procedure comes from the work of Suomi et al. (1974), who found that exposure to conspecifics ("therapist" monkeys) subsequent to isolation rearing can rectify deficits in the social behavior of rhesus monkeys. Thus, temporally displacing the exposure to normally occurring stimuli can, to varying degrees, ameliorate the effects of prior experiential attenuation.

These categories of manipulations provide a framework within which most experimental investigations of behavioral development can be placed. However, they should not be taken to represent rigid categories of mutually exclusive research strategies, for components characteristic of a particular category can overlap with those of another (e.g., substitution implies attenuation of a particular form of experience; attenuation of some stimuli may tend to enhance the extent to which an animal will attend to nonattenuated stimuli). The categories should be considered as somewhat overlapping, especially because it is often *post facto* of a manipulation that we have a handle on the nature of the relevant versus irrelevant (or less relevant) experience of which a particular behavior is a function (see also Bateson 1976).

NORMAL DEVELOPMENT

The experimental study of normal behavioral development involves manipulating certain environmental variables that fall within the range of variability characteristic of a species to ascertain the extent to which such variables influence the course of development. Thus, to embark on such an investigation necessitates some knowledge about what is typical for the species. This ultimately leads us back to the importance of having normative baseline data sampled across several environments (McCall 1977; Miller 1977a).

Aspects of normal development can be experimentally elucidated in the laboratory; one need not necessarily do experiments in the field. What one does to an organism is probably more important than where one does it (although for certain types of problems the latter can also be quite important, especially when working with species that do not adapt well to laboratory environments). In order experimentally to control variables that are believed to influence subsequent behavioral development, some degree of captivity is usually essential. One should be aware, however, that the combined effects of experimental manipulation and artificial environmental rearing and testing can interact to influence functionally behavioral outcomes that deviate from the norm. Thus, if one is interested in studying normal development, the rearing and testing conditions should be as naturalistic as possible (see also the discussion by Suomi & Harlow 1977 on maintaining animals in adequate laboratory environments). Providing animals with biologically relevant stimuli in a captive environment can often reveal modal aspects of a species's repertoire that would otherwise be obscured (e.g., Pinel & Treit 1978). In addition to the usual considerations of temperature, light/dark cycle, and dietary requirements, other physical and social conditions should be considered to the extent that they are not involved in the actual manipulation (e.g., cage size, group versus individual rearing). (Although these considerations may seem obvious to most investigators, it is equally obvious to referees of journal articles and grant proposals that such factors are not always keenly appreciated by many researchers. The ever-increasing literature on biological constraints on learning is, it is to be hoped, fostering a better appreciation of what might otherwise seem to be apparent.)

Most often, the manipulation employed in the study of normal development is experiential attenuation – depriving the animal of some form of normally occurring experience in early development and later assessing the behavioral outcome. If a particular type of normally occurring experience is attenuated under otherwise adequate rearing conditions and the developing organism later fails to develop a species-typical behavior at the appropriate time, it is generally safe to conclude that the attenuated experience plays a role, either directly or indirectly, in normal behavioral development (albeit the role may be of either a general or specific nature, as discussed by Bateson 1976). Experience can have several types of effects on behavioral development. At the weakest level, experience can maintain ongoing developmental states or particular endpoints; at a moderate level, experience can have a facilitative effect by quantitatively or temporally influencing the course of development; at the strongest level, experience can induce or determine whether or not a given species-typical neural feature or behavioral activity will manifest itself later on in development (Gottlieb 1976a; see also Chap. 1).

For purposes of illustration, I shall briefly discuss two different programs of experimental research that typify the conceptual strategy of elucidating factors of normal behavioral development. The first comes from the literature on bird song ontogeny (see also Chap. 20). A number of experimental tactics have been employed on a diverse range of species to gain an understanding of the species-typical parameters influencing the development of normal adult vocalizations. Most of these investigations are firmly rooted in the field in terms of having assessed the range of variation typical of normal adult song. This has provided a normative data base against which to compare the songs of birds whose early experiences have been altered in some way. The most typical experiential manipulations have been isolation rearing (to determine if the developing bird must have access to an external adult model), isolation combined with tutoring (to determine the characteristics of a vocal model that are important in normal song development), deafening (to eliminate and assess the role of auditory feedback), and rearing in loud white noise (a partially reversible procedure that greatly attenuates auditory feedback in early life but permits feedback while singing as an adult upon termination of the white noise).

The effects of such manipulations vary considerably depending on the species under scrutiny, even among closely related species (see reviews by

Marler 1975, 1976; Marler & Mundinger 1971; Nottebohm 1970). An extensive review of the findings of such studies is well beyond the scope and nature of the present chapter. Suffice it to say that the experiential attenuation of normally occurring stimuli (i.e., lack of external model and/or auditory feedback) has profound effects on normal vocal development in some species and little or no effects in other species, and that the extent to which such effects are present may have implications pertaining to the evolution of this form of communicative behavior (Nottebohm 1970), as well as the evolution of developmental strategies vis-à-vis constraints on learning (Marler 1975). In some species, young males must be able to hear their own voice and an external conspecific model to develop normal adult song; other species need only hear their own voices with no external model; still others develop normal species-typical vocalizations without having heard themselves or an external model. Perhaps even more remarkable is the fact that some species (e.g., the Arizona junco) can develop normal adult song provided they have general social stimulation only from agemates (as opposed to adult models) (Marler 1975), and other species (e.g., the bullfinch and zebra finch) rely on a social bond with the father (i.e., the bird that fed them in the nestling and fledgling stages) (Immelmann 1969; Nicolai 1959). Thus, with the exception of those birds that develop normal adult vocalizations without having obviously profited from self-produced or externally administered auditory stimulation or from social relationships with conspecifics (e.g., chickens and doves), some form of normally occurring stimulation has been experimentally identified as playing a significant role in the ontogeny of these vocal motor patterns. The vocalizations of those species that appear to develop in the absence of relevant experience still pose an intriguing developmental problem that may best be handled via comparative-developmental auditory neuroanatomical and physiological investigations.

The other example of normal development pertains to the development of perceptual preferences (as opposed to motor output) extending into the embryonic period. Naturalistic observation of early parent–offspring interactions in waterfowl, primarily wood ducks and mallard ducks, has revealed that the female utters a species-typical maternal call while incubating her eggs and brooding her young (Gottlieb 1963a, 1963b, 1965; Miller & Gottlieb 1976, 1978) and that this vocalization is virtually identical (with only some quantitative differences) to the call that she utters while calling the young off the nest a day or two after hatching (see especially Miller & Gottlieb 1978). These maternal vocalizations promote approach and/or following on the part of the young in nature. Laboratory tests with recordings of these vocalizations (summarized by Gottlieb 1971) have revealed that maternally naive (i.e., incubator-hatched) ducklings are selectively attracted to the maternal call of their species in advance of exposure to the call and that (in the case of domestic mallards) this fine tuning is manifest prior to hatching. (Such postnatal preferences for conspecific vocalizations have been found in a number of precocial avian species, such as ring-billed gulls [Evans 1973], domestic chickens [Gottlieb 1971], bobwhite quail [Heaton et al. 1978], and ring-necked pheasants [Heinz 1973].) Additional laboratory experiments on domestic mallard ducklings (summarized in Gottlieb 1971) have revealed that certain normally occurring species-typical stimulation (i.e., the ducklings' own embryonic and neonatal vocalizations) greatly influences the ontogeny of the auditory preference. Moreover, recent experiments (Gottlieb 1976b, 1978) have elucidated the nature of the acoustic self-stimulation that influences the perceptual preference for conspecific auditory stimuli at certain ages (i.e., repetition rate and dominant frequency). Postnatal laboratory experiments with maternally naive wood ducklings also suggest the importance of self-produced auditory stimulation on the development of a preference for conspecific maternal vocalizations (Gottlieb 1974).

By employing the tactic of experiential attenuation, the above studies on the ontogeny of bird song and the development of species identification have demonstrated how experimental manipulation, within the framework of a firm naturalistic background, has elucidated the course of species-typical behavioral development as a function of the perception of normally occurring stimuli in early life. Studies involving experiential transposition, though few in number, can also directly assess normal behavioral development, as in the previously cited investigations by Emlen (1969, 1970) on stellar orientation. However, it is conceivable that such a manipulation, if carried to an extreme, may demonstrate plasticity more than normality depending on the exact nature of the transposition.

A similar precaution must be raised with regard to the displacement procedure. Although sensitive phases in development no doubt exist (i.e., normally occur), the normal nature of these phases may differ from what has been portrayed in many laboratory investigations, especially with regard to the duration of the period of maximum sensitivity (see Chap. 14). Sensitive phases may be longer than previously believed (e.g., Brown 1974; Eiserer 1978; Gaioni et al. 1978). As pointed out in Chapter 14, certain discrepancies may arise due to the use of biologically irrelevant stimuli in the determination of sensitive phases.

Manipulations involving experiential enhancement or substitution typically render findings that would be difficult to interpret in the framework of normal development. These types of manipulation reflect the contributory roles of normally occurring experience on species-typical behavioral development only in light of the extent to which the enhancement or substitution falls within the range of normally occurring variability. Providing an animal with forms of experience (via enhancement or substitution) that it would not encounter in nature more directly elucidates varying degrees of plasticity. Indirectly, however, certain inferences with regard to normal development can be made from such studies. The extent to which this is possible will be discussed in the section "Modal species atypicality."

Before leaving this section on normal development, I should mention investigations that explicitly involve abnormal development (i.e., behavioral disorders or pathologies). Most studies of abnormal development (usually involving humans and nonhuman primates) have a definite applied character in which the ultimate goal seems to be prevention and/or treatment of the abnormalities under scrutiny. By identifying the factors involved in producing abnormalities and by elucidating the most effective therapy for these deviations, such studies are in actuality pointing out the factors that are important in normal development, albeit indirectly. The research by Harlow and his associates is a case in point. Separating infant rhesus monkeys from their mothers causes varying degrees of abnormality that persists into adulthood, the extent of the abnormality depending upon the actual rearing conditions employed (e.g., Ruppenthal et al. 1976). One can conclude from such studies that the stimulus (e.g., rhesus mother) of which the organism was deprived has an important influence on normal behavioral development to the extent that the absence of the stimulus results in behavioral deficits.

In this way, studying abnormal behavior is compatible with studying normal behavior. *Plasticity*, as defined earlier in this chapter, is not synonymous with *abnormal* in the sense that *abnormal* refers to behavioral disorders or gross behavioral deficiencies or deviances (i.e., maladaptations). The difference between behavioral plasticity and abnormal behavior is unfortunately subtle but exceedingly important. Plasticity refers to a range of behavior potentials that are not realized in the course of normal development but that, via experimental manipulation, could be realized and would be considered as adaptive with respect to the demands set forth vis-à-vis the manipulation (see also Kuo 1976). Abnormal behavior is typically nonadaptive (or maladaptive) in reference to a population or species-typical norm. (It should be recognized, however, that such behavior patterns may be intrinsically adaptive insofar as they may somehow functionally benefit the individual. But such behavior patterns have little or no adaptive value for the species and, therefore, are either not selected for or possibly are selected against, as would be the case, for example, with regard to human psychoses and other severe physical and/or mental disorders.) Instead of representing a potential extension of the range of normality vis-à-vis behavioral neo-phenotypes (see "Behavioral plasticity"), grossly abnormal behavior is, in fact, diametrically opposed to behavioral adaptations that fall within the range of normality. Thus, to the extent that one can assume that the presence of a given stimulus or experience promotes normal development whereas its absence promotes abnormal development, the concepts of normal and abnormal are compatible within the realm of experimental manipulation involving experiential attenuation.

BEHAVIORAL PLASTICITY

Studies of behavioral plasticity (as defined previously) are just as important as studies of normal development. As will be discussed later, one important reason for studying atypical plasticity is that such investigations may provide initial evidence of a process or phenomenon that exists within the range of normality for subsequent experimental verification involving aspects of species-typical stimuli and behavior patterns.

Another reason for studying behavioral plasticity pertains to the evolutionary argument that if plasticity is present in the system, it must have been selected for. The fact that such plasticity exists but does not appear to play a role with regard to the particular phenomenon under scrutiny may suggest a lack of contemporary selective pressures for its manifestation (but see the discussion below). Nevertheless, as long as plasticity continues to be selected for (or at least not selected against), future selective pressures may enable the species to incorporate into its range of species-typical variability aspects that at present are outside the range of variability observed in natural habitats. This is actually the main point behind Kuo's (1976) concepts of *behavioral potentials* and *behavioral neo-phenotypes.* According to Kuo, neonates possess a wide range of possibilities or potentialities of behavior patterns within the limits of species-typical morphological constraints, and the neonate is born with far more behavioral potentials than would be actualized in real behavior patterns during its lifetime. It is on the basis of these behavioral potentials that behavioral neo-phenotypes can be created, which are new behavior patterns within the range of behavior potentials that become actualized via experimental manipulation. Kuo argues that the study of these behavior patterns that are contemporarily either not commonly found or nonexistent in nature can yield valuable information about potential evolutionary pathways. In other words, as long as one can demonstrate a potential for behavioral modifiability in development by creating behavioral neo-phenotypes, it is possible that at some later point in evolution selection pressures may, so to speak, call upon this plasticity and incorporate new behavior patterns in the species-typical repertoire. It is, perhaps, of historical interest that the premise underlying the concept of behavioral neo-phenotypes is basic to two other tenets articulated earlier in this century in the framework of interrelating ontogeny and phylogeny in a manner counter to Lamarckian interpretation – the *Baldwin effect* (Baldwin 1902; Simpson 1953) and Waddington's demonstration of the *genetic assimilation of an acquired character* (Waddington 1953). The essence of these principles is that certain characters having a low incidence of occurrence in a population can, via specific selection, become typical features of the population in subsequent generations. Similar principles were expounded independently by two of Baldwin's contemporaries, C. L. Morgan and H. F. Osborn (Baldwin 1902; Simpson 1953). Only recently has the interrelationship between Baldwin and Waddington been appreciated (Gottlieb 1979).

Although the above scheme depicting the relationship between behavioral neo-phenotypes and evolution seems plausible in terms of long-range evolutionary change, other interpretations falling within a more contemporary framework are also likely. For example, it is possible that plasticity may actually be employed contemporarily for purposes other than that under experimental study.

The experimental analysis of the development of behavioral plasticity usually involves either experiential enhancement or experiential substitution. Regarding the notion of enhancement, an interesting point has been raised by Daly (1973) that bears repeating here. Compared to the natural habitat of certain rodent species, laboratory conditions can, in a sense, be considered as overstimulative, rather than impoverished, for an infant rodent. For example, compared to a constantly dark, sound-attenuated burrow in nature (i.e., a species-typical environment for infant rats), laboratory rats are usually maintained at least partially in light and exposed to sounds and temperature fluctuations that would not typically occur in nature. In other words, studies involving developmental aspects of infant rats that are maintained under such enhancing conditions may be interpretable only with regard to the conceptual strategy of behavioral plasticity inasmuch as they have been subjected to neonatal experiences far outreaching the limits of normal variability encountered in the species-typical habitat.

Although Daly's reinterpretation of the early rodent experience literature is compelling, one should bear in mind that the extent to which a set of stimulating conditions can be classified as overstimulative or understimulative depends upon what is being measured. Using cortical development in adult rats as a dependent variable, for example, Rosenzweig (1971) and his associates have found that rats reared in an enriched laboratory cage have greater brain development than rats reared in a standard cage, which in turn have greater cortical development than rats reared in an impoverished cage. However, what is strikingly important is that rats reared in a seminatural outdoor enclosure have significantly greater cortical development than rats reared in the enriched laboratory condition (Rosenzweig et al. 1972; Rosenzweig & Bennett 1976). Using nature as a baseline, the enriched condition employed by these investigators is merely another form of impoverishment with respect to brain development. Moreover, it has been suggested that the differential effect on brain size in enriched versus impoverished rats is more directly a function of the debilitating effects that isolation has on neural development rather than the facilitative effects of enrichment (Cummins et al. 1977). Such an interpretation is also consistent with the finding that seminaturally reared rats have larger brain sizes than rats reared under the so-called enriched condition.

Studies involving experiential substitution have provided a wealth of data demonstrating how organisms can come to redirect their social preferences to other species or artificial objects via crossfostering (e.g., Immelmann 1972a, 1972b; Mason & Kenney 1974). Perhaps the best prototype of experiential substitution is the experimental study of imprinting, both filial and sexual.

Konrad Lorenz (1937), one of the pioneers of the imprinting concept, was primarily concerned with how species that do not recognize conspecifics instinctively come to recognize them vis-à-vis the imprinting process. Interestingly, however, all species tested to date for instinctive conspecific preferences (i.e., in advance of exposure to conspecifics) have shown such preferences (see also the discussion by Gottlieb 1976a). This is not to rule out, however, the possibility that imprinting acts as a fail-safe mechanism to assure proper conspecific species identification or that it plays a facilitative role in the sharpening of already existing preferences. Imprinting may also promote individual recognition of conspecifics and thereby serve to facilitate recognition of parents by young and to regulate the extent of inbreeding and outbreeding within a population (Bateson 1978, 1979; Miller 1979).

Whereas the intent of Lorenz and others was to elucidate the process by which normal species identification occurs, many investigators seem to have veered away from the biological relevance aspect of imprinting (cf. Immelmann 1975a, 1975b) and focused instead on factors that contribute to preference formation in general and on the general learning process. Although this line of research has provided interesting data on behavioral plasticity, one must be cautious in overgeneralizing these data to account for normal species identification. One of the greatest problems with overgeneralizing pertains to the choice of highly artificial (species-atypical) stimuli in such experiments. It may be tempting to assume that there is a generality of process across a wide range of stimuli ultimately including species-typical stimuli. However, similar assumptions have led psychologists astray in their search for general laws of learning without (until relatively recently) taking into consideration the concept of biological constraints on learning (e.g., Bolles 1970, 1973; Seligman 1970).

A case can be made for initially approaching problems akin to species identification and mate selection interspecifically. For example, an assessment of the extent to which an organism identifies or recognizes conspecifics necessitates a simultaneous choice test involving a conspecific stimulus versus a heterospecific stimulus. However, such an assessment does not elucidate the ontogenetic basis of how the organism comes to identify its own species or why it may prefer to mate with certain individuals over others. Because the mode in nature is for animals to pair and mate only with conspecifics (i.e., to avoid hybridization), it would seem that ultimately the most compelling way to demonstrate the contribution of an imprinting process to normal species identification would be to study experimentally the problem intraspecifically whereby species-typical variables are manipulated. A number of investigators are pursuing the problem in this fashion (e.g., Bateson 1978; Cooke 1978; Cooke et al. 1976; Gallagher 1976; Gottlieb 1974; Immelmann et al. 1978; Miller 1979); however, the abundance of data that has accumulated on imprinting over the past three decades has more direct bearing on behavioral plasticity as such than on the problem of species identification (Gottlieb 1976a; Miller 1980).

INTERRELATIONSHIP OF NORMAL DEVELOPMENT AND PLASTICITY

The conceptual strategies of elucidating normal development and assessing the extent of atypical plasticity represent equally valid approaches to answering different ontogenetic questions. To the extent that the questions and issues are kept clear, one need not address one conceptual strategy while working within the framework of the other. However, there are many instances when an interrelationship between the two approaches would prove most desirable, as, for example, in attempting to relate the wealth of data on imprinting that has been collected within the framework of behavioral plasticity to the original question of the development of normal conspecific preferences.

Figure 2.1 depicts the interrelationship of the two conceptual strategies with regard to answering a hypothetical research problem. The standard curve at the top represents the range of species-typical environmental and behavioral variation as assessed via normative observational–descriptive studies or naturalistic observation. The lower abscissa reflects the extent of species-typicality with respect to the normal curve at the top. The ordinate portrays the conceptual strategies of behavioral plasticity and normal behavioral development. The regions of the curve marked A, B, and C represent types of studies that elucidate these particular strategies and points in between. Some types of investigations (type A) illustrate only behavioral plasticity in that they involve stimuli and/or assess motor patterns beyond the range of species-typical variation. Other types of investigations (type C) directly elucidate normal behavioral development by working well within the limits of species-typical variability. Studies of the sort portrayed in region B are transitional and serve to bridge the gap between the two conceptual strategies.

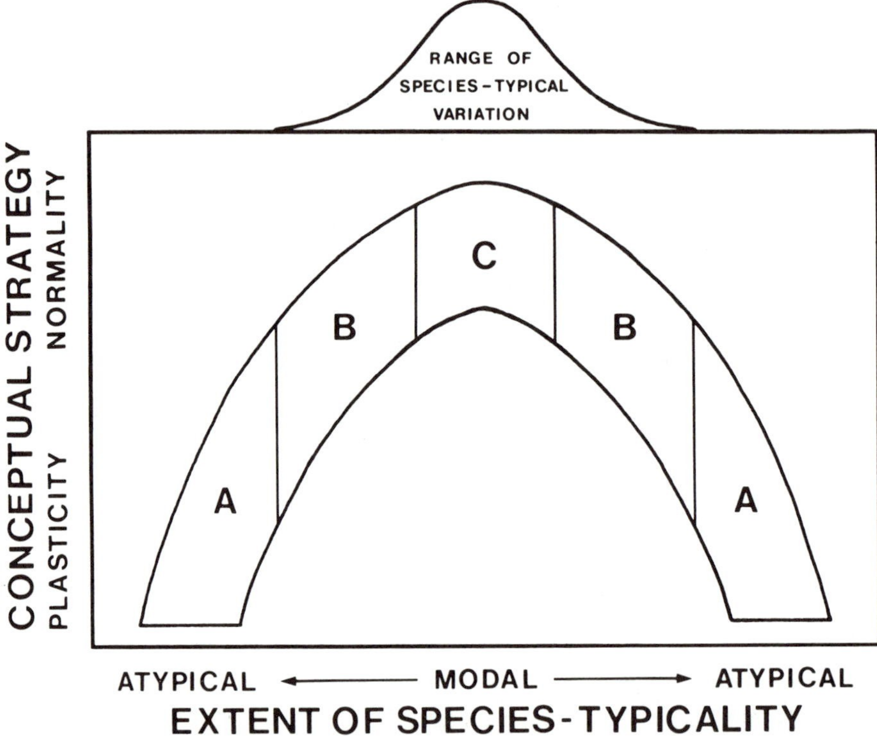

Figure 2.1. A model depicting the manner in which different types of investigations (A, B, and C) fall within the framework of, and elucidate the interrelationship between, the conceptual strategies of normal development and behavioral plasticity. See text for explanation.

The model portrayed in Figure 2.1 may best be explained by considering, for example, the experimental study of imprinting. Most laboratory studies of imprinting have involved assessing the preferences of a particular species for objects or other species that they normally would not prefer (or even encounter) in nature (i.e., a type A investigation). Such studies have provided useful information on the process of imprinting, especially with regard to such issues as sensitive periods and reversibility versus irreversibility. However, the ultimate issue of relating such data to normal species identification necessitates moving from investigation type A to type B and eventually to type C. If the results are similar across all three types (or at least between types A and C), one can then conclude that the process is a general one. In the case of sexual imprinting, for example, research programs involving interspecific cross fostering (type A) can gradually pave the way for an assessment of intraspecific variables of a rather gross nature (type B; e.g., intraspecific cross fostering of different color morphs that have a low incidence of interbreeding in nature) and gradually refine the analysis of preferences vis-à-vis the most modal aspects of species-typical variation (type C; e.g., by assessing preferences for subtle color variations within a color morph). In other words, by gradually refining the analysis to incorporate aspects that fall within the range of species-typical variability (as determined by normative assessment), studies that illustrate behavioral plasticity can, indeed, come to elucidate the course of normal behavioral development.

One example of such an approach is the study of olfactory imprinting and homing in salmon (recently reviewed by Hasler et al. 1978). Laboratory and field studies (type A), wherein young coho salmon were exposed to an artificial (species-atypical) chemical stimulus, revealed that these animals retain and use such chemical information to achieve successful homing. Subsequent field studies (type C) revealed that salmon home successfully when the only chemical cues present are those that normally occur in the natural water of the rearing stream. Whereas the type A studies employing artificial stimuli showed that salmon can use chemical cues to home successfully, the type C studies revealed that salmon actually do use such cues as they normally occur, thereby corroborating the role of olfactory imprinting in the development of normal homing behavior.

Another example that illustrates the interrelationship between the two strategies pertains to song learning in male zebra finches. Immelmann (1969) found that young male zebra finches that are kept with their father until 80 days of age develop a song that is a fairly close match to the father's. However, young males isolated from their fathers before day 40 develop a song that has some similarity to the father's song but is far from being a good copy. Interestingly, in the wild, young male (and female) zebra finches typically leave the parents between days 30 and 40. Thus, the experiment in which young males are kept with their father until day 80 demonstrates a remarkable degree of plasticity that falls beyond the range encountered in nature, whereas the experiment in which birds are isolated from the father within the range of species typicality directly reveals the extent to which young male zebra finches incorporate elements of their father's song into their own repertoire.

This example is also relevant to Kuo's (1976) concept of behavioral neo-phenotypes. The experimental demonstration of behavioral neo-phenotypes is clearly an example of behavioral plasticity. But Kuo would forecast that contemporary behavioral neo-phenotypes can, in future evolution, be a manifest component of the species-typical repertoire, given the appropriate selective pressures. The fact that organisms have a degree of plasticity that exceeds the range typically occurring in nature suggests that evolution has favored maintaining a fairly open system (e.g., a young male zebra finch has the potential of almost perfectly duplicating his father's song, even though there is no contemporary selective pressure to do so). Of course, as previously mentioned, it is possible that plasticity can be used for different ends and that a particular experimental manipulation (e.g., rearing with the father until day 80) may only reveal the existence of plasticity that has adaptive functions other than that being assessed. In other words, a young male zebra finch may be plastic for this period of time for reasons other than song learning.

One explanation for the evolutionary advantage of selecting for a high degree of plasticity that exceeds the contemporary environmental demands imposed upon the species pertains to possible sudden ecological fluctuations that may, for example, reduce the population of a species-typical prey. If the predator in question was not able to adjust rapidly to such environmental demands, it would face the possibility of extinction, as has happened in a number of species that have overspecialized in feeding and/or nest-site selection habits. In most species, it is possible that natural selection has favored a degree of plasticity exceeding the range typically employed or exhibited by the species under contemporary ecological conditions, thereby favoring survival in the face of changing ecological demands. It is within this ecological and evolutionary framework that the conceptual strategies of normal development and behavioral plasticity may be most compatible.

MODAL SPECIES ATYPICALITY

One premise that is basic to the theme of this chapter is that the development of species-typical behavior is best elucidated within the framework of manipulating species-typical stimuli. An implicit assumption behind this approach is that species-typical stimuli are the most optimal stimuli for eliciting species-typical behavior. There are instances, however, in which the most modal aspects of species-typical stimuli are not necessarily the most effective elicitors of species-typical behavior (e.g., Hogan et al. 1975; King & West 1977; Snodderly 1978; Tinbergen 1951:44–46). Such supernormal stimuli usually differ from the mode along some quantitative dimension, such as size or wavelength. The preferential responsiveness to supernormal versus modal stimuli is an interesting phenomenon, and there has even been speculation as to its possible evolutionary significance (Staddon 1975). Nevertheless, this phenomenon remains a product of experimental manipulation inasmuch as supernormal stimuli do not typically occur in nature (see also Baerends & Kruijt 1973).

An intriguing illustration of a species-typical response to a species-atypical stimulus comes from recent studies on female cowbird responsiveness to male cowbird song (King & West 1977; West et al. 1979). Under laboratory playback situations, these investigators found that laboratory-raised and wild-caught female cowbirds are more responsive (as evinced by the display of a species-typical copulatory posture) to an abnormal song (i.e., one uttered by a male reared in social isolation) than to the song of a normal male. The extent to which this example illustrates normal behavior or behavioral plasticity on the part of the female remains unclear, as normative field data on the male's use of song and the female's response to it in different contexts are lacking – a point recognized by these investigators.

It is important to recognize the possibility that the isolate song may actually be the modal song in the species. Cowbirds are nest parasites. The young are, therefore, reared by species other than their own. Because the developmental mode in nature is for young cowbirds to be reared apart from conspecifics, self-stimulation may play an important role in song development (Gottlieb 1973). Adjunctive auditory stimulation provided in the laboratory by conspecifics may, in fact, represent a form of experiential enhancement that results in the development of songs that are atypical and are therefore less attractive to the female, or at least are less effective in communicating a purely sexual message (King & West 1977).

ERRONEOUS CONCLUSIONS

Throughout this chapter, I have advocated a conceptual framework that distinguishes the extent to which developmental data elucidate normal behavioral development as opposed to behavioral plasticity beyond the range of species-typical variability. I have tried not to attach value judgments to these conceptual strategies. Both approaches are relevant to the study of ontogeny. I do feel, however, that we must be chary about overgeneralizing data collected within the framework of the strategy of behavioral plasticity to account for normal developmental phenomena.

A legitimate question can be raised regarding the extent to which we have been misguided by failing to recognize the distinction between these conceptual strategies. Has a lack of normative data and/or the use of species-atypical stimuli in experimental manipulations led to erroneous conclusions?

This question is rather difficult to answer because there are few studies that address the issue explicitly. The paucity of such studies may stem from the unwillingness of the scientific establishment to accept radically different ideas or data that are contrary to contemporary dogma, as discussed by Revusky (1977:53–71). There are, however, a number of studies that I find sufficiently compelling to warrant an appreciation of these strategies.

There is a growing body of literature that addresses the issue of the optimality of stimuli in eliciting species-typical behavioral responses. For example, the most optimal imprinting objects are those that most closely approximate the most modal aspects of species-typical, intraspecific stimuli (e.g., Gallagher 1978; Gossop 1974; Gottlieb 1971; Griswold 1971; Hess 1973). The issue of reversibility versus irreversibility of preferences is a case in point; the choice of stimuli can lead to rather different conclusions. The preferences of animals initially imprinted on species-atypical stimuli tend to be reversible upon subsequent exposure to species-typical stimuli; however, if the initial imprinted stimulus is a species-typical one and the subsequent stimulus is atypical, the initial preference is usually irreversible (e.g., Gallagher 1978; Hess 1973). Thus, one can easily be led to the wrong conclusions regarding stability of preferences depending on the nature of the imprinted stimulus (see also Chap. 14).

There are two examples of possible erroneous conclusions arising from inadequate normative assessment, both concerning primate social organization. The first example pertains to a theory posited by Zuckerman (1932), who suggested that sexuality is the binding force of primate social organization. Zuckerman believed that higher primates are distinguished from all other mammals by their uninterrupted sexual life. Unfortunately, this theory, which dominated thought in primate sociobiology for over a quarter of a century (Lancaster & Lee 1965; Wilson 1975:514–515), was founded on observations of captive hamadryas baboons at the London Zoological Gardens. Subsequent field studies on a variety of primate species proved Zuckerman's theory wrong (e.g., Kummer 1968; Lancaster & Lee 1965). Indeed, some primate species have been found to possess distinct breeding seasons, and many aspects of primate social organization are quite independent of sexual behavior.

The above example illustrates how erroneous conclusions can be drawn when attempting to build general theories of behavior based largely upon observations of captive animals. However, one must be equally cautious about overgeneralizing on the basis of inadequate naturalistic observation. If a species inhabits various types of niches in nature, it is important to collect normative data in each of these niches, for failure to do so could result in erroneous conclusions. This criticism has been raised by Curtin and Dolhinow (1978) regarding alleged infanticide in the gray langur monkey. Hrdy (1977) proposed an evolutionary model according to which adult male langurs routinely kill infants as an adaptation to competition for females. However, Hrdy's field observations were based largely on a colony of langurs at a location in India that has been greatly altered by humans. The monkeys at this site, according to Curtin and Dolhinow, are overcrowded and greatly affected by agriculture and urbanization. These authors believe that the evidence for infanticide as an evolutionary strategy is weak and that Hrdy's observations of one-male troops and male takeovers of troops do not represent normal langur social organization but rather "a symptom of the failure of the multi-male troop structure to endure environmental conditions far different from those in which it evolved" (1978:475).

It seems apparent from the above examples that adequate normative assessment combined with experimental manipulation of biologically relevant stimuli is essential to gain a valid picture of normal behavioral development. The following concluding statement was written with respect to the langurs of India. I feel, however, that it could aptly apply to the study of any species.

> In the last few thousand years, at most, civilization has transformed India, and there now are langurs living under conditions that simply did not exist ten thousand years ago. To study the evolution of langur behavior, we must consider carefully the whole range of behavior that exists today. Behaviors that appear everywhere, or almost everywhere, and that exist in habitats little altered by man are those most likely to have survived from the evolutionary past. Behaviors that occur only at selected sites and only under novel environmental conditions are quite likely to be artifacts of modern conditions. These new patterns of behavior are of great interest – not because they reveal the course of langur evolution, but because they demonstrate the disturbing results when even a remarkably adaptable species is pushed beyond the range of its flexibility. [Curtin & Dolhinow 1978:475]

SUMMARY

The study of behavioral development necessitates both normative assessment and experimental manipulation. A pivotal question concerns the extent to which experimental manipulation elucidates normal (i.e., species-typical) behavioral development (i.e., what the animal does) as opposed to a kind of behavioral plasticity beyond the range of species-typical variability (i.e., what the animal can do).

There are five modes of analysis that can be employed in the experimental manipulation of behavioral events: (1) experiential attenuation (i.e., reducing normally occurring stimulation); (2) experiential transposition (i.e., rearranging normally occurring stimuli); (3) experiential enhancement (i.e., increasing stimulation above the norm); (4) experiential substitution (i.e., replacing normally occurring stimuli with species-atypical stimuli); and (5) displacement (i.e., temporally shifting the administration of stimuli). The study of normal behavioral development usually involves attenuation and transposition, whereas the study of behavioral plasticity involves enhancement and substitution. Displacement can address either strategy depending on the nature of the manipulation.

A model is presented depicting the potential relationship between the two conceptual strategies. Studies that initially involve species-atypical stimuli can come to elucidate normal behavioral development by subsequently incorporating stimuli and behavioral events that fall within the most modal range of species-typical variability as defined by normative assessment. There are only a few cases in which the most modal aspects of species-typical stimuli are not necessarily the most optimal in eliciting species-typical behavior patterns.

Although the conceptual strategies of normal development and behavioral plasticity are equally valid approaches to the study of behavioral ontogeny, it is important for investigators to avoid overgeneralizing from one to the other, for doing so can lead to erroneous conclusions insofar as normal development is concerned. The necessity of adequate normative assessment and the experimental use of biologically relevant stimuli renders the study of normal behavioral development a tedious as well as an exciting area of inquiry.

ACKNOWLEDGMENTS

Many of the ideas expressed in this chapter by no means originated with me. Similar points of view have been expressed in the writings of individuals from diverse theoretical and conceptual backgrounds (e.g.,Lorenz, Tinbergen, Schneirla, Lehrman, Kuo). I have personally profited from numerous discussions with Gilbert Gottlieb, to whom I am indebted for being a continuing source of intellectual stimulation. I am also grateful to the following individuals who, through discussion and criticism of an earlier draft, have sharpened my thinking considerably: Russell P. Balda, George W. Barlow, P. P. G. Bateson, Gordon M. Burghardt, Victor H. Denenberg, Stephen E. Glickman, Timothy D. Johnston, Klaus Immelmann, Donald E. Kroodsma, David L. G. Noakes, Ronald W. Oppenheim, Jay S. Rosenblatt, Gene P. Sackett, Sverre Sjölander, and Stephen J. Suomi. Of course, I assume full responsibility for all shortcomings in this Chapter. I also thank Linda L. Miller for helping formulate the model in Figure 2.1 and for patiently preparing the figure.

This chapter was prepared while I was supported by a fellowship from the Alexander von Humboldt-Stiftung and by Research Grant HD-00878 from the National Institute of Child Health and Human Development.

REFERENCES

Adam, J. H., & S. J. Dimond. 1971. Influence of light on the time of hatching in the domestic chick. *Animal Behaviour* 19:226–229.

Baerends, G. P., & J. P. Kruijt. 1973. Stimulus selection. *In:* R. A. Hinde & J. Stevenson-Hinde (eds.), *Constraints on learning*. Academic Press, New York, pp. 23–50.

Baldwin, J. M. 1902. *Development and evolution*. Macmillan, New York.

Barlow, G. W. 1968. Ethological units of behavior. *In:* D. Ingle (ed.), *The central nervous system and fish behavior*. University of Chicago Press, Chicago, pp. 217–232.

1977. Modal action patterns. *In:* T. A. Sebeok (ed.), *How animals communicate*. Indiana University Press, Bloomington, pp. 98–134.

Bateson, P. P. G. 1976. Specificity and the origins of behavior. *In:* J. S. Rosenblatt, R. A. Hinde, E. Shaw & C. Beer (eds.), *Advances in the study of behavior*, vol. 6. Academic Press, New York, pp. 1–20.

1978. Sexual imprinting and optimal outbreeding. *Nature* 273:659–660.

1979. How do sensitive periods arise and what are they for? *Animal Behaviour* 27:470–486.

Boice, R. 1977. Burrows of wild and albino rats: effects of domestication, outdoor raising, age, experience, and maternal state. *Journal of Comparative and Physiological Psychology* 91:649–661.

Bolles, R. C. 1970. Species-specific defense reactions and avoidance learning. *Psychological Review* 77:32–48.

1973. The comparative psychology of learning: the selective association principle and some problems with "general" laws of learning. *In:* G. Bermant (ed.), *Perspectives on animal behavior*. Scott, Foresman, Glenview, Illinois, pp. 280–306.

Bradshaw, A. D. 1965. Evolutionary significance of phenotypic plasticity in plants. *In:* E. W. Caspari & J. M. Thoday (eds.), *Advances in genetics*, vol. 13. Academic Press, New York, pp. 115–155.

Bronfenbrenner, U. 1977. Toward an experimental ecology of human development. *American Psychologist* 32:513–531.

Brown, R. T. 1974. Following and visual imprinting in ducklings across a wide age range. *Developmental Psychobiology* 8:27–33.

Callaway, W. R., Jr. 1970. Modes of biological adaptation and their role in intellectual development. *PCD Monographs* 1:1–34.

Capretta, P. J., J. T. Petersik, & D. J. Stewart. 1975. Acceptance of novel flavours is increased after early experience of diverse tastes. *Nature* 254:689–691.

Collias, N. E., & E. C. Collias. 1967. A field study of the red jungle fowl in North-Central India. *Condor* 69:360–386.

Cooke, F. 1978. Early learning and its effect on population structure. Studies of a wild population of snow geese. *Zeitschrift für Tierpsychologie* 46:344–358.

Cooke, F., G. H. Finney, & R. F. Rockwell. 1976. Assortative mating in lesser snow geese (*Anser caerulescens*). *Behavior Genetics* 6:127–140.

Cummins, R. A., P. J. Livesey, J. G. M. Evans, & R. N. Walsh. 1977. A developmental theory of environmental enrichment. *Science* 197:692–694.

Curtin, R., & P. Dolhinow. 1978. Primate social behavior in a changing world. *American Scientist* 66:468–475.

Daly, M. 1973. Early stimulation of rodents: a critical review of present interpretations. *British Journal of Psychology* 64: 435–460.

de Beer, G. 1958. *Embryos and ancestors*, 3rd ed. Oxford University Press, London.
Dethier, V. G. 1978. Other tastes, other worlds. *Science* 201:224–228.
Dewsbury, D. A. 1975. Diversity and adaptation in rodent copulatory behavior. *Science* 190:947–954.
Eiserer, L. A. 1978. The effects of tactile stimulation on imprinting in ducklings after the sensitive period. *Animal Learning and Behavior* 6:27–29.
Emlen, S. T. 1969. The development of migratory orientation in young indigo buntings. *Living Bird* 8:113–126.
1970. Celestial rotation: its importance in the development of migratory orientation. *Science* 170:1198–1201.
1975. Migration: orientation and navigation. *In:* D. S. Farner & J. R. King (eds.), *Avian biology*, vol 5. Academic Press, New York, pp. 129–219.
Evans, R. M. 1973. Differential responsiveness of young ring-billed gulls and herring gulls to adult vocalizations of their own and other species. *Canadian Journal of Zoology* 51:759–770.
Gaioni, S. J., H. S. Hoffman, P. DePaulo, & V. N. Stratton. 1978. Imprinting in older ducklings: some tests of a reinforcement model. *Animal Learning and Behavior* 6:19–26.
Gallagher, J. 1976. Sexual imprinting: effects of various regimens of social experience on mate preference in Japanese quail (*Coturnix coturnix japonica*). *Behaviour* 57:91–115.
1978. Sexual imprinting: variations in the persistence of mate preference due to difference in stimulus quality in Japanese quail (*Coturnix coturnix japonica*). *Behavioral Biology* 22:559–564.
Gossop, M. R. 1974. Movement variables and the subsequent following response of the domestic chick. *Animal Behaviour* 22:982–986.
Gottlieb, G. 1963a. "Imprinting" in nature. *Science* 139:497–498.
1963b. A naturalistic study of imprinting in wood ducklings (*Aix sponsa*). *Journal of Comparative and Physiological Psychology* 56:86–91.
1965. Components of recognition in ducklings. *Natural History* 74:12–19.
1971. *Development of species identification in birds.* University of Chicago Press, Chicago.
1973. Neglected developmental variables in the study of species identification in birds. *Psychological Bulletin* 79:362–372.
1974. On the acoustic basis of species identification in wood ducklings (*Aix sponsa*). *Journal of Comparative and Physiological Psychology* 87:1038–1048.
1976a. The roles of experience in the development of behavior and the nervous system. *In:* G. Gottlieb (ed.), *Neural and behavioral specificity.* Academic Press, New York, pp. 22–54.
1976b. Early development of species-specific auditory perception in birds. *In:* G. Gottlieb (ed.), *Neural and behavioral specificity.* Academic Press, New York, pp. 237–280.
1977. The development of behavior. *In:* K. Immelmann (ed.), *Grzimek's encyclopedia of ethology.* Van Nostrand Reinhold, New York, pp. 579–606.
1978. Development of species identification in ducklings. 4. Change in species-specific perception caused by auditory deprivation. *Journal of Comparative and Physiological Psychology* 92:375–387.
1979. Recent history of comparative psychology and ethology. *In:* E. Hearst (ed.), *The first century of experimental psychology.* Erlbaum, Hillsdale, New Jersey, pp. 147–176.
Griswold, J. G. 1971. Initial perceptual status of chicks with respect to parental objects and changes of status with increasing age. Unpublished Ph.D. dissertation, Pennsylvania State University, University Park, Pennsylvania.

Harlow, H. F., M. K. Harlow, & S. J. Suomi. 1971. From thought to therapy: lessons from a primate laboratory. *American Scientist* 59:538–549.

Halser, A. D., A. T. Scholz, & R. M. Horrall. 1978. Olfactory imprinting and homing in salmon. *American Scientist* 66:347–355.

Heaton, M. B., D. B. Miller, & D. G. Goodwin. 1978. Species-specific auditory discrimination in bobwhite quail neonates. *Developmental Psychobiology* 11:13–22.

Heinz, G. 1973. Responses of ring-necked pheasant chicks (*Phasianus colchincus*) to conspecific calls. *Animal Behaviour* 21:1–9.

Hess, E. H. 1973. *Imprinting*. Van Nostrand Reinhold, New York.

Hogan, J. A., J. P. Kruijt, & J. H. Frijlink. 1975. "Supernormality" in a learning situation. *Zeitschrift für Tierpsychologie* 38:212–218.

Hrdy, S. B. 1977. Infanticide as a primate reproductive strategy. *American Scientist* 65:40–49.

Immelmann, K. 1969. Song development in the zebra finch and other estrildid finches. *In:* R. A. Hinde (ed.), *Bird vocalizations*. Cambridge University Press, Cambridge, pp. 61–74.

1972a. The influence of early experience upon the development of social behaviour in estrildine finches. *Proceedings of the 15th International Ornithological Congress* 15:316–338.

1972b. Sexual and other long-term aspects of imprinting in birds and other species. *In:* D. S. Lehrman, R. A. Hinde, & E. Shaw (eds.), *Advances in the study of behavior*, vol. 4. Academic Press, New York, pp. 147–174.

1975a. Ecological significance of imprinting and early learning. *Annual Review of Ecology and Systematics* 6:15–37.

1975b. The evolutionary significance of early experience. *In:* G. Baerends, C. Beer, & A. Manning (eds.), *Function and evolution in behavior: essays in honor of Professor Niko Tinbergen, F.R.S.* Oxford University Press, London, pp. 243–253.

Immelmann, K., H.-H. Kalberlah, P. Rausch, & A. Stahnke. 1978. Sexuelle Prägung als möglicher Faktor innerartlicher Isolation beim Zebrafinken. *Journal für Ornithologie* 119:197–212.

Keeton, W. T. 1974. The orientational and navigational basis of homing in birds. *In:* D. S. Lehrman, J. S. Rosenblatt, R. A. Hinde, & E. Shaw (eds.), *Advances in the study of behavior*, vol. 5. Academic Press, New York, pp. 47–132.

King, A. P., & M. J. West. 1977. Species identification in the North American cowbird: appropriate responses to abnormal song. *Science* 195:1002–1004.

King, J. A. 1956. Social relations of the domestic guinea pig living under semi-natural conditions. *Ecology* 37:221–228.

Kramer, L. I., & M. E. Pierpont. 1976. Rocking waterbeds and auditory stimuli to enhance growth of preterm infants. *Journal of Pediatrics* 88:297–299.

Kummer, H. 1968. *Social organization of Hamadryas baboons: a field study.* University of Chicago Press, Chicago.

Kuo, Z.-Y. 1976. *The dynamics of behavior development*, enlarged ed. Plenum Press, New York.

Lancaster, J. B., & R. B. Lee. 1965. The annual reproductive cycle in monkeys and apes. *In:* I. DeVore (ed.), *Primate behavior*. Holt, New York, pp. 486–513.

Lauber, J. K., & J. V. Shutze. 1964. Accelerated growth of embryo chicks under the influences of light. *Growth* 28:179–190.

Leiderman, P. H., S. R. Tulkin, & A. Rosenfeld (eds.). 1977. *Culture and infancy: variations in the human experience.* Academic Press, New York.

Lehrman, D. S. 1970. Semantic and conceptual issues in the nature–nurture problem. *In:* L. R. Aronson, E. Tobach, D. S. Lehrman, & J. S. Rosenblatt (eds.),

Development and evolution of behavior: essays in memory of T. C. Schneirla. Freeman, San Francisco, pp. 17–52.

Lorenz, K. 1937. The companion in the bird's world. *Auk* 54:245–273.

1965. *Evolution and modification of behavior*. University of Chicago Press, Chicago.

Marler, P. 1975. On strategies of behavioural development. *In:* G. Baerends, C. Beer, & A. Manning (eds.), *Function and evolution in behaviour: essays in honor of Professor Niko Tinbergen, F.R.S.* Oxford University Press, London, pp. 254–275.

1976. Sensory templates in species-specific behavior. *In:* J. C. Fentress (ed.), *Simpler networks and behavior*. Sinauer, Sunderland, Massachusetts, pp. 314–329.

Marler, P., & P. Mundinger. 1971. Vocal learning in birds. *In:* H. Moltz (ed.), *The ontogeny of vertebrate behavior*. Academic Press, New York, pp. 389–450.

Mason, W. A. 1979. Social ontogeny. *In:* J. G. Vandenbergh & P. Marler (eds.), *Social behavior and communication*. Plenum Press, New York, 2–28.

Mason, W. A., & M. D. Kenney. 1974. Redirection of filial attachments in rhesus monkeys: dogs as mother surrogates. *Science* 183:1209–1211.

McBride, G., I. P. Parer, & F. Foenander. 1969. The social organization and behaviour of the feral domestic fowl. *Animal Behaviour Monographs* 2:125–181.

McCall, R. B. 1977. Challenges to a science of developmental psychology. *Child Development* 48:333–344.

McKay, H., L. Sinisterra, A. McKay, H. Gomez, & P. Lloreda. 1978. Improving cognitive ability in chronically deprived children. *Science* 200:270–278.

Miller, D. B. 1977a. Roles of naturalistic observation in comparative psychology. *American Psychologist* 32:211–219.

1977b. Early parent–young interactions in red jungle fowl: earlobe pecking. *Condor* 79:503–504.

1977c. Social displays of mallard ducks (*Anas platyrhynchos*): effects of domestication. *Journal of Comparative and Physiological Psychology* 91:221–232.

1978. Species-typical and individually distinctive acoustic features of crow calls of red jungle fowl. *Zeitschrift für Tierpsychologie* 47:182–193.

1979. Long-term recognition of father's song by female zebra finches. *Nature* 280:389–391.

1980. Beyond sexual imprinting. *Proceedings of the 17th International Ornithological Congress, Berlin* 17: in press.

Miller, D. B., & G. Gottlieb. 1976. Acoustic features of wood duck (*Aix sponsa*) maternal calls. *Behaviour* 57:260–280.

Miller, D. B., & G. Gottlieb. 1978. Maternal vocalizations of mallard ducks (*Anas platyrhynchos*). *Animal Behavior* 26:1178–1194.

Nicolai, J. 1959. Familientradition in der Gesangsentwicklung des Gimpels (*Pyrrhula pyrrhula* L.). *Journal für Ornithologie* 100:39–46.

Nottebohm, F. 1970. Ontogeny of bird song. *Science* 167:950–956.

Pinel, J. P. J., & D. Treit. 1978. Burying as a defensive response in rats. *Journal of Comparative and Physiological Psychology* 92:708–712.

Revusky, S. 1977. Learning as a general process with an emphasis on data from feeding experiments. *In:* N. W. Milgram, L. Krames, & T. M. Alloway (eds.), *Food aversion learning*. Plenum Press, New York, pp. 1–71.

Rood, J. P. 1972. Ecological and behavioural comparisons of three genera of Argentine cavies. *Animal Behaviour Monographs* 5:1–83.

Rosenzweig, M. R. 1971. Effects of environment on development of brain and behavior. *In:* E. Tobach, L. R. Aronson, & E. Shaw (eds.), *The biopsychology of development*. Academic Press, New York, pp. 303–342.

Rosenzweig, M. R., & E. L. Bennett. 1976. Enriched environments: facts, factors, and fantasies. *In:* L. Petrinovich & J. L. McGaugh (eds.), *Knowing, thinking, and believing: Festschrift for Professor David Krech*. Plenum Press, New York, pp. 179–213.
Rosenzweig, M. R., E. L. Bennett, & M. C. Diamond. 1972. Brain changes in response to experience. *Scientific American* 226:22–29.
Ruppenthal, G. C., G. L. Arling, H. F. Harlow, G. P. Sackett, & S. J. Suomi. 1976. A 10-year perspective of motherless-mother monkey behavior. *Journal of Abnormal Psychology* 85:341–349.
Sales, G., & D. Pye. 1974. *Ultrasonic communication by animals*. Chapman & Hall, London.
Seligman, M. E. P. 1970. On the generality of the laws of learning. *Psychological Review* 77:406–418.
Simpson, G. G. 1953. The Baldwin effect. *Evolution* 7:110–117.
Snodderly, D. M., Jr. 1978. Eggshell removal by the laughing gull (*Larus atricilla*): normative data and visual preference behaviour. *Animal Behaviour* 26:487–506.
Staddon, J. E. R. 1975. A note on the evolutionary significance of "supernormal" stimuli. *American Naturalist* 109:541–545.
Suomi, S. J., & H. F. Harlow. 1977. Early separation and behavioral maturation. *In:* A. Oliverio (ed.), *Genetics, environment, and intelligence*. Elsevier/North-Holland Biomedical Press, Amsterdam.
Suomi, S. J., & M. A. Novak. 1974. Reversal of social deficits produced by isolation rearing in monkeys. *Journal of Human Evolution* 3:527–534.
Tees, R. C. 1976. Perceptual development in mammals. *In:* G. Gottlieb (ed.), *Neural and behavioral specificity*. Academic Press, New York, pp. 281–326.
Tinbergen, N. 1951. *The study of instinct*. Oxford University Press, New York.
Tunnell, G. B. 1977. Three dimensions of naturalness: an expanded definition of field research. *Psychological Bulletin* 84:426–437.
Vidal, J. M. 1975. Influence de la privation sociale et de "l'autoperception" sur le comportement sexuel du coq domestique. *Behaviour* 52:57–83.
von Uexküll, J. 1934. Streifzüge durch die Umwelten von Tieren und Menschen. Springer, Berlin. Translated in C. H. Schiller (ed.), *Instinctive behavior*. International Universities Press, New York, pp. 5–80.
Waddington, C. H. 1953. Genetic assimilation of an acquired characteristic. *Evolution* 7:118–126.
West, M. J., A. P. King, D. H. Eastzer, & J. E. R. Staddon. 1979. A bioassay of isolate cowbird song. *Journal of Comparative and Physiological Psychology* 93:124–133.
Wilson, E. O. 1975. *Sociobiology: the new synthesis*. Harvard University Press, Cambridge, Massachusetts.
Yodlowski, M. L., M. L. Kreithen, & W. T. Keeton. 1977. Detection of atmospheric infrasound by homing pigeons. *Nature* 265:725–726.
Zuckerman, S. 1932. *The social life of monkeys and apes*. Routledge & Kegan Paul, London.

3

CONTINGENCY EXPERIENCE IN BEHAVIORAL DEVELOPMENT

JOHN S. WATSON

Six years ago, I proposed a hypothesis about the onset of attachment and sexual imprinting in humans. Briefly, the proposal was that infants are informed as to what constitutes social stimuli for humans by experience they obtain in early response–stimulus contingencies that normally arise in gamelike interactions with people. Repeated exposure to these clear contingency experiences engenders the constituent physical stimuli with the power to elicit unconditioned social responses (e.g., smiling, cooing, heightened attentional regard). In short, the infant initially identifies an object as an appropriate target of social behavior not so much by how it appears as by how it behaves. If its behavior is responsive to (contingent upon) the infant's behavior, then the infant's perception of this contingency will cause the object to be classed as social – that is, the object will begin to manifest the power to elicit social responses.

Publication of that proposal (Watson 1972) received considerable attention from colleagues in developmental psychology. The attention was gratifying, but disconcerting has been the fact that reference to the proposal has often been accompanied by some misrepresentation of it. Therefore, at the risk of reducing the attractiveness that may have depended on its ambiguity, I will use this opportunity to clarify the hypothesis of "the game" while discussing the broader implications of this hypothesis for the general analysis of behavioral development in man and other animals. Let us begin by considering the basic assumption that contingency experience can have a direct affect on behavior or development.

CONTINGENCY EXPERIENCE AS A STIMULUS FOR BEHAVIOR OR DEVELOPMENT

Imagine you are walking in the evening. You hear a sound in the darkness. You stop moving. There is silence. You move again, and soon you hear the sound again. At three consecutive corners, you alternate the direction of your turns. The sound continues with you. Its pattern clearly is not an echo of your footsteps, yet you can perceive that this sound is linked to your behavior very closely. That perception would very likely arouse some apprehension if you could think of no good reason for something to be following you.

What stimulates the onset of wariness? Perception of the sound? That seems hardly likely because the particular physical characteristics of the sound have not been specified in the example. Clearly a basic ingredient in this behavioral reaction is the perceived relationship (contingency) between the occurrence of the sound and one's movement. The point illustrated is that a contingency experience can function as a stimulus to behavior in a manner that does not depend much on the specific nature of the physical stimuli or the responses involved in the contingency. In this example it would seem that the provocative stimulus is the contingency per se.

In light of the preceding example, it seems surprising that the potentially direct role of contingency experience in stimulating behavior or development has not been formally acknowledged until recently. Previously, attention was given exclusively to the physical composition of stimuli and responses, with contingency being important only indirectly as it might affect the animal's learning of associations between those physical stimuli and responses (as in operant conditioning of specific behaviors or the perceptual learning of movement-produced visual stimulation; Held and Hein 1963). However, as will be illustrated below, the past decade has brought forth a variety of evidence that would implicate contingency as a determinant in its own right. The evidence is not vast, but notably it derives from disparate classes of behavior and from a reasonable variety of species. Consider first the evidence from human infants.

An example in human infancy: the game hypothesis

In a set of studies of early instrumental learning (Watson 1972; Watson and Ramey 1972), 8-week-old infants were provided a means of controlling the movement of a mobile over their cribs. Movement of an infant's head on a special pressure-sensing pillow caused the mobile to turn for 1 second. This contingency experience was presented for 10 minutes each day for 2 weeks. The infants learned to control their mobiles but, unexpectedly, after the initial few days of exposure their mothers reported that they also began exhibiting vigorous smiling and cooing to the mobile. By contrast, in other experimental conditions in which no control over the mobile was possible, including one condition in which the mobile turned periodically on its own, mothers of the infants did not report a similar increase of these social responses to the mobile. This contrasting reaction to contingent versus noncontingent mobile stimulation has been corroborated in a follow-up study in which the smiling rate was formally assessed by a trained observer (Watson 1979). Possibly the first researchers to make special note of this reaction to early contingency experience were Hunt and Uzgiris (1964), who observed heightened smiling among a few infants in their sample who were able to gain control of a mobile's movement by shaking their cribs.

One might interpret this reaction as the expression of joy of control or mastery. Although the game hypothesis at times has been interpreted as incorporating such a notion, it quite explicitly does not. Other attributes of the smiling reaction in this age period of 2 to 4 months diminish the need for an assumption that the vigorous smiling that occurs at this age is primarily the expression of positive affect. An unresponsive facial configuration (mask or real) can repeatedly provoke smiling at this age if presented en face but not in profile (Spitz and Wolf 1946) and if presented in alignment with the infant's face but notably less in 90° rotation (Watson 1966; Watson et al. 1979). If smiling is the expression of positive affect, then why does it not occur with equal vigor to profile or 90° faces, which are apparently associated with the joys of feeding as much as en face 0° faces are associated with the joys of mastery (Watson 1967)? If smiling requires the specific joy of mastery, then why is the smile repeatedly elicitable from the 3-month-old even when a properly aligned face is not presently accompanied by an opportunity to control anything? The most one could say of the latter smiles is that they recall the joys of mastery associated with the face stimulus in the past.

Although not doubting that smiles may have some function in relation to expressing or signaling states of affective arousal (Sroufe and Waters 1976) or doubting that infants often enjoy and even pursue mastery of instrumental contingencies, I would yet emphasize the seemingly obvious fact that the smile has evolved in terms of its effectiveness as a stimulus to the behavior of fellow humans. Unlike most specialized behaviors that can serve useful functions when directed toward nonsocial as well as social objects (e.g., grasping), the special muscular reaction of the smile would seem to be evolved uniquely for application to fellow members of the species. Smiles will neither move trees nor stop tigers. Therefore, when infants begin smiling vigorously and repeatedly at an object, it seems likely that they are telling us as much about their category of "social" as they are telling us about their joy of mastery, state of arousal, or affective evaluation of the world around them.

For the immediate purpose of the present discussion of contingency as a determinant of behavior or development, it is not crucial that the reader accept my view of the smiling reaction's primarily social significance. For now, the point to be noted is more empirical than theoretical. The smiling that erupted to our contingent mobiles, whatever its meaning and however mediated, was apparently some function of the young infant's exposure to a contingent relation between its behavior and activation of the mobile. Smiling did not affect the mobile's movement. In noncontingent conditions of these studies, neither the physical stimulus of the turning mobile nor the response activity of the subject was a strong elicitor of the smile. Rather, vigorous smiling was provoked by the mobile stimulus only after some repeated exposure to the contingency.

Some examples from research with animals

Social reactions in rats. Latané and his colleagues have carried out a series of studies on the stimulus control of social attractiveness in rats (Latané and Hothersall 1972; Latané et al. 1972; Werner and Latané 1974). They observed that social orienting toward the experimenter's hand increased with experience in interactive handling. The social reactions of nuzzling and burrowing under were eventually directed to the hand as they normally would be to another rat. This social orienting did not occur to a variety of static physical stimuli that in various ways (e.g., shape, smell, furriness) represented the physical stimulus attributes of "ratness." It would seem that the potential for interaction with a stimulus holds a special attraction that far outweighs that of various static physical dimensions associated with the biological structure of rats. These researchers have concluded that interaction with the rat's behavior is itself a major, possibly the primary, determinant of the rat's social orientation. The point to be emphasized is stated succinctly by Werner and Latané in summary of their observations:

> Rats were very attracted to other rats but, when allowed to become familiar with the hand, were equally attracted to and showed similar reactions to it... Such results cannot be explained by theories that attribute rodent sociability to attraction to physical characteristics only. [Werner & Latané 1974:328]

It is important to note that in Latané's experiments with rats, as in my experiments with infants, the surrogate social object apparently obtained social significance solely by presentation in a context where contingent relations existed between the subject's behavior and available stimulation. On the basis of available data, it seems doubtful that the contingencies experienced were directly conditioning the social behavioral displays by either instrumental or classical conditioning. Rather, it would appear that contingency experience was the effective variable that led the surrogate stimulus to acquire the power to elicit social responses.

If one distinguishes between a stimulus to behavior and a stimulus to development, the evidence in Latané's and my work would support a claim that contingency experience can function as a stimulus to development of a subject's social responsiveness to a previously neutral stimulus (the hand, the mobile). That is, in both examples, contingency appears to function as a stimulus to development (of the subject's social responsiveness to the contingent stimulus), but it remains unclear as to whether contingency is subsequently continuously required as an ingredient of the stimulus to behavior (of the social action) or whether, once established, the physical event and its context can elicit social behavior even in instances when the event is not contingent. I assume that once the event is established as a social stimulus, it will continue to function for some time in the absence of contingency. For the purpose of the present discussion, it does not matter much whether I am right or wrong in that assumption. The basic point to keep in mind here is that contingency may have a direct impact upon a subject - an impact that is separate from the impact of the physical stimulus or the response involved in the contingency experience.

Territorial defense reactions in the white-crowned sparrow. Petrinovich and his colleagues have performed an extensive series of studies of the role of habituation in the establishment and maintenance of the territorial behavior of the Nuttall subspecies of the white-crowned sparrow (e.g., Petrinovich & Peeke 1973; Petrinovich et al. 1976; Petrinovich & Patterson 1980; see also Chap. 4). The basic method involved entering the natural habitat of these birds and assessing their reactions (e.g., flights, flutters, songs, "chink" sounds, visual presentations) to the repeated playing of a recorded male song. In general, these birds do habituate to the recorded songs, but the rate of decline in responsiveness varies significantly as a function of a number of factors, such as the reproductive condition of the female and the sex of the bird.

Two recent findings by Petrinovich and Patterson (1980) are of special interest to our present discussion. The usual method of stimulus presentation in habituation research is scheduling the stimulus (e.g., the 2-second song) to be given every so often without regard for the subject's behavior. That is, the stimulus is presented noncontingently. Petrinovich and Patterson altered this standard procedure in one study. Here, they made the recorded song contingent on the male bird's singing. Ten songs were played to attract the male. Then the contingency began such that each time the resident male sang, a recorded song was presented within 1 or 2 seconds of the end of his song. Although habituation was statistically significant in this condition, the absolute amount (or rate) of response decrement for the various indices was far less than under the noncontingent presentation procedure. It would seem that the impact on the male of response-contingent song is functionally distinct from noncontingent song and that this is so for a variety of territorial behaviors other than the one upon which the contingency was established (singing).

The female's reaction was also notable. Her response decrement was more generalized (i.e., evident in more indices) than under the usual noncontingent procedure. Because the contingency was not established with respect to her behavior, one must assume that she was affected either by the male's reaction to the contingency or by her perception of this special stimulus-contingent stimulation; novel male song is less arousing (more easily habituated to) when it is contingent upon familiar male song. Anthropomorphically, it seems reasonable and perhaps even adaptive for the female to be less sustaining of her responsiveness to a novel male who is clearly under the control of her mate. However fancifully one interprets the finding, the essential point for our present discussion is that the territorial behaviors of this species of bird appear to be influenced by the contingency as well as the physical features and/or familiarity of a male song.

Reproductive development of female ring doves. Friedman (1977) has recently uncovered evidence that the direct effects of contingency may not be limited to behavioral reactions but may extend to basic physiological processes as well. Specifically, Friedman found that the development of the reproductive tract of the female ring dove is maximally stimulated by male vocalizations if those vocalizations are contingent in some way upon her courtship behavior. It was known from previous research that the sight and sound of courting males could stimulate the female to lay eggs (Erickson & Lehrman 1964; Lehrman 1965), but it was not known that the response-contingent nature of this stimulation was important. Friedman points out that this discovery extends the perspective taken by Lorenz (1950) and Tinbergen (1951), who proposed that the species-typical reactions of an animal to the stereotyped behavior of a conspecific involve the activation of feature detectors in the sensory system of the reacting animal. In Friedman's words,

> The female must recognize that the male's behavior is contingent upon her own for maximal ovarian development... Contrary to various previous proposals [Lambe & Erickson 1973; Lorenz 1950], this hypothesis implies that the female's brain is not just a passive accumulator of redundant feature-detection events during courtship but that it must detect stimuli from the male that are contingent upon her own efferent activity. [Friedman 1977:1415]

It should be noted that on the basis of the evidence reported by Friedman, it is not clear whether the effect of contingency is limited to special forms of physical stimulation, for example, certain sights and sounds of males. Given that a contingency is established, how distant from conspecific features can the contingent stimulus be and still function? The same question arises for the study of contingent song stimulation by Petrinovich. The observations reported above from my work with infants and Latané's with rats would imply that, for those cases at least, contingency with surrogate stimulation for social orienting can function with stimulus features that are quite distinct from those functioning under natural conditions.

A judicious guess would be that when contingency has a direct role in behavioral development, most empirical cases will fall between complete independence and complete dependence on specific physical stimulation. That is, the stimulation within the contingency probably will be free to vary, but not without limit, from the naturally occurring range of stimulus features that normally serve the function. Of course, speculation is cheapest when relevant data are rare. Yet it seems safe to say at least that investigators of animal and human behavior will be well advised to keep one eye on contingency experience as a potential determinant of behavioral development.

SUMMARY

This chapter has two objectives. One is to clarify a specific hypothesis termed "the game," which proposes that human infants discover the physical stimulus features of their conspecifics by noting the stimulus context in which they perceive their first clear control over external stimulation. Common games of interaction are presumed to provide the natural setting for this perception and its generation of positive social responses - smiling, cooing, visual attention.

The second objective of the chapter is to note the potential generalization of the game hypothesis - that other behavioral developments in man and other species may likewise be directly influenced by behavior-stimulus contingencies. Some potential examples are drawn from research on social orienting in rats, territorial defense in sparrows, and sexual development of doves.

REFERENCES

Erickson, C. J., & D. S. Lehrman. 1964. Effect of castration of male ring doves upon ovarian activity of females. *Journal of Comparative and Physiological Psychology* 58:164–166.

Friedman, M. B. 1977. Interactions between visual and vocal courtship stimuli in the neuroendocrine response of female doves. *Journal of Comparative and Physiological Psychology* 91:1408–1416.

Held, R., & A. Hein. 1963. Movement-produced stimulation in the development of visually guided behavior. *Journal of Comparative and Physiological Psychology* 56:872–876.

Hunt, J. McV., & I. Uzgiris. 1964. Cathexis from recognitive familiarity: an exploratory study. Paper presented at the 1964 Convention of the American Psychological Association, Los Angeles (September).

Lambe, F. R., & C. J. Erickson. 1973. Ovarian activity of female ring doves (*Streptopelia risoria*) exposed to marginal stimuli from males. *Physiological Psychology* 1:281–283.

Latané, B., & D. Hothersall. 1972. Social attraction in animals. *In:* P. C. Dodwell (ed.), *New horizons in psychology*, vol. 2. Penguin Books, New York.

Latané, B., V. Joy, J. Meltzer, & B. Lubell. 1972. Stimulus determinants of social attraction in rats. *Journal of Comparative and Physiological Psychology* 79:13–21.

Lehrman, D. S. 1965. Interaction between internal and external environments in the regulation of the reproductive cycle of the ring dove. *In:* F. A. Beach (ed.), *Sex and behavior.* Wiley, New York.

Lorenz, D. 1950., The comparative method in studying innate behaviour patterns. *Symposia of the Society for Experimental Biology* 4:221–268.

Petrinovich, L., & T. L. Patterson. 1980. Field studies of habituation. III. Playback contingent on the response of the White-crowned Sparrow. *Animal Behaviour* 28:742–751.

Petrinovich, L., T. L. Patterson, & H. V. S. Peeke. 1976. Reproductive condition and the response of White-crowned Sparrows (*Zonotrochia leucophrys nuttalli*) to song. *Science* 191:206–207.

Petrinovich, L., & H. V. S. Peeke. 1973. Habituation to territorial song in the White-crowned Sparrow (*Zonotrochia leucophrys*). *Behavioral Biology* 8:219–226.

Spitz, R. A., & K. M. Wolf. 1946. The smiling response: a contribution to the ontogenesis of social relations. *Genetic Psychology Monographs* 34:57–125.

Sroufe, L. A., & E. Waters. 1976. The ontogenesis of smiling and laughter: a perspective on the organization of development in infancy. *Psychological Review* 83:173–189.

Tinbergen, N. 1951. *The study of instinct.* Oxford University Press, New York.

Watson, J. S. 1966. Perception of object orientation in infants. *Merrill-Palmer Quarterly* 12:73–94.

1967. Why is a smile? *Trans-action* (May):36–39.

1972. Smiling, cooing, and "The Game." *Merrill-Palmer Quarterly* 18:323–339.

1979. Perception of contingency as a determinant of social responsiveness. *In:* E. B. Thoman (ed.), *The origins of the infant's social responsiveness.* Erlbaum, Hillsdale, New Jersey.

Watson, J. S., L. A. Hayes, P. Vietze, & J. Becker. 1979. Discriminative infant smiling to orientations of talking faces of mother and stranger. *Journal of Experimental Child Psychology.* 28:92–99.

Watson, J. S., & C. Ramey. 1972. Reactions to response-contingent stimulation in early infancy. *Merrill-Palmer Quarterly* 18:219–227.

Werner, C., & B. Latané. 1974. Interaction motivates attraction: rats are fond of fondling. *Journal of Personality and Social Psychology* 29:328–334.

4

A METHOD FOR THE STUDY OF DEVELOPMENT

LEWIS PETRINOVICH

In this chapter, I have tried to draw on my knowledge of general psychology, statistics, and the ethological study of birds, and the fruit of extensive methodological musings, to outline some possible solutions to the problems involved in the study of development as I have come to understand them.

First, a general research scheme will be laid out within the context of the Brunswikian lens model (Brunswik 1952, 1956). Then, classic systematic design will be discussed and compared with and contrasted to representative design – the approach advocated here. The logic of multiple regression–correlation analysis will be developed because these statistical methods are well suited for representative research designs that embody features of the lens model. A case history based on a study of habituation to the playback of song to birds will be presented to demonstrate how the conceptions offered can be used to test predictions of a deductive theory, to understand research data, to generate new hypotheses, and to establish an active data archive system.

A strategy for studying behavior at the individual level will be developed. The analytic statistics appropriate for this approach will be outlined and a technique will be discussed that allows the clustering of individuals on the basis of profile similarities. Finally, a strategy will be offered that extends the above principles to the study of development at the level of the individual subject.

The sections of the chapter are intended to form an integral whole, each part of which follows from and extends the previous sections. It is possible, however, to utilize multiple regression models as they are outlined here without adopting the Brunswikian model, for example. Similarly, one can use the methods suggested here to study development with a strict adherence to the controlled situation of the laboratory rather than using the representative design suggested here. One can believe in the principles of representative design without rejecting laboratory research as the method of choice or accepting a final position on whether or not natural laws are probabilistic. Also, one can utilize multiple regression models and strategies in the laboratory as well as in the field. Yet this argument is presented in a manner that is intended to stress the unity of the approach.

A GENERAL RESEARCH MODEL TO STUDY BEHAVIOR

The lens model

Before discussing systematic and representative designs, let us consider the Brunswikian lens model, which will be used to represent the conceptual framework around which research is organized. A more detailed development and presentation of the Brunswikian system can be found in several sources: Brunswik 1952, 1956; Hammond 1966, 1976; Petrinovich 1973, 1976, 1979; Postman & Tolman 1959. Space is devoted here to the nature of the lens model because it is a general system that has been applied in diverse areas of investigation. The cited sources speak to this generality, and the present chapter indicates yet another extension of the method.

Ward Edwards (1971:640) expressed the opinion that Brunswik was probably the most underrated psychologist of the 1937–55 period: "It wouldn't surprise me if, 100 years from now, he were seen as the most important psychologist of the first half of the 20th century." I concur with this evaluation and for the reason that Edwards goes on to develop:

> He saw that psychology is not only about people who emit behavior – it is also, perhaps more importantly, about the tasks that elicit that behavior. That is, he saw that the task-relevant characteristics of the environment are a necessary part of every process theory in psychology... My own guess is that most successful models now available are successful exactly because of their success in describing tasks, not people. If so, Brunswik is the father of successful psychological theorizing, since he was the first to make explicit and clear the fact that modelling tasks is different from modelling people, to hunt for tools for modelling tasks, and to provide linkages between models of tasks and models of people. [Edwards 1971:640–641]

The lens model (Fig. 4.1) is a pictorial representation of the functional unit of behavior. I have modified and extended Brunswik's model for presentation here. The major change is the inclusion of two lenses, one on the stimulus side and the other on the motor side. I have also included what I have called *process detail* arrays and a feedback arc from the distal achievement (*A*) to the central region (*C*), and another from *C* to the peripheral sensory region (*E*). These details were not included by Brunswik, but I have added them to make the model more comprehensive and inclusive.

It should be made clear, at the outset, that the lens model as used here is not a theory of behavior. It is a method that can aid the scientist's attempts to construct a theory of behavior. The model can give some insights into the problems that one is faced with in general, and should influence the choice of variables and the specific testing and analytic strategies to be used. Beyond this, its value will be no greater than the substantive scientific decisions made by the investigator.

There are several regions of geographical reference in the model: remote, distal, proximal, peripheral, and central. This functional unit is conceived as if it operates by means of a double-convex lens transmitting a widespread array of influences that issue from a distal stimulus through the interposition of the perceptual apparatus on the stimulus side. On the response side, there is

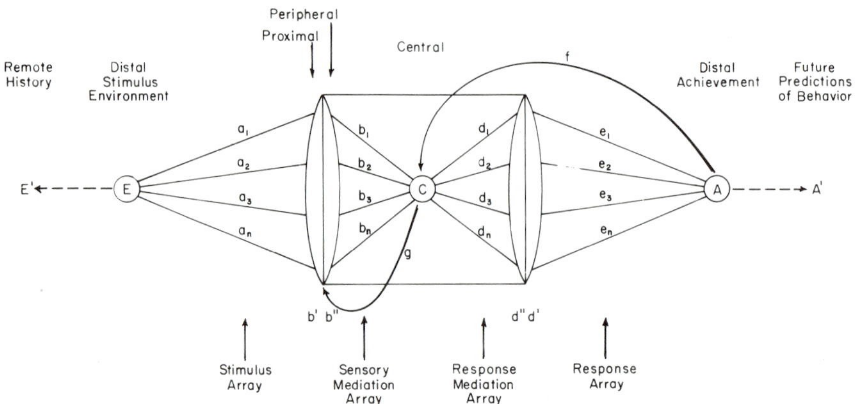

Figure 4.1. A modified version of Brunswik's system of regional reference and the lens model. (From Petrinovich, 1979)

another array of influences representing the means–end apparatus of the organism, and this array is focused on a distal functional achievement. There are two separate lenses: one on the stimulus side that receives distal sensory input and is focused centrally, and one on the motor side that receives central input and is focused distally.

At the left side of the diagram (the stimulus side), region E' represents the remote developmental history of the organism (both ontogenetic and phylogenetic). Region E represents the focal distal stimulus in the environment. Region b represents the proximal stimulus, the physical energy impinging on the receptors of the organism. (This can be divided into a proximal region, b', defined in stimulus terms and a peripheral region, b'', defined in terms of the effective physiological stimulation of the receptor.) A double convex lens can be considered to operate at the peripheral region; the distal event in the environment scatters its effects, and the organism recombines them.

The process detail arrays ($a_1 - a_n$) that emanate from the distal stimulus vary in terms of their trustworthiness. Some stimuli are highly trustworthy as indicators of the distal event (they have a high ecological validity) or are highly salient, whereas others are not as trustworthy or may have a low saliency. These vicarious stimuli will be hierarchically ordered by the organism in terms of their trustworthiness and saliency. Thus, there are many ways to construe the same situation, and there are many stimuli that emanate from a distal situation.

As we proceed from left to right through the diagram, we find another array, $b_1 - b_n$. This represents the physiological channels that mediate the peripheral signals for central processing. Again, this is multiple and is arrayed vicariously and hierarchically. The central region is an inferential one that represents the decision regarding the nature of the stimuli and the decision regarding the appropriate functional end state and how to attain it. The central region could be treated both as the physical central nervous and endocrine systems and as an inferential state construct. This is the region where many of our classical inferential processes lurk (e.g., memory, judgment, perception, motives, emotion, expectancy).

The array to the right of the central area represents the response side and mirrors that for the stimulus events; $d_1 - d_n$ represent efferent channels to the periphery. The various hierarchically organized response modes are represented by $e_1 - e_n$ and converge on the distal functional achievement (A). There are many ways to act appropriately in the same place and in response to the same judgmental event. For completion we can add a remote A', which refers to the prediction of behavior in future times.

A feedback arc (g) extends from the central region to the peripheral sensory region, and another feedback arc (f) extends from the distal achievement to the central region. The sensory arc reflects the influence of central states on the information-processing channels, and the achievement arc reflects the influence of the functional achievement on the central state. It should be pointed out that the feedback arcs and the remote regions could be ignored if one is using the model to characterize the contemporaneous structure of reality because they imply a time dimension. The unit exists at a particular time, and the structure of the events can be frozen and described. One could thus move on to another time and characterize the state of the elements at that time. The model will be used in that fashion, in fact, when it is extended to the study of development. Viewed in this perspective, the remote history, future predictions, and feedbacks could be ignored and their effects represented by the structural elements of the model.

Two basic concepts of representative design can be developed at this point: *ecological validity* and *functional validity*. I should note, parenthetically, that the ideas of ecological and functional validity are presented in an oversimplified manner. For example, as the model is presented there are at least three functional validities; one relates to the way in which stimuli are utilized (E to C), and another relates to the way in which means are utilized (C to A). There is a third overreaching arch relating distal stimulus events (E) to achievement (A). The last meaning is closest to that of Brunswik. In a complete explication and development of the model, these aspects should be developed in detail. The first concept refers to the structure of the environment and the second to the organism's utilization of that structure. Aspects of any situation ($a_1 - a_n$) vary in stability from time to time. This variability will affect the value of a particular stimulus as a veridical indicator of the distal situation. The extent of this veridicality is referred to as *ecological validity*. If a_1 is always present when distal event E occurs and seldom present when E does not occur, then it will have a high ecological validity as an indicator of E. If a_2 is present only half of the times that event E occurs and is often present when E does not occur, then a_2 will have a low validity as an indicator of E. If a_3 occurs half of the times, and those times are the same as when a_2 occurs, then we consider a_2 and a_3 to have a perfect intraecological correlation, and they are completely redundant in terms of the information they carry regarding event E. It should be added that an efficient organism utilizes stimuli to the extent that they are ecologically valid.

The manner in which the organism utilizes the arrays impinging on it is referred to as *functional validity*. Organisms vary in the consistency with which they use different stimuli. The degree to which stimuli in the array are actually utilized is defined as *functional validity.* A stimulus can have a high ecological validity and a low functional validity; the organism does not use it even though it is a good stimulus. Conversely, a stimulus with a low ecological validity can have a high functional validity (at least for a restricted period of time); the organism utilizes it consistently and in spite of its lack of usefulness. (The same analysis can be made of the means-end routes, $e_1 - e_n$.)

The various elements in the stimulus array ($a_1 - a_n$) can be thought of as being dimensions within a single sensory system (visual angle, brightness, hue, etc.) or as consisting of bundles across different sensory systems (a_1, a bundle of visual stimuli; a_2, a bundle of auditory stimuli; a_3, a bundle of odors, etc.). In this case, each of these bundles could be further broken down into its constituent array of stimuli. Similarly, on the response side, each of the means-end routes ($e_1 - e_n$) could represent a different way to achieve the same goal (run, crawl, swim, etc.) or could be a distinct and qualitatively different mode of response (fly, attack, remain stationary, approach, etc.), each of which could be broken down into sets of movements.

This way of viewing behavior is a dynamic one. Stimuli and means differ in the trustworthiness with which they mediate distal events. The organism places a bet when it utilizes the stimuli and the means–end routes. It arrays these stimuli and means in a hierarchical fashion, and the pattern of utilization should be related to their salience and trustworthiness. Because each member of the array has some degree of trustworthiness, it will be utilized with a differing probability (or hierarchically organized) by the organism, and, with luck, in the long run, this probability of utilization (functional validity) will reflect the degree of actual trustworthiness (ecological validity).

In short, this model recognizes that variability characterizes, and is an essential part of, the behavior styles of organisms. Brunswik (1952) considered "vicarious functioning" of this kind to be the essence of behavior. The analysis of behavior, he argued, should be viewed in terms of receiving or sending messages through redundant channels – the aim of the organism being to reduce the probability of error.

McFarland (1976:59) has expressed the same view in a discussion of the form and function of the temporal patterns of behavior: "Animals make decisions almost every minute of their lives. The decisions concern what the animal ought to do in a given situation, where many courses of action are possible. The various actions differ in their consequences, and have different costs and benefits attached to them."

Systematic design

The favored research paradigm in behavioral science is what Brunswik has called *systematic design* (see Petrinovich 1979), and he contrasts this to the ideal of *representative design.* I will discuss the ideals of systematic and representative designs as though they represent a dichotomy. Clearly, systematic design can be made more representative than I will characterize it, and representative design can be adapted in ways that employ some of the advantages of systematic experimentation. The case is exaggerated here to highlight the differences between the two modes of approach, even at the risk of creating something of a caricature.

To control variables other than the one (or ones) the experimenter deems to be of interest, the organism is isolated from the action of unwanted extraneous variables. This is done most easily by performing the experiment in a controlled laboratory environment that permits a maximum degree of control. Subjects are drawn from a relatively homogeneous population, and random assignment is used to eliminate differences due to uncontrolled (and unwanted) variability among subjects.

The consequent pattern of results is judged against the null hypothesis that the observed differences between the various groups are a mere function of chance sampling variablility. If this hypothesis is found to be unlikely at a satisfactory level of significance, then some alternative hypothesis is accepted and it is presumed that the treatment had some significant effect. In principle, it is assumed that total variance would be completely explained by between-group effects if the general laws of behavior could be freed from uncontrolled influences and that the within-group variance (called *error*) is due to difficulties in measurement and in the manipulation of variables (e.g., Hull 1943; Postman 1955; Underwood 1957). This method, then, is designed to detect whether or not a particular variable (or variables) has any systematic effect on behavior.

Representative design

Representative design is based on the assumption that to understand the behavior of organisms, it will be necessary not only to study the organism and its adjustment capacities when faced with different stimuli but also to understand the situations in which stimuli are encountered.

If the necessity to understand the normal interplay of environmental and organismic variables is taken seriously and if the environmental variables are admitted into the behavioral equation, then the probabilistic nature of environmental circumstances will be accurately reflected. This, then, requires a representative sampling of situations from the organism's ecology, and the variables studied should remain correlated as they are in the environment. The only control exerted in a truly representative study is the nonintrusive one of actuarial registration of the values of relevant variables as the behavior occurs.

The use of this strategy implies that the choice of the variables themselves should be based on their biological or psychological relevance. Thus, to understand behavior it will be necessary to establish ecological validities. This will then make it possible to move to an understanding of functional validities. Merely studying the organism and the action of isolated stimuli and responses will not suffice.

The analytic methods used should be those that allow us not only to test the significance of hypotheses but also to determine the size of the effects of the different independent variables that have differing degrees of correlation with one another. The statistical methods appropriate to this task, multiple regression–correlation, will be discussed later.

A comparison of systematic and representative designs

The discussion and comparison of systematic and representative designs will be organized around Table 4.1, which is a summary of the characteristics of the

Table 4.1. *Summary of the characteristics of systematic and representative design related to some key issues in experimentation*

Issue	Systematic design	Representative design
Subjects	Random sampling	Random sampling
Situations	Controlled	Random sampling
Stimulus variables	Controlled range and covariance	Natural range and covariance
Response variables	Relatively few; selected by experimenter	Many and comprehensive; actuarially registered
Statistical procedures	Analysis of variance	Multiple regression–correlation
Individual differences	Error variance	Primary data
Explanatory model	Nomothetic	Probabilistic

two designs related to some key research issues. The discussion will follow the organization of the table, briefly describing each issue and then characterizing each of the designs in terms of the issue. Again, the issues are presented as exaggerated polarizations. An extended discussion of the characteristics of the two designs will be found in Petrinovich (1979).

Subject sampling

One of the first issues any investigator must face is that of defining a subject population and then drawing representative samples from it. There is no inherent difference between the designs considered here; both rely on randomization to select subjects and to form groups if a group design is used. Both designs could be used to study an individual subject, of course. Brunswik (1956) has done this using a single subject and a representative sampling of situations. Skinner (1938) has advocated the use of single subjects and a systematic sampling of conditions.

Situation sampling

Both subject and situation sampling refer to what Campbell and Stanley (1963) call *external validity*. This is the question of generalizability: To what populations, settings, treatment variables, and measurement variables can an effect be generalized? Both designs take care to establish the conditions essential to permit a generalization across subjects. The essence of systematic design involves the control of extraneous situational variables in the interest both of replicability and of making statements concerning the functional relationship of an independent variable (or variables) to a dependent variable with all other variables held constant or eliminated by randomization.

The ideal of systematic design, especially as exemplified in the laboratory experiment, precludes situation sampling. Occasionally, situational variables may be included in the design, but this is almost always done to the accompaniment of the control and manipulation of variables in a synthetic environment. The focus is on an experimental task, and a representative sample of subjects from the population is tested. The degrees of freedom for the statistical tests are based on the number of subjects in the study.

One of the major premises of representative design is that situational variables play a major role in determining the behavior of organisms and in regulating its course. If one subject is tested many times in a standard situation, the results can be generalized to the behavior of that subject in that particular situation. If the focus is on the one subject, a representative sample of the population of situations might be taken and the subject could be tested in each of them. Brunswik (1956) has conducted studies of this type, and that is the approach that will be advocated here.

A problem does arise, however, when one takes representative samples of situations. The results can vary greatly from one situational sample to another as a result of differences in the composition of the social groups and the physical characteristics of the ecology. Often the behavior of the same sample of subjects in the same situation is found to differ over successive years. This variation complicates the issue because one must engage in a further search to establish the representative range of variables. One must test more samples of subjects in a broader range of situations, over more years, and include more dependent variables. This variation might be considered a drawback by the frustrated scientist seeking to resolve the ambiguities that arise. On the other hand, it can be taken as a signal that more relevant variables await uncovering.

Stimulus variables

The term *stimulus variables* will be used to refer loosely to anything that is used as an independent variable in a research study. The essence of systematic design, as outlined above, involves the controlled presentation of relatively few stimuli that are manipulated by the experimenter in a preconceived manner. The question of whether the range of stimuli chosen for the experiment are from a range of values that have any ecological or biological significance is usually not confronted. Stimuli are commonly presented within a controlled range, and the covariation of the different stimuli is set at zero. This guarantees equal cell densities at each stimulus value and with each combination of values and, thereby, makes it easier to interpret the pattern of results. The price of this gain in interpretability is the loss of the natural correlational texture of the environment. As Brunswik (1956:70) has so nicely phrased it, "Mostly there is little technical basis for telling whether a given experiment is an ecological normal, located in the midst of a crowd of natural instances, or whether it is at the fringes of reality, as are bearded ladies and other freakish creatures, or whether it perhaps is like a mere homunculus of the laboratory out in the blank."

The aim of representative design is to study those variables that are relevant to the organism's adjustment and survival. The ideal is to let all stimulus variables naturally covary by identifying a large and comprehensive set of variables, then taking random samples of the ecology of the organism. The research is conducted in the natural cultural habitat of the organism. This strategy increases the likelihood that the variables chosen will be those that have some biological and social relevance to the particular organism and to the species, rather than being selected primarily on the basis of their importance to the theoretical interests of the experimenter.

Response variables

When using systematic design, the responses the organism is permitted are usually circumscribed by the nature of the testing situation. Typically the experimenter records only that aspect of the response system in which there is an a priori theoretical interest. Often behaviors are chosen for study because they are salient and easy to observe and record, there is a good transducer available to measure them, or other investigators have studied them. Thus, behaviors are studied because of concerns relating to the experiment and the experimenter rather than to the behaving organism in its environment. The ideal of representative design is to permit the organism a free range of behavior and to rely on actuarial registration of a completely representative sample of the organism's behavior. Of course, this ideal cannot be completely attained because it is not possible to avoid some selection and coding of variables.

Statistical procedures

The analytic statistics tend to differ depending on which design is used. When using systematic design, the preferred statistic is the fixed effect analysis of variance, often employing a factorial design. (A tabulation by Edgington [1974] of the types of statistical analyses used in those American Psychological Association journals primarily concerned with original empirical research supports this statement.) When one uses this approach, it is desirable to have either an equal or a proportional number of observations in each cell throughout the matrix of cells for computational efficiency and to avoid the spurious correlations among independent variables that occur as a result of disproportionate cell frequencies. In experimental research, then, the emphasis is on the study of the main effects and interaction of a set of variables that are preconceived as theoretically important. Traditionally, little attempt is made to represent the interaction of subjects, stimuli, or situations as they are found in nature.

The essence of representative design, on the other hand, is the analysis of variables as they occur in the natural setting. "Many issues in behavioral sciences are simply inaccessible to true experiments, and can only be addressed by the systematic observation of phenomena as they occur in their natural flux" (Cohen and Cohen 1975:8). In such nonexperimental settings the independent and dependent variables have an inescapable messiness that is not characteristic of those variables found in controlled experiments.

A more extended discussion of the nature and application of multiple regression–correlation to representative design will be presented later in this chapter. The essential point here is that the nonexperimental nature of the variables and the mixture of experimental and nonexperimental variables in the same research study make the traditional analysis of variance inappropriate and require the use of the more general multiple regression–correlation analysis.

It should be emphasized that both analysis of variance and multiple regression are special cases of the general linear model. Multiple regression, as it will be outlined in the next section, is a special case of the canonical generalization, and analysis of variance is a special case of the more general multiple regression. However, as Kerlinger and Pedhazur (1973) have pointed out, multiple regression is the superior or the only appropriate method to use in situations in which (1) an independent variable is continuous, or (2) there are both continuous and categorical independent variables, or (3) the cell frequencies in a factorial design are unequal and disproportionate, or (4) trends in data are being studied.

Individual differences

In the standard schemes of systematic design, individual differences are usually assigned to the error term (within-groups variance) against which the size of the main effect and interactions (between-groups variance) will be evaluated to determine the statistical significance of the effects. The intent is to discover the general and universal laws that govern behavior and to determine the form of the functional relationships between manipulated independent variables and the dependent variable, with the effects of individual differences between subjects removed as a factor.

The essence of representative design is to determine lawful relationships between a representative sample of independent variables and the functional attainments of individuals. Subjects can then be grouped according to their response styles, as will be illustrated in the section "A design model using individual regression analysis." Viewed in this way, individual differences become the primary data of focus.

Explanatory model

The aim of systematic design is nomothetic – to write a set of universal and general laws that govern behavior. If one fails to attain this end, "proponents of the nomothetic point of view see the difficulty in inadequate knowledge of antecedent conditions, while retaining their belief in the essential uniformity of the behavioral laws; proponents of the probability view believe that the laws themselves must be stated in probability terms" (Postman 1955:222).

The probabilistic nature of representative design is partly a result of the recognition that environmental influences are complex and interacting, and that the causes of behavior are multiple. This suggests that one should use a research strategy that allows the essential probabilistic nature of the general laws describing the relationship between organisms and the distal environment to express itself. It can be argued even further (Petrinovich 1976) that this probabilism is an inherent property of the biological processes on which behavior depends.

Multiple regression/correlation analysis

The approach to research advocated here is one that has had appeal to many theorists and researchers for some years. It has not had many adherents in actual practice, however, because there were no analytic models equal to the task of dealing with the complexity of the conceptual framework. With the advent of the high-speed computer the field of multivariate statistics has proceeded apace; standard "canned" computer programs are available for all of the techniques discussed here. These developments have been incorporated into a general data analytic model that can be applied to data in almost any form. In this presentation I have placed heavy reliance on two recent texts that develop the multiple regression/correlation (MRC) models at a level that is intelligible for the nonmathematical reader. In particular, these texts take pains to outline the applications of these models to the data of behavioral science. I wish to express my debt to the authors (and hope that they do not feel either that I borrowed too freely from them or that I have done violence to the elegance of their presentations by this brief treatment) and urge anyone not familiar with these methods to study both books carefully. One of these books is *Multiple Regression in Behavioral Research* by Kerlinger and Pedhazur (1973), and the other is *Applied Multiple Regression/Correlation Analysis for the Behavioral Sciences* by Cohen and Cohen (1975).

I will begin with a quotation from Cohen and Cohen, followed by one from Kerlinger and Pedhazur, to give the reader the flavor of their enthusiasm for these methods. "In short, and at the risk of sounding like a television commercial, MRC is a versatile, all-purpose system for analyzing the data of the behavioral, social, and biological sciences and technologies" (1975:4). "Within the decade we will probably see the virtual demise of one-variable thinking and the use of analysis of variance with data unsuited to the method. Instead, multivariate methods will be well-accepted tools in the behavioral scientist's and educator's armamentarium" (1973:vi).

MRC is a general data analytic system that can be used with any combination of variables in any quantitative form. It is appropriate with continuously measured independent variables (IVs) that represent some construct (scores on a personality test), attribute (height, weight), or manipulated variables (intensity of a light, amount of weight loss). It can be used with categorical variables of any kind (sex, race, religion, social class, passing vs. failing a test). The dependent variable (DV) can be in any continuous form (the logic has been extended to categorical variables, as well), and there is no problem with any combination of types of IVs and DVs. In addition, sets of IVs can be formed from the individual variables at the discretion of the researcher, and the set is then treated as a single variable if the logic of the problem permits it. The methods can be used with any form of relationship between the IVs and the DVs – linear or curvilinear, although the latter requires a model of greater complexity. The system is flexible enough to study the interaction of variables and to analyze results that have missing data for some individuals on some of the variables. Finally, it can be used with experimental and nonexperimental data or a combination of data in one matrix. The general model permits the analysis of multiple IVs and multiple DVs – a canonical generalization – but the discussion here will be restricted to multiple IVs and a single DV.

Basic concepts

The MRC model is an extension and generalization of the general linear regression model. The basic equation to be generalized is the simple linear regression equation to predict one variable (Y) from another (X): $Y' = A + bX$, where Y' is the predicted value of Y; A is the intercept constant that gives the predicted value of the DV when the IV value is zero; b is the slope constant (also called the *regression coefficient*) that indicates how much of a change in Y' occurs with one unit change in X.

The regression equation itself does not provide the best way to characterize how well it can be used to predict Y' from X. The best way to express the predictive efficiency of a regression equation is to calculate the Pearsonian r between the predicted Y values (Y') and the obtained Y values (Y). Thus r^2 describes how much variance is shared between the Y' and Y variables.

A conceptual leap must be made to understand multiple regression, which is a generalization of this basic equation. If one were to calculate a Pearsonian r between the residuals ($Y - Y'$) and the original X values, it would always be zero. However, this does not mean that the variance of the residuals cannot be explained by some other predictor. We have obtained a minimal value for $\Sigma(Y - Y')^2$ where $Y' = A + b_1X_1$. $\Sigma(Y - Y')^2$ can be rewritten as $\Sigma[Y - (A + bX_1)]^2$. To include more than one IV, the equation can be expanded as follows: $Y' = A + b_1X_1 + b_2X_2$. Then $\Sigma(Y - Y')^2 = \Sigma[Y - (A + b_1X_1 + b_2X_2)]^2$. The effect of incorporating the additional variables (X_2) is to further minimize the residual left after the first variable (X_1) has been entered. The X_2 variable is brought into play by substituting the $Y - Y'$ value for Y and X_2 for X_1. This, then, substitutes the residuals for the original values and a second IV (X_2) for the first IV (X_1). After mathematical manipulation, the formula is $Y' = A + b_1X_1 + b_2X_2$. The procedure can be repeated again for a third variable or, within reasonable limits, for as many predictors as the experimenter needs to consider.

The predictive efficiency of the multiple regression formula can be stated in the same way it was in the simple linear case. The square of the correlation between Y and Y' can be calculated and expressed as R^2. This number represents the proportion of variance in the Y scores that is accounted for by a linear composite of the X scores.

The basic equation, then, can be written in a form that can be extended to any number of IVs: $Y' = A + b_1X_1 + b_2X_2 + b_3X_3 + \ldots + b_kX_k$ where b_1 is the weight given to variable X_1 when variables X_2 through X_k are also in the equation. In this equation b is a partial regression coefficient that expresses the optimal (i.e., least squares) linear estimates of Y when all of the X variables are used in combination.

How are equations of this kind applied to research problems? Assume that we are interested in studying the factors that contribute to the level of maternal sensitivity. Assume, also, that we have been able to scale sensitivity in a reliable fashion (say, on a scale from 1 to 7) and that the validity of the characterization has also been found to be acceptable. In other words, assume that we have a continuously scaled criterion variable, Y. The theoretical proposition of interest is that the gaze of the mother and the gaze of the infant are important indicators of maternal sensitivity when the mother and infant are in close interaction.

To obtain data bearing on this point, the looking behaviors of each have

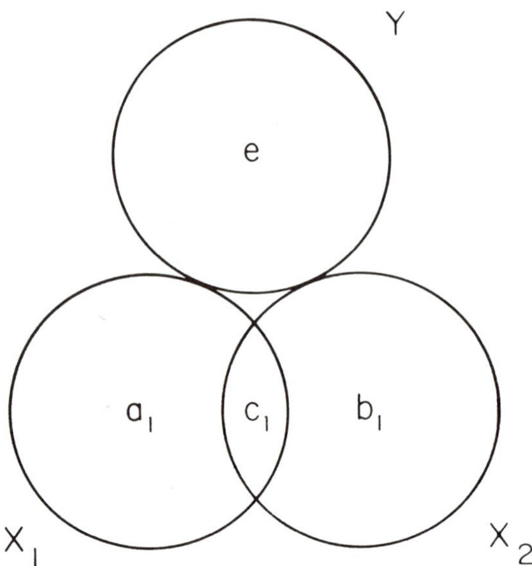

Figure 4.2. Ballantine in which variables X_1 and X_2 are correlated but neither is correlated with Y.

been recorded in a representative sample of situations in which mother and infant encounter one another. The data are in the form of continuous recordings over 15-minute periods of how many seconds the infant looks at the mother (X_1) and how many seconds the mother looks at the infant (X_2), and they have been recorded with the time entered so that the number of seconds the mother and infant engage in mutual gaze can be determined (X_1 intersection X_2). We would like to know whether or not, and to what extent, gaze (X_1, X_2, $X_1 \cap X_2$) is related to maternal sensitivity (Y). Let us assume that none of the variance in Y is related to X_1 or X_2, but that X_1 is correlated with X_2. This could be represented by what is called the *ballantine* by Cohen and Cohen: The variance of each variable is represented by a circle of unit area. The overlapping of two circles represents their relationship, which is expressed as r^2, the proportion of variance in one variable that is shared with the other.

The situation is represented in Figure 4.2.

None of the area e is overlapped by a_1, b_1, or c, the areas representing X_1, X_2, and X_1 intersection X_2, respectively. Hence R^2, the proportion of the Y variance shared with the optimally weighted IVs, is zero. The variance shared by X_1 and X_2 is represented by area c, and this represents the proportion of the time that the infant and mother are looking at each other at the same time.

Let us now assume a weak relationship between X_1, X_2, and $Y(R^2 = 0.10)$ and that X_1 is still correlated with X_2. This situation is represented in Figure 4.3.

Now, Y is overlapped by X_1 and X_2 and the total area of Y covered by the X_1

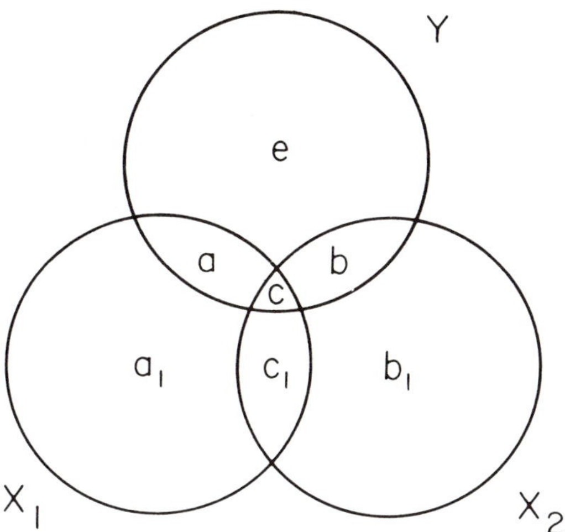

Figure 4.3. Ballantine in which variables X_1 and X_2 are correlated and both are correlated with Y.

and X_2 areas (a, b, c) represents the proportion of the variance of Y accounted for by X_1 and $X_2 (R^2 = 0.10)$. The R^2 can be analyzed into three separate components: area a, the proportion of Y overlapped uniquely by X_1 (a), the proportion of Y overlapped uniquely by X_2 (b), and the proportion of Y overlapped simultaneously by X_1 and X_2 (c).

This can also be expressed as follows (the figures in parentheses are, of course, hypothetical). $R^2 = a + b + c = 0.10$. This 0.10 can be broken into the three separate components mentioned above, and these three proportions express the amount of the total variance in Y uniquely accounted for by each variable: called the squared *semipartial* rs, sr^2

$$sr_a^2 = \frac{a}{a+b+c+e} = \frac{a}{1} = (0.01)$$

$$sr_b^2 = \frac{b}{a+b+c+e} = \frac{b}{1} = (0.03)$$

$$sr_c^2 = \frac{c}{a+b+c+e} = \frac{c}{1} = (0.06)$$

$$R^2 = \frac{a+b+c}{a+b+c+e} = \frac{a+b+c}{1} = (0.10)$$

We can see that 0.01 of the variance in maternal sensitivity is uniquely related to the amount of time the infant looks at the mother (X_1); 0.03 is uniquely related to the amount of time the mother looks at the infant (X_2); 0.06 of the variance is uniquely related to the amount of time the baby and the mother are looking at each other at the same time ($X_1 \cap X_2$).

We could also express these relationships in terms of the amount of variance uniquely accounted for by each variable and not by any other: the squared *partial r*, pr^2.

$$pr_a^2 = \frac{a}{a+e} \left(\frac{0.01}{0.91} = .011\right)$$

$$pr_b^2 = \frac{b}{b+e} \left(\frac{0.03}{0.93} = .032\right)$$

$$pr_c^2 = \frac{c}{c+e} \left(\frac{0.06}{0.96} = .0625\right)$$

Several things should be pointed out: (1) pr^2 is always larger than sr^2 if there is any relationship between the IVs and the DV; the partial r is expressed as the proportion of the unexplained Y variance, and the semipartial r is expressed as the proportion of the total Y variance; (2) the model presented here is a simultaneous one in the sense that all IVs have been considered equally and at the same time; (3) this strategy could be used to include any number of IVs.

We could use an alternative strategy to treat these data, specifying an a priori hierarchy by which we wish to examine the data. For example, we might be primarily interested in the influence of the amount of time the infant looks at the mother (X_1). We could enter it first in the regression equation, giving it all of the X_1 variance ($a + c$), and then enter X_2, which will then be assigned only area b. The point is that the logic of the research can determine the priority with which the variables are treated, and the analysis will follow dutifully along as our theory and insight demand.

It is hoped that this brief excursion into the nature of MRC will provide at least an idea of the procedures. To summarize some of its characteristics:

1 It is a general data analytic system that "operates like a detective searching for clues rather than like a bookkeeper seeking to prove out a balance" (Cohen & Cohen 1975:15).
2 It is appropriate for information in any scalar form.
3 It can be applied to data that are of either functional shape, linear or curvilinear.
4 It can be used with either correlated or uncorrelated IVs.
5 It is more versatile than factorial analysis of variance, which is constrained to treat research factors in a nominal form and which assumes orthogonal factors.

As Cohen and Cohen (1975) have also pointed out, MRC is designed to answer a set of specific questions:

1 How well does a particular group of IVs estimate Y? The answer is contained in the squared coefficient of multiple correlation (R^2).
2 How much does any single IV add to the estimation of Y that has already been accomplished by other variables? The answer is in terms of incremental validities.
3 What is the relationship between any given IV and Y when the other IVs have been taken into account? The answer is in terms of partial correlation. (It is no problem to eliminate the effect of a variable by partialing out its effects: A generalization of the analysis of covariance that has the useful property that

the required assumption of equal regression of the DV on the covariate across all groups can be tested.)

4 What is the amount of change in Y' associated with a unit change in each of the IVs when all variables are expressed in standard score units? The answer is in terms of standard partial regression weights (β).

What are the assumptions of the model as it has been presented? In its simplest and most straightforward application, the model as described assumes linearity of regression of each variable on Y. (This is not a necessary restriction because one can – especially if there is a theoretical reason to do so – detect, represent, and study curvilinear relationships within the confines of linear MRC; see Cohen & Cohen 1975, Chap. 6.)

For testing statistical significance of the components of MRC, one should be able to assume a normal distribution around the mean of X and of Y with equal variates of Y on each conditional value of X *in the population* (the assumption of homoscedasticity). If this assumption is questionable, then appropriate scale transformations should be applied. The significance tests used have been found to be very robust, and little error of inference occurs when the data are treated as if these assumptions were valid. The errors produced by violations of assumptions tend to be in the conservative direction because almost all violations examined decrease both the estimates of association and the likelihood of detecting significant differences.

When using MRC the IVs are combined additively. This is defensible in two regards. First, it has been found that when the linear model is applied to different sets of data, the R^2 is more reliable from instance to instance. One might catch the special characteristics of a particular set of data by some other combinatorial principle, but another principle would capitalize heavily on chance relationships in the data. When the same complex regression weights are applied to an independent sample (cross-validated), these chance factors are not present and the R^2 is found to drop. The linear model has been found to be less subject to this shortcoming (see Wiggins 1973).

Second, overwhelming support has been obtained for the adequacy of the linear model as a representation of human judgment in such diverse realms as clinical inference (Hammond et al. 1964), multiple cue probability learning (Kahnemann & Tversky 1973), and human social judgment (Brehmer 1976b; Hammond et al. 1975) (see Wiggins 1973 for a review of this literature). Slovic and Lichtenstein (1971) have surveyed the human information-processing literature and found that the linear additive model accounts for about 0.50 of the variance in adult human judgments that have been studied. Thus, the procedures advocated here are quite satisfactory even when dealing with some of the most complex human processes.

Some cautions are in order regarding problems that will be encountered when MRC models are used with the kinds of data usually available to those studying development – especially data from longitudinal studies. A major problem has to do with the number of IVs relative to the number of subjects. If one is engaged in long-term intensive studies of a few subjects, then as much information is usually gathered as possible.

Having gathered information, one is loath to ignore it because of the dictates of the Protestant ethic and the desire to be certain that all substantive aspects of the issue have been dealt with. The temptation is, then, to add all of the IVs possible in the prediction equation in the interest of thoroughness and obsessiveness. Cohen and Cohen (1975) suggest that, in such instances, variables should be purged of redundancy. It might be best to exclude peripheral variables and to combine redundant variables into a sum, an index, or a factor score. Such combinations will increase reliability and the power of the test on each IV because fewer degrees of freedom will be lost as a result of the large number of IVs. Cohen and Cohen (1975:16) express this principle as "less is more – more statistical test validity, more power, and more clarity in the meaning of results." One not only obtains more power by combining variables in this way, but less shrinkage (reduction) of the R^2 occurs when the regression system is tested on an independent sample of subjects.

Cohen and Cohen (1975) also recommend that research factors should be ordered according to their centrality to the theoretical model being investigated. Those factors of least relevance should be appraised last when using a hierarchical MRC model of inference, and the results obtained regarding these variables should be taken as indicators rather than conclusions. They name this principle "least is last."

MULTIPLE REGRESSION AND REPRESENTATIVE DESIGN

How does the MRC scheme relate to the conception of the lens model discussed earlier? One can consider the separate aspects of the data arrays in the lens model (e.g., $a_1 - a_n$) to be separate IVs that are focused on a criterion variable (e.g., *E* or back into *C*) (see fig. 4.1). The applicability of MRC to data in this form is readily apparent. Each ray is represented as an IV in an MRC scheme and is used to predict the state of *Y*, which could be a trait (*E*), a judgment (*C*), or a functional attainment (*A*). As long as *A*, *C*, and *E* can be reliably scaled in some quantitative fashion, no matter how crudely, MRC analysis can be used.

Different classes of variables could be combined into the same analysis. For example, it would be possible to attempt to predict a response outcome, such as the rate of habituation of a response over time (an *A* variable), using stimulus variables such as strength, modality, frequency, and patterning of stimulation, and attribute variables such as physiological state of the organism, age, and excitability level. These predictions could be simple linear associations or, if theory demands it, curvilinear functions of some of the variables. All of these variables could then be entered as IVs to determine the proportion of total variance accounted for and the proportion of unique variance in *Y* that can be attributed to each variable when all other variables are in the equation.

It would probably make more sense, however, to use some hierarchical analytic procedure whereby one enters the variables in some rational order dictated by theory. First, one might want to enter the number of stimulus presentations, because according to Thompson's theory of habituation this is the variable of singular importance (see Thompson et al. 1973). Next, the quadratic component (indicative of curvilinearity) of the number of presentations could be entered to detect whether or not there is an initial inflection in the response curve, as habituation theory predicts. Then the cubic might be entered to determine whether or not there is a second inflection that would reveal the predicted asymptotic level for some of the curves. Next, the attribute variables, physiological condition, age, and excitability level might be entered, and then the manipulated variables, type, modality, and patterning of stimulation. Rather than continue the discussion in the abstract, it might be instructive to consider some data from a research project that uses representative design conceptions and MRC strategies in conducting the study in the attempt to understand the data.

A CASE HISTORY IN REPRESENTATIVE DESIGN USING MRC ANALYSIS

Although these data are not strictly developmental, they involve a broad sampling of behavior in the natural environment, bear on a systematic theoretical issue, and illustrate some of the potential positive characteristics of representative design. The study does deal with the analysis of a time-dependent process, habituation, and some of the methods utilized would be applicable to the study of short-term developmental processes. The research program is described primarily to illustrate and consolidate the principles discussed up to this point. The specific long-term developmental applications of the model will take a different approach from the strategies utilized here.

The experiments to be considered are designed to help us understand the role of habituation in the territorial behavior of the Nuttall subspecies of the white-crowned sparrow (*Zonotrichia leucophrys*). Several reports of this work have been published (Petrinovich & Peeke 1973; Petrinovich et al. 1976; Patterson & Petrinovich 1979; Petrinovich & Patterson 1979, 1980), so few details will be presented here. I will concentrate, instead, on the major aspects of the study as they relate to the methodological questions at hand.

These experiments are done in the field with breeding pairs. The substantive focus of the research is the role of habituation in the establishment and maintenance of the territorial system in this species. The aim is to establish the factors that determine the level of the response to the recorded playback of song and to determine the factors regulating the rate of change in those responses.

Consider some aspects of the life history of the species. This sedentary subspecies is territorial. The male patrols the boundaries of the territory (which is usually a little over 1,000 square meters in size) from about March through July. The pairs are monogamous for life and spend the time from January through July almost entirely in the territory. Following pair formation in January, the male does not sing much. This quiet period usually lasts until March. Then typically one male sings and the other males fly about and respond to the song, all staying within their respective territorial boundaries. Early in the season, frequent territorial conflicts marked by physical encounters occur between males. By the time the breeding season starts, the territorial conflicts are reduced to bouts of singing and countersinging between the neighboring males.

In early April the female builds a nest, the pair copulates, and the female lays a clutch of about three eggs, one per day. The young hatch after about 13 days, and the nestlings are fed insects, mainly by the female at first, with the male assisting more near the end of the nestling period (about 9 days long). When the young fledge, they stay in the region of the nest for about 20 to 30 days, with the male assuming major responsibility to feed the young during the latter part of the period. A few days after the young of the early broods fledge, the female begins a new nest and the whole cycle starts again, continuing until the pair have two broods or until sometime in July, when feeding flocks of juveniles and adults can be seen foraging through the territories and the territories begin breaking down. The young suffer heavy predation from both land and aerial predators; only about 30% of the eggs produced result in a fledgling (Patterson & Petrinovich in preparation).

Each male usually has one song that is about 2 seconds long and is repeated every 11 seconds during a bout of singing. There are pronounced regional dialect groups (Baptista 1975; Marler & Tamura 1962), which are stable from year to year. The songs of these groups are composed of similar elements, but they are combined in different orders.

Why is habituation being studied? This time-dependent process has been demonstrated to exist in a wide range of species, from invertebrates to humans. The characteristics of habituation have been studied intensively by Richard Thompson and his associates (e.g., 1973) using both intact animal preparations and the isolated spinal cord in cats. They have provided a broad spectrum of parametric data with which our results can be compared.

When a song is played in a territory, the male and female almost immediately appear, respond by flying about, and perform aggressive displays such as rapid wing flutters and trills. The female, under some circumstances, will emit rapid "chinks" and the male will begin to sing. These responses seem to be less intense and long-lasting to the familiar song of the immediate neighbors than they are to unfamiliar songs. It has been suggested that habituation is involved in maintaining the territorial system in some species of birds (e.g., Falls & Brooks 1975; Krebs 1977) and in fish (Peeke & Peeke 1973).

Habituation is defined as "the relatively permanent waning of a response as a result of repeated stimulation which is not followed by any kind of reinforcement. It is specific to the stimulation and is relatively enduring" (Thorpe 1963:61). Thompson et al. (1973) have identified several factors that influence habituation, and Thompson (1976) suggests that these are characteristics that have wide generality across species, preparations, and situations.

The research to be outlined here investigates the characteristics of habituation to the playback of recorded song in the field. I have chosen to work in the field because all variables that influence the birds are present as background and the correlation texture of all variables can be preserved. Thus, I do not have to worry about the effect of artificial and atypical backgrounds against which the experimental variables are displayed. The animals are not maintained in confined, aberrant circumstances. The experimenters intrude on the organisms to a minimal degree, maintaining a discreet distance and occasionally presenting song at a normal rate through a loudspeaker. The birds are permitted a free range of behavior, and all observable behavior is recorded for a period of 3 to 4 hours.

One prevalent belief is that using such naturalistic conditions is fine for framing hypotheses and identifying important variables, but that in the face of all of the uncontrolled variance present in the field, one cannot isolate and manipulate variables sufficiently adequately to test the parameters of quantitative behavior theory. To do this, it is argued, one must move into the laboratory. I hope to demonstrate that this presumption is not necessarily true.

To avoid misunderstanding, it should be made clear that there are many tasks facing behavioral science whose solution almost demands laboratory investigation. For example, if one seeks to understand mediational processes, then systematic laboratory study is the method of choice. Also, if a representative study is to be undertaken, it is wise to conduct a series of preliminary systematic studies aimed at identifying those variables that possibly influence the behaviors in question. Those variables can then be included in a study that seeks to determine the relative probabilities of the IVs in conjunction with the behavior. "It is necessary to establish possibility, but a complete and sufficient science will arrive at a statement of the probable importance of variables in the determination of behavioral outcomes" (Petrinovich 1979:383.). "Indeed, the laws which govern the isolated fragments of behavior studied in contrived laboratory situations may be of a different order than the laws which govern behavior in more complex naturalistic settings" (Wiggins 1973:4).

Thus, a systematic, organism-centered science is not *the* enterprise, nor is it adequate to all tasks. Just as molecular genetics has not replaced evolutionary biology, so the study of physiological processes cannot replace functional psychology. The physiological psychologist and the biological or psychological psychologist focus on different data domains that may require different types of principles.

The attempt to understand systems by analyzing them at the level of the most basic elements is quite prevalent and of unquestionable value. However, analysis at the molecular level is only one approach and not the final goal. "The past history of biology has shown that progress is equally inhibited by an anti-analytical holism and a purely atomistic reductionism. A healthy future for biology can be guaranteed only by a joint analytical and systems approach" (Mayr 1964:72).

The research program

In 1974 the nests of 22 mated pairs of birds were located and the territories were mapped (Petrinovich & Patterson 1979). A given pair was subjected to the playback of the song of a territorial male of the same dialect group. The initial portion of the playback (which is all that will be considered here) was presented in a series of eight trials. Each trial is constructed as follows: ten 2-second long songs with a fixed 11-second intersong interval, a 1-minute silent period, another 10 songs as before, and a 5-minute silent period. Each trial, then, contains 20 songs, and there is a total of 160 songs over 4,784 seconds, or a song about every 30 seconds. One IV, then, is the trial number.

A preliminary regression analysis indicated that the reproductive condition of the female (whether she was brooding eggs [E], feeding nestlings [N], or

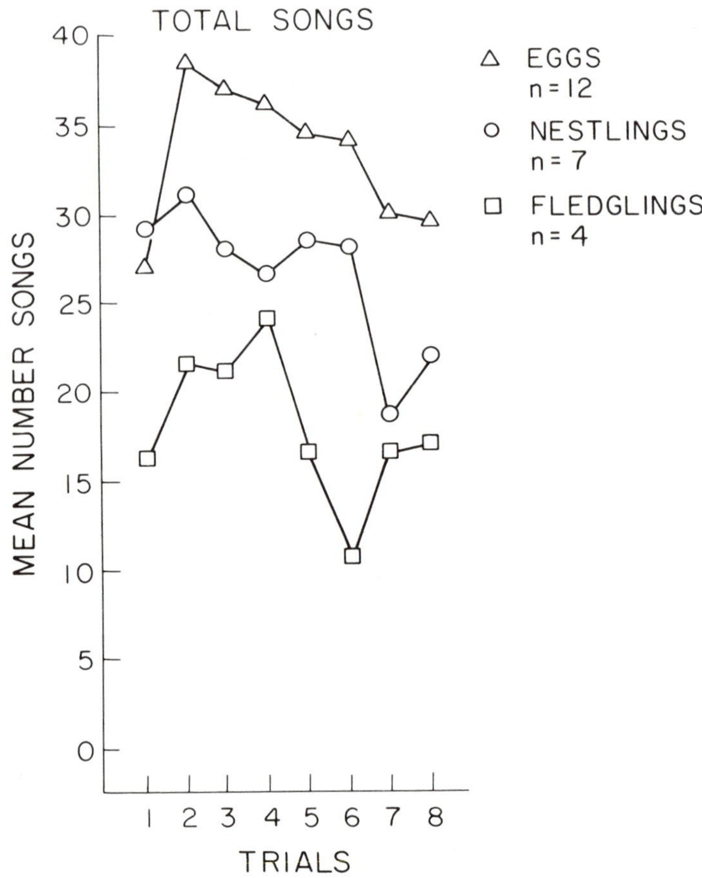

A

feeding fledglings [F] was a variable of considerable importance. Because of this finding, reproductive condition was used to create an IV and the pairs were classified into three groups: E, n = 11; N, n = 7; F, n = 4. Incidentally, the decreasing n reflects the structure of the population. The experimental mortality is just that. The E group can be tested as the nests are found, it is necessary to wait until eggs hatch to test them as nestlings, and the nests suffer predation during this interval. Even greater predation occurs if one must wait until the nestlings fledge to test them. This could be considered a drawback in view of the decreasing *n*s; however, I consider it to represent the reality of the situation.

All observable behaviors were recorded, and each was used as a DV in a separate regression analysis. The male behaviors recorded are: full songs, partial songs, intersong interval, flights, fright chinks, trills, flutters, attacks on other birds, and distance from the speaker. The female behaviors recorded are: flights, fright chinks, trills, flutters, and time (in seconds) in view (the females do not ordinarily sing).

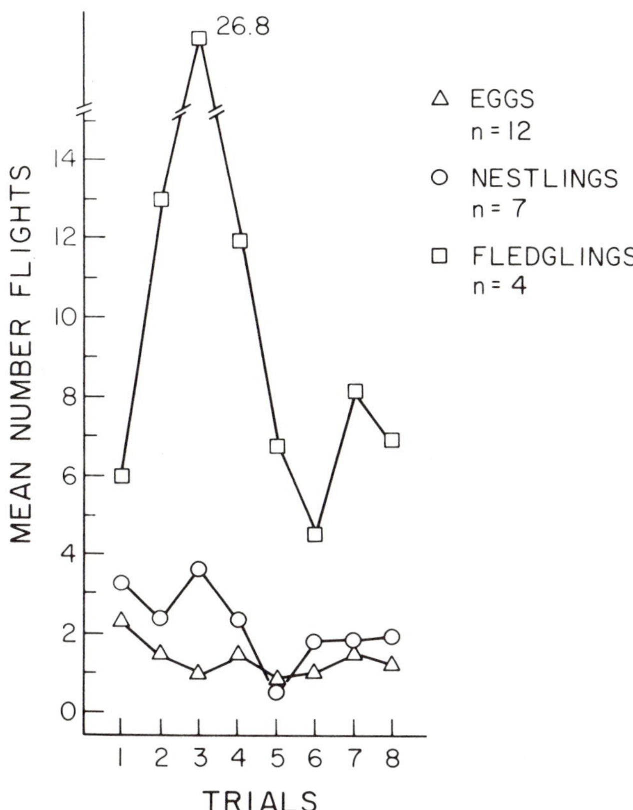

B

Figure 4.4. *A*. Number of male songs, and *B*. number of female flights during the playback periods. Eleven pairs were tested with eggs (triangles), seven pairs were tested with nestlings (circles), and four pairs were tested with fledglings (squares).

A regression analysis was done separately for each DV over the eight trials using reproductive condition as a classificatory variable to form three groups. This analysis allows the determination of whether or not the regression lines across trials for the three groups are parallel (a test for a common regression coefficient), whether the response levels of the groups to be compared differ significantly (a test of intercept), and whether the change across trials is significant for each group (a test of slope constants).

For example, consider the results for two of the variables. The data for male total songs are plotted in Figure 4.4A. A regression analysis indicates that the regression lines are parallel for the three groups, there is a significant difference between response rates of the three groups, and the rate decreases significantly over trials for all groups. The data for female flights are plotted in Figure 4.4B, and the analysis indicates that the regression system is not common over the three groups and therefore cannot be described using a single regression line. This means that there is an interaction over trials: The females with fledglings (F) fly significantly more and the level decreases across trials, whereas the females in the E and N groups fly very little and their rate remains constant over trials.

The pattern for the different DVs is a bit overwhelming and bewildering at first glance. However, it becomes clear upon close examination. During the playback, the complex pattern is easy to comprehend in the context of the ongoing behavior during the different states of the reproductive cycle. When the female is brooding eggs, she does not come into view a great deal. Having no young to warn, she issues practically no fright chinks, but she does trill and flutter in response to the playback on those occasions when she does come into view. These last two behaviors seem to serve an aggressive function for both males and females. The male whose female is brooding eggs does not chink, but he trills and flutters at the outset and ceases to do so as the playback progresses.

With fledglings, the female is in view most of the time and flies about, issuing a large number of chinks. The fledglings tend to cease moving and to stop emitting begging calls when either the male or female chinks; this behavior enhances the concealment of the young. The female also flutters and trills at a fairly high rate. The male sings less than in the other two conditions; the interval between songs is longer; he flies less; he initially flutters but stops doing so as the trials progress. At this stage the male is taking a more active role in the care of the fledglings, and chinks and trills drop out as trials progress; the male often begins to forage for insects to feed the fledglings during the later playback trials.

The message is that it is difficult to understand either the patterning of response levels for the different variables or the amount of change in level unless something is known of the appropriateness of the different behaviors in the context of the environmental demands. Further, the major variable by which the groups were classified (reproductive condition) could not have been recognized in a laboratory setting because this species, like many, does not reproduce in the laboratory. The naturalistic strategies followed here have led to an appreciation of the importance of a physiological mechanism that can now be systematically investigated in the laboratory.

Several conclusions are important in the present context. First, the choice of response measure is an important consideration because the effects on the different measures are so complex. A response decrement does occur to the repeated playback of recorded song for some responses, but not for others. If I had arbitrarily chosen only one or a selected few of these variables for study, it would be possible to argue that there are no differences in response level as a function of reproductive condition (male flutters, trills, and attacks), that there is a large difference in level (female trills, time in view), that birds with eggs respond more than those with young (male flights and partial song), or that birds with fledglings respond more than any other group (female time in view). Similarly, by selecting variables, I could conclude that response level does not change over trials (male flight, female trill, female time in view), or that it decreases over trials (full and partial song, male and female chinks). By allowing the animals to behave freely, I have arrived at some understanding of the organization of their behavior in the context of the entire behavioral repertoire, where all ecological determinants and supports are present.

One of the most serious problems in the use of representative design is the proper choice of variables. Because we are dealing with stimulus and response systems in the environment, and because environmental situations can alter the organism's hierarchy of stimuli and means, we must study representative environments as systematically as we study representative organisms.

To proceed, I have suggested that we mount a three-pronged attack (Petrinovich 1979):

1 A laboratory and field study of the organism's capacities: to determine the stimuli to which it is receptive; to determine what responses are available in its repertoire; to determine the extent to which it is able to associate stimuli and responses.
2 A study of the natural history of the species: to determine behaviors that occur given different stimulus situations and to understand the possible adaptive significance of these behaviors. An ethogram should be constructed to discover what the animal does in selected representative contexts.
3 A study of the quantitative and qualitative aspects of the environment and situations in which the behaviors of interest occur.

Following this initial stage of analysis, we can move to a level of synthesis. Here we control and manipulate variables in a laboratory setting to determine the array of variables that are of possible importance in controlling the behaviors of interest and to identify the behaviors that are likely to appear in the face of controlled situational factors.

After the stages of analysis and synthesis, we can proceed to the primary task with which we are involved: to determine the relative potential importance of the variables that we have identified in the control of behavior in the natural environment.

In the case of the study to which we have been referring, this approach seems to have a satisfactory degree of power. Out of 17 tests of parallelism, 2 were significant (indications of an interaction between trials and group). These 2 significant systems yielded 6 significant differences out of a possible 12. The 15 parallel systems yielded 11/15 significant intercept differences and 6/15 significant slope differences. (Because some of the DVs are highly intercorrelated, caution must be used to evaluate the meaning of the sheer number of significant results.)

From 12 to 18% of the total variance in song, female chinks, and time in view was accounted for by only two variables – the number of trials and reproductive condition of the female. In a later experiment, one new variable was added (general responsiveness of the male), and this accounted for as much as 54% of the total variance.

In 1975 and 1976, 27 pairs of birds were studied using a slightly different playback regime to study other characteristics of habituation (Patterson & Petrinovich 1979). The patterning of responses was similar to those found with the distributed schedule in relation to the stage of the breeding cycle, thereby providing a cross-validation of the general conclusions of the first study.

Next, an attempt was made to allow a more natural set of conditions to prevail during the playback (Petrinovich & Patterson 1980). In the previous two paradigms, the playback occurred once every 11 seconds (with silent periods interspersed). In nature, the territorial neighbors would behave toward one another in a different manner. Two males may engage in a bout of singing. If one of them flies to another portion of his territory, the other usually stops singing and the countersinging bout ends. With the standard playback procedure, the song runs according to a preplanned schedule and is not responsive to the subject bird's behavior.

In this new study the playback was contingent on the response of the resident male. Ten songs were played to attract the male. After that, the playback was contingent on the song of the resident male. Each time he sang, a playback was presented within 1 or 2 seconds of the end of his song. If he did not sing for a period of 2 minutes, one song was presented, and this occurred every 2 minutes if the male was unresponsive. This procedure continued for 120 minutes. Twelve pairs with eggs were tested in 1976.

Because of the large number of playback trials created with this paradigm (20, because there are no silent periods), there was a large number of significant differences; 16/21 variables showed a significant decrement at the 0.05 level of confidence or greater. However, the amount of the variance accounted for by the trials effect (which indicates the amount of response decrement) is extremely small. The significant response decrements account for as little as 0.5%, increasing to a maximum of only 7.7% of the total variance.

During the experiment, both observers (who were responding to the songs of the male rather than passively recording behavior in response to automatically programmed stimulation) had the impression that there were two types of males. Some seemed to respond at a high rate, and others seemed to be almost completely inactive. This impression led to a secondary analysis of the data.

The median number of songs was used to classify the males into two groups, high singers and low singers. There was a significant difference between the groups and a significant response decrement for both. The interesting finding was that the high singers were significantly higher on all variables than were the lows, and the response level decreased across trials for the highs on all variables except attacks (which almost never occurred in this experiment).

The grouping was done on the basis of the male's behavior. What about the females? The female response levels decreased across trials for four of the five responses, an unusually large number when compared to the results obtained with the other playback regimes. The high-low effect, however, was found on only two variables, female chinks and flutters, and the second variable was in the opposite direction from the male behavior. That is, the females paired with high-responding males fluttered significantly less. These experiments indicate that the behavior of the male is influenced by the reproductive stage of the female. The females, in turn, show a greater response decrement on more behaviors when the male is responding to a contingent playback, even though there is no contingency involving her own behavior. The general activity of the female, however, is not related to that of the male.

Adding the number of male songs as a continuous vector in a regression analysis increased the proportion of variance accounted for from the previous 0.5% to 7.7% range to a new range of 3.6% (female flutters) to a high of 54.4%

(male flights). This is a substantial amount of variance to account for with only two variables entered as IVs: number of full songs and trials (with reproductive condition controlled). An exploratory analysis was done using a stepwise multiple regression, entering all of the other behaviors to predict the level of male singing. This analysis accounted for 67% of the total variance with nine variables and 62% with only four. The data from the first and second studies were also analyzed in terms of the high–low difference; the general pattern of results is the same, only not so striking. These two analyses provide a retrospective cross-validation of the high–low effect.

These findings are encouraging. The general representative design used in these studies seems to have much to recommend it. It was found that the reproductive condition of the female had a major influence on the nature of the responses of both the male and the female, and the effect was replicated in a second experiment. In the last study, yet another factor was identified that exerts a strong influence on the pattern of results: the general responsiveness of the male. This appears to be a state variable that may reflect the action of short-term environmental factors or result from some acute or chronic physiological variable of the bird. One of the next tasks is to inquire into the nature of this variable.

I am now at a point where I can examine some precise aspects of the two processes presumed by Thompson to be involved in determining responsiveness over time: habituation and sensitization. I can now remove statistically influences that cloud the expression of these processes and use the computer to generate predictions about the nature of these underlying functions. These functions can be generated by using the data reported here, along with those from two further experiments done to study the effects of varying the characteristics of the playback regime. The more salient, interesting, or counterintuitive predictions can be tested with new experiments.

It could be argued that such influences as those I have uncovered – reproductive condition, number of trials, and so on – could have been eliminated by using controlled laboratory procedures. If I had chosen to do these experiments in the laboratory, I would quite likely have remained unaware of the action of these influences, however. I am exerting control through statistical procedures, the animal is allowed free behavioral expression, all behaviors that can be observed are recorded, normal ecological factors are undisturbed as much as possible, and there is minimal intrusion into the situation. It is my belief that the potential heuristic value of the methods and the richness of the data base justify the rather large initial expenditure of time and effort required to pursue research in this manner.

A DESIGN MODEL USING INDIVIDUAL REGRESSION ANALYSIS

A number of investigators seem to agree that it is necessary to analyze data at the level of the individual subject if we are to understand the development of behavior in any detail. Some years ago, Estes (1956) questioned the adequacy of using averaged group curves to represent the nature of the learning function. He demonstrated that the shape of an averaged curve might be completely different in form from all the individual curves of which it is composed. For example, each individual might learn in one trial, but the particular trial at which the learning occurs could differ from subject to subject. The resulting group curve would appear sigmoid rather than reveal the underlying step function.

Wohlwill (1973) has argued that studies of development should center on attributes of the developmental patterns of individuals rather than on a characterization derived from the intercorrelation of patterns of a group of individuals at two different times. He has argued the necessity of gathering longitudinal data based on intensive study of individuals if we are interested in any of four things (1973:140): "(1) to preserve information as to the shape of the developmental function: (2) to provide information on change and patterning of change: (3) to relate earlier behavior to later, and (4) to relate earlier conditions of life to subsequent behavior."

Dennenberg (1978), though advocating a general systems approach to the study of development, has come to the conclusion that information can be gained from the study of individuals that cannot be gained from group averaging procedures, and he advocates single subject research.

McCall (1977:337) has emphasized this point in a succinct review of conceptual and methodological issues in developmental psychology: "But, if a primary mission is to discern ontogenetic change within individuals, the sequence and timing of developmental transitions, and the changing social and environmental factors that permit development to occur, then we must use longitudinal, not cross-sectional, approaches to our subject matter."

The model that is developed here can be used to analyze data at the level of the single subject as well as to study data obtained from groups of subjects as it has been discussed up to this point. The appropriate methods have been developed and used extensively to understand the nature of clinical prediction – that is, how a clinician combines information to make a judgment about some criterion behavior or state (e.g., Brehmer 1976a; Hammond et al. 1964; Hoffman 1960; Wiggins & Hoffman 1968; see Wiggins [1973] for an overview of such studies).

Let us consider, first, the hypothetical study of maternal sensitivity that was used as an illustration earlier. Before, the analysis was done on a group of mother-infant dyads. Here it will be used to illustrate how the analysis can be focused on a single dyad. The IVs in that example were the number of seconds an infant looked at the mother (I → M; X_1), and the number of seconds the mother looked at the infant (M → I; X_2), and we will now create a separate variable to represent the number of seconds they are mutually looking (I ⇄ M; X_3). These three IVs will be used to predict maternal sensitivity (Y) on a seven-point scale.

To obtain the data, we could have the M–I pair observed for 2 hours. One observer records the looking behavior of each of the pair for 5 minutes while an independent observer records a maternal sensitivity score for the total 5-minute period. This is done throughout the 2 hours, thereby resulting in 24 5-minute periods during each of which there is a score in seconds for I → M (X_1), M → I (X_2), I ⇄ M (X_3), and a criterion score (Y). These repeated measures are entered in the standard linear regression equation based on a least-squares solution for a single case (in this instance, a dyad). As Zedek (1977) has pointed out, the equation is determined for an individual as opposed to a sample of subjects. The equation describes how the DV is related to the IVs for each individual.

A multiple correlation coefficient is calculated for each dyad that estimates the degree to which the behavior can be predicted by a linear combination of the IVs. The individual points on which R is based are a repeated series of measurements of the IVs and the DV of a dyad. When this analysis is completed, each dyad can be characterized by R^2 (which tells how much of the outcome variable the IVs have captured) and a regression equation (which characterizes the relative weight each IV has for each dyad). This method of analysis can be used with categorical variables, continuous variables, or a mix of the two. One could include higher powers of any of the variables to test for the presence of curvilinearity in the functional relationships. (For a discussion of curvilinearity see Cohen & Cohen 1975, Ch. 6, and Kerlinger & Pedhazur 1973, Ch. 9).

The regression model, then, has been extended from data based on a group of subjects to the study of the individual case. It would be useful to take one further step. There is a series of R^2 values and a series of regression equations, one for each dyad. Can anything further be done with them to obtain a more parsimonious description of the reality? Christal (1968a) presents a method called *judgment analysis* (*JAN*), an iterative technique that clusters individuals on the basis of the homogeneity of their regression equations. Bottenberg and Christal (1968) have generalized the method to group optimally a set of criteria, each of which may be predicted from a single set of predictors. Christal (1968b) has extended the procedure to categorical variables. Zedeck (1977) has used the model to study the factors that influence the preference of students for jobs that vary on several dimensions. He has also examined the job preferences of persons at different life and career stages. In the former study, 91 subjects could be described as three clusters, and the clustering accounted for 34% of the variance. In the second study, 233 individuals could be described as four clusters, and the clustering accounted for 45% of the variance.

Briefly, the method clusters individuals on the basis of the homogeneity of their regression equations so that the grouping results in the least loss of predictive efficiency as raters are combined. The aim is to maintain a balance between overall predictive efficiency and a minimal number of regression equations. First, a single R^2 is calculated when a separate least-squares regression equation is used for each of the individuals being studied. The two individuals with the most homogeneous regression equations and whose combination results in the smallest loss of predictive efficiency (i.e., the value of R^2 drops the least) are then selected. Thus, if there are 10 subjects, the overall R^2 indicates the predictive efficiency of a system with 10 different equations. The second R^2 is the predictive efficiency of nine systems (one cluster of the two most homogeneous subjects and the other eight individuals). The next step is to reduce the number of systems to eight. This is accomplished either by adding a third subject to the existing cluster and maintaining seven individual systems or by forming a second cluster and retaining six individual systems. This process continues until a final R^2 is determined with all subjects considered as one system.

In the study by Zedeck (1977), for the first sample of 91 subjects, when 91 different policies were considered, the $R^2 = 0.53$. When the 91 subjects were all considered as one cluster, the $R^2 = 0.21$. Zedeck concluded that three clusters best described the data, $R^2 = 0.34$. In his second study, based on 233 subjects, the 233 different policies resulted in an R^2 of 0.67. When all subjects were combined into one cluster $R^2 = 0.23$. Again, three clusters were used to best characterize the data, $R^2 = 0.42$. The number of clusters chosen can be based on a priori theoretical hypotheses regarding the research factors, or one can use the number of clusters that precedes the largest loss in predictive efficiency, or the decision can be made on the basis of the cumulative loss in predictive efficiency as equations are combined (Christal 1968a; Zedeck & Kafry 1977). There is an appropriate F test for common parameter regression coefficients that permits the test that the regressions are homogeneous (Bottenberg & Christal 1968). Following the clustering procedure, one can then use some significance testing models, such as a multivariate analysis of variance (MANOVA), to test for differences in the weight of the clusters formed.

Let me recapitulate the statistical argument to this point before attempting to extend it to the study of developmental problems. The basic logic of MRC allows one to study the effects of a set of IVs on some criterion variable. First, the extent to which the overall set of IVs can account for the variance in the DV (the R^2) can be determined. Then, these multiple determinants of behavior can be examined to discover the relative weight of the individual variables and their patterns of interaction. The analysis can be done using either a group of subjects or individual subjects as outlined above. If one studies individual subjects, it is possible to determine the R^2 and the regression equation for each subject and then to group the subjects into clusters that have a similar profile of regression weights.

One point will be developed briefly. There has been legitimate concern expressed in the literature (e.g., Keppel 1973) regarding the uncritical interpretation of R^2 values to determine the magnitude of experimental effects. It has been pointed out that the coarseness or fineness of the selected levels of the variables within the experimental conditions will influence the size of the obtained R^2 values. This criticism is valid when using systematic design but is not a telling point when representative design is employed. The choice of the magnitudes of the stimulus variables is not arbitrary in representative design; they are the magnitudes that exist in the natural environment. Therefore, the R^2 does faithfully reflect effect size in natural settings. (I am grateful for a discussion with Geoff Keppel that led me to understand the problem and its resolution.)

Another instance in which one need not be concerned with selected levels is in any applied setting where the value of the variables (e.g., salary range as a variable in a study of job preference) is established by practical considerations dictated by the reality of the situation. The same might hold true when the properties of an a priori theory are being explored.

AN EXTENSION TO THE STUDY OF DEVELOPMENT

The problem that appears at the outset when one considers the study of development is that whatever complexity already exists is immediately compounded with the addition of time as a necessary consideration. The model that has been developed in this chapter has promise for developmental studies because it will accommodate the complexity involved and can be used to advantage with individual subjects.

The strategy I suggest for using the model to study development essentially involves freezing the situation at selected times in development rather than studying change directly. Although, at first glance, this might seem to be an undesirable aspect of the model, close reflection reveals that such freezing is essential in any study of development. Even if one is studying change directly, one must measure variables at selected points in time. These points of measurement are inescapably static at the instant the measurement is made; reality is frozen and registered for the selected time.

The important thing is to be able to reconstruct the developing reality in such a way that its dynamic nature can be captured. This has been attempted through the use of change scores (see Harris 1967 and Cohen & Cohen 1975, Ch. 6 for discussions of the problems in measuring change), autocorrelations, factor analysis (Baltes & Nesselroade 1973), and time trend analysis. All of these methods require the investigator to freeze the situation, and most of them possess the inherent disadvantage that the analysis is not done on the individual case.

The major problem is to choose the times when the sampling should be done and to determine the relative sampling frequency that will be required. The only guidelines that can be offered must come from the investigator's own depth of knowledge of the behavioral processes of interest. The variables chosen for study must be identified on the basis of intensive observation of the developing organism in those situations in which the behaviors occur. Time must be devoted to the codification and quantification of the critical aspects of the environment, the changes occurring within the organism, the stimulation to which the organism is responsive, and the behaviors that normally occur in a representative sampling of situations. Then, objective criteria must be developed that relate to the construct (DV) under consideration. Following this phase, the investigator will be in a position to make some educated guesses about the proper times to draw samples: those periods just before and just after some particularly interesting changes in the pattern or organization of behavior, changes in behavioral capacity, or qualitative leaps in modes of functioning. The times to sample might also be chosen because it is known that structural or physiological changes are taking place that might be related to the developmental dimension under consideration. These structural and functional clues should guide the investigator to those times when meaningful changes are occurring. No statistical or design method can tell the scientist when to sample the behavior. If the methods are adequate, they can only allow the investigator to determine patterns of similarities and differences and to make some estimates regarding the magnitude of the effects. It might also be useful to employ occasional cross-sectional groups to evaluate the extent of any effects of repeated testing.

Assuming that a choice of variables has been made and that a sampling strategy has been adopted, the study could then focus on any of the arrays of interest: the *a* stimulus dimension, the *b* or *d* mediation dimensions, or the *e* response dimension (see Fig. 4.1). How are these sets of multiple cues to be analyzed? Each individual should be studied at time 1 (t_1) and again at time 2 (t_2). These times should be chosen to bracket some developmental period of theoretical or descriptive interest. For each of these times, the regression weights for each IV (or sets of IVs if there are many IVs and one is interested in economy of expression) should be determined using an appropriate criterion variable as Y.

These regression weights (when standardized and expressed as β) are partial regression coefficients, and the squared partial coefficient expresses the proportion of the total Y variance that is accounted for by a variable and that is not estimated by the other IVs in the equation. These weights and the R^2 can be determined at t_1 and t_2 for each subject. If the regression weights for the subject have not changed, then a set of common regression weights could be used to express the systems.

The hypothesis of no change can be tested statistically (see Kerlinger & Pedhazur 1973:206 ff., 237). If the significance test reveals a significant difference, this means that the regression system for the two times can be considered different. If the test does not reveal a significant difference, this means that the weights at the two times can be considered to be the same. One can also then test the significance of the partial coefficients for each IV (Cohen & Cohen 1975:111–113) and whether or not the two R^2 values are significantly different (Overall & Klett 1972:424).

Significance of different outcome patterns

I. If the pattern of β values for t_1 and t_2 can be considered to be the same and the R^2 value is insignificant or so low that it can be considered uninteresting, then one would question whether or not an appropriate selection of IVs has been made and whether or not the quantification of the DV is adequate (instance I in Table 4.2). This would lead to a search for new IVs, a refinement of the measurement characteristics of the current ones, and a careful consideration of the reliability and validity of the Y measure.

II. If the β values for $t_1 = t_2$ and R^2 are significant, large enough, and similar for both times, then it could be argued that the measurement system is adequate, that it represents the relative weights of variables in the determination of Y, and that within the confines of the study, little of developmental significance has occurred (instance II in Table 4.2). In this case, attention should be directed to a later time t_3, another sample should be taken, and so forth.

III. If the relative patterning of the β values is the same across t_1 and t_2 but the R^2 values differ significantly, then one should examine the situation carefully because something of developmental significance has occurred. The variables are receiving the same relative weights, but the level of predictability based on those weights has changed. If the R^2 is larger at t_2, this means that the organism is being more closely regulated by the IVs relative to those things producing the unexplained variance (instance III in Table 4.2). When any difference of this kind occurs, the investigator should study other subjects and take additional time slices between t_1 and t_2, as well as repeat the t_1 and t_2 measurements. This

Table 4.2. *Hypothetical results illustrating the possible outcomes of a developmental study of the type advocated here*

Instance	Variable	t_1 β	t_1 R^2	t_2 β	t_2 R^2	Decision
I	X_1	0.03		—		Seek new and better variables
	X_2	0.02		—		and test at t_1 again
	X_3	0.01	0.005	—	—	
	X_4	0.01		—		
II	X_1	0.20		0.25		Move on to other *t*s until some
	X_2	0.10		0.09		change occurs
	X_3	0.06	0.16	0.05	0.17	
	X_4	0.04		0.02		
III	X_1	0.20		0.30		Test another S and take
	X_2	0.10		0.15		additional time slices between t_1
	X_3	0.06	0.16	0.09	0.36	and t_2 to locate change more
	X_4	0.04		0.06		precisely
IV	X_1	0.20		0.25		Test another S and take
	X_2	0.10		0.10		additional time slices between t_1
	X_3	0.06	0.16	0.05	0.36	and t_2
	X_4	0.04		0.20		
V	X_1	0.20		0.01		Test another S and take
	X_2	0.10		0.09		additional time slices between t_1
	X_3	0.06	0.16	0.05	0.16	and t_2
	X_4	0.04		0.25		
VI	X_1	0.20		0.02		Test another S and take
	X_2	0.10		0.03		additional time slices between t_1
	X_3	0.06	0.16	0.01	0.008	and t_2; seek new variables
	X_4	0.04		0.03		

will provide an independent replication of the effect, and the additional slice (or slices) between t_1 and t_2 will help to locate exactly the time when the change is taking place.

IV. If the β values for t_1 differ from those for t_2 and R^2 increases, this means that the predictive efficiency and the relative weighting of the variables in the hierarchy have changed (instance IV in Table 4.2). This means, again, that something of developmental significance has occurred, and one should attempt to account for the change in pattern and take additional time slices using independent subjects between t_1 and t_2 as before.

V. If the β values change significantly between t_1 and t_2 and the R^2 value remains at the same level, then the same variable set is accounting for the same proportion of variance but the relative weighting of the variables has shifted (instance V in Table 4.2). This indicates that something of developmental significance has occurred. The organism is still being regulated by the IVs, but their relative importance has shifted. Again, additional time slices should be taken between t_1 and t_2 and the effect should be replicated with additional subjects.

VI. If the β weights for t_1 differ from those for t_2 and the R^2 drops significantly (instance VI in Table 4.2), this could mean that (1) a variable not being measured has entered the system or (2) the organism has moved into a state that cannot be predicted by our set of IVs. If this occurs, one should take additional time slices between t_1 and t_2 to replicate and to find where it all happened, and then search for new variables related to the behavior.

A hypothetical illustrative experiment

Let me now represent instances II to VI by graphing the results that might be obtained from a hypothetical experiment (Fig. 4.5). (Instance I is of no interest because the variables were not accounting for enough of the total variance in Y.) Remember that each of the data points plotted is based on results obtained with repeated measures of one individual infant.

Assume that the DV, Y, is the number of seconds the infant smiles in a 2-minute period. The IVs are as follows: X_1 is the rate at which a looming red disc is moved from a 1-m distance to a distance of 0.33 m at five different standardized rates. X_2 is the amount of overt motoric behavior the infant engages in. X_3 is the amount of time since the infant had its last meal. X_4 is the presence of the mother at a 1-m distance from the infant; the mother is present on half of the test occasions in a random order. The infant is exposed to this set of conditions 60 times when it is 4 weeks of age and 60 times when it is 8 weeks of age in a 1-day testing session in a standard situation. It would be desirable to include a range of representative situations in which the testing occurs as one of the experimental variables, but that is not included in this example in the interest of ease of exposition.

The weighting of variables is plotted in a standardized form (β) for t_1 and t_2 (Fig. 4.5). The state of affairs at t_1 will be kept the same across all instances. At t_1 the $R^2 = 0.16$ (which is significantly different from zero). The patterning of the variables indicates that smiling is related most to the rate at which the disc is moved (X_1), next to the time since the last meal (X_3), and least to the presence of the mother (X_4).

Instance II. The relative weighting of the variables and the R^2 is similar at t_2 and the next test with the infant would be made at t_3, say at an age of 12 weeks. If there is still no change, we could continue testing at greater and greater ages. If the state of affairs persists, we would conclude that we are measuring nothing of developmental interest. If a change occurs, we would follow the strategy of instance III, IV, V, or VI.

Instance III. The R^2 has increased from 0.16 to 0.36, and the only significant change in pattern is that X_1 has increased. This is of mild interest. It attests to the overall stability of the system and indicates that the rate of looming (X_1) accounts for more of the variance in Y. This could mean that there is an increasing sensitivity to visual stimuli. In this instance one could, if sufficiently

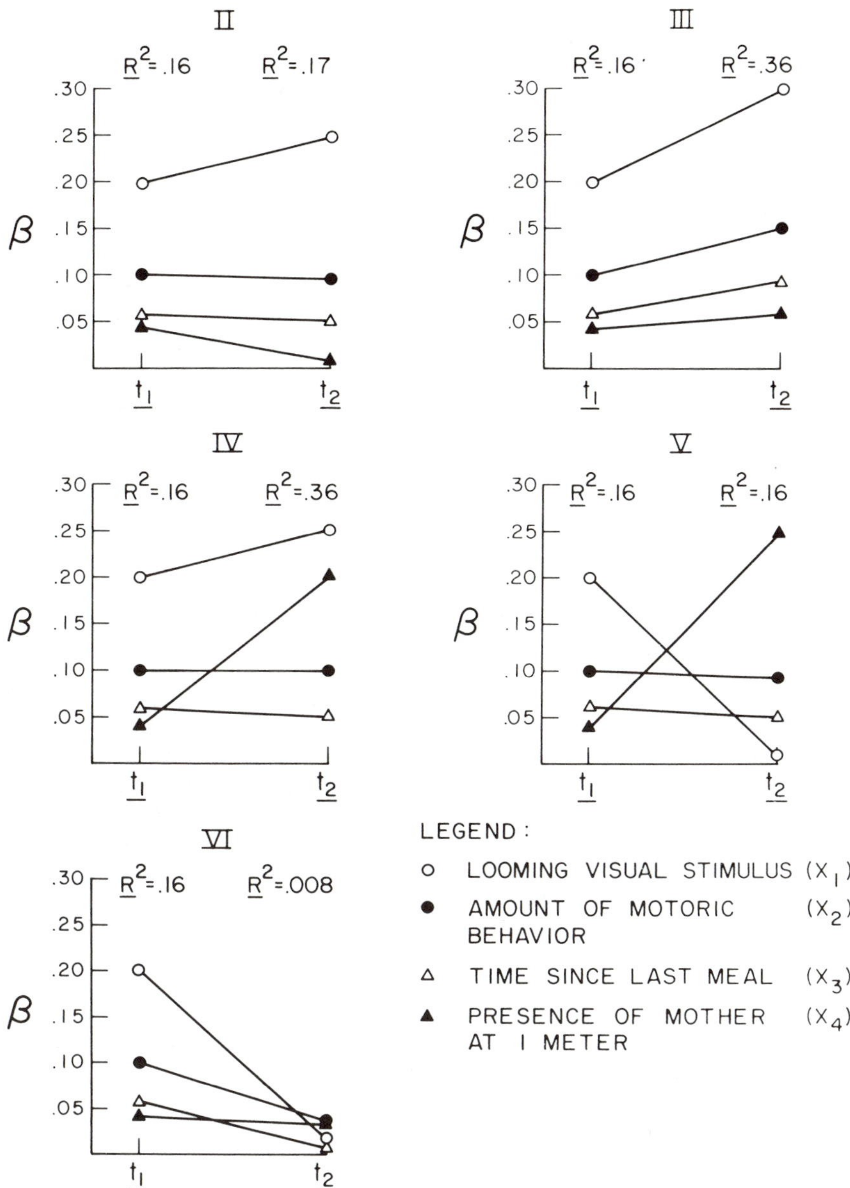

Figure 4.5. Outcomes of a hypothetical experiment. See text for explanation.

interested in visual perception, test a new subject at an intermediate time, t_1. If the pattern discussed in instance IV is found at a later time, t_3, then this would lend credence to the hypothesis that the change is due to an increase in visual sensitivity (as long as the effects of repeated testing can be ruled out).

Instance IV. The weighting of the variables changes and the R^2 increases from 0.16 to 0.36; assume it is a significant amount. X_1, the rate of looming, commands an increasing proportion of the variance. X_2 and X_3 stay at their same levels, whereas the infant smiles more in the presence of the mother, X_4, which moves from 0.04 to 0.20. Thus we can account for 20% more of the variance at t_2 than we could at t_1. It appears that the infant is slightly more responsive to the looming disc and much more responsive to the presence of the mother. This suggests that visual stimulation is becoming more potent as a factor influencing smiling. This should lead us to do several things.

First, test the same infant at t_3 to determine whether or not the system is stable. If it is stable, we could move to t_4 (say, 16 weeks); if it is not, we would test another subject at t_3', say at 10 weeks.

Second, test another infant at t_1 and again at t_1', 6 weeks, and then at t_2. If we wished, we could systematically narrow the time interval and find, using different subjects, where the change occurs between t_1 and t_2. Each time we test a subject at t_1, t_2, and so on, that constitutes a replication of the results of the preceding subject. In this way, a richer and richer archive of data at a series of times is accumulated. Such an archive would consist of identical data for all subjects at several times.

Third, when enough data have been amassed, we can then cluster individuals on the basis of their similarity of regression patterns as discussed above, using age as a means to categorize the individuals, or we can cluster them on the basis of their similarity at the successive testings, ignoring age. When the clusters have been established in this second way, we can test whether or not the different clusters differ in age (or on any other variable) using MANOVA, in which any numbers of IVs and any number of DVs can be used. It is possible to use MANOVA to determine whether the means of the DVs are equal when they are considered simultaneously. In this way, it is possible to investigate the different effects of the IVs on the DVs. (This approach could be used at any step in the analysis if the results seem interesting enough to warrant it.)

Fourth, a separate study of the characteristics of the visual system would be in order to identify any changes in visual capacity that have occurred, to determine whether the child's style of interacting with all visual stimuli has altered, or to decide whether or not the importance of the mother as a social stimulus has suddenly increased drastically.

Instance V. Although the R^2 is the same, variable X_1 has dropped nearly to zero and X_4 has increased over sixfold. This could mean that the infant is not now responding to isolated visual stimulation but is suddenly sensitive to social stimulation. This could lead to: (1) testing other subjects at t_1', as before, to identify the time of the change; (2) conducting an experimental investigation of the social stimulation hypothesis.

Instance VI. The R^2 has dropped to zero. This could mean that the infant's smiling in this situation is no longer predictable by the variables being investigated. In this case, we should check the level of the Y variable to make sure that the criterion level has not dropped to zero, for example. If this is found to be the case, the level of smiling in other situations should be examined to determine whether the change is general or is specific to the conditions of the test. If we can assume that the drop in the level of Y is a real one, we would wish to look for some overriding change in state or general responsiveness. If the level has not changed, then we should consider carefully the behavior of the infant to discover whether or not we can identify some new variable, which can then be included as a predictor variable.

This rather trite example should make it clearer how the method can be used, what kind of measurement procedures would be used, and what strategies can be employed to understand the analyses. Further, even through this example the possible heuristic value of the endeavor becomes evident. It is possible continually to generate new hypotheses that can be evaluated through the addition of new variables to the standard test situation (often ones that have always been present and can be added through mere actuarial registration) or by experimental probes directed at interesting epochs in development.

SUMMARY OF ADVANTAGES OF THE METHOD

This method has several characteristics that provide distinct advantages over many other methods.

First, the individual is used as the unit of analysis. This makes it possible to detect developmental changes in individuals, and these changes are not time-locked. Change in either the pattern of weights for a given individual or the total R^2 value is the key to halve the time interval. The fact that these changes may occur at different absolute times will make no difference. If the changes are reflecting a regular behavioral trend, each individual can be characterized in terms of age at the times of change, and a developmental scale can thereby be drawn up. The method also permits one to cluster the individuals and to look for meaningful differences between the clusters either on the set of IVs or on some supplementary variables on which information exists or can be obtained. It should be possible to apply this method to the interaction of mother–infant dyad data of the kind obtained by Lewis and Lee-Painter (1974).

Second, the clustering technique can be used to cluster individuals at t_1 and then again at t_2. The membership in the different clusters at each time can be examined to identify which individuals are grouped together at t_1 and then at t_2. Those individuals who move from one cluster to another might be a subgroup of great interest, and a more intensive study of their characteristics might reveal some interesting functional relationships.

Third, the variables used can be of any nature – experimental or nonexperimental; stable attribute, physiological, ecological, or manipulated – and they can be scaled in any way, categorically or continuously.

Fourth, the system is, basically, a longitudinal one, although it relies on a semi-cross-sectional approach. The cross sections are not arbitrarily fixed and unchanging. As the pattern of differences and similarities begins to emerge, the analysis of subsequent subjects will reflect what has been learned from the preceding ones. Thus the system has high heuristic value and is self-correcting, continually providing feedback on the tactics to be used on the next subject.

If the times between the successive samples become very great, then one might want to resort to some strategy of testing a number of individuals as a cohort. This problem has received a great deal of attention, but McCall (1977) has pointed out that many of the presumed historical effects on research of this type do not seem to be of very great magnitude in those studies that have investigated their effect systematically. McCall doubts as well that the effects of repeated testing constitute a major problem. He points out that the effects of repeated tests are often large between the first and second tests but minimal thereafter. If there are effects due to repeated testing, they can be partialed out using the procedures advocated here. If they are found to be large, it might be possible to use a warm-up test to reduce the magnitude of the problem. It will probably always be necessary to test new subjects at two different times to assess directly whether or not there are effects due to repeated testing.

Fifth, one of the most important requirements in using a correlational system such as this is that all results must be replicated. In any complex data field, such as the ones generated here, there will always be patterns of chance correlations that will distort the results. The heart of this system is the continual replication that occurs every time a subject is added and whenever a group of individuals is clustered. No attention has been paid to corrections for shrinkage that are required when there is a large number of variables relative to the number of subjects. In representative designs of this longitudinal variety, it is inevitable that the number of measurements will be larger than ideal relative to the number of subjects. Longitudinal subjects are hard to come by, whereas measurements are cheap. The procedure of cross validation satisfies the concerns of those who advocate MRC analyses. "The surest way of assessing how well a regression equation predicts is to apply it to a new set of data. Particularly when the original n is small, or the scatter of Y values is skewed or unequal for different sets of X_1, or stepwise regression has been used, cross validation to a new sample is strongly indicated" (Cohen & Cohen 1975:115). Cohen and Cohen also point out that cross validation is mandatory when the IVs are highly interrelated (high multicollinearity).

Finally, these procedures will permit the development of an active data archive. All variables are registered for every subject over a variety of times and epochs. After a number of subjects have been studied, the resulting data archive permits the retrospective testing of new hypotheses regarding the interaction of variables or sets of variables. For example, the bird habituation study discussed earlier has produced just such an archive. When it was noticed that the males in the contingent playback study seemed to vary in their degree of overall responsiveness, it was possible immediately to cross-validate the finding on the two independent groups of subjects that had been studied earlier. This type of retrospective cross validation is especially satisfying because one always worries about the possibility of observer bias in recording field data. Obviously, if the hypothesis had not been conceived at the time the data were collected, such a bias could not have been operative.

I realize that I have presented the developmental model with a great deal of enthusiasm and optimism. I am convinced of the value of the system by the historical and logical analysis, by the structure of the MRC methods on which the approach is based, and by its success in accounting for the most complex clinical and social judgments. My own experience using the MRC system to understand habituation of birds in a field experimental setting has also emboldened me.

As an afterthought (and a thought for the future), I would like to suggest that this general strategy might prove to be useful as a general model for cross-species and cross-cultural comparisons. For example, if we can identify factors such as reproductive success, parental caregiving, pair bonding, infant handling, and relations to authority as being of universal importance at the functional level, then we could describe how any particular culture or species expresses the variable and proceed to substitute the value of each cultural or species expression for t_1, t_2 and so on, in order to make direct comparisons of the kind that have been outlined here.

To close on a slightly different note: Wohlwill (1973:87) has proposed a set of criteria that he considers to be necessary if one is to decide on a behavioral dimension suitable for tracing the course of developmental changes: (1) systematic shifts with age occur on the dimension; (2) the dimension should be meaningful in terms of its reference to known or postulated developmental processes; (3) the dimension is defined in terms that yield measures based on a constant unit of measurement or are a unidimensional set; (4) the dimension should be defined in general terms, sufficiently situation independent to yield a valid as well as stable measure of developmental status. I believe that the system proposed here can lead to the delineation of these dimensions and will provide the analytic tools adequate to let us understand the interplay of such dimensional systems throughout the course of development.

ACKNOWLEDGMENTS

I am grateful to George Barlow, Jack Block, Berndt Brehmer, Dave Carter, Steve Glickman, Gunnar Goude, Curt Hardyck, Rick Jacobs, Mary Main, Arnold Sameroff, and John Watson. They all wrestled with an earlier version of this paper and their comments and criticisms have improved the paper greatly. The research reported here was supported by a University of California Intramural Grant and by NICHHD Grant HD04343.

REFERENCES

Baltes, P. B., & J. R. Nesselroade. 1973. The developmental analysis of individual differences on multiple measures. *In:* J. R. Nesselroade & H. W. Reese (eds.), *Life-*

span developmental psychology/methodological issues. Academic Press, New York, pp. 219–251.

Baptista, L. F. 1975. Song dialects and demes in sedentary populations of the White-crowned Sparrow (*Zonotrichia leucophrys nuttalli*). *University of California Publication in Zoology* 105:1–52.

Bottenberg, R. A., & R. E. Christal. 1968. Grouping criteria – a method which retains maximum predictive efficiency. *Journal of Experimental Education* 36:28–34.

Brehmer, B. 1976a. Note on clinical judgment and the formal characteristics of clinical tasks. *Psychological Bulletin* 83:778–782.

1976b. Social judgment theory and the analysis of interpersonal conflict. *Psychological Bulletin* 83:985–1003.

Brunswik, E. 1952. The conceptual framework of psychology. *In: International Encyclopedia of Unified Science*, vol. 1, no. 10. University of Chicago Press, Chicago.

1956. *Perception and the representative design of psychological experiments.* University of California Press, Berkeley.

Campbell, D. T., & J. C. Stanley. 1963. Experimental and quasi-experimental designs for research on teaching. *In:* N. L. Gage (ed.), *Handbook of research on teaching.* Rand McNally, Skokie, Illinois, pp. 171–246.

Christal, R. E. 1968a. JAN: A technique for analyzing group judgment. *Journal of Experimental Education* 36:24–27.

1968b. Selecting a harem – and other applications of the policy-capturing model. *Journal of Experimental Education* 36:35–41.

Cohen, J., & P. Cohen. 1975. *Applied multiple regression/correlation analysis for the behavioral sciences.* Lawrence Erlbaum, Hillsdale, New Jersey.

Dennenberg, V. H. 1978. Paradigms and paradoxes in the study of behavioral development. *In:* E. B. Thoman (ed.), *The origins of the infant's social responsiveness.* Erlbaum, Hillsdale, New Jersey.

Edgington, E. S. 1974. A new tabulation of statistical procedures used in APA journals. *American Psychologist* 29:25–26.

Edwards. W. 1971. Bayesian and regression models of human information processing – a myopic perspective. *Organizational Behavior and Human Performance* 6:639–648.

Estes, W. K. 1956. The problem of inference from curves based on group data. *Psychological Bulletin* 53:134–140.

Falls, J. B., & R. J. Brooks. 1975. Individual recognition by song in white-throated sparrows. 2. Effects of location. *Canadian Journal of Zoology* 53:1412–1420.

Hammond, K. R. 1966. Probabilistic functionalism: Egon Brunswik's integration of the history, theory, and method of psychology. *In:* K. R. Hammond (ed.), *The psychology of Egon Brunswik.* Holt, New York, pp. 15–80.

1976. The social implementation of cognitive theory. *In:* L. Petrinovich & J. L. McGaugh (eds.), *Knowing, thinking, and believing.* Plenum Press, New York, pp. 245–260.

Hammond, K. R., C. Hursch, & F. Todd. 1964. Analyzing components of clinical inference. *Psychological Review* 72:438–456.

Hammond, K. R., T. R. Stewart, B. Brehmer, & D. O. Steinmann. 1975. *Social judgment and decision processes: formal and mathematical approaches.* Academic Press, New York, pp. 271–312.

Harris, C. W. (ed.). 1963. *Problems in measuring change.* University of Wisconsin Press, Madison.

Hoffman, P. J. 1960. The paramorphic representation of clinical judgment. *Psychological Bulletin* 57:116–131.

Hull, C. L. 1943. *Principles of behavior.* Appleton, New York.

Kahneman, D., & A. Tversky. 1973. On the psychology of prediction. *Psychological Review* 80:237–251.

Keppel, G. 1973. *Design and analysis: a researcher's handbook.* Prentice-Hall, Englewood Cliffs, New Jersey.

Kerlinger, F. N., & E. J. Pedhazur. 1973. *Multiple regression in behavioral research.* Holt, New York.

Krebs, J. R. 1977. The significance of song repertoires: the Beau Geste hypothesis. *Animal Behaviour* 25:475–478.

Lewis, M., & S. Lee-Painter. 1974. An interactional approach to the mother–infant dyad. *In:* M. Lewis & L. A. Rosenblum (eds.), *The effect of the infant on its caregivers.* Wiley, New York.

Marler, P., & M. Tamura. 1962. Song "dialects" in three populations of White-crowned Sparrows. *Condor* 64:368–377.

Mayr, E. 1964. From molecules to genetic diversity. *Federation Proceedings* 23:1231–1235. Reprinted in E. Mayr, *Evolution and the diversity of life.* Harvard University Press, Cambridge, Massachusetts, 1976.

McCall, R. B. 1977. Challenges to a science of developmental psychology. *Child Development* 48:333–344.

McFarland, D. J. 1976. Form and function in the temporal organization of behaviour. *In:* P. P. G. Bateson & R. A. Hinde (eds.), *Growing points in ethology.* Cambridge University Press, Cambridge, pp. 55–93.

Overall, J. E., & C. J. Klett. 1972. *Applied multivariate analysis.* McGraw-Hill, New York.

Patterson, T. L., & L. Petrinovich. 1979. Field studies of habituation. 2. The effect of massed stimulus presentation. *Journal of Comparative and Physiological Psychology* 93:351–359.

In preparation. The White-crowned Sparrow: ecology, territorial behavior, and reproductive success.

Peeke, H. V. S., & S. C. Peeke. 1973. Habituation in fish with special reference to intraspecific aggressive behavior. *In:* H. V. S. Peeke & M. J. Herz (eds.), *Habituation. 1. Behavioral studies.* Academic Press, New York, pp. 59–83.

Petrinovich, L. 1973. Darwin and the representative expression of reality. *In:* P. Ekman (ed.), *Darwin and facial expression.* Academic Press, New York, pp. 223–256.

1976. Molar reductionism. *In:* L. Petrinovich & J. L. McGaugh (eds.), *Knowing, thinking, and believing.* Plenum Press, New York, pp. 11–27.

1979. Probabilistic functionalism: a conception of research method. *American Psychologist* 34:373–390.

Petrinovich, L., & T. L. Patterson. 1979. Field studies of habituation. 1. The effects of reproductive condition, number of trials, and different delay intervals on the responses of the White-crowned Sparrow. *Journal of Comparative and Physiological Psychology* 93:337–350.

1980. Field studies of habituation. 3. Playback contingent on the response of the White-crowned Sparrow. *Animal Behaviour* 28:742–751.

Petrinovich, L., T. L. Patterson, & H. V. S. Peeke. 1976. Reproductive condition and the response of White-crowned Sparrows (*Zonotrichia leucophrys nuttalli*) to song. *Science* 191:206–207.

Petrinovich, L., & H. V. S. Peeke. 1973. Habituation to territorial song in the White-crowned Sparrow (*Zonotrichia leucophrys*). *Behavioral Biology* 8:219–226.

Postman, L.,1955. The probability approach and nomothetic theory. *Psychological Review* 62:218–226.

Postman, L. & E. C. Tolman. 1959. Brunswik's probabilistic functionalism. *In:*

S. Koch (ed.), *Psychology: a study of a science*, vol. 1. McGraw-Hill, New York, pp. 502–564.

Skinner, B. F. *The behavior of organisms*. New York: Appleton, 1938.

Slovic, P., & S. Lichtenstein. 1971. Comparison of Bayesian and regression approaches to the study of information processing in judgment. *Organizational Behavior and Human Performance* 6:649–744.

Thompson, R. F. 1976. Introduction. *In:* A. H. Riesen & R. F. Thompson (eds.), *Advances in psychobiology*, vol. 3. Wiley, New York, pp. xi–xv.

Thompson, R. F., P. M. Groves, T. J. Teyler, & R. H. Roemer. 1973. A dual-process theory of habituation: theory and behavior. *In:* H. V. S. Peeke & M. J. Herz (eds.), *Habituation:* 1. *Behavioral studies*. Academic Press, New York, pp. 239–271.

Thorpe, W. H. 1963. *Learning and instinct in animals*. Methuen, London.

Underwood, B. J. 1957. *Psychological research*. Appleton, New York.

Wiggins, J. S. 1973. *Personality and prediction: principles of personality assessment*. Addison-Wesley, Reading, Massachusetts.

Wiggins, J. S., & P. J. Hoffman. 1968. Three models of clinical judgment. *Journal of Abnormal Psychology* 73:70–77.

Wohlwill, J. 1973. *The study of behavioral development*. Academic Press, New York.

Zedeck, S. 1977. An information processing model and approach to the study of motivation. *Organizational Behavior and Human Performance* 18:47–77.

Zedeck, S., & D. Kafry. 1977. Capturing rater policies for processing evaluation data. *Organizational Behavior and Human Performance* 18:269–294.

5

ON EVOLUTIONARY AND ONTOGENETIC ADAPTATION: TOWARD A PSYCHOBIOLOGICAL APPROACH

GUNNAR GOUDE

A wide range of psychological research follows the SOR paradigm: Given a stimulus (S), an organism (O) responds (R) in a certain way. The first part of the relation involves questions of how the organism gets information about the environment and is studied in perception psychology. The other part describes how the organism behaves in light of the information it gets and falls under the general heading of cognitive psychology, which covers a series of areas such as choice behavior, decision making, and problem solving.

In the following discussion, the word *event* (E) will be used instead of *stimulus* to emphasize that the organism is interacting with the environment, not just reacting to stimuli. The information the organism gets about the actual event will be regarded as percepts or cues and symbolized as c. The actual behavior will be denoted R. With these symbols we will describe an individual's reaction to or interaction with the environment as a sequence composed of two steps: the first perceptual, the second cognitive: (In this chapter *cognition* is used in a very general sense, and neither *cognition* nor *perception* will be restricted to conscious processes.)

$$E_i \xrightarrow{\text{perception}} c_j \xrightarrow{\text{cognition}} R_k \qquad (1)$$

The event–cue concept was used by Brunswik (1952) in his development of the lens model conception of behavior, in which the organism is considered to focus on a certain event or set of events and to actualize a set of cues, which are then used to select the appropriate behavior (Fig. 5.1). A full presentation of this lens model is given in Chapter 4.

The lens model has been developed and used by a number of psychologists. Hammond et al. (1964) and Hursch et al. (1964) have quantified the theory in terms of correlational statistics. Bjorkman (1967) has developed a probabilistic version. The theory has been widely used in various areas of psychology; see for example Brehmer's (1979) studies of the learning of cue–event relations.

Our way of using the model differs slightly from that of the Brunswik tradition. One difference concerns the concept of *cue,* which we treat as a percept, whereas in the traditional approach *cue* is a property of the stimulus.

The model is employed here in its probabilistic version. This model has been elaborated to cover the general situation, common in psychological experi-

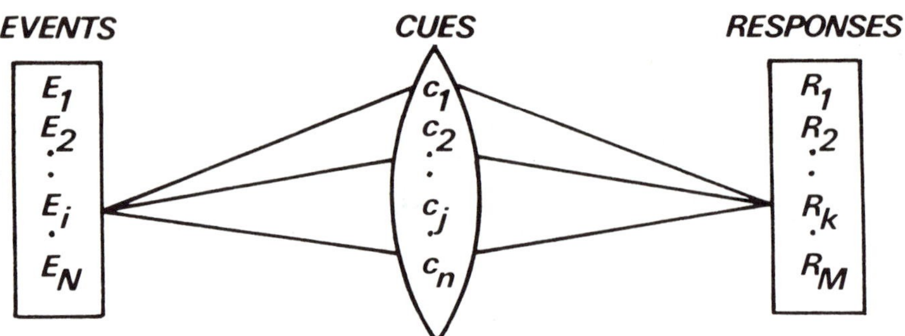

Figure 5.1. Graphic representation of Brunswik's lens model with events (E), percepts (c), and behaviors (R).

ments, where cues are given to a subject who is instructed to predict an event. After each prediction the event is shown as a feedback. This means that the model uses the conditional probabilities of an event (E) or of a response (R) that occur when a certain cue (c) is given: $P(E/c)$ or $P(R/c)$. For our purpose, it is adequate to follow the direction indicated by the arrows in equation 1. This version of a probabilistic lens model is developed and used in Goude (1979) and discussed in a theoretical overview by Bjorkman (1979). The probabilistic version of the lens model is presented in the next section, together with an illustrative example for a simple case with two events, two cues and two behaviors. We will later use this model for a general description of the behavior of an organism and expand it to apply to social interactions between individuals. In this expanded form, the model is then used for a description of a social contest situation in terms of a game, with the payoff values defined by reproductive success or fitness. In the model a strategy is regarded as a combination of two parts, one perceptual and one cognitive. We will study the survival value of different strategies using the concept of an evolutionarily stable strategy (ESS). This leads us to a problem of equifinality, which means that one strategy that is an ESS may be composed of many different combinations of perceptual and cognitive substrategies. We will introduce further restraints on the interpretation of an ESS and then discuss ecological and psychological restrictions.

A PROBABILISTIC VERSION OF THE LENS MODEL

The illustrative example concerns the picking behavior of a stone-picker. The stone-picker lives in a forest where there are only two types of stones, big (E_1) and small (E_2). The big stones are not that big and the small ones not that small. In fact, the stone-picker has some difficulty seeing the difference. If a stone is big (E_1), he will see it as big (c_1 = looks big) in 80% of the cases and incorrectly as small (c_2) in 20%. If a stone is small (E_2), he will see it as small (c_2) correctly in 70% of the cases and mistakenly as big (c_1) in 30%. The accuracy of his perceptual system can be described thus:

	c_1	c_2
E_1	0.80	0.20
E_2	0.30	0.70

(2)

where the values in the matrix describe conditional probabilities for percepts c_1 and c_2 given event E_1 or E_2 [$P(c_j/E_i)$; $i, j = 1, 2$].

When the stone-picker walks around in the forest, doing what stone-pickers generally do, he employs a very simple, straightforward strategy. He ignores (R_1) every stone that looks big (c_1) and picks (R_2) every stone that looks small (c_2). A psychologist would say that the stone-picker has a cognitive strategy that is called *differential maximizing* (see Bjorkman 1967). The efficiency of the stone-picker's cognitive system could be described as follows, where the values in the matrix are the conditional probabilities for behaviors R_1 and R_2 given the percepts c_1 and c_2:

	R_1	R_2
c_1	1.00	0.00
c_2	0.00	1.00

(3)

To describe the conditional probabilities for the occurence of R_1 and R_2 at the two events, E_1 and E_2, we can simply multiply matrices 2 and 3:

$$\begin{array}{c|cc} & c_1 & c_2 \\ \hline E_1 & 0.80 & 0.20 \\ E_2 & 0.30 & 0.70 \end{array} \times \begin{array}{c|cc} & R_1 & R_2 \\ \hline c_1 & 1.00 & 0.00 \\ c_2 & 0.00 & 1.00 \end{array} = \begin{array}{c|cc} & R_1 & R_2 \\ \hline E_1 & 0.80 & 0.20 \\ E_2 & 0.30 & 0.70 \end{array} \qquad (4)$$

If there is a small stone (E_2), the probability of the stone-picker ignoring it (R_1) is 30%. [From the matrix multiplication: $P(R_1/E_2) = 0.30 \times 1.00 + 0.70 \times 0.00 = 0.30$.] The *E–R* matrix in equation 4 describes a strategy that consists of two parts, one perceptual (the *E–c* matrix) and the other cognitive (the *c–R* matrix).

So far we have ignored the fact that the forest may contain different numbers of big and small stones. Suppose, now, that in this forest 90% of the stones are big and 10% are small, and that what interests us is the relative number of times the stone-picker takes or ignores big and small stones. Multiplying the first row in the *E–c* matrix by 0.90 and the second row by 0.10 gives us the probability for the joint occurrence of *E* and *c*. Keeping the cognitive matrix unchanged (the stone-picker still uses the given information for his decision) and multiplying the two matrices then gives the probabilities for the joint occurrence of *E* and *R*:

$$\begin{array}{c|cc} & c_1 & c_2 \\ \hline E_1 & 0.72 & 0.18 \\ E_2 & 0.03 & 0.07 \end{array} \times \begin{array}{c|cc} & R_1 & R_2 \\ \hline c_1 & 1.00 & 0.00 \\ c_2 & 0.00 & 1.00 \end{array} = \begin{array}{c|cc} & R_1 & R_2 \\ \hline E_1 & 0.72 & 0.18 \\ E_2 & 0.03 & 0.07 \end{array} \qquad (5)$$

Assuming that adequate behavior for a stone-picker is to ignore big stones and pick small stones, his achievement is 0.79 (showing adequate behavior in 79% of the cases in equation 5). He gets small stones in 7% of the cases and takes the big ones by mistake in 18% of the cases. Can he do better than this? Apart from ignoring the perceptual mechanism, he could change the cognitive strategy. If, for example, he picked every stone regardless of size, he would obtain small stones in 10% of the cases but would also have 90% big stones. This strategy, known as *maximizing,* decreases his achievement from 79 to 10%. If he maximized the other way, always ignoring all stones, he will admittedly never get any stones, but his achievement rises to 90%. So if the purpose was just to predict the size of the stones, we might expect him to use this strategy.

One drawback to the lens model is that it does not allow for differences in the value of the various E-R combinations. Let us introduce some risks and benefits in the life of a stone-picker by assuming that picking a small stone yields him a positive value V, picking a big stone deprives him of a value D ($D > 0$), and ignoring stones yields nothing. With risks and benefits introduced, the value of different strategies will depend on the values of V and D. Let us use α as a measure of the relative loss and gain, with $\alpha = D/V$. For the example given in equation 5, differential maximizing will result in an average value of $0.07V - 0.18D$, which is positive for $\alpha < 7/18$. Differential maximizing is also the best strategy in terms of the average value, when $3/72 < \alpha < 7/18$. For $0 < \alpha < 3/72$ the loss when picking big stones is so small that maximizing (picking all stones) is the best strategy. When $\alpha > 7/18$, the best strategy is to ignore all stones, which of course gives the stone-picker nothing. The only possibility of securing a positive value in this case would be to change the perceptual mechanism. We will come back to this later.

Let us now leave the stone-picker for a while. We met him to learn something about the probabilistic version of the lens model. We have seen how this model can describe a strategy as consisting of two mechanisms, one perceptual and one cognitive. We have also suggested a way of using the model in games with risks and benefits included.

We will now apply the expanded lens model to a case of social interaction that is very close to the social contest situation used by Maynard Smith and Parker (1976) in their studies of ESS. The strategies will be evaluated in terms of survival value (fitness) and the evaluation will be in the form of tests for evolutionary stability, using the ESS model. A short description of the ESS model is given below.

A MODEL OF EVOLUTIONARILY STABLE STRATEGIES

The original ESS model applies to a social contest situation treated as a game with the behavior of individuals described as strategies, which in turn are connected to a set of defined payoff values. The model tests whether a certain strategy, in use at the moment in a population, will succeed in keeping an intruding new strategy out of the population or whether the new one will take over. This is an evolutionary game played over generations. The model is developed under the general assumptions of nonsexual reproduction, with no overlap between generations, and infinite populations with random meeting between individuals. The strategies are assumed to be genetically inherited and the payoff values of different strategies are defined in terms of fitness, which can be thought of roughly as a gain in the number of offspring in the next generation. The intruding strategy (the one tested against) is called by Maynard Smith the *mutant* strategy. We will follow Maynard Smith's denotations and represent the existing strategy by I, which is tested against a mutant strategy J. The value of playing I is denoted $E(I)$, which is a weighed sum of the value of

	Dove	*Hawk*
Dove	$\frac{V}{2}$	0
Hawk	V	$\frac{V-D}{2}$

Figure 5.2. Average payoff values for the two strategies *Hawk* and *Dove* (to the left) in different types of contests. V is the value of winning and $-D$ the value of being injured.

playing I against another I-player, $E_I(I)$, and the value of playing I against a mutant J-player, $E_J(I)$. The value $E(J)$ is defined in the same way. The weights are simply the probabilities of meeting the two types of player. The proportion of I-players and J-players in the population is p and q, respectively. So, $E(I)$ and $E(J)$ are defined thus:

$$\begin{gathered} E(I) = pE_I(I) + qE_J(I) \\ E(J) = pE_I(J) + qE_J(J) \\ \text{with } p + q = 1 \end{gathered} \tag{6}$$

Strategy I is an ESS if for all alternative strategies (J) in the game

$$E(I) > E(J) \tag{7}$$

Because q is small compared to p (J is the mutant intruder), we see from equation 6 that criterion 7 is fulfilled if

$$E_I(I) > E_I(J) \tag{8}$$

or

$$E_I(I) = E_I(J) \text{ and } E_J(I) > E_J(J) \tag{9}$$

So far we have considered what are known as *pure strategies,* where a particular player always adheres to one and the same strategy. But the same criteria 7 to 9 also yield mixed strategies, where a player applies two or more strategies randomly, with a specified probability for each strategy.

Let us look at an example for Maynard Smith and Parker (1976), the "hawk and dove" game. Playing hawk is always to attack and continue to attack until *a* one is injured, in which case one would retreat, or *b* the opponent retreats: *a* gives a loss of D and *b* a gain of V. When two hawk-players meet, each wins with a probability of 0.50, giving an average payoff of $(V-D)/2$. Playing the dove is always to display and *a* to retreat if the opponent attacks, or *b* to settle the contest by social agreement if the opponent also displays. *a* results in zero gain and *b* results in V in 50% of the cases. (V and $D > 0$.) The payoff matrix for the three cases of competition is shown in Fig. 5.2. The matrix denotes the outcome for row meeting column and not vice versa.

Assume that strategy I is a mixed strategy of hawk and dove, with the probability P for playing hawk and $1-P$ for playing dove. If I is an equilibrium, the expected gain of an individual who is playing hawk against I must equal the expected gain of one who is playing dove against I:

$$P\frac{V-D}{2}+(1-P)V=(1-P)\frac{V}{2}$$

or

$$P=\frac{V}{D} \tag{10}$$

To test strategy I against an alternative mixed strategy, J, with the probability P' for playing hawk, it is then enough to show that $E_J(I) > E_J(J)$ or

$$E_J(I)-E_J(J)>0 \text{ for all } P' \ (P' \neq P) \tag{11}$$

The actual payoff values inserted in equation 11 gives

$$E_J(I)-E_J(J)=(P-P')\left(P'\frac{V-D}{2}+(1-P')\frac{V}{2}\right) \tag{12}$$

Equation 12 is always positive for $P = P'$ and we can conclude that I is an ESS for $P = V/D$. If $V > D$ then $P = 1$, which means that when the value of winning exceeds the loss from being injured, the ESS is always to play hawk. When the value of winning is exceeded by the loss from injury, say for example $V = 0.25\,D$, then the ESS is to play hawk with the probability ($P = V/D$), which in this case is to play hawk in 25% and dove in 75% of the meetings. It is important to observe that the concept of mixed ESS is interpreted here in the context of a monomorphic population with all individuals playing the same mixed strategy (and not a dimorphic population with two types of players, each type playing a pure strategy) (cf. Maynard Smith and Parker 1976:161).

ESS IN TERMS OF THE LENS MODEL

Maynard Smith and Parker (1976) analyze a situation called an *asymmetric contest with incomplete information* that is based on the two types of strategy defined in the hawk and dove game. Let us use this situation in a slightly modified form in the following example. In terms of the lens model, we will denote the two behaviors R_1 (play dove) and R_2 (play hawk). The events in this situation of social interaction are the two participating individuals, each one being the event for the other. Assume that the population comprises two types of individual, big (E_1) and small (E_2). The subjectively perceived size of the opponent is denoted c, with c_1 = "seems perceptually to be big" and c_2 = "seems perceptually to be small." An individual has no information about his own size. The perceptual accuracy, $P(c_1/E_1)$ and $P(c_2/E_2)$, will be denoted p_1 and p_2, respectively. The probability to display (play dove) when the opponent seems to be big is P_1, and the probability to attack (play hawk) when the opponent seems to be small is P_2. In the original hawk and dove game, the probability of winning when both attack was assumed to be 0.50 for each of the combatants. This is also the case here when two big or two small individuals meet. But for the case where one big and one small individual attack each other (both playing hawk), we will assume that the probability of the bigger one winning is P_w (and we might expect $P_w > 0.50$). The payoff values will be the same as those given in

Figure 5.2, where V is the value of winning and D is the loss (damage) when injured.

The example is now explicated in a way that makes it possible to define the strategy in terms of the lens model. We also have enough information to test the strategy for evolutionary stability with different specifications of the variables. Before doing this, let us refresh our memories with a brief summary of the conditions:

1 Ecological conditions. Individuals in the population are either big (E_1) or small (E_2). The relative frequency of big ones is $P(E_1)$, and that of small ones is $P(E_2)$. $P(E_1) + P(E_2) = 1$.

2 Perceptual strategy. Each individual can perceive the size of the opponent with an accuracy of $P(c_1/E_1) = p_1$ and $P(c_2/E_2) = p_2$ (with c_1 = "looks big" and c_2 = "looks small").

3 Cognitive strategy. The hawk and dove strategies are used. If the opponent seems to be big, the individual plays dove with the probability $P(R_1/c_1) = P_1$, and if the opponent seems to be small, it plays hawk with the probability $P(R_2/c_2) = P_2$.

4 Evolutionary payoff. The payoff matrix is based on the one used in the original hawk and dove game. V is the gain if one wins and D is the loss if injured. V and D are defined in terms of fitness.

	R_1	R_2
R_1	$V/2$	0
R_2	V	$(V - D)/2$

(13)

As a measure of the relative seriousness of the situation, we will use $\alpha = D/V$.

5 Secondary condition of an asymmetry. In a contest between one big and one small individual, both of whom are playing hawk, the big one wins with a probability of P_w.

Say that we are mainly interested in the cognitive strategy, defined by the two parameters P_1 and P_2, and how the efficiency of this strategy depends on the seriousness of the situation, defined by α. Assume that there are as many big individuals as there are small ones in the population ($P(E_1) = P(E_2) = 0.50$), that the individuals have perfect discrimination ($p_1 = p_2 = 1$), and that $P_w = 1$. Let us repeat the specifications and then use them to calculate a numerical example.

$$P(E_1) = P(E_2) = 0.50 \tag{14}$$

$$P(c_1/E_1) = P(c_2/E_2) = 1 \tag{15}$$

$$p_w = 1 \tag{16}$$

The lens model description of the total strategy (cf. equation 5) with specifications 14 to 16 is

$$\begin{array}{r|c|c|} & c_1 & c_2 \\ \hline E_1 0.5 \times & 1 & 0 \\ \hline E_2 0.5 \times & 0 & 1 \\ \hline \end{array} \times \begin{array}{r|c|c|} & R_1 & R_2 \\ \hline c_1 & P_1 & 1 - P_1 \\ \hline c_2 & 1 - P_2 & P_2 \\ \hline \end{array} = \begin{array}{r|c|c|} & R_1 & R_2 \\ \hline E_1 & P_1/2 & (1 - P_1)/2 \\ \hline E_2 & (1 - P_2)/2 & P_2/2 \\ \hline \end{array} \tag{17}$$

Let us now test the strategy in equation 17 for evolutionary stability. Call this strategy I, with P_1, P_2, to be tested against another strategy J, with P_1 and

Table 5.1. Strategies (P_1, P_2), *which are an ESS at different values of* α

P_1	P_2	α
0	1	α 1/3
$(3\alpha - 1)/\alpha$	1	$1/3 < \alpha < 1/2$
1	1	$1/2 < \alpha < 2$
1	$2/\alpha$	$2 < \alpha$

P_1, conditional probability of displaying when an opponent seems to be big; P_2, conditional probability of attacking when an opponent seems to be small; $\alpha = (D/V)$, measure of the relative seriousness of the contest. Visual accuracy = 1.

P'_2 ($P'_1 = P_1$ and $P'_2 = P_2$). According to the criterion given in equation 8, we calculate the values of $E_I(I)$ and $E_I(J)$. If the difference between these two values $E_I(I) - E_I(J)$ is positive, then strategy I is an ESS. Knowing the rules for the game, the probabilities from the right-hand matrix in equation 17, and the payoff values given in equation 13, we can see that when two big individuals meet, each will have the following value:

$$(P_1/2)^2 V/2 + 0 + [(1 - P_1)/2(P_1/2]V + [(1 - P_1)/2)^2(V - D)/2] \qquad (18)$$

If to expression equation 18 we add the average value for a small meeting a big, a big meeting a small, and a small meeting a small, we get the total average value, $E_I(I)$. The $E_I(J)$ value is calculated in the same way. The difference $E_I(I) - E_I(J)$ is studied with the two parts J_1 and J_2 of strategy J separated. J_1 is the strategy (P'_1, P_2) and J_2 is the strategy (P_1, P'_2).

$$E_I(I) - E_I(J_1) = \frac{V}{4}(P_1 - P'_1)\,[P_2 - 2 + \alpha(1 - P_1 + 2P_2)] \qquad (19)$$

and

$$E_I(I) - E_I(J_2) = \frac{V}{2}(P_2 - P'_2)\,(3 - P_1 - \alpha P_2) \qquad (20)$$

The result of the ESS test is interpreted graphically in Figure 5.3.

Table 5.1 and Figure 5.3 show that if the injury is relatively slight, $D < V/3$, it is an ESS always to attack even if the opponent seems to be big ($P_1 = 0$). When the loss at injury is more serious, $1/3 < \alpha < 1/2$, it is an ESS always to attack (play hawk against) an opponent who seems to be small, but only at a certain proportion $(3\alpha - 1)/\alpha$ is it an ESS to attack those who seem big. If the relative seriousness is greater than 1/2 but less than 2, it is an ESS always to display against opponents who seem big and always to attack those who seem small. [illegible] the consequences become still more serious, $\alpha > 2$, the ESS is to display against those who look big and at a certain proportion $(2/\alpha)$ to attack those who seem small.

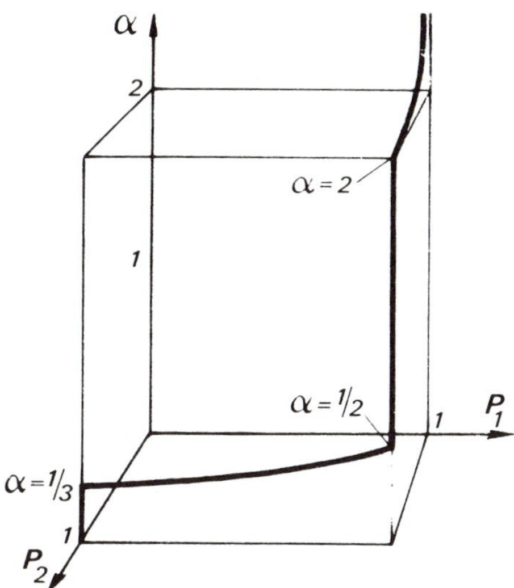

Figure 5.3. Different combinations of P_1 and P_2 that are an ESS, depending on the relative seriousness of the contest ($=\alpha$). See Table 5.1.

A PROBLEM OF EQUIFINALITY

The strategy used in the above example concerns an individual with perfect perception, and the question was which cognitive strategy would lead to an ESS at different degrees of seriousness (α). The same technique can be used to study the perceptual mechanism, keeping the cognitive strategy constant. Say that we want to know which perceptual mechanism (strategy) will result in an ESS when the individual has a totally rigid cognitive strategy. Assume that this individual will always display against opponents who look big and always attack opponents who look small ($P_1 = P_2 = 1$) (differential maximizing). The lens model description of the strategy is now

$$\begin{array}{r} \\ E_1\,0.5\times \\ E_2\,0.5\times \end{array}\begin{array}{c|c|c|} \multicolumn{1}{c}{c_1} & \multicolumn{1}{c}{c_2} \\ \hline p_1 & 1-p_1 \\ \hline 1-p_2 & p_2 \\ \hline \end{array} \times \begin{array}{c|c|c|} & \multicolumn{1}{c}{R_1} & \multicolumn{1}{c}{R_2} \\ \cline{2-3} c_1 & 1 & 0 \\ \cline{2-3} c_2 & 0 & 1 \\ \cline{2-3} \end{array} = \begin{array}{c|c|c|} & \multicolumn{1}{c}{R_1} & \multicolumn{1}{c}{R_2} \\ \cline{2-3} E_1 & p_1/2 & (1-p_1)/2 \\ \cline{2-3} E_2 & (1-p_2)/2 & p_2/2 \\ \cline{2-3} \end{array} \qquad (21)$$

The strategy to be tested has its probabilistic content given in the E–R matrix in equation 21. We use these probabilities together with the payoff values from equation 13 in exactly the same way as in the previous example. The E–R matrix in equation 21 is identical to the matrix in equation 17, with p instead of P. The solutions given in Table 5.1 and Figure 5.3 also hold for the test of the perceptual strategies. From Figure 5.3 we can see that if the injury is relatively slight, $D < V/3$, it is an ESS to see all opponents as small. This means that it is an ESS to follow a totally rigid cognitive strategy combined with a visual system with no accuracy at all (no discriminatory ability); all opponents seem small. As α increases, it starts paying to discriminate. When α is greater than $1/2$ but less than 2, it is an ESS to have perfect perceptual accuracy ($p_1 = p_2 = 1$). When the consequences become still more serious, it is an ESS to see small ones as small in $2/\alpha$ of the cases. For very high α values it is an ESS to have hardly any perceptual accuracy – to see almost all individuals as big.

We have found that for each α we have two ESSs. In a case where both the cognitive and the perceptual systems are free to adapt, there will be an infinite number of combinations of perceptual and cognitive parameters that all give the same *E–R* matrix, as we have seen in equations 13 and 21. From this it follows that for each given α there is an infinite number of combinations of perceptual and cognitive systems that constitute one and the same ESS. This does not mean that the lens model and the ESS model lack scientific discriminatory power. It must not be forgotten that in our example there is also an infinite number of combinations of perceptual and cognitive systems that are not an ESS. In the next few pages let us discuss some ways of using existing knowledge to raise the predictive power of the lens–ESS model.

SOME FOCUSING RESTRAINTS

The preceding section showed that there is a need for further restrictions on the plausible variation of the two parts of the lens model. Because we are mainly concerned with the interdisciplinary possibilities, the discussion will be confined to the perceptual part, about which it is easy to find information from psychological as well as biological research. Four aspects will be discussed, the first three being mainly theoretical and the fourth more empirical.

Functional generality of the perceptual system

There are good reasons for supposing that a perceptual system has a higher degree of generality than a cognitive strategy. Take, for example, a visual perception system similar to our own visual system. The phylogenetic and ontogenetic adaptations of this system have not served only one single purpose. On the contrary, the visual system should provide information on which to base a series of very different types of choice, decision, and behavior. We can think of the visual system as a general informing organ that has been adapted to discriminate those light energy distributions in the environment that are of special importance for living in the niche to which the actual organism is adapted. We might conclude that there are two types of restraints on the visual system: first, a demand for generality regarding the many different cognitive strategies it should serve; second, a demand for ecological validity in the sense that it should be highly related to the general characteristics of the actual niche. One simple explication of this would be to expect that the phylogenetic and ontogenetic test situation for a perceptual system in lens model terms is:

$$\begin{array}{c|c|c|} & c_1 & c_2 \\ \hline E_1 & a & b \\ \hline E_2 & c & d \\ \hline \end{array} \times \begin{array}{c|c|c|} & R_1 & R_2 \\ \hline c_1 & 1 & 0 \\ \hline c_2 & 0 & 1 \\ \hline \end{array} = \begin{array}{c|c|c|} & R_1 & R_2 \\ \hline E_1 & a & b \\ \hline E_2 & c & d \\ \hline \end{array} \qquad (22)$$

where the E–c and E–R matrices describe the probabilities of joint occurrence ($a + b + c + d = 1$; cf. equation 21).

Equation 22 indicates that the cognitive systems or behaviors concerned with the adaptation of the perceptual system should, on the average, be a sort of identification and differentiation of the events, with the important condition that the events are representative of the actual niche (in a broad sense). Equation 22 states that the perceptual system is adapted with a cognitive criterion of differential maximizing, which is the strategy that always gives the highest achievement when $a > c$ and $d > b$.

One may wonder why we should not always expect that $a + d = 1$. One answer is that there are always biological restrictions on what can be developed (in the form of genetic information, biological building material, etc.). Another answer is that the stimuli E_1 and E_2 can always be chosen to be so similar that it is nearly impossible to detect a difference. This type of situation is in fact typical for many of the experiments in perception psychology, in what are known as *discrimination tests.*

Ecological veridicality

Let us return to the stone-picker and have a look at his perceptual system. His perceptual matrix is (see equation 5)

	c_1	c_2	Σ
E_1	0.72	0.18	0.90
E_2	0:03	0.07	0.10
Σ	0.75	0.25	1.00

(23)

In equation 23 we have the sums of rows and columns. In the forest where the stone-pickers live there are 90% big stones (E_1) and 10% small stones (E_2). However, a stone-picker who counts what he sees will think that the forest contains 75% big stones and 25% small stones. As far as stone-picking behavior is concerned, it could pay to overestimate the proportion of small stones. But if the perceptual system is also used for many other behaviors, there is reason to expect that it will have been adapted to a state that gives correct information about the relative numbers of things in the environment. This means that we could ask for the following restriction on the perceptual system:

$$P(c_i) = P(E_i) \tag{24}$$

We will refer to equation 24 as a condition of *ecological veridicality.*

Symmetric perceptual systems

Let us take yet another look at the perceptual system of the stone-picker. Compare the probability that he will see a big stone (perceptually) when it is there with the probability that there is a big stone when he sees one (perceptually). The probability of the first instance, $P(c_1 / E_1)$, is $0.72/0.90 = 0.80$ (see equation 23). The second one, $p(E_1 / c_1)$, is $0.72/0.75 = 0.96$. He has a perceptual accuracy of 0.80 but a predictive cue validity of 0.96 for big stones. This can be highly effective under special circumstances, but from a general point of view we could expect that the perceptual system should have the same capacity in both cases.

In ethology we sometimes distinguish between two types of behavior: consummatory behavior and searching behavior (see for example Tinbergen 1951 and Thorpe 1963). Let us use these words more loosely than usual and say that *consummatory behavior* is a direct, quick response to a given stimulus, in contrast to *searching behavior,* which is a slower process with the percept given and with the goal of finding the event (stimulus) that matches the percept. We could then conclude that these two types of behavior seem to have different conditional probabilities, $P(c/E)$ and $P(E/c)$, which are of interest for the evaluation of the efficiency. There are reasons to expect these two probabilities to be identical. Assume that the perceptual system is ecologically veridical, as stated in equation 24. It then follows directly from Bayes's theorem, that is,

$$P(E_i/c_j) = \frac{P(E_i)\,P(c_j/E_i)}{P(c_j)} \tag{25}$$

that for $i = j$

$$P(c_i/E_i) = P(E_i/c_i) \tag{26}$$

Let us for a moment accept assumption 24. For the "two events–two cues" case we know that

$$P(E_1/c_1) = 1 - P(E_2/c_1) \tag{27}$$

and

$$P(c_1/E_2) = 1 - p(c_2/E_2)$$

Using transformations 27 and assumption 24 in Bayes's theorem 25 we find that

$$P(c_1/E_1) = \frac{P(E_2)}{P(E_1)}P(c_2/E_2) + \frac{P(E_1) - P(E_2)}{P(E_1)} \tag{28}$$

and

$$P(c_2/E_1) = \frac{P(E_2)}{P(E_1)}P(c_1/E_2) \tag{29}$$

Equation 28 shows that if the perceptual system is adapted so that the percepts are veridical in the sense expressed in equation 24, then the perceptual accuracies, $P(c_1/E_1)$ and $P(c_2/E_2)$, are related linearly, and their relation is determined entirely by the relative frequency of the events in the environment. Equation 28 is a law that specifies the ecological restrictions and possibilities for the set of perceptual accuracies that the phylogenetic and ontogenetic adaptations can reach. If the relative frequencies of events in the environment are stable, the improvement of perceptual accuracy has to follow the straight line defined by equation 28. We also see that if the distribution of events in the environment is changed, then the perceptual accuracy in general will also change (there are exceptions to this principle).

Equation 29 shows the relation between the probabilities for inadequate perception, for example, seeing a big thing as small and a small thing as big. This relation is linear too, and the line goes through the origin, which means that the probabilities for inadequate perception could both reach zero even if

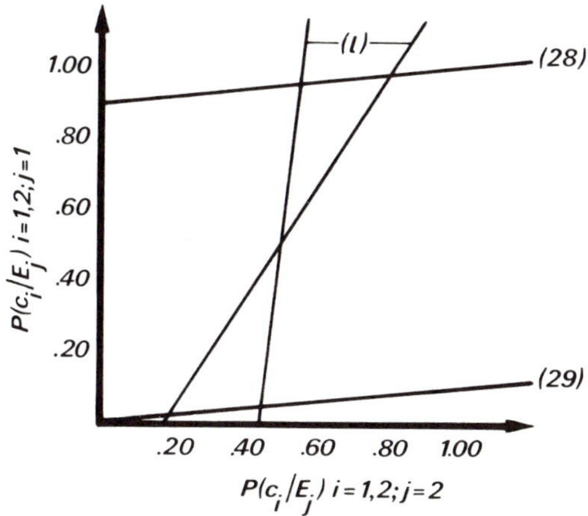

Figure 5.4. Graphic illustration of possible perceptual accuracies, $P(c_i/E_i)$ and inaccuracies, $P(c_i/E_j)$ with $i \neq j$, at the ecological distribution: $P(E_1) = 0.90$ and $P(E_2) = 0.10$. The possible cases are found as the intersections between the rotating line l, and the two lines *28* and *29*. See text and equations 28 and 29 for further information.

$P(E_1) \neq P(E_2)$. Equation 29 specifies the environmental restrictions on the possibility of adapting the perceptual system to a state with certain acceptable levels of error. The two lines defined by equations 28 and 29 are parallel, which means that the accuracy and inaccuracy levels cannot be mutually independent. The accuracy cannot be increased without also decreasing the risk of failure. The exact relation between this increase and decrease can be seen in Figure 5.4, where the two lines 28 and 29 are represented graphically for a certain ecological distribution [$P(E_1) = 0.90$ and $P(E_2) = 0.10$]. Because $P(c_1/E_i) = 1 - P(c_2/E_i)$, the possible combinations of $P(c_i/E_j)$ can be found as the intersection of a straight line through (0.50; 0.50) and the two lines 28 and 29. In Figure 5.4 two different positions of the rotating line give two examples of possible combinations of $P(c_i/E_j)$.

The relations shown in Figure 5.4 also hold for the predictive cue validity, $P(E/c)$. Because the event distribution in Figure 5.4 is the same as in the stone-picker example, we can now easily see which possible combinations of $P(c/E)$ and $P(E/c)$ an adapted stone-picker could have.

Empirical investigation of the perceptual system

The last type of restraint concerns the possibility of studying the *E-c* matrix empirically. Much information is available about perception in the numerous studies from physiology, psychology, and zoology. We might, for instance, be able to find published data on the accuracy of a perceptual system of a certain species. In practice, however, it is often difficult to find studies that have been conducted in an environment that is biologically relevant for the species in question. The events employed are seldom representative for the natural environment or the natural behavior of the animal (cf. Chapter 4). In terms of the lens model, Brunswik has developed the arguments for the necessity of representative design in psychological experiments (Brunswik 1955). In spite of the large body of empirical studies on perception, there is still a need for experiments and observations of the perceptual systems in adequate situations.

SUMMARY

This chapter investigates some possibilities of applying evolutionary and ecological criteria to a psychological model of behavior. The psychological model studied is known as the lens model. It consists of two parts: one perceptual, giving the organism information about events in the environment, and the other cognitive, describing how the organism uses the information to decide what to do. The lens model is expanded to yield social interaction between two individuals, and a possibility is introduced of assigning values to the different types of behaviors or strategies. The lens model is used to describe an asymmetric contest situation with incomplete information about the opponent and with the payoff defined in terms of fitness. Different strategies are tested for evolutionary stability, using the ESS model. There were an infinite number of combinations of perceptual and cognitive strategies, all constituting one and the same ESS, which raises *a* problem of equifinality. This problem leads us to ask whether the predictive power of the lens–ESS model could be increased by introducing further restrictions into the model. Four possible restraints on the perceptual system are discussed, with the tentative conclusion that the perceptual system should be (1) functionally general, (2) ecologically veridical, (3) symmetric, and (4) empirically investigated. Applying these criteria drastically restricted the body of plausible alternatives in our sample.

REFERENCES

Bjorkman, M. 1967. Stimulus–event learning and event learning as concurrent processes. *Organizational behavior and human performance* 3:219–235.

1979. The Bayesian paradigm and Brunswik's model: toward a synthesis.

Brehmer, B. 1979. Single-cue probability learning: a general review of results.

Brunswik, E. 1952. The conceptual framework of psychology. *International Encyclopedia of Unified Science* 1:1–102.

1955. Representative design and probabilistic theory in a functional psychology. *Psychological Review* 62:193–217.

Goude, G. 1979. Psychobiological aspects of the function of base-rate in subjective probability estimation.

Hammond, K. R., C. J. Hursch, and F. J. Todd. 1964. Analyzing the components of clinical inference. *Psychological Review* 71:438–456.

Hursch, C. J., K. R. Hammond, and J. Hursch. 1964. Some methodological considerations in multiple-cue probability studies. *Psychological Review* 71:42–60.

Maynard Smith, J., and G. A. Parker. 1976. The logic of asymmetric contests. *Animal Behaviour* 24:159–175.

Thorpe, W. H. 1963. *Learning and instinct in animals.* Methuen, London.

Tinbergen, N. 1951. *The study of instinct.* Clarendon Press, Oxford.

PART II

EARLY PROCESSES AND GENETICS

INTRODUCTION

GEORGE W. BARLOW

The preceding part dealt with a variety of issues, either theoretical or methodological, but all general. In this part, we turn to basic processes of special import to early development. In fact, the first two chapters here dwell mostly on events taking place during embryonic development, though with obvious relevance to later stages. The last two chapters embrace all phases of life, from conception to senescence, but at the basic level of its genetic substrate. Thus this part encompasses material at a fundamental level that has been pivotal to the nature/nurture argument. Though that argument never erupts in this book in its formerly counterproductive and at times vitriolic form, all four chapters here are obviously relevant to that issue.

Studying behavioral development to discern how behavior comes to be has its frustrations. A case in point is the examining of ever earlier stages to see how motor behavior first appears and progresses to its definitive form. It was this approach that led to exploration of the behavior of embryos because the degree of development at birth or hatching varies so greatly among species (see Chapter 18).

In a sense, this process consists of looking for continuity between the first jerky movements of the embryo and its spontaneous waves of activity, then the relatively coordinated actions that become increasingly evident near term, and finally the motor behavior of early postnatal life. This is the theme of the admirably concise Chapter 6, by Anne Bekoff. Concentrating on birds and mammals, this chapter initially defines the levels of progression in embryonic motor competence. It then poses questions about the functional significance of such activities and gives the available evidence. After presenting that information, the chapter argues that there is continuity from beginning to end. Embryonic activities, however, may serve the immediate needs of the embryo, on the one hand, and prepare the neural circuitry, on the other. Repeatedly, the stumbling block in interpreting the behavioral data is our lack of information about the developing circuitry; the next chapter addresses that fundamental question.

In Chapter 7, by J. R. Wolff, we get an in-depth view of the most difficult questions facing the developmental neurobiologist. To aid the reader, the material is first divided into an inquiry into the nature of the basic units: How are neurons produced, how are they then distributed into a functional arrangement, and how do they further develop? Next, the nature of the connections between the units is dealt with in the treatment of synaptogenesis: How are connections formed, how do they differentiate, and how do they become integrated into a functional system? In closing, the chapter reflects on the problems of behavioral plasticity in relation to the dynamics of neural substrates of plasticity, its relationship to age, and its possible role in sensitive phases.

The next two chapters might seem at first to be out of place because they involve the genetics of behavior. All the other chapters in this book take the genetics of behavior either as given or as lying outside the subject of development. Yet when ethology was in its ascendancy during the 1950s and 1960s, ethologists argued forcefully that students of behavior, including its development, ought to pay more attention to the genetics of behavior. It matters not, for the moment, that in the beginning their conception of genetics concentrated on differences between species rather than between individuals. The point is that there emerged from the nature–nurture polemic an appreciation of the importance of behavior genetics. The field of behavior genetics then grew by leaps and bounds, and a journal by that name was founded.

The odd thing is that behavior genetics has had so little tangible effect on the study of behavior, and vice versa. It is difficult to say why this should be. Certainly, we editors have no special insight into the problem. From our naive view, however, a large part of the separation seems due to the choice of behavior for analysis whose evolutionary relevance is, to put it charitably, unclear. Given the need to process large samples for rare mutations, or to obtain ample sets of data for polygenic traits, geneticists have favored behaviors that lend themselves to rapid screening or to quick and simple quantification, an understandable tactic. However, that has led them to uninteresting behavior such as audiogenic seizure and rate of defecation. For their part, the ethologists have done little to involve themselves in genetics; nor have they tried to provoke the geneticists, or aid them, to work with behavior whose adaptive significance is more apparent.

Perhaps the greatest casualty here has been in understanding the genetics of behavioral development. Just as the geneticists have moved away from relevant behavior, so have the behavioral developmentalists from genetics. The main thrust in developmental studies has been to comprehend the role of the environment. And that, too, is understandable. The two chapters on genetics that follow, however, have as their objectives stimulating investigators to bring the genetic approach to the study of development and exposing geneticists to a more meaningful and rich source of behavior for analysis, again in a developmental context.

The Bielefeld experience proved that most students of behavior have a poor grasp, and many none, of genetics beyond the basic paradigm of a dihybrid cross. For that reason, both chapters deal with fundamentals at first. Chapter 8, by George W. Barlow, takes up the molecular nature of the gene, how it produces proteins, and how genes are switched on and off during development; it also outlines the major analytical approaches. But the main thrust of the chapter is that a more meaningful genetics of behavioral development can be obtained by analyzing interindividual and intraindividual variation in modal action patterns (MAPs). The ontogeny of MAPs can be tracked, and differences are clearly apparent within and between individuals. That makes it possible to analyze the dynamics of gene activation in different or changing environments during ontogeny.

Chapter 9, by Robert Plomin, has as its main theme the understanding of differences between individuals. That theme was developed, at least in part, as an antidote to the view prevailing in some circles that what is important in the genetics of human behavior is human universals. Emphasizing the central role of stabilizing selection, the chapter explains why it is selectively advantageous to have multiple alleles for genes, hence a rich source of individual genetic variation. Coupled with genotype–environment interactions and correlations, it illustrates how this approach can lead to a better appreciation of the development of within-family and between-family differences and the ontogeny of wariness. The chapter also points out that "the difficulties of studying humans are a disguised blessing in that we are forced to work with naturally occurring genetic and environmental variation."

6

BEHAVIORAL EMBRYOLOGY OF BIRDS AND MAMMALS: NEUROEMBRYOLOGICAL STUDIES OF THE DEVELOPMENT OF MOTOR BEHAVIOR

ANNE BEKOFF

Over the past 100 years, many neuroembryologists, including Preyer (1885), Coghill (1929), Windle (1940), and Hamburger (1963, 1973), have focused attention on the embryonic development of the nervous system and its relationship to the development of motor behaviors (for recent reviews see Hamburger 1973; Oppenheim 1974). In addition to providing insight into mechanisms of neural development, their studies served to point out that the behavioral repertoire of an animal begins to develop, not at birth or hatching, but with the first movements of the embryo. In this chapter I will review some of the neuroembryological studies of the ontogeny of motor behavior in birds and mammals, concentrating on those that provide some insight into the relationship between embryonic motor behavior and the development of postnatal behavior (see also Chap. 11).

AN INTRODUCTION TO EMBRYONIC MOTOR BEHAVIOR

On the basis of their extensive observations of the normal embryonic repertoire of spontaneously performed behaviors in chick embryos and rat fetuses, Hambuger and co-workers recognized three categories of motor behaviors, Types I, II, and III (Hamburger 1963, 1975; Hamburger & Oppenheim 1967; Narayanan et al. 1971). These same categories can be recognized from the descriptions given in earlier studies of embryonic behavior, although they were not explicitly named (e.g., Windle & Griffin 1931; Windle et al. 1933, 1935; Orr & Windle 1934; Barcroft & Barron 1939).

Type I behavior is characterized by its jerky and uncoordinated appearance. The movements consist primarily of irregular, spasmodic twitches of the limbs, head, neck, and trunk, beak clapping and eyelid and tongue movements. Various body parts (wings, legs, head, etc.) often move simultaneously, but in unpredictable combinations. Behavioral observations reveal no coordination among body parts.

Type II behavior consists of spontaneous startles in which a wave of jerky activity passes rapidly through the body. Type II behavior is much more similar in appearance to Type I than to Type III behavior and may be found to represent a subclass of Type I when the underlying neural mechanisms are analyzed. Because Types I and II embryonic behaviors occur under the same conditions and have not been found to respond differently to any of the experimental procedures that have been applied to embryos so far, they will be treated together in this chapter.

Type III behavior differs markedly in appearance from Types I and II because it consists of movements that are smooth and coordinated. Moreover, Type III behaviors bear a clear resemblance to postnatal goal-directed motor behaviors in that coordinated patterns of movement can be recognized. That is, legs, wings, and head move in predictable sequences relative to one another. In addition, Type III behaviors often appear to be used to achieve specific goals, and therefore several different Type III behaviors have been recognized and named according to their function. For example, the chick embryo must tuck its head underneath its right wing in a specific orientation in order to attain the proper hatching position and thereby maximize its chances of successful hatching. This is achieved by performing tucking, a series of bouts of Type III behavior in which the right wing is raised and the head is rotated to the right, up under the wing (Hamburger & Oppenheim 1967).

SPONTANEITY

A striking characteristic of embryonic behavior in all birds and mammals studied to date is that, after an early quiescent stage, the embryo becomes active (for reviews, see Hamburger 1963, 1973; Narayanan et al. 1971; Oppenheim 1974). For example, at 5 days of incubation, soon after the chick embryo first begins to move, it is active about 15% of the time, performing 3 to 4 movements per minute. The amount of activity rises to a maximum of 21 to 22 movements per minute, and the chick embryo is active 75 to 80% of the time at 12 days. Activity decreases to lower levels again near the time of hatching (21 days) (Oppenheim 1972a, 1972b). Typically these embryonic movements are performed spontaneously, that is, in the absence of obvious external stimulation. Spontaneity remains a prominent characteristic of embryonic behaviors throughout development (Hamburger 1963, 1973; Oppenheim 1974). A similar pattern of initial low levels of spontaneous activity increasing to a maximum and then decreasing somewhat near birth is also seen in fetal mammals (Edwards & Edwards 1970; Narayanan et al. 1971).

To learn more about the neural mechanisms underlying spontaneous activity, experiments were performed in which the spinal cords of embryonic chicks and fetal mammals were transected (Barcroft & Barron 1937; Bekoff, unpublished observations of rat fetuses; Hamburger et al. 1965; Hooker & Nicholas 1930; Oppenheim 1975; Provine & Rogers 1977). Spinal transections have been made at both cervical and thoracic levels, and observations have been made on both chronically and acutely spinalized animals. In all cases the results were similar in that spontaneous activity continued both above and below the cut. These results indicate that spontaneous activity is a property that is either distributed throughout the nervous system or has several initiation sites.

Furthermore, it has been shown that in chick embryos that have been both deafferented and spinalized, spontaneous movements continue in the absence of both sensory and descending input (Hamburger et al. 1966). Neural activity has also been recorded in the completely isolated lumbosacral spinal cord of the chick embryo (Sharma et al. 1970). Thus, in the chick embryo at least, the spontaneous activity must result from endogenous activity of spinal cord neurons. However, the neural mechanism underlying this spontaneous activity has not been identified. It is not even known whether the activity is a property of individual neurons or of neural circuits. Nevertheless, in view of its importance to the embryonic development of motor behavior, the mechanism involved deserves further investigation.

It has been suggested that spontaneous activity is necessary to ensure adequate neural activity, muscular activity, or both during embryonic stages when sensory stimulation might be limited (Bekoff 1981; Hamburger 1968). The embryo is often thought to exist in a state of sensory deprivation (Bradley & Mistretta 1975; Reynolds 1962). It floats in a pool of amniotic fluid that keeps it buffered from rapid chemical or temperature changes. In addition, visual, auditory, and tactile stimuli are limited or attenuated by this environment. However, stimuli are not entirely absent, as shown, for example, by the studies of Bradley and Mistretta (1975), Gottlieb (1968, 1979), Oppenheim (1972a, 1972b), and Vince (1979).

The availability of stimuli may not be sufficient to conclude that they have an effect on motor behavior, however. For example, Oppenheim (1972a) has shown that even when tactile and proprioceptive stimuli are increased experimentally in chick embryos, little increase in activity is seen, suggesting that under normal circumstances these stimuli are not likely to be major sources of stimulus-evoked motor activity. The mechanism responsible for the failure of these stimuli to evoke additional movement is not known, but it may be due to inherent fatigability of embryonic sensory receptors or to habituation. Rapid failure to respond to repeated stimuli seems to be a common characteristic of embryonic sensory systems and has also been found in work on taste receptors (Bradley & Mistrettra 1975) and on cortical responses to visual stimulation (Sedláček 1971) in mammalian fetuses. Thus, the limited intensity and frequency of sensory stimuli that impinge on the embryo, coupled with rapid decreases in responsiveness to the stimuli that are available, may reduce the probability of stimulus-evoked motor activity to unacceptably low levels. Under these conditions, spontaneously generated activity would be called for to provide sufficient motor activity.

The argument that spontaneous behavior is needed to assure adequate motor activity assumes, of course, that embryonic motor activity is important to normal development. Evidence suggesting the importance of embryonic movement comes from studies in which drugs were used to block muscle activation in chick embryos. As little as 48 hours of paralysis has been found to result in permanent malformation of joints and atrophy of muscles (Drachman & Coulombre 1962; Hall 1975; Oppenheim et al. 1978). After 60 hours of immobility, changes are seen in motor neuron development as normal motor neuron cell death is delayed (Pittman & Oppenheim 1979). It is obvious that irreversible damage to joints and muscles will adversely affect subsequent behavior. Thus, complete suppression of activity for as little as 10% of the incubation period can have a serious effect. It is interesting to note, however, that a decrease in activity levels by 40 to 50% continuously from 10 to 16 days of incubation does not result in joint or muscle damage (Oppenheim et al. 1978). This suggests that there is a relatively high safety factor for muscle and joint development. Nevertheless, none of these studies has assayed for more subtle effects of reduced motor activity on neural development and synaptogenesis. Moreover, in all of the studies mentioned above, it has been assumed but not proven that only neuromuscular junctions were blocked and that normal spontaneous neural activity continued as usual.

The effect of experimentally blocking neural activity on the development of the neural circuits involved in generating coordinated motor behaviors is unknown in birds and mammals. However, some suggestive data are available from tissue culture studies. Normal synapses are known to develop among neurons in tissue cultures that have been treated with various drugs that block neural activity (Crain et al. 1968; Model et al. 1971; Obata 1977). However, this situation does not provide information on whether or not normal, adaptively organized neural circuits would develop in vivo in the absence of neural activity.

Studies of chloretone-anesthetized amphibians suggest that normal synaptic connections and normal neural circuits for locomotion can develop in the absence of neural activity because these animals were observed to swim normally after removal from the anesthetic (Harrison 1904; Matthews & Detwiler 1926; Carmichael 1926,1927). Nevertheless, these studies are still ambiguous because neural activity was not monitored and therefore the extent to which neural activity was reduced is not known. It would be worthwhile to repeat these experiments with adequate monitoring of neural activity.

REFLEXES

In addition to spontaneous behavior, reflexes have also been extensively studied in chick and mammalian embryos. These will be dealt with as a separate category of behavior because they can be studied separately. However, it should be noted that it is not yet clear to what extent reflexes contribute to spontaneous embryonic behavior (Bekoff 1981). Certainly, as discussed above, it is clear that spontaneous behavior can continue, apparently unchanged, in the absence of sensory feedback in the chick embryo (Hamburger et al. 1966). On the other hand, the role of reflexes in normal embryonic movement has not been analyzed.

It has been found that in mammals a reflex response can be obtained at the same time that spontaneous movements first appear (e.g., 15 days in rat embryos), and there is therefore no prereflexogenic period of motor activity. However, in chick embryos spontaneous coordinated leg movements appear at 6.5 days, preceding the appearance of reflex responses, which can first be elicited at 7.5 to 8 days (Bekoff et al. 1975). Thus, in the chick embryo the earliest leg movements appear to be produced by a central pattern-generating circuit and are not dependent on sensory feedback. Nevertheless reflex responses can be elicited throughout most of embryonic development in both chick embryos and mammalian fetuses.

By applying tactile or proprioceptive stimulation to embryos during periods of inactivity, the time of development of various reflex responses can be charted (e.g., chick: Oppenheim 1972a; Orr & Windle 1934; rat: Narayanan et al. 1971; Windle et al. 1935; Windle & Baxter 1936; guinea pig: Carmichael 1934; cat: Windle & Griffin 1931; Windle et al. 1933). Reflex responsiveness typically begins in the anterior part of the body earlier than in the posterior part, but sensitivity to stimulation spreads rapidly. Early reflex responses are generalized, often involving many body parts – the so-called total body movements. These appear similar to spontaneous Type I behavior (Narayanan et al. 1971), suggesting that sensory input at these stages is activating the circuits responsible for generating Type I activity. Nevertheless, in the only two studies that have attempted to analyze the development of reflex responses using electromyogram (EMG) recordings, it was found that early responses in guinea pigs (Ånggard et al. 1961) and sheep (Bergström et al. 1962) were uncoordinated. In other words, whereas the response to stretch of the gastrocnemius muscle in adults is a selective activation of gastrocnemius and its agonists and inhibition of its antagonists, in fetuses at early stages, the response is generalized activation of both agonists and antagonists. This stands in contrast to the finding that EMG recordings during Type I activity in chick embryos show coordinated activation of muscles. Until EMG recordings are made from either chick embryos or mammalian fetuses during both reflex responses and spontaneous activity, the relationship of the neural circuits generating motor activity reflexively to those used in spontaneous activity will remain unclear.

After the period of generalized responses to sensory stimulation, the responses become more and more restricted until they reach the localized adult form. This happens at different times in different parts of the body, and some reflex responses may not be fully mature until several days after birth (Narayanan et al. 1971). There does not appear to be a good correlation between reflex restriction and the appearance of Type III behavior, although again EMG recordings during reflex responses as well as Type III behavior in chick embryos might be instructive.

RELATIONSHIP OF TYPES I AND II BEHAVIOR TO TYPE III BEHAVIOR

Most of the spontaneous embryonic motor behavior in birds and mammals is Type I. Type II behavior, or startles, is present but less common during this period. Based on behavioral observations alone, it is difficult to recognize any direct relationship between the jerky Type I and II embryonic movements and later-appearing, coordinated Type III behaviors. Nevertheless, EMG recordings in chick embryos have shown that the neural circuitry that will later produce the leg movements of hatching (a Type III behavior) begins developing at least as early as 6.5 to 7 days of incubation when the first leg movements are observed (Bekoff et al. 1975). For example, ankle muscles are activated in a pattern similar to the pattern that will be used in hatching. Muscles that act as agonists during hatching are coactivated at 6.5 to 7 days, and muscles that act as antagonists during hatching are activated alternately at these early stages. Moreover, from at least 9 days on, knee muscle activity is coordinated with ankle muscle activity during Type I activity; again, the motor output pattern is similar to that seen during hatching (Bekoff 1976).

It is clear, then, that the muscles within a limb are activated in the same pattern as during hatching. Thus, it has been shown that, in the chick embryo, the Type I leg movements are produced by a neural circuit that has many of the same properties as the neural circuit that produces the Type III leg movements of hatching (Bekoff 1976). Based on this observation, it can be suggested that the same neural circuit is used during both Types I and II behaviors and Type III behaviors.

According to this view, throughout most of embryonic development the neural circuit that patterns the muscle contractions of one leg is activated in such a way that the leg movements appear jerky, and there is little or no coordination of that neural circuit with circuits for other body parts. Thus the neural circuit is activated in the Type I activity pattern. This Type I behavior is spontaneously generated and fullfills the embryonic need for sufficient activity to ensure normal neural and/or muscular development. However, when specific goals must be achieved by the movements, the same circuit is activated in such a way that smooth movements are produced and its activity is coordinated with circuits for other body parts. This then produces a Type III behavior pattern such as hatching.

If the leg movements of Type I and II behaviors and Type III behaviors are all produced by the same (or parts of the same) neural circuits, then one obvious question is, why do they appear so different? One of the proximate reasons may be that, although the leg movements during Type I behavior are produced by coordinated contraction of muscles within a leg, the muscles of the two legs may not be coordinated. This has not been tested with EMG recordings; but based on behavioral observations, one of the most distinctive characteristics of Type I behavior is the apparent absence of coordination between body parts. Provine (1980) has shown an increase in synchronous movements (but not necessarily an increase in coordination) of right and left wings in the last third of the incubation period, but he did not distinguish between Type I, II, and III behaviors.

The other major defining characteristic of Type I and II behaviors, the jerkiness of the movements, may possibly be a result of activating the neural circuits with a different pattern of input than is used during Type III behaviors.

The ultimate explanation for the differences between Type I and II behaviors and Type III behaviors, despite the common use of some neural circuitry, may lie in the different functions that they seem to perform. As suggested earlier, the role of the Type I and II behaviors during embryonic stages may be to ensure adequate neuromuscular activity to permit normal development. Because Type I and II behaviors do not seem to play a role in locomotor, hatching, or other goal-oriented behaviors, it may be that jerky movements with little or no coordination between body parts are sufficient to fulfill the developmental need for activity. Smooth movements and coordination between body parts (Type III behavior) are needed only later, when goal-directed behavior is required.

If this is the case, then one can also ask why the Type I and II behaviors are coordinated at all. The answer may simply be that it is more expedient to make functionally appropriate synapses initially than to make them randomly at first and then later rearrange them.

RELATIONSHIP BETWEEN TYPE III EMBRYONIC BEHAVIOR AND POSTNATAL BEHAVIOR

In addition to the arguments presented above for the continuity at the level of neural circuits of Type I and II behaviors and Type III behavior, a case can also be made for continuity between Type III behaviors in the embryo and certain postnatal behaviors. The spontaneous Type III movements, which appear smooth and coordinated, bear a clear resemblance to behaviors seen postnatally. These Type III behaviors typically appear near the end of the incubation or gestation period. For example, in the chick embryo, Type III movements are first recognized at 17 days of incubation during tucking, when they serve to tuck the head under the right wing in the tucked or hatching position (Bekoff 1976; Hamburger & Oppenheim 1967; Oppenheim 1973). Thus, in the chick embryo at least, Type III movements are used when the movements have a goal such as a specific change in position or escape from the shell. This has also been observed in a variety of other birds and in some reptiles (see Oppenheim 1973 for review).

In mammals, Type III behavior is seen only rarely and has been recognized as walking or running-type movements or as righting behavior. In cat fetuses, coordinated leg movements similar to walking have been seen only under conditions of anoxia (Brown 1915; Windle & Griffin 1931). In rat fetuses, under nonanoxic conditions, they were not recognized until frame-by-frame analyses of videotape records were carried out (Narayanan et al. 1971; Bekoff & Lau 1980). They emerged as short sequences of smooth, coordinated limb movements that appeared similar to the trotting or swimming pattern seen in newborn rats (Bekoff & Trainer 1979). The relative paucity of Type III movements in mammalian fetuses in comparison to birds and reptiles may be related to the more passive role played by mammalian fetuses during birth.

In mammalian fetuses many of the short and rarely occurring sequences of Type III behavior resemble postnatal walking. It seems reasonable to assume, therefore, that they represent a prenatal antecedent to postnatal walking in the sense that they are produced by the neural pattern-generating circuit that will be used for locomotion after birth.

In chick embryos the situation is different because the Type III movements are needed to play a role in prehatching and hatching behaviors. These behaviors do not, at first glance, appear to be direct precursors to any posthatching behaviors. Nevertheless it has been suggested that, despite the obvious differences in postural configuration and rhythmicity between hatching and walking, the same, or elements of the same, neural pattern-generating circuitry may be used to produce both behaviors (Bekoff 1978).

RELATIONSHIP OF TYPE I AND II BEHAVIORS TO POSTNATAL BEHAVIOR

If the arguments presented above are valid, then Type I and II behaviors are related to postnatal behavior by virtue of the fact that the same, or elements of the same, neural circuits for leg movements are used during Type I and II behaviors, the Type III behavior of hatching, and posthatching walking. Presumably similar results would be found if the motor output of other body parts was analyzed. This scheme is still to some degree speculative, of course, because the actual neural circuits involved have been identified only indirectly, by their motor output patterns.

In addition, it is possible, though untested, that the Type I behavior seen during embryonic life may be related to rapid-eye-movement (REM) sleep movements after birth or hatching (Hamburger 1975; Narayanan et al. 1971). The Type I movements of rat fetuses and the movements of newborn rats during REM sleep are similar in appearance (Bekoff unpublished observations). Little work has been done to identify or characterize the neural circuits that are activated to produce the movements of REM sleep. It is not known whether the limb movements, for example, involve coordinated sequences of muscle contractions or not. In the only study I can find in which EMG recordings have been made from limb muscles (in the cat) during REM sleep (Gassel et al. 1964), the published records are similar to recordings from chick embryos during Type I activity (Bekoff 1976). However, it is not possible to determine from the published records whether or not the muscle contractions are coordinated. Further work in this area would undoubtedly be rewarding.

CONCLUSION

Despite distinct differences in form and function, the various types of embryonic behavior appear to be related to one another in the sense that they are generated by activation of the same, or elements of the same, neural circuits. The differences in appearance may be related to the different ways in which the same neural circuits are activated and to the differing degrees to which neural circuits controlling the movements of the various body parts are coordinated with one another.

Moreover, embryonic motor activity probably should not be treated as entirely distinct and unrelated to postnatal behaviors. During the performance of embryonic behaviors that fulfill purely embryonic functions, it appears that neural circuits are activated that will later be reused to perform postnatal functions. Thus it will be necessary to examine early embryonic motor activity in order to understand the mechanisms by which the neural circuits underlying at least some postnatal behaviors, such as walking, are assembled (Bekoff 1981 in press).

SUMMARY

A brief and selective review of some of the studies of the embryonic development of motor behaviors in birds and mammals is presented. The relationship among the three types of embryonic motility patterns is explored as well as the relationship of embryonic to postnatal motor activity. The argument is made that, despite the obvious differences in appearance between the jerky Type I and II embryonic behaviors, in which coordination between body parts is apparently absent, and the smooth, coordinated Type III embryonic behaviors, they are produced by activation of some of the same neural circuits. Evidence for this view is provided by EMG recordings from chick embryo leg muscles, which show patterns of motor output with many similar characteristics during Type I and II behaviors and during Type III hatching behavior (Bekoff et al. 1975; Bekoff 1976).

The suggestion is also made that some of the neural circuitry used in Type III embryonic behaviors may be reused in postnatal behaviors such as walking. In addition, a possible relationship between Type I and II behaviors and the movements seen during REM sleep is discussed.

Although further studies are needed to clarify certain points, it may be profitable to consider embryonic motility as representing both an adaptation to the embryonic need for spontaneous motor activity and a prenatal antecedent of postnatal behavior in the sense that the same, or elements of the same, neural circuits are used in both. This view stresses the continuity between prenatal and postnatal behaviors.

ACKNOWLEDGMENTS

I would like to thank Marc Bekoff and Robert C. Eaton for useful comments on the manuscript. My work has been generously supported by grants from the National Science Foundation and the University of Colorado Council on Research and Creative Work and a fellowship from the Alfred P. Sloan Foundation.

REFERENCES

Änggård, L. R., R. Bergström, & C. G. Bernhard. 1961. Analysis of prenatal spinal reflex activity in sheep. *Acta Physiologica Scandinavica* 53:128–136.

Barcroft, J., & D. H. Barron. 1937. Movements in midfoetal life in the sheep embryo. *Journal of Physiology* 91:329–351.

1939. The development of behavior in foetal sheep. *Journal of Comparative Neurology* 70:477–502.

Bekoff, A. 1976. Ontogeny of leg motor output in the chick embryo: a neural analysis. *Brain Research* 106:271–291.

1978. A neuroethological approach to the study of the ontogeny of coordinated behavior. *In:* G. M. Burghardt & M. Bekoff (eds.), *The development of behavior: comparative and evolutionary aspects*. Garland Press, New York, pp. 19–41.

1981. Embryonic development of the neural circuitry underlying motor coordination. *In:* W. M. Cowan (ed.), *Topics in developmental neurobiology: essays in honor of Viktor Hamburger*. Oxford University Press, Oxford. In press.

Bekoff, A., & B. Lau. 1980. Interlimb coordination in 20-day-old rat fetuses. *Journal of Experimental Zoology* 214:173–175.

Bekoff, A., P. S. G. Stein, & V. Hamburger. 1975. Coordinated motor output in the hindlimb of the 7-day chick embryo. *Proceedings of the National Academy of Sciences U.S.A.* 72:1245–1248.

Bekoff, A., & W. Trainer. 1979. Development of interlimb coordination during swimming in postnatal rats. *Journal of Experimental Biology* 83:1–11.

Bergström, R. M., P.-E. Hellström, & D. Stenberg. 1962. Studies in reflex irradiation in the foetal guinea-pig. *Annales Chirurgiae Gynaecologiae Fenniae* 51:171–178.

Bradley, R. M., & C. M. Mistretta. 1975. Fetal sensory receptors. *Physiological Reviews* 55:352–382.

Brown, T. G. 1915. On the activities of the central nervous system of the unborn foetus of the cat; with a discussion of the question whether progression (walking, etc.) is a "learnt" complex. *Journal of Physiology (London)* 49:208–215.

Carmichael, L. 1926. The development of behavior in vertebrates experimentally removed from the influence of external stimulation. *Psychological Review* 33:51–58.

1927. A further study of the development of behavior in vertebrates experimentally removed from the influence of external stimulation. *Psychological Review* 34:34–47.

1934. An experimental study in the prenatal guinea pig of the origin and development of reflexes and patterns of behavior in relation to the stimulation of specific receptor areas during the period of active fetal life. *Genetic Psychology Monographs* 16:337–491.

Coghill, G. E. 1929. *Anatomy and the problem of behavior.* Hafner, New York.

Crain, S. M., M. B. Bornstein, & E. R. Peterson. 1968. Maturation of cultured embryonic CNS tissues during chronic exposure to agents which prevent bioelectric activity. *Brain Research* 8:363–372.

Drachman, D. B., & A. J. Coulombre. 1962. Experimental clubfoot and arthrogryposis multiplex congenita. *Lancet* 2:523–526.

Edwards, D. D., & J. S. Edwards. 1970. Fetal movement: development and time course. *Science* 169:95–97.

Gassel, M. M., P. L. Marchiafava, & O. Pompeiano. 1964. Phasic changes in muscular activity during desynchronized sleep in unrestrained cats. An analysis of the patterns and organization of myoclonic twitches. *Archives Italiennes de Biologie* 102:449–470.

Gottlieb, G. 1968. Prenatal behavior of birds. *Quarterly Review of Biology* 43:148–174.

1979. Development of species identification in ducklings. 5. Perceptual differentiation in the embryo. *Journal of Comparative and Physiological Psychology* 93:831–854.

Hall, B. K. 1975. A simple, single injection method for inducing long-term paralysis in embryonic chicks and preliminary observations on growth of the tibia. *Anatomical Record* 181:767–778.

Hamburger, V. 1963. Some aspects of the embryology of behavior. *Quarterly Review of Biology* 38:342–365.

1968. 4. Emergence of nervous coordination. Origins of integrated behavior. *Developmental Biology Supplement* 2:251–271.

1973. Anatomical and physiological basis of embryonic motility in birds and mammals. *In:* G. Gottlieb (ed.), *Behavioral embryology.* Academic Press, New York, pp. 52–76.

1975. Fetal behavior. *In:* E. S. E. Hafez (ed.), *The mammalian fetus.* Charles C. Thomas, Springfield, Illinois, pp. 68–81.

Hamburger, V., M. Balaban, R. Oppenheim, & E. Wenger. 1965. Periodic motility of normal and spinal chick embryos between 8 and 17 days of incubation. *Journal of Experimental Zoology* 159:1–14.

Hamburger, V., & R. Oppenheim. 1967. Prehatching motility and hatching behavior in the chick. *Journal of Experimental Zoology* 166:171–204.

Hamburger, V., E. Wenger, & R. Oppenheim. 1966. Motility in the chick embryo in the absence of sensory input. *Journal of Experimental Zoology* 162:133–160.

Harrison, R. G. 1904. An experimental study of the relation of the nervous system to the developing musculature in the embryo of the frog. *American Journal of Anatomy* 4:197–220.

Hooker, D., & J. S. Nicholas. 1930. Spinal cord section in rat fetuses. *Journal of Comparative Neurology* 50:413–467.

Matthews, S. A., & S. R. Detwiler. 1926. The reactions of *Amblystoma* embryos following prolonged treatment with chloretone. *Journal of Experimental Zoology* 45:279–292.

Model, P. G., M. B. Bornstein, S. M. Crain, & G. D. Pappas. 1971. An electron microscopic study of the development of synapses in cultured fetal mouse cerebrum continuously exposed to xylocaine. *Journal of Cell Biology* 49:362–371.

Narayanan, C. H., M. W. Fox, & V. Hamburger. 1971. Prenatal development of spontaneous and evoked activity in the rat (*Rattus norvegicus albinus*). *Behaviour* 40:100–134.

Obata, K. 1977. Development of neuromuscular transmission in culture with a variety of neurons and in the presence of cholinergic substances and tetrodotoxin. *Brain Research* 119:141–153.

Oppenheim, R. W. 1972a. An experimental investigation of the possible role of tactile and proprioceptive stimulation in certain aspects of embryonic behavior in the chick. *Developmental Psychobiology* 5:71–91.

1972b. Embryology of behavior in birds: a critical review of the role of sensory stimulation in embryonic development. *Proceedings of the 15th International Ornithological Congress*, 283–302.

1973. Prehatching and hatching behavior: a comparative and physiological consideration. *In:* G. Gottlieb (ed.), *Behavioral embryology*. Academic Press, New York, pp. 163–244.

1974. The ontogeny of behavior in the chick embryo. *In:* D. S. Lehrman, R. A. Hinde, & E. Shaw (eds.), *Advances in the study of behavior*, vol. 5. Academic Press, New York, pp. 133–172.

1975. The role of supraspinal input in embryonic motility: a re-examination in the chick. *Journal of Comparative Neurology* 160:37–50.

Oppenheim, R. W., R. Pittman, M. Gray, & J. L. Maderdrut. 1978. Embryonic behavior, hatching and neuromuscular development in the chick following a transient reduction of spontaneous motility and sensory input by neuromuscular blocking agents. *Journal of Comparative Neurology* 179:619–640.

Orr, D. W., & W. F. Windle. 1934. The development of behavior in chick embryos: the appearance of somatic movements. *Journal of Comparative Neurology* 60:271–285.

Pittman, R., & R. W. Oppenheim. 1979. Cell death of motoneurons in the chick embryo spinal cord. 4. Evidence that a functional neuromuscular interaction is involved in the regulation of naturally occurring cell death and the stabilization of synapses. *Journal of Comparative Neurology* 187:425–446.

Preyer, W. 1885. *Specielle physiologie des embryo.* Grieben, Leipzig.

Provine, R. R. 1980. Development of between-limb movement synchronization in the chick embryo. *Developmental Psychobiology* 13:151–163.

Provine, R. R., & L. Rogers. 1977. Development of spinal cord bioelectric activity in spinal chick embryos and its behavioral implications. *Journal of Neurobiology* 8:217–228.

Reynolds, S. R. M. 1962. Nature of fetal adaptation to the uterine environment: a problem of sensory deprivation. *American Journal of Obstetrics and Gynecology* 83:800–808.

Shedláček, J. 1971. Cortical responses to visual stimulation in the developing guinea pig during prenatal and perinatal period. *Physiologia Bohemoslovoca* 20:213–220.

Sharma, S. C., R. R. Provine, V. Hamburger, & T. T. Sandel. 1970. Unit activity in the isolated spinal cord of chick embryo, *in situ. Proceedings of the National Academy of Science, U.S.A.* 66:40–47.

Vince, M. A., 1979. Postnatal effects of prenatal sound stimulation in the guinea pig. *Animal Behaviour* 27:908–918.

Windle, W. F. 1940. *Physiology of the fetus: origin and extent of function in prenatal life.* Saunders, Philadelphia.

Windle, W. F., & R. E. Baxter. 1936. Development of reflex mechanisms in the spinal cord of albino rat embryos. Correlations between structure and function, and comparisons with the cat and the chick. *Journal of Comparative Neurology* 63:189–204.

Windle, W. F., & A. M. Griffin. 1931. Observations on embryonic and fetal movements of the cat. *Journal of Comparative Neurology* 52:149–188.

Windle, W. F., W. L. Minear, M. F. Austin, & D. W. Orr. 1935. The origin and early development of somatic behavior in the albino rat. *Physiological Zoology* 8:156–185.

Windle, W. F., J. E. O'Donnell, & E. E. Glasshagle. 1933. The early development of spontaneous and reflex behavior in cat embryos and fetuses. *Physiological Zoology* 4:521–541.

7

SOME MORPHOGENETIC ASPECTS OF THE DEVELOPMENT OF THE CENTRAL NERVOUS SYSTEM

J. R. WOLFF

In recent years numerous articles and books have presented excellent reviews of various aspects of developmental neurobiology (e.g., Stent 1977; Corner et al. 1978; Cotman 1978; Edds et al. 1979). Jacobson (1978), in particular, offers a comprehensive overview and evaluation of the expansive literature in this field. It makes no sense, therefore, to add yet another review. Instead, I shall try to (re)arrange some well-known findings together with more recent data – partly from my own laboratory.

The objective is to highlight general trends in the developmental process and to isolate some morphogenetic aspects that lie submerged in the flood of observations, experimental data, and hypotheses. I will not give a detailed description of isolated developmental mechanisms, such as the proliferation, migration, and differentiation of neurons; these can be found in the reviews and original papers cited. I will focus, instead, on some typical variables of brain structure, such as the polarity, number, and position of neurons and the differentiation of excitatory and inhibitory neurons. The temporospatial structure of processes that determine these properties may help us to understand long-term alterations of complex central nervous system (CNS) functions, such as behavior, following interference with early brain development.

The classical neuron theory portrays the nervous system as a set of polarized cellular units (neurons) that communicate through intercellular contacts (synapses). As discussed in "Polarity of neurons," this is an oversimplification, but it preserves many essential and characteristic properties of nervous systems. Accordingly, the developmental process will be split into two major aspects: (1) the production and distribution of cellular units with appropriate properties, that is, processes leading to neurogenesis and cytodifferentiation; and (2) the formation of specific neuronal connections, the synapses, that allow rapid interneuronal communication. The treatment will be restricted to synaptogenesis, because the actual neuronal processes underlying behavior depend predominantly on the rapid synaptic information transfer. Other factors such as hormones, trophic factors, and other substances may fundamentally influence the development and function of the CNS. For simplicity, they are not included. However, much of their influence on the CNS development might be mediated by modifying some aspects of synaptogenesis.

NEUROGENESIS AND CYTODIFFERENTIATION

Neuronal populations show a number of properties that may vary more or less independently from each other. In the following discussion, the development of some variables of the brain structure will be described. These examples have been selected to demonstrate developmental processes with a variable temporo-spatial structure and different types of decisions regulating epigenesis.

Number of neurons

The number of neurons existing in any given region of the adult brain is determined in a complex series of morphogenetic decisions. The continuous proliferation of germinative cells causes an exponential increase in the number of cells. The ultimate number of such mitotic cycles determines the maximum number of neurons that can develop in a specific brain.

For unknown reasons, the angle between the plane of the mitotic cleavage and the apical surface of the neuroepithelium varies (Smart 1973). This variation causes a fraction of the mitotic cycles to produce two different daughter cells. One daughter cell, losing the characteristic epithelial polarity of the germinative epithelium, seems to give rise to a glioblast that leaves the proliferation zone (Fig. 7.1; Rickmann & Wolff 1977). The fate of the other daughter cell is yet to be established. Here a binary morphogenetic decision is taken by introducing a threshold (contact with the apical surface) into a continuously varying process (orientation of the cleavage plane). Almost nothing is known about the decisive factor producing postmitotic preneurons, except that it also causes a binary decision occurring in the proliferation zone during one mitotic cycle.

Because neurons lose their ability to proliferate, the number, time, and location of these last mitotic cycles determine the number of preneurons that can be provided to a specific brain region. A number of teratogenic agents interfering with cell proliferation cause behavioral changes. Depending on the time of application, these effects vary greatly, being either more severe during early postnatal periods than later and even absent in adults, or vice versa (see Hutchings 1978). This indicates that numerical deficits in specific neuron populations cannot be compensated for during synaptogenesis.

On the other hand, the number of neurons provided by proliferation is generally higher than the definite number of neurons found in the same region or the same brain of an adult (e.g., Katz & Lasek 1978). This also holds true for those nervous systems of invertebrates that contain a rather small and constant number of neurons (Sulston & Horvitz 1977). This discrepancy depends on the amount of cell death occurring at various stages of development.

Recent studies have demonstrated that neuronal cell death is not a uniform phenomenon. In some cases death seems to be preprogrammed, because it happens before any functional contacts with target cells are established. Other neurons seem to die as a consequence of interactions with the target organ and/or other neurons, for example, as part of those processes involved in

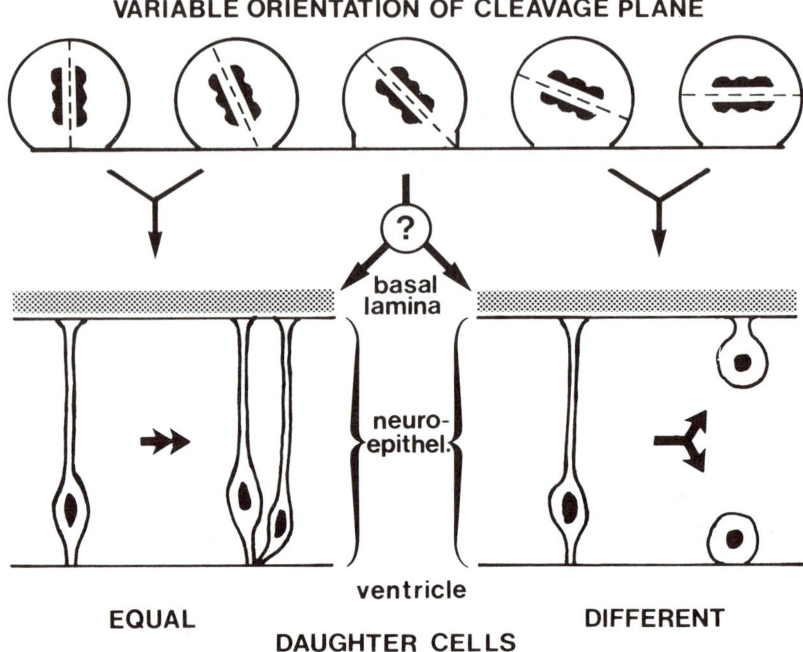

Figure 7.1. Diagram demonstrating how in germinative cells a continuous variation of the cleavage plane (broken line) results in a binary decision producing different types of daughter cells. The upper row represents dividing cells in telophase at a somewhat higher magnification than below. The question mark indicates that small changes of the angle and irregularities in the cleavage plane might induce a different result from mitosis.

matching neuronal populations and their connectivity (Oppenheim et al. 1978; Pittman & Oppenheim 1979; Rager 1978).

As mentioned above, the development of behavior might be different depending on whether the size of a neuron population is reduced by interference with proliferation or by physiological cell death. This suggests that at least some of the eliminated cells play an important role during synaptogenesis (see "Sensitive phases and imprinting"). Some neurons, furthermore, seem to die throughout life, certainly in brains of advanced age. At present, we cannot exclude the possibility that the reduction of neurons during aging is an effect of those morphogenetic processes that continue in the adult brain.

In summary, the definitive size of a neuron population is determined stepwise. Factors stimulating and terminating proliferation regulate the size of a primary neuron population. This population is reduced secondarily by physiological factors that induce cell death and determine its time, amount, and location. There is indirect evidence that eliminated cells might play a temporary role in morphogenesis of the brain and its connectivity. Thus, the production of neurons seems to be related to the development of behavior in at least two ways. First, the overall number of neurons in a nervous system or in one of its subsystems obviously is one of the factors delimiting the behavioral repertoire and variability. Second, certain neurons being formed during specific periods of ontogenesis seem to influence fundamentally the organization of connectivity. Although these neurons apparently cannot be replaced in their morphogenetic function, they may or may not be eliminated during further development.

Position of neurons

After determinative mitosis, postmitotic preneurons leave the site of production by migrating along certain guiding structures. These structures, called *radial glial cells*, guide preneurons to their definitive position in the CNS (Rakic 1972; see also Jacobson 1978).

In the anlage of the cerebral cortex, two types of radial glial cells have been found. The long ones terminate at the outer mesodermal surface of the brain and guide preneurons to the outermost layer of the anlage. This set of guiding structures causes an inside-out mode of cell deposition (see Rakic 1975). Recently, it has been recognized that scattered neurons represent a separate subpopulation and probably follow another sort of guide. Short radial glial cells terminate at the inner mesodermal surfaces of the brain, that is, at the intracerebral blood vessels. Migration along these guidelines might cause the diffuse mode of deposition (Rickmann et al. 1977; Wolff et al. 1978a). Diffusely deposited cells develop exclusively into nonpyramidal neurons, whereas pyramidal neurons seem to be deposited according to the inside-out principle (Chronwall & Wolff 1978a).

Thus, migration in fact determines the ultimate position of a neuron in the brain and even influences its chance to differentiate into a certain type of neuron. Immediately after their production, the neuronal populations of various brain regions are separated by a different course of their migration guides. The subdivision of the brain into subunits (centers, nuclei, areas, laminae, etc.), therefore, seems to be determined by the temporospatial characteristics of growth (site of origin within the proliferation zone) and vascularization of the early brain anlage (Wolff 1978).

Polarity of neurons

The nervous systems of all species, beginning with the Coelenterata, contain neurons that are polarized between presynaptic and postsynaptic elements. The majority of them form specific interneuronal contacts, often chemical synapses (Bullock & Horridge 1965). Increasing knowledge about specific neuronal systems, however, has revealed that not all types of neuronal communication can be described in terms of transmission via chemical synapses (Dismukes 1977; Shepherd 1972). Therefore, I will separate three basic aspects of neuronal polarity: secretion/receptors, presynaptic/postsynaptic elements, axon/dendrites. Because all these aspects are cytologically unique for neurons, we must first ask about the polarity of the cellular material from which neurons develop.

Loss of primordial polarity. Neurons always seem to be derived from ectodermal epithelium (Lentz 1968), that is, from cells with an apicobasal polarization. The development of neural anlages can be traced back to the stage of gastrulation. In many species the third germ layer, the mesoderm, is formed between ectoderm and entoderm during this period. This process has been called internation (Remane 1956), because it internalizes cellular material into a space that is completely enclosed by cells of the embryo. Ectodermal epithelial cells are then polarized between a cell apex confronted with extracorporal space and a cell base directed toward the intracorporal space. The presence of a space completely controlled by the embryo and/or the polarization between extracorporal and intracorporal spaces (see row 1, Table 7.1) seems to be important for neural development.

In vertebrates the apicobasal polarization is preserved during the following neurulation. However, the cell apex of the neuroepithelium is introverted and now faces the lumen of the neural tube. The cells of the neural anlage are then polarized between two spaces both controlled by the embryo itself. The lumen of the neural tube is ultimately filled with cerebrospinal fluid that is formed by derivatives of the neural anlage. Hence, the neuroepithelium may be characterized by its polarization between a transneural space and the extraneural mesoderm (see row 2, Table 7.1).

Finally, preneurons (neuroblasts) are formed by a process that causes them to lose the apicobasal polarity of the neuroepithelium (neurogenesis; see Jacobson 1978). These developmental processes can be summarized as a sequence of introversions that progressively exclude extracorporal influences on the neural anlage. Consequently, the environment of newly formed apolar preneurons is restricted to the intercellular space that is monitored by the neural anlage itself.

A new polarity. In spite of their highly variable shapes, all neurons develop basically into dendritic cells (Lassmann 1966). Unlike compact cells, dendritic cells distribute their cytoplasm and surface membrane in a space that is much larger than their own volume (Fig 7.2). Such cells influence or monitor that space either by secretory products or by receptors (e.g., connective tissue cells and chromatophores). In contrast to other dendritic cells, neurons develop both mechanisms to a high degree of specificity. They synthesize and release transmitter substances that interact with specific receptor molecules localized in plasma membranes of neurons and nonneuronal effector cells.

Neurons are born as isolated cellular individuals without specialized contacts that would hinder their migrating to definite positions in the CNS anlage. The beginning of neuronal differentiation is signaled structurally by the appearance of one to several processes. For most neurons of the vertebrate nervous system, these processes can be classified early as axons and dendrites (see Jacobson 1978). Thus, the axodendritic polarization seems to be a fundamental property for the majority of neurons in vertebrates and also of some invertebrate neurons.

Electrophysiologically the new polarity is detectable by the appearance of action potentials. These originate from the initial segment of the axon or somewhere in its vicinity, when gradual changes of the membrane potential

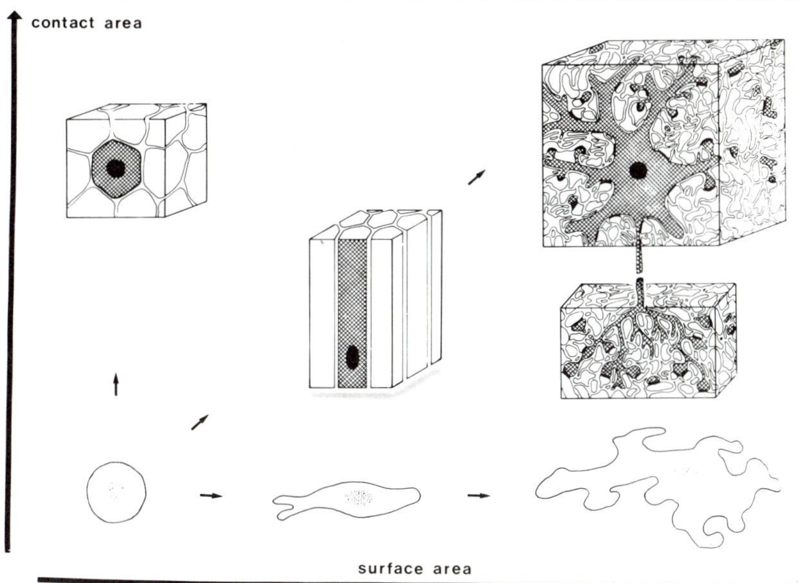

Figure 7.2. Two possibilities by which cells can change their relation to the environment. Variations of the surface area can be realized either as variations of the free cell surface or as variations of that surface fraction that is in contact with other cells. In neurons, both free and adherent surfaces are very large.

pass over a threshold. It is unknown which factors cause shifts of the membrane potential and spontaneous firing activity in the earliest developmental stages of neurons. However, there is indirect evidence that extrasynaptic receptor molecules appear in neuronal membranes before synapses are formed.

The maturation of axons and dendrites creates multiple possibilities for neuronal connections provided suitable devices for communication develop. Most neurons begin to form chemical synapses as early as the appearance of the first dendrites. This indicates that the new polarity establishes its function mainly through synaptic communication among neurons and between neurons and effector cells.

In many neurons a good topographical correlation develops between the axodendritic polarity and the polar aggregation of presynaptic and postsynaptic elements (Fig. 7.3). However, there are important exceptions to this correlation. In some neurons, even nonsynaptic mechanisms for modulating neuronal activity seem to exist (see "Functional polarity and neuron theory"). Thus, the most general feature of neuronal polarity is probably the polarization between secretion and reception of specific molecules.

Whatever mechanism is used for communication, the maturation of each neuron is regulated progressively by its incorporation into multicellular and functional units. Even the simplest reflex mechanism depends on the cooperation of at least two neurons. Beginning with interactions between local neuron populations, the connectivity becomes more and more complex. During this

Table 7.1. *Sequence of introversions during CNS development*

Process	Introverted material	Product (anlage of:)	New cellular polarity of (A) between (B) and (C)
1. Gastrulation	Mesoderm	3 Germ layers (organism)	(A) Ectodermal epithelium (B) Extracorporal space (C) Intracorporal mesoderm
2. Neurulation	Neuroectoderm	Neural tube, etc. (central nervous system)	(A) Neuroepithelium (B) Lumen of the neural tube (C) Extraneural mesoderm
3. Neurogenesis	(Pre)neurons	Local neuron populations (neuronal subsystems)	(A) Preneurons (B) Intraneural space surrounding soma and growing dendrites (C) Microenvironment of growing axon
4. Synaptogenesis	Transmitter effects	Presynaptic and postsynaptic offerings and synapses (adult connectivity of brain)	(A) Neurons (B) Afferent synaptic spectrum (C) Efferent synaptic spectrum
a. Slow synaptogenesis	Spontaneous activity and effects of microenvironment	Randomly formed synaptic contacts (self-stabilized connectivity)	(A) Neurons (B) Foreign synaptic influences (C) Own synaptic effects

b. Rapid synaptogenesis	Synaptically driven activity and feedback	Selectively stabilized synapses (primary connectivity of functional systems)	(A) Neurons (B) Primary species-specific input (C) Primary species-specific output
c. Primary neuroplasticity	Activity changed by sensory input (and learning?)	Selectively stabilized synapses (connectivity adapted to functional requirements)	(A) Neurons (B) Accommodated input (C) Adapted output
d. Secondary neuroplasticity	Activity changed by degeneration of presynaptic and postsynaptic elements	Selectively exchanged synapses (stabilized abnormal connectivity)	(A) Neurons (B) Reoptimized input (C) Reoptimized output

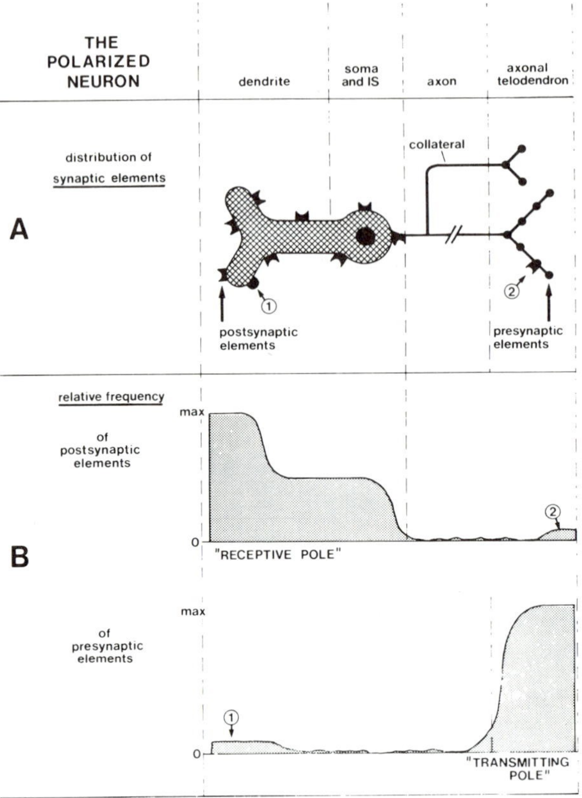

Figure 7.3. Schematic representation of a neuron with axodendritic polarity. Note that some presynaptic and postsynaptic elements may occur in an unusual position forming (1) dendrodendritic or (2) axoaxonal synapses. This does not change the polarized interaction of the neuron within a neuronal network, indicating that the synaptic polarization is not necessarily a topographical one. Although a coincidence between axodendritic and synaptic polarity frequently exists in vertebrate neurons, it is virtually absent in unipolar neurons of invertebrates.

process the nervous centers, subsystems, and systems gain access to input from the intracorporal space. This input is produced not only by receptors in muscles, tendons, and viscera but also by sensory organs. The latter then extend the influences on central neurons to those from the extracorporal space. Thus, after synaptogenesis, neuronal polarity is no longer a cellular phenomenon but involves many neurons. It must then be defined functionally as a polarization of neuronal networks between input and output (see row 4, Table 7.1).

In summary, the development of neuronal polarity between secretion and reception forms the base from which interneuronal communication evolves. Beginning locally, the interactions between neurons become increasingly complex and include, finally, the extracorporal space as a source of input and a target of output. On a cellular level, this part of CNS development can be regarded as a progressive extroversion, recruiting transneuronally input from more and more distant parts of the nervous system and finally from the extracorporal space.

Functional polarity and neuron theory. The fundamental polarity between secretion and reception is common to all secretory systems inside and outside the nervous system. Nevertheless, this most primitive state persists in some mature cells that develop from the neural anlage, for example, epinephrine-producing cells of the adrenal medulla and neurosecretory neurons.

The exclusively neuronal character of this polarity develops when the specific receptors are no longer restricted to nonneuronal effectors (muscle and glandular cells) but are also localized on neurons. This localization allows the secretory product to be utilized as a transmitter for specific interneuronal communication.

The polarity between broadcasting and receiving is independent of whether or not synaptic contacts are formed. For example, a nonsynaptic release of neurotransmitters has been suggested on the basis of morphological evidence for some monoaminergic neuronal systems of the adult CNS (see Chan-Palay 1977). Presynaptic elements without contact to postsynaptic elements are found in the peripheral nervous system called *synapses par distance* and also at some monoaminergic axons in the CNS (Descarries et al. 1977). Certain neurons of the substantia nigra presumably release dopamine not only from axon terminals as a typical synaptic transmitter but additionally from soma and dendrites by some hypothetical nonsynaptic mechanism (see Dismukes 1977; Glowinski et al. 1978). Many receptors for transmitter molecules are located in postsynaptic membranes, the *synaptic receptors.* However, in many innervated neurons, additional *extrasynaptic receptors* have also been demonstrated; they bind the same substances that act as synaptic transmitters.

These examples demonstrate that the polarization between presynaptic and postsynaptic elements represents a further specialization of the general polarity between secretion and receptors. However, this does not mean that the synaptic polarity has completely replaced more primitive types of communication in highly developed brains. Synaptic and nonsynaptic transmission coexist in the invertebrate CNS as well as in highly organized brains, although the vast majority of presynaptic elements in the vertebrate brain seem to make contact with postsynaptic elements. As described above, most vertebrate neurons develop separate axons and dendrites. Again, the majority of presynaptic elements are located on axons, the majority of postsynaptic elements on dendrites and somata.

In spite of this statistical correlation between synaptic and axodendritic polarity, there are dendrodendritic and axoaxonal synapses (Fig. 7.3). This fact indicates that the location of the secretory and receptive poles may vary independently from the axodendritic polarization. The factors regulating the position of presynaptic and postsynaptic elements on the neuronal surface are unknown. However, as long as neurons show receptors and the secretion of transmitter molecules, there is no reason for changing the general principle of the neuron theory. This also holds for neurons without axons (*amacrine cells;* see Shepherd 1972) if the definitions of polarity are extended.

The mechanisms for interneuronal transmission and communication, then, clearly show various levels of differentiation. They vary from nonsynaptic release and reception to synaptic transmission that shows a highly organized topography on neurons. There is, however, no evidence that these various levels follow each other during ontogenesis; they coexist in the same brain, possibly even on the same neuron, and seem to serve different functions. In the vertebrate CNS, synaptic and axodendritic polarization of neurons prevail. This fact suggests that with increasing complexity of the nervous systems, information transfer prefers channels that localize the effects of transmission (synapses) and separate spatially transmitters and receptors (axons/dendrites).

Choice of transmitter

Several substances are selectively produced by certain neurons and can specifically change the membrane potentials of neurons. It is not important whether these substances (e.g., acetylcholine, monoamines, amino acids, peptides) are actually utilized in synaptic transmission or are released nonsynaptically. Each neuron has to choose among various possibilities at some point in its differentiation.

Recent experiments on neurons derived from the neural crest have elegantly demonstrated in vivo and in vitro that this choice is induced or regulated by external factors (Bunge et al. 1978; Le Douarin et al. 1977; Patterson 1978). For example, adrenergic neurons of sympathetic ganglia seem to be affected by an adrenergic conditioning factor during their migration. However, they need electrical activity imposed from spinal neurons to express definitely the adrenergic character. On the other hand, the same class of neurons seems to remain responsive to a cholinergic conditioning factor, if spinal neurons do not impose electrical activity on them. Thus, the determination of the transmitter used by one of these neurons seems to depend on several environmental factors and on the sequence of their action during ontogenesis.

Excitatory and inhibitory neurons

Little is known about the factors influencing the functional differentiation of preneurons into different classes of neurons. As mentioned above, the spatial distribution of neurons produced in the neocortex by different migration guides apparently somehow affects neuronal differentiation. Pyramidal cells with apical dendrites terminating in the first layer seem to follow the inside-out layering of deposition (Wolff et al. 1978a), whereas none of them develops the biochemical properties of inhibitory GABA-ergic neurons. However, some nonpyramidal neurons, following the diffuse mode of deposition, attain the ability to accumulate GABA (γ-aminobutyric acid, the probable inhibitory transmitter substance of the neocortex) and synthesize the GABA-producing enzyme (Chronwall and Wolff 1978b; Ribak 1978).

Because this fact indicates that not all nonpyramidal neurons become GABA-ergic, migration, although separating two populations of cortical neurons, does not directly determine the production of a specific transmitter. Prospective inhibitory neurons of the neocortex can already be detected during the embryonic period. They develop the high-affinity uptake of GABA before they receive a reasonable number of synapses, if any, and before their axons can be recognized (Chronwall & Wolff 1979).

Whether a neuron acts to excite or inhibit does not depend exclusively on the release of a specific transmitter. This transmitter, by binding to a receptor, has to open the corresponding ionic channel in the postsynaptic membrane. Therefore, the development of inhibitory neurons cannot be determined by an isolated decision in the presynaptic neuron (choice of transmitter) but rather has to coincide with a specific differentiation of the postsynaptic neuron (choice of receptor–ion channel combination). The final step in the development of excitatory or inhibitory interactions between neurons, therefore, has to be a cooperative effect between at least two neurons.

The preceding sections demonstrated that general and essential features of nervous systems are determined during early stages of neuronal cytodifferentiation. However, the temporospatial course of neurogenesis, cytodifferentiation, and cell death also determines variable properties of nervous systems that characterize species differences. These are, for example, the size of the total neuron population in a brain, its subdivision and separation of regional subpopulations and, finally, the differentiation of neurons with long axons that organize the functional systems in the CNS by interconnecting specifically the various subdivisions (centers, nuclei, areas, laminae, etc.).

Temporal interference with these early developmental processes can produce major defects (e.g., microcephaly, agenesis of various parts of the CNS) but can also disturb the internal organization of functional systems. The resulting abnormalities of behavior may or may not be compensated for later. This possibility for compensation indicates that the further development and maturation of nervous systems not only allow neurons to interact randomly within a predetermined framework but also create a great many specific adaptations in synaptogenesis.

SYNAPTOGENESIS AND DIFFERENTIATION OF CONNECTIVITY

In a restricted sense, *synaptogenesis* denotes the formation of synaptic contacts between presynaptic and postsynaptic elements. However, we have to adopt a broader definition of synaptogenesis when asking about the probability of connections being formed between two specific neurons or sets of neurons. Differentiated nervous systems are characterized by nonrandom connectivity between neurons. This indicates that synaptogenesis is to some degree selective. Thus, a broader formulation of synaptogenesis includes factors that regulate the direction and the amount of growth and branching in axons and dendrites and the factors that influence the distribution and amount of presynaptic and postsynaptic elements formed on each neuron. For simplicity, the migration of neurons will be excluded from the present considerations, although it influences the position and arrangement of axonal and dendritic modules.

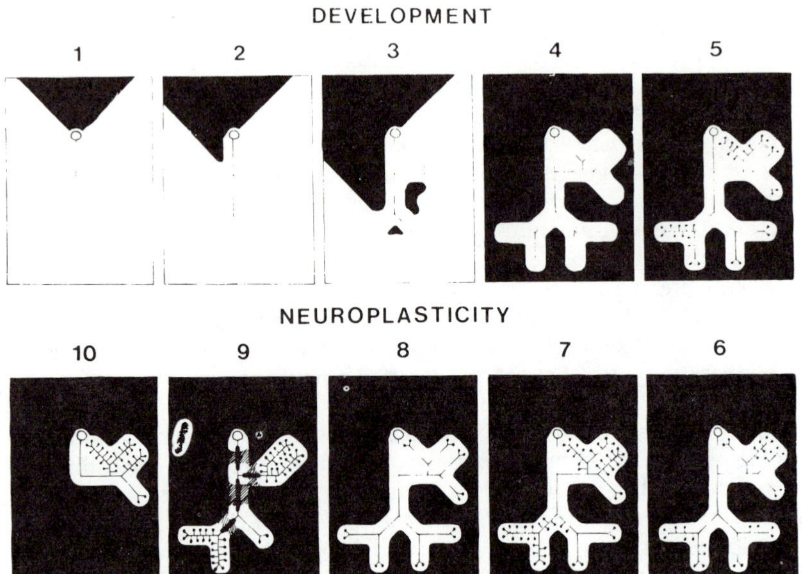

Figure 7.4. Schematic representation of a neuron (soma = circle) and its axon, including terminal branches and presynaptic elements (dots). The probability of making synapses is indicated (white: > 0; black: = 0). During ontogenesis the period of axonal growth and branching (1–4) can be described as increasing the space within which it is unlikely to receive contacts from this neuron (black). The distribution and number of synapses existing at the end of the growth period (5) can be varied within the space of possible synaptic connections (6–8). Later, this space shrinks as soon as axon branches degenerate because axonal growth is prevented in adults. Degeneration of axonal branches does not necessarily reduce the overall number of synapses (10 = 5 = 6). The number of synapses might increase (7) or decrease (8) within axonal territories of normal size. Shaded zones in 9 indicate that the myelin sheath also excludes the formation of presynaptic elements except for the nodes of Ranvier (white). The dendritic module is disregarded in the figure (see Fig. 7.5).

Axon and presynaptic elements

In most neurons the development of the axon is one of the first morphological events during cytodifferentiation (see Jacobson 1978). The directed growth of axons reduces the probability, for the greater part of the nervous system, of receiving synapses from the neuron concerned (Fig. 7.4: 1–4). This restrictive consequence of the directed growth of axons is a fundamental and definitive step toward nonrandom connectivity. Whatever mechanisms guide the course of axons and determine the basic structure of neuronal networks (see Jacobson 1978), their wiring can secondarily be changed by the breakdown of axonal branches (Fig. 7.4: 9) or of the main axon (Fig. 7.4: 10) or even by cell death (see above and also below).

Growing axons show a relatively weak tendency to form synapses. Additionally, these synapses formed early may be broken down after the growth cone passes on. Hence, regions through which axons pass do not necessarily remain sites of synaptic connections. However, these regions maintain a certain probability of receiving contacts as long as the axon and its branches or collaterals survive as unmyelinated fibers. Myelination, that is, the formation of a myelin sheath, as a side effect greatly reduces the probability of synaptogenesis along an axon, because presynaptic elements can be formed only at naked axon positions, the nodes of Ranvier (e.g., Saito 1979; Fig 7.4: 9). Apart from this restriction, whether or not a CNS region penetrated by an axon is innervated may be decided much later during ontogenesis.

For most axonal systems, growth stops at the latest with the end of general brain growth. From this stage on, the probability of receiving synaptic connections from a certain neuron remains zero when the respective part of the nervous system does not contain at least one branch of the axon concerned. Some monoaminergic neuronal systems, however, preserve the capacity to grow and branch, even in the adult brain (e.g., Nygren et al. 1971); these axons penetrate more or less diffusely a great part of the CNS.

Most axons form several branches near their beginning (e.g., recurrent collaterals) and before they terminate (*telodendron,* Bodian 1967; compare Figs. 7.3 and 7.5). Geometric figures circumscribing these parts of axons have been called *axonal modules* (see Szentágothai 1975, 1977). The reason for this tendency toward localized branching is unknown. Its effect, however, is that the length of axons per unit of volume (specific length) increases, as does the probability of making synaptic contacts. The latter finally is regulated by the number of presynaptic elements that develop per unit length of axon and by their chances of making synaptic contacts.

Again, certain monoaminergic axons are exceptions. These axons form many transmitter-releasing varicosities that are devoid of contact with postsynaptic elements in the adult brain. It is unknown whether they form synapses par distance, as in the peripheral nervous system, and/or play a nonsynaptic role in the CNS (Descarries et al. 1977).

These axons indicate that sites called *presynaptic elements,* which produce, accumulate, and/or store and release transmitter substances, can develop independently of the presence and availability of postsynaptic elements. A serious inadequacy of our current knowledge is the complete lack of information about the factors inducing and influencing the formation of presynaptic elements. At present, there are no answers to questions such as the following: On which parts of axons can presynaptic elements be formed, and how many? Why do some axons form mainly synapses en passant (e.g., about 10^2 varicosities on the two branches of the T-shaped parallel fibers in the cerebellar cortex; Eccles et al. 1967; Palay & Chan-Palay 1974), whereas other axons are studded with axon terminals, the boutons terminaux (Ramón y Cajal 1911)? How is the total number of presynaptic elements related to that on the various axonal branches? Is the total number of synapses fixed for each neuron, and which factors can change it? The process of synaptogenesis cannot be analyzed without answering these questions. There is some evidence that the mean activities of neurons that are related to RNA and protein synthesis (see

Berry et al. 1978) can influence the size of the telodendron (axonal module) at least during early postnatal periods (e.g., Schatz & Stryker 1978) and even the number of synapses (Lee et al. 1979). In the adult CNS at least short terminal branches and presynaptic elements can be formed, called *terminal sprouting* (see "Neuroplasticity").

Dendrites and postsynaptic elements

The formation of main dendrites is often preceded by thin filopodia that form few synapses but may make small adhesions (intermediate junctions) with other cell processes, including axons. Definitive dendrites and dendritic branches develop at about the time when the first single synapses appear together with some vacant postsynaptic structures. These free postsynaptic densities resemble the postsynaptic densities of Gray's type 1 or asymmetric synapses. It has been suggested that they represent potential postsynaptic sites that mature in the absence of contacts with presynaptic elements (Hinds & Hinds 1976). As for axons, information is missing about factors that promote the formation of stem dendrites and dendritic branches or determine their position, number, and orientation (Berry et al. 1978). Corresponding to axonal modules, *dendritic modules* may be regarded as those geometrical spaces circumscribing all dendrites of neurons (Szentágothai 1975, 1977; Fig. 7.5). Dendritic spines represent a specific type of postsynaptic element that characterizes certain types of neurons and is more or less missing on others. Spines bearing free postsynaptic thickenings can form on Purkinje cells in the absence of presynaptic elements (see Sotelo 1978).

It is not known which factors induce the formation of spines and/or free postsynaptic thickenings during normal development. Recent studies on the neocortex indicate that inhibition might be involved (Wolff et al. 1978a, 1979b; Chronwall & Wolff 1979). In adult sympathetic ganglia, γ-aminobutyric acid or sodium bromide can induce the formation of free postsynaptic thickenings in addition to the normal innervation. Both substances suppress the ganglionic excitability and activity (Joó et al. 1979; Wolff et al. 1979a). If these membrane thickenings represent potential postsynaptic sites, these results indicate that the number of postsynaptic offerings for synaptic contacts is not constant but might be regulated by the average activity of inhibition or by the relation between inhibition and excitation on each neuron. Such regulation is consistent with Sotelo's (1978) observation that the number of spines increases on the dendrites of cerebellar Purkinje cells after destruction of the excitatory climbing fibers that innervate predominantly these parts of the dendritic tree.

Formation of synaptic contacts

In spite of the observation that presynaptic as well as postsynaptic elements can develop independently, neither usually occurs as separate units; rather, they are combined in synaptic contacts. In the normal brain this coincidence of independent elements could be explained in different ways (see Stent 1977). For example, presynaptic and postsynaptic elements behaving as offerings develop independently from each other, and each is stabilized by forming a

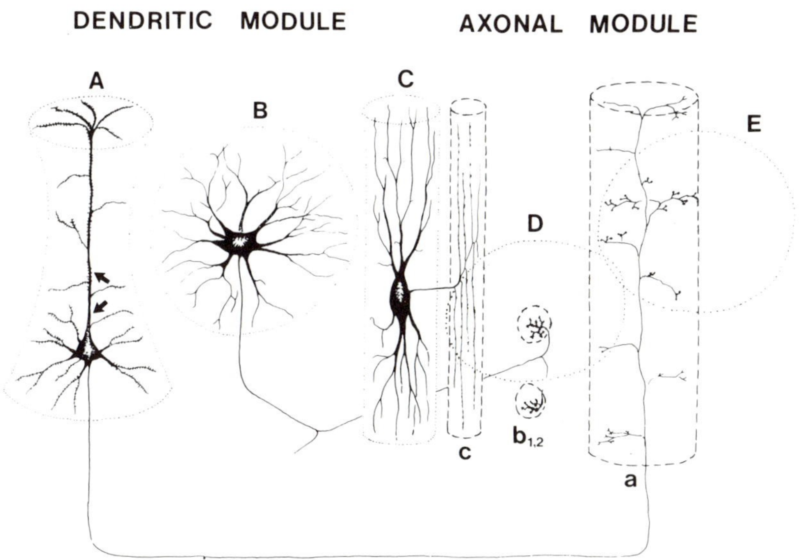

Figure 7.5. Dendritic (*A–E*) or axonal (*a–c*) modules represent geometric figures circumscribing the spaces in which all dendrites or axonal branches of one neuron are distributed. Outside these modules, the probability of making synaptic contacts is zero for the neuron concerned. Therefore, the probability of synaptic contacts being established between two neurons is limited by the amount of overlapping of their dendritic and axonal modules (*D* and *E* with *a*, b_1, *c*). Specific affinities seem to play an important role in promoting the realization of probable contacts, as indicated, for example, by the variable density of dendritic spines on different sections of the same dendrite (arrows) and by the local accumulation of terminals on axons (b_1, 2).

synapse with an adequate partner that has to be found by chance. With incompatible partners, the offerings cannot be used and are broken down after a short time. Another possibility is that synaptic contacts have to be selectively stabilized (Changeux & Mikoshiba 1978) if they are to persist.

Neuromuscular synapses in vitro were shown to be transient with mean lifetimes of about 7 to 55 hours (Puro et al. 1977). Classical experiments demonstrated that synaptic connections of retinal fibers are shifted from the rostral to the caudal part of the optic tectum while the axons grow (see Jacobson 1978). Thus, it is possible that a rather high turnover of presynaptic and postsynaptic elements exists during development, a possibility required for the explanation of synaptic contact formation mentioned above.

Recent experiments in the chronically isolated neocortex (Teuchert et al. 1979) suggest that neuroplastic reinnervation might not be primarily selective but that the stabilized connections are secondarily selected from newly formed synapses. Whatever the mechanism regulating the formation of stable synapses, it has to be a cooperative process between presynaptic and postsynaptic offerings and/or presynaptic and postsynaptic neurons.

A number of observations and experiments, mentioned above, fit the hypothesis that activated neurons increase the number of presynaptic offerings along their axons or even the size of their telodendron (e.g., Lee et al. 1979; Schatz & Stryker 1978). On the other hand, inhibited (or not excited, e.g., denervated; see "Neuroplasticity") neurons might increase the number of postsynaptic offerings on their dendrites (see Joó et al. 1979; Wolff et al. 1978c, 1979a). Inhibited cells seem to seek type I synapses that often can be correlated with excitatory synapses. Activated neurons can increase their presynaptic representation only when they find vacant postsynaptic offerings. This type of synaptogenesis offers the possibility for establishing associations between two different neurons by including inhibitory interneurons in the circuit. On the other hand, activated cells, by increasing their presynaptic representation on inhibitory interneurons, could negatively feed back on themselves via axon collaterals and countercurrent connections.

The production of presynaptic and postsynaptic offerings could, then, be regarded as an extroversion of a neuron's recent changes of activation and inhibition. The utilization of these offerings by forming synaptic contacts, on the other hand, could be viewed as an introversion of these conditioned offerings. The new synapses, by changing the input on the cell, will be stabilized only if a new equilibrium of excitation and inhibition is established (Fig. 7.6). This description of synaptogenesis as a cycling of extroversions and introversions of presynaptic and postsynaptic offerings is highly speculative. Using essential components of the selective stabilization hypothesis (see Changeux & Mikoshiba 1978), it explains the process of stabilization by changes in the probability of synaptogenesis. This approach has heuristic value because it allows the design of experiments and prediction of results.

Probability of synaptogenesis

The beginning of synaptogenesis is characterized by the appearance of axons among more or less undifferentiated neurons. The formation of synaptic contacts then depends on the appearance of postsynaptic offerings that are formed spontaneously or are induced by interactions with extrasynaptic receptors (Wolff et al. 1979a). All the factors described in the preceding three sections influence synaptogenesis in that they determine the overall probability of synaptic contacts being formed per unit volume and per unit time. Sensory dysfunctions (e.g., deprivation) can make qualitative changes in neuron types and topography and quantitative changes in synaptogenesis. These changes are not restricted to connections between the first and second neurons of sensory projections but occur transneuronally in stations of higher order in the central sensory systems. The excitatory and inhibitory interactions of neurons driven by sensory input seem, therefore, to influence the probability of synaptogenesis during the early postnatal peak. Additionally, nonneuronal factors such as hormones seem to play an important role in regulating the probability of synaptogenesis (e.g., thyroxine and cortisone; see Jacobson 1978).

In many parts of the brain, the overall probability differs from the actual synaptogenesis between specific neurons or groups of neurons. The complexity of conditions influencing synaptogenesis suggests that there might be more

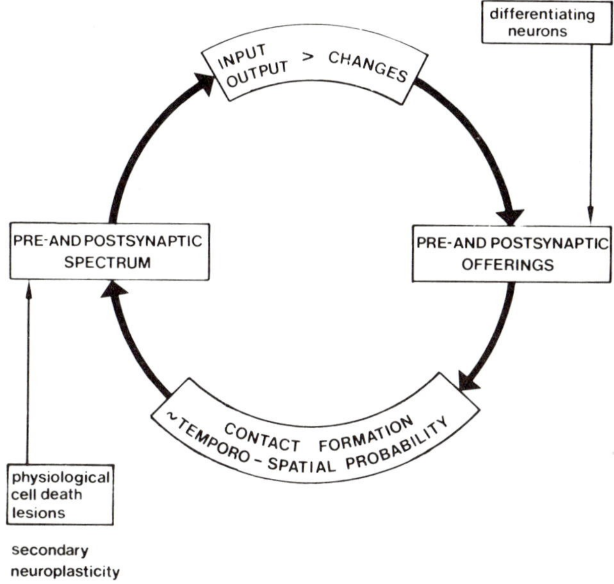

Figure 7.6. The hypotheses presented here describe synaptogenesis as a cyclic process that, according to probability, forms synaptic contacts between presynaptic and postsynaptic offerings, that is, potential or vacant presynaptic and postsynaptic elements. The number of offerings depends on recent changes in excitation and/or inhibition induced by changing input and/or changing efficiency to produce output activity. The actual synaptogenic probability is then determined by the collective number of presynaptic and postsynaptic offerings made by various neurons at a certain time in a limited part of the nervous system. Synaptic contacts are formed by chance. Newly formed synaptic contacts become part of the presynaptic or postsynaptic spectrum of the neurons concerned and change their output efficiency and their input, respectively. This, in turn, will change the number of presynaptic and postsynaptic offerings, and so on. The spatial distribution of offerings is limited for each adult neuron by the size, shape, and position of the axonal and dendritic modules (see Fig. 7.5). The synaptogenic probability changes permanently as long as axons and dendrites grow during ontogenesis. This is the time when changed sensory input can cause primary neuroplasticity. In adults the probability can change irreversibly only when neurons degenerate within the network, causing additional offerings at denervated neurons and possibly reinnervation by secondary neuroplasticity. It is conceivable, however, that shifts of the synaptogenic probability can be stabilized in a new dynamic equilibrium.

than one way to make synaptogenesis specific. A heterochronic differentiation of neurons might, for example, cause one type of axon to increase its presynaptic offerings more than other types during a certain period and in a specific part of the CNS. This axonal system will make preferential contacts with those dendrites that increase their postsynaptic offerings at the same time. If there is a turnover of synapses, then specific presynaptic offerings, increasing in number, can replace preexisting synaptic connections by competition for postsynaptic offerings. Thus, time and space can be used in more than one way to increase the probability of producing specific neuronal connections (*timing hypothesis;* see Jacobson 1978).

In recent experiments, the application of inhibitory agents resulted in a formation of what were interpreted as postsynaptic offerings (Wolff et al. 1978c, 1979a; see "Dendrites and postsynaptic elements"). Hence, changes of neuronal activity might also be used to make synaptogenesis more specific (cf. Berry et al. 1978). Such changes may be initiated by increasing sensory input or may be a consequence of the formation of new synapses. Thus, synaptogenesis itself might change the conditions for further synaptogenesis on the neurons concerned.

There are several possible ways in which neuronal activity might contribute to specifying the developing connections. In spite of some differences, two hypotheses agree in that they propose a poststabilization of specific connections, either by *functional verification* (Wiesel & Hubel 1974) or by *selective stabilization* (Changeux et al. 1973; for both references, see Changeux & Mikoshiba 1978). Redundant connections might or might not be removed. All these hypothetical mechanisms of selective formation or selective stabilization allow a wide range of adaptive modifications in synaptogenesis that might serve to change the synaptic spectrum of a neuron according to recent variations in its average activity. Such changes of synaptogenesis are, however, limited by the position, orientation, size, and shape of the dendritic and axonal modules and their overlap with other afferent and efferent modules, which were determined stepwise during earlier stages of development (Fig. 7.5). Consequently, all adaptive changes in the synaptic connectivity of a neuron have to be limited by its specific biographic character. It can also be predicted that the extent of adaptive changes that can be induced in adult neurons decreases with the amount of changes that occurred before, that is, with age.

According to the above hypothesis, the quantitative variations and increasing specificity of synaptogenesis occurring during ontogenesis can be explained as shown in Table 7.1 (4a–c). Synaptogenesis would initially be low as long as the majority of neurons are weakly connected and show low and spontaneous activity. It would rapidly increase when more and more neurons drive each other and are directly or transneuronally driven by sensory input. Finally, synaptogenesis would slow down when the driven activity is not further increased and inhibition is fully developed. This fits well the time course of synaptogenesis in the mammalian CNS. Here, the formation rate of synapses increases from low prenatal values to a maximum during the perinatal period and decreases toward the end of brain growth. The actual time of the peak varies to some extent between different brain regions as well as between prococial and insessorial species. However, in all regions studied, the time course has been essentially of the same type.

Neuroplasticity

The term *neuroplasticity* denotes various types of long-lasting or permanent changes in the reactivity of neurons to specific stimuli or changes in neuronal connectivity (see Cotman 1978; Jacobson 1978). Such changes can be produced in at least two different ways: (1) abnormal sensory input during an early postnatal period (*critical period* of Hubel & Wiesel 1970; see Pettigrew 1978) causes permanent changes in the structure and function of neurons in the central part of the corresponding sensory system; (2) the destruction of neurons and/or axons, followed by anterograde degeneration of the respective presynaptic elements, causes a neuroplastic reinnervation of certain postsynaptic neurons whenever the denervation is induced throughout life. This classification disregards the functional plasticity of neurons that is reversed in relatively short periods of time (minutes) and, therefore, probably does not represent structural changes.

Functionally induced neuroplasticity seems to be restricted to the ontogenetic period during which the essential part of synaptogenesis takes place. It is possibly related to the type of competitive interactions between presynaptic and postsynaptic elements described above.

The local synaptogenetic probabilities change permanently and rapidly as long as axons and dendrites grow, that is, as long as new axonal and dendritic modules penetrate each other (Fig. 7.5). During rapid brain growth, changed functional activity might, therefore, change the formation of certain synapses, either in time or in space, so that they might be formed, say, too late, that is, at the wrong postsynaptic elements. In fact, the most vulnerable period for various external influences (e.g., hormonal influences) on brain development is always the period between the stage when the number of neurons is complete and the end of growth in the respective brain region (see Jacobson 1978). Thus these changes seem to be inducible only during the primary development of adult patterns of connectivity. For simplicity, therefore, we can call this phenomenon *primary neuroplasticity*. It should not be regarded as pathological and degenerative (Pettigrew 1978). Rather, primary neuroplasticity is the physiological process that adapts the primordial connectivity (a product of self-organization in the CNS) to the sensory input.

The cellular and molecular mechanisms of the primary neuroplasticity are unknown. One could speculate that the permanence of the effects is caused by changes in the telodendron of certain neuron classes, that is, changes in the probability of their interaction (cf. Fig. 7.4: 9 and 7). Recent experimental evidence suggests an important role for monoamines and inhibition (Kasamatsu & Pettigrew 1979).

Most studies show that neuroplasticity based on degeneration occurs not only during development but also in adults (Eccles 1976; Merrill & Wall 1978). Usually, however, the effects are more severe if the lesions are applied in early developmental stages than later. According to a probabilistic type of synaptogenesis, temporary functional changes in the adult CNS could temporarily change synaptic connections, but these changes should be gradually replaced by the former connectivity as long as axonal and dendritic probabilities are unchanged (Fig. 7.4, 5–8). Consequently, in the adult brain neuroplasticity is mainly observed after partial denervation. Because this type of neuroplasticity changes the already established dominant connectivity, it might be called *secondary neuroplasticity*.

In the normal CNS a great number of neurons degenerate, predominantly in early stages of development. Some of these neurons show driven activity and die under conditions that are regulated by functional interaction with target cells (Pittmann & Oppenheim 1979). The death of such neurons may cause transneuronal degeneration of the synaptic partners (Beresfold 1965) and/or a rewiring of the surviving neurons. Thus, some sort of secondary neuroplasticity seems to participate in the normal morphogenesis of the CNS (see "Sensitive phases and imprinting").

In adults, axonal growth and regeneration are apparently missing even during secondary neuroplasticity (Eccles 1976; Merrill & Wall 1978). Therefore, every branch of an axon that is more than about 100 μm long is lost forever when it degenerates. An important source of secondary neuroplastic rewiring is, therefore, the great number of very thin unmyelinated axons that exist in the normal adult CNS. These are apparently somehow suppressed and form only a few terminals in the normal brain. In secondary neuroplasticity some of them increase drastically the number of presynaptic elements. This increase is called *terminal sprouting* (see Teuchert et al. 1979; Wolff et al. 1978b) and is evidence for the statement of Merrill and Wall (1978:110) that neuroplastic "responses are simply an exaggeration of what already exists in the intact animal."

In experimental and pathological conditions, mature neurons reveal a considerable capacity for neuroplastic reactions. One might, however, doubt whether this potential is utilized in natural conditions after the brain reaches its adult size and a quantitative equilibrium of synaptic density. There is some evidence that synapses are rearranged in the adult neocortex.

For example, the commissural connections between the visual cortex of cats are primarily much more extended than in adults (Innocenti 1979). Preliminary observations suggest that in rats the characteristic columnar and regional patterns of commissural connections do not develop before 6 weeks after birth, although the cortex stops growing by 4 weeks (Böttcher & Wolff unpublished). These results fit other observations on the human brain indicating that the myelination of corticocortical connections continues for 2 to 3 decades, although the brain reaches its adult weight between 4 and 6 years of age (Yakovlev & Lecours 1967).

The increasing myelination indicates that the regional remodeling of commissural connections is accompanied by a redistribution of synapses along the axons (Wolff & Záborsky 1979c). During this process the connections of some neurons seem to be strengthened at the cost of others. Finally, many neurons are completely displaced from the interhemispheric connectivity either by retracting axon branches or by cell degeneration (Innocenti 1979). Although there is not much cell degeneration during this remodeling period, at least in rats, the possibility that the disseminated cell death occurring in brains of advanced age is caused by this type of progressive morphogenesis cannot be excluded.

Sensitive phases and imprinting

Such a great diversity of phenomena has been related to imprinting (see Chap. 14) that one cannot expect all these phenomena to be based on a common neurobiological mechanism. One may, however, ask about the types of developmental processes that could be involved.

A common feature of various imprinting processes is the *sensitive phase*, that is, a postnatal period during which the nervous system is highly sensitive to the imprinting stimulus. The sensitivity is limited in time and appears independent of the imprinting stimulus. Various sensory systems can develop sensitive phases, and sometimes multisensory input is most effective. Another typical property of imprinting is that the behavioral effects are usually long-lasting, sometimes permanent.

The long persistence of imprinted behavior suggests that changes in neuronal connectivity are involved. Recent experiments seem to confirm this assumption (Bateson, personal communication). The sensitive phase could then be a period during which the synaptogenic probability is locally increased, probably by increasing the number of postsynaptic offerings. These offerings could be utilized to make specific synaptic contacts if the imprinting stimulus caused terminal sprouting on specific axons, for example, by increasing their firing activity (see Lee et al. 1979). Synapses formed according to such a concept, finally, must be stabilized against competitive replacement by other presynaptic elements. If primary neuroplasticity is the mechanism underlying imprinting, the sensitive phase should be induced, for example, by hormones, (e.g., monoamines; see Kasamatsu & Pettigrew 1979). Additionally, the newly formed synapses must be selectively stabilized.

Secondary neuroplasticity should also be taken into account. Physiological cell death of synaptically connected neurons could initiate the sensitive phase, for example, by causing a denervation hypersensitivity of neurons in certain regions of the CNS. The newly formed synapses might be as stable as those synapses that were replaced.

Preliminary observations confirm some of the predictions that can be derived from the second speculation: (1) in various sensory systems physiological cell death includes innervated neurons; (2) physiological degeneration of axon terminals coincides to some extent with the sensitive phases; (3) this terminal generation varies in time between incessorial zebra finches and precocial ducks (Wolff et al. unpublished).

CONCLUSIONS

The proposed model of synaptogenesis (Fig 7.6) indicates the following conclusions: The development of the whole nervous system can be regarded as a process determining stepwise the local probability of synaptogenesis that goes on throughout life. The overall synaptogenesis can be subdivided as follows:

1 Pre-sensory self-organization of neuronal networks. Interference with this process may cause fundamental changes of wiring and performance of the CNS, that is, in the viability or behavior of the individual.
2 Primary neuroplastic adaption to sensory input forms the neurobiological base of the profound influence of early experience.
3 Connectivity is probably optimized throughout life.
4 Secondary neuroplastic rearrangement of synapses results in permanent changes of connectivity. These remain within the limits of ontogenetic determination if induced in adults. They may, however, produce associations

that are improbable if induced during the growth period, for example, sensitive phases for imprinting.

SUMMARY

The objective of this chapter is to point out some characteristic trends in the morphogenetic process that determine typical variables of brain structure, in particular, its connectivity. The developmental process is divided into cellular and communicative aspects: (1) neurogenesis and cytodifferentiation and (2) synaptogenesis and differentiation of connectivity.

The size of neuron populations is determined by the sequence of proliferation and physiological cell death. Some of the eliminated neurons seem to play a transitory role in synaptogenesis.

Neurons reach their ultimate positions within the CNS by migrating along two kinds of guiding structures terminating at the meningeal surface and at intracerebral blood vessels, respectively. The arrangement of pyramidal and nonpyramidal neurons in the adult neocortex, being determined by the two models of cell deposition, therefore is related to growth and vascularization of the anlage.

The epithelial polarization of the neuroectoderm is lost during neurogenesis, resulting in apolar preneurons that are completely surrounded by an intercellular space monitored by the neural anlage. The basic neuronal polarity between secretion and reception of specific transmitter or modulator molecules develops secondarily. It may be combined to a variable degree with the polarization between presynaptic and postsynaptic elements and with the axodendritic polarity.

Some neurons choose their transmitter under the influence of external factors (chemical, electrical). Inhibitory neurons of the neocortex are determined before they receive and make synapses.

Synaptogenesis is defined as the formation of synaptic contacts according to the probability of vacant presynaptic and postsynaptic elements (offerings) to coexist in space and time. The basic decisions are, therefore, made during neurogenesis and early cytodifferentiation (number and position of neurons, course of axons).

The number of presynaptic and postsynaptic offerings seems to be related to the firing activity of the neuronal membranes and to excitation and/or inhibition of the postsynaptic membranes, respectively. This apparent relationship indicates the strategic importance of inhibitory neurons and sensory input.

Because synaptic contacts show a turnover, it is suggested that they are selectively stabilized by stabilizing the equilibrium of excitation and inhibition, that is, the formation of presynaptic and postsynaptic offerings of the neurons concerned. Hence, synaptogenesis is described as a cycling process that transforms induced activity of neurons into adaptive changes of their connectivity that, in turn, reduce their sensitivity for further changes by the same input.

The probability of synaptogenesis in the adult CNS is progressively determined through all stages of development, maturation, adulthood, and aging. During the embryonic period the rules for pre-sensory self-organization of connectivity are worked out. During the postnatal period their primordial connectivity is adapted to sensory input by a process called primary neuroplasticity. During the rest of life the connectivity seems to be optimized in a quantitative equilibrium of synapses. Secondary neuroplasticity rearranges the connectivity after degeneration of stabilized connections, irrespective of whether it is caused by physiological or pathological degeneration of axon branches or whole neurons. Following physiological death of connected neurons, the preformed connectivity may be permanently changed. This process is proposed as a possible basis for sensitive phases and behavioral imprinting during perinatal periods.

ACKNOWLEDGMENT

I am indebted to my co-workers and to Drs. Franz Huber, Werner Noodt, Patrick Sourander, and Gertracid Teuchert for valuable comments and criticism and to Gisela Kotte and Ursula Wurl for preparing the manuscript. Most of our work was supported by grants SFB 33: E3, E4, and E5 of the Deutsche Forschungsgemeinschaft.

REFERENCES

Beresfold, W. A. 1965. A discussion on retrograde changes in nerve fibres. *Progress in Brain Research* 14:33–56.

Berry, M., P. B. Bradley, & S. Borges. 1978. Environmental and genetic determinants of connectivity in the central nervous system – an approach through dendritic field analysis. *Progress in Brain Research* 48:133–148.

Bodian, D. 1967. Neurons, circuits and neuroglia. *In:* G. C. Quarton, Th. Melnechuck, & F. O. Schmitt (eds.), *The neurosciences: a study program.* Rockefeller University Press, New York, pp. 6–23.

Bullock, T. H., & G. A. Horridge. 1965. *Structure and function of the nervous system of invertebrates*, vol. 1. Freeman, San Francisco, London.

Bunge, R. P., M. Johnson, & C. D. Ross. 1978. Nature and nurture in development of the autonomic neurons. *Science* 199:1409–1416.

Changeux, J.-P., & K. Mikoshiba. 1978. Genetic and "epigenetic" factors regulating synapse formation in vertebrate cerebellum and neuromuscular junction. *Progress in Brain Research* 48:43–68.

Chan-Palay, V. 1977. *Cerebellar dentate nucleus.* Springer-Verlag, Berlin.

Chronwall, B. M., & J. R. Wolff. 1978a. Aspects of the development of non-pyramidal neurons in the neocortex of rat. *Zoon* 6:145–148.

1978b. Classification and location of neurons taking up ^{3}H-GABA in the visual cortex of rats. *In:* F. Fonnum (ed.), *Amino acids as chemical transmitters*. Plenum Press, New York, pp. 297–303.

1980. On the pre- and postnatal development of GABA-accumulating cells in the occipital neocortex of rat. *Journal of Comparative Neurology* 190:187–208.

Corner, M. A., R. E. Baker, N. E. Van de Poll, D. F. Swaab, & H. B. M. Uylings (eds.). 1978. *Progress in brain research*. Vol. 48, *Maturation of the nervous system*. Elsevier, Amsterdam.

Cotman, C. W. (ed.). 1978. *Neuronal plasticity*. Raven Press, New York.

Descarries, K., K. C. Watkins, & Y. Lapierre. 1977. Noradrenergic axon terminals in the cerebral cortex of rat. 3. Topometric ultrastructural analysis. *Brain Research* 133:197–222.

Dismukes, K. 1977. Two-faced neurons. *Nature* 269:104–105.

Eccles, J. C. 1976. The plasticity of the mammalian central nervous system with special reference to new growths in response to lesions. *Naturwissenschaften* 63:8–15.

Eccles, J. C., M. Ito, & J. Szentágothai. 1967. *The cerebellum as a neuronal machine*. Springer, New York.

Edds, M. V., Jr., R. M. Gaze, G. E. Schneider, & L. N. Irwin. 1979. Specificity and plasticity of retinotectal connections. *Neuroscience Research Program Bulletin* 17:243–375.

Glowinski, J., A. Nieoullion, & A. Cheramy. 1978. Regulations of activity of the nigrostriatal dopaminergic systems. *In:* A. Karlin, V. M. Tennyson, & H. J. Vogel (eds.), *Neuronal information transfer*. Academic Press, New York, pp. 35–46.

Hinds, J. W., & P. L. Hinds. 1976. Synapse formation in the mouse olfactory bulb. 2. Morphogenesis. *Journal of Comparative Neurology* 169:41–62.

Hubel, D. H., & T. N. Wiesel. 1970. The period of susceptibility to the physiological effects of unilateral eye closure in kittens. *Journal of Physiology (London)* 206:419–436.

Hutchings, D. E. 1978. Behavioural teratology: embryopathic and behavioural effects of drugs during pregnancy. *In:* G. Gottlieb (ed.), *Early influences*. Academic Press, New York, pp. 3–35.

Innocenti, G. M. 1979. Adult and neonatal characteristics of the callosal zone at the boundary between areas 17 and 18 in the cat. *In:* J. S. Russell, M. W. van Hof, & G. Berlucchi (eds.), *Structure and function of cerebral commissures*. Macmillan, London.

Jacobson, M. 1978. *Developmental neurobiology*, 2nd ed. Plenum Press, New York, London.

Joó, F., W. Dames, & J. R. Wolff. 1979. Effect of prolonged sodium bromide administration on the fine structure of dendrites in the superior cervical ganglion of adult rat. *Progress in Brain Research* 451:109–115.

Kasamatsu, T., & J. D. Pettigrew. 1979. Preservation of binocularity after monocular deprivation in the striate cortex of kittens treated with 6-hydroxydopamine. *Journal of Comparative Neurology* 185:139–162.

Katz, M. J., & R. J. Lasek. 1978. Evolution of the nervous system: role of ontogenetic mechanisms in the evolution of matching populations. *Proceedings of the National Academy of Sciences of the USA* 75:1349–1352.

Lassmann, G. 1966. Einige Bemerkungen über die dem peripherischen Nervensystem zugeordneten Dendritenzellen. *Wiener Klinische Wochenschrift* 78:293–295.

Le Douarin, N. M., M. A. Teillet, & C. Le Lièvre. 1977. Influence of the tissue environment on the differentiation of neural crest cells. *In:* J. W. Lash & M. M. Burger (eds.), *Cell and tissue interactions*. Raven Press, New York, pp. 11–27.

Lee, K., M. Oliver, F. Schottler, R. Creager, & G. Lynch. 1979. Ultrastructural effects of repetitive synaptic stimulation in the hippocampal slice preparation: a preliminary report. *Experimental Neurology* 65:478–480.

Lentz, T. L. 1968. *Primitive nervous systems.* Yale University Press, New Haven, Conn.

Merrill, E. G., & P. D. Wall. 1978. Plasticity of connections in the adult nervous system. *In:* C. W. Cotman (ed.), *Neuronal plasticity.* Raven Press, New York, pp. 97–112.

Nygren, L.-G., L. Olson, & A. Seiger. 1971. Regeneration of monoamine-containing axons in the developing and adult spinal cord of the rat following intraspinal 6-OH-dopamine injections or transsections. *Histochemie* 28:1–15.

Oppenheim, R. W., I. W. Chu-Wang, & J. L. Maderdrut. 1978. Cell death of motoneurons in the chick embryo spinal cord. 3. The differentiation of motoneurons prior to their induced degeneration following limb-bud removal. *Journal of Comparative Neurology* 177:87–112.

Palay, S. L., & V. Chan-Palay. 1974. *Cerebellar cortex: cytology and organization.* Springer, Berlin, Heidelberg, New York.

Patterson, P. H. 1978. Environmental determination of neurotransmitter function. *Trends in Neurosciences* 1:126–132.

Pettigrew, J. D. 1978. The paradox of the critical period for striate cortex. *In:* C. W. Cotman (ed.), *Neuronal plasticity.* Raven Press, New York, pp. 311–330.

Pittman, R., & R. W. Oppenheim. 1979. Cell death of motoneurons in the chick embryo spinal cord. 4. Evidence that a functional neuromuscular interaction is involved in the regulation of naturally occurring cell death and the stabilization of synapses. *Journal of Comparative Neurology* 187:425–446.

Puro, D. G., F. G. de Mello, & M. Nirenberg. 1977. Synapse turnover, the formation and termination of transient synapses. *Proceedings of the National Academy of Sciences of the USA* 74:4977–4981.

Rager, G. 1978. Systems-matching by degeneration. 2. Interpretation of the generation and degeneration of retinal ganglion cells in the chicken by a mathematical model. *Experimental Brain Research* 33:79–90.

Rakic, P. 1972. Mode of cell migration to the superficial layers of fetal monkey cortex. *Journal of Comparative Neurology* 145:61–84.

1975. Timing of major ontogenetic events in the visual cortex of the rhesus monkey. *In:* M. Buchwald & M. Brazier (eds.), *Brain mechanisms in mental retardation.* Academic Press, New York, pp. 3–40.

Ramón y Cajal, S. 1911. *Histologie du système nerveux de l'homme et des vertébrés,* 2 vols. (L. Azonlay, trans.). Mason, Paris.

Remane, A. 1956. *Die Grundlagen des natürlichen Systems der vergleichenden Anatomie und Phylogenetik,* 2nd ed. Akademische Verlagsgesellschaft, Leipzig.

Ribak, C. E. 1978. Spinous and sparsely-spinous stellate neurons contain glutamic acid decarboxylase in the visual cortex of rats. *Journal of Neurocytology* 35:313–323.

Rickmann, M., & J. R. Wolff. 1977. Morphological constellation of the initial step of glial differentiation in the neocortex of rat. *Folia Morphologica* 25:231–234.

Rickmann, M., B. M. Chronwall, & J. R. Wolff. 1977. On the development of non-pyramidal neurons and axons outside the cortical plate: the early marginal zone as a pallial anlage. *Anatomy and Embryology* 151:285–307.

Saito, K. 1979. Branchings at the central node of Ranvier, observed in the anterior horn and Clarke's nucleus of the cat. *Neuroscience* 4:391–399.

Schatz, C. J., & M. P. Stryker. 1978. Ocular dominance in layer IV of the cat's visual cortex and the effects of monocular deprivation. *Journal of Physiology* 281: 267–283.

Shepherd, G. M. 1972. The neuron doctrine: a revision of functional concepts. *Yale Journal of Biology and Medicine* 45:584–599.

Smart, I. H. M. 1973. Proliferative characteristics of the ependymal layer during the early development of the mouse neocortex. *Journal of Anatomy* 116:67–91.

Sotelo, C. 1978. Purkinje cell ontogeny: formation and maintenance of spines. *Progress in Brain Research* 48:149–170.

Stent, G. S. (ed.). 1977. *Function and formation of neural systems.* Abakon Verlagsgesellschaft, Berlin.

Sulston, J. E., & H. R. Horvitz. 1977. Post-embryonic cell lineages of the nematode *Caenorhabditis elegans. Developmental Biology* 56:110–156.

Szentágothai, J. 1975. The "module-concept" in the cerebral cortex architecture. *Brain Research* 95:475–496.

1977. The neuron network of the cerebral cortex: a functional interpretation. *Proceedings of the Royal Society of London B* 201:219–248.

Teuchert, G., M. Holzgraefe, & J. R. Wolff. 1979. Neuroplasticity of cortico-cortical connections in the isolated sensory cortex of adult rats. Submitted for publication.

Wolff, J. R. 1978. Ontogenetic aspects of cortical architecture: lamination. *In:* M. Brazier & H. Petsche (eds.), *Architectonics of the cerebral cortex.* Raven Press, New York, pp. 159–173.

Wolff, J. R., B. M. Chronwall, & M. Rickmann. 1978a. Morphogenetic relations between cell migration and synaptogenesis in the neocortex of rat. *In:* V. Neuhoff (ed.), *Proceedings of the European society for neurochemistry*, vol. 1. Verlag Chemie, Weinheim, New York, pp. 158–173.

Wolff, J. R., M. Holzgraefe, & G. Teuchert. 1978b. On plastic changes of the synaptology in the isolated cortex of rats. *Neuroscience Letters, Suppl.* 1:S48.

Wolff, J. R., F. Joó, & W. Dames. 1978c. Plasticity in dendrites shown by continuous GABA administration in superior cervical ganglion of adult rat. *Nature* 274:72–74.

Wolff, J. R., F. Joó, W. Dames, & O. Fehér. 1979a. Induction and maintenance of free postsynaptic membrane thickenings in the adult superior cervical ganglion. *Journal of Neurocytology* 8:549–563.

Wolff, J. R., N. Rickmann, & B. M. Chronwall. 1979b. Axo-glial synapses and GABA-accumulating glial cells in embryonic neocortex of rats. *Cell & Tissue Research* 210:239–248.

Wolff, J. R., & L. Záborszky. 1979c. On the normal arrangement of fibres and terminals and limits of plasticity in the callosal system of the rat. *In:* J. S. Russell, M. W. van Hof, & G. Berlucchi (eds.), *Structure and function of cerebral commissures.* Macmillan, London, pp. 147–154.

Yakovlev, P. I., & A.-R. Lecours. 1967. The myelogenetic cycles of regional maturation of the brain. *In:* A. Minkowski (ed.), *Regional development of the brain in early life.* Blackwell, Oxford, Edinburgh, pp. 3–70.

8

GENETICS AND DEVELOPMENT OF BEHAVIOR, WITH SPECIAL REFERENCE TO PATTERNED MOTOR OUTPUT

GEORGE W. BARLOW

There are three major points I want to make in this Chapter. Each is aimed at moving toward a better understanding of how behavior develops. The first is that gene action must be thought of in terms of differences during the course of development. The second is that stereotyped motor output is perhaps the best trait for tracking the development of behavior. The last is that using stereotyped motor output for the analysis of developmental genetics offers the best hope for a genetics of behavior meaningful to ethologists.

Most investigators agree that the inheritance of traits can be analyzed only in terms of differences between individuals (Lehrman 1970; Waddington 1975). With that understanding came a better conceptualization of the nature–nurture issue. That conceptualization, however, has detracted from our appreciation of the role of genes in development. Pushed to an extreme, the argument that only between-individual differences are relevant suffers in two ways. One tacit assumption could be that all genes are equally active in an individual, which is an unrealistic and uninformed position. Another possible assumption is that only the endpoint in the ontogeny of the phenotype is worth considering. Both assumptions are antidevelopmental.

Development is organized change through time. A comparison between stages in development reveals measurable differences. One can relate such change to genetic differences (large, small, or none), just as one can do in estimating heritability between individuals. By no means, however, can this position be equated with genetic determinism, for it does not deny the rich interaction with the environment.

What it boils down to is this: Ignoring the role that genetic information plays in the ontogeny of behavior has hindered our understanding of gene–environment interaction in development. The position has been one of focusing on environmental factors, accepting the organism as an otherwise passive biological vessel.

In my year at Bielefeld, I was impressed by how little information from genetics has filtered into the field of behavior development. At best, some researchers appreciate Mendelian genetics. Only a few understand how genetic information is translated into developmental processes. For that reason, I devote considerable space to basic problems such as gene expression, chromosomal morphology, sexual mosaics and fate maps, timing of gene action, and neurogenetics. I have tried to give an overview, but I have been selective, emphasizing those concepts necessary for comprehending things to follow. Where possible, I have used as examples studies focusing on patterned motor output. But because the genetics of patterned output have not received much attention, I have often resorted to other behavioral traits.

Throughout the Chapter I refer to patterned motor output and to modal action patterns, or MAPs (Barlow 1968, 1977), interchangeably, though MAPs are a subset of patterned output. By *MAPs* I mean the chunks of behavior animals perform that have a statistically recognizable pattern, as in displays, specialized feeding behavior, and some actions involved in bodily care.

Ethologists commonly use MAPs as their units when studying behavior quantitatively (Barlow 1968, 1977). When they do ontogenetic studies, it is usually the appearance, change, and disappearance of MAPs that are reported. It is surprising, therefore, that so little is known about the genetics of MAPs. This is the more puzzling when one considers that a genetic analysis might illuminate the reality of MAPs as units in quantitative models of behavior. MAPs are also useful in seeking the neurological substrates of behavior.

The advantage of MAPs to a developmental geneticist is the wealth of material they offer. Any species of modest complexity has a variety of MAPs. They emerge at fairly regular points in development and become integrated into functional sequences. Their actual form is subject to variation within and between individuals, as are their ontogenetic emergence and integration. The chances are that a large portion of that variation results from genetic differences, but information is scanty. That is one reason I devote considerable space to the findings from hybrids.

Hybrids are useful for a number of reasons. First, they show easily detected heritable differences in almost all aspects of their behavior. Second, much of the evidence concerning the genetics of MAPs comes from hybrids. Third, hybrids present provocative material for developmental ethologists. And finally, hybridization may open up the process of maturation to environmental influences.

Our knowledge of the variation in MAPs that is due to environmental influences is meager. The available information suggests that visual MAPs are not obviously shaped through experience, though their elicitation, sequencing, and orientation often are (Barlow 1977). Studies of bird song and its acquisition, in contrast, are exemplars of how experience affects motor output (Hinde 1969; Chap. 20). Although there are obvious constraints and predispositions in song learning, there has been no formal genetic analysis of differences to complement the investigations of the role of experience. But the differences between species in what they will learn, and in the basic structure of the song, appear to be due to genetic differences.

MAPs thus seem to offer the best type of behavior for the study of development in which genetic and experiential factors are integrated. By using hybrids, including subspecies with salient dissimilarities, abundant genetic differences can be produced. As I hope to persuade you, although such material may seem messy to a geneticist, it provides challenging and stimulating problems to those with a truly epigenetic view.

GENE ACTION

Recent years have seen a remarkable growth in molecular genetics, an elucidation of the nature of genes and how they behave. Though the fundamental research has been done primarily on bacteria and bacteriophages, the broader principles seem to apply to all plants and animals. Higher organisms, however, are yet more complex and promise many surprises (Wilt 1972). Most of this information is routinely presented to biology students today, but many investigators of behavioral development have only fragmentary knowledge in this area. The following synopsis is offered to establish some points basic to the essay. Stein et al. (1975) provide a readable review.

Structure of genes

Chromosomes consist of nucleic acids and proteins, together called *nucleoproteins,* arrayed in pairs of long helical molecules. The backbone of each molecule consists of DNA (deoxyribonucleic acid) arranged in small groups of deoxyribose sugar and a phosphate. Each group has four bases: adenine, guanine, thymine, and cytosine. The bases extend toward the axis of the helix and pair with their complementary bases, adenine with thymine and guanine with cytosine, and thereby hold the paired DNA molecules together. These base pairs are the code of the genes. Each triplet set of base pairs codes for one of the 20 amino acids. A gene is a segment of the long helical molecule. It is thought to consist of about 1,000 base pairs because the average polypeptide has slightly more than 300 amino acids.

Functions of genes

Genes can be considered to have two functions. One is to replicate themselves reliably, free of errors (barring the odd mutation). In the process, genes pass on their information to daughter cells. Replication through cleavage occurs in each DNA molecule and in the chromosome that bears it. This is heredity in the narrow sense, whether in the process of generating reproductive cells (meiosis) or of producing somatic cells within an individual (mitosis).

The other function of genes is the regulation of biochemical processes. They send out chemical information for the structuring of tissues and organs, that is, the differential reproduction of the cells that produce organs and tissues. In the same way, their chemicals regulate the activities of their own behavior or that of genes in other cells. In short, the genes preside over the development of their embodiment in an organism, and also over the physiological processes at all levels within that organism. That is not to say that genes express their actions free of their environment. A closer understanding of how genes act will help to make this clear.

A gene expresses itself as follows: Ribonucleic acid (RNA) transcribes the base sequence of that gene's part of the DNA chain, producing a complementary sequence. The RNA then leaves the cell nucleus to join a ribosome, which translates the triplet code of base sequences into the amino acid. A number of amino acids then link to form a polypeptide, that is, a complex protein molecule. In eukaryotes, two RNA molecules may unite before translation; in such instances, a gene can be considered to consist of noncontiguous segments (Darnell 1978).

Most mutations alter only one amino acid, not the entire gene. Thus a given gene can give rise to numerous alleles through the alteration of constituent amino acids. The consequence is a variety of similar proteins, each produced by a different allele.

The proteins provide the enzymes that regulate the development of structures and the crucial metabolic pathways. It is only through the regulation of transcription and translation that development occurs.

Regulation of genes

Each and every cell in an organism contains all the genes of the genome. All genes cannot be active at all times, however, any more than could all neurons in our nervous system be firing continuously. That would produce total disorganization. There must be some way of regulating the genes that regulate physiological processes.

During development, different genes turn on and off at the right moments. As cells become differentiated into specific types with limited functions, they have to call upon different genes to regulate their specific tasks. A cell in the thyroid has to manufacture thyroxin, one in a muscle, myoglobin.

Generally, only about 10% of the information in the genome is used at a given time. The rest of the DNA is said to be *transcriptionally inactive*. The activity, however, is greater in a vigorously developing embryo than in an adult. In several adult tissues, the complexity of RNA was found to be less than 35% that in the embryo. In terms of genomic information, therefore, the demands of development are high (Davidson 1977).

One model of development holds that at the very beginning all genes are active. As differentiation proceeds, various genes are switched irreversibly off. That some genes appear to become inactive, then later again active, is explained by claiming that such genes had remained on, that is, available for transcription; for various reasons they were active only at low, virtually undetectable levels (Caplan & Ordahl 1978). The appearance of genes as alternately on, off, and on again, however, is an empirical observation that does not depend on this model or the more widely known one that now follows.

Most of the genes are inactivated by histone proteins called *repressors*, which are coded by sites termed *operators*, next to the genes they control. When DNA replication occurs, there is a necessary cessation of the production of histones. When replication is over, more histones are produced to hold the new DNA in check. The trick, then, is to determine how the repressor is removed to permit the gene to express itself.

Activation appears to be accomplished by another type of protein that is associated with the chromosome, called collectively *nonhistone proteins*. Unlike histones and DNA, which are fairly stable in composition and in amount per cell, the nonhistones are at least partly in a state of dynamic flux. The nonhistones, moreover, are structurally noteworthy for their heterogeneity. They vary among cell types and show considerable species differences. Further, when the gene activity in one cell type changes, one usually detects a change in the nonhistone proteins. Some of them, though not all, are thought to be responsible for switching genes on.

The production of nonhistone proteins is itself controlled by genes. These feed back within the confines of a given cell, as a consequence of other chemical activity, such as pathways of oxidative metabolism; these are the "housekeeping" proteins. Of more interest to us, nonhistones could come from other cells, or their production could be triggered within the cell by other types of chemical signals received from other cells. In the final analysis, the regulation of the level of transcription is the basic process underlying differentiation and development (Davidson 1977).

The action of steroid hormones, such as estrogen and hydrocortisone, is a case in point; they bind to the nuclei of the target tissue and thereby alter the pattern of gene transcription into RNA. Several steroids have been shown to produce changes in the composition and metabolism of nonhistone chromosomal proteins.

Localization

Although genetic regulation is pervasive, it is not the single determining factor. As the fertilized egg, the zygote, progresses from the blastula to the gastrula, it becomes rapidly complex and irreversibly differentiated, though its structure is still simple compared to later stages. Cell lineages appear that are already fated to develop along certain paths. They can be identified by their location, hence the term *localization.*

In some species, patterns of localization occur even before the first cell division; in others, the patterns are established progressively. The perpetuation of cell lineages could be accomplished through qualitative regional sequestration of special sets of proteins, maternal RNA, or regulatory products of genes. "The localization phenomenon is particularly interesting to students of development because it suggests that specific programs of development are sequestered in the egg cytoplasm" (Davidson 1976:247). Thus cell lineage is an interactional source of information of some significance to further development.

The contrast of localization moves the discussion in the direction of embryogenesis and the vast complexities of tissue interaction. Fundamental to us as that subject is, a consideration of it exceeds the scope of this Chapter.

Summary

Viewed just from the perspective of gene action, then, development consists of two processes. One is the replication of the genome, assuring that each and every daughter cell has all the DNA of its forebearer. The other is the regulation of the production of proteins, which in turn regulate life processes.

In this latter activity, genes are like notes on an instrument, played through time by an epigenetic "hand" (whose nature we only dimly perceive) that the genes themselves have had a central role in producing. But it is a hand whose chemical fingers also reach from other cells that are becoming ever more differentiated. The tune played derives from a vast number of notes, and it depends on the arrangement of genes within the chromatin as well as the specific molecular identity of the genes. That is the subject of the next section.

DIVERSITY AND ARRANGEMENT OF GENES

One of the most noteworthy findings of modern genetics is that the genome contains so many genes, even though the bacteriophage MS 2 has but a paltry 3-gene RNA system whereas T 4 has around 80 genes. With bacteria, we jump to roughly 1,000 genes. The fruit flies of the genus *Drosophila* have about 5,000 genes, and mammals have approximately 100,000 genes in every cell (Wyman 1976).

The electrophoretic study of the genes' products, the polypeptides or enzymes, has revealed that not only are they produced in great variety but, not surprisingly, their occurrence across individuals of the same species is highly variable. Plomin and Kuse (1979) gave a range of genetic differences within species of from 25 to 75%. They further stated, with regard to humans, that "just considering eight enzymes with known polymorphisms, Harris (1970) has shown that the probability that two randomly selected individuals would have exactly the same combination of enzyme types is only about 1 in 200" (p. 190).

The major purpose of the article by Plomin and Kuse was to point out that the work of King and Wilson (1975) has been misinterpreted to reach a contrary conclusion about genetic variability. King and Wilson wrote that "the average human polypeptide is more than 99 percent identical to its chimpanzee counterpart" (pp. 114–115). Their analysis indicated that of the 1,012 amino acid sites of eight proteins, two were different. Bear in mind that the number of different proteins and enzymes in the human body has been estimated to be as high as 100,000. Thus the conclusion by Washburn (1978:415) that humans and chimps "share 99% of their genetic material," and further that humans "share, in fact, more than 99% of their genes," appears unwarranted (Plomin & Kuse 1979).

Ayala (1980) reached almost the opposite conclusion based on the above and on newer molecular evidence derived from a variety of sources: Humans, chimpanzees, and gorillas are apparently about equally genetically differentiated, and to a degree "similar to that observed between species of the same genus in other groups of organisms" (Ayala 1980:147). (Note that these three hominoids are conventionally placed in two separate families rather than in the same genus.) Ayala further reported that the genetic variability among humans and other mammals is about twice that so far reported for any other primate, whether ape or monkey.

Recent evidence suggests that a substantial portion of this genetic richness in animals is unused (Ohno 1973). At the level of traditional genetics, Dobzhansky (1970) demonstrated an enormous amount of concealed variability through breeding to produce organisms homozygous at many loci. A fair number of such genes are lethal when homozygous. The information potentially available in an organism appears to exceed by far that necessary for the fertilized egg, the zygote, to develop into a competent adult (see Lewontin 1974).

Genes mutate from time to time; by analyzing their proteins, it is possible to show that they change slowly through geologic time. One may therefore speak of a particular protein, or its gene, evolving. Curiously, protein evolution and morphological evolution may proceed at different rates. Wilson et al. (1974a) made this point by comparing frogs and mammals (the comparison is uneven because frogs constitute an order, mammals a class).

Frogs arose 150 million years ago but have remained anatomically conservative. The eutherian mammals are only half as old as a group, but they have radiated anatomically into forms as diverse as bats, moles, whales, sloths, cheetahs, and humans. Morphologically, chimpanzees and humans (within the order Primates) differ more from one another than do the most widely unrelated frogs (Cherry et al. 1978; but see the exchange between Findley 1979 and Cherry et al. 1979). Genetically, the frogs are much more divergent than are mammals in spite of the frogs' less variable phenotypes. Within frogs and within mammals, the degree of difference in proteins is consistent with a steady time-dependent change in genes.

A different picture emerges when the chromosomes of frogs and mammals are compared (Wilson et al. 1974b). Mammals have evolved different numbers of chromosomes about 20 times faster than have frogs. Because the amount of DNA per cell has nonetheless remained about the same, changes in chromosomal number must have been accomplished by a rearrangement of chromosomal structure rather than by a gain or loss in DNA. That can be accomplished by chromosomes joining one another or breaking apart. Ploidy, the splitting of one set of chromosomes into two, is an extreme but demonstrable case. Even without changing numbers, chromosomes may rearrange their genes through inversions, a process in which a piece of the chromosome is reversed end for end.

Wilson et al. (1974b) reasoned that the reshuffling of genes produces a new genetic environment. That environment has a powerful influence on the regulatory processes of development. Furthermore, chromosomal rearrangement might allow large jumps in evolution.

The evidence from hybridization is relevant here. Frogs hybridize relatively easily, even across generic boundaries, whereas mammalian hybrids are successful only between closely related species (Wilson et al. 1974a). Ostensibly this is so because frogs have a tolerably similar chromosomal architecture whereas different mammals do not, even though frogs have greater differences in kinds of genes.

It is possible to hybridize somatic cells from incredibly different species, such as an invertebrate and a mammal. Such cells manage to function, in spite of the extreme dissimilarities in genes. Wilson et al. (1974a) pointed out that the reason for this success is that somatic cells merely have to stay alive; they do not have to develop; "housekeeping" metabolism is therefore sufficient. The difficulties arise when a hybrid zygote is formed, one that then proceeds to differentiate. In such organismal hybrids the paternal and maternal loci come into conflict when development starts; the more distant the relationship between the hybrids, the greater the problem. This suggests that the right chromosomal environment for a gene is an essential prerequisite for its developmental interactions.

In this section I have stressed the importance of the chromosomal arrangement of genes in determining their contribution to development. By doing so, I did not mean to imply that selective influences on the effects of individual genes are therefore unimportant. On the contrary, most students of behavior are familiar with the effects of gene differences (if not, see the excellent introductory overview by Plomin and McClearn 1979), but few appreciate the significance of the chromosomal environment.

MATERNAL EFFECT

Ocassionally some aspects of the offspring consistently favor the mother more than the father, a phenomenon called *matrocliny*. It is seen in certain reciprocal crosses between two different genotypes. A male of type A is mated with a female of type B, abbreviated mA × fB, and reciprocally mB × fA. The expectation from classic genetics is that the progeny from the reciprocal crosses will not differ. In some cases, however, the offspring of mA × fB are more like female B, whereas those of mB × fA are closer to female A. Two explanations are possible, sex-linked genes and cytoplasmic inheritance.

Maternal bias can be observed in males when they are the heterogametic sex. In the fruit fly *Drosophila,* for instance, the males have only one sex chromosome (XO) or an X and a relatively inert Y chromosome, as in mammals. Thus most if not all sex-linked genes come from the mother. The homogametic females have two sex chromosomes (XX), so they have both complements of parental genes in the reciprocal crosses. To the extent that the genes for the trait are borne on the X chromosome, matrocliny among male offspring is possible. When the female is the heterogametic sex, the possibility then exists for paternal bias.

Instances of maternal bias have also been reported irrespective of the sex chromosomes. These biases result from extrachromosomal inheritance (Subtelny & Konigsberg 1979). The ovum of the female contains the cytoplasm and particles that provide the environment in which the chromosomes lie, and thus in which development commences. The maternal influence can be fleeting or trivial, as in pigments in the cytoplasm, or enduring and significant, perhaps mediated by DNA in the ribosomes. The actual mechanisms involved, however, are poorly understood.

Keeping in mind the principles of gene expression and the importance of the chromosomal cytoplasmic environment, we can turn to the well-established methods of analyzing genetic differences.

METHODS OF GENETIC ANALYSIS

Underlying all genetic analyses is the simple logic of correlating traits found in the parent with those found in the offspring. Traditionally, this has involved pedigrees, as in hair patterns or hemophilia in humans. Ideally, however, correlations are obtained when the environment is held constant and the phenotypes produced by different genotypes are then compared. The differences in the phenotypes are attributable to the differences in the genotypes. But even if the environment varies, it is possible to assess genetic influence at the population level (Lehrman 1970) or across individuals, using powerful statistical techniques derived from linear models of analysis of variance (DeFries & Plomin 1978).

A major difficulty in this research area is that no one organism has enough desirable characteristics to give a totally satisfactory answer to the questions we would like to pose. And only a few species have enough desirable features to make them attractive enough for one to invest years of research labor in them.

The animals that offer the best array of features are the tiny fruit flies of the genus *Drosophila.* They have only four chromosomes, including giant ones in their salivary glands, an exceedingly short reproductive cycle, breed readily in small flasks, and have complex mating and grooming behavior. They have been used by geneticists for years. As a consequence, they are available as inbred, thus nearly completely homozygous, strains. A large number of mutations are known and have been mapped to specific chromosomal loci. Of particular value to neurogeneticists, they produce sex mosaics (of which more later).

Another species attractive to neurogeneticists is a tiny nematode worm, *Caenorhabditis elegans.* It also has a short reproductive cycle, only six chromosomes, and breeds readily in small containers. Specific mutations, including a number of behavioral ones, are well known. That it has but 260 neurons is a commendable feature, and those neurons have now been almost totally mapped (Ward 1977). However, their nervous system is already enormously complex, and the neurons are too small for single-cell recording and stimulation; the latter feature, in particular, seems to preclude for now any expectation of further progress.

Other favorites of geneticists include bacteria and bacteriophages, especially for gene action; the ciliate protozoan *Paramecium;* and crickets, because of their simple neural network and large neurons. Of most interest to the likely readers of this book, however, is the work done with mice (see Broadhurst et al. 1974).

There are now over 100 inbred strains of mice that are nearly genetically homozygous. Their life cycle is short, they breed in small cages, and several interesting behavioral mutants are known. More importantly, they have behavior relevant to investigators concerned with the complex interactive development of parent–offspring relationships and their consequences. Unfortunately, they lack the genetic simplicity of creatures such as *Drosophila* and *Ceanorhabditis.*

Overlooked is an outstanding, naturally occurring genetic experiment. I refer to clones of lizards such as those in the genus *Cnemidophorus.* Some females have been shown to reproduce parthenogenetically (Cole 1975). Thus mothers, daughters, and sisters are genetically identical. These lizards, found in the southwestern United States, have conspicuous stereotyped displays.

Comprehending gene–environment interaction in its fullest expression requires an optimistic tolerance of long jumps from one type of organism to another. In large part this is a result of our impatience, our hurry to know. Given time and new techniques, it should be possible to achieve a reasonably full understanding of the genetics of behavior in mammals.

Mendelian genetics: major genes

Classical textbook or Mendelian genetics originally depended on each gene having a major, discrete phenotypic effect. In the simplest case, one gene has two alleles. Classically, one allele is dominant, the other recessive, though the logic is applicable to polygenic systems (see "Polygenic systems").

The genetic analysis of Mendelian traits consists of pairing an animal having one (or more) trait with a conspecific animal that differs in that trait. In this case, all the offspring, the F_1 generation, are phenotypically like the parent that has the dominant allele. When the offspring are mated with one another, they produce an F_2 generation in which the dominant allele and the recessive allele are expressed in the classic 3:1 ratio.

Another analytical step is to mate the F_1 offspring with the paternal genotype in one instance and the maternal in the other. This backcrossing produces different predictable ratios depending on which parent carries the recessive and which the dominant allele. The techniques of producing F_2 generations and backcrosses are fundamental to parsing the phenotype and its genetic basis, whether in simple Mendelian crosses or in more complex polygenic systems.

Few naturally occurring behaviors have such a simple monofactorial basis. Evidently these behaviors are due to switch genes controlling the expression of a complex ensemble of genes. An often cited example was provided by Rothenbuhler (1964) in his study of hygienic behavior in honeybees (*Apis mellifera*). Two recessive genes assort independently, one controlling the behavior of uncapping an infected larval cell, the other the behavior of cleaning out the diseased cell.

Similarly, two major genes control gentleness and aggressiveness (readiness to sting) in the Italian and African strains of the honeybee (Stort 1975). The Italian queens have two dominant genes for gentleness, and their workers sting relatively seldom. The African form has only the recessive alleles and stings frequently.

In general, it is probably true that when monofactorial control of MAPs is indicated, there are actually switch genes controlling a multifactorial system. In addition, Ewing and Manning (1967) cautioned that multifactorial control can mimic monofactorial control (see also Whitney 1973). The two cases can be distinguished only through a careful program of genetic analysis.

Induced mutations

One of the more powerful techniques for assessing the effects of single genes is that of inducing mutations. This is done by exposing the parental stock to sublethal doses of X-rays or treating them with chemical mutagens, such as ethyl methanesulfate, now commonly administered in the animals' food or water. Because mutations are so frequently recessive, they are often sought in the F_2 generation.

Mutants in *Drosophila* were first detected by their altered morphology, such as eye or body coloration, or vestigial wings. Now many behavioral mutants are also known, ranging from altered chemotaxis in bacteria and nematodes to abnormal mating in *Drosophila* and peculiar gaits in mice. Most of the mutants receive mnemonic codes, some of which are delightful. A nonlearning mutant *Drosophila* is called *Dunce;* one that responds with peculiar movements to ether is called *Ether-a-go-go.* My favorite is *Lot,* a mutant that tolerates unusually high levels of salt in its drinking water.

Such mutants must be evaluated cautiously. The behavioral effect we observe might be simply the secondary consequence of a morphological defect. Take, for example, a white-eyed mutant *Drosophila* that mates slowly, apparently because its visual system is defective (Sciandra & Bennett 1976). Additionally, and importantly, the mutation might have broader pleiotropic effects to the degree that the change in behavior has little relevance to its normal causation (a pleiotropic gene is one that influences a number of different traits).

Thus, induced one-gene mutations share many of the difficulties that exist in evaluating the effects of lesions in the nervous system. Whereas a lesion or mutation has a predictable effect, and usually a deleterious one, other information is needed to understand the significance of the alteration.

One of the main limitations of this approach lies in detecting the mutants. The mutagenic treatment is blind, damaging DNA molecules seemingly at random. Probably most of the mutations go undetected because of the necessarily biased methods of screening or because no detectable difference results. Usually the investigator searches for a specific kind of change, and to that end some ingenious techniques have been devised.

Falk and Atida sought mutant flies that would tolerate high salt solutions in their drinking water; they put a red dye into the solution and could thereby see at a glance which fly among hundreds had drunk the saline water because the red shows through the body (in Ward 1977). Bentley (1975) sought cricket mutations with defective receptors, ones unresponsive to puffs of air; over thousands of crickets, he passed a device that delivered a puff of air and was followed by a vacuum cleaner. The normal crickets jumped and were sucked away, leaving the few mutants behind.

Using such screening techniques, it is possible to assemble a number of different mutations that have defects similar enough to be sorted out together. One simple method of obtaining flightless flies is to release them at the bottom of a glass column, retaining those that cannot fly out. But there can be a host of defects causing impaired flight, leaving aside those patently defective in morphology. Homyk (1977; Homyk & Sheppard 1977) carried out at least six kinds of behavioral tests on flight-related behavior. Forty-eight mutants at 34 loci were identified; and one has the feeling that further analysis would uncover yet more.

Once mutations have been found, they are usually verified as being unique through *complementation.* To do this, mutations with the same phenotypic change are mated. If the sources of the defects lie at different loci, their normal alleles will complement the defective ones and override their effects. In a similar way, one can identify different alleles at the same loci.

Many easily detected but benign mutations become useful as *markers.* The mutation for coral-colored eyes, for example, permits the experimenter to select out fruit flies that will have a particular chromosome on which coral eyes are linked to some other gene on the same chromosome.

Chromosomal mapping

A signal advance in understanding genetic mechanisms was made by A. H. Sturtevant in the first quarter of this century (Benzer 1973). He deduced how to map the location of genes on chromosomes by taking advantage of the phenomenon of *crossing over.*

During meiosis when homologous chromosomes come together, they sometimes exchange pieces. The closer together two genes lie on the chromosome, the more likely they are to remain linked together. The farther apart they are, the more likely they will become unlinked during a cross-over. Each locus can therefore be mapped linearly in terms of probability of being separated during a cross-over: The lower the probability, the closer together they lie.

Genetic mosaics and fate maps

Sturtevant recognized the possibility of applying the same logic to the origin of traits in the early embryo, though he never published his data (Benzer 1973). Benzer appreciated that mapping blastodermal origins of traits was a vital link in tracing the effect of a particular gene on a given piece of behavior. He reasoned that it should be possible to go from the one-dimensional array of information on the linear chromosome; to the two-dimensional array of cells on the blastoderm (the surface of the blastula); to the three-dimensional arrangement of sense organs, integrated neural networks, and muscles; and ultimately to the four-dimensional realm of behavior. Finding the embryological foci of behaviors promised to provide a crucial piece of the puzzle.

Embryologists have long been concerned with *fate maps.* Cells are marked in various ways early in development so that they can be followed and their destinies determined. From a number of experiments using various cells, one can project a map backward in time onto the blastoderm, a map showing the origins of the various adult tissues and organs.

The exciting twist that Benzer (1973) and his associates (e.g., Hotta & Benzer 1972) exploited was the utilization of genetic mosaics of *Drosophila.* An understanding of this procedure is essential to what follows. The female fruit fly is the homogametic sex, whereas the male is X0. Some females have an unstable X chromosome called *ring-X* (X_R). X_R is often (not always) lost as early as the first cell division of development. When that happens, half the cells develop as male (X0) and the rest as female (XX_R). They become *sexual mosaics.* If X_R is lost later in development, fewer male cells result.

This process enabled the investigators to exploit the system in a clever way. First, they produced a homozygous strain of fruit flies. Second, by appropriate matings, they put on the normal X chromosome a recessive marker, yellow external color, linked to a recessive behavioral mutation; this chromosome became X*. When X_R was lost, the cells without it could be recognized on the surface of the fly by their yellow color. Further, the behavioral mutation had its origins within the same embryological tissues as did the yellow surface. One more piece of information is necessary to understand how this phenomenon can be exploited.

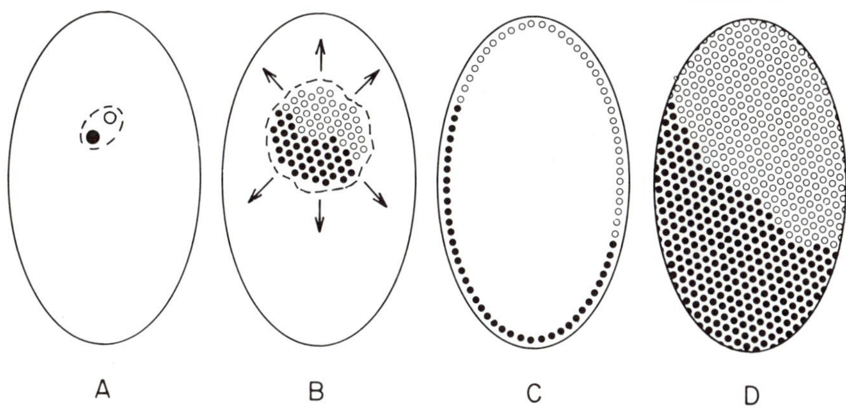

Figure 8.1. The formation of a mosaic fly by loss of one X chromosome. The initial egg is female, containing one X_R and one X* chromosome. X_R is lost in about 35% of the X^*X_R eggs at the first division of the zygote nucleus (*A*) producing one X^*X_R nucleus (solid circle) and one X*0 nucleus (open circle). Nuclei divide in cluster (*B*) and then migrate to the egg cortex, where cell membranes form to produce a blastoderm one cell thick (*C*). *D* shows the surface as seen from outside; part of the blastoderm area is covered by each cell type; the mosaic boundary separates the two areas. This is a simplified sketch. (From Hotta & Benzer 1972)

The line of the first cell division is at random with respect to the long axis of the embryo, which becomes established soon thereafter. Thus the boundary between normal and mutant sectors of the fly might divide it into a front and rear half, two sides, or anything in between (Fig. 8.1). The divisions need not be equal. It is possible to have a fly, say, with just a small part of its head male, the rest of the body being female (Fig. 8.2).

With such information, and many flies, it is possible to calculate the blastodermal focus of any trait by using the same logic as in chromosomal mapping. Now, because the blastoderm is two-dimensional, three points are needed. At first, Hotta and Benzer did such analyses only for features on the surface of the fly. Three features, say A, B, and C, which could be two legs and a wing, are compared pair-wise and scored for how often each is either normal or mutant. The closer together they are, the higher the probability that they originated near one another on the blastoderm. By measuring the distances between all pairs of features of interest, it is possible to map them onto the blastoderm. The calculation becomes more complicated when working with bilateral features, but the logic is the same.

The resulting map (Fig. 8.3) yields the embryonic foci of the trait. One focus might be in the mesoderm and produce muscle, another in that part of the ectoderm that gives rise to the brain, or in another case any one of the thoracic ganglia. By using the linkage between the marker and the behavior, one can locate the blastodermal focus of the change in behavior. If the behavioral defect involves flying, for instance, one can quickly decide from its focus whether this change was in the muscles, their innervation, local neural ganglia, the brain, or elsewhere.

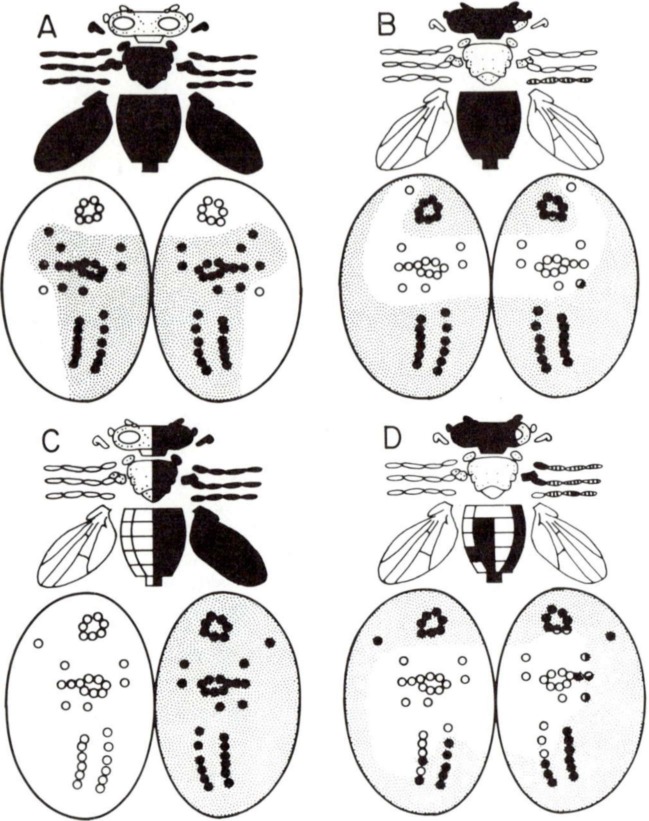

Figure 8.2. Orientations of the boundaries in four mosaic flies (*A–D*), deduced from the genotypes of body landmarks and behavioral foci; seen in dorsal view. Solid circles indicate normal sites; open circles denote mutant (X*) ones. A plausible dividing line has been drawn in each case. (From Hotta & Benzer 1972)

The beauty of this technique is that it also enables the researcher to rule out pleiotropic effects, or behavioral changes that are merely secondary consequences of morphological changes that are not obvious. Furthermore, knowing the focus directs one's attention to the structure most likely to be defective.

Caption to Figure 8.3 (*cont.*)
halving the distance measured between two homologous contralateral sites. The size of the circle used to represent a site is proportional to the frequency with which the corresponding structure is itself split by the mosaic boundary. *B.* A pictorial sketch of the external parts of the eventual right half of the adult fly derived from various sites on the blastoderm, based on the fate map. Dotted lines indicate areas that, according to embryological studies, give rise to the nervous system and the mesoderm. (From Hotta & Benzer 1972)

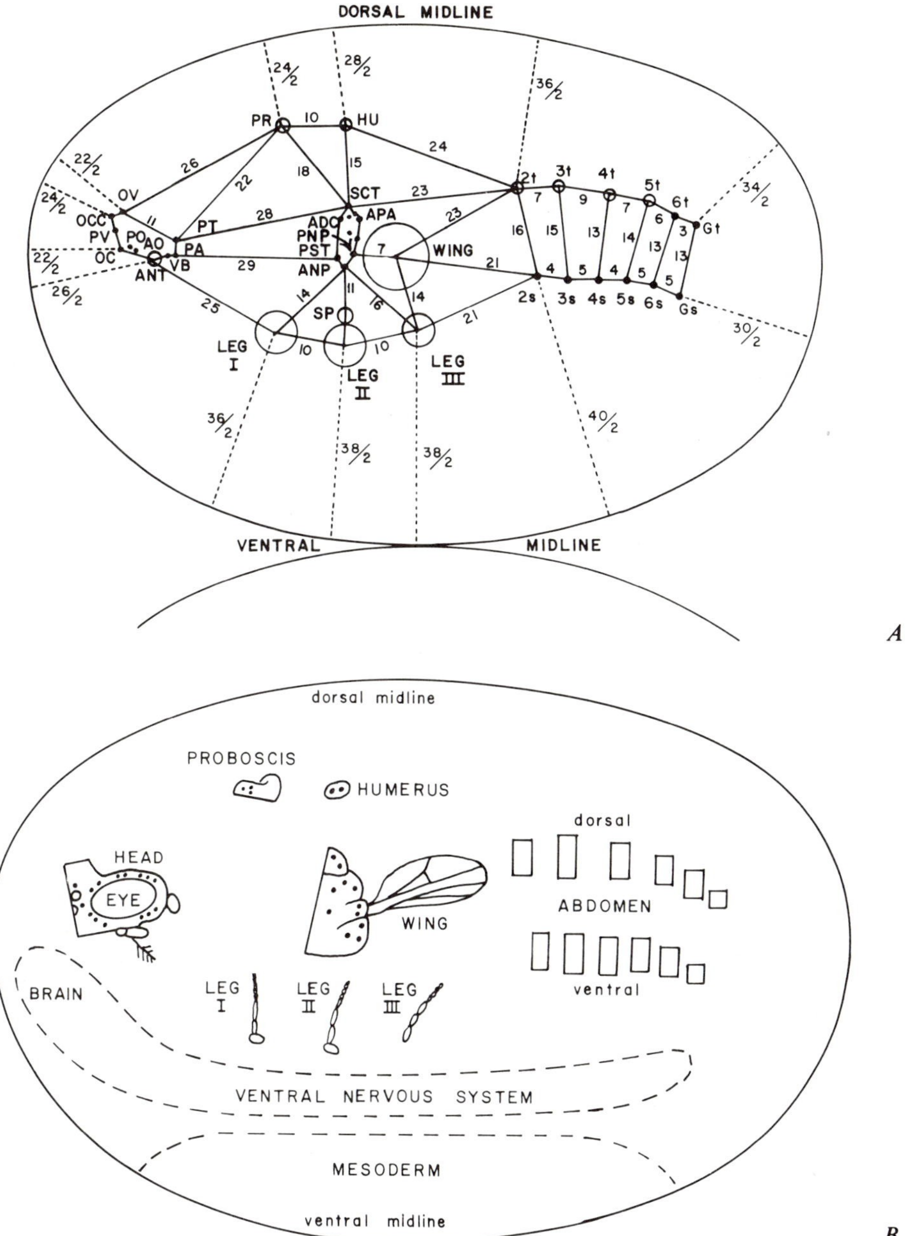

Figure 8.3. *A*. A fate map of the blastoderm of *Drosophila melanogaster* predicting adult external body parts, constructed by mosaic mapping. The map is a projection of the right half of the blastoderm (bilaterally symmetrical) as seen from inside the egg, showing sites of cells that will eventually develop into the indicated parts of the right side of the fly. Distances between pairs of sites are indicated in "sturts" (short for Sturtevant). Dotted lines indicate distances to the nearest midline, as obtained by

An example makes the point. Two different mutations can cause the fruit fly to hold its wings up. That posture could result from improper innervation, faulty muscles, or some more remote factor. For one, a change in hormones could alter the threshold of the neuromuscular junctions. The foci for both mutants, however, lie in the ventral midline of the blastula; that is the source of mesoderm for muscles.

Histological examination of the wing muscles showed that the two mutations cause different defects. In one, the muscles develop normally, then degenerate. In the other, the myoblasts fuse so that there are no muscle fibrils. A fly having both mutations holds the wings normally but cannot fly because its muscles are still defective. The other muscles are not affected by the mutations.

Enzyme mutations have now been found on the X chromosome, making it possible through staining to identify cells not on the surface. Furthermore, such cell lineages can be tracked during development to observe how they interact with other cells, normal or mutant. This staining technique has proved instructive in unraveling the source of a visual deficiency. In this case, the photoreceptor cells originate from a different area than do the neurons of the lamina to which they project. One mutation affects the receptor, the other the lamina (Benzer 1973).

Genetic mosaics of *Drosophila* provide a powerful analytical tool for tracing the effects of a mutation in a major gene from its position on the chromosome, to its anlage in the embryo, to the adult tissue, and on to the behavior. Eventually it should enable us to understand the developmental processes involved, particularly when individual cells can be marked by their enzymes. So far, that understanding remains for the future.

POLYGENIC SYSTEMS: QUANTITATIVE BEHAVIORAL GENETICS

In the analytical techniques covered above, we were considering single-gene differences with relatively massive effects. In the case of induced mutations, most of the effects are detrimental. In contrast, the genetics of naturally occurring behavior reveals continuous variation around a mode. The problem is almost reversed: Single-gene differences often have such small effects that they are difficult to detect (Franck 1974). That is because behavioral traits are influenced by a large number of genes and hence are polygenic (Dobzhansky 1970, 1972). As a consequence large, or qualitative, differences in behavioral traits are difficult to demonstrate in naturally occurring populations.

Unitary action of sets of genes

Manning (1975) raised the issue of whether and to what degree the analysis of such polygenic behavioral traits sheds light on their seemingly unitary genetic basis. I should make clear here, however, that *unitary* is used loosely and refers only to the phenotype. It draws attention to the general finding that behavior appears to be organized hierarchically into functional groups consisting of subgroups, which consist of further subgroups, down to neuromuscular units (Dawkins 1976).

There is no evidence, so far, that this hierarchical organization corresponds to some type of genetic organization. Nonetheless, it is tempting to look for ensembles of genes that underlie functional sets of behavior at various hierarchical levels. One might further suppose that, once evolved, such ensembles might be conserved, as through the action of switch or super genes, pleiotropy, or epistasis. Ohno (1973) suggested that linkage might be especially important here.

Plomin (personal communication), however, pointed out that it is not generally true that an essential ensemble of genes requires linkage for protection. "It seems to be true only if there are epistatic interactions among alleles at different loci. If the effects of the genes are additive, it shouldn't matter on which chromosome they are located."

Supporting Plomin's statement, Manning (1975) reviewed a number of studies whose findings argue for nonlinkage in a variety of seemingly unitary behavioral traits (see also Bentley & Hoy 1972) as revealed, for example, by the independent assortment of the components in the F_2 generation. Manning then suggested that this problem might best be tackled using MAPs.

Polygenic systems underlying behavior thus present the investigator with formidable problems of analysis. The differences in behavior within a species are apt to be small, making it difficult to screen rapidly large groups of animals. And because the differences are likely to involve thresholds of responding, the measurement of a trait may require statistical characterization even when the behavior can be seen to be different. There are ways around such difficulties. One is to magnify the differences by using hybrids.

Hybrids

In this approach, two closely related species are mated. They are chosen because they have some clear difference in a behavior they have in common, such as a call in crickets or nest building in birds.

In most instances, though by no means all, the behavior of the hybrids is intermediate. The genetically interesting results are obtained in the F_2 and backcross generations. In particular, one can estimate the degree to which the behavior and its component acts are inherited intact, fractionate into components, or vary continuously. Unfortunately, hybrids are often sterile, precluding F_2 and backcross offspring, especially in birds and mammals.

Interspecific hybridization lacks genetic elegance, informative as it can be. Consequently geneticists favor cleaner methods that I will now mention. Also, the most interesting work on hybrids gets us prematurely into a discussion of the genetics of MAPs (see "Genetics of modal action patterns").

Strain differences

For some time, geneticists have produced inbred strains in animals such as *Drosophila* and mice. The objective is to create organisms that are homozygous at all loci. The basic procedure consists of making successive brother–sister matings on the premise that alleles are lost at each pairing until only one remains at each locus.

Producing and maintaining homozygous strains is an expensive, time-consuming task. It is complicated by the expression of recessive lethal genes that have to be eliminated. Not surprisingly, there are only three mammals for which homozygous strains are available. These are rabbits, rats, and mice; there are several strains of the last. For mice, it takes about 20 generations, roughly 5 years, to produce a strain that is 98% homozygous. But once produced, such strains become a valuable resource made available to other researchers.

It is now conceptually possible to produce a fully homozygous mammal in one generation. Markert and Petters (1977) have microsurgically removed the pronucleus from a mouse egg before fertilization, creating a haploid egg. The egg was then chemically stimulated to start development, producing a homozygous female embryo (males would die, having only a Y sex chromosome). Other investigators have had 30 to 50% success in implanting normal eggs at the blastocyst stage. So, completely homozygous females may yet be produced in one generation, lethal loci permitting.

Homozygous strains demonstrate that distinct behavioral differences between strains are attributable to genetic differences. That is no longer an exciting finding. The importance of homozygous strains lies in their utility in more sophisticated analyses.

Diallel analysis

This approach takes advantage of the homozygous strains and is sensitive to small differences in behavior. Three or more strains are chosen and all possible crosses and their reciprocals are made, producing n^2 sets of F_1 offspring. Each set is scored for one or more frequently occurring behaviors. The data field is analyzed with factor-analysis models and analysis of variance (e.g., Royce et al. 1975), from which one can estimate epistasis, directional dominance, heritability, and maternal effects.

Selection for traits

One need only spend an afternoon perusing the periodical *Behavior Genetics* to gain the impression that it must be possible to breed selectively for almost any behavioral difference. In mice or flies, significant differences can be produced in speed of mating, aggressiveness, maze solving, activity in an open field, or positive or negative phototaxis or geotaxis. And the heritability of the trait need not be great (*heritability* is the proportion of variation between the progeny that is attributable to the genetic component; see Chap. 9). Heritability initially as low as 4 to 9% can produce a dramatic change in 10 to 30 generations when selection is intense (Dobzhansky 1972; see also DeFries below).

There are several refinements to these experiments, such as avoiding inbreeding, bidirectional selection, using more than one line per trait for reliability, and control lines. The chief danger for us, however, is not so much procedural as it is one of interpretation.

When an investigator selects for mating speed, different behavioral changes might produce the same outcome. Manning (1976) found in one experiment on *Drosophila* that slow mating resulted from interference due to a raised level of

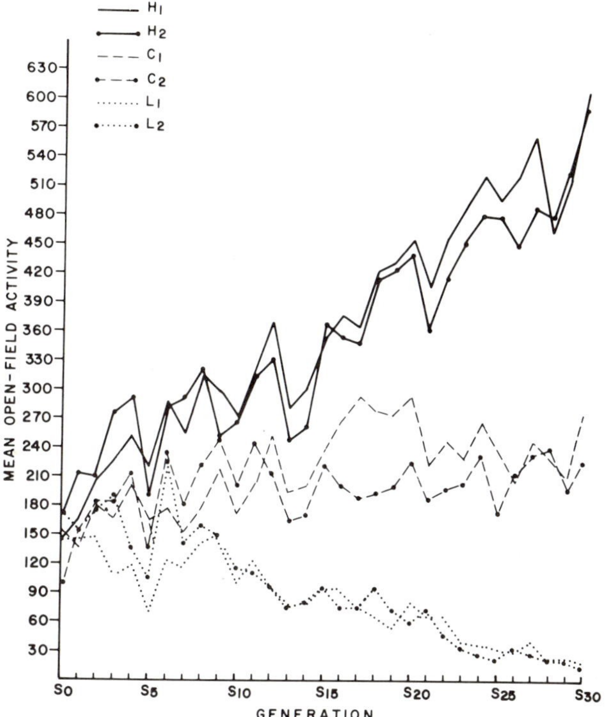

Figure 8.4. Mean open-field activity scores of six lines of mice. Two lines were selected for high open-field activity (H_1 and H_2), two were selected for low activity (L_1 and L_2) and two were randomly mated within line to serve as controls (C_1 and C_2). (From DeFries 1979)

general activity. In another selection experiment, delayed mating and depressed activity were associated. In each experiment, however, mating had indeed been retarded.

The utility of this method is nicely illustrated by the investigations of DeFries and his co-workers on the open-field behavior of mice (DeFries 1980). Open-field behavior is often equated with emotionality. The fewer photocells of a grid the mouse activates as it moves around, and the more often it defecates, the more emotional the mouse is said to be (we need not trouble ourselves here with the reality of the term *emotional*).

The experiment started with an emotional and an unemotional inbred strain of mice. There was about a tenfold difference in activity and an eightfold difference in defecation scores between the parental strains. The derived F_1, F_2, F_3 and backcrosses showed a nearly perfect dose–response relationship to selection for high and low activity (Fig. 8.4).

The heritability was moderately low, about 0.25 and 0.10 for activity and defecation, respectively. But there was a large negative correlation of 0.80

between activity and defecation, indicating that individual differences in activity and defecation are influenced by many of the same genes.

DeFries calculated that the minimum mean number of loci responsible for the strain differences was about 3.2 for activity and 7.4 for defecation. It thus follows that both characters are influenced by genes at many loci and are polygenic.

Although defecation scores were not selected for, the high- and low-activity lines showed a marked change in such scores. Starting with an F_3 founder stock, 30 generations of selection produced a mean defecation score for the low-activity line that was seven times that of the high-activity line, further proof that the differences share some genetic basis.

The study by DeFries and his associates illustrates well the information available through the technique of recombining strains, then selecting for a trait. I have reported only part of what they found. Nonetheless, this and all the other techniques mentioned here rely on the same basic principle of observing correlations between parents and offspring.

GENETICS OF MODAL ACTION PATTERNS

The reason the genetics of modal action patterns (MAPs) is so seldom mentioned in reviews is probably that the study of MAPs has not progressed far. The few genetic treatments of MAPs concern insect song, as will be described below. Most of our information comes from interspecific hybrids, not from the more refined genetic approaches. Consequently, most of this research has been done by ethologists, not behavior geneticists.

Hybrids

It is tempting to select one or two studies as exemplars, showing some clear conclusions about the behavior of hybrids. I have done this to some degree, but with misgivings. Although there are some examples permitting uncomplicated but cautious conclusions, such is often not the case. Perhaps when more research has been done it will be possible to reach more confident conclusions while accounting for departures from the general rules. Nonetheless, a few themes emerge.

Behavioral collages and omissions

It has seemed to be a challenge to naturalists to produce hybrids between animals as distantly related as possible. Such hybrids are regularly infertile and usually have reduced viability. Their behavior suggests that their disparate genomes are incompatible to a large degree during development. Sexual behavior is often lacking, as in a duck × goose hybrid (Poulson 1950), which failed to produce many MAPs of the parent species.

Hybrids between widely unrelated species often produce peculiar collages, as though the two sets of genes elaborate both parental behavior patterns in the nervous system, though also omitting some (see also Hinde 1956). Examples include hybrids between a lion and a tiger (Leyhausen 1950), a duck and a goose (Poulson 1950), and a goosander and a shellduck (Lind & Poulson 1963).

Collages can also appear when dealing with closely related, that is, at least congeneric, species. This appearance probably results from having sets of genes at different loci for the different traits. Heinrich's (1967) observations on cichlid fishes of the genus *Tilapia* (*sensu lato*) are instructive. Some of these fishes lay eggs that adhere to the bottom, and they fan and protect the eggs. In most species, however, the female broods nonadhesive eggs and larvae in her mouth. Hybrids between a substrate brooder, *T. tholloni,* and a mouth brooder, *T.* (= *Sarotherodon*) *nilotica,* executed MAPs of both parental species in a disorganized sequence. Eggs were alternately fanned or mouthed and spit out.

Another example, and one often cited, is Dilger's (1962b) analysis of the nest-building behavior of hybrids between two small parrots, *Agapornis roseicollis* and *A. fischeri. A. roseicollis* cuts strips of plant leaves (paper, in the laboratory) for its nest; several strips are successively tucked into the rump plumage, and then the bird flies to its nest. In *A. fischeri* the strip is picked up, then simply held in the beak during flight. The hybrid is frustrated by having both patterns of behavior. It tries to tuck the strip but will not let go. Thus in closely related species with fundamentally different behavior for the same function, the MAPs (or parts of them) may be developed but fail to be integrated into a functional routine.

One of the few studies done in satisfying detail on the MAPs of hybrids and their parent species is that by Helversen and Helversen (1975a, 1975b). They used two species of grasshoppers, *Chorthippus biguttulus* and *C. mollis.* These insects are so closely related they can hardly be distinguished by their morphology. Their calls, however, are highly distinctive and serve as species-isolating mechanisms for these sympatric insects. Both sexes produce the calls, which can be conveniently recorded, transduced to audiospectograms, and thereby analyzed in exquisite quantitative detail.

The calls (Fig. 8.5) can be resolved hierarchically into the basic *pulse* (the simplest unit), a *chirp* (a cluster of pulses), and a *phrase* (a cluster of chirps in *C. biguttulus*) or a *buzz* (a string of chirps in *C. mollis*). Each pulse is produced by rubbing a file on the femur against a pad on the front wing in a quick succession of down–up movements (see Chap. 17). It is possible to track these leg movements photoptically and display them visually simultaneously with the audiospectograms (Helversen & Elsner 1977; Chap. 17).

Four relevant conclusions emerged: (1) there is great variation in calling between individual hybrid siblings; (2) each hybrid is much more complex than the parent species; (3) typically, the hybrids have calls that indicate they are producing both parental calls at the same time, that is, they are superimposed; some hybrids, however, tended to favor one parent type, whereas the calls of others approached the other parent type; and (4) the basic pulses, nonetheless, remained the same. An analysis of the calls of the females, which are more difficult to obtain and more variable, yielded similar results. In a further study, a few males were found that sometimes simultaneously produced the call of one species with one leg while emitting the other species's song with the other leg (Helversen & Helversen 1975b). The Helversens concluded that the hybrid grasshoppers had developed, in parallel, the neural equipment for both parent species' calls. They reasoned that the separate development occurred because their genes were not "homologous" (*sic*).

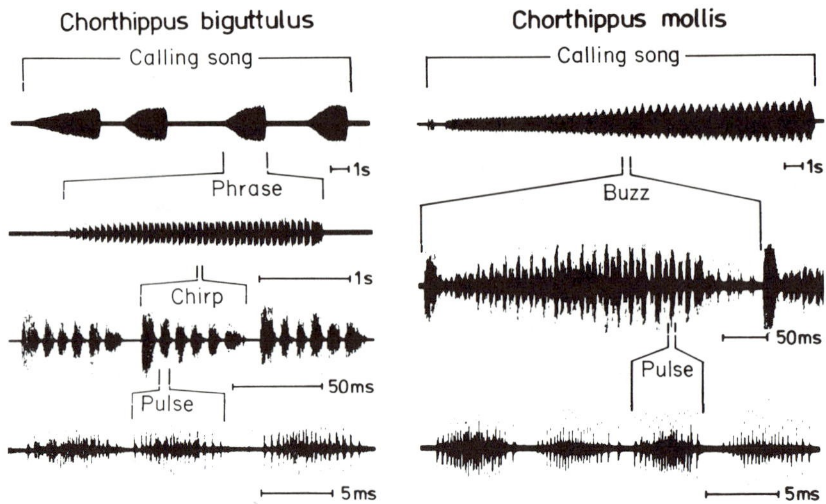

Figure 8.5. Sound pulse patterns in the calling songs of the grasshoppers *Chorthippus biguttulus* and *C. mollis,* illustrating how pulses are combined into chirps, chirps into phrases or buzzes, and these into the calling songs. (From Helversen & Helversen 1975a)

The pulses, however, were held to be regulated by alleles of the same genes and thus were intermediate between those of the parent species (which differed only slightly). That led to the conclusion that the pulses are organized by a different set of genes than those underlying the formation of the chirps, phrases, and buzzes.

Hybrid intermediacy and dominance

When species have similar behavior for the same function, chances seem good that the behavior of the hybrid will be intermediate to that of the parents (e.g., Alexander 1968; Blair 1955, 1956; Hinde 1956). There are some remarkable exceptions, however, including apparent dominance. Also, different aspects of a MAP, or different MAPs, may show different kinds of control in the same individual.

The reported push-up display of a hybrid *Anolis* lizard (Gorman 1969) provides an example of hybrid intermediacy and also of apparent dominance. The bursts of tail flicking were intermediate to those of the parent species, as was the pattern of head bobbing. But the number of bobs was as in one parent species, whereas the duration of a string of bobs was like that of the other. Apparent dominance has also been noted by Peters and Brestowsky (1961) in hybrids of two tilapias, a male *Sarotherodon mossambicus* paired with a female *Tilapia tholloni.* The duration and frequency of contacting the mother was as in *S. mossambicus* fry.

One of Peters's students (Bauer 1968) extended this observation, analyzing

Table 8.1. *Mean lengths of bowing displays of doves of the genus* Streptopelia, *measured, in seconds, from films*

Species	Number of individuals	Number of bows	Mean of mean length of bowing cycle	Mean of standard deviations
Barbary	5	33	2.19	0.15
Necklace	3	25	1.12	0.08
Turtle	2	48	0.76	0.06
Senegal	2	31	0.51	0.07
Neck. × Barb.	2	18	1.07	0.12
Barb. × Neck.	3	23	1.26	0.11
Seneg. × Barb.	3	26	1.36	0.20
Seneg. × Turt.	2	15	1.10	0.23

Source: Condensed from Davies (1970), Table 5.

contacting in fry from F_1, F_2, and backcrossed generations. As is so often unfortunately the case, in only one pair type, *S. niloticus* × *S. heudeloti,* were the hybrids fertile and of both sexes. Reciprocal crosses to produce those hybrids gave conflicting results. In one, the F_1 hybrids favored *S. heudeloti;* in the other, they were intermediate. The F_2 fry were also intermediate. The backcrosses resembled the parent species used in the cross, with some favoring of *S. heudeloti.* Although obviously polyfactorial, the duration of contacting appears to be controlled by relatively few genes (Bauer 1968).

Davies (1970) compared the bowing of five species of doves (*Streptopelia*) and some of their hybrids (Table 8.1). The duration of bowing was intermediate in one hybrid (Senegal × Barbary), favored the necklace dove in its three hybrid crosses, and may have been additive in the Senegal × Turtle hybrid. (The hybrids may also have been more variable; $p = 0.057$, u test.)

The form of the display differed in noteworthy ways, as well, in the hybrid doves. Davies commented particularly on the position at the top and bottom of the bow. Commonly the top was like that of one parent species and the bottom like that of the other, but the situation was often more complicated. The bow regularly looked like a new type of bowing, and hybrid intermediacy was not the rule.

The distress calls of hybrids from a chicken × pheasant mating also show a mixture of determining factors (McGrath et al. 1972). The duration of the call is intermediate, though closer to that of the pheasant. The upward inflection of frequencies, however, is patterned as in the pheasant. This led to the suggestion that simple Mendelian dominance might be involved.

When hybrids are formed from the fruit flies *Drosophila melanogaster* and *D. simulans,* their wing-beat frequency is intermediate. The interpulse interval of the male courtship song, however, is the same as that of the mother species, *D. simulans.* Schilcher and Manning (1975) presumed that the dominance is due to sex linkage.

A certain amount of care must be taken in assessing intermediacy when the behavioral trait under analysis is involved in a feedback relationship, as during courtship between two animals. When a male parrot of the genus *Agapornis* courts a female, he often displays a MAP called *switch-sidling*. Males of *A. roseicollis* spend 32% of the time switch-sidling during courtship, whereas those of *A. fischeri* spend 51% of the time so engaged (Dilger 1962b). Hybrid males switch-sidled 40% when courting hybrid females, a nicely intermediate value. However, hybrid males switch-sidled 33% to *A. roseicollis* females and 50% to *A. fischeri* females. The females control the amount of switch-sidling, and the hybrid female is intermediate (Dilger 1962b). The female's behavior is assessed through the male's conspicuous display, which could have been mistakenly interpreted.

An exemplar of hybrid intermediacy was reported by Bentley and Hoy (Bentley 1971; Bentley & Hoy 1972; Hoy 1974) on calling in two sympatric crickets, *Teleogryllus commodus* and *T. oceanicus*. Only the males of these insects call, by rubbing their wings together, producing a hierarchically organized pattern of pulses, chirps, and trills. In contrast to the grasshopper hybrids, these hybrids did not vary much among themselves, producing a relatively uniform class. The backcrosses, too, were uniform. The genetic analysis suggested to Bentley and Hoy (1972) that many genes are involved, and that they are distributed across the many chromosomes. This is also borne out by the intermediacy of the hybrids (Fig. 8.6), though hybrids between strains can be intermediate when only one gene is involved (Gwadz 1970; Plomin personal communication). The situation is further complicated by maternal bias.

Maternal effects

In most of the hybrid studies there have been too few subjects to examine the data for matroclinous effects, though in many cases the investigators did not present their data in a way that would reveal maternal bias. Bentley and Hoy (1972), however, did a careful genetic analysis of cricket song, employing reciprocal crosses and backcrosses; matroclinous effects were easily detected (Fig. 8.6).

Of the eight characteristics of cricket calling that Bentley and Hoy analyzed, three showed maternal bias. These were the duration and variability of the intertrill interval and the variability of the phrase-repetition rate.

Because the male has X0 sex chromosomes, they hypothesized that the maternal effect resulted from sex linkage. These crickets have 29 chromosomes, so that would be a considerable degree of localization. The traits were not totally like the maternal stock that supplied the X chromosomes, so some of their genes must have been distributed on the autosomal chromosomes as well. They did not consider extrachromosomal inheritance; nor did Hoy et al. (1977) when they reached the unexplained conclusion that the responses of hybrid females to the male's song is also controlled by sex-linked genes.

Helversen and Helversen (1975a, 1975b) also found maternal effects. Grasshoppers have one advantage over crickets, in such studies, in that both males and females sing. If the matrocliny were sex-linked, one would expect the males (X0) to show the effect but not the females (XX). The females, however,

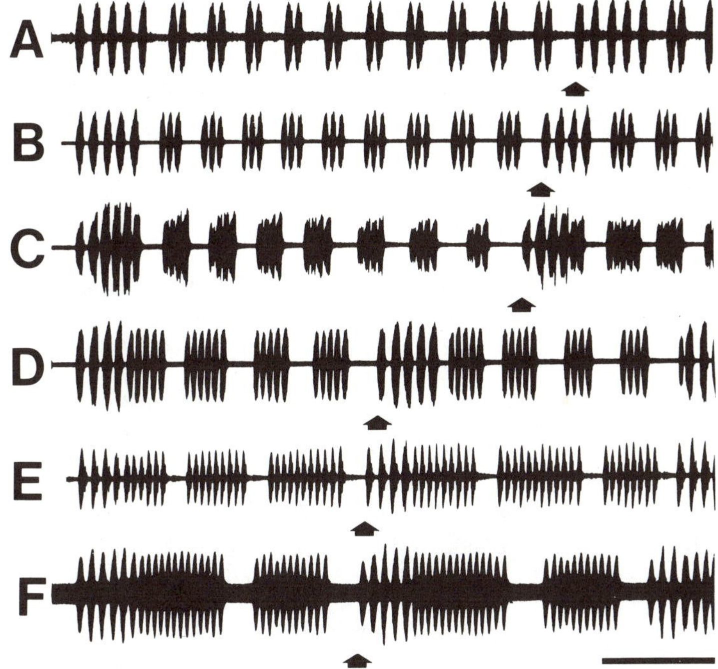

Figure 8.6. Sound pulse patterns in the calling song of *Teleogryllus* wild types and hybrids. Each record begins with a single four- to six-pulse chirp, followed by a series of trills containing 2 to 14 sound pulses, depending on genotype. Chirps and trills are arranged in a repeating phrase. Records start with a complete phrase. Arrows mark the onset of the second phrase. Records are as follows: *A* = wild type of *T. oceanicus; B* = backcross of ♀ *T. oceanicus* × ♂ F_1 (shown in *C*); *C* = F_1 of ♀ *T. oceanicus* × ♂ *T. commodus; D* = ♀ *T. commodus* × ♂ *T. oceanicus; E* = backcross of ♀ *T. commodus* × ♂ F_1 (shown in *D*); *F* = wild type of *T. commodus.* (From Bentley 1971; copyright 10 December 1971 by the American Association for the Advancement of Science)

were also matroclinous; this suggests that the effect could be due to extrachromosomal factors. Further analysis is needed, using F_2 and backcrossed progeny.

Because in grasshoppers and crickets the parents have no contact with their developing eggs or young, the effects of maternal care can be ruled out. In mammals, in contrast, the embryo has a relatively long life in the uterus. Effects of the uterine environment might confound genetic differences. It has been suggested, however, that hybrid offspring of inbred strains may be less susceptible to differences between intrauterine environments.

DeFries et al. (1967) took this suggestion as a point of departure, asking explicitly if the nature of the hybrid's womb might reduce the apparent susceptibility. Using two inbred strains of mice, one black and one white, they surgically arranged hybrid females with ovaries of black females in some individuals, and with ovaries of white females in others, while retaining their own "hybrid" uterus. Hybrid females with "black" ovaries were inseminated by black males, those with "white" ovaries by white males. The effects of the uterine environment were slight, as judged by an open-field test; only for defecation by black mice was the score significantly different from black controls, and the difference was small. The large between-strain differences remained. All mice developed in hybrids' wombs were larger than the controls, however; that could lead to differences later in life, as in dominance relations.

It is well appreciated that parental care after birth or hatching can influence the course of behavioral development. What is often overlooked is that the parent behaves as a buffer against a variable environment. In effect, the parent acts as a homeostatic agent, providing a relatively predictable environment for its offspring. And because each species or strain may provide characteristic differences in such a relationship, it is easy to assume, mistakenly, that such differences are genetic.

Concluding here, hybrids between species present the observer with many differences in MAPs – their form, sequential integration, and orientation. One sometimes encounters difficult problems of analysis and interpretation in relation to conventional genetic models, depending on the degree of difference between the species (which do not detract from their interest as developmental problems). Those difficulties are lessened when one can find different populations of the same species showing distinctive dissimilarities in MAPs. There are many examples of this phenomenon, and one family of fishes springs to mind, the Goodeidae.

Exploiting differences between populations

The Goodeidae are confined to the plateau of Mexico. They are small viviparous fishes that breed readily in aquaria and reach reproductive maturity quickly, attractive features to a geneticist. One advantage of studying them is the possibility of establishing the adaptive significance of the behavior analyzed.

For example, Fitzimons (1976) has found in the genus *Xenotoca* that when two species occur together their displays (MAPs) tend to diverge, and new displays may be added. Where they occur alone, their repertoire of displays differs less from those of isolated populations of the other species.

Within one species males of one population have four major displays, whereas those of another population have two additional displays for a total of six. Numerous differences exist, too, in the forms of the displays: the lack of a sigmoid component and a tilt more or less out of the vertical, for example. Such species present a rare opportunity for genetic analysis of MAPs.

Coevolved traits

All the studies of the genetic basis of patterned motor output indicate highly polygenic systems. Nonetheless, it is tempting for the evolutionist to look for *genetic coupling* of traits. (I use *coupling* loosely here to refer to any genetic mechanism, such as linkage, inversion, or pleiotropy, that would increase the probability of two traits varying together in an adaptive fashion.) One could argue that a MAP used as a signal should be coupled with that signal's detector system. Or particular display movements should be coupled with markings or morphological features that accent them, or with taxes that assure the proper orientation. Or MAPs should be connected in their most effective sequence. Most of the evidence suggests the contrary, however.

Because both morphology and behavior are often intermediate in the offspring, it should not be surprising to find them in a seemingly functional relationship in the hybrid. For example, the Senegal dove has a dark mark on the underside of its neck, and it does not bow deeply, keeping the mark exposed. In contrast, the Barbary dove has its marking on the back of its neck and it bows deeply, showing its neck mark to best advantage. The hybrid has the marking on the side of its neck, and its bow is on intermediate depth (Davies 1970). More characteristically, however, Lind and Poulson (1963) found no correlation between structure and behavior in hybrid waterfowl. And Clarke et al. (1954) noted that a backing-display, and the sword it presents, are independently assorted in platyfish × swordtail hybrids.

Sharpe and Johnsgard (1966) have made the most direct and planned investigation on the question of whether morphology and MAPs are controlled by common genetic factors. Using anatid ducks, which are ideal animals for this purpose, they bred F_1 and F_2 progeny from a pintail × mallard cross. Each of the eleven F_2 males was assigned two scalar values for degree of resemblance to pintail or mallards, one value being for courtship displays and the other for plumage. The remarkable result was that morphology and behavior were highly correlated ($r = +0.76$). That indicates a substantial degree of joint inheritance, whatever the genetic mechanism.

There was appreciable evidence, however, for independent assortment of MAPs. For example, a mallardlike F_2 duck showed both pintail and mallard MAPs. Apparently a number of such mixtures occurred. Thus the positive correlation is clearly statistical and is not the result of genetic coupling.

Uncoupling of a MAP from its taxis has been seen in hybrids. In courtship, the hybrid swordtail male of *X. montezumae* × *X. helleri* expresses the sword-bending characteristic of *X. montezumae*. But it lacks the appropriate and rigid spatial orientation that *X. montezumae* maintains relative to the female (Franck 1970). Likewise, tucking of nest material in hybrid love birds becomes disoriented; the female tucks throughout her plumage, not just in her rump feathers (Buckley 1969).

The sequencing of MAPs can also become scrambled in closely related hybrids with homologous displays. Ramsay (1961) observed three individual hybrid ducks (*Anas*); he found sequences that never appeared in the adults. Comparable findings have been reported by Lorenz (1958), by Sharpe and Johnsgard (1966), and by Kaltenhäuser (1971) for other hybrid anatid ducks.

The issue of coupling, however, has drawn the most attention in the joining of signals and the perception of them. Obviously, signal and receiver must coevolve if communication is to continue to occur during speciation. Alexander (1962) wrote that more rapid speciation would be possible if the signal and its reception were determined by the same mechanism.

That thought has been expressed by avian ethologists (e.g. Marler 1973) with more regard to processes relating motor output, such as song, to its perception. If the motor program shared its pattern-processing system with the feature detector, or auditory template, then they would stay in step, even in hybrids and their derivative crosses. Does the evidence lend support? First, consider two cases not centering on acoustical signals.

Female love birds (*Agapornis*) select their mates. If cross fostered, they pair as adults with males of the species that had been their siblings in the nest. Hybrid females, however, always pick only hybrid males of the same origin, even if the female had been raised by a species other than her parents' and with her foster parents' offspring serving as siblings (Buckley 1969). It is not known whether her choice is based on different displays, calls, coloration, or other attributes of the hybrid male. Note that this is not an adequate test of the hypothesis. Whatever the attribute of the male and the response of the female, each could be a result of hybrid intermediacy in noncoupled polygenic traits.

Fitzimons (1976) has shown that goodeid fishes of the genus *Xenotoca* raised in isolation select their own species for mates. Hybrids, however, respond to either parent species.

A direct test, and initially an apparent confirmation, of the hypothesis of coupling of signal and receiver was made using hybrid crickets. Females were tested by observing their turning toward (Hoy & Paul 1973) or approach to (Hoy et al. 1977) the broadcast calling songs of males. Females were of two types, from reciprocal crosses of *Teleogryllus commodus* and *T. oceanicus*. The songs offered to them were variously from both parental males and from the two types of hybrid males. The results were clear.

Females preferred the songs of hybrid males from their own specific reciprocal cross. It was concluded that there is genetic coupling, probably pleiotropy, between the processes of perception and generation of the song. "Genetic control could be achieved by identical sets of genes acting on the same neuron types in both male and female" (Hoy et al. 1977:83). However, those experiments did not exclude convergent hybrid intermediacy of feature detector and pattern generator.

A recent experiment on *T. oceanicus* by Pollack and Hoy (1979) has ruled out genetic coupling, in the sense they proposed. They found that females recognize their species's song from temporal pattern alone. The females flew toward synthesized songs in which the sequential order of intervals was random but that retained the characteristic statistical distribution of intervals. The oscillographic patterns show how different are the structures of the synthesized and normal songs. The crickets' neuronal pattern generator cannot therefore be acting as a perceptual template. Rather, the feature detector seems to be following some simple rule about the distribution of intervals, as in thermal coupling in frogs (see below).

Perdeck (1958) noted that female hybrid grasshoppers (*Chorthippus brunneus* × *C. biguttulus*) approach songs of hybrid males. But they also move toward songs of one or even both males of the parent species. The females of the parental species do not respond to the hybrid males' songs. Helversen and Helversen (1975b) extended this study, using a different combination of species. About half of the hybrid females (*C. biguttulus* × *C. mollis*) responded to both parent species' songs. The others responded more to one parent's songs or to the other's. Although individuals were consistent, there was appreciable variation among them.

In contrast to the cricket studies of Bentley and Hoy, the hybrid grasshopper females responded only weakly to the songs of hybrid males, even of their own brothers. Recall, however, that the songs of the hybrid males differed greatly from male to male. One hybrid male was as effective as the parent species in attracting females. Experiments with artificial, synthesized songs give an insight into why that might be.

Helversen and Helverson (1975b) wanted to know if the hybrid females would respond best to a synthesized song with properties intermediate to those of the parent species. As mentioned, songs of the hybrid males were not intermediate but were rather an odd mixture of their parents' songs. Early work by one of the Helversens had shown that for species recognition the key feature of the song is the ratio of chirp length to interchirp interval in *C. biguttulus;* indications are that the same applies to *C. mollis,* but with a different ratio. None of the hybrid females preferred the synthesized songs with intermediate ratios, but they responded well to the synthesized songs of their parents.

Helversen and Helversen (1975b) also pointed out that the ratio of chirp to interchirp interval is the one characteristic of calling that remains the same when the temperature changes. It has long been known that the rate of calling in heterothermic animals, such as amphibians and insects, decreases as the temperature falls, and vice versa; the receptor system of the female changes in parallel. This has been termed *temperature coupling* (Gerhardt 1978). If the signal generator and the receptor system rely on some temperature-independent or compensating feature as in the ratio here, or in the stable ratio of pulse-repetition rate and pulse duration in the gray tree frog (Gerhard 1978), there is no need to propose a unitary system for output and receptors to account for thermal stability.

In addition, the Helversens presented the hybrid female grasshoppers with a synthetic call that was a precise combination of the calls of both species. (The calls of the hybrid males combined both species calls, but they were also special in many ways and thus different from the synthetic calls.) The hybrid females went to the synthetic combined calls just as they had to their parents' calls.

From these experiments the Helversens concluded that the females have developed two apparently separate receptor systems, one from each parent species. These results parallel their study of the generation of the calls (Helversen & Helversen 1975a). Taken alone, however, these results do not conclusively disprove the coupling of generator and perceiver. For that, it is necessary to examine the call of each female in relation to that female's preference. If the systems are coupled, there should be a high positive correlation.

The calls emitted by 22 females were compared to their preferences for type of call. The correlation was weak ($r = 0.21$; no p value given) and could be accounted for by matrocliny. Most importantly, some females produced a call nearly the same as that of one species but preferred the call of the other.

This study by the Helversens seems to resolve the issue, at least for those grasshoppers. Actually, however, it does not altogether. Their evidence is persuasive that each individual has the genetic information for developing both calls and for perceiving both of them. This is relevant to those females that emitted one species's call but preferred the other's. One would want to know whether some accident of development has differentially altered the threshold of activation on the motor side and the perceptual side of the same system. That is, the input–output systems could be coupled, but during development the output side of one system could interfere with the other, and vice versa. The question of differential threshold of expression is relevant here (see "Threshold differences").

All the evidence, therefore, favors the view that the generator and the perceiver are polygenic coadapted systems that develop independently. Some evidence does exist, however, for certain behavioral traits having many genes in common, for example, open-field activity and defecation in mice (DeFries 1979).

Threshold differences

As mentioned in passing, one of the major difficulties in dealing with the genetics of MAPs is that the threshold of expression plays a vital role. This is illustrated by Manning's (1959) analysis of the courtship behavior of two closely related fruit flies, *Drosophila melanogaster* and *D. simulans.* They differ in behavior more in degree than in kind, for they share the same MAPs.

One species, *D. simulans,* is less reactive and only rarely shows wing vibrating, a display performed just before attempting copulation and associated with high excitation; wing scissoring, however, is displayed frequently; it is a low-threshold MAP that grades into vibrating. The other species, *D. melanogaster,* vibrates when moderately stimulated, and therefore frequently; scissoring is relatively rare. Manning argued that the dissimilarities are due to differences in threshold of the MAPs. The more active, excitable species, *D. melanogaster,* performs more high-threshold displays.

Baerends and Blockzijl (1963) concluded that differences in the displays of two closely related cichlid fishes, *Sarotherodon niloticus* and *S. mossambicus,* can be explained by differences in threshold. Both sexes of each species can perform most of the displays, but the males usually express a number of them that the females do not; this difference was also accounted for in terms of thresholds.

These types of changes can be better related to genetics by examining hybrids between species. A good example has been provided by Franck (1970), using hybrids of the swordtail fishes *Xiphophorus helleri* and *X. montezumae cortezi.* When the hybrid males are not strongly stimulated in courtship, they show the MAPs characteristic of *X. montezumae.* But when strongly stimulated, they display the apparently higher-threshold MAPs of *X. helleri* (Franck 1970).

Helversen and Helversen (1975a) made a number of relevant observations on hybrid grasshoppers. One was parallel to the switch-over in swordtails just mentioned: A few males emitted a call similar to that of *Chorthippus biguttulus* during spontaneous singing or when in contact with rival males; during courtship their call came to resemble that of *C. mollis.* Comparing the parental species, *C. mollis* has a prolonged calling phrase during courtship, but *C. biguttulus* can go quickly into the precopulatory phase of countersinging, even omitting calling. Thus *C. biguttulus* can be compared to the more excitable, lower-threshold *D. melanogaster* and *C. mollis* to the less quickly activated, higher-threshold *D. simulans*. The hybrid males that showed the switch followed this relationship.

Not all hybrid grasshopper males behaved that way, however. Some persisted for long periods with the call of *C. biguttulus*. On the other hand, some hybrid males never called at all, others rarely. Noncallers occasionally showed intention movements of the femur, as though to start calling, but stopped short. Some of those males could be stimulated to call briefly in answer to other males calling. Their thresholds were apparently so high that calling could only rarely be evoked.

Unexpressed behavioral potential

Organisms appear to have more information in their genome than they normally express. This is sometimes revealed in behavior that is ordinarily never seen, but that emerges when a species is stimulated in an unusual way, or in the so-called primitive behavior of interspecific hybrids. Manning (1975) stressed the theoretical significance of so-called atavistic MAPs. They indicate that the complex polygenic basis of a MAP may be carried intact in the genome long after selective forces have ceased to operate on them. Unfortunately, most of the evidence is anecdotal.

Hybrid individuals have been reported to perform displays never observed in their parent species, but that do occur in species presumed to be ancestral. The implication is that the parent species once performed those MAPs but that their expression has been selected against. Conceivably, both parents could have the genetic system to develop a MAP in question, or only one parent does, but the system is suppressed by a supergene; or parts of the information are combined from the two parental genomes in a complementary way.

The most frequently discussed cases come from the displays of waterfowl (e.g., Kaltenhäuser 1971; Lind & Poulson 1963; Lorenz 1958; Sharpe & Johnsgard 1966), and the nest-building activities of love birds (Buckley 1969; Dilger 1962a, 1962b).

Apparently, however, some investigators (e.g., Kaltenhäuser 1971) have uncritically concluded that unusual MAPs in hybrids are ancestral or primitive. Wall (1963) has taken a more cautious view in studies of hybrid ducks. Franck (1974) suggested that the correspondence to primitive behavior could be due to a chance resemblance: The judgment that MAPs are atavistic is made in some cases because the behavior appears simpler and relatively unritualized. That could be merely the consequence of a less complex expression of an inadequately developed MAP. We need careful comparisons with presumed ancestral species, should they be extant. Critical quantitative studies of the visual displays of hybrids, their parents, and related species do not exist.

Should some displays of hybrids prove to be ancestral (proof may be impossible), a question still remains: Do the parental species have the genetic information but not develop the organic substrates of the behavior? Or do they develop the neuromuscular equipment but never express the MAP?

Species may actually develop behavior that they never use. Of particular interest is the next example. It shows how a MAP develops, has no opportunity for expression, and then disappears.

Most tilapia are mouth-breeding fishes. After hatching, the larvae are retained in the parent's mouth for varying amounts of time. When the young fish, the fry, are finally released, they typically swim to the parent and make contacting movements. The larvae of *Sarotherodon melanotheron* are retained much longer than in other species, and they emerge at a more advanced stage of development. The fry depart from the parents quickly. Contacting is either weakly developed or not expressed at all.

Brestowsky (1968) performed a revealing experiment on these fry. He took larvae of *S. melanotheron* from the mouth of their parent at an age when the young of other tilapia species were contacting. The larvae could not swim because of their large yolk sacs. Brestowsky delicately punctured the sacs and removed the yolks. This enabled the larvae to swim. They then showed well-developed contacting behavior. Because the results are so remarkable and the response is susceptible to different interpretations, this work should be replicated.

Parallel cases of unused behavior patterns are known for human infants. Premature babies, for example, have distinct grasping behavior in their toes and other rudimentary responses (Peiper 1963).

Latent MAPs are known for adult birds such as doves and rails. According to Poulsen (1953), bird species in these groups are primarily ground nesters. Those species that nest on the ground retrieve their eggs as does a goose, placing the bill on the far side of the egg and hooking it back into the nest. Those species that are secondarily tree nesters, however, never have an opportunity to show such behavior. An egg out of the nest falls to the ground.

Suspecting that tree nesters might still have the behavior to retrieve an egg, Poulsen constructed collarlike platforms around the nests of some of the species. He placed an egg on the platform, and the bird in the nest retrieved the egg as do ground nesters. Thus the response and its form have remained intact over great spans of time and in the absence of selective pressure to maintain the behavior.

Artificial selection

Selecting for or against a trait is one of the most powerful approaches in the behavior geneticists' armamentarium (DeFries 1979); it has never been used scientifically to alter a MAP. Although the approach is generally difficult to apply, there may be felicitous situations nonetheless. For the moment, we have only indirect or anecdotal information. All of it arises from the time-honored practice of domestication, in which behavior patterns are selected for and against. Breeders have long utilized the method of selective inbreeding to produce desired behaviors, such as singing in canaries or pointing in bird dogs.

It is sometimes proposed that in the process of selecting for some desirable trait, degenerative changes occur in other traits. The most common behavioral example cited is the omission of displays in ducks (reviewed by Miller 1977). A recent naturalistic study of the Peking duck, a white domestic form of the mallard, revealed, however, that it has retained all the displays of the wild form (Miller 1977); the usual conditions of captivity were thought to inhibit the displays and thus to explain why the notion of degeneration cropped up.

Desforges and Wood-Gush (1976) made parallel observations on another strain of domesticated mallard, the Aylesbury. They also observed the ducks in a seminatural situation, and they made time-based control observations on mallards. The Aylesbury showed most of the displays, though ritualized drinking failed to appear; their vocalizations were also aberrant, and the down–up display was said to be less intense and occurred far less frequently. Furthermore, the Aylesbury drakes engaged in many more forced copulations, and pair bonding was weak or missing. Thus, upon closer examination, this strain showed a number of deficiencies as a consequence of domestication, probably through the well-known phenomenon of inbreeding depression.

Animal breeders have practiced artificial selection for behavioral traits for centuries. In many cases the behavior has been complex, including surveillance and the ability to perceive relationships and to learn, as in sheep dogs. Selection for MAPs has been practiced less often, but its results are common enough. Dogs provide examples, as in setting or pointing. Trotting and pacing in horses might be included. The most striking cases, however, are the elaborate, prolonged crows of roosters, upon which money is wagered in Belgium, and the different types of singers among canaries.

Nicolai (1976) has recently taken up this problem in pigeons. Their domestication can be traced back to the Arabs in the sixteenth century, and special strains are still being produced. A main theme of Nicolai's study is that the bizarre behaviors are all exaggerations of behavior existing in rock pigeons, their wild precursors.

Pouting is merely extended crop inflation, derived from normal courtship and nest calling. Emphatic wing clapping and "parachuting" have been derived from the normal aerial display. Likewise, circle clapping, in which the male jumps up and claps his wings while circling the female, is an exaggeration and combining of circle bowing and jumping with clapping. The origin of aerial tumbling, also called *rolling,* was not so obvious and has baffled pigeon fanciers, including Charles Darwin and me.

Tumblers, when flying, suddenly fall through the air somersaulting backward. Tumbling resembles no known pigeon behavior. By observing its ontogeny, Nicolai established that tumbling has been derived from aerial display, which normally consists of two or three wing claps followed by a slightly wing-up glide (Fig. 8.7a); one kind of pouter shows this behavior in the extreme (Fig. 8.7b).

Initially, the young tumbler starts to wing clap, throwing the wings back. Shortly, gliding is added with the wings held very high and the body inclined upward. As tumbling emerges from this maneuver, clapping disappears, and the aerial acrobatic loses all resemblance to the original display (Fig. 8.7c).

Nicolai has looked at a number of hybrids between these special breeds and normal pigeons. Hybrid intermediacy is the rule, making it likely that the traits are polygenic. Darwin and others had proposed that tumbling is due to a brain

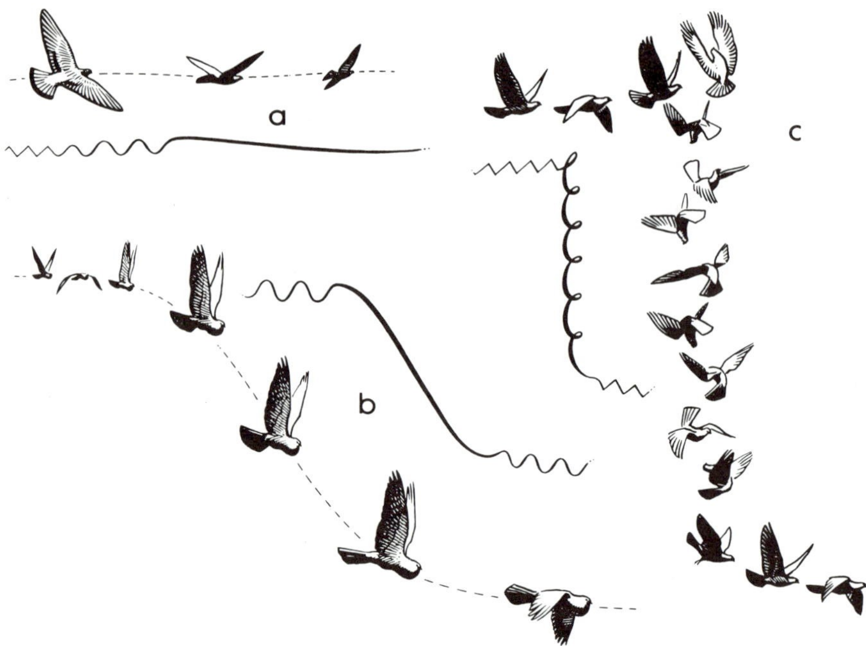

Figure 8.7. Derivation of tumbling (rolling) in the domestic pigeon. (a) Gliding phase of display flight in the wild progenitor, the rock dove. (b) Gliding with wings held very high, and descending, in a pouter. (c) Tumbling in the Birmingham roller. The zigzag lines indicate tail steering, the wavy lines the wing-beating phase, and the thickened lines the glide phase. (After Nicolai 1976)

defect. It would be tempting, if so, to presume that a single-locus mutation were responsible, one with a lesionlike effect. However, hybrids from tumbler × nontumbler crosses produced a marvelously intermediate half tumble (Fig. 8.8).

Conclusions and prospects

An understanding of the genetics of MAPs is still in a relatively primitive stage. Yet MAPs offer potentially the best material for tracking the development of behavior from the genome through embryogenesis to the adult. The reasons the genetics of MAPs has been so little studied are easy to recognize. The main difficulty is that altered MAPs seem difficult to screen; only a few have been picked up with nonobservational techniques for filtering large numbers of individuals.

It is also not enough to record simply the presence or absence of MAPs, as has usually been done with hybrids. That presupposes a genetically unitary basis, which is unlikely from what we know. It is therefore essential that MAPs be analyzed in detail, which is time-consuming enough in the parental stocks, not to mention screening the progeny for differences.

Figure 8.8. A pigeon that was a hybrid between a tumbling and a nontumbling strain. It started to tumble, then returned to normal flight. This intermediate performance remained unchanged throughout the life of the bird. (From Nicolai 1976)

The significance of such studies would also be enhanced if functional systems of MAPs were analyzed, such as courtship and mating, aggression, and grooming. Obvious genetic differences could be produced, starting with hybrids. An experienced observer could probably filter out mutagen-induced differences within a species, and these subjects could then be the founders of strains for closer analysis. Or different inbred strains of mice or *Drosophila* could be characterized and subjected to selective-breeding methods of analysis. Then we could begin to answer critical questions about the genetics of MAPs.

How are the components of stereotyped hybrid MAPs assorted in F_2 and backcrosses? Are there genetic assemblages that approach one or a few genes, the smaller the portion of the MAP? Or are the assemblages pleiotropic across different components, or both? And what is the nature of genetic control when differences in clearly graded movements are involved? Is the coupling of the components, the phase relationship, affected in the same ways? The answers to all of these questions are to be sought in careful quantitative studies of the fine structure of MAPs.

NEUROGENETICS AND BEHAVIOR

Behavior is a physiological consequence of the structure and function of tissues and organs acting as an integrated whole. Although underlying gross structure is necessary, much of it does not differ interestingly between individuals and species that behave differently. These behavioral dissimilarities are produced by the nervous system, whether they are to be attributed to obvious structural divergences in the nervous system, to subtle functional differences, or to modulation by hormones. In understanding the development of behavior, therefore, the genetics of neuronal organization assumes central importance (review by Ward 1977).

The goal in neurogenetics is to make the connection between the biochemical product of a gene, its consequences in the ontogeny of the nervous system, and the influence on behavior. In no case can we yet make that connection, though that day is probably not far off. But even when it comes, the utility of such a finding will be limited. It will suggest little about the way the nervous system is elaborated. That will require working out the complex interaction of the multiple genes underlying the trait within the embryonic environment and all its relationships, and will take some time.

For the moment, the main concern in neurogenetics is to produce single-gene mutations with large, easily identified effects. In principle, it is using genes to make neurological lesions by causing malfunctions. Just as in neurosurgery, such lesions are informative in revealing how a dysfunction in part of the network can perturb the system and consequently its behavior.

Taken alone, however, such mutations offer some difficulties of interpretation. The perceived defect could result secondarily from another defect. Benzer (1973) used the example of a visually inadequate fruit fly. Its impairment would be assumed to be in the eyes, but it might actually stem from the inability of the gut to absorb vitamin A. Genetic mosaics provide a way around this difficulty.

Sexual mosaics

In a mosaic fly it is possible to localize the suspected defect and to observe a number of flies that have that defect in combination with all other wild-type organs and tissues. In Benzer's example, flies would be created with defective eyes but functional guts to rule out the digestive system as the source of the impairment. Mosaics are further useful in that mapping the focus directs the search for structural defects in the nervous system because the defects are sometimes subtle or not visible.

Hotta and Benzer (1976) have used sexual mosaics to analyze the major steps in the sequence of male courtship in a fruit fly. These are, highly simplified: (1) orient toward and follow the female, (2) tap the female's abdomen, (3) extend and vibrate one wing (sound produced), (4) lick the female's genitalia, and (5) attempt to copulate. The female provides the stimuli and indicates her acceptance. If not receptive, she avoids the male or kicks him away.

In the genetic analysis, the male's behavior was broken down into follow, vibrate, attempt to copulate, and copulate. Following and vibrating co-occurred in the mosaics, being either both present or both absent; their foci in the head were either indistinguishably close together or the same; they could be a cluster of neurons that develop only in male tissue or a group of neuroendocrine cells that influence nearby neurons in the brain.

Attempting to copulate occurred only in flies that followed and vibrated. Its focus is in the thoracic ganglion, thus downstream from this insect's brain. The focus for copulation itself lies in the abdomen and may be related to the presence of a male genitalium. Some flies had the male focus for courtship but were otherwise entirely female, including their receptors, external surfaces and wings, genitalia, and thoracic ganglia; but they still performed the male display of vibrating.

Unfortunately, no MAPs were examined for interesting differences within them, such as whether vibrating was sometimes scissoring. If such differences exist, the technique of mapping may lack the resolution necessary to distinguish between separate foci. If the difference between such MAPs is a matter of thresholds, there is no reason to suspect that the MAPs themselves should have different foci.

Hotta and Benzer (1972) and Benzer (1973) have provided a host of such examples, including alterations in visual systems, brain structure and function, neuromuscular junctions, and fine structure of muscles. In short, they have located genetically the foci for the three major pieces of a behavioral system: the input, the integration and the output.

Cricket calls

Crickets are attractive to neurogeneticists because of the relatively simple arrangement of the neuromuscular system used in calling and the large size of the neurons. The call is generated endogenously by a small cluster of neurons in the paired thoracic ganglia. "Most of the muscles involved have only one to three hierarchically arranged fast motor units, each of which is activated in a one-to-one manner by a single motor neuron" (Bentley 1971:1140). The timing of bursts of impulses from these motor neurons determines the pattern of the sound pulse: Multiple-impulse bursts produce a loud chirp, whereas a single impulse results in softer trill pulses.

> For most single motor units, activity corresponding to a trill pulse is only a single impulse, so the difference between the output of homologous neurons in *T. oceanicus* and the backcross is only a single action potential per trill. Therefore, genetically stored information is capable of specifying the output of single neurons with resolutions approaching the theoretical maximum - single impulse increments.
>
> [Bentley 1971:1140]

This study speaks for itself. It is the best example, perhaps the only one, in which the smallest resolvable element of a MAP can be shown to be under genetic control.

Mouse tails

Hegmann (1975) took advantage of inbred strains of mice to look for differences in the velocity of neural conduction. He anesthetized mice, electrically stimulated the near end of the tail, then recorded distally the speed of the impulse in the caudal nerve. The genetic differences among six strains accounted for about 15% of the variance. Hybrids conducted impulses about 15% faster than the parental strains. It also proved possible to select for velocity of conduction (Hegmann 1975). The noteworthy thing about this research is that it involved a polygenic system. The analysis did not rely on induced deleterious mutations or on interspecific hybrids. Although this study did not employ overt behavior, it dealt with the genetic basis of the neurological substrate of motor output.

Neurological mechanisms

Neurogenetics can also yield information about the organization of the nervous system. In some cases the results can be shown to be consistent with neurophysiologial investigations, as in the calls of hybrid grasshoppers (Helversen & Helversen 1975a). Another example would be the calls of hybrid crickets of the genus *Gryllus,* the analysis of which supported the hypothesis that two separate neural oscillators control the organization of calling (Bentley & Hoy 1972).

A recent study of a fruit fly by Jan and Jan (1978) has implicated a mutation in the enhancement of long-term facilitation of a paralytic response to being banged about. The evidence suggests that there are two separate types of facilitation of this response, short-term and long-term, with separate biochemical mechanisms. The mutation is thought to work its effect selectively on the long-term process through a change in the transport of sodium across a neural membrane.

Another approach to neurogenetics is overtly developmental. It is the production of neurological chimeras. Part of the embryonic brain anlage of one species is removed and replaced with the homologous part from a closely related species with different behavior. The objective is to observe to what degree the foreign tissue responds to its new neural environment. It is a problem in developmental genetics. It bears on such things as the timing of irreversibility of cell lineages and the role of intercellular feedback.

As one example, Rössler (1976) exchanged hindbrain tissue between two species of frogs during early neurulation. The tadpoles of one species, *Xenopus laevus,* rhythmically pump water to filter out microplankton for food. The other species's tadpoles, *Hymenochirus boettgeri,* fixate small prey, then "gulp" them into their mouth. Of the surviving gulpers that had received tissue from pumper hindbrains, 42% showed the pumping behavior of the donor. Some of those gulpers, however, also fixated and snapped up individual prey, indicating that the gulping mode of feeding is organized outside of the hindbrain. Such experiments point the way to potentially more revealing studies.

These few examples suffice to make the point that genetic manipulation can illuminate the neurophysiological mechanisms generating overt behavior. Only a little imagination and a lot of hard work is needed to apply those approaches to developmental problems.

TIMING OF GENETIC ACTIVITY

I have already made the point that development during embryogenesis is directed by genes switching on and off. The genes, in turn, operate in an interlocking feedback relationship with the buffered environment they have largely produced and whose very nature depends on this relationship. Consequently, the beginning of an analysis of development depends on the appreciation that genes act at different times during development.

Little is known about the sequential activation of genes during postembryonic development, though much could be said by inference. Most readers would want to be assured, nonetheless, that there is evidence for sequential genetic activation after birth or hatching, though in a phylogenetic framework birth or hatching are arbitrary events in ontogeny (Chap. 18).

Several papers indicate that genetic differences result in time- or age-dependent differences in behavior (Broadhurst & Jinks 1963; McClearn 1970). A mutation in mice, for instance, produces a distinct peak around 21 days of age in susceptibility to audiogenic seizure. Learning is age-specific in some strains of mice, but not in others. Similarly, alcohol preference drops abruptly at 9 weeks in one strain of mice, but not in others. Whitney (1970) discovered different time courses between strains of mice in the likelihood of vocalizing when picked up by the tail.

Wilson (1972) produced developmental profiles for human infants, using the Bayley mental score. Monozygotic twins showed a much higher concordance of profiles than did dizygotic twins (see also Chap. 9). Wilson hypothesized that the monozygotic twins were more in phase, sharing more genes for a programmatic series of spurts and lags in development.

The most striking example of timing of gene expression is that of the mutant called drop dead in a fruit fly (Benzer 1973). The fly appears normal, but within a few hours after emerging as an adult it falls over dead. Using sex mosaics and fate mapping, the defect was localized in the brain. Histological examination showed that the brain was at first normal in appearance, then began to deteriorate shortly before death.

Similar breakdowns occur in humans. Huntington's chorea is a heritable trait in people. It results from neural degeneration and is often accompanied by psychotic behavior (McClearn 1970). Its onset occurs around the ages of 35 to 39, appearing a little earlier in women than in men and just after each sex has entered its postreproductive phase, suggesting relaxed natural selection (Medawar 1957:66).

Hormones and reproductive behavior

The control of sexual behavior by hormones provides the best material for considering how genes act discontinuously during development. It is now well known that steroid hormones interact with the nervous system shortly before or after birth in mammals, depending on the species; this interaction sets the behavioral system as male or female (Young et al. 1964). At puberty, the level of sex hormones rises and sexual behavior and secondary sex characters develop.

Hormone action is gene regulated (McEwen & Pfaff 1973). The hormones themselves affect their target tissues, such as the uterus or a site in the hypothalamus, by direct action on the cells' nuclei. The hormone may have multiple effects, including transcription by RNA and translation (Hamilton 1968). Thus the classical experiments of endocrinology, removing glands and administering hormones, have mimicked the expression of genetic activity.

That the onset of puberty can be changed genetically has long been known. Stone and Barker (in McClearn 1970) selected for early and late puberty in rats. The mean age of puberty in the early line was 47.6 days for males and 43.0 for females. In the late line the ages were 61.2 and 56.9 for males and females, respectively, for this polygenic trait.

The onset of sexual receptivity in insects such as flies and their relatives, the Diptera, is regulated in the female by a hormone from the corpus allatum. Differences in the timing of activity of the corpus allatum are genetically determined in the mosquito *Aëdes atropalpua.* Females from two geographic strains were compared. The mean age of receptivity for one race was 38 hours; for the other it was 120 hours. The progeny of their reciprocal crosses were intermediate to the parents but did not differ from one another; the backcross progeny shifted toward the parental race in mating. The simplest explanation here was that the difference in timing of receptivity was set by a single semidominant autosomal gene (Gwadz 1970). A remarkably parallel example is provided by a small poeciliid fish.

A pair of alleles at one locus on the X chromosome produces three age classes in the development of sexual maturity in males of the platyfish *Xiphophorus maculatus.* When the alleles are homozygous for "early," maturity occurs within 10 to 16 weeks of age. Individuals homozygous for "late" take 20 to 32 weeks, and the heterozygotes mature in 16 to 25 weeks. Because the males stop growing when they mature, three size groupings result (Kallman & Schreibman 1973).

That raises a question of interest to developmental biologists. What is the feedback that tells the genome to switch on the reproductive machinery? It could be age, or it could be size. Sohn and Crews (1977) addressed that question using another poeciliid, the platyfish. Their data indicate that size is the key factor for that fish.

There is reason to believe that size could also be a significant variable for mammals, including humans (Frisch 1974, 1978). Whether size, age, or both are involved poses different questions about feedback control of the genome. This also serves to remind us that age may be a less relevant variable than is sequential attainment of a given stage of development.

Experimental approaches

When is behavior organized? The age at which a behavior appears can be misleading with regard to its development. It is fairly common, for example, to produce the MAPs of adult sexual behavior in immature animals. A recent example involves domesticated ducklings that were given testosterone propionate (Balthazart 1974; Balthazart & Stevens 1975). One-month-old ducklings were induced to produce nod-walking, and 5-month-old birds performed almost all the adult displays. In such studies, some caution is needed when reaching conclusions about the role of hormones because very young animals, such as domestic chicks, are competent to produce copulatory behavior without hormonal treatment if stimulated in the right way (Andrew 1963).

Highly organized behavior can therefore exist in the nervous systems long before it is called into use, as by threshold lowering brought on by hormones or through unusual stimulation. The most convincing example is to be found, again, in Bentley's work on crickets (see also Chap. 17).

After hatching, crickets progress as nymphs through 9 to 11 molts before becoming adults. They do not fly or stridulate until adulthood, even when fighting. Areas in the mushroom bodies of the brain, when lesioned, disinhibit stridulation in adults. Lesions in the brains of last-instar nymphs produce the exact motor pattern of the complex calling of the adults, showing that the system is ready to go but is suppressed (Bentley & Hoy 1970).

Cricket nymphs as young as the seventh instar can be stimulated to assume the highly differentiated flight posture of the adults if they are suspended in a wind tunnel. That flight program can be "read" from their muscles by means of implanted electrodes. In that way Bentley and Hoy (1970) tracked the gradual emergence of neural activity separately for fore and hind wings and their progressive coordination. Because that neuromuscular system is not ordinarily in use until the cricket becomes an adult, the orderly development of the motor program probably reflects the sequential activation of genes. The approach of Bentley and Hoy provides an opportunity to examine how and to what extent environmental feedback is involved in this motor development and which environmental variable might play a role.

Temperature as a tool. One of the advantages of working with heterothermic animals is that the temperature at which they develop can be moved up or down. Each species has a normal range of permissive temperatures within which development can proceed. Outside of that range, development is adversely affected; the animal may be abnormal or die at those restrictive temperatures.

The interference of low temperatures generally involves disruption of the more general metabolic pathways, whereas high temperatures tend to produce a number of more interesting effects. Thus the research here usually consists of inducing mutations in fruit flies or nematodes, then screening for defects upon exposure to some higher temperature, but one that is still permissive in the broad sense.

Ideally, two strategies are employed (Ward 1977). One is to turn a gene on or off to assess its role in development. The other, basically the same, is to sample from time to time to establish whether a gene is now switched on (see Hirsh and Vanderslice 1976 for a model program).

Suzuki (1970, 1974) has made great use of temperature-sensitive mutants in the study of behavior. By shifting flies from 22° to 29° C, he and his colleagues discovered 11 temperature-sensitive mutants distributed across three loci. One has to wonder about the sense of humor of anyone who has the patience to screen 1,350,000 flies to find thermally induced paralytic individuals. But my faith was restored by their naming a staggering fly stoned^{ts} (stn^{ts}) and a paralytic mutant shi^{ts} (in Japanese, *shibire* means paralyzed).

In the typical case, as in the mutant para^{ts}, the fly is paralyzed within minutes at 29° C; some of them recover if left at that temperature, and most do if returned to 22°. Shi^{ts} is usually lethal to flies left at 29°C. During a brief exposure, flies with stn^{ts} still move a bit at 29°C but recover within 15 to 60 minutes when removed. Closer analysis of these mutants is informative.

The temperature-sensitive mutants are affected most as embryos, but also as adults. In shi^{ts}, for instance, there are at least six periods when the postembryonic fly is vulnerable, that is, when the paralytic gene or its complement is active. There is also sexual dimorphism, with one sex having a long period of vulnerability but the other only a short one. Further, in one mutant the thermal response is triggered more by change in temperature, and the magnitude of the response is greater after larger thermal steps. Although the behavior here is uninteresting, the diversity of phasic activity it has indicated suggests the potential for broader application.

Regeneration. Another unorthodox approach to development involves removing organs or tissues and observing their regeneration. So far, it is limited to those heterothermic vertebrates and invertebrates known to have regenerative powers, such as crabs replacing their legs and lizards their tails. At the level of morphology, the pattern of events during regeneration is essentially the same as that during normal development, but speeded up (Edwards & Palka 1976); that also applies to neural tissue, the substrate of behavior.

The implication, then, is that during regeneration the genetic program is reactivated, and through more powerful environmental guidance its time course is hastened. Where such organs or tissues are crucial to some behavior, it would be of interest to see how that behavior is restored.

A Milk Model. Dealing with temperature-triggered paralysis, regenerating legs, and the like seems to carry us far from the familiar world. I would like to mention a mundane phenomenon that brings home the reality of phasic activity of the genome in a provocative way.

The babies of all mammals get milk from their mothers (a trait that defines the class), and it is their only food at first. To digest the milk sugar, lactose, the baby must have the enzyme lactase. Almost magically, lactase appears in the digestive system of the baby at birth and disappears after weaning; the gene(s) for lactase is switched on when needed, then permanently turned off.

The situation for some populations of humans is different. Among non-Caucasian populations, 60% to 100% of the adults lack lactase and therefore cannot digest milk (galactosemia). Within populations of northern Europeans, however, 80% to 100% of the adults possess the gene(s) for switching lactase permanently on (Gottesman 1975).

Among northern Europeans, then, a process that is of crucial importance to infants has been extended throughout life. Put another way, there has been a deactivation of the regulator gene that in most mammals suppresses the gene for lactase after weaning.

One need only think of the arguments about the uniqueness of human behavior in relation to the prolonging of infant and juvenile processes (Mason 1979). It might take only a few genes to slow down the rate of repression of infant or juvenile features. One obvious candidate, though surely not the only one, is the hormonal system regulating the onset of sexual behavior. All that is needed is a prolongation of the repression of hormonal activity, perhaps through raised thresholds to feedback.

The basic argument is that through a small genetic change it might be possible to extend greatly the entire ensemble of immature behavior. The change could well be one that simply makes the system more sensitive to feedback. To return to the milk model, consider the case of an individual who cannot produce lactase as an adult. A mutation in its offspring might change the control of the switch-off gene such that lactase would continue to be produced past infancy, so long as milk was ingested. External feedback would now end the immature condition. Small genetic differences could prolong the period that the system is open to receiving information from the environment. That brings us full circle to gene–environment interaction.

GENE–ENVIRONMENT INTERACTION

The literature in developmental genetics of behavior is disappointing because most of it consists of observations establishing only that both the environment and the genome contribute to differences in the phenotype. Although that is a necessary first step, what is lacking is a vigorous analysis of the progression through time of that interactive relationship, to shed light on the dynamic processes involved in development. Perhaps it is asking too much at this time, because such a program is a prodigious undertaking. It is at least a start to demonstrate that both the environment and the genome contribute to the variation in the phenotype.

The interaction of environment and genome can be maddeningly difficult to disentangle in exactly those places where we most want to know, as in mental illness. Recently there has been a growing appreciation that many forms of mental illness may be facilitated genetically (DeFries & Plomin 1978; Omenn 1976). But it is also apparent that the expression of this disposition depends on the environmental circumstance.

The difficulties of sorting out the contributions of genome and environment, and of assessing their interaction, have been emphasized by Erlenmeyer-Kimling (1975). Formal experiments on humans are out of the question, so one can deal only with correlations derived from existing conditions. The problem of covariation of environment and genome is difficult but not insurmountable (see Chap. 9).

Take the incidence of schizophrenia. It occurs at a higher rate in lower economic classes. That could be the consequence of an unfavorable social environment facilitating the syndrome, hence an interaction between environment and genome. Or it could result from downward social mobility of those who are genetically disposed toward schizophrenia; thus a covariation (Erlenmeyer-Kimling 1975). In the framework of Plomin et al. (1977; see also Chap. 9), this would be an example of reactive genotype–environment correlation.

Working with animals, it is at least possible to plan experiments to sort out the relative contributions of genome and environment. Such studies have an unreal quality, however, because the estimates depend so much on the method of gathering data, the particular genotype, and the specified environment.

Genome and environment as independent variables

One of the most illustrative experiments here is also one of the earlier ones. Freedman (1958) employed four known breeds of dogs as subjects. Breed was thus one dimension; treatment was the other. One group was reared from the third week of life under a disciplined regimen, the other under an indulgent one. The data came from a test in which a bowl of food was placed before the young dog. When it ate, it was punished and admonished. The experimenter left the room, and the dog was secretly observed to see if it then returned to the food.

Among the beagles and fox terriers, the dogs that had had a disciplined upbringing ate sooner than did the indulged ones. Apparently, early experience was more important than the genetic differences between the strains. However, the basenjis of both the disciplined and indulged groups ate quickly. Not only that, the shetlands of both rearing groups were greatly inhibited, some not eating at all. In the latter two cases, genetic differences prevailed over experience. There are now many studies showing that the effects of experience depend greatly on the genetic constitution, and vice versa (see Chap. 9).

Differences in fighting between strains of mice are influenced by the amount of handling during infancy (Porter 1972). One can effectively select for building large or small nests in mice, but lowering the temperature causes both lines to make larger nests (Lynch & Sanchez 1975). Male chickens selected for frequent or infrequent mating are differentially responsive to androgen after castration, the low line showing the larger response (McCollom et al. 1971). Vale et al. (1972) tested the effect of administering exogenous androgen to neonatal female mice. Ordinarily, only male mice fight as adults. In this case, the treated females from the aggressive strain were fighters as adults, but the treated females from two unaggressive strains were largely unaffected by androgen.

Experiments such as these demonstrate that responsiveness to the environment must be considered in relation to the genotype. But they do not tell us much about the way environment and genotype interact. Nor is it easy to extract from such data information about the processes involved. More useful here are experiments that seek to isolate especially pregnant events.

The environmental hand on the genetic switch

The two experiments that immediately follow have an air of the artificial about them. They serve, however, as useful models for experiments that might be cast in a more natural context.

Environmental priming. Some inbred strains of mice have seizures when they are exposed to loud sounds, for example, over 100 dB for a minute. Pretreatment in certain strains increases the susceptibility to this audiogenic seizure. Deckard et al. (1976) selected bidirectionally for high and low responders. The mouse pups were exposed to loud sound (primed) at age 19 days, then tested with sound at 22 to 27 days. Seizures were eliminated in the low line. They occurred in the high line, but only after priming. Deckard et al. suggested that the priming and the seizure itself are mediated by separate genetic mechanisms. If so, priming is a genetically controlled form of plasticity.

Suzuki (1974) reported a similar case of environmental priming in a fruit fly. The mutant stonedst gives a jump response when the light is turned off. It fails to do so if reared in the dark and then briefly exposed to light. The jump response requires one 30-minute exposure to light before it appears.

Naturally occurring environmental switches. The world is full of examples, but they are seldom recognized for what they are. One of the most familiar examples is pregnancy, in which the embryo triggers a host of genetic switches regulating the mother's physiology. In a complementary way, the mother provides an environment for the fetus that is rich in maternal chemical signals that trigger genetically mediated responses in the embryo. Womb mates occur in many mammals, and these can communicate chemically to one another's genomes, as in the case of sex-altered calves, the freemartins.

Sequentially hermaphroditic fishes, of which there are many kinds, provide a spectacular example of behavioral control of gene expression. In the cleaner wrasse, *Labroides dimidiatus,* one male dominates a small harem of females within his territory. Within a day or so after his removal, the dominant female begins to behave like a male; about a week later, she is well on her way to having functional testes and atrophied ovaries (Robertson 1972).

A poeciliid fish provides a constructive example here for comparison with the work of Kallman and Schreibman (1973) on the platyfish mentioned in the preceding section. Recall that the genetic differences between three combinations of two alleles were correlated with three sizes at which the male fish matured and grew no more. In a related poeciliid, *Xiphophorus variatus,* males also stop growing when they mature. But here the timing of maturation is a response to social feedback. When a fish is subordinate, it forestalls sexual maturity and continues to grow until it becomes dominant by virtue of larger size. Consequently, each next subordinate grows progressively larger, leapfrogging the dominant fish in the social group (Borowsky 1973).

Thus, in closely related fishes it is possible in the one case to have an internally controlled timing of switching to the sexual mode – one's own size provides the signal. In the other species the information to become reproductive derives from the social environment, which would seem more adaptive. But the best strategy of development for one species may not be the best for another.

Environmental masking. One last piece of evidence must be considered in the gene–environment issue. We tend to think of the environment as a rich source of variation, providing the impetus for development to run off this way or that in a Waddingtonian epigenetic landscape. In fact, the environment in which the laboratory subject develops can be so impoverished that development becomes enormously canalized, concealing the genetic differences between individuals. Henderson's studies have nicely illustrated this point. (See also Chap. 9 for an example of differences that are minimal in impoverished and rich environments but large in an intermediate situation.)

Henderson (1970) utilized six inbred strains of mice for a diallel analysis of the parental strains and 30 F_1 crosses. Representatives of all groups were raised in either a standard (impoverished) or an enriched environment. The test consisted of solving a maze with ladders and tubes that shared some features with the enriched environment. Not surprisingly, enriched mice were best at solving the maze.

The noteworthy outcome of Henderson's study was that in the case of the standard mice the genetic differences accounted for only 10% of the variation; for the enriched mice 40% of the variation was genetic. Using only the standard cage, an investigator could well have concluded that genetic variation was of no consequence, which would have been correct for that environment. But "investigators must be aware of the possibility that early environmental interactions with genotype may limit the validity of their findings to their own unique laboratory situation" (Henderson 1970:510–511).

CLOSING COMMENTS

The goal of most developmental studies of behavior appears to be to illuminate the effects of experience. The genetic part of the system becomes a given; indeed, it is commonly buried in euphemisms such as "maturation" or "biological basis." Too often, the genetic system is regarded in the same way that we do weather: Because you can't do anything about it, just accommodate to it.

This attitude is inherent in the logical distinction that relegates genetics to differences between individuals and the effects of experience to differences within the life of an individual (Lehrman 1970). But even though development may be assessed across individuals, the natural and prudent approach is to analyze the development of individuals (Chap. 4).

The time has come for students of behavior to face the reality that development is truly epigenetic. It is likely that within a few years it will be possible to switch genes on and off during ontogeny in order to assess their roles in development. Using an experimental approach in which gene action and environment are manipulated in a balanced design, and with a time base, we should be able to make progress in the analysis of development. I will return to this point in closing, after considering some other issues pertinent to the interaction of genes and environment.

Is it possible to alter a genetically canalized behavior such that it becomes susceptible to experience with the external environment? If so, we would have a marvelous tool for exploring developmental processes.

In an early paper, Hinde (1956:209) made passing note of the "exceptional imitative abilities" of some bird hybrids. He suggested that the tendency of the parent species to constrain song learning to their own cardueline finch species had been upset in the hybrids. One wonders how general this characteristic might be (recall the plasticity of switch-sidling in hybrid male *Agapornis* [Dilger 1962b] and the greater variability of hybrid *Streptopelia* doves [Davies 1970]).

Waddington (1975:82) reflected on the finding that some traits can be more canalized (buffered against environmental influences) in one genome than in another. He then suggested that a change in a major gene might open up that trait to the environment by destabilizing the developmental processes. Waddington had in mind selecting for resistance to the harmful effect of high temperature on the eye facets of *Drosophila.* The nature of the developmental processes, and how they might work, was left unexplained.

Hybrid grasshoppers in Waddington's epigenetic landscape

I am struck with the possibility of exploiting hybrids such as grasshoppers and their songs (Helversen & Helversen 1975a, 1975b). Recall that the hybrids of both sexes were highly variable in the F_1 generation. The variation took the form of each individual expressing the calls for both parent species, but in varying mixtures; the same applied to the perception of calls. In addition, there was a wide range in readiness to respond; that suggested a separate system for thresholds and one that results from a mixture, even an inhibition, of the mechanism from the two parent species.

I was reminded of Waddington's epigenetic landscape. He presented the analogy for development of a ball rolling down a valley in a landscape. The flatter the valley, the easier it is to dislodge the ball from its path by means of extraneous forces (i.e., not greatly canalized). The deeper the valley, the more inevitable the trajectory of development (buffered, canalized). At times the ball encounters a Y-junction; presumably the two pathways represent alternative routes of development.

The hybrid grasshoppers seem to have had two separate landscapes, developing both communicatory systems and expressing bits of each. However, it is possible that they had developed in a truly hybrid landscape, with many more pathways down which to roll. The ball would have trundled down now a valley of one species, now that of the other. Perhaps hybridization tended to flatten the hybrid epigenetic landscape.

I realize that this is only an analogy. Furthermore, calling and responding in grasshoppers is a highly canalized system. So, it may be asking too much to expect the hybrids to be more open to the postembryonic environment. The interesting environmental effects probably occur during embryogenesis.

The choice of behavior

Most of us, with apologies to the embryologists and their fascinating research, are concerned with the role of the environment that is external to the animal. That is a variable source of information, largely independent of the information in the developing organism's genome (related organisms and products of one's own behavior, such as nests, are only partly nondependent). Consequently, we concentrate on experience that is received via functioning sensory systems. Sensory competence develops fairly late in the embryo's life, and at different rates in different modalities (Gottlieb 1976). All of this means that we are mainly interested in experience after hatching or birth, or shortly before (but see Chap. 6).

Waddington argued that when the environment is highly predictable, and when it is also important that an animal respond during development to that environment, then canalization will produce a threshold or switch-on response to meet that environmental situation. But when a switch mechanism exists, there is the chance that the wrong stimulus may activate it.

> As the canalization will only have been built up by natural selection if there is an advantage in regular production of the optimum response, there will be a selective value in such a suppression of the environment by the even more regularly acting gene. *Such a gene must always act before the normal time at which the environmental stimulus was applied,* otherwise its work would already be done for it, and it could have no appreciable selective advantage. [Waddington 1975:21; italics added]

For the most part, visual displays of animals seem to fall into the kind of behavior that completes its development before it is called into use (Barlow 1977; Bentley & Hoy 1970; Edwards & Palka 1976). However, other types of MAPs show progressive changes during ontogeny, suggesting the possibility of continuing gene–environment interaction. Good examples are the development of MAPs used in food handling among birds (e.g., Kear 1962; Smith 1972) and mammals (e.g., Eibl-Eibesfeldt 1956a, 1956b). Moreover MAPs used in displays are often made up of elements that are less than absolutely coupled, and considerable refinement of coordination may occur. The MAPs themselves are often linked to varying degrees with other MAPs (e.g., Wyman & Ward 1973). The connectivity of the elements, and of MAPs, should be particularly fertile ground in the search for effective environmental factors.

The concept of rate-limiting processes may be pertinent here. Because MAPs most likely develop before they emerge, they act as though their expression is denied until some other process is completed. A simple example would be reproductive behavior that does not surface until facilitated by sex hormones.

Soll (1979) has put forth a program for distinguishing between three different models of rate-limiting processes, termed *simple, sequential,* and *parallel.* Testing is done by comparing the time taken to develop from one stage to another at different temperatures. The approach could be applied nicely to the development of behavior in poikilotherms such as fishes and lizards. Combined with genetic differences, as in populations of the goodeid fishes *Xenotoca,* such an undertaking could be most revealing.

Attack–escape behavior. An ideal system for longitudinal study of its MAPs is the attack–escape system, often called *agonistic behavior.* In animals that grow up in a social group, such behavior starts to emerge remarkably early; it can lead to dominance relations among nursing kittens, puppies, and swine, and between nestling birds, often while they are motorically weak and have their eyes still shut (e.g., Ewer 1961; McBride 1963). In what is one of the finest but seldom cited papers in behavioral development, Kruijt (1964) described the early separate appearances of escape and attack in chicks and their subsequent integration. Ohm (1964) presented data on the very first appearance of each of the numerous MAPs of agonistic behavior in a school of young cichlid fish; some MAPs emerged singly, others in clusters.

Agonistic behavior has the further advantage that its MAPs are distinctive and numerous, occur often, and are frequently incorporated into the sexual behavior of the adult, thus widening the scope and significance of such ontogenetic studies. Yet, little is known about such ontogeny, even descriptively; experiments on the role of experience here are almost nonexistent. Genetic differences, furthermore, are unstudied. And beyond the role of sexual hormones, nothing is known about sequential gene action in this pattern or about gene–environment interaction.

One disadvantage of agonistic MAPs is that they involve two individuals, even if one is only a mirror image. That greatly complicates matters. But if one wants to study the development of interactions themselves, there is no better system. MAPs and their orientation provide salient events to measure, whether in and of themselves or as indicators of relationships.

Grooming. I originally discounted the utility of grooming because it is such a complex behavior with appreciable within-individual variation. A number of points led me to reconsider, however.

Grooming is a good choice for several reasons: (1) it is frequent, which enables screening for differences; (2) it is self-directed, which removes as a source of variation another individual (see Chap. 12); (3) it consists of simple, repetitive elements; (4) the elements occur in sequences segmented into bouts that appear to have relatively straightforward rules of relationships (Chap. 12), or grammar (Dawkins & Dawkins 1976); (5) it seems to be a nice blend of centrally generated patterning and functional feedback control from the periphery; and (6) it occurs throughout the life of an individual, so its ontogeny can be tracked.

The obvious organisms to study are fruit flies and mice. Fruit flies have the advantage that their genetics is well known and genetic engineering is feasible. Their grooming behavior is relatively uncomplicated (Szebenyi 1969), so screening for differences is realistic.

Also, Dawkins and Dawkins (1976) have established in another fly some fairly simple rules of grammar for grooming, and some individuals showed promising differences in replaceability of elements. There exists, therefore, a lability in the connectivity of the elements that might prove exploitable. (It is unclear just how responsive grooming is to external stimulation; the article by Heinz [1949] is sometimes cited as evidence that the behavior is insensitive to peripheral input, but a closer reading of his paper suggests that the question remains open.)

Mice have their advantages. The main one is that grooming shows a distinct ontogenetic progression after birth (Chap. 12).Therefore, there is scope for manipulation. The other advantage is that grooming is responsive to external stimulation. (But if mouse grooming were actually annointing, as in gerbils (Thiessen personal communication), one would predict that peripheral input would be less salient because there could be a program for the most effective method of spreading the secretion.)

The most attractive feature of mouse grooming, however, is that the behavior might be both a series of MAPs and a kind of behavior that Turvey et al. (1978) would consider under action theory (see also Lashley 1951; Chap. 12). Action theory deals with motor output that seems guided by a higher-order goal, as in making the letter *A* with a pen held in the hand, or with a foot, or by the mouth. A MAP, in contrast, implies a central motor program that is specific to the effectors involved. In the final analysis, their neurological organization may not be so different, but action-theory behavior is clearly more open to experiential influence.

To return to the mouse, Golani (Chap. 13) observed a pup grooming its face. The normal free action of one arm was blocked by another pup. To accommodate, the pup moved its entire body up and down, deriving the motion from leg and shoulder movements, to produce the rotary relationship between paw and face. That was clearly a goal-directed modification of a MAP. Because that was a unique observation, one cannot know if the MAP was open only at that stage, which would be the more interesting if it were.

Analyses of grooming in flies and the ontogeny of grooming in mice could be made especially meaningful by introducing genetic differences. These exist in inbred strains and in known mutants. Such differences should be further sought, selected for, analyzed genetically, and tested during development in different environments.

Other systems. Criteria for the choice of other behavioral subsystems include the presence of a number of MAPs or their components, early appearance and progressive development, and sufficiently wide distribution across species and higher taxa to allow relevant generalizations; various methods of food handling are obvious candidates. Some systems are limited in occurrence but offer other advantages, such as being found in highly inbred strains. A good case in point is nest building in mice. It emerges early in ontogeny, consists of a complex set of behaviors, and shows clear developmental differences between strains (Oortmerssen 1970).

Using genetics to open development to experience

I am particularly taken by the milk model because it is so tangible, and because it suggests another way to open behavior to environmental modification. Phase-specific learning is an obvious kind of behavior to think about in this context. How could one manipulate when and how long the "window" for learning is open? Hybrids could provide the answer.

We need a hybrid between a species that shows sexual imprinting and one that does not. Ideally, derivative F_2 and backcross generations would be viable. Among anatid ducks one would seek a monomorphic species as one parent because both sexes imprint; the other parent would be a highly dimorphic species, with exclusively female parental care, so that the females do not imprint sexually (Schutz 1965). Parallel cases might be found in monogamous and lekking species of gallinaceous birds, or in finches (e.g., Sonnemann & Sjölander 1977).

It is impossible to predict whether the hybrids would be intermediate or a mixture. The F_2 generation should provide a rich spectrum of various degrees of imprintability and independence from experience. One could only imagine how phenomena such as length and timing of the sensitive period would sort out, and how one could select for differences.

Comparable analyses could be done using hybrids from poeciliid fishes. One parent could have a fixed time for the onset of sexual maturity, the other an open time, that is, be timed by social interaction.

MAPs could still be involved and provide perhaps the best material. Bird songs are ideal in that they are stereotyped, species-specific, and rendered quantitative by audiospectrograms. Learning is involved in all the species so far studied (Kroodsma 1977; Chap. 20). In some species, most of the song is learned; in others, experience seems to fill in an already existing template (Hinde 1969). If strains of domestic canaries differ in the degree to which their songs are learned, they would be ideal subjects. Unfortunately, interspecific hybrids of song birds are often difficult to produce or are sterile.

Imagine, nonetheless, the genetic recombinations possible for what is most likely a polygenic system. Birds might be produced with distinctly different dependence on learning, and even for different characteristics of the songs. The phasing of the behavior might also be opened up. An individual might learn novel songs but still show savings when learning one parent type. The motor program for song and its perceptual filter might become completely uncoupled. I can conceive of a bird having a filter for one song and a motor program for another. How would it behave as it developed its song? Could it teach itself the wrong song?

This idea has appeal because it would mean studying the genetics of constraints and predispositions in learning. It would make meaningful the dictum that behavior is the outcome of a complex genome–environment interaction.

It is tempting at this point to describe the ideal program for a developmental genetic analysis of MAPs. One would want systematically to vary the genome and the experience while tracing the developmental trajectory of some bit of aggressive behavior or of the grammar of grooming. Genetic or surgical mosaics would locate the source of the behavior, and the biochemical products of the genetic loci would be followed into the complexities of physiology. Meanwhile, the genes would be switched on and off physically, and in relation to the developmental stage and the environmental surround. It might even be possible to insert single genes into a zygote (Marx 1978), the reverse of knocking genes out.

That state of scientific nirvana is a long way off, and this chapter is becoming too long. I will end it with a few comments about the genetics of human behavior, in keeping with the interdisciplinary spirit of this volume.

Developmental genetics of human behavior

Experiments, in the strict sense, are out of the question. We can, however, parasitize the experiments that society unwittingly provides in the form of adoptions, which are free-form cross-fostering experiments (DeFries & Plomin 1978). These studies do not yet deal with MAPs, but they could in the future.

The pedigree method is helpful for some human traits. But then such traits usually stem from differences in major genes. They are thus often deleterious, and commonly they are sex-linked. I know of none that provides information about MAPs. And because MAPs in humans, as in our rich facial expressions or the numerous distinctive actions of infants, are doubtless polygenic, the pedigree method is too slow to be of use. Some behavior in infants, however, might be controlled by switch genes. I think here of crawling versus sliding on one's bottom for first locomotion in some infants; the pedigree method might be applicable for such memorable differences.

In this realm, then, we are tempted to resort to inference by analogy. That can be dangerous. It is true that there is a remarkable universality of genetic mechanisms in all living organisms, and this holds in exquisite detail among mammals. Yet the phenotypic expressions can be so different that we dare not overgeneralize. That is why the study of development is so fascinating. How can such conservative genetic machinery, and probably basic developmental processes, produce the vast array of plants and animals that populate the earth, of which we humans are only one?

SUMMARY

This chapter was written to persuade the reader to accept three conclusions: (1) genetic differences during development are fundamental to development; (2) stereotyped motor output is the best trait for tracking behavior through ontogeny; (3) the analysis of stereotyped motor output will provide a more meaningful behavioral genetics than presently exists.

Genes express themselves through their products, proteins, which regulate metabolic activity and the process of development. All cells have all genes, but at any time only a few genes are active; the highest levels of genetic activity occur early, during rapid development. Otherwise, genes are repressed by histone proteins. A variety of feedback relationships are set up as different cell lineages appear and develop along fated paths.

For each gene there are usually alternate forms, alleles, which sometimes exist in large numbers in a population. Much of this richness appears to be unused. Further, genetic differences are greatly augmented by altering the chromosomal environment, as through crossing over between chromosomes and the loss or duplication of some or parts of them. That males and females have distinct sex chromosomes accounts in large measure for the maternal (or paternal) bias in the inheritance of some traits, though other mechanisms also exist.

There are several methods of genetic analysis. These include the traditional crossing experiments, together with backcrossing and the production of a second-generation progeny of siblings. In some instances mutations are chemically induced. Analysis is also helped through chromosomal mapping, using frequency of crossing over. Mapping studies were precursors to the exciting use of fate maps in sexual mosaics in the fruit fly.

Behavioral traits are polygenic, so quantitative methods of analysis are often required because changes in one gene are usually so hard to detect, though major or switch genes may mimic simple Mendelian inheritance. Hybrids between species, however, provide abundant obvious behavioral differences. At a more sophisticated level, inbred homozygous strains provide more manageable genetic differences in behavior. Three or more such strains can be bred in all possible reciprocal crosses (diallel analysis) to produce considerable information about mode of inheritance. Another powerful technique is that of selecting for differences, sometimes starting with a founder stock made by crossing two inbred strains.

There is considerable evidence demonstrating that differences in stereotyped motor patterns result from genetic differences. (Regularly recurring motor performances, as in displays and grooming, are called modal action patterns, or MAPs.) Hybrids illustrate how the form, orientation, and sequencing of MAPs correlate with genetic differences. Hybrids also raise questions of interest to developmental ethologists, as when two motor (or sensory) systems appear to compete for expression in the phenotype. The evidence from hybrids negates the idea that a signal (MAP) and its sensory detector are genetically coupled. Differences in MAPs are also found between populations of the same species, providing a splendid opportunity for research.

An intriguing observation is that individuals in some species have the potential to express behavior that they ordinarily do not. How is such information maintained in the genome? And what does it tell us about genetic ensembles for behavior traits? On the other hand, intensive inbreeding of the type often practiced in domestication may lead to inbreeding depression.

There have been some attempts to link genetic effects on the nervous system to changes in behavior. So far, a number of mutations have been uncovered or produced that have large effects, almost always detrimental ones. More informative have been sexual mosaics in *Drosophila.* However, genetic "lesions" of the nervous system have in some cases been refined to an exceptional degree.

Of more interest to development are studies on the timing of genetic activity. Some mutants show distinct temporal peaks in sensitivity to altered environments. Normal sexual maturation is an excellent example of a timed genetic activation of a system and how it responds to environmental differences. Studies of immature animals, using hormones and other techniques, indicate that the forms of MAPs have been laid down in the organization of the central nervous system before they are called into play. Also noteworthy is the possibility of switching certain genes on and off during development by manipulating temperature. Finally, feedback from the environment can be decisive in switching genes on or off or in keeping them on.

Thus gene–environment interaction becomes central to understanding development. This position has been generally advocated but interpreted too often to mean studying experiential factors without regard to genetic differences. Treating genome and environment as independent variables in the same experiment has proved highly informative about the production of the phenotype.

Hybrids are attractive here because of the evidence, admittedly fragmentary, that they may be more open than their parent species to environmental effects during development. They also present challenges in other ways. For example, a hybrid or a selected descendant might have a predisposition on the sensory side to attend to one MAP, for example, a song but a motor predisposition to produce a different one.

The best behavioral system for ontogenetic analysis should have a large repertoire of MAPs, at least some of which should appear early. The system should also be found in most higher animals for comparative studies and for understanding the differences. By these criteria, the attack–escape system is the preferred one, but it is complicated by the need for interaction between two individuals. Grooming has some features that recommend it; for example, it can be done by a single subject. Human behavior could be approached in the same way, using large samples and adoption studies.

ACKNOWLEDGMENTS

For their patience in reading this chapter and for their thoughtful suggestions for its improvement, I am grateful to Gordon Burghardt, Stephen E. Glickman, David L. G. Noakes, Lewis Petrinovich, Robert Plomin and David B. Wake. I would also like to express my warm thanks to Gerta M. Barlow for her understanding, and for translating my obscure handwriting into the first typewritten draft. Colin G. Barnett, Terrance M. Lim, and William Rogers helped in filtering out the numerous technical defects, for which aid I gladly thank them.

REFERENCES

Alexander, R. D. 1962. Evolutionary change in cricket acoustical communication. *Evolution* 16:443–467.

1968. Life cycle origins, speciation, and related phenomena in crickets. *Quarterly Review of Biology* 43:1–41.

Andrew, R. J. 1963. Effects of testosterone on the behavior of the domestic chick. *Journal of Comparative and Physiological Psychology* 56:933–940.

Ayala, F. J. 1980. Genetic and evolutionary relationships of apes and humans. *In:* H. Markl (ed.), *Evolution of social behavior: hypotheses and empirical tests.* Verlag Chemie, Deerfield Beach, Florida, pp. 147–162.

Baerends, G. P., & G. J. Blockzijl. 1963. Gedanken über das Entstehen von Formdivergenzen zwischen homologen Signalhandlungen verwandter Arten. *Zeitschrift für Tierpsychologie* 20:517–528.

Balthazart, J. 1974. Short-term effects of testosterone propionate on the behaviour of young intact male domestic ducks (*Anas platyrhynchos*). *Psychologica Belgica* 14:1–10.

Balthazart, J., & M. Stevens. 1975. Effects of testosterone propionate on the social behaviour of groups of male domestic ducklings *Anas platyrhynchos* L. *Animal Behaviour* 23:926–931.

Barlow, G. W. 1968. Ethological units of behavior. *In:* D. Ingle (ed.), *The central nervous system and fish behavior.* University of Chicago Press, Chicago, pp. 217–232.

1977. Modal action patterns. *In:* T. A. Sebeok (ed.), *How animals communicate.* Indiana University Press, Bloomington, pp. 98–134.

Bauer, J. 1968. Vergleichende Untersuchungen zum Kontaktverhalten verschiedener Arten der Gattung *Tilapia* (Cichlidae, Pisces) und ihrer Bastarde. *Zeitschrift für Tierpsychologie* 25:22–70.

Bentley, D. R. 1971. Genetic control of an insect neuronal network. *Science* 174:1139–1141.

1975. Single gene cricket mutations: effects on behavior, sensilla, sensory neurons, and identified interneurons. *Science* 187:760–764.

Bentley, D. R., & R. R. Hoy. 1970. Postembryonic development of adult motor patterns in crickets: a neural analysis. *Science* 170:1409–1411.

1972. Genetic control of the neuronal network generating cricket (*Teleogryllus gryllus*) song patterns. *Animal Behaviour* 10:478–492.

Benzer, S. 1973. Genetic dissection of behavior. *Scientific American* 229(6):24–37.

Blair, W. F. 1955. Mating call and stage of speciation in the *Microhyla olivacea - M. carolinensis* complex. *Evolution* 9:469–480.

1956. The mating calls of hybrid toads. *Texas Journal of Science* 8:350–355.

Borowsky, R. L. 1973. Social control of adult size in males of *Xiphophorus variatus. Nature* 245:332–335.

Brestowsky, V. M. 1968. Vergleichende Untersuchungen zur Elternbindung von *Tilapia*-Jungfischen (Cichlidae, Pisces). *Zeitschrift für Tierpsychologie* 25:761–828.

Broadhurst, P. L., D. W. Fulker, & J. Wilcock. 1974. Behavioral genetics. *Annual Review of Psychology* 25:389–415.

Broadhurst, P. L., & J. L. Jinks. 1963. The inheritance of mammalian behavior re-examined. *Heredity* 54:170–176.

Buckley, P. A. 1969. Disruption of species-typical behavior patterns in F_1 hybrid *Agapornis* parrots. *Zeitschrift für Tierpsychologie* 26:737–743.

Caplan, A. I., & C. P. Ordahl. 1978. Irreversible gene repression model for control of development. *Science* 201:120–130.

Cherry, L. M., S. M. Case, & A. C. Wilson. 1978. Frog perspectives on the morphological difference between humans and chimpanzees. *Science* 200:209–211.

Cherry, L. M., S. M. Case, J. G. Kunkel, & A. C. Wilson. 1979. Comparisons of frogs, humans, and chimpanzees. *Science* 204:435.

Clarke, E., L. R. Aronson, & M. Gordon. 1954. Mating behavior patterns in two species of xiphophorin fishes; their inheritance and significance in sexual isolation. *Bulletin of the American Museum of Natural History* 103:141–225.

Cole, C. J. 1975. Evolution of parthenogenetic species of reptiles. *In:* R. Reinboth (ed.), *Intersexuality in the animal kingdom.* Springer, New York, pp. 340–355.

Darnell, J. E., Jr. 1978. Implications of RNA-RNA splicing in the evolution of eukaryotic cells. *Science* 202:1257–1260.

Davidson, E. H. 1976. *Gene activity in early development,* 2nd ed. Academic Press, New York.

Davies, S. J. J. F. 1970. Patterns of inheritance in the bowing display and associated behavior of some hybrid *Streptopelia* doves. *Behaviour* 36:187–214.

Dawkins, R. 1976. Hierarchical organisation: a candidate principle for ethology. *In:* P. P .G. Bateson & R. A. Hinde (eds.), *Growing points in ethology.* Cambridge University Press, Cambridge, pp. 7–54.

Dawkins, R., & M. Dawkins. 1976. Hierarchical organisation and postural facilitation: rules for grooming in flies. *Animal Behaviour* 24:739–755.

Deckard, B. S., J. M. Tepper, & K. Schlesinger. 1976. Selective breeding for acoustic priming. *Behavior Genetics* 6:375–383.

DeFries, J. C. 1980. Genetics of animal and human behavior. *In:* G. W. Barlow & J. Silverberg (eds.), *Sociobiology: beyond nature/nurture?* American Association for the Advancement of Science Selected Symposium Number 35, Westview Press, Boulder, Colorado, pp. 273–294.

DeFries, J. C., & R. Plomin. 1978. Behavioral genetics. *Annual Review of Psychology* 29:473–515.

DeFries, J. C., E. A. Thomas, J. P. Hegmann, & M. W. Weir. 1967. Open-field behavior in mice: analysis of maternal effects by means of ovarian transplantation. *Psychonomic Science* 8:207–208.

Desforges, M. F., & D. G. M. Wood-Gush. 1976. Behavioural comparison of Aylesbury and mallard ducks: sexual behaviour. *Animal Behaviour* 24:391–397.

Dilger, W. C. 1962a. Behavior and genetics. *In:* E. L. Bliss (ed.), *Roots of behavior.* Harper, New York, pp. 35–47.

1962b. The behavior of lovebirds. *Scientific American* 206:88–98.

Dobzhansky, T. 1970. *Genetics of the evolutionary process.* Columbia University Press, New York.

1972. Genetics and diversity of behavior. *American Psychologist* 27:523–530.

Edwards, J. S., & J. Palka. 1976. Neural generation and regeneration in insects. *In:* J. C. Fentress (ed.), *Simpler networks and behavior.* Sinauer, Sunderland, Massachusetts, pp. 167–185.

Eibl-Eibesfeldt, I. 1956a. Über die ontogenetische Entwicklung der Technik des Nüsseoffnens vom Eichhörnchen (*Sciurus vulgaris* L.). *Zeitschrift für Säugetierkunde* 21:132–134.

1956b. Angeborenes und Erworbenes in der Technik des Beutetotens (Versuche am Iltes, *Putorius putorius* L.). *Zeitschrift fur Saugetierkunde 21:135–137.*

Erlenmeyer-Kimling, L. 1975. Commentary I. *In:* K. W. Schaie, V. E. Anderson, G. E. McClearn, & J. Money (eds.), *Developmental human behavior genetics.* Heath, London, pp. 25–31.

Ewer, R. F. 1961. Further observations on suckling behavior in kittens, together with some general considerations of the interrelations of innate and acquired responses. *Behaviour* 17:247–260.

Ewing, A. W., & A. Manning. 1967. The evolution and genetics of insect behaviour. *Annual Review of Entomology* 12:471–494.

Findley, J. S. 1979. Comparisons of frogs, humans and chimpanzees. *Science* 204:434–435.

Fitzimons, J. M. 1976. Ethological isolating mechanisms in goodeid fishes of the genus *Xenotoca* (Cyprinodontiformes, Osteichthyes). *Bulletin of the Southern California Academy of Science* 75:84–99.

Franck, D. 1970. Verhaltensgenetische Untersuchungen an Artbastarden der Gattung *Xiphophorus* (Pisces). *Zeitschrift für Tierpsychologie* 27:1–34.

1974. The genetic basis of evolutionary changes in behaviour patterns. *In:* J. H. F. van Abeelen (ed.), *The genetics of behaviour.* North Holland, Amsterdam, pp. 119-140.

Freedman, D. G. 1958. Constitutional and environmental interactions in rearing of four breeds of dog. *Science* 127:585–586.

Frisch, R. E. 1974. Critical weight at menarche, initiation of the adolescent growth spurt, and control of menarche. *In:* M. M. Brumbach, G. D. Grave, & F. E. Mayer (eds.), *Control of onset of puberty.* Wiley, New York, pp. 443–457.

1978. Population, food intake, and fertility. *Science* 199:22–29.

Gerhardt, H. C. 1978. Temperature coupling in the vocal communication system of the gray tree frog, *Hyla versicolor. Science* 199:992–994.

Gorman, G. C. 1969. Intermediate territorial display of a hybrid *Anolis* lizard (Sauria: Iguanidae). *Zeitschrift für Tierpsychologie* 26:390–393.

Gottesman, I. I. 1975. Possible directions for developmental human behavior genetics. *In:* K. W. Schaie, V. E. Anderson, G. E. McClearn, & J. Money (eds.), *Developmental human behavior genetics.* Heath, London, pp. 221–225.

Gottlieb, G. 1976. Conceptions of prenatal development: behavioral embryology. *Psychological Review* 83:215–234.

Gwadz, R. W. 1970. Monofactorial inheritance of early sexual receptivity in the mosquito *Aëdes atropalpus. Animal Behaviour* 18:358–361.

Hamilton, T. H. 1968. Control by estrogen of genetic transcription and translation. *Science* 161:649–661.

Harris, H. 1970. *The principles of human biochemical genetics.* American Elsevier, New York.

Hegmann, J. P. 1975. The response to selection for altered conduction velocity in mice. *Behavioral Biology* 13:413–423.

Heinrich, W. 1967. Untersuchungen zum Sexualverhalten in der Gattung *Tilapia* (Cichlidae, Teleostei) und bei Artbastarden. *Zeitschrift für Tierpsychologie* 24:684–754.

Heinz, H. J. 1949. Vergleichende Beobachtungen über die Putzhandlungen bei Dipteren im allgemeinen und bei *Sarcophaga carnaria* L. im besonderen. *Zeitschrift für Tierpsychologie* 6:330–371.

Helversen, O. von, & N. Elsner. 1977. The stridulatory movements of acridid grasshoppers recorded with an opto-electronic device. *Journal of Comparative Physiology* 122:53–64.

Helversen, D. von, & O. von Helversen. 1975a. Verhaltensgenetische Untersuchungen am akustischen Kommunikationssystem der Feldheuschrecken (Orthoptera, Acrididae). 1. Der Gesang von Artbastarden zwischen *Chorthippus biguttulus* und *Ch. mollis. Journal of Comparative Physiology* 104:273–299.

1975b. Verhaltensgenetische Untersuchungen am akustischen Kommunikationssystem der Feldheuschrecken (Orthoptera, Acrididae). 2. Das Lautschema von Artbastarden zwischen *Chorthippus biguttulus* und *Ch. mollis. Journal of Comparative Physiology* 104:301–323.

Henderson, N. D. 1970. Genetic influences on the behavior of mice can be obscured by laboratory rearing. *Journal of Comparative and Physiological Psychology* 72:505–511.

Hinde, R. A. 1956. The behaviour of certain cardueline F_1 inter-species hybrids. *Behaviour* 9:202–213.

(ed.). 1969. *Bird vocalizations.* Cambridge University Press, Cambridge.

Hirsh, D., & R. Vanderslice. 1976. Temperature-sensitive developmental mutants of *Caenorhabditis elegans. Developmental Biology* 49:220–235.

Homyk, T. 1977. Behavioral mutants of *Drosophila melanogaster.* 2. Behavioral analysis and focus mapping. *Genetics* 87:105–128.

Homyk, T., & D. E. Sheppard. 1977. Behavioral mutants of *Drosophila melanogaster.* 1. Isolation and mapping of mutations which decrease flight ability. *Genetics* 87:95–104.

Hotta, Y., & S. Benzer. 1972. Mapping of behavior in *Drosophila* mosaics. *Nature* 240:527–535.

1976. Courtship in *Drosophila* mosaics: sex-specific foci for sequential action patterns. *Proceedings of the National Academy of Sciences U.S.A.* 73:4154–4158.

Hoy, R. R. 1974. Genetic control of acoustic behavior in crickets. *American Zoologist* 14:1067–1080.

Hoy, R. R., J. Hahn, & R. C. Paul. 1977. Hybrid cricket auditory behavior: evidence for genetic coupling in animal communication. *Science* 195:82–84.

Hoy, R. R., & R. C. Paul. 1973. Genetic control of song specificity in crickets. *Science* 180:82–83.

Jan, Y. N., & L. Y. Jan. 1978. Genetic dissection of short-term and long-term facilitation at the *Drosophila* neuromuscular junction. *Proceedings of the National Academy of Sciences U.S.A.* 75:515–519.

Kallman, K. D., & M. P. Schreibman. 1973. A sex-linked gene controlling gonadotrop differentiation and its significance in determining the age of sexual maturation and size of the platyfish *Xiphophorus maculatus. General and Comparative Endocrinology* 21:287–304.

Kaltenhäuser, D. 1971. Über Evolutionsvorgänge in des Schwimmentenbalz. *Zeitschrift für Tierpsychologie* 29:481–540.

Kear, J. 1962. Food selection in finches with special reference to interspecific differences. *Proceedings of the Zoological Society of London* 138:163–204.

King, M. C., & A. C. Wilson. 1975. Evolution at two levels in humans and chimpanzees. *Science* 188:107–116.

Kroodsma, D. E. 1977. A re-evaluation of song development in the song sparrow. *Animal Behaviour* 25:390–399.

Kruijt, J. P. 1964. Ontogeny of social behaviour in Burmese red junglefowl (*Gallus gallus spadiceus*) Bonnaterre. *Behaviour Supplement* 12:1–201.

Lashley, K. S. 1951. The problem of serial order in behavior. *In:* L. A. Jeffress (ed.), *Cerebral mechanisms in behavior.* Wiley, New York, pp. 112–136.

Lehrman, D. S. 1970. Semantic and conceptual issues in the nature–nurture problem. *In:* L. R. Aronson, E. Tobach, D. S. Lehrman, & J. S. Rosenblatt (eds.), *Development and evolution of behavior.* Freeman, San Francisco, pp. 17–52.

Lewontin, R. C. 1974. *The genetic basis of evolutionary change.* Columbia University Press, New York.

Leyhausen, P. 1950. Beobachtungen an Löwen-Tiger-Bastarden mit einige Bemerkungen zur Systematik der Grosskatzen. *Zeitschrift für Tierpsychologie* 7:46–83.

Lind, H., & H. Poulsen. 1963. On the morphology and behaviour of a hybrid between goosander and shelduck (*Mergus merganser* × *Tadorna tadorna*). *Zeitschrift für Tierpsychologie* 20:558–569.

Lorenz, K. 1958. The evolution of behavior. *Scientific American* 199:67–78.

Lynch, C. G., & E. R. Sanchez. 1975. Selection and genotype–environment interaction for nest-building in *Mus musculus. Behavior Genetics* 5:100–101.

Manning, A. 1959. The sexual behaviour of two sibling *Drosophila* species. *Behaviour* 15:123–145.

1975. Behaviour genetics and the study of behavioural evolution. *In:* G. P. Baerends, C. R. Beer, & A. Manning (eds.), *Essays on function and evolution in behaviour: Festschrift for Professor Niko Tinbergen.* Clarendon, Oxford, pp. 71–91.

1976. The place of genetics in the study of behaviour. *In:* P. P. G. Bateson & R. A. Hinde (eds.), *Growing points in ethology.* Cambridge University Press, Cambridge, pp. 327–343.

Markert, C. L., & R. M. Petters. 1977. Homozygous mouse embryos produced by microsurgery. *Journal of Experimental Zoology* 201:295–302.

Marler, P. 1973. Learning, genetics, and communication. *Social Research* 40:293–310.

Marx, J. L. 1978. Successful transplant of a functioning mammalian gene. *Science* 202:610.

Mason, W. 1979. Ontogeny of social behavior. *In:* J. G. Vandenbergh & P. Marler (eds.), *Social behavior and communication.* Plenum Press, New York, pp. 1–28.

McBride, G. 1963. The "teat order" and communication in young pigs. *Animal Behaviour* 11:53–56.

McClearn, G. E. 1970. Genetic influences on behavior and development. *In:* P. H. Mussen (ed.), *Charmichael's manual of child psychology,* 3rd ed., Vol. 1. Wiley, New York, pp. 39–76.

McCollom, R. E., P. B. Siegel, & H. P. van Krey. 1971. Responses to androgen in lines of chickens selected for mating behavior. *Hormones and Behavior* 2:31–42.

McEwen, B. S., & D. W. Pfaff. 1973. Chemical and physiological approaches to neuroendocrine mechanisms: attempts at integration. *In:* W. F. Ganong & L. Martini (eds.), *Frontiers in neuroendocrinology.* Oxford University Press, New York.

McGrath, T. A., M. D. Shalter, W. M. Schleidt, & P. Sarvella. 1972. Analysis of distress calls of chicken × pheasant hybrids. *Nature* 237:47–48.

Medawar, P. B. 1957. *The uniqueness of the individual.* Basic Books, New York.

Miller, D. B. 1977. Social displays of mallard ducks (*Anas platyrhynchos*): effects of domestication. *Journal of Comparative and Physiological Psychology* 91:221–232.

Nicolai, J. 1976. Evolutive Neuerungen in der Balz von Haustaubenrassen (*Columbia livia* var. *domestica*) als Ergebnis menschlicher Zuchtwahl. *Zeitschrift für Tierpsychologie* 40:225–243.

Ohm, D. 1964. Die Entwicklung des Kommentkampfverhaltens bei Jungcichliden. Ein ethologischer Vergleich zwischen *Aequidens latifrons* und *Ae. portalegrensis. Zeitschrift für Tierpsychologie* 21:308–325.

Omenn, G. W. 1976. Inborn errors of metabolism: clues to understanding human behavioral disorders. *Behavior Genetics* 6:263–284.

Oortmerssen, G. A. van. 1970. Biological significance, genetics and evolutionary origin of variability in behaviour within and between inbred strains of mice (*Mus musculus*). *Behaviour* 38:1–92.

Peiper, A. 1963. *Cerebral function in infancy and childhood.* Pitman, London.

Perdeck, A. C. 1958. The isolating value of specific song patterns in two sibling species of grasshoppers (*Chorthippus brunneus* Thunb. and *C. biguttulatus* L.). *Behaviour* 12:1–75.

Peters, H. M., & M. Brestowsky. 1961. Artbastarde in der Gattung *Tilapia* (Cichlidae, Teleostei) und ihr Verhalten. *Experientia* 17:261.

Plomin, R., J. C. DeFries, & J. C. Loehlin. 1977. Genotype–environment interaction and correlation in the analysis of human behavior. *Psychological Bulletin* 84:309–322.

Plomin, R., & A. R. Kuse. 1979. Genetic differences between humans and chimps and among humans. *American Psychologist* 34:188–190.

Plomin, R., & G. McClearn. 1979. Behavioral genetics. *In:* M. E. Meyer (ed.), *Foundations of contemporary psychology.* Oxford University Press, New York.

Pollack, G. S., & R. R. Hoy. 1979. Temporal pattern as a cue for species-specific calling song recognition in crickets. *Science* 204:429–432.

Porter, R. H. 1972. Infantile handling differentially effects (*sic*) inter-strain dominance interaction in mice. *Behavioral Biology* 7:415–420.

Poulsen, H. 1950. Morphological and ethological notes on a hybrid between a domestic duck and a domestic goose. *Behaviour* 3:99–103.

1953. A study of the incubation responses and some other behaviour patterns in birds. *Videnskabelige Meddelelser Dansk Naturhistorisk Forening* 115:1–131.

Ramsay, A. O. 1961. Behaviour of some hybrids in the mallard group. *Animal Behaviour* 9:104–105.

Robertson, D. R. 1972. Social control of sex reversal in a coral-reef fish. *Science* 177:1007–1009.

Rössler, E. 1976. Übertragung von Verhaltensweisen durch Transplantation von Anlagen neuroanatomischer Structuren bei Amphibien larven. 1. Xenoplastischer Austausch von Nachhirnanlagen zwischen *Xenopus laevus* und *Hymenochirus boettgeri* (Amphibia, Anura). *Zeitschrift für Tierpsychologie* 41:244–265.

Rothenbuhler, W. C. 1964. Behavior genetics of nest cleaning in honey bees. *American Zoologist* 4:111–123.

Royce, J. R., T. M. Holmes, & W. Poley. 1975. Behavior genetic analysis of mouse emotionality. 3. The diallel analysis. *Behavior Genetics* 5:351–372.

Schilcher, F. von, & A. Manning. 1975. Some aspects of sexual behavior in hybrids between *Drosophila melanogaster* and *Drosophila simulans*. *Behavior Genetics* 5:395–404.

Schutz, F. 1965. Sexuelle Prägung bei Anatiden. *Zeitschrift für Tierpsychologie* 22:50–103.

Sciandra, R. J., & J. Bennett. 1976. Behavior and single gene substitution in *Drosophila melanogaster*. 1. Mating and courtship differences with, *w*, *cn*, and *bw* loci. *Behavior Genetics* 6:205–218.

Sharpe, R. S., & P. A. Johnsgard. 1966. Inheritance of behavioral characters in F_2 mallard × pintail (*Anas platyrhynchos* × *Anas acuta*) hybrids. *Behaviour* 27:259–272.

Smith, S. M. 1972. The ontogeny of impaling behaviour in the loggerhead shrike, *Lanius ludovcianus* L. *Behaviour* 42:232–247.

Sohn, J. J., & D. Crews. 1977. Size-mediated onset of genetically determined maturation in the platyfish, *Xiphophorus maculatus*. *Proceedings of the National Academy of Sciences U.S.A.* 74:4547–4548.

Soll, D. R. 1979. Times in developing systems. *Science* 203:841–849.

Sonnemann, P., & S. Sjölander. 1977. Effects of cross-fostering on the sexual imprinting of the female zebra finch *Taeniopygia guttata*. *Zeitschrift für Tierpsychologie* 45:337–348.

Stein, G. S., J. S. Stein, & L. J. Kleinsmith. 1975. Chromosomal protein and gene regulation. *Scientific American* 232(2):46–57.

Stort, A. C. 1975. Genetic study of the aggressiveness of two subspecies of *Apis mellifera* in Brazil. 4. Number of stings in the gloves of the observer. *Behavior Genetics* 5:269–274.

Subtelny, S., & E. R. Konigsberg (eds.) 1979. *Determinants of spatial organization.* Thirty-seventh Symposium of the Society for Developmental Biology. Academic Press, New York.

Suzuki, D. T. 1970. Temperature sensitive mutations in *Drosophila melanogaster*. *Science* 170:695–706.

1974. Behavior in *Drosophila melanogaster*. A geneticist's view. *Canadian Journal of Genetic Cytology* 16:713–735.

Szebenyi, A. L. 1969. Cleaning behaviour in *Drosophila melanogaster*. *Animal Behaviour* 17:641–651.

Turvey, M. T., R. E. Shaw, & W. Mace. 1978. Issues in the theory of action: degrees of freedom, coordinative structures and coalitions. *In:* J. Requin (ed.), *Attention and performance VII.* Erlbaum, Hillsdale, New Jersey, pp. 557–595.

Vale, J. R., D. Ray, & C. A. Vale. 1972. The interaction of genotype and exogenous neonatal androgen: agonistic behavior in female mice. *Behavioral Biology* 7:321–334.

Waddington, C. H. 1975. *The evolution of an evolutionist.* Edinburgh University Press, Edinburgh.

Wall, W. von de. 1963. Bewegunsstudien an Anatiden. *Journal für Ornithologie* 104:1–15.

Ward, S. 1977. Invertebrate neurogenetics. *Annual Review of Genetics* 11:415–450.

Washburn, S. L. 1978. Human behavior and the behavior of other organisms. *American Psychologist* 33:405–418.

Whitney, G. 1970. Ontogeny of sonic vocalizations of laboratory mice. *Behavior Genetics* 1:269–273.

1973. Vocalization of mice influenced by a single gene in a heterogeneous population. *Behavior Genetics* 3:57–64.

Wilson, A. C., L. R. Maxon, & V. M. Sarich. 1974a. Two types of molecular evolution: evidence from studies of interspecific hybridization. *Proceeding of the National Academy of Sciences U.S.A.* 71:2843–2847.

Wilson, A. C., V. M. Sarich, & L. R. Maxon. 1974b. The importance of gene rearrangement in evolution: evidence from studies on rates of chromosomal, protein, and anatomical evolution. *Proceeding of the National Academy of Sciences U.S.A.* 71:3028–3030.

Wilson, R. S. 1972. Twins: early mental development. *Science* 175:914–917.

Wilt, F. H. 1972. The impact of molecular biology on study of cell differentiation. *In:* J. A. Behnke (ed.), *Challenging biological problems.* Oxford University Press, Oxford, pp. 81–109.

Wyman, R. J. 1976. A simple network for the study of neurogenetics. *In:* J. C. Fentress (ed.), *Simpler networks and behavior.* Sinauer, Sunderland, Massachusetts, pp. 153–166.

Wyman, R. L., & J. A. Ward. 1973. The development of behavior in the cichlid fish *Etroplus maculatus* (Bloch). *Zeitschrift für Tierpsychologie* 33:461–491.

Young, W. C., R. W. Goy, & C. H. Phoenix. 1964. Hormones and sexual behavior. *Science* 143:212–218.

9

ETHOLOGICAL BEHAVIORAL GENETICS AND DEVELOPMENT

ROBERT PLOMIN

When I began this chapter, I planned to consider ways in which behavioral genetics might be useful to ethologists interested in behavioral development. However, it quickly became apparent that an interdisciplinary *ethological behavioral genetic* approach would result in hybrid vigor with benefits to behavioral genetics as well as ethology. For this reason, the chapter has metamorphosed into an examination of the interface between the two disciplines. I shall consider three major differences in viewpoint that have caused ethology and behavioral genetics to keep their distance. These concern (1) differences between and within species, (2) the relationship between evolution and genetic variability, and (3) interaction between genes and environment. In the course of this discussion, I hope to illuminate the reasonableness of combining the techniques of ethology and behavioral genetics to advance our understanding of behavioral development.

DIFFERENCES BETWEEN AND WITHIN SPECIES

We may approach the study of behavior from one of three perspectives (Table 9.1). It is important to emphasize that perspectives are useful to varying degrees for various purposes – they are not right or wrong. The first perspective recognizes no important differences between or within species. Such a position is implied by classic psychological research in learning and is typified in titles of books such as *The Behavior of Organisms* (Skinner 1938). This view has largely given way to the second perspective, which recognizes differences between species. It characterizes comparative psychology and, indirectly, much current research on human behavior. Researchers interested in human behavior often study humans rather than other animals because they assume the existence of important species differences. The third perspective, which recognizes variability between and within species, is reflected in the focus of behavioral genetics.

These different perspectives may each be useful for particular purposes. However, it is my belief that a powerful science of behavior must recognize and explain the ubiquitous differences within as well as between species. The three perspectives are something like powers of a microscope. To a Martian landing on earth for the first time, we humans may not appear all that different from

Table 9.1. *Three approaches to the study of behavior*

Perspective	Examples
No important differences between or within species	Classical learning theories Molecular biology
Differences between but not within species	Ethology Comparative psychology
Differences between and within species	Behavioral genetics "Differential" psychology

Source: Adapted from Hirsch (1963).

squirrels. Humans are bigger and have somewhat less fur, but both have a brain, a heart, and four limbs. When we examine these species with a higher power setting on our microscope, differences emerge quickly. At this next power setting, however, all humans may seem much the same. For example, nearly all humans walk and talk. In the domain of behavior, this power setting has yielded some important information concerning common features of development in perception, cognition, and personality. However, it is important that some behavioral scientists switch their microscope to the highest resolving power in order to study differences within species, particularly the human species, because the questions that most often confront us are those involving such differences.

Although ethology need not be limited to any one of the three perspectives, most ethological research has focused on behavioral differences between species in its attempts to trace the evolutionary origins of such behavioral differences. Behavioral genetics, on the other hand, tends to focus on differences within species, attempting to determine the genetic and environmental origins of such differences in behavior. There is much to be gained by cross-fertilization between these two fields. Ethology will profit from a recognition of differences within species, and behavioral genetics will benefit from the evolutionary between-species focus of ethology.

Overshadowing the relationship between ethology and behavioral genetics, however, is sociobiology, and a brief digression is necessary to dispel the shadow. Although some proponents of sociobiology claim that it encompasses all fields from biology to sociology (Wilson 1975), sociobiology arose in reaction to Wynne-Edwards's (1962) group-selection explanation of altruistic behavior. Sociobiology (Hamilton 1964) countered with kinship-selection theory, which expanded Darwinian fitness of an individual to inclusive fitness of an individual's genes. Although the novelty of this explanation of altruism as selfish genes stimulated a burst of evolutionary theory and research, the unique feature of sociobiology is the concept of inclusive fitness.

Sociobiologists, like ethologists, tend to focus on average differences between species, describing the behavior of a species typologically, as if there were no variability within species. However, the theory rests on the coefficient of genetic relationship, which requires genetic variability within species. The coefficient of genetic relationship refers to the fact that parents and their offspring share roughly half of their segregating genes, full siblings share half, half siblings share one-quarter, cousins share one-eighth, and so on. The word *segregating* in the previous sentence needs to be emphasized. If there were no genetic variability within a species, all members of a species would have the same coefficient of genetic relationship and kinship would not matter because all members of the species would be identical genetically. Thus, although sociobiologists emphasize typological differences between species, the theoretical foundation of kinship selection and inclusive fitness rests on genetic variability within species. This is a critical point in understanding sociobiology and its relationship to ethology and behavioral genetics and merits some examples.

Kinship-selection and inclusive-fitness theories have been used to explain why bees, ants, and wasps have a nonreproductive worker caste (Hamilton 1964); why adult zebras defend their calves but wildebeests do not (West-Eberhard 1975); why male mountain bluebirds respond the way they do to adultery, whereas other species do not (Barash 1976); why parental investment differs between species (Trivers 1972); and why parent–offspring conflict occurs in mammalian species (Trivers 1974). Occasionally, sociobiological research has focused on populations within a species – for example, why paternal behavior of hoary marmots differs in isolated family units and in populous colonies (Barash 1975). Nonetheless, the perspective is typological and assumes invariant behavior within populations. For humans, it has been argued that "sociobiology deals with biological *universals* that may underlie human social behavior" (Barash 1977:278). But we know that these behaviors are not invariant. Obviously, all human families with the same-aged children do not experience the same degree of parent–child conflict. Similarly, humans tend to be monogamous and to show enhanced paternal care compared to other species, but the striking differences within the human species cannot be denied.

Given that many such behaviors may be found to vary when they are studied from a less typological point of view, it is necessary to determine the extent to which such variability is genetic in origin. If genetic differences do not affect a particular behavior, then evolutionary theory does not apply. However, there is a distressing tendency among sociobiologists to assume that all behavior related to altruism is of genetic origin. In contrast, the goal of behavioral genetics is to study this very question – in fact, to describe the extent of all behavioral (not just altruistic) differences and to ascribe these differences to genetic and/or environmental causes. It is important to note that most behaviors in mice and men studied by behavioral geneticists are influenced by both genetic and environmental factors. Although genetic influences are found, they often do not account for a majority of the observed variance.

Although ethologists have not developed systematic genetic theories of evolution, their emphasis on between-species differences tends to be compatible with the between-species perspective of most sociobiologists. Thus, ethologists are likely to be susceptible to a view of evolution that focuses on genetic variability between, but not within, species – a view quite different from that of behavioral genetics. For this reason, the next section addresses the relationship between evolution and genetic variability.

EVOLUTION AND GENETIC VARIABILITY

Differences in perspective between ethology and behavioral genetics are tied to different views of evolution and its relationship to genetic variability. Darwin had considerable difficulty reconciling his theory of natural selection with the prevailing blending theory of inheritance. He knew that variability was the key to natural selection, yet he realized that blending inheritance would halve variability in each generation. He halfheartedly accepted Lamarck's notion of the law of use and disuse as a source of continuing variability.

It is ironic that, in Darwin's office, a copy of Mendel's manuscript was left uncut (Allen 1975). Mendel's theory, of course, solved the riddle of variability by demonstrating that the units of inheritance are discrete – that is, they do not blend. After the rediscovery of Mendel's laws of transmission, there was considerable disagreement as to their applicability to complex, quantitatively varying traits that did not show qualitative Mendelian segregation ratios. The issue was resolved in 1918 when the theory of quantitative genetics was advanced by R. A. Fisher, who demonstrated that small, additive effects of many genes can produce a normal distribution.

We now know that genetic variability, the ultimate source of which is mutation, is the raw material of evolution with respect to both single-gene and polygenic characters. However, the relationship between evolution and genetic variability is often fuzzy. Fisher's (1930) "Fundamental Theorem of Natural Selection" pointed out that directional selection, that is, selection in the direction of an extreme phenotype, diminishes additive genetic variability. Additive genetic variability is that part of genetic variability that breeds true as compared to the rest of genetic variability, which is called *nonadditive* (see Plomin et al. 1979 for details). In other words, if selection is directional, alleles (alternate forms of a gene) favoring the selected characteristic tend to become locked into the species or population, thus reducing additive genetic variability.

This view of natural selection fosters an emphasis on differences between rather than within species, because selection keeps chipping away at deviations from the ideal genetic constitution of a species. However, directional selection is not the only kind of selection, and there are reasons why it is necessary to consider other strategies of selection.

During the past decade, it was somewhat of a surprise to population geneticists to find that at least a third of all loci are polymorphic in most species. Population geneticists now recognize substantial genetic variability within species, although there are differing opinions concerning the importance of selection in maintaining that variability. Neutralists (e.g., Kimura & Ohta 1971) argue that much of the variability is selectively neutral. Selectionists (e.g., Dobzhansky 1970), however, argue that variability is actively maintained by stabilizing selection (balanced polymorphisms). Stabilizing selection creates a selective edge for moderate levels of a trait, thus balancing the phenotypic extremes.

Although both positions are probably correct to some extent for some characters (e.g., Lewontin 1974), several interesting examples of stabilizing selection (such as heterozygote advantage, frequency-dependent selection, and frequency-dependent sexual selection) have been discovered in recent years (e.g., Clarke 1975). Stabilizing selection provides an important evolutionary

Table 9.2. *Examples of directional and stabilizing selection*

		Relative fitness	
Genotype	Frequency	Directional selection	Stabilizing selection
AA	p^2	1	0
Aa	$2pq$	1	1
aa	q^2	0	0

link connecting studies of genetic differences between species and studies of genetic differences within species.

Perhaps because artificial selection is nearly always directional, we have become accustomed to thinking about natural selection as directional. However, this view is changing. Stabilizing selection is not nearly as dramatic as directional selection, but it is surely more common in nature. E. O. Wilson (1975:132) noted that "examples of counteracting [stabilizing] selection forces are easy to find in nature" and described aggressive behavior, dominance systems, and sexual behavior as examples. Crow and Kimura, in their book on population genetics, concluded:

> Several times in this book we have noted that for almost any metrical trait (except fitness itself) the most fit individuals are likely to have an intermediate value for the trait. If size is the trait, the species typically has a characteristic size and individuals that are too large or too small are less viable or fertile, and similarly for other quantitative traits. [Crow & Kimura 1970:293]

Because directional selection squeezes out genetic variability, it leads to typological thinking about differences between species. It has even been argued that traits showing substantial genetic variability within species are "genetic junk" - that is, unimportant evolutionarily. However, stabilizing selection provides an alternative for relating genetic variability within species to evolution. In addition to maintaining the mean of a population, stabilizing selection can maintain genetic variability. In the polygenic case, there is likely to be some reduction of variability; however, this is a complex issue depending on the extent to which homozygotes or heterozygotes have the selective edge, as described by Crow and Kimura (1970:293–294). For example, stabilizing selection occurs for human birth weight, but substantial variability remains for this polygenic character (Cavalli-Sforza & Bodmer 1971). When heterozygotes have a selective advantage, genetic variability is clearly maintained.

Examples of directional selection and stabilizing selection are compared in Table 9.2 and Figure 9.1 for a single-locus, two-allele character. The first column of Table 9.2 shows the three possible genotypes, and the second column shows the frequency of the three genotypes in a stable population (the genotypic segregation ratio described as Hardy-Weinberg equilibrium). The frequencies of the two alleles (*A* and *a*) sum to 1.0, as do the genotypic frequencies ($p^2 + 2pq + q^2$). In the absence of selection (and other forces that change gene frequencies), the genotypic frequencies remain the same genera-

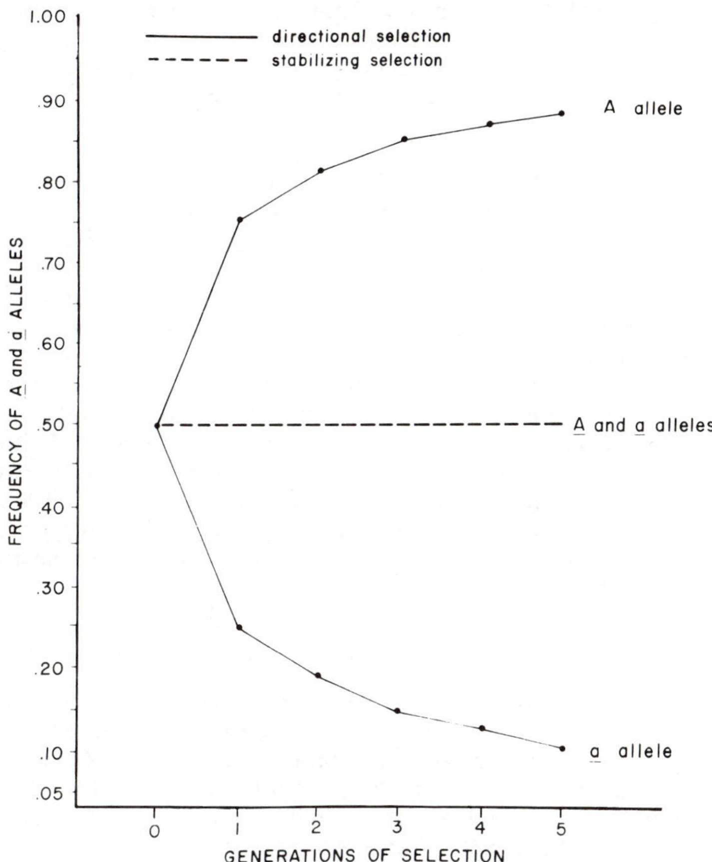

Figure 9.1. Effects of directional and stabilizing selection on genetic variability. This illustration is based on examples given in Table 9.2.

tion after generation, thus maintaining the genetic variability that is referred to as *Hardy-Weinberg equilibrium.* Selection, however, can change relative rates of reproduction and thus change allelic and genotypic frequencies in subsequent generations.

Directional selection

Directional selection implies selection against one genotype. In other words, the other genotypes have greater relative fitness. In the example in Table 9.2, the relative fitness of the *aa* homozygote is 0, which means that individuals with this genotype produce no offspring. Although this is an extreme example, the conclusions to be drawn would not be different if selection were less extreme. If *Aa* heterozygotes also did not reproduce, the *a* allele would be eliminated in one generation and the frequency of the *A* allele would be 1.0. Thus, selection of this type would drastically reduce genetic variability. The *Aa* heterozygote in Table 9.2 has the same relative fitness as the *AA* homozygote. This situation would occur, for example, if dominance were complete (which means that the *Aa* heterozygote is indistinguishable phenotypically from the *AA* homozygote).

The relative contribution of each genotype to the next generation is the genotypic frequency weighted by its relative fitness. It should be clear that, if the *aa* genotype does not reproduce, the frequency of the *a* allele will decrease greatly. Because the *a* allele is represented in the *Aa* heterozygote, matings between heterozygotes will continue to produce some *aa* homozygotes. However, the frequency of the *a* allele will be reduced each generation that selection of this type continues.

For example, if the frequency of the *a* allele at a particular locus is 50% (and the *A* frequency is also 50%), the frequency of the genotypes is 25% *AA*, 50% *Aa*, and 25% *aa*. After one generation of directional selection as in Table 9.2, the frequency of the *a* allele will be 25%. After five generations of such selection, the *a* frequency will be 11%, and the frequency of the *A* allele will thus be 89% (Fig. 9.1). If selection stopped at this point, the frequency of the three genotypes would be 79% *AA*, 20% *Aa*, and 1% *aa*. Thus, allelic and genotypic variability can be greatly diminished by directional selection.

Stabilizing selection

Stabilizing selection, on the other hand, maintains genetic variability. The example of stabilizing selection in Table 9.2 is in the form of a heterozygote advantage. If selection operates against both homozygotes, *AA* and *aa* (that is, if the relative fitness of the *Aa* heterozygote is greater than that of the homozygotes), then genetic variability will be maintained by this form of selection. Using the same extreme example as before, assume that the frequencies of *A* and *a* are equal (50%) and selection operates against both homozygotes. Only the heterozygotes reproduce, and their offspring are 50% *Aa*, 25% *AA*, and 25% *aa*. Thus, the frequencies of the alleles remain the same, and therefore genetic variability remains the same (Fig. 9.1). Even if the selection coefficients are different for the two homozygotes, genetic variability will nonetheless be maintained. For example, we could show that, if selection against the *AA* homozygote is 75% and selection against the *aa* homozygote is 5%, the frequency of the *a* allele will stabilize at 60%.

In summary, directional selection reduces genetic variability, whereas stabilizing selection in the form of a heterozygote advantage maintains it. For completeness, it should be mentioned that there is a third (unusual) type of selection, referred to as *disruptive*. Disruptive selection favors both extremes, thus leaving the mean unchanged but greatly increasing genetic variance.

Heritability

A brief digression is necessary to relate these concepts to *heritability*, which has become something of a bad word in recent years. If properly defined and employed, heritability is a useful statistic describing the ratio between genetic variance and phenotypic (observed) variance in a particular population at a particular point in time. For example, when we say that the heritability of height is about 80%, we mean that about 80% of the observed individual differences in height are due to genetic differences among individuals in the population. An analogous statistic has been labeled *environmentality* (Fuller & Thompson 1978) – the proportion of phenotypic variance caused by nongenetic factors. Because of the confusion surrounding these statistics, it is necessary to emphasize what they are not: They are not constants or immutable; they do not refer to a single individual; and they do not imply more precision than other descriptive statistics (Plomin et al. 1979).

Thus, heritability is a descriptive statistic referring to variability within a species. If a character shows no variability within a species – such as binocular vision or bipedal locomotion in humans – heritability is an inappropriate statistic. However, most characters that interest behavioral scientists are highly variable; moreover, in the world outside the laboratory, questions concerning individual differences and their etiology are of prime importance.

One still encounters the misconception that behaviors that are important evolutionarily will have high heritabilities. To the contrary, a trait that has been and continues to be highly selected in a directional sense will show low heritability because directional selection diminishes additive genetic variance, as discussed in the previous section. At the extreme, genetic variability can be eliminated except for new mutations; but in less extreme conditions, genetic variability that remains will display nonadditivity (*dominance*) as its mode of inheritance. This fact can provide a tool for isolating behavioral characters that have been subjected to severe directional selection. However, as we have seen, directional selection has been overemphasized in our evolutionary thinking. Substantial genetic variability – that is, heritability – can be maintained for traits subject to stabilizing selection.

In summary, there are important empirical and conceptual reasons for considering genetic variability within as well as between species. It has been sarcastically said of behavioral scientists that they have finally become aware of Darwin but have not yet been introduced to Mendel, implying that behavioral scientists have begun to recognize the evolutionary origins of differences between species but have not yet comprehended the within-species variability caused by the genetic reshuffling inherent in sexual reproduction. Meiosis suggests a picture of a biological system that is not just tolerant of trivial differences from a species prototype – the system generates differences, insists upon them. Genetic differences within species are the sine qua non of evolution.

The most immediate gains from the hybridization of ethology and behavioral genetics will come from studies of differences within species. The next section reviews some basic concepts related to analyses of genetic influences within species. The section can also be read as a list of possible intersections between ethology and behavioral genetics.

GENES AND ENVIRONMENT

One reason for the reluctance to merge ethology and behavioral genetics has been widespread misunderstanding of the roles of genes and environment in behavioral development. In an attempt to clear up some of these misconceptions, I shall discuss some basic concepts in this section, although it is assumed that the reader has already been exposed to some of these concepts in Chapter 8.

It is an empty truism that there can be no behavior without both genes and environment. Although it is fashionable nowadays to proclaim the nature-nurture issue dead, considerable misunderstanding remains. Frequently, the mistaken notion of nature versus nurture has been replaced with the equally mistaken interactionist view that the separate effects of heredity and environment cannot be analyzed. This problem will not be resolved with jingoism. The relationship between genes and environment in behavioral evolution and development is fundamental.

Genes

Genes do not cause behavior. They do not constitute a homunculus within us, pulling our strings as if we were puppets, which is the image that comes to mind when some people talk about innate behavior. There are no genes for behavior, just as there are no genes for bones. The schemas in Figure 9.2 illustrate some common misconceptions about the ways in which genes influence behavior. Although no one explicitly espouses these views, they are so prevalent in an implicit way that they should be mentioned.

The view shown in Figure 9.2*a* is obviously naive; genes do not directly code for any behavior. As indicated in Figure 9.2*b,* genes code for proteins. However, proteins do not directly cause behavior, although a malfunctioning protein may well have drastic effects on a certain behavior. As illustrated in Figure 9.2*c,* each protein is not directly linked to a specific behavior. Any given behavior is likely to be influenced by many different proteins. Examples of single-gene influences on behavior are only demonstrations that a single-gene mutation leading to a malfunctioning protein can have a profound effect on a certain behavior; they do not imply that the behavior is explained completely by that single gene. Figure 9.2*d* indicates that there are many steps between the proteins coded by genes and the behaviors. It is only through the intermediaries, representing organ systems and physiological processes, that genes indirectly affect behavior. These points have become much clearer in the last few years from behavioral genetic studies of simple systems such as bacteria (Parkinson 1977), paramecia (Kung et al. 1975), nematodes (Ward 1977), and *Drosophila* (Hall 1977). Furthermore, even though Fisher demonstrated over 50 years ago that single-gene, Mendelian theory can be generalized to a theory of polygenic inheritance, some people still have the impression that single genes somehow affect behavior more directly than do polygenic influences. That is not true.

Environment

Even the level of complexity represented in Figure 9.2*d* does not tell the whole story. Environmental influences must also be considered (Fig. 9.3). When we talk about genetic influences on behavior, we do not mean robotlike hard wiring but rather an indirect and complex path between genes and behavior via

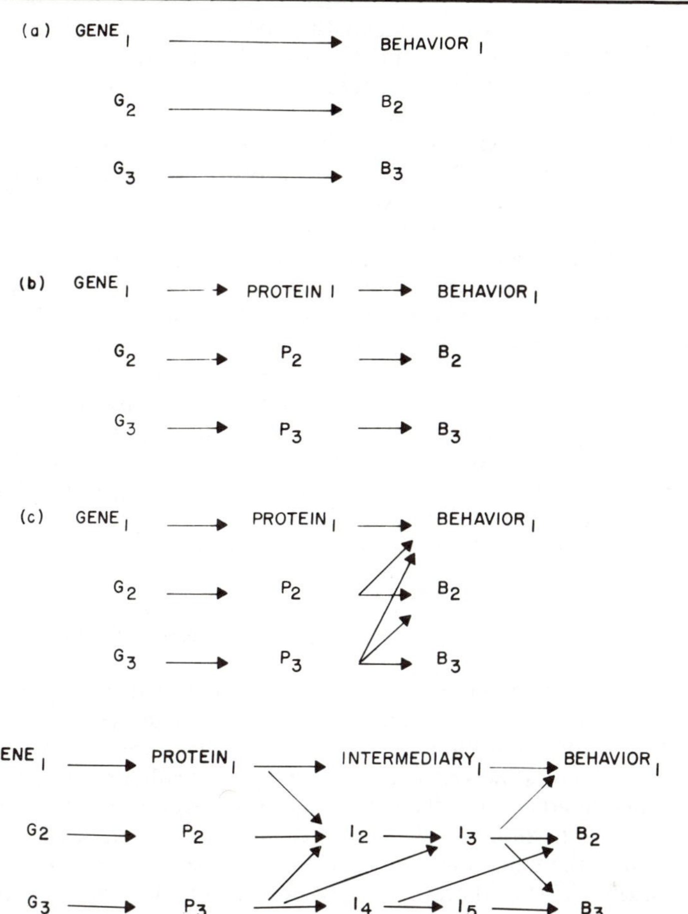

Figure 9.2. Schemas illustrating some common misconceptions about the ways in which genes influence behavior.

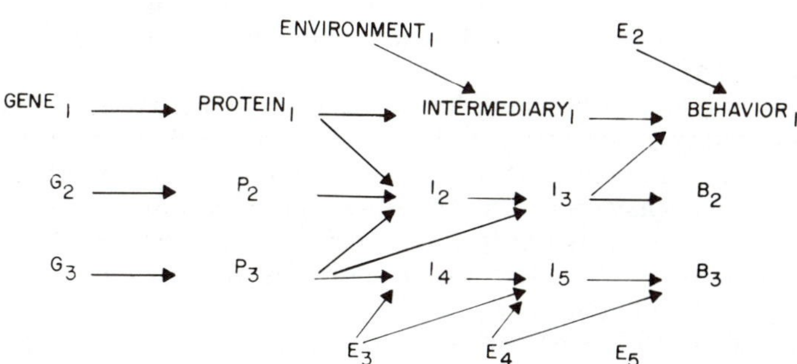

Figure 9.3. Schematic illustration of genetic environmental influences on behavior.

proteins and physiological systems that are also affected by environmental factors. Innate behaviors are no exception. Mayr (1974) distinguished *closed behavioral programs* from *open behavioral systems* to replace the hopelessly confused attempts to distinguish between instinctive and learned behavior. Closed behavioral programs are relatively impervious to individual experience, whereas open behavioral systems are more susceptible to environmental influences. However, genes operate no more directly for closed behavioral programs than for open behavioral systems.

Part of the confusion in the nature–nurture controversy stemmed from a definition of *environment* that was too broad. Hebb (1966) has suggested several categories of environmental forces. The major distinction is between *species-constant* and *species-variable* environmental influences. Species-constant factors are those biological and sensory influences that are normally inevitable for all members of the species (see Chap. 2). This concept is related to the environment of evolutionary adaptedness. Species-variable environmental influences are those experiences that vary from one member of the species to another. Although Hebb considered only exogenous environmental forces, we can also speak of the environmental milieu in the nucleus of a cell and in the extranuclear cell, as well as within physiological systems.

Interactions between genes and environment

Species evolve in response to the environment that the species normally encounters. Thus, a species's genetic architecture is influenced by exposure to species-constant environmental factors (the environment of evolutionary adaptedness), and it makes no sense to talk about either genes or environment alone. Such interaction at the species-constant level makes it clear that *innate* does not mean *unmodifiable.* Numerous deprivation studies have been conducted to show that manipulation of the environment can affect behavioral development. These studies typically deprive the developing organism of a species-constant factor and then demonstrate developmental changes. If we go to the extreme in a deprivation study, it is always possible to show that the environment affects development. There is no behavior, or anatomical characteristic, for that matter, that cannot be influenced by the environment. On the other side of the coin, there is probably no behavior or anatomical feature that cannot be influenced by manipulation of genes through interference with DNA.

Just as it is interesting to consider between-species behavioral differences, it is also interesting to consider genetic and environmental effects at the species-constant level. However, when we talk about the effects of genes and environment on behavior, we are most often concerned about those genetic and environmental factors that vary among members of a species. Typically, we observe behavioral differences within a species and are curious about the etiology of those differences.

Behavioral geneticists set out to answer these questions of the etiology of behavioral differences within a species by developing methodologies directed to both genetic and environmental sources of variance underlying phenotypic variance. Behavioral genetics describes behavioral differences and ascribes the differences to genetic and environmental influences, given the mix of genetic variation and environmental variation at a particular time in a particular population. If the genetic mix or the environmental mix changes, the relative impact of genes and environment will change. In other words, behavioral geneticists describe what is; they do not predict what could be. It seems to be a reasonable first step in understanding behavioral differences within species to ask about the relative contributions of genetic and environmental sources of variance.

The fact that there can be no behavior without both genes and an environment is just as true at the species-variable level as at the species-constant level. Although it is impossible to separate genetic from environmental influences upon the behavior of single individuals, we must not adopt the discouraging interactionist point of view. That would mean that we could not study the effects of genetic factors on behavior because they are hopelessly enmeshed with the effects of environment. It would also mean that we could not isolate environmental effects because they are inseparable from genetic effects.

Our solution to the problem is that individual differences in a population can be ascribed to genetic or environmental influences. Environmental differences may be expressed when genetic differences do not exist, just as genetic differences may be expressed in the absence of environmental differences. Furthermore, interactions between genes and environment, due to the nonlinear combination of genetic and environmental effects, may be revealed.

Genotype–environment interaction and correlation and their effects on behavioral genetic analyses have been discussed by Plomin et al. (1977). Because these concepts are important in understanding the role of genes, environment, and their coaction in behavioral development, I shall briefly describe them.

Genotype–environment (*GE*) *interaction* refers to the possibility that individuals of different genotypes may react differently to the same environment. Another way of looking at it is to say that an environment may be differentially effective for different genotypes. The extent to which genetic and environmental influences interact is an empirical question to be answered by statistical analyses of behavioral data.

GE interaction has been considered in studies of nonhuman animals (Erlenmeyer-Kimling 1972). The best-known of these studies is Cooper and Zubek's (1958) experiment in which maze-bright and maze-dull rats (rat lines selectively bred for maze-running ability) were reared in three different environments. The results (Fig. 9.4) indicate GE interaction. It can be seen that the question as to the effect of restricted and enriched environments on maze-running ability has no simple answer. The answer is, it depends. It depends on the genotype of the animal, and it depends on the environment in which the animal was reared. Another well-known example of GE interaction (Freedman 1958) showing differential effectiveness of discipline on different breeds of dogs was discussed in the previous chapter.

The general design of GE interaction studies with nonhuman animals is depicted in Table 9.3. This is a 2×2 design in which one independent variable is the genotype, the other is some aspect of the environment, and the dependent variable is some measured behavior.

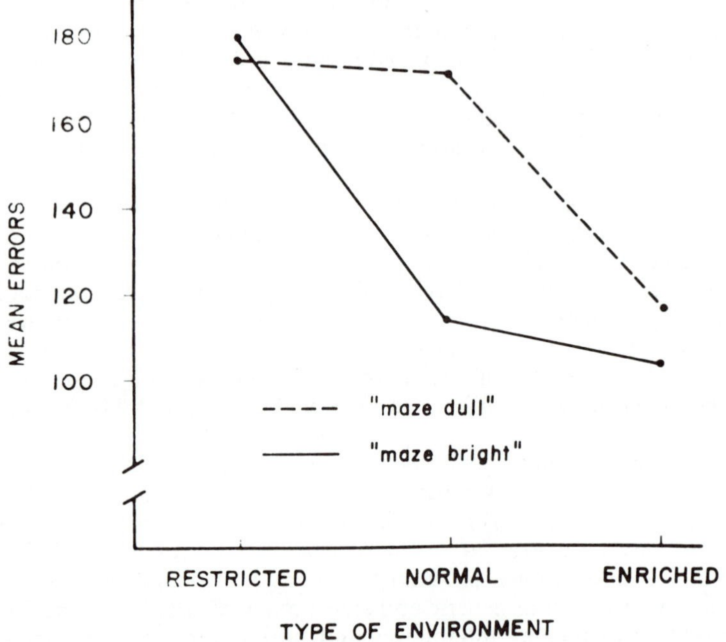

Figure 9.4. An example of genotype–environment interaction. (Adapted from Cooper & Zubek 1958)

Table 9.3. *Simplified design for testing genotype-environment interaction*

	Environment	
Genotype	Low	High
Low	1	2
High	3	4

Adoption studies permit a similar analysis of human behaviors. The genotype of adopted children can be estimated from information about their biological parents. Their environment can be any measurable environmental variable, such as some characteristic of the adoptive parents. The dependent variable is some measured aspect of their behavior. As in the animal studies, a 2 × 2 analysis of variance may reveal genetic influences independent of the environmental measure, the effect of environmental influences independent of genotype, and GE interaction. If genes do not make a difference for the particular behavior, there will be neither a genetic effect nor any GE interaction. It should be noted that the simplified design shown in Table 9.3 is for illustrative purposes only. Rather than arbitrarily dichotomizing continuously distributed variables, one actually uses a multiple regression technique in such analyses.

At the Institute for Behavioral Genetics of the University of Colorado at Boulder, Professors DeFries and Vandenberg and I are collecting data from a prospective longitudinal adoption study that includes many measures of behavior of biological parents, their adopted-away children, and the adoptive parents of these children, as well as extensive assessments of the adopted children's environment. No previous studies have collected such extensive data. When the limited data available from previous adoption studies are analyzed according to the above design, no evidence for GE interaction is revealed (Plomin et al. 1977). Nonetheless, the use of adoption data to screen for GE interaction is an unusually promising tool for the more refined analysis of environmental effects on behavior.

Reaction range, or *norm of reaction,* is a concept related to GE interaction. *GE interaction,* like other quantitative genetic terms, is descriptive. It describes the extent to which there are nonlinear interactions between genes and environment for the particular mixture of genetic and environmental sources of variance that exist in a population at a particular point in time. *Reaction range,* on the other hand, considers what could be rather than describing what is. It also tends to be interpreted in terms of an individual rather than of individuals in a population. I personally find the concept vague and not useful, and believe it lends itself to considerable misinterpretation. A common misinterpretation is that genes somehow provide a propensity toward some phenotypic range and that the environment determines the actual level of behavior within that range. One could just as easily suggest that a given environment allows a certain range of behaviors and that genetic variation among individuals accounts for fluctuations within that range. Neither of these polarized views is correct. For any given environment genetic variability is possible. Similarly, for any genotype, environmental differences can create variablity. Also, there may be certain unique, nonlinear interactions between genotypes and environments. In my opinion, the popular concept of reaction range does not add anything except confusion to the concepts of genetic variability, environmental variability, and GE interaction.

Genotype–environment (GE) correlation refers to the differential exposure of genotypes to environments. It is a function of the frequency with which certain genotypes and certain environments occur together. In another paper (Plomin et al. 1977), I suggested three types of GE correlation (passive, reactive, and active), as summarized in Table 9.4. The most frequently mentioned type is *passive,* in that individuals are considered passive recipients of parental genes and environment that are both favorable (or unfavorable) for the development of a trait. Although passive GE correlation has been discussed much more than other types, it is not the only, nor perhaps the most common, form of GE correlation. A second type can be called *reactive,* in that people may react differently to individuals of different genotypes. In short, people may

Table 9.4. *Three types of genotype–environment correlation*

Type	Description	Pertinent environment
Passive	Individuals are given genotypes linked to their environments	Natural parents and siblings
Reactive	Individuals are reacted to on the basis of their genotypes	Anyone
Active	Individuals contribute to and/or seek an environment appropriate to their genotypes	Anything

Source: Plomin et al. (1977)

respond to genotypic differences among individuals in such a way that they provide an environment that reflects and correlates with those genotypic differences. *Active* GE correlation occurs when an individual contributes to his or her own environment and may actively seek one related to genetic propensities.

The trichotomy of passive, reactive, and active GE correlation is merely for conceptual convenience. Many real-life cases of GE correlation are intermediate, ambiguous, or mixed in character. Nonetheless, this approach provides a useful perspective for thinking about the relationship between genes and environment in behavioral development. Adoption studies would also be useful in isolating specific GE correlations for human behavior, but no data yet exist to provide such a test.

BEHAVIORAL GENETICS AND DEVELOPMENT

Each of these quantitative genetic concepts can be extended to a developmental analysis over time. The relative mix of genetic and environmental influences is likely to change as an organism develops. For example, as children begin to make their way in the world, interacting with peers and other extrafamilial environmental influences, we might expect environmental factors to contribute more heavily to observed behavioral differences among them, and thus predict that heritability will decline during development. However, one could also speculate that heritability might increase as more genes are turned on during development. Investigations of these possibilities could use cross-sectional analyses, but longitudinal investigations would be even more interesting. For example, developmental change can be analyzed as a phenotype to determine the extent to which such change is genetically or environmentally mediated. Age-to-age changes over many points of observation can be analyzed by means of a repeated-measures profile analysis. In the longitudinal Louisville twin study, analyses of age-to-age changes in cognitive development during the first 6 years of life indicated genetic influence (Wilson 1978).

One of the more dramatic conceptual shifts within developmental psychology during the last decade has been the recognition of an issue that most developmentalists refer to as the *direction of effects in socialization* (Bell 1968). GE correlation, particularly the reactive and active varieties, is related to this concept. The direction-of-effects issue concerns the extent to which observed correlations between environmental factors and behaviors of children can be interpreted in one causal direction or the other. That is, have certain environmental influences caused the behavioral differences, or do the environmental influences merely reflect genetically mediated behavioral differences? GE correlation analyses can estimate the extent to which genetic differences among children lead to differences in the environment to which they are exposed.

In addition to developmental analyses of genetic and environmental variance, and of GE interaction and correlation, multivariate quantitative genetic analyses can also be fruitfully applied in the developmental context. Until recently, nearly all behavioral genetic analyses were univariate; they examined the phenotypic variance of single behavior. It is now clear that multivariate analyses can also be applied to behavioral genetic data. Rather than analyzing the variance of a single behavior, one can analyze the covariance among behaviors. Any behavioral genetic method that can untangle genetic and environmental influences for the variance of a single behavior can also be used to separate genetic and environmental influences on the covariance among behaviors (Plomin & DeFries 1979). In the bivariate case, we can ask whether the phenotypic covariance between two behaviors is genetically or environmentally mediated. In the multivariate case, where we are used to analyzing phenotypic factor structures, we can now also consider the structure of genetic influences and the structure of environmental influences for a set of behaviors.

Developmentally, multivariate GE analyses have interesting implications that have not yet been explored. Consider first a cross-sectional design. Even though the relative contributions of genetic and environmental variance may not change from one developmental period to another, the structure of genetic influences and the structure of environmental influences may be different in the two developmental periods. Discontinuities in development may reflect such a process of genetic or environmental restructuring. Environmental restructuring will occur if the various environmental factors influencing behaviors in early childhood change quantitatively or qualitatively in terms of their relative importance in later childhood. Similarly, on the genetic side, some of the many genes influencing behavior in early childhood may not be so important later.

If cross-sectional analyses reveal differences in phenotypic structure in different developmental periods, it would be interesting to study the genetic and environmental restructuring underlying these phenotypic differences. Even if the phenotypic structure shows no dramatic developmental differences, the underlying genetic or environmental structure may still change. In a longitudinal design, phenotypic correlations among behaviors across time can be analyzed using multivariate GE techniques to test whether continuity across various developmental periods is genetically or environmentally mediated. In the bivariate case, this simply means that the phenotypic correlation for a certain behavior between one developmental period and another (i.e., the correlation between phenotype X at time 1 and time 2) can be broken down into genetic covariance and environmental covariance over time. When this is done for several behaviors simultaneously, we are essentially dealing with longitudinal factor analysis. Additional food for thought comes from the possible application of idiographic multiple regression and clustering techniques, as proposed by Petrinovich (Chap. 4) to developmental behavioral genetic analyses.

ETHOLOGY'S CONTRIBUTION TO BEHAVIORAL GENETICS

Because I am a behavioral geneticist, I have emphasized possible contributions of behavioral genetics to ethology. However, as I indicated at the beginning of this chapter, the benefits of a combined ethological behavioral genetic approach to development also flow in the other direction. The major contribution of ethology to behavioral genetics will be to provide tools for isolating ecologically and evolutionarily meaningful units of behavior. Although it seems surprising that scientists who study behavioral evolution and genetic differences between species sometimes do not consider genetic differences within species, it is just as surprising that those who focus on genetic differences within species do not often consider the evolutionary context of behavior.

Early behavioral genetic studies of nonhuman animals focused almost exclusively on *Mus musculus* and *Drosophila.* During the last 2 decades, comparisons of inbred strains of mice and selection studies have demonstrated that genetic influences on behavioral differences within species are ubiquitous. Fascination with this finding has worn off, and it is necessary to ask what it means in an evolutionary context. However, the evolutionary implications of previous research are limited because evolution was not considered in the design of these studies – neither with respect to the investigation of genetic and environmental variability nor in the selection and analysis of behaviors. Using terms discussed by Petrinovich (Chap. 4), previous research in behavioral genetics tended to be *systematic* rather than *representative.*

Genetically, there are over 100 inbred strains of mice, but the commonly used strains derive from a very few animals obtained from mouse fanciers. Even though crosses of these inbred strains can be used to produce genetically heterogeneous stocks, it is unlikely that the genetic variability among these animals is nearly as great as (or nearly representative of) the genetic variability of wild *Mus musculus.* The behavior of wild mice, and even of their offspring reared from birth in a laboratory environment, is radically different from that of inbred strains and crosses among inbred strains (Plomin & Manosevitz 1974). Thus, from the standpoint of genetic variability, it would be useful for behavioral geneticists to consider genetic variability in an evolutionary context. Additional studies of the behavior of wild mice might be most informative.

Environmentally, nearly all behavioral genetic studies with mice have investigated behavior under standard laboratory conditions. One would expect that the variability of such an environment would be considerably different from that of the environments in which mice evolved. Although it may be necessary to study mice in controlled settings, no one would argue with the suggestion that there is much room for behavioral genetic studies of mice to swing in the direction of ecologically valid environments (see Chap. 2).

An ethological perspective will make the greatest contribution to behavioral genetic analyses in terms of selection and analysis of behavior. Most research, particularly on mice, has relied on convenient but ethologically unpalatable measures such as open-field activity, running-wheel activity, and performance in various learning devices such as the shuttle box. This sort of approach made sense when our goal was to demonstrate only that genes can influence behavior, because automated measures are useful for the large sample sizes required for quantitative genetic analyses. The particular behaviors chosen were almost irrelevant. However, now that genetic differences within species are common knowledge, the next phase of research is to specify the genetic and physiological mechanisms in greater detail. This work has begun, but ethologically refined behavioral analysis is certainly another important direction for further research. Ethology will assist behavioral genetics by pointing to behaviors that are more appropriate in an evolutionary sense, as stated in Chapter 8.

What about the human animal? Clearly, humans are one of the most difficult organisms for genetic analyses. Their generation time is long, experimental control is next to impossible, and selective breeding is out of the question. *Drosophila* kindly provided geneticists with very short generations, easy maintenance, and interesting genetic phenomena such as mosaics – which, when combined with mutations, permit powerful developmental analyses (Benzer 1973). Mice, at least, are small and easily maintained mammals. However, the difficulties in studying humans are a disguised blessing in that we are forced to work with naturally occurring genetic and environmental variation. This necessity is a critical difference between human and animal studies and one that has not previously been emphasized.

Human behavioral genetic analyses assess phenotypic differences in a population and ascribe the differences to genetic and environmental sources of variance in that population at that point in time. Some critics of behavioral genetics have pointed out that we are studying only a small subset of all conceivable genotypes and environments. However, the genotypes and environments that exist in extant human populations represent no trivial and arbitrary subset. The human genotypes that exist today are the endpoint of a long evolutionary history, and the environments to which humankind is exposed are important in continually shaping the human gene pool. Furthermore, current environments and genetic differences are those that potentially affect behavioral development. Thus, it seems more appropriate to study such influences rather than to speculate about other possible genotypes and environments.

Although human behavioral geneticists by necessity consider naturally occurring genetic and environmental variability, we are free to select the behaviors to be studied. Most of our choices would not please an ethologist. The first twin study (Merriman 1924) measured intelligence quotient (IQ), and the vast majority of twin and adoption studies since that time have used paper-and-pencil measures of cognitive abilities or personality. As a result of this reliance on written tests, there have been few studies of the early stages of development in humans. Thus, naturalistic observations in appropriate environmental contexts would seem the most appropriate ethological behavioral approach to the study of human development at this time.

ETHOLOGICAL BEHAVIORAL GENETICS OF HUMAN DEVELOPMENT

I shall briefly describe a behavioral genetic study of social behavior in infants (Plomin & Rowe 1978, 1979) that demonstrates the usefulness of this approach. The study was meant to be a first step in the investigation of social behavior of 1- and 2-year-old children. Although the sample included 92 children (members of 21 identical twin pairs and 25 same-sex fraternal twin pairs), it was too small for any sophisticated quantitative genetic analyses.

Despite extensive studies of social behavior in infancy, little is known about the etiology of individual differences in proximity seeking, reactions to strangers, play behavior, cuddliness, and children's reactions to brief separations from their mothers. The wide range of individual differences in social behaviors is not often recognized, and the possibility that genetic differences among children underlie some of these observed differences in social behavior is seldom considered. Furthermore, it is usually assumed that environmental influences salient to the development of social behavior operate between families, although there is little evidence supporting this assumption. If the environment works in this way, then children in the same family should be more similar to one another than they are to members of other families. This is referred to as *between-family environmental variance.* However, in a study of 850 pairs of adolescent twins, Loehlin and Nichols (1976) found that the significant environmental impact of personality lies within, not between, families.

Infants' social behavior was studied in their home in seven standardized situations that permitted the comparison of social responding to the mother and to a stranger. Two raters were employed, one for each twin, and behavior was evaluated in terms of both time-sampled observations of specific behaviors and more global ratings. The standardized situations included a warm-up session, approach by stranger, play with stranger, play with mother, cuddling with mother, cuddling with stranger, and separation from mother. In situation 1, the infants had 5 minutes to warm up to the stranger. During the warm-up, the project was explained to the mother and her questions were answered, but the stranger did not interact with the children. In situation 2, the stranger enticed the infants to play with him. In situation 3, the stranger played with the infants using a standard toy. The mother played with her infants in the same way in situation 4, and she cuddled them in situation 5. In situation 6, the infants were cuddled by the stranger. Finally, the mother was briefly separated from her infants in situation 7.

All of the behaviors showed substantial individual differences. Correlational analyses indicated that this variability was reliable at least in terms of interrater agreement and internal consistency. Twin analyses compare identical twins to same-sex fraternal twins. If a trait is not influenced by genes, the twofold greater genetic similarity of identical twins should not make them more similar phenotypically than fraternal twins. If, however, genes influence a trait, identical twins will show greater phenotypic resemblance. Although the twin method is often criticized for its assumption of equal environment for the two types of twins, a recent review suggests that the equal environments assumption is reasonable (DeFries & Plomin 1978).

Intraclass correlations were computed for all behaviors. The most conservative indication of heritable influences is obtained by testing the significance of the difference between identical and fraternal twin correlations. The most notable finding was that social behavior toward the stranger was heritable in several situations, but social behavior toward the mother was not. This finding suggests the intriguing possibility that genetic influences are more important in the development of social responsiveness to strangers than to familiar persons. It underlines the need to consider the context of behavior in behavioral genetic studies. The finding is particularly exciting because it corresponds to other behavioral genetic data that suggest that social responsiveness to unfamiliar persons may be the most heritable aspect of personality (Horn et al. 1976). Another recent observational study of 30-month-old twins counted incidents of attachment (defined as seeking the mother's proximity, attention, and help) in the home and in a laboratory situation (Lytton et al. 1977). These investigators did not include assessments of social behavior directed toward a stranger. As in our study, attachment behavior directed toward the mother was not heritable.

How does this finding relate to evolution? As discussed earlier, the traditional view of directional selection would look for reduced genetic variability for evolutionarily important characteristics. However, social behavior directed toward a stranger may be an example of stabilizing selection. Stabilizing selection confers a selective advantage for moderate levels of a character, thus balancing against either phenotypic extreme and maintaining genetic variability. Bowlby (1969) speculated that the evolutionary underpinnings of attachment are not intrinsic to the affectional relationship between mother and child but rather to predator pressure favoring wariness toward novel stimuli. If fear of strangers is part of such general wariness, it seems reasonable to speculate that stabilizing selection rather than directional selection was the more likely evolutionary strategy. At either extreme, wariness can be maladaptive; too much wariness is debilitating, overwhelming exploration, and too little wariness can lead to predatory pressure, as suggested by Bowlby. Thus, significant heritability for infants' reactions to a stranger is not incompatible with speculations about its evolutionary heritage.

The second major finding of the study requires a brief introduction. In the past, behavioral genetic analyses have estimated the influence of genetic factors and ascribed all remaining phenotypic variability to environmental variance plus error. Obviously, individual differences that are not substantially influenced by heredity must be primarily determined by environmental factors. However, it is possible to separate the influences of the environment into two distinct categories. One category operates between families to make family members similar to one another but different from members of other families. The other category (by definition, the rest of the environmental influences) includes those factors that operate within families to make family members different from one another. This includes systematic within-family environmental influences, such as birth order, as well as stochastic events, which may be called *error*.

The importance of within-family environmental factors can be assessed by the differences within pairs of identical twins. Because such twins are identical genetically, differences within pairs can be caused only by environmental factors that make family members different from one another. Between-family environmental variance can be estimated by subtracting the within-family environmental component from the total environmental variance. However, this method is hazardous with sample sizes numbering less than hundreds of pairs. Thus, a more conservative procedure was used. We noted each social behavior that was significantly correlated in both identical and fraternal twin samples (suggesting between-family influence), but with no significant difference in correlations between types of twins (suggesting that the between-family influences are environmental rather than genetic). Because these behaviors show between-family similarity but no significant heritable influence, they were tentatively identified as primarily under the influence of between-family environmental variables (although they involved within-family environmental influences as well).

Our most notable finding was the relatively small effect of between-family environmental factors on social behaviors. In the twin study by Lytton et al. (1977), more evidence was found for between-family influences; however, a single observer recorded behavior of both twins at the same time, and this may well have inflated the similarity of the twins. Our data are in accord with Loehlin and Nichols's conclusion: "In short, in the personality domain we seem to see environmental effects that operate almost randomly with respect to the sorts of variables that psychologists (and other people) have traditionally deemed important in personality development" (1976:92).

The results suggest that serious attention needs to be paid to the possibility of a major role for environmental influences that make family members different from (rather than similar to) one another. Although the only systematic within-family environmental variable that has been considered extensively is birth order, the potency of its effect on personality is questionable. Other variables that may have systematic within-family environmental effects include changes in parenting with an increase in the number of children in a family, as well as contrast and labeling effects within a family. However, we need to keep an open mind regarding the radical possibility that "there are no broad systematic environmental influences in personality development. The environmental variance may come about as the child makes his idiosyncratic way through the world, experiencing many slightly different situations" (Buss & Plomin 1975:224).

In summary, this twin study of 1- and 2-year-old children observed in their homes suggests that heredity affects individual differences in social responding to unfamiliar persons more than to familiar persons. The study also suggests that the substantial influence of environment in the development of social behavior may occur primarily *within* families (making members of the family different from one another) rather than *between* families (making family members similar to one another), as is widely assumed.

CONCLUSIONS

It is safe to predict that ethological behavioral genetics will significantly advance understanding of behavioral development in both human and nonhuman animals. Ethologists and behavioral geneticists often have different perspectives on variations between and within species, the relationship between evolution and genetic variability, and interactions between genes and environment in development. However, these differences in viewpoint provide strengths on both sides that will have synergistic effects upon the two disciplines.

Ethology will profit from considering variability within species. The ubiquity of within-species genetic variability suggests that more thought should be given to adaptations involving stabilizing selection rather than directional selection. The theory and tools of quantitative genetics, including mutivariate GE analyses and concepts such as GE interaction and correlation, will be useful in guiding the search for the influence of genes and environment in behavioral development. Behavioral genetics will benefit from the evolutionary perspective of ethology. Furthermore, the observational expertise of ethology will contribute greatly to behavioral genetic methodology when behavioral geneticists begin to study behavior per se rather than use behavior as just another phenotype for genetic analysis. Together, ethology and behavioral genetics promise much for the study of behavioral development.

SUMMARY

My purpose has been to ease the way for a rapprochement between ethology and behavioral genetics in the study of development. Ethology and behavioral genetics tend to differ in their perspectives on three issues: (1) differences between and within species, (2) the relationship between evolution and genetic variability, and (3) the relationship between environment and genes.

In the past, ethology has emphasized average differences between species, whereas behavorial genetics has focused on variability within species. Although the between-species perspective is useful in some contexts, behaviors are almost always found to vary within species when they are studied from a less typological point of view. The goal of behavioral genetics is to study the etiology of such within-species behavioral variability.

The between-species perspective is related to a view of evolution that holds that natural selection chips away at genetic variability within a species so that members of the species eventually become identical. Directional selection (selecting for an extreme of a dimension) does, in fact, winnow genetic variability in this way. However, directional selection has been overemphasized at the expense of stabilizing selection, which creates a selective edge for moderate levels of a character and thus maintains genetic variability within a species. We now know that most species display considerable genetic variability; over a third of their loci vary from one member of the species to another. Stabilizing selection may be the mechanism responsible for this wealth of genetic diversity within species.

Although it is fashionable to proclaim the nature–nurture issue dead, the relationship between genes and environment is fundamental. Genes do not directly cause behavior. They control the production of proteins and indirectly affect behavior via physiological intermediaries and environmental circumstances. It is an empty truism that there can be no behavior without both genes and environment. Behavior evolves in response to the environment that the species normally encounters. Behavioral genetics describes behavioral variability within a species and ascribes the variability to genetic and environmental influences, given the mix of genetic variation and environmental variation at a particular time.

GE interaction refers to the possibility that the effect of an environmental influence can be modulated by the genotype of an individual. For both human and nonhuman animals, the presence of GE interaction can be detected, and tests of such interactions are a promising tool for the more refined analysis of environmental effects on behavior. GE correlation refers to the differential exposure of individuals of different genotypes to environments. Three types have been identified: passive, reactive, and active. These behavioral genetic concepts can be extended to multivariate analyses of continuities and discontinuities in development.

The effect of ethology on behavioral genetics will be to provide tools for isolating ecologically and evolutionarily meaningful units of behavior. In the past, behavioral genetic research has emphasized the study of inbred strains under standard laboratory conditions using behavioral measures selected for their convenience rather than for their evolutionary significance. Although studies of human behavior have been more representative in terms of genetic and environmental variance, most human behavioral genetic research has employed paper-and-pencil tests.

As an example of the usefulness of an ethological perspective in behavioral genetic studies of development, a twin study of infant social behavior was described. The children's social behaviors directed toward their mother and toward a stranger were observed in semistructured situations in the twins' homes. The most notable finding was that social behavior toward the stranger was heritable in several situations, but social behavior toward the mother was not. The evolutionary implications of this finding were discussed in relation to Bowlby's theory of attachment. The second major finding was that environmental influences salient to the development of social behavior in infants operate primarily within families (making family members different from one another) rather than between families (making family members similar to one another), as is widely assumed.

ACKNOWLEDGMENTS

I wish to acknowledge the support of the W. T. Grant Foundation, the Spencer Foundation, and NICHD research grant HD-10333. I thank Rebecca G. Miles for her excellent editorial assistance in the preparation of this chapter.

REFERENCES

Allen, G. 1975. *Life science in the twentieth century.* Wiley, New York.

Barash, D. P. 1975. Ecology of paternal behavior in the hoary marmot (*Marmota caligata*): an evolutionary interpretation. *Journal of Mammalogy* 56:612–615.

1976. The male response to apparent female adultery in the mountain bluebird, *Sialia currocoides:* an evolutionary interpretation. *American Naturalist* 110:1097–1101.

1977. *Sociobiology and behavior.* Elsevier, New York.

Bell, R. Q. 1968. A reinterpretation of the direction of effects in studies of socialization. *Psychological Review* 75:81–95.

Benzer, S. 1973. Genetic dissection of behavior. *Scientific American* 229:24–73.

Bowlby, J. 1969. *Attachment.* Basic Books, New York.

Buss, A. H., & R. Plomin. 1975. *A temperament theory of personality development.* Wiley-Interscience, New York.

Cavalli-Sforza, L. L., & W. F. Bodmer. 1971. *The genetics of human populations.* Freeman, San Francisco.

Clarke, B. 1975. The causes of biological diversity. *Scientific American* 233:50–60.

Cooper, R. M., & J. P. Zubek. 1958. Effects of enriched and restricted early environment on the learning ability of bright and dull rats. *Canadian Journal of Psychology* 12:159–164.

Crow, J. N. F., & M. Kimura. 1970. *An introduction to population genetics theory.* Harper, New York.

DeFries, J. C., & R. Plomin. 1978. Behavioral genetics. *Annual Review of Psychology* 29:473–515.

Dobzhansky, T. 1970. *Genetics of the evolutionary process.* Columbia University Press, New York.

Erlenmeyer-Kimling, L. 1972. Gene–environment interactions and the variability of behavior. *In:* L. Ehrman, G. Omenn, & E. Caspari (eds.), *Genetics, environment and behavior: implications for educational policy.* Academic Press, New York.

Fisher, R. A. 1918. The correlation between relatives on the supposition of Mendelian inheritance. *Transactions of the Royal Society of Edinburgh* 52:399–433.

1930. *The genetical theory of natural selection.* Clarendon Press, Oxford.

Freedman, D. G. 1958. Constitutional and environmental interaction in rearing of four breeds of dogs. *Science* 127:585–586.

Fuller, J. L., & W. R. Thompson. 1978. *Foundations of behavioral genetics.* Mosby, St. Louis.

Hall, J. C. 1977. Behavioral analysis in *Drosophila* mosaics. *In:* W. J. Gehring (ed.), *Genetic mosaics and cell differentiation.* Springer, New York.

Hamilton, W. D. 1964. The genetical theory of social behaviour (I and II). *Journal of Theoretical Biology* 7:1–52.

Hebb, D. O. 1966. *A textbook of psychology.* Saunders, Philadelphia.

Hirsch, J. 1963. Behavior genetics and individuality understood. *Science* 142: 1436–1442.

Horn, J. M., R. Plomin, & R. Rosenman. 1976. Heritability of personality traits in adult male twins. *Behavior Genetics* 6:17–30.

Kimura, M., & T. Ohta. 1971. *Theoretical aspects of population genetics.* Princeton University Press, Princeton, New Jersey.

Kung, C., S. Y. Chang, Y. Satow, J. Van Houten, & H. Hansma. 1975. Genetic dissection of behavior in *Paramecium. Science* 188:898–904.

Lewontin, R. C. 1974. *The genetic basis of evolutionary change.* Columbia University Press, New York.

Loehlin, J. C., & R. C. Nichols. 1976. *Heredity, environment and personality.* University of Texas Press, Austin.

Lytton, H., N. G. Martin, & L. Eaves. 1977. Environmental and genetical causes of variation in ethological aspects of behavior in two-year-olds. *Social Biology* 24:200–211.

Mayr, E. 1974. Behavior programs and evolutionary strategies. *American Scientist* 62:650–659.

Merriman, C. 1924. The intellectual resemblance of twins. *Psychological Monographs* 33 (whole no. 152).

Parkinson, J. S. 1977. Behavioral genetics in bacteria. *Annual Review of Genetics* 11:397–414.

Plomin, R., & J. C. DeFries. 1979. Multivariate behavioral genetic analysis. *Behavioral Genetics* 9:505–517.

Plomin, R., J. C. DeFries, & J. C. Loehlin. 1977. Genotype–environment interaction and correlation in the analysis of human behavior. *Psychological Bulletin* 84:309–322.

Plomin, R., J. C. DeFries, & G. E. McClearn. 1980. *Behavioral genetics: a primer.* Freeman, San Francisco.

Plomin, R., & M. Manosevitz. 1974. Behavioral polytypism in wild *Mus musculus. Behavior Genetics* 4:145–157.

Plomin, R., & D. C. Rowe. 1978. Genes, environment, and development of temperament in young human twins. *In:* G. M. Burghardt & M. Bekoff (eds.), *The development of behavior.* Garland Press, New York.

1979. Genetic and environmental etiology of social behavior in infancy. *Developmental Psychology* 15:62–72.

Skinner, B. F. 1938. *The behavior of organisms: an experimental analysis.* Appleton, New York.

Trivers, R. L. 1972. Parental investment and sexual selection. *In:* B. Campbell (ed.), *Sexual selection and the descent of man.* Aldine, Chicago.

1974. Parent–offspring conflict. *American Zoologist* 14:249–264.

Ward, S. 1977. Invertebrate neurogenetics. *Annual Review of Genetics* 11:415–450.

West-Eberhard, M. J. 1975. The evolution of social behavior by kin selection. *Quarterly Review of Biology* 50:1–33.

Wilson, E. O. 1975. *Sociobiology: the new synthesis.* Harvard University Press, Cambridge, Massachusetts.

Wilson, R. S. 1978. Synchronies in mental development: an epigenetic perspective. *Science* 202:939–948.

Wynne-Edwards, V. C. 1962. *Animal dispersion in relation to social behaviour.* Hafner, New York.

PART III

THE DEVELOPMENT OF PATTERN

INTRODUCTION

GEORGE W. BARLOW

Historically, ethologists have shown considerable interest in the structure of behavior, whether they were dealing with patterned motor output or with the interaction between two individuals. This interest has usually been expressed in the investigation of the behavior of adult organisms. The chapters in this part illustrate the value of analyzing the changing structure of behavior that occurs during the course of development. The first two chapters confront the challenge offered by play behavior; the last two are concerned with the developmental dynamics of grooming and of nonplay dyadic interactions.

Chapter 10, by Patrick Bateson, hearkens back initially though briefly to the theme of continuity and discontinuity that marked the close of Part II. This chapter considers three criteria for recognizing discontinuity and some of the difficulties inherent in them. It then discusses play in kittens. The objective is to use play to explore the more general question in ontogeny occasioned by major behavioral reorganization, for example, at weaning. This chapter also inquires into ultimate factors - why is the reorganization coincident with weaning, whether weaning occurs early or late? - in order to point out the adaptiveness of such plasticity during ontogeny. Finally, the chapter touches upon some of the many functions that have been suggested for play, as does the next chapter, and presents the author's own insights.

Chapter 11, by Marc Bekoff and John A. Byers, is directed to play among mammals and its significance in behavioral development. It is an extensive review that is abundantly documented and argued in detail. But before the review begins, the problem of defining play is considered. The authors had been understandably reluctant to define play in Bielefeld. But we urged them at least to delimit the problem and to discuss the difficulties of formulating a definition - and that they have done. The review itself is organized around three themes: (1) How is the intent to play communicated? (2) What are the functions of play? Because play is energetically costly and done at some risk, there must be some selective pressure favoring its retention. (3) What is the nature of the spatiotemporal structure of play, and how does it vary across species? The last theme, though not the last in the chapter, has obvious ties to Chapters 12 and 13.

Chapter 12, by John C. Fentress, treats the development of behavior as an emerging structure. At one level, it analyzes the ontogeny of grooming in solitary mouse pups. That rich material provides the opportunity to comment on many issues in the development of behavior, including the meaning of continuity. The ontogenetic progression of the appearance of individual movements, their integration into higher-order sets, and the development of sequences are noted. As the mice grow, shifts in rules of connectivity and of contextual associations occur. The chapter reflects on whether such higher-order aspects of behavior may be more unitary and more evident than their components. It also takes up interindividual rules of movement and spatial relationship in two wolves and the ontogeny of those rules. It draws parallels, through analogy, to higher-order rules of relationships between limb segments of an individual as compared to relationships between individuals. Parallels with the development of speech are also mentioned, as well as other issues of general import.

The common ground between Chapter 13, by Ilan Golani, and Chapter 12 is apparent, which is not surprising considering that Golani and Fentress have worked together. Yet Chapter 13 is distinctly different. Much of it is devoted to developing a sophisticated methodology for visualizing behavior as a temporally dynamic structure with a highly quantified geometry. From this it seeks to derive subsystems that can be characterized and recognized as organizational stability while avoiding premature designation of atomistic units. The ultimate goal is to draw inferences about the organization of the neural substrates of the behavior. The relevance to ontogeny is obvious: The methodology provides a means of quantifying and visualizing reorganization of behavior during the course of development, whether in the patterned motor output of an individual or in the structure of interindividual encounters.

10

DISCONTINUITIES IN DEVELOPMENT AND CHANGES IN THE ORGANIZATION OF PLAY IN CATS

PATRICK BATESON

A butterfly has been a caterpillar; a limpet has led a mobile life as a delicate planktonic larva; and a frog has been a tadpole. It is commonplace that individual animals have within them the ability to lead utterly different kinds of lives. The expression of a particular capacity may be dependent on environmental circumstances. A locust will become migratory only if the population has been crowded for several generations. So, an individual animal may never express all the capacities of which it is capable.

These examples of animals having special capacities for particular stages or particular circumstances in their life cycle have been familiar to biologists for a long time. By degrees the biological evidence has impinged on studies of child psychology particularly through the writings of Piaget (see also Oppenheim 1980). It was a step forward that the behavior of a child should no longer be treated as though it were necessarily a miniature or less complicated version of adult behavior. Clearly, suckling is not an incompetent form of adult eating, and it seems entirely proper to treat many of the social skills of a child as adaptations to the special conditions in which it has to live. The clear implication for studies of the developmental process is that continuities from an early to a late stage should not always be expected.

Most of us have been brought up on an intellectual tradition that places great emphasis on the long-term effects of early experience. At first, it is not easy to accept that what happens to a young animal has little influence on its behavior as an adult. But as we warm to the idea, the possibility of a behavioral equivalent to metamorphosis can become so entrancing that it seems to dominate all other possible explanations for an apparent discontinuity in development. At this point, the enthusiasm for the analogy needs to be countered by some admonitions to consider alternative explanations for the evidence.

The most direct evidence for a discontinuous change in development comes from descriptive studies in which it is observed that a qualitatively new pattern of behavior emerges at a certain stage in the growth of the individual. The behavior may consist of something relatively straightforward, like grooming, or it may be an integrated series of actions that imply the development of a cognitive strategy, such as Piaget's *object permanence.*

The taxonomic problems of deciding when a "new" pattern of behavior really is new for that individual are not trivial. May it not be fundamentally equivalent to something that went before? This question is sidestepped by a different approach to discontinuity, namely, to look for changes in rates of change. For example, the growth spurt before puberty is sometimes regarded as a discontinuity in development. The assumption is, of course, that the intervals of the same value at different parts of the scale of measurement are equivalent. This assumption may be reasonable for height, but it is much more questionable for most indices of behavior. In any event, few patterns of behavior can be easily measured in the same way at widely different stages of development because of differences in size, general changes in rates of movement, and so forth. These difficulties mean that evidence for discontinuities in behavioral development tends to come from a different quarter.

A discontinuity is often presumed to have occurred when a given event exerts an influence at one stage of development and subsequently its effects cannot be detected. For instance, abnormally treated children can show differences in behavior from normally treated children at one stage of their development, but under certain conditions no differences can be found when their behavior is examined later in life (Clarke & Clarke 1976; Dunn 1976; Sameroff 1975).

Another line of evidence for discontinuities comes from longitudinal studies in which the same pattern of behavior is measured repeatedly in a group of subjects through development and the rank order on a measure at one stage is correlated with the rank order at another stage. The rank on a measure at one stage may successfully predict the rank at successive stages, and then the correlation suddenly falls away to insignificance (see Fig. 10.1). So long as the rank order is dependent on new sources of variation or fluctuates randomly, extreme values tend to regress toward the mean. As a result, correlations between behavior at one stage and behavior at successive stages tend to diminish with time. Nevertheless, a particularly rapid reduction in the strength of a correlation such as is shown in Figure 10.1 seems to require additional explanation - even though it is necessary to provide clear criteria for what is meant by a particularly rapid reduction.

It should be clear that the result such as that shown in Figure 10.1 might arise for a trivial reason. For instance, the scale of measurement might have a ceiling, so that in a case in which the average value of the population was rising with age, there might come a point when the variance within the population started to decline rapidly. This would lead to a sharp drop in correlation between measurements made earlier and measurements made at the point where the ceiling effect was obtained. Sometimes enhanced vulnerability to external influences or internal reorganization may produce a temporary reordering of individuals with respect to a particular measure. However, as compensatory mechanisms come into operation or the period of reorganization passes, the old rank order may return (Bateson 1978). This recovery would be detected only if measurement were continued for a long enough period of the subjects' lives.

The cases of greatest relevance to the discontinuity discussion are those in which a new internal or external source of variation becomes evident at a certain stage so that a permanent change is produced in the ranking of individuals. Before we allow theory to race too far ahead, it is necessary to

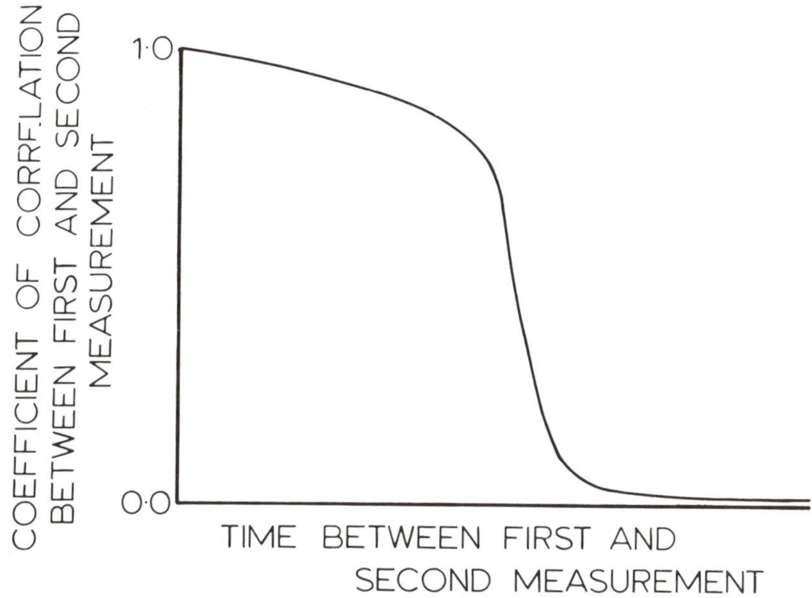

Figure 10.1. A hypothetical set of correlations between a measure taken at one stage of development and measures taken at successive stages. A discontinuity in development might be inferred if the correlation coefficients suddenly dropped at a given stage, as they do here.

know that at least one new source of variation is responsible for a discontinuity in behavioral development and that other explanations can be excluded. I have discussed these issues at greater length elsewhere (Bateson 1978), and they are also considered in Chapter 1. Here I should simply like to reiterate that the health of a subject can only benefit from considering as many alternative explanations as possible. I want to turn now from these generalities to the specific issue of the reorganization of play that occurs shortly after weaning in domestic cats.

THE DEVELOPMENT OF PLAY IN CATS

In recent years an increasing number of attempts have been made to understand the nature and function of play. These have been hampered by the fragmented character of the evidence (see Bruner et al. 1976; Weisler & McCall 1976; Bekoff 1978; Chap. 11). In response to the appeals for quantitative data, we started a study on the development of play in cats at Madingley (Barrett & Bateson 1978), focusing on quantitative analysis of potentially distinct facets of play from the fourth to the twelfth week after birth. Ideally, a descriptive approach that preserved information about the sequential structure of play should have been used. However, at a practical level, such a fine-grained approach is immensely time-consuming in terms of both data collection and

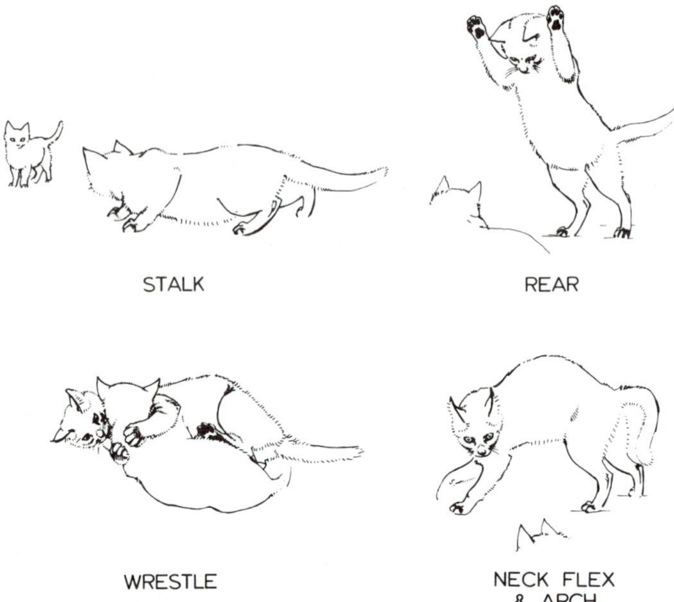

Figure 10.2. Aspects of play in the young domestic cat. (From Barrett & Bateson 1978)

subsequent analysis. So we compromised, measuring the frequency of behavior patterns that were relatively easy to record and analyze but that, nevertheless, would provide a reasonably detailed picture of changes with age in the kittens' playful activity.

Definitions of play are notoriously difficult even though the observer has a strong subjective sense of certainty about when an animal is playing; Chapter 11 discusses the issues in detail. In dealing with gray areas where obvious play grades into something else, we were sometimes able to use the criteria for recognizing play suggested by Loizos (1967). Play was also indicated when bites and pats delivered to another kitten did not elicit flight, agonistic behavior, or vocalization – in other words, when they did not seem to hurt or annoy the recipient. However, such criteria could not be applied to every observed account of supposedly playful activity. To a large extent, we had to rely on contextual cues. The occurrence of a particular action was recorded if it was given just after the animal had been behaving in a way that did fit the rigorous criteria for play. It seemed better to do that than to exclude a large number of otherwise uncertain events. In practice, we observed only a few momentary changes from a playful to a serious state in circumstances in which we were observing the kittens. Interestingly these serious incidents seemed to occur more frequently in the older animals, and I shall return to this point later.

Five of the categories of play are illustrated in Figure 10.2. Detailed definitions are given in Barrett and Bateson (1978). In addition, we recorded

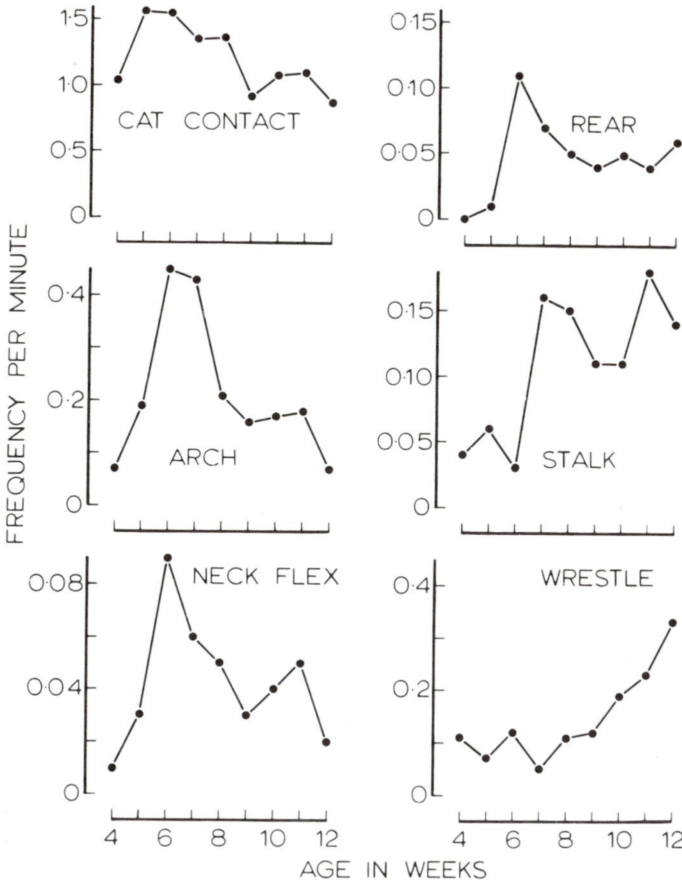

Figure 10.3. Changes with age in the frequencies of six measures of play in cats. The scores are the means for 28 kittens. (From Barrett & Bateson 1978)

the frequency with which kittens, by batting with their forepaws or by biting, made contact with each other (Cat Contact) or with objects (Object Contact). Despite the alleged difficulties of identifying play, most of these categories were not hard to recognize, and the performance of one observer correlated well with that of another observer (see Caro et al. 1979). Also, we had measures of the kittens' cries, their timidity, their general activity, and the distance between them and their mother.

The frequencies per minute for each category of play are shown in Figures 10.3 and 10.4 for a sample of 28 kittens. Cat Contact, Arch, Neck Flex, and Rear initially increased significantly and then fell away in frequency significantly after the seventh week. Stalk, Wrestle, and Object Contact increased significantly from the 4-to-7-week period to the 8-to-12-week period. (Object Contact, in particular, increased dramatically from the seventh to the eighth

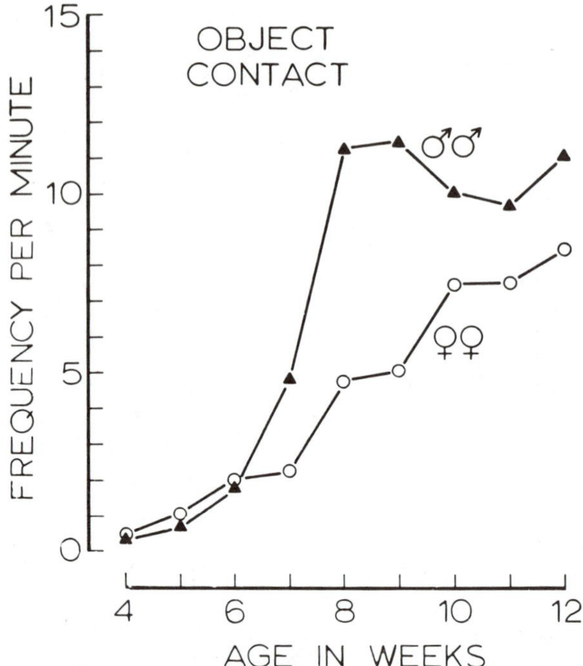

Figure 10.4. Changes with age in the frequencies of Object Contacts in cats. The scores are the means for 14 males and 14 females. (From Barrett & Bateson 1978)

week, which was why the data were split for purposes of analysis at that point.) Confirmation of the general trends has come from a study by Caro (1981), who also recorded details of social and predatory behavior. This study and an earlier one (Bateson & Young 1979) showed that Object Play in female kittens did not increase as dramatically as it did in males. However, the sex difference was obtained only if females were reared in a litter without a male in it (see Table 10.1). If the female had a brother, the frequencies of Object Contact in the two sexes were indistinguishable. We were able to show that females from mixed litters behaved like males in the absence of their brothers (Bateson & Young 1979), so the influence of the male on the female (if that is what it was) was relatively long-lasting. At present, we have no further insight into how the difference between females with and without brothers is generated.

The analysis of play frequencies suggests that some kind of reorganization takes place between 7 and 8 weeks after birth. This impression is corroborated by two other pieces of evidence. First, six out of the seven measures of play obtained in the 4-to-7-week period are poor predictors of the same measure in the 8-to-12-week period. Only in the case of Cat Contact is the correlation between the measure in the 4-to-7-week period and that in the 8-to-12-week period statistically significant. Second, the correlations between the various measures of play drop significantly from the 4-to-7-week period to the 8-to-12-

Table 10.1. *Object contact (mean frequency per minute and SEM) at 8 to 12 weeks in male and female domestic cats in litters of same sex and of mixed sexes*

	Males	Females
With same sex	10.94 ± 1.57 ($N = 8$)	4.14 ± 0.86 ($N = 6$)
With other sex	10.85 ± 1.07 ($N = 6$)	8.09 ± 1.35 ($N = 8$)

Source: Data from Barrett & Bateson (1978).

week period. For instance, the Spearman correlation coefficient between Cat Contact and Wrestle is 0.80 in the 4-to-7-week period and 0.23 in the 8-to-12-week period. When all possible correlations between the categories of play are calculated, none is negative in the 4-to-7-week period and the mean is 0.35. By contrast, four correlations are negative in the 8-to-12-week period and the mean is reduced to 0.19. For comparison, the mean correlation between the nonplay measures is 0.07 in the 4-to-7-week period and changes to 0.01 in the 8-to-12-week period. It would be foolish of me (and inconsistent) to deny that some of these results might have arisen from ceiling, floor, or other clumping effects on the various scales of measurement. Nevertheless, I do not think all the low correlations can be explained away so easily – particularly when the variances of the correlated measures are the same (see also Caro 1981).

The developmental trends and the lack of association between most of the categories of play, particularly after 7 weeks, suggest that output from a variety of separately controlled systems may be commonly lumped under the general heading of "play." Object Contact, in particular, seems to be the output from a different system from those influencing other measures of play. Comparison between the developmental trends in the measures of play and those of the other measures indicates that none of the changes in the categories of play can be readily accounted for in terms of changes in general attributes of behavior such as activity, timidity, or distress. These impressions were substantiated by a failure to find correlations between the play and nonplay measures (see Barrett & Bateson 1978). So, three points emerge from this descriptive study:

1 Play is heterogeneous, and it seems likely that the factors controlling one system of play are not the same as those controlling another.
2 None of the systems of play can be linked simply to general attributes of behavior such as gross motor activity. So, there is something special about each system of play.
3 Substantial reorganization in the control of play seems to take place between the seventh and eighth weeks after birth.

The precise nature of the reorganization in play taking place between 7 and 8 weeks after birth is not yet known. One explanation is that the kittens become more exploratory at this stage. As a result, object manipulation increases and, through competition for available time, other categories of play drop in frequency. Some support for this view comes from the work of Dodwell et al. (1976), who found that dark-reared kittens started to manipulate a panel that turned on a light shortly after the age at which we obtained a sharp increase in Object Contact (see also Timney et al. 1979). Equally, their results could have been generated by an increase in object play or both types of behavior could depend on a third and, as yet, unidentified developmental change.

Another explanation for the reorganization in play is that some kind of behavioral differentiation takes place, and as this happens the various measures of play come increasingly under separate types of control. These new controlling factors could be the ones that influence distinct systems of adult behavior so that, for example, Arch becomes increasingly associated with agonistic behavior and Object Contact becomes increasingly associated with exploration and prey catching.

Caro (1980b) has measured various aspects of play and predatory behavior and found, among other things, that the correlations between Arching, Rearing, and playful chasing, on the one hand and predatory behavior on the other, declined from before 8 weeks to afterward. Interestingly, approaching and biting siblings became more strongly correlated with predatory measures over the same period of development. These findings raise some important issues about the functional interpretation of play; I shall discuss these later.

Here, it is worth noting that an observer experiences the greatest difficulty in categorizing the intermediates between obvious play and serious activity after the eighth week. Furthermore, Egan (1976) found that the stimuli that were most effective in eliciting Object Play were those most closely resembling natural prey objects. She found this after the eighth week but unfortunately did not look at it in younger kittens. There is a strong implication that, at least in the older animal, some overlap of control exists between specific systems of play and specific systems of nonplayful activity.

The principle that there may be some degree of overlap between one activity and another is not difficult to grasp; indeed, it is likely to be a common feature of behavioral systems (see Fentress 1973, 1976). In practice, partial overlap of control between two systems can enormously complicate the problems of motivational analysis. Furthermore, as Fentress (1973) pointed out, it creates considerable problems when attempts are made to categorize behavior – an all too familiar problem in the study of play.

An obvious developmental milestone that might be linked to some reorganization in play is weaning, which starts about 6 weeks after birth. If the reorganization is a move toward a more adultlike state, the adaptive links with weaning would be obvious. However, a functional link need not necessarily imply a causal link in the ontogeny of each individual.

In looking for such a link, we have been examining the possibility that early weaning might accelerate the reorganization of behavior (Bateson & Young 1981). Around the 5th week after birth, before weaning normally ends, two kittens from a litter of four were removed from the mother and reared together in another room. They were hand-reared until they could take solid food of their own accord. The separated kittens lost weight but eventually caught up and continued to grow at the same rate as the kittens left with the mother.

Throughout this period and the period in which they were observed, each separated kitten was kept with its separated sibling. We scored the frequency of each measure of play as the separated kittens and their siblings remaining with the mother grew older.

Some of these measures indicated that, indeed, the changes in play occurred at an earlier age in the separated kittens. An unexpected finding was that the separated kittens played significantly more than those in the control group. In part this was because they were more active, but when the play data were corrected for general activity differences, the separated kittens were still found to have played more. The early-weaned kittens not only developed more quickly but also seemed to follow a different developmental course.

Obviously it is not possible, on the basis of a preliminary study, to state precisely what is causing the changes in behavioral development in the prematurely weaned kittens. It might be the change in the diet; it might be the stress produced by the end of suckling; it might be many things. Nevertheless, it does seem reasonable to infer that the change in organization of play is induced by some aspect of weaning. As a result, propensities lying concealed within the developing animal emerge.

Even though the behavior is reorganized, play done before the change may still influence adult behavior. It is possible that the perceptual or motor skills acquired in the course of play prior to the reorganization of behavior are used in newly emerging behavioral systems that will eventually be of service to the adult animal. These matters of use and service raise an entirely different question from the one I have been considering so far. What is play for? The functional issue of the adaptiveness of play can no longer be avoided.

FUNCTIONS OF PLAY

I have argued elsewhere that it is useful to distinguish between development of behavior and behavior used in development (Bateson 1976:411; Oppenheim 1980). Although it is not exclusively a feature of juvenile behavior, play does occur predominantly in young animals. This is certainly the case in the domestic cat (Koepke & Pribram 1971; West 1974; Caro 1980). So, it is reasonable to suppose that play is part of the scaffolding required to build the edifice of adult behavior. In other words, this form of behavior is required in the processes of developing adult behavior and may even be needed to gather specific kinds of information.

Although some people have argued that play has no biological function of this kind, most who have written about the subject have assigned a specific role to play in the assembly of adult behavior. However, the variety of roles that have been suggested is remarkable. Baldwin and Baldwin (1977), in their excellent review of the literature, listed 30 biological functions attributed to exploration and play. As they pointed out, several of these overlap and the list can be shortened. Chapter 11 discusses ways in which it can be further reduced.

It is worth emphasizing that some consequences of play may be beneficial without having been particularly decisive in shaping the evolution of play. (For a discussion of this point, see Hinde 1975 and Bateson & Hinde 1976:319.) For instance, it is patently unnecessary to play in order to recognize members of the social group, acquire knowledge of local culture, or become accustomed to strange features of the environment because many species are able to do these things without obviously playing. Nevertheless, kin recognition and many other possibilities are plausible, beneficial outcomes of play when it does occur. We need to look for consequences of play on which strong selection pressures are likely to have more than compensated for the undoubted costs. I believe that those features of play that allow simulation of potentially dangerous situations arising in adult life were probably the most important in the course of evolution. In this view, attention should be focused on the effects of play on fighting and on catching dangerous prey.

With these thoughts in mind, it is not difficult to reduce the list of functions for play to a manageable length without postulating unduly vague or general consequences on which natural selection is supposed to have acted. Even so, I see no special need to reduce the list to a single candidate which is *the* role for play. Our study of play in cats suggests that it is a mistake to treat play as a unitary category.

If the various play systems are causally distinct, why should different systems have evolved? A reasonable answer is that they are concerned with different functions. Some aspects of play could be concerned with the better prediction of future rivals' behavior, some with increasing predatory skills, and so forth. If this is correct, the discontinuity in object play occurring after the seventh week could reflect the changing ecology of the kitten as it is weaned and moves out of the nest. It would be efficient to concentrate play concerned with social behavior into a time when the kittens are in enforced contact with each other, and to step up play with the physical environment as the kittens' ties to the natal area are gradually broken.

A separate functional issue is why the changes in the organization of play should be linked causally to weaning. It may be the simplest way of coping with individual variation in mothers. A kitten that changed to the postweaning state at 50 days after birth when its mother had stopped producing milk 20 days beforehand might well be at a disadvantage compared with a kitten whose development was responsive to the milk-producing capacity of the mother. The late-developing kitten would behave inappropriately in the new circumstances generated by changes in diet and the mother's behavior and by the move out from the den where it was born.

An even more cogent argument for kittens having a facultative response to the time of weaning would arise if the mother herself adjusted the time of weaning according to environmental conditions. Take the simple case shown in Figure 10.5, in which a mother is capable of producing two litters in her lifetime and the parental resources spent on the first litter eventually influence the chances of survival of the second litter. The best strategy for producing the maximum number of surviving offspring in a lifetime is to wean the first litter before the kittens have extracted all the possible benefits they could from the mother.

The curves shown in Figure 10.5 are for a particular set of environmental conditions. If the conditions at the time of the first breeding are bad, then the mother may not be able to produce so much milk and, as a consequence, the number of offspring surviving from that litter might fall. The optimal time for

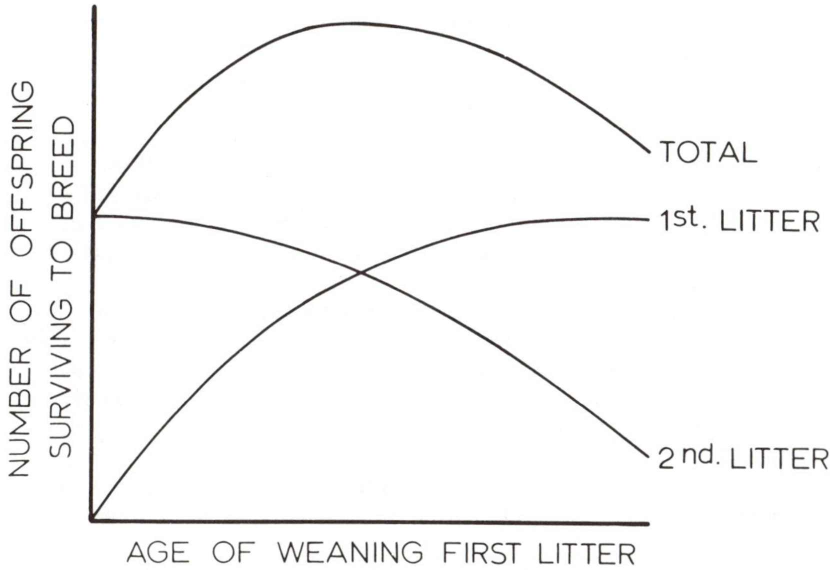

Figure 10.5. The hypothetical numbers of offspring surviving to breed in the first and second litters plotted against the time of weaning of the first litter.

weaning the first litter could be altered so that it would pay the mother to adjust weaning time according to the nature of the environmental conditions. In general, the effect of worse than usual conditions in the first breeding season would be to reduce the age at which the first litter was weaned. However, if the conditions were so bad that the mother herself was unlikely to survive to breed again, the optimal age of weaning might then increase dramatically so that the mother devoted all that she was able to give to her first (and only) litter.

As with all such modeling attempts, the precise predictions would depend on the details of the model. It would be possible to explain away any set of results by fiddling with the parameters of the model. The only point I want to make is that a facultative adjustment of weaning time by the mother to environmental conditions is possible. If it does happen, the kittens would have to be able to change to the postweaning state whenever the mother chose to wean them.

CONCLUSION

At the beginning of this chapter, I suggested that analogies with metamorphosis and latent migratory abilities in insects have a certain use in the understanding of behavioral development in much more complicated animals. I pointed out that an apparent discontinuity in behavioral development was not a sufficient justification for employing such analogies. It is important to consider alternative explanations for the evidence. Even with this caution in mind, the substantial changes in the play of cats taking place shortly after weaning do seem to reflect the outcome of new mechanisms coming into operation at a particular stage in development. Furthermore, preliminary evidence suggests that these changes are induced by weaning.

If the metamorphosis analogy is used for the reorganization of the play of cats after they have been weaned, what precisely are the implications? Are we to suppose that the reorganization involves the wiping out of all the effects of previous experience? If this were so, it would mean that play prior to weaning was simply required for that stage of life and had no influence on adult behavior – a conclusion that does not seem plausible. So, where does that leave a crude application of the metamorphosis concept?

It is worth noting, first, that even some insects can carry over the effects of experience from larval to adult life (Manning 1967; Thorpe & Jones 1937). Second, the reorganization of behavior could be radical without implying the dissolution of previously stored information. For instance, previously linked behavior patterns could become part of separate systems. It is not hard to employ another metaphor and imagine that reorganization involves the transfer of subroutines from one general program to others. It is much more difficult to test such ideas, but that should not inhibit the airing of them.

Many of the rapidly occurring changes after weaning may simply reflect the fivefold increase in Object Play. This increase may displace other mutually exclusive forms of play and so generate a misleading impression that everything is happening at the same point in development. The presumed transfer of skills acquired during play before weaning to systems of behavior required by the adult may take place over a much longer period of time. That change need not be anything as explosive in character as the sudden increase in Object Play.

Understanding the nature of what happens during a period of behavioral reorganization in ontogeny is distinct from asking why the rules for development evolved in the first place. Nevertheless, some interaction can and does take place between the two independent lines of theoretical activity (e.g., Fagen 1977; Bateson 1981). Several functional explanations can be given for why the reorganization in play might be linked to weaning. One states simply that the cat has to start growing up at this point; so, the skills gathered through play prior to weaning have to be transferred to the serious systems of behavior required by the adult. This is the growing-up hypothesis. Another functional explanation is that weaning represents a change in the ecology of the kitten as its food and, increasingly, its surroundings change; therefore a change must occur in the kinds of information that can be usefully gathered from the environment. This is the optimal instruction time hypothesis.

It seems likely that the relative plausibility of these functional explanations will depend on what is known about the precise changes occurring at weaning. Conversely, a liking for one of the functional explanations would focus attention on particular aspects of the developmental process. For my part, I do not think the functional explanations are mutually exclusive. It may well turn out that the reorganization of play involves both a redistribution of old skills and a preparation for gathering new information.

SUMMARY

Analogies between aspects of behavior development in complex animals and metamorphosis and latent migratory ability in insects can be helpful. However, an apparent discontinuity in development may arise for a number of reasons, some of which are trivial.

Substantial reorganization in the play of cats takes place around 50 days after birth. Preliminary evidence suggests that the change is induced by weaning.

The descriptive evidence suggests that play in cats is heterogeneous and that the factors controlling one system of play are not the same as those controlling another.

Social play occurring before the behavioral reorganization at around 50 days may simulate potentially dangerous aspects of adult social encounters such as fighting. Social play may start before weaning because the opportunities for contact with siblings are particularly great at this stage.

Object Play may increase after weaning as the ecology of the kitten changes and it moves out from the natal area. This play may simulate potentially dangerous aspects of catching prey and dealing with the physical environment.

The sudden increase of Object Play after weaning may give the misleading impression that at exactly the same stage, skills gathered during social play are transferred to the systems of behavior required by the adult. Such transference may be a much slower process than increasing the frequency of one form of play.

ACKNOWLEDGMENTS

I am indebted to the following for their comments on earlier drafts of the manuscript: George W. Barlow, Tim Caro, Judy Dunn, Klaus Immelmann, and Michelle Young. I am particularly grateful to Tim Caro for much useful discussion and for allowing me to quote some of his unpublished data. The work done on cats at Madingley by Michelle Young and myself was supported by a grant to me from the Science Research Council.

REFERENCES

Baldwin, J. D., & J. I. Baldwin. 1977. The role of learning phenomena in the ontogeny of exploration and play. *In:* S. Chevalier-Skolnikoff & F. E. Poirer (eds.), *Primate bio-social development*. Garland, New York, pp. 343–406.

Barrett, P., & P. Bateson. 1978. The development of play in cats. *Behaviour* 66:106–120.

Bateson, P. P. G. 1976. Rules and reciprocity in behavioural development. *In:* P. P. G. Bateson & R. A. Hinde (eds.), *Growing points in ethology.* Cambridge University Press, Cambridge, pp. 401–421.

1978. How does behaviour develop? *In:* P. P. G. Bateson & P. H. Klopfer (eds.), *Perspectives in ethology,* vol. 3. Plenum Press, New York, pp. 55–66.

Bateson, P. P. G. 1981. Behavioural development and evolutionary processes. *In:* King's College Sociobiology Group (eds.), *Current problems in sociobiology.* Cambridge University Press, Cambridge.

Bateson, P. P. G., & R. A. Hinde. 1976. *Growing points in ethology.* Cambridge University Press, Cambridge.

Bateson, P., & M. Young. 1979. The influence of male kittens on the object play of their female siblings. *Behavioral and Neural Biology* 27:374–378.

Bateson, P. G., & M. Young. 1981. Separation from the mother and the development of play in cats. *Animal Behaviour* 29.

Bekoff, M. 1978. Social play: structure, function, and the evolution of a co-operative social behavior. *In:* G. M. Burghardt & M. Bekoff (eds.), *The development of behavior.* Garland, New York, pp. 367–383.

Bruner, J. S., A. Jolly, & K. Sylva (eds.). 1976. *Play: its role in development and evolution.* Penguin Books, Harmondsworth, Middlesex.

Caro, T. M. 1980. Effects of the mother, object play and adult experience on predation in cats. *Behavioral and Neural Biology,* 29:29-51.

1981. Predatory behaviour and social play in kittens. *Behaviour* 76.

Caro, T. M., R. Roper, M. Young, & G. R. Dank. 1979. Inter-observer reliability. *Behaviour* 69:303–315.

Clarke, A. M., & A. D. B. Clarke. 1976. *Early experience.* Open Books, London.

Dodwell, P. C., B. N. Timney, & V. F. Emerson. 1976. Development of visual stimulus-seeking in dark-reared kittens. *Nature (London)* 260:777–778.

Dunn, J. 1976. How far do early differences in mother–child relations affect later development? *In:* P. P. G. Bateson & R. A. Hinde (eds.), *Growing points in ethology.* Cambridge University Press, Cambridge, pp. 481–496.

Egan, J. 1976. Object-play in cats. *In:* J. S. Bruner, A. Jolly, & K. Sylva (eds.), *Play: its role in development and evolution.* Penguin Books, Harmondsworth, Middlesex, pp. 161–165.

Fagen, R. M. 1977. Selection for optimal age-dependent schedules of play behavior. *American Naturalist* 111:395–414.

Fentress, J. C. 1973. Specific and nonspecific factors in the causation of behavior. *In:* P. P. G. Bateson & P. H. Klopfer (eds.), *Perspectives in ethology,* vol. 1. Plenum Press, New York, pp. 155–224.

Fentress, J. S. 1976. Dynamic boundaries of patterned behaviour: interaction and self-organisation. *In:* P. P. G. Bateson & R. A. Hinde (eds.), *Growing points in ethology.* Cambridge University Press, Cambridge, pp. 135–169.

Hinde, R. A. 1975. The concept of function. *In:* G. Baerends, C. Beer, & A. Manning (eds.), *Function and evolution of behaviour.* Clarendon Press, Oxford, pp. 3–15.

Koepke, J. E., & K. H. Pribram. 1971. Effect of milk on the maintenance of sucking behaviour in kittens from birth to six months. *Journal of Comparative and Physiological Psychology.* 75:363–377.

Loizos, C. 1967. Play behaviour in higher primates: a review. *In:* D. Morris (ed.), *Primate ethology.* Weidenfeld & Nicholson, London, pp. 176–218.

Manning, A. 1967. "Pre-imaginal conditioning" in *Drosophila. Nature (London)* 216:338–340.

Oppenheim, R. W. 1980. Metamorphosis and adaptation in behavior of developing organisms. *Developmental Psychobiology* 13:353–356.

Sameroff, A. J. 1975. Early influences on development: fact or fancy? *Merrill-Palmer Quarterly* 21:267–294.

Thorpe, W. H., & F. G. W. Jones. 1937. Olfactory conditioning and its relation to the problem of nest selection. *Proceedings of the Royal Society, B,* 124:56–81.

Timney, B. N., V. F. Emerson, & P. D. Dodwell. 1979. Development of visual stimulus-seeking in kittens. *Quarterly Journal of Experimental Psychology* 31: 63–81.

Weisler, A., & R. B. McCall. 1976. Exploration and play: resumé and redirection. *American Psychologist* 31:492–508.

West, M. 1974. Social play in the domestic cat. *American Zoologist* 14:427–436.

11

A CRITICAL REANALYSIS OF THE ONTOGENY AND PHYLOGENY OF MAMMALIAN SOCIAL AND LOCOMOTOR PLAY: AN ETHOLOGICAL HORNET'S NEST

MARC BEKOFF AND JOHN A. BYERS

If there is one problem area that has suffered from a plethora of gross description by behavioral scientists and a corresponding dearth of quantitative documentation, it is play behavior. When coupled with the difficulty of studying ontogenetic processes in general (Bekoff 1977a; Symons 1978), analysis of the role of play in development may be an arduous task. As we show below, and as has also been demonstrated before, play is an analyzable behavioral phenotype in both ontogenetic and phylogenetic frameworks and may indeed be acted upon by natural selection (Bekoff 1977a; Fagen 1977; Symons 1978). And, with the revitalization of the view that many questions of ontogeny are ultimate (evolutionary) ones (Alexander 1975, 1977; Appleton 1910; Bekoff 1978a; Fagen 1977; Gould 1977; Hall 1906; Immelmann 1975; Lorenz 1965; Tinbergen 1963), it should be only a matter of time until studies of play will shed the proximate veil that has cloaked the vast majority of efforts. Furthermore, as will become apparent below, analyses of play will have to deal with different levels of organization, ranging from neurobiological processes to overt motor patterns (Welker 1971).

This chapter includes a fairly broad survey of literature that relates to play.[1] It becomes immediately obvious that play research requires multidisciplinary input. We shall selectively review diverse studies of mammals (for reviews of avian play, see Armstrong 1965 and Ficken 1977) that provide evidence bearing on three major research foci of social and locomotor play, namely, communication, structure, and function. We shall briefly discuss self-play, but object play will not be considered in detail. We shall not be directly concerned with the proximate factors that encourage and permit play to occur, such as weather, terrain or habitat, and nutrition (Berger 1978; Gard & Meier 1977; Gentry 1974; Hinde 1971; Jungius 1971; van Lawick-Goodall 1968; Richard & Heimbuch 1975; Sussman 1977; Zimmerman 1975). Nor shall we discuss the relationship between play and classical ethological drive theory (see M. Bekoff 1976; Ewer 1968; Leyhausen 1973).

PLAY AND DEVELOPMENT

To anyone who has observed young mammals, it will not come as a surprise to find a chapter devoted to play in a book whose subject is behavioral ontogeny.

As Beach (1945) has pointed out, play progresses as part of ontogeny, and play and postnatal development cannot be teased apart. And, as Lowenfeld (1967) noted, play is not an accident but an essential function of childhood. There might be a relationship between postnatal play and prenatal motor activity as well (see "Prenatal motility and postnatal play: functional continuity?"). In addition, young individuals in the majority of the few mammalian species for which play has been described devote considerably more time and energy to play activities than do adult conspecifics and are persistent in seeking out possibilities for play.[2] There is also evidence that play has immediate as well as delayed benefits (Fagen 1977). That is, the social organization of young individuals may be affected by within-group play associations, and there may also be cumulative effects on later behavior stemming from early play interactions (M. Bekoff 1977b; Harlow & Harlow 1969; Owens 1975a; Wilson 1973). Last, the periods of maximal play and maximal growth coincide; in most mammals this is during early life when the developing young are free to play.

Because natural selection operates at all ages (Fishbein 1976; Williams 1966) and does not bypass ontogeny, play may be viewed as an ontogenetic adaptation and need not be studied only with respect to adult behavior. The young of many species appear programmed to move, and the direction and consequences of their actions depend to a large extent on external stimulation and reinforcement. Although we recognize that behavior at one age may be a poor predictor of behavior at a later age and that there may be developmental discontinuity in certain aspects of ontogeny (Barrett and Bateson 1978; Bateson 1976; Kagan 1978; Plooij in press), we feel that differential early play experience most probably can affect subsequent individual development and reproductive fitness.

DEFINITION

Play is a blanket term that covers a wide range of behavior patterns. The word is used with reference to social interactions, interactions with inanimate objects, situations in which an individual(s) moves vigorously about as if it has been bitten by a bug in its "activity center," and even interactions with a god (Moltmann 1972; Neale 1969; Rahner 1972). The absence of a good definition of play, however, has not been an impediment to solid research. Although we are to some extent in agreement with Gentry (1974:402) that "play research can adequately proceed without a global definition of the term," the existence of what we believe to be careless and loose definitions (e.g., Levy 1978) prompts us to make an effort to define play, with full recognition that our definition may be no better than that of others. The analogies that we draw below are only suggestive and are meant as no more than new possibilities that should be considered along with others.

Play is a recognizable phenomenon, yet it has proven difficult to develop a comprehensive definition that is applicable to even the relatively few mammalian species in which some form of play has been described. As more species are studied, the difficulty of coming up with a satisfactory definition will undoubtedly increase logarithmically. Definitions based on structure pose a problem, because play assumes such different forms in different mammalian

Table 11.1. *Some defining characteristics of mammalian social play that may be used to distinguish play from nonplay behavior (see text); not all characteristics are necessarily present in any given species*

Characteristic	Representative studies
Activities from a variety of contexts are linked together sequentially	Aldis 1975; Bekoff 1972, 1974; Henry & Herrero 1974; Loizos 1966; Poole 1978; Rudnai 1973; Symons 1978
Specific sets of signals, gestures, postures, facial expressions, gaits, and vocalizations are important in the initiation of play (though their function has only rarely been demonstrated)	Aldis 1975; Altmann 1967; Bekoff 1972, 1974, 1977d; Berger 1978; Eibl-Eibesfeldt 1974; Henry & Herrero 1974; Jungius 1971; McGrew 1972; Poole 1978; Sade 1973; Symons 1978; Tembrock 1957; Wilson 1973; Wilson & Kleiman 1974
Certain behaviors, such as threat and submission, are absent or occur infrequently	Bekoff 1972; Blurton Jones 1967, 1972; Goldman & Swanson 1975; van Hooff 1974; Jungius 1971; McGrew 1972; Owens 1975a; Smith & Connolly 1972; Symons 1978
There are breakdowns in dominance relationships, role reversals, changes in chase–flee relationships and contact time, and individuals engage in self-handicapping	Barnett 1975; Bekoff 1978a; Eibl-Eibesfeldt 1974; Loizos 1969; Miller 1975; Owens 1975b; Poole 1978; Symons 1978
There are detectable changes in individual motor acts and differences in sequential variability	See text

orders; definitions based on function are, at this time, impossible, because the function(s) of play largely remains a mystery. The enormity of the problem of definition is evidenced by the fact that the word *play* itself is used in definitions of play, and moreover, in works that consider (critically, in some cases) previous definitions under the heading "definitions of play" or "what is play," no further definition or insights are offered.

Table 11.1 presents some of the characteristics of play that have been found in a number of studies on a few, but diverse, mammals. Not all of the characteristics apply to all species, nor is it presently possible to say that at least two or three must apply in order for the activity to be play. It is clear, however, that play is readily characterized and is different from other behaviors that it resembles. It should also be stressed that social play in infants or juveniles is not only distinguishable when compared to adult activities. Rather, play may be clearly separated from other activities performed by the same young individuals (Hill & Bekoff 1977). It is important to make this point; one can get into the trap of assigning no function to play because young individuals are only borrowing adult activities from other contexts with a corresponding loss of adaptive function(s).

Prenatal motility and postnatal play: functional continuity?

In an attempt to define postnatal play, it may be instructive to begin with a brief discussion of prenatal motor behavior, or motility (for reviews, see A. Bekoff 1976, 1978; Hamburger 1963, 1973; Oppenheim 1972, 1974), especially from a neuroethological perspective (A. Bekoff 1978). That there may be a link between prenatal locomotor activity and postnatal locomotor play (M. Bekoff et al. 1980) may not be so frivolous an idea as it first seems, given the fact that both activities share a number of common characteristics, at least at the level of overt behavior. Also, it is well known that prenatal experience can affect postnatal behavior (e.g., Impekoven 1976; Impekoven & Gold 1973; Joffe 1969), and in humans, postnatal repetition of prenatal activity sequences has been studied in great detail (e.g., Humphrey 1969). Rosenblatt (1971) has related fetal movements in cats to postnatal nursing activities such as head turning and mouth opening.

Prenatal motility. It now appears that all vertebrate fetuses studied to date exhibit spontaneous overt motility during development, and in most cases, spontaneous motility is mediated by the nervous system (neurogenic, not myogenic, in origin; Oppenheim 1974). That is, movements are not dependent on sensory stimulation for their initiation or maintenance, and in many cases, external stimulation does not alter them (Oppenheim 1972). Furthermore, chemical suppression of motility in chick embryos for a short time during development does not modify the development of subsequent motility, reflex responses, or interfere with hatching (Oppenheim et al. 1978). In a sense, prenatal movements appear to be functionless by-products of neural activity.

One of the most interesting findings, and the one that is most relevant to the present discussion, is that although overt motility at different stages of chick embryonic development does not resemble later perinatal or postnatal behaviors such as hatching or walking, it has been found that there is a strong resemblance in the covert patterns of muscle activation and coordination between early and later motility and between hatching and walking, as demonstrated by electromyographic (EMG) recordings (A. Bekoff 1976, 1978; A. Bekoff et al. 1978). These findings do not necessarily mean that motility and later behaviors are functionally isomorphic, nor do they attend to the important issue of whether or not the later (ontogenetically speaking) behavior patterns are really the same as ones that appeared earlier in development (Bateson 1978a). Rather, the discovery that the underlying neuromuscular patterning of both prenatal and postnatal behaviors may be the same, coupled with experimental documentation that prenatal movements are spontaneous or endogenous, provides us with a new perspective from which we can view postnatal play behavior.

Postnatal play. The perspective provided by consideration of prenatal development is that outwardly purposeless motor activity is a regular feature of vertebrate ontogeny that seems to have reached the peak of its expression in mammals, in which it is continued long after birth as play. The point we wish to make is that it seems as if early activation of the developing neuromuscular system was selected for at some point in vertebrate evolution and that this requirement for activity became more pronounced, elaborate, and longer-lived (ontogenetically speaking) as the vertebrate neuromotor system became more complex.

Because prenatal life is basically nonsocial and opportunities for motor activity are limited, likely benefits of prenatal activity include the facilitation of neuromuscular development. We tend to be highly suspicious of claims that such behaviors are unavoidable, nonfunctional expressions of the developing nervous system, because nonfunctional energy expenditure is usually selected against (see "The concept of function in relation to play"). In this view, therefore, the phylogenetically oldest function of postnatal outwardly purposeless motor behavior (play) was probably the facilitation of neuromuscular development (see "Play as motor training").

At this point, natural selection probably began to mold this postnatal behavior in response to a number of selection pressures that were most likely consequences of a species adaptive syndrome (e.g., its size, habitat, and food habits) and its degree of adult neuromuscular and behavioral complexity. The result, as we observe it today, is play. As more descriptions of play in many different mammalian orders become available, we will be able to fill out a phylogenetic tree of play and thus may be able to deduce its evolutionary history more precisely.

Therefore, there are two possible avenues of continuity between prenatal and postnatal motor activities. The first is phylogenetic, in that embryonic motility may be ancestral in evolution to postnatal play. Many vertebrates that show prenatal motility do not play (e.g., fish, amphibians, reptiles, birds, and perhaps a large number of mammals). The second is ontogenetic, in that there may be functional continuity between prenatal motility and postnatal play.

A DEFINITION OF PLAY

When one scans the literature on play, it becomes apparent, as indicated above, that there are some similarities between prenatal motility and postnatal play. Both appear to be functionless, and in many cases play (like prenatal motility) appears to be spontaneous (Ewer 1968). One characteristic of locomotor play is that of sudden, persistent, frantic motor activity (such as locomotor-rotational movements; Wilson & Kleiman 1974) that may include undirected protean flight (see Driver & Humphries 1966; Humphries & Driver 1967, 1970). It is almost as if the animals are responding to some internal force and asking themselves, "What should I do with this discharge that will help me and for which I won't have to pay severe penalties?" In fact, it seems that virtually all postnatal activities in nondeprived settings that appear functionless are referred to as play.

Having clarified these points, we shall now define play as it is seen in natural conditions or in settings that closely simulate them. *Play* is all motor activity performed postnatally that appears to be purposeless, in which motor patterns from other contexts may often be used in modified forms and altered temporal sequencing. If the activity is directed toward another living individual, it is called *social play;* if it is directed toward an inanimate object(s), it is called *object play;* if the activity carries the individual in a seemingly frantic flight about its environment, it is called *locomotor play*. Both social and object play can be locomotory in nature, and what has been referred to as *self-play* could include object and locomotor play. We would also like to include in our definition the idea that there may be an "impulse to exercise" (Appleton 1910), and that in some cases, play may be "involuntary" (Ewer 1968). Many of the first interactions of young mammals, either with littermates, parents, or objects, seem to develop almost reflexively from fidgeting and mouthing.[3] For example, early rooting and mouthing movements used in nursing, when transferred to the leg or face of a littermate, are usually called *play*.

Are these early behaviors simply the result of endogenous neural activity (as has been found in invertebrates)? Are the movements nonspecific reflexes that are channeled by whatever is available (e.g., nipple or limb)? Why do individuals engage in self-play?

The emergence of high-energy play from more subtle forms of interaction suggests that the phenotype of play that is observed at a given moment is dependent on the motor and sensory abilities of the developing individual. Accordingly, it is necessary to trace longitudinally, in detail, the development of motor activity from birth until the emergence of adultlike coordinated behavior (e.g., Altman & Sudarshan 1975; Fox 1966; Pepin & Baron 1978; Scott & Fuller 1965). And, just because the earliest vestiges of play may be involuntary, this is not to suggest that with increasing experience (social and otherwise), play is not modifiable. Of course, it is. As Bateson (1976) has suggested, developmental control mechanisms may themselves be modifiable by the environment in which an organism grows up.

In sum, the apparent lack of purpose of play activity, its spontaneity, and its emergence from early fidgeting movements suggest that there may be some continuity between prenatal motility and postnatal play. Whether the two activities simply look discontinuous because of the differences between prenatal and postnatal environments is beyond the scope of this discussion. The outward purposelessness of both suggests that there has been selection for early rehearsal of certain motor activities. Although the apparent lack of purpose of play is an important defining characteristic, it really is not functionless at all (see "Hypothesized functions of play").

SELF-PLAY

In addition to play with other individuals and objects, many mammals engage in self-play (Bekoff 1972, 1974; Ferron 1975; Mason 1965), even in the presence of other potential partners. Ferron (1975), studying red squirrels (*Tamiasciurus hudsonicus*), suggested that a relationship might exist between the degree of sociability and the relative proportion of solitary and social play activities, the more social species engaging in less solitary play. Although this is an interesting suggestion, it may be of limited applicability. In infant canids, for example, the amount of self-play seems to depend almost entirely on the desire of other available individuals to engage in play, regardless of species. Pairs of infant beagles (*Canis familiaris*), infant wolves (*C. lupus*), and infant coyotes (*C. latrans*) were observed for equal amounts of time between 21 and 50 days of age. If one ranked them in degree of species-typical sociability, the order would be, from highest to lowest, beagles, wolves, coyotes. The frequency of occurrence of self-play for each species was 553, 134, and 319 instances, respectively (Bekoff 1974). The beagles, the most social of the observed species, engaged in much more self-play than did the coyotes. It is really not worthwhile to carry speculations about self-play further; more data are needed.

COMMUNICATION

Because play resembles other activities, it is important to consider the ways in which play intention may be communicated. Little research has been done in the area of social play since the last reviews (Bekoff 1977d, 1978a), so there is no use repeating at length what is already known. Briefly:

1 Most mammals that engage in social play have evolved specific and often very subtle visual, olfactory, auditory, and/or tactile signals that are used in the initiation (and possible maintenance) of social play (Altmann 1962, 1967; Bekoff 1972, 1974, 1975, 1977d; Chevalier-Skolnikoff 1974; Jungius 1971; Poole 1978; Redican 1975; Sade 1973; Stern 1974; Symons 1978; Tembrock 1957; Wilson 1973; Wilson and Kleiman 1974; but see Wemmer & Fleming 1974).

2 These signals appear stereotyped (Bekoff 1977d) and in various canids, at least, seem to be modified little, if at all, during ontogeny.

3 Although these signals appear to be important in the generation of a play mood, this fact is more accepted on faith than on solid evidence. There have been only two demonstrations, to our knowledge, that play signals are, in fact, functional (Bekoff 1975; Berger 1978).

4 There is no evidence that play signals serve as punctuation (Hailman and Dzelzkalns 1974), though they often serve to call attention to the performer.

5 There is no evidence that visual play signals serve to maintain a play mood (but see Stern 1974), though it is much more difficult to study this for other modalities. Because social play differs structurally from other activities anyway, Symons (1978) suggests that play signals are not even necessary, because the individuals should be able to "read" the differences. However, in a number of species, play signals are repeated throughout playful interactions (Bekoff 1976, 1977d; Poole 1978). Poole (1978) found that during polecat play, play signals occupied about one-half the time spent in social play, but he did not provide evidence that the signals were functional or even necessary to maintain the play mood.

A comment on the term *metacommunication* is in order. This word has often been used to refer specifically to play signals. However, as has been pointed out by Hailman (1977), such signals are merely syntactic in that they provide aid to interpretation of other signals by the recipient. When used specifically to refer to play signals, the term is too restrictive, because any signals with syntactic content are, in fact, metacommunicative (Bekoff 1978a; Hailman 1977; Smith 1977). We suggest simply dropping the term and dealing with the phenomenon.

In addition to initiating social play in which the signaler is involved, it has also been demonstrated (Byers 1978) that play signals can be used to facilitate solitary play in other individuals. Siberian ibex (*Capra ibex sibirica*) females stimulate locomotor play in kids by performing play movements that always contain a rotational component. Mothers show a strong tendency to stimulate selectively only their own offspring, and they tend to do it after a period of time during which the kids have not engaged in play. There are probably benefits to the young partaking in play (Byers 1977), although there are also high risks of falling and serious injury. Byers presented evidence that physical training effects have shaped the evolution of play in the ibex. In addition to this interesting finding, maternal facilitation of play in young also points to the fact that the term *play signal* should be extended to include behaviors that may elicit solitary play as well as social play. Play is a contagious activity, and perhaps play signals in a wider variety of mammals function in stimulating play in individuals other than the signaler.

THE TERMINATION OF SOCIAL PLAY

Although there has been a good deal of emphasis on the question of how play begins, questions about how play ends (e.g., the message, "this is no longer play") are also interesting. Few data are available on the termination or control of play (M. Bekoff unpublished data; Blurton Jones 1967; Carpenter 1934; Henry & Herrero 1974; Jungius 1971; van Lawick-Goodall 1968; McGrew 1972; Owens 1975a; Symons 1978). Size, strength, and individual rank seem to play important roles. In play between male baboons (*Papio anubis*), larger individuals have a greater role in determining the amount of play that occurs (Owens 1975a). In reedbucks (*Redunca arundinum*), the stronger males control playfighting (Jungius 1971). In infant coyotes, among whom there were clear-cut dominance relationships, play was terminated 82.9% of the time by the more dominant individual (Bekoff unpublished data). In human children, as in other mammals, there is a difference between the way in which rough-and tumble play and agonistic behavior terminates (Blurton Jones 1967; McGrew 1972). After agonistic interactions, the participants usually separate and do not continue interacting. After rough-and-tumble play, the children remain in closer proximity and often only become temporarily separated by joining a group. Future studies will have to concentrate on both ends of an interaction, as it may be just as important to know that "this is play" as it is to know that "this is no longer play."

STRUCTURE

It is essential to have a solid grasp of what individuals do when they play.[4] Indeed, structure and function are inextricably tied together. A complete analysis of play structure would entail consideration of neural maturation (see above: Altman et al. 1973; Anokhin 1964; Bekoff & Fox 1972; Kilmer 1975; Nadel et al. 1975), physical development, and events such as weaning (Chap. 10), as well as anatomical (motor and sensory) abilities and constraints (Bekoff 1977d; Gambaryan 1974; Jenkins & Camazine 1977; Lehner 1978; Symons 1978). Other factors that may affect play structure, especially in the field, include individual nutritional state, the availability of different types of playgrounds, and the nature of the terrain (Berger 1978; Gentry 1974; Sussman 1977; Symons 1978; Fig. 11.1).

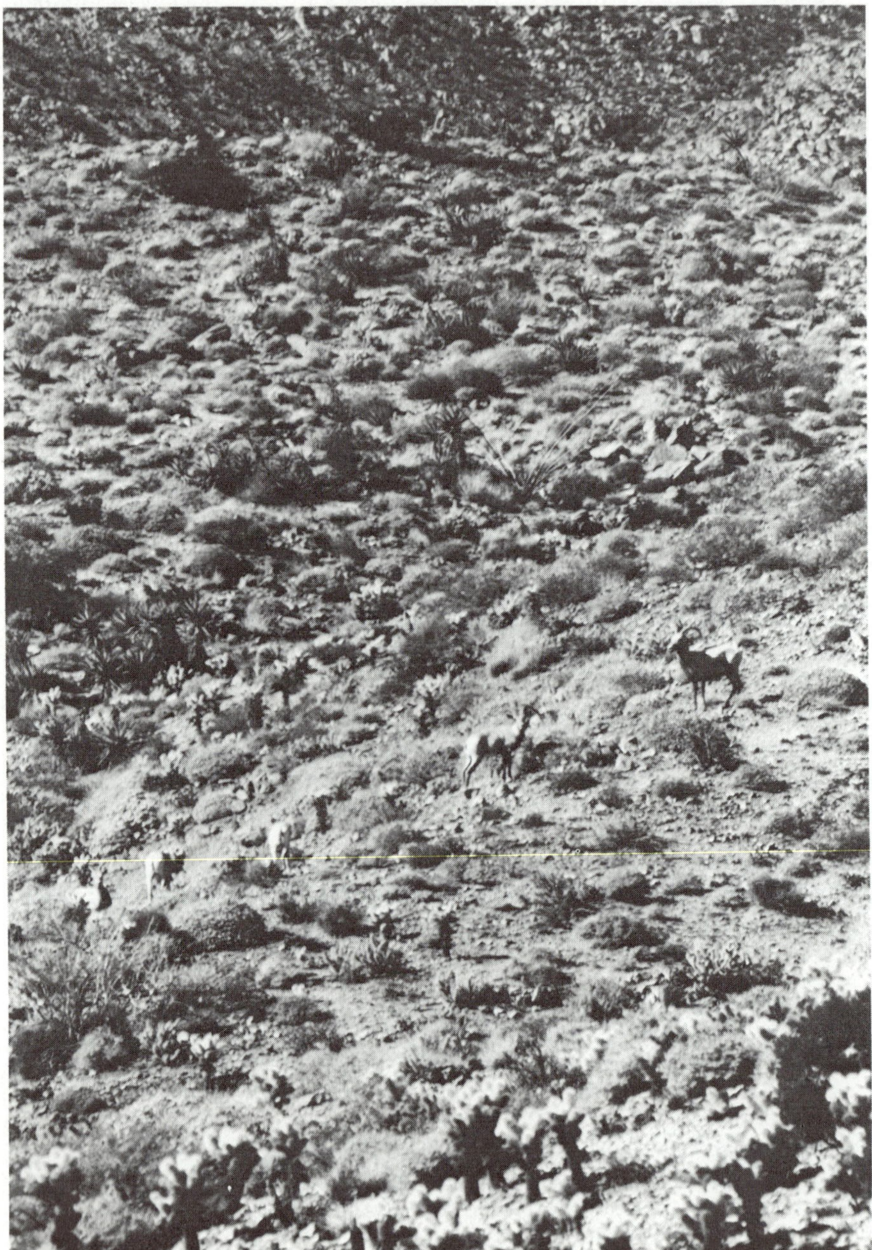

Figure 11.1. Typical habitat of mountain sheep, *Ovis canadensis,* living in the Santa Rosa Mountains, outside of Palm Desert, California. Note the presence of Cholla, *Opuntia* spp., cacti. Because of the abundance of this plant, play is more risky than in montane populations of sheep in the Chilcotin, British Columbia, Canada, where

We would like now to consider some representative studies that present quantitative data bearing on play structure. A number of questions can be asked. For example, how closely does play resemble the other categories of behavior from which it borrows motor acts? In addition to this general inquiry, we can examine the acts themselves and ask (1) are the acts actually the same? (2) are there predictable changes in the frequency or rate of performance in duration, variability, form, and/or sequential coupling?

The general phenotype of social play

One fairly reliable characteristic of mammalian social play (Table 11.1) is the incorporation of actions from different contexts (e.g., predatory, antipredatory, agonistic, sexual; but see Wilson 1974) into a continuous interaction (with the exception of play-soliciting signals; see "Communication") (Fig. 11.2). The motor patterns seem to lack the function of the acts they resemble. In many species, agonisticlike actions prevail (Ewer 1968; Gentry 1974; Henry & Herrero 1974; Hrdy 1977; Owens 1975a, 1975b; Poole 1978; Poole & Fish 1976; Rowe-Rowe 1978; Symons 1978).

Indeed, play may grade into agonism, but not as frequently as is often believed (Bekoff 1978a; Symons 1978). From an analysis of 6 minutes of social play in hybrid polecats, F_1 *mustela putorius* × *M. furo,* Poole (1978) found that social play resembled uninhibited fighting and predatory behavior, but that it was most closely related to the former. In both uninhibited fighting and play, for example, the majority of attacks (68% in play and 80% in fighting) were directed toward the neck, and the greatest amount of biting was on the neck. For 14- to 18-week-old polecat hybrids, agonistic behavior patterns accounted for 45.1% of play acts observed. The general structure of play, not unexpectedly, varies from species to species. For example, whereas some carnivores, primates, and rodents tend to perform predominantly agonistic and predatory actions during play, other mammals, especially ungulates, tend to perform behaviors that are used in antipredatory behavior (Berger 1978; Ewer 1968; Symons 1978).

The next level of analysis entails an examination of the motor patterns themselves and the changes, if any, that accompany their incorporation into social play. There have been few detailed analyses that bear on this issue. The problem of measurement is particularly difficult when comparing young individuals to adults (e.g., Henry & Herrero 1974; Poole 1966, 1978), and it would be best, if possible, to compare same-age individuals, or the same

Caption to Figure 11.1 (*cont.*)
there are more suitable play habitats such as sandbowls and grassy fields. There were differences in both the structure and frequency of occurrence of play in the desert. Desert yearlings were never observed to engage in locomotor play, and play was observed significantly less frequently in the desert. This study is a good example of the necessity for fieldwork on allopatric conspecifics. Speaking about play in the mountain sheep per se would be misleading; the functions and consequences of play may be different in the two environments. (From Berger 1978)

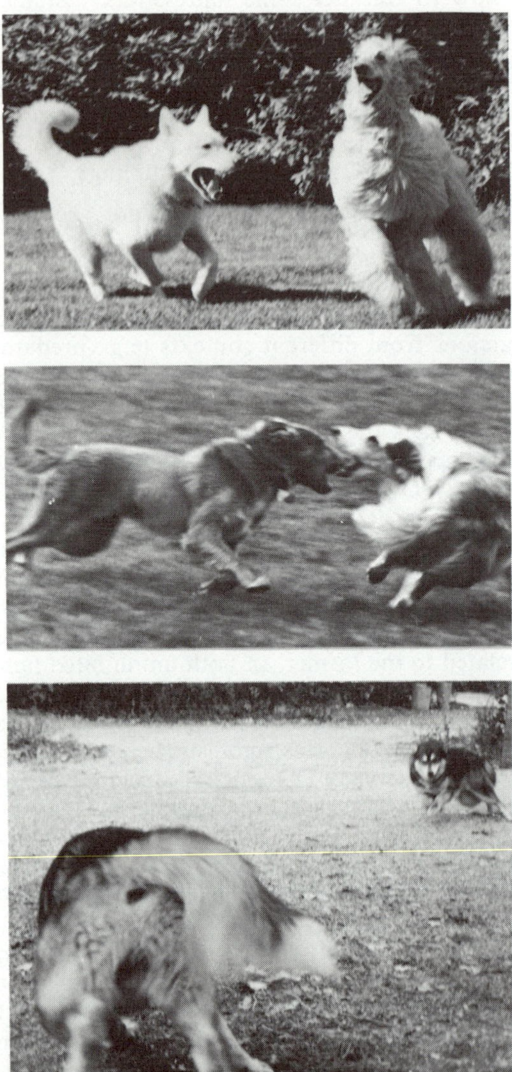

Figure 11.2. One of the most reliable characteristics of mammalian social play involves the incorporation of actions from different contexts into a continuous interaction. *Top:* The malemute on the left shows a threat face; the lips are drawn up vertically, and the teeth are bared. This was a prelude to an inhibited neck bite. The afghan on the right is wearing a play face; the lips are drawn back horizontally, and the mouth and eyes are open wide. *Middle:* Reciprocal threat faces during chase play. Note the small mouth; these dogs were also snarling at one another. *Bottom:* a dog's-eye view of the play bow from behind. Bows may be performed at the beginning or during play interactions. Bows performed during play interactions are very stereotyped in both duration and form. Compared to bows performed at the

individuals, that engage in social play as well as in the behaviors from which social play borrows its constituent actions.

Along these lines, three motor components of social play and agonistic behavior were analyzed in infant Eastern coyotes (*Canis latrans* var.) (Hill & Bekoff 1977). Play and agonism emerge at about the same time ontogenetically, although there are differences in frequencies of performance (Bekoff et al. 1975). The three actions that were analyzed were standing over, scruff biting, and general body biting (see Bekoff 1978b for descriptions). The initial intent of the study was to determine if the fluid, smooth actions performed during play were exaggerated when compared to the same actions performed in a nonplay situation. Duration was used as a measure of exaggeration, following the example of Henry and Herrero (1974). We did not find this to be the case (see *"Coyotes"*). Neither did Henry and Herrero.

There is a problem in interpretation associated with the use of the rather imprecise term *exaggeration.* Henry and Herrero (1974) compared play in young American black bears (*Ursus americanus*) to agonistic behavior in adults. And, as Poole (1978) pointed out, use of the term *exaggerated* can be misleading if it implies that an exactly equivalent behavior is performed by adults and that this behavior is not exaggerated. However, there is no reason to make this assumption at all. Comparison of the same individuals (same age) in different contexts is all that is required (Hill & Bekoff 1977). Furthermore, the term *exaggeration* need not imply that any comparison is being made. For example, actions used in the solicitation of play that are observed in virtually no other context appear to be performed in a loose, bouncy, exaggerated manner (Altmann 1967; Bekoff 1972, 1974; Symons 1978; Wilson and Kleiman 1974). Another problem stems from the use of the term *exaggeration* to refer to a variety of characteristics such as duration, rate of performance, or form. Yet, the term has been used in general to define play, without regard to any property of the motor pattern(s). For example, Poole and Fish (1976:251) define play as follows: "Play is defined as *any* [our emphasis] activity involving exaggerated movements and inhibited attacks." We believe that the term *exaggerated* is a useful expression for the initial characterization of motor patterns either for comparative purposes or for a behavior itself. However, if the term is used in a comparative manner, measurements of defined characteristics must be presented (Henry & Herrero 1974; Hill & Bekoff 1977). As more precise studies are done, the specific features that lend an exaggerated appearance should become apparent.

Social play, play fighting, and real fighting

Because social play so closely resembles real fighting in many species, we can ask what characteristics specifically separate the two. Of course, detailed

Caption to Figure 11.2 *(cont.)*
beginning of play bouts, however, bows occurring during play bouts for some canids show more variability in duration but are essentially the same in form (Bekoff 1977d). The canid bow apparently has been shaped by natural selection and, as a result, amibiguity in the communicated message has been reduced.

studies of agonistic behavior as well as of social play are required (Poole 1974; Tembrock 1962) if meaningful comparisons are to be made. A number of characteristics such as the presence or absence of specific signals or motor acts, changes in the acts themselves (duration, frequency, rate, form), differences in sequential coupling of individual acts, and changes in interaction patterns (e.g., contact time, chase–flee relationships, role reversals) may be observed and contrasted. Once again, few data are available for such comparisons. A consideration of some of these studies will show that social play and/or play fighting can be teased apart from real agonism with careful study.

Polecats. In polecats, although play fighting may grade into real aggression and it is not possible to draw a distinction at any developmental stage between the cessation of aggressive play and the commencement of ritualized aggression, differences between the two are still clearly detectable (Poole 1966, 1967, 1974, 1978). A summary of Poole's work is as follows: During play fighting (as compared to real fighting), biting is inhibited, there are role reversals, patterns that may intimidate or immobilize the partner are absent, self-handicapping is observed, there are more chase–flee interactions, the open-mouth play face is worn, and play-soliciting actions are performed. In aggression there is a slower tempo, with sustained attack and intimidation of the opponent.

American black bears. In a seminal and detailed study focusing on subtle aspects of behavior, Henry and Herrero pointed to a number of ways in which juvenile play and adult agonism could be separated (Henry & Herrero 1974). (An analysis of same-age individuals should also be done.) Even low-intensity and high-intensity play fighting could be differentiated with respect to the variability in duration of the bouts (see their Table 1; mean duration did not differ, but there was significantly more variability in low-intensity play fighting; based on our calculations of coefficients of variation). Some characteristics of play, in contrast to aggression, are these: Play is usually nonvocal, with the exception of respiratory sounds; biting and clawing are inhibited, and there is greater variability in their orientation; there are characteristic facial expressions (open mouth, puckered-lip face) and ear positions (crescent-shaped or partially flattened); there are no attempts to pin down the partner; there are rearing–pawing matches; several motor patterns are observed almost exclusively during social play (head butting, muzzle seizure, play nip, and hindleg clawing), and many motor patterns are performed in an incomplete fashion.

Coyotes. Both coyotes and Eastern coyotes (Bekoff et al. 1975; Hilton 1978) are useful for comparing social play and agonistic behavior because infants show high frequencies of both types of behavior and cross-age comparisons are not necessary (Bekoff unpublished data; Hill & Bekoff 1977). In Eastern coyotes, an analysis of three actions, standing over, scruff biting, and general body biting, showed that all of them lasted longer and showed greater variability in agonistic behavior. There were no differences in rates of biting or in the form of biting (Bekoff unpublished data), although stand overs in play differ with respect to the rigidity of the extended forelegs on the back of the partner

Table 11.2. *Frequency distribution of play signals during social play by a pair of infant coyotes (21–50 days of age)*

	Action unit[a,b]												
	1	2	3	4	5	6	7	8	9	10	Total	χ^2	p
Male	25	2	5	3	3	6	1	2	4	0	51	91.9	0.001
Female	14	2	5	4	2	2	2	2	2	1	36	36.8	0.001

[a] Because play bouts differed in duration, division of bouts into equal time units could not be done. Therefore, individual bouts were divided into 10 "action units" such that an equal number of movements were performed per unit. The number of movements in corresponding units (e.g., lst, 2nd ... 10th) of all observed bouts was summed to give a "super sequence," and the frequency of occurrence of each act, in this case play signals, was determined for each unit. For further information, see Ainley (1974) and Bekoff, et al. (1979).

[b] Using this type of analysis, one is able to look at the distribution of acts and compare it to a random model as well as compare individuals using a Wilcoxon matched-pairs signed ranks test. In this example, the individuals did not differ from one another.

(Bekoff 1978b). Analyses of the form of other behaviors (using high-speed motion pictures) used both in play and nonplay are currently being undertaken. In addition to looking at the acts themselves, we have also been concerned with the frequency distribution of different motor patterns during ongoing interactions (e.g., where they occur, as the first, second, third, or *n*th act) and with sequential variability.

In coyotes, approximately 90% of all play bouts are previously solicited by an observable play-soliciting action (Bekoff 1974; Vincent & Bekoff 1978). These actions are almost never observed outside of the context of play and are nonrandomly distributed in the beginning (first 10%) of all interactions, usually occurring as the first act (Table 11.2).

The distribution of three acts associated with agonistic behavior was also investigated, namely, threat vocalizations, distress vocalizations, and passive submission (see Bekoff 1978b and Lehner 1978 for descriptions). During social play, these three behaviors occurred rarely, and they were randomly distributed. In some cases, however, passive submission occurred most frequently toward the end of an interaction and, in fact, the termination of a playful interaction was often facilitated by the performance of the behavior. Likewise, threat vocalizations, if they occurred with any notable frequency, came at the end of an interaction and typically elicited passive submission and consequent termination of the interaction. During agonistic interactions, however, threat vocalizations, distress vocalizations, and passive submission occurred up to 10 times as frequently, appeared earlier in the interaction, and continued at a high frequency throughout. Finally, an analysis of the frequency of occurrence and distribution of face biting, scruff biting, and body biting showed that there were no differences between social play and agonistic behavior. So, in infant coyotes, Eastern coyotes, and other canids (Bekoff unpublished data), social

Table 11.3. *Sequential variability, in terms of two-act coupling, in the social play and agonistic behavior of pairs of infant canids (21–50 days of age)*

	Coefficients of variation[a]	
Species	Social play	Agonistic behavior
Coyote	98.02 (0.69)[b]	72.27 (0.67)
Coyote	89.32	58.79
Wolf	76.43	51.96
Wolf	83.67	43.82
Dog (beagle)	121.77	78.98
Dog (beagle)	107.79	74.32

[a]Coefficients of variation were determined for the conditional (transitional) probabilities of two-act transitions in complete transition matrices. See Bekoff 1977c for a discussion and rationale of this method.

[b]All differences were statistically significant; because of the lack of stationarity of our data (Bekoff 1977c:28–30), we did not calculate the measure of conditional uncertainty. The numbers in parentheses were calculated by R. Fagen and represent normalized variability ($H_{B}/_{A}H$). Note that the results are consistent, although the assumptions for the use of the latter technique have not been met.

play and aggression can be differentiated with respect to the duration, variability, frequency of occurrence, and distribution of individual motor acts, especially those used in play soliciting and agonism.

The next level of analysis involves consideration of the way in which individual motor acts are assembled into sequences. In infant canids (Table 11.3) as well as in ferrets (Fagen 1978), play sequences are significantly more variable than agonistic sequences.[5] Indeed, it is the protean nature of play that seems to catch the eye of most observers, although there are species differences. In fact, only a very limited number of species (three canids, ferrets; Fagen 1978), Norway rats, *Rattus norveigicus* (Poole & Fish 1975, 1976), and Hamadryas baboons, *Papio hamadryas* (LeResche 1976) have been studied quantitatively. The reason for species differences is not at all clear and probably will not be explicable until more data are available. The possible adaptive significance of increased behavioral diversity in social play will be discussed (under "Hypothesized functions of play"). With respect to the communication of play intention, it has been suggested that greater variability as well as other differences in temporal sequencing may be functional during play interactions in maintaining the play mood (Bekoff 1977d).

Nonhuman primates. As in other mammalian orders, there are consistent differences between social play and aggression among nonhuman primates. These include play-specific facial expressions (Chevalier-Skolnikoff 1974; van Hooff 1974; Hrdy 1977; Redican 1975; Symons 1978); for a comparative discussion of the "play face" see Poole (1978) and postures and gaits (Altmann 1967; Sade 1973; Symons 1978), differences in chase–flee relationships (Loizos 1969; Owens 1975b), role reversals, the absence of specific acts such as threat expressions and submission (van Hooff 1974; Owens 1975b; Symons 1978) changes in contact and chase durations (Owens 1975b), different biting orientations (Owens 1975b), and inhibited biting. The reader is referred to van Hooff (1974), Owens (1975b), and Symons (1978) for excellent and exemplary models of the types of analysis that are needed. Van Hooff's principal component and concordant analyses provide nice examples of the use of multivariate procedures in play research.

Human children. Although there have been many studies of human play, especially in children, it is perhaps not surprising to find that the most detailed studies in terms of structure (at least to our knowledge) have been done by scientists with ethological training (e.g., Blurton Jones 1967, 1972; Blurton Jones & Konner 1973; McGrew 1972; Sharpe 1973; Smith 1973, 1974; Smith & Connolly 1972). Although there are many similarities between social play in humans and nonhumans, the most striking difference is the absence of mouthing in human play (Aldis 1975:274). Aldis suggested that the lack of mouthing by humans is related to the disappearance of biting as a form of attack.

It has been shown that various forms of play can be separated from other categories of behavior by factor or principal component analyses (Blurton Jones 1972; Smith 1973; Smith & Connolly 1972). With respect to the distinction between play fighting and rough-and-tumble play, there is also a fairly clear difference between the two, although there are some shades of gray (Blurton Jones 1972; McGrew 1972). Blurton Jones (1972) showed that behaviors used in rough-and-tumble play, such as laugh, play face, run, jump, hit at, and wrestle, loaded more highly on a different factor than did behaviors associated with aggression, such as frown, hit, push, and take-tug-grab (see pp. 104–106 in his article for descriptions).

Blurton Jones stresses two important points, both of which are pertinent to studies of nonhumans as well. First, there are exceptions to the rule, in that there is an occasional individual who does not perform as if he or she has read the way things are supposed to be. But occasional exceptions do not necessarily render one's findings meaningless. Rather, they should stimulate research to determine the ways in which these individuals play and fight. Second, it remains possible that the distinctions that are evident at one age may change as a function of social experience.

McGrew (1972) also provided a detailed ethogram of child play, and his results can be summarized as follows. When comparing agonistic interactions and rough-and-tumble play (McGrew referred to rough-and-tumble play as *quasi-agonistic* behavior; however, quasi-agonistic behavior so closely resembles what other researchers call *rough-and-tumble play* that we think that comparison would be easier if the same terminology were used) to nonagonistic behavior, McGrew found that there were no differences in mean duration or mean number of behavior patterns exhibited per interaction. Also, 18 behaviors occurred significantly more frequently in agonistic and rough-and-tumble play than in nonagonistic interactions, 7 occurred more frequently in nonagonistic interactions, and for 39 behaviors there was no difference between the two categories (see McGrew 1972, Tables 5.6, 5.7, and 5.8). Four agonistic behaviors were absent from rough-and-tumble play. Blurton Jones's (1967) and McGrew's categorizations of rough-and-tumble play do not differ from one another. It is unfortunate that McGrew did not do more detailed analyses of the differences between agonistic and rough-and-tumble interactions.

In conclusion, it is clear that social play, play fighting, and real fighting are analyzable and different with respect to a number of measurable attributes and that individuals are able to read these differences. It is no longer necessary to characterize play as what it is not (or ever was), because play has its own defining properties, regardless of whether a neatly packaged definition can be devised.

THE CONCEPT OF FUNCTION IN RELATION TO PLAY

Study of the function of play seeks to answer the question Why do animals play? from the viewpoint of ultimate causation. In other words, it is a study of the process through which natural selection shaped this behavioral phenotype. As such, it is different from a study of proximate causation, which seeks to define the immediate stimuli and physiological mechanisms that control play. We repeat this truism here (one would think it repeated enough already; see Alcock 1975; Altmann 1974; Baker 1938; Barash 1977; Byers 1977; Moynihan 1973; Wilson 1975) because it is evident, from recent publications and presentations at scholarly meetings about play, that the point has not yet sunk in. As Beer (1975) correctly noted, at some point in the analysis of behavior, proximate and ultimate questions are woven together; however, we are not yet at that point in the analysis of play. Mammalian play is a complex phenomenon that has repeatedly resisted facile, all-encompassing explanations, and a distinction between proximate and ultimate questions about play is the first step that must be taken toward credible analyses; it will involve the formulation and testing of clearly defined, falsifiable hypotheses.

We must also consider some nuances of the term *function.* Function has been clearly discussed by Hinde (1975) and Williams (1966) and, with specific reference to play, by Symons (1978). The main point is that not all of the beneficial consequences of a behavior pattern constitute its function. By function, we mean the specific consequences of a behavior pattern that have resulted in its fixation in a species's repertoire by natural selection. This is a simple issue, theoretically, but there are often several equally plausible hypotheses about the function of a behavior pattern (Beer 1975), and it may be difficult to design studies or experiments to distinguish between them. In the case of play, it often seems likely that one motor pattern has several functions or that several motor patterns together have one function. The problem here is to reconstruct the evolutionary history of play so that we may know in what form, and why, mammalian play originally appeared and what modifications have since occurred. As in functional morphology, evidence from ontogeny and comparative anatomy should be useful in this analysis.

Play is a fascinating activity from an evolutionary point of view because it often involves risks and a substantial energy outlay but appears to confer no immediate beneficial results upon the player.

As far as we are aware, no one has measured the proportion of an animal's daily energy output spent in play, but it is clear that in several species play comprises the bulk of a young animal's vigorous activity (Fagen & George 1977; Symons 1978; Byers personal observation). Because natural selection often acts in a finely tuned way to curtail needless energy expenditures (e.g., biochemical pathways that produce specific compounds may not be developed or retained when these compounds become a stable component of a species's diet; Lehninger 1975) and also to reduce risks wherever possible (e.g., ritualized fighting among males during the mating season has evolved in many species; see Walther 1974), we assume that play would have been eliminated, or never would have evolved, unless it had beneficial results that outweighed its disadvantages. This argument is especially true for young mammals, which must devote a large amount of energy to growth and proportionally more energy than adults to thermoregulation. Young animals are in the worst possible position for superfluous or slightly adaptive energy expenditures, but they play more than other age groups.

The risk of physical injury in play has been documented by Byers (1977), Symons (1978) and Welles and Welles (1961). Because they are prereproductive, young mammals are also selected to take as few unnecessary risks as possible, but some regularly take risks in play (Symons 1978 found that rhesus monkeys fell from trees only during play). This means that play should confer substantial advantages upon the player. Symons (1978:2–3) has come to the same conclusion: "If play were not functional, animals that played would be at a selective disadvantage compared to non-playing animals that husbanded their resources, used their time more profitably, and avoided the inevitable risks of injury and exposure to predators."

What, then, may be some functions of play? Clearly, play has immediate effects on young individuals in that the activity could possibly maintain, facilitate, or induce certain developmental processes, both physiologically and behaviorally (see Gottlieb 1976 for a discussion of the effects of stimulation on development). For adults, play may be important in developing and maintaining social bonds (e.g., during courtship), as well as for physical training and exercise. In addition, there is evidence that rhesus monkeys (*Macaca mulatta*) sometimes use social play in a manipulative fashion to achieve immediate goals (Breuggeman 1976). However, it appears likely that social manipulation is a derived and not an original consequence of play (Symons 1978), and available evidence strongly suggests that in most instances play is a cooperative social venture (Bekoff 1978a).

Given that play has immediate benefits, one is still faced with the fact that play (like all other behavior patterns occurring before reproductive age) also must have delayed, cumulative consequences as well, specifically for individual reproductive fitness. That is, natural selection has favored behaviors of direct significance to young (or pre-adult) prereproductive individuals, and subsequent reproductive benefits may literally be consequences and not direct functions of play (Crook personal communication). The immediate benefits may be of a physical or social nature, or both (Table 11.4), and later reproductive benefits may accumulate from previous individual experience, of which play would constitute one type. However, an important and largely unconsidered question concerns the ages at which the maximum benefits of individual play motor patterns are realized. For instance, in many ungulate species, running play may increase endurance and thus have an immediate and cumulative benefit in terms of individual survival. However, butting-type play in males may result in enhanced competitive skill, which appears to be of little consequence to juveniles but of enormous importance for adults during competition for mates.

In the next section, we review major hypotheses about functions of play. Then we present the available evidence for these hypotheses, and in the final section we suggest methods that may be useful in future analyses of play.

HYPOTHESIZED FUNCTIONS OF PLAY

Many different beneficial consequences have been proposed as the function of play (see Baldwin & Baldwin 1977; Symons 1978). Although there are distinctions among play hypotheses, all those that seem to be worth considering may be placed in one of three categories. The fact that we establish these categories does not mean that finer differentiations within each should not be made. Indeed, anyone seeking to demonstrate a function of play should try to define his or her questions as precisely as possible. The three categories listed below are simply a start toward the goal of clear definition of the functions of play.

Play as motor training

Repetition of varied and vigorous motor activity generally has four physiological results in mammals: (1) bones thicken and become remodeled in response to the specific stresses imposed by the activity; (2) muscles that are used in the activity hypertrophy and show cellular and biochemical changes associated with an increased ability to do work; (3) cardiopulmonary capacity, efficiency increase, and metabolic pathways are altered so that the mammal shows increased endurance; (4) the smoothness, or economy of action or efficiency of the motions that are repeated, increases.[6] However, as Geist (1978:4) pointed out, any motor activity, including play, can become stressful and have negative effects on growth (see also Batzli et al. 1977 and Viitala 1977 for discussions of the effects of social factors on maturation). Also, excessive repetition may, in itself, impede learning (Haldane, cited in Hutt 1966).

Points 1, 2, and 3 comprise the *training response* defined by exercise physiologists. Fagen (1976) discussed the exercise literature in relation to play

Table 11.4. *Evidence for functions of play*

Authors[a]	Species/group	Study conditions	Function proposed	Evidence
Bekoff 1977a	*Canis* spp.	Captive	Social bonding	Degree of sociality of canid species positively correlated with the amount of social play performed and negatively correlated with the appearance of aggression before play
Birch 1945	Chimpanzees	Captive	Generic learning	Play with sticks improved later ability to use sticks in reaching food
Byers 1977	Siberian ibex	Captive	Motor training	Locomotor play occurred predominantly on steep slopes, despite risk (serious falls were observed during play)
Fagen & George 1977	Ponies	Captive	Motor training	Play comprised 65% of all running exercise and more than 95% of all fast turns
Sylva 1974	Humans	Experimental/captive	Generic learning	Prior play with the components of a problem improved later ability to solve the problem
Symons 1974, 1978	Rhesus monkeys	Wild	Motor training	Structure of play appropriate for motor training in fighting and predator avoidance; structure not appropriate for learning species-specific communication patterns
Vincent & Bekoff 1978	Coyotes	Captive	Motor training	Evidence against: prey-killing success not correlated with prior play experience
Wilson 1973	Voles	Captive	Social bonding	Spring-born voles played frequently, were subsequently tolerant of each other and new young; autumn-born males did not play and were subsequently intolerant of each other and new young (spring litters possessed a glandular secretion that stimulated play, whereas autumn litters did not)

[a]Only studies in which a function is proposed and evidence is presented are listed.

and made the important point that young mammals often show larger and more complete training responses than do older individuals, and that training responses attained at an early age often persist into adulthood. Fagen (1976) defined the process through which effects 1, 2, and 3 occur as *physical training* and, using the findings of the exercise physiologists, went on to predict what structure play should have if it is designed to provide physical training.

Symons (1978) discussed points 2 and 4 and their relation to play. He defined the process through which effects 2 and 4 occur as *practice* (Groos 1898) and showed that the classical characteristics of play established by Loizos (1966), Meyer-Holzapfel (1956), and others are congruent with the structure that juvenile activity should assume in order to provide practice. Symons's work is a beautifully clear example of how the structure of play may be used to make inferences about its function. However, use of the term *practice* should be avoided in favor of a more precise term. As Symons (1978:101) noted, "practice" implies repetition "in order to learn or become proficient." This is ambiguous because the term does not imply the domain (e.g., motor activity, social skills, cognitive skills) in which proficiency is gained.

The principal difference between Fagen's (1976) and Symons's (1978) treatment of this issue is that Symons emphasized point 4, the development of economy, precision, and smoothness of movements through repetition—"The components of a complex activity no longer require conscious attention for their performance and become automatic or reflex like" (Symons 1978:103). Compare this to a passage from Eccles's (1973) discussion of the function of the cerebellum:

> So, quite clearly, each side of the cerebellum is concerned in the smooth and reliable control of movement... on that side... What you do with ordinary movements is to give a general command – such as "place finger on nose," or "write signature," or "pick up glass" – and the whole motor performance goes automatically... You just give the general command from the cerebrum and let the cerebellum take over in order to give the fine characteristic details... It is my thesis that the cerebellum is concerned in all this enormously complex organization and control of movement, and that throughout life, particularly in the earlier years, we are engaged in an incessant teaching program from the cerebellum. [Eccles 1973:122–123]

Eccles may have been more daring than other neurophysiologists in his generalizations about cerebellar function, but we quote the passage to emphasize that the increased smoothness and efficiency of motor patterns gained through repetition is, in part due to selective training responses of the nervous system. For instance, human electromyelograms change as performance of a motor task becomes more skilled (Person 1958; Kamon & Gormley 1968) and exercise in young mice (B6D2F) and monkeys (*Macaca fasicularis*) results in cellular changes in the cerebellum (Floeter & Greenough 1979; Pysh & Weiss 1979). Thus, there is no reason to consider point 4 as separate from points 1, 2, and 3; all represent aspects of the developmental process leading to the proficient performance of complex motor activities. In order for an adult animal to perform a demanding motor task, its skeletal system must be strong enough to support the stresses produced by the activity, its muscles must be strong enough to drive the motion, it must have the necessary endurance (this becomes important mainly in prolonged activity), and it must have the ability to send precise motor commands to the appropriate muscles.

Thus, it is important to mention here that the play-as-motor-training hypothesis does not imply that normal adult motor patterns of coordination will fail to develop without play; rather, it suggests that play enhances the ability of animals to perform certain patterns of activity well. Indeed, most of the basic patterns of motor coordination that characterize the natural behavior of a species do develop in individuals reared in social isolation (Marler 1975).

It is therefore likely, for species in which play has evolved as a form of motor training, that play should mimic adult activities that (1) are closely related to survival; (2) involve considerable motor skill; and (3) occur relatively rarely compared to other patterns. Furthermore, by combining actions from various contexts in play, regardless of the variability of the sequencing, individuals may be assessing what works in a given situation and what routines and subroutines fit together (Bruner 1974a, 1974b; White 1959). In other words, the individuals may be looking for the optimal goodness of fit (Klopfer 1970) of individual behavior patterns in situations in which they do not have to pay severe consequences for mistakes. They also may be learning to make fine movements from more global actions involving many muscles and body parts (Gibson 1977). Even if the behaviors used in play differ from their adaptive counterparts in aggression, predation, or reproduction, it is possible that EMG patterns are similar and that this is the level at which training has its effects. It must also be stressed that the distinction between motor and cognitive training is murky (see "Play as cognitive training") and that benefits may accrue from both types.

The reviews provided by Fagen (1976) and Symons (1978) showed that repetition of motor patterns does result in skeletal and neuromuscular adaptations designed to achieve the above goals and that, in some cases, the repetition has more pronounced effects for young animals than for mature ones. The question, then, is not whether play provides repetitive exercise (there is no doubt that in many species it does) but whether the training responses produced by this type of exercise conferred a selective advantage that led to the evolution of play in animals.

Play as socialization

Most of the hypotheses about play fall into this category. The essential idea behind all of them is that young animals may enhance their ability to interact adaptively with some, or all, conspecifics by engaging in social play when they are young. In addition, the nature of play (or its absence) may be a useful diagnostic tool in monitoring social development (Axline 1969; Hutt & Hutt 1970; Leach 1972; Kalverboer 1977, personal communication). Three examples from this category state that play helps young animals learn species-specific communication skills (Dolhinow 1971; Jolly 1972); enhances the development of social bonds among individuals (Bekoff 1977b; Bowlby 1969; Carpenter 1934, 1974; Ross & Goldman 1977; Schaeffer & Emerson 1964; Watson 1972; Wilson 1973); helps young animals learn to control aggression (Suomi & Harlow 1971). Baldwin and Baldwin (1977) and Symons (1978) presented more extensive lists. It is difficult to find many socialization hypotheses that are specific enough to have predictive value. Most, as Symons (1978) noted, are so vague as to be untestable.

Most of the play-as-socialization hypotheses, and indeed, most of the writing about play in general, comes from the primate literature, where sweeping generalizations and anthropomorphic statements about play abound. Although detailed studies of primate play are rare, most authors of general descriptions of primate social behavior have felt obliged to include a cursory description of play and a guess about its function. This is unfortunate, because most of the well-known primates show a very complex and probably somewhat derived form of play that is not likely to be tractable to intuitive analysis. We do not imply that the subject should be avoided, but we wish to stress that the complexity of primate play demands extremely careful description and quantification (this has been accomplished by van Hooff 1974; Owens 1975a, 1975b; and Symons 1978) and that other mammalian orders in which play is simpler and more stereotyped should not be overlooked. In fact, other primate families in which play may be simpler also deserve more attention; the family Cercopithecidae is greatly overrepresented in the primate play literature.

Solid evidence for play as socialization is scarce. Most authors interested in this subject point out that play often seems to be structured to provide certain types of socialization but offer only vague descriptions of play. Once again, as for the play-as-motor-training hypothesis, the question is not whether play provides early social experience (unquestionably, in many species it does) but whether the social experience provided by play has been a selective force in the establishment of play and/or the evolution of its structure. It is not yet clear whether, in some species, such as some primates that show complex play, it will be possible to collect the evidence necessary to distinguish between, for instance, motor training and socialization as the primary selective forces for play. In some cases, it may be possible, but most socialization hypotheses will have to be tightened up considerably before it becomes evident what data are required.

The most clearly stated socialization hypothesis is the one that proposes play to be a mechanism through which social attachments are formed and social bonds strengthened and maintained (Bekoff 1977b, 1979; Happold 1976; Schaeffer & Emerson 1964; Watson 1972; Wilson 1973, 1974). The developmental time course of the discriminative abilities of infants and the types of stimulus–response contingencies that must be established through play may also apply to adult individuals, for example, during courtship. Also, in species in which play occurs in high frequencies among young individuals, there may be a cumulative effect that may reduce and delay the tendency for dispersal (Barash 1974; Bekoff 1977b). Struhsaker (1975) suggested that intergroup mobility of red colobus monkeys (*Colobus badius tephosceles*) may depend on the strength of the ties to the group during the juvenile stage of life, which in turn may depend on the amount of attention the individual previously received from group members.

The possibility that there are cumulative effects of early play experience stems from three sources. First, in some species and genera, there is a correlation between the sociality of adults and the amount of social play performed by young (Bekoff 1974, 1977b; Wilson 1973). Second, there is mounting evidence that aggression is not always the reason for emigration by individuals from a group (Bekoff 1977b; Michener & Sheppard 1972). Third, much experimental work shows that early experience may exert a profound influence on subsequent social preferences and relationships (Bateson 1978b; Bowlby 1969; Gilbert 1974; Harlow 1969; Harlow & Harlow 1969; Immelmann 1972; Porter et al. 1978; Sackett & Ruppenthal 1973; Scudo 1976; Sluckin 1973). These observations, and the fact that play may account for a substantial portion of a young animal's active social interactions, suggest that play may function as a mechanism through which social bonds are formed and maintained and, thus, cohesive adult social organization established.

An extention of this idea is that play (and other forms of early experience) may facilitate the development of the recognition of kin or of other group members (Bekoff 1978a, 1979; Freedman 1974; Horwich 1972; Wilson 1974; Wilson & Kleiman 1974). In the absence of a high degree of relatedness among all group members, some mechanism of kin recognition is required to explain the evolution of aid-giving behavior through kin selection. Such recognition is strongly expressed by most mammalian mothers in nursing; offspring are suckled and alien young are not. It is therefore reasonable to ask whether mechanisms for sibling recognition (the coefficient of genetic relatedness, r, = 0.5 on the average for siblings and exactly 0.5 between parents and their offspring) or recognition of more distant relatives exist and, if so, what they might be (see Bateson 1978b; Bekoff 1981; Gilder & Slater 1978).

Because littermates in many mammalian species are in close contact during early life and may grow up in social groups in which there is a high degree of genetic relatedness among group members (Bekoff 1978a), most early interactions, especially those that may serve to strengthen bonds among individuals, would involve siblings and other kin. Therefore, the ability to recognize kin and show later preferences toward these individuals may develop simply through early experience and sustained preference for familiar individuals (Bekoff 1981). That is, there would be nothing magical about kin recognition and there would be no need to postulate the existence of recognizer genes. It is also possible that kin recognition may be based on some innate ability to recognize related individuals that may be subsequently augmented by play. Wu et al. (1981) have found that infant pigtail macaques (*M. nemestrina*) isolated from all kin at birth are able to discriminate between half-siblings and nonkin and preferentially orient toward the former in choice tests.

In summary, there are some observations that make it reasonable to suggest that play may have certain socialization functions. Most current socialization hypotheses, however, are neither predictive nor testable and need to be restated in more precise terms. Solid evidence to implicate socialization effects as a selective force in the evolution of play may be difficult to obtain but should be possible if questions are stated clearly and studies are carefully designed.

Play as cognitive training

Hypotheses of this sort assert that young mammals may, through play, adaptively influence their ability to deal with the nonsocial environment through sensorimotor training. The most familiar of these postulates is that play serves to generate novel, adaptive behavior, such as object manipulation and tool use (Bastian & Bermant 1973; Beck 1978, 1980; Birch 1945; Buchholtz 1973; Caplan & Caplan 1973; Fagen 1974, 1976; Piaget 1971; Thorpe 1963; Vandenberg 1978; Wilson 1975). According to this hypothesis, new behavior is generated in play, and the new patterns that are adaptive are retained by learning.

Symons (1978) made two important points in a critique of this hypothesis. He noted that the invention of novel adaptive behavior through play has never been observed in a wild, unprovisioned population, and he argued that the novelty hypothesis is inconsistent with what is known about strategies of behavioral development. We will not summarize his arguments here but refer the reader to Symons (1978:ch. 8) for an interesting treatment of this complex issue.

Another cognitive training hypothesis has asserted that play may facilitate generic learning involving the extraction of predictive description (rule, model, hypothesis, or coding system) from a set of examples (Fagen 1974; see also Bruner 1972 and Sylva et al. 1974). Chevalier-Skolnikoff (1977) implicated play as a means of advancement through Piagetian states of cognitive development.

These hypotheses are usually discussed in relation to humans or nonhuman primates, but they may have applicability to other mammalian orders. However, because our biological knowledge of animal cognition is so primitive (compared, for instance, to our biological knowledge of neuromuscular or skeletal development), it is difficult to evaluate hypotheses that postulate play as a form of cognitive training. Also, the separation between cognitive and motor training is difficult to make, because both are undoubtedly important in making a decision about what an animal can and cannot do.

For instance, in the acrobatic locomotor play of the Siberian ibex (Byers 1977), kids may be developing the neural basis for rapid, coordinated movements over steeply sloped areas. Cognition does not seem to be involved. However, the ibex kids could also be said to be learning the types of jumps that are possible, the kinds of maneuvers that can be performed on slopes of a given angle, and so on. In other words, they might be said to be engaging in visual-motor action-contingent (e.g., Held 1968; Held & Hein 1963) generic learning about rapid locomotion over precipitous terrain.

It would be extremely difficult, if not impossible, at this time to obtain evidence to implicate generic learning as a selective force in the evolution of this kind of play. The problem is that there appear to be no operational definitions of what constitutes cognition or cognitive development that are applicable to mammals in general.

Evidence for hypotheses about the functions of play

Solid evidence for any of the hypotheses discussed above is scarce. In Table 11.4 we list all the studies of which we are aware that propose a function for play and provide some evidence for it. This list is far too short to allow us to draw any conclusions. The most remarkable feature of the table is that most of the cited studies are quite recent. Note also that some of the studies have used rather simple observational techniques; there is nothing intrinsically difficult about studying play.

FUTURE RESEARCH

Mammalian play studies are now off to a productive, if belated, start. In this section, we shall outline research strategies that have already been used and seem likely to be useful in the future, and we shall also suggest some other techniques that have not yet been used but that should be valuable in analyzing function. Multidisciplinary approaches will undoubtedly produce the most useful results. Also, field studies are essential because captive studies may, in fact, underestimate the complexity of play patterns that occur in nature (Hinde 1971), especially when captive conditions do not replicate those found in the field.

Phylogenetic studies

Nothing is known about play in most mammalian species. We do not even know whether most mammals exhibit play. Work on primates and carnivores, orders that comprise about 11% of all mammalian species, dominates the play literature. Descriptions of play, however brief, exist for less than 20 of the 1,687 species of rodents. Almost nothing is known about play in bats. Similarly, our knowledge about play in monotremes, marsupials, edentates, insectivores, cetaceans, hyrocoideans, and sirenians is extremely sketchy.

Descriptions of play in more diverse species will greatly assist our thinking about functional hypotheses in several ways. First, knowledge about the broad phylogenetic distribution of play structures should provide some clues about the evolution of play. Second, a comparison between the structure of play and the adaptive syndromes exhibited by various mammalian groups will provide inferential support for functional hypotheses. Third, it will be interesting to know the mammalian species in which play does not exist. A comparison of the ecology and social organization of these species to those of closely related playing species should tell us something about the forces that select for play. Fourth, detailed comparisons of the structure of play within families or genera in which a range of adaptive syndromes is seen should provide evidence about the function and evolution of the structure of play. Fifth, a comparison of play in precocial and altricial mammals should reveal something about the role of play on ontogeny and would provide evidence for the oft-repeated maxim that play is most prominent and important in mammals that have a lengthy period of development.

Ecological comparisons

Some mammalian species, such as langurs (Dolhinow 1972), rhesus monkeys (Southwick et al. 1965), and bighorn sheep (Geist 1971; Berger 1978) occupy markedly different habitats across their ranges. Where intraspecific differences in social organization exist because of habitat differences, a comparison of play between populations could yield inferential evidence about play's functions.

Berger (1978) made such a comparison between desert and mountain bighorn sheep and found substantial differences in play in the two environments. A comparison of closely related species that have recently undergone adaptive radiation should be equally useful.

Natural variation

There may be considerable individual, population, or yearly variation in the amount of play performed within a species (Baldwin & Baldwin 1974; Bekoff 1976, 1977b; Byers 1977; Gentry 1974; Shackleton 1973). In some cases, it may be possible to demonstrate by longitudinal studies of identified individuals that animals that play less are in some way less fit than high-level players. No such correlations have been found yet (see Baldwin & Baldwin 1974; Vincent & Bekoff 1978). However, if, as Symons (1978) suggested, the issue with regard to play is not whether behaviors develop or not but how proficiently they are performed, studies of individual variation will have to measure proficiency with care.

This brings up the problem of interpreting negative data. Where no correlation between play and proficiency is found, the results could be due to insufficient sensitivity in the proficiency measure. Symons's (1978) review of the human motor development literature showed that proficiency may be divided into a number of discrete, measurable components. The same should be true for measurement of social proficiency. Studies that attempt to correlate the amount of play performed with subsequent competence will probably have to look for subtle differences and should therefore carefully consider the aspects of proficiency that are measured.

Predictions from structure

It is often possible to predict aspects of the structure that play should assume in order to fulfill a hypothesized function (see Byers 1977; Fagen & George 1977). As Byers (1977) pointed out, there may be difficulties of interpretation, because more than one function may be congruent with the observed structure. This problem should not be serious as long as investigators carefully consider what kinds of structural data are necessary to distinguish between functional hypotheses. Help may also be provided if the consequences of certain play structures are considered. For instance, when terrain or locale preferences in play result in the risk of injury (Byers 1977; Symons 1978), motor training is distinctly implicated. Although socialization of cognitive training effects could result in risk taking only through tortuous evolutionary paths, it is easy to see how selection for enhanced motor training can result in a moderate level of risk taking in play.

An advantage of outlining elements of play structure in detail, as we have done above, is that predictions about each can be made from functional hypotheses. The socialization hypothesis, for instance, might predict that social play should occur before aggression in highly gregarious species. So far, no play studies have systematically made predictions about each of the structural elements discussed above, starting from a functional hypothesis.

Such studies have much promise, however, for investigation of the function of play. The greater the number of structural elements that are congruent with predictions from a specific function, the stronger the evidence for that function.

Experimental studies

It should be possible to conduct meaningful experimental studies of play.

Deprivation. Most authors believe that play deprivation studies (there are two questionable ones in the literature; see Bekoff 1976) hold no promise for studies of function, because it is difficult to deprive an animal of play without depriving it of other normal experiences. However, Baldwin and Baldwin (1976), in a laboratory simulation of the feeding ecology of a nonplaying troop of squirrel monkeys (*Saimiri sciureus*), virtually eliminated play in captive monkeys by requiring them to feed in a tedious, time-consuming manner (see also Oakley & Reynolds 1976). This is a relatively noninterventionist technique, and it may prove to be useful. Large individual differences in play might be produced in this manner, and the play-deprived animals could then be compared to normal individuals. More careful analysis of the technique is necessary, however, before the results of such studies can be wholeheartedly accepted. The frequencies of other social or nonsocial behaviors may also be affected.

A variant of wholesale play deprivation is to deprive animals of certain structural features of typical play. For instance, Byers (1977) interpreted the steeply sloped terrain preferences of playing Siberian ibex kids as evidence for play as a form of motor training. Presumably, the kids obtained the best motor training for locomotion over steep surfaces (the species-typical predator-avoidance response) by playing on these surfaces. It might be interesting to deprive kids solely of the opportunity to play on steep slopes. This could easily be done, because play occurs exclusively at dawn and dusk in this species. Experimental kids would be allowed access to slopes during the day but kept in flat areas from dusk through dawn. As more structural details of play in other species become known, it should be possible to design similar partial deprivation techniques.

Selection for high- and low-playing strains. This technique is suggested by the success of behavioral geneticists in selecting for divergent strains that differ in their expressions of particular traits. As far as we know, no one has attempted to select for high- and low-playing strains of a mammal. Such an attempt would be worthwhile for several reasons. First, it would be interesting to observe the general behavior of high- and low-playing strains, to see what other behavioral features are influenced along with selection for or against play. Second, high- and low-playing lines could be assessed on various measures of proficiency, or sociality, according to the functional hypothesis of interest. Third, it might be possible to determine if there are genetically separable components of play. Fourth, cross fostering between high- and low-playing lines could yield information about the relative importance of genetic and social factors in the expression of play. Points three and four are of functional interest in that they bear upon mechanisms of the evolution of play.

Neurobiological studies of play. Extremely useful information will be gathered by comparing the patterns of neuromuscular activation in actions used in play and their counterparts in aggression, predation, and reproduction. Training may have its maximal effects at this level, facilitating the performance of complex coordinated behavior composed of a variety of simpler motor acts. Seiler (1973) has done an EMG study to analyze the functions of facial muscles in different behavioral situations in five species of macaques. His work provides a nice example of the application of EMG techniques to social biology.

Play energetics. Play may be a high-energy activity. An immediate cost of play, in addition to the risks involved, may be the energy requirement and consequent depletion of a limited energy store. In some species, it may be the case, as previously suggested by Bekoff (1978a), that caregivers that provide direct aid to developing young may curtail play activities in order to conserve energy in developing individuals. Along these lines, it would be interesting to compare the amount of play in which young (and old) partake under differing conditions of food availability. It would also be important to gather data on the energy costs of different types of locomotory play, as has been done for other forms of locomotion (see Goldspink 1977 and references therein). Although play may have some immediate benefits in terms of motor and cognitive training and socialization, too much of a good thing may have negative effects as well.

CONCLUSIONS AND SUMMARY

Play has proven to be one of the most difficult behavioral phenotypes with which to deal from ontogenetic and phylogenetic perspectives. The concluding quotation from George C. Williams's excellent book, *Sex and Evolution,* is applicable to both the present chapter and the field in general.

> I am sure that many readers have already concluded that I really do not understand the role of sex in either organic or biotic evolution. At least I can claim, on the basis of conflicting views in the recent literature, the consolation of abundant company. Clearly the contest of ideas on these fundamental problems has only just begun. History has afforded a rare opportunity to ardent participants and alert spectators in the years ahead. [Williams 1975:169]

In this chapter, we suggest that there may be ontogenetic functional continuity between prenatal motor behavior (motility) and postnatal play. Specifically, natural selection may have favored the early rehearsal of motor activities during ontogeny to facilitate complete neuromuscular development. Furthermore, we consider the possibility that prenatal motility is a phylogenetic precursor to postnatal play. We then consider the ways in which play intention may be communicated. Next, we discuss the structure of play. It is clear that careful, rigorous analyses of play are mandatory in order to demonstrate that play can be differentiated from nonplay activities it closely resembles.

It is also important to consider the functions of play. The energy and the risks involved in play indicate that it should have some adaptive function(s). Current evidence suggests that play most probably has immediate functions and benefits and delayed consequences. Three major categories of hypotheses about the functions of play are recognized, namely, motor training, socialization, and cognitive training. Evidence for any of these suggestions is slim. Our ability to deal with functional hypotheses about play is severely limited by our ignorance of the distribution of this behavior within mammals.

Some questions that should be considered in future comparative research include: (1) How can play be studied more rigorously to explicate developmental processes at different levels of organization? (2) What is the adaptive significance of social play in a wide variety of species inhabiting different environments, living in different age/sex groups, and having different life histories? (3) What about species that do not play? Are there functional counterparts to play, or are they even necessary? (4) In what species would play be expected to occur? (5) What kinds of laboratory and field experiments can be conducted to help to clarify the role of social play both in behavioral development and for adult individuals? As Bronfenbrenner (1977) has stressed, field studies of humans are needed in addition to contrived studies done in conditions of captivity. Such studies, as well as cross-cultural analyses (e.g., Blurton Jones & Konner 1973; Eibl-Eibesfeldt 1974), will undoubtedly tell us much about the role of play in human evolution and the natural history of different human cultures. (6) How important are individual, sex, and age differences in social play? (7) Do differences in litter size and age/sex ratios affect play?

The list can go on and on. Speculations about human play, entailing rather precarious jumps across phylogenetic lines and among the diversity of activities that are labeled *play,* must be supported by detailed description, relevant experimentation, and quantitative analyses. Researchers must realize that social play is a crucially important behavioral phenotype, a full understanding of which will have a significant effect on our understanding of the ontogeny and phylogeny of behavioral processes in general. Exchange of ideas across disciplines will aid the quest for knowledge about one of behavior's enigmas and will help to distinguish between science fiction and nonfiction in play research. "Science fiction predictions, then, are something like a broken clock. After all, a broken clock is correct twice each day. There have been so many science fiction stories full of 'predictions' that some were bound to come true" (Bova 1978:viii).

NOTES

1 The play literature is growing rapidly. For other reviews of play in diverse areas see Aldis 1975; Bekoff 1972, 1976; Bruner et al. 1976; Caplan & Caplan 1973;

Ellis 1973; Fabri 1973; Fagen 1976, 1977; Herron & Sutton-Smith 1971; Garvey 1977; Lancy & Tindall 1976; Lowenfeld 1967; Loizos 1966, 1967; McLellan 1970; Millar 1968; Müller-Schwarze 1971, 1978; Sleet 1971; Stephenson 1967; Symons 1978; Tizard & Harvey 1977; Welker 1971; Winnicott 1971.

2 Adults do play with infants in many species (see Breuggeman 1976 for a review). However, adult–adult play in some species is rare and may be locale-specific (Richard & Heimbuch 1975). Symons (1978), for example, observed no adult–adult play in the population of rhesus monkeys that he studied. Likewise, Harrington (1975) observed no adult–adult play in the lemurs (*Lemur fulvus fulvus*) he watched.

3 The idea that adaptive behavior might develop from simple motor activity, or locomotion, has been suggested by Barlow (1977). Barlow notes that many social displays are derived from locomotory behavior and are little more than ritualized locomotion.

4 Most analyses of structure, function, and communication will require detailed study of motion picture film (perhaps even coupled with EMG analyses; see Barlow 1977 and A. Bekoff 1978). These techniques are time-consuming and tedious; there are no shortcuts. Ample literature is available that may be used as guides (e.g., Barlow 1977; A. Bekoff 1976, 1978; Bekoff 1977c, 1977d; Eaton et al. 1977; Seiler 1973; Symons 1978). Although videotape analyses may, in the long run, be less expensive than movie film analyses, the former are usually less precise because of the difficulty of maintaining an accurate time base. Also, longitudinal single-subject research may be involved. A book that is devoted to these types of analyses has recently been published, and we highly recommend it (Kratochwill 1978).

5 Play is not necessarily more variable in all species (LeResche 1976: Müller-Schwarze 1971; Poole & Fish 1975), nor does it have the same structure for different conspecific age groups (Poole & Fish 1976). Furthermore, it should be stressed that standard analyses of behavioral sequences may not be applicable if the assumption of stationarity cannot be met (see Bekoff 1977c:28–30 and Slater 1973 for discussion). This problem is particularly acute in developmental studies in which repertoire size may change with age and during which time social relationships are being formed.

6 The vestibular stimulation resulting from motor activity may also affect the development of gross motor skills (e.g., Clark et al. 1977).

ACKNOWLEDGMENTS

We thank Dion McMain and Becky Kallem for typing the manuscript and Drs. George W. Barlow, Benjamin Beck, Anne Bekoff, Craig Black, John H. Crook, Stephen Glickman, Klaus Immelmann, Ronald Oppenheim, and Brian Vandenberg for providing very helpful (and in some cases rather biting) comments on an earlier draft of this chapter. We remain responsible for the final version.

Addendum: After this chapter was completed, R. Fagen's book, *Animal play behavior* (1981, Oxford University Press, New York) appeared. It provides a comprehensive review of many aspects of play behavior from a broad comparative perspective.

REFERENCES

Ainley, D. G. 1974. The comfort behaviour of Adélie and other penguins. *Behaviour* 50:16–51.

Alcock, J. 1975. *Animal behavior: an evolutionary approach.* Sinauer, Sunderland, Massachusetts.

Aldis, O. 1975. *Play fighting.* Academic Press, New York.

Alexander, R. D. 1975. The search for a general theory of behavior. *Behavioral Science* 20:77–100.

1977. Natural selection and the analysis of human sociality. *In:* C. E. Goulder (ed.), *The changing scenes in the natural sciences.* Philadelphia Academy of Natural Sciences Special Publication 12, pp. 283–337.

Altman, J., R. L. Brunner, & S. A. Bayer. 1973. The hippocampus and behavioral maturation. *Behavioral Biology* 8:557–596.

Altman, J., & K. Sudarshan. 1975. Postnatal development of locomotion in the laboratory rat. *Animal Behaviour* 23:896–920.

Altmann, S. A. 1962. A field study of the sociobiology of rhesus monkeys, *Macaca mulatta. Annals of the New York Academy of Science* 102:338–435.

1967. The structure of primate social communication. *In:* S. A. Altmann (ed.), *Social communication among primates.* University of Chicago Press, Chicago, pp. 325–362.

1974. Baboons, space, time and energy. *American Zoologist* 14:221–248.

Anokhin, P. 1964. Systemogenesis as a general regulator of brain development. *Progress in Brain Research* 9:54–86.

Appleton, L. E. 1910. *A comparative study of the play activities of adult savages and civilized children.* University of Chicago Press, Chicago.

Armstrong, E. A. 1965, *Bird display and behaviour.* Dover, New York.

Axline, V. M. 1969. *Play therapy.* Ballantine Books, New York.

Baker, J. R. 1938. The evolution of breeding seasons. *In:* G. R. deBeer (ed.), *Evolution.* Oxford University Press, London.

Baldwin, J. D., & J. I. Baldwin. 1974. Exploration and social play in squirrel monkeys (*Saimiri*). *American Zoologist* 14:303–315.

1976. Effects of food ecology on social play: a laboratory simulation. *Zeitschrift für Tierpsychologie* 40:1–14.

1977. The role of learning phenomena in the ontogeny of exploration and play. *In:* S. Chevalier-Skolnikoff & F. Poirier (eds.), *Primate bio-social development.* Garland Press, New York, pp. 343–406.

Barash, D. P. 1974 The evolution of marmot societies: a general theory. *Science* 185:415–420.

1977. *Sociobiology and behavior.* American Elsevier, New York.

Barlow, G. W. 1977. Modal action patterns. *In:* T. A. Sebeok (ed.), *How animals communicate.* Indiana University Press, Bloomington, Indiana, pp. 98–134.

Barnett, S. A. 1975. *The rat.* University of Chicago Press, Chicago.

Barrett, P., & P. P. G. Bateson. 1978. The development of play in cats. *Behaviour* 66:106–120.

Bastian, J., & G. Bermant. 1973. Animal communication: an overview and conceptual analysis. *In:* G. Bermant (ed.), *Perspectives on animal behavior.* Scott, Foresman, Glenview, Illinois, pp. 307–357.

Bateson, P. P. G. 1976. Rules and reciprocity in behavioural development. *In:* P. P. G. Bateson & R. A. Hinde (eds.), *Growing points in ethology.* Cambridge University Press, New York, pp. 401–421.

1978a. How does behavior develop? *In:* P. P. G. Bateson & P. H. Klopfer (eds.), *Perspectives in ethology,* vol. 3. Plenum, New York, pp. 55–66.

1978b. Early experience and sexual preferences. *In:* J. B. Hutchinson (ed.), *Biological determinants of sexual behaviour.* Wiley, London, pp. 29–53.

Batzli, G. O., L. L. Getz, & S. S. Hurley. 1977. Suppression of growth and reproduction of microtine rodents by social factors. *Journal of Mammalogy* 58:583–591.

Beach, F. A. 1945. Current concepts of play. *American Naturalist* 79:523–541.

Beck, B. B. 1978. Ontogeny of tool use by nonhuman animals. *In:* G. Burghardt & M. Bekoff (eds.), *The development of behavior: comparative and evolutionary aspects.* Garland Press, New York.

1980. *Animal tool behavior.* Garland Press, New York.

Beer, C. G. 1975. Multiple functions and gull displays. *In:* C. G. Beer & A. Manning (eds.), *Function and evolution in behaviour.* Oxford University Press, New York, pp. 16–54.

Bekoff, A. 1976. Ontogeny of leg motor output in the chick embryo: a neural analysis. *Brain Research* 106:271–291.

1978. A neuroethological approach to the study of the ontogeny of coordinated behavior. *In:* G. Burghardt & M. Bekoff (eds.), *The development of behavior: comparative and evolutionary aspects.* Garland Press, New York, pp. 19–41.

Bekoff, A., M. Nusbaum, & A. Silver. 1978. Prenatal antecedents to postnatal behavior: a comparison of hatching behavior and walking in chicks. Paper presented at the Animal Behavior Society meetings, Seattle.

Bekoff, M. 1972. The development of social interaction, play, and metacommunication in mammals: an ethological perspective. *Quarterly Review of Biology* 47:412–434.

1974. Social play and play-soliciting by infant canids. *American Zoologist* 14:323–340.

1975. The communication of play intention: are play signals functional? *Semiotica* 15:231–239.

1976. Animal play: problems and perspectives. *In:* P. P. G. Bateson & P. G. Klopfer (eds.), *Perspectives in ethology,* vol. 2. Plenum, New York, pp. 165–188.

1977a. Socialization in mammals with an emphasis on nonprimates. *In:* S. Chevalier-Skolnikoff & F. E. Poirier (eds.), *Primate bio-social development.* Garland Press, New York, pp. 603–636.

1977b. Mammalian dispersal and the ontogeny of individual behavioral phenotypes. *American Naturalist* 111:715–732.

1977c. Quantitative studies of three areas of classical ethology: social dominance, behavioral taxonomy, and behavioral variability. *In:* B. A. Hazlett (ed.), *Quantitative methods in the study of animal behavior.* Academic Press, New York, pp. 1–46.

1977d. Social communication in canids: evidence for the evolution of a stereotyped mammalian display. *Science* 197:1097–1099.

1978a. Social play: structure, function, and the evolution of a cooperative social behavior. *In:* G. Burghardt and M. Bekoff (eds.), *The development of behavior: comparative and evolutionary aspects.* Garland Press, New York, pp. 367–383.

1978b. Behavioral development in coyotes and Eastern coyotes. *In:* M. Bekoff (ed.), *Coyotes: biology, behavior, and management.* Academic Press, New York, pp. 97–126.

1981. Mammalian sibling interactions: insightful (inciteful) genes, facilitative environments, and the coefficient of familiarity. *In:* D. Gubernick & P. H. Klopfer (eds.), *Parental behavior in mammals.* Plenum Press, New York, pp. 307–346.

Bekoff, M., D. G. Ainley, & A. Bekoff. 1979. The ontogeny and organization of comfort behavior in Adélie penguins. *Wilson Bulletin* 91:255–270.

Bekoff, M., J. A. Byers, & A. Bekoff. 1980. Prenatal motility and postnatal play: Functional continuity? *Developmental Psychobiology* 13:225–228.

Bekoff, M., & M. W. Fox. 1972. Postnatal neural ontogeny: environment-dependent and/or environment expectant? *Developmental Psychobiology* 5:323–341.

Bekoff, M., H. L. Hill, & J. B. Mitton. 1975. Behavioral taxonomy in canids by discriminant function analysis. *Science* 190:1223–1225.

Berger, J. 1978. Social ontogeny and reproductive strategies in bighorn sheep. Ph.D. dissertation, University of Colorado, Boulder, Colorado.

Birch, H. G. 1945. The relationship between previous experience to insightful problem-solving. *Journal of Comparative Psychology* 38:367–383.

Blurton Jones, N. 1967. An ethological study of some aspects of social behaviour of children in nursery school. *In:* D. Morris (ed.), *Primate ethology.* Anchor Books, New York, pp. 437–463.

1972. Categories of child–child interaction. *In:* N. Blurton Jones (ed.), *Ethological studies of child behaviour.* Cambridge University Press, New York, pp. 97–127.

Blurton Jones, N., & M. J. Konner. 1973. Sex differences in behaviour of London and Bushman children. *In:* R. P. Michael & J. H. Crook (eds.), *Comparative ecology and behaviour of primates.* Academic Press, New York, pp. 689–750.

Bova, B. 1978. Introduction. *In:* G. L. Verschuur (ed.), *Cosmic catastrophes.* Addison-Wesley, Reading, Massachusetts, p. viii.

Bowlby, J. 1969. *Attachment.* Basic Books, New York.

Breuggeman, J. 1976. Adult play behavior and its occurrence among free-ranging rhesus monkeys (*Macaca mulatta*). Ph.D. dissertation, Northwestern University, Evanston, Illinois.

Bronfenbrenner, U. 1977. Toward an experimental ecology of human development. *American Psychologist* 32:513–531.

Brownlee, A. 1954. Play in domestic cattle in Britain: an analysis of its nature. *British Veterinary Journal* 110:48–68.

Bruner, J. S. 1972. Nature and uses of immaturity. *American Psychologist* 27:687–708.

1974a. Nature and uses of immaturity. *In:* K. J. Connolly & J. S. Bruner (eds.), *The growth of competence.* Academic Press, New York, pp. 11–48.

1974b. The organisation of early skilled action. *In:* M. P. M. Richards (ed.), *The integration of a child into a social world.* Cambridge University Press, New York, pp. 167–184.

Bruner, J. S., A. Jolly, & K. Sylva (eds.). 1976. *Play: its role in development and evolution.* Basic Books, New York.

Buchholtz, C. 1973. *Das Lernen bei Tieren.* Gustav Fischer Verlag, Stuttgart.

Byers, J. 1977. Terrain preferences in the play behavior of Siberian ibex kids (*Capra ibex sibirica*). *Zeitschrift für Tierpsychologie* 45:199–209.

1978. Selective play facilitation by Siberian ibex mothers. Submitted for publication.

Caplan, F., & T. Caplan. 1973. *The power of play.* Anchor Press, New York.

Carpenter, C. R. 1934. A field study of the behavior and social relations of howling monkeys. *Comparative Psychology Monographs* 10:1–168.

1974. Aggressive behavioral systems. *In:* R. L. Holloway (ed.), *Primate aggression, territoriality, and xenophobia.* Academic Press, New York, pp. 459–496.

Chevalier-Skolnikoff, S. 1974. The primate play face: a possible key to the determinants and evolution of play. *Rice University Studies* 60:9–29.

1977. A Piagetian model for describing and comparing socialization in monkey, ape, and human infants. *In:* S. Chevalier-Skolnikoff & F. E. Poirier (eds.), *Primate bio-social development.* Garland Press, New York, pp. 159–187.

Clark, D. L., J. R. Kreutzberg, & F. K. W. Chee. 1977. Vestibular stimulation influence on motor development in infants. *Science* 196:1228–1229.

Darlington, P. J. 1978. Altruism: its characteristics and evolution. *Proceedings of the National Academy of Science* 75:385–389.

Dolhinow, P. J. 1971. At play in the fields. *Natural History* (Dec.):66-71.

1972. The north Indian langur. *In:* P. J. Dolhinow (ed.), *Primate patterns.* Holt, New York, pp. 181–238.

Driver, P. M., & D. A. Humphries. 1966. Protean behaviour: systematic unpredictability in interspecific encounters. University of Michigan, Mental Health Research Institute, Ann Arbor, Michigan, preprint 197.

Eaton, R. C., R. A. Bombardieri, & D. I. Meyer. 1977. The Mauthner-initiated startle response in teleost fish. *Journal of Experimental Biology* 66:65–81.

Eccles, J. C. 1973. *The understanding of the brain.* McGraw-Hill, New York.

Eibl-Eibesfeldt, I. 1974. The myth of the aggression-free hunter and gatherer society. *In:* R. L. Holloway (ed.), *Primate aggression, territoriality, and xenophobia.* Academic Press, New York, pp. 435–457.

Ellis, M. J. 1973. *Why people play.* Prentice-Hall, Englewood Cliffs, New Jersey.

Ewer, R. F. 1968. *Ethology of mammals.* Plenum, New York.

Fabri, K. 1973. To the problem of play in animals. *Bulletin of the Moscow Society of Naturalists, Section on Biology* 78:137–147 (in Russian).

Fagen, R. M. 1974. Selective and evolutionary aspects of animal play. *American Naturalist* 108:850–858.

1976. Exercise, play, and physical training in animals. *In:* P. P. G. Bateson & P. H. Klopfer (eds.), *Perspectives in ethology,* vol. 2. Plenum, New York, pp. 189–219.

1977. Selection for optimal age-dependent schedules of play behavior. *American Naturalist* 111:395–414.

1978. Evolutionary biological models of animal play behavior. *In:* G. Burghardt & M. Bekoff (eds.), *The development of behavior: comparative and evolutionary aspects.* Garland Press, New York.

Fagen, R. M., & T. K. George. 1977. Play behavior and exercise in young ponies (*Equus caballus* L.). *Behavioral Ecology and Sociobiology* 2:267–269.

Fedigan, L. 1972. Social and solitary play in a colony of vervet monkeys (*Cercopithecus aethiops*). *Primates* 13:347–364.

Ferron, J. 1975. Solitary play of the red squirrel (*Tamiasciurus hudsonicus*). *Canadian Journal of Zoology* 53:1495–1499.

Ficken, M. 1977. Avian play. *Auk* 94:573–582.

Fishbein, H. D. 1976. *Evolution, development, and children's learning.* Goodyear, Pacific Palisades, California.

Floeter, M. K., & W. T. Greenough. 1979. Cerebellar plasticity: modification of purkinje cell structure by differential rearing in monkeys. *Science* 206:227–229.

Fox, M. W. 1966. *Canine pediatrics.* Thomas, Springfield, Illinois.

Freedman, D. G. 1974. *Human infancy: an evolutionary perspective.* Erlbaum, Hillsdale, New Jersey.

Gambaryan, P. O. 1974. *How mammals run.* Wiley, New York.

Gard, G. C., & G. W. Meier. 1977. Social and contextual factors of play behavior in subadult rhesus monkeys. *Primates* 18:367–377.

Garvey, C. 1977. *Play.* Harvard University Press, Cambridge, Massachusetts.

Geist, M. 1971. *Mountain sheep: a study in behavior and evolution.* University of Chicago Press, Chicago.

1978. On weapons, combat, and ecology. *In:* L. Krames, P. Pliner, & T. Alloway (eds.), *Aggression, dominance, and individual spacing.* Plenum, New York, pp. 1–30.

Gentry, R. 1974. The development of social behavior through play in the stellar sea lion. *American Zoologist* 14:391–403.

Gibson, K. R. 1977. Brain structure and intelligence in macaques and human infants from a Piagetian perspective. *In:* S. Chevalier-Skolnikoff & F. E. Poirer (eds.), *Primate bio-social development.* Garland Press, New York, pp. 113–157.

Gilbert, B. K. 1974. The influence of foster rearing on adult social behavior in fallow deer, *Dama dama. In:* V. Geist & F. Walther (eds.), *The behaviour of ungulates and its relation to management.* IUCN, Morges, Switzerland, pp. 247–273.

Gilder, P. M., & P. J. B. Slater. 1978. Interest of mice in conspecific male odours is influenced by degree of kinship. *Nature* 274:364–365.

Goldman, L., & H. H. Swanson. 1975. Developmental changes in pre-adult behavior in confined colonies of golden hamsters. *Developmental Psychobiology* 8:137–150.

Goldspink, G. 1977. Energy cost of locomotion. *In:* R. McN. Alexander & G. Goldspink (eds.), *Mechanics and energetics of animal locomotion.* Halsted Press, New York, pp. 153–167.

Gottlieb, G. 1976. The roles of experience in the development of behavior and the nervous system. *In: Neural and behavioral specificity.* Academic Press, New York, pp. 25–54.

Gould, S. J. 1977. *Ontogeny and phylogeny.* Harvard University Press, Cambridge, Massachusetts.

Groos, K. 1898. *The play of animals.* Appleton, New York.

Hailman, J. 1977. *Optical signals: animal communication and light.* Indiana University Press, Bloomington, Indiana.

Hailman, J., & J. J. I. Dzelzkalns. 1974. Mallard tail-wagging: punctuation for animal communication? *American Naturalist* 108:236–238.

Hall, G. S. 1906. *Youth.* Appleton, New York.

Hamburger, V. 1963. Some aspects of the embryology of behavior. *Quarterly Review of Biology* 38:342–365.

1973. Anatomical and physiological basis of embryonic motility in birds and mammals. *In:* G. Gottlieb (ed.), *Behavioral embryology.* Academic Press, New York, pp. 52–76.

Happold, M. 1976. The ontogeny of social behaviour in four conilurine rodents (Muridae) of Australia. *Zeitschrift für Tierpsychologie* 40:265–278.

Harlow, H. F. 1969. Age-mate or peer affection system. *Advances in the Study of Behaviour* 2:333–383.

Harlow, H. F., & M. K. Harlow. 1969. Effects of various mother–infant relationships on rhesus monkey behaviors. *In:* B. M. Foss (ed.), *Determinants of infant behaviour,* vol. 4. Methuen, London, pp. 15–35.

Harrington, J. E. 1975. Field observations of social behavior of *Lemur fulvus fulvus* E. Geoffroy 1812. *In:* I. Tattersall & R. W. Sussman (eds.), *Lemur biology.* Plenum, New York, pp. 259–279.

Held, R. (discussion leader). 1968. Action contingent development of vision in neonatal animals. *In:* D. P. Kimble (ed.), *Experience and capacity.* New York Academy of Sciences, New York, pp. 31–111.

Held, R., & A. Hein. 1963. Movement-produced stimulation in the development of visually guided behavior. *Journal of Comparative and Physiological Psychology* 56:872–876.

Henry, J. D., & S. M. Herrero. 1974. Social play in the American black bear: its similarity to canid social play and examination of its identifying characteristics. *American Zoologist* 14:371–389.

Herron, R. E., & B. Sutton-Smith (eds.). 1971. *Child's play.* Wiley, New York.

Hill, H. L., & M. Bekoff. 1977. The variability of some motor components of social play and agonistic behaviour in infant Eastern coyotes, *Canis latrans* var. *Animal Behaviour* 25:907–909.

Hilton, H. 1978. Systematics and ecology of the Eastern coyote. *In:* M. Bekoff (ed.), *Coyotes: biology, behavior and management.* Academic Press, New York, pp 209–228.

Hinde, R. A. 1971. Development of social behavior. *In:* A. M. Schrier & F. Stollnitz (eds.), *Behavior of nonhuman primates,* vol. 3. Academic Press, New York, pp. 1–68.

1975. The concept of function. *In:* C. G. Beer & A. Manning (eds.), *Function and evolution in behaviour.* Oxford University Press, New York, pp. 3–15.

Hooff, J. A. R. A. M. van. 1974. A structural analysis of social behaviour of a semi-captive group of chimpanzees. *In:* M. von Cranach & I. Vine (eds.), *Social communication and movement.* Academic Press, New York, pp. 75–162.

Horwich, R. H. 1972. The ontogeny of social behavior in the gray squirrel (*Sciurus carolinensis*). *Zeitschrift für Tierpsychologie,* Suppl. 8.

Hrdy, S. B. 1977. *The langurs of Abu: female and male strategies of reproduction.* Harvard University Press, Cambridge, Massachusetts.

Humphrey, T. 1969. Postnatal repetition of human prenatal activity sequences with some suggestions of their neuroanatomical basis. *In:* R. J. Robinson (ed.), *Brain and early behavior.* Academic Press, New York, pp. 43–84.

Humphries, D. A., & P. M. Driver. 1967. Erratic display as a device against predators. *Science* 156:1767–1768.

1970. Protean defence by prey animals. *Oecologia* 5:285–302.

Hutt, C. 1966. Exploration and play in children. *Symposium of the Zoological Society of London* 18:61–81.

Hutt, C., & S. J. Hutt. 1970. Stereotypes and their relation to arousal: a study of autistic children. *In:* S. J. Hutt & C. Hutt (eds.), *Behaviour studies in psychiatry.* Pergamon Press, New York.

Immelmann, K. 1972. Sexual and other long-term aspects of imprinting in birds and other species. *Advances in the Study of Behavior* 4:147–174.

1975. The evolutionary significance of early experience. *In:* G. Baerends, C. Beer, & A. Manning (eds.), *Function and evolution in behaviour.* Oxford University Press, New York, pp. 243–253.

Impekoven, M. 1976. Responses of laughing gull chicks (*Larus atricilla*) to parental attraction- and alarm-calls, and effects of prenatal auditory experience on the responsiveness to such calls. *Behaviour* 56:250–278.

Impekoven, M., & P. S. Gold. 1973. Prenatal origins of parent–young interactions in birds: a naturalistic approach. *In:* G. Gottlieb (ed.), *Studies on the development of behavior and the nervous system.* Academic Press, New York, pp. 325–356.

Jenkins, F. A., & S. M. Camazine. 1977. Hip structure and locomotion in ambulatory and cursorial carnivores. *Journal of Zoology* (*London*) 181:351–370.

Joffe, J. M. 1969. *Prenatal determinants of behaviour.* Pergamon Press, New York.

Jolly, A. 1972. *The evolution of primate behavior.* Macmillan, New York.

Jungius, H. 1971. The biology and behaviour of the reedbuck (*Redunca arundinum* Boddaert 1785) in the Kruger National Park. *Mammalia Depicta,* Verlag Paul Parey, Hamburg and Berlin.

Kagan, J. 1978. Continuity and stage in human development. *In:* P. P. G. Bateson & P. H. Klopfer (eds.), *Perspectives in ethology,* vol. 3. Plenum, New York, pp. 67–84.

Kalverboer, A. 1977. Measurement of play: clinical applications. *In:* B. Tizard & D. Harvey (eds.), *The biology of play.* Lippincott, Philadelphia, pp. 100–122.

Kamon, E., & J. Gormley. 1968. Muscular activity pattern for skilled performance and during learning of a horizontal bar exercise. *Ergonomics* 11:345–357.

Kilmer, W. 1975. Biology of decisionary and learning mechanisms in mammalian CA3-hippocampus: a review. *International Journal of Man-machine Studies* 7:413–437.

Klopfer, P. H. 1970. Sensory physiology and esthetics. *American Scientist* 58:399–403.

Kratochwill, T. R. (ed.). 1978. *Single subject research: strategies for evaluating change.* Academic Press, New York.

Lancy, D. F., & B. A. Tindall (eds.). 1976. *The anthropological study of play: problems and prospects.* Leisure Press, Cornwall, New York.

Lawick-Goodall, J. van. 1968. The behaviour of free-living chimpanzees in the Gombe Stream Reserve. *Animal Behaviour Monographs* 1:161–311.

Leach, G. M. 1972. A comparison of the social behaviour of some normal and problem children. *In:* N. Blurton Jones (ed.), *Ethological studies of child behaviour.* Cambridge University Press, New York, pp. 249–281.

Lehner, P. N. 1978. Coyote communication. *In:* M. Bekoff (ed.), *Coyotes: biology, behavior, and management.* Academic Press, New York, pp. 127–162.

Lehninger, A. L. 1975. *Biochemistry.* Worth, New York.

LeResche, L. A. 1976. Dyadic play in Hamadryas baboons. *Behaviour* 57:190–215.

Levy, J. 1978. *Play behavior.* Wiley, New York.

Leyhausen, P. 1973. On the function of the relative hierarchy of moods. *In:* K. Lorenz & P. Leyhausen, *Motivation of human and animal behavior.* Van Nostrand Reinhold, New York, pp. 144–247.

Loizos, C. 1966. Play in mammals. *Symposium of the Zoological Society of London* 18:1–9.

1967. Play behaviour in higher primates: a review. *In:* D. Morris (ed.), *Primate ethology.* Anchor Books, New York, pp. 226–282.

1969. An ethological study of chimpanzee play. *Proceedings of the 2nd International Congress of Primatology* 1:87–93.

Lorenz, K. 1965. *Evolution and modification of behavior.* University of Chicago Press, Chicago.

Lowenfeld, M. 1967. *Play in childhood.* Wiley, New York.

Marler, P. 1975. On strategies of behavioural development. *In:* G. Baerends, C. Beer, & A. Manning (eds.), *Function and evolution in behaviour.* Oxford University Press, New York, pp. 254–275.

Mason, W. A. 1965. The social development of monkeys and apes. *In:* I. Devore (ed.), *Primate behavior.* Holt, New York, pp. 514–543.

McGrew, W. C. 1972. *An ethological study of children's behavior.* Academic Press, New York.

McLellan, J. 1970. *The question of play.* Pergamon Press, New York.

Meyer-Holzapfel, M. 1956. Das Spiel bei Säugetieren. *Handbuch der Zoologie* 8:1–36.

Michener, G. R., & D. H. Sheppard. 1972. Social behavior between adult female Richardson's ground squirrels (*Spermophilus richardsonii*) and their own and alien young. *Canadian Journal of Zoology* 50:1343–1349.

Millar, S. 1968. *The psychology of play.* Penguin Books, Baltimore.

Miller, F. L. 1975. Play activities of black-tailed deer in northwestern Oregon. *Canadian Field-Naturalist* 89:149–155.

Moltmann, J. 1972. *Theology of play.* Harper, New York.

Moynihan, M. H. 1973. The evolution of behavior and the role of behavior in evolution. *Brevoria* 415:1–29.

Müller-Schwarze, D. 1971. Ludic behavior in young mammals. *In:* M. B. Sterman, D. J. McGinty, & A. M. Adinolfi (eds.), *Brain development and behavior.* Academic Press, New York, pp. 229–249.

(ed.). 1978. *Evolution of play behavior.* Dowden, Stroudsburg, Pennsylvania.

Nadel, L., J. O'Keefe, and A. Black. 1975. Slam on the brakes: a critique of Altman,

Brunner, and Beyer's response-inhibition model of hippocampal function. *Behavioral Biology* 14:151–162.

Neale, R. E. 1969. *In praise of play*. Harper, New York.

Oakley, F. B., & P. C. Reynolds. 1976. Differing responses to social play deprivation in two species of macaque. *In:* D. F. Lancy & B. A. Tindall (eds.), *The anthropological study of play: problems and prospects.* Leisure Press, Cornwall, New York, pp. 179–188.

Oppenheim, R. 1972. An experimental investigation of the possible role of tactile and proprioceptive stimulation in certain aspects of embryonic behavior in the chick. *Developmental Psychobiology* 5:71–91.

1974. The ontogeny of behavior in the chick embryo. *Advances in the Study of Behavior* 5:133–172.

Oppenheim, R., R. Pittman, M. Gray, & J. L. Maderut. 1978. Embryonic behavior, hatching, and neuromuscular development in the chick following a transient reduction in spontaneous motility and sensory input by neuromuscular blocking agents. *Journal of Comparative Neurology* 179:619–640.

Owens, N. W. 1975a. Social play behaviour in free living baboons, *Papio anubis. Animal Behaviour* 23:387–408.

1975b. A comparison of aggressive play and aggression in free-living baboons, *Papio anubis. Animal Behaviour* 23:757–765.

Pepin, F-M., & G. Baron. 1978. Développement postnatal de l'activité motrice chez *Microtus pennsylvanicus. Canadian Journal of Zoology* 56:1092–1102.

Person, R. S. 1958. Electromyographical study of coordination of the activity of human antagonist muscles in the process of developing motor habits. *Jurn. Vys'cei. nervn. dejat.* 8:17–27.

Piaget, J. 1971. *Biology and knowledge.* University of Chicago Press, Chicago.

Plooij, F. X. in press. How wild chimpanzee babies trigger the onset of mother–infant play and what the mother makes of it. *In:* M. Bullowa (ed.), *Before speech: the beginning of human communication.* Cambridge University Press, Cambridge.

Poole, T. B. 1966. Aggressive play in polecats. *Symposium of the Zoological Society of London* 18:23–44.

1967. Aspects of aggressive behaviour in polecats. *Zeitschrift für Tierpsychologie* 24:351–369.

1974. Detailed analysis of fighting in polecats (Mustelidae) using cine film. *Journal of Zoology* (*London*) 1973:369–393.

1978. An analysis of social play in polecats (Mustelidae) with comments on the form and evolutionary history of the open mouth play face. *Animal Behaviour* 26:36–49.

Poole, T. B., & J. Fish. 1975. An investigation of playful behaviour in *Rattus norvegicus* and *Mus musculus* (Mammalia). *Journal of Zoology* (*London*) 175:61–71.

Poole, T. B., & J. Fish. 1976. An investigation of individual, age, and sexual differences in the play of *Rattus norvegicus* (Mammalia: Rodentia). *Journal of Zoology* (*London*) 179:249–260.

Popper, K. R. 1972. *Objective knowledge: an evolutionary approach.* Oxford University Press, New York.

Porter, R. H., M. Wyrick, & J. Pankey. 1978. Sibling recognition in spiny mice (*Acomys cahirinus*). *Behavioral Ecology and Sociobiology* 3:61–78.

Pysh, J. J., & G. M. Weiss. 1979. Exercise during development induces an increase in Purkinje cell dendritic tree size. *Science* 206:230–232.

Rahner, H. 1972. *Man at play.* Herder & Herder, New York.

Redican, W. K. 1975. Facial expressions in nonhuman primates. *Primate Behavior: Field and Laboratory Research* 4:103–194.

Richard, A. F., & R. Heimbuch. 1975. An analysis of the social behavior of three groups of *Propithecus verreauxi*. *In:* I. Tattersall & R. W. Sussman (eds.), *Lemur biology*. Plenum, New York, pp. 313-333.

Rosenblatt, J. S. 1971. Suckling and home orientation in the kitten: a comparative developmental study. *In:* E. Tobach, L. Aronson, & E. Shaw (eds.), *The biopsychology of development*. Academic Press, New York, pp. 354–410.

Ross, H. S., & B. D. Goldman, 1977. Establishing new social relations in infancy. *In:* T. Alloway, P. Pliner, & L. Krames (eds.), *Attachment behavior*. Plenum, New York, pp. 61–79.

Rowe-Rowe, D. 1978. Reproduction and post-natal development of South African mustelines (Carnivora: Mustelidae). *Zoologica Africana* 13:103–114.

Rudnai, J. 1973. *The social life of the lion*. Washington Square East, Wallingford, Pennsylvania.

Sackett, G. P., & G. C. Ruppenthal. 1973. Development of monkeys after varied experiences during infancy. *In:* S. A. Barnett (ed.), *Ethology and development*. Lippincott, Philadelphia, pp. 52–87.

Sade, D. S. 1973. An ethogram for rhesus monkeys. 1. Antithetical contrasts in posture and movement. *American Journal of Physical Anthropology* 38:537–542.

Schaeffer, H. R., & P. E. Emerson. 1964. The development of social attachments in infancy. *Monographs of the Society for Research in Child Development* 29: 1–77.

Scott, J. P., & J. L. Fuller. 1965. *Genetics and the social behavior of the dog*. University of Chicago Press, Chicago.

Scudo, F. M. 1976. "Imprinting." Speciation and avoidance of inbreeding. *Evolutionary Biology* (*Prague*) 1976:375–392.

Seiler, R. 1973. On the function of facial muscles in different behavioral situations. A study on muscle morphology and electromyography. *American Journal of Physical Anthropology* 38:567–572.

Shackelton, D. W. 1973. Population quality and bighorn sheep (*Ovis canadensis canadensis* Shaw). Ph.D. dissertation, University of Calgary, Calgary, Alberta.

Sharpe, E. M. 1973. An analysis of activities of children during free play in nursery schools. Ph.D. dissertation, Washington University, St. Louis, Missouri.

Slater, P. J. B. 1973. Describing sequences of behavior. In: P. P. G. Bateson and P. H. Klopfer (eds.), *Perspectives in ethology*, vol. 1. Plenum, New York, pp. 131–153.

Sleet, D. A. 1971. *Interdisciplinary research index on play*. University of Toledo, Toledo, Ohio.

Sluckin, W. 1970. *Early learning in man and animal*. Schenkman, Cambridge, Massachusetts.

1973. *Imprinting and early learning*. Aldine, Chicago.

Smith, P. K. 1973. Temporal clusters and individual differences in the behaviour of preschool children. *In:* R. P. Michael & J. H. Crook (eds.), *Comparative ecology and behaviour of primates*. Academic Press, New York, pp. 751–798.

1974. Ethological methods. *In:* B. Foss (ed.), *New perspectives in child development*. Penguin Books, Baltimore, Maryland, pp. 85–137.

Smith, P. K., & K. Connolly. 1972. Patterns of play and social interaction in pre-school children. *In:* N. Blurton Jones (ed.), *Ethological studies of child behaviour*. Cambridge University Press, New York, pp. 65–95.

Smith, W. J. 1977. *The behavior of communicating: an ethological approach*. Harvard University Press, Cambridge, Massachusetts.

Southwick, C. H., M. A. Beg, & M. R. Siddiqi. 1965. Rhesus monkeys in north India. *In:* I. Devore (ed.), *Primate behavior: field studies of monkeys and apes*. Holt, New York, pp. 111–159.

Stephenson, W. 1967. *The play theory of mass communication*. University of Chicago Press, Chicago.

Stern, D. N. 1974. Mother and infant at play: the dyadic interaction involving facial, vocal, and gaze behavior. *In:* M. Lewis & L. A. Rosenblum (eds.), *The effects of the infant on its caregiver.* Wiley, New York, pp. 187–213.

Struhsaker, T. T. 1975. *The red colobus monkey.* University of Chicago Press, Chicago.

Suomi, S. J., & H. F. Harlow. 1971. Monkeys at play. *Natural History* (Dec.):72–75.

Sussman, R. W. 1977. Socialization, social structure, and ecology of two sympatric species of *Lemur. In:* S. Chevalier-Skolnikoff & F. E. Poirer (eds.), *Primate biosocial development.* Garland Press, New York, pp. 515–528.

Sylva, K. 1974. The relationship between play and problem-solving in children 3–5 years old. Ph.D. dissertation, Harvard University, Cambridge, Massachusetts.

Symons, D. 1974. Aggressive play and communication in rhesus monkeys (*Macaca mulatta*). *American Zoologist* 14:317–322.

1978. *Play and aggression: a study of rhesus monkeys.* Columbia University Press, New York.

Tembrock, G., 1957. Spielverhalten beim Rotfuchs. *Zoologische Beiträge, Berlin* 3:424–496. (English translation by B. Piddack.)

1962. Versuch einer Analyse des Imponiersverhaltens beim Rotfuchs, *Vulpes vulpes* (L.). *Zeitschrift für Tierpsychologie* 19:577–585.

Thorpe, W. H. 1963. *Learning and instinct in animals.* Harvard University Press, Cambridge, Massachusetts.

Tinbergen, N. 1963. On aims and methods of ethology. *Zeitschrift für Tierpsychologie* 20:410–433.

Tizard, B., & D. Harvey. (eds.). 1977. *Biology of play.* Lippincott, Philadelphia.

Vandenberg, B. 1978. Play and development from an ethological perspective. *American Psychologist* 33:724–738.

Viitala, J. 1977. Social organization in cyclic subarctic populations of the voles *Clethrionomys rufocanus* (Sund.) and *Microtus agrestis* (L.). *Annals Zoologica Fennici* 14:53–93.

Vincent, L. E., & M. Bekoff. 1978. Quantitative analyses of the ontogeny of predatory behaviour in coyotes, *Canis latrans. Animal Behaviour* 26:225–231.

Walther, F. 1974. Some reflections on expressive behaviour in combats and courtship of certain horned ungulates. *In:* V. Geist & F. Walther (eds.), *The behaviour of ungulates and its relation to management.* IUCN, Morges, Switzerland, pp. 56–106.

Watson, J. S. 1972. Smiling, cooing, and "the game." *Merrill-Palmer Quarterly of Behavior and Development* 18:323–339.

Welker, W. I. 1971. Ontogeny of play and exploratory behaviors: a definition of problems and a search for conceptual solutions. *In:* H. Moltz (ed.), *The ontogeny of vertebrate behavior.* Academic Press, New York, pp. 171–228.

Welles, R. E., & F. B. Welles. 1961. *The bighorn of Death Valley.* U.S. National Park Service Fauna Series, No. 6.

Wemmer, C., & M. J. Fleming. 1974. Ontogeny of playful contact in a social mongoose, the meerkat, *Suricata suricatta.* American Zoologist 14:415–426.

White, R. W. 1959. Motivation reconsidered: the concept of competence. *Psychological Review* 66:297–333.

Williams, G. C. 1966. *Adaptation and natural selection.* Princeton University Press, Princeton, New Jersey.

1975. *Sex and evolution.* Princeton University Press, Princeton, New Jersey.

Wilson, E. O. 1975. *Sociobiology: the new synthesis.* Harvard University Press, Cambridge, Massachusetts.

Wilson, S. 1973. The development of social behaviour in the vole *Microtus agrestis. Zoological Journal of the Linnaean Society* 52:45–62.

1974. Juvenile play of the common seal *Phoca vitulina vitulina* with comparative notes on the grey seal *Halichoerus grypus*. *Behaviour* 48:37–60.

Wilson, S., & D. G. Kleiman. 1974. Eliciting and soliciting play. *American Zoologist* 14:341–370.

Winnicott, D. W. 1971. *Playing and reality*. Basic Books, New York.

Wu, H. M. H., W. G. Holmes, S. R. Medina, & G. P. Sackett. 1980. Kin preference in infant *Macaca Nemestrina*. *Nature* 285:225–227.

Zimmerman, R. R. 1975. Behavior and malnutrition in the rhesus monkey. *Primate Behavior: Field and Laboratory Research* 5:241–306.

12

ORDER IN ONTOGENY: RELATIONAL DYNAMICS

JOHN C. FENTRESS

A major task for analysts of the development of behavior is to determine rules of order in expression and control that apply systematically to the organism over its life span. Two important issues are: (1) how we divide behavior (and/or its underlying control processes) into meaningful dimensions, so that both these dimensions and the rules of relation between them can be assessed; (2) how we capture the dynamic-process aspects of organization, rather than artificially freeze-framing them into static abstractions.

My aim in this chapter is to explore these issues. The perspective toward which I am working is summarized under the heading of *relational dynamics*. This combination of terms reminds us that an important goal for future research is to find ways of joining the relatively short time frames of behavioral integration with the broader temporal perspectives of ontogeny (e.g., Fentress 1978a; Hinde 1970; Tinbergen 1963).

I look first at the problem of order in its general aspects, and then specifically with respect to ethological research. I next examine ordered movements in individual animals and then explore whether similar principles might be applied to social behavior. I conclude with a brief discussion of biosocial mechanisms.

ORDER AS A CONCEPT

My basic premise is that order is a concept that is fundamental to both the description and interpretation of behavioral development. As Bohm (1969:18) has emphasized from his perspective as a theoretical physicist, "order is something that is more fundamental and more universal than most of what has previously been generally regarded as basic in our thinking. This is because order is common not only to physics and biology, but also to all that we can know and all that we can perceive." The reason for stressing the conceptual aspects of order is that there are potentially a large (perhaps infinite?) number of ways to construct taxonomies in behavior, and our explanatory models derive as much from these initial taxonomies as they do from the data we examine. As Lorenz (1973) has emphasized, it is important for ethologists to acknowledge their own constraints when seeking order in the behavior of others (cf. Bronowski 1978; Laszlo 1973; Piaget 1971).

Order as prediction

Order implies predictability, that is, rules of the game. If we know only part of an ordered universe, we can account for parts that are not yet known. If we know the length of one side of a triangle plus its two adjacent angles, we can account for the unobserved angle and the two remaining sides. Of course, we have to understand that we are looking for a triangle, which is a major problem. If we, as ethologists, know several acts in an understood sequence, we can often account for the remaining acts, at least statistically. Prediction is not always perfect, but that fact can reflect either the degree of order or our grasp of it.

Order by degree

It is possible to rank (order) orders from a given perspective. From his definition of order as "similar differences," Bohm (1969) defined a straight line as "first order" (each successive chord is arranged similarly), a circle as "second order" (each change in chord angle is similar), a spiral as "third order," and so on. By this type of definition, behavior appears as very high order. This is one reason why ethologists have been wise to concentrate upon relatively stereotyped (fixed) action patterns. It also suggests dangers in extrapolation, such as to cases involving higher-level stochastic processes (e.g., Fentress 1972; Slater 1973).

Order by level

The situation can often be simplified by ranking order according to (ordered) levels, such as in the hierarchical models of ethology (e.g., Tinbergen 1951; Dawkins 1976). Thus individual kinematic details can be combined into facial grooming strokes in mice, which in turn are combined into higher-order sets, and so on (Fentress & Stilwell 1973). A difficulty is to determine how these different levels of order relate to and influence one another. One possibility I develop more fully below is that higher-order levels of behavior may in some respects be more fundamental (and simple) than the lower orders of which they are composed (cf. Bertalanffy 1969; Fentress 1980; Gerard 1969; Pattee 1970; Simon 1962; Weiss 1967).

Order in time

Order in time defines both behavior and development in their most fundamental aspect (process). I list it for two reasons. The first is to emphasize the need to think in terms of dynamic order. Control boundaries may shift within, and between, defined classes of expression even in the relatively short time scale of behavioral integration (e.g., Fentress 1973a, 1976a). The problem is more obvious when we consider development. The second reason is to make explicit the concept that time frames also can be hierarchically ordered. This raises the problem of how we should think about rules of connectivity between these (temporal) levels.

Order of perspective

Ethologists have long recognized that classifications of behavior by form, antecedents, or consequences can yield different ordering principles (e.g., Hinde 1970). Less frequently recognized is the fact that classifications of behavior by form can vary markedly from one descriptive perspective to another. This variance can alter one's views of mechanism. For example, Golani (1976) has shown that descriptions of the same movement with reference to the animal's own body, a fixed point in the environment, or a social partner can give different pictures of both descriptive order and inferred control priorities. The relevance to models of development is clear: If we assume we already know what is controlled, we may stop hunting for other possible mechanisms (e.g., Kagan 1971; White 1978).

"Bootstrap" order

As presently explored in the physical sciences, properties of relations may be not only a product of the properties of pieces but perhaps also the reverse (e.g., Bohm 1969; Capra 1976; Pattee 1970; Shrader-Frechette 1977). This fact blurs the distinction between elements (pieces) and relations in nature. A similar problem may occur in defining systems and their relations in behavioral integration. The defining boundaries of a given system can be influenced by its interactions with other systems (e.g., Fentress 1976a, 1978b). Developmental biologists are beginning to face similar dilemmas (e.g., Weiss 1967; Davidson 1976; Jacobson 1978).

ORDER IN ETHOLOGY

Ethologists have employed a variety of descriptive terms in an attempt to capture the idea of order in behavior. Obvious examples include *unit* (e.g., Barlow 1977), *bout* (e.g., Machliss 1977), *pattern* (e.g., Fentress 1977a), *hierarchy* (e.g., Dawkins 1976), and even *species-characteristic* (e.g., Tinbergen 1963). The goal has been to divide behavior into dimensions that are internally consistent and separable (Fentress, 1980). Even as descriptors, however, these terms present certain difficulties.

First, homogeneity within a category typically involves a statistical distribution rather than absolute unity. Barlow's (1977) discussion of limitations of the early *fixed action pattern* concept is an illustration. Second, the distinction between categories is often imperfect, for example, Machlis's (1977) examination of temporal boundaries that separate one bout from another. Third, the boundary conditions used to define a category may shift in time. Although this is true even over relatively short-term patterns of behavior (e.g., Fentress 1977a), it is particularly troublesome in developmental studies (e.g., Fentress 1978a). Fourth, most methods of classification are multidimensional. It is easy to shift the weighting of different criteria from instant to instant without an awareness that one has done so (e.g., Golani 1976). These problems are accentuated when causal or functional implications are drawn from initial descriptions of form (e.g., Hinde 1970).

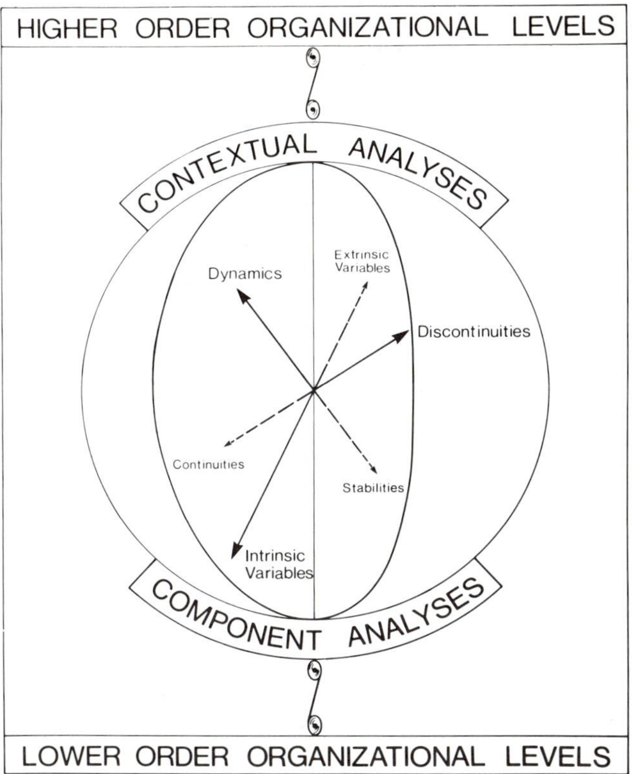

Figure 12.1. Schematic summary of basic dimensions used to determine order in species-characteristic behavior. (1) Discontinuities–continuities refers to the clarity with which a line of demarcation between events can be drawn. (2) Dynamics–stabilities refers to the extent to which given measures change over time. (3) Intrinsic variables–extrinsic variables refers to the relative importance of processes that originate within a system as opposed to processes external to it. Each of these dimensions represents a vector rather than simple dichotomy. (4) Contextual analyses and component analyses refers to the double strategy of looking both "upstream" and "downstream" from one's initial level of inquiry. A contextual perspective at one level of inquiry can refer to components at another level of inquiry, and vice versa. These perspectives, in turn, can change one's evaluation of the discontinuities–continuities, dynamics–stabilities, and intrinsic–extrinsic dimensions. (From Fentress 1976b)

Dimensions of order

Examination of the ethological literature suggests three dimensions upon which conclusions about order in behavior and development rest (Fig. 12.1).

Continuity–discontinuity. From a descriptive perspective, this dimension refers to the clarity of separation between events. Notes in a bird song appear discontinuous in comparison to the gradual tonal modulations in a wolf howl. Decisions still must be put in relative terms and anchored to a particular descriptive perspective. Thus, whereas Fentress and Stilwell (1973) could divide facial grooming strokes of mice into several heuristically distinct categories, Woolridge (1975) found that particular features such as movement duration yielded a relatively continuous data distribution.

From a causal perspective, the continuity–discontinuity dimension refers to the extent to which antecedent events are shared among discriminated products. This concept normally is conceptualized in terms of control specificity (e.g., Fentress 1973a, 1976a). However, specificity can be relative (rather than all or none), it can shift in time, and it can depend upon one's initial taxonomic perspective (ibid). The continuity–discontinuity dimension extended to development focuses upon necessary and sufficient ontogenetic precursors (e.g., Kagan 1971; Chapters 1 and 10).

Change-stability. Individual linguistic terms with which we construct our models of behavior are static, but behavior is not. The extent to which behavior is stable as opposed to changing over time is at the heart of developmental analyses. Changes can be relative and depend upon the particular perspective taken. In human language, individually articulated phonemes may be perceived as being constant by the listener, but through acoustical analysis they prove to vary between contexts (e.g., Studdert-Kennedy 1976; Lieberman 1977). Chomsky's (e.g., 1968) ideas of *deep structure* in human language represent a further attempt to find stabilizing rules that account for changes in expression from one instant to the next. Models of motivation in ethology share a similar goal (e.g., Fentress 1978b). An early discussion by Weiner (1961:50) on invariants and transformations in the construction of physical laws is also useful in this context (cf. Chap. 13).

In terms of causal analyses of behavior, most investigators view control system boundaries in fixed terms (e.g., "a drive is a drive is a drive"). However, this may reflect a limited perspective (e.g., Fentress 1976a). When behavioral analyses are applied to development, perspectives that permit the idea of changing control boundaries gain in importance.

Intrinsic–extrinsic. Descriptively, this dimension is equivalent to the distinction between inside and outside. Assuming that the boundaries are clear (discontinuous) and stable, there is not much difficulty. Still, inside from one perspective can be outside from another. The dimension of intrinsic-extrinsic is critical when control systems are considered. The nature-nurture debate in behavioral development shows how (1) different perspectives can generate different conclusions, and (2) simple dichotomies can obscure rather than clarify research efforts (e.g., Bateson 1976; Lehrman 1970).

All control systems must both interact with their surroundings and have properties of intrinsic order (e.g., Bernard 1865; Bertalanffy 1969; Laszlo 1973; Miller 1978; Nicolis & Prigogine 1977; Oster et al. 1973; Weiss 1967). It is the balance between interactive and self-organized modes of operation that is critical. This balance can shift in time, with different interactions taking place from one instant to the next. The above statements apply both to the organism and its environment viewed in toto and to every control system defined as being within the organism. This is why rules of relation between different classes of behavior during ontogeny are important to examine (cf. Gottlieb 1976).

Contextual and component analyses

The three conceptual dimensions isolated above are interdependent. Previous debates about nature and nurture in ontogeny have stemmed not only from the relative evaluation of intrinsic and extrinsic factors but also from individual investigators' perspectives on the degree of continuity versus discontinuity and stability versus change in the system chosen for investigation. It is necessary to view these dimensions together.

Evaluation also depends upon the level of inquiry. With more molecular perspectives, factors initially included within (intrinsic to) a system may now fall outside of the newly defined system. Further, apparently continuous features may now be separable, and seemingly stable features may appear in flux.

Ethologists have developed an important strategy of analysis that to date has not received the recognition it deserves. In the best ethological research, investigators frequently go in two opposite directions from their initial level of inquiry. The first is examining the broader context within which one or more classes of event occur. The second is dividing the initial phenomena into component parts, each of which is explicitly examined in its context. This is an approach of major importance. It permits one explicitly to compare rules of order as they are expressed at different levels (Fentress 1980). Comparison, in turn, permits the possible extrapolation of common themes of order (cf. Holton 1978) that apply to distinct levels.

In the remaining sections of this chapter, I shall explore possible thematic commonality in certain features of behavior at several levels of order. I shall concentrate on rules of relation in time among divisions of behavior at these different levels. The purpose is to explore the possibility that ordering principles of integrated behavior and its development might emerge in terms of relations and dynamics at hierarchical levels.

MOVEMENT RELATIONS IN INDIVIDUAL ANIMALS

In this section, I examine aspects of the expressive context, component structure, and control of relatively simple movement sequences in individual animals. My primary focus is upon the integration of ontogeny of facial grooming movements in rodents. These movement patterns are broadly distributed among Rodentia, with close parallels found in other small Eutheria and even among some smaller Metatheria; their precursors and significance thus appear to be deeply rooted in phylogeny.

For the present purpose, their value is that they occur frequently and in predictable contexts (e.g., Barnett 1963; Bolles 1960; Eisenberg 1963; Ewer 1966; Fentress 1968a, 1968b), have a component structure that can be defined (e.g., Fentress 1972; Fentress & Stilwell 1973; Woolridge 1975), show systematic changes during ontogeny (e.g., Fentress 1973b, 1978a; Stilwell et al. unpublished observations), and provide convenient material for determining relations among intrinsic and extrinsic control mechanisms (e.g., Dunn et al. 1979; Fentress 1972, 1978a; Hopkins 1970; Woolridge 1975).

Contextual relations

Adult behavior. Grooming in adult rodents commonly occurs during transitions between protracted active and inactive states, as well as between various forms of goal-directed behavior (e.g., feeding, drinking, fighting; Bolles 1960; Ewer 1966; Fentress 1972, 1978a). Total grooming in an observation period can sometimes be facilitated by moderate activation of other functionally defined behavior systems but is suppressed by strong activation of these same systems (e.g., Fentress 1968a, 1968b, 1972, 1978a). This cross-system facilitation of grooming is most reliable when the animals are placed in small and simple environments that do not encourage the expression of other goal-directed activities.

The form as well as the amount of grooming is contextually dependent. When animals are recovering from stimuli that produce fleeing or freezing, or are placed in novel environments, grooming sequences are often abbreviated, with the most highly stereotyped movements predominating (e.g., Fentress 1972, 1978a; Woolridge 1975). Further, the control of grooming is contextually dependent. Denervation of the face by sectioning sensory branches of the trigeminal nerve alters relaxed grooming observed in the home cage but not the more frantic-appearing sequences that occur in novel environments (e.g., Fentress 1972, 1978a). Together, these observations indicate that (1) context is a predictor for grooming, and (2) there are dynamic rules of relation among systems that control certain aspects of grooming and other behavioral classes.

A general model I have proposed previously (Fentress 1973a, 1976a, 1980) is that integrative systems that control various activities are relatively undifferentiated (continuous) at early stages of activation and/or with low activation, and tightly focused (discontinuous) at later stages and/or with greater activation (Fig. 12.2). Similar models have been developed for the control of certain motor patterns in man (e.g., Gelfand et al. 1971; Luria 1976; Turvey 1977), although in each case precise titration of the trade-off between the timing and quantity of system activation deserves further analysis (cf. Fentress 1978a). As a speculative point, increased specification may involve neural mechanisms similar in function to surround inhibition in sensory systems.

Related comparisons to surround-inhibition models in their quantitative and temporal aspects have now been applied to questions of progressive differentiation in development (e.g., Gierer 1977) and to other aspects of self-organization in biology (e.g., Eigen 1971; Glansdorff & Prigogine 1971; Jones 1977; Nicolis & Prigogine 1977; Oster et al. 1973). Although precise mechanisms differ in particular cases, formal parallels between increased specification during behavioral activation and ontogeny deserve further investigation. To illustrate, cortical sensory cells frequently respond to a wider range of inputs during low central nervous system (CNS) activation (e.g., under

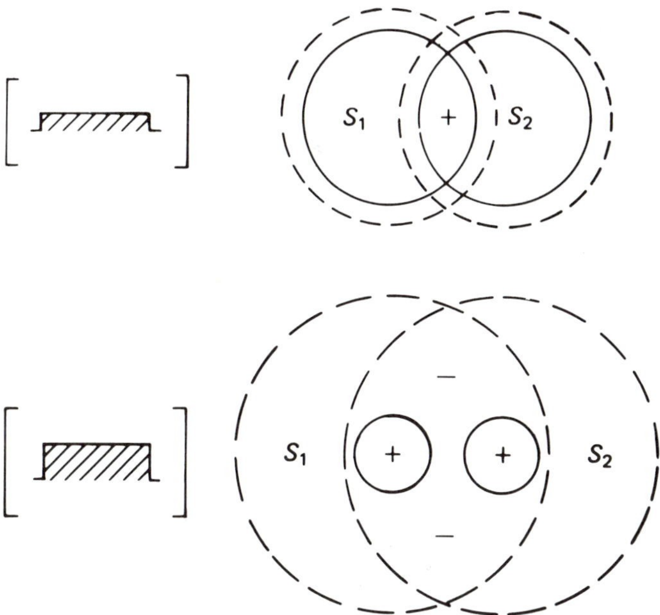

Figure 12.2. Representation of two control systems (S_1 and S_2) as a function of the extent to which they are activated (height of bars on the left side of the figure). For schematic purposes, the systems are drawn as if they have an excitatory center and an inhibitory surround. The model is that with low amounts of activation the excitation of a given system is relatively nonspecific, and its concurrent inhibition upon other systems is minimal. This can lead to mutual facilitation among these systems. With greater amounts of activation the excitation of a system is viewed as more specifically focused, and the inhibitory surround is viewed as more widespread. Under these conditions, the same two systems may be mutually antagonistic. The amount of activation is a hypothetical construct. It can depend upon imperfectly understood relations among qualitative, quantitative, and temporal variables. (From Fentress 1973a)

anaesthesia) than during alert states (e.g., Durelli et al. 1978) and prior to extensive developmental experience (e.g., Pettigrew 1974).

Ontogeny. Contextual relations of grooming in young rodents take on a somewhat different form, perhaps due in part to the fact that protracted goal-directed sequences of activity are less commonly observed. In particular, mice up to the age of approximately 2 weeks often show abbreviated facial grooming movements if their forepaws fortuitously pass near their faces during locomotion (Fentress 1972), swimming (Fentress 1978a), and so on (cf. observations by Lind 1959 on *transitional action* and Dawkins & Dawkins 1976 on *postural facilitation*).

Ilan Golani and I have recently pursued the question of contextual associations in ontogeny. If one places a newborn mouse in an adultlike grooming posture, a series of strokes oriented to the vicinity of the face can be elicited. Further, once the young animal is trapped by its postural set (either spontaneous or imposed by the observer), grooming can be facilitated through the application of various stimuli, such as light pinches on the tail. Strong tail pinches block rather than facilitate grooming.

This process forms a simplified analogy to rules of relation among higher-order control systems previously found to facilitate grooming in adults, that is, where weak activation of a functionally distinguishable behavioral system can sometimes facilitate rather than block grooming. The basic difference is that in adult animals contextual relations appear to follow the lines of functionally integrated units, more or less independently of the specific physical form of expressed activity, whereas in infant animals transitions by physical form, regardless of functional expediency, are the rule. Thus, as the animals get older, simple motor and postural contingencies become less effective in generating grooming, and one gets the impression that higher-order functions, and transitions among them, take over.

With the assistance of Terry Jones and Nancy Mohler, I have found that deactivation of the cortex of adult mice through topical application of potassium chloride (KCl) can, in some respects, produce a return to the infant pattern of transitional action (Table 12.1). Teitelbaum and his associates (e.g., Golani et al. 1979; Chap. 13) have found analogous parallels between motor dependencies in young rats and in animals recovering from lateral hypothalamic lesions. Although such parallels between CNS disruption and infantile forms of expression are obviously imperfect in detail, they suggest converging ways to dissect successive levels of order that may operate during ontogeny (cf. Doty 1976).

Comparison to other systems. An implication of these observations is that rules of connectivity among different classes of behavior can be traced at many levels. The relative importance of these different levels may shift during ontogeny and as a function of behavioral state. Luria's (1976) research on human neurolinguistics provides an informative parallel. He documented contextual infusions in speech at various linguistic levels (e.g., semantic, phonetic) in normal adults and individuals with CNS disturbances. One analytical technique employed by Luria was to condition the subject when he or she utters or is exposed to one linguistic feature and then to trace the extent to which this conditioned response generalizes to other linguistic features. The strength of higher-order semantic connections observed in normal adults is often reduced in relation to lower-order phonetic connections in brain-damaged and stressed patients.

My suggestion is that this reduction occurs in a manner analogous to the shifting balance between higher integrative transitions and simple movement transitions found in our animals. As Luria pointed out, there are also some interesting (though not perfect) analogies to speech ontogeny in that levels of linguistic connectivity shift in their relative predominance (cf. Piaget 1971). Luria's emphasis upon "multidimensional simultaneous structure" in speech

Table 12.1 *Number of times grooming was seen to occur as a transitional behavior as opposed to part of a more highly integrated sequence of activities in six normal adult DBA/2J mice, six 10-day-old infant mice, and six adult mice whose cortices were inactivated by KCl application*[a]

	Motor transitions	Integrative transitions	Total
Adult normal	7 (2/6)	113 (6/6)	120
10-day infant	37 (6/6)	54 (4/6)	91
Adult KCl	29 (5/6)	68 (6/6)	97
Total	73	235	308

[a]Each animal was tested individually in a small Plexiglas container (12 × 18 × 20 cm high) for four contiguous 15-minute sessions (each marked by momentary lifting and placing of the animal in the container). Every occurrence of grooming that was isolated from a previous episode by more than 10 seconds was scored as a separate event. In the relevant adult group 25% KCl was administered bilaterally to the cortical surface through small holes in the skull at the beginning of each 15-minute session. A transitional behavior is one in which similarity in the form of one movement to another (e.g., locomotory circling in young mice in which the forepaw passes near the face and facial grooming behavior) can lead to an abrupt transition between functionally distinct behavior classes (e.g., locomotion, grooming). Integrative transitions refer to switches between functional groupings of behavior that do not necessarily share motor similarities. In both young mice and mice with cortical deactivation, transitional actions are relatively common, but this is not so in normal adults. The number of mice showing each form of behavior is given in parentheses (e.g. 2/6), with the total number of observations for each type of transition listed above.

(1976:31), as well as Piaget's warning that in developmental studies "the establishment of relationships, is at once central and hard to demarcate" (1978:xviii), suggests that rules of contextual association between classes of behavior at different levels may provide future ethology with promising material for developmental analysis (cf. Bregman 1977; Posner 1978; Turvey 1977).

Component relations

Adult behavior. Rodent grooming is not a unitary action. It can be subdivided in terms of the form, consequences, and control of movement components. These components can then be examined for rules of temporal connectivity rather like the individual notes and pauses in a musical composition or the phonemes and syllables in human speech (e.g., Fentress 1978a). The simplest

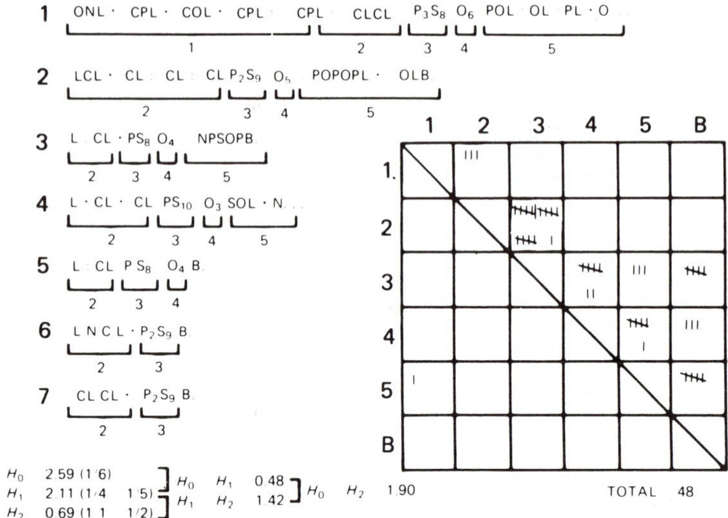

Figure 12.3. Face-grooming sequences for DBA/2J mice were divided into seven basic components, as indicated by the individual letters in rows 1–7. (B represents body grooming, the eighth component in the total grooming sequence examined.) When sequential analyses are made for the six most common face-grooming components in adult mice, events can be predicted on the assumption that each event is equally likely (H_0), from the actual probabilities of individual components (H_1). When the previous component is known (H_2), one can predict components with a probability of more than 50% (1/1–1/2). It is also possible to find higher-order groupings (face-grooming sets 1–5 and body grooming) whose sequential relations are indicated in the matrix (the first set in a pair is represented on the vertical axis). Note that individual components may be found in more than one set, and like words in a language, the sets are defined from the sequential relations between components. (From Fentress & Stilwell 1973)

division is in terms of movements oriented to the face, the belly, and the back. In extended grooming these movements tend to occur in sequence. It is an error to think of these divisions as being independent in their control. For example, application of mild irritants such as water or air puffs to the back will initially elicit face and belly grooming as the animal works its way to back grooming. Although total face and belly grooming can be increased by such manipulations, the proportion of time spent grooming the back versus other body regions is also increased. When a strong irritant such as ether is applied to the back, the animal orients immediately, and total face and belly grooming are then decreased. We see a facilitory–inhibitory relation between control systems, such as noted above for grooming as a whole.

Facial grooming can be divided into stroke types that from a descriptive perspective are arranged hierarchically (Fig. 12.3). Several points of interest arise here. First, when strokes are categorized by criteria that encompass both kinematic details and contact pathways between forepaws and face, interobserver reliability approaches 100% (i.e., the categories are discontinuous), whereas when single measures such as stroke duration, velocity, pathway circumference, and area are abstracted, the lines of demarcation are often less clear (Fentress 1972; Fentress & Stilwell 1973; Woolridge 1975; Golani & Fentress unpublished). One is reminded of problems involving categorical perception in human speech, in which the isolated phonemes are less easily recognized than when they form part of a higher-order articulatory grouping (e.g., Lenneberg 1967; Lieberman 1977; Luria 1976; Studdert-Kennedy 1976). Perceptual constancy is an ethological problem of interest for the observer.

Second, the sequential ordering of recognized stroke types does not follow an invariant statistical distribution (e.g., ABC, ABC, ABC) but changes at specifiable locations (e.g., ABC, ABC, ACD). This change permits consideration of a descriptive hierarchical structure (as if they were letters, words, and phrases). Further, these higher-order sets are often easier for the observer to recognize than are individual strokes (Woolridge 1975). Also, these sets (words), unlike the elements of which they are composed, follow one another in an almost invariant temporal order (phrases). This progression raises the possibility that sets, and their sequential connections, are in some respects more fundamental than are the elements of which they are composed. It is as if the adult animals will misspell words but form reliable phrases (just as the previous material might suggest they can produce recognizable words with misshapen letters). Lower levels of order are not necessarily simpler levels of order, even in a descriptive sense.

A third point is that characteristics used to define individual stroke types can vary within limits as a function of strokes that precede and follow. Fentress and Stilwell (1973) found that duration of licking movements could be used as a predictor of which paw movements were likely to occur next. Woolridge (1975) has shown that the duration of licking movements is related to the amplitude and duration of immediately preceding strokes. Similarly, when the same stroke is repeated in a sequence, its duration and amplitude may change. These observations invite comparisons to the issue of coarticulation in human speech with the implication that the control is shared among descriptively distinguishable elements (cf. Lieberman 1977; Studdert-Kennedy 1976). It would be of interest to see whether some of the variation in modal action patterns (Barlow 1977) may be related to differences of context within which these action patterns occur.

In summary, (1) adult grooming can be divided into components, (2) these components can be arranged hierarchically in terms of their order of expression, (3) higher levels of order may appear more simple (predictable) than lower levels, and (4) this appearance may reflect constraints on component structure by relations among components. These points together indicate limitations of beads-on-a-string models of animal behavior, similar to the limitations found for human skills and language (e.g., Bregman 1977; Chomsky 1970; Cooper & Shepard 1973; Lenneberg 1967; Lieberman 1977; Luria 1976; Piaget 1971; Posner 1978; Studdert-Kennedy 1976; Turvey 1977).

My conclusion is that an important part of the programming of behavior may be relations among components, relations that remain constant in important ways even though the components vary – rather like the constant relations among sides of a rotated triangle. Lashley (1951) long ago attempted to discuss such issues in terms of *motor equivalence,* that is, the combined action of individual movements can lead to a constant endpoint even though the individual components of movement vary.

Recent neurophysiological research and work on motor skills suggest that nervous systems indeed may be at least as concerned with relations among components as with the individual components. To illustrate, Kots and Syrovegin (1966) showed that when human subjects are asked to flex or extend their wrists, along with flexion and extension of the ipsilateral elbow, the individual movements can vary over a wide range, but with only a small number of ratios between the two movement components. Most recently, Polit and Bizzi (1979) have provided evidence that movements in monkeys are programmed in terms of ratios of coactivation of agonist and antagonist muscles rather than muscles as individual units.

Components are real, but perhaps only in their context. Because both components and context may change during development, the importance of a multilevel as well as dynamic perspective is clear. The following discussion will elucidate this point further.

Ontogeny. By postnatal day 10, infant mice show fairly protracted periods of grooming in which both component strokes and their higher-order groupings, as defined originally for adult animals, can be recognized. Recognition makes it possible to trace the subsequent ontogeny of these strokes and their connections (Fentress 1978a). One can then ask whether individual strokes develop prior to their higher-order combinations, rather like words prior to complete phrases in children's language acquisition. Frances Stilwell and I have examined this question by extrapolating several tens of thousands of feet of filmed groomings (32 and 64 fps) into more than 1,500 illustrations of basic profiles.

Two easily distinguished stroke types of adults are *singlestrokes,* in which the paws move with an alternative asymmetry along the side of the face at 8 to 10 strokes per second, and large-amplitude *overhands,* which are of much longer duration and pass over the midline of the snout. Although each of these strokes can form various combinations with others, there is one phase (set 3; Fentress & Stilwell 1973) in which at least eight singlestrokes occur in sequence, followed immediately by an overhand series (set 4).

In 10-day-old mice, singlestrokes and overhands are distinct categories, but with considerable variation in form, fewer repetitions in a sequence than in adults, longer intervals between successive strokes in a sequence, and less precise alternation between major and minor paw excursions. The cycle time of an individual singlestroke in set 3 is the same as that for an adult, but pauses between successive singlestrokes provide the illusion that the movements are slowed. Overhand strokes (set 4) follow singlestrokes as in adults, but in infants other stroke combinations may intervene.

By day 16 most of the individual strokes have taken on adult form, most intervals between successive strokes are eliminated, there is a nearly perfect

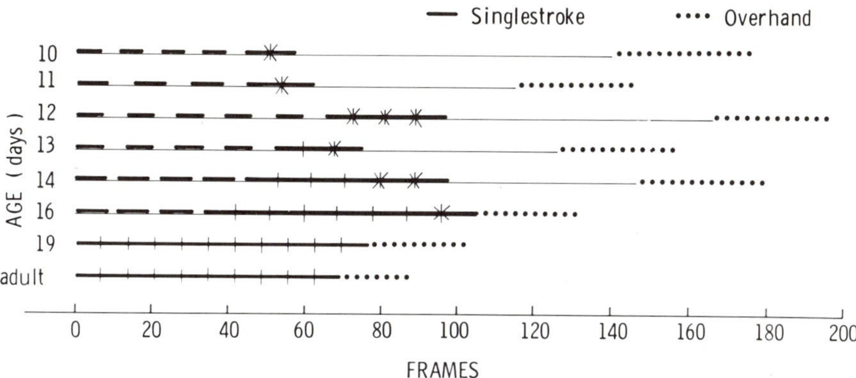

Figure 12.4. Developmental profile of singlestroke series (hierarchical set 3) and overhand stroke series (hierarchical set 4) and their sequential connections in 10-day-old to adult mice. The length of the bars indicates mean duration of individual strokes (64 fps). Gaps between singlestrokes indicate pauses. Xs on singlestrokes indicate failure to alternate between major and minor limb movements. Gaps between singlestroke series as a whole and first overhand most frequently indicate interspersing of stroke combinations not expected from adult observations. Note that gaps and failures to alternate were each spaced randomly throughout the sequence; the segregated representation here is for schematic convenience. (From Fentress 1978a; Stilwell & Fentress unpublished)

alternation between major and minor paw excursions, and the overhand series follows immediately after the singlestroke series, as in adults (Fig. 12.4; see Fentress 1978a for further details). The perfection of individual movements developmentally is accompanied by the perfection of higher-order sets, as well as the sequencing of these sets. The maturation of component strokes and their relations is not clearly separable.

Facial grooming stroke types that can be unambiguously classified earliest during ontogeny, via adult criteria, bear no obvious relation to their mature location within a grooming sequence (cf. Bekoff 1978). Rather, strokes that are simplest in form (e.g., singlestrokes) appear to fit adult classificatory criteria before more complex strokes (e.g., overhands) do. This sequence might be expected from taxonomic considerations alone. The general sequence of face-belly–back (i.e., anterior to posterior) grooming in adults is reflected in ontogeny, however (cf. Richmond and Sachs 1980).

A major problem is to decide whether an infant movement that is unlike an adult movement should be classified as immature, or whether it should be viewed on its own terms (e.g., Anokhin 1964; Kagan 1971; White 1978). At least part of this difficulty is that any given movement can be described from a variety of perspectives (e.g., with reference to the animal's own body, or vis-à-vis an external referent; cf. Golani 1976), and changes along different axes may have different rules. For example, if one asks whether a grooming movement becomes more stereotyped during development, the answer might depend on whether one's taxonomy emphasizes the contact pathways between the

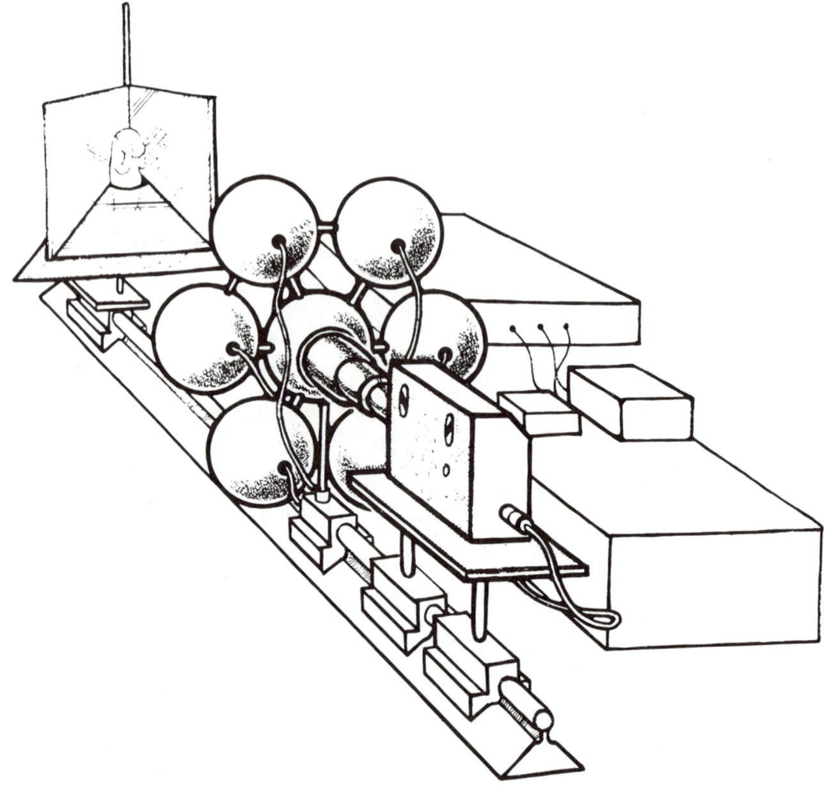

Figure 12.5. Mirrored filming chamber with stroboscopic illumination to permit kinematic analysis of mouse grooming strokes from postnatal day 1 and from orthogonal perspective. The infant mice could be made to groom by being supported in an upright position with the bottom mirror. Films were taken at 100 fps with a LoCam camera. (From Fentress 1978a; Golani & Fentress unpublished)

forepaws and the face or the kinematic details of any given limb segment's motion in space.

Contact pathways between the forepaws and face that define functional grooming result from the combined action of individual limb segments (e.g., head, neck, upper arm, lower arm, wrist). Golani (1976) has previously adapted the Eshkol–Wachmann method of choreography to behaving animals to describe planar, rotational, and conical limb segment movements with reference to one another and to points in the external environment. This permits one to compare relative invariances in behavior from different perspectives.

By placing infant mice into a mirrored filming chamber that provided them with necessary back support (Fig. 12.5), we were able to trace in orthogonal perspective the movements of individual limb segments involved in grooming from postnatal day 1. Detailed analysis of more than 250,000 film frames are being analyzed for publication elsewhere. Here I shall only outline some major changes in limb-segment kinematics and contact pathways that we observed over the first 10 postnatal days.

Up to approximately 5 days, there is a large variation in individual limb segment movements during grooming and imperfect coordination between them. Resulting contacts between the forepaws and face are variable and apparently fortuitous. This, of course, makes functional definitions of grooming difficult in young animals. However, certain invariances such as orientation of the head toward the midline, rotation of the forepaws from a horizontal to a vertical plane, and rhythmicity, plus occasional facial contacts, make it reasonable that these movements are antecedents of later grooming sequences.

The loose symmetry between the two limbs, as well as the imperfect coordination of kinematic details within a limb, can be seen in the simplified representation of grooming in a 3-day-old mouse in Figure 12.6. The rectangular "staircase" ascending strokes seen in the right forelimb are due to the animal's failure to combine raising of the lower arm and rotation of the upper arm in the more normal fashion represented by the left forelimb. Thus there is much richness of grooming movements in the animal's early development but an overall looseness of structure.

Between days 5 and 10, there is a simplification of individual limb segment movements performed in the filming chamber, plus improved coordination between both ipsilateral and contralateral limb segments. This means that if the observer has information about the motions of one limb segment, it is possible to account for the actions of other limb segments; that is, rules of order have become clear. Also, contact pathways between forepaws and face are now more regular, but their extent is reduced. Head movements that are in the opposite direction to paw movements in adults are not normally seen before day 10. Until that time the head is held in a fixed midline position.

By day 9 or 10, the contact pathways between the forepaws and the face begin to take on predictability from sequence to sequence. In contrast to the previous phase, a given contact pathway can be performed through alternative kinematic routes. The combined action of individual limb segments now leads to predictable results even though the kinematic details of each individual limb segment vary widely; the constancy is in the relations.

Kinematic details among adjacent limb segments during face grooming intersplice in complex coordinated patterns from day 12 or so. For example, the ascending movements involve raising of the lower arm that overlaps to varying degrees with raising of the upper arm and also upper arm rotations. During the lowering phase, the forearm is lowered while the upper arm continues to rise (bringing the paws out in a relatively horizontal plane). The upper arm then drops while at the same time rotating. The extent of arm movements can be compensated for by the extent of antagonistic head movements, and so on.

Comparison to other systems. If we take contact pathways to be the goal of grooming, we can make comparisons with previous ethological work showing that movement form may develop prior to orientation (e.g., opening of nuts by

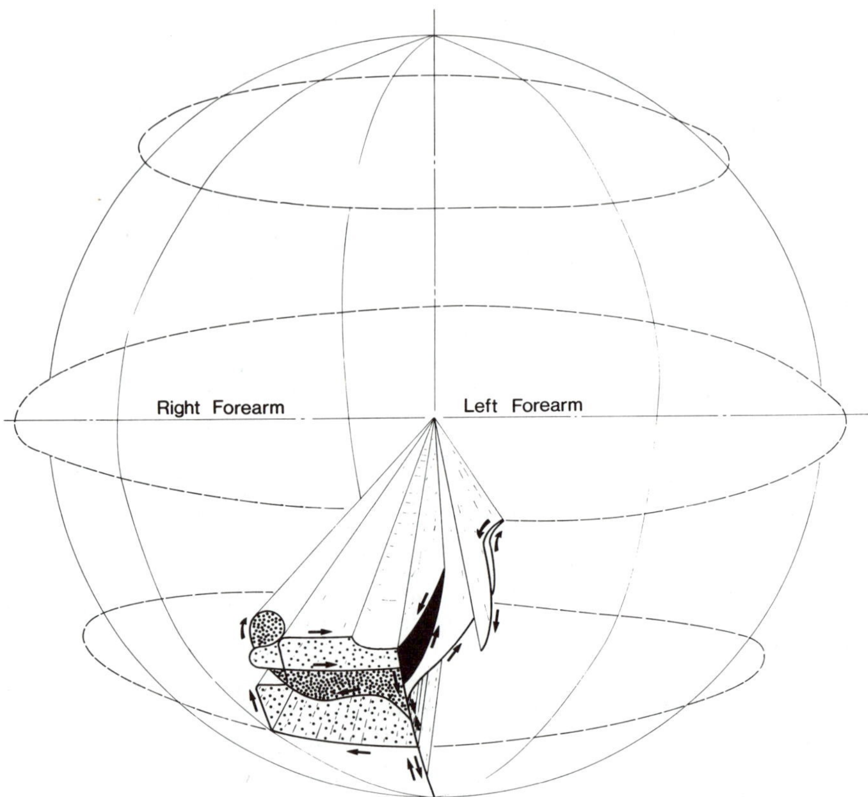

Figure 12.6. Representation of facial grooming strokes in a 3-day-old mouse, derived from the Eshkol–Wachmann movement notation system. Each forelimb is viewed as tracing movement patterns along the surface of a sphere from within, thereby depicting the relative continuity of ipsilateral limb movements and basic asymmetry between the two forelimbs at this ontogenetic phase. The figure is drawn as if the two shoulders are superimposed on a single spot at the center of the sphere for purposes of schematic simplification. (From Fentress 1978a; Golani & Fentress unpublished)

red squirrels, Eibl-Eibesfeldt 1951; pouncing in a wolf pup, Fentress 1967). Grooming is recognized in mice from postnatal days 1 to 5 largely because the form of forepaw sweeps is similar to that found in adults, even though contact with the face is fortuitous. A second comparison is to the simplification of grooming from postnatal days 5 to 10 and subsequent elaboration. Similar findings have been reported, such as by Hines (1942) in her analysis of the development and regression of reflexes and postures in macaque monkeys.

The relative stereotypy of behavior during ontogeny depends not only upon when one looks at the animal but also upon where one looks. In certain respects, contact pathways of grooming in mice become more predictable with age in terms of their temporal regularities. At the same time, the individual kinematic articulations that result in these regularities become more flexible. This pattern recalls the literature on development of action strategies in children, where one finds an analogous progressive flexibility of kinematic details in reaching a goal after orientation is initiated successfully (e.g., Piaget 1971).

Bernstein (1967) argued that a major feature of motor development is the restriction on degrees of freedom in expression (cf. Turvey 1977). Simon (1962) noted that complex systems can develop from simple systems much more effectively if there are stable intermediate forms where previously independent pieces become part of a higher-order interconnected unit. Pattee (1970) and others maintain that when this type of hierarchical arrangement occurs in biological systems, the expression of parts becomes highly constrained by regularities of the superordinate system(s). One can see each of these features in the ontogeny of grooming movements.

Aspects of control

Although space does not permit a detailed analysis of mechanism, certain aspects of control in grooming deserve mention. The first is that grooming ontogeny is relatively independent of feedback sources one might assume to be critical. If contact between the forepaws and face is eliminated at birth by surgical removal of the lower arms, the probability and sequencing of grooming strokes (as judged by upper arm rotations) are remarkably normal (Fentress 1973b). Normally observed rhythmic closure of the eyes and extension of the tongue in licking are also retained. The animals do make some adjustments, however, such as in their sitting posture and in licking other animals at the termination of a grooming sequence (as if to obtain expected feedback on their tongues).

As noted above, denervation of the face of adult mice through sectioning sensory branches of the trigeminal nerve has little effect upon the vigorous and stereotyped phases of grooming seen in novel environments, although elaborate grooming in the home cage is clearly altered. Removal of proprioceptive input from one or both forelimbs by sectioning dorsal roots in adult mice has little effect upon the performance of grooming, particularly more stereotyped movements, when other forms of forelimb use (e.g., patting the sides of the cage) are eliminated. In both integration and ontogeny, careful dissection of the data demonstrates that intrinsic and extrinsic factors contribute in amounts that vary with the particular aspect and context of the behavior examined (cf. Bentley & Konishi 1978; Fentress 1976b, 1977a, 1980).

One way to think about control is in terms of priorities among participating systems. Thus the ontogeny of grooming can be viewed in terms of the emergence of priority of symmetrical contact pathways of the forepaws across the face, with kinematic details being subservient to these pathways. Golani (see Chap. 13) has documented a case of a 10-day-old mouse in its nest that maintained the symmetry of contact pathways between the forepaws and face even though one limb was made relatively immobile due to its position under the animal. The symmetry of contact pathways was made possible by the adjustment of limb segments through the animal's body. Thus the 10-day-old animal demonstrates what Lashley (1951) termed *motor equivalence*. In subsequent work I have found that younger mice do not make these adjustments; that is, distortion of the kinematic profiles of one limb segment can lead to asymmetrical facial contact, to contact restricted to one side of the face, or to no grooming at all.

One can also perturb part of the system, such as by applying an extrinsic load on the forelimbs, and then trace the limits to which other parts of the system (or other systems; this is semantic) will adjust. Ilan Golani and I found that when one forelimb of a grooming mouse is pulled gently from the face with a thread, the other limb, instead of maintaining its normal contact with the face, will move out to a position symmetrical to that of the displaced limb. The limbs may then continue to perform several strokes in front of the face.

Michael Woolridge, in my laboratory (unpublished), asked whether the degree of endogenous programming varies with different phases of the grooming cycle. When one or both limbs are displaced outward from the face during slow and elaborate phases of grooming, the animals characteristically stop grooming almost immediately. However, when the animals have entered the highly stereotyped and vigorous singlestroke phase of grooming, they complete the entire sequence of eight or more strokes even though their paws never once touch their face, and even though this sequence takes nearly a full second to complete. Similar techniques of extrinsic disturbance applied to animals at different stages of development could be most revealing.

MOVEMENT RELATIONS IN SOCIAL BEHAVIOR

My purpose in this section is to explore whether useful parallels might be drawn between the way one thinks about relations among movements in an individual's behavior and movements in social behavior. Again, I shall suggest that relational aspects of behavior may be of primary importance, with individual components being in some sense secondary, and I shall emphasize both contextual and component aspects. It should now be clear that these are relative terms; that is, one person's context may be another person's component. What is important is the attempt to look both "upstream" and "downstream" from one's initial level of inquiry.

Context of component structure

My first example is wolf vocal behavior. Wolves make a variety of sounds that can be broadly classified as howls, growls, barks, and social squeaks (e.g., Fentress 1967; Fentress et al. 1978). Within each of these categories there is much variation, both between and within animals. Schassburger (1978) described 45 vocalizations, some of which are composites that cluster together (e.g., woof–bark–growl). He considered 10 vocalizations to be major. Most investigators use fewer categories (e.g., Cohen & Fox 1976; Field 1978; Harrington 1975, Harrington & Mech 1978; Mech 1970).

Although the four basic vocalization types are unambiguous in adult animals, this is not true in pups. Mech (1970; see also Harrington & Mech 1978) has attempted to trace adult howling sounds from pup vocalizations that he classified as whines. These share characteristics of adult squeaks as well as howls. Within categories, pup vocalizations are marked by their variability. Field (1978, 1979; see also Fentress et al. 1978) took a series of quantitative measures on social squeaks in pups and found them to show greater variability than in adults in such characteristics as syllable duration and frequency fluctuation (Fig. 12.7; cf. Gautier & Gautier 1977 on variability of vocalizations during ontogeny in Old World monkeys). Further studies in which individual animals are traced systematically throughout development would be of considerable interest. One is reminded of early grooming strokes in mice, in which adult categories are not easily applied to infant animals partially because of the initial variability of behavioral expression in infants.

Much of the variation within wolf vocalization categories can be accounted for by looking at the precise context within which the sounds are emitted. For example, social squeaks emitted during pack howling sessions or agonistic encounters tend to be of longer duration and greater structural complexity than are squeaks emitted when a familiar animal approaches (Fentress et al. 1978; Field 1979). Fentress (1967) reported that howls emitted from a hand-reared wolf also differed with a change of context. Thus, just as some of the variation within grooming stroke categories can be accounted for by examining the broader framework within which they are expressed, the form of social vocalization appears constrained by the system of relations within which it is found.

Young wolves' responses to standardized vocal signals change as a function of the broader context within which the signals occur. Also, when they are manipulated into a particular behavioral set (compare to mouse grooming posture), their responses to taped vocalizations are elicited in a highly reliable fashion (Shalter et al. 1977) – much more so than are the responses of adults. Although these findings are difficult to articulate precisely, one gains the impression that the young animals are trapped by a lower-order structure, rather like the mice who are trapped into grooming through transitional motor actions (cf. Lind 1959). Stereotypy versus flexibility of defined social responses as a function of the range of factors attended to by an animal at different ages might provide an interesting assay for future research (cf. sensorimotor versus later stages in Piaget's writings, e.g., 1971, 1978).

Animal pairs as a system

The next level of extrapolation involves looking at rules of relation between animals as the fundamental unit rather than activities defined within the animal. Golani (1976) has shown how the basic logic of examining adjacent limb segments in individual animals can be extended to pairs of animals in a social group. The question of interest is whether there are regularities in the relations of two (or more) animals not apparent in the behavior of each animal as an individual. Two animals might maintain a fixed orientation to one another even though each moves through space in an irregular manner. If constraints are between animals, then the behavior can be defined as truly social. The ontogeny of these constraints can then be examined.

Gregory Moran (1978; see also Moran & Fentress 1979) has amplified upon

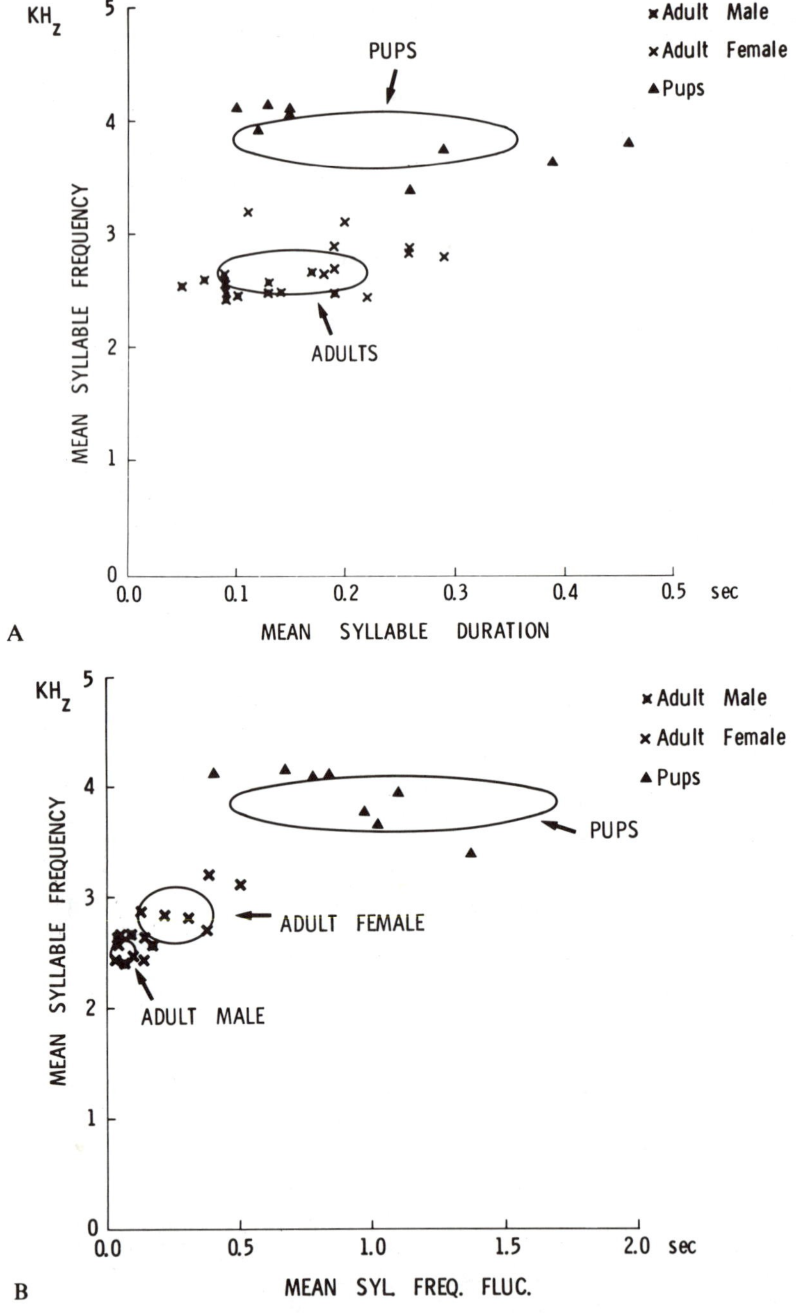

Figure 12.7. Measures of wolf social squeaks obtained by digitizing X, Y coordinates on sound spectrograms. Coordinate mean values for pairs of spectral measurements were plotted for each vocalization phrase. The ellipses represent a grand mean coordinate for all phases from a particular animal or group of animals, with the bound-

Golani's methodology in an extensive study of wolf social behavior. Figures 12.8 and 12.9 depict a mating-season interaction filmed by our co-worker, Heather Parr, that illustrate regularities at this level. The movements of the male and female with respect to each other show a clear escalating oscillation. Note that changes of orientation of one animal (A) with respect to the other (B) can come about through movements of A, or B, or A and B together.

Moran (1978; Moran et al. in press) has taken this logic of analysis one step further in a detailed examination of supplanting (agonistic) interactions. His primary metric was the coordination among three separate measures of the relation of one animal in terms of the other. These measures were distance between the animals, angle of orientation of each animal with respect to the other, and closest anatomical point of one animal as measured on the body surface of the other. From this metric he constructed a three-dimensional interaction space (see also Chap. 13).

Two important findings emerged. First, fixations of the two animals with respect to each other fell into two distinct clusters. Second, transitions between these fixation points occurred along five highly restricted pathways within the total interaction space, two in one direction and three in the other. Thus, most of the theoretically available interaction space (represented by animal distances × angles of orientation × nearest contact points) was unused. Both the relational fixations and the routes of transitions between them were highly regular, although the behavior measured for each animal often varied.

These observations are analogous to the previously reviewed data on grooming in mice in which rules of relation among limb segments can be clearly ordered even though the movements of these same segments through environmental space vary widely. Attempts to extrapolate this logic to larger groupings of animals would be of obvious interest.

The question of development of social relations in wolf pups has been taken up by Zvika Havkin (1977), who performed quantitative measures of contact symmetry among wolf pups at various ages. The idea of these symmetry measures was to see the extent to which contact of pup A with pup B was reciprocated. Symmetry is another relational measure. Particular contact points can occur from a variety of specific actions by each pup. Havkin found that for pups a few weeks old, reciprocal contacts were "loosely symmetrical," whereas in older animals these contacts differentiated into distinct, highly symmetrical and asymmetrical categories (Fig. 12.10). Once more we see analogies to mouse grooming, in which early coupling between the forelimbs is loosely symmetrical, with clear patterns of symmetry and asymmetry developing later.

Caption to Figure 12.7 (*cont.*)

aries of the ellipses defined as one standard deviation on each side of the grand mean for a given axis. *A* plots mean syllable frequency versus mean syllable duration for two adult animals and two pups. In *B* the mean syllable frequency is plotted against the mean syllable frequency fluctuation within a phrase. The figures represent a total of 256 syllables of squeaking that occurred in the context of an approaching caretaker. These squeaking sounds are frequently heard during friendly interactions between wolves. In both syllable duration and syllable frequency fluctuation, the pups showed greater variability than did the adults. (From Fentress et al. 1978; Field 1979)

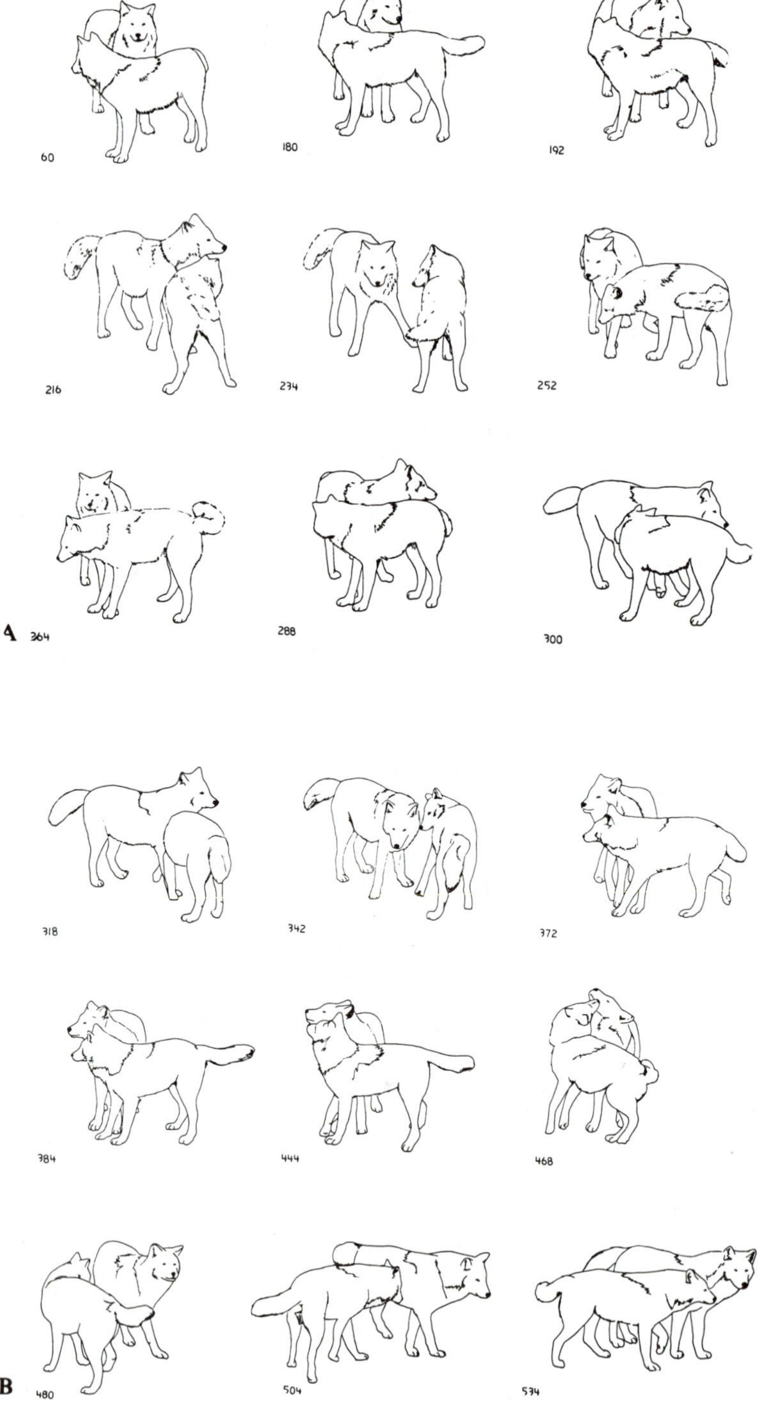
60
180
192
216
234
252
364
288
300
A
318
342
372
384
444
468
480
504
534
B

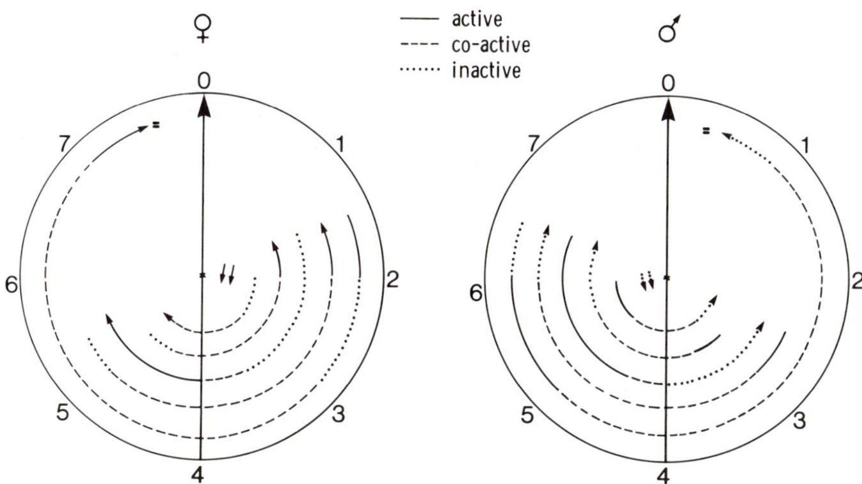

Figure 12.9. A schematic representation of the sequence in figure 12.8 showing changes in relative orientation for both wolves. An active movement means that the animal in question was moving in absolute space; a coactive movement means that each animal was moving; an inactive movement means that only the animal's partner was moving (which still produces a change in relative orientation). Movements for the female are on the left, for the male on the right. The longitudinal axis of the social partner is represented by the 0–4 axis in each diagram; the head is at 0, the tail at 4. The arrows trace the movements of the subject relative to this fixed referent much as an imaginary compass needle. Movements are represented chronologically outward, with the first movement of the sequence closest to the center. The size of each movement is equal to the angle of arc traversed. Movements in a single direction that are not interrupted by more than 0.25 second are represented by a continuous arc. The contribution of each animal to the dynamics of this particluar relation is evident. (From Moran & Fentress 1979)

Although it is apparent that detailed comparisons of the emergence of rules of order in individual animals and animals in social groups must not ignore their obvious differences, intriguing parallels can thus be found. In each case, relations among individually defined dimensions in time are often at least as clearly ordered as is each dimension on its own. The simple building up of higher levels of behavior from the summed articulation of lower levels has its logical, and probably biological, limitations (cf. Hinde & Stevenson-Hinde 1976).

Figure 12.8. Breeding season sequence filmed by H. Parr and drawn by M. Gordon. The male is the larger animal facing the reader. The selected frames (numbered, 24 fps) represent a series of movements of the two animals in relation to each other. The frame number indicates a fixed location in absolute space. The regularities of cyclical movements involving these two animals are apparent. (From Moran & Fentress 1979; for further details see Moran 1978)

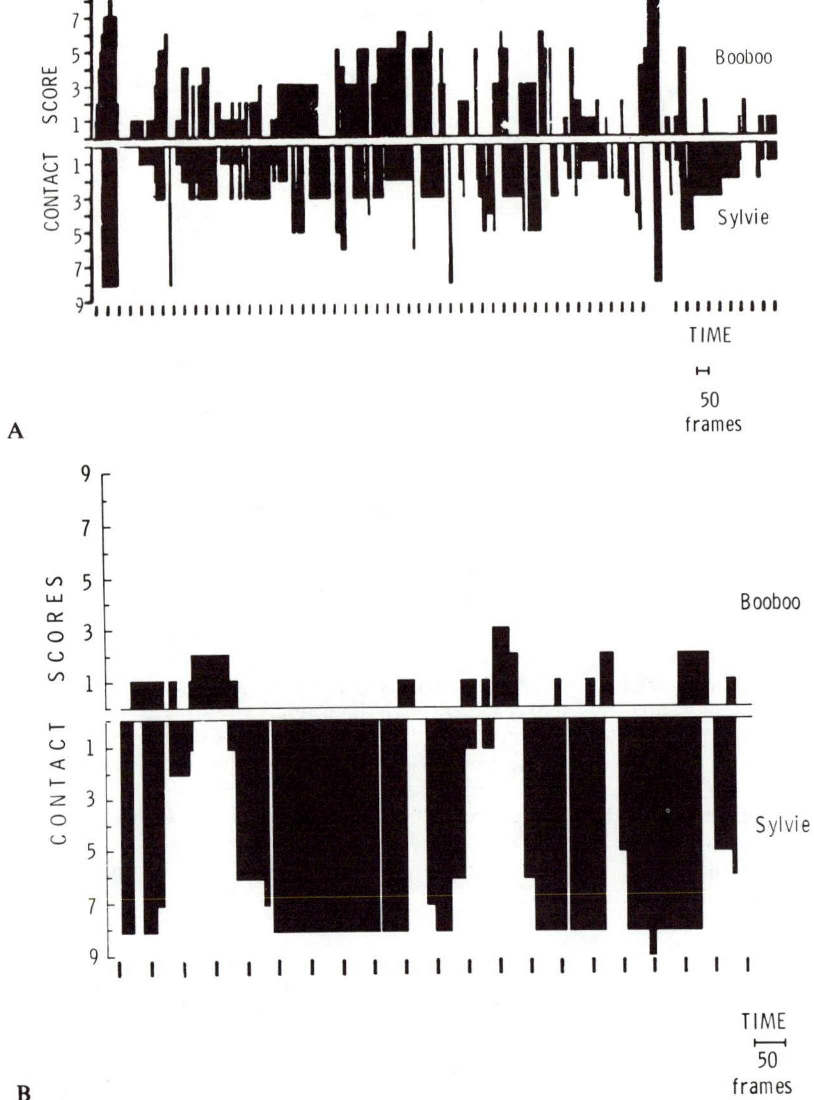

Figure 12.10. A highly symmetrical (*A*) and asymmetrical (*B*) interaction of two wolf pups at 11 weeks of age as measured by the reciprocity of their snout contacts on the body surfaces of one another. For analytical purposes the animals were schematically divided into nine bands, with 1 representing their rostral aspects and 9 their caudal aspects. Films were taken at 24 fps. *A* is a sequence of 3,165 frames; *B* is a sequence of 1,005 frames. Quantitative measures of asymmetry based on the unsigned differences between the two corresponding contact orientation scores were 0.992 and 4.405, respectively. In 5- to 6-week-old pups, neither this clear symmetry nor asymmetry were observed; rather, the mutual contact scores were loosely symmetrical. (From Havkin 1977)

FUNCTIONAL RELATIONS AND MECHANISM

My argument in this closing section is simple. If functional units in behavior and biology are the fundamental focus of natural selection (e.g., Mayr 1970), and if we find that these units are based upon ordered relations among potentially changing components (e.g., Pattee 1970; Weiss 1967), then the search for rules of connectivity among individually defined actions may provide important clues with respect to the operation of mechanism. It is tempting to think that components of a system will generate simpler problems for analysis than do the various combinations of these components, but this may not always be the case (Fentress 1980).

At the behavioral level, Gottlieb (1976) has recently made a similar point. In terms of neural circuits, Jacobson (1978:376) has argued that "there is some indication, but no firm evidence, that the elementary functional and structural unit is also the developmental unit of the system." As a single example, Woolsey and Wann (1976) have found that neuron "barrels" in the fourth layer of the somatosensory cortex of mice not only serve as functional units that receive input from individual mystacial hairs but also develop as an essentially unitary package.

Similar thinking can be found in the search for order of function at the molecular level. As stated by Lwoff: "The functioning of each cell is controlled by the organism as a whole... In a protein, no individual function can be assigned to any isolated amino acid or group of animo acids. Their functional value depends on the sequence of all amino acids. The unit of function is the whole protein molecule" (Lwoff 1962:5, 23; cf. Jacob 1976).

In behavior a functional unit may encompass modes of both sensory processing and motor action that are physically distinct. Thus there may be important developmental routes of "cross talk" among aspects of behavior that are quite distinct in terms of their descriptive form. I raise this issue here because there is a common tendency among research workers to expect that rules of developmental connectivity will generalize across physical form (e.g., pecking for food, pecking in fights) rather than across dimensions that are physically distinct but normally occur together (e.g., pecking and kicking during fights). In short, developmental analyses characteristically adopt the strategy of a transitional action perspective rather than a functional unit perspective. The correctness and possible limitations of this strategy deserve further examination.

We are left finally with the kinds of interactions as well as the extent of interaction(s) we expect between experience and genetic substrates in behavior. Most models of behavioral development can be defined as instructional models in which behavior mirrors in a more or less one-to-one fashion the details of experience (e.g., learning of bird song). In other areas of biological inquiry (e.g., Cowan 1978; Davidson 1976; Jerne 1967) selection models have gained predominance, that is, models in which experience helps the organism gain access to potentialities (e.g., through gene regulation) that are in some sense already encoded within it, and potential pathways that do not receive sufficient support are often eliminated (e.g., through competition). As Jerne (1967) has correctly emphasized, instruction at one level of inquiry might be reinterpreted as selection at another level.

One can find in the behavioral literature potential limitations of strict instruction models, such as in the fact that brief exposure to an imprinting stimulus may facilitate subsequent preferences for different stimuli (e.g., Kilham et al. 1968) or that certain song bird species such as the Arizona junco sing more perfected adult songs after exposure to juvenile songs than they do when reared in social isolation (e.g., Marler 1975, 1976). Certainly mice do not have to be instructed how to groom, nor wolves how to pounce, howl, or dig dens (Fentress et al. unpublished), nor children how to crawl. As Bruner (1957:title) has nicely put it, developing organisms, including human organisms, have the capacity to go "Beyond the Information Given" through experience.

In some respects these speculations renew the emphasis upon genetic mechanisms in development, but only as these mechanisms interact with the environment that surrounds them (cf. Bateson 1976). It remains easy to think in terms of either/or dichotomies, or conversely, to treat the world as so much homogeneous soup. The idea of relational dynamics developed here shares much with ideas of dynamic pattern formation in biophysics (e.g., Katchalsky et al. 1974) in that it stresses the importance of interaction in defining systems that in turn display important qualities of intrinsic organization. Certainly if there are general rules in developmental biology, they are that determination and differentiation necessarily depend upon relations among components (e.g., cells) in time, and that once this determination and differentiation take place, the resulting systems become relatively immune to further influence by the very extrinsic factors that led to their occurrence (e.g., Davidson 1976; Edwards & Palka 1976; Jacobson 1978; Kimmel & Eaton 1976).

I have argued above, and previously (e.g., Fentress 1973a, 1976a, 1977a, 1977b), that analogous processes may operate among behavioral systems during an integrated performance. Several systems may interact to produce a behavior. But while the behavior is being expressed, it may be impervious to further action by these systems. An initially interactive system can become self-organized.

If these parallels hold, even in part, the general perspective of *relational dynamics* in behavior will have proved its utility. Questions concerning the extent to which they hold at different levels of order should provide stimulus for future research. The constructs of relation and change, and particularly their connection, have historically provided major conceptual as well as analytical challenges to the understanding of organisms (e.g., Whitehead 1929). The effort, however, is critical. Entities may be easier to understand than relations, and things may appear more manageable than processes, but in the study of behavior and its development, both relational and dynamic issues must somehow be faced. As summed up by Weiner (1961:58), organisms are in many respects comparable to metastable Maxwell demons, where "the stable state of a living organism is to be dead." That remains the challenge of analyzing relational dynamics in development: an order of the day from the past and for the future.

SUMMARY

Models of order in behavioral ontogeny depend ultimately upon the divisions we make in describing behavioral events and their underlying control systems, as well as upon the rules of relation among these divisions that we subsequently seek. The problem of order is thus conceptual as well as empirical. Three primary dimensions in our models of order are: (1) the relative continuity versus discontinuity of phenomena selected for analysis, (2) the degree to which these phenomena appear stable or change in time, and (3) the balance between intrinsic and extrinsic operational constraints. Each of these dimensions can be applied to successive levels of biological and behavioral order.

In this chapter, I argue that two particularly important aspects of order in behavior are (1) rules of relation among different dimensions, and (2) changes in both these dimensions and their relations through time. I am particularly interested in bringing together the relatively short-term changes in integrated patterns of behavior and the more extended time frames of development by looking for rules to account for changes in relationships. This perspective is called *relational dynamics.*

Data on the context, components, development, and control of facial grooming behavior in rodents show that divisions can be made at a variety of levels, each of which has its own rules of order. However, in each case, our understanding of what I have termed *components* depends in part upon the rules of relation among these components. Indeed, relations may impose constraints upon the formation of components, as well as the reverse. Further, rules of relation among components can be more consistent than are the components viewed in isolation. One can see analogies here to aspects to human speech, as well as to other forms of skilled performance.

During development, both the components of grooming and their relations reach a mature form of expression at approximately the same time. Thus, the question of whether pieces mature before connections among pieces do can be misleading. More refined analyses of kinematic details in grooming and their resulting contact pathways between the forepaws and face demonstrate that initially loose order in expression becomes simplified, then elaborated. The question of whether behavior becomes more or less stereotyped during ontogeny cannot be answered in absolute but only in relative terms.

In social behavior, rules of relation between the behavior of individual animals may also be as fundamental as are the activities defined for each animal on its own. Data on vocal behavior and other social behavior in wolves demonstrate that broad themes of relational dynamics in ontogeny previously articulated for rodent facial grooming may be applicable at this level as well. For example, early loose symmetry in the expression of components can lead to subsequent highly symmetrical and asymmetrical relations.

These data together emphasize the value of examining broad functional units of behavior at different levels of expression. The role of experience in perfecting these functional units may be selective as well as instructional. The dynamics of *interactive and self-organizing systems* in behavior suggest that similar properties of order may operate in both the short and long (development) time frames.

ACKNOWLEDGMENTS

The preparation of this chapter was aided by a research grant (A9787) from the Natural Sciences and Engineering Research Council of Canada plus funds from Graduate Studies at Dalhousie University. The research reviewed was funded in part by those sources plus U.S. Public Health Service Grants MH-16887 and MH-16955. I thank Ilan Golani, Zvika Havkin, Terry Jones, Nancy Mohler, Gregory Moran, Heather Parr, Jenny Ryon, Frances Stilwell, and Michael Woolridge for their cooperation in various phases of this research, and for letting me refer to some of their previously unpublished efforts. George Barlow, Victor Denenberg, Stephen Glickman, David Noakes, Heather Parr, and John Watson provided particularly helpful comments on an earlier version of this manuscript. I also benefited from stimulating conversations by many conference participants. My special thanks to the warm hospitality of Klaus Immelman and his colleagues. Mary MacConnachie meticulously typed the manuscript in its various states of order. Special thanks also to Heather Parr, Sarah Taurmini, and Lisa Arian for opening my eyes to some of the more exciting features of human behavioral development.

REFERENCES

Anokhin, P. K. 1964. Systemogenesis as a general regulator of brain development. *Progress in Brain Research* 9:54–86.

Barlow, G. W. 1977. Modal action patterns. *In:* T. A. Sebeok (ed.), *How animals communicate.* University of Indiana Press, Bloomington, pp. 94–125.

Barnett, S. A. 1963. *A study in behaviour.* Methuen, London.

Bateson, P. P. G. 1976. Rules and reciprocity in behavioral development. *In:* P. P. G. Bateson & R. A. Hinde (eds.), *Growing points in ethology.* Cambridge University Press, Cambridge, pp. 401–421.

Bekoff, M. 1978. A field study of the development of behavior in Adelie Penguins: univariate and numerical taxonomic approaches. *In:* G. M. Burghardt & M. Bekoff (eds.), *The development of behavior: comparative and evolutionary aspects.* Garland Press, New York and London, pp. 177–202.

Bentley, D., & M. Konishi. 1978. Neural control of behavior. *Annual Review of Neuroscience,* 1:35–59.

Bernard, C. 1865. *Introduction to the study of experimental medicine* (H. C. Greene, translator, 1927). Macmillan, reissued by Dover Press, New York.

Bernstein, N. 1967. *The co-ordination and regulation of movements.* Pergamon, London.

Bertalanffy, L. V. 1969. Chance or law. *In:* A. Koestler & J. R. Symthies (eds.), *Beyond reductionism.* Beacon Press, Boston, pp. 56–76.

Bohm, D. 1969. Some remarks on the notion of order. *In:* C. H. Waddington (ed.), *Towards a theoretical biology,* vol. 2, *Sketches.* Aldine, Chicago.

Bolles, R. C. 1960. Grooming behavior in the rat. *Journal of Comparative and Physiological Psychology* 53:306–310.

Bregman, A. S. 1977. Perception and behavior as compositions of ideals. *Cognitive Psychology* 9:250–292.

Bronowski, J. 1978. *The origin of knowledge and imagination.* Yale University Press, New Haven and London.

Bruner, J. S. 1957. Going beyond the information given. *In:* J. S. Bruner et al. (eds.), *Contemporary approaches to cognition.* Harvard University Press, Cambridge, Massachusetts.

Capra, F. 1976. *The tao of physics.* Fontana, Bungay, Suffolk.

Chomsky, N. 1968. *Language and mind.* Harcourt, New York.

1970. Problems of explanation in linguistics. *In:* R. Borger & F. Cioffi (eds.), *Explanation in the behavioral sciences.* Cambridge University Press, Cambridge, pp. 425–451.

Cohen, J. A., & M. W. Fox. 1976. Vocalizations in wild canids and possible effects of domestication. *Behavioural Processes* 1:77–92.

Cooper, L. A., & R. N. Shepard. 1973. Chronometric studies of the rotation of mental images. *In:* W. G. Chase (ed.), *Visual information processing.* Academic Press, New York, pp. 75–176.

Cowan, W. M. 1978. Selection and control in neurogenesis. *In:* F. O. Schmitt and F. G. Worden (eds.), *The neurosciences: fourth study program.* MIT Press, Cambridge, Massachusetts, pp. 59–79.

Davidson, E. H. 1976. *Gene activity in early development,* 2nd ed. Academic Press, New York.

Dawkins, R. 1976. Hierarchical organisation: a candidate principle for ethology. *In:* P. P. G. Bateson & R. A. Hinde (eds.), *Growing points in ethology.* Cambridge University Press, Cambridge, pp. 7–54.

Dawkins, R., & M. Dawkins. 1976. Hierarchical organization and postural facilitation: rules for grooming in flies. *Animal Behaviour* 24:739–755.

Doty, R. W. 1976. The concept of neural centers. *In:* J. C. Fentress (ed.), *Simpler networks and behavior.* Sinauer, Sunderland, Massachusetts, pp. 251–265.

Dunn, A. J., E. J. Green, & R. L. Isaacson. 1979. Intracerebral adrenocorticotropic hormone mediates novelty-induced grooming in the rat. *Science* 203:281–283.

Durelli, L., E. M. Schmidt, J. S. McIntosh, & M. J. Bak. 1978. Single-unit chronic recordings from the sensorimotor cortex of unrestrained cats during locomotion. *Experimental Neurology* 62:580–594.

Edwards, J. S., & J. Palka. 1976. Neural generation and regeneration in insects. *In:* J. C. Fentress (ed.), *Simpler networks and behavior.* Sinauer, Sunderland, Massachusetts, pp. 167–185.

Eibl-Eibesfeldt, I. 1951. Beobachtungen zur Fortpflanzungsbiologie und Jungendentwicklung des Eichörnchens. *Zeitschrift für Tierpsychologie* 8:370–400.

Eigen, M. 1971. Self-organization of matter and the evolution of biological macromolecules. *Naturwissenschaften* 58:465–523.

Eisenberg, J. F. 1963. The behavior of heteromyid rodents. *University of California Publications in Zoology* 69:1–114.

Ewer, R. F. 1966. The behavior of the African giant rat (*Cricetomys gambianus,* Waterhouse). *Zeitschrift für Tierpsychologie* 24:6–79.

Fentress, J. C. 1967. Observations on the behavioral development of a hand-reared male timber wolf. *American Zoologist* 7:339–351.

1968a. Interrupted ongoing behaviour in two species of vole (*Microtus agrestis* and *Clethrionomys britannicus*). 1. Response as a function of preceding activity and the context of an apparently "irrelevant" motor pattern. *Animal Behaviour* 16:135–153.

1968b. Interrupted ongoing behaviour in two species of vole (*Microtus agrestis* and *Clethrionomys britannicus*). 2. Extended analysis of motivational variables underlying fleeing and grooming behaviour. *Animal Behaviour* 16:154–167.

1972. Development and patterning of movement sequences in inbred mice. *In:*

J. Kiger (ed.), *The biology of behavior.* Oregon State University Press, Corvallis, Oregon, pp. 83–132.

1973a. Specific and nonspecific factors in the causation of behavior. *In:* P. P. G. Bateson & P. H. Klopfer (eds.), *Perspectives in ethology.* Plenum, New York, pp. 155–224.

1973b. Development of grooming in mice with amputated forelimbs. *Science* 179:704–705.

1976a. Dynamic boundaries of patterned behaviour: interaction and self-organization. *In:* P. P. G. Bateson & R. A. Hinde (eds.), *Growing points in ethology.* Cambridge University Press, Cambridge, pp. 135–169.

(ed.). 1976b. *Simpler networks and behavior.* Sinauer, Sunderland, Massachusetts.

1977a. The tonic hypothesis and the patterning of behavior. *Annals of the New York Academy of Sciences* 290:370–395.

1977b. Opening remarks: constructing the potentialities of phenotype. *Annals of the New York Academy of Sciences* 290:220–225.

1978a. Mus musicus: the developmental orchestration of selected movement patterns in mice. *In:* G. M. Burghardt & M. Bekoff (eds.), *The development of behavior: comparative and evolutionary aspects.* Garland Press, New York and London, pp. 321–342.

1978b. Conflict and context in sexual behaviour. *In:* J. Hutchinson (ed.), *Biological determinants of sexual behavior.* Wiley, New York and London, pp. 579–614.

1980. How can behavior be studied from a neuroetholgical perspective? *In:* H. M. Pinsker and W. D. Willis, Jr. (eds.), *Information processing in the nervous system.* Raven Press, New York, pp. 263–283.

Fentress, J. C., R. Field, & H. Parr. 1978. Social dynamics and communication. *In:* H. Markowitz & V. J. Stevens (eds.), *Behavior of captive wild animals.* Nelson Hall, Chicago, pp. 67–106.

Fentress, J. C., & F. P. Stilwell. 1973. Grammar of a movement sequence in inbred mice. *Nature* 244:52–53.

Field, R. 1978. *Vocal behavior of wolves (Canis lupus): variability in structure, context, annual, diurnal patterns, and ontogeny.* Sc.D. thesis, Johns Hopkins University, Baltimore.

1979. A perspective on syntactics of wolf vocalizations. *In:* E. Klinghammer (ed.), *The behavior and ecology of wolves.* Garland Press, New York, pp. 182–205.

Gautier, J. P., & A. Gautier. 1977. Communication in Old World monkeys. *In:* T. A. Sebeok (ed.), *How animals communicate.* Indiana University Press, Bloomington, pp. 890–964.

Gelfand, I. M., V. S. Garfinkel, M. L. Tsetlin, & M. L. Shik. 1971. Some problems in the analysis of movements. *In:* I. M. Gelfand, V. S. Garfinkel, S. V. Fomin, & M. L. Tsetlin (eds.), *Models of the structural-functional organization of certain biological systems.* M.I.T. Press, Cambridge, Massachusetts.

Gerard, R. W. 1969. Hierarchy, entitation, and levels. *In:* L. L. Whyte, A. G. Wilson, & D. Wilson (eds.), *Hierarchical structures.* American Elsevier, New York, pp. 215–228.

Gierer, A. 1977. Biological features and physical concepts of pattern formation exemplified by hydra. *Current Topics in Developmental Biology* 11:16–59.

Glansdorff, P., & I. Prigogine. 1971. *Thermodynamic theory of structure, stability and fluctuations.* Wiley, New York.

Golani, I. 1976. Homeostatic motor processes in mammalian interactions: a choreography of display. *In:* P. P. G. Bateson & P. H. Klopfer (eds.), *Perspectives in ethology,* vol. 2. Plenum, New York, pp. 69–134.

Golani, I., D. Wolgin, & P. Teitelbaum. 1979. A proposed natural geometry of recovery from akinesia in the lateral hypothalamic rat. *Brain Research* 164:237–267.

Gottlieb, G. 1976. Conceptions of prenatal development: behavioral embryology. *Psychological Review* 83:215–234.

Harrington, F. H. 1975. *Response parameters of elicited wolf howling.* Ph.D. thesis, State University of New York at Stony Brook.

Harrington, F. H., & L. D. Mech. 1978. Wolf vocalization. *In:* R. L. Hall & H. S. Sharp (eds.), *Wolf and man: evolution in parallel.* Academic Press, New York and London, pp. 109–132.

Havkin, G. Z. 1977. *Symmetry shifts in the development of interactive behaviour of two wolf pups (Canis lupus).* M.A. dissertation, Dalhousie University, Halifax, Nova Scotia.

Hinde, R. A. 1970. *Animal behaviour: a synthesis of ethology and comparative psychology,* 2nd ed., McGraw-Hill, New York.

Hinde, R. A., & J. Stevenson-Hinde. 1976. Towards understanding relationships: dynamic stability. *In:* P. P. G. Bateson & R. A. Hinde (eds.), *Growing points in ethology.* Cambridge University Press, Cambridge, pp. 451–479.

Hines, M. 1942. The development and regression of reflexes, postures and progression in the young macaque. *Contributions to embryology, Carnegie Institution, Washington* 30:153–204.

Holton, G. 1978. *The scientific imagination: case studies.* Cambridge University Press, Cambridge.

Hopkins, D. A. 1970. *The neural basis of grooming behavior in the rat.* Ph.D. dissertation, McMaster University, Hamilton, Ontario.

Jacob, F. 1976. *The logic of life: a history of heredity.* Vantage Books, Random House, New York.

Jacobson, M. 1978. *Developmental neurobiology,* 2nd ed. Plenum, New York.

Jerne, N. K. 1967. Antibodies and learning: selection versus instruction. *In:* G. C. Quarton, T. Melnechuk, & F. O. Schmitt (eds.), *The neurosciences study program,* vol. 1. Rockefeller University Press, New York, pp. 200–205.

Jones, D. D. 1977. Entropic models in biology: the next scientific revolution? *Perspectives in Biology and Medicine* Winter 1977:285–299.

Kagan, J. 1971. *Change and continuity in infancy.* Wiley, New York.

Katchalsky, A. K., V. Rowland, & R. Blumenthal. 1974. Dynamic patterns of brain cell assemblies. Neurosciences Research Program Bulletin, vol. 12, no. 1. Boston, Massachusetts.

Kilham, P., P. H. Klopfer, & H. Oelke. 1968. Species identification and colour preferences in chicks. *Animal Behaviour* 16:238–244.

Kimmel, C. B., & R. C. Eaton. 1976. Development of the Mauthner cell. *In:* J. C. Fentress (ed.), *Simpler networks and behavior.* Sinauer, Sunderland, Massachusetts, pp. 186–202.

Kots, Ya. M., & A. V. Syrovegin. 1966. Fixed set of variants of interactions of the muscles of two joints in the execution of simple voluntary movements. *Biophysics* 11:1212–1219.

Lashley, K. S. 1951. The problem of serial order in behavior. *In:* L. A. Jeffress (ed.), *Cerebral mechanisms in behavior.* Wiley, New York, pp. 112–136.

Laszlo, E. 1973. *Introduction to systems philosophy: toward a new paradigm of contemporary thought.* Torchbook ed. Harper, New York.

Lehrman, D. S. 1970. Semantic and conceptual issues in the nature-nurture problem. *In.* L. R. Aronson, E. Tobach, D. S. Lehrman, & J. S. Rosenblatt (eds.), *Development and evolution of behavior.* Freeman, San Francisco, pp. 17–52.

Lenneberg, E. H. 1967. *Biological foundations of language.* Wiley, New York.

Lieberman, P. 1977. The phylogeny of language. *In:* T. A. Sebeok (ed.), *How animals communicate.* Indiana University Press, Bloomington and London, pp. 3–25.
Lind, H. 1959. The activation of an instinct caused by a "transitional action." *Behaviour* 14:123–135.
Lorenz, K. 1973. *Behind the mirror: a search for a natural history of human knowledge.* (Translated by R. Taylor.) English translation copyright 1977 by Methuen, New York and London.
Luria, A. R. 1976. *Basic problems of neurolinguistics.* Mouton, The Hague.
Lwoff, A. 1962. *Biological order.* M.I.T. Press, Cambridge, Massachusetts.
Machlis, L. 1977. An analysis of the temporal patterning of pecking in chicks. *Behaviour* 63:1–70.
Marler, P. 1975. On strategies of behavioural development. *In:* G. Baerends, C. Beer, & A. Manning (eds.), *Function and evolution in behaviour: essays in honour of Professor Niko Tinbergen, F.R.S.* Clarendon, Oxford, pp. 254–275.
1976. Sensory templates in species-specific behavior. *In:* J. C. Fentress (ed.), *Simpler networks and behavior.* Sinauer, Sunderland, Massachusetts, pp. 314–329.
Mayr, E. 1970. *Populations, species, and evolution.* Belknap Press of Harvard University Press, Cambridge.
Mech, L. D. 1970. *The wolf: the ecology and behavior of an endangered species.* Doubleday, Garden City, New York.
Miller, J. G. 1978. *Living systems.* McGraw-Hill, New York.
Moran, G. A. 1978. The structure of movement in supplanting interactions in the wolf. Ph.D. dissertation, Dalhousie University, Halifax, Nova Scotia.
Moran, G. A., & J. C. Fentress. 1979. A search for order in wolf social behavior. *In:* E. Klinghammer (ed.), *The behavior and ecology of wolves.* Garland Press, New York, pp. 245–283.
Moran, G., J. C. Fentress, & I. Golani, 1981. A description of relational patterns of movement during 'ritualized fighting' in wolves. *Animal Behaviour,* in press.
Nicolis, G., & I. Prigogine. 1977. *Self organization in nonequilibrium systems.* Wiley, New York.
Oster, G., A. Perelson, & A. Katchalsky. 1973. Network thermodynamics: analysis of biophysical systems. *Quarterly Review of Biophysics* 6:1–138.
Pattee, H. H. 1970. The problem of biological hierarchy. *In:* C. H. Waddington (ed.), *Towards a theoretical biology.* 3. *Drafts.* Aldine, Chicago, pp. 117–136.
Pettigrew, J. D. 1974. The effect of visual experience on the development of stimulus specificity by kitten cortical neurons. *Journal of Physiology (London)* 237:49–74.
Piaget, J. 1971. *Biology and knowledge.* University of Chicago Press, Chicago.
1978. *Behavior and evolution.* Random House, New York.
Polit, A., & E. Bizzi, 1979. Characteristics of motor programs underlying arm movements in monkeys. *Journal of Neurophysiology* 42:183–194.
Posner, M. I. 1978. *Chronometric explorations of mind.* Erlbaum, Hillsdale, New Jersey.
Richmond, G., & B. D. Sachs. 1980. Grooming in Norway rats: the development and adult expression of a complex motor pattern. *Behaviour* 75:82–96.
Schassburger, R. M. 1978. *The vocal repertoire of the wolf: structure, function and ontogeny.* Ph.D. thesis, Cornell University, New York.
Shalter, M. D., J. C. Fentress, & G. W. Young. 1977. Determinants of response of wolf pups to auditory signals. *Behaviour* 60:98–114.
Shrader-Frechette, K. 1977. Atomism in crisis: an analysis of the current high energy paradigm. *Philosophy of Science* 44:409–440.
Simon, H. A. 1962. The architecture of complexity. *Proceedings of the American Philosophical Society* 106:467–482.

Slater, P. J. B. 1973. Describing sequences of behavior. *In:* P. P. G. Bateson & P. H. Klopfer (eds.), *Perspectives in ethology,* vol. 1. Plenum, New York, pp. 131–153.

Studdert-Kennedy, M. 1976. Speech perception. *In:* N. J. Lass (ed.), *Contemporary issues in experimental phonetics.* Academic Press, New York, pp. 243–293.

Tinbergen, N. 1951. *The study of instinct.* Clarendon, Oxford.

1963. On aims and methods of ethology. *Zeitschrift für Tierpsychologie* 20:410–433.

Turvey, M. T. 1977. Preliminaries to a theory of action with reference to vision. *In:* R. Shaw & J. Bransford (eds.), *Perception, action, and comprehension towards an ecological psychology.* Erlbaum, Pontiac, Maryland, pp. 211–265.

Weiner, N. 1961. *Cybernetics.* (2nd ed.) M.I.T. Press, Cambridge, Massachusetts.

Weiss, P. 1967. One plus one does not equal two. *In:* G. C. Quarton, T. Melnechuk, & F. O. Schmitt (eds.), *The neurosciences: a study program,* vol. 1. Rockefeller University Press, New York, pp. 801–82.

White, S. J. 1978. Are LASSes (language acquisition socialization systems) better than LADs (language acquisition devices)? *Annals of the New York Academy of Sciences* 318:53–64.

Whitehead, A. N. 1929. *Process and Reality.* Macmillan, New York.

Woolridge, M. W. 1975. *A quantitative analysis of short-term rhythmical behaviour in rodents.* D. Phil., Oxford University, Oxford.

Woolsey, T. A., & J. R. Wann. 1976. Areal changes in mouse cortical barrels following vibrissae damage at different postnatal ages. *Journal of Comparative Neurology* 170:53–66.

13

THE SEARCH FOR INVARIANTS IN MOTOR BEHAVIOR

ILAN GOLANI

The title of the present chapter involves an apparent contradiction: How can the concept of invariance be used in the study of motor behavior, even more so in a developing organism? Both movement and development imply transience and change, and it is not at all apparent from the outset how motor ontogeny can be explained in such terms as invariance, stability, and homeostasis. In order to show that this is possible, it will be shown first that these concepts can be fruitfully used in the study of motor behavior in general. Most examples in this chapter are drawn from adult animals because their well-integrated behavior exhibits many invariant properties. The chapter ends on a developmental note that suggests how concepts of invariance or stability can also be applied in ontogenetic studies.

That developmental processes can be approached from a morphogenetic point of view has been shown by Waddington (1962) and Thom (1975). The present chapter describes an attempt to apply a morphogenetic approach to the study of motor behavior. *Morphogenesis* is here defined as the coming into being of characteristic and specific form in living organisms (see Waddington 1970). In order to study motor behavior from such a point of view, it is necessary to isolate the variables that generate and maintain forms of movement. Such variables are described in the present chapter as *relevant variables,* meaning that they are relevant for behavioral morphogenesis.

THE ISOLATION OF RELEVANT VARIABLES

The overwhelming complexity and variety of animal behavior have often forced ethologists to take a first-approximation approach to its description. Frequently this has meant that the flux of behavior is divided into individual acts or patterns that are then classified, labeled, and placed on a list – the ethogram.

Ethograms do give a relatively quick overview of the behavioral repertoire of a species. They are sufficient for answering certain kinds of questions, and there is no better testimony to their usefulness than the progress ethology has made in the last few decades.

Such lists of items have, however, one fundamental disadvantage that should be taken into account in the establishment of a rigorous science. Every behavior pattern has many variables that might themselves be part of possible dynamic systems. The initial chopping of the flux into atomistic units often conceals relevant variables that interact to generate behavior. In some studies, it might prove more fruitful to start by listing the candidate variables that might prove relevant to the observed motor structure, instead of listing behavioral patterns as such.

With some behaviors, such listing is relatively easy. For instance, in social interactions both the distance and the angle between the interactants are likely to be relevant variables. In the structuring of grooming behavior, contact pathways on the face and body may prove to be a relevant variable, as might the kinematic relations between the various limb and body segments (cf. Chapter 12). However, in other studies the discovery of relevant variables may prove to be the result of the study rather than its beginning.

One probable reason for the difference in status between physiology and ethology is that in physiology many of the relevant variables have already been isolated. Some examples are body temperature, hormone level, and electrical activity of nerve cells. The physiologist need only choose the relevant variables for a specific study and then examine their interaction. This is not the case in the study of the morphology of behavior, in which we usually do not even know what the relevant variables are.

Because movement is a spatiotemporal process, it has often been suggested (e.g., Baerends & Baerends-van Roon 1950) that a continuous recording of spatiotemporal patterns must involve a description of muscular activity. Such statements deterred ethologists, who preferred to observe behavior in freely moving animals with their eyes, rather than become involved with cumbersome electromyogram recordings in restrained animals. However, motor behavior, although mediated by muscular activity, involves movements of limb and body segments in relation to each other. For ethologists, studying these movements means staying on the observable level. This kinematic level, although as legitimate as any other biological level, has for some reason been studied least.

The relevant kinematic variables must be by definition geometrical. If behavioral morphology is ever to become as rigorous a science as physiology, and if movement is to be studied as a process in its own right, then the geometrical variables must be isolated and measured and their interaction used for a dynamic interpretation of the process of morphogenesis of motor behavior. The isolation of geometrical variables can now be achieved by the use of the Eshkol–Wachmann movement notation (Eshkol & Wachmann 1958; Golani 1976).

In this chapter, I shall discuss several behavioral geometrical variables. For clarity of exposition, I shall first discuss the behavior of some familiar physiological variables and then show that the geometrical ones behave similarly.

THE BEHAVIOR OF RELEVANT VARIABLES: POINT STABILITIES IN PHYSIOLOGY

Body temperature is a good example of a physiological variable. When measured continuously in an endotherm, it takes a particular value and maintains it for relatively long periods. Movements away from this value are immediately followed by a return to it. The system is described as stable: Its dynamic behavior consists not only of the maintained value but also of all the unidimensional trajectories along the dimension of temperature that repeatedly lead to this value from both higher and lower values. In a unidimensional graphic representation of this system, all the trajectories lead to a point. The stability of the system is referred to as *point stability,* and the point itself is termed a *set point* or *point attractor.*

The discovery of such stability suggested that body temperature is actively maintained invariant by subservient processes. As a result, a whole series of initially fragmentary and seemingly unrelated phenomena become tied together: metabolic rate, peripheral vasodilatation and vasoconstriction, perspiration, shivering, and so on. All of these variables are coupled together within one unitary, self-regulatory structure. The structure is defined as homeostatic because of the relatively invariant maintenance of body temperature. The relevant variables of the structure are all the variables involved in the management of body temperature, including body temperature itself.

A similar process of isolation of a managed relevant variable, identification of point stabilities along it, and a description of the subservient variables coupled together to manage and maintain these point stabilities can now be used to study motor behavior.

RELEVANT VARIABLES AND POINT STABILITIES IN MOTOR BEHAVIOR

As suggested earlier, a rigorous study of the spatiotemporal structure of movement should involve the isolation of the observable variables that underlie and explain motor morphogenesis. In some forms of social behavior, one reasonable candidate for a relevant variable is body contact with a partner.

When a pair of Tasmanian devils (*Sarcophilus harrisii*), marsupial carnivores, engages in precopulatory behavior, the mates move around each other in ways that were formerly spliced and classified into behaviors such as circling, wrestling, rolling, performing mutual upright, revolving in a T posture, and so on. However, when examined from the point of view of body contact, it becomes apparent that both animals are shifting the contact point with the partner on their own bodies to particular locations. Once these contact points are reached, they are actively maintained by both interactants for a considerable amount of time. Thus, in spite of, or rather as a result of, the vigorous and rich movements of both interactants, the point of contact on each participant's body surface is maintained invariant.

Because the fixation of these points on the bodies of both partners acquires priority, a so-called joint is formed between them. The two animals twist, lift, lower, wag, and drag each other through it without exerting any actual physical force (Eisenberg & Golani 1977; Golani 1976). The whole interaction involves the successive establishment, maintenance, and disappearance of such joints, which structure a significant part of the social encounter (see Figs. 13.1 & 13.2).

The kinematics of the process involve antagonistic and self-compensatory movements of some or all of the limb and body segments of one or both

Figure 13.1. A pair of Tasmanian devils engages in precopulatory behavior. During most of the interaction (frames 005–217), a cheek-to-cheek joint is maintained between the two interactants. Such simultaneous maintenance of point stabilities on the body surface is common in social interactions of a variety of animal classes. Drawings were made from a 16-fps film. Numerals indicate frame numbers of drawings and are attached to a constant position on the floor.

interactants. Small shifts away from the preferred contact points are immediately compensated for by appropriate movements toward them. Geometrically, such contact points are two-dimensional attractors on the body surface; one can circumscribe their basins of attraction – their *draining areas,* so to speak – by drawing the contact trajectories that lead toward them. Thus, body surface is not a space evenly populated with contact points and trajectories, but rather a set of areas where contact never occurs and other areas that form basins into which trajectories drain and then coalesce to form dense, invariant, two-dimensional point stabilities.

The joint example involves the maintenance of point stabilities on body surfaces. However, motor behavior abounds with homeostatic processes that

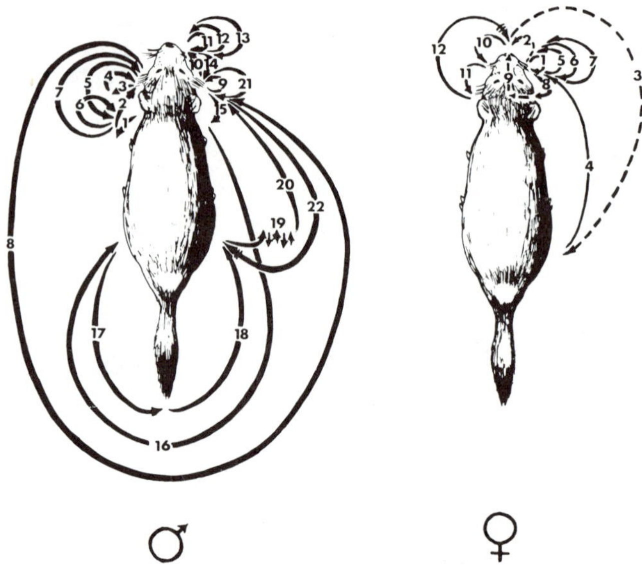

Figure 13.2. A schematic representation of contact pathways on the body surface of a pair of Tasmanian devils during a particular precopulatory interaction. Arrows describe the shift of the contact point with the partner on each animal's own body and are drawn away from the body to allow proper exposition. Arrows that start and end at about the same location on the body surface indicate steadily maintained contact points. As is shown, these points are concentrated on the head. The diagram, which represents only the horizontal aspect of contact shifts, was extracted from an Eshkol–Wachmann movement notation motor score obtained from a 16-fps film.

involve the maintenance of a body or limb segment in an invariant geometrical position in space. For example, when the head of an animal rotates through a certain angle to the right and the eyes move simultaneously on the head to the left through the same angle, the net result of the two antagonistic and self-compensatory movements is that the eyes fixate in relation to the environment, that is, they are maintained invariant on a particular angular coordinate.

The angular horizontal position of the eyes in relation to the environment may be treated as a relevant variable and the coordinates in which fixations occur as point stabilities on it. Such stabilities may involve antagonistic and self-compensatory movements of the head on the neck, neck on the torso, torso on the pelvis, and so on. The steady gaze is generated by specific bodywise movements, themselves the relevant variables that, in their interaction, maintain another variable steady.

By using geometrical invariance as the culling rule for the classification of motor behavior into relatively independent stable processes, a large number of otherwise unrelated activities prove to be structurally similar: Vestibular head fixation, leading with the head in quadruped locomotion, contact fixation of a rodent's snout with the ground, and the kinematics of breathing in man are all examples of motor processes that involve the invariant maintenance of body segments in a particular coordinate in space.

Fixation of the head's position in relation to the vertical involves compensatory vertical movements of the various limb and body segments. As we know, the invariant vertical position of the head is mediated by the vestibular and visual systems.

When a quadruped changes its direction of progression, it first moves its neck toward the preferred direction. Then it fixates the neck in this direction by performing antagonistic and self-compensatory movements of the neck on the torso and of the torso in relation to the ground (Golani 1976).

During exploratory behavior a rat keeps invariant the minimal distance between its snout and the ground by coupling the movements of the lower, middle, and upper torso and the neck and head (contact fixation). A change in the tilt of any of the above body segments in the vertical domain involves simultaneous antagonistic changes in the vertical tilt of some or all of the other serially connected segments, so that the sum total of the movements results in the snout's maintaining steady light contact with the ground (Golani et al. 1979).

When humans brêathe, chest expansion would involve a shift of the center of gravitation forward, except for a homeostatic synergism of the various body segments that counters this result by appropriate movements in opposite directions (Gurfinkel et al. 1971). In these examples, the invariant coordinates and the geometry of the subservient kinematic processes have been defined rigorously (Golani 1976; Robinson 1964). The neurophysiological processes that mediate eye fixation, vertical head fixation, and the kinematics of breathing have been partly described (e.g., Gurfinkel et al. 1971; Kornhuber 1974; Robinson 1974).

All the examples cited above involve unidimensional or two-dimensional point stabilities of motor behavior, because one or at the most two coordinates are maintained. When plotted in time, they are represented graphically by a line that runs parallel to the time axis. In this respect, they are linear and involve quasi-static stability in the sense implied by Cannon's concept of homeostasis (Iberall 1969). However, as we now know, not all homeostatic processes are of this nature.

Often stability takes the form of a nonlinear limit cycle, whereby a managed variable runs cyclically and repetitively through a series of specific values. In the following section, I shall first discuss some physiological limit cycles and then describe a behavioral one.

LIMIT CYCLE STABILITIES IN PHYSIOLOGY

One common physiological limit cycle is that of the heartbeat as measured and represented by the electrocardiogram (EKG) trace. The EKG runs cyclically and repetitively through a series of electrical values. The trace immediately returns to its highly specific trajectory after any electrical perturbation (providing it does not exceed certain bounds). When plotted in time, the attractor is in the form of a trajectory rather than a point. Because each value along this trajectory is momentarily stable in the sense that at that particular

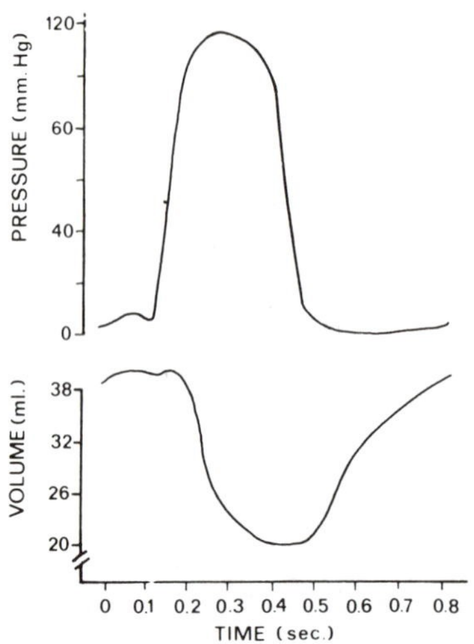

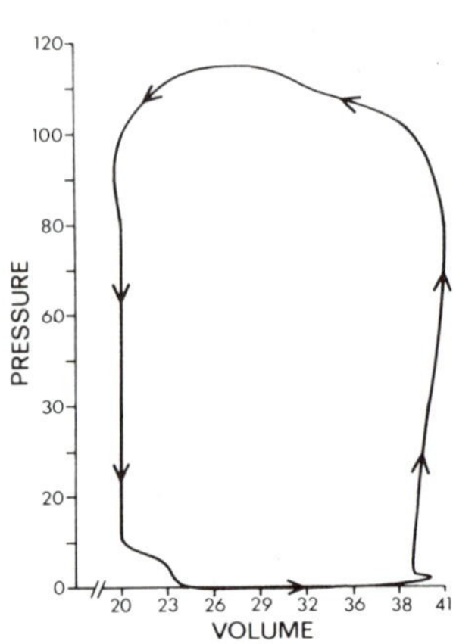

Figure 13.3. The two graphs on the left describe the pressure and volume in the dog's left ventricle, in time, throughout one heartbeat cycle. The graph on the right represents the same information, but the time axis is eliminated, as pressure is plotted against volume. The space thus created is termed a *phase space.* The graph plotted within it can be obtained from the two graphs on the left by plotting successively simultaneous values of pressure and volume. Each pair of pressure and volume values is represented by a point # – the so-called representative point. When plotted successively, the representative points form a closed cycle termed a *limit cycle.*

moment a perturbation is followed by a return to that value, the process is said to be stable in relation to a limit cycle. The limit cycle is unidimensional because only one variable is measured and represented.

The same kind of stability can be seen in two dimensions when cardiac volume is plotted against cardiac pressure throughout the heartbeat complex. At every point in the phase space thus created, there is a vector of two coordinates giving a specific volume and a specific pressure. When the actual pairs of volume and pressure are plotted successively, a closed cycle is obtained (Fig. 13.3).

As before, the dynamic behavior of the system consists not only of the cycle itself but also of all the trajectories leading to it from inside and outside the cycle. The process is stable because any drift away from the cyclical trajectory is immediately corrected and the trajectory is seemingly sucked into the same cycle. Whereas in the case of quasi-static stability oscillations occur around a static point, here oscillations occur around a more complicated geometric object, namely a closed trajectory, which is nevertheless structurally invariant. This type of stability had been termed *homeokinetic* to indicate the more dynamic nature of the regulation (Iberall 1969). Similar physiological limit cycles have been shown to operate within cells (Goodwin 1963) as well as on the level of the whole organism, ranging in time scale from 0.1 second per cycle (neural spikes) through 24 hours (circadian rhythms) to a month or so (menstrual cycle) (Iberall 1969).

LIMIT CYCLE STABILITY IN MOTOR BEHAVIOR

The step cycle in walking, the hand stroke cycle in face grooming in rodents, and scratching in many species of mammals represent typical motor cycles that are most probably structured around limit cycles. I will now analyze one example of face grooming in mice to show that it is indeed a limit cycle process. It is taken from work done in collaboration with John Fentress on the ontogeny of grooming in mice (see also Chapter 12). The analysis of this behavior was made from a high-speed film using the Eshkol–Wachmann movement notation.

A 10-day-old mouse sits in the nest and leans on a sibling with its adducted left elbow so that its left paw is high up in the air, away from its face. The mouse has to establish paw contact on both sides of its face in order to groom. On the right side, face contact can be established by flexing the lower arm on the upper arm and by a slight raising of the upper arm. However, on the left side, the elbow is anchored to the sibling and the mouse supports itself on it. Therefore the face must be brought to the paw to establish face-to-paw contact. This involves coordinated movements of the ankle, knee, hip, and shoulder joints. In spite of the totally different kinematic processes on the right and on the left, contact is established on both sides of the face simultaneously and symmetrically, and two symmetrical descending contact pathways are generated and terminated at the same time. Highly similar contact pathways are generated three times recursively on both sides of the face, involving two completely different kinematic strategies.

The recursive performance of almost identical contact pathways suggests that the contact pathways are limit cycle attractors. This aspect of the behavior is maintained invariant throughout the cycle. The two paws of the mouse are seemingly sucked into two symmetrical orbits. The two different kinematic strategies may be described as two subservient motorically equivalent groups of movements, because, when transformed into contact pathways, they generate almost identical geometrical orbits.

Invariant motor transients

Given that there are specific point and limit cycle stabilities around which motor behavior is organized, what are the routes along which animals move from one such stability to the next? For instance, by what route does a male Tasmanian devil shift the female's snout from one stable contact point on one cheek to the next stable contact point on the other cheek? The records show that such shifts, when they occur, proceed along specific trajectories under the chin of the male, or along the flank of the body, via the hindquarters and back along the other flank of the body to the other cheek. Contact never shifts along a different pathway, for example, along the frontal aspect of the face. Similarly, when contact is shifted on the female's body from a joint on her snout to a joint on the dorsal aspect of her neck, the pathway always proceeds under the line

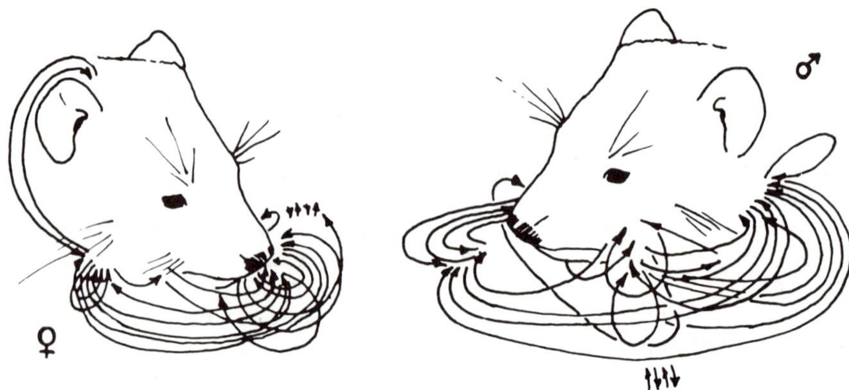

Figure 13.4. A diagram of contact pathways on the heads of a pair of Tasmanian devils during two precopulatory interactions. Arrows that start and end at about the same location stand for steadily maintained contact with the partner. Other arrows describe the pathways along which contact shifted. These contact pathways are species-specific and differ for both sexes. Note the total lack of contact pathways within the head surface enclosed by an imaginary line connecting the ears, genal and mystacial vibrissae, and snout. Extracted from an Eshkol–Wachmann movement notation motor score obtained from a 16-fps film.

connecting the mouth and the cheek, around and behind the ear, up to the dorsal aspect of the neck (Fig. 13.4).

In general, contact pathways from one fixated contact point to the next follow a few highly specific routes. They are by no means the shortest ones; it is surprising to see how seemingly convenient routes are avoided. Furthermore, as soon as one animal is introduced or introduces itself into the vicinity of another, it is immediately sucked into one of these specific trajectories and travels along it until it reaches a point stability. Then, as this stable point disappears and a new one emerges, it again travels along such a route to the next stable point, and so on. This may occur simultaneously for both animals.

In Tasmanian devils this process involves actual contact, but in higher mammals, such as jackals, similar pathways may be traversed in close proximity without any physical contact (pathways of opposition). In both cases, it is as though each animal's body surface is surrounded by a highly differentiated network composed of preferred orbits and point stabilities. Once the two animals enter each other's sphere of attraction, they "go into orbit" and revolve within each other's preferred orbits until they reach a point stability on their own bodies. Because sooner or later both reach such points, a joint is formed between them.

All the opposition and contact trajectories that we have observed coalesce into such preferred orbits, which then connect either to other such orbits or directly to point stabilities. Social interactions are bounded within such orbital constellations in much the same way as astronomical interactions are bounded within gravitational fields or interactions between atomic particles are

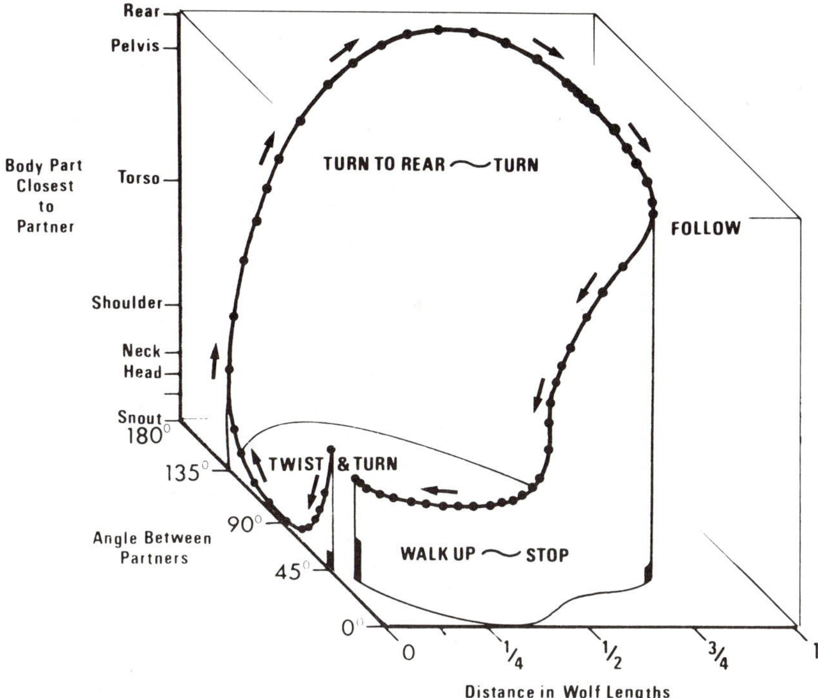

Figure 13.5. Part of a specific interaction between two female wolves is represented by a kinematic graph. The cubic phase space defines the configurational interaction space of the two animals. Each point on the graph represents a specific configurational relationship between the two wolves in terms of interanimal distance, angle, and body part closest to the partner. This last variable relates to only one of the animals. The graph is composed of representative points that describe the temporal succession. Arrows indicate the direction of flow. Black bars on the bases of the cube indicate the amount of time spent in a particular configuration. The represented part of the interaction includes two three-dimensional point stabilities and two transients that connect them. The two wolves start with a "twist or turn" fixation, which they maintain for some time, then shift to a "follow" fixation through a "turn to rear ~ turn" transient, then shift again to a "twist and turn," through a "walk up ~ stop" transient. (Adapted from Moran 1978)

bounded within electromagnetic fields. The limit network thus created expresses the force exchange configurations between the atomisms in the system (see also Goodwin 1970; Iberall & McCulloch 1969).

HIGHER-DIMENSIONAL MOTOR LIMIT NETWORKS

Up to now I have described point, limit cycle, and limit transient stabilities of up to two dimensions (as on body surface). Now I will describe higher-dimensional motor stability (Fig. 13.5).

To describe the changing relations between two interacting quadrupeds so that the spatiotemporal structure of social configurations can be reconstructed from it, it is sufficient to record continuously the distance between the interactants, the relationship of opposition, and the angle between them (partnerwise orientation). Greg Moran did such recording in his study of extended supplanting interactions in wolves (Moran et al. in press).

In this investigation (see also Chap. 12) the choice of the relevant variables was made at the outset, because it made sense that when a wolf interacts with a partner, it regulates simultaneously the distance, the orientation, and the body part facing the partner. When verbalized, such a description may run as follows: "Wolf A keeps wolf B in front of his snout (relationship of opposition) facing in the same direction (partnerwise orientation) at a distance of approximately one-half wolf length. Then, the distance between the two animals decreases to zero, and wolf B is shifted clockwise to the right shoulder of wolf A as the relative angle between the two animals increases clockwise for 315°." The time course for the change in each variable is specified in the score.

The description discloses the changing relationships between the two wolves without taking into account the contribution of each wolf to the change. This contribution is obtained from a description of the behavior of each animal in relation to the environment (e.g., the distance between the two animals may decrease due to the movement of one, or the other, or both, in the same or in opposite directions).

A cubic phase space, the coordinates of which are the above relative variables, comprises a set of points, each of which is a vector of three numerals that describe distance, orientation, and body part facing the partner in a particular theoretically possible configuration. The cube includes all the theoretically possible configurations, but the wolves actually use only a subset of this set of points. By tracing the representative point – the point that describes successive actual configurations – one can draw a kinematic graph that describes the social interaction as it proceeded in sequence from one configuration (vector) to the next. After drawing all notated interactions within the cube, we get a graphic representation of extended supplanting interactions.

Moran has shown that within the cube there are four specific classes of configurations contained within two spatial subregions, that, once arrived at, are maintained homeostatically for long periods. Every point stability represents the simultaneous homeostatic maintenance of three variables. For instance, the wolves may move around and circle while maintaining an antiparallel orientation at a distance of one-half the wolf length and a relationship of opposition of A's snout to B's hindquarters; or they may revolve while maintaining a perpendicular orientation touching each other and an opposition relationship of neck to shoulder, and so on.

When the wolves move from one such three-dimensional point stability to the next, they do so through a specific three-dimensional transient. There are five such classes of transients that connect the four classes of point stabilities. The members of each class of transients are topologically similar in the sense that the graphs that describe them have the same form, that is, the same set of points of singularity. Each of these transients is itself a preferred orbit in that the wolves seemingly get sucked into it upon entering its neighborhood.

As in the case of opposition pathways, here too the limit network thus created expresses the force exchange configurations of the social system. Both wolves employ a variety of movements to maintain a nonvariant limit network. These movements are at the same time part of subservient lower-level point, limit cycle, and transient stabilities that operate at the level of the individual animal. The limit network is the skeleton, around which the interaction is organized. Behaviors such as bristling, growling, shifting to plantigrade locomotion on hindlegs, performing various facial expressions, and so on switch on at particular points along the network and off at other points.

With this view of motor behavior as organized around attractor limit networks, stability and invariance are no longer vague concepts. Rather, they imply a hierarchy of specific homeostatic and homeokinetic structures embedded within structures of a similar nature.

The advantage of the attractor concept, and the inadequacy of the prevailing distinction between goal and strategy, are apparent here: Whereas it might sometimes prove useful to view point stabilities as goals, the more intricate the geometrical form of the attractor becomes, the less useful the concept of goal becomes. To claim that the goal of the system is running through the limit network is not informative.

PREFERRED ORBITS IN INDIVIDUAL MOTION SPACE

The limit network described above may also be referred to as the *social motion space* of wolves during extended supplanting. Is *individual* motion space organized similarly around preferred orbits? Our work on motor recovery from severe lateral hypothalmic (LH) lesions in rats suggests that it might (Golani et al. 1979).

Recovery from brain damage, like ontogeny, provides an opportunity to observe motor structures as they emerge, in relative isolation, before new structures are superimposed upon them to produce normal adult behavior. In recovery, exploratory movements occur along several relatively independent dimensions that appear successively. Lateral scanning movements of the head, which is carried on top of other moving limb and body segments, recover first. At about the same time or later, longitudinal (backward–forward) movements begin to appear. As movements along these two dimensions increase in amplitude and involve the whole body, vertical (dorsal–ventral) scanning movements of the head with snout contact (along vertical surfaces) appear and increase gradually in amplitude.

Body support and management of limb and body segments' contact with the ground also recover relatively independently. In addition, the rat recapitulates the process of recovery in each sequence of movements after pronounced immobility. As the rat starts to move after an arrest, its head travels along small lateral orbits. Then, as these orbits increase in amplitude, it starts to move along longitudinal orbits and along trajectories with both lateral and longitudinal components. Still later, it starts to move along vertical orbits with contact, as well as along orbits with lateral, longitudinal, and vertical components. Snout contact with the substrate is maintained throughout. Finally, the head starts to move along vertical orbits without contact.

The interesting thing is that the rat cannot move along a longitudinal orbit before it travels along a lateral one; it cannot move along a vertical before travelling along a longitudinal, and so on. It is as though the rat has to weave its own space, step by step, every time it moves. In this context, to move means to construct a motor manifold and to move along it within specific ordered orbital constellations.

Seven relevant variables account for the morphogenesis of the observed behavior: Four are actual spatial dimensions of movement, as measured in relation to the longitudinal axis of the rat's body; support and contact are two additional spatial variables; and the seventh is the position of the actual movement in the sequence.

For some time, motion space is organized only around the animal's own body. Then it becomes coupled to the environment. For instance, arrests and grooming occur at a specific location. In unexplored areas, only lateral and longitudinal movements are performed. During successive visits to previously explored areas, vertical movements appear with increasing amplitudes: Locomotion away from the site of arrest involves a slow, low gait (plantigrade), toward the site a fast, high (digitigrade) gait, and so on (for more details see Golani et al. 1979). The modulation of the basic organization of motion space around the body by a higher-level organization in relation to the environment often conceals the lower-level one. In a study of the emergence of organizations in recovery and in ontogeny, underlying invariance can be revealed.

Once the relevant variables of movement have been isolated, their subservient kinematics can be studied. In the recovering rat, the head is carried along the motion space described above by specific kinematic synergisms that involve progressive cephalocaudal recruitment of all limb and body segments. The LH animals show a characteristic delay in the recruitment of the next causal limb segment, in comparison to normal rats (straitjacket phenomenon). The underlying neurophysiological organization of some of these motor subsystems has already been described (Jung & Hassler 1960).

The subject of the Golani et al. study was the recovery of exploratory behavior. Because telereceptors are concentrated in the head, the structured movements of the head through space suggest the possibility that the observed organization also involves a hierarchy of attention. It is possible, for instance, that the lateral and longitudinal movements, which recover first, involve primarily tactile and olfactory processes. Similarly, vertical head movements away from surfaces, which appear later, may involve specific visual processes and so on. If this is so, motor invariance may sometimes indicate the emergence of perceptual processes in recovery as well as in ontogeny.

ONTOGENY: DEVELOPMENTAL PROCESSES CAN BE STUDIED WITHOUT RERERENCE TO ADULT BEHAVIOR

Once behavior is conceived of as a sequence of items called *behavior patterns,* development becomes the process whereby each item on the ethogram acquires its final shape while the number of items on the list increases with time. New patterns that emerge in ontogeny are then described and examined with reference to what is identified as their complete form shown in adulthood. Such reference has its obvious power of explanation, because development implies a process of becoming, and it is always helpful to compare developing structures to their final form. On the other hand, if we accept the view that organisms must have some integration and stability of their own throughout ontogeny, then it should be possible to describe and explain motor development in terms of integrated processes in their own right, without reference to their future form and function. Such integrated processes can be uncovered by isolating the relevant variables and by studying their behavior with a search image for emerging attractors. Clearly, the emergence of an attractor indicates the establishment of a new behavioral subsystem.

THE ISOLATION OF RELEVANT VARIABLES IN ONTOGENY

Sometimes the isolation and follow-up of a variable can be instructive in uncovering some aspects of developmental processes. For instance, Hines (1942) has shown that in ontogeny, support of the body, as expressed in terms of the degree of extension of the legs during locomotion and the degree of arching of the torso, develops excessively in infant rhesus monkeys before it regresses to normal adult support behavior. This and other similar findings led her to title her paper "The development and regression of reflexes, postures and progression in the young macaque." Our own work on recovery from LH akinesia in rats has uncovered a similar trend of excessive development and subsequent reduction along the variables of support, lateral and longitudinal movements, and duration of bouts of activity between arrests. It might be of interest to examine motor ontogeny of rats to see whether similar trends are manifested there as well.

The systematic recording of face contact during the ontogeny of face grooming in mice uncovered another general trend (Golani & Fentress in preparation; see also Chap. 12). Up to day 5 postnatally, infants generate a whole variety of contact pathways on their face. These range from stationary points to long pathways that may start on the forehead and terminate at the tip of the snout. The number of successive strokes varies from 1 to 10. The pathways are sometimes simultaneous and symmetrical, at other times alternately symmetrical, and at still other times asymmetrical. Pathways may be discontinued in the middle of their performance, and often the hand stroke is performed in the air, without actually touching the face.

From day 5 to day 9 or so, only one type of pathway is generated. This is a symmetrical, simultaneous, short (from mystacial vibrisae and down) pathway. Then, from day 10 or 12 on, the pathways seen during the first period reappear, but this time as part of a well-orchestrated activity yielding a predictable variety of elaborate short and long, symmetrical and alternatively symmetrical pathways. In this example, the measured variable has excessively low values temporarily.

To sum up, in ontogeny, the values of a specific variable may become temporarily excessively high, as in the examples cited in the previous paragraph, or excessively low, as in the contact pathways example. Such ontogenetic trends may disclose important dynamic properties of the developing motor sub-systems involved.

In adults, the balance between the various attractors is already established. Ontogeny provides an opportunity to examine the various attractors before the establishment of such balance.

The emergence of attractors

One measure of an animal's integrative powers is its homeostatic and homeokinetic capacities. In ontogeny these capacities increase in number and range of action, thereby increasing the stability of the developing animal. Within the framework of the present chapter, motor ontogeny can be understood as the study of the emergence of homeostatic and homeokinetic structures. At one level, these structures can be defined in terms of attractors and basins of attraction, and at another lower level in terms of their subservient kinematic processes. On the one hand, it is easier to uncover such stable processes in the adult, where behavior is well integrated, that is, organized around well-defined attractors. On the other hand, in the adult, several attractors are often superimposed on each other, so that their isolation becomes difficult or even impossible. Ontogeny provides an opportunity to discover attractors as they emerge, in relative isolation, before they become tightly coupled to each other.

Ethologists have shown that in ontogeny the form of a behavior often develops before its orientation (Hinde 1970, ch. 19). Our own study on the ontogeny of egg-smashing behavior by Egyptian vultures has shown that the well-coordinated throwing of stones develops long before the vulture orients the throw at the ostrich egg. In fact, a vulture may show extensive throwing before it is ever exposed to an egg. Orientation then becomes superimposed on the already perfected throw (Marder et al. unpublished results).

In the language of the Eshkol–Wachmann movement notation, the so-called form refers mainly to the kinematic relations between the limb segments of the body (bodywise description), whereas the so-called orientation refers to kinematic regularities in relation to the environment (description in the absolute). Within the framework of the present chapter, the ontogenetic primacy of form over orientation may mean that bodywise kinematic attractors often develop before absolute attractors. The last ones may involve telereception or contact.

Our study of the ontogeny of face grooming in infant mice (Golani & Fentress in preparation) also suggests that in development contact attractors are superimposed on the previously established bodywise kinematic regularity. As stated earlier, up to day 5 postnatally, contact pathways on the face are fortuitous, whereas the kinematics of grooming show regularity. From day 5 on, contact pathways seemingly canalize into simple preferred orbits, which from approximately day 12 on become progressively more elaborate and highly structured. In development, both the kinematics and the contact pathways become more elaborate and predictable. Yet their partial independence, and the time lag in their development, provide aspects of organization not available in the adult.

It is possible that in adults two attractor cycles, a kinematic and a contact one, operate simultaneously, thereby structuring at least some phases of grooming behavior. For instance, when a forepaw of an adult grooming mouse is pulled forward and downward by a string tied to its wrist, both paws may perform several parallel simultaneous and symmetrical circular pathways in the air, in front of its nose: Upon forced release of face contact in one paw, the mouse immediately abandons paw-to-face contact with the free paw and prefers to maintain the kinematic spatiotemporal relationship with the constrained paw. The free paw is seemingly sucked into an orbit parallel to that of the constrained paw, and it abandons the highly specific, regularly performed contact orbit on the face (Golani & Fentress in preparation). Such experimental perturbations in adults may uncover attractors first noticed in ontogenetic studies.

In general, two or more organizing attractors may operate simultaneously and thereby structure the behavioral landscape in the same way that in a geographical landscape the draining of water is structured by the simultaneous attraction of several attractors, such as valleys and riverbeds. Such an approach to behavior is similar to Waddington's and Thom's approach to structural stability in that it explains the structure of behavior in terms of the organization of the structure itself (Thom 1975; Waddington 1962). It also explains the inadequacy of the conceptual dichotomy between goal and strategy: It is inadequate to define contact pathways as goals and kinematic trajectories as strategies. Rather, both may exert organizing forces on behavior, and the relative attraction of each may change in ontogeny, as well as with the different circumstances in which the behavior is performed. In one case, as in functional grooming, priority may be given to contact pathway attractors; in another, as in displacement grooming, to kinematic ones.

The last examples clarify another important aspect of the integrative approach suggested in this chapter: that the mechanics of a behavior can be obtained from a description in one frame of reference (a description of the movements of each segment in relation to the next serially connected one – bodywise description), whereas its consequences can be obtained by a description of it in a different frame of reference (a description of the movements of each segment in relation to contact, to the environment, or to a partner – contactwise, absolute, or partnerwise descriptions). Within this framework, mechanics and consequence, causality and finality, are merely two aspects of structure; it is only by juxtaposing these different aspects of the same behavior that one can obtain an intimate grasp of it.

CONCLUSION

The kinematic invariants together with their associated kinematic variables specify self-regulatory motor subsystems embedded in motor behavior. Described in terms of observables, they offer representations that (1) disclose the organization of motor behavior, and (2) allow the visualization of complex behavior in one's own mind in much the same way that a musical score allows a musician to "hear" the music upon sight-reading it.

Because all the variables are geometrical, the obtained organization is described exclusively in real or configurational space. It is constructed independently of the underlying lower-level processes that are coupled to it.

For the physiologist, the discovery of each invariant indicates the existence of a relatively independent neural subsystem that mediates it. Therefore, a final statement about the structure of motor behavior should be based on measurements along all the levels involved – kinematic, biodynamic, muscular, neurophysiological, and electrophysiological. However, it is necessary to isolate and describe a subsystem before subjecting it to a multilevel study. Such subsystems can sometimes be identified by anecdotal observations and inspired guesses. However, the time is ripe for a rigorous, disciplined method of isolating them. Motor behavior is like an unexplored land that abounds with variables and invariants waiting to be discovered, and the Eshkol–Wachmann movement notation is a most appropriate technology for their isolation.[1]

The details of application of this technology have been described elsewhere (Golani 1976), and they are beyond the scope of this chapter. Essentially, the analysis involves a full kinematic description of a specific behavior in one particular frame of reference, and then transformations to other frames of reference. Invariance is then disclosed in one description, and the relevant variables associated with it in other descriptions of the same behavior.

SUMMARY

This chapter describes an integrative approach to the study of behavioral morphogenesis. It shows how the organization of motor behavior can be obtained by the exclusive recording and examination of kinematic observables.

In the representations obtained by the use of this method, motor behavior appears to be composed of a class of relatively independent, self-regulatory subsystems that interact with each other. These subsystems provide the skeleton around which behavior is organized.

The isolation of subsystems is achieved in the following way: First the kinematics of movement are described in Eshkol–Wachmann movement notation. The positions and movements of all the limb and body segments are described in a specific polar coordinate system in relation to the next serially connected segment. Then, the same behavior is transformed into other polar coordinate systems, also in relation to the next serially connected segment, but so that the coordinates are determined by the environment or a partner. Such transformational analysis allows the viewing of the same behavior from different angles. One view discloses what is kept steady for some time during movement, whereas other views disclose the mechanics associated with the process of maintenance.

The kinematic value or series of values that are kept steady are described as invariants, and the kinematics associated with them are described in terms of relevant variables. Each subsystem comprises an invariant and a group of associated variables.

The concepts of stability, homeostasis, relevant variables, and invariance, fruitfully used in physiology, can now be applied to the study of motor behavior.

The emergence of an invariant in ontogeny indicates the establishment of a new stability – a new homeostatic subsystem. Ontogeny provides an opportunity to study the various subsystems as they emerge, in relative isolation, before they become indistinguishably coupled in adult behavior.

NOTE

1 The Eshkol–Wachmann movement notation publications can be obtained in the United States and Canada from Dr. Annaliz Hoymans, Department of Physical Education, University of Illinois at Urbana–Champaign, Illinois. In other countries publications can be obtained from the Movement Notation Society, 75, Arlozorov St., Holon 58327, Israel.

ACKNOWLEDGMENTS

Part of the research reported here was supported by a grant from the United States–Israel Binational Science Foundation (BSF), Jerusalem, Israel. Dr. Greg Moran of the Department of Psychology, University of Western Ontario, London, Canada, kindly gave permission to use some of his unpublished Ph.D. thesis results. Thanks are due to Prof. Evelyne Satinoff for her critical reading of the manuscript.

REFERENCES

Baerends, G. P., & J. M. Baerends-van Roon. 1950. An introduction to the study of the ethology of cichlid fishes. *Behaviour Supplement* 1:1–242.

Eisenberg, J. F., & I. Golani. 1977. Communication in metatheria. *In:* T. A. Sebeok (ed.), *How animals communicate.* Indiana University Press, Bloomington, pp. 575–599.

Eshkol, N., & A. Wachmann. 1958. *Movement notation.* Weidenfeld & Nicholson, London.

Golani, I. 1976. Homeostatic motor processes in mammalian interactions: a choreography of display. *In:* P. P. G. Bateson & P. H. Klopfer (eds.), *Perspectives in ethology,* vol. 2. Plenum, New York, pp. 69–134.

Golani, I., D. L. Wolgin, & P. Teitelbaum. 1979. A proposed natural geometry of recovery from akinesia in the lateral hypothalmic rat. *Brain Research* 164:237–267.

Goodwin, B. C. 1963. *Temporal organisation in cells.* Academic Press, London.

1970. Biological stability. *In:* C. H. Waddington (ed.), *Towards a theoretical biology,* vol. 3, *Drafts.* Edinburgh University Press, Edinburgh, pp. 1–17.

Gurfinkel, S. V., Y. M. Kots, E. I. Paltsev, & A. G. Fel'dman. 1971. The compensation of respiratory disturbances of the erect posture of man as an example of the organisation of interarticular interaction. *In:* I. M. Gelfand, V. S. Gurfinkel, S. V. Fomin, & M. L. Tsetlin (eds.), *Models of the structural-functional organization of certain biological systems.* M.I.T. Press, Cambridge, Massachusetts.

Hinde, R. A. 1970. *Animal behaviour: a synthesis of ethology and comparative psychology.* McGraw-Hill, New York.

Hines, M. 1942. The development and regression of reflexes, postures and progression in the young macaque. *Contributions to Embryology* 3:155–205.

Iberall, A. S. 1969. New thoughts on bio-control. *In:* C. H. Waddington (ed.), *Towards a theoretical biology,* vol. 2., *Sketches.* Edinburgh University Press, Edinburgh, pp. 166–178.

Iberall, A. S., & W. S. McCulloch. 1969. The organising principle of complex living systems. *Journal of Basic Engineering* (June):290–294.

Jung, R., & R. Hassler. 1960. The extrapyramidal system. *In:* J. Field et al. (eds.), *Handbook of physiology,* section 1, *Neurophysiology,* vol. 2. American Physiological Society, Washington, D.C., pp. 863–927.

Kornhuber, H. H. (ed.). 1974. *Vestibular system,* part 1, *Basic mechanisms.* Springer-Verlag, Berlin.

Moran, G. 1978. The structure of movement in supplanting interactions in the wolf. Ph.D. dissertation, Dalhousie University, Nova Scotia, Canada.

Moran, G., J. C. Fentress, & I. Golani. In press. A description of relational patterns of movement during 'ritualized fighting' in wolves. *Animal Behaviour*

Robinson, D. A. 1964. The mechanics of human saccadic eye movement. *Journal of Physiology (London)* 174:245–264.

1974. The effect of cerebellectomy on the cats' vestibulocular integrator. *Brain Research* 71:195–207.

Thom, R. 1975. *Structural stability and morphogenesis.* Benjamin, Reading, Massachusetts.

Waddington, C. H. 1962. *New patterns in genetics and development.* Columbia University Press, New York.

1966. *Principles of development and differentiation.* Macmillan, New York.

1970. Concepts and theories of growth, development, differentiation and morphogenesis. *In:* C. H. Waddington (ed.), *Towards a theoretical biology,* vol. 3, *Drafts.* Edinburgh University Press, Edinburgh, pp. 177–197.

PART IV

PHASE SPECIFICITY

INTRODUCTION

KLAUS IMMELMANN

This group of chapters is devoted to a discussion of privileged periods during the development of behavior. Inevitably, the authors of this section must refer to a problem already addressed in this volume, that of continuity versus discontinuity in development. Whereas the majority of developmental processes have been considered to be continuous throughout life, others are characterized by discontinuities. But, as our authors have already indicated (see Chap. 1; Section II), this is a controversial area. One of the reasons may be that clear-cut discontinuities are difficult to find; total continuity and abrupt discontinuity are two ends of a continuum with many intermediates.

Evidence for discontinuities comes from two sources. One is the occurrence of qualitatively new patterns of behavior at a certain age, as in species that have a metamorphosis within their ontogeny. The other is the existence of privileged periods in the development of some behaviors, that is, periods in which environmental influences are of great importance to developmental processes.

Evidence for privileged phases comes from behavioral phenomena that have been called *imprinting*. Research on imprinting and discussion of its theoretical implications have always played a major role in the work of ethologists. Konrad Lorenz introduced the term in his frequently cited Kumpan paper (1935), which was based in part on observations made by Spaulding as early as 1873 and by Heinroth early in this century. Lorenz provided the first general description of imprinting, listing its peculiar characteristics and comparing it to other learning processes.

Lorenz's paper was followed by numerous studies of filial imprinting. These studies demonstrated that the two main criteria Lorenz mentioned as characterizing imprinting – the existence of a sensitive phase for learning and the high degree of stability of the results of the early learning process – can indeed by found, especially in filial imprinting. However, differences in the species studied, the experimental methods used, and an obvious inability of authors to repeat each others' experiments caused remarkably different conclusions to be drawn from these studies. The phenomenon was further broadened when sensitive phases and stability were found to exist in a variety of other developmental processes, nonsocial as well as social. Certain aspects of human development were also said to fall within the concept of imprinting. As a consequence, the concept of imprinting became so broad and general that the question of whether phase specificity in development is a real phenomenon was raised; it is worthy of further study in animals and humans.

New data and clarifying reviews and overviews have gradually softened the intense controversy of the earlier period. But the reader comparing the three chapters in this section will recognize that differences in viewpoint still exist. This section starts with two chapters dealing with the phenomena of imprinting and sensitive phases in general. The first one is by Klaus Immelmann and Stephen J. Suomi, two authors with entirely different scientific backgrounds. Their chapter (14) provides a critical overview of the imprinting literature and emphasizes evolutionary considerations that have in general been neglected. They take a slightly more conventional view than does Chapter 15, by Patrick Bateson, which offers some new theories of the regulation and possible functions of sensitive phases.

The reader will also notice that there is not complete agreement regarding the most appropriate term for the stage of enhanced sensitivity. In Chapter 14, a rationale is offered for introduction of the term *sensitive phase*. In Chapter 15, the expression *sensitive period* has been retained; this term is more commonly used in the literature on imprinting.

Chapter 16, by P. Herbert Leiderman, makes a critical statement about the possible occurrence of sensitive phases in human development. It takes a skeptical view and thus provides a counterbalance to some recent literature that has either overstated or understated the role of sensitive phases. Leiderman feels that it is unlikely that "for such a complex organism as man, fixing of an essential bond might occur only in the brief period following childbirth." If one looks at present-day *Homo sapiens,* this conclusion appears correct. There are, however, those who argue on evolutionary grounds that there may be a phase of heightened sensitivity in humans and nonhuman primates shortly after birth. Such a sensitive phase would provide a means of facilitating the mother-child bond in prehuman social organization. Vestiges of that former adaptation could still be present in the development of humans. Evidence for or against such an assumption, however, can be gained only through careful investigations of early human development, for which Chapter 16 is an excellent example.

The question of phase specificity in development will also be addressed in other chapters of the book, mainly in Chapters 19, 20, and 21, as well as in Chapters 7 and 18.

14

SENSITIVE PHASES IN DEVELOPMENT

KLAUS IMMELMANN AND STEPHEN J. SUOMI

In the literature on behavior development in both animals and man, much attention has been given to the possible occurrence of sensitive phases in development. Many investigators studying many different species claim to have found a variety of developmental processes to be characterized by phase specificity, that is, by stages during which steps of particular importance are taken. An area in which examples of sensitive phases seem to be particularly clear-cut is the influence of environmental factors, social as well as nonsocial, on development. Here, special attention has been directed to demonstrating the importance of early experience upon adult patterns of preference and behavior. (Use of the term *sensitive phase,* however, is not restricted to behavior ontogeny. Classically, the term has been applied to any event that has a greater influence at some stages of development than at others; see under "imprinting phenomena.")

The first indication of phase specificity came from early research on imprinting in birds. Unfortunately, very strict and rather narrow definitions of what were then called *critical periods* gave the impression that sensitive phases are brief and invariant and that environmental influences during those stages lead to results that are completely buffered against subsequent alterations. This view, in turn, created some doubts whether – despite increasing evidence of phase specificity in development – the concept of the sensitive phase, and even of imprinting in general, was valid and, above all, whether it could be generalized to mammalian species, including nonhuman primates and man. Very different opinions ranging from general acceptance of this notion of generalization (e.g., Bowlby 1969; Hofman & Ratner 1973) to strict rejection (e.g., Harlow et al. 1972) have been expressed.

The main arguments against the existence of critical, or sensitive, phases (for discussion of terminology, see "A note on terminology") are that they may be artifacts of experimental procedure. Reality, as usual, seems to be found somewhere between the opposite notions. Brief sensitive phases for early learning clearly represent only one end of a continuum. And the sequence of developmental processes certainly does exert an important influence. This is evidenced by the wide diversity of sensitive-phase phenomena that have been reported in the literature. In addition to the well-documented cases of filial and sexual imprinting, there is evidence that sensitive phases can exist for the establishment of food and habitat preferences and/or aggressive behavior patterns. Moreover, sensitive-phase phenomena are not limited to a few species of birds; instead, they have been reported in various insects as well as in certain mammalian species, including man and many other primates. Representative examples of this great diversity will be presented under "Imprinting phenomena."

The essential point, however, is the fact that there exists such a wide variety of phase specificity between organisms. Among different, sometimes closely related species, marked differences in the onset and duration of sensitive stages occur. Even within a species, different developmental processes may have their maximum sensitivity to environmental influences at different ages (see "Nature of sensitive phases"). We assume, therefore, that like all characteristics of living organisms, the specific time and age programs for learning reflect adaptations to the species' particular environment and have developed, by natural selection, during the course of evolution. Sensitive phases, therefore, are convergent phenomena, instanced by many analogies across species. Consequently, a comparative discussion, in which close attention is paid to the biology as well as to the behavior of the particular species, may clarify controversial issues.

THE CAUSES OF SENSITIVE PHASES

Explanation of terms

The first step one could take during this process of clarification is to ask questions about both the possible functions and benefits sensitive phases may have and the mechanisms responsible for their regulation. In the biological sciences, a clear distinction is made between these two types of causes, which are termed *ultimate* and *proximate,* respectively. This distinction is seldom addressed in the psychological literature, but it is of the greatest importance for the understanding of phase specificity. An introductory discussion and explanation of terms therefore seems to be appropriate here, even though this issue is also dealt with in Chapter 11.

The terms *ultimate* and *proximate causes* were first introduced by Baker (1938) in connection with the study of breeding seasons of birds. Thomson (1950) called them *ultimate* and *proximate factors,* terms that have since been commonly used in the literature on annual periodicity in birds and other species. The original reason for differentiating between the two terms is as follows. The breeding seasons of birds have evolved mainly in relation to the requirements of the young, each species being adjusted to breed at the time of the year at which the resulting young can be most effectively cared for. Both before and after leaving the nest, birds hatched at less advantageous times suffer a heavier mortality and rarely survive the reproductive age. The gene complexes of those pairs producing young at the wrong time of the year should, therefore, be reduced or eliminated by natural selection (for a review, see Immelmann 1971).

The selective pressures on the birds will therefore operate toward the end of the reproductive period, and this produces a problem in timing. There may be no problem in some mainly tropical and subtropical areas where environmental conditions are sufficient for raising young during a large part of the year: There the birds can rely on the improvement of environmental factors (e.g., food supply) and utilize these immediate changes as signals to begin to reproduce (cf. Ashmole 1971). In the vast majority of natural environments, however, periods of optimum conditions are usually rather brief, and direct dependence on changes in environmental factors is insufficient. This is because the entire reproductive cycle, starting with gonad growth and including courtship, nest building, and incubation, requires several weeks or months. Thus, depending on the developmental rate of the species, reproductive changes must be initiated well in advance of such optimum periods. In order to be able to do so, the organism must receive some forewarning, signaling the impending favorable season, that guides the necessary physiological and behavioral preparations for reproduction to occur at the appropriate time (cf. Farner 1970).

As a consequence, environmental factors exerting the selection pressure for well-adapted reproductive seasons and those providing the necessary information for the early stages of the cycle as a rule are not identical. A major selective factor, for example, is an adequate food supply. The most important source of environmental information, on the other hand, is provided by changes in day length, at least in temperate zones (for a review, see Farner & Lewis 1971). Those causes that have led, through natural selection, to the evolution of species-specific breeding periodicities have been called *ultimate factors,* whereas those that keep the adapted organism in conformity with the periodicity of its environment are termed *proximate factors.*

An exception to the rule of diversity between selective factors on the one hand and regulatory factors on the other hand is provided only in the above-mentioned cases of very extended breeding seasons. Here, the occurrence of an adequate food supply may also act as a triggering stimulus, and thus ultimate and proximate factors may be identical.

Since the two terms were introduced, it has become increasingly clear that the distinctions between ultimate, selective factors leading to specific adaptations and proximate, informative factors actually regulating the individual's behavior can be applied not only to reproductive periodicities but also to a variety of other phenomena (for detailed discussion, see Mayr 1961). A well-known example is provided by habitat selection, especially the selection of a suitable site for reproduction. Ultimate factors are those that influence the survival rates and reproductive success of individuals living or breeding in different environments. Proximate factors, on the other hand, are those characteristics (e.g., color and structure of soil, density and character of vegetation, shape and size of leaves) that provide the necessary signals for the individual to recognize and return to the appropriate environment (Immelmann 1971; Orians 1971). Other examples of differences between selective and regulatory factors can be found in mating systems (e.g., duration and nature of the pair bond), in reproductive strategies (e.g., dispersal mechanisms of the young at the end of the breeding season), in the determination of clutch size in birds (Klomp 1970), and in group structures of social animals (Crook 1970; Kummer 1971; Kurland 1977) (including mechanisms of incest avoidance; for a review, see Bischof 1972), as well as in many aspects of migratory behavior (Berthold 1975).

The same distinction between ultimate and proximate factors is important in the consideration of sensitive phases in behavioral development. Because ignorance of this distinction may be one reason for many misunderstandings in discussions about the existence or nonexistence of sensitive phases, a brief outline of the different possible causes will be presented in this section.

Ultimate factors in sensitive phases

With regard to sensitive phases, the essential question to ask is, what are the selective factors that during the course of evolution have led to the formation of privileged periods of learning? The answer to this question must be found in the life history of the species because, as mentioned above, there exist major species differences with respect to how sharply defined in time and effect these phases may be. Under natural conditions, the opportunities to learn and/or to develop specific behavior patterns and habits may be quite different during different stages of life. These differential opportunities are especially evident in those species of birds that have intensive parental care and whose young disperse as soon as they have reached nutritional independence. It is obvious that the young animal's opportunities to gain knowledge in the social (species-specific characteristics, such as plumage characters and vocalizations) and nonsocial (food, habitat) spheres from conspecifics who share a large proportion of its genes are much greater early in life than after it has left the family. In addition, later social experiences might not only be more difficult to obtain but might also be wrong.

In the Australian zebra finch (*Taeniopygia guttata*), for example, the young stay close to the nest only for the first days after fledging (which occurs around the twenty-first day of life); later on, they meet with young birds from other nests and form small groups of their own (Immelmann 1962). Because many Australian finches breed in mixed colonies or neighborhoods, these groups may consist of young from different species. The young zebra finches would then come into close social contact with members of other species. A brief sensitive phase that brings the learning of species-specific characteristics more or less to a close before the young leave their parents may, therefore, prevent the birds from learning inappropriate social signals from nonconspecifics.

Similar suggestions have been made by Evans (1970) for the ring-billed gull (*Larus delawarensis*), which also breeds in mixed colonies. This species likewise shows an early termination of the sensitive phase, ensuring attachment to parents and siblings before the onset of a degree of mobility that could be sufficient to bring young chicks in close contact with another species and thus could bring about the danger of the wrong kind of social information. In species in which the young remain with their parents for a longer period of time or in which there is no close proximity to other species, no such selection pressure favoring an early end of the sensitive phase need occur. An example almost opposite to the zebra finch is that of the grey-lag goose (*Anser anser*), in which the parent–offspring bond is known to last for about 10 months and to break apart only shortly before the onset of the following breeding season. For this species, the sensitive phase for sexual imprinting has been found to last at least until the 150th day of life (Schutz 1969).

Among mammals, the period of time infants spend with their parents (especially with the mother in most species) is usually longer than that found in most avian species. Correspondingly, the duration of sensitive phases for establishing the most elementary patterns of social behavior are usually longer, with less well-defined endpoints as well. Nevertheless, these sensitive phases usually overlap almost entirely with the chronological period during which the infant remains in close contact with its closest blood relatives. This is true even in the higher primates, which have notoriously long periods of infant care. Among rhesus monkeys (*Macaca mulatta*), the primary period for development of basic social skills occurs during months 2 to 6, a period when infants of both sexes typically remain in close proximity to their mothers (e.g., Hinde & Spencer-Booth 1967; Lindburg 1973).

Another example in which ultimate factors controlling sensitive phases become apparent is song learning in birds. This is dealt with in greater detail in Chapter 20 (see also Thielcke 1969; Thompson 1970).

An example from the nonsocial sphere is provided by the early termination of the sensitive phase that has been found in the indigo bunting (*Passerina cyanea*) with regard to its learning of star patterns. This early termination ensures that it is really the pattern of the bird's own birthplace that is learned in order to be used, the following spring, as an orientation mechanism during the return migration to the breeding grounds (Chap. 19).

From the few examples given, it becomes apparent that in many species and for different functional systems, strong selection pressures that favor great sensitivity to certain environmental stimuli and a maximum of learning during early stages of life may well exist. They may also favor great stability of the results of such early experience, providing some kind or degree of protection against some later possible influences on the individual. In addition, it becomes apparent that differences in such specific needs and demands between species are almost certainly responsible in large part for the enormous diversity in the degree of stability and in the duration and characteristics of sensitive phases, as will be discussed later.

Differences between functional systems may also reflect their different requirements. For example, filial imprinting has to take place quickly in order to provide the hatchling with the template of the object it has to follow shortly afterward. Sexual imprinting, on the other hand, provides information that is needed only when the animal has reached sexual maturity. Therefore, the whole period during which the young animal stays with its parent(s) may be used for learning the characteristics of its close kin. As a consequence, sensitive phases for filial and sexual imprinting may be different even within a species, as Schutz (1965) suggested for mallards (*Anas platyrhynchos*). (This statement does not imply that the sensitive phases are completely separate in time; rather, a certain amount of overlap and connection may well exist; see the discussion in Andrew 1964; Bateson 1979; Vidal 1976.)

Taken together, the evidence suggests that different ultimate factors have not resulted in a uniform sensitive phase phenomenon but rather have produced a variety of specific adaptations. More examples of such adaptations will be provided later in the chapter. At this point, we only want to demonstrate that there can be a definite need for specific stages of enhanced sensititivity during development (for further discussion, see Bateson 1979).

Proximate factors for sensitive phases

So far, we have discussed some possible selective factors responsible for the adaptive character of sensitive phases. Now that we have thus specified the problem, the question of how it is solved arises. In order to serve the purpose for which sensitive phases have been selected, there must be a system of mechanisms that actually regulates the increase and decline of sensitivity in the individual. In the biological literature, such mechanisms, as mentioned above, are generally called *proximate causes* or *proximate factors,* whereas in the psychological (and sometimes also in the biological) literature they are referred to as *immediate causes, psychological factors, social factors, regulating factors,* or just *mechanisms.*

The search for such determinants presents a more difficult task than does formulating plausible explanations for different ultimate factors. One problem is that sensitive phases, most probably, are not regulated by a single factor but rather by a joint operation of several variables. Other difficulties arise from another consideration. There might be situations in which there is no need for specific proximate factors because the regulatory mechanism can take advantage of conditions or developments already in existence. This would parallel those cases of reproductive activities of birds in which the individual can rely on the selective factor of an adequate food supply to serve as a triggering factor as well. Thus the ultimate factor could at the same time represent the main proximate factor (see "Explanation of terms"). In the regulation of sensitive phases, a comparable situation exists if during the normal course of development there are developmental stages and events that can provide a starting point for the onset of sensitivity without being especially selected to serve this purpose.

For example, in filial imprinting, the increase in locomotor ability has sometimes been thought to be a main factor determining the beginning of sensitive phases (for details and further discussion, see Bateson 1966, 1972; Hess 1973). The age at which this increase occurs, however, is most likely a consequence of general developmental speed, which in turn is the result of the interplay of a number of selective pressures, leading to an adaptation to the young precocial bird's specific needs at various developmental stages. It is unlikely, though, that the onset of sensitivity is a major factor to which the specific age of occurrence of such increase is adjusted, unless it can be shown that in different species of ducks in which the onset of sensitive phases has been found to be different, there are parallel differences in motor development.

In other birds, the determination of subsequent social preferences seems to start as soon as the sensory organs have reached a developmental state that allows the nestling to acquire the information necessary for the establishment of such preferences. In the zebra finch, for example, the sensitive phase has been found to begin before the fourteenth day of life (see "Nature and intensity of stimuli"). The eyes are not fully open before the eighth or ninth day of life (Sossinka 1970), so that visual imprinting may start as soon as the birds are able to perceive and process optical stimuli (Immelmann 1972b). A similar correlation with the development of sensory discriminatory abilities has been discussed for the following responses of precocial birds (cf. Hinde 1962; Kovach et al. 1966; Strobel et al. 1968). Again, it does not seem likely that opening of the eyes at this particular age has evolved to serve as a mechanism to enable visual imprinting to occur. Rather, it is probably an adaptation to the specific needs of the growing nestling.

In the cases mentioned, the sensitive phase for filial or sexual imprinting thus seems to start as early as possible, that is, as soon as the relevant motor and sensory capacities are developed. Here, no special proximate factors are necessary. (This, of course, does not mean that in such cases the onset of the sensitive phase cannot be influenced by natural selection: If it were important for filial or sexual imprinting to occur earlier, presumably there would have been selection pressures against the constraints on that happening.) In other instances, gross steps in developmental sequence just do not occur at the particular age at which, for reasons discussed above, sensitivity should start or end. This is especially true for the end of the sensitive phase, which frequently is preceded by a rather long phase of gradual decline in sensitivity. The gradual decline does not seem to be correlated with events as dramatic as opening the eyes or obtaining locomotor ability. Furthermore, the temporal differences in optimum sensitivity often found between related species obviously are not correlated with any apparent differences in the overall course of development.

This lack of correlation is the case, for example, within the avian group of finches (Fringillidae) for which timing of the sensitive phase for song learning has been found to be different in different species even though the overall speed of ontogenetic development is similar (for details, see Chap. 20). Obviously the species-specific termination of sensitivity reflects specific demands, presumably correlated with peculiarities of the species' reproductive biology.

In these cases, therefore, the need for proximate factors specifically selected for regulating sensitive phases becomes obvious. (Here, of course, ultimate factors are involved again, as they have determined, during the course of evolution, which timing mechanisms, in terms of providing optimum survivial value, are best suited for the particular species or functions.)

There are two general regulatory systems in the organism, the hormonal system and the central nervous system, that are likely candidates for the focus of such timing mechanisms, and some preliminary evidence of their function in regulating sensitivity is indeed available. For filial imprinting, Landsberg and Weiss (1976) have shown that an increase of the corticosterone level in the blood is one of the factors limiting the sensitive phase in ducklings (although the corticosterone level itself may be influenced by neural changes that, in turn, are consequent on experience, e.g., stress). Sexual imprinting and song learning in birds may also be under hormonal control, as may several other aspects of filial imprinting. The data available from this field of research, however, are still limited and rather controversial, partly because of differences in the methods applied (for a review, see Landsberg 1981).

Much more promising results have been obtained for the central nervous system, both from biochemical and from neuroanatomical work. Bateson et al. (1969, 1973, 1975, 1978) have reported that in domestic chicks, there is a correlation between the effects of visual experience in the imprinting situation and the incorporation of radioactive amino acids into protein in different regions of the brain, which may reflect accelerated protein synthesis in those regions. The findings of Laudien and Iken (1977) in the fruit fly *Drosophila melanogaster* likewise suggest a correlation between imprinting and the protein biosyntheses in the central nervous system. If it can be shown that other learning is not affected in the same locus, it can be assumed that the capacity for a specific developmental rate of the particular brain region is adapted to this ultimately selected learning process and thus represents a specific regulatory mechanism.

Recent neuroanatomical studies indicate that great sensitivity early in life may be correlated with the formation of new synapses and dendritic branching, with the rearrangement of synapses optimizing the probability of contact for some neurons, and/or with the disconnection of neurons and their physiological death (cf. Greenough 1975; Rosenzweig et al. 1972; see also Chap. 7). The next step to take would be to answer the question of whether different brain loci, correlated with temporally different learning processes, show correlated temporal differences in development.

It seems possible, therefore, that some kind of phase specificity can be observed even without any specifically evolved proximate control. Such specificity would be a consequence of the normal course of behavior development. Thus, if the onset of an apparent sensitive phase were determined merely by motor, sensory, and/or neural maturation and its offset were determined by limits on the neural space available for a given function, the term *sensitive phase* would merely be a description of the normal development of some behavior pattern. If, on the other hand, the increase and decrease of sensitivity were contingent on the level of hormone flow or the rate of dendritic branching, then *sensitive phase* would refer to a distinct, specialized process evolved to fulfill a particular function. Hormonal and/or neural control of sensitivity offers the advantage of being able – through slight temporal changes or local specialization in particular loci of the brain – to serve the needs for increases and declines in specific sensitivities to the environment without affecting the gross course of development. From the ultimate reasoning, this form of control seems to be possible or likely. At this time, however, no definite conclusion about the kind and degree of its involvement can be drawn. Clearly, therefore, the rapidly occurring biochemical changes in the brain and the possible phase specificity in its neuroanatomy represent a promising field of research in this area (cf. Chap. 7).

The obvious advantages of the neural and/or hormonal control of sensitivity do not exclude the possibility that other mechanisms might be involved in such control. Reviews of the regulation of sensitive phases, including discussions of many other possible factors (e.g., increase in emotionality, onset of fear and avoidance reactions), are treated in Chapter 15, as well as by Bateson and Reese (1969), Hess (1973), Moltz (1960, 1963), and Sluckin (1973).

IMPRINTING PHENOMENA

In the previous section, we pointed out that diversity in sensitive phases is to be expected because different ultimate factors and control mechanisms are operating in the development of different functional systems in different species. We now present a more comprehensive examination of the range and characteristics of sensitive-phase phenomena.

As mentioned, the first evidence for phase specificity in behavior development came from research on imprinting. (Because there is no universally accepted definition of *imprinting,* we would like – for reasons that will become clear later – to adopt a rather broad view and define it as an early learning process with a rather stable result.) Indeed, the existence of a sensitive phase has always been regarded as a necessary precondition for imprinting. In view of the close correlation between sensitive phases and imprinting phenomena, it seems worthwhile to give a brief overview of contemporary imprinting research and concepts. This appears especially important because recent findings have arrived at a view of imprinting that is considerably different from earlier conceptions. (It has to be stressed again, however, that sensitive phases are not restricted to the development of behavior but also occur in other contexts. The characterization of sensitive phases in terms of the occurrence of imprinting, therefore, is valid only within the context of behavioral aspects of development.)

Perceptual preferences

Most studies of imprinting have centered on observations that specific stimuli encountered during a restricted period of the organism's lifetime continue to be preferred, even in the case of more extended exposure to other stimuli of the same general class. Demonstrations of imprinting usually involve preference tests in which the subject is given the opportunity to choose among several stimuli, to one of which it has had previous exposure, usually during an early stage of development.

From the very beginning, imprinting was thought to be largely a characteristic of birds, perhaps because most studies on filial and sexual preferences were (and still are) conducted with birds. Such prevalence of bird studies may be due to birds' rather rapid ontogenetic development: Birds may reach their adult size and weight within about 1% of their total life expectancy, whereas some mammals need 30% and more (cf. Frazer 1977; Hendrichs 1978), as is the case for most of the higher primates, including man. Such speed in general development, which has been understood as an adaptation to a quick acquisition of the ideal ratio between body weight and a constant wing surface (Mayr 1963), must necessarily also involve some behavioral and cognitive characteristics of birds, including the development of learning and memory. It is certainly not by chance, therefore, that imprinting, being a comparatively rapid and early learning process, not only was first discovered but is also especially widespread in avian species.

Most evidence still comes from studies of the two classical cases of imprinting: filial imprinting, which establishes a preferred target for the following response of the young precocial bird, and sexual imprinting, which determines subsequent mating preferences. Extensive reviews of both kinds of imprinting in birds have been published by Bateson (1966), Hess (1973), Hoffman and Immelmann (1972b), Klinghammer (1967), Ratner (1973), and Sluckin (1973). These reviews summarize and discuss the available data and conclusions, so no further specification seems to be necessary in this chapter.

In other groups of animals, there presently exists much less clear-cut evidence for preferences and attachments meaningfully analogous to avian filial and sexual imprinting. Data that have become available in recent years nonetheless point to interesting parallels.

In mammals, an extensive experimental study of sexual imprinting has been carried out with two species of North American lemmings (*Dicrostonyx groenlandicus* and *Lemmus trimucronatus*) by Huck and Banks (1980). It revealed that cross-fostered males preferred the species odor of their foster mother and that the influence of the mother in this respect seems to be more profound for males than for females.

Fallow deer (*Dama dama*) were separated from their mothers between 1 and 48 hours after birth and either foster-reared by goats or bottle-fed. In a series of tests carried out 4 to 7 years later, Gilbert (1975) found sexual approaches to goats or a strong attachment to humans, respectively, the degree of which was highly correlated with the age within this period at which the fawns were removed from their mothers. These data indicate that adult attachment resulted from processes initiated during the first hours of life.

In addition, sexual or social preferences resulting from early experience with another species or with a human caretaker have been observed in a number of rodents, ungulates, and some other species, although in many of these latter cases, the evidence has been based on casual observations of only a small number of individuals (cf. Bateson 1978; Immelmann 1972). Altogether, however, the data suggest that processes comparable to sexual imprinting in birds do occur in mammals, and they appear to be more common than supposed in the early literature on imprinting.

Even for members of advanced primate species, long-term preferences for specific social stimuli encountered early in life have been reported. Sackett et al. (1965) measured the relative preferences of 4-year-old rhesus monkeys for a peer, an adult female human, or an empty compartment. Some of these monkeys had spent their first 6 months of life in physical and visual isolation from conspecifics and humans, others had been physically isolated from conspecifics but hand-fed by an adult female human, and the remaining subjects had been reared with peers. Sackett et al. found that the peer-reared subjects preferred the peer stimulus animal, the isolates preferred the empty compartment, and the hand-reared monkeys preferred the adult female human, even though all subjects had interacted extensively with conspecifics during the 3.5-year interval between rearing manipulation and preference testing. Similar findings have been obtained by Suomi and Baysinger (in preparation) for adolescent monkeys raised on surrogate mothers during their first 6 months, but with no subsequent exposure to those surrogates before preference tests. Strong preferences for surrogates similar in design and size to the original rearing surrogates were displayed over surrogates that more closely resembled the adolescent peers they were living with at the time of preference testing.

Some recent experimental studies of several species of fish have suggested sexual and other social, species, and color morph preferences based on early experience. These patterns closely resemble the preferences obtained through interspecific and intraspecific cross fostering in fishes (Fernö & Sjölander 1973, 1976; Kop & Heuts 1973; Sjölander & Fernö 1973).

In insects, finally, an experimental study has been carried out by Mainardi (1968) with *Drosophila melanogaster.* The results indicate that courtship preferences can be affected by early experience. Although not immediately comparable, the results obtained by Jaisson (1975) with the ant, *Formica polyctena,* at least point in the same direction: If separated from the mother colony on the day of hatching and given contact with cocoons of a different species during the first 15 days of life, the worker ants will subsequently accept and tend cocoons only of this other species, even if it belongs to another genus.

Apart from filial and sexual imprinting, certain other preferences have been found to be strongly influenced by early experience in some species. Hence their establishment has been compared to imprinting. These phenomena include preferences for a specific type of habitat, a certain type of food, selection of home area or, in parasitic animals, selection of specific hosts. Even the way in which some migratory birds use the star compass for orientation can be learned only during a brief sensitive phase before they start their first autumnal migratory season (Chap. 19). Although experimental data available at present are limited, it seems that such cases of ecological imprinting, for reasons to be discussed below, do have some characteristics in common with filial and sexual imprinting (for reviews, see Hasler 1966; Immelmann 1975; Klopfer & Hailman 1965; Thorpe 1963).

Other behavior patterns

As well as demonstrations of preferences for specific stimuli, there exist a wide range of other phenomena that strongly suggest that early experience has lasting consequences for the organism's interaction with its environment. These include phenomena as distinct as the development of normal copulatory behavior, the development of contact behavior, the organization of maternal behavior, and the degree of socialization, as well as the early and rapid song learning occurring in some species of passerine birds and perhaps even human language (see Chaps. 20 and 21).

To illustrate, in many mammals, including canine, rodent, and primate species, the degree of aggressive behavior displayed toward conspecifics in adulthood can be related to the opportunities a subject has for interaction with peers during particular periods before or during adolescence; the same opportunities presented either earlier or later appear to be far less systematically related to adult levels of aggression (Ågren & Meyerson 1979; Scott 1962; Suomi & Harlow 1977). In beagle dogs, the period of from 3 to 14 weeks is seen as particularly crucial in determining sociability versus wildness (Scott et al. 1974). In rhesus monkeys, the form, target, and chronological peaks of social contact behavior can be related to specific social experiences during the infant's first 3 months of life (Harlow & Harlow 1969). The quality of maternal behavior in this same species appears to be disproportionately influenced by experiences with one's own mother as well as by experiences during the first days of care for previous offspring (Ruppenthal et al. 1976). In rhesus monkeys, male sexual competency likewise appears to be highly dependent on particular experiences during months 3 to 9 of life (Goy et al. 1974; Harlow & Lauersdorf 1974).

Other investigators have argued that the normal development of social attachment in monkeys is consistent with an imprinting model (e.g., Hoffman & Ratner 1973; Mason 1970). Indeed, according to Bowlby (1969), the processes by which human infants acquire specific social attachments can be viewed in an imprinting perspective:

> So far as is at present known, the way in which attachment behavior develops in the human infant and becomes focused on a discriminatory figure is sufficiently like the way in which it develops in other mammals and in birds, for it to be included, legitimately, under the heading of imprinting. [Bowlby 1969:223]

Finally, psychoanalysts have traditionally assumed that the long-term effects of certain experiences are due to the fact that they occurred at crucial points during the individual's childhood or adolescence (e.g., Freud 1953).

CRITERIA FOR IMPRINTING

Three conclusions can be drawn from the evidence presented in the previous section:

First, for many behaviors across many different species, within several classes of animals, there exist phases during which specific kinds of experiences disproportionately affect not only future patterns of preference in free-choice situations but also frequencies of exhibition or even the presence or absence of particular patterns of behavior. Most of these phases occur relatively early in the lifetime of the organism.

Second, something special takes place during the restricted period, something that does not occur to the same extent during other periods of the organism's lifetime. The evidence brings these phenomena into some relationship with the classical cases of imprinting. Indeed, the terms *imprinting, imprinting-like process,* or *learning process akin to imprinting* have frequently been used in the literature in describing and discussing these phenomena.

Third, a considerable broadening of the original concept of imprinting has occurred over the years. One might ask, therefore, whether there exist any common distinguishing characteristics that justify continued use of the term *imprinting* itself. If so, how might these characteristics compare to those used for the original definition of the term by Lorenz (1935) and to those described in the subsequent literature on imprinting? The criteria for imprinting that were originally developed by Lorenz, and that have frequently been cited and discussed in the literature, are as follows: (1) imprinting can take place only during a restricted time period in the individual's life, the critical (sensitive) period; (2) it is irreversible, that is, it cannot be forgotten; (3) it involves learning of supraindividual, species-specific characters; (4) it may be completed at a time when the appropriate reaction itself is not yet performed.

The sensitive-phase criterion has traditionally been regarded as the most important one, due in part to the fact that most of the early studies had been performed on the following reactions of young precocial birds, in which sensitive phases are more prominent than in any other imprinting process. It also reflects the fact that phase specificity does indeed seem to be the determining attribute of imprinting, characteristic of all imprinting processes. This will be discussed under "Nature and intensity of stimuli."

The criterion of irreversibility has been less frequently dealt with but has nonetheless led to many controversial discussions. The disagreements have been based in large part on misinterpretations of Lorenz's original statement, which emphasized from the outset that imprinting always affects a preferential rather than an exclusive response to social stimuli. Therefore, any conclusions about the possible existence and extent of irreversibility of following or sexual responses can be drawn only if the animal is tested in a free-choice situation. Despite such misinterpretations, many preferences have been found to be less persistent and more open to subsequent changes than one would have predicted from Lorenz's original view (see "Stability of phenomena established during sensitive phases").

The third criterion, generalized learning, applies to sexual imprinting, to host selection, and also to food and habitat imprinting, in which the young animal learns to recognize a certain class of objects rather than only one specific object. It does not apply to filial imprinting, in which preferences as a rule are restricted to one particular individual.

The fourth criterion of imprinting – its completion at a time when the appropriate reaction itself is not yet performed – is, as Lorenz stated from the beginning, applicable only to sexual imprinting and perhaps to some cases of host imprinting and song learning. In other imprinting processes the reaction itself is more or less fully developed during the sensitive phase. Therefore, these latter two criteria should not be considered to be general characteristics of all imprinting phenomena.

Several further possible features of imprinting have been mentioned and discussed during the years following the publication of Lorenz's Kumpan paper. They include the effort expended by an animal during imprinting, the effect of punishment, and the influence of drugs (for a review, see Hess 1973). These criteria are more specific, however; they apply to or have been tested only for particular kinds of imprinting, mainly for filial imprinting of precocial birds. As a consequence, in all probability these claims cannot be made for a characterization of imprinting in general.

To summarize, there is only one criterion, except for an enhanced degree of stability, that seems to hold true for a general characterization of imprinting: the existence of sensitive phases. In all the phenomena that have been called imprinting or been compared to it, some developmental and learning processes are favored in one way or the other during certain, usually early, periods of the individual's lifetime. In the nature of such phases, however, large differences exist. These will be discussed in the next section.

NATURE OF SENSITIVE PHASES

Species-specific and individual aspects

Like the term *imprinting,* the concept of *sensitive phases* has changed considerably over the years. In the earlier studies of imprinting, for reasons mentioned in the introduction, sensitive phases were believed to be short, well defined, and rigid in their beginning and end (for a review, see Fabricius 1964). These characterizations were expressed by the term *critical period,* which at that time was commonly used in reference to imprinting phenomena.

Such strict requirements have long since been relaxed, inasmuch as the available empirical data now show that sensitive phases (1) in most cases are fairly extended; (2) are never sharply defined but instead are rather gradual as far as their onset and especially their termination are concerned; (3) differ in duration from species to species, between functional systems, and between individuals; (4) depend on the nature and intensity of environmental stimuli both during the sensitive phase itself and during the time preceding that period. Nevertheless, the discrepancy between earlier claims in the literature that sensitive phases are of short duration and the more recent data, which indicate that in certain cases the actual duration of these phases can be long, may be more apparent than real. We would like to explain the factors that contribute to this conclusion (for further discussion, see Chap. 15).

One main reason for the obvious complications in evaluating the duration of sensitive phases, and for the wide spectrum found in the literature, seems to lie in the question of whether the term *sensitive phase* refers to the species or to the individual. This question has been seen differently by different authors, although explicit statements as to how the term is used are seldom found in the literature.

The answer to the question is that both aspects of sensitive phases, the species-specific and the individual, should be considered. Comparative studies of several species have revealed species differences in the onset and duration of sensitive phases. In those experimental studies, however, in which it was possible to use a large number of test animals, individual differences became readily apparent. Obviously, therefore, it is only the outer age limits of sensitivity that are largely species-specific. Within those limits, environmental (and perhaps also genetic) factors can determine at which time the establishment of a preference takes place in a particular individual.

The term *sensitive phase,* if applied to a species, thus refers to a longer period of time than if applied to the individual, who in general requires only a small portion of the overall phase of sensitivity. For example, at the species level, the sensitive phase for sexual imprinting in grey-lag geese is of longer duration than it is in the mallard (Schutz 1965, 1970), and it is of slightly longer duration in the Bengalese finch (*Lonchura striata* f. domestica) than it is in the zebra finch (Immelmann, unpublished data). A statement like this, however, does not provide any information about the age at which a particular individual actually establishes a preference, nor can it tell us the specific age at which that individual, as a consequence of the amount and kind of its own experience, becomes insensitive to subsequent contact with different social stimuli. In nature, where the social conditions to which the growing organism is exposed are presumably fairly stable, the age at which actual imprinting takes place may be comparably uniform throughout the species or population (but see also "Individual variation"). In the laboratory, on the other hand, where conditions can be changed rather drastically, individuals may become imprinted earlier or later.

With respect to the species-specific aspect, the literature indicates that most sensitive phases are fairly extended and often much longer than was originally thought. This is clearly the case for sexual imprinting, in which the sensitive phase usually extends over a period of several weeks for species such as mallards, mourning doves (*Zenaidura macroura*), and zebra finches, or even as long as several months for species such as the grey-lag goose and bullfinch (*Pyrrhula pyrrhula*) (for a comprehensive review, see Klinghammer 1967). Sensitive phases of similar extended duration have been reported for song learning in some birds (cf. Chap. 20). Even in filial imprinting, in which the duration of sensitive phases was often thought to be just a few hours (for a review, see Hess 1973; Sluckin 1973), subsequent investigations have also revealed longer periods (which in the mallard, for example, may exceed 1 week) during which the establishment of social preferences is possible (Fabricius 1962, 1964).

It is in these outer age limits of the sensitive phase for a given behavior in a given species that such formation of preferences takes place in the individual. The length of exposure actually needed for the process can be remarkably brief, and this is the main reason for the above-mentioned statements about brief sensitive phases. In mallards, for example, the shortest exposure time on record that led to the establishment of definite preferences lasting for at least 5 days was about 1 minute, and the shortest exposure time leading to a preference maintained over 103 days, that is, up to the end of the following reaction, was 4 minutes 49 seconds (Schutz 1972).

There is also evidence that among some primates, exposure to relevant stimuli need not be continuous throughout the whole of the sensitive phase. For example, in rhesus monkeys affectional relationships with peers are usually established during the first 6 months of life (Harlow 1969; Harlow & Harlow 1965). However, Rosenblum (1961) has shown that species-appropriate peer relationships can be established during this period with as little as 20 minutes of daily exposure to peers. Thus, the actual length of exposure to appropriate stimuli required to establish the preference or behavior pattern in question need not be synonymous with the duration of the chronological period during which such a preference or pattern can be and, under normal conditions, is established.

The discrepancy between the long duration of sensitivity within a given species and the shorter time of exposure needed to establish a preference in a given individual means that there is room for individual variation. Theoretically it is possible that an individual can form a stable preference early or late during the period of sensitivity, or somewhere between the two extremes. The end of the sensitive phase for the species and the end of the imprinting process for the individual are thus not identical.

Such variation has been found in several instances. It may be due to genetic and/or environmental factors. For example, it seems possible that within a species there is some genetically determined variation in the duration of sensitivity or in the age at which maximum sensitivity occurs in the individual. It also seems possible that the nature and time of occurrence of relevant stimuli determine the exact age at which a particular preference is established. At least for the determining influence of environmental factors, much evidence has become available during recent years, but there are also some indications that genetically determined differences may also be involved. Both groups of factors will be discussed after some details about the nature of the termination of sensitivity are presented. (For further discussion of factors influencing imprinting, see Bateson 1978b.)

Termination of sensitive phases

As stated above, early sensitivity does not come to an end abruptly but rather in a gradual way. Quantitative evidence comes, among others, from three studies of adolescent male zebra finches misimprinted on Bengalese finches. In the first study, zebra finches were raised by another species of estrildid finch, the Bengalese finch. The young zebra finches were separated from their foster parents, and all other birds, when they reached nutritional independence, that is, when they were able to feed by themselves without supplements from their foster parents. When the males became sexually mature, they were tested in a series of double-choice experiments with a conspecific female and a female Bengalese finch. All zebra finch males in this study courted the Bengalese females almost exclusively (Immelmann 1969).

In a second study, foster-reared zebra finch males were deprived of any further visual and acoustic contact with the foster parents' species after weaning, but they were provided with a conspecific female and with nesting facilities. Most of these males eventually mated with the females and jointly raised one or several broods. After several months or years, they were separated from their conspecific mates and tested again in a double-choice situation. The results of these tests revealed the same preference for the Bengalese finch females as was observed before the period of intraspecific contact, indicating that the brief contact with the foster parents early in life clearly exerted a longer-lasting influence than did social contact of long-term duration during adult life (Immelmann 1972a).

A third study investigated whether the same degree of irreversibility observed in adult birds can also be demonstrated in adolescents. Zebra finches were again foster-raised by Bengalese finches. But instead of being kept in isolation after separation from the foster parent, they were first given intraspecific experience by being put into a cage with several zebra finch females. Four series of experiments were run with 3, 7, 30, and 60 days of intraspecific contact. The age at which the birds were transferred from the Bengalese foster parents to the zebra finch females varied from the twenty-seventh to the seventy-third day.

The results of the study can be summarized as follows. For adolescent males, in contrast to adults, it was still possible to alter a previously established preference and to reimprint the birds on their own species. The success of such

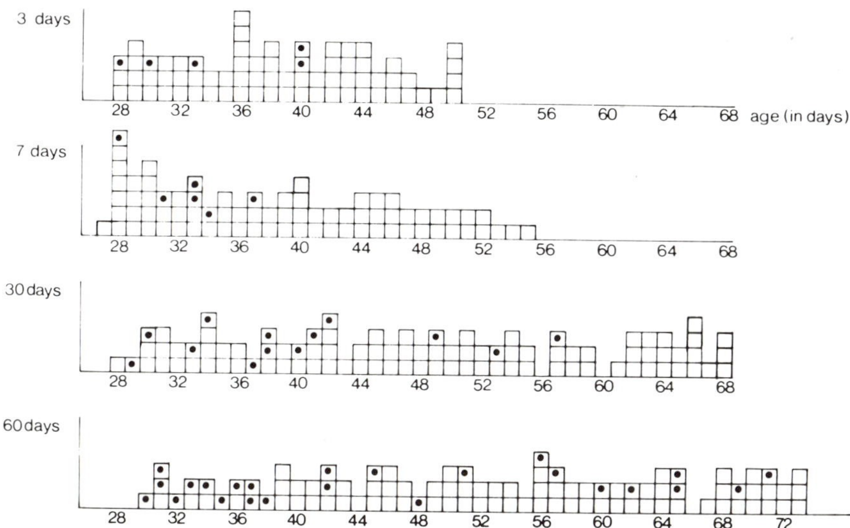

Figure 14.1. Sexual preferences of male zebra finches reared by Bengalese finch foster parents and subsequently exposed to conspecific females for 3, 7, 30, or 60 days. The abscissa gives the age (in days) of transfer from the foster parents to the conspecific females. An empty square represents an individual that retained the preference for Bengalese females; a dotted square represents a male that in the double-choice tests showed a preference for zebra finch females.

attempts, however, depended on two variables: the age of the bird and the duration of social contact with its own species. If only 3 or 7 days of intraspecific contact were permitted, such contact had to begin before or at the fortieth day of life in order to have any permanent effect on subsequent sexual preferences. On the other hand, when 30 or 60 days of contact were provided, changes in preference were still achieved when the bird was placed together with the conspecific females as late as 57 or 71 days, respectively. This means that the older the adolescent bird is, the more social contact is necessary to change a previously established social preference. Thus, with increasing age the social effort necessary to establish new preferences becomes greater. This process, as a comparison of the four series indicates, is a gradual one. Therefore, the sensitivity to those social stimuli responsible for establishing permanent social preferences decreases by degrees and comes to an end gradually rather than abruptly. The results of this study are published in greater detail elsewhere (Immelmann 1979).

Other data in the literature also point to a gradual close of certain sensitive phases. Guinea pigs (*Cavia aperea* f. porcellus), for example, are more sensitive to olfactory imprinting during the period from 1 to 3 days of age than during later 3-day exposure periods (Carter & Marr 1970). (For reviews of further examples, see Fabricius 1964; Sluckin 1974; for examples from song learning in birds, see Chap. 20.)

On a scale of considerably longer durations, some recent primate data suggest that sensitive phases for the development of some social behavior patterns may be extended over months, even years, under certain stimulus conditions. For example, although a large body of data has repeatedly demonstrated that the optimal period for development of initial peer relationships in rhesus monkeys is from 3 to 6 months of age, the relationships can be established in individuals socially isolated from all conspecifics for as late as 15 months of age (Baysinger 1975; Suomi et al. 1974). Similarly, although almost a century's worth of data has revealed that orphanage-reared children deprived of essential social stimuli during the first 2 years of life generally have a poor prognosis for normal social and cognitive development, recent findings have indicated that good foster care can result in little or no deficit in subsequent social and cognitive endeavors (Clarke & Clarke 1972; Dunn 1976; Rutter 1972, 1977).

Individual variation

The studies of sexual preferences in zebra finches not only revealed the gradual way that sensitivity to social stimuli comes to its close but also showed an unexpectedly high degree of individual variation. To illustrate, some males proved to be so strongly imprinted on the species of their foster parents that even 60 days of intraspecific contact produced no change in their subsequent preference for Bengalese finches. In other individuals, however, such preferences could be reversed with only 3 days of intraspecific contact at the age of 40 days.

Because the experimental conditions under which these birds were bred, kept, and tested were identical for all males, the conclusion seems to be justified that, in this case, the individual differences were genetically determined. Cross-breeding experiments with early imprinters and late imprinters are planned that, we hope, will provide definitive evidence.

The biological significance of individual differences is not yet known. One might speculate, however, that it is correlated with a problem discussed in more detail by Bateson (1978a; Chap. 15) concerning the balance between inbreeding and outbreeding within a given population. If sexual imprinting contributes to the achievement of an optimal degree of such balance, individual differences in the duration of sensitive phases may provide an alternative mechanism to the principle of *optimal discrepancy* described by Bateson. Those males that establish early and strong preferences will probably try to mate with a female as similar as possible to their mother. Those individuals, on the other hand, that remain "open" for a longer period of time, for example, up to the time when they leave their parents and come in contact with other members of the breeding colony, could still make small changes in their primary preference due to social interactions with other birds. These birds might prefer to mate with individuals somewhat different from their mother and could thus be responsible for the necessary degree of outbreeding.

In the two color morphs of the lesser snow goose (*Anser caerulescens caerulescens*), Cooke (1978) found a similar amount of individual variation in the influence of early experience on subsequent mate choice: Whereas most birds chose a mate similar in color to their own family, about 11% of the offspring with parents of one color were found to be paired with a mate of the opposite color. Cooke assumed that such differences are due to genetic variation in selectivity, with narrowly selective individuals choosing familial color and with broadly selective individuals using those species-specific cues for mate selection that are common to both morphs. Similar to the individual differences found in the duration of sensitive phases in zebra finches, variation in the degree of selectivity might contribute to maintaining a balance between panmixis and assortative mating.

In mammals, the degree of variability in duration of sensitive phases across individuals is probably even greater than in avian species, in which the necessity for comparatively brief sensitive phases results in stronger limits to such variability. Individual differences may be greatest among the higher primates, especially man.

Nature and intensity of stimuli

If individual differences do serve a biological function in the above-mentioned examples, or in any other way, it can be expected that such variation also exists under natural conditions. Unfortunately, relevant data are not yet available.

Evidence is available, however, in a slightly different direction. The extensive laboratory research on imprinting and imprintinglike processes over the years has shown that in addition to possibly genetically determined differences between individuals, similar differences in the duration of sensitivity and the strength of preferences may also be caused by the nature and intensity of the stimuli to which the young animals are exposed. Again, data come from another study with zebra finches.

In this experiment, the young zebra finches were allowed to hatch in their parents' nest and were fed by their parents for the first days. Afterward they were transferred, at different ages, to a nest of Bengalese finch foster parents, which reared them to independence. When tested in a double-choice situation, all birds transferred to the Bengalese finches before their fourteenth day of life preferentially courted Bengalese females. All birds transferred after their twenty-second day of life preferred the zebra finch females. In the intermediate group, however, both kinds of preference occurred. Because the birds did not have any intraspecific contact between transfer and test, all the individuals that showed a sexual preference for zebra finch females must have established the preference before they were transferred. They must have had a preference for their own species at an age as young as 14 days, and they must have retained that preference even in the light of close subsequent contact with the foster parents' species.

For most birds of this experimental group, the sensitive phase for sexual imprinting had to end within the first 2 to 3 weeks of life. That is substantially earlier than in the birds treated the opposite way (intraspecific contact not before but after the contact with another species), some of which still changed their preferences as late as 10 weeks of age (Fig. 14.1). Obviously, in these cases, the stimuli provided by conspecific parents exerted a stronger influence than did those from foster parents of another species. Other experiments indicate

Table 14.1. *Sexual preferences of males reared successively by their own parents and by Bengalese finch foster parents*

Day of transfer	B	B > Z	Z > B	Z
6	1	—	—	—
7	1	—	—	—
8	1	—	—	—
10	2	—	—	—
11	4	—	—	—
12	1	—	—	—
13	1	2	—	—
14	4	2	2	2
15	3	—	1	1
16	1	1	3	—
17	1	3	1	2
18	—	1	1	3
19	—	—	2	1
20	3	—	—	—
21	—	1	—	1
22	—	2	2	1
23	—	—	—	1
24	—	—	1	1
25	—	—	—	1

B, number of males courting only Bengalese finch females; B > Z, number of males preferring Bengalese finch females; Z > B, number of males preferring zebra finch females; Z, number of males courting only zebra finch females.

that such differences are due to genetically mediated preferences for one's own species that facilitate intraspecific imprinting and make imprinting on a strange species more difficult. The nature and significance of such unlearned preferences will be discussed elsewhere (Immelmann, in preparation).

Other data from the imprinting literature are basically consistent with these findings. Most species have been found to imprint most easily on their own species. If no conspecifics are available, they imprint on similar species more easily than on dissimilar ones (cf. Gray 1963; Guiton 1966). Imprinting on humans, on the other hand, that is, on a very dissimilar object, usually proves to be far less stable. Many hand-reared animals have been reported to show only a slight preference for humans and also to direct sexual behaviors toward other objects (Guiton 1962; Hess & Hess 1969; Scott 1962; Smith 1969). The same applies to birds imprinted on unnatural dummies (for a review, see Immelmann 1972b).

This evidence indicates that the most effective stimuli that can lead to a quick establishment of preferences are usually provided by normal, that is, species-specific characteristics. In contrast, with unnatural objects such preferences often take longer to develop, and the animal will remain open to subsequent environmental stimuli for a more extended period of time. This is almost certainly one of the reasons why those workers who observed responses to fairly natural stimuli under somewhat natural conditions arrived at different conclusions about the duration of sensitive phases than did those who performed experiments under highly artificial laboratory conditions with, from the biological point of view, relatively poor and inadequate stimulation.

Of course, both approaches have their specific merits: The first yields conclusions about the ways in which imprinting works under natural conditions; the second shows how far the system can be pushed around and thus may lead to some insights into the degree of variability and the immediate regulation of sensitive phases. When drawing any general conclusions, however, one should be aware that for the reasons mentioned, the results of these two approaches may well differ in many ways and that seemingly conflicting evidence does not necessarily mean that one or the other approach will yield wrong results or conclusions. This issue is discussed in Chapter 2.

In addition, there might be another set of environmental factors that could contribute to individual differences in the onset and duration of sensitive phases. These are the environmental stimuli that precede the age at which sensitivity to a certain social signal begins and that therefore might play a role in initiating and accelerating it. The time between onset of incubation and hatching of the young bird, for example, is not rigidly fixed but varies according to various environmental factors. Individuals of the same posthatch age may, therefore, be of different developmental ages.

It follows that the amount of stimulation that occurs when the young bird is still in the egg and that has proved to have a significant influence, for example, on the perfection of auditory perceptual mechanisms (Gottlieb 1971) may be different for different individuals; really comparable data can be obtained only if both developmental and posthatch ages are known and are considered (cf. Gottlieb 1961; Landsberg 1976). Analogous effects have been reported in the prematurity literature for humans (e.g., Parmalee & Sigman 1976) and other primates (e.g., Sackett et al. 1976). Here, the discrepancy between the postconceptual age of prematures and full-term infants of the same postnatal age may be a significant factor in their apparent differences in sensitivity to various environmental stimuli. Another contribution to a better understanding of intraspecific variability, therefore, could probably be made if more attention were paid to pre-sensitive-phase conditions and behaviors.

Finally, differences in maximum sensitivity occur not only between different species, individuals, and functional systems but also between different sensory modalities. In filial imprinting, for example, Gottlieb and Klopfer (1962) found that the optimal phase for visually imprinting ducks occurred later than the optimal phase for auditory imprinting. Similar results were obtained by Fabricius (1951).

The evidence given above demonstrates that – in contrast to many statements still to be found in the literature – sensitive phases are neither a unitary nor a strictly age-dependent phenomenon. Instead, they depend in various ways on direct influences from the environment. It follows that the early descriptions of sensitive phases for filial imprinting covered only a small part of age restrictions in the sensitivity to environmental stimuli. It does not follow, however, that sensitive phases are so vague and nonuniform that the concept has to be given up. There is still one important characteristic common to all sensitive phases described in the literature. This characteristic is the relative ease of establishing stability during those periods.

STABILITY OF PHENOMENA ESTABLISHED DURING SENSITIVE PHASES

The concept of *stability* refers to the tendency for preferences or behavioral patterns established during sensitive phases to be maintained by the organism, even in the face of new experiences or activities. This concept can be traced back to Lorenz's ideas about the irreversibility of imprinting phenomena. Demonstrating once again his knack of discovering exceptionally clear-cut examples of a general principle, Lorenz (1935) presented cases of preferences established during critical periods that remained intact even though his subjects subsequently received extensive exposure to other social stimuli. In those cases, use of the term *irreversible* was apt and appropriate. Unfortunately, the term came to be viewed as a general characteristic of all imprinting phenomena, not necessarily limited to the classic cases described by Lorenz. Thus, when later studies demonstrated that under certain experimental conditions preferences for imprinted objects could be altered, the credibility of the concept of imprinting itself came under attack (e.g., Harlow et al. 1972).

We now know that irreversibility, in the original Lorenzian sense, represents only one extreme of relative stability. The majority of the phenomena based on sensitive phases can, in fact, be altered, suppressed, or even superseded by other preferences or behaviors, given the appropriate experimental paradigm. However, even under such contrived conditions, they are usually more resistant to modification than are comparable phenomena that become established outside of the sensitive phases. At any rate, the concept of stability, like the concepts of imprinting and sensitive phases, has to be modified considerably from earlier, popularly accepted, formulations.

Assessment of relative stability cannot be achieved through naturalistic observation alone; observation must be complemented by experimentation. Traditionally, tests of stability of preference have involved measurement of the subject's reactions when it is exposed, in a free-choice situation, to its imprinting objects along with other familiar and/or novel stimuli. Stability of a given behavioral pattern established during a sensitive phase has usually been assessed by comparing the degree to which its basic characteristics can be changed by environmental manipulations, relative to changes seen in other behavior patterns developed outside of the sensitive phase.

Even a cursory view of the recent literature indicates considerable diversity in the degree of stability demonstrated for various imprinting phenomena. Such diversity can be seen across different species and for different functional systems. Inasmuch as different ultimate factors undoubtedly have contributed to the establishment of different sensitive phase phenomena, it should not be surprising to find considerable variation in their relative stability.

At one end of any scale of relative stability is the form of irreversibility popularized by Lorenz. Here, preferences established during sensitive phases may indeed remain unchanged for periods of time that may actually exceed the average life expectancy of the species. A case in point is the previously described finding that zebra finches raised by Bengalese finches retain their preference for their foster parents' species even after 7 years of intervening exposure to conspecifics only. Because the average life expectancy of these small finches is considerably less than 7 years, this means that complete stability of preference for the imprinted species has been demonstrated for a period longer than the natural life expectancy for the species (Immelmann 1972a).

However, some recent findings indicate that even these lasting preferences are not entirely resistant to change. If tested in a double-choice situation within only a few days after separation from the conspecific female, some of the zebra finch males preferred to court an unfamiliar zebra finch female and paid less attention to or ignored the Bengalese finch female. However, subsequent daily tests, between which the birds were kept isolated, revealed that such preferences gradually decreased and finally disappeared. In contrast, the preference for the foster species reappeared and increased again over the same time span. Finally, after a number of days or weeks, the Bengalese finch females were again courted preferentially or exclusively, just as they had been before the zebra finch males' period of intraspecific contact (Immelmann 1979).

It follows that even in individuals with irreversible preferences, a new preference can be established in adult life. The point is, however, that this new preference will be lost in the absence of continual exposure or reinforcement, whereas the original preference established during the sensitive phase should be retained indefinitely even without any further reinforcement. Similar results have recently been obtained in filial imprinting in quails by Cherfas and Scott (1981).

Thus, even real irreversibility is not as total as some earlier results seemed to indicate. What may be permanent is the subject's memory of (or ability to recognize) the imprinted stimulus. In the absence of that stimulus, the subject may well develop new preferences among other stimuli to which it has subsequently been exposed. However, these new preferences will be relatively transient, disappearing after withdrawal of the relevant stimuli. In contrast – and this is the point about extreme stability that remains – if the original imprinting stimulus is reintroduced, the subject will again display a strong preference for it. At any rate, it can be argued that this distinction is parallel to that now evident in modern-day nature–nurture controversies (e.g., Eibl-Eibesfeldt 1976): Even extreme cases of inherited qualities can be modified under unnatural environmental conditions, but such qualities reappear in their original form as soon as environmental conditions permit them to be expressed. It is not known whether, in other cases of irreversibility reported in the literature, a similar temporary change in preferences is possible, or whether in some instances an absolute irreversibility in the original Lorenzian sense can be observed.

More common are cases in which the preference or behavior pattern is semipermanent. Here, if the general environment of the subject changes little from that experienced during the sensitive phase, the preference or behavior pattern will remain stable throughout the subject's lifetime. Under different environmental conditions, however, the preference or behavior pattern can be modified in form, magnitude, and/or direction. Still, it will reappear whenever conditions exist that permit it to be expressed.

For instance, in foster-reared adolescent zebra finches, it has been possible – up to a certain age – to change sexual preferences through subsequent contact with conspecific females. If tested in a double-choice situation with a Bengalese finch and a third species of estrildid finch, however, even those males that apparently have developed a new preference for their own species will continue to prefer Bengalese females. It follows that the primary reaction to Bengalese finches is still there; it has only been superseded by the secondary experience with conspecifics. As soon as the secondary stimulus is no longer present, it becomes visible again.

Near the other end of the stability continuum are those cases in which a preference or behavior pattern established during a sensitive phase diminishes or disappears later in life but can be reinstated if environmental conditions similar to those that existed during the sensitive phase are presented to the subject and/or the subject is put under conditions of stress. This type of stability seems to be more common among mammals. Ågren and Meyerson (1979) have provided a case in point on long-term effects of social deprivation during early adulthood in Mongolian gerbils (*Meriones unguiculatus*). Gerbils isolated between 90 and 200 days of age showed increased agonistic behavior compared with controls living in pairs during comparable periods. This difference disappeared when subjects were subsequently housed with a cagemate. A secondary period of isolation late in life, however, resulted in a more rapid onset of agonistic behavior in the early isolates than in the controls. It was concluded that the early isolation had a lasting influence that became apparent only after renewed isolation treatment.

Another example can be seen in studies of rhesus monkeys that experienced periods of social separation from their mothers (Hinde & Spencer-Booth 1971; Mitchell et al. 1967) or from peers (Suomi et al. 1970) during infancy. If reunited with their respective attachment objects, such individuals may well display relatively normal social development through adolescence and into adulthood. However, if such individuals are again separated from social partners later in life, they generally exhibit far more severe separation reactions than do individuals without a prior history of social separations during infancy (Suomi et al. 1981; Young et al. 1973). Similar findings regarding predisposing effects of early separations on reactions to separations later in life appear in the human literature (e.g., Bowlby 1973; Brown et al. 1977; Heinicke & Westheimer 1966; Seligman 1975).

Thus, there exists considerable cross-species variability in the stability of the effects of sensitive phases. Differences between functional systems have also been found with regard to the stability of sensitive-phase phenomena. In the case of sexual imprinting, some remarkable instances of stability have been reported. Hand-reared male turkeys proved to be imprinted on humans at 5 years of age, when they still preferred to court humans even in the presence of female turkeys (Schein 1963). The same reaction was observed in a red junglefowl cock (*Gallus gallus*) (Hess 1959). Mallards that had been foster-reared by other species of ducks and geese still preferred to pair with members of their foster parents' species at the age of 9 years (Schutz 1969). As mentioned, zebra finch males foster-reared by Bengalese finches still showed the same strong preference for Bengalese females even if they had been kept together with conspecific females for 7 years (Immelmann 1972a).

A similar persistence of preferences has been found in the locality imprinting of North Pacific salmons, which, after spending 1.5 to 7 intervening years at sea, returned to the tributaries in which they hatched, using chemical cues that they learned during rather precise sensitive phases early in life (Hasler et al. 1978; Scholz et al. 1976).

A parallel case in birds has been described for the short-tailed shearwater (*Puffinus tenuirostris*) in eastern Bass Strait. When these birds first start breeding at the age of 5 years, they return to their natal islands on an extensive transequatorial migratory circuit. Egg-transfer experiments have shown that homing of the young birds has no hereditary basis but is due to locality imprinting that takes place during a restricted sensitive phase when the young begin their nocturnal emergence from the burrows (Serventy 1967).

For food imprinting, most preferences have, unfortunately, been followed up only for days or weeks, and only a few data are available that cover a period of several months. The durability of early food preferences, therefore, in most cases still remains obscure. However, Hess (1973:303) concluded that in domestic chicks, modification of pecking preferences during the sensitive phase is "apparently permanent." For locality and habitat imprinting, finally, several long-term studies have shown that a high degree of persistence can be found with regard to site tenacity at least during the reproductive period (for a review, see Immelmann 1975).

Thus the relative stability of sensitive-phase phenomena depends considerably on the species and the function under study. Obviously, the degree of persistence is correlated with the specific and functional systems. In sexual imprinting, for which the characteristics of the object, that is, of the conspecific mate(s), remain the same for the whole life span of the imprinted animal, great stability is strongly selected for in order to promote sexual isolation. In host imprinting of parasitic animals, a high degree of persistence may be advantageous, too. In so-called food imprinting, on the other hand, because of possible changes in the food situation, rigid invariability would be disadvantageous. In locality and habitat imprinting, the situation seems to be somewhat intermediate. In highly stable habitats, and in particular during the reproductive period, strong persistence, though perhaps not as rigid as in sexual imprinting, could be advantageous. Outside this period, a higher degree of variability may be permissible, although even then many cases of habitat and site tenacity have been described (Immelmann 1975, McNicholl 1975).

In addition to the differences between species and functional systems, other findings indicate that even within species and functions, considerable variability in stability can occur across different post–sensitive-phase environments. Moreover, most measures of stability can clearly be influenced by such factors as choice of comparison stimuli and test settings or housing conditions prior to the time of testing (see Bateson 1979; Suomi et al. 1974; Chap. 1). Any comparison of the relative stability of sensitive phases between species, functional systems, or individuals should therefore take into account the test conditions that yield the various comparative data.

SENSITIVE PHASES AS POTENTIAL RESEARCH TOOLS

The concept of sensitive phases clearly provides a broader developmental framework than that encompassed by earlier critical period formulations. Included in this framework are not only the classic cases of Lorenzian imprinting but also diverse phenomena for which the sensitive periods are neither brief nor have well-defined endpoints and that can be readily altered in subsequent environments. However, this does not mean that sensitive phases represent a basic characteristic of all developmental processes, an inevitable consequence of all qualitative change in structure (be it anatomical, behavioral, or social), as Scott et al. (1974) have argued. Rather, sensitive phases are characteristic of only those developmental processes for which selective pressures for privileged periods of learning have existed. Moreover, because this often involves different ultimate and proximate factors in different species and functional systems, sensitive phases must be viewed as convergent phenomena, analogous rather than homologous with one another.

It should also be clear from the preceding discussions that meaningful study of sensitive phases is far from easy or straightforward. The criteria required for delineation of chronological periods that can legitimately be termed sensitive phases are extensive (see Chap. 1); in terms of the time and effort required to satisfy them, they are often prohibitively expensive as well. Moreover, attempts to measure such basic features as time of onset or total duration of a sensitive phase will never yield absolute values because these basic parameters can vary considerably as a function of the subject's living and/or test environment. Hence, only relative values can be obtained, values that may well be inaccurate for other experimental settings.

Given these various problems, one might reasonably ask whether it is profitable to invest research time and effort in any study of sensitive-phase phenomena. Instead, should one simply use the concept as a heuristic device and direct his or her research interests elsewhere? We believe that this would be a mistake, because knowledge of the existence of a sensitive phase for a given preference or behavior can serve as a valuable research tool for a variety of purposes. Such knowledge can be employed in the formulation of hypotheses regarding ultimate factors. It can be used to facilitate the study of proximate factors that underlie the preference or behavior in question. In addition, such knowledge can be useful in applied areas of study.

A recurring problem in the search for ultimate factors has been that analysis of evolutionary mechanisms that shape specific behavioral tendencies in most birds and mammals is largely speculative. This is so because the time span needed to track the evolution of a given behavioral characteristic is often greater than the life span, let alone the interest span, of any one investigator.

Thus, the study of ultimate factors is typically approached by correlating specific patterns of behavior with postulated adaptive needs of the species. Such a research strategy can be improved, of course, by a comparative perspective that searches for behavioral differences in closely related species. These differences can then be related to possible differences in adaptive needs. The problem is that there may well be several plausible ways by which such differences might have evolved.

Now, sensitive phases owe their existence to selective pressures that favor restricted periods of optimal sensitivity. Knowledge that a sensitive phase exists for a given preference or behavioral pattern can very likely reduce the number of plausible pathways for the evolution of the particular phenomenon. Knowledge that differences in sensitive phases exist between closely related species might well provide the insight needed for deducing the basis for species differences in the preference or behavioral pattern in question.

For example, comparative studies of the following response of several species of ducks have revealed interesting differences (cf. Bjerke & Bjerke 1970; Fabricius 1951; Schutz 1965) that seem to be correlated with breeding biology (see the discussion in Klopfer 1959; see also Gottlieb 1968). A clear example is offered by two closely related species of ducks, the redhead (*Aythya americana*) and the canvasback (*A. valesineria*). In both species visual imprinting occurs. But only in canvasbacks are the responses selectively enhanced by calls presented in the absence of the visual stimulus. Such differences in strategies can easily be understood: In the nonparasitic canvasback, strong responses to maternal calls when the mother is heard but not seen could facilitate cohesion of the family unit, whereas in the semiparasitic redhead, a reduced auditory responsiveness could help to create the preconditions for the necessary subsequent separation of the young from members of the foster species (Mattson & Evans 1974).

A different kind of example can be found in the comparison of social structure, behavioral patterns, and sensitive phases between two closely related species of macaques: rhesus monkeys and pigtail macaques (*Macaca nemestrina*). Rhesus monkeys live in multimale groups that are organized basically along matriarchal lines, although there are many interactions between members of different family groups, especially those involving infants and juveniles (Harlow & Lauersdorf 1974; Kaufmann 1966; Lindburg 1973; White & Hinde 1975). Pigtail macaques have a social structure in which single adult males are associated with small groups each consisting of an adult female and several generations of her offspring. Male offspring typically remain in their natal clan until late adolescence (Rosenblum 1971b). What might be the basis for such differences in social structure?

It is unlikely that the basis lies in the mother–infant relationships found in the two species, for they are highly similar. Both rhesus and pigtail females are possessive mothers, seldom allowing other females to inspect or handle their infants (Rosenblum 1971a). Both rhesus and pigtail offspring develop strong attachments with their mothers over the same time period. And the infants of both species are prone to severe depression if separated from their mothers during the first year of life. In each of these areas of comparison, the two species are closer to each other than they are to most other species of macaques.

Similarly, differences between pigtail and rhesus monkeys with respect to adult male–infant interactions also appear to be slight, at least in terms of existing comparative data for other macaques (Hrdy 1977; Redican 1976).

However, a possible basis for differences in social structure is suggested by the discovery that the two species differ considerably with respect to sensitive phases for the formation of social bonds between peers. Extensive laboratory research has demonstrated that rhesus monkey infants denied the opportunity to interact with peers during their first 9 months have great difficulty subsequently establishing stable peer relationships; instead, they tend to become hyperaggressive and sexually incompetent (e.g., Harlow & Harlow 1969). Pigtail macaque infants isolated from peers under comparable conditions for their first 9 months have much less difficulty forming and maintaining subsequent peer relationships (Sackett et al. 1975). It can be argued that the sensitive phase for rhesus infants helps insure that peer bonds will be formed with and limited to troop members. In contrast, interactions with individuals outside of the troop, usually occurring after the end of the sensitive phase, will generally be aggressive in nature; the troop will remain distinct and cohesive. Pigtail macaques, lacking such a well-defined sensitive phase for peer relationships, will more readily accept strangers as they mature; social groupings beyond the family clans will likely be less distinct and probably less cohesive.

Thus knowledge of differences in the existence of particular types of sensitive phases among closely related species may be useful in identifying different selective factors that may be operating on these various species for characteristics as broad as social structure. In this respect, the existence versus nonexistence of a sensitive phase may provide a basis for testing the viability of postulated ultimate factors operating on the behavioral characteristic under examination.

Knowledge of the existence of sensitive phases can also be put to profitable use in the study of possible proximate factors that underlie a given behavior pattern or preference. For example, the brain of the young of many species is characterized by a high degree of equipotentiality prior to major environmental influences. Early experiences might therefore be more readily incorporated because the brain at that time has not been preempted, as might be the case later in development. Here, information about sensitive phases could be used to identify chronological periods that encompass major perceptual, neuroanatomical, biochemical, and/or psychophysiological changes for the organism. This is because the occurrence of sensitive phases is usually indicative of changes in the direction and/or rate of maturation for some underlying system (e.g., Mason 1979; Scott et al. 1974). Thus, one might expect to find larger differences in the system just before versus just after the onset of a sensitive phase than would be found between any other pair of chronological points spanning a like period of real time. Because changes of large magnitude are usually easier to detect than are changes of minute magnitude, a researcher's search for physiological, anatomical, and/or biochemical correlates of developmental changes in behavior and/or preference patterns is made that much easier. Moreover, discovery of changes that reliably precede or follow the onset of sensitive phases may suggest lines of causality among the various systems.

To illustrate, an investigator interested in the mechanisms underlying perceptual development in precocial birds might do well to focus initial studies on the chronological period that brackets the onset of a sensitive phase for imprinting. The choice of such a time period for study would likely encompass a period during which qualitative changes in the subject's perceptual capabilities might well be taking place, enhancing an investigator's likelihood of detecting developmental changes relative to those that might be found during a similar period at some other point in development.

In addition to facilitating the study of ultimate and proximate influences on behavior, knowledge about the existence of sensitive phases in certain species under specified environmental conditions may have considerable practical utility. Such knowledge might well be used to make decisions about procedures for the care and maintenance of captive colonies of subjects. For example, investigators who must move their populations into new laboratory environments, or who must develop optimal procedures for rearing the young in artificial settings, might well profit from knowledge of specific sensitive phases in planning their procedures. Individuals concerned with domestication might find that certain extra precautions taken during these crucial periods may make taming attempts more successful. Similarly, animal trainers might use information about sensitive phases in their choice of not only procedures but also times at which to carry out training for optimal learning. Finally, therapeutic approaches whose purpose is to change deviant behavior could include information about sensitive phases in the formulation of possible etiologies. Such information could then be used to plan rehabilitative strategies.

Knowledge of sensitive phases and the age at which they occur may also have some practical implications with regard to wildlife conservation. If the decrease of a particular species in a given area is due to the destruction of its specific habitat, some offspring of that population could be raised in captivity and have imprinted on them the features of another safer type of habitat; subsequently they could be released into this new type of environment. This is at present done in eastern Austria with the great bustard (*Otis tarda*) (Lukschanderl 1971).

Knowledge of sensitive phases can even be of economic importance. A prominent example is provided by the studies by Hasler and his co-workers on homing in the Pacific salmon, which after spending intervening years at sea return to the home tributary in which they were raised, irrespective of the rivers from which their parents came (Hasler et al. 1978; Scholz et al. 1976). They showed that the fish are able to discriminate successfully between the chemical differences of various streams and can retain a particular stream odor in their memory. Hasler argued that the young salmon becomes imprinted on the odor of its natal stream and that such olfactory imprinting is an essential mechanism employed by the sexually mature fish during the return river migration, when it swims against the current and rejects all odors until it finally arrives at the home riverlet. Such sensitivity to early olfactory stimulation provides an excellent tool for introduction of salmon into areas where they were not native or from transplantations from one river system to another.

A NOTE ON TERMINOLOGY

As a final point, some statement should be made about terminology. In the literature, *critical period, sensitive period, sensitive phase, susceptible period,* and *optimal phase* have been used most frequently (see Hess 1973). We prefer *sensitive phase* for the following reasons.

At the outset, the term *critical period* was borrowed from embryology, in which it was and continues to be used to describe those periods during early ontogeny when rapid changes in the organization of embryos occur (cf. Chap. 16). Because any experimental interruption of the normal sequence of events during those periods has been found to have profound and irreversible effects on the structural and functional development of the organism, those periods are indeed critical.

The first cases of imprinting described in the literature, mainly by Lorenz (1935), also gave the impression that the establishment of stable social preferences is indeed possible only during a brief period in ontogeny. At that time, therefore, usage of the term seemed to be justified because such periods appeared to be critical steps in the development of the organism. For the same reason, human psychologists used the term, especially for periods during development that were found to be critical in the formation of the adult personality.

As the wealth of information that now exists about imprinting and imprintinglike phenomena clearly indicates, stability in many cases is far less rigid than assumed in the beginning, and, as a consequence, the early stages are perhaps not so critical. Thus we prefer the term *sensitive* which indicates an enhanced degree of receptiveness to environmental stimuli without the slightly negative suggestion of the word *critical.*

Sensitive should also be preferred to *optimal* not only because it has been used more frequently and thus is more accepted but also because *optimal,* in a strict sense, refers only to the – rather brief – time of optimum sensitivity within the overall period of enhanced sensitivity (for further discussion of terms, see also Fabricius 1964).

With respect to the terms *period* and *phase,* an interesting difference in usage exists in the English and German languages. In English, *period* is defined as "a course or extent of time" (*Oxford English Dictionary,* 1971), whereas in German, *Periode* is referred to as "eine in räumlichen oder zeitlichen Abständen auftretende Wiederholung bestimmter Erscheinungen" (a repetition of events occurring at regular spatial or temporal intervals) (*Brockhaus Enzyklopädie,* 1972). The German *Periode* does not at all apply, of course, to sensitive phases for imprinting, the most important characteristic of which is that they occur only once in a lifetime. Because the term was introduced first in the German language literature, and because in both languages identical terms should be used, we propose to abandon the term *period* and to speak of *sensitive phases* in development.

SUMMARY

The data presented in this chapter indicate that sensitive phases in development exist for a variety of functional systems across a wide range of organisms. Such phases appear to be characterized by enhanced responsiveness on the part of the organism to certain types of stimulation. Moreover, preferences and behavior patterns established during sensitive phases are generally more stable, that is, more resistant to subsequent modification, than are preferences and/or behavior patterns established outside of the sensitive phases.

It is true that in some species, for some functional systems, the relevant sensitive phases are relatively brief, with well-defined chronological points of onset and termination. In many of these cases, the resulting preferences or behavior patterns are exceedingly stable throughout the rest of the subject's life. However, these cases should not be considered as representative of sensitive-phase phenomena in other species and/or for other functional systems, as they often have been in the literature to date. Rather, they should be considered as extreme cases of a much more general and widespread phenomenon characteristic of many developmental processes. Along the same lines, given the diversity in form and stability of sensitive-phase phenomena, one should expect wide diversity in both ultimate and proximate factors across species and functions. In fact, this has generally been found to date, although the present literature is limited.

Because sensitive phases are so diverse in form, duration, stability, and cause, one might question the utility of the concept for problems of development. We argue instead that such diversity is in itself useful in establishing the basis for differences in closely related species, in identifying proximate factors of certain developmental processes, and in making practical decisions about the form and timing of environmental changes imposed on populations. We believe that in spite of its obvious diversity, the concept of sensitive phases will continue to be useful in the study of developmental problems and – referring to a well-introduced term – will retain its didactic value.

ACKNOWLEDGMENTS

We are indebted to Patrick Bateson, for his comments on an earlier draft of the manuscript. We would also like to thank Ragna Pröve, who did most of the double-choice experiments with zebra finches and Bengalese finches described in the chapter.

REFERENCES

Ågren, G., & B. J. Meyerson. 1979. Long term effects of social deprivation during early adulthood in the Mongolian gerbil (*Meriones unguiculatus*). *Zeitschrift für Tierpsychologie* 47:422–431.

Andrew, R. J. 1964. The development of adult responses from responses given during imprinting by the domestic chick. *Animal Behaviour* 12:542–548.

Ashmole, N. P. 1971. Sea bird ecology and the marine environment. *In:* D. S. Farner & J. R. King (eds.), *Avian biology,* vol. 1. Academic Press, New York, pp. 223–286.

Baker, J. R. 1938. The evolution of breeding seasons. *In:* G. R. de Beer (ed.), *Essays on aspects of evolutionary biology*. Oxford University Press, London and New York, pp. 161–177.

Bateson, P. P. G. 1966. The characteristics and context of imprinting. *Biological Reviews of the Cambridge Philosophical Society* 41:177–220.

1972. The formation of social attachments in young birds. *Proceedings of the 15th International Ornithological Congress,* The Hague, 1970, pp. 303–315.

1978a. Sexual imprinting and optimal outbreeding. *Nature* 273:659–660.

1978b. Early experience and sexual preferences. *In:* J. B. Hutchinson (ed.), *Biological determinants of sexual behaviour.* Wiley, London, pp. 29–53.

1979. How do sensitive periods arise and what are they for? *Animal Behaviour* 27:470–486.

Bateson, P. P. G., G. Horn, & S. P. R. Rose. 1969. Effects of an imprinting procedure on regional incorporation of tritiated lysine into protein of chick brain. *Nature* 223:534–535.

1975. Imprinting: correlations between behaviour and incorporation of (^{14}C) uracil into chick brain. *Brain Research* 84:207–220.

Bateson, P. P. G., G. Horn, & B. J. McCabe. 1978. Imprinting and the incorporation of uracil in the chick brain: a radioautographic study. *Journal of Physiology* 275:70 P.

Bateson, P. P. G., & E. P. Reese. 1969. The reinforcing properties of conspicuous stimuli in the imprinting situation. *Animal Behaviour* 17:692–699.

Bateson, P. P. G., S. P. R. Rose, & G. Horn. 1973. Imprinting: lasting effects on uracil incorporation into chick brain. *Science* 181:576–578.

Baysinger, C. M. 1975. Effects of chloropromazine on rhesus monkeys reared in social isolation. Unpublished M.A. thesis, University of Wisconsin - Madison.

Berthold, A. 1975. Migration: control and metabolic physiology. *In:* D. S. Farner & J. R. King (eds.), *Avian biology,* vol. 5. Academic Press, New York, pp. 77–128.

Bischof, N. 1972. Inzuchtbarrieren in Säugetiersozietäten. *Homo* 23:330–351.

Bjerke, I., & L. G. Bjerke. 1970. Imprintability of goldeneyes (*Bucephala clangula*). *Psychological Reports* 27:981–982.

Bowlby, J. 1969. *Attachment.* Basic Books, New York.

1973. *Separation.* Basic Books, New York.

Brown, G. W., T. Harris, & J. R. Copeland. 1977. Depression and loss. *British Journal of Psychiatry* 130:1–18.

Carter, C. S., & J. N. Marr. 1970. Olfactory imprinting and age variables in the Guinea-pig, *Cavia porcellus. Animal Behaviour* 18:238–244.

Cherfas, J. J., & A. M. Scott. 1981. Impermanent reversal of filial imprinting. *Animal Behaviour* 29:301.

Clarke, A. D., & A. M. Clarke. 1972. Consistency and variability in the growth of human characteristics. *In:* W. Wall & V. Varma (eds.), *Advances in educational psychology.* Barnes and Noble, New York.

Cooke, F. 1978. Early learning and its effect on population structure: studies of a wild population of snow geese. *Zeitschrift für Tierpsychologie* 46:344–358.

Crook, J. H. 1970. Social organization and the environment: aspects of contemporary social ethology. *Animal Behaviour* 18:197–209.

Denenberg, V. H., G. A. Hudgens, & M. X. Zarrow. 1963. Mice reared with rats: modification of behavior by early experience with another species. *Science* 143:380–381.

Dunn, J. 1976. How far do early differences in mother–child relations affect later development? *In:* P. P. G. Bateson & R. A. Hinde (eds.), *Growing points in ethology.* Cambridge University Press, Cambridge.

Eibl-Eibesfeldt, I. 1976. Phylogenetic and cultural adaptation in human behavior. *In:* G. Serban & A. Kling (eds.), *Animal models in human psychobiology.* Plenum Press, New York.

Evans, R. M. 1970. Imprinting and mobility in young ring-billed gulls, *Larus delawarensis. Animal Behaviour Monographs* 3:193–248.

Fabricius, E. 1951. Zur Ethologie junger Anatiden. *Acta Zoologica Fennica* 68:1–178.

1962. Some aspects of imprinting in birds. *Symposia of the Zoological Society, London* 8:139–148.

1964. Crucial periods in the development of the following response in young nidifugous birds. *Zeitschrift für Tierpsychologie* 21:326–337.

Farner, D. S. 1970. Predictive functions in the control of annual cycles. *Environment Research* 3:119–131.

Farner, D. S., & R. A. Lewis. 1971. Photoperiodism and reproductive cycles in birds. *In:* Arthur C. Giese (ed.), *Photophysiology,* vol. 6. Academic Press, New York, pp. 325–370.

Fernö, A., & S. Sjölander. 1973. Some imprinting experiments on sexual preferences for colour variants in the platy fish (*Xiphophorus maculatus*). *Zeitschrift für Tierpsychologie* 33:417–423.

1976. Influence of previous experience on the mate selection of two colour morphs of the convict cichlid, *Cichlasoma nigrofasciatum. Behavioural Processes* 1:3–14.

Frazer, J. F. D. 1977. Growth of young vertebrates in the egg or uterus. *Journal of Zoology London* 183:189–201.

Freud, S. 1953. Three essays on sexuality. *In:* J. Strackey (ed.), *S. Freud, the standard edition of the complete psychological works.* Hogarth Press, London. (First German edition: 1905).

Gilbert, B. K. 1975. The influence of foster rearing on adult social behavior in the fallow deer (*Dama dama*). *In:* V. Geist (ed.), *Determinants of behavior.* University of Alberta Press, Calgary.

Gottlieb, G. 1961. Developmental age as a baseline for determination of the critical period in imprinting. *Journal of Comparative and Physiological Psychology* 54:422–427.

1968. Species recognition in ground-nesting and hole-nesting ducklings. *Ecology* 49:87–95.

1971. *Development of species identification in birds.* University of Chicago Press, Chicago.

Gottlieb, G., & P. H. Klopfer. 1962. The relation of developmental age to auditory and visual imprinting. *Journal of Comparative and Physiological Psychology* 55:821–826.

Goy, R. W., K. Wallen, & D. A. Goldfoot. 1974. Social factors affecting the development of mounting behavior in the male rhesus monkey. *In:* W. Montagna & W. Sadler (eds.), *Reproductive behavior.* Plenum Press, New York.

Gray, P. H. 1963. The descriptive study of imprinting in birds from 1873–1953. *Journal of General Psychology* 68:333–346.

Greenough, W. T. 1975. Experimental modification of the developing brain. *American Scientist* 63:37–46.

Guiton, P. 1962. The development of sexual responses in the domestic fowl, in relation to the concept of imprinting. *Symposia of the Zoological Society, London* 8:227–234.

1966. Early experience and sexual object-choice in the brown leghorn. *Animal Behaviour* 14:534–538.

Harlow, H. F. 1969. Agemate or peer affectional system. *In:* D. Lehrman, R. Hinde, & E. Shaw (eds.), *Advances in the study of behavior,* vol. 2. Academic Press, New York, pp. 333–383.

Harlow, H. F., J. O. Gluck, & S. J. Suomi. 1972. Generalization of behavioral data from nonhuman and human animals. *American Psychologist* 27:709–716.

Harlow, H. F., & M. K. Harlow. 1965. The affectional systems. *In:* A. Schrier, H. Harlow, & F. Stollnitz (eds.), *Behavior of nonhuman primates.* Academic Press, New York.

1969. Effects of various mother–infant relationships on rhesus monkey behaviors. *In:* B. M. Foss (ed.), *Determinants of infant behavior,* vol. 4. Methuen, London, pp. 15–36.

Harlow, H. F., & H. E. Lauersdorf. 1974. Sex differences in passion and play. *Perspectives in Biology and Medicine* 17:348–360.

Hasler, A. D., A. T. Scholz, & R. M. Horrall. 1978. Olfactory imprinting and homing in salmon. *American Scientist* 66:347–355.

Heinicke, C., & I. Westheimer. 1966. *Brief separations.* International Universities Press, New York.

Hendrichs, H. 1978. Die soziale Organisation von Säugetierpopulationen. *Säugetierkundliche Mitteilungen* 26:81–116.

Hess, E. H. 1959. Imprinting. *Science* 130:133–141.

1973. *Imprinting.* Van Nostrand, New York.

Hess, E. H., & D. B. Hess. 1969. Innate factors in imprinting. *Psychonomic Science* 14:129–130.

Hinde, R. 1962. Some aspects of the imprinting problem. *Symposia of the Zoological Society London* 8:129–138.

Hinde, R., & V. Spencer-Booth. 1967. The behavior of socially living rhesus monkeys in their first two and a half years. *Animal Behaviour* 15:169–196.

1971. Effects of brief separations from mothers on rhesus monkeys. *Science* 173:111–118.

Hofman, H. S., & A. M. Ratner. 1973. A reinforcement model of imprinting: implications for socialization in monkeys and men. *Psychological Review* 80: 527–544.

Hrdy, S. 1977. *The langurs of Abu.* Harvard University Press, Cambridge, Mass.

Huck, U. W., & E. M. Banks. 1980. The effects of cross fostering on the behavior of two species of North American lemmings. *Dicrostonyx groenlandicus* and *Lemmus trimucronatus. I.* Olfactory preferences. *Animal Behaviour* 28:1046–1052.

Immelmann, K. 1962. Beiträge zu einer vergleichenden Biologie australischer Prachtfinken (Spermestidae). *Zoologische Fahrbücher Systematik* 90:1–196.

1969. Ueber den Einfluß frühkindlicher Erfahrungen auf die geschlechtliche Objektfixierung bei Estrildiden. *Zeitschrift für Tierpsychologie* 26:677–691.

1971. Ecological aspects of periodic reproduction. *In:* D. S. Farner & J. R. King (eds.), *Avian biology,* vol. 1. Academic Press, New York, pp. 341–389.

1972a. The influence of early experience upon the development of social behaviour in estrildine finches. *Proceedings of the 15th International Ornithological Congress,* The Hague, 1970, pp. 316–338.

1972b. Sexual and other long-term aspects of imprinting in birds and other species. *Advances in the Study of Behavior* 4:147–174.

1975. Ecological significance of imprinting and early learning. *Annual Review of Ecology and Systematics* 6:15–37.

1979. Genetical constraints on early learning: a perspective from sexual imprinting in birds. *In:* J. R. Royce (ed.), *Theoretical advances in behavior genetics.* Shinthoff & Noordhoff, Alphen van de Rijn.

Jaisson, P. 1975. L'Imprégnation dans l'ontogenèse des comportements de soins aux cocons chez la jeune fourmi rousse (*Formica polyctena* Forst.). *Behaviour* 52:1–37.

Kaufmann, J. H. 1966. Behavior of infant rhesus monkeys and their mothers in a free ranging band. *Zoologica* 51:17–27.

Klinghammer, E. 1967. Factors influencing choice of mate in altricial birds. *In:* H. W. Stevenson (ed.), *Early behavior: comparative and development approaches.* Wiley, New York, pp. 5–42.

Klomp, H. 1970. The determination of clutch-size in birds. *Ardea* 58:1–124.

Klopfer, P. H. 1959. An analysis of learning in young Anatidae. *Ecology* 40:90–102.

Klopfer, P. H., & J. P. Hailman. 1965. Habitat selection in birds. *Advances in the Study of Behavior* 1:279–303.

Kop, P. P. A. M. & B. A. Heuts. 1973. An experiment on sibling imprinting in the jewel fish *Hemichromis bimaculatus. Revue de Comportement Animal* 7:63–76.

Kovach, J. K., E. Fabricius, & L. Fält. 1966. Relationship between imprinting and perceptual learning. *Journal of Comparative and Physiological Psychology* 61:449–454.

Kummer, H. 1971. Immediate causes of primate social structures. *Proceedings of the 3rd International Congress on Primatology,* Zürich 1970. Karger, Basel, pp. 1–11.

1971. *Primate societies.* University of Chicago Press, Chicago.

Kurland, J. A. 1977. Kin selection in the Japanese monkey. *Contributions to Primatology.* Karger, Basel, New York.

Landsberg, J. W. 1976. Posthatch age and developmental age as a baseline for determination of the sensitive period for imprinting. *Journal of Comparative and Physiological Psychology* 90:47–52.

1981. Hormones and filial imprinting. *Proceedings of the 7th International Ornithological Congress,* Berlin 1978 (in press).

Landsberg, J. W., & J. Weiss. 1976. Stress and increase of the corticosterone level prevent imprinting in ducklings. *Behaviour* 57:173–189.

Laudien, H., and H. H. Iken. 1977. Ökologische Prägung und Protein-biosynthese. *Zeitschrift für Tierpsychologie* 44:113–129.

Lindburg, D. G. 1973. The rhesus monkey in North India: an ecological and behavioral study. *In:* L. A. Rosenblum (ed.), *Primate behavior,* vol. 2. Academic Press, New York, pp. 1–106.

Lorenz, K. 1935. Der Kumpan in der Umwelt des Vogels. *Journal für Ornithologie* 83:137–213, 289–413.

Lukschanderl, L. 1971. Zur Verbreitung und Oekologie der Groβtrappe (*Otis tarda*) in Österreich. *Journal für Ornithologie* 112:70–93.

Mainardi, M. 1968. Su alcuni fattori etologici determinanti accopiamenti assortativi in *Drosophila melanogaster.* Instituto Lombardo (Rendiconti Classe di Scienze).

Mason, W. A. 1970. Early deprivation in biological perspective. *In:* V. H. Denenberg (ed.), *Education of the infant and young child.* Academic Press, New York.

1979. Social ontogeny. *In:* J. Vandenberg & P. Marler (eds.), *Social behavior and communication.* Plenum Press, New York.

Mattson, M. E., & R. M. Evans. 1974. Visual imprinting and auditory discrimination learning in young of the canvasback and semi-parasitic redhead. *Canadian Journal of Zoology* 52:421–427.

Mayr, E. 1961. Cause and effect in biology. *Science* 134:1501–1506.

1963. The role of ornithological research in biology. *Proceedings of the 13th Ornithological Congress,* Ithaca, New York, 1962, pp. 27–38.

McNicholl, M. K. 1975. Larid site tenacity and group adherence in relation to habitat. *Auk* 92:98–104.

Mitchell, G. D., H. F. Harlow, G. A. Griffin, & G. W. Møller. 1967. Repeated maternal separation in the monkey. *Psychonomic Science* 8:197–198.

Moltz, H. 1960. Imprinting: empirical basis and theoretical significance. *Psychological Bulletin* 57:291–314.

1963. Imprinting: an epigenetic approach. *Psychological Review* 70:123–138.

Orians, G. 1971. Ecological aspects of behavior. *In:* D. S. Farner & J. R. King (eds.), *Avian biology,* vol. 1. Academic Press, New York, pp. 513–546.

Parmalee, A. H., & M. Sigman. 1976. Development of visual behavior and neurophysical organization in preterm and full-term infants. *In:* A. Pick (ed.), *Minnesota symposium on child psychology.* University of Minnesota Press, Minneapolis.

Redican, W. K. 1976. Adult male-infant interactions in nonhuman primates. *In:* M. Lamb (ed.), *The role of the father in child development.* Wiley, New York.

Rosenblum, L. A. 1961. The development of social behavior in the rhesus monkey. Unpublished Ph.D. dissertation, University of Wisconsin-Madison.

1971a. Kinship interaction patterns in pigtail and bonnet macaques. *In: Proceedings of the 3rd International Congress in Primatology.* Karger, Basel.

1971b. The ontogeny of mother–infant relations in macaques. *In:* H. Moltz (ed.), *The ontogeny of vertebrate behavior.* Academic Press, New York.

Rosenzweig, M. R., E. L. Bennet, & M. C. Diamond. 1972. Brain changes in response to experience. *Scientific American* 226:22–29.

Ruppenthal, G. C., G. L. Arling, H. F. Harlow, G. P. Sackett, & S. J. Suomi. 1976. A ten-year perspective of motherless-mother monkey behavior. *Journal of Abnormal Psychology* 85:341–348.

Rutter, M. 1972. *Maternal deprivation: reassessed.* Penguin Books, Harmondsworth.

1977. *Maternal deprivation: revisited.* Penguin Books, Harmondsworth.

Sackett, G. P., M. Porter, & H. Holmes. 1965. Choice behavior in rhesus monkeys: effect of stimulation during the first month of life. *Science* 147:304–406.

Sackett, G. P., G. A. Griffin, C. L. Pratt, W. D. Joslyn, & G. C. Ruppenthal. 1967. Mother–infant and adult female choice behavior in rhesus monkeys after various rearing experiences. *Journal of Comparative and Physiological Psychology* 63:376–381.

Sackett, G. P., R. Holm, & S. Landesman-Dwyer. 1975. Vulnerability for abnormal development: pregnancy outcome and sex differences in macaque monkeys. *In:* N. Ellis (ed.), *Aberrant development of infancy: human and animal studies.* Halstead Press, New York.

Sackett, G. P., R. Holm, & G. C. Ruppenthal. 1976. Social isolation rearing: species differences in behavior of macaque monkeys. *Developmental Psychology* 4:283–288.

Schein, M. W. 1963. On the irreversibility of imprinting. *Zeitschrift für Tierpsychologie* 20:462–467.

Scholz, A. T., R. M. Horrall, J. C. Cooper, & A. D. Hasler. 1976. Imprinting to chemical cues: the basis for home stream selection in salmon. *Science* 192:1247–1249.

Schutz, F. 1965. Sexuelle Prägung bei Anatiden. *Zeitschrift für Tierpsychologie* 22:50–103.

1969. Triebstrukturen und Fehlleitungen der Sexualität bei Tieren. *In:* A. Schelkopf (ed.), *Sexualität, Formen und Fehlentwicklungen.* Vandenhoeck and Ruprecht, Göttingen, pp. 33–54.

1970. Zur sexuellen Prägbarkeit und sensiblen Phase von Gänsen und der Bedeutung der Farbe des Prägungsobjektes. *Zoologischer Anzeiger Supplementband* 33:301–306.

1972. Früherfahrung und Verhalten. *Verhandlungen der Schweizerischen Naturforschenden Gesellschaft* pp. 71–84.

Scott, J. P. 1962. Critical periods in behavioral development. *Science* 138:949–958.

Scott, J. P., J. M. Stewart, & V. J. DeGhett. 1974. Critical periods in the organization of systems. *Developmental Psychobiology* 7:489–513.

Seligman, M. E. P. 1975. *Helplessness.* Freeman, San Francisco.

Serventy, D. C. 1967. Aspects of the population ecology of the short-tailed shearwater *Puffinus tenuirostris. Proceedings of the 14th International Ornithological Congress,* Oxford 1966, pp. 165–190.

Sjölander, S., & A. Fernö. 1973. Sexual imprinting on another species in a cichlid fish, *Haplochromis burtoni. Revue de Comportement Animal* 7:77–81.

Sluckin, W. 1973. *Imprinting and early learning,* 2nd ed. Aldine, Chicago.

Smith, F. V. 1969. *Attachment of the young: imprinting and other developments.* Oliver and Boyd, Edinburgh.

Sossinka, R. 1970. Domestikationserscheinungen beim Zebrafinken (*Taeniopygia guttata castanotis* Gould). *Zoologische Fahrbücher Systematik* 97:455–521.

Strobel, M. G., G. M. Clark, & G. E. MacDonald. 1968. Ontogeny of the approach response: a radio sensitive period during embryological development of domestic chicks. *Journal of Comparative and Physiological Psychology* 65:314–318.

Suomi, S. J., & H. F. Harlow. 1977. Early separation and behavioral maturation. *In:* A. Oliverio (ed.), *Genetics, environment, and intelligence.* Elsevier/North Holland Press, Amsterdam.

Suomi, S. J., H. F. Harlow, & C. J. Domek. 1970. Effect of repetitive infant–infant separation of young monkeys. *Journal of Abnormal Psychology* 76:161–172.

Suomi, S. J., H. F. Harlow, & S. Mineka. 1981. Social separation in monkeys as viewed from several motivational perspectives. *In:* P. Teitelbaum & E. Satinoff (eds.), *Handbook of behavioral neurobiology: motivation.* Plenum Press, New York (in press).

Suomi, S. J., H. F. Harlow, & M. A. Novak. 1974. Reversal of social deficits produced by isolation-rearing in monkeys. *Journal of Human Evolution* 3:527–534.

Thielcke, G. 1969. Geographic variation in bird vocalizations. *In:* R. A. Hinde (ed.), *Bird vocalizations.* Cambridge University Press, Cambridge, pp. 331–339.

Thompson, W. L. 1970. Song variation in a population of indigo buntings. *Auk* 87:58–71.

Thomson, A. L. 1950. Factors determining the breeding seasons of birds: an introductory review. *Ibis* 92:173–184.

Thorpe, W. H. 1963. *Learning and instinct in animals,* 2nd. ed. Methuen, London.

Vidal, J.-M. 1976. Empreinte filiale et sexuelle - réflexions sur le processus d'attachement d'après une étude expérimentale sur le coq domestique. Docteur dès Sciences Thèse, University of Rennes.

White, L. E., & R. A. Hinde. 1975. Some factors affecting mother–infant relations in rhesus monkeys. *Animal Behaviour* 23:527–542.

Young, L. D., S. J. Suomi, H. F. Harlow, & W. T. Kinney. 1973. Early stress and later response to separation. *American Journal of Psychiatry* 130:400–405.

15

CONTROL OF SENSITIVITY TO THE ENVIRONMENT DURING DEVELOPMENT

PATRICK BATESON

The conviction that experience can exert a greater influence at some times of life than at others is deeply rooted in conventional thinking about ourselves and other animals. Nevertheless, the disturbing picture of a child missing the developmental bus by not being treated in a particular way at specific times has been strongly challenged (e.g., Clarke & Clarke 1976). In many instances, it is possible to resolve the apparent contradiction between the view that the young are especially susceptible to particular experiences at particular times and the view that adults can be rehabilitated (Bateson 1979). This is because a sensitive period for instruction from the environment can arise not so much through an incapacity to learn as through an unwillingness to do so outside the period of sensitivity. When such unwillingness can be overcome, it is possible for the older animal to learn about new things once again. It is important therefore to deal with the evidence for sensitive periods separately from the mechanisms that control the timing of increases and decreases in sensitivity. An understanding of the mechanisms can explain why, under certain circumstances, the evidence for sensitive periods seems to evaporate. In this chapter, I shall consider the specific case of imprinting in birds in order to illustrate how it is possible to move toward some understanding of the underlying processes.

The ways in which *sensitive period* or one of its many synonyms were first used have been reviewed by Hess (1973). Many embryologists thought of it as a stage in development when an embryo is most vulnerable to disruption by external factors (e.g., Stockard 1921). However, it was also taken to mean a stage when the developing system is most susceptible to instruction from outside. The first sense carries with it no necessary functional implications; a *critical moment* in Stockard's usage might simply correspond to a period of rapid reorganization when immunity from disruption is lowered. The second sense, which is the one employed in the imprinting literature, has the obvious evolutionary implication that this is a time when particular information from the environment is best obtained.

THE NATURE OF IMPRINTING

Imprinting is the process or set of processes by which various kinds of preferences can be determined by experience (reviewed by Bateson 1966;

Sluckin 1972; Hess 1973; Hoffman & Ratner 1973a; Rajecki 1973). Generally it is thought of as narrowing preexisting preferences. I shall be considering filial and sexual preferences in this chapter, but the narrowing of habitat preferences, feeding preferences, and so forth has also been subsumed under the general heading of imprinting. The concept itself is surrounded by a certain amount of controversy. The argument is partly about inference. Is it or is it not a special kind of learning? I have been embroiled in this debate and can hardly claim to have a detached view. Nevertheless, I think it is fair to say that the outcome remains inconclusive because what is meant by a special process is vague. Does it refer to some aspect of information storage, to the perceptual mechanisms involved, or to state factors with which storage might be associated? To settle issues about the nature of these and other subprocesses involved in the acquisition of information from the environment requires knowledge about the underlying machinery that is simply not available at the moment.

Undoubtedly filial imprinting can be placed in a framework in which an initially significant aspect of an imprinting stimulus is regarded as necessary for subsequent selective responsiveness to initially neutral aspects; in other words, the process can be likened to that involved in classical conditioning (James 1959; Hoffman & Ratner 1973a; Hoffman & de Paulo 1977). Many unconditioned stimuli in a classical conditioning procedure can also be used as reinforcers in an operant conditioning procedure, and certainly stimuli that are effective for filial imprinting are also effective as reinforcers (Bateson & Reese 1969). On the other hand, a familiar object remains effective as a reinforcer long after responsiveness has become selective to it (Hoffman et al. 1966), so in that sense the reinforcing effects of a stimulus can be dissociated from its preference-narrowing effects.

Even if the imprinting process turns out to be associative, the procedure used in studies of filial imprinting is not. It simply involves exposing a bird to a single stimulus without explicit pairing of neutral and significant events. Subsequently the bird is given a choice between the object to which it was exposed and something different. If, in a balanced experiment, birds exposed to object A are more likely to approach it in a choice between A and B than birds exposed to object B, it is usually supposed that filial imprinting has taken place. Such a conclusion can be suspect unless the stimuli were as well balanced as the experimental design, because exposure may facilitate the expression of preexisting preferences (cf. Klopfer 1965). This is particularly obvious if one object elicits a great deal more social behavior during the period of exposure than the other.

If the process has generated most argument and the procedure has elicited most ingenuity, the social context of imprinting probably excites most interest – at least in the eyes of the nonspecialist. In the natural world, imprinting does not only reduce the number of individuals that are likely to be approached; it can influence whom the animal feeds with, whom it escapes to in times of danger, and so on (see Hinde 1974:160). The process of establishing a close and special relationship, attachment in a word, has many facets that are easily forgotten in the relentless pursuit of mechanism and precise measurement.

A superficially worrying aspect of the work on imprinting is the apparent inability of experimentalists to repeat each other's results. Some get beautifully defined sensitive periods (e.g., Hess 1959; Gottlieb 1961; Rubel 1970); others get hardly any effect whatsoever (e.g., Smith & Nott 1970; Vidal 1971; Brown 1975a). Now, it is possible to draw various conclusions from all this, but the most likely explanation is that our conception of what is going on is far too simple. We seem to expect straightforward results from an exceedingly complex and delicately balanced system. It is already obvious from many careful studies of domestic chicks and mallard ducklings that a large number of factors can affect the outcome of an imprinting experiment. The possibilities for surprising interactions are enormous. We should expect contradictory evidence from a system such as this if everything has not been standardized – and it has not been.

PROXIMATE CONTROL OF INCREASING SENSITIVITY

Some evidence does suggest that the onset of sensitivity to stimuli that can trigger the filial imprinting process is dependent on the general developmental state of the bird. Gottlieb (1961), making use of variation in the time of development when hatching occurs, studied how easy it was to imprint ducklings at different times after hatching. His intention was to separate the influence of the developmental state from that of the many experiences occurring at and after hatching. He found that the extent to which Peking ducklings would narrow their preferences to a moving model was markedly affected by their age calculated from the beginning of embryonic development. He went on to argue that the sensitive period was better measured in terms of developmental age than age from hatching. Indeed, when he expressed his data in terms of age from hatching, the sensitive period looked much less clear-cut and quite unlike the much reprinted figure presented by Hess (1959). Gottlieb's conclusion was accepted by many people, including myself. However, it was subsequently criticized by Williams (1972) because the four time bins for developmental age spanned 48 hours, whereas the five time bins for posthatch age spanned only 24 hours. In other words, the seemingly unimportant influence of posthatch age could be attributed to the smaller age range that was sampled.

Some reconciliation between the studies of Hess and Gottlieb was achieved by Landsberg (1976). Following Gottlieb, he made use of the different stages of development at which ducks hatch and varied independently the time to imprinting from hatching and from the beginning of embryonic development. His technique differed from Gottlieb's in a way that could be important. Whereas Gottlieb had tested his ducklings at a constant posthatch age, Landsberg kept the time from training to testing constant so that the age of testing varied with posthatch age. Landsberg's results, which are summarized in Figure 15.1, showed that both age from the beginning of embryonic development and age from hatching were significant sources of variation. In other words, it seems that the general state of development of the bird plays a part in the onset of sensitivity but that the events associated with hatching or the experience subsequent to hatching also play their part. Once again, the

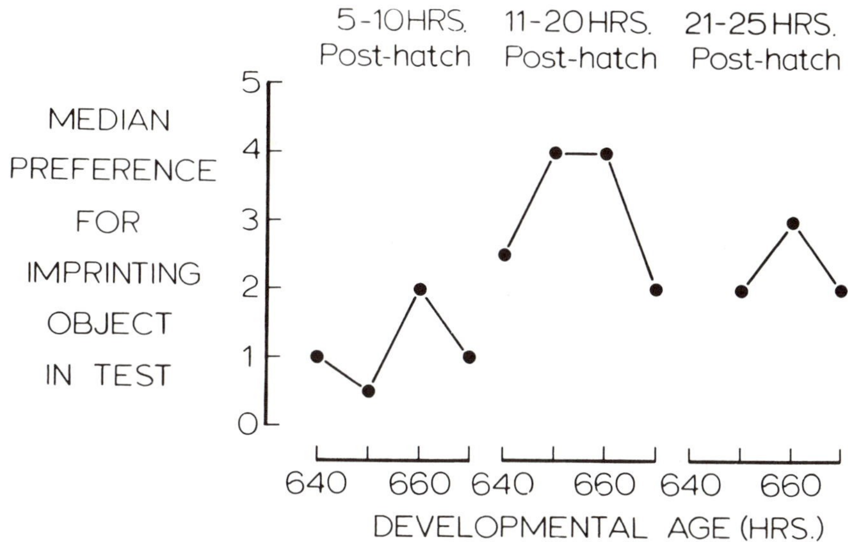

Figure 15.1. The median preference of different groups of ducklings for an imprinting object to which they were exposed for 30 minutes at the specified developmental and posthatch ages. Their preferences for the object were measured 24 hours after exposure. (Data from Landsberg 1976)

story turned out to be more complicated than the partial accounts had led us to expect.

Part of the increase in sensitivity is attributable to changes in the efficiency of the visual system (Paulson 1965), and here the interaction between internal control and external experience is particularly easy to understand. Visual experience with patterned light has a general facilitating effect on the development of visually guided behavior (see the review in Bateson 1976; Tees 1976; also Cherfas 1977, 1978) and may well serve to strengthen neural connections in relevant underlying systems (see reviews in Horn et al. 1973; Riesen 1975; Cotman 1978). Other changes in internal state, particularly in levels of corticosterones, appear to be associated with the changes in sensitivity (Martin 1975: Landsberg & Weiss 1976; Weiss et al. 1977), but the extent to which they are dependent on preceding external events is not yet known.

Finally, a general increase in the level of arousal, frequently suggested as being important in imprinting (e.g., Fischer 1970; Kovach 1970; Martin & Schutz 1974), may be a consequence of the other changes already mentioned or may reflect an endogenous increase in the excitability of the central nervous system.

DECLINE IN SENSITIVITY

The evidence for some endogenous control over the ending of the sensitive period is much less satisfactory. By contrast, the powerful influence of external

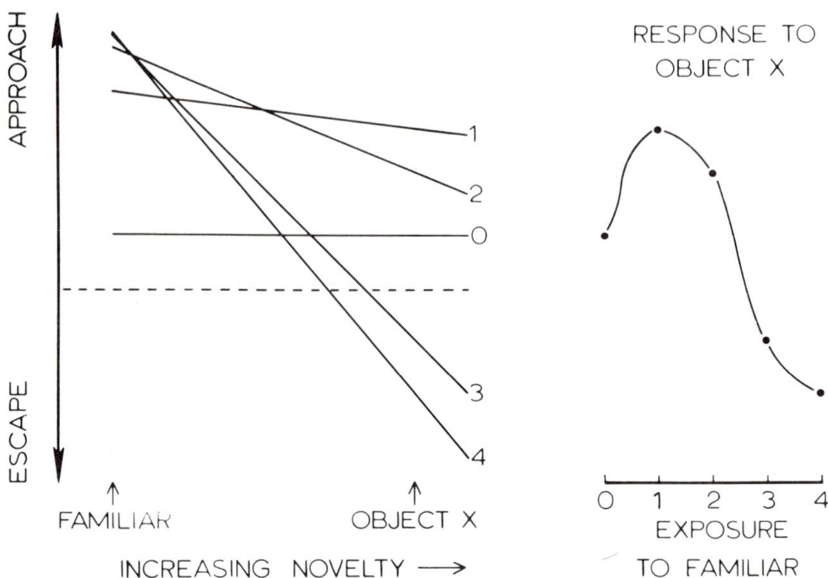

Figure 15.2. The postulated interaction between the general facilitating influences of a conspicuous visual stimulus and the specific narrowing effects on filial preferences in dark-reared birds such as domestic chicks. The diagram on the right shows how the approach to a standard novel object (object X) would first increase as a function of exposure to the familiar and then decline. (From Bateson 1979)

experience is compelling. Imprinting is a preemptive, self-terminating process in the sense that it narrows social preferences to those that are familiar and therefore tends to prevent fresh experience from further modifying those social preferences. Moreover, although some stimuli are much more effective in restricting preferences than others, birds can eventually form social preferences for suboptimal stimuli such as the static cages in which they have been isolated (e.g., Bateson 1964a; Evans 1970). It follows that if some birds are reared with near optimal stimuli such as their siblings and some are reared in isolation, it should be possible to imprint the isolated birds with a novel object at an age when the socially reared birds escape from or are unresponsive to new things. This has been demonstrated in chicks and ducklings (Guiton 1959; Sluckin & Salzen 1961; Asdourian 1967; Smith & Nott 1970). Furthermore, when a bird's experience is attenuated experimentally, the age at which it will respond socially to novel objects can be greatly extended (Moltz & Stettner 1961; MacDonald 1968). Such results seem to contrast to, for instance, those of Polt and Hess (1964, 1966), who found that relatively short periods of light and social experience facilitated the approach to novel objects. This paradox indicates that stimulation can have both general and specific effects. It can initially raise responsiveness to all objects but then, as the bird becomes increasingly familiar with a particular form of stimulation, responsiveness is restricted to it. The net effect is shown diagrammatically in Figure 15.2 –

omitting, it must be stressed, the further complication of a preference for slight novelty (e.g., Bateson & Jaeckel 1976).

It has frequently been suggested that one reason for the reduction in readiness to learn with increasing age is that the birds are becoming more fearful. Hoffman and Ratner (1973b) have argued that familiarity with one object is not a sufficient condition for the onset of such fearfulness. Because fearful birds do not escape from familiar objects (e.g., Rubel 1970), the point should be put another way: Does the motor system by which escape is accomplished develop later than the recognition system that controls when escape should occur? Hoffman and Ratner's reason for thinking that it does was based on their observation that ducklings would prefer to approach a familiar object even when the novel object did not elicit any distress. However, it can equally well be argued that the bird has a number of responses to novelty, ranging from reduced social behavior through indifference to flight. Just how it responds will depend on how different the novel object is from the familiar and how strong a preference the bird has formed for the familiar object. So, Hoffman and Ratner's observations could be explained in terms of insufficient exposure of the ducklings to the familiar object, too close a similarity between familiar and novel objects, or habituation of the escape responses to the novel object. The issue of whether or not escape develops later than familiarization remains open, as does another possibility: that in birds kept in a suboptimal environment, the readiness to respond socially to all objects declines. It seems likely that the efficiency of receptors would fall off under conditions of deprivation, the level of arousal would sink, and so forth. One further possible complication should be mentioned. Millikan (1972) suggested, on the basis of his experiments with ducklings, that sensitivity might decline as a result of nonspecific stimulation.

The complexities lurking in the wings notwithstanding, the influence of external events on the ending of the sensitive period is hard to deny. People have difficulty in getting older birds to respond socially to an object at least in part because the birds have developed a preference for something else. The precise degree of difficulty will obviously depend on how strange the object seems to the bird. As Brown (1975a) pointed out, this almost certainly explains why he was able to demonstrate imprinting across a wide age range (see also Brown 1975b; Brown & Hamilton 1977). Although the development of new preferences is initially prevented by escape from novelty or by the low level of social responsiveness to unfamiliar things, enforced contact may wear down these behavioral constraints to the point where the bird does develop a new preference. Escape from novel objects can undoubtedly be habituated (Bateson 1964b; Ratner & Hoffman 1974), and also chicks that have developed a preference for object A can be induced to prefer object B by a sufficiently long period of exposure to it (Salzen & Meyer 1968; Cherfas & Scott 1979). As Evans (1970) pointed out, this flexibility could be of some functional importance in colonial nesting species such as gulls. In the absence of parents, for which the young bird forms its strongest preference, the bird may still be able to survive by responding socially to other adults and inducing them to feed it. This flexibility also has implications for a distinction that has sometimes been drawn between the period when filial behavior can be elicited by a novel

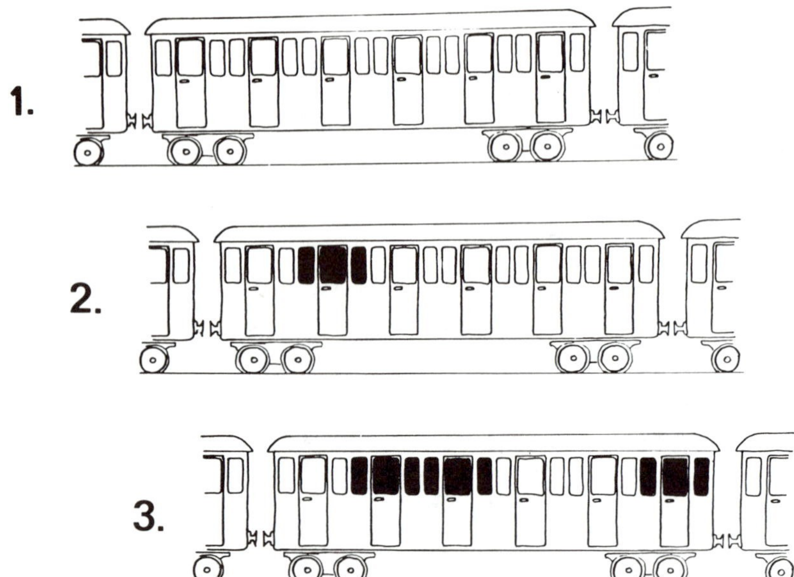

Figure 15.3. The developmental train, which has opaque windows for purposes of the sensitive period analogy, is traveling from Conception to an indeterminate place where it disappears off the tracks. At a certain stage (2), a window to a particular compartment opens. This is necessary for the beginning of a specific sensitive period. The sensitive period could end because the compartment window closes later in development. However, in this case the window stays open and the end of the sensitive period results from changes in the occupants. At stage 3 the window of another compartment opens, marking the start of another specific sensitive period. (From Bateson 1979)

object and the period when filial imprinting can occur (e.g., Fabricius 1964). If social responsiveness to novel objects implies a capacity to learn about them as indeed is suggested by Salzen and Meyer's (1968) results, then the distinction evaporates (see, however, Cherfas & Scott 1979).

WHAT KIND OF INTERACTION?

The picture emerging from studies of filial imprinting is that the sensitive period is multiply determined and arises from interactions between many internal and external factors – a point frequently emphasized by Hinde (e.g., 1962, 1970). In terms of an analogy with a train that I have proposed elsewhere (Bateson 1979), the window of the filial compartment in the developmental train opens at a particular stage in the journey and then stays open (Fig. 15.3). As a result of what they learn about the outside world, the occupants subsequently avert their gaze from anything strange. Because they can learn nothing until the window does open, the timing of the ending of the sensitive period is also dependent on the internal processes responsible for opening the window in the first place. If this analogy can be pressed just a little further, it looks as though the occupants can, under certain circumstances, be persuaded to study strange things outside the train later in the journey, and when they do so, they are influenced by what they see. I expressed these ideas in more formal terms in another paper and showed by computer simulations that the model can behave remarkably like a real bird (Bateson 1978a). The model showed some of the possible ways in which early experiences can exert a long-term effect on adult behavior in the face of potentially disruptive intervening experience. Although the protective devices generate a sensitive period in development, the simulations showed how dependent such a description is on the parameter values of a particular experiment. In other words, it emphasizes what is already obvious from empirical data: It is meaningless to give a precise figure for the optimal time for imprinting without specifying the conditions under which the measurements were obtained.

The working model also showed how, long after the apparent end of sensitivity, prolonged exposure to a novel object can lead to the development of a preference for that object. It should be noted that in that model, previous memories were erased when a new preference was formed. The stable preference had to be manifest; it could not lie latent while the animal responded preferentially to another object. I am convinced that the simplification was excessive; it prevents the model from simulating the data obtained by Immelmann (1969). He found that male zebra finches reared in early life with Bengalese finches, and subsequently kept with their own species, would breed successfully with female zebra finches. However, when given the chance, they would court Bengalese finches in preference to zebra finches. The preference for the foreign species surfaced despite the birds' considerable sexual experience with their own species. Incidentally, a period of isolation can be crucial for the latent preferences to show themselves (see Chap. 14). If the male zebra finches are given a choice between a female of their own species and a Bengalese finch without being isolated, they may initially prefer the zebra finch. As the days of isolation pass by, the preference for the Bengalese finch gradually emerges (see also the experiment on filial imprinting in chicks by Cherfas & Scott 1979).

In order to explain Immelmann's (1969) results, it is necessary to postulate that the store of information about a particular object can be uncoupled from the expression of a preference for that object under certain conditions. Second, it is necessary to postulate the rules stating the priority that will be given to different familiar objects, all of which have been responded to socially at some time or other. As in all such modeling attempts, it is possible to produce a number of different solutions to the given problem. Ideally, the theorist should present in print several alternatives making different predictions so that the empirically minded can run competitions between the alternatives. This is a counsel of perfection for the writer (and indeed, the reader!); besides, a lot of possibilities are rejected before they are fully articulated – perhaps because their inadequacies seem so obvious. Anyway, I do not present a formal model here. I merely provide verbal sketches of some possibilities that I find attractive.

The main suggestion is that imprinting involves two kinds of plasticity: one

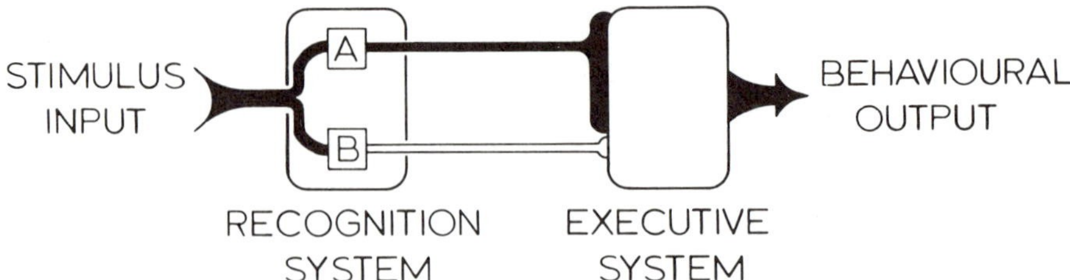

Figure 15.4. Two linked systems postulated to show plasticity during imprinting. The recognition system has a larger capacity and can be linked to many different executive systems according to the animal's state. The input to the executive system is limited and, given sufficient exposure, can be entirely captured by the subsystem recognizing one object. (Any resemblance between this input and a synapse is entirely coincidental.) Here the subsystem responding to the first object with which the animal was imprinted (A) has captured 80% of the available input.

of enormous capacity to deal with the storage of information about familiar objects, and one of restricted capacity to deal with the link between that recognition system and an executive part of the central nervous system concerned with the patterning of social behavior. (It is worth comparing this idea with the two-stage model of discrimination learning proposed by Sutherland and Mackintosh [1971].) The observed restriction of responsiveness to familiar objects can be attributed to the connection from a particular store in the recognition system gradually dominating access to the executive part controlling social behavior. Such a preemptive effect of one kind of experience need not be wholly irreversible providing that another object can gain access to the executive system. The situation might be as shown in Figure 15.4: Object A would be preferred to object B, but if A were not available, the connections between the B recognition subsystem and the executive system would be strengthened and, simultaneously, those required by A might be weakened – particularly if maintenance of contact were necessary to keep the connections in a functional state. Suppose, for instance, that prior exposure to A has led to capture of 80% of the available connections to the executive system. After prolonged exposure to B, the remaining 20% of the available connections are captured by the B recognition subsystem. Meanwhile, as a result of the absence of stimulation, 90% of the A connections have become inactive. The net result is that only 8% of the functional connections to the executive system come from A. So, B will be preferred. Now, consider what will happen as a result of isolation. The number of functional B connections will drop until only 2% of those connections to the executive system come from B. (The assumption is that the proportion of functional connections from B will fall to the same steady state as those from A.) It is obvious that a time will come when A is once again preferred to B.

In neural terms, this model is not inherently unreasonable because evidence for the maintenance of neural connections as a result of use is extensive (Horn et al. 1973; Riesen 1975; Cotman 1978). Nevertheless, the model might indicate a decrease of responsiveness as a result of isolation, which may not be wholly

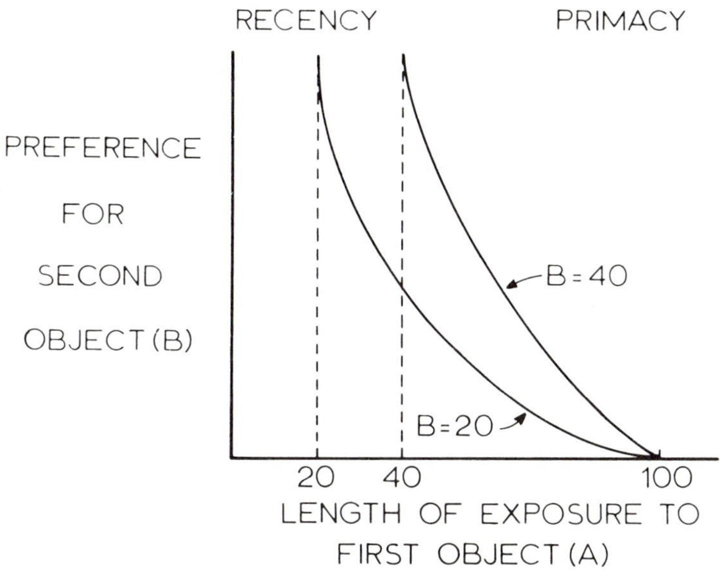

Figure 15.5. The hypothetical preference for the second of two objects in a choice between them given after exposure to first A and then B. All the connections from A and B recognition subsystems are assumed to be functional at the time of the test. Different lengths of exposure to A are given for two lengths of exposure to B. The numbers are percentages of the minimum length of exposure to the first object (A) required to produce an unmodifiable preference for that object.

realistic. A different approach would be to postulate inhibition of competitors by connections from the recognition subsystem that has been activated in the recent past. If this were the case, it would be possible to simulate Immelmann's (1969) zebra finch data if the inhibition were gradually lifted as a result of isolation.

I should be the first to admit that many details of sexual imprinting are left unexplained by the model. What I like about it, though, is that the first experience received at the optimal stage of development does not necessarily generate the dominant preference, even though it will often do so. This might have been deduced on commonsense grounds even if the misleading connotation of imprinting as an instantaneous, all-or-nothing process was still accepted. Even for an extremely rapid process, it should still be possible to find a length of exposure that was sufficiently short to leave no impact. So, in an experiment like Immelmann's in which exposure to object A is followed by exposure to object B and then by isolation, it should be possible to reduce the length of exposure to A to the point at which the most recent experience with B generated the dominant preference. I have shown diagrammatically what might happen in Figure 15.5. Such a curve would not be absolute for all conditions and combinations of stimuli. For example, increasing the stimulus value of the second object (B) relative to the first (A) or increasing the length of exposure to B should move to the right the line separating recency from primacy effects.

Evidence for a stable preference lasting from early life into old age does not exclude the possibility of other preferences being established later in life. The major virtue of the work done on filial imprinting and, increasingly, on sexual imprinting is that it begins to reconcile the observation that preferences can be narrowed more readily at some stages of development than at others with the evident capacity for changes of those preferences later in life. It indicates that the notion of the powerful determining influence of early experience can coexist with that of subsequent rehabilitation.

RELATIONS BETWEEN FILIAL AND SEXUAL PREFERENCES

An important feature of the theoretical approach developed elsewhere (Bateson 1978a) and discussed briefly here is the postulation of an internal change in state specific to a modifiable preference. The precise timing of an increase in intrinsic responsiveness would surely be influenced by a number of general environmental factors such as temperature, patterned light, and so forth. Nevertheless, the idea that a particular window in the developmental train opens at a particular stage in the journey is central. The evidence has so far been drawn largely from the work on filial imprinting. Filial behavior usually drops out of an animal's repertoire by the time it is an adult and the enduring influences of early experience are shown in the mating preferences of adults (see reviews in Klinghammer 1967; Immelmann 1972; Bateson 1978a). So, the question is raised of what connection there may be between filial and sexual imprinting. How much does the opening of one window in the developmental train influence the occupants of other compartments? Is there a draft of wind, so to speak, from the filial compartment to the sexual one? Is it right even to think of them as separate compartments?

Evidence for some sharing of control between filial and sexual behavior came from the studies in which young birds were trained so that they formed a filial attachment to a particular object. Precocious sexual responsiveness was induced by injecting the birds with the male hormone testosterone and giving them a choice test. They were found to direct their sexual behavior toward the object that was familiar from the filial context (Bambridge 1962; Guiton 1966; Salzen 1966). In apparent contrast, Schutz (1965) argued that in the mallard, filial and sexual imprinting were distinct processes and sexual imprinting started considerably later. His major reason for drawing this conclusion was that some of his drake mallards showed a sexual preference for species to which they had been first exposed up to 3 weeks after hatching. Schutz may have had an exaggerated respect for the old concept of sensitive periods. This idea implied that a decline with age in readiness to learn the characteristics of an object in a period of 15 minutes indicated an absolute decline in readiness to develop a preference for that object even if the period of exposure was extended to more than 6 weeks. In any event, the interpretation of Schutz's data is not straightforward because he varied at least three factors – namely, onset of exposure, length of exposure, and type of companion – and the numbers of birds represented in the various possible subgroups are very different. Probably the strongest conclusion that can be drawn from his study is that if exposure is started within the first 3 weeks, the duration of the exposure is the most important factor that determines whether or not male mallards will subsequently show a sexual preference for the species to which they were exposed. A 6-week exposure period started at some time during the first 3 weeks might well have ensured that the time when a change in state specific to sexual preferences occurred lay within the period of exposure, regardless of precisely when exposure was started. So, Schutz's conclusion that sexual imprinting was different from filial imprinting could still be right.

An inference similar to that of Schutz was drawn by Gallagher (1977) on the basis of work with Japanese quail. He exposed quail chicks for 10 days to an albino female, starting the period of exposure at different ages. Males whose exposure started 5 days after hatching subsequently showed a stronger mating preference for albino females than those whose exposure started at earlier and later ages. However, the difference from the males whose exposure was started on the first day after hatching was not statistically significant. So, the distinction between filial and sexual imprinting could still be questioned.

The clearest indication that sexual imprinting might be at least partly dissociated from filial imprinting comes from a study of domestic cockerels by Vidal (1976a,b). He exposed cockerels to a moving model from 0 to 15 days, 16 to 30 days, or 31 to 45 days after hatching. Subsequently they were isolated or reared with a female until they became adults. Starting at 150 days they were given a series of choice tests. Of his various findings, the one of greatest interest here is that the chicks that had been exposed for 31 to 45 days and then isolated showed the strongest sexual preference for the model. These birds had shown the least amount of filial behavior to the model during the period of exposure.

Before concluding that the details of sexual preferences tend to be determined later in development than those filial preferences, the influence of filial imprinting on precocially induced sexual preferences still needs to be explained. One consequence of filial imprinting is that strange objects are avoided; avoidance of novel test objects might ensure that the only outlet for sexual behavior is the object for which a filial preference had been previously formed. A more subtle possibility is that the mechanisms involved in parental recognition do influence sexual preferences, but that further modification of those preferences can take place when a change in state specific to sexual responsiveness occurs later in development. This may prove to be the most satisfactory explanation for the partial overlap of control between filial and sexual behavior. For the remainder of this chapter, I shall assume that the overlap is only partial and that in many species marked modification of sexual preferences does indeed occur later than initial narrowing of filial preferences.

If filial and sexual imprinting occur at different times, it is fair to ask whether they are different processes. Put in such a general way, the answer must surely be "yes," but the question needs to be refined. Are the plastic processes involved in acquiring an ability to recognize parents, and an ability to recognize grown-up siblings, different from each other, and, for that matter, are they different from the plastic processes involved in other forms of recognition? Or are filial and sexual imprinting examples of state-dependent learning (see Overton

1974)? It seems likely that the willingness to learn and the output from the plastic recognition systems are dependent on specific state factors, such as hormonal level or neural activity of a particular kind.

FUNCTIONS OF SENSITIVE PERIODS FOR IMPRINTING

Why should it be adaptive for sexual imprinting to occur later than filial imprinting? In order to answer that question, it is necessary to speculate on the functional significance of filial and sexual imprinting. It has become increasingly apparent over the years that neither process plays an essential role in species recognition, because a bird can show a predisposition to respond to members of its own species – even when it has had no direct previous experience with any of them except itself (Gottlieb 1971; Immelmann 1969; Schutz 1965). The simplest but least satisfying explanation is that imprinting represents the development of a fail-safe system that provides a backup for other mechanisms involved in species recognition. Another suggestion is that in a species in which external characteristics are changing rapidly, imprinting provides the means of automatically and appropriately shifting preferences as bodily appearance changes in the course of evolution (Bateson 1966; Immelmann 1975). However, this explanation brackets together filial and sexual imprinting and so does not provide any access to the problem, if problem it be, of why the processes should occur at different stages of development. The most promising possibility is that both filial and sexual imprinting have evolved to enable birds to recognize their close kin – but the necessity for kin recognition is different in the young and adults.

The young bird needs to discriminate between the parent that cares for it and other members of its species because parents discriminate between their own offspring and other young of the same species and may actually attack young that are not their own. Adult behavior of this kind is well known in mammals, such as sheep, and has also been documented in many species of bird (e.g., Tinbergen 1953:227; Davies & Carrick 1962; Burtt 1977). In most cases, the parent that cares exclusively for its own young will be more likely to rear them to fledgling than a parent that accepts and cares for all the stray young that come up to it. In other words, the phenotypic character of caring for young, with all its attendant advantages, is more likely to be transmitted from one generation to the next by genetic means if the behavior is directed exclusively at close kin. Note, however, some interesting exceptions like the eider and the shelduck – both of which form creches of young ducklings under certain conditions. In essence, the general suggestion is that filial imprinting is required for individual recognition of parents and is a secondary consequence of the selective pressures on parents to discriminate between their own and other young (see Bateson 1966:198 and more especially Evans 1970:217).

The evolutionary pressures that gave rise to sexual imprinting are, I believe, quite different. Briefly, the suggestion is that sexual imprinting enables an animal to learn the characteristics of its close kin, and subsequently it can choose a mate that appears slightly different (but not too different) from its parents and siblings. The advantage of behaving in this way arises because of the evolutionary pressures to strike an optimal balance between inbreeding and outbreeding. The selection pressures for outbreeding are widely accepted (e.g., Bischof 1975). One commonly held view is that a pressure derives from the advantages of producing variety in offspring so that one or another of them is able to cope with fluctuations in the environment. Another is that outbreeding reduces the probability of lethal recessive genes being expressed. The value of these and other ideas is disputed (see Maynard Smith 1978), but the existence of some kind of pressure for outbreeding is not. The selection pressures for inbreeding are more familiar to botanists than zoologists (see Jain 1976); nevertheless, it is as important to an animal as it is to a plant to transmit its own adaptive characteristics to its offspring. Any recombination arising from sexual reproduction that might break apart coadapted complexes of genes could be disadvantageous. Mather (1943) perceived clearly the opposing pressures in the evolution of mate selection that on the one hand drive toward outbreeding and variety in offspring, so that some of them at least may cope with an alteration in the environment, and on the other hand drive toward inbreeding and offspring that are all as well adapted as their parents. The optimal balance between negative and positive assortative mating will clearly depend on how rapidly the environment changes. If the environment is relatively stable, the pressure should be for a greater degree of inbreeding than if the environment is rather labile. This expectation is based on a particular set of theories about the nature of opposed pressures for outbreeding and inbreeding—theories that Maynard Smith (1978) would not necessarily accept. The essential point is that, whatever the opposed pressures may be, an optimal solution to the problem can be that mates should be related to a certain extent. For the sake of argument, suppose the optimal mate is a first cousin. How does an animal know what a cousin looks like? Only a small number of individuals will be cousins for one individual, and they will be cousins for very few others. So, in finding a mate, each individual has a problem virtually unique to itself. The solution, I suggest, is for each individual, using the sexual imprinting process, to learn the characteristics of its parents and siblings and, when it is an adult, to choose a mate that looks a bit different from its immediate kin. The underlying assumption is, of course, that there is a correlation between relatedness and similarity of external appearance.

The principle of optimal discrepancy crops up in many studies of animal and human behavior (e.g., McClelland & Clark 1953; Berlyne 1960; Thomas 1971; Bateson 1973). In the present context the postulated standard for mate selection is learned, and the optimal degree of discrepancy from that standard is presumably determined by an inherited rule that in turn depends on the evolutionary history of the species.

How can my hypothesis account for the facts of sexual imprinting? Taking Immelmann's (1969) experiments, for instance, how is the explanation compatible with the evidence that when zebra finches have been reared as young Bengalese finches, they subsequently prefer to mate with Bengalese finches? The answer lies, I suggest, in the way that tests of mating preferences are normally carried out. The differences between the options are generally gross, and it seems highly probable that in many cases the optimal stimulus is more like the familiar than the novel one, as shown in Figure 15.6. Certainly

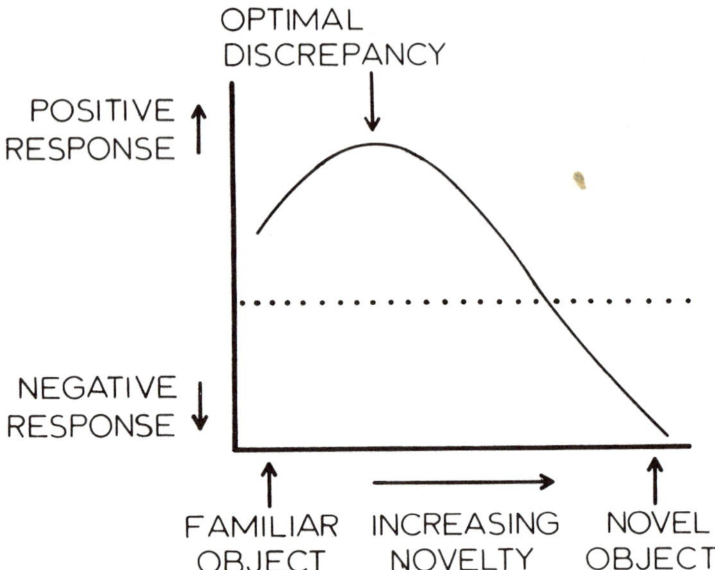

Figure 15.6. The postulated relationship between the sexual response to an individual and its degree of novelty relative to familiar objects that would be kin under natural conditions. A positive response means sexual approach, and a negative response could mean escape. (From Bateson 1978b)

male Japanese quail preferred to mate with a female of a familiar white plumage type rather than one with grossly different brown plumage (Gallagher 1976, 1977), and conversely, they preferred a known brown female to an unknown white one (Bateson 1978b). However, when they were given a choice between a female with which they had grown up and a novel female of the same brown plumage, they preferred the novel one (Bateson 1978b).

If all the theorizing is correct, some sense can be made of why sexual imprinting might occur later than filial imprinting. In order for a bird to maximize its chances of recognizing close kin, it should delay learning about them until its siblings are old enough for their juvenile characteristics to provide a strong indication of their adult appearance. I have reviewed elsewhere the evidence suggesting that this may, indeed, be the case (Bateson 1979). So, it does seem quite likely that the timing of sexual imprinting is associated with the development of adult plumage, which is what would be expected if each bird needs to learn about the adult appearance of its siblings. In those species in which the young disperse before they have developed adult plumage, an individual could get information about the visual appearance of close kin only from its parents. In such cases, the arguments that I have advanced for sexual imprinting occurring late in development would not apply.

In summary, it is possible to argue with some plausibility that different types of selection pressure have shaped the timing of the increase in intrinsic responsiveness specific to filial imprinting and that specific to sexual imprinting. Taking filial imprinting first, in each generation, individuals will differ in the state of development when their filial responsiveness to parentlike objects first increases. Those that do it too early obtain inappropriate or insufficient information about their parents. They might not, for instance, have adequate opportunities to explore all facets of their parent and so fail to recognize it quickly enough later on when quick recognition is important. Those that do it too late respond in a friendly way to hostile members of their own species and consequently suffer. In these different ways, the optimal timing for the increase in intrinsic responsiveness could have evolved. It would be critically affected by how rapidly the parents learned to discriminate between their own young and other young. In the case of sexual imprinting, the optimum was, I suggest, achieved in a different way. Those birds that tune the reference point for their mating preferences too early simply get misinformation from their siblings. Alternatively, they might have their preferences erased in the drastic reorganization of behavior that may occur, for other good reasons, as they change from a juvenile to a more adultlike state (Campbell & Spear 1972). Those birds that have their mating preferences determined too late in development do so after the family group has broken up or after they have been exposed to too many other individuals that are not their kin. Here again, the optimal time for an increase in intrinsic responsiveness represents some balance between opposing pressures.

CONCLUSIONS

It would be nice to argue that the considerations applying to imprinting in birds apply to all other processes associated with descriptive sensitive periods. Nice – but almost certainly false. It just does not seem very plausible that, say, the onset of language acquisition is brought about in the same way as the onset of maternal sensitivity to newborn young. Nor, for that matter, is the development of a preemptive preference bringing a period of particular behavioral plasticity to an end likely to be the same as a developmental change, such as a slower growth rate, reducing vulnerability to the long-term effects of starvation. In other words, I do not think there is much sense in talking about *the* theory of sensitive periods on the basis of what is known about imprinting – or anything else, for that matter. Even if no general principles can be derived, some useful lessons have, nevertheless, been learned.

The first lesson from the work on imprinting is that a sensitive period can arise not so much through an incapacity to learn as through an unwillingness to do so. If the various systems making an adult animal unready to respond to novelty are silenced, by habituation for example, the animal may then learn about new things once again. It should be obvious that the more powerful are the protective mechanisms, the more stable will be the consequences of the initial experience and the more robust will be the sensitive period phenomenon. The imprinting work suggests that the extent to which a sensitive period is replicated may frequently depend on the degree to which the conditions in which it was first described are copied. Even small changes can cause the evidence to evaporate. These alterations in conditions are worth investigating because they probe the systems normally protecting the consequences of early experience from subsequent modification. In other words, they open the way to adult rehabilitation. The lesson that sensitivity may end not so much through a lack of capacity to learn as through a lack of willingness is worth bearing in mind, especially in cases in which humans are found to acquire certain skills more easily at some stages of development than at others.

The second lesson is more subtle. A sensitive period for imprinting is not something that can be manipulated independently of the learning process. A sensitive period is the outcome of interactions between a number of different factors, one being developmental age and another experience – resulting in imprinting and the narrowing of preferences. So, it is highly confusing to argue, as is often done, that imprinting did or did not occur because exposure was inside or outside the sensitive period. The likelihood that an event, such as exposure to a particular object, will have a long-term effect should be related to factors that can be independently varied. When this is done, the mental fog starts to lift.

The third point relates to the implacable opposition between those who see the sensitive period as the expression of inflexible endogenous rules (e.g., Scott 1962) and those who regard development as a continuous interaction between the animal and its environment (e.g., Schneirla & Rosenblatt 1963). In an interesting paper, Kovach (1970) argued that these represent alternative modes of thought, both of which are needed to cope with the real world. The lesson I draw from the imprinting work is that the debate represents a confusion of different levels of operation – identification and analysis. Scott (1962) had a view of sensitive periods that can be criticized – rightly, in my view. However, it does not follow that, because alternative interpretations can be found for the evidence, the phenomena are therefore suspect. The general point is that if a sensitive period has been characterized by varying the age at which a particular treatment is given, the job remains of discovering how the results were generated.

The fourth point is concerned with the adaptiveness of opening particular behavioral systems to instruction from the environment at particular stages of development. Plausible suggestions can, I believe, be made for why timing is both different and functionally important in the cases of filial and sexual imprinting. The fact that in some circumstances the effects of experience can be overridden by subsequent events does not alter the adaptive significance of either the timing or the mechanisms that normally protect preferences from subsequent disruption.

The final point also raises a functional issue. A powerful determining influence on behavior at one stage need not affect behavior later in life. Filial imprinting may, for instance, be adapted to the needs of the young, whereas sexual imprinting occurring later in development is adapted to adult life. Clearly, a great deal of a developing animal's behavior is required for the specific problems that beset it while it is young. Wholesale reorganization of behavior can occur as the ecology of the animal changes with age – the most dramatic examples being the metamorphosis of many insects and amphibia. So, the experiences that exert such a profound effect on behavior at one stage may fail totally to carry over into adulthood.

The punning use of *sensitive period* or one of its synonyms does have a number of disadvantages. It can easily be taken to mean that the effects of treatments are always measured at the same point in development and are always stable throughout life. Neither is the case. A common term can also imply a common mechanism that, as I have already argued, seems highly implausible. Finally, it can suggest a common function. Even in the cases of filial and sexual imprinting this is probably wrong, and it may even be quite misleading to suggest that some descriptively defined sensitive periods have any function whatsoever. They may, for instance, represent a time of rapid reorganization when the developing animal is more easily destabilized by deprivation or environmental insult. Because these conclusions may seem a little too cautious, it is worth emphasizing that the description of sensitive periods remains, nevertheless, an important first step in the analysis of the processes underlying development.

SUMMARY

The sensitive periods for filial and sexual imprinting in birds are dependent on many factors. The onset of sensitivity to particular stimuli is determined by a change in state specific to the system of social behavior involved; in some species the change specific to sexual preferences seems to occur later than that specific to filial behavior. The end of sensitivity comes about because imprinting narrows preferences to familiar objects and, for want of anything better, birds do narrow their preferences to suboptimal stimuli.

The first preferences to be established are protected, at least in part, by responses such as escape from or indifference to novel objects. Under certain conditions, such as prolonged exposure to novelty, these protective devices can be overcome. So, the existence of a sensitive period does not necessarily mean that further preferences cannot be established later in development.

The influences of experiences, occurring early and late in development, on sexual preferences suggest that two forms of neural plasticity may be involved. The first is associated with learning about the characteristics of familiar objects, and the second is associated with establishing and maintaining links between the recognition system and the executive part of the central nervous system concerned with the patterning of particular social behavior.

When filial and sexual imprinting normally occur at different stages of development, the different evolutionary selection pressures operating on the timing mechanisms can be attributed to the different functions of filial and sexual imprinting. Filial imprinting is probably needed in order to avoid neglect or damage from an adult of the same species that can tell the difference between its own and other young. Sexual imprinting is probably needed in order to set the standard by which an individual can select a mate that is optimally related to itself.

A general explanation for sensitive periods should not be derived from the studies of imprinting. Nevertheless, these studies have refined the questions that can be asked about other instances of sensitive periods in development.

REFERENCES

Asdourian, D. 1967. Object attachment and the critical period. *Psychonomic Science* 7:235–236.

Bambridge, R. 1962. Early experience and sexual behavior in the domestic chicken. *Science* 136:259–260.

Bateson, P. P. G. 1964a. Effects of similarity between rearing and testing conditions on chicks' following and avoidance responses. *Journal of Comparative and Physiological Psychology* 57:100–103.

1964b. Changes in chicks' responses to novel moving objects over the sensitive period for imprinting. *Animal Behaviour* 12:479–489.

1966. The characteristics and context of imprinting. *Biological Reviews* 41:177–220.

1973. Internal influences on early learning in birds. *In:* R. A. Hinde & J. Stevenson Hinde (eds.), *Constraints on learning.* Academic Press, London, pp. 101–116.

1976. Specificity and the origins of behavior. *In:* J. Rosenblatt, R. A. Hinde, & C. Beer (eds.), *Advances in the study of behavior,* vol. 6. Academic Press, New York, pp. 1–20.

1978a. Early experience and sexual preferences. *In:* J. B. Hutchison (ed.), *Biological determinants of sexual behavior.* Wiley, London, pp. 29–53.

1978b. Sexual imprinting and optimal outbreeding. *Nature* 273:659–660.

1979. How do sensitive periods arise and what are they for? *Animal Behaviour* 27:470–486.

Bateson, P. P. G., & S. B. Jaeckel. 1976. Chicks' preferences for familiar and novel conspicuous objects after different periods of exposure. *Animal Behaviour* 24:386–390.

Bateson, P. P. G., & E. P. Reese. 1969. The reinforcing properties of conspicuous stimuli in the imprinting situation. *Animal Behaviour* 17:692–699.

Berlyne, D. E. 1960. *Conflict, arousal and curiosity.* McGraw-Hill, New York.

Bischof, N. 1975. Comparative ethology of incest avoidance. *In:* R. Fox (ed.), *Biosocial anthropology.* Malaby, London, pp. 37–67.

Brown, R. T. 1975a. Following and visual imprinting in ducklings across a wide age range. *Developmental Psychobiology* 8:27–33.

1975b. Discrepancy from rearing conditions affects chicks' behavior in a novel situation. *Developmental Psychobiology* 8:187–191.

Brown, R. T., & A. S. Hamilton. 1977. Imprinting: effects of discrepancy from rearing conditions on approach to a familiar imprinting object in a novel situation. *Journal of Comparative and Physiological Psychology* 91:784–793.

Burtt, E. H. 1977. Some factors in the timing of parent-chick recognition in swallows. *Animal Behaviour* 25:231–239.

Campbell, B. A., & N. E. Spear. 1972. Ontogeny of memory. *Psychological Reviews* 79:215–236.

Cherfas, J. J. 1977. Visual system activation in the chick: one-trial avoidance learning affected by duration and patterning of light exposure. *Behavioral Biology* 21:52–65.

1978. Simultaneous colour discrimination in chicks is improved by brief exposure to light. *Animal Behaviour* 26:1–5.

Cherfas, J. J., & A. M. Scott. 1981. Impermanent reversal of filial imprinting. *Animal Behaviour* 29:301.

Clarke, A. M., & A. D. B. Clarke. 1976. *Early experience: myth and evidence.* Open Books, London.

Cotman, C. W. 1978. *Neuronal plasticity.* Raven Press, New York.
Davies, S. J. J. F., & R. Carrick. 1962. On the ability of crested terns, *Sterna bergii,* to recognise their own chicks. *Australian Journal of Zoology* 10:171–177.
Evans, R. M. 1970. Imprinting and mobility in young ring-billed gulls, *Larus delawarensis. Animal Behaviour Monographs* 3:193–248.
Fabricius, E. 1964. Crucial periods in the development of the following response in young nidifugous birds. *Zeitschrift für Tierpsychologie* 21:326–337.
Fischer, G. J. 1970. Arousal and impairment: temperature effects on following during imprinting. *Journal of Comparative and Physiological Psychology* 73:412–420.
Gallagher, J. 1976. Sexual imprinting: effects of various regimens of social experience on mate preference in Japanese quail *Coturnix coturnix japonica. Behaviour* 57:91–114.
Gallagher, J. E. 1977. Sexual imprinting: a sensitive period in Japanese quail (*Corturnix coturnix japonica*). *Journal of Comparative and Physiological Psychology* 91:72–78.
Gottlieb, G. 1961. Developmental age as a baseline for determination of the critical period in imprinting. *Journal of Comparative and Physiological Psychology* 54:422–427.
1971. *Development of species identification in birds.* University of Chicago Press, Chicago.
Guiton, P. 1959. Socialization and imprinting in brown leghorn chicks. *Animal Behaviour* 7:26–34.
1966. Early experience and sexual object-choice in the brown leghorn. *Animal Behaviour* 14:534–538.
Hess, E. H. 1959. Imprinting. *Science* 130:133–141.
1973. *Imprinting.* Van Nostrand Reinhold, New York.
Hinde, R. A. 1962. Sensitive periods and the development of behaviour. *In:* S. A. Barnett (ed.), *Lessons from animal behaviour for the clinician.* National Spastics Society, London, pp. 25–36.
1970. *Animal behaviour,* 2nd ed. McGraw-Hill, New York.
1974. *Biological bases of human social behaviour.* McGraw-Hill, New York.
Hoffman, H. S., & P. de Paulo. 1977. Behavioral control by an imprinting stimulus. *American Scientist* 65:58–66.
Hoffman, H. S., & A. M. Ratner. 1973a. A reinforcement model of imprinting: implications for socialisation in monkeys and men. *Psychological Reviews* 80:527–544.
1973b. Effects of stimulus and environmental familiarity on visual imprinting in newly hatched ducklings. *Journal of Comparative and Physiological Psychology* 85:11–19.
Hoffman, H. S., J. L. Searle, S. Toffey, & F. Kozma, Jr. 1966. Behavioral control by an imprinted stimulus. *Journal of the Experimental Analysis of Behaviour* 9:177–189.
Horn, G., S. P. R. Rose, & P. P. G. Bateson. 1973. Experience and plasticity in the central nervous system. *Science* 181:506–514.
Immelmann, K. 1969. Ueber den Einfluss frühkindlicher Erfahrungen auf die geschlechtliche Objektfixierung bei Estrildiden. *Zeitschrift für Tierpsychologie* 26:677–691.
1972. Sexual and other long-term aspects of imprinting in birds and other species. *In:* D. S. Lehrman, R. A. Hinde, & E. Shaw (eds.), *Advances in the study of behavior,* vol. 4. Academic Press, New York, pp. 147–174.
1975. The evolutionary significance of early experience. *In:* G. Baerends, C. Beer, & A. Manning (eds.), *Function and evolution in behaviour.* Clarendon Press, Oxford, pp. 243–253.

Jain, S. K. 1976. The evolution of inbreeding in plants. *Annual Review of Ecology and Systematics* 7:469–495.

James, H. 1959. Flicker: an unconditioned stimulus for imprinting. *Canadian Journal of Psychology* 13:59–67.

Klinghammer, E. 1967. Factors influencing choice of mate in altricial birds. *In:* H. W. Stevenson, E. H. Hess, & H. I. Reingold (eds.), *Early behavior. Comparative and developmental approaches.* Wiley, New York, pp. 5–42.

Klopfer, P. H. 1965. Imprinting: a reassessment. *Science* 147:302–303.

Kovach, J. K. 1970. Critical period or optimal arousal? Early approach behavior as a function of stimulus, age, and breed variables in chicks. *Developmental Psychology* 3:73–77.

Landsberg, J.-W. 1976. Posthatch age and developmental age as a baseline for determination of the sensitive period for imprinting. *Journal of Comparative and Physiological Psychology* 90:47–52.

Landsberg, J.-W., & J. Weiss. 1976. Stress and increase of the corticosterone level prevent imprinting in ducklings. *Behaviour* 57:173–189.

MacDonald, G. E. 1968. Imprinting: drug-produced isolation and the sensitive period. *Nature* 217:1158–1159.

McClelland, D. C., & R. A. Clarke. 1953. Discrepancy hypothesis. *In:* D. C. McClelland, J. W. Atkinson, R. A. Clarke, & E. L. Lowell (eds.), *The achievement motive.* Appleton-Century-Crofts, New York, pp. 42–66.

Martin, J. T. 1975. Hormonal influences on the evolution and ontogeny of imprinting behaviour in the duck. *In:* W. H. Gispen, Tj. B. Van Wimersma Greidanus, B. Bohus, & D. de Wied (eds.), *Hormones, homeostasis and the brain: progress in brain research,* vol. 42. Elsevier, Amsterdam, pp. 357–366.

Martin, J. T., & F. Schutz. 1974. Arousal and temporal factors in imprinting in mallards. *Developmental Psychobiology* 7:69–78.

Mather, K. 1943. Polygenic inheritance and natural selection. *Biological Reviews* 18:32–64.

Maynard Smith, J. 1978. *The evolution of sex.* Cambridge University Press, Cambridge.

Millikan, G. C. 1972. The development of filial behaviour in ducklings. *Behaviour* 43:13–47.

Moltz, H., & L. J. Stettner. 1961. The influence of patterned light deprivation on the critical period for imprinting. *Journal of Comparative and Physiological Psychology* 54:279–283.

Overton, D. A. 1974. Experimental methods for the study of state-dependent learning. *Federation Proceedings* 33:1800–1813.

Paulson, G. W. 1965. Maturation of evoked responses in the duckling. *Experimental Neurology* 11:324–333.

Polt, J. M., & E. H. Hess. 1964. Following and imprinting: effects of light and social experience. *Science* 143:1185–1187.

1966. Effects of social experience on the following response in chicks. *Journal of Comparative and Physiological Psychology* 61:268–270.

Rajecki, D. W. 1973. Imprinting in precocial birds: interpretation, evidence, and evaluation. *Psychological Bulletin* 79:48–58.

Ratner, A. M., & H. S. Hoffman. 1974. Evidence for a critical period for imprinting in khaki campbell ducklings (*Anas platyrhynchos domesticus*). *Animal Behaviour* 22:249–255.

Riesen, A. H. 1975. *The developmental neuropsychology of sensory deprivation.* Academic Press, New York.

Rubel, E. W. 1970. Effects of early experience on fear behaviour of *Coturnix coturnix. Animal Behaviour* 18:427–433.

Salzen, E. A. 1966. The interaction of experience, stimulus characteristics and exogenous androgen in the behaviour of domestic chicks. *Behaviour* 26:286–322.

Salzen, E. A., & C. C. Meyer. 1968. Reversibility of imprinting. *Journal of Comparative and Physiological Psychology* 66:269–275.

Schneirla, T. C., & J. S. Rosenblatt. 1963. "Critical periods" in the development of behavior. *Science* 139:1110–1115.

Schutz, F. 1965. Sexuelle Prägung bei Anatiden. *Zeitschrift für Tierpsychologie* 22:50–103.

Scott, J. P. 1962. Critical periods in behavioral development. *Science* 138:949–958.

Sluckin, W. 1972. *Imprinting and early learning*, 2nd ed. Methuen, London.

Sluckin, W., & E. A. Salzen. 1961. Imprinting and perceptual learning. *Quarterly Journal of Experimental Psychology* 13:65–77.

Smith, F. V., & K. H. Nott. 1970. The "critical period" in relation to the strength of the stimulus. *Zeitschrift für Tierpsychologie* 27:108–115.

Stockard, C. R. 1921. Developmental rate and structural expression: an experimental study of twins, "double monsters" and single deformities, and the interaction among embryonic organs during their origin and development. *American Journal of Anatomy* 28:115–275.

Sutherland, N. S., & N. J. Mackintosh. 1971. *Mechanisms of animal discrimination learning*. Academic Press, New York.

Talmon, Y. 1964. Mate selection in collective settlements. *American Sociological Review* 29:491–508.

Tees, R. C. 1976. Perceptual development in mammals. *In:* G. Gottlieb (ed.), *Neural and behavioral specificity: studies on the development of the nervous system*, vol. 3. Academic Press, New York, pp. 281–326.

Thomas, H. 1971. Discrepancy hypothesis: methodological and theoretical considerations. *Psychological Review* 78:249–259.

Tinbergen, N. 1953. *The herring gull's world*. Collins, London.

Vidal, J. -M. 1971. Expérience préliminaire de déclenchement tardif des réactions de poursuite chez le poulet domestique (*Gallus domesticus*). *Compte rendu de l'Académie des Sciences*. Paris, 272:626–628.

1976a. *Empreinte filiale et sexuelle – réflexions sur le processus d'attachement d'après une etude expérimentale sur le coq domestique*. Docteur des Sciences Thèse, University of Rennes.

1976b. L'Empreinte chez les animaux. *La Recherche* 63:24–35.

Weiss, J. , W. Köhler, & J.-W. Landsberg. 1977. Increase of the corticosterone level in ducklings during the sensitive period of the following response. *Developmental Psychobiology* 10:59–64.

Williams, J. T., Jr. 1972. Developmental age and the critical period for imprinting. *Psychonomic Science* 27:167–168.

16

HUMAN MOTHER–INFANT SOCIAL BONDING: IS THERE A SENSITIVE PHASE?

P. HERBERT LEIDERMAN

BACKGROUND

The sensitive or critical period hypothesis[1] for particular developmental phases has intrigued biological scientists since its introduction by embryologists around the turn of the century (see Spemann 1938; Child 1941; Grobstein 1969). Like many hypotheses developed in the physical and biological sciences, the sensitive phase hypothesis was adopted by behavioral scientists, modified, perhaps inadvertently distorted, and gradually embedded in the discipline of developmental psychology. Though this is not the place to provide a detailed history of the introduction of the critical period hypothesis into the behavioral sciences, it should be noted that one of the earliest contributors was Freud (1935), undoubtedly influenced by German embryologists, who suggested a critical period phenomenon in his thesis that the sequence of developmental stages relates to the sensitivity of the erogenous zones (oral, anal, and genital) in infants and children (see Sutherland 1963). Freud postulated that the child's relationship to important individuals (e.g., mother, father, and others) was influenced by the primacy of these erogenous zones in the course of early development, especially the genital phase, ages 4 through 7 years, during which the triadic Oedipal complex is thought to emerge. The development of the child's erogenous zones, and the subsequent fixation thereon that sometimes ensued, was thought to be related to psychopathology and/or certain character traits that emerged later in childhood. Thus, these early developmental periods were critical in the formation of the adult personality.

American biopsychological researchers, possibly following the earlier embryological researchers, used the sensitive phase hypothesis in studies of the effects of endocrinological and temperamental responses in the development of rats (see Denenberg 1964; Rosenblatt 1975; Smotherman et al. 1976 as a summary of this work). However, its more general use in the behavioral sciences was for understanding early social development (see Scott 1962; Scott et al. 1974). Scott, in his work on the development of the social behavior of canine pups, was undoubtedly influenced by the ethologist Konrad Lorenz (1970), who utilized the concept in his study of imprinting in precocial birds. In a series of experiments with the greylag goose, he found that the period about 24 hours after hatching was critical for the development of following behavior.

Other European ethologists (Tinbergen 1951; Hess 1959, 1973; Chap. 14) elaborated on Lorenz's earlier findings. Thus, by the mid-1960s the hypothesis became an integral part of the study of developmental psychology in the United States as well as in Europe.

The hypothesis was recognized as possibly relevant to human studies (see Gray 1958; Moltz 1960; Ambrose 1963), an application summarized in a paper by Caldwell (1962). As applied to humans, the critical period hypothesis was studied in terms of the effect on the infant, particularly the development of the infant's social relationship to an adult figure. The possible bias of considering the development of social interaction as unidirectional was not recognized despite Sears's 1951 warning about the incompleteness of a theory that posits only the effects of the parent on the child. Sears's general theoretical statement about human interaction was made more specific for mother–infant relationships by Gewirtz (1961) in a critique of Bowlby's (1969) and Ainsworth's (1973) attachment theory. Gewirtz suggested that infants learn or are reinforced by maternal behavior, and similarly, that mothers may learn or be reinforced by infant behavior. The evidence for the reciprocality of human interaction was summarized in a paper by Bell (1968). Finally, the temporal dimension in reciprocality of human mother–child interaction was added by Barnett et al. (1970), Klaus et al. (1972), and Brazelton et al. (1974). In these papers, the effect of a time delay in contact between a mother and her infant in the newborn period was used to evaluate the possibility of a sensitive phase in mother–infant social bonding.

Thus the concept of a sensitive phase, developed originally in connection with the behavior of an immature organism in relationship to a mature organism, was now extended to include the converse, the relationship of a mature organism to its offspring. This subtle but quite reasonable extension of the sensitive phase hypothesis implied an equivalence of the mother–infant and infant–mother relationships and ignored the obvious discrepancy in developmental state, prior experience, and biopsychological requirements of the two individuals. The question quite properly raised was, though the sensitive phase hypothesis might be appropriate for describing the development of the infant–mother relationship, is it appropriate for describing the development of the mother–infant relationship?

This chapter will deal primarily with the sensitive phase hypothesis as it applies to the mother–infant relationship. I shall emphasize studies of human social behavior, utilizing information from mammalian studies when appropriate.

MAMMALIAN STUDIES

What is the evidence for a sensitive phase in the development of social bonding or attachment between a mother and her infant? Rosenblatt (1975), one of the most productive researchers in the endeavor to answer this question, demonstrated in his study of parturient and postpartum behavior in rats that both hormonal and environmental events influence the onset and continuance of maternal behavior. He found that hormonal control of maternal behavior in the prepartum and immediate postpartum phases facilitates nest building, lactation, and infant retrieval. He delineated a second phase following parturition, controlled by stimulus conditions in the environment (e.g., the immaturity of the rat pups and stimulation by nursing pups), that precipitates appropriate maternal behavior. Whereas the hormonal events surrounding birth initiate certain maternal behaviors, others are dependent upon the behavior of the pups. Rosenblatt further discovered that behaviors associated with nurturance became evident in the 4-day period following the birth of the rats. This 4-day span was found to be the sensitive phase for maternal development in the rat, the period during which environmental events – in this case, the presence and behavior of immature rats – modified and shaped the behavior of the mother toward them. The major studies of sensitive phases for social behavior in larger mammals were done by Hersher et al. (1963a, 1963b). They found that maternal behavior in sheep and goats was modified by separation of the mother and infant in the immediate neonatal period. Periods of separation as short as 30 minutes modified maternal behavior 3 months afterward. Goats and sheep that have been separated from their infants following birth were more likely partially to reject their infants when tested after 3 months or to be indiscriminately accepting of strange kids and lambs when compared with normal ewes and dams, highly unusual behavior for these species. The sensitive phase for development of the maternal bond was 3 hours after birth. The evidence is that at least three mammalian species – rat, sheep, and goats – have a sensitive phase for the formation of maternal caretaking functions and the development of mother–infant social bonds. Adequately rigorous studies of primates, however, leave the question of a sensitive phase unanswered for the higher mammals (see Suomi et al. 1972; Mason & Kenney 1974).

HUMAN STUDIES

Early contact

Kennell and Klaus (Kennell et al. 1975; Klaus et al. 1975; Klaus and Kennell 1976; Newman et al. 1976), the major proponents of the hypothesis of a sensitive phase in humans, performed an experiment in which the amount of contact between a mother and her infant was varied in the immediate postpartum period. They studied primiparous mothers with normal full-term infants. One group of 14 mothers was permitted to hold their babies for 1 hour during the first 2 hours after birth and for 5 extra hours on each of the next 3 days. The other group of 14 mothers received care that is routine in most United States hospitals – a glimpse of the baby at birth, brief contact for identification at 6 to 8 hours, and then 20 to 30 minutes during feeding every 4 hours. The two groups were matched for age, marital and socioeconomic status (SES), and gender and weight of the infant. Random selection was used in assigning each subject to a group. Each mother returned to the hospital some 29 to 32 days following discharge for a follow-up study consisting of three types of observations: (1) standardized interviews, (2) observations of the mother's behavior during a physical examination of the infant, and (3) a film study of the mother feeding her infant. At 1 month after the birth, mothers in the extended-contact group were reported to be more reluctant to leave their infants with someone else, stood and watched carefully during the physical examination, and showed more soothing behavior when the infant cried. The analysis of the film showed more fondling and en face behavior – that is, eye-to-eye contact – for the extended-contact group.

At 1 year, the extended-contact group was found to spend a greater percentage of time assisting the physician when he examined the infants and soothing the infants when they cried. At 2 years of age, five mothers were selected from each group and the linguistic behavior of the mother toward her infant was evaluated. The extended-contact mothers asked twice as many questions using more words per proposition, fewer content words, more adjectives, and fewer commands than the control mothers. Such verbal behavior was thought to suggest closer social bonding of the mother to her infant.

At 5 years, the children of the extended-contact mothers had significantly higher intelligent quotients (IQ) and more advanced scores on two language tests when compared to the mothers of the routine-contact group. To quote Klaus and Kennell (1976:59): "These findings suggest that just 16 extra hours of contact within the first three days of life affect maternal behavior for one year and possibly longer and offer support for the hypothesis of maternal sensitivity."

My more cautious conclusion would be that under the conditions of this hospital-based study, women who are predominantly unmarried, black, of relatively low SES, and who receive social and psychological support from hospital and clinical researchers, when given the opportunity for early contact with their infants do modify their subsequent behavior toward them. Further, this increased contact and great involvement with the child appears to improve the child's performance on cognitive tests at 5 years of age.

The question still remains as to whether early contact is necessary as well as sufficient to modify maternal behavior and whether or not other factors, such as marital status and lower SES, affect the generalizability of the result. This latter point is especially important because other studies have shown that SES does influence maternal behavior (Tulkin 1973a, 1973b). The issue of whether this early contact constitutes a sensitive phase is not addressed in Kennell and Klaus's papers, as there are no data on early deprivation and then later contact over an extended period for comparison.

Klaus and Kennell continued their studies in Guatemala. Infants in two hospitals were allowed to stay with their mothers for a 45-minute period immediately after birth. The control group was permitted the usual care, very much like that in United States hospitals: routine separation of mother and infant for 8 to 12 hours after birth. Klaus and Kennell (1976) reported that the experimental group breast-fed more and that the infants gained more weight and had fewer infections. Although such factors as SES of the father and weight of the infant were not equivalent in the two groups, the findings were interpreted to support the hypothesis that there may indeed be a sensitive phase immediately postpartum for mother–infant social bonding.

Because of the possible effects of marital status, ethnicity, and SES in the Klaus and Kennell studies, the studies of de Chateau (1976) using a middle-class northern Swedish population became important. De Chateau permitted one group of mothers to have tactile contact during the infant's first 30 minutes of life. Maternal and infant behaviors were evaluated 3 months later by personal interview and home observation. The early-contact mothers reported that they breast-fed for longer periods, adapted more easily to the infant, and had fewer problems with night feeding. Early-contact mothers were also observed to look more steadily en face and to kiss the infants more often. The infants of the early-contact mothers were observed to cry less and smile more. These behaviors are consistent with the social bonding of mother to infant and perhaps infant to mother. One possible caveat to this study is that the early-contact mothers participated more in an instructional program prior to the birth of the child. This finding might indicate that these mothers were highly committed to their infants and felt more at ease with the hospital setting even before the birth of their infants. As in the Klaus and Kennell studies, the specific issue of a sensitive phase was not examined.

The evidence presented by these two research groups appears to support the notion that early contact influences subsequent maternal behavior and is consistent with the possibility of a sensitive phase immediately following birth for mother–infant social bonding. As yet, the question of the duration of the sensitive phase has not been addressed. To examine this proposition, the studies of Leiderman et al. (1973) become relevant.

Separation

The findings of influence of early contact on mother–infant social bonding are not directly relevant to the issue of the duration of a sensitive phase. This issue can be addressed only by studies comparing mothers who have been delayed in early contact and then reestablished it after a period of time with mothers who have not been separated.

My work, begun in 1966, focused on the influence of the infant on maternal behavior, in particular how the absence of the infant in the neonatal period might shape subsequent maternal attitudes and behavior. My colleagues and I utilized the then extant practice of separating a premature infant from its mother until just before it was to be discharged from the hospital. To create an experimental situation, we modified the nursery procedure to permit one group of mothers to participate in the caretaking of their infants while the other group was routinely separated. Mothers in the contact group began their touching and/or caretaking within 1 to 3 days following the infant's birth. This group of mothers was compared to a group of mothers of prematures who experienced the typical separation, generally 2 to 3 months in duration. Both groups were compared to a full-term sample. In this way, we could examine the question of whether an 8- to 12-week separation might constitute a sensitive phase. This experimental manipulation of contact allowed us to determine whether the sensitive phase for mother–infant bonding extended up to and beyond the first 3 months following birth.

In all, 72 mothers, fathers, and their infants were included in this study. Basic observations consisted of interviews and questionnaires of the mothers and, in some cases, the fathers. In these interviews, we were particularly interested in learning about the family relations, the commitment of the mother and father to the infant, and their feelings of competency in caretaking activities. In a measure more directly related to maternal social bonding or attachment behavior, we observed the maternal behaviors in the hospital and in the home at periodic intervals for 21 months after discharge from the hospital. We also measured the infants' physical and psychological growth during the same period, on the assumption that maternal behavior might be reflected in some of these performance tasks. Finally, as a longer-term follow-up, we interviewed as many mothers as were available in the San Francisco Bay Area 5 to 8 years after our last contact. We paid particular attention to the social relationship of the mother to her child, the mother's perception of the child's school performance, the mother's disciplinary techniques, and the infant's physical health and growth, an index of maternal social bonding behavior and attitudes.

The results have been reported in a series of papers (Leiderman et al. 1973; Leiderman and Seashore 1975; Leifer et al. 1972; Seashore et al. 1973). To summarize briefly, we found that the early separation of mother and infant did affect maternal attitude; for example, there was less commitment and self-confidence in the mothers of the separated group. These differences disappeared by 1 month after discharge from the hospital. Maternal behavior was also modified, with less ventral–ventral contact between mother and infant in the separated group. These differences disappeared by approximately 1 year after discharge. For the same time period, it was noted that the SES of the family, play behavior of the infant, and gender of the infant became more important factors in differentiating maternal behavior of the contact and noncontact mothers than the initial experience of nonseparation or separation. The only independent effects were: (1) mothers of boys touched and attended to their infants more than mothers of girls; (2) infants who were more mobile elicited more smiling from their mothers; (3) infants who played more received more attention from their mothers; and (4) mothers of higher SES paid more attention to their infants. However, the amount of variance, a statistical estimate of predictability, accounted for by all these variables for each of the maternal behavior categories, ranged from 21% for looking behavior to 40% for smiling behavior. Thus, there is ample opportunity for other variables not measured in our study to account for differences in maternal behavior.

In the 21-month posthospital discharge evaluations, we found that all differences in maternal behavior among the three groups – premature separated, premature contact, and full term – had disappeared, except that the mothers of prematures, whether or not involved in early contact, touched and attended to their children more than mothers of full terms. Separated mothers of prematures seemed to be especially attentive to their infants. No other maternal behaviors were differentiated either by prematurity or by the early separation experience. Differences in behavior attributed to SES and gender of the infant that were found at 1 year had also disappeared by 21 months. It would appear that other circumstances in the infants' first 2 years, rather than the initial separation, were the major influence in reducing the difference we had found among the three groups at the end of the infants' first year.

In another approach to finding out the effects of separation, we did a multiple regression analysis using initial conditions, maternal attitudes, maternal behaviors, and family status to predict motor and mental performance scores of the infant on the Bayley infant test. For motor performance, we found no independent effect of any of these variables at 21 months. For mental performance, we found that female infants performed better than males, and that infants of high SES performed better than infants of low SES. On maternal attitude and behavior variables, infants whose mothers felt closer to them (dyadization) and held them more closely did less well on infant mental tests. Early separation, prematurity, parity, and birth weight did not predict the mental performance score. The findings suggested that nonsocial variables such as SES and gender are important in accounting for later infant performance and maternal behavior. And when the social variable – dyadization – was considered, mothers who felt more closely tied to their infants, regardless of initial separation or contact conditions, had infants who performed less well on cognitive tests. This finding suggested overprotection by the mothers rather than age-appropriate maternal attachment to their infants.

The inescapable conclusion is that even after the initial 2 to 3 months of separation from their premature infants, mothers do establish social bonds that cannot be differentiated from the bonds established by the mothers of prematures and full-term mothers who initially were not separated from their infants. We concluded from our studies that the sensitive phase of mother–infant social bonding extends at least beyond the first 3 months after birth.

The maternal experience of the early separation, however, did have some measurable later effects – more on the family than on the mother–infant relationship. We found high marital discord, often leading to separation or divorce, in the 2-year period following hospital discharge for the families of infants who were initially separated from their mothers. Gender of the infant, birth order, and family SES did not have a major influence on the parents' marital harmony. After the first 2 years, there was an increase in divorce for families of both the full-term and premature contact groups.

The importance of the mother–infant separation on family stability appears clear. The delay of contact in the neonatal period has a major effect on family dynamics, with much less evidence of disruption of the mother–infant tie. This finding speaks for the desirability of looking beyond the neonatal period and examining the mother–infant relationship in a wider social context. The conclusion is consistent with observations of Clarke-Stewart (1978), who showed the importance of triadic interrelationships among the father, mother, and infant during the infant's first 30 months of life.

Our follow-up study 5 to 8 years after hospital discharge is not conclusive; child observations were not available. Information was obtained only through the mothers' reports. The data indicate that there were no outstanding differences between these two groups on selected child and familial variables as reported by the mother. Whatever the initial effects had been, early contact with or separation from infants, in this sample of 24 mothers, 10 of whom were separated from their infants in the neonatal period, there were no differences between the separated and contact groups.

I conclude from all these data that early contact, that is, contact beginning within 24 to 36 hours after birth, does not produce major changes in maternal behavior and attitudes by 2 and certainly by 5 years after hospital discharge in predominantly middle-class suburban families. Other elements affecting the child from the time of birth – specifically SES of the family, parity of the mother, and gender of the child – seem to play a much larger role in predicting mother and infant behavior. Prematurity and early separation, however, do place the family at greater risk for maintenance of familial bonds, leading to greater likelihood for dissolution of family ties. Thus, factors unrelated to the initial birth contact of the mother with her infant play a larger role in the determination of maternal behavior and later child development than do the events immediately following parturition. A sensitive phase, if it does exist, is at least 3 months in duration and not only influences the mother–infant bond but extends to the familial network.

COMPARISON AND CRITIQUE

The three sets of studies should be compared because the findings are somewhat at variance with one another. Klaus and Kennell and de Chateau were concerned with the first hours of contact after birth. The rationale for emphasizing this period lies in the clinical observation (Klaus and Kennell 1976:66) that infants born of unanesthetized mothers are in a quiet alert state in the first hours after birth and later become less alert. Thus, in the first hour after birth, the infant is presumably in an optimal situation to engage its mother in a social relationship and thus solidify the social bonding between them. In our study, we were not concerned with this initial hour and therefore our studies are not strictly comparable, though the fact remains that the mothers in our study did become socially bonded whether or not initially separated.

Further differences between the Klaus and Kennell and Leiderman studies is the noncomparability in the populations being studied. One can visualize that the East Cleveland urban population is at one end of a continuum for nuclear family organization and the middle-class Stanford Hospital population is at the other. (In the Stanford study, all mothers were married and living with their husbands at the time of entry into the study.) The same contrast holds in an economic dimension. Thus, some of the differences in results between the Klaus and Kennell and Leiderman studies could be attributed to the greater potential for gain by an economically and socially deprived urban group (Cleveland and Guatemala), in which a relatively small modification in the hospital environment could have a very large subsequent effect. In contrast, the potential for gain in the predominantly middle-class population could be much less; therefore, there was less benefit to be gained for this group from changes in hospital practice.[2]

A third point to be considered in comparing the studies in Sweden, Cleveland, Guatemala, and Palo Alto is the emphasis by Klaus and Kennell and de Chateau on breast feeding as an index of social bonding. Breast feeding was absent in our study. There is no evidence that breast feeding per se can be conceived as an index of social bonding, because it is a derivative of cultural values, social and economic conditions in the family, and individual preference. For example, in traditional societies, economic and social conditions dictate breast feeding for all young infants; considerable variations in the social bonding process develop despite the presence of breast feeding. Breast feeding in Western cultures may facilitate social bonding, but it should not be construed as an index of social bonding. Because the evidence in the studies reported by Klaus and Kennell and de Chateau is most clear on the point of prolonged breast feeding by mothers having early contact with their infants, the importance of early contact for the adequate function of a biopsychological process such as breast feeding is obvious. No conclusions about social bonding, however, should be drawn.

For a final comparison between these three studies, it should be noted that Klaus and Kennell's observations were made chiefly in the hospital, whereas de Chateau's observations were made in the hospital and at home. Observations made in a single setting should be carefully evaluated because the importance of contextual and situational variables on human behavior is well known. This factor becomes especially important for the effect of early experience, because imprinting on the environment as well as social object has been reported (see Chap. 14 for a discussion of sensitive phases and imprinting on the environment).

What conclusions can be derived from these studies? The data suggest that although close contact in the immediate neonatal period encourages social bonding for some populations, events occurring later and experience within the family are equally important. The thesis that brief moments of contact in the immediate postpartum period are the most important element in mother-infant social bonding is probably not supported. Yet it is possible that such brief early contact might be sufficient to carry a socially deprived mother above some threshold for social bonding with her infant, though such an experience might have relatively little influence on mothers from less deprived backgrounds. But early contact does not necessarily facilitate social bonding; the data only suggest that this possibility exists for some individuals. The question regarding the length of the sensitive phase remains unanswered.

FUTURE APPROACHES

We have not addressed the question of whether the onset of the sensitive phase for social bonding is initiated at birth or develops before birth. In studies by Bibring (1959; Bibring et al. 1961) of pregnant women who were undergoing psychoanalysis, it was found that some women became strongly attached to their infant at the time of quickening, that is, approximately 5 months into pregnancy. This observation raises the issue of individual differences in maternal attitude toward pregnancy and its influence on the initiation of social bonding. Pertinent to this point on maternal response to an unborn infant is an unpublished study done at Stanford Hospital on unmarried women who had given birth and planned to give their infants up for adoption. Three of five women wanted to see and hold their infants before giving them up; two did not, feeling that in so doing they would become too attached. This clinical observation illustrates the highly individual reactions of mothers to their newborn infants. And from it one could not deduce that the mothers who wanted to see and hold their infants were any more closely bonded than the mothers who did not for fear of becoming too attached to them. This point of individual differences in social bonding behavior in animals is emphasized in Chapter 14.

Another approach to separating the influence of the birth process itself from the psychological concomitants (i.e., social bonding) consists of studying the effects of the father's participation in the birth of the child. The father, of course, would not have the biological experience of childbirth, with the concomitant hormonal changes, but he would experience the arousal effects of participation (see Hoffman and DePaulo 1977). In a recent work by Peterson et al. (1979), the father's attachment and commitment to the infant were examined. By means of interviews and home observations, we studied fathers who participated in the home or hospital birth of their infants and compared their reaction with that of fathers whose first contact with their infant was through the window of the newborn nursery. We found that fathers who were present at the birth of their infant either at home or at the hospital, and who held their infant in the immediate postpartum period, appeared to have greater personal commitment, as measured by both subjective reports and behavioral observations 4 and 8 months later at home. Observations consistent with these findings were reported by Parke (1974) and Greenberg and Morris (1974). We concluded that observation of the infant's birth and contact with the infant immediately postpartum can trigger the attachment process for fathers. The duration of this sensitive phase for fathers, as for mothers, is unknown. We do know, on the basis of clinical reports and naturalistic observations, that the potential for social bonding continues for fathers at least for months, if not years, and is independent of the father's participation in early child care.

Additional evidence that could help elucidate the experiential, temporal, and situational components in the ontogenesis of mother–child social bonding might be the study of mothers of adopted children. Because parents adopt children of different ages, one could test the hypothesis that the onset of the sensitive phase for social bonding of a mother to her child varies according to the age of the child. Partially relevant to this point is research by Kadushin (1967). He found that in children adopted after age 5, the social and behavioral outcome, as measured by school records and parental reports, was successful in over 80% of the sample when evaluated during adolescence. Presumably these children had adequate parenting by the adoptive mother (and father), sufficient for the majority to make an adequate adjustment to school and society. Still other approaches might be to compare parental behavior of adoptive parents with that of natural parents and behavior of mothers and fathers who have both natural and adoptive children. These studies could aid in disentangling the complex series of events bound up in childbirth, early contact, feeding practices, and sensitive phases in early social bonding. Through such studies, we could test whether the sensitive phase continues throughout the greater part of the adult life cycle or becomes attenuated with the passage of time and/or the involvement with other family members.

SUMMARY AND CONCLUSIONS

In summary, there is no doubt that the sensitive phase hypothesis has been heuristically valuable in stimulating research on important events in the development of human social behavior. The ontogeny of social bonding between mother and infant is one important example. The available evidence indicates that for some mothers, early contact is sufficient to modify maternal behavior and, in all likelihood, later mother–infant interaction, although the duration of the effect is not known. These observations indicate that the exposure of the mother to the infant in the period immediately after birth can release appropriate maternal social behavior. Although we do not know that the biological processes in the pregnant, parturient, or postpartum woman condition or influence this behavior, we do have some suggestion of the environmental circumstances that facilitate social behavior. However, the duration, if any, of the sensitive phase following birth for human social bonding remains unknown. Available evidence suggests that it is longer than 3 months and may well continue throughout much of the life cycle. Perhaps even grandmotherhood may retrigger maternal social bonding; as for the social processes involved in grandfatherhood, almost nothing is known. (For a beginning on some aspects of grandparenthood see Epstein 1978; Feldman et al. 1979.)

Although the sensitive phase hypothesis does excite the imagination of ethologically oriented pediatricians, psychologists, and psychiatrists, unqualified acceptance of it can lead to the false assurance that more has actually been proven than is properly warranted. Particularly dangerous is the belief that if proper mother–infant contact is not made in the neonatal period, and if the early mother–infant bond is deficient, subsequent social bonding to other individuals is more difficult. Such a belief may encourage the premature surrender of efforts made by mothers and (fathers) to establish appropriate social bonds with their infant beyond the neonatal period. In other words, the sensitive phase hypothesis does not and should not be construed to predict later social behavior; it can only define some of the influences upon it.

The evolutionary significance of a sensitive phase for human social bonding should at least be mentioned. It is unlikely, for such a complex organism as man, that fixing of an essential bond would occur only in the brief period following childbirth. On the contrary, it is more likely for humans, in whom dependency of a child lasts for years, if not decades, that social bonding systems will have sufficient redundancy to ensure activation of attachment of the mother (and father) to the child.[3] If the social bonding systems are not activated at birth in the normal course of events, then they would quite likely be activated within the infant's first months or years of life. Perhaps the more important issue for the researcher is not to elucidate whether or not there is a sensitive phase for the initiation of social bonds in humans but rather to determine the necessary and sufficient conditions to maintain these bonds once they have been formed. On this point, for humans at least, much additional research has yet to be done.

NOTES

1 For a detailed discussion and comparison of the terms *sensitive, critical,* and *optimum period,* see Hess 1959, 1973 and Chapter 14. In this chapter, the term

sensitive phase will be used and should be understood to include the concept of the critical and optimum periods. (*Critical period,* when used, will indicate historical use of the term by others.)

2 However, this argument would not hold for the de Chateau study, which sampled a predominantly married, middle-class Swedish population.

3 This redundancy is particularly plausible for human mothers, in whom social bonding to several individuals over a lifetime is typical. This prolonging of the sensitive period for mother–infant bonding is consistent with the longer sensitive period for sexual imprinting, absent in some avian species, in contrast to the relatively short sensitive phase for filial imprinting, in which bonding by the immature organism is to a single individual.

ACKNOWLEDGMENTS

The initial empirical research on premature and full-term infants was supported by grants from the U.S. Public Health Service (Hd 02636 and MH 20162/A1) and from the W. T. Grant Foundation, New York.

Follow-up studies on these infants and mothers were supported by funds from the Boys Town Center for Youth Development, Stanford University. However, the opinions expressed or the policies advocated herein do not necessarily reflect those of the Boys Town Center.

My thanks to Dr. David Feigal for interviewing mothers in the follow-up study, to Dr. Marjorie Seashore and Ms. Rowena Hardin for statistical analyses, to Ms. Sue Thiemann for research assistance, to Ms. Joan Wolfe for preparation of this manuscript, and to Prof. Klaus Immelmann and Prof. Carl Corter for a critique of an earlier version of the chapter.

Portions of this chapter appeared in *Early Developmental Hazards: Predictors and Precautions,* edited by Frances D. Horowitz, American Association for Advancement of Science Symposium 19, Westview Press, Boulder, Colorado, 1978.

REFERENCES

Ainsworth, M. D. S. 1973. The development of infant–mother attachment. *In:* B. M. Cardwell & H. N. Riccuti (eds.), *Review of child development research,* vol. 3. University of Chicago Press, Chicago.

Ambrose, J. A. 1963. The concept of a critical period for the development of social responsiveness. *In:* B. M. Foss (ed.), *Determinants of infant behavior II.* Methuen, London.

Barnett, C. R., P. H. Leiderman, R. Grobstein, & M. H. Klaus. 1970. Neonatal separation, the maternal side of interaction deprivation. *Pediatrics* 45:197–205.

Bell, R. Q. 1968. A reinterpretation of the direction of effects in studies of socialization. *Psychological Review* 75:81–93.

1974. Contributions of human infants in caregiving and social interaction. *In:* M. Lewis & L. A. Rosenblum (eds.), *The effect of the infant on its caregiver.* Wiley, New York, pp. 1–20.

Bibring, G. 1959. Some considerations of the psychological processes in pregnancy. *Psychoanalytical Study of the Child* 14:113–121.

Bibring, G., T. F. Dwyer, D. S. Huntington, & A. F. Valenstein. 1961. A study of the psychological processes in pregnancy and the earliest mother–child relationship. *Psychoanalytical Study of the Child* 16:9–27.

Bowlby, J. 1969. *Attachment and loss,* vol. 1. Hogarth, London.

Brazelton, T. B., B. Koslowski, & M. Main. 1974. *In:* M. Lewis & L. A. Rosenblum (eds.), *The effect of the infant on its caregiver.* Wiley, New York, pp. 49–76.

Caldwell, B. M. 1962. The usefulness of the critical period hypothesis in the study of filiative behavior. *Merrill-Palmer Quarterly* 8:229–242.

Chateau, P. de. 1976. Neonatal care routines: influences on maternal and infant behavior and on breast feeding. *Umea University Medical Dissertations,* New Series #20. Umea, Sweden.

Child, C. M. 1941. *Patterns and problems of development.* University of Chicago Press, Chicago.

Clarke-Stewart, & K. Alison. 1978. And daddy makes three: the father impact on mother and young child. *Child Development* 49:466–478.

Denenberg, V. H. 1964. Critical periods, stimulus input and emotional reactivity: a theory of infantile stimulation. *Psychological Review* 71:335–351.

Epstein, A. L. 1978. *Ethos and identity.* Tavistock, London.

Feldman, S., S. Nash, & S. C. Nash. 1979. Sex differences in responsiveness to babies among mature adults. *Developmental Psychology* 15:430–435.

Freud, S. 1935. *A general introduction to psychoanalysis.* Doubleday, Garden City, New York.

Gewirtz, J. L. 1961. A learning analysis of the effect of normal stimulation, privation and deprivation in the acquisition of social motivation and attachment. *In:* B. M. Foss (ed.), *Determinants of infant behavior,* vol. 1. Methuen, London.

Gray, P. H. 1958. Theory and evidence of imprinting in human infants. *Journal of Psychology* 46:155–166.

Greenberg, M., & N. Morris. 1974. Engrossment: the newborn's impact upon the father. *American Journal of Orthopsychiatry* 44:520–531.

Grobstein, C. 1969. Critical periods in development. *In:* N. Kretchmer & D. N. Walcher (eds.), *Environmental Influences on Genetic Expression.* Fogarty International Proceedings, 2:5–7.

Hersher, L., J. B. Richmond, & A. U. Moore. 1963a. Modifiability of critical period for the development of maternal behavior in sheep and goats. *Behavior* 20:311–319.

1963b. Maternal behavior in sheep and goats. *In:* H. Rheingold (ed.), *Maternal behavior in animals.* Wiley, New York.

Hess, E. 1959. The relationship between imprinting and motivation. *In: Nebraska Symposium on Motivation.* University of Nebraska Press, Lincoln, Nebraska, pp. 44–77.

1973. *Imprinting: early experience and the developmental psychobiology of attachment.* Van Nostrand Reinhold, New York, pp. 36–64, 324–350, 351–423.

Hoffman, H. S., & P. DePaulo. 1977. Behavioral control by an imprinting stimulus. *American Scientist* 65:58–66.

Kadushin, A. 1967. Reversibility of trauma: a follow-up study of children adopted when older. *Social Work* 12:23–33.

Kennell, J. H., M. A. Trause, & M. H. Klaus. 1975. Evidence for a sensitive period in the human mother. *Ciba Foundation Symposium #33, Parent–Infant Interaction.* Elsevier, Amsterdam.

Klaus, M. H., B. S. Jerauld, N. C. Kreger, W. McAlpine, M. Steffa, & J. H. Kennell. 1972. Maternal attachment: importance of the first postpartum days. *New England Journal of Medicine* 286:460–463.

Klaus, M. H., & J. H. Kennell. 1976. *Maternal–infant bonding: the impact of early separation or loss on family development.* Mosby, St. Louis.

Klaus, M. H., M. A. Trause, & J. H. Kennell. 1975. Does human behavior after delivery show a characteristic pattern? *Ciba Foundation Symposium #33, Parent–Infant Interaction.* Elsevier, Amsterdam.

Leiderman, P. H., A. D. Leifer, M. J. Seashore, C. R. Barnett, & R. Grobstein. 1973. Mother–infant interaction: effects of early deprivation, prior experience and sex of infant. *In:* J. I. Nurnberger (ed.), *Biological and environmental determinants of early development. ARNMD* vol. 51. Williams & Wilkins, Baltimore.

Leiderman, P. H., & M. J. Seashore. 1975. Mother–infant separation: some delayed consequences. *Ciba Foundation Symposium #33, Parent–Infant Interaction.* Elsevier, Amsterdam.

Leifer, A. D., P. H. Leiderman, C. R. Barnett, & J. A. Williams. 1972. Effects of mother–infant separation on maternal attachment behavior. *Child Development* 43:1203–1213.

Lorenz, K. Z. 1970. *Studies in human and animal behaviour,* vol. 1. Harvard University Press, Cambridge, Massachusetts.

Mason, W. A., & M. D. Kenney. 1974. Redirection of filial attachments in rhesus monkeys: dogs as mother surrogates. *Science* 183:1209–1211.

Moltz, H. 1960. Imprinting: empirical basis and theoretical significance. *Psychological Bulletin* 57:291–314.

Newman, L. F., J. H. Kennell, & J. M. Schrieber. 1976. *Early human interactions: mother and child in primary care, clinics in office practice.* Saunders, Philadelphia, pp. 491–506.

Parke, R. 1974. Father–infant interaction. *In:* M. H. Klaus, T. Leger, & M. A. Trause (eds.), *Maternal attachment and mothering disorders: a round table panel.* Johnson & Johnson, Sausalito, California.

Peterson, G. H., L. E. Mehl, & P. H. Leiderman. 1979. The role of some birth related variables in father attachment. *American Journal of Orthopsychiatry* 49:330–338.

Rosenblatt, J. S. 1975. Prepartum and postpartum regulation of maternal behavior in the rat. *Ciba Foundation Symposium #33, Parent–Infant Interaction.* Elsevier, Amsterdam.

Scott, J. P. 1962. Critical periods in behavioral development. *Science* 38:949–958.

Scott, J. P., J. H. Stewart, & V. DeChett. 1974. Critical periods in the organization of systems. *Developmental Psychobiology* 7:489–513.

Sears, R. R. 1951. A theoretical framework for personality and social behavior. *American Psychologist* 6:476–483.

Seashore, M. J., A. D. Leifer, C. R. Barnett, & P. H. Leiderman. 1973. The effects of denial of early mother–infant interaction on maternal self-confidence. *Journal of Personality and Social Psychology* 26:369–378.

Smotherman, W. P., J. Wiener, S. P. Mendoza, & S. Levine. 1976. Pituitary–adrenal responsiveness of rat mothers to noxious stimuli and stimuli produced by pups. *Ciba Foundation Symposium #45, Breast-Feeding and the Mother.* Elsevier, Amsterdam.

Spemann, H. 1938. *Embryonic development and induction.* Yale University Press, New Haven.

Suomi, S., H. Harlow, & W. McKinney. 1972. Monkey psychiatrists. *American Journal of Psychiatry* 128:927–932.

Sutherland, J. D. 1963. The concepts of imprinting and critical period from a psychoanalytic viewpoint. *In:* B. M. Foss (ed.), *Determinants of infant behavior II.* Wiley, New York.

Tinbergen, N. 1951. *The study of instinct.* Oxford University Press, New York.

Tulkin, S. R. 1973a. Social class differences in infant's reactions to mother's and stranger's voice. *Developmental Psychology* 8:137–141.

1973b. Social class differences in attachment behaviors of ten-month old infants. *Child Development* 44:171–174.

PART V

COMPARATIVE ASPECTS

INTRODUCTION

GEORGE W. BARLOW and
LEWIS PETRINOVICH

Comparative studies of behavior seem to have passed out of fashion. Yet the information gained by systematically comparing different species can be enormously valuable. It is hard enough, at present, to find developmental studies of behavior for single species, not to mention programmatic phyletic or ecological analyses. One can only hope that as the field grows, more investigations of the diversity of developmental strategies within and between related taxa or guilds will appear. The first two chapters of this part are steps in the right direction. One treats crickets and grasshoppers, whereas the other covers a wide range of fish species. Of the two chapters dealing with birds, one is on song and the other on orientation. The last chapter searches for the roots of human speech.

In organizing the Bielefield Project, it was hard to find biologists studying the development of behavior but easy to find psychologists. Most of the readers of this book will probably be interested in human behavior and they might be tempted to pass over broadly comparative reports of animal behavior, particularly of insects and fishes. All of these chapters, however, make significant contributions to the general problems of behavioral development.

Chapter 17, by Norbert Elsner, explains the relevance of the study of insect behavior to that of mammals. In the past, some important neurophysiological mechanisms of behavior were first discovered in the invertebrates. Those discoveries provided models that guided the search for their counterparts in the nervous systems of mammals, with rewarding results. Chapter 17 lays out the reasons insects are suited for further research and discoveries. The insects studied, crickets and grasshoppers, have a wealth of stereotyped motor patterns. This fact facilitates the task of relating those patterns to their neurophysiological substrates. Such behavior is readily elicited in the laboratory, and the insects will perform even when wired up with numerous electrodes in their central nervous system, effectors, and receptors. In addition, ontogeny consists of a succession of discrete intervals marked by molts, which simplifies questions of developmental stages. One of the clearest results of this research is the phenomenon of forward reference. Repeatedly, these insects develop the neurological organization for complex motor behavior well before the behavior appears.

Chapter 18, by David L. G. Noakes, approaches the development of behavior in fishes from the opposite end of the spectrum. Rather than examining behavior and the nervous system in detail, it searches for broad evolutionary themes that appear to transcend the animals under immediate consideration. This is done by comparing fishes within an ecological classification instead of the traditional phyletic scheme.

Chapter 18 relies on two concepts. One is that development can be regarded as consisting of five periods from the embryo to the adult; such events as birth or hatching do not define the periods. The chapter asks whether the application of this developmental classification might not be appropriate to comparisons across other animal groups as well. For example, the human infant might best be considered as an extension of the embryonic period; the behavioral reorganization (discontinuity) that characterizes later development of the infant (see Chap. 22) might mark the onset of a new period.

The other concept is that of reproductive guilds. Their use compels a consideration of the ecological circumstances promoting an early occurrence of hatching or birth (altriciality) as contrasted to a later occurrence when the organism is better developed (precociality). An understanding of the demographic relationships is relevant to the developmental strategies of all animals and should be kept in mind when reading the other chapters that follow.

Chapter 19, by William T. Keeton, on bird orientation is tightly focused. This pithy chapter first reviews the major findings on the development of the ability of songbirds to use stars to guide their migratory flights. Then it covers the phenomenon of homing in pigeons and its development. The same broad array of factors found in other developmental studies emerges, including early sensitive phases, maturational constraints, and fine tuning through continual experience. For instance, pigeons learn to integrate information about time, direction, and azimuth of the sun in perfecting their sun compass; that information is integrated with magnetic cues. The study of navigation among birds has had a history of long, slow, and uneven progress. Analyzing its development has greatly accelerated that progress.

Chapter 20, by Donald E. Kroodsma, contains an overview of one of the most promising fields of comparative developmental study: the ontogeny of bird song. That ontogeny is characterized, at one extreme, by species that show a rigid sequence of development that requires little stimulus input and, at the other extreme, by a plastic, stimulus-dependent mechanism that exhibits many aspects of other phase-specific mechanisms. The chapter considers both proximate and ultimate explanations of vocal imitation, the importance of improvisation, studies of selective learning, the possible role of female choice in mate selection, and the neurophysiology of vocal ontogeny. The specific questions raised are considered in light of Kroodsma's research on the nature of song development in the marsh wren.

One of the central questions in song development concerns the existence of learned dialectical differences among several species of songbirds. The chapter emphasizes the importance of understanding patterns of mating and dispersal to resolve the controversies that have arisen in this area. Finally, it reviews the interesting research that suggests there is neural lateralization in some species of songbirds, a pattern analogous to that found in the human language system.

This theme is developed at some length in Chapter 21, by the psycholinguist Michael Studdert-Kennedy.

At the editors' behest, Studdert-Kennedy has attempted the difficult task of characterizing the nature of language at a level comprehensible to investigators not familiar with the complexities and niceties of linguistics and phonetics. Chapter 21 reviews his research on acoustic feature detectors and considers a highly developed human signaling system - nonvocal mammalian sign language. It concludes that the research on training apes to communicate by means of artificial symbols is more useful in teaching us about the evolutionary origins of mind than of language. The theme stated in Chapter 20 is reiterated: The analogues of bird song might be more useful in providing insight into the origins of language than are the possible homologues of ape signs. This conclusion rests on the distinction argued in Chapter 2: The species atypicality of ape language suggests that it should not be compared to the species-typical human language systems.

17

DEVELOPMENTAL ASPECTS OF INSECT NEUROETHOLOGY

NORBERT ELSNER

During the last decade, insects have increasingly attracted both ethologists and neurobiologists who are interested in the ontogeny of behavior and its underlying neuronal mechanisms. Insects produce a rich variety of behaviors ranging from simple locomotory activities such as walking or flying to complex patterns such as stridulation and courtship displays. To the ethologist, in particular, communicative behavior of orthopterans (crickets, katydids, grasshoppers) is of interest because the acoustic and visual displays provide excellent examples of action patterns called *Erbkoordination* by Konrad Lorenz and more recently *Modal Action Patterns* by Barlow (1968, 1977). These clearly favor developmental studies because the stereotyped adult behavior serves as a standard against which the growing pattern can be measured (Bentley & Hoy 1970).

To the neurobiologist, insect behavior provides an important advantage: It can easily be elicited in the laboratory, even under the conditions of electrophysiological recording. Techniques have been developed to record the activities of central nervous and neuromuscular units during the performance of elaborate behavior. This effort has led to considerable progress in revealing the functions and interactions of nerve cells, receptors, and effector organs underlying behavior. A new term, *neuroethology,* is used for this field of research, which combines the ethological and neurophysiological approaches to the understanding of animal behavior (reviews and books: Fentress 1976; Hoyle 1970; Huber 1975; Usherwood & Newth 1975).

One of the most attractive and promising aspects of neuroethology is that it is not restricted to the study of behavior of adult and fully grown animals. As in classical ethology, developmental, genetic, and evolutionary aspects are taken into consideration. This chapter focuses on the neuroethology of insect stridulation and flight, with particular emphasis on ontogenetic questions. It is not a comprehensive review, but rather an introduction to the neuroethological approach to the development of animal behavior. The reader will find more and detailed information in the reviews by Bentley (1973), Elsner and Popov (1978), Kutsch (1977), Wilson (1968), and Young (1973) (see also Chap. 8, which covers the genetic aspects of the development of motor patterns).

A NEUROETHOLOGICAL APPROACH TO STRIDULATION AND FLIGHT OF ORTHOPTERAN INSECTS

Sound production of crickets and grasshoppers

Orthopteran insects are known for their highly developed acoustic behavior. Genetically mediated sound patterns are used during intraspecific communication and are especially important in pair formation and territorial behavior. There are numerous review articles and books covering the field, in which one can find detailed information (Bennet-Clark 1971; Busnel 1963; Elsner & Huber 1973; Elsner & Popov 1978; Huber 1975; Michelsen & Nocke 1974). For the convenience of the reader, a few remarks are made on the acoustic behavior of those orthopterans mainly used for neuroethological studies.

Crickets (Grylloidea) and katydids (Tettigonioidea) have developed an elytroelytral mechanism of sound production: A row of sclerotized teeth on the undersurface of one forewing (elytron) is scraped sonorously past the inside edge (plectrum) of the other. In most cricket species, sound is produced only during the inward (closing) movement of the elytra, whereas in many katydids both directions of movement may be sonorous.

For a long time, neuroethological work has been concentrated almost exclusively on the European field cricket *Gryllus campestris* and some closely related species (Huber 1975). More recently, these studies have been extended to species native to the southern Soviet Union (Popov et al. 1974; see Fig. 17.1) and to species found in the Southern Hemisphere such as *Teleogryllus commodus* and *T. oceanicus* (Bentley & Hoy 1970). In all these species, as well as in most other crickets and katydids, only the males stridulate. They have developed a rich acoustic repertoire containing several distinct types of songs. These genetically mediated sound patterns are produced in different behavioral contexts and, therefore, have been named according to their biological context. Calling song, for example, is emitted by single males to attract conspecific females. As soon as a female has approached, the male changes to courtship song, which precedes mating. As part of the territorial and fighting behavior in male-to-male-interactions, a high-intensity rivalry song is produced. The calling song patterns of several cricket species are shown in Figure 17.1.

Among grasshoppers and locusts (Acridoidea), many species belonging to the subfamily Gomphocerinae have evolved extremely complex acoustic behavior. In contrast to crickets, these orthopterans are unique in that they employ simultaneously two stridulatory elements, that is, the two hindlegs each rubbing its femoral row of stridulatory pegs against a vein of the ipsilateral elytron (femuroelytral method). The two legs move with a distinct phase lag. Surprisingly in some species, different patterns are produced simultaneously by the two hindlegs. From time to time the legs change their part (Elsner 1974; see Fig. 17.5B).

As in crickets, the males produce several species-specific song patterns that have distinct behavioral significance. Due to the rapid speciation this group has undergone, the stridulatory patterns are often complex and contain several layers of rhythmicity. In some species, courtship behavior has been elaborated beyond song in that hindleg stridulation is accompanied by movements of

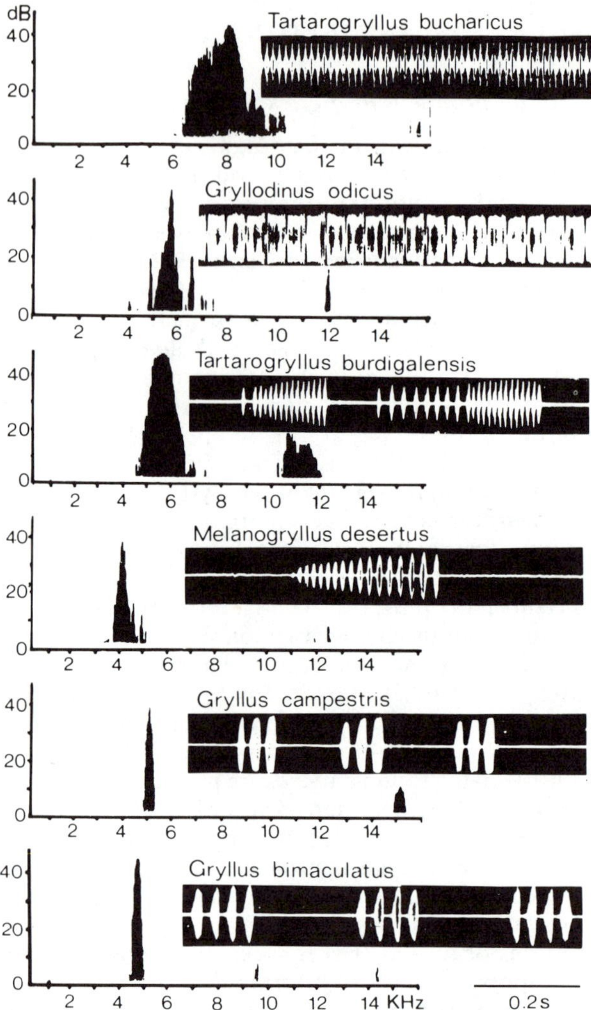

Figure 17.1. Calling song patterns and frequency spectra of cricket species native to the southern Soviet Union. (From Elsner & Popov 1978)

other parts of the body, for example the head, the palps, and the antennae (Jacobs 1953; Elsner 1968). Remarkably, not only the males but also the females (at least, as long as they are virgins) produce sounds in response to male stridulation.

Flight in orthopteran insects

Compared with stridulation, flight patterns appear primitive, because there is only one continuous rhythm that is not further modulated. Wing-beat rate depends on the size of the insect. In the large migratory locust *Locusta migratoria* it is about 18 to 20 Hz, whereas it is 50 to 55 Hz in small gomphocerine grasshoppers such as *Chorthippus biguttulus* (see Wilson 1968).

Some aspects of the neuromuscular basis and the central nervous control of stridulation and flight

If one wants to study the neuronal basis of complex behavior such as orthopteran stridulation, and even flight in these insects, one is confronted with a fundamental technical problem: Normally, recordings of nervous activity require a tethered animal with its nervous system exposed for microelectrode recordings. To the ethologist, at first sight, this must be a horrifying situation because it seems to prevent the performance of any reliable behavioral activity.

Further problems arise in the case of developmental studies: Cricket stridulation and flight in all orthopteran insects are impossible during larval life because the wings are not developed before the animals molt to adulthood. Is it possible to follow the ontogeny of motor patterns that are not expressed as visible movements during their development? Two methods have been developed to overcome these difficulties.

First, if the brain is stimulated mechanically or electrically, stridulatory motor patterns can be evoked in larval and adult crickets and grasshoppers (Bentley & Hoy 1970; Huber 1955, 1960). During these performances, recordings can be made from neurons that belong to the central networks generating the motor output for stridulation (Bentley 1969; Hedwig unpublished; Otto unpublished). Of course, the combination of two sophisticated techniques (focal brain stimulation and selective recordings from the central nervous system) is not easy and, therefore, has not yet become an everyday lab routine. For many neuroethological questions another method might be more favorable, one that allows electrophysiological work in almost freely moving animals.

Second, instead of recording directly from the central nervous system, one may start at the periphery, that is, record first the pattern of motor activity that is sent from the central nervous system to the effector organs. Hoyle (1964) invented an elegant method to monitor indirectly this pattern in unrestrained and normally behaving insects via flexible wire electrodes implanted in the muscles involved in the behavior of interest. The motoneuronal (i.e., central nervous) activity on which muscle excitation is based can be deduced from such recordings because a fixed one-to-one relationship exists between the action potential of muscle fibers and the motoneurons driving them. Even in small gomphocerine grasshoppers, up to 30 electrodes can be implanted without restraining their behavior (Fig. 17.2A). The electrodes can be left chronically implanted up to 6 weeks, a feature that is essential for developmental studies.

This technique has been widely used to monitor the patterns of central nervous output underlying insect behavior – for example, flight in locusts (Wilson & Weis-Fogh 1962), crickets (Bentley & Hoy 1970; Kutsch 1969) and saturniid and sphingid moths (Kammer 1968) and stridulation in crickets and grasshoppers (Elsner 1968, 1975; Huber 1965; Kutsch 1969). There is not enough space to describe these patterns in detail; therefore, the reader is

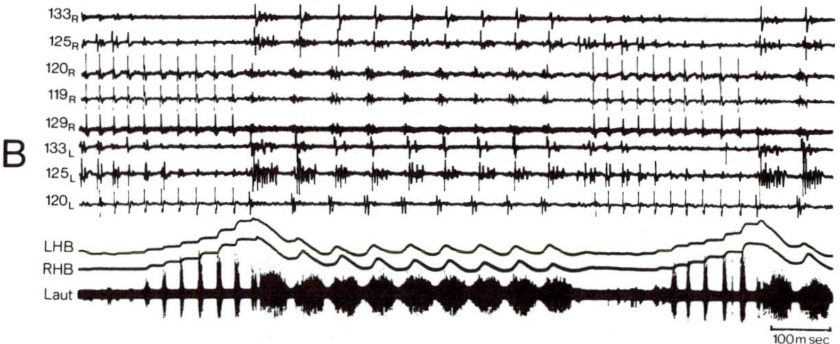

Figure 17.2. *A*. The alpine grasshopper, *Stenobothrus rubicundus,* sonorously beating its wings during courtship behavior. Twenty-five flexible wire electrodes have been chronically implanted in the muscles in order to monitor the underlying neuromuscular activity.
B. Simultaneous recordings of the sound pattern (Laut), the stridulatory movements of the left (LHB) and right (RHB) hindlegs, and the neuromuscular activity during courtship song of the grasshopper *Stauroderus scalaris*. 125, 133: depressor muscles; 119, 120, 129: elevator muscles; L, R: left side, right side. (*B* from Koppers 1977)

referred to Figures 17.2 to 17.5. Because of the small number of motoneurons that supply each insect muscle, and because of the surprisingly high selectivity of the recordings, it is possible to identify electrophysiologically individual motor units (Elsner 1967, 1975). Thus, one can describe complex behavior such as stridulation in terms of the activity of a known group of motoneurons. With regard to the neuroethological goal of these investigations, it is important that this technique can be combined with other methods of monitoring behavior. In stridulating grasshoppers, for instance, we have simultaneously recorded (1) the sound pattern, (2) the corresponding hindleg movements, and (3) the underlying neuromuscular activity pattern (Fig. 17.2B).

Knowing the pattern of central nervous output underlying flight and stridulation, one has an excellent basis for further investigations in various directions. As one example, one can ask whether these motor patterns are autonomously generated by central nervous networks or whether their production also depends on sensory feedback. Recording the neuromuscular activity is a useful tool for attacking this problem because the motor patterns can be monitored even after operations that eliminate any visible behavior.

In crickets and grasshoppers, the stridulating elytra and hindlegs were fixed in various positions, loaded, or even cut off. Nevertheless, these animals continued to stridulate normally at the neuromuscular level, that is, the normal neuromuscular stridulatory motor pattern could be recorded. One can hardly get a better impression of what is called a *centrally programmed motor pattern* than by studying electrophysiologically a cricket or a grasshopper singing without stridulatory organs. Despite these severe peripheral ablations, by which all possible proprioceptive feedback was destroyed, the central nervous system continued to produce the specifically patterned stridulatory motor activity. The temporal pattern remained basically unchanged, at least over the short term (Elsner & Huber 1969; Kutsch & Huber 1970). Such ablation experiments show what the central nervous system is capable of doing autonomously. Of course, they do not exclude the possibility that a centrally generated rhythm is modulated by sensory influence (Wendler 1974, 1978).

DEVELOPMENT OF FLIGHT AND STRIDULATORY MOTOR PATTERNS

Some general remarks

Recordings of the movements and the underlying neuromuscular activity have shown that insect flight and stridulation are precisely structured behavior patterns, predominantly programmed by the central nervous system. Remarkably, except for a gradual increase in flight frequency that occurs during the first 3 weeks of adult life in orthopterans (see "Orthoptera"), the patterns are already complete at the time of their first performance in adult animals. Even the most elaborate songs of crickets and grasshoppers are perfectly structured species-specifically at the moment of their emergence in adults, and no further practice is needed to improve the patterns. Thus, one has to look at larval life when investigating the ontogeny of these behaviors.

At first sight, it seems impossible to follow the development of behaviors produced by the wings, for example, insect flight and cricket stridulation. During larval life, insects lack the wings to perform flight or singing movements. Therefore, even if there exist premature forms of such behavior, there is no possibility of monitoring them with conventional methods. Fortunately, recordings of the patterns of neuromuscular activity underlying flight and stridulation are a way to solve this crucial problem. Originally, this technique was designed mainly to get an insight into the central nervous control of behavior. Beyond that, however, it is a useful tool for developmental studies. The experiments reviewed briefly above have demonstrated that it is possible to monitor behavior (in terms of neuromuscular activity) even if it is not expressed as visible movements. Given that one succeeds in stimulating the developing neuronal networks appropriately, larval flight and stridulatory motor patterns can be monitored. In other words, the neurophysiological technique makes it feasible for the investigator to approach the otherwise invisible development of insect behavior.

Development of flight motor patterns

Orthoptera. Crickets, grasshoppers, and locusts belong to the group of hemimetabolous insects, that is, they undergo a gradual metamorphosis. The larvae hatching from the eggs already resemble the adults in most characters except that they still lack the wings and have only immovable pads. The number of larval stages – each separated from the next by a molt – varies: In European grasshoppers it is 4, whereas migratory locusts go through 5 and crickets through 10 to 12 stages. In all groups, it is not until final ecdysis that the wings are drawn out of the pads, spread, and hardened. First flights are performed 1 to 2 days after reaching adulthood.

We know that in hemimetabolous insects such as grasshoppers and crickets the neuronal motor system is almost complete in early instars, as far as the number of neurons is concerned. In contrast, the number of sensory fibers increases by a factor of 10 to 100 during larval life (Edwards & Palka 1973). In both systems the complex of dendritic arborization increases enormously during this period. At what age are the connections among motor neurons and between the motor and sensory systems formed to enable the generation of patterned activity?

Bentley and Hoy (1970) implanted wire electrodes in the flight muscles of larval crickets (*Teleogryllus commodus*) and held the animals in the warm air stream of a wind tunnel. The larvae displayed the typical flight posture of adults: The forelegs and middle legs were drawn to the body and the hindlegs were straight, parallel to the body axis. The first definite signs of flight motor activity were detected in nymphs of the seventh instar, that is, in larvae that have to undergo four more molts before becoming adults equipped with wings. In the seventh and eighth instars a regular activity of some depressor muscles, at about half the flight frequency, were observed (Fig. 17.3A/a–b). This pattern developed further by the recruitment of antagonistic muscles in the ninth instar (Fig. 17.3A/c); however, the phase relationship between the two sets was not yet stable. In the final larval instar (tenth stage) all flight muscles were recruited and coordination among them was correct, although the repetition rate remained lower than in adult flight (Fig.17.3A/d). Apart from this detail, the neuronal network generating the flight motor pattern appeared to be almost fully matured before the animal reached adulthood.

Findings such as those of Bentley and Hoy (1970) reinforced the popular belief that the development of behavior in insects proceeds without significant

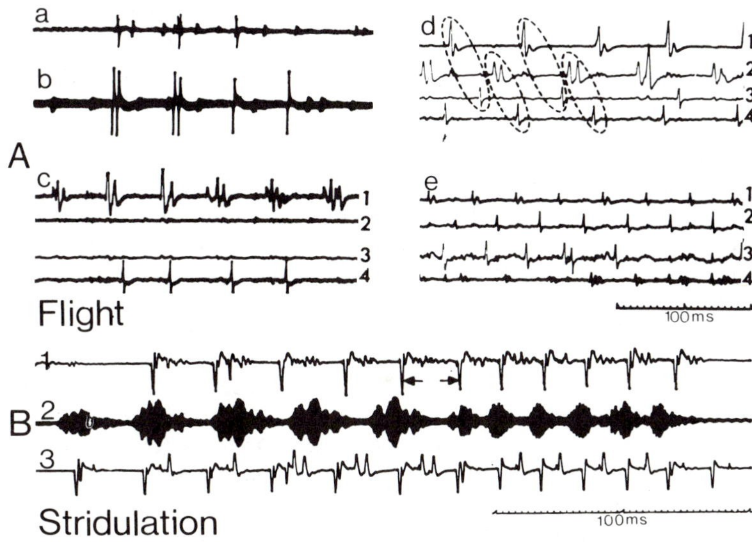

Figure 17.3. *A*. The progressive development of the flight motor patterns in nymphal crickets (*Teleogryllus commodus*). Oscillograms a, b, c: fourth, third, and second to last instar stages; oscillogram d: last instar; oscillogram e: adult cricket. The recordings are from a hindwing depressor muscle (a, b; trace 1 in c, d, e), a hindwing elevator (trace 2 in c, d, e), a forewing depressor (trace 3), and a forewing elevator (trace 4).
B. Comparison of the stridulatory motor output pattern (traces 1 and 3) of a cricket nymph with the actual song of an adult (trace 2). (From Bentley & Hoy 1970)

effects of experience. However, Weber (1972, 1974) has shown that within that short period, experience can influence the precision of such larval flight motor patterns to some degree. When nymphs of the eighth instar of the cricket *Gryllus campestris* were held in a windstream, they produced, just like *Teleogryllus* larvae, a rhythmic neuromuscular pattern of activity that could be identified as the motor pattern of adult flight. In the first "flight" this larval pattern was unstable, that is, the variance of the spike intervals (corresponding to the wing stroke intervals in adults) was higher than in adults. However, during subsequent performances the variance decreased considerably from one larval flight to the next. But this stabilization effect did not persist; after a 10-minute rest between performances, the variance of the spike intervals became as low as before.

In larval locusts (*Schistocerca gregaria, Locusta migratoria, Chortoicetes terminifera*), experiments similar to those with crickets were performed (Altman 1975; Altman & Tyrer 1974; Kutsch 1971, 1977). As in crickets, nymphs of early stages could be induced to display the typical flight posture when exposed to a windstream. However, regular flight motor rhythm could not be recorded from the muscles. With the exception of *Chortoicetes,* in which short sequences of alternating activity could occasionally be observed shortly before final ecdysis, antagonistic muscles were activated synchronously and not in antiphase, as in adult flight. Apparently, all the main features of the flight motor pattern are developed within a short period just before and/or after molting into adulthood.

At the beginning of adult life, the wing beat rate is only half of its final value, which is then gradually reached within the ensuing 2 to 3 weeks. Kutsch (1971, 1974, 1977) carefully studied all possible mechanisms underlying this phenomenon and demonstrated that the increase of flight frequency in locusts during early adult life is a purely central nervous phenomenon and does not depend on experience or maturation of sensory mechanisms.

Lepidoptera. Premature flight motor patterns have been observed not only in hemimetabolous (e.g., crickets) but also in holometabolous insects such as Lepidoptera (butterflies and moths). These insects undergo a complete metamorphosis with three distinct stages: the larva (caterpillar), the pupa, and the imago. During the pupal period the larval structures are transformed into those of the imago. That means that completely new appendages, organs, and behavior patterns have to be developed.

Kammer and Rheuben (1976) inserted sterile wire electrodes in developing pupal muscles of several saturniid (*Antheraea polyphemus, A. pernyi*) and sphingid (*Manduca sexta*) moths. The electrodes were implanted chronically and recordings were made daily. Normal development of the muscles and of other structures was not noticeably impaired. Although the pupae looked quiescent, motor patterns resembling behavior of adult moths were recorded from the developing muscles. These patterns were identified as flight and preflight warm-up (shivering), the latter being distinguished from the former by synchronous activation of antagonistic flight muscles (see Kammer 1967, 1968). In the pupae these two patterns were produced spontaneously and occurred intermittently at various times of the day (Fig. 17.4).

The first signs of phasic muscle activity were recorded on the sixth day of the pupal stage. Six to 7 days later, activity was produced more rhythmically and for longer periods, with antagonistic muscles regularly alternating. On the fifteenth day, that is, still 6 days before adult eclosion, fully developed flight and warm-up patterns were seen that were distinguished from the adult patterns only by a longer cycle time and a greater spike-interval variance.

Larval "stridulation" in crickets and in grasshoppers

Crickets. As with flight, stridulation is impossible in larval crickets because the nymphs lack fully developed forewings. Nevertheless, by using neuromuscular recording techniques, one can attack the question of how far the neuronal mechanisms generating song motor patterns have developed at that time. Cricket nymphs of the last stage, with electrodes implanted in various muscles, were confronted with conspecific males or females, that is, placed in natural situations that would normally elicit aggressive or courtship song. At first, the results of such experiments were disappointing: In nymphs of *Teleogryllus commodus* no signs of any stridulatory motor activity could be detected (Bentley 1973; Bentley & Hoy 1970). In *Gryllus campestris* the situation seemed

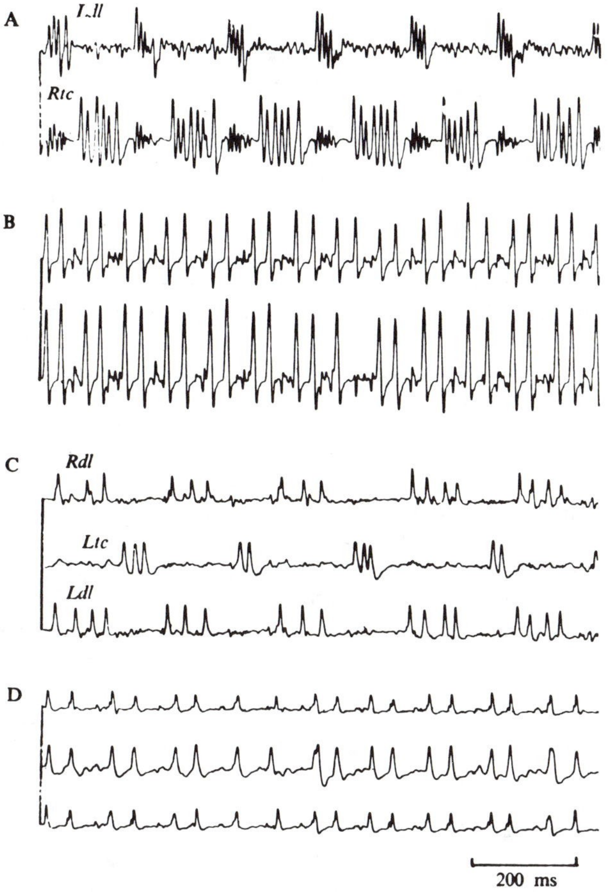

Figure 17.4. Flight (*A, C*) and warmup (*B, D*) motor patterns in adult (*A, B*) and pupal (*C, D*) *Antherae polyphemus.* Recordings are from the left and right dorsal longitudinal (Rdl, Ldl) and the left and right posterior tergocoxal muscles (Ltc, Rtc). (From Kammer & Rheuben 1976)

similar at first. However, in 2 of 40 aggressive interactions between conspecific males, motor patterns were finally recorded in last instar nymphs; they clearly resembled the patterns of neuromuscular activity underlying adult rivalry song (Weber 1974). The question arose as to whether these two animals were exceptional with regard to the maturation of the neuronal pattern generator or to the elicitation of already fully developed stridulatory patterns.

Bentley and Hoy (1970) presented clear evidence for the latter alternative. By making heat lesions in the mushroom bodies of the supraesophageal ganglion (an operation known to elicit stridulation in adult crickets; Huber 1955) they evoked stridulatory motor patterns in last instar nymphs of *T. commodus* (Fig.

17.3B). In several cases, all three patterns were released, that is, the motor programs for calling, courtship, and rivalry song. Obviously, the neuronal pattern generators are already fully developed before the final molt to adulthood, but they are normally under strong inhibition exerted from the brain. This inhibition, unfortunately, impedes detailed investigation of the maturation of the song pattern-generating networks because it is difficult to make precise lesions in the brains of younger instars. Therefore, the pioneer study of Bentley and Hoy (1970) has so far not been carried into earlier stages.

Grasshoppers. Whereas neurophysiological recording techniques, and sometimes even neurosurgical methods such as brain lesions, are necessary for studying developing flight and stridulatory motor patterns in cricket nymphs, the investigator is in a more favorable position when looking for larval forms of grasshopper stridulation. As part of their normal behavior, the larvae of acridid grasshoppers perform rhythmic hindleg movements (Jacobs 1949, 1953; Smit & Reyneke 1940; Weih 1951).

These movements are normally produced by the third and fourth (last) stage instar nymphs in response to the songs of adult males (Fig. 17.6A), but they may also be elicited by other acoustic (e.g., artificial sounds) and tactile or optic stimuli. Larval "stridulation" begins in the middle of the third stage. Weih (1951) studied the responsiveness of male *Chorthippus biguttulus* larvae to songs of conspecific adult males. The first responses were seen on the eighth day of the third stage; thereafter the probability of response increased and decreased rhythmically according to the molting cycle (Fig. 17.5A).

Because the larvae still lack the forewings, against which the hind femura are rubbed sonorously in the adults, these larval stridulations are silent, although the larval hindlegs are already equipped with a file of stridulatory pegs. Therefore, until recently, it remained unclear whether these behaviors are really larval forms of adult species-specific stridulatory patterns and not merely unspecific movements. To answer this question, Halfmann and Elsner (1978) recorded corresponding movement patterns of adult and larval grasshoppers in the genus *Chorthippus* (Gomphocerinae) by using a new opto-electronic device (Helversen & Elsner 1977).

These recordings showed that a few days before final ecdysis to adulthood, fourth (last) stage nymphs of *Chorthippus mollis, Ch. biguttulus,* and *Ch. brunneus* display rhythmic hindleg movements that strongly resemble the adult species-specific stridulatory patterns (Figs. 17.5, 17.6). For example, adult males of *Ch. mollis* and *Ch. biguttulus* are known to produce different patterns with each hindleg (Elsner 1974). It has now been shown that these features are already present in the larvae: In *Ch. mollis* stridulatory sequences are composed of subunits that by one leg are initiated by a steep downstroke (Fig. 17.5B, arrow) followed by a vibratory period. The other hindleg omits the downward movement, producing only the vibratory part. Adult and larval stridulations correspond well in these specific features, although the general course of the movement curves still may be somewhat different.

As in *Ch. mollis,* the movements of *Ch. biguttulus* nymphs resemble adult stridulation in that different species-specific patterns are produced by each hindleg. In both larval and adult sequences the subunits can be easily

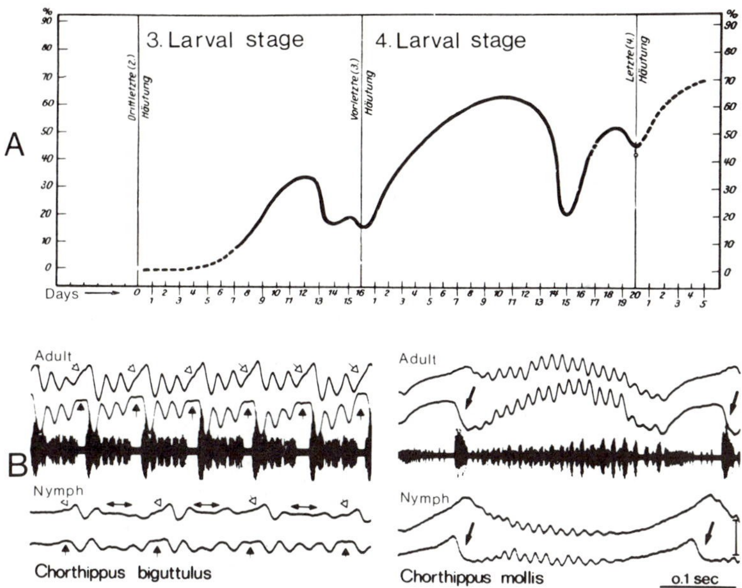

Figure 17.5. *A*. Responsiveness to adult song of the third and fifth stage instar nymphs of *Chorthippus biguttulus*.
B. Comparison of adult and larval stridulatory movements in *Ch. biguttulus* and *Ch. mollis*. For further explanation, see text. (*A* from Weih 1951, modified; *B* from Halfmann & Elsner 1978)

recognized because they are characteristically marked by pauses in the movements of one leg (Fig. 17.5B, black arrows) and by prolonged upward movements of the contralateral leg (Fig. 17.5B, white arrows). As in *Ch. mollis*, the legs may change their role from one sequence to the next. Stridulations of adult male *Ch. biguttulus* and fourth stage instar nymphs are different: The larvae do not persistently perform the higher-frequency oscillatory movements during the middle parts of the subunits (Fig. 17.5B, horizontal arrows).

In *Ch. brunneus*, the development of larval stridulatory patterns has been followed in some detail (although not yet completely) throughout the third and fourth stages (Halfmann 1977). Such studies are particularly favorable in this species because adult and larval male *Ch. brunneus* display a characteristic anaphonetic behavior. Therefore, larval stridulation can be easily evoked. The larvae respond to adult song as precisely as do adult males (Fig. 17.6A).

The adult stridulations of this species are characterized by two rhythms, a slower one (with high amplitude) of about 20 to 25 Hz and a faster one (with lower amplitude). The faster rhythm is usually superimposed upon the slower, but it may occur alone at the beginning or end of each sequence (Fig. 17.6B/7, arrows).

As in the case of *Ch. biguttulus*, the first larval stridulations were observed in the middle of the third instar stage. The movement patterns of these early songs were irregular and not well coordinated (Fig. 17.6B/1). Similar primitive

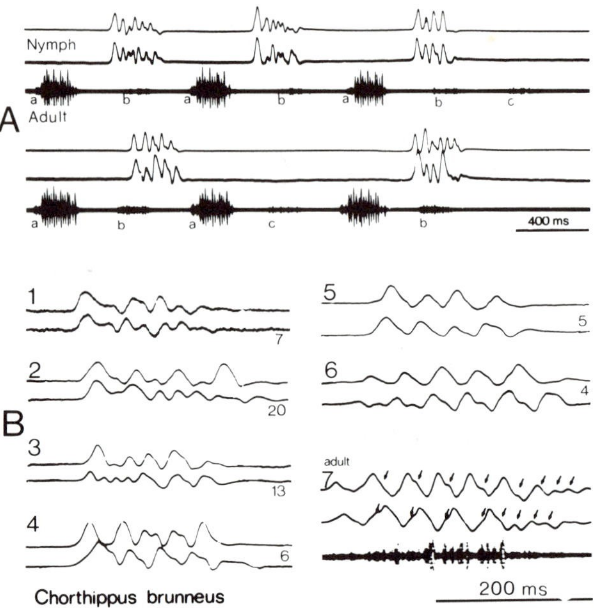

Figure 17.6. *A*. Duetting between larval and adult *Chorthippus brunneus*. Top and middle traces: Stridulatory movements of a fourth instar larva responding to the song of an adult male (a). Bottom trace: Sound recording of the songs of the adult males (a, b, c) that are responding to each other.
B. Stridulatory movements of third (oscillogram 1) and fourth stage instar nymphs (oscillograms 2–6) of *Ch. brunneus* in comparison with the movement and the sound pattern of an adult male (oscillogram 7). The small numbers at the right of each oscillogram indicate the day (prior to the next molt) on which the record was made. (From Halfmann 1977)

stridulatory patterns were recorded at the beginning of the fourth (last) stage (Fig. 17.6B/2). The two rhythms were still produced irregularly, and the left and right hindlegs moved almost independently of each other. At the beginning of the last week before final ecdysis, however, larval stridulations more and more resembled the adult movement pattern in that a regular 25 Hz rhythm was produced (Fig. 17.6B/3–5). Furthermore, the coordination of the two hindlegs became stable. Finally, a few days before molt to adulthood, the nymphs displayed stridulations that could hardly be distinguished from the adult movement patterns (Fig. 17.6B/6).

FINAL REMARKS

Research on the ontogeny of insect behavior and its underlying neuronal mechanisms is only beginning, and therefore it is difficult to draw firm conclusions. Nevertheless, the reader – especially if he is a human psychologist or an ethologist working on higher vertebrates – will wonder about the general virtue of these studies. What are the essential features of the neuroethological approach to the development of insect behavior?

1 Besides "primitive" locomotory activities, insects display remarkably complex communicative behavior patterns, for example, a rich variety of species-specific songs.
2 Even these elaborate behaviors are genetically mediated. The environment has been shown to be of little importance for their development and performance.
3 By the use of neuroethological techniques (e.g., brain lesions, recordings of the neuromuscular activity), the development of these patterns can be investigated even before the corresponding morphological structures (e.g., wings) are developed.

Higher vertebrate and human behavior is far from being exclusively genetically mediated, though there is little doubt that it contains inherent components. Therefore, one should look for model systems suitable for the investigation of the underlying neuronal mechanisms and their development. As far as basic neuronal principles of adult patterns are concerned, invertebrates have already served this function: Numerous types of synaptic transmission and interaction were first detected in molluscs, crustaceans, and insects and only later found in vertebrates. Knowing already which types of neuronal mechanisms exist somewhere in the animal kingdom, vertebrate neurophysiologists were in a much more favorable position than before because they then knew what to look for in the enormously more complex vertebrate nervous systems.

Research on the development of behavior and its neural basis has not yet reached that state. However, one can assume that our knowledge will increase in the future because the motor patterns of insects are ideal objects of ontogenetic studies. Not only can growing patterns be easily evoked in the laboratory, they can be investigated with neuroethological techniques, which even allow one to record behavior that has not yet been expressed as movements of appendages. Thus, we can hope to find general principles of motor-pattern development in insects that can then be looked for in higher phyla.

SUMMARY

This chapter describes the neuroethological approach to the ontogeny of insect flight and stridulation. These behaviors are genetically mediated and are developed during larval life. Except for a few details, they are completed by the time of their first performance in the adult animals. In grasshoppers, the development of stridulation can easily be followed because the larvae display species-specific stridulatory movements with their hindlegs when responding to the songs of adult males. This premature stridulation remains silent because larval grasshoppers – like all larval insects – lack the wings against which the hindlegs are rubbed sonorously in the adults. The ontogeny of insect flight and of stridulation in crickets (which sing by rubbing the forewings against each other), on the other hand, is impossible to analyze with conventional methods because no visible movements can be produced as long as the wings have not been developed. However, by the use of appropriate stimulation techniques, premature flight and stridulatory motor patterns are elicited in the larvae and can then be recorded electrophysiologically via electrodes chronically inserted in the muscles.

ACKNOWLEDGMENTS

I thank George W. Barlow and Klaus Immelmann for their helpful criticism of the manuscript.

REFERENCES

Altman, J. S. 1975. Changes in the flight motor pattern during development of the Australian plague locust, *Chortoicetes terminifera. Journal of Comparative Physiology* 97:127–142.

Altman, J. S., & M. N. Tyrer. 1974. Insect flight as a system for the study of the development of neural connections. *In*: L. B. Browne (ed.), *Experimental analysis of insect behaviour.* Springer, Berlin, pp. 159–179.

Barlow, G. W. 1968. Ethological units of behavior. *In*: D. Ingle (ed.), *The central nervous system and fish behavior.* University of Chicago Press, Chicago, pp. 217–232.

1977. Modal action patterns. *In*: T. A. Sebeok (ed.), *How animals communicate.* Indiana University Press, Bloomington, pp. 98–134.

Bennet-Clark, H. C. 1971. Acoustics of insect song. *Nature* 234:255–259.

Bentley, D. R. 1969. Intracellular activity in cricket neurons during the generation of song patterns. *Zeitschrift für Vergleichende Physiologie* 62:267–283.

Bentley, D. R., & R. R. Hoy. 1970. Postembryonic development of adult motor pattern in crickets. A neural analysis. *Science* 170:1409–1411.

1973. Postembryonic development of insect motor systems. *In*: D. Young (ed.), *Developmental neurobiology of arthropods.* Cambridge University Press, London, pp. 147–177.

Busnel, R. G. (ed.). 1963. *Acoustic behaviour of animals.* Elsevier, Amsterdam.

Edwards, J. S., & J. Palka. 1973. Neural specificity as a game of cricket: some rules for sensory regeneration in *Acheta domesticus. In*: D. Young (ed.), *Developmental neurobiology of arthropods.* Cambridge University Press, London, pp. 131–146.

Elsner, N. 1967. Muskelaktivität und Lauterzeugung bei einer Feldheuschrecke. *Zoologischer Anzeiger, Suppl.* 31:592–601.

1968. Die neuromuskulären Grundlagen des Werbeverhaltens der roten Keulenheuschrecke *Gomphocerippus rufus* L. *Zeitschrift für Vergleichende Physiologie* 60:308–350.

1974. Neuroethology of sound production in gomphocerine grasshoppers. I. Song pattern and stridulatory movements. *Journal of Comparative Physiology* 88:67–102.

1975. Neuroethology of sound production in gomphocerine grasshoppers. II. Neuromuscular activity underlying stridulation. *Journal of Comparative Physiology* 97:291–322.

Elsner, N., & F. Huber. 1969. Die Organisation des Werbegesanges der Heuschrecke *Gomphocerippus rufus* L. in Abhängigkeit von zentralen und peripheren Bedingungen. *Zeitschrift für Vergleichende Physiologie* 65:389–423.

1973. Neurale Grundlagen artspezifischer Kommunikation bei Orthopteren. *Fortschritte der Zoologie* 22:1–48.

Elsner, N., & A. V. Popov. 1978. Neuroethology of acoustic communication. *Advances in Insect Physiology* 13:229–355.

Fentress, J. C. (ed.). 1976. *Simpler networks and behavior.* Sinauer, Sunderland, Mass.

Halfmann, K. 1977. Adulte und larvale Stridulationsmuster bei Feldheuschrecken der Gattung *Chorthippus.* Dissertation, University of Cologne.

Halfmann, K., & N. Elsner. 1978. Larval stridulation in acridid grasshoppers. *Naturwissenschaften* 65:265.

Helversen, D., & N. Elsner. 1977. The stridulatory movements of acridid grasshoppers recorded with an opto-electronic device. *Journal of Comparative Physiology* 122:53–64.

Hoyle, G. 1964. Exploration of neuronal mechanisms underlying behavior in insects. *In*: R. F. Reiss (ed.), *Neural theory and modeling.* Leland Stanford Junior University, Palo Alto, California, pp. 346–376.

1970. Cellular mechanisms underlying behavior - neuroethology. *Advances in Insect Physiology* 7:349–444.

Huber, F. 1955. Sitz und Bedeutung nervöser Zentren für Instinkthandlungen beim Männchen von *Gryllus campestris* L. *Zeitschrift für Tierpsychologie* 12:12–48.

1960. Untersuchungen über die Funktion des Zentralnervensystems und insbesondere des Gehirns bei der Fortbewegung und der Lauterzeugung der Grillen. *Zeitschrift für Vergleichende Physiologie* 44:60–132.

1965. Aktuelle Probleme der Physiologie des Nervensystems der Insekten. *Naturwissenschaftliche Rundschau* 18:143–156.

1975. Principles of motor co-ordination in cyclically recurring behaviour of insects. *In*: P. N. R. Usherwood & D. R. Newth (eds.), *Simple nervous systems.* Arnold, London, pp. 381–413.

Jacobs, W. 1949. Über Lautäusserungen bei Insekten, insbesondere bei Heuschrecken. *Entomon* 1:100–107.

1953. Verhaltensbiologische Studien an Feldheuschrecken. *Beiheft I zur Zeitschrift für Tierpsychologie* 10.

Kammer, A. 1967. Muscle activity during flight in some large lepidoptera. *Journal of Experimental Biology* 47:277–295.

1968. Motor pattern during flight and warm-up in lepidoptera. *Journal of Experimental Biology* 48:89–109.

Kammer, A., & E. Rheuben. 1976. Adult motor pattern produced by moth pupae during development. *Journal of Experimental Biology* 65:65–84.

Koppers, S. 1977. Die neuromuskulären Grundlagen des Gesangs der Feldheuschrecke *Stauroderus scalaris.* Staatsarbeit, Master's thesis, University of Cologne.

Kutsch, W. 1969 Neuromuskuläre Aktivität bei verschiedenen Verhaltensweisen von drei Grillenarten. *Zeitschrift für Vergleichende Physiologie* 63:335–378.

1971. The development of the flight pattern in the desert locust, *Schistocerca gregaria. Zeitschrift für Vergleichende Physiologie* 74:156–168.

1974. The development of the flight pattern in locusts. *In*: L. B. Browne (ed.), *Experimental analysis of insect behaviour*. Springer, Berlin, pp. 149–158.

1977. Ontogeny of rhythmic behavioural pattern in orthoptera. *Journal de Physiologie* 73:593–616.

Kutsch, W., & F. Huber. 1970. Zentrale versus periphere Kontrolle des Gesangs von Grillen (*Gryllus campestris*). *Zeitschrift für Vergleichende Physiologie* 67:140–159.

Michelsen, A., & H. Nocke. 1974. Biophysical aspects of sound communication in insects. *Advances in Insect Physiology* 10:247–296.

Popov, A. V., V. F. Shuvalov, I. D. Svetlogorskaja, & A. M. Markovich. 1974. Acoustic behaviour and auditory system in insects. *In*: J. Schwartzkopff (ed.), *Mechanoreception*. Westdeutscher Verlag, Opladen, pp. 281–306.

Smit, C. J. B., & A. L. Reyneke. 1940. Do nymphs of Acricidae stridulate? *Journal of the Entomological Society of South Africa* 3:72–75.

Usherwood, P. N. R., & D. R. Newth (eds.). 1975. *Simple nervous systems*. Arnold, London.

Weber, Th. 1972. Stabilisierung des Flugrhythmus durch Erfahrung bei *Gryllus campestris* L. *Naturwissenschaften* 59:366.

1974. Elektrophysiologische Untersuchungen zur Entwicklung und zum Verlauf von Verhaltensweisen bei *Gryllus campestris* L. Dissertation, University of Cologne.

Weih, A. S. 1951. Untersuchungen über das Wechselsingen (Anaphonie) und über das angeborene Lautschema einiger Feldheuschreckenarten. *Zeitschrift für Tierpsychologie* 8:1–41.

Wendler, G. 1974. The influence of proprioceptive feedback on locust flight co-ordination. *Journal of Comparative Physiology* 88:173–200.

1978. Lokomotion: das Ergebnis zentral-peripherer Interaktion. *Verhandlungen der Deutschen Zoologischen Gesellschaft* 71:80–96.

Wilson, D. M. 1968. The nervous control of insect flight and related behaviour. *Advances in Insect Physiology* 5:289–338.

Wilson, D. M., & T. Weis-Fogh. 1962. Patterned activity of co-ordinated motor units, studied in flying locusts. *Journal of Experimental Biology* 39:643–667.

Young, D. (ed.). 1973. *Developmental neurobiology of arthropods*. Cambridge University Press, London, pp. 131–146.

18

COMPARATIVE ASPECTS OF BEHAVIORAL ONTOGENY: A PHILOSOPHY FROM FISHES

DAVID L. G. NOAKES

Ethology, like evolution, proceeds in an opportunistic manner. As Bateson (1976) has pointed out, theories of behavioral development have not been especially coherent, because information bearing on questions such as filial imprinting in waterfowl, sexual imprinting in birds, nursing in mammals, and song development in birds is more or less scattered. I hope to show some advantages for the study of behavioral ontogeny in fishes and sketch its relation to a more general consideration of behavioral development.

I will provide a general overview and synthesis with some details of early behavior in fishes because studies of fishes are not so widely known as those in birds or mammals.

THE EVIDENCE FROM FISHES

Classification by reproductive guilds

Fishes are a large, diverse evolutionary assemblage (Greenwood et al. 1966, 1967), but they may be categorized into four major living groups (Fig. 18.1). These groups indicate phyletic relationships in general terms (Lagler et al. 1977; Nelson 1976), but in this chapter I will use the terms *primitive* and *advanced* only with reference to presumed evolutionary grade (level). That is, *primitive* indicates a condition presumed to be closer to the ancestral condition, whereas *advanced* indicates a more specialized or derived condition. This usage does not imply phyletic descent or any direct relationship between primitive and advanced groups.

Fishes are much more diverse in their reproductive habits than other vertebrates (Noakes 1978a), and several authors have attempted to categorize them on this basis (e.g., Breder & Rosen 1966; Wickler 1966). I prefer the system of reproductive guilds (Balon 1975a), in which *guild* indicates a group distinguished by a specific mode of life (Table 18.1).

These guilds are ecologically based, with no necessary relationship to conventional Linnean categories. All fishes fall into one of six subsections (the actual guilds proposed by Balon are further subdivisions of these subsections but are unnecessarily detailed for my purpose). Each guild is defined on the basis of ecological (where and when fish spawn), embryological (amount and

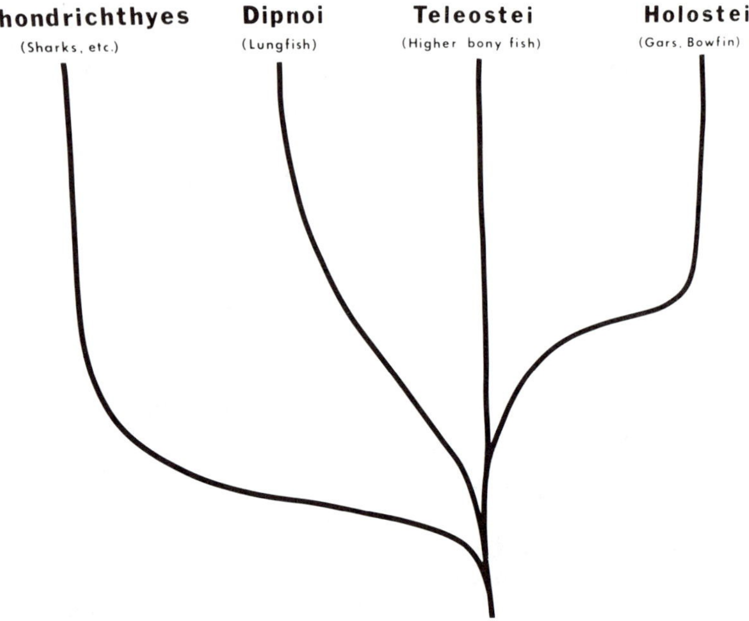

Figure 18.1. Hypothetical relationships of four major groups of living fishes. (Adapted from Lagler et al. 1977)

Table 18.1. *Proposed classification of living teleost fishes according to reproductive guilds*

Guild section	Guild subsection
A. Nonguarders	A.1. Open spawners
	A.2. Brood hiders
B. Guarders	B.1. Substrate choosers
	B.2. Nest spawners
C. Bearers	C.1. External brooding
	C.2. Internal brooding

Source: Simplified from Balon (1975a).

quality of yolk in each embryo), and ethological (patterns of mating and/or parental behavior) information. The guilds range from primitive (nonguarders) to advanced (bearers) (see the discussion of these and related suggestions in Balon 1975a, 1977, 1980; Barlow 1974; Wickler 1966).

Reproductive behavior has a central importance in the life of fishes. It will determine the social behavior of adults for at least some part of their life and

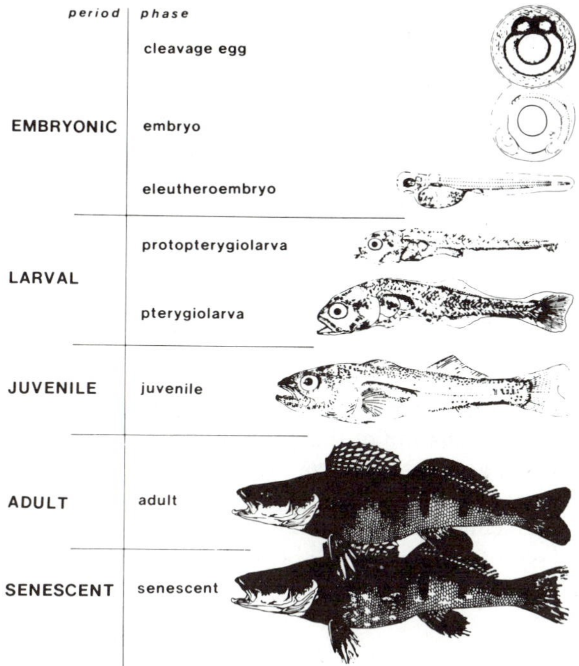

Figure 18.2. Developmental intervals in a typical teleost fish (*Stizostedion* sp., family Percidae). The overall developmental periods are divided into phases, which in turn consist of stages (not named here). (From Balon 1975b, with permission)

will likely have a general influence on the social system of the species. It will have a major effect on early embryonic development and therefore on early behavioral development. (I have implied that reproductive behavior has a cause-and-effect relationship with these other life history features only as a convenient shorthand to detailed considerations of cause and effect.)

Some unified terminology for development

Meaningful comparisons consistent for all categories and across such strikingly different species require a unified scheme of terminology to apply to developmental intervals of fishes. The suggestion that the life of an animal is composed of a number of stages is by no means new. I have adopted this proposal, even though there is by no means universal acceptance of any of the alternative terminologies (Balon 1975b, 1976; Richards 1976). There appears to be agreement that definite stages occur during development. Disagreement centers on the precise definition and nomenclature for these intervals.

Developmental periods. The life of any fish consists of five periods (Fig. 18.2) from the time of fertilization until death (Balon 1975b). Significantly, hatching (or birth) as a process or incident does not enter into the definition of any of these periods. Some broader implications for such a consideration of birth will come later.

The embryonic period is initiated by the fusion of gametes (or triggering of cell division in parthenogenetic species) and is characterized by endogenous nutrition (either from the yolk or through specialized absorptive organs). The larval period begins with the transition to exogenous feeding and lasts until the median fins have differentiated and the axial skeleton is formed. The juvenile period follows and terminates with the beginning of the first maturation of gametes. This process characterizes the initiation of the adult period, which includes reproduction. The senescent period follows after gametes are no longer produced, and growth is much reduced (see also Crowe & Crowe 1969:176).

There are large variations in the development of young in different fishes, as these periods may be variously compressed or extended (see Balon 1980 and Gould 1977a for a discussion of this phenomenon of heterochrony). Because hatching may occur at different stages in different species, it is misleading as an indicator of developmental age. The salmonids (family Salmonidae) and the mouth-brooding cichlids (family Cichlidae), for example, both lack the larval period. The developments that would occur during the larval period now take place during the embryonic period, and the juvenile period is correspondingly modified.

Examples and comparisons from reproductive guilds

I will outline briefly some examples from each of the major reproductive guilds to illustrate the relationships for subsequent considerations of early development.

Nonguarders. The embryos may be scattered widely in the planktonic drift of open lakes or oceans, as in many open spawning nonguarders. There is no social attachment between parent and offspring and, initially at least, not likely to be any such association among the young. These species tend to have relatively high fecundity and altricial young (Balon 1975a, 1977, 1980). The young hatch after a relatively short time (a few days) and are altricial, but usually with special features such as those related to buoyancy or light-oriented reactions. They undergo further development, often including a larval transformation, after hatching.

The schooling behavior in young of a nonguarding open spawner, the silverside *Menidia menidia* (family Atherinidae), develops gradually over a period of several weeks, after an initial period of approach and orientation (Shaw 1960, 1961). Maturational changes in the lateral line vibration receptors are associated with this increasing schooling tendency (Shaw 1970). Nursall (1973) has also reported that the schooling behavior of young yellow perch *Perca flavescens* (family Percidae), another nonguarder species, develops progressively during early ontogeny.

Brood-hiding nonguarders such as salmon and trout (family Salmonidae) have relatively fewer, larger eggs, and their young emerge in a somewhat more precocial condition. The parents deposit embryos beneath the gravel substrate, where they complete their embryonic and larval growth and differentiation to the juvenile condition before they emerge into the open waters of the lake or stream (Noakes 1978a, 1978b). The protection afforded by the gravel, coupled with a compressed embryonic and larval development and a larger yolk supply, allows attainment of a relatively advanced condition by the time of emergence.

As several hundred fertilized eggs are deposited in each nest, young salmonids develop in close association with conspecifics (siblings or others). Their behavior on emergence varies from schooling to strongly territorial, depending on the species (Ellis 1977; Hoar 1976; Noakes 1980). The onset of early behaviors such as feeding and agonistic responses, and of emergence itself, do not appear to be affected by most environmental manipulations (Bams 1969; Cole 1976; Dill 1969; Dill & Northcote 1970; Mason 1976; Twongo & MacCrimmon 1976). There are some indications of maturational changes, at least in agonistic responses (Chiszar et al. 1975; Cole 1976; Dill 1977; Noakes 1978a), but these are relatively minor in the present context.

Probably the best-known example of salmonid behavior affected by early experience is the precise home stream selection by adults when they return to spawn in freshwater (Hara 1975; Hasler et al. 1978; Scholz et al. 1976). Local adaptations or responses to pheromones may also be involved (Bams 1976; Doving et al. 1973; Nordeng 1971), but these would likely serve to complement the effects of early chemical experience under normal circumstances.

The two guild sections, guarders and bearers, both have some form of parental behavior (in the generally accepted sense). I will give one example of a nest-spawning guarder, and one each of an internal and external bearer, to compare with the previous accounts of the nonguarder species (nest-spawning guarders and substrate-choosing guarders differ little as far as the present discussion is concerned).

Guarders. Substrate-brooding cichlids (Baerends & Baerends-van Roon 1950; Barlow 1974) are the best-known examples of nest-spawning guarders. The young hatch after only a few days and develop through at least embryonic and larval periods under parental care (Barlow 1976; Noakes & Barlow 1973a; Ward & Wyman 1977).

The young have extremely close social contact with both parents and siblings as a family unit at this time. One or both parents remain close to the young, and interactions between parents and young may be bidirectional and relatively complex (e.g., Barnett 1977; Baylis 1974; Cichocki 1977; Cole & Ward 1969, 1970; Kuenzer & Kuenzer 1962; Kühme 1963; McKaye & Barlow 1976; Myrberg 1966, 1975; Noakes & Barlow 1973a, 1973b; Quertermus & Ward 1969; Timms & Keenleyside 1975; Ward & Barlow 1967; Ward & Wyman 1977; Weber 1970; Wyman & Ward 1973). This has been the basis for a number of studies of both early behavior and sensory capabilities of the young (e.g., Baerends & Baerends-van Roon 1950; Baerends et al. 1960; Brestowsky 1968; Kuenzer 1968; Kühme 1962; Myrberg 1964; Ohm 1964; Peters 1963, 1965).

Some studies have been directed to the question of possible long-term consequences of this early social experience, especially the possibility of imprinting, but the results are either inconclusive or somewhat contradictory (e.g., Barlow et al. 1977; Barlow & Rogers 1978; Fernö & Sjölander 1976; Weber & Weber 1976). We can anticipate sexual imprinting in rapidly evolving groups, as well as in situations in which several closely related and similar species occur in the same area, based on findings in birds (Immelmann 1972). Cichlids are a speciose, rapidly evolving group, and the occurrence of several polymorphic species in some situations enhances the appeal of the suggestion of sexual imprinting in these fish (e.g., Barlow & Munsey 1976; Fryer & Iles 1972; Loiselle 1977; Lowe-McConnell 1975; Miller 1976).

Bearers. Early behavior of the young of bearers has been studied infrequently, probably because they are precocial and in many cases do not act much different from adults. Examples from mouth-brooding cichlids (family Cichlidae) as external bearers, and surfperches (family Embiotocidae) and platyfish (family Poeciliidae) as internal bearers, clearly show this.

Mouth-brooding cichlids and a number of other fishes (Oppenheimer 1970) carry their developing young in the buccal cavity. In a manner somewhat reminiscent of the brood-hiding salmonids, they pass through their accelerated embryonic and larval development protected, in this case inside the parent's mouth. Young may or may not be taken back into the parent's mouth once they are released, depending on their developmental age (Balon 1977; Brestowsky 1968; Goude et al. 1972a, 1972b; Ohm 1964; Oppenheimer 1970; Oppenheimer & Barlow 1968).

Comparisons between substrate- and mouth-brooding cichlids (but see Noakes 1978a; Trewavas 1973) have shown that some species of young mouth brooders go through at least some of the same phases in early behavior as do young substrate brooders (Brestowsky 1968). Young mouth brooders that do not normally show social cohesion toward the parents, if taken from the parent's mouth as embryos and enabled to swim prematurely by puncturing the yolk sac to release some of the heavy yolk material, will show the same attachment for later social cohesion as do young substrate brooders. They do not normally show this behavior because they pass through the sensitive phase (for forming the social attachment) while they are still inside the parent's mouth.

Similarly, even though young *Labeotropheus* sp., another mouth-brooding cichlid, do not normally return to the mother's mouth after they are released, they will do so and will be actively retrieved by the mother if they are forced out by accident or experiment earlier in the embryonic period (Balon 1977). During the embryonic period, these young have behavioral responses (e.g., strong photophobia) that serve to keep them within the buccal cavity.

It is tempting to designate the apparent persistence (but nonfunctioning) of the social cohesion phase in these mouth brooders as atavistic behavior (see Chap. 8). This implies a retention of a behavior typical of the ancestral condition, as there is general agreement that substrate brooding is the ancestral condition to mouth brooding (Balon 1975a, 1977; Barlow 1974; Oppenheimer 1970; Wickler 1966). However, atavism (in the sense of recapitulation) is unlikely unless the situation involves hypermorphosis (i.e., an extension of the embryonic or juvenile period and delayed onset of the adult period) (Gould 1977a). If anything, the embryonic development of mouth brooders is compressed (i.e., accelerated) compared to substrate brooders (Balon 1977). Mouth brooders lack a larval period, for example, but direct comparisons between species are complicated by the fact that the actual time spent in each period is often different (and is not usually clearly defined in behavioral studies).

The young of internal bearers receive the greatest direct protection from the parent during their early development. I include here only those species that bear embryos inside the body until they are full-grown juveniles, the true live bearers (Balon 1975a). In the surfperches (family Embiotocidae) of the temperate North Pacific, young of some species are sexually mature and reproductively active within weeks of their birth (Bryant 1977; Shaw et al. 1974). In platyfish (family Poeciliidae) (*Xiphophorus maculatus*) sexual maturity is reached 10 to 20 weeks after birth, depending on the genotype and social environment (Sohn 1977).

An earlier age of first reproduction has a profound effect on the rate of population growth, and so they may act to shift a species more toward an *r*-selected condition (see below), probably imposed secondarily on an otherwise *K*-selected species in this case. Young live bearers may be born singly or in broods of up to about 50 (Balon 1975a), and so they may or may not have much early social contact with siblings. Social contact with parents is typically nonexistent, as these young are independent and precocial. Their behavior is presumably similar to that of adults, with the obvious exception of sexual behavior.

GENERAL CONSIDERATIONS

Reproductive guilds and r–K considerations

I will leave this detailed treatment of individual case histories to focus on a more general discussion of what may be a useful synthesis of information from ecological, evolutionary, and embryological considerations. Extensive treatments of the related topics to which I will refer are given in Balon (1977, 1980), Gould (1977a), Krebs (1978), and Pianka (1978).

The apparent parallel between reproductive guilds and the more widely known ecological terms *r* and *K* (Pianka 1978) deserves further comment. For the widely used logistic growth curve (Fig. 18.3), *r* is the instantaneous rate of increase (slope of the curve) and *K* the upper asymptote (often referred to as the *carrying capacity of the environment).*

Species usually accepted as having *r*-selected features typically have large litter sizes (increased fecundity), reduced parental care, and altricial young. The same features correspond to nonguarder guilds. On the other hand, bearers have features typically associated with *K*-selected species, for example, reduced litter size (decreased fecundity), increased parental care, and precocial young (Balon 1975a), although this association requires clarification.

This comparison is intended only in general terms and does not deny the dissociation of some features (e.g., fecundity and parental care) in more restricted comparisons of closely related species (Williams 1959). Although it may be tempting to look upon either reproductive guilds or *r–K* life history

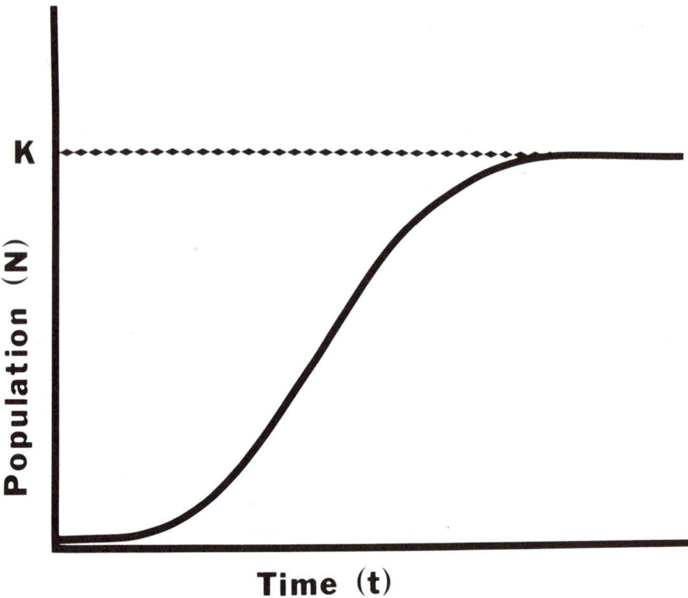

Figure 18.3. Logistic growth curve for a hypothetical population showing changes in population size (N) over time (t), with the upper asymptote of the curve (K) representing the carrying capacity of the environment. (Adapted from Pianka 1978)

features as a panacea, I will shortly elaborate on reasons for exercising caution in grasping at either for simple explanations.

R- and K- species. In habitats that have less temporal stability, greater unpredictability of resources, and less stringent competition, we can expect animals to be more *r*-selected. Such species have life-history features that tend to maximize reproduction and hence population growth (r tends toward r_{max} for the population). Conversely, animals tend to be more *K*-selected (with more stable population numbers) in environments that have greater temporal stability, more predictable and stable resources, and more stringent competition. These species have life-history features that tend to favor individuals in competition for limited resources, and population numbers tend to remain fairly constant (near the carrying capacity of the environment).

As mentioned, the sequence of reproductive guilds represents a progression in evolutionary grades from primitive (nonguarders) to advanced (internal bearers). The same general argument has been made for *r* and *K*, from primitive (*r*) to advanced (*K*) conditions. In this context, primitive and advanced do not (necessarily) imply an ancestral–descendent (phyletic) relationship, and there is good evidence of species secondarily evolving life-history features typical of primitive conditions (*r*-selected, or nonguarder).

Some predictions. From this brief and necessarily simplified overview, several important points emerge. From a knowledge or consideration of some life-history features of a species, we should be able to make some inferences as to its likely behavioral development. We should also be able to make certain predictions, perhaps in a more general sense, regarding our expectations of fishes in given environments or in relation to phyletic history.

As an example, we might expect fishes from tropical communities to be more likely *K*-selected and/or belong to a more advanced guild, on the assumption that there is a general trend for tropical communities to be more stable and complex and to have more stringent competition (Lowe-McConnell 1975; Pianka 1978). Conversely, we would expect fishes from temperate communities to be more likely *r*-selected or to belong to more primitive guilds.

As an admittedly simplistic assumption that the amount of time available would affect the progression in an evolutionary sequence (from primitive to advanced), we would consider phylogenetically older species (i.e., species less changed over time) more likely to be *K*-selected and to belong to a more advanced guild. Some examples from fishes may illustrate the point.

Salmonids are relatively recent north temperate species (Balon 1980; Cavender & Miller 1972; Nelson 1976), so we would expect them to belong to a primitive guild. They are nonguarders, but they do have some degree of specialization in that embryos are hidden (a step in the evolutionary progression of guilds) and development is accelerated by compression of the larval period (another step in progression).

Sharks are characterized by internal fertilization, an evolutionarily advanced feature otherwise found only in some recent specialized teleosts. The proposed scheme of reproductive guilds does not include sharks (or any chondrichthyan fishes). But as Wourms (1977) has outlined, sharks clearly follow the same general pattern. All species have internal fertilization, but reproduction ranges from oviparous (primitive) to live bearing (advanced) in several different evolutionary lines.

It would seem that sharks, as an ancient evolutionary line (several hundred million years old), have had time to evolve this degree of reproductive specialization (internal fertilization). Similarly, lungfishes (subclass Dipnoi) are very old species (essentially unchanged for at least 100 million years), characterized by well-developed parental care and advanced reproductive features. Examples can be extended to include the well-developed parental care in the bowfin (*Amia calva*) and mouth brooding in the arawana (*Osteoglossum bicirhossum*), both primitive species. I must hasten to add, however, that not all primitive species belong to advanced reproductive guilds. Other species of osteoglossids (e.g., *Hiodon alosoides*) are open-spawning nonguarders.

These instances of such obviously advanced and specialized forms of reproduction in otherwise primitive species have usually drawn attention only as intriguing paradoxes rather than as part of an overall trend. Of course, as mentioned, the correlation between phyletic age and reproductive behavior is by no means a necessary one, and certainly not so in a causal sense. Phylogeny may be important, but the ecology of a species must also be considered.

Particular habitats, such as the open pelagic zone of the ocean, provide few opportunities for reproduction other than internal (or possibly external) bearing or nonguarding open spawning. In the first case the species would be more likely to be *K*-selected, in the second more *r*-selected, so other factors might well tip the balance. Often it is not so easy to visualize the most likely, or possible, reproductive strategies.

Considerations of the evolution of both particular families of fishes and fish communities in general have demonstrated the utility of the guild concept in ecological and evolutionary investigations (Balon 1978; Balon et al. 1977). Sale (1978) has outlined a model of reproductive strategies for some coral reef fishes that favors adaptations for (apparent) *r*-selection, despite appearances that the fish should be *K*-selected (tropical, diverse community, intense competition). These species produce large numbers of small, altricial young and show little if any parental care, in a numbers game Sale calls a *lottery for living space.* There can be little doubt that these species (e.g., pomacentrids) are relatively recent specialized teleosts, yet they show secondary reproductive adaptations of an otherwise primitive nature. In this situation, selection has apparently acted to favor individuals that can rapidly colonize unpredictable territories as they become available on the reef.

Altricial and precocial young

The terms *altricial* and *precocial* have been derived from and continue to be used most frequently in reference to birds, although they are commonly applied to mammals as well. Altricial animals are characterized by large litters, rapid development, brief gestation, and the birth of relatively undeveloped, helpless young. Precocial animals are characterized by small litters, slow development, extended gestation, and the birth of relatively well-developed, capable young (Gould 1977a). Because these definitions rely explicitly on birth (or hatching) as indicative of developmental age, they do not fit my proposed frame of thinking very well. I shall return to this point presently.

There have been suggestions by some authors (see the discussion in Gould 1977b) that the important (dominant) trend in mammalian evolution has been toward the *K*-selection pattern, including a more precocial mode of ontogeny. Although this may be true in the sense that *K*-selection represents the advanced and *r*-selection the primitive grade, I think it is not likely correct if we assume it means a necessary correlation between the phyletic status of species and their life-history attributes.

The great diversity of reproductive behavior (and consequently early development) among fishes presents opportunities for studying evolutionary questions related to behavioral development, especially because most theories have been derived from consideration of birds and mammals. Consideration of altricial and precocial young seems particularly relevant.

In fishes there seems to be correspondence between the series from altricial to precocial and from nonguarders to bearers. Parental care increases along this continuum so that parents give little if any care to altricial young and most care to precocial young. This situation seems to be in contrast to birds and mammals, in which parents (usually) appear to give more care to altricial young.

In mammals, it seems that the altricial condition is secondarily derived from the precocial one, with humans (*Homo sapiens*) representing the extreme case

(Gould 1977a; Balon 1978). There is good evidence (see the discussion in Gould 1977a, 1977b) that humans have achieved their evolutionary success largely as a result of neoteny and features associated with it.

The extension of the embryonic period in humans involves a prolonged period of parental care. In fact, there is good evidence that the human embryonic period extends for some months after parturition (Gould 1977b), even though parturition is usually taken, explicitly or implicitly, as the end of the embryonic period.

It would be interesting, and perhaps illuminating, to consider mammals and birds categorized by reproductive (and developmental) features, as I have suggested for fishes. A unitary system of terminology of developmental intervals in fishes has proven useful and informative, not just to systematize our knowledge but to allow comparisons across otherwise divergent forms. Hatching in birds and birth in mammals might be as artificial as the corresponding processes in fishes, in general terms, for defining developmental periods across species.

Obviously birth in mammals or hatching in birds is a striking and in some ways traumatic event in the animal's life. It involves major changes in almost every external factor impinging on the individual, and these may be paralleled by corresponding alterations in many internal systems. Nevertheless, this event is not likely to have general significance as a reference point for comparisons among species, because it occurs at very different developmental times in different species. The recognition of altricial young is a reflection of this fact.

Surely it would be more relevant to define developmental periods than to assume the moment of birth as a reference point for interspecies comparisons. There is a growing body of evidence (e.g., Gottlieb 1976) to suggest that hatching in birds may also have a residue of ambiguity.

The implicit adherence to a basic Linnean classification (conventional species and higher taxonomic categories) has an obvious utilitarian purpose. But it might limit or even misdirect our attention when we consider behavioral development. In searching for models or parallels in behavioral ontogeny, perhaps we should look not at the closest (phyletic) relatives but at the most similar (ecological) forms.

The study of widely different species, whether in fishes or other groups, with basically different developmental patterns (e.g., altricial versus precocial young) should provide some useful insights as to how development of early behavior has been altered or adapted to these differences. It should be possible, for example, to select species that belong to the same reproductive guild, but in one case as a secondary adaptation, to see if early behavior differs and how. If, as Gould (1977a) suggested, much of evolution has occurred through heterochronies, such comparative studies become extremely interesting. It would be important, of course, to understand behavioral development in a particular species, but it might be equally or more important to appreciate related species in terms of alterations of early behavior.

Some thoughts about humans

As mentioned, humans are almost certainly one of the species most affected in this regard, in being markedly neotenic. Perhaps we should consider early human development in a more comparative light. As Gottlieb (1976:232) said, "It may be that retention of embryonic or neonatal plasticity into later stages of ontogeny is what distinguishes the behavioral development of higher from lower forms."

In considerations of early behavioral development in humans, there may well be some principles of general interest and importance, as I have tried to illustrate. Most notably there is a need for a more formal designation of developmental intervals. We have to acknowledge not only the possibility but also the probability that humans are still embryos for some time after parturition. In a number of studies (see Chaps. 3 and 22), there seems to be a correspondence in findings of common discontinuities within the first year after parturition. There are independent means for assessing developmental stages in terms of anatomical or morphological development (e.g., absolute or relative growth or differentiation rates of brain or somatic tissue). Such estimates allow us to suggest when developmental boundaries occur and whether the periods should be called *embryonic, larval,* or whatever label is appropriate for the species.

Comparisons of developmental studies of humans and other species may not be sufficient without such a calibration because such comparisons tend to imply some degree of evolution through recapitulation in humans. If humans are neotenic, then our development is slower than in related forms, and so our ontogeny is by no means a recapitulation. If anything, it is only an exaggerated section of a much longer sequence, to put the matter somewhat crudely (e.g., see Geist 1971). The appropriate comparison, therefore, would have to take into account not only the direction but the rate of probable changes, so that a comparison might be made between a postpartum human infant and a nonhuman primate at some time prior to parturition.

A second point, which follows from this one, is that we should expect, and perhaps specifically look for, some correspondence between developmental processes in behavior and those in the more usual embryonic (i.e., anatomical) features (e.g., Oppenheim 1974). We would expect to find a general correspondence in that behavior could occur only if the necessary motor and/or receptor pathways exist, but also that discontinuities in development should be synchronized, at least to some extent. The acquisition of sensory or motor capabilities related to some greater degree of independence from the mother, for example, should be correlated with corresponding behavioral changes. In some cases, a knowledge of developmental anatomy (embryology) will be the key to suggest that we look for particular behavioral developments. In others, however, it may be a knowledge of behavioral development that directs a search for corresponding changes in underlying mechanisms.

SUMMARY

The early development and behavior of fishes was presented as a possible model for studies in other species. A terminology, based on developmental stages, was offered to allow meaningful comparisons among species with very different patterns of early development. A second scheme, in this case classifying all fishes according to their reproductive behavior and early development, was presented with examples to illustrate the major categories.

The classification of fishes by these criteria draws attention to features of their early development and emphasizes similarities between species with similar features, rather than species that may be the closest phyletic relatives.

The concept of birth (or hatching) as a feature of general significance in the early development of animals is discounted. Altricial and precocial young are discussed, particularly with reference to these concepts as they have been developed from studies of birds and mammals. The evidence available from fishes suggests that the relationship between this altricial–precocial continuum and the amount of parental care given by adults may follow a different pattern than that seen in other vertebrates.

It is suggested that application of these two concepts, reproductive guilds, and a more precise terminology of developmental intervals could profitably be applied to other species, including primates and man. Also, the interrelationships of reproductive strategies, early developmental patterns, and the relative *r–K* features of a species are suggested as an area with promise for future studies of early development. In particular, the potential of these factors as predictive relationships is emphasized.

Various ecological factors may act on a species to shift its relative *r–K* features and therefore alter the pattern of its early development as well. Because there also seems to be a general trend toward the *K*-selected condition and internal bearing as a reproductive strategy, a consideration of the phyletic history of a species will be important in terms of its early development.

ACKNOWLEDGMENTS

Much of what I have said here is not original, either in thought or in presentation. Perhaps my repetition will serve to reinforce what I consider some important points. My debt to Eugene Balon goes beyond my obvious dependence on his published works to the influence of his discussions, constructive criticisms, and relentless enthusiasm on the subject. I am indebted to my colleagues at the Bielefeld Project who took the time and effort to review critically an earlier version of this manuscript and did their best to improve it with their suggestions. I must especially thank George W. Barlow, Gordon Burghardt, John H. Crook, Stephen E. Glickman, Gunnar Goude, Klaus Immelmann, and Sverre Sjölander in this regard. Of course, the responsibility for the final product remains mine. My research activities in the area of behavioral ontogeny have been sustained during my studies of salmonid fishes by the National Research Council of Canada and the Ontario Ministry of Natural Resources.

REFERENCES

Baerends, G. P., & J. M. Baerends-van Roon. 1950. An introduction to the study of the ethology of cichlid fishes. *Behaviour Supplement* 1:1–242.

Baerends, G. P., B. E. Bennema, & A. A. Vogelzang. 1960. Ueber die Aenderung der Sehschärfe mit dem Wachstum bei *Aequidens portalagrensis* (Hensel) (Pisces, Cichlidae). *Zöologische Jahrbuche* 88:67–78.

Balon, E. K. 1975a. Reproductive guilds of fishes: a proposal and definition. *Journal of the Fisheries Research Board of Canada* 32:821–864.

1975b. Terminology of intervals in fish development. *Journal of the Fisheries Research Board of Canada* 32:1663–1670.

1976. A note concerning Dr. Richard's comments. *Journal of the Fisheries Research Board of Canada* 33:1254–1256.

1977. Early embryology of *Labeotropheus* Ahl, 1927 (Mbuna, Cichlidae, Lake Malawi), with a discussion on advanced protective style in fish reproduction and development. *Environmental Biology of Fishes* 2:147–176.

1978. Reproductive guilds and the ultimate structure of fish taxocenes: amended contribution to the discussion presented at the mini-symposium. *Environmental Biology of Fishes* 3:149–152.

1980. Comparative ontogeny of charrs: principles of heterochrony in evolution. *In:* E. K. Balon (ed.), *Charrs: salmonid fishes of the genus Salvelinus.* Junk, The Hague, pp. 703–720.

Balon, E. K., W. T. Momot, & H. A. Regier. 1977. Reproductive guilds of percids: results of the paleogeographical history and ecological succession. *Journal of the Fisheries Research Board of Canada* 34:1910–1921.

Bams, R. K. 1969. Adaptations of sockeye salmon associated with incubation in stream gravels. *In:* T. Northcote (ed.), *Symposium on salmon and trout in streams.* Institute of Fisheries, University of British Columbia, Vancouver, pp. 71–88.

1976. Survival and propensity for homing as affected by presence or absence of locally adapted paternal genes in two transplanted populations of pink salmon (*Oncorhynchus gorbuscha*). *Journal of the Fisheries Research Board of Canada* 33:2716–2725.

Barlow, G. W. 1974. Contrasts in social behavior between Central American cichlid fishes and coral-reef surgeon fishes. *American Zoologist* 14:9–34.

1976. The Midas cichlid in Nicaragua. *In:* T. B. Thorson (ed.), *Investigations of the ichthyofauna of Nicaraguan lakes.* University of Nebraska Press, Lincoln, pp. 333–358.

Barlow, G. W., & J. W. Munsey. 1976. The Red Devil–Midas–Arrow cichlid species complex in Nicaragua. *In:* T. B. Thorson (ed.), *Investigations of the ichthyofauna of Nicaraguan lakes.* University of Nebraska Press, Lincoln, pp. 359–369.

Barlow, G. W., & W. Rogers. 1978. Female Midas cichlids' choice of mate in relation to parents' and own color. *Biology of Behavior* 3:137–145.

Barlow, G. W., W. Rogers, & R. V. Capeto. 1977. Incompatibility and assortative mating in the Midas cichlid. *Behavioral Ecology and Sociobiology* 2:49–59.

Barnett, C. 1977. Aspects of chemical communication with special reference to fish. *Biosciences Communications* 3:331–392.

Bateson, P. P. G. 1976. Rules and reciprocity in behavioural development. *In:* P. P. G. Bateson & R. A. Hinde (eds.), *Growing points in ethology.* Cambridge University Press, Cambridge, pp. 401–422.

Baylis, J. R. 1974. The behavior and ecology of *Herotilapia multispinosa* (Pisces, Cichlidae). *Zeitschrift für Tierpsychologie* 34:115–146.

Breder, C. M., & D. E. Rosen. 1966. *Modes of reproduction in fishes.* Natural History Press, Garden City, New Jersey.

Brestowsky, M. 1968. Vergleichende Untersuchungen zur Elternbindung von *Tilapia*-Jungfischen (Cichliden, Pisces). *Zeitschrift für Tierpsychologie* 25:761–828.

Bryant, G. L. 1977. Fecundity and growth of the tule perch, *Hysterocarpus traski*, in the lower Sacramento-San Joaquin delta. *California Fish & Game* 63:140–156.

Cavender, T. M., & R. R. Miller. 1972. *Smilodonichthys rastratus*, a new Pliocene salmonid fish from the Western United States. *Bulletin of the Museum of Natural History, University of Oregon (Eugene)* 18:1–44.

Chiszar, D., R. W. Drake, & J. T. Windell. 1975. Aggressive behavior in rainbow trout (*Salmo gairdneri* Richardson) of two ages. *Behavioral Biology* 13:425–431.

Cichocki, F. 1977. Tidal cycling and parental behavior of the cichlid fish, *Biotodoma cupido. Environmental Biology of Fishes* 1:159–169.

Cole, J. E., & J. A. Ward. 1969. The communicative function of pelvic fin flickering in *Etroplus maculatus* (Pisces, Cichlidae). *Behaviour* 36:1–31.

1970. An analysis of parental recognition of the young of the cichlid fish, *Etroplus maculatus* (Bloch). *Zeitschrift für Tierpsychologie* 27:156–176.

Cole, K. S. 1976. Social behaviour and social organization of young rainbow trout, *Salmo gairdneri*, of hatchery origin. M.Sc. thesis, zoology, University of Guelph, Guelph, Ontario.

Crowe, A., & A. Crowe, 1969. *Mathematics for biologists*. Academic Press, London.

Dill, L. M. 1969. The sub-gravel behavior of Pacific salmon larvae. *In:* T. Northcote (ed.), *Symposium on salmon and trout in streams*. Institute of Fisheries, University of British Columbia, Vancouver, pp. 89–99.

Dill, L. M., & T. G. Northcote. 1970. Effects of gravel size, egg depth, and egg density on intragravel movement and emergence of coho salmon (*Oncorhynchus kisutch*) alevins. *Journal of the Fisheries Research Board of Canada* 27:1191–1199.

Dill, P. A. 1977. Development of behaviour in alevins of Atlantic salmon, *Salmo salar*, and rainbow trout *S. gairdneri. Animal Behaviour* 25:116–121.

Doving, K. B., P. S. Enger, & H. Nordeng. 1973. Electrophysiological studies on the olfactory sense in char (*Salvelinus alpinus* L.). *Comparative Biochemistry and Physiology* 45A:21–24.

Ellis, D. V. 1977. The fish: an ethogram for survival. *In:* D. V. Ellis (ed.), *Pacific salmon management for people*, vol. 13. Western Geographical Series, University of Victoria, British Columbia, pp. 35–67.

Fernö, A., & S. Sjölander. 1976. Influence of previous experience on the mate selection of two colour morphs of the convict cichlid, *Cichlasoma nigrofasciatum* (Pisces, Cichlidae). *Behavioural Processes* 1:3–14.

Fryer, G., & T. D. Iles. 1972. *The cichlid fishes of the great lakes of Africa*. T.F.H. Publications, Neptune City, New Jersey.

Geist, V. 1971. *Mountain sheep: a study in behavior and evolution*. University of Chicago Press, Chicago.

Gottlieb, G. 1976. Conceptions of prenatal development: behavioral embryology. *Psychological Review* 83:215–234.

Goude, G., B. Edlund, U. Enqvist-Edlung, & M. Andersson. 1972a. Approach and withdrawal in young of *Tilapia mossambica* (Cichlidae, Pisces) as a function of age and onset of stimulation. *Zeitschrift für Tierpsychologie* 31:60–77.

1972b. Approach and withdrawal in young of *Tilapia mossambica* (Cichlidae, Pisces) as a function of age and social experience. *Scandinavian Journal of Psychology* 13:89–97.

Gould, S. J. 1977a. *Ontogeny and phylogeny*. Belknap Press, Cambridge, Massachusetts.

1977b. *Ever since Darwin*. Norton, New York.

Greenwood, P. H., G. S. Myers, D. E. Rosen, & S. H. Weitzman. 1967. Named main divisions of teleostean fishes. *Proceedings of the Biological Society of Washington* 80:227–228.

Greenwood, P. H., D. E. Rosen, S. H. Weitzman, & G. S. Myers. 1966. Phyletic studies of teleostean fishes, with a provisional classification of living forms. *Bulletin of the American Museum of Natural History* 131:339–455.

Hara, T. J. 1975. Olfaction in fishes. *Progress in Neurobiology* 5:271–335.

Hasler, A. D., A. T. Scholz, & R. M. Horrall. 1978. Olfactory imprinting and homing in salmon. *American Scientist* 66:347–355.

Hoar, W. S. 1976. Smolt transformation: evolution, behavior and physiology. *Journal of the Fisheries Research Board of Canada* 33:1233–1252.

Immelmann, K. 1972. The influence of early experience upon the development of social behaviour in estrildine finches. *Proceedings of the 15th International Ornithological Congress,* pp. 316–338.

Krebs, C. J. 1978. *Ecology,* 2nd ed. McGraw-Hill, New York.

Kuenzer, P. 1968. Die Auslösung der Nachfolgereaktion bei erfahrungslosen Jungfischen von *Nannacara anomala* (Cichlidae). *Zeitschrift für Tierpsychologie* 25:257–314.

Kuenzer, P., & P. Kuenzer. 1962. Untersuchungen zur Brutpflege der Zwergcichliden *Apistogramma reitzigi* und *A. borelli. Zeitschrift für Tierpsychologie* 19:56–83.

Kühme, W. 1962. Das Schwarmverhalten elterngeführter Jungcichliden (Pisces). *Zeitschrift für Tierpsychologie* 19:513–538.

1963. Chemisch ausgelöste Brutpflege und Schwarmreaktionen bei *Hemichromis bimaculatus* (Pisces). *Zeitschrift für Tierpsychologie* 20:688–704.

Lagler, K. E., J. Bardach, R. R. Miller, & D. R. M. Passino. 1977. *Ichthyology,* 2nd ed. Wiley, New York.

Loiselle, P. V. 1977. Colonial breeding by an African substratum spawning cichlid fish, *Tilapia zilli. Biology of Behaviour* 2:129–142.

Lowe-McConnell, R. H. 1975. *Fish communities in tropical freshwater: their distribution, ecology and evolution.* Longmans, London.

Mason, J. C. 1976. Some features of coho salmon, *Oncorhynchus kisutch,* fry emerging from simulated redds and concurrent changes in photobehavior. *Fishery Bulletin* 74:167–175.

McKaye, K. R., & G. W. Barlow. 1976. Chemical recognition of young by the Midas cichlid, *Cichlasoma citrinellum. Copeia* 1976:276–282.

Miller, R. R. 1976. Derivation of the Central American freshwater fish fauna. *In:* T. B. Thorson (ed.), *Investigations of the ichthyofauna of Nicaraguan lakes.* University of Nebraska Press, Lincoln, pp. 125–156.

Myrberg, A. A. 1964. An analysis of the preferential care of eggs and young by adult cichlid fishes. *Zeitschrift für Tierpsychologie* 21:53–98.

1966. Parental recognition of young in cichlid fishes. *Animal Behaviour* 14:565–571.

1975. The role of chemical and visual stimuli in the preferential discrimination of young by the cichlid fish *Cichlasoma nigrofasciatum* (Günther). *Zeitschrift für Tierpsychologie* 37:274–297.

Nelson, J. S. 1976. *Fishes of the world.* Wiley, New York.

Noakes, D. L. G. 1978a. Ontogeny of behavior in fishes: a survey and suggestions. *In:* G. M. Burghardt & M. Bekoff (eds.), *Comparative and evolutionary aspects of behavioral development.* Garland Press, New York, pp. 103–125.

1978b. Early behaviour in fishes. *Environmental Biology of Fishes* 3:321–326.

1980. Social behavior in young charrs. *In:* E. K. Balon (ed.), *Charrs: salmonid fishes of the genus Salvelinus.* Junk, The Hague, pp. 683–702.

Noakes, D. L. G., & G. W. Barlow. 1973a. Ontogeny of parent-contacting in young *Cichlasoma citrinellum* (Pisces, Cichlidae). *Behaviour* 46:221–255.

1973b. Cross-fostering and parent–offspring responses in *Cichlasoma citrinellum* (Pisces, Cichlidae). *Zeitschrift für Tierpsychologie* 33:147–152.

Nordeng, H. 1971. Is the local orientation of anadromous fishes determined by pheromones? *Nature* 233:411–413.

Nursall, J. R. 1973. Some behavioral interactions of spottail shiners (*Notropis hudsonicus*), yellow perch (*Perca flavecens*), and northern pike (*Esox lucius*). *Journal of the Fisheries Research Board of Canada* 30:1161–1178.

Ohm, D. 1964. Die Entwicklung des Kommentkampverhaltens bei Jungcichliden. Ein Ethologischer Vergleich zwischen *Aequidens latifrons* und *Ae. portalegrensis. Zeitschrift für Tierpsychologie* 21:308–325.

Oppenheim, R. W. 1974. The ontogeny of behavior in the chick embryo. *Advances in the Study of Behavior* 5:133–172.

Oppenheimer, J. R. 1970. Mouthbreeding in fishes. *Animal Behaviour* 18:493–503.

Oppenheimer, J. R., & G. W. Barlow. 1968. Dynamics of parental behavior in the black-chinned mouthbreeder, *Tilapia melanotheron* (Pisces: Cichlidae). *Zeitschrift für Tierpsychologie* 25:889–914.

Peters, H. M. 1963. Untersuchungen zum Problem des angeborenen Verhaltens. *Naturwissenschaften* 22:677–686.

1965. Angeborenes Verhalten bei Buntbarschen. 2. Das Problem der erblichen Grundlage des Kontaktverhaltens. *Umschau* 22:711–716.

Pianka, E. 1978. *Evolutionary ecology,* 2nd ed. McGraw-Hill, New York.

Quertermus, C. J., & J. A. Ward. 1969. Development and significance of two motor patterns used in contacting parents by young orange chromides (*Etroplus maculatus*). *Animal Behaviour* 17:624–635.

Richards, W. J. 1976. Some comments on Balon's terminology of fish developmental intervals. *Journal of the Fisheries Research Board of Canada* 33:1253–1254.

Sale, P. F. 1978. Coexistence of coral reef fishes – a lottery for living space. *Environmental Biology of Fishes* 3:85–102.

Scholz, A. T., R. M. Horrall, J. C. Cooper, & A. D. Hasler. 1976. Imprinting to chemical cues; the basis for home stream selection in salmon. *Science* 192:1247–1249.

Shaw, E. 1960. The development of schooling behavior in fishes. *Physiological Zoology* 33:79–86.

1961. The development of schooling behavior in fishes, 2. *Physiological Zoology* 34:263–272.

1970. Schooling in fishes: critique and review. *In:* L. R. Aronson, E. Tobach, D. S. Lehrman, & J. S. Rosenblatt (eds.), *Development and evolution of behavior.* Freeman, San Francisco, pp. 452–480.

Shaw, E., J. Allen, & R. Stone. 1974. Notes on a collection of shiner perch, *Cymatogaster aggregata,* in Bodega Harbor, California. *California Fish & Game* 60:15–22.

Sohn, J. J. 1977. Socially induced inhibition of genetically determined maturation in the platyfish, *Xiphophorus maculatus. Science* 195:199–201.

Timms, A. M., & M. H. A. Keenleyside. 1975. The reproductive behavior of *Aequidens paraguayensis* (Pisces, Cichlidae). *Zeitschrift für Tierpsychologie* 39:8–23.

Trewavas, E. 1973. On the cichlid fishes of the genus *Pelmatochromis* with the proposal of a new genus for *P. congicus;* on the relationship between *Pelmatochromis* and *Tilapia* and the recognition of *Sarotherodon* as a distinct genus. *Bulletin of the British Museum of Natural History, Zoology* 25:1–26.

Twongo, K. T., & H. R. MacCrimmon. 1976. Significance of the timing of initial feeding in hatchery rainbow trout, *Salmo gairdneri. Journal of the Fisheries Research Board of Canada* 33:1914–1921.

Ward, J. A., & G. W. Barlow. 1967. The maturation and regulation of glancing off the parents by young orange chromides (*Etroplus maculatus;* Pisces, Cichlidae). *Behaviour* 29:1–56.

Ward, J. A., & R. L. Wyman. 1977. Ethology and ecology of cichlid fishes of the genus *Etroplus* in Sri Lanka: preliminary findings. *Environmental Biology of Fishes* 2:137–147.

Weber, P. G. 1970. Visual aspects of egg care behaviour in *Cichlasoma nigrofasciatum* (Günther). *Animal Behaviour* 18:688–699.

Weber, P. G., & S. P. Weber. 1976. The effects of female color, size, dominance, and early experience upon mate selection in male convict cichlids, *Cichlasoma nigrofasciatum* Günther (Pisces, Cichlidae). *Behaviour* 54:116–135.

Wickler, W. 1966. Sexualdimorphismus, Paarbildung und Versteckbrutten bei Cichliden (Pisces: Perciformes). *Zoologische Jahresbuche* 93:127–164.

Williams, G. C. 1959. Ovary weights of darters: a test of the alleged association of parental care with reduced fecundity in fishes. *Copeia* 1959:18–24.

Wourms, N. J. 1977. Reproduction and development in chondrichthyan fish. *American Zoologist* 17:379–410.

Wyman, R. L., & J. A. Ward. 1973. The development of behavior in the cichlid fish *Etroplus maculatus* (Bloch). *Zeitschrift für Tierpsychologie* 33:461–491.

19

THE ONTOGENY OF BIRD ORIENTATION

WILLIAM T. KEETON

One of the most intriguing aspects of the biology of birds is the ability of many species to find their way across hundreds or even thousands of miles of often unfamiliar territory. This orientational ability is manifest both in round-trip migratory journeys and in homing behavior, the latter especially well developed in such species as shearwaters, albatrosses, petrels, swallows, and homing pigeons. The many hazards (e.g., storms, unfavorable winds, predators) encountered during migration or homing flights result in heavy losses, but surely many other deaths of individual birds can be attributed to errors of orientation. When the distances to be flown are great, even small angular errors may mean that the goal is missed by a wide margin. In view of such intense selection pressures, then, it is not surprising that the interplay between inherited and experiential factors in the ontogeny of avian orientational behavior is apparently subject to tight constraints. This means, in my opinion, that the development of orientation behavior can serve as a valuable model in the study of behavioral development in general, especially in the case of behavior that requires such precision that errors of learning would ordinarily be highly deleterious to the organism.

I shall not attempt in this brief chapter to give a thorough review of research on the ontogeny of orientation behavior in birds. Rather, I shall focus on a few selected topics that will, I hope, convince the reader that my enthusiasm for this subject has some objective basis.

DEVELOPMENT OF THE STAR COMPASS

About 30 years ago, Gustav Kramer (1949, 1951) observed that several species of nocturnal migrants spontaneously exhibited oriented migratory restlessness (*Zugunruhe*) in circular cages under clear night skies. Later, Sauer (1957) found that such nocturnal orientation depended on the stars; caged birds in a planetarium would even orient relative to artificial stars projected on the planetarium dome (Sauer & Sauer 1960). Sauer thought that the star compass would require time compensation, that is, that the birds would have to keep track of the passage of time in order to correct for the changes in the stars' positions during the night. However, in a detailed study of the orientation of the indigo bunting (*Passerina cyanea*), Emlen (1967a, 1967b) found that this

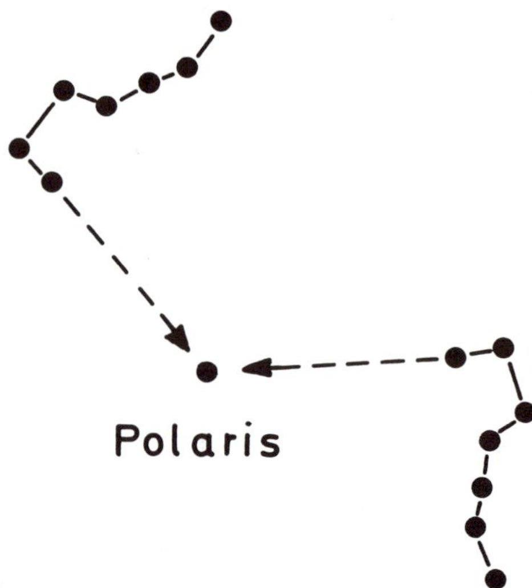

Figure 19.1. An example of how north can be located by star patterns. If an arrow is drawn through two stars in the cup of the constellation Ursa Major (the big dipper), it will point toward Polaris. Although the positions of the constellations change during the night (two positions are shown here), the same stars always determine an arrow pointing toward Polaris (i.e., toward north, or the pole of the celestial rotation); hence, directions can be determined without the need for time compensation. Many different star patterns could be used for direction finding in this way.

species uses star patterns to determine directions, a process that does not require time compensation (Fig. 19.1). There is now abundant evidence, moreover, that the birds derive only compass information from the stars, even though they could potentially be used in true bicoordinate navigation (Emlen 1975a, 1975b).

Emlen (1972) later found that there is a brief sensitive phase during which young buntings must learn to read the star compass. If the buntings have had a view of the starry sky during the weeks preceding the start of their first autumnal migration season, they can orient properly when that season begins in September. But if they have not seen the night sky until after the migration season has begun, they never learn to use the star compass, no matter how often they see the sky thereafter. Obviously, therefore, there has been, during evolution, a strong selection pressure favoring an early end of the sensitive phase in order to avoid the acquisition of wrong information at a later time when the bird has left its breeding grounds (cf. Chap. 14).

Emlen (1970, 1972) also showed that, in learning to read the star compass, young buntings respond initially to the apparent rotation of the starry sky during the night. The axis of this rotation is north–south, hence it itself can provide compass information. But detecting the celestial rotation probably takes considerable time; it is unlikely that the rotation could be determined at a glance. It is understandable, therefore, that the birds do not long depend on the axis of rotation per se; rather, they soon learn star patterns that will indicate

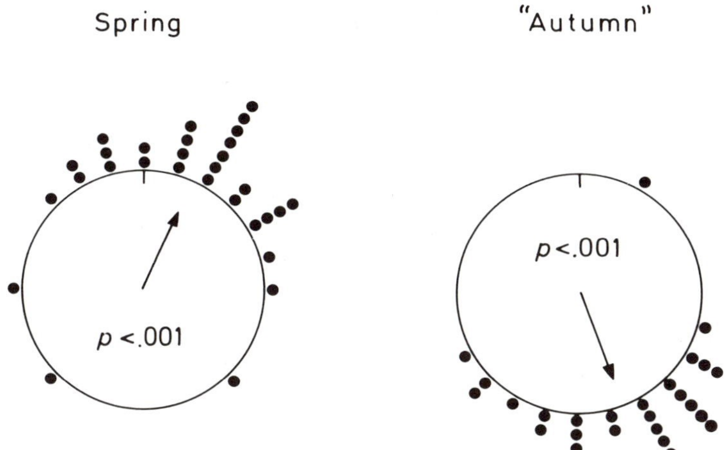

Figure 19.2. The orientation under a spring planetarium sky of indigo buntings in "spring" and "autumnal" physiological conditions. The birds in the spring condition oriented north–northeast, the usual direction for this species, whereas the birds brought artificially into the autumnal condition oriented south–southeast. (In this and later figures showing bearings, the direction chosen by each bird is shown by a small symbol on the outside of the circle. The mean vectors are shown as arrows whose length is proportional to the tightness of clumping of the bearings; that is, the longer the vector, the better oriented the sample of bearings; north is at the top of the circle. The uniform probability under the Raleigh test is given inside each circle.) (Redrawn from data in Emlen 1975a)

where the axis is, and thereafter they rely exclusively on those patterns (primarily ones within 35° of the celestial pole). In other words, the axis of rotation functions in ontogeny only as the reference against which the star compass is initially calibrated. Thus, when Emlen exposed hand-reared young buntings to a planetarium sky rotating around an incorrect axis – one for which Betelgeuse was the pole star – the buntings learned to use the stars in the circum-Betelgeuse portion of the sky, and consequently, they oriented in an inappropriate (but experimentally correct) direction when later tested under a normal sky. When retested a year later, after extensive exposure to the normal sky, they had not corrected their orientation; what they had learned during the sensitive phase in their early life still dominated their behavior.

Emlen (1969) has pursued the question of whether the seasonal differences in the temporal positions of the stars determine southward orientation by migratory birds in autumn and northward orientation in spring, or whether the differences in orientation result from corresponding differences in the physiological condition of the birds. By manipulating photoperiods, he contrived to bring one group of male indigo buntings into an autumnal condition at the same time that another group was in a spring condition. He then tested both groups simultaneously under a spring sky in the planetarium. The birds in the autumnal condition oriented southward, whereas those in the spring condition oriented northward (Fig. 19.2). Because the two groups saw identical star patterns, Emlen concluded that their different directions of orientation were due to their physiological conditions, not to the environmental stimuli. He predicted that the important factor would be found to be hormonal.

Later studies by Martin and Meier (1973) supported Emlen's prediction by showing that the orientation of white-throated sparrows (*Zonotrichia albicollis*) in circular cages can be reversed by altering the temporal pattern of administration of prolactin and corticosterone. Thus birds given injections of prolactin 4 hours after injections of corticosterone orient southward, whereas birds given the prolactin 12 hours after corticosterone orient northward.

It would now be of great interest to use the 12-hour corticosterone–prolactin treatment on young buntings during the sensitive phase for learning the star compass. Would such birds learn to read the star compass backward, and in later years orient northward in autumn and southward in spring? Or would they learn the compass correctly and orient with reversed polarity only while under hormonal treatment?

DEVELOPMENT OF THE SUN COMPASS

In the years since Kramer (1952) first showed that birds can derive directional information from the sun, a huge amount of research has been devoted to this topic. As in the case of the star compass, the preponderance of evidence indicates that solar cues are used by birds only as a simple compass, not as a basis for bicoordinate navigation (Keeton 1974a, 1974b). But unlike the star compass, a correct reading of the sun compass does require time compensation by the birds because the sun, being a single body, does not provide suitable pattern information. That birds do indeed couple their internal clock (circadian rhythm) with their observation of the sun's azimuth in determining compass directions was clearly demonstrated by Kramer (1953) and by Hoffmann (1954), working with caged birds, and later by Schmidt-Koenig (1960) working with free-flying homing pigeons. Schmidt-Koenig showed that pigeons whose internal clocks have been experimentally shifted 6 hours out of phase with true sun time choose initial bearing roughly 90° different from those of control pigeons when released at a distant test site (Fig. 19.3). Their clocks have been shifted a quarter of a day and, as a consequence, they misread the sun compass and choose bearings a quarter of a circle different from those of the controls. Thus the way birds read the sun compass differs fundamentally from the way they read the star compass.

Although the sun compass is a dominant cue in the navigation system of homing pigeons, it is not essential for proper orientation by experienced birds. Such birds can orient accurately homeward from distant, unfamiliar sites under heavy overcast (Keeton 1969). In the absence of solar cues, the birds appear to rely on information from the earth's magnetic field; in other words, they can use the sun compass and the magnetic compass interchangeably (Keeton 1971). But this is not true of very young pigeons on the first homing flight of their life (Keeton & Gobert 1970); when released under total overcast, these first-flight birds usually depart randomly (Fig. 19.4). Moreover, first-flight youngsters also appear to require magnetic cues; they usually depart randomly, even on sunny days when wearing bar magnets attached to their

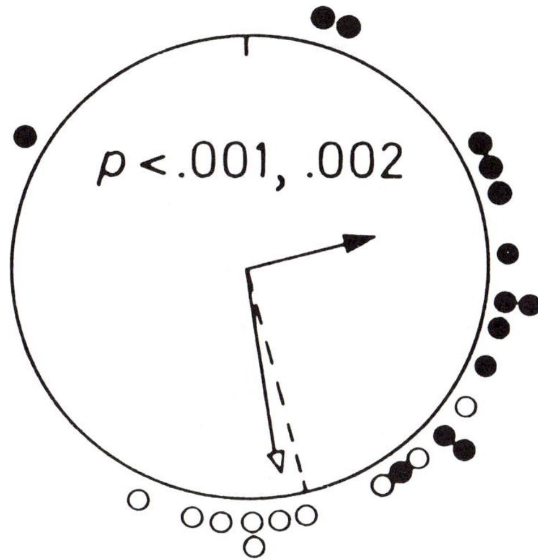

Figure 19.3. A comparison of the vanishing bearings of pigeons that have been clock-shifted 6 hours fast with those of control pigeons on normal time. The home direction is indicated by a dashed line. The bearings of the control birds (open symbols) are tightly clumped, and their mean vector (arrow with open head) points in the proper homeward direction. By contrast, the bearings of the clock-shifted birds (filled symbols) are deflected roughly 90° counterclockwise, and their mean vector points eastward.

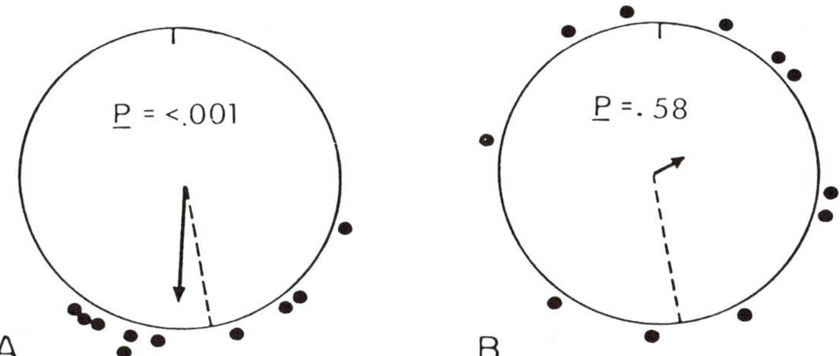

Figure 19.4. A comparison of the orientation of experienced and first-flight pigeons released under total overcast on the same day at the same site. The bearings of the experienced pigeons (*A*) were well oriented homeward, whereas those of the first-flight birds (*B*) were random.

backs (Fig. 19.5; Keeton 1971, 1972). In short, the first-flight birds need both sun and magnetic cues, whereas experienced pigeons need only one or the other. It seems, then, that these young, inexperienced pigeons are integrating cues in a manner quite different from experienced pigeons. Perhaps the effect of experience is to enable them to get by with less information. Alternatively,

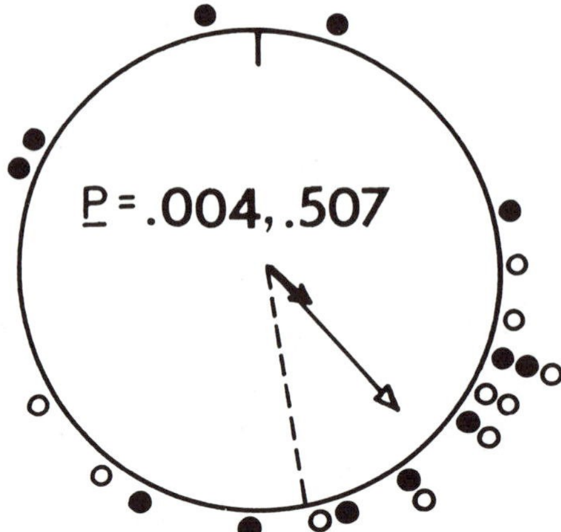

Figure 19.5. Bearings on a sunny day of first-flight pigeons wearing nonmagnetic brass bars (open symbols) or magnet bars (filled symbols) glued to their backs. The control birds wearing brass bars were oriented, whereas the magnet-laden birds vanished randomly.

the experience may help them establish a hierarchy of choice, so that they can later deal with situations in which two or more cues give conflicting information.

In some cases, the effects of experience and of increasing age may be essentially interchangeable. Thus R. Wiltschko (in press) reports that first-flight pigeons less than 10 weeks old seldom respond to 6-hour clock shifts by choosing bearings deflected 90° from those of control birds, as older pigeons do, but Keeton and Brown (in preparation) have found that even pigeons as young as 7 weeks respond to clock shifts like experienced adults if they have had previous homing flights or have trained themselves by flying unusually vigorously during their daily exercise flights (the vigorous flying often includes ranging away from the vicinity of the loft). Birds that have neither flown unusually vigorously nor had previous homing flights but are more than 18 weeks old respond to clock shifts like experienced adults. In other words, either flight experience or increasing age can result in maturation of orientational responsiveness to clock shifts.

We have seen that young first-flight pigeons normally require both solar and magnetic cues for proper orientation. But what of young pigeons raised without ever having had a chance to see the sun? Wiltschko et al. (in preparation) have tested such no-sun youngsters (the birds were flown for exercise at the loft only on totally overcast days) and found that they could orient perfectly well when released under total overcast for their first homing flight, even though their siblings, which had been permitted some view of the sun and thus served as controls, vanished randomly. Having never viewed the sun, the no-sun pigeons had not incorporated it into their navigation system and hence had no difficulty orienting when it was missing. Experiments are

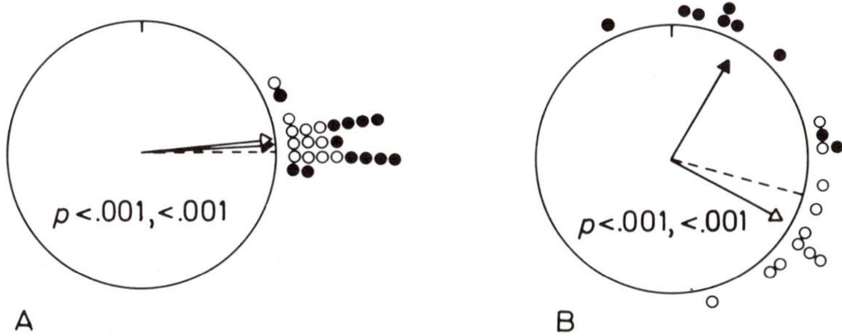

Figure 19.6. Bearings of young pigeons raised under a "permanent" 6-hour-slow clock shift. (*A*) While still living under the shifted photoperiod, the experimental birds (filled symbols) oriented like the controls (open symbols) toward home. (*B*) When retested 5 days after being moved to a normal photoperiod, the experimental birds chose bearings deflected roughly 90° counterclockwise from those of the controls. (From Wiltschko et al. 1976)

now underway at Cornell University to discover whether there is a sensitive phase for learning the sun compass, as we have seen there is for the star compass. Already there is evidence that when the birds are at their most responsive age, a very brief exposure to the sun is sufficient to induce complete maturation of sun-compass behavior.

Studies of the ontogeny of the sun compass in pigeons have also revealed that the coupling of time, directions, and sun azimuths is not inherited but must be learned (Wiltschko et al. 1976). Thus young pigeons raised under a permanently 6-hour-slow clock-shifted photoperiod orient normally, with no indication of the deflection seen in ordinary clock shifts (Fig. 19.6A). The birds appear to have learned that the "morning" sun is in the south, the "noon" sun in the west, and so on. When these birds are moved to a normal photoperiod and retested after 5 or 6 days, they then show bearings deflected 90° from the controls (Fig. 19.6B); being put in a normal photoperiod has the same effect on them as a 6-hour-fast clock shift has on normal pigeons. These results indicate that the sun compass must be calibrated, which suggests that it may be a derivative compass – that there may be some other more fundamental directional cue that functions as the reference for calibration during ontogeny. One current line of research is the attempt to determine what that reference cue might be.

This short discussion has focused on several studies of the ontogeny of star and sun compass orientation in birds. Another active area of research, mentioned here only in passing, deals with the development of route knowledge in young migratory birds. Such birds, without any migratory experience, appear to exhibit in test cages seasonal changes in orientation that are appropriate to the real course changes in the migratory route of their species (Gwinner & Wiltschko 1978). Still other topics could be mentioned here, but these few suffice, I hope, to show that studies of the ontogeny of orientation behavior are both a powerful way of teasing apart the many interacting elements in avian orientation systems and a promising approach to understanding the interplay among inheritance, experience, age, and hormonal condition in the development of animal behavior in general.

SUMMARY

Birds do not inherit a knowledge of star patterns or of the path of the sun across the sky. Both of these must be learned if the birds are to derive orientational information from the stars or the sun. But in both cases, the birds appear to be especially sensitive at an early age to critical aspects of the celestial environment that permit rapid, very specific, and perhaps irreversible learning. As would be expected, however, both intensity of experience and changing hormonal state can probably influence both what is learned and at what age it is learned. Further studies of the ontogeny of avian orientational behavior promise to be fruitful both in helping to unravel the details of the amazingly complex navigation system of birds and in contributing to an understanding of more general questions of behavioral development.

ACKNOWLEDGMENTS

Many parts of this chapter have been excerpted, with little change, from a longer article by the author entitled "Avian orientation and navigation: new developments in an old mystery," to be published in the *Proceedings of the International Ornithological Congress,* Berlin. The author's research is supported by grants from the National Science Foundation.

REFERENCES

Emlen, S. T. 1967a. Migratory orientation of the indigo bunting, *Passerina cyanea.* Part 1. Evidence for use of celestial cues. *Auk* 84:309–342.

1967b. Migratory orientation of the indigo bunting, *Passerina cyanea.* Part 2. Mechanism of celestial orientation. *Auk* 84:463–489.

1969. Bird migration: influence of physiological state upon celestial orientation. *Science* 165:716–718.

1970. Celestial rotation: its importance in the development of migratory orientation. *Science* 170:1198–1201.

1972. The ontogenetic development of orientation capabilities. *In:* S. R. Galler, K. Schmidt-Koenig, G. J. Jacobs, & R. E. Belleville (eds.), *Animal orientation and navigation* (NASA SP-262). U.S. Government Printing Office, Washington, D.C., pp. 191-210.

1975a. Migration: orientation and navigation. *In:* D. S. Farner & J. R. King (eds.), *Avian biology,* vol. 5. Academic Press, New York, pp. 129–219.

1975b. The stellar-orientation system of a migratory bird. *Scientific American* 233:102–111.

Gwinner, E., & W. Wiltschko. 1978. Endogenously controlled changes in migratory direction of the garden warbler *Sylvia borin. Journal of Comparative Physiology* 125:267–273.

Hoffmann, K. 1954. Versuche zu der im Richtungsfinden der Vögel enthaltenen Zeitschätzung. *Zeitschrift für Tierpsychologie* 11:453–475.

Keeton, W. T. 1969. Orientation by pigeons: is the sun necessary? *Science* 165:922–928.

1971. Magnets interfere with pigeon homing. *Proceedings of the National Academy of Science* 68:102–106.

1972. Effects of magnets on pigeon homing. *In:* S. R. Galler, K. Schmidt-Koenig, G. P. Jacobs, & R. E. Belleville (eds.), *Animal orientation and navigation* (NASA SP-262). U.S. Government Printing Office, Washington, D.C., pp. 579–594.

1974a. The orientational and navigational basis of homing in birds. *Advances in the Study of Behavior* 5:47–132.

1974b. The mystery of pigeon homing. *Scientific American* 231:96–107.

Keeton, W. T., & A. Gobert. 1970. Orientation by untrained pigeons requires the sun. *Proceedings of the National Academy of Science* 65:853–856.

Kramer, G. 1949. Ueber Richtungstendenzen bei der nächtlichen Zugunruhe gekäfigter Vögel. *In:* E. Mayr & E. Schüz (eds.), *Ornithologie als biologische Wissenschaft.* Winter, Heidelberg, pp. 269–283.

1951. Eine neue Methode zur Erforschung der Zugorientierung und die bisher damit erzielten Ergebnisse. *Proceedings of the 10th International Ornithological Congress,* Uppsala, pp. 271–280.

1952. Experiments on bird orientation. *Ibis* 94:265–285.

1953. Die Sonnenorientierung der Vögel. *Verhandlungen Deutsche Zoologische Gesellschaft, Freiburg* 1952:72–84.

Martin, D. D., & A. H. Meier. 1973. Temporal synergism of corticosterone and prolactin in regulating orientation in the migratory white-throated sparrow (*Zonotrichia albicollis*). *Condor* 75:369–374.

Sauer, E. F. G. 1957. Die Sternorientierung nächtlich ziehender Grasmücken (*Sylvia atricapilla, borin* und *curruca*). *Zeitschrift für Tierpsychologie* 14:29–70.

Sauer, E. F. G., & E. M. Sauer. 1960. Star navigation of nocturnal migrating birds: the 1958 planetarium experiments. *Cold Spring Harbor Symposium for Quantitative Biology* 25:463–473.

Schmidt-Koenig, K. 1960. Internal clocks and homing. *Cold Spring Harbor Symposium for Quantitative Biology* 25:389–393.

Wiltschko, W., R. Wiltschko, & W. T. Keeton. 1976. Effects of a "permanent" clock-shift on the orientation of young homing pigeons. *Behavioral Ecology and Sociobiology* 1:229–243.

20

ONTOGENY OF BIRD SONG

DONALD E. KROODSMA

The diversity of adult singing behaviors among different songbird species is matched by an equally impressive diversity of developmental strategies. Herein lies the frustration of the developmental biologist who wishes to generalize from studies of a single species, but this same diversity of behaviors, ontogenies, and life styles among species fuels the comparative approach that has proven so useful in clarifying proximate and ultimate factors (for definition of these terms, see Chap. 14) involved in evolution.

One of the most fundamental aspects of song ontogeny is whether the adult song arises through improvisation (invention) or imitation (for reviews, see Nottebohm 1970; Konishi & Nottebohm 1969; Marler & Mundinger 1971). Does the young male imitate the precise details of a model song, does he imitate some details but improvise others, or is no model necessary for him to develop fully normal, wild-type songs (i.e., is song innate)? (The female usually does not sing. This in itself is a fascinating subject for further study; see below and Kern & King 1972.) Songs are complex vocalizations that probably evolved from simpler calls (Thielcke 1966); many calls develop normally even if the juvenile bird has had no exposure to a model, and undoubtedly fairly simple songs that develop in this fashion will eventually be studied as well. At present, though, juvenile males of all songbird species that have been thoroughly studied must hear the songs of adults in order to develop fully normal, wild-type songs (Kroodsma 1977).

Even when the adult song is acquired primarily through imitation, a variety of strategies are still possible. For example, when will the vocal imitation occur? Selection for the timing of the learning phase during the life cycle of the individual has not been uniform. For example, greenfinches (*Chloris chloris*) may continue to modify their song repertoire as adults (Güttinger 1977). The phase of song learning is more limited in chaffinches (*Fringilla coelebs;* Thorpe 1958) and in cardinals (*Cardinalis cardinalis;* Dittus & Lemon 1969), which learn songs or song elements during both the first fall and the following spring. On the other hand, Marler (1970a; Marler & Tamura 1964) found a more restricted sensitive phase in white-crowned sparrows (*Zonotrichia leucophrys*). Here, males could learn the details of model songs presented between 8 and 28 or between 35 and 56 days of age, but males exposed to songs before 8 or after

56 days of age did not develop fully normal songs. Immelmann (1969) found a similarly limited sensitive phase in zebra finches (*Poephila guttata*); juvenile males acquired the details of their adult song before day 80.

Also, if imitation is to occur, what guides the learning process? What cues are available to insure that the juvenile learns the correct, species-specific song(s)? Occasional errors in song learning are documented among free-living birds; for example, in Oregon I studied two house wrens (*Troglodytes aedon*) that had learned extensive portions of the song repertoires of Bewick's wrens (*Thryomanes bewickii;* see Kroodsma 1973). Other examples of such miscopying exist (Baptista 1974; Baptista & Wells 1975; Kroodsma 1972) but such mistakes rarely appear. (For an entirely different aspect of heterospecific vocal imitation, see Nicolai 1969; Payne 1973; and Sullivan 1976 for work on parasitic indigo birds and finch hosts.) Social interaction with adults may in some instances guide song learning, but various sensory or motor constraints could also restrict imitation to appropriate sounds.

A multitude of other questions for which answers are few involve various spin-offs from the improvisation versus imitation options, the timing of song learning (sensitive phases), and the aspect of selective learning. How, for instance, are the diverse developmental strategies and adult singing behaviors adapted to differing life styles of the animals involved? What features of a life style influence the timing of song learning, where that song imitation will take place, from whom the young male will copy his songs, or how many different songs the young male will develop?

Finally, what are the proximate factors that influence or control song development? Nottebohm and Arnold (e.g., 1976) have made some exciting contributions in understanding the neurophysiology of vocal behavior, and advances in understanding the ontogeny of song are imminent.

What about the female? In most temperate species, she does not sing; yet if she is implanted with testosterone, she may be able to produce a song that is indistinguishable from the male song (see Kern & King 1972). If the female makes the final choice in mate selection (see Orians 1969), it is conceivable that her songs (even if they remain unuttered) could play a role in that mate selection. Such a mechanism could insure that the female will mate with males from a fairly small localized area near her birthplace, but with the possibility of differing sensitive phases and/or dispersal times for the two sexes, inbreeding certainly need not be the evolutionary goal. The ontogeny and evolutionary role of this female song are totally unknown, yet there is some exciting potential here for further studies.

Beyond these rather basic questions of differing developmental strategies and life styles, one faces the difficult question, why imitate songs at all? And why does this imitation occur so extensively among the songbirds? The parallels with the development of human speech are truly remarkable: (1) both babies of *Homo sapiens* and young of many songbird species imitate sounds of adults; (2) babies babble and juvenile songbirds subsing; (3) hearing (i.e., auditory feedback) is fundamental for normal vocal development; (4) neural lateralization exists in vocal control of both humans and birds, and (5) vocal learning is maximal during a sensitive phase early in life. Nowhere else in the animal kingdom, not even among the nonhuman primates, have such parallels with the development of human speech been uncovered (see Marler 1970b, 1976, 1978; Petrinovich 1972; Chap. 21).

Having outlined the major ideas and questions that are at the forefront in studies of the ontogeny of bird song, I shall address in greater depth several of these topics: (1) the nature of vocal imitation and the sensitive phase, (2) the role of improvisation and imitation in ontogeny, (3) studies of selective learning, and (4) the neurophysiology of vocal ontogeny. Data and speculation will be cast within an ontogenetic/phylogenetic or proximate/ultimate framework where possible.

VOCAL IMITATION (= SONG LEARNING) AND THE SENSITIVE PHASE

Overview of vocal imitation

The list of oscine species in which song learning has been documented under laboratory conditions is constantly growing. Examples of species that learn the details of song types presented over loudspeakers include the chaffinch (*Fringilla coelebs;* Thorpe 1958), the white-crowned sparrow (*Zonotrichia leucophrys;* Marler 1970a; Marler & Tamura 1964), the swamp sparrow (*Melospiza georgiana;* Kroodsma unpublished data; Marler & Peters 1977), the cardinal (*Cardinalis cardinalis;* Dittus & Lemon 1969), and the house finch (*Carpodacus mexicanus;* Mundinger personal communication).

In addition to such laboratory documentation for song learning, field data for numerous species indicate that song types of neighboring males are often very similar to one another but, to varying degrees in different species, they are different from those of males in neighboring populations; such local variation, when investigated, has proven to result from song imitation among males (e.g., Dittus & Lemon 1969; Kroodsma 1974; Marler & Tamura 1964).

Yet, other than the fact that imitation is a prevalent factor in song ontogeny among oscines, we know very little of its evolutionary significance. Marler and Tamura (1964), Nottebohm (1969a), and more recently Baker (1975a, 1975b; Baker & Mewaldt 1978) have provided some exciting ideas and data that indicate that vocal imitation, together with a limited sensitive phase for song learning in some *Zonotrichia* populations, may actually promote inbreeding and prevent mixing of populations from adjacent dialect areas. Such results from intensively studied species or populations are an encouragement to those biologists working with less well-known species.

In other species, vocal imitation may occur at an age that insures interacting conspecifics will share like songs. In the Bewick's wren, young males probably are capable of imitating the songs of the father, but after dispersal during the second month of life, these are rejected or dropped in order to match the songs of adult males with which the juvenile will interact for the remainder of his life; after 100 days, then, songs within the repertoire of a given male are very stable (Kroodsma 1974). In other species, though, song imitation may continue throughout life; both indigo birds (*Vidua chalybeata;* Payne personal communication) and saddlebacks (*Philesturnus carunculatus;* Jenkins 1978) can disperse when older than 1 year of age and alter their song repertoires to match the songs of males at the new location. Jenkins (1978) has even proposed for the saddleback that familiarity with songs of the father and the "home dialect" repel the juvenile from his home area, leading to dispersal to other dialect areas; this would promote outbreeding, just the opposite of the Marler–Nottebohm–Baker model for *Zonotrichia.* Although it is certainly possible that systems could function in such a diametrically opposed manner, Jenkins's data do not, I believe, overwhelmingly support his speculations; he studied five father–son combinations and found that initially all of the sons dispersed to a dialect area different from that of the father. However, in its second season, one of the sons returned to breed adjacent to the father; with only four dialect areas and five father–son pairs, determining the significance of any dispersal pattern is not possible. Until more is learned of both the behavior and the ecology of species with different combinations of learning phases, site fidelity, and so on, the adaptive significance of such variability will remain unclear.

Details of an early sensitive phase

Even though some species are capable of learning during their entire life, many species that have been studied in the laboratory have fairly well-defined sensitive phases. However, the details of relative abilities to learn songs throughout this sensitive phase are lacking. The dynamics of this song-learning process are also unstudied: Does social interaction play a prominent role, and if so, how can studies of song ontogeny in the laboratory be related to song development in nature?

Furthermore, what are the proximate causes or factors involved in controlling the sensitive phase? Clues come from Nottebohm (1969b), Pröve (1974), and Arnold (1975), who found that castration and presumably testosterone may affect song development differently in the chaffinch and zebra finch. In the one chaffinch studied by Nottebohm (1969b), castration delayed song imitation until the male was 2 years old and high levels of testosterone were administered exogenously; in the zebra finch, however, gonadal androgens appear to influence song development in a less dramatic fashion. Singing in adults is testosterone-dependent (Pröve 1978), and song development can be advanced in young males by early administration of exogenous testosterone (Sossinka et al. 1975); however, castration of young males does not block song development entirely but only appears to retard it by days or weeks (Arnold 1975; Pröve 1974). Certainly more work with chaffinches is necessary, but it is possible that temperate species, such as the chaffinch, would rely more heavily on day length and levels of gonadal androgens in regulating song and its development than would subtropical species such as the zebra finch.

The typical juvenile oscine male in temperate zones must become independent of parents, imitate songs, subsing as practice, molt (postjuvenile or prebasic I), and migrate, not necessarily in that order or in a nonoverlapping sequence; do these different events affect, limit, or interfere with one another in any way? Also, a juvenile of a migratory species that is hatched early in the year faces considerably different light–dark schedules, and before migrating south he may have twice the amount of time to complete song imitation, molting, and so on of a young male hatched near the end of the breeding season. We know that, in several species, young hatched later in the year disperse further (see Dhondt & Huble 1968), but is the timing of the song-learning phase then different as well? In addition to interspecies differences, it is highly possible that there are significant intrapopulational and interpopulational differences within species as well.

In order to address some of these questions, I chose the marsh wren (*Cistothorus palustris*) for an intensive study of the timing and processes of song learning. Welter (1935), Kale (1965), and Verner (1964, 1965) have studied many details of the life history of this species, providing an excellent background for an examination of the male song, which appears to play such a prominent role in the breeding biology of the species. Furthermore, Verner's recent (1975) study of the singing behavior of eastern Washington populations reveals that (1) males may sing well over 100 different types of songs (2) neighboring males within a population have repertoires of nearly identical song types, and (3) males interact by countersinging with the same song type. The large repertoire size may at first seem too cumbersome for laboratory studies; on the contrary, as will be seen, a tremendous amount of information about song learning and its sensitive phase can be gleaned from a single individual, far more than from species in which males learn a single song type. It is true that analysis of data for a given male becomes a greater burden, but with continuous spectrum analyzers becoming increasingly available, the advantages of working with large-repertoire species greatly outweigh the disadvantages. The repertoire size of song types, degree of theme matching during countersinging (Verner & Kroodsma in preparation), and several aspects of marsh wren population ecology (Kale 1965; Verner 1964; Welter 1935) vary geographically, making the marsh wren an intriguing subject for an evolutionary and comparative study.

To test some of the general features of song learning, in July 1974 two marsh wren males were collected and raised from about 10 days of age. Three tutor tapes were prepared, each with nine different song types. The two males were then exposed to one set of nine songs between the ages of 15 and 65 days, to another set of nine songs between 65 and 115 days, and to the third set of nine songs the following spring. Both of the males learned (i.e., imitated) all 9 of the song types to which they were exposed before 65 days of age but none of the 18 songs heard after that age; neither male improvised any song types, so each of the two males had identical song type repertoires.

In order to refine this experiment and to determine the relative sensitivity to song learning throughout these first couple of months of life, nine young male marsh wrens, beginning at ages 6 to 15 days were exposed over a 72-day period to 44 different song types (see Fig. 20.1A). On each of the 72 days, the subjects heard 1,000 repetitions of each of three different song types; however, some song types were presented for 3 successive days (song types 1 to 24; Fig. 20.1A), some for 6 days (types 25 to 36), and some for 9 days (types 37 to 44).

Males were adept at imitating song types that were heard over 3- as well as 9-day periods and learned an average of 15.6 song types each ($n = 9$; range 9 to 20). In addition to these songs heard and learned from the tutor tape, males

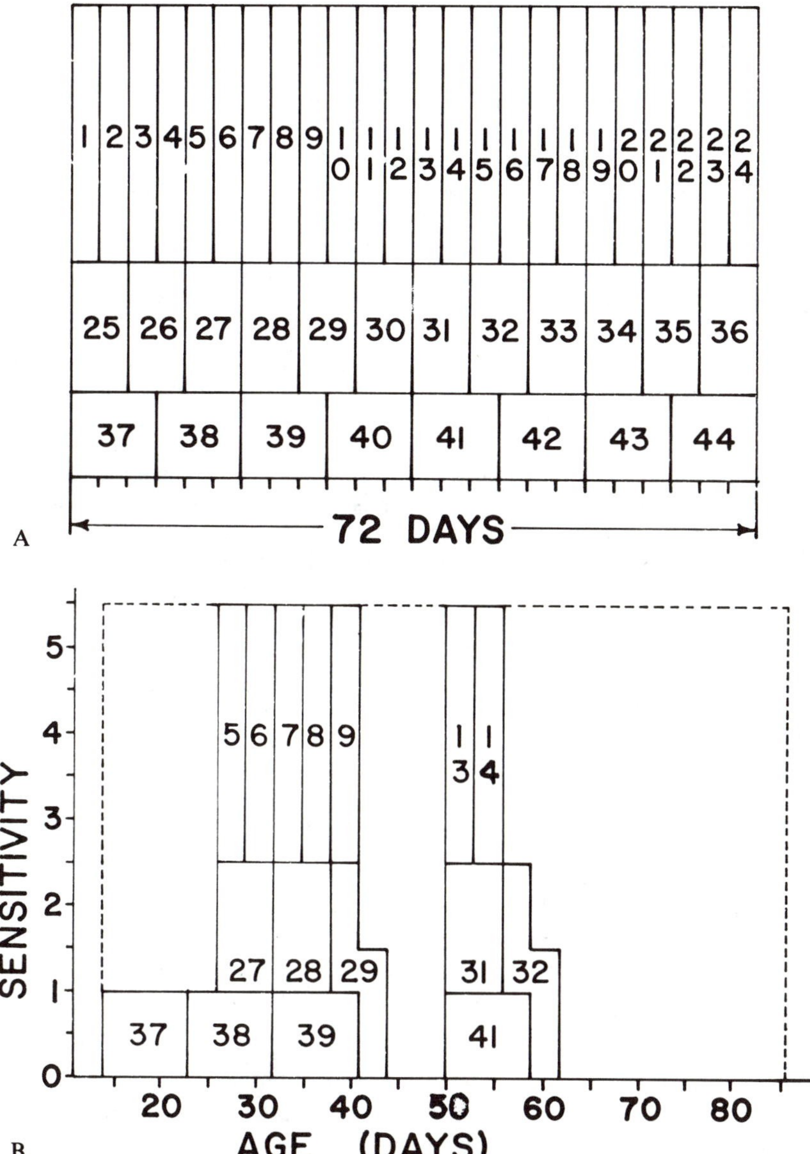

Figure 20.1. Determining the sensitive phase in the marsh wren, a typical songbird with a large repertoire of song types. *A*. Over a period of 72 days, 44 different song types are presented to each male. Song types 1 to 24 are presented over 3-day periods, 25 to 36 over 6-day periods, and 37 to 44 over 9-day periods. *B*. Cells representing song types that were imitated remain in this figure, and portions of cells (here, 29 and 32) are dropped to the abscissa in order to yield the histogram appearance of a typical sensitive phase for an individual marsh wren male. The dashed line indicates the maximum sensitivity to song learning that this male could have achieved if he had learned all song types presented to him at a given age.

averaged 2.4 improvised song types in their repertoires (range 0 to 6). Thus, the average repertoire size for the nine males the following spring, when about 300 days old, was 18 song types (range 10 to 23).

Data for the sensitive phase of a typical male with 16 learned song types appear in Figure 20.1B. Song types presented over 9, 6, and 3 days give increasingly finer resolution as to the exact age when a song type was learned; arbitrary units of sensitivity have been used, and the rectangular areas for all learned song types are equal (thus, 9 days × 1 sensitivity unit = 6 days × 1.5 sensitivity units = 3 days × 3 sensitivity units = 9 day-sensitivity units). Data for the male in Figure 20.1*B* indicate an overall sensitive phase confined to the age of 14 to 62 days, with peak learning occurring between 26 and 56 days. The data suggest a bimodal learning curve, with a phase of maximum sensitivity occurring in the mid-30s and the early 50s but a minimum sensitivity at about 45 days of age.

When the data for all nine males are combined (see Kroodsma 1978), these general features of the sensitive phase persist. There is a gradual increase and decrease in the ability to learn songs from a tutor tape, with apparent peaks of sensitivity at roughly 33 and 54 days and a minimum of sensitivity at 45 days. Thus, the sensitive phase in the marsh wren is not sharply defined but has a gradual onset and termination (see also Chap. 14). The apparent dip in sensitivity to song learning was probably caused by the dispersal of the young birds from one location to another during the experiment. The first tutor tape heard at the new location involved song types 11, 30, and 40; types 30 and 40 were learned by a few, but type 11 was not learned by any of the nine males. The minimum sensitivity at day 45 was then an artifact of housing conditions, but it may be a biologically significant artifact. In nature juveniles disperse at roughly this age, and learning songs during dispersal may be suppressed by a similar mechanism.

Also, as outlined in Chapter 14, the duration of the sensitive phase for song learning may depend on the nature and intensity of the stimuli. Male marsh wrens can learn song types from loudspeakers, but this is a relatively sterile tutor technique compared to the dynamic interactions that the juvenile male may experience in nature. In the Bewick's wren, meager evidence in the field indicated that the social interaction with neighboring territorial adults determined the song types that the juvenile would sing as an adult (Kroodsma 1974). Among marsh wrens, song learning can occur as late as 80 days of age, indicating that marsh wrens are also capable of postdispersal song learning.

In order to test the flexibility of the sensitive period for song learning in the juvenile marsh wren, I devised several experimental conditions in which juveniles were exposed first to 20 song types via a tutor tape and loudspeaker from day 15 to day 45 and then later that same fall or the next spring to varying amounts of social interaction with adult males that had repertoires of song types entirely different from those on the tutor tape. This social interaction occurred, then, (1) during the fall, about 2 weeks after the juvenile was independent of adult care and therefore capable of dispersing and/or (2) during the following spring, when the young male returned from the wintering grounds to the breeding marshes.

Overall, the experimental data for 13 males indicate a flexibility in the timing of song learning for a juvenile marsh wren. A sizeable repertoire may be acquired before day 45, after day 45 during the first fall, or apparently even the following spring after a young male returns from his first year on the wintering grounds. However, song learning during the young male's first spring seems to require stimulation from an adult singing male, for at this time I have had no success in tutoring young males ($n = 6$) in new song types via a loudspeaker. The caveat that working with artificial stimuli (here, songs over loudspeakers) may lead to erroneous conclusions about the nature of a learning process has been echoed in Chapter 14.

IMITATION VERSUS IMPROVISATION

For humans, Jerison (1973, 1976) and Freedle and Lewis (1977) argue persuasively that social interaction was the key to language evolution (phylogeny) and remains essential for language acquisition (ontogeny). Likewise, the quality of the social interaction among different bird species has probably been the focus of natural selection in the evolution of differing degrees and time periods for the ability to learn songs. In those bird species in which marked philopatry to a given location is demonstrated, a sensitive phase terminating soon after the establishment of site fidelity insures that interacting males will possess like songs; marsh wren, white-crowned sparrow, swamp sparrow, cardinal, and Bewick's wren males all remain in or return repeatedly to the same territory, and sensitive phases in these species appear to terminate during the first year of life. On the other hand, the social environment of some species may change dramatically, and the ability to alter vocalizations throughout life may coevolve as a means of insuring that interacting conspecifics will possess like communication signals. An indigo bird, for example, may move from one dialect area to another, and the male may change his entire song repertoire during such a move (Payne personal communication). Vocal learning among cardueline finches includes call notes, and Mundinger (1970) has demonstrated that call learning and modification throughout life are crucial in maintaining cohesiveness of both the breeding pair and the nonbreeding flock. And the long-lived (see Lill & Snow 1974) duetting species in the tropics also demonstrate this ability to modify and learn vocalizations throughout life; such vocal flexibility presumably is essential for maintaining and reinforcing the pair bond within these species (Thorpe 1972).

Conversely, the sedge wren (*Cistothorus platensis*) has emerged as an exemplar species in which (1) imitation plays a minor role in song development and (2) philopatry is poorly expressed. Breeding populations of the sedge wren may arrive or leave in the middle of the breeding season, they may be present or absent in a given year, and adult males may or may not return yearly to the same territory to breed. Thus, interactions with a given individual may occur for only several weeks; here, development of a large repertoire does not involve imitation, as in the more sedentary and/or philopatric marsh wren. Rather, a large song type repertoire appears to develop largely through improvisation; all songs are unmistakably those of the sedge wren, but neighboring males do not share similar song types (Kroodsma & Verner 1978). Thus, the generalized song developed by the sedge wren may actually facilitate the mixing of individuals from different geographical locations within the range of the species.

Counter examples for the above reasoning undoubtedly exist, but where are the species with precise vocal imitation, well-defined sensitive phases for song imitation, and high mobility (i.e., low philopatry)? In species in which individuals demonstrate such high mobility, interactions with a given conspecific or within a given population are relatively brief. I would predict that in these mobile species, sensitive phases and precise vocal imitation of adult conspecifics are less likely to evolve or be maintained than in more philopatric populations, in which an extended period of interaction with a limited number of individuals is the rule. The highly sedentary *nuttalli* race of the white-crowned sparrow may represent one extreme of the continuum, for here vocal imitation during a brief sensitive phase and remarkable philopatry and low dispersal rates apparently lead to a correlation of dialect areas with populations of individuals that are genetically similar to one another (Baker 1975a, 1975b; Baker & Mewaldt 1978; Marler 1970a).

This may be the essence of the difference in migratory and nonmigratory populations of several species in North America. For example, the rufous-sided towhee (*Pipilo erythrophthalmus*) of the western United States is sedentary, and neighboring males have very similar song type repertoires; precise song imitation during a limited sensitive phase probably is involved (Kroodsma 1971). Eastern populations, on the other hand, are migratory, and the songs of neighboring males are usually dissimilar; adults do return yearly to the same territories (Ewert personal communication), so either the young do not return to the same location where they imitated the details of adult songs, or else improvisation plays a greater role in song development among eastern birds. Laboratory studies of the ontogeny of song in males from these two populations should reveal the answer.

Eastern and western populations, again migratory and resident, respectively, of the red-winged blackbird (*Agelaius phoeniceus;* Zimmer & Morton personal communication) and the white-crowned sparrow (Baptista 1975, 1977; Marler & Tamura 1964) also differ. Eastern red-wings did not demonstrate an overwhelming ability to imitate tutor songs (Marler et al. 1972), but negative results could indicate that some element of the tutoring regime may have been inadequate (e.g., lack of social interaction, which is required in some species, or perhaps tutoring during a nonsensitive phase in the juvenile's life). Eastern populations do not have song dialects (Zimmer personal communication). However, marked song dialects do exist in some western nonmigratory populations (Morton personal communication), and imitation must therefore occur.

Selection for precise song imitation, whether during a relatively brief sensitive phase or later in life, seems to be prevalent in species in which birds are highly likely to interact with a given conspecific or group of conspecifics over an extended period of time. Social interaction, so dominant in the phylogeny and ontogeny of human language (Feedle & Lewis 1977; Jerome 1973, 1976) appears to be a key element in the evolution of vocal imitation in songbirds as well.

SELECTIVE LEARNING

Song imitation among oscines permits the rapid change of a communication signal and may serve to enhance reproductive isolation in a rapidly evolving population (see Marler 1970b; Nottebohm 1972). At the same time, however, this flexibility in the developmental process presents a hazard to the individual that must, usually during a limited sensitive phase, be exposed to and acquire the vocalizations of conspecific adults. Because examples of misimprinting in nature are extremely rare (see Introduction), we must infer that the young male (and perhaps the female) possesses a relatively fail-safe mechanism that guides song learning along species-typical pathways.

In some species, it seems that a social bond between juvenile and parent may insure learning of the proper vocalizations. Juvenile male zebra finches learn the songs of either conspecific or heterospecific grassfinch parents but do not learn songs merely broadcasted from a loudspeaker (Immelmann 1969; Price personal communication). And in the short-toed treecreeper (*Certhia brachydactyla;* Thielcke 1970), males apparently do not learn from loudspeakers either, but they can learn the song of another male within earshot (but out of visual contact). Thielcke speculated that it was the call note of the adult male that guided the song learning of the juvenile male.

And, of course, selectivity does not seem to be a problem with habitual mimics, such as the mockingbird (*Mimus polyglottos*) of North America. However, even the mockingbird may be selective, for interesting differences in the amount of heterospecific imitation occur throughout the range of the species, with more intraspecific and less interspecific imitation occurring where mockingbird populations are most dense. Numerous deprivation experiments in the laboratory, where juvenile males are exposed to none or an insufficient number of vocalizations from their own species, have also revealed that the young male of several oscine species may be capable of imitating diverse sounds; however, given a choice of its own or other species vocalizations, it usually favors conspecifics. Myna birds (*Gracula religiosa*), for example, are renowned mimics in captivity, but in the wild only the calls and vocalizations of conspecific males or females are imitated (Bertram 1970). Lanyon (1957) also demonstrated that meadowlarks will learn songs of other species if deprived of their own songs. And the occasional examples of miscopying among free-living birds may be natural deprivation experiments, with a juvenile raised in relative isolation from other members of its species; such isolation could occur near the edge of a species's range, in populations of low density, or near the end of the breeding season when conspecific adults may not be singing.

But for those species that are able to copy the details of tutor songs from loudspeakers, what cues are used during the song-learning process? If these cues are to be found within the song itself, then in species in which songs are highly variable, the cues must be found in those features of the song that are constant and on which the tremendous variability is superimposed.

Two experiments examining various aspects of selective learning among *Cistothorus* wrens and *Melospiza* sparrows have revealed an array of selective learning among these species. Among the wrens, the sedge wren learned nothing from the array of songs, but rather improvised fairly good wild-type songs on his own (see above). The marsh wren, on the other hand, selectively imitated marsh wren song trills, with a probability exponentially related to the number of marsh wren components in the song (Kroodsma 1979). Among the sparrows, the song sparrows (*M. melodia*) seemed unable to distinguish song from swamp sparrow (*M. georgiana*) song components, learning an equal number of each, whereas the swamp sparrows learned only the song components of conspecific songs, regardless of their context and rate of temporal delivery.

Thus, there is quite a range of abilities in discriminating songs of conspecifics and heterospecifics. Aside from the possible coevolution of nomadism and the ability to improvise a generalized song type in the sedge wren (see "Imitation versus improvisation"), the significance of different abilities in the sparrows and the marsh wren is not immediately clear. Perhaps as more studies are conducted, both the evolutionary significance of this range of abilities and the cues that the discriminating juvenile uses will become clear.

THE NEUROPHYSIOLOGY OF VOCAL ONTOGENY

Important progress has been achieved in recent years in revealing underlying neurophysiological processes occurring during ontogeny of vocalizations in songbirds. The syrinx of birds includes two separate sound sources: the internal tympaniform membranes, which are controlled by muscles in the right and left syringeal halves and innervated by branches of the right and left hypoglossal nerves, respectively. By unilaterally severing branches of either the right or left hypoglossal nerves, the Nottebohms (1971, 1976) have demonstrated that in the canary (*Serinus canarius*), chaffinch, and white-crowned sparrow, it is the left half of the syrinx that produces the majority of sound during vocalization. Furthermore, in the chaffinch, if the left hypoglossal nerve is severed before the juvenile male has fully developed his song, the song will not be abnormal, but the right hemisphere of the brain can assume dominance via the right hypoglossus, leading to normal song development.

Other recent discoveries also provide exciting avenues for research in the ontogeny of bird song. Male song is under the control of circulating testosterone levels in many songbirds, and in the chaffinch it has been demonstrated that the nucleus intercollicularis of the midbrain accumulates testosterone at higher levels than other brain areas (Zigmond et al. 1973). Furthermore, in canaries and zebra finches, the sexual dimorphism of four vocal control areas in the brain appear well correlated with vocal behavior. Three of the vocal control areas are larger in males than in females. The fourth is well developed in males of both species, less well developed in female canaries, and absent in female zebra finches. Males of both species learn songs in their environment and sing during courtship, whereas females normally do not sing. Exogenous testosterone will induce female canaries to sing, but not female zebra finches (Nottebohm & Arnold 1976). Study of the ontogeny of this adult sexual dimorphism in the brain will prove exciting and should reveal some of the fundamental processes occurring during vocal ontogeny.

CONCLUSIONS

My goal throughout this brief chapter has been less to document the known than to reveal the unknown. Careful reflection on what is known about the ontogeny of bird song reveals many loose ends. Pointed questions about those loose ends are raised throughout the text and, it is hoped, will stimulate further research by others.

Specific areas where research is likely to make major advances in the near future include:

1 The ontogeny and the role of female song in mate selection
2 Proximate and ultimate factors involved in sensitive phases
3 Understanding the clues used by juveniles in order to recognize conspecific songs and/or song components
4 The significance of imitation versus improvisation in different life styles
5 The neural and physiological mechanisms involved in vocal ontogeny

With such a diversity of behaviors in species with different life-history strategies, our understanding of the proximate and ultimate factors involved in the evolution of different vocal ontogenies must proceed on a broad front. We must examine divergent or convergent behaviors in closely related or distantly related species before we can arrive at general principles with wide applicability.

ACKNOWLEDGMENTS

I thank Roberta Pickert for help with data analyses and colleagues at Rockefeller University for valuable discussion. Research reported here was funded in part by grants BNS 76–02753 and BNS 78–02753 from the National Science Foundation.

REFERENCES

Arnold, A. P. 1975. The effects of castration on song development in zebra finches (*Poephila guttata*). *Journal of Experimental Zoology* 191:261–278.

Baker, M. C. 1975a. Genetic structure of two populations of white-crowned sparrows with different song dialects. *Condor* 76:351–356.

1975b. Song dialects and genetic differences in white-crowned sparrow (*Zonotrichia leucophrys*). *Evolution* 29:226–241.

Baker, M. C., & L. R. Mewaldt. 1978. Song dialects as barriers to dispersal in white-crowned sparrows, *Zonotrichia leucophrys nuttalli*. *Evolution* 32:712–722.

Baptista, L. F. 1974. The effects of songs of wintering white-crowned sparrows on song development in sedentary populations of the species. *Zeitschrift für Tierpsychologie* 34:147–171.

1975. Song dialects and demes in sedentary populations of the white-crowned sparrow (*Zonotrichia leucophrys nuttalli*). *University of California Publications in Zoology* 105:1–52.

1977. Geographic variation in song and dialects of the Puget Sound white-crowned sparrow. *Condor* 79:356–370.

Baptista, L. F., & H. Wells. 1975. Additional evidence of song-misimprinting in the white-crowned sparrow. *Bird Banding* 46:269–272.

Bertram, B. 1970. The vocal behaviour of the Indian Hill Mynah, *Gracula religiosa*. *Animal Behavior Monographs* 3:79–192.

Dhondt, A. A., & J. Huble. 1968. Fledging-date and sex in relation to dispersal in young great tits. *Bird Study* 15:127–134.

Dittus, W. P. J., & R. E. Lemon. 1969. Effects of song tutoring and acoustic isolation on the song repertoires of cardinals. *Animal Behavior* 17:523–533.

Freedle, R., & M. Lewis. 1977. Prelinguistic conversations. *In: Interaction, conversation, and the development of language*. M. Lewis & L. A. Rosenblum (eds.), Wiley, New York.

Güttinger, H. R. 1977. Variable and constant structures in Greenfinch songs (*Chloris chloris*) in different locations. *Behaviour* 60:304–318.

Immelmann, K. 1969. Song development in the zebra finch and other estrildid finches. *In:* R. A. Hinde (ed.), *Bird vocalizations*. Cambridge University Press, London.

Jenkins, P. F. 1978. Cultural transmission of song patterns and dialect development in a free-living bird population. *Animal Behavior* 26:50–78.

Jerison, H. J. 1973. *Evolution of the brain and intelligence*. Academic Press, New York.

1976. Paleoneurology and the evolution of mind. *Scientific American* 234:64–79.

Kale, H. W., II. 1965. Ecology and bioenergetics of the long-billed marsh wren *Telmatodytes palustris griseus* (Brewster), in Georgia salt marshes. *Publications of the Nuttall Ornithology Club* 5:1–142.

Kern, M. D., & J. R. King. 1972. Testosterone-induced singing in female white-crowned sparrows. *Condor* 74:204–209.

Konishi, M., & F. Nottebohm. 1969. Experimental studies in the ontogeny of avian vocalizations. *In:* R. A. Hinde (ed.), *Bird vocalizations*. Cambridge University Press, London.

Kroodsma, D. E. 1971. Song variations and singing behavior in the rufous-sided towhee, *Pipilo erythrophthalmus oregonus*. *Condor* 73:303–308.

1972. Variations in songs of vesper sparrows in Oregon. *Wilson Bulletin* 84:173–178.

1973. Coexistence of Bewick's wrens and house wrens in Oregon. *Auk* 90:341–352.

1974. Song learning, dialects, and dispersal in the Bewick's wren. *Zeitschrift für Tierpsychologie* 35:352–380.

1977. A re-evaluation of song development in the song sparrow. *Animal Behaviour* 25:390–399.

1978. Aspects of learning in the ontogeny of bird song: where, from whom, when, how many, which, and how accurately? *In:* G. Burghardt & M. Bekoff (eds.), *Comparative and evolutionary aspects of behavioral development*. Garland Press, New York.

1979. Vocal dueling among male marsh wrens: evidence for ritualized expressions of dominance/subordinance. *Auk* 96:506–515.

Kroodsma, D. E., & J. Verner. 1978. Complex singing behaviors among *Cistothorus* wrens. *Auk* 95:703–716.

Lanyon, W. E. 1957. The comparative biology of the meadowlark (*Sturnella*) in Wisconsin. *Publications of the Nuttall Ornithology Club* 1:1–67.

Lill, A., & D. W. Snow. 1974. Longevity records for some neotropical land birds. *Condor* 76:262–267.

Marler, P. 1970a. A comparative approach to vocal learning: song development in white-crowned sparrows. *Journal of Comparative and Physiological Psychology* 71:1–25.

1970b. Birdsong and speech development: could there be parallels? *American Scientist* 58:669–673.

1976. Sensory templates in species-specific behavior. *In:* J. Fentress (ed.), *Simpler networks and behavior.* Sinauer, Sunderland, Massachusetts.

1978. Perception and innate knowledge. *In: Proceedings of the 13th Nobel Conference on "The Nature of Life,"* 111–139.

Marler, P., & P. Mundinger. 1971. Vocal learning in birds. *In:* H. Moltz (ed.), *Ontogeny of vertebrate behavior.* Academic Press, New York.

Marler, P., P. Mundinger, M. S. Waser, & A. Lutjen. 1972. Effects of acoustical stimulation and deprivation on song development in red-winged blackbirds (*Agelaius phoeniceus*). *Animal Behaviour* 20:586–606.

Marler, P., & S. Peters. 1977. Selective vocal learning in a sparrow. *Science* 198:519–521.

Marler, P., & M. Tamura. 1964. Culturally transmitted patterns of vocal behavior in sparrows. *Science* 146:1483–1486.

Mundinger, P. C. 1970. Vocal imitation and individual recognition of finch calls. *Science* 168:480–482.

Nicolai, J. 1964. Der Brutparasitismus der Viduinae als ethologisches Problem. *Zeitschrift für Tierpsychologie* 21:129–204.

Nottebohm, F. 1969a. The song of the chingolo, *Zonotrichia capensis,* in Argentina: description and evaluation of a system of dialects. *Condor* 71:299–315.

1969b. The "critical period" for song learning in birds. *Ibis* 111:386–387.

1970. Ontogeny of bird song. *Science* 167:950–956.

1971. Neural lateralization of vocal control in a passerine bird. 1. Song. *Journal of Experimental Zoology* 177:229–261.

1972. The origins of vocal learning. *American Naturalist* 106:116–140.

Nottebohm, F., & A. P. Arnold. 1976. Sexual dimorphism in vocal control areas of the songbird brain. *Science* 194:211–213.

Nottebohm, F., & M. E. Nottebohm. 1976. Left hypoglossal dominance in the control of canary and white-crowned sparrow song. *Journal of Comparative Physiology* 108:171–192.

Orians, G. 1969. On the evolution of mating systems in birds and mammals. *American Naturalist* 103:589–603.

Payne, R. B. 1973. Behavior, mimetic songs and song dialects, and relationships of the parasitic indigobirds (*Vidua*) of Africa. *Ornithology Monographs* 11:1–333.

Petrinovich, L. 1972. Psychobiological mechanisms in language development. *Advances in Psychobiology* 1:259–285.

Pröve, E. 1974. Der Einfluß von Kastration und Testosteronsubstitution auf das Sexualverhalten männlicher Zebrafinken (*Taeniopygia guttata castanotis* Gould). *Journal für Ornithologie* 115:338–347.

1978. Quantitative Untersuchungen zu Wechselbeziehungen zwischen Balzaktivität und Testosterontitern bei männlichen Zebrafinken. (*Taeniopygia guttata castanotis* Gould). *Zeitschrift für Tierpsychologie* 48:47–67.

Sossinka, R., E. Pröve, & H. H. Kalberlah. 1975. Der Einfluß von Testosteron auf den Gesangsbeginn beim Zebrafinken (*Taeniopygia guttata castanotis*). *Zeitschrift für Tierpsychologie* 39:259–264.

Sullivan, G. A. 1976. Song of the finch *Lagonostricta senegala:* interspecific mimicry by its brood-parasite *Vidua chalybeata* and the role of song in the host's social context. *Animal Behaviour* 24:880–888.

Thielcke, G. 1966. Ritualized distinctiveness of song in closely related sympatric species. *Philosophical Transactions of the Royal Society of London,* Series B, 251:493–497.

1970. Lernen von Gesang als möglicher Schrittmacher der Evolution. *Zeitschrift für zoologische Systematik Evolutionsforschung* 8:309–320.

Thorpe, W. H. 1958. The learning of song patterns by birds, with special reference to the song of the chaffinch, *Fringilla coelebs. Ibis* 100:535–570.

1972. Duetting and antiphonal song in birds. Its extent and significance. *Behaviour,* Suppl. 18.

Verner, J. 1964. Evolution of polygamy in the long-billed marsh wren. *Evolution* 18:252–261.

1965. Time budget of the male long-billed marsh wren during the breeding season. *Condor* 67:124–139.

1975. Complex song repertoire of male long-billed marsh wrens in eastern Washington. *The Living Bird* 14:263–300.

Welter, W. A. 1935. The natural history of the long-billed marsh wren. *Wilson Bulletin* 47:3–34.

Zigmond, R. E., F. Nottebohm, & D. W. Pfaff. 1973. Androgen-concentrating cells in the midbrain of a songbird. *Science* 179:1005–1007.

21

THE BEGINNINGS OF SPEECH

MICHAEL STUDDERT-KENNEDY

Man's life is diverse. The range of habitats, natural and man-made, to which he has adapted is incomparably wider than that of any other species. This is so because man evolved capacities for rapid cultural evolution to augment the lengthier biological processes of adaptive radiation. These capacities have permitted him to create new and unpredictable patterns of behavior in the face of both old and new contingencies. The nature of these capacities is unknown. But we can be sure that language is among them, and that an understanding of its biology would take us a long way toward understanding the history of man and the earth during the past 10,000 years.

Unfortunately, "the development of human speech represents a quantum jump in evolution comparable to the assembly of the eucaryotic cell" (Wilson 1975:556). Whatever the lost links in phyletic evolution since the first hominids diverged from the apes, presently living species offer few analogies and even fewer homologies with language. In fact, the most fruitful approaches to its biology seem to be those that have been followed for many years by developmental psycholinguists (for reviews, see Brown 1973; Dale 1976; Ferguson & Slobin 1973) and by students of neurophysiology (e.g., Lenneberg 1967; Lenneberg & Lenneberg 1975; Whitaker & Whitaker 1976): first, study of its ontogeny, with particular attention to similarities within and across language communities; second, study of its pathology in childhood and adult aphasia.

The present chapter makes no attempt to review the vast resulting literature. Instead it undertakes to examine critically several tempting analogies with language in the great apes and in the song learning of oscine birds. Analogies often have the heuristic value of leading us to look at familiar facts from a fresh viewpoint. Moreover, they may be instructive even if they prove to be false.

THE NATURE OF LANGUAGE

If we compare language with other animal communication systems, it is by its breadth of function that we are struck. The flashing white rump of the fallow deer denotes alarm; the "peep" of the squirrel monkey indicates that it is alone and wishes it wasn't; the song of the chaffinch informs the interested listener of its species, sex, local origin, personal identity, and readiness to breed or fight.

Even the elaborate dance of the honeybee merely conveys information about the direction, distance, and quality of a nectar trove. But language can convey information about all these matters and many more besides. In fact, it is the peculiar property of language to set no limits on the possible topics of discourse.

More exactly, no language consists of a finite number of sentences. This fact may be demonstrated by formal proof (Chomsky 1956) or by the persuasive calculation that a single rendering of all grammatical English sentences of up to, say, 20 words in length would last several hundred years (Miller et al. 1960:146). In fact, no normal speaker of a language – no matter how limited his vocabulary or tedious his conversation – speaks by rote or constructs an utterance by drawing its components from a store of ready-made phrases.

How does language achieve this openness or productivity? There are several crucial features to its design (Hockett 1960). First, language is learned; it develops under the control of an open rather than a closed genetic program (Mayr 1974). Transmission of the code from one generation to the next is therefore discontinuous; each individual re-creates the system for himself. There is ample room here for creative error – probably a central factor in the evolution of language and in the constant process of change that all languages undergo (Kiparsky 1968). One incidental consequence is that the universal properties of language (whatever they may be) are largely masked by the surface variety of the several thousand languages now spoken in the world, not to mention their thousands of dialects and idiolects.

A second condition of productivity is that linguistic signals are arbitrary. With a few onomatopoeic exceptions, only by coincidence does a sign share any property with its referent. Of course, many other animal signals are arbitrary: the courtship rituals of the great-crested grebe, the abdomen of the egg-laden stickleback, the blush of a shamed human. But under the surface of such instances, some unknown physiological necessity is at work. These are not the arbitrary signs of convention by which *bird, oiseau, Vogel,* and *uccello* are equivalent. Notice that if signs were iconic rather than arbitrary, the number of possible referents would be limited by the signaling organism's physical capacity to represent or depict.

A third, closely related condition of productivity is that signals are discrete rather than analog (Marler 1963). To be precise, signals are perceived as discrete, even if they are not physically separable. Here again, if signals were not categorized by the receiver and if changes of meaning required changes of degree along some continuous scale, the number of possible signals would be limited by the number of possibly and perceptibly variable dimensions of the signal.

A final condition of productivity, and the one to which we will give most attention, is that language has two hierarchically related levels of structure: Its signal elements are combined according to two more or less independent systems of rules. At the lower level of each language, that of phonology or sound system, a small set (usually between 20 and 60) of meaningless phonemes (consonants and vowels) is specified, together with rules for their combination into morphemes (meaningful units that, for present purposes, we may treat as roughly equivalent to words). These are the rules that permit a vast, if not infinite, lexicon to be constructed by permutation and combination of a few dozen alphabetic units.

At a second level of structure, that of syntax, the rules for combining words into meaningful sentences are specified. These are the rules that permit us to predicate relations among objects or events. Central to the syntax of every language are recursive rules by which a sentence may be treated as a component in another sentence. This capacity to embed a sentence within a sentence means that the set of all possible sentences in a language is infinite (Chomsky 1956). Moreover, it is through this device that we can extend our communicative reach by constructing complex sentential names for referents not represented in our lexicon, a trick already in the armory of many 3-year-olds: "I want the one Mary's got" (Limber 1973). Incidentally, it is this central, inventive (though commonplace) use of language that Premack (1976:15) thinks it "absurd" to expect of the chimpanzee.

IMPLICATIONS OF DUAL STRUCTURE

We begin to apprehend the importance of a dual structure if we imagine a language with only one level, say that of sound (cf. Liberman & Studdert-Kennedy 1978). Such a language would consist of meaningless elements (perhaps consonants and vowels) combined into lexical items, a set of words each with a different referent. Its users would presumably be confined to ostensive definition. For even if they were able to conceive of absent objects ("the bear we met yesterday") or abstract ideas ("the solar year") and were able to construct, from their phonetic resources, new lexical items to refer to them, they would be quite unable, lacking discursive speech, to establish the new meanings with their fellows. It is only by means of syntax that we are able to deploy old (known) words into new (previously unknown) statements – such as those that define new words. In short, rules for syntactic structure are a sine qua non of linguistic productivity.

The lack of a sound structure, on the other hand, would be less crippling. For even if we were to replace every word in the lexicon with an arbitrary number (as might be done if the lexicon were stored in a computer), the syntactic structure of any particular utterance would be preserved despite the total loss of phonetic equivalences. (It is for this reason that linguists sometimes describe a language as an abstract system of communication, independent of its medium of expression.) Each lexical item would then be a totally distinct sign, lacking any systematic physical relation to any other. Of course, the number of such irreducible, holistically distinct signals that humans are capable of recalling, producing, and identifying at even a moderate rate – let alone the 50 bits per second typical of much speech – is certainly small, and it is not surprising that most vertebrate communication systems dispose of no more than 10 to 40 signals (Wilson 1975:183). However, a small lexicon does not preclude a productive syntax. That is why Premack (1976) and Rumbaugh (1977) saw no need for a formational structure in the visual symbols they devised for their pongid pupils.

Nonetheless, having granted that phonological (or word formational) structure is not, in principle, necessary for productive language, we must next acknowledge that every known language does, in fact, display it. The extra level of sound structure – which perhaps was prior to syntax in phyletic evolution, as it is in ontogeny – must therefore fulfill some function.

That function, as we have already suggested, is to facilitate the formation of a lexicon. Whether or not the lexical, or naming, function is at the root of language, as is sometimes argued (e.g., Lancaster 1968), most linguistic communities do have – in addition to their everyday lexicon of several thousand words – large, more or less specialized vocabularies, crucial to their cultural elaboration of the environment. This is as true of "primitive" peoples, such as the Hanunoo of the Philippines with their vast inventories of flora and fauna (Levi-Strauss 1968), as of a modern industrial society with its proliferation of technical terms and subculture jargon. Thus, the seemingly trivial discovery that an essentially unlimited lexicon could be constructed from a small alphabet of sounds may have been the catalyst that set linguistic development in motion by providing an interface between man's intellect and his peripheral anatomic structure (Liberman 1970; Mattingly 1975). Certainly, it is at the level of the signaling system (that is, of speech), rather than of the abstract syntactic and semantic structure, that we find the clearest traces of biological adaptation, and it is therefore primarily with speech that the following sections are concerned.

THE SIGNALING SYSTEM

The sounds of any language can be viewed as the product of a sound source and a resonant filter. The sound source is usually either the voice produced by rapid pulsing of the vocal cords (as in the final sounds of *be* and *do*), the hiss of air blown through a narrow constriction (as in the initial and final sounds of *safe* and *thrush*), or both (as in the final sounds of *leave* and *bees*). The resonant filter is the vocal tract, that is, the cavities of the pharynx, mouth, and nose.

The pulsing of the vocal cords at fundamental frequencies of roughly 90 to 250 Hz for males, 150 to 350 Hz for females, and somewhat higher for small children yields a signal rich in harmonic frequencies (multiples of the fundamental). Relatively slow variations in fundamental frequency over the course of an utterance yield the characteristic melody or intonation of speech. Taken with systematic variations in intensity, rate, and rhythm, this melody is the basis of speech prosody and plays an important role in communicating the emotional tone of an utterance as well as, to some extent, its syntactic structure (e.g., question, statement, imperative). To the unfamiliar listener (whether infant or foreigner), the slow variations of prosody are probably more salient than the rapid patter of consonant–vowel syllables. But it is primarily by syllables that the distinctively linguistic (lexical and syntactic) information is carried. That, incidentally, is why writing systems encode phonetic segments, but not prosody.

For the most part, this distinctively linguistic information is conveyed by systematic variations in the tuning of the vocal tract. The curved column of air in the tract, like that in an alpine horn, resonates in characteristic frequency bands (or formants) when set in motion by air from some vibrating source, with the result that some of the source frequency components are amplified whereas

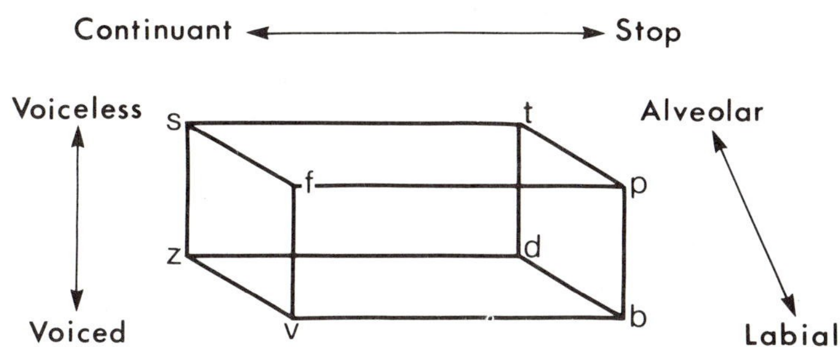

Figure 21.1. A three-dimensional binary feature space, excerpted from the multidimensional feature space that describes the English phonological system.

others are attenuated. If we vary the size and shape of the resonating tract by shifting the relative positions of the articulators, especially the tongue, lips, jaw, and soft palate, the resulting shifts in the formants yield the various sound spectra characteristic of particular phonetic segments. The reader may find it instructive to monitor the position and shape of his tongue as he runs it around the vowel triangle: *eat, it, et, at, aht, ought, oot.*

THE SOUND PATTERN OF LANGUAGE

Here we must introduce the concept of a sound system or phonology. Each language forms its words from a relatively small alphabet of distinctive phonetic segments, termed *phonemes.* These are its consonants and vowels, and in English there are about 35 of them, depending on dialect. The phonemes are not chosen randomly. Each may be described in terms of the small set of binary features (usually a dozen or so) deployed in a particular language. The phonemes may then be classified according to their shared features and the resulting classes contrasted to one another on the basis of their feature oppositions. A basic division, observed in every language, is between consonants, formed by a more or less complete constriction of the vocal tract, and vowels, formed with a relatively open tract. From their contrastive combination is formed the fundamental unit of all spoken language, the consonant–vowel syllable. It is the repeated opening and closing of the tract and the consequent repetitive frequency and amplitude modulation, or syllabic beat, that establishes the characteristic rhythms of human speech.

We may draw further contrasts among the phonemes (Fig. 21.1). For example, in English we may draw contrasts between voiced (*/b,d,v,z/*) and voiceless (*/p,t,f,s/*), between continuant (*/s,f,z,v/*) and stop (*/t,p,d,b/*), between constriction at the alveolar ridge behind the upper front teeth (*/s,z,t,d/*) and constriction at the lips (*/f,v,p,b/*). Taken together, these eight phonemes, formed from three binary contrasts, constitute a little system within the large system of English phonology.

The particular selection of features used in any language is largely determined by phonetic drift over time and by a complex of historical and social forces. But the universal stock of phonetic features is presumably constrained by human anatomy and physiology: They must be drawn from the (as yet unspecified) intersection of what we can articulate with what we can perceive. The goal of much work (e.g., Chomsky & Halle 1968; Jakobson et al. 1963; Ladefoged 1971) has been to define the smallest set of universal features (perhaps fewer than 20) that will include all features that may be distinctive in any language.

But there is more to the phonology of a language than the structure of its phonemic system. Each language also disposes of more or less elaborate rules for combining phonemes into words: These are the rules of its syllable structure. For example, in English the basic syllable structure can be represented as *(C) (C) (C) V (C) (C) (C) (C)*, where *C* = consonant, *V* = vowel, and parentheses indicate that the slot may or may not be filled. Thus, the simplest syllable is an isolated vowel. But in most syllables the required vowel is preceded by up to three consonants and followed by up to five consonants (the latter only in a few rare words such as *triumph'st;* Abercrombie 1967).

Moreover, there are strict limits on the permissible consonant clusters. For example, in English, if two obstruents (stops or fricatives) occur together, the voicing of the second must match the voicing of the first. Accordingly, English words may begin with *sp-, st-,* or *sk-,* but not with *sb-, sd-,* or *sg-*. Hence, too, the plurals in *-s* or *-z* (*apes, lions*), the present indicatives in *-s* or *-z* (she *raps,* she *loves*), and the past in *-t* or *-d* (*rapped, loved*). A subsidiary rule states that, if the two obstruents are formed by closure at roughly the same point in the vocal tract, a neutral vowel (the so-called schwa) must be inserted between them, giving the plural, *roses,* the present indicative, *she kisses,* and the past, *she hated.* Most normal children growing up among English speakers have unconsciously learned these rules by the age of about 6 and therefore have no difficulty in forming the correct plural, present, and past forms of words they have never heard before (Berko 1958).

The point of this example is to make it clear that much more is required to learn the sound structure of a language than the capacity to listen and to imitate. In fact, as we shall see ("The infant as pattern seeker"), even within its first year of life, the infant has begun to discover and apply rules.

THE FUNCTION OF PHONETIC FEATURES

We have defined features up to this point in articulatory terms. In part, this is because precise acoustic description, drawing on spectrographic analysis, has proved intractable. But it is principally because articulation is, in fact, prior to the acoustic signal. Indeed, it has been plausibly argued that the feature structure of spoken language was primarily a solution to the problem of getting high-speed articulatory performance out of low-speed articulatory machinery (Liberman et al. 1967). The feature structure permits a shift from one phoneme to the next by a change of no more than one or a few articulatory features. The value of articulatory ease is attested to by the universal phenomenon of assimilation. Every language has many rules by which certain sounds or classes of sounds take on features of neighboring sounds, permitting a lazier and so more rapid articulation. For example, the final *n* of the prefix *syn-* (*synthesis, synechdoche*) becomes *m* in *symbiosis* and *sympathy*, taking on the labial articulation of the following consonant. Similarly, normally voiced *l*, sounded with laryngeal pulsing in *light*, takes on the voiceless feature of *s* in a word such as *slight*.

Of course, a gain for the speaker may be a loss for the listener. It is precisely such shifts in articulation and the consequent subtle shingling of the acoustic properties of neighboring phonemes that have thwarted attempts at automatic speech recognition and given rise to the central problems for a theory of speech perception. Parallel (or co-) articulation of consonant and vowel in the integral ballistic gesture of the syllable (Stetson 1952) gives rise to an acoustic signal in which the cues to a particular phoneme vary widely as a function of context and in which the boundaries between successive phonemes are obliterated. The tempting model that language might have been expected to offer for the division of motor behavior into natural units is thus a mirage. The units are not to be found either in the articulation or in the acoustic signal. The problem of segmentation appears to be solved by perceptual fiat. Not surprisingly, this has encouraged theorists of speech perception to invoke exotic perceptual mechanisms such as analysis-by-synthesis (Stevens & Halle 1967; cf. Liberman et al. 1967) and "dedicated" property or feature-detecting devices (see "Templates and feature detectors").

Perhaps specialized perceptual mechanisms have indeed evolved to match the specialized motor mechanisms. There is strong evidence in vocal tract morphology, in tongue and lip innervation, in mechanisms for breath control during speech, and so on, that extensive adaptations for speech did occur (Du Brul 1977; Lenneberg 1967; Lieberman 1972). Perhaps these and matching perceptual adaptations (including specialized sensorimotor processes for imitation) underlie the evolution of language. However, once the capacity for language had evolved, man was able to deploy it in another mode. What is interesting is that, when he does so, as in American Sign Language, the formal structure of the system remains largely unchanged.

AN ALTERNATIVE SIGNALING SYSTEM: MANUAL SIGN LANGUAGE

Visual and tactile finger-spelling, like alphabetic and syllabic writing, are parasitic on speech: They simply transpose its units into another modality. However, some visual languages are independent of spoken language: for example, the sign languages of the American Plains Indians (West 1960), of the Australian aborigines (Umiker-Sebeok & Sebeok 1977), and of countless deaf communities in the various countries of the world (Stokoe 1974). The signs of these languages do not necessarily correspond to the words of any particular spoken language, nor do the rules for their combination follow the syntax of any spoken language.

Consider, as an example, because it has been the most extensively studied, American Sign Language (ASL). ASL is a derivative of the French sign language (SL) introduced by Gallaudet to the United States in 1817. Users of Ameslan today understand French SL better than British SL – evidence for the independence of sign and spoken languages. The first dictionary of ASL (Stokoe et al. 1965) contains over 2,000 signs. Many of them seem iconic, but usually not until one knows what they mean – just as one may not recognize the metaphor in, say, "The road *runs* west" until it is pointed out. Other signs are indexical; pronouns, for example, are often formed by pointing. However, pantomime is rare. The overwhelming majority of signs is arbitrary or, if once iconic, has now lost much of the iconicity (Frishberg 1975).

Signs may require the use of one or two hands and may vary along at least three orthogonal dimensions: shape, position within the signing area (a rough circle around the head and chest, centered below the chin), and movement. Stokoe et al. (1965) have analyzed the values along these dimensions into some 55 *cheremes,* a number well within the phonemic count of spoken languages. Later work (e.g., Battison 1974; Klima & Bellugi 1979; Lane et al. 1976) has demonstrated that formational rules govern the possible combinations of cheremes into signs, just as the phonological rules of a language govern the combination of phonemes into words. Finally, ASL has a grammar with various inflections and a syntax, that is, a set of rules governing the spatial and temporal ordering of signs into sentences (Klima & Bellugi 1979; Siple 1978). In short, ASL displays all the distinctive properties of a human language, including a dual pattern of shape and syntax.

The significance of this recent work on ASL is twofold. First, it underlines the link between hand and mouth and the likely importance of a rapid, informationally dense signaling system for efficient linguistic communication, a point to which we return below. Second, it demonstrates the abstractness of the capacities underlying language development. So far as we know, no other animal has developed a capacity for essentially equivalent communication in two different sensorimotor systems.

THE GREAT APES

Recent successes in training apes to communicate by means of artificial symbol systems (Premack 1976; Rumbaugh 1977) or a natural sign language (Ameslan) (Gardner & Gardner 1969, 1975; Patterson 1978; Terrace et al. 1976a, 1976b) have shown that the cognitive, representational, and perhaps even linguistic capacities of chimpanzees and gorillas, though vastly inferior, are nonetheless much closer to those of man than was once thought. Given the close genetic relation between man and chimpanzee (King & Wilson 1975) and their very different ecologies, one may wonder whether these apparently similar behavioral capacities in man and ape may not be homologous capacities derived by genetic transmission from a common ancestor.

Unfortunately, the degree of similarity and its evolutionary implications are difficult to assess because none of the supposedly linguistic behaviors of the apes seems to occur naturally. All have required intervention by animals of another species in the form of systematic operant conditioning. This is particularly striking in the work of Premack (1976) and Rumbaugh (1977), in which chains of behavior are established by direct shaping and primary reinforcement of hundreds of responses with food, drink, bodily contact, and so on. For the signing chimpanzees, such as Washoe (Gardner & Gardner, 1975) and Nim (Terrace et al. 1976a, 1976b), the social reward of trainer approval is more usual. Nonetheless, even here the fundamental training procedure has been operant shaping and molding of specific behaviors. In other words, language learning in the great apes does not proceed without the establishment of stimulus–response contingencies.

By contrast, the human infant apparently has a disposition to learn language even in the absence of specific response shaping and reinforcement. Although it too may require the generalized social reinforcement of a partner's attention, the infant does not require shaping and reinforcement of particular responses. On the contrary, as Brown (1973) has remarked, parents tend to reinforce the truth value but not the form of their children's utterances. In other words, language appears to develop in spite of the absence of stimulus–response contingencies.

Particularly striking in this context is the recent work of Feldman et al. (1977) on the spontaneous development of signing in deaf children. They studied six deaf children, over an age span of 1 year and 5 months through 4 years and 6 months whose parents were following the oralist practice recommended by some authorities in the United States. These authorities believe that signing to congenitally deaf children lowers their motivation to lip-read and articulate English; they therefore urge parents and siblings of such children to avoid all gestures, formal or informal. According to Feldman et al. the families of their six subjects were largely successful in following this practice.

The procedure of the study was to videotape each child playing and passing time with its mother and the experimenter during several standardized home visits. In the course of playing with the toys and games introduced by the experimenter, every child devised its own *home-signs,* that is, a characteristic set of motor–iconic gestures to refer to objects, actions, and predicates. Moreover, each child gradually began to combine these signs into two-, three-, and even six-sign sequences, creating its own semantically based syntax, including systematic deletion rules of the kind observed in a normal hearing child's telegraphic speech. This last point is particularly interesting, because telegraphic signing was not produced by the adults conversing with the children any more than is telegraphic speech under normal circumstances. The authors end their lengthy analysis with the conclusion that "there are significant internal dispositions in humans that guide the language acquisition process" (Feldman et al. 1977:132).

There is, of course, no evidence for such dispositions in the ape. This argues that the cognitive capacities now being discovered in the apes are general rather than specifically linguistic. The adaptive functions of these capacities are not always obvious. For example, how does the wild chimpanzee use its capacity to symbolize? Or is this capacity perhaps a *neo-phenotype* (Kuo 1976; Chap. 2), an item of general behavioral plasticity not normally deployed but available for use in the face of the right selective pressures?

Another general capacity, impressively displayed in recent language projects, does have obvious utility, namely, the capacity to learn a new motor response by observation and imitation. This capacity requires that the animal, first, be able to parse perceived behavior into action components and, second, have sensorimotor connections by which the parsed patterns may be mapped into motor commands (cf. Terrace et al. 1976a:21). Field observations attest to the role of imitation in the young chimpanzee's learning to fish for termites, for example, or to build its nest (van Lawick-Goodall 1971).

Yet a third chimpanzee capacity, essential to linguistic communication, has recently been demonstrated by Premack & Woodruff (1978) – the attributing of intention to the behavior of another organism. Here again, the capacity, whatever its linguistic worth, obviously contributes to the development of social intelligence. In fact, laboratory studies of ape language acquisition probably have more to teach us about the evolutionary origins of mind than of language. Certainly, as Limber (1977) suggests, conversational chimpanzees may offer an experimental approach to the study of relations between language and thought (for example, does naming facilitate problem solving?), but the focus would then be on thought rather than on language. For insight into the origins of language, the frank analogues of bird song may have more to offer than the possible homologues of ape signs.

THE SONGBIRDS

Templates and feature detectors

Unlike observational learning of other motor behavior, vocal learning can have no value beyond its use in communication. The analogous appearance of vocal learning in both man and bird is therefore of special interest (Marler 1970, 1975; Nottebohm 1970, 1975). Indeed, Marler has proposed as "a significant evolutionary step toward... the strategy of speech development of *Homo sapiens"* the emergence of "new sensory mechanisms for processing speech sounds" as well as "neural circuitry... to modify patterns of motor outflow so that sounds generated can be matched to preestablished auditory templates" (Marler 1975:32–33). As we shall see, the evidence for "new sensory mechanisms" or "auditory templates" in humans is weak, but there is good evidence for specialized sensorimotor processes.

Birds and other animals. Species-specific templates were proposed by Marler (1963) and Konishi (1965) to account for the fact that many songbirds learn only the songs of their own species. Even if they are deprived of conspecific song during the sensitive phase and are exposed to the songs of closely related species (e.g., Marler & Peters 1977), they do not learn them.

The form of these templates "lying in the auditory pathway" (Marler 1975:26) has never been specified. However, presumably they could consist of networks of specialized neurons tuned to particular properties of the species's song. Cortical neurons sensitive to changing frequencies were reported for cats ("miaow cells") by Whitfield and Evans (1965). Cells tuned to species calls have been reported for the bullfrog (Capranica 1965; Frishkopf & Goldstein 1963), the squirrel monkey (Wollberg & Newman 1972), several species of echolocating bat (Neuweiler 1977), and the starling (Leppelsack & Vogt 1976).

Humans. A possible analogy between species-specific call or song detectors and phonetically relevant acoustic feature detectors was not lost on students of speech perception (e.g., Abbs & Sussman 1971; Liberman et al. 1967; Studdert-

Kennedy 1974). The feature detector promised to solve at a single blow a variety of problems in speech perception, including that of syllable segmentation. Moreover, the notion of feature with its roots in ethology, linguistics, and pattern recognition was attractive to biologically inclined students of language looking for signs of an innate acquisition device (e.g., Stevens 1975). Unfortunately, the several lines of evidence and speculation seem to have converged on an error.

The story begins with the phenomenon of categorical perception (Liberman et al. 1967; Studdert-Kennedy et al. 1970). Early work with speech synthesizers showed that it was a simple matter to construct acoustic tokens of opponent phonetic types by manipulating a single acoustic variable. For example, by varying the interval between plosive release and the onset of laryngeal pulsing, that is, voice onset time (VOT), one could construct a continuum of, say, a dozen tokens ranging in equal acoustic steps from /*ba*/ to /*pa*/ or from /*da*/ to /*ta*/.

If listeners were asked to identify these tokens, they showed a strong tendency to call any particular stimulus by the same name (e.g., /*ba*/) every time they heard it. There were few, if any, ambiguous tokens. Furthermore, if they were asked to discriminate between neighboring pairs of tokens, they tended to do badly if they judged the two tokens to be members of the same phoneme class but well if they judged the tokens to be members of opponent phoneme classes – even though the acoustic interval between pairs was identical in the two cases. This phenomenon, dubbed *categorical perception,* seemed to be a useful process for speech perception. After all, one cannot afford to judge a word to be more or less *bat* or more or less *pat*. One must categorize it instantly as one or the other: Classification is a crucial process in phonetic perception.

The next event in the story was the demonstration by Eimas et al. (1971), using a nonnutritive sucking habituation procedure, that 1- and 4-month-old infants could discriminate between two tokens differing by 20 milliseconds along a voice onset time continuum, providing they were tokens that adults normally classified as different phonemes. But the infants could not discriminate between tokens that adults normally classified as the same phoneme. Similar results for a variety of synthetic speech continua were reported in due course for infants growing up in other language communities (see Eimas 1975 for a review).

The suspicion that these results reflected categorical perception mediated by specially tuned, innate feature detectors was not easy to resist – particularly because the phylogenetic emergence of such detectors might then be the evolutionary step that carried hominids from a graded to a categorical communication system (cf. Marler 1975). The hunt for independent evidence of such detectors operating in human adults began, and by 1973 Eimas and Corbit were able to report success.

They modified a procedure with a long history in visual studies: adaptation. The paradigm is simple enough. For example, prolonged fixation of a red patch of light adapts or fatigues a red detector cell and relatively sensitizes its opponent green detector cell, so that upon looking at a white screen, the viewer sees a relatively unsaturated green patch the same shape as the red adaptor.

Related effects in form and tilt also occur. Such effects have frequently been taken as evidence for the operation of opponent feature detectors.

Eimas and Corbit (1973) asked listeners to categorize members of a synthetic voice onset time continuum and demonstrated that the perceptual boundary between voiced and voiceless categories along that continuum was shifted by repeated exposure to (that is, adaptation with) either of the endpoint stimuli: There was a decrease in the frequency with which stimuli close to the original boundary were assigned to the adapted category and a consequent shift of the boundary toward the adapted stimulus. They took the effect to be evidence for the operation of an opponent feature-detecting system. Several dozen studies over the next 5 years replicated the effect on several other synthetic speech continua (see Ades 1976 for reviews; Cooper 1975; Eimas & Miller 1978).

Thus, the chain of inference and speculation from percept to detector was complete. Unfortunately, each link in the chain has proved weak. First, several studies have shown that categorical perception is not peculiar to speech, or even to audition. For example, Pastore et al. (1977) demonstrated categorical perception of critical flicker, with a sharp boundary at the flicker–fusion threshold. Second, other studies (e.g., Carney et al. 1977) have demonstrated that the degree of categorical perception varies with the experimental method used to measure it: Listeners can be trained to hear a supposedly categorical continuum noncategorically or to shift category boundaries from one point on a VOT continuum to another. Finally, cross-language studies have found that speakers of different languages may place phonetic boundaries at different points along the same acoustic continuum, demonstrating that acoustic-phonetic categories are linguistically rather than physiologically determined (for a review of cross-language studies, see Strange & Jenkins 1978).

The demise of categorical perception as a specialized phonetic process also cuts the other links in the chain. Thus, instances of what appears to be infant categorical perception will doubtless find a straightforward explanation in terms of auditory psychophysics, similar to that developed for the adult case. In fact, Pisoni (1977) has already developed such an explanation for VOT.

By the same token, we no longer need opponent process feature detectors to account for a general psychophysical phenomenon – particularly because there are other reasons for doubting the opponent detector model. Most obvious is the model's lack of behavioral or neurological motivation. For although the facts of additive color mixture and retinal neurophysiology make an opponent detector account of aftereffects entirely plausible, the facts of perceived stop consonant onset and cochlear neurophysiology certainly do not. However, an adequate discussion of speech adaptation is well beyond the scope of this chapter, and it must suffice to remark that plausible accounts of the effects in terms of stimulus range (Rosen 1979), auditory contrast (Simon & Studdert-Kennedy 1978), or other general psychophysical processes (Remez 1979) have already begun to appear.

We must conclude that we now have no evidence for the operation in speech perception of specialized sensory mechanisms analogous to the auditory templates postulated for certain songbirds.

Lateralization and the sensorimotor device

Birds. One of the most remarkable discoveries in recent years is the lateralization of neural function in bird song (Nottebohm 1971, 1972, 1977) – at present, the only securely attested-to instance of lateralized behavior apart from man (although see Dewson 1977 and Petersen et al. 1978). The typical songbird syrinx, as instanced by that of the canary (Nottebohm 1977), has two independently innervated and functionally separate halves. Sections of the right and left halves (or of their innervating hypoglossal branches) have very different effects: right-side sections lead to the loss of no more than 0 to 15% of preoperative song syllables, whereas left-side sections lead to a 90 to 100% loss. Similar effects of peripheral lesion have been observed in the chaffinch and the white-crowned sparrow (Nottebohm 1971, 1972). For the canary, Nottebohm (1977) has also traced motor pathways from the syrinx to the associated brain structures: Unilateral brain lesions indicate that the left hemisphere contributes radically more to song control than does the right.

All these effects are motor, and no perceptual lateralization has been demonstrated. However, it is of interest that the principal motor control center lies next to the telencephalic auditory projection, where processes involved in establishing the species-specific song template are believed to occur. Indeed, it was Nottebohm's (1970) original notion that lateralization might be associated with complex learned behaviors. This view has been thrown into question by the discovery of peripheral lateral equipotentiality in the orange-winged Amazon parrot (Nottebohm 1976), a bird well known for its vocal plasticity, and of left lateralization in the domestic fowl (Youngren et al. 1974), a bird of equally well-known vocal stereotypy. Nonetheless, current research on the canary is attempting to chart links between the two centers, that is, to establish the sensorimotor connection presumably essential to song learning (Nottebohm 1977).

Humans. It has been known for many years that the left cerebral hemisphere contributes more to language function than the right in most normal humans. The bulk of our knowledge comes from studies of aphasia, induced by stroke, tumor, or gunshot wound (e.g., Hécaen & Albert 1978; Jenkins et al. 1975) and, more recently, from studies of split-brain patients, whose cerebral hemispheres have been surgically separated by section of the connecting pathways for relief of epilepsy (e.g., Zaidel 1978a, 1978b). The latter condition permits an investigator to assess the linguistic capacities of each hemisphere independently.

Of particular interest, in light of the bird song findings, is that left hemisphere specialization seems to be primarily for control of the articulatory apparatus and for perceptual analysis of spoken words into their phonetic segments. The human larynx and its associated articulatory structures (tongue, velum, jaw) are bilaterally innervated but unilaterally controlled. Thus, *verbal apraxia,* or aphasic disturbance of articulation, is associated with damage to motor areas of the left hemisphere. As a corollary, the right hemisphere, despite a fair capacity for understanding speech, is essentially (that is, apart from a limited capacity for expletive and nonpropositional utterance) mute. Interestingly, skilled manual movements (Kimura & Archibald 1974) and nonverbal oral movements (Mateer & Kimura 1977) also tend to be impaired in cases of nonfluent aphasia. Moreover, disturbances of sign language in the deaf are associated with left-hemisphere damage (Kimura et al. 1976). From a review of such evidence, Kimura (1976:154) suggests that "the left hemisphere is particularly well adapted, not for symbolic function *per se,* but for the execution of some categories of motor activity which happened to lend themselves readily to communication."

However, more than specialization is involved. Studdert-Kennedy and Shankweiler (1970) concluded, from a study of normal subjects' performance on a test in which competing nonsense syllables were presented simultaneously to left and right ears, that the left hemisphere was specialized for phonological analysis of spoken language. Recent work with split-brain patients has confirmed this conclusion (Zaidel 1978a). The dissociated right hemisphere of such a patient has a sizeable auditory lexicon and a rudimentary syntax sufficient for understanding phrases of up to three or four words in length. However, it is incapable of identifying nonsense syllables or of recognizing that, say, *rose* rhymes with *toes* (Levy 1974). In other words, the right hemisphere is not only mute but is organized by meaning rather than by linguistic structure: Unlike the left hemisphere, it perceives language holistically, seizing meaning from the "auditory contours" of words rather than by phonological analysis. If, as we suggested earlier, the characteristic feature structure of speech sounds derives from articulatory constraints, we should perhaps not be surprised to discover that their perception is linked neurologically to their production.

Direct evidence for a sensorimotor link in the left hemisphere comes from the work of Sussman and MacNeilage (1975). They devised a bizarre tracking task in which a sinusoidal waveform, fed into one ear, could be tracked (i.e., copied) by lateral movements of the tongue, jaw, or hand. The results of the tracking movements, electronically multiplied into the audio-frequency range, were then fed to the opposite ear. In three experiments, Sussman and his colleagues showed that tracking movements made by a speech articulator (tongue, jaw) were more accurate if auditory feedback from the movements came to the right ear (i.e., left hemisphere) rather than to the left ear. There was no ear difference if the tracking movements were made by hand. The authors concluded that the results reflected "a lateralized, speech-related, auditory-sensorimotor integration mechanism" (1975:139).

The ultimate function of such a mechanism is, of course, unknown. However, if anything is to be made of the analogy with bird song, we may speculate that unilateral control is necessary for motor coordination of a bilaterally innervated apparatus (cf. Liberman 1974; Marler 1970). This might be achieved either by assigning execution primarily to one side of the peripheral apparatus and therefore to lateralized control centers in the brain (as seems to be done in the canary) or by assigning to one side of the brain central coordination of a symmetrically innervated peripheral apparatus (as seems to be done in humans). Lateralization of the associated perceptual center would then follow to facilitate sensorimotor learning. In humans, evolution of the sensorimotor mechanism led to the development of a lateralized syntactic device, itself perhaps motoric in origin and specialized for precise temporal coordination of hierarchically ordered structures. The result is that the left hemisphere "does seem to possess an innate and highly specialized linguistic mechanism whose paradigmatic functions are phonetic and syntactic encoding and analysis" (Zaidel 1978a:196).

Finally, in humans, lateralized control of the vocal apparatus seems to have been laid down on the neural substrate of manual lateralization, already evolved for tool use and/or gestural communication (Levy 1976). Semmes (1968) has provided an account of the association by arguing (from a lengthy series of gunshot lesions) that the left hemisphere is focally organized for fine motor control, the right hemisphere diffusely organized for broader control. More generally, Zaidel (1978b:263) has suggested that "each hemisphere specializes for a different style of information processing," and Levy (1976) proposes that hemispheric specialization may achieve functional dissociation of neurologically incompatible behaviors. But the important point here is not the possible complementary functions of the cerebral hemispheres (Zangwill 1960). Rather it is the notion, developed by Kimura (1976) and touched on in our discussion of manual sign language, that the origin of cerebral lateralization for language is in the control of skilled movement rather than in any higher symbolic processes.

What is puzzling, of course, is that, unlike song lateralization in birds, which has been observed in virtually every individual studied (Nottebohm 1977), human lateral specializations are neither uniform across the population nor perfectly associated. The incidence of right-handedness in the U.S. population is estimated at roughly 89% (Levy 1976) and the incidence of left dominance for language at roughly 95% among the right-handed, 60% among the left-handed (Milner et al. 1964). If such figures prove reliable across the human population, the network of lateralized functions would seem to offer an instance of an *evolutionarily stable strategy* (Maynard Smith & Price 1973:15), a balanced polymorphism that it will be a challenge to explain.

SENSITIVE PHASES

Birds. Many songbirds can learn their species song only if they are exposed to that song during a sensitive phase. The phase may range from as little as 40 days for the white-crowned sparrow, to 10 months for the chaffinch, to as long as 2 years for the Oregon junco. In some birds, such as the white-crowned sparrow or the marsh wren, there may be two distinct phases separated by weeks or even months: an input phase for perceptual learning and an output phase for subsong and learning to sing. In other birds, such as the chaffinch, the two phases may overlap, with elements of subsong appearing before the input phase has ended. Presumably such variations have adaptive value and can be related to the ecologies and life histories of the different species. In fact, Chapter 14 points out that it is precisely the systematic variations in temporal patterns of song learning that validate the concept of a sensitive phase and prove it to be more than a handy descriptive term for a process begun by maturation and ended by song acquisition. Much recent work is therefore aimed at pinning down the ultimate selective pressures (Chap. 20).

However, the proximate mechanisms controlling the onset and offset of sensitive phases are not well understood. Hormone levels are often suggested (e.g., Bateson 1973). Nottebohm (1967) castrated a male chaffinch during its first winter, thus precluding either the learning or the singing of song during its first spring. In its second spring the bird was implanted with a testosterone pellet and proved able to learn two tutor songs, but no more. Nottebohm suggests that "the ability to develop song for the first time is not age-dependent" (1967:278). However, *age* is a cover term for aspects of physical maturity as well as for the mere passage of time. Because castration may have delayed, if not halted, normal maturational processes, the experiment does not rule out physical maturation as the determinant of the onset of song learning. Moreover, because a total of two songs falls within the normal chaffinch repertoire range of 2 to 6 songs (Nottebohm 1967), we might reasonably hypothesize that song learning had ceased when the available neural space was filled (cf. Bateson 1973; Kroodsma in press). The point here is that, as noted in Chapter 14, specialized proximate mechanisms beyond physical maturation and neural preemption may not always be necessary for delimitation of a sensitive period in songbirds.

Humans. Lenneberg (1967:125–187) was the first to postulate a *critical period* for language learning. He was careful to make clear that he was offering no more than an analogy with the critical periods (or sensitive phases) of filial imprinting and song learning in birds. He placed the period roughly between the end of the second year and the beginning of the twelfth. Broadly, his argument is based on (1) the regularity of the time of onset of speech across cultures; (2) the different effects on language of various pathologies, particularly cerebral insult and deafness, as a function of age; in general, the younger the child at the time of the brain injury or the older the time of onset of deafness, the better the prognosis for language development; (3) the commonly observed increased difficulty of learning a foreign language after puberty – at least without appreciable interference from already known languages. Within the critical period, Lenneberg argued, languages are fully learned by mere exposure; after the critical period, they are learned less well and with increasing difficulty – an analogy with song learning in the zebra finch (Immelmann 1969).

Lenneberg attributes onset of the critical period to general maturation of the central nervous system. Cerebral structure (cell density, dendritic arborization) and chemical composition, as well as characteristic brain wave rhythms measured by electroencephalography, have reached roughly 75% of their adult asymptotic values by the age of 2 years. Thus, Lenneberg does not propose, nor is there any evidence for, a specialized onset mechanism analogous to the changes in hormone levels postulated for some birds.

The lateness of the proposed onset is largely a matter of definition. Because Lenneberg regarded syntax as the distinctive property of language, he identified language onset with the first putting together of words. This typically occurs between 18 and 28 months. Moreover, Lenneberg specifically denied the importance of experience during the first 2 years, largely on the grounds that children deafened as late as the end of their second year find it no easier to learn language than do those who have been deaf since birth. However, his evidence is drawn entirely from informal personal observation, and it seems unlikely that the orderly progression during the first year of life from prespeech oral play through cooing, intonation, and babbling is devoid of functional value. If we take the presence of language-specific structure in infant babble at roughly 8 months (Mehler personal communication) or even the prespeech lip and tongue movements in train with a mother's behavior (Trevarthen et al. 1976) as evidence that language sensitivity has begun, we may place the onset of the sensitive phase in the second half of the first year or even as early as the second month of life. The factors controlling this onset may still then be, as Lenneberg proposed, a combination of physical maturation and appropriate environmental stimulation.

The difficulty of learning a language after puberty is commonly known. Formal evidence for the likelihood of both grammatical and articulatory defects in a second language learned as an adult comes from Oyama (1973, cited by Krashen 1975). Evidence for even greater defects in a first language learned after puberty has recently come from Genie, a California "wild child" (Curtiss 1977). When discovered at the age of 13.5 years, after nearly 12 years of brutal undernourishment and isolation in a silent back room, Genie had virtually no language. Five years later, she had learned some language by mere exposure without specific training. Interestingly, her capacity for phonetic perception was normal, perhaps because her isolation had not begun until 20 months, when the phonetic groundwork has already been laid and she had begun to speak a few words. But her speech was severely distorted and her syntax deficient – for example, she could not use any *wh-* question words, verbal auxiliaries, or embedded structures. In other words, she learned language far less well than a normal child, as Lenneberg would have predicted.

The factors controlling offset at puberty are not known. Lenneberg proposed a loss of cerebral plasticity due to completed lateralization of function – without, however, offering any suggestion as to why language should be lateralized. His argument was based on clinical evidence of recovery from aphasia as a function of age. The picture has been confused by recent work suggesting that lateralization may be present from birth (Glanville et al. 1977; Molfese et al. 1975) and essentially complete by 5 years – roughly coinciding with the time when first language acquisition is approaching completion (Krashen 1975). But the question of an offset mechanism is important if the concept of a sensitive phase for language learning is to retain validity.

This question is important because we cannot justify the concept of sensitive phase by referring to interspecies differences of the kinds observed in songbirds, or by reference to its onset mechanism, because this appears to correlate with general physical maturation. If, further, its offset mechanism were merely preemption of neural space, as the articulatory, syntactic, and even lexical interference between earlier and later learned languages perhaps suggests, we might be dealing with a general loss of cerebral plasticity and with a process common to other classes of behavior rather than one peculiar to language. In short, the validity of the concept may rest on the demonstration that the offset mechanism is directed specifically at language learning. At present, we have no evidence that this is so.

Finally, we must ask what the function of a sensitive phase for language might be. First, following Immelmann (1976:152), we must distinguish between the period during which a behavior can be learned and the period during which it normally is learned. It is on the offset of the former that we might expect selective pressures to bear. If offset were early, roughly contemporaneous with release of offspring into a peer world, the language learned would be that of the parents, and we might reasonably suspect that dialect serves to attract sexual partners from ecologically similar backgrounds. Dialects might then, indeed, be "signs of incipient speciation" (Marler 1963:796; cf. Armstrong 1963:chap. 5). Such a function is unlikely in humans, despite the presumably high correlation between inbreeding and dialect in, say, the highlands of New Guinea or Austria, because many more salient features (such as habitat and body ornament) serve to isolate human breeding populations.

In fact, offset in humans is relatively late, well beyond the point when the child has abandoned the nuclear family for its peers. Accordingly, whether a child learns the dialect of its parents rather than of its peers (as is said of some English upper-class children thrown, by the accidents of war, among lower-class peers), or of its peers rather than of its parents (as do the children of non-English-speaking immigrants to Australia or the United States), may sometimes depend on social rather than directly biological factors. An echo in the behavior of Bewick's wren, which learns the song not of its father but of neighbors in its newly chosen breeding site (Kroodsma 1974), suggests that social bonding may be among the biological functions of dialects in both bird song and language (see Chap.4).

Whether this function is important enough to account for a sensitive phase in language learning is doubtful. In fact, given the weakness of this function and the lack of any clear evidence for proximate controlling mechanisms directed specifically at language, one may be tempted to conclude that a critical period for human language acquisition is more apparent than real, a mere matter of cerebral maturation in its onset and of neural preemption (or atrophy) in its offset.

THE INFANT AS PATTERN SEEKER

In song birds, both the species-specific template and sensitive phases are adapted to the same end, namely, acquisition of the species song within a few months of birth. The song to be learned is relatively brief and simple. A template ensures that from the varied songs around it, the young bird will learn to recognize (if female) as well as to practice and execute (if male) the song of its own species, whereas a sensitive phase usually confines learning to the weeks before dispersal from the home site and/or to the weeks soon after the bird has settled among its breeding peers. Nonetheless, not all birds that learn to sing have either a template or a sensitive phase. Indeed, certain mimics, such as the North American mockingbird, learn, presumably without a template and even late in life, the songs of species quite unrelated to themselves. Perhaps it is among such generalized, all-purpose song learners that we should look for an analogy with the human infant.

In any event, far from being constrained to learn the sound pattern of its language within a few months of birth, the human newborn has before it some 2 years of infancy. Moreover, what it must learn is not merely to imitate the sounds of the speakers around it – important though this undoubtedly is – but also to perceive and deploy their characteristic sound system. Rather than narrowly defined templates, we might therefore expect the infant – and its caretakers – to have evolved broad behavioral programs that will encourage vocal interchange and facilitate discovery of the spoken pattern. The general process seems, in fact, to be one of gradual differentiation: sound from silence, voice from sound, mother's voice from stranger's, intonation from monotone, syllabic beat from intonated melody, consonant from vowel, perhaps feature from phoneme.

One-day-old infants will suck a pacifier to turn on music and soon begin to prefer voices to music (Friedlander 1970). Indeed, within a few days of birth, they have learned to turn toward a voice, twisting the mouth as if in expectation of a nipple and crying when none is there (Alegria & Noirot 1977). By 20 to 30 days the infant has learned to recognize its mother's voice, as she reads from behind a screen, and will suck more rapidly for her voice than for a stranger's (Mills & Melhuish 1974) – provided she speaks with her customary intonation rather than reads backward from a text (Mehler et al. 1978).

From around the second month, the infant becomes accessible to "conversations" with its mother, watching her eyes (humans are the only animals with permanently visible whites to their eyes, contrasting to the iris), smiling, moving its lips and tongue in apparent imitation of the mother (*prespeech*), and gurgling (Trevarthen et al. 1975). With the child's discovery that events in the external world – particularly the vocalizations, touches, and gestures of its mother – may be contingent on its own behavior, the way is opened for games (e.g., peekaboo), rhythmic interactions, cooing, and laughter (Papousek & Papousek 1975; Watson 1979). The very precise temporal patterning of mother–infant interaction, with its alternating vocalizations, pauses, exaggerated facial displays, and so on, lays the groundwork for later social interchange (Stern et al. 1975). Freedle and Lewis (1977) find that vocalization occupies a special place in early mother–infant interaction: It is more likely to accompany playing, looking, holding, or touching than changing, feeding, or rocking. Moreover, vocalization by one partner is the most likely behavior to follow vocalization by the other, leading to the conclusion that "vocalization is the central behavior which maintains interaction" (Freedle & Lewis 1977:160). However, this interactive pattern is not specific to the vocal modality: For deaf children growing up as signers, signing occupies the privileged position (Feldman et al. 1977). From this we may conclude that mother–infant interaction is broadly adapted to the development, not simply of speech, but of any communicatively viable signaling system. This, in turn, suggests that the infant's discovery of speech may be guided more by the pattern of input from its environment than by the triggering of tuned detectors.

Of interest here is the nature of the mother's vocalizations, that is, of what has come to be called *baby talk (BT),* the style of speech used by adults, and even young children, when addressing infants (as well as animals and lovers). Baby talk has been studied in many cultures and is characterized by what Ferguson (1978) has termed a *simplified register.* The principal acoustic characteristics of this register are, according to Sachs (1978), an overall higher pitch, a wider frequency and intensity range, and a more markedly regular rhythmic structure (cf. nursery rhymes). In short, BT exaggerates the acoustic contrasts on which speech is based. Although it is unlikely that any single property of the speech addressed to the infant is essential to normal development (cf. Newport et al. 1978), it is equally unlikely that a culturally widespread phenomenon such as BT is devoid of function. If function can be inferred from structure, the function of BT is to draw the infant's attention to important acoustic contrasts in speech (cf. Garnica 1978) and to launch it on its search for pattern. Thus, we may see BT as the exogenous auditory counterpart of the endogenously controlled eye movements and head turning with which the human newborn searches for visual contour (Haith 1979).

What the infant has learned perceptually about its native language begins to emerge in babble around the sixth to ninth month. Jakobson (1968) dismisses babble as irrelevant to language acquisition on the grounds that it is primarily a motor activity devoid of linguistic import. He is correct inasmuch as normal perception of speech and language, as well as a highly educated level of reading and writing, can be developed, by prolonged and careful instruction, even when articulation has been pathologically precluded since birth (e.g., Fourcin 1975). But this does not mean that, under normal circumstances, babble contributes nothing to perceptual or especially expressive development. Indeed, it is unlikely that a behavior so regular in its time of onset and developmental course should altogether lack function.

Babble offers an obvious analogy with subsong, the low-intensity, generalized singing that precedes true song in many songbirds. Here, too, function is in doubt, largely because subsong recurs each year, as though it might simply reflect lower motivation early in the season (Thorpe 1956:373). Moreover, the female learns to recognize the male's song even though she herself (like the pathological humans cited above) never engages in subsong. Nonetheless, subsong does last longer in the bird's first year and bears several interesting analogies with babble – enough to suggest that both activities may be necessary to normal motor, if not to normal perceptual, development.

In the chaffinch, for example, subsong seems to be a poorly differentiated version of the species song with a much greater frequency range. Learning involves dropping unwanted elements and organizing the remaining notes into the correct rhythm (Thorpe 1956:374), presumably to accord with the inborn template, as modified during the early months of the sensitive phase. In the human, babble also seems to begin as a poorly differentiated stream, with many more components than will eventually be used. Gradually, over the course of 2 or 3 months, the stream begins to take on properties of the native language, presumably revealing what the infant learned perceptually during its first months of life. Just what these properties are is not yet known, partly because reliable phonetic transcription is difficult. Intonation is the most obvious, and characteristic pitch contours can be traced in spectrograms (e.g., Nakazima 1962), but language-specific consonant–vowel syllables may also be present (Huxley & Ingram 1971;162ff.; Kewley et al. 1974). In any event, Mehler (personal communication) has found that French-speaking adults can reliably identify infant babble, even in the second month of babbling, as French or not-French.

All this is consistent with the view that babble and subsong enable the organism to discover the limits of its vocal apparatus and to establish necessary sensorimotor links. Here, however, parallels between bird and infant cease. For whereas the end of subsong is true song, the use of which does not have to be learned, the end of babble is a modest articulatory repertoire, already language-specific but enough for no more than a start on the discovery of a linguistic system.

The process of discovery is, so far as we know, without parallel in the communication system of any other animal. The infant does not simply imitate, matching a particular utterance to a particular type of situation. Rather, it searches out contrasts among components of its own repertoire and uses them to signal contrasts in its desires, experience, or behavior. Often the contrasts, in both signal and message, are entirely novel and without counterpart in the adult system.

The process is well illustrated in a recent study by Menn (1978). She followed the development of intonation (pitch contour) in the babble and early speech of an American English boy between the ages of about 13 and 15 months. She classified his behavioral routines into categories such as greeting, curiosity, narrative, desiderative, and donative. Then she classified the pitch levels of babble in these situations as either moderate or high and the pitch contours as either rising or falling. Finally, she correlated pitch levels and contours with behavioral routines.

Among the outcomes, predicted from adult speech and observed in the data, were that narrative routines were accompanied by falling contours, whereas curiosity or desiderative routines were almost always accompanied by rising contours. However, the most interesting finding was that rising desiderative contours, addressed to adults, were split according to absolute pitch levels into high (peak above 550 Hz) and moderate (peak below 450 Hz), according to whether the child was seeking an object (e.g., food, toy) or social interaction (e.g., play). In other words, at a stage of his linguistic development when isolated words were still rare and word combinations did not occur at all, this boy had constructed a subclassification of his own rising pitch contours into moderate for sociable occasions and high for object-seeking occasions. Because adult speakers of American English do not use absolute pitch to contrast the uses they wish to make of other people, we must conclude that the child has created its own "erroneous" rules of intonation (Menn 1978).

Such invention is not without a precursor. The process of discovering meaning, and of seeking its correlates in the gestures or vocalizations of others, probably begins with the earliest mother–infant interchanges (cf. Bruner 1975; MacNamara 1972). In due course the infant chances upon such correlates in its own vocal repertoire and, with recognition of the first contrasts in intonation, there begins the slow discovery of sound pattern that will end, several years later, in a full and intricate phonological system. For this and for the parallel processes of syntactic development we find no analogues among birds or apes.

CONCLUSIONS AND QUESTIONS

A language is an open system, adapted by its dual structure of sound pattern and syntax for unlimited communication. If, as was argued, the dual structure evolved to interface man's intellect with his peripheral anatomy, it is unlikely that analogous duality of patterning will be found in animals of appreciably lower cognitive complexity.

A dual structure is also found in manual sign languages. That sign languages are manual emphasizes the importance of rapid articulatory gesture to effective linguistic communication. So far as we know, no other animal has developed a capacity for essentially equivalent communication by means of two different sensorimotor systems.

Because none of the supposedly linguistic behavior of the great apes occurs in a natural environment, recent successes in training them to communicate symbolically have little bearing on the origins of language. However, laboratory studies of the apes may lend insight into the evolution of intelligence and relations between language and thought.

The capacity for vocal learning has no value beyond its use in communication, its appearance (and pivotal social role) in both man and songbird is of great interest. However, of several possible analogies between bird song - and language-learning - auditory templates, sensitive phases, and lateralized sensorimotor mechanisms - only the last invites fruitful speculation. Lateralized motor control of bird song, as well as the association of speech, right-handedness, and manual sign language with left hemisphere mechanisms in humans, suggests that the origin of cerebral lateralization for language may be in the control of skilled movements. Further work might profitably explore functional relations among manual skills and the perception and production of both speech and sign language, in an attempt to establish the extent of neural overlap.

The long period of human infancy, taken with the diversity of human languages (both spoken and signed), suggests that adaptations for language learning are likely to be behavioral rather than tightly neurophysiological. Study of these behavioral adaptations, particularly mother–infant interaction during the first year of life, may bring fuller understanding of language and of how it is learned.

REFERENCES

Abbs, J. H., & H. M. Sussman. 1971. Neurophysiological feature detectors and speech perception: a discussion of theoretical implications. *Journal of Speech and Hearing Research* 14:23–36.

Abercrombie, D. 1967. *Elements of general phonetics.* Chicago: Aldine.

Ades, A. E. 1976. Adapting the property detectors for speech perception. *In:* R. J. Wales & E. Walker (eds.), *New approaches to language mechanisms.* North-Holland, Amsterdam.

Alegria, J., & E. Noirot. 1977. Neonate orientation behaviour towards the human voice. Paper read before the 15th International Ethological Conference, Bielefeld, August 22–31.

Armstrong, E. A. 1963. *A study of bird song.* Oxford University Press, London.

Bateson, P. P. G. 1973. The imprinting of birds. *In:* S. A. Barnett (ed.), *Ethology and development.* Spastics International Medical Publications (with Heinemann Medical Books), London.

1979. How do sensitive periods arise and what are they for? *Animal Behaviour* 27:470–486.

Battison, R. 1974. Phonological deletion in American Sign Language. *Sign Language Studies* 5:1–19.

Berko, J. 1958. The child's learning of English morphology. *Word* 14:150–177.

Brown, R. W. 1973. *A first language: the early stages.* Harvard University Press, Cambridge, Massachusetts.

Bruner, J. S. 1975. From communication to language – a psychological perspective. *Cognition* 3:255–287.

Capranica, R. R. 1965. *The evoked vocal response of the bullfrog.* M.I.T. Press, Cambridge, Massachusetts.

Carney, A. E., G. P. Widin, & N. F. Viemeister. 1977. Noncategorical perception of stop consonants differing in VOT. *Journal of the Acoustical Society of America* 62:961–970.

Chomsky, N. 1956. Three models for the description of language. *IRE Transactions on Information Theory* IT-2:113–124.

Chomsky, N., & M. Halle. 1968. *The sound pattern of English.* Harper, New York.

Cooper, W. E. 1975. Selective adaptation of speech. *In:* F. Restle, R. M. Shiffrin, N. J. Castellan, H. Lindman, & D. B. Pisoni (eds.), *Cognitive theory,* vol. 1. Erlbaum, Hillsdale, New Jersey.

Curtiss, S. 1977. *Genie: a psycholinguistic study of a modern-day "wild child."* Academic Press, New York.

Dale, P. S. 1976. *Language development,* 2nd ed., Holt, New York.

Dewson, J. H., III. 1977. Preliminary evidence of hemisphere asymmetry of auditory function in monkeys. *In:* S. Harnad, R. W. Doty, L. Goldstein, J. Jaynes, & G. Krauthamer (eds.), *Lateralization in the nervous system.* Academic Press, New York, pp 63–74.

DuBrul, E. L. 1977. Origin of the speech apparatus and its reconstruction in fossils. *Brain and Language* 4:365–381.

Eimas, P. D. 1963. The relation between identification and discrimination along speech and non-speech continua. *Language and Speech* 6:206–217.

1975. Speech perception in early infancy. *In:* L. B. Cohen & P. Salapatek (eds.), *Infant perception.* Academic Press, New York.

Eimas, P. D., & J. D. Corbit. 1973. Selective adaptation of linguistic feature detectors. *Cognitive Psychology* 4:99–109.

Eimas, P. D., & J. L. Miller. 1978. Effects of selective adaptation on the perception of speech and visual patterns. *In:* R. D. Walk & H. L. Pick, Jr. (eds.), *Perception and experience.* Plenum, New York.

Eimas, P. D., E. R. Siqueland, P. Jusczyk, & J. Vigorito. 1971. Speech perception in infants. *Science* 171:303–306.

Entus, A. K. 1977. Hemispheric asymmetry in processing dichotomically presented speech and nonspeech stimuli by infants. *In:* S. J. Segalowitz & F. A. Gruber (eds.), *Language development and neurological theory.* Academic Press, New York, pp. 64–73.

Feldman, H., S. Goldin-Meadow, & L. Gleitman. 1977. Beyond Herodotus: the creation of language by linguistically deprived deaf children. *In:* A. Lock (ed.), *Action, gesture and symbol: the emergence of language.* Academic Press, New York.

Ferguson, C. A. 1978. Baby talk as a simplified register. *In:* C. E. Snow & C. A. Ferguson (eds.), *Talking to children.* Cambridge University Press, Cambridge.

Ferguson, C. A., & D. I. Slobin. 1973. *Studies of child language development.* Holt, New York.

Fourcin, A. J. 1975. Language development in the absence of expressive speech. *In:* E. H. Lenneberg & E. Lenneberg (eds.), *Foundations of language development,* vol. 2. Academic Press, New York, pp. 263–268.

Freedle, R., & M. Lewis. 1977. Prelinguistic conversations. *In:* M. Lewis & L. A. Rosenblum (eds.), *Interaction, conversation and the development of language.* Wiley, New York, pp. 157–186.

Friedlander, B. A. 1970. Receptive language development in infancy. *Merrill-Palmer Quarterly* 16:7–51.

Frishberg, N. 1975. Arbitrariness and iconicity: historical change in American Sign Language. *Language* 51:696–719.

Frishkopf, L., & M. Goldstein. 1963. Responses to acoustic stimuli in the eighth nerve of the bullfrog. *Journal of the Acoustical Society of America* 35:1219–1228.

Gardner, R. A., & B. T. Gardner. 1969. Teaching sign language to a chimpanzee. *Science* 165:664–672.

1975. Early signs of language in child and chimpanzee. *Science* 187:752–753.

Garnica, O. K. 1978. Some prosodic and paralinguistic features of speech to young children. *In:* C. E. Snow & C. A. Ferguson (eds.), *Talking to children.* Cambridge University Press, Cambridge, pp. 63–88.

Glanville, B. B., C. T. Best, & R. Levenson. 1977. A cardiac measure of asymmetries in infant auditory perception. *Development Psychology* 13:54–59.

Haith, M. M. 1979. Visual competence in early infancy. *In:* R. Held, H. Leibowitz, & H. L. Teuber (eds.), *Handbook of sensory physiology,* vol. 8. Springer-Verlag, Berlin.

Hardyck, C., & L. Petrinovich. 1977. Left-handedness. *Psychological Bulletin* 84:385–404.

Hécaen, H., & M. L. Albert. 1978. *Human Neuropsychology.* Wiley, New York.

Hockett, C. F. 1960. The origin of speech. *Scientific American* 203:89–96.

Huxley, R., & E. Ingram (eds.). 1971. *Language acquisition: models and methods.* Academic Press, New York.

Immelmann, K. 1969. Song development in the zebra finch and estrildid finches. *In:* R. A. Hinde (ed.), *Bird vocalizations.* Cambridge University Press, London.

1976. Sexual and other long-term aspects of imprinting in birds and other species. *In:* D. S. Lehrman, R. A. Hinde, & E. Shaw (eds.), *Advances in the study of behavior,* vol. 4. Academic Press, New York.

Jakobson, R. 1968. *Child language, aphasia and phonological universals.* Mouton, The Hague.

Jakobson, R., G. Fant, & M. Halle. 1963. *Preliminaries to speech analysis.* M.I.T. Press, Cambridge, Massachusetts.

Jenkins, J. J., E. Jimenez-Pabon, R. E. Shaw, & J. W. Sefer. 1975. *Schuell's aphasia in adults,* 2nd ed. Harper, New York.

Kelley, D. B., & F. Nottebohm. 1979. Projections of a telencephalic auditory nucleus - Field L - in the canary. *Journal of Comparative Neurology* 183:455–470.

Kewley-Port, D., & M. Preston. 1974. Early apical stop production: a voice onset time analysis. *Journal of Phonetics* 2:195–210.

Kimura, D. 1976. The neural basis of language *qua* gesture. *In:* H. Whitaker & H. A. Whitaker (eds.), *Studies in neurolinguistics,* vol. 3. Academic Press, New York.

Kimura, D., & Y. Archibald. 1974. Motor functions of the left hemisphere. *Brain* 97:337–350.

Kimura, D., R. Battison, & B. Lubert. 1976. Impairment of nonlinguistic hand movements in a deaf aphasic. *Brain and Language* 4:566–571.

King, M. C., & A. C. Wilson. 1975. Evolution at two levels in humans and chimpanzees. *Science* 188:107–116.

Kiparsky, P. 1968. Linguistic universals and linguistic change. *In:* E. Bach & R. T. Harms (eds.), *Universals in linguistic theory.* Holt, New York, pp. 170–202.

Klima, E. S., & U. Bellugi. 1979. *The signs of language.* Harvard University Press, Cambridge, Massachusetts.

Konishi, M. 1965. The role of auditory feedback in the control of vocalization in the white-crowned sparrow. *Zeitschrift für Tierpsychologie* 22:770–783.

Krashen, S. D. 1975. The critical period for language acquisition and its possible bases. *In:* D. Aaronson & R. W. Rieber (eds.), *Developmental psycholinguistics and communication disorders.* New York Academy of Sciences, New York, pp. 211–224.

Kroodsma, D. E. 1974. Song learning, dialects and dispersal in the Bewick's Wren. *Zeitschrift für Tierpsychologie* 35:352–380.

In press. Song learning and its sensitive period in the Marsh Wren. (*Cistothorus palustris.*)

Kuo, Z. -Y. 1976. *The dynamics of behavior development,* enlarged ed. Plenum, New York.

Ladefoged, P. 1971. *Preliminaries to linguistic phonetics.* University of Chicago Press, Chicago.

Lancaster, J. B. 1968. Primate communication systems and the emergence of human language. *In:* P. C. Jay (ed.), *Primates.* Holt, New York.

Lane, H., P. Boyes-Braem, & V. Bellugi. 1976. Preliminaries to a distinctive feature analysis of handshapes in American Sign Language. *Cognitive Psychology* 8:263–289.

Lenneberg, E. H. 1967. *The biological foundations of langauge.* Wiley, New York.

Lenneberg, E. H. & E. Lenneberg. 1975. *Foundations of language development,* vols. 1 and 2. Academic Press, New York.

Leppelsack, H. J., & M. Vogt. 1976. Responses of auditory neurons in the forebrain of a songbird to stimulation with species-specific sounds. *Journal of Comparative Physiology* 107:263–274.

Levi-Strauss, C. 1968. *The savage mind.* University of Chicago Press, Chicago.

Levy, J. 1969. Possible basis for the evolution of lateral specialization of the human brain. *Nature* 224:614–615.

1974. Psychobiological implications of bilateral asymmetry. *In:* S. J. Dimond & J. G. Beaumont (eds.), *Hemisphere function in the human brain.* Elek, London.

Liberman, A. M. 1970. The grammars of speech and language. *Cognitive Psychology* 1:301–323.

1974. The specialization of the language hemisphere. *In:* F. O. Schmitt & F. G. Worden (eds.), *The neurosciences: third study program.* M.I.T. Press, Cambridge, Massachusetts, pp. 43–56.

Liberman, A. M., F. S. Cooper, D. P. Shankweiler, & M. Studdert-Kennedy. 1967. Perception of the speech code. *Psychological Review* 74:431–461.

Liberman, A. M., & M. Studdert-Kennedy. 1978. Phonetic perception. *In:* R. Held, H. W. Leibowitz & H. -L. Teuber (eds.), *Handbook of sensory physiology,* vol. 8, *Perception.* Springer-Verlag, New York, pp. 143–178.

Lieberman, P. 1972. *The speech of primates.* Mouton, The Hague.

Limber, J. 1973. The genesis of complex sentences. *In:* T. Moore (ed.), *Cognitive development and the acquisition of language.* Academic Press, New York.

1977. Language in child and chimp. *American Psychologist* 32:280–295.

MacNamara, J. 1972. Cognitive basis of language learning in infants. *Psychological Review* 79:1–13.

Marler, P. 1963. Inheritance and learning in the development of animal vocalizations.

In: R. G. Busnel (ed.), *Acoustic behavior of animals.* Elsevier, Amsterdam, pp. 228–243, 794–797 (addendum).

1970. Birdsong and speech development: could there be parallels? *American Scientist* 58:669–673.

1975. On the origin of speech from animal sounds. *In:* J. F. Kavanagh & J. E. Cutting (eds.), *The role of speech in language.* M.I.T. Press, Cambridge, Massachusetts.

Marler, P., & S. Peters. 1977. Selective vocal learning in a sparrow. *Science* 198:519–521.

Mateer, C., & D. Kimura. 1977. Impairment of nonverbal oral movements in aphasia. *Brain and Language* 4:262–276.

Mattingly, I. G. 1975. The human aspect of speech. *In:* J. F. Kavanagh & J. E. Cutting (eds.), *The role of speech in language.* M.I.T. Press, Cambridge, Massachusetts, pp. 63–72.

Maynard-Smith, J., & G. R. Price. 1973. The logic of animal conflict. *Nature* 246:15.

Mayr, E. 1974. Behavior programs and evolutionary strategies. *American Scientist* 62:650–659.

Mehler, J., J. Bertoncini, M. Barrière, & D. Jassik-Gerschenfeld. 1978. Infant recognition of mother's voice. *Perception* 7:491–497.

Menn, L. 1978. Pattern, control and contrast in beginning speech. Indiana University Linguistics Club, Bloomington.

Miller, G. A., E. Galanter, & K. Pribram. 1960. *Plans and the structure of behavior.* Holt, New York.

Mills, M., & E. Melhuish. 1974. Recognition of mother's voice in early infancy. *Nature* 252:123.

Milner, B., C. Branch, & T. Rasmussen. 1964. Observations on cerebral dominance. *In:* A. V. S. deRueck & M. O'Connor, (eds.), *Disorders of language.* Churchill, London, pp. 200–214.

Molfese, D. L., R. B. Freeman, & D. S. Palermo. 1975. The ontogeny of brain lateralization for speech and non-speech stimuli. *Brain and Language* 2:356–368.

Nakazima, S. 1962. A comparative study of the speech developments of Japanese and American English in childhood 1. A comparison of the developments of voices at the prelinguistic period. *Studia Phonologica* 2:27–46.

1975. Phonemicization and symbolization in language development. *In:* E. H. Lenneberg & E. Lenneberg (eds.), *Foundations of language development,* vol. 1. Academic Press, New York, pp. 181–187.

Neuweiler, G. 1977. Recognition mechanisms in echolocation of bats. *In:* T. H. Bullock (ed.), *Recognition of complex acoustic stimuli.* Dahlem Konferenzen, Berlin, pp. 111–126.

Newport, E. L., H. Gleitman, & L. R. Gleitman. 1978. Mother, I'd rather do it myself: some effects and non-effects of maternal speech style. *In:* C. E. Snow & C. A. Ferguson (eds.), *Talking to children.* Cambridge University Press, Cambridge.

Nottebohm, F. 1967. The role of sensory feedback in the development of avian vocalizations. *Proceedings of the 14th International Ornithological Conference,* Oxford, 1966, pp. 265–280.

1970. Ontogeny of bird song. *Science* 167:950–956.

1971. Neural lateralization of vocal control in a passerine bird. 1. Song. *Journal of Experimental Zoology* 177:229–261.

1972. Neural lateralization of vocal control in a passerine bird. 2. Subsong, calls and a theory of vocal learning. *Journal of Experimental Zoology* 179:35–49.

1975. A zoologist's view of some language phenomena with particular emphasis on vocal learning. *In:* E. H. Lenneberg & E. Lenneberg (eds.), *Foundations of language development: a multi-disciplinary approach,* vol. 1. Academic Press, New York.

1976. Phonation in the orange-winged Amazon parrot, *Amazona amazonica. Journal of Comparative Physiology* 108:157–170.

1977. Asymmetries in neural control of vocalization in the canary. *In:* S. Harnad, R. W. Doty, L. Goldstein, J. Jaynes, & G. Krauthamer (eds.), *Lateralization in the nervous system.* Academic Press, New York, pp. 23–44.

Nottebohm, F., & M. E. Nottebohm. 1976. Left hypoglossal dominance in the control of canary and white-crowned sparrow song. *Journal of Comparative Physiology* 108:171–192.

Oyama, S. 1973. A sensitive period for the acquisition of a second language. Unpublished Ph.D. dissertation, Harvard University, Cambridge, Massachusetts.

Papoušek, H., & M. Papoušek. 1975. Cognitive aspects of preverbal social interaction between human infants and adults. *In:* M. O'Connor (ed.), *Parent–infant interaction.* Elsevier, Amsterdam, pp. 241–260.

Pastore, R. E., W. A. Ahroon, K. J. Baffuto, C. Friedman, J. S. Puleo, & E. A. Fink. 1977. Common factor model of categorical perception. *Journal of Experimental Psychology: Human Perception and Performance* 3:686–696.

Patterson, F. G. 1978. The gestures of a gorilla: language acquisition in another pongid. *Brain and Language* 5:72–97.

Penfield, W., & L. Roberts. 1959. *Speech and brain mechanisms.* Princeton University Press, Princeton, New Jersey.

Petersen, M. R., M. D. Beecher, S. R. Zoloth, D. B. Moody, & W. C. Stebbins. 1978. Neural lateralization of species-specific vocalizations by Japanese macaques (*Macaca fuscata*). *Science* 202:324–327.

Petrinovich, L. 1972. Psychobiological mechanisms in language development. *In*: G. Newton & A. H. Riesen, (eds.), *Advances in psychobiology*, vol. 1. Wiley, New York.

Pisoni, D. B. 1977. Identification and discrimination of the relative onset of two component tones: implications for the perception of voicing in stops. *Journal of the Acoustical Society of America* 61:1352–1361.

Premack, D. 1976. *Intelligence in ape and man.* Erlbaum, Hillsdale, New Jersey.

Premack, D., & G. Woodruff. 1978. Chimpanzee problem-solving: a test for comprehension. *Science* 202:532–535.

Remez, R. E. 1979. Adaptation of the category boundary between speech and non-speech: a case against feature detectors. *Cognitive Psychology* 11:38–57.

Rosen, S. M. 1979. Range and frequency effects in consonant categorization. *Journal of the Acoustical Society of America.*

Rumbaugh, D. (ed.). 1977. *Language learning by a chimpanzee.* Academic Press, New York.

Sachs, J. 1978. The adaptive significance of linguistic input to prelinguistic infants. *In*: C. E. Snow & C. A. Ferguson, (eds.), *Talking to children.* Cambridge University Press, Cambridge, pp. 51–62.

Semmes, J. 1968. Hemispheric specialization: a possible clue to mechanism. *Neuropsychologia* 6:11–26.

Simon, H. J., & M. Studdert-Kennedy. 1978. Selective anchoring and adaptation of phonetic and nonphonetic continua. *Journal of the Acoustical Society of America* 64:1338–1368.

Siple, P. (ed.). 1978. *Understanding language through sign language research.* Academic Press, New York.

Stern, D. N., J. Jaffe, B. Beebe, & S. L. Bennett. 1975. Vocalizing in unison and in alternation: two modes of communication within the mother–infant dyad. *In:* D. Aaronson & R. W. Reiber (eds.), *Developmental psycholinguistics and communication disorders.* New York Academy of Sciences, New York, pp. 89–100.

Stetson, R. H. 1952. *Motor phonetics.* North Holland, Amsterdam.

Stevens, K. N. 1975. The potential role of property detectors in the perception of consonants. *In*: G. Fant & M. A. A. Tatham (eds.), *Auditory analysis and perception of speech.* Academic Press, New York, pp. 303–330.

Stevens, K. N., & M. Halle. 1967. Remarks on analysis by synthesis and distinctive features. *In*: W. Wathen-Dunn (ed.), *Models for the perception of speech and visual form.* M.I.T. Press, Cambridge, Massachusetts.

Stokoe, W. C., Jr. 1974. Classification and description of sign languages. *In*: T. A. Sebeok (ed.), *Current trends in linguistics*, vol. 12(1). Mouton, The Hague, pp. 345–371.

Stokoe, W. C., Jr., D. C. Casterline, & C. G. Croneberg. 1965. *A dictionary of American Sign Language on linguistic principles.* Gallaudet College Press, Washington, D.C.

Strange, W., & J. J. Jenkins. 1978. The role of linguistic experience in the perception of speech. *In:* H. L. Pick, Jr., & R. D. Walk (eds.), *Perception and experience.* Plenum, New York.

Studdert-Kennedy, M. 1974. The perception of speech. *In:* T. A. Sebeok (ed.), *Current trends in linguistics,* vol. 12(4). Mouton, The Hague, pp. 2349–2385.

1976. Speech perception. *In:* N. J. Lass (ed.), *Contemporary issues in experimental phonetics.* Academic Press, New York.

1977. Universals in phonetic structure and their role in linguistic communication. *In:* T. H. Bullock (ed.), *Recognition of complex acoustic signals.* Dahlem Konferenzen, Berlin.

Studdert-Kennedy, M., A. M. Liberman, K. S. Harris, & F. S. Cooper. 1970. The motor theory of speech perception: a reply to Lane's critical review. *Psychological Review* 77:234–249.

Studdert-Kennedy, M., & D. P. Shankweiler. 1970. Hemispheric specialization for speech perception. *Journal of the Acoustic Society of America* 48:579–594.

Sussman, H. M. 1970. A laterality effect in lingual auditory tracking. *Journal of the Acoustical Society of America* 49:1874–1880.

Sussman, H. M., & P. F. MacNeilage. 1975. Studies of hemispheric specialization for speech production. *Brain and Language* 2:131–151.

Sussman, H. M., & J. R. Westbury. 1978. A laterality effect in isometric and isotonic labial tracking. *Journal of Speech and Hearing Research* 21:563–579.

Terrace, H. S., L. Petitto, & T. G. Bever. 1976a. *Project Nim: progress report 1.* Columbia University, New York.

1976b. *Project Nim: progress report 2.* Columbia University, New York.

Thorpe, W. H. 1956. *Learning and instinct in animals.* Harvard University Press, Cambridge, Massachusetts.

Trevarthen, C., P. Hubley, & L. Sheeran. 1975. Les activités innées du nourrisson. *La Récherche* 56:447–458.

Umiker-Sebeok, D. J., & T. A. Sebeok. 1977. Aboriginal sign "Languages" from a semiotic point of view. *Ars Semeiotica* 1:69–97.

van Lawick-Goodall, J. 1971. *In the shadow of man.* Collins, London.

Watson, J. S. 1979. Perception of contingency as a determinant of social responsiveness. *In:* E. B. Thoman (ed.), *The origins of the infant's social responsiveness.* Halsted Press, New York.

West, LaM., Jr. 1960. The sign language: an analysis. Unpublished Ph.D. dissertation, Indiana University, Bloomington.

Whitaker, H., & H. A. Whitaker. 1976. *Studies in neurolinguistics,* vols. 1, 2, 3. Academic Press, New York.

Whitfield, I. C., & E. F. Evans. 1965. Responses of auditory cortical neurons to stimuli of changing frequency. *Journal of Neurophysiology* 28:655–672.

Wilson, E. O. 1975. *Sociobiology.* Belknap Press, Cambridge, Massachusetts.

Wollberg, Z., & J. D. Newman. 1972. Auditory cortex of squirrel monkey: response patterns of single cells to species-specific vocalizations. *Science* 175:212–214.

Youngren, O. M., F. W. Peek, & R. E. Phillips. 1974. Repetitive vocalizations evoked by local electrical stimulation of avian brains. *Brain, Behavior and Evolution* 9:393–421.

Zaidel, E. 1978a. Lexical organization in the right hemisphere. *In:* P. A. Buser and A. Rougeul-Buser (eds.), *Cerebral correlates of conscious experience.* Elsevier/North-Holland Biomedical Press, Amsterdam, pp. 177–197.

1978b. Concepts of cerebral dominance in the split brain. *In:* P. A. Buser and A. Rougeul-Buser (eds.), *Cerebral correlates of conscious experience.* Elsevier/North-Holland Biomedical Press, Amsterdam, pp. 263–285.

Zangwill, O. 1960. *Cerebral dominance and its relation to psychological function.* Oliver & Boyd, Edinburgh.

PART VI

SOCIAL PROCESSES IN HUMAN INFANTS

INTRODUCTION

MARY MAIN

This part of the book is organized into two sections. The first deals with emotions and communication. The second deals with infant–adult relationships.

The first section opens with Chapter 22, by two researchers who are clinicians – Robert N. Emde and Theodore Gaensbauer. The chapter offers three models of emotion in human infancy and marshals some persuasive arguments against views of emotion held until recently (e.g., that emotions are essentially nameless states of activation). It argues, first, that we must admit that, as humans, we have some knowledge of the meaning of emotions; thus a purely behavioristic approach will miss much in terms of depth of understanding. Evidence is offered for the existence of developmental discontinuities in emotional organization in the first year of life (see Chap. 10), with two great periods of reorganization occurring at 2 months and at 7 to 9 months of age. The chapter shows that the number of dimensions along which infant emotions are interpreted alters with age, and it argues that emotions are complexly organized rather than simple; ongoing rather than sudden and disruptive; and far from unidimensional. These arguments are illustrated with a unique study of the emotions of normal and neglected infants undergoing the same laboratory procedures.

Aggression in infancy and childhood is the topic of Chapter 23, by Tore Bjerke. This chapter reviews studies of aggressive behavior in both human and nonhuman primates, and presents new data on aggression in human infants. He has found sex differences in aggressive behavior (higher in boys) in infants as young as 1 year of age. The chapter discusses studies of sex differences in terms of both environmental and hormonal control mechanisms. These would seem to explain some of the observed differences, but the chapter argues against the popular view that boys (because they are more aggressive) must receive more rewards (positive reinforcement) for aggression. Both the author's own observations and his reflections on primate sex differences lead him to conclude that we may actually strengthen aggression in boys through negative reinforcement. Thus, our sex-trait stereotypes may cause us to expose boys to more aversive stimuli with a view to reducing their "natural" aggressiveness. However, this aversive stimulation is often withdrawn when boys behave aggressively, thus strengthening aggressive behavior through negative reinforcement.

Chapter 24 by Glyn M. Collis, the final chapter in this section, discusses a topic that most students of social development will find highly original. This is communication through and about objects, as opposed to the more common studies of communication through face-to-face interaction (which, it is argued, is actually less common). This chapter discusses communication through and about objects in animals and in human infant–mother pairs studied in the laboratory. It describes the development of the pointing gesture by the infant, and the way in which the mother and infant together integrate pointing and naming. Because maternal speech is closely integrated with shared attention and joint action with objects, the phenomenon may provide useful cues for the acquisition of language. The larger message, however, is one that most developmental psychologists have missed: Communication often involves more than just the participating individuals and their behavior.

The section on infant–adult relationships opens with Chapter 25, by Everett Waters, a discussion of three models of infant–adult attachments – as traits, behavioral systems, and relationships. Most attachment research has implicitly involved an outmoded causal trait model of the attachment construct. This has led to an unfortunate emphasis on individual differences in strength of attachment, a concept that has not stood up to examination. (New formulations of *traits* exist but have yet to be applied to attachment.) It is shown how attachment can be conceived of as a behavioral system, a property of an individual that serves to integrate attachment behavior with exploratory behavior and that is strongly sensitive to context. At the same time, the infant–adult tie can profitably be conceived of as a relationship, and dyadic relationships rather than individuals can then be conceived of as the unit of analysis. All three models of the tie call for further descriptive research; our understanding of attachment will be enlarged by this and by cross-paradigm communication.

Chapter 26, the second chapter in this section, by Mary Main, presents and discusses the phenomenon of avoidance of attachment figures. Avoidance occurs following stressful long-term separations in most infants, and following even very brief laboratory separations in infants who have experienced rejection by the attachment figure. The phenomenon is intriguing, because both attachment theory and recent sociobiological interpretations of infant–parent relations lead to the prediction that only increased attachment behavior rather than avoidance should be shown by infants following separation. A number of explanations of the phenomenon can be ruled out on the basis of studies already conducted. But several are left open. Avoidance may be a matter of self-control or organization. Alternatively, following ethological studies of avoidance of social partners in nonhuman animals, we may see avoidance as a (deceptive) signal that renders the performer nonthreatening and/or as a means of reducing flight or aggressive tendencies in the performing animal. In this case avoidance may be a secondary strategy for proximity maintenance.

Strong avoidance of attachment figures is a relatively uncommon occurrence in laboratory separation studies conducted in the United States (and recently in England and in Italy). Chapter 27, a research note by Klaus and Karin Grossmann, shows that strong avoidance of the parent is, in contrast, common in the infants in the authors' middle-class Bielefeld sample. It is possible that this behavior is more common in their sample because Bielefeld parents may stress obedience training. What else avoidance means for Bielefeld infants can only be determined by the further studies in which the Grossmanns are now engaged.

Chapter 28, the final chapter in this section, by Ross D. Parke and Steven J. Suomi, discusses adult male–infant relationships. Parke is a developmental psychologist working with human dyads, Suomi a psychologist specializing in the study of nonhuman primates. There is considerable variation across primate species in modal degree of adult male involvement with infants; otherwise, there are striking similarities. Adult males can take over maternal roles when necessary in particular cases. Otherwise, their roles tend to complement those of the mother. Males are more likely to play with infants than are females; they become more involved with infants as they age; and they are more responsive to sex differences. Infants can and do develop strong and distinct relationships with adult males as well as with females, even though there may be relatively fewer interactions. There is little doubt that the infant–adult male relationship plays an important role in social development.

22

SOME EMERGING MODELS OF EMOTION IN HUMAN INFANCY

ROBERT N. EMDE and
THEODORE GAENSBAUER

This chapter considers three models of emotion that have emerged from our developmental research with human infants. Although they are descriptive, we believe these models raise interesting questions for students of animal behavior. To what extent are they limited to man or primates? To what extent are they applicable to other animals? These are intriguing questions to us, but before presenting our infancy models, we would like to share some thoughts about evolution and about models in general. These thoughts, stimulated by dialogues begun in Bielefeld, provide a necessary context for our attempts to understand and model those complex processes that we call emotions in humans.

SOME THOUGHTS ABOUT EVOLUTION

The high degree of organized complexity in human functioning forms a background for our thinking about development. As Platt (1966) so cogently stated, an evolutionary perspective reveals man to be the most complex thing in the universe. For scientists, this complexity forever insures a large degree of indeterminancy and privacy with respect to human behavior. With the best of measures and the best of models, we simplify and distort, and we can understand only so much. So it is with human emotions. As aspects of an individual's complex functioning, they often elude precise definition.

Still, this background makes more salient the fact that we, as clinicians, find emotions at the center of our everyday work. However difficult they are to define in the abstract, emotional expressions are useful. They provide empathic points of orientation for ongoing diagnostic assessment; they provide organismic clues about motivational states; and they often allow for prediction.

Although many ethologists have found emotions to be unnecessary or even burdensome concepts, there are others, particularly those working with primates, who have found such concepts useful. Emotional terms have been found to offer shortcuts for description, allowing for global judgments in the absence of scientific detail. Hebb, in his work with chimpanzees, found that verbal descriptions of emotional states offered intelligible and useful guides for behavior (Hebb 1946); they often captured intuitive judgments not yet accessible from compilations of detailed observations. Caretakers needed emotional terms for telling each other about basic features of individual animals that were important for safety, and researchers made use of emotional terms (even frankly anthropomorphic ones) as a starting point for the process of scientific specification. Similarly, Bowlby (1969), following Ryle (1949), used emotional words as *dispositional adjectives,* words that could offer great convenience in the vernacular language of feeling.

But are emotional terms merely inexact shortcuts for description? To put this question in another form: Because all constructs are conveniences, are emotional constructs purely artifacts of researchers? Are they totally in the eye of the beholder, representing algorithms for description? We think there is more to it. We assume, along with Darwin (1872) and many others (e.g., Tomkins, Izard, Ekman, Kaufman and Rosenblum, and Chevalier-Skolnikoff), that emotional states represent complex systems of organized functioning inherent in the human person. As such, they are useful to the individual and to the species, and we should therefore be able to trace their evolutionary history.

One aspect of this evolutionary history has been discussed by Hamburg (1963), who emphasizes the close ties between emotions and social life. According to Hamburg, group living has been a powerful adaptive mechanism over the course of evolution of primates, such that the formation of social bonds is experienced as pleasurable and its disruption as unpleasurable. Not surprisingly, the unpleasant disruption of social bonds is associated with profound psychophysiological changes and with instrumental behaviors that are designed to restore them. Thus, human emotions may have evolved because of their selective advantage in facilitating social bonding.

The programmatic research of Myers (1976) offers compelling experimental evidence for close biological connections between emotions and social life in free-ranging and laboratory macaques. Emotional and social behaviors are controlled by the same forebrain areas (prefrontal, anterotemporal, and orbitofrontal cortex), and when these areas are surgically ablated, those facial expressions and vocalizations that are ordinarily used in emotional behavior and in social communication cannot be used. Ablated animals, after being released from captivity, pass through their social groups without interacting with other conspecifics; indications are that they do not survive in the free-ranging condition, in what amounts to an emotionless and isolated state.

Another aspect of the evolutionary history of human emotions is provided by recent research on facial expressions. Although Darwin (1872) suggested long ago that emotional responses are patterned, that they express qualitatively distinct messages, and that they are centered in the facial region in both animals and man, recent cross-cultural work on human facial expressions has given new life to this area of investigation. Evidence strongly suggests that a number of discrete facial expressions representing qualitatively different emotional response systems are universally recognized and expressed throughout the human species (Ekman 1971; Ekman et al. 1972; Izard 1971, 1972, 1977). Thus, even for those animal behaviorists who object to imputing emotions to animals, questions about evolutionary antecedents of these facial expressions have a new excitement (see Ekman 1973).

Interestingly, the evolution of facial expression in primates may have occurred concomitant with the enhancement of visual capacity, which in turn brought advantageous functions of social communication for group-living species. In one way or another, this view has been offered by Andrew (1964), van Hooff (1962), Hamburg (1963), Bowlby (1969), and especially by the excellent review of Chevalier-Skolnikoff (1973). This review points out that in monkeys there is a traceable shift from the prosimians to the Old World monkeys (macaques) and beyond – a shift marked by increasing facial expressiveness and visual function along with decreasing emphasis on olfaction, touch, and sound reception. This shift corresponds to a movement from a nocturnal to a diurnal ecological niche and to involvement in more complex social worlds.

In the evolutionary step to man, facial muscles undoubtedly became differentiated in association with the increased functions of speech. Chevalier-Skolnikoff (1973) offers the interesting speculation that the number of basic emotional states may have stayed the same in the progression from apes to man, with social communication of more subtle internal states occurring primarily through language instead of through emotional expression. We would add that in human infancy, without language, emotional expressions are prominent. In fact, they provide a medium of peremptory messages in the infant–caregiver system – messages that are necessary for the infant's survival.

SOME THOUGHTS ABOUT MODELS

Our approach shares some common strategies with the ethological tradition. We place high importance on adequate description before experimental manipulation in order to insure both naturalistic and clinical relevance. We have an interest in heuristic models, yet we realize there is a risk in their being taken too seriously by those less familiar with the data sources. Because they simplify, they cannot, by definition, do justice to individual differences or organized complexity. Worse yet, such models can be reified or pulled out of their human context. Developing man is part of a social process, and attempts to abstract aspects of his behavior are likely to freeze and distort interactional realities.

We feel that models of emotion should be neither so simple as to do violence to the organized complexity of humans nor so all-encompassing as to become impractical or yield circular explanations. As we consider the results of the extraordinary negentropic changes brought about by evolution, as we look at complex behavior in mammals and primates, we are struck by our increasing dissatisfaction with purely external or behavioristic explanations. They are too simple. Not only can less be explained by S–R models, but less can be explained by fixed action patterns and related concepts. Barlow (1977) has pointed out that contemporary ethologists would consider that there is a continuum between precisely patterned movements that are relatively independent of external influence and patterned behavior that varies in accordance with momentary changes in the environment. But even *modal action patterns* (a refinement of the *fixed action patterns* concept allowing for statistical variability) are difficult to delineate in primates. In primates, social signaling displays are likely to be more complex, environmentally flexible and, from an individual subjective point of view, more idiosyncratic. Partly as a consequence of increasingly organized complexity, species-typical experiences are more varied, there is a greater impact of ontogenetic experience and, above all, individual differences are more prominent. Hebb, in his already cited 1946 report, made an emphatic point about individual differences: The researcher needed to become familiar with individual chimpanzees over time in order to make reliable and valid predictions from momentary emotional displays. The same conclusion about longitudinal observations for taking into account individual differences was reached in a study of rating human emotional expressions in a psychiatric setting (Hamburg et al. 1958).

Although this chapter focuses on emotional expressions, we tend to think of human emotions more broadly as motivational states involving appraisal, cognition, and memory elements. On the stimulus side, these internal states involve amplification, attenuation, and sometimes redirection of stimulus input. On the response side, they involve action tendencies or plans. Their centered aspects involve relations to pleasure and unpleasantness. With such complexity, we would expect such internal states to reflect considerable individual differences. But there are species-wide biological features. These include a tendency for certain patterns of behavior, phylogenetically derived and found useful in certain experiential realms, to be experienced as pleasurable and rewarding and therefore more likely to occur in given stimulus conditions. Such a *response bias* is probably true for social behavior in general. We also feel that species-wide features include built-in central nervous system (CNS) *affect programs* for a number of discrete emotions (see Izard 1977). However, we cannot assume a one-to-one correspondence between an external expression and an internal state that might reflect such a program. For any inference about an internal state, especially an emotional one, we feel there should be convergent measures from a number of realms. In addition, we share the problem of how to choose meaningful behavioral units with all ethologists. Therefore, our models are multiple and reflect multiple measures; they use different units of behavioral observation and represent different levels of complexity. In this way, we hope to generate schemes that have both naturalistic and experimental relevance. If we are successful, new questions will lead to new and better models.

AN ORGANISMIC MODEL: SCHEMATIZING TWO BIOBEHAVIORAL SHIFTS IN DEVELOPMENT, ONE AT 2 MONTHS AND ANOTHER AT 7 TO 9 MONTHS

A first model relating to the emotions places them within a developmental perspective. Attempts to find continuities in development have often not been successful and have pointed to the fact that development is not continuous in any simple way. At certain times there are major shifts in organization, resulting in qualitative transitions in behavior. New behaviors and functions emerge, with which shifts in affective expression are intimately entwined. We have previously detailed how information from our own research and that of many others has led to the inference of two major developmental shifts in the first year (Emde et al. 1976; Emde 1977). We will summarize some of this information.

A developmental shift at 2 months

After 2 months, behavior cannot be easily accounted for by endogenous rhythms and internal state. There is a shift away from endogenous control with more time spent in wakefulness and less in sleep. As Dittrichova and Lapackova have put it (1964), "Wakefulness becomes used a new way."

For parents, the shift from endogenous to exogenous control is most obvious in affective development. There is little in life more quietly dramatic than the onset of their baby's social smile soon after 2 months. This regular social smile, however, is not without antecedents. Prior to it, there is a period of irregular smiling followed by an upsurge of smiling to stimuli in a wide variety of modalities (Emde & Harmon 1972). Moreover, before the social smile becomes predominant, another form of smiling is seen. This form occurs as a concomitant of rapid eye movement (REM) state physiology (Emde & Koenig 1969a, 1969b; Emde & Metcalf 1970) and occurs more often in the premature, where it has a negative correlation with gestational age (Emde et al. 1971). We refer to this form of smiling as *endogenous smiling;* it declines during the normal newborn period during the same time that *exogenous smiling,* that form of smiling elicited by outside stimulation, increases. This developmental change is also a concomitant of the decline in nonhunger (or endogenous) fussiness. The decline in fussiness has been documented by many, including Brazelton (1962) and two longitudinal studies of our group (Tennes et al. 1972; Emde et al. 1976). Dittrichova and Lapackova (1964) have also pointed to the decline of fussiness during this time and an upsurge of babbling and exploratory behaviors.

In our longitudinal research we found an increase in wakefulness occurring during the first 2 months. This was followed by a plateau, which was then followed by a further increase in wakefulness preceding 7 to 9 months, followed in turn by a second plateau. These data are represented in Figure 22.1, where they provide the shape for a more general schematization of findings to be discussed later.

Numerous other changes occur during the first 2 months. Quiet sleep (N-REM) increases markedly (Dittrichova & Lapackova 1969; Parmelee et al. 1967). There is a decrease in behavioral activity during sleep and behaviorally undifferentiated REM states diminish (Emde & Metcalf 1970). Sleep distribution is altered, with an increase in the ability to sustain long periods of sleep and a shift to a diurnal pattern of nighttime sleep (Parmelee et al. 1967). The pattern of sleep onset also shifts from active REM to quiet N-REM.

In terms of perception, significant scanning of the face begins to develop around 7 weeks of age, when there is a prominent scanning of the eye region (Bergman et al. 1971; Haith 1976), a finding that corresponds to naturalistic observations (Robson 1967) (see also the work of Salapatek 1969; Mauer & Salapatek 1976). There also appears to be a change in organization around 2 months with respect to orienting and attentiveness, as demonstrated by heartrate responsiveness and visual attention (see the emphasis of Kagan 1970a and 1970b).

In conditioning and habituation studies, results are different before and after

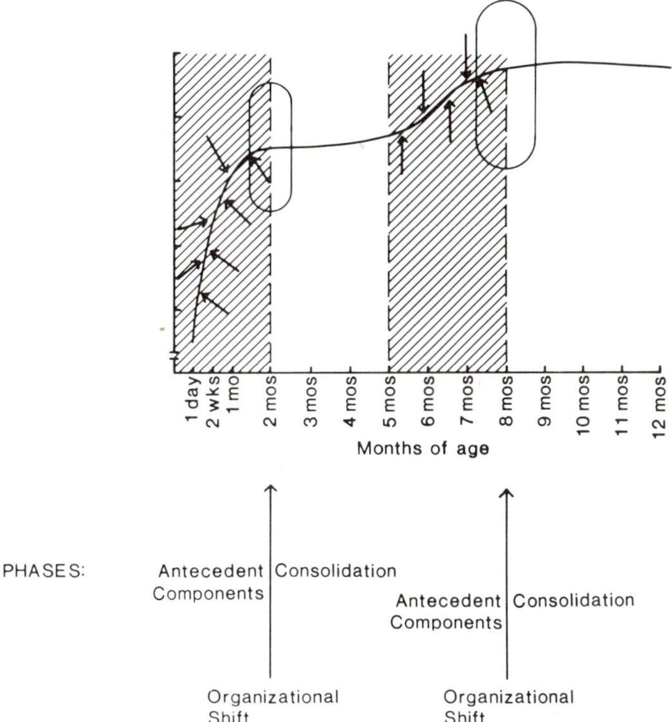

Figure 22.1. Schematic representation of two biobehavioral shifts occurring in the first year of life.

2 months. Before 2 months classical avoidance conditioning is very difficult to bring about, and operant conditioning effects are short-lived. After 2 months this is not the case. Similarly, with habituation, almost heroic measures are needed before 2 months for a successful experiment. After that time, habituation can readily be established in auditory and visual modalities.

A host of neurological reflexes are active within the first 2 months that decline thereafter; this decline is thought to reflect the postnatal maturation of forebrain inhibitory areas (see reviews in Paine 1965; Parmelee & Michaelis 1971; Peiper 1963). The visual cortical evoked response (Ellingson 1960) undergoes rapid maturational change between 4 and 8 weeks.

A developmental shift at 7 to 9 months

Another biobehavioral shift occurs between 7 and 9 months. In social–affective development, differential responsivity to strangers and caregivers, with fearfulness shown to strangers, is most prominent. Indeed, the emergence of this differential affective response to caregivers is so striking that it has often been regarded as marking the onset of the capacity for specific attachments. From studies with approaching strangers, with the visual cliff, and with other stimulus conditions (see summaries in Emde et al. 1976; Scarr & Salapatek 1970) there is evidence that a capacity for fearful responding begins at this time. As with smiling, we have found that fearfulness of strangers emerges with antecedents. An increment in wakefulness precedes this time of developmental shift. Further, longitudinal study has shown that certain behaviors (comparing faces and sobering to the approach of a stranger) regularly precede the onset of stranger distress (Emde et al. 1976).

There are other changes during this developmental shift that involve cognition, sleep state organization, and heartrate organization (Campos et al. 1975; Emde et al. 1976).

Contrary to what we had thought, these times of developmental shift cannot be conceptualized simply as times of rapid change. For each there are approximately 2 months of preparation during which components of new behavior appear. These become integrated into a new emergent organization at nodal times and are followed by periods of developmental consolidation. This process is illustrated schematically in Figure 22.1. The schema is superimposed on a data graph from our longitudinal study of mean hours of daily wakefulness during the first year (Emde et al. 1976). Component changes, indicated by arrows, appear before the nodal times of shift, which are indicated by circles. The latter represent new fields of emergent organization. Plateaus, representing times of consolidation, follow each shift.

In a recent symposium, two other investigators found a major qualitative transition in infant behavior at similar age periods. McCall (1977), in reanalyzing data from the Berkeley Growth Study, found qualitative transitions at precisely these two age points. Kagan (1977), in summarizing his research program on cognitive development, presented compelling evidence for a behavioral reorganization at the time of the second shift.

A SOCIAL SIGNALING MODEL: SCHEMATIZING THE ORGANIZATION OF INFANT EMOTIONAL EXPRESSIONS

As psychiatrists engaged in infant research, we continually confront a difficult question: How do we know that what we are calling *emotional* in babies is meaningful and related to the emotional experience that we find central in our clinical work? We were reassured (1) by observations from our longitudinal studies indicating that caregivers rarely mistook the meaning of certain infant expressions and (2) by regularities in cross-cultural work in adults, where there was dramatic agreement about emotional expressions using still photographs of the face (Ekman et al. 1972; Izard 1971). Because of this, we embarked on a research program designed to learn more about the expression, recognition, and contextual meaning of emotions within the caretaker–infant system.

One approach we have used involves multidimensional scaling (Shepard

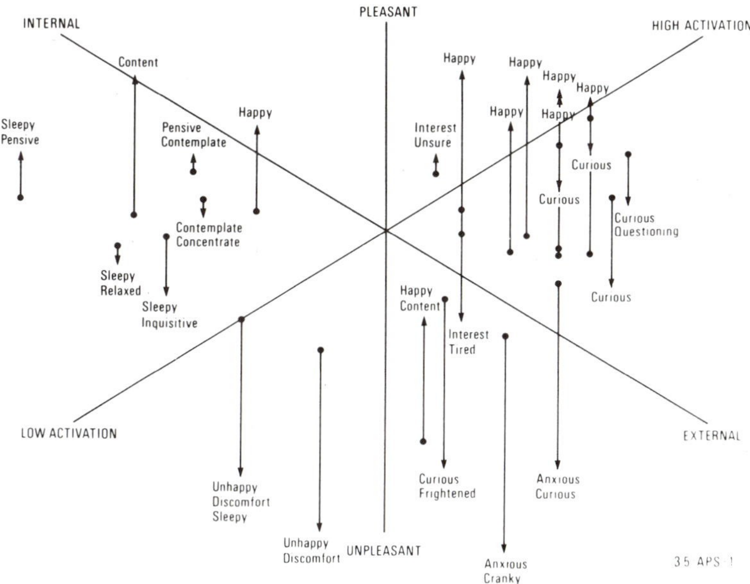

Figure 22.2. Three-dimensional solution from multidimensional scaling resulting from judgments of infant pictures taken at 3 months.

1962a, 1962b, 1974), in which 25 judges are asked to sort stimulus cards (either infant pictures or verbal responses of mothers to their own infants' pictures) into one or more piles, putting those that seem to belong together in the same pile. In studies so far, all judges have been women experienced with children. The original photographs of infant expressions were taken in standardized home sessions, involving sampling both with and without social and nonsocial stimulation. Similarity sortings have been done for infants' expressions at 2, 3, 4, and 12 months of age. To summarize, at 2 months, scaling solutions have been two-dimensional, with the first dimension easily characterized as *hedonic tone* and the second probably best characterized as *state.* At 3 months, three-dimensional scaling solutions predominate, and three dimensions are characteristic of all our solutions at 4 and 12 months. In the three-dimensional solution, hedonic tone carries the most variance, activation appears as the second dimension, and an internally oriented/externally oriented dimension appears as well. Figure 22.2 displays a three-dimensional plot from our 3-month-old infant picture-sorting data. Not only are the results internally consistent but, after 3 months, the suggested pattern of results shows consistency with studies of adult emotional expression. In fact, there is a history, containing striking regularities consistent with these results, that includes Spencer (1890), Wundt (1896), Freud (1915), Woodworth and Schlosberg (1954), Engen, Levy, and Schlosberg (1958), Gladstone (1962), Abelson and Sermat (1962), Frijda and Philipszoon (1963), Osgood (1966), and Frijda (1970). As in our results, *pleasantness–unpleasantness* emerges as the major dimension, *activation* or *intensity* is next, and a third dimension is often suggested but frequently difficult to interpret. This third dimension is sometimes called *acceptance-rejection, control,* or *expressed feeling versus inner feeling.* Based on this literature and on our preliminary multidimensional scaling of infant data, we propose that these dimensional properties are manifest soon after the neonatal period (i.e., after our first biobehavioral shift), remain throughout the life span, and reflect a structure for biologically adaptive messages. A neurophysiological substrate for the first two dimensions could involve diencephalic–reticular core brain structures, including reward and aversion systems, mediating hedonic tone (Olds & Olds 1963) and the reticular activating system, mediating activation (Lindsley 1951). As Bergstrom (1969) has documented, core brain structures involve a variety of homeostatic survival systems, and these tend to mature early in ontogenesis.

We also consider it a basic characteristic of human affect expressions that they are biologically organized in such a way as to communicate discrete categories of information, although such information often occurs in combinations or blends and usually at much less than peak intensity. From an evolutionary standpoint, these categories, because they appear to be universal, must also represent biologically meaningful messages. Based on our own longitudinal and cross-sectional studies (Campos et al. 1975; Emde & Harmon 1972; Emde et al. 1976; Emde et al. 1978b) and on extensive literature of similar observations by others (e.g., Bayley 1969; Bridges 1933; Gesell & Amatruda 1945; Hetzer & Wolf 1928; Spitz 1965; Spitz & Wolf 1946) we conclude that discrete affect expressions are not present at birth but appear according to an epigenetic sequence.

Neurophysiologically, it would seem that underlying structures mediating these discrete affect expressions would require complex feedback relationships between multiple brain centers and forebrain areas for cognition; as such, they would be presumed to develop later. After early infancy, there are increasingly intimate relationships among cognitive, motivational, and affective sectors of development. Our experience in a longitudinal study (Emde et al. 1976) corresponds to that of Sroufe (1977) in finding that affect expressions of fear, surprise, and anger become prominent in development only toward the second half of the first year. Recently, we have had corroboration of this finding in a cross-sectional study. Using our photograph sampling technique, infant expressions were judged in the categories of surprise, fear, and anger by multiple raters at 12 months, whereas there were none in these categories at 3 months. Current work includes a components analysis of facial movements involved in these expressions in infancy (see Ekman & Friesen 1975; Oster & Ekman 1977).

Because experiential factors have increasing importance as the child gets older, we would not expect discrete affect expressions to emerge suddenly as fully developed during the first 2 years, at least in the sense in which they are measured by Ekman and Friesen (1975). We assume that context is especially important in attributing message value to early affect expressions. We also assume that the epigenetic process is such that before their complete emergence, components of expressions would be seen as developmental antecedents, as our previous organismic model highlights.

A DYNAMIC MODEL: SCHEMATIZING INFANT EMOTIONS IN A STANDARDIZED PLAYROOM SITUATION

In the pursuit of discrete, measurable units of behavior, we must remind ourselves that all aspects of human functioning are part of ongoing processes. Emotional aspects are no exception; they represent continuous processes in our lives. Whether we view them as appraisal mechanisms, motivating forces, or expressive modes, we assume they function in an ongoing, dynamic way to facilitate the organism's adaptation to changing environmental conditions. If our view that emotions reflect qualitatively distinct elements of CNS organization is valid, such discrete entities should be capable of being reliably identified in a dynamic situation. Furthermore, as discrete emotions are expressed over time, we might expect blends of emotions to occur, as well as changing interrelationships among them, depending on varying stimulus contexts and the previous experience of the infant.

Based on this dynamic model, we had several expectations about how, in optimal circumstances, specific emotions might be expressed. An infant should have a capacity to "turn on" a particular emotion promptly, given an appropriate stimulus, and to sustain it for an appropriate length of time, again depending on the context. Correspondingly, an infant should be capable of effectively modulating, or "turning off," emotional reactions as conditions change. Considerable variability would be expected in these characteristics, both between infants and within a given infant. In addition, different combinations of emotion blends might be seen in different individuals as a result of a variety of constitutional or environmental factors. At the same time, if such reactions are to be adaptive, there should be a degree of predictability as to the likelihood of specific emotions being evoked by specific situations.

To study emotions from a dynamic point of view, we have used an experimental paradigm modified from the Strange Situation used by Ainsworth and others (Ainsworth & Wittig 1969). The infant is exposed to a sequence of changing stimulus conditions, with each situation expected to highlight a different emotion or set of emotions. The situations are ordered in such a way as to allow for an ebb and flow of reactions to potentially pleasant and unpleasant experiences and to observe such reactions over time. Following an initial free play period with the mother and infant alone in the playroom, there is an entrance, graduated approach, and eventual picking up of the infant by a stranger/experimenter. Then, after an abbreviated Bayley developmental test and a brief play period, the mother leaves the room. After her return, the experimenter leaves the room; the sequence ends after the experimenter's return. The entire session lasts between 45 and 60 minutes and is videotaped through a one-way mirror for subsequent rating.

Six emotions have been chosen for study – pleasure, interest, fear, anger, sadness, and distress. A nine-point scale is used to rate the presence and intensity of each of the six emotions. Ratings of interest are divided into three subcategories: interest in the mother, interest in the stranger, and interest in the inanimate environment, for example, toys. Ratings are based on specific be-

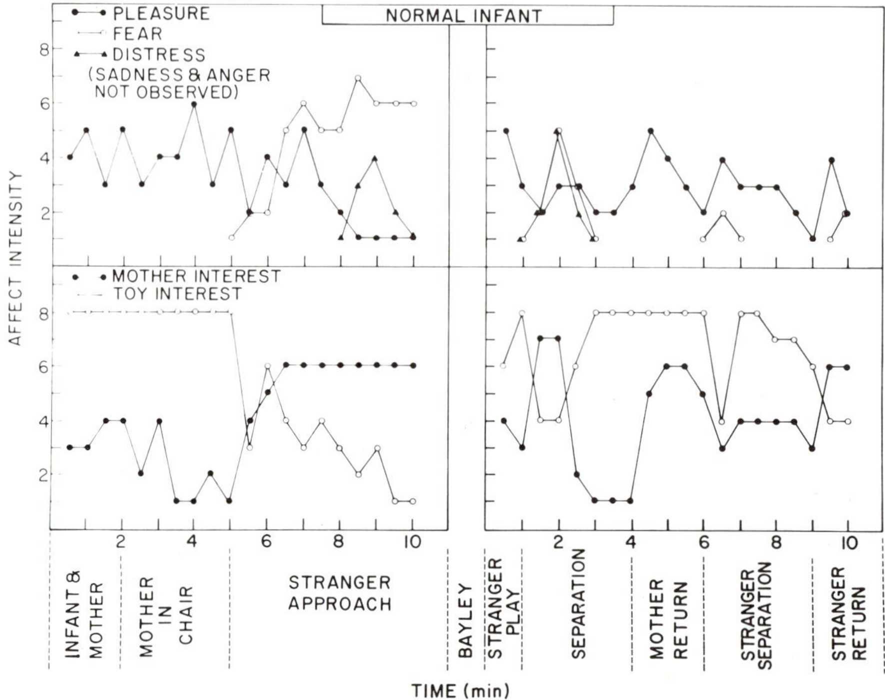

Figure 22.3. Patterning of affective expression in a 12-month-old normal infant.

havioral criteria involving the presence and intensity of characteristic facial expressions and motoric behaviors during 30-second intervals. For each rating interval, two independent and naive raters score the intensity of each emotion, resulting in a total of eight ratings per interval and permitting the scoring of emotional blends.

To date we have reported on a total of 60 normal infants in groups of 20 at ages 12, 15, and 18 months, as well as 12 infants in the same age range who were referred to us for a psychosocial evaluation following suspected or documented abuse and/or neglect (Gaensbauer et al. 1979; Gaensbauer in press). To illustrate our points regarding the dynamic nature of the emotions, we would like to present data taken from two infants, a 12-month-old infant from our normal group and a 12-month-old infant referred to us for psychosocial evaluation because of documented parental neglect.

Figure 22.3 shows the data obtained for the normal infant. The top part of the graph shows the fluctuation in the emotions of pleasure, fear, and distress. Sadness and anger were not observed during the session. The bottom half of the graph displays the ratings for toy-interest and mother-interest. To facilitate reading of the graph, ratings for stranger-interest have not been included; these were found to be highest during the stranger approach and mother separation sequences.

In the normal infant, there is a considerable variety and range of emotions expressed, though with a preponderance of pleasurably toned emotions. There is an evident capacity to sustain emotional reactions during those intervals when stimulus conditions are relatively constant, as shown most notably by the sustained pleasure and toy-interest during the initial free play period, even though there is some variability from interval to interval. At the same time, each of the emotions is quite responsive to changing circumstances. This is seen especially with the stranger entrance and approach. As the stranger gradually approaches over a 4-minute period, there is a decline in pleasurable responses, a decrease in toy-interest, an increase in mother-interest, and an increase in fear responses (defined as a fearful facial expression and/or avoidance). Distress responses (defined as whimpering or crying) were seen only at the most stressful point of the approach, when the stranger picked up the infant; in rating, a clear distinction can be made between fear and distress. When the mother leaves, toy-interest falls initially, pleasurable responses decrease, and there is a brief period of increased fear and distress. There is some sustained interest in the mother following her departure (as indicated by search behaviors) and a heightened interest in her for the next 2 minutes after her return. Interestingly, a considerable increase in mother-interest is precipitated by the stranger's return at the end of the sequence, which is likely motivated by a wish for the security of the mother's presence.

Although capable of expressing fear and distress, the normal infant also shows a capacity to modulate or turn off these negative emotional responses. During maternal separation, they do not disrupt the infant's interest in the current situation (note high toy-interest), nor do they interfere with its capacity to greet the mother with expressions of interest and pleasure on her return.

An additional point illustrated by Figure 22.3 is the occurrence of emotional blends in varying combinations over the course of the session. In practically every rating interval, two or more emotions are judged to be present. Often the patterns of combinations shown by the discrete emotions appear to complement each other, for example, during the stranger approach, when fear and mother-interest are observed to increase together. At other times, there is a suggestion of competing emotional states; this was most notable during the stranger approach and briefly during the maternal separation, when the emotions of pleasure and fear were observed during the same rating intervals.

Implicit in this dynamic model of the emotions is the notion that they would be profoundly affected by the infant's caretaking environment. Under conditions of extreme stress, one might anticipate that some infants might show considerable distortion in their affective expression that would be revealed in altered dynamic patterns. Our study of a group of abused/neglected infants has supported the usefulness of this way of thinking about emotions. A recent paper (Gaensbauer and Mrazek in press) describes several different affective behavior patterns observed in an abused/neglected sample.

Figure 22.4 illustrates one kind of distorted responding observed in these infants, tracing the emotional responses of a 12-month-old neglected infant.

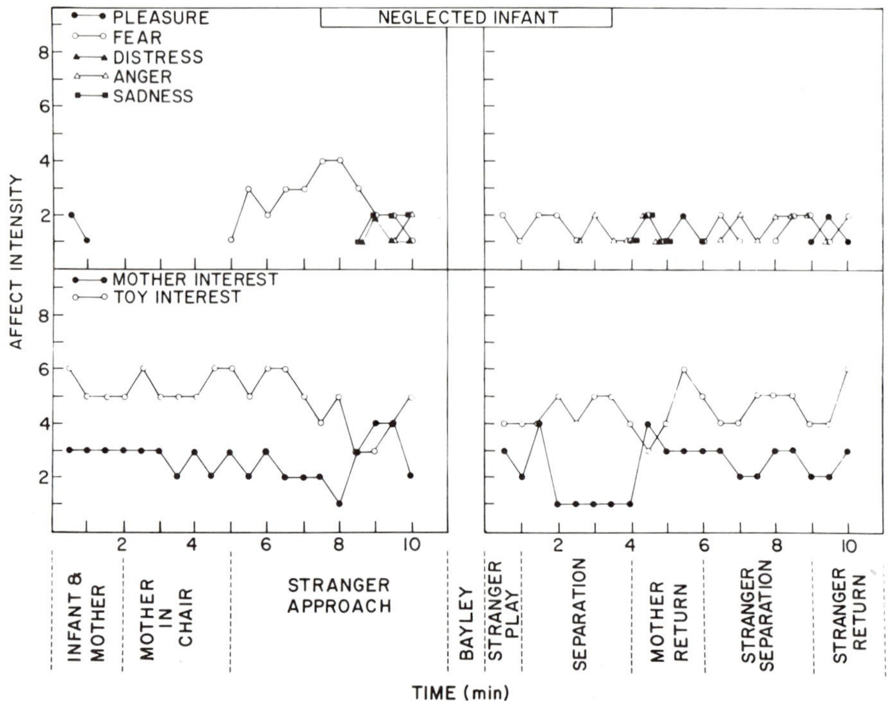

Figure 22.4. Patterning of affective expression in a 12-month-old neglected infant.

This infant scored within the normal range on developmental testing and did not appear to be clinically depressed. Perhaps the most impressive aspect of this child's record is what we have considered emotional blunting. Each of the emotions, if rated as present at all, is found at the low end of the intensity scale. Most importantly, there is a very narrow range of expression, with little or no change in response to changing stimulus events. Pleasurable responses are essentially absent. Interest in the mother remains low throughout the session and does not change appreciably even in response to such salient events as the stranger's approach or the mother's return following the brief separation. The same is true of toy-interest, which is initially somewhat lower than in the normal infant but is sustained with striking consistency despite a variety of changing situations. Though there is a degree of fearfulness during the stranger approach, there does not seem to be much heightening in the course of the approach, and in contrast to the normal infant's response, there is no increased mother-interest during this time. Except for this phase, negative emotional expressions are also absent, as are positive ones. The neglected infant appears to be affectively withdrawn from her environment, particularly from other people. Her impoverished affective life stands in contrast to the rich and responsive affective expression of the normal infant.

SOME CONCLUDING THOUGHTS ABOUT THE ADAPTIVE NATURE OF EMOTIONS

There are two views of emotion that no longer seem compelling in light of our infancy research. One is the *activation* view (Mandler 1975; Schachter & Singer 1962) in which all emotions are physiologically nonspecific, requiring only activation and a specific cognitive context for their special character. Aside from problems related to the fact that this is a peripheralist view, with activation conceptualized in terms of the autonomic nervous system instead of the CNS, such an idea is inconsistent with a behavioral biology of development in which there are species-specific patterned emotional responses that not only appear in infancy but, from a social signaling point of view, have crucial survival functions. There is every reason, because of their early organized appearance and importance, to view infant emotions as rooted in biology and as central to biobehavioral development from the outset.

Another view that loses its usefulness is the drive-reduction or *tension* view of pleasure and unpleasure. In our dimensional studies activation becomes abstracted as an independent dimension of emotional expression; there can be high activated or low activated pleasure. The same is true for unpleasure. That pleasure and unpleasure cannot be equivalent to the increase and decrease of tension is also dramatized by the social smile of a 3-month-old. When the adult approaches, the infant shows a build-up of behavioral activation. There is a "bicycling" of the arms and legs, and the smile continues or broadens as the face seems to light up, with sparkling eyes that engage the adult directly. Consistent with this picture of increasing activity, we have recently shown that infant smiling tends to be associated with increased rather than decreased heartrate, as the tension-reduction model would predict (Emde et al. 1978a).

Above all, we feel convinced that emotions are not unidimensional. They are multidimensional and complex. Further, the biological structures underlying emotions have sufficiently organized built-in constraints so that there are qualitatively distinct emotions with qualitatively different patterns of behavior and experience.

Emotional states reflect organized CNS mechanisms for arousing and sustaining adaptive behavior within both the self and other conspecifics. As such, emotional states are ongoing and dynamic rather than intermittent. They are not, in general, disruptive or disorganizing. Although it is true that they are apt to be less organized at their extremes and may even appear to disrupt patterned responses, this feature is hardly surprising when one considers the inverted U-shaped curves that usually characterize measures of activation and performance.

Our models highlight the concept that emotions are adaptive. This concept is buttressed by our clinical experience, in which all meaningful social relationships are seen to be affective (see Emde 1978; Rangell 1967). It is given developmental emphasis by similar thoughts about the infant–caregiver relationship. Affects are continuous factors in the lives of both infant and caregiver and provide a medium for their developing relationship. Over the course of constantly recurring sequences of interaction, mother and infant normally establish modes of reciprocal adjustment that leave both of them with a preponderance of pleasurable and positively toned expectations rather than negative ones. Where there is early separation, as in modern day-care nurseries, and where the opportunity for mutually rewarding affective reciprocity is denied the infant and caregiver, the incidence of battering and child neglect is increased (Elmer & Gregg 1967; Shaheen et al. 1968). Further, correction of early separation can enhance affective parent–infant relations (de Chateau & Wiberg 1977a, 1977b; Klaus et al. 1972; Klaus & Kennell 1976). In our own research, the adaptive importance of early infant affect expressions is underscored by the deviant development of Down's syndrome children, in whom, because of CNS defects, initial smiling is dampened and parents suffer disappointment, which often inaugurates further grieving for the normal child who was expected but not born (Emde & Brown 1978).

To the extent that an infant is unable to tune in flexibly and adaptively to the affective communications of the caretaker, such an infant may contribute to its own deficit in caretaking (Sameroff & Chandler 1976; Gaensbauer & Sands 1978). In the case of abused/neglected infants, this process may not only reflect biological individual differences in temperament but may also be a consequence of the interactional experience itself. After a period of interactional deprivation or aberrant parenting, infants can suffer a derailment in their development such that affective patterns of response are unappealing or provocative. Milowe and Lourie (1964) and Gil (1970) have directed attention to the fact that some children are abused in more than one home, and a number of other authors have enumerated infant factors that may lead to abuse in particular children (Friedrich & Boriskin 1976; Green et al. 1974; Klein & Stern 1971; Lynch 1976; Parke & Collmer 1975). Certainly the infant illustrated in Figure 22.4 would not show the same appeal or give the same satisfaction to a caregiver as the affectively responsive infant in Figure 22.3. A recent paper summarizes our experience thus far with distorted affective communications in abused/neglected infants along with their potential impact on caretakers (Gaensbauer & Sands 1978).

Dysynchrony in affective states, either in real life or in our playroom situation, can certainly be viewed as emanating from either infant or parent and is often a reflection of disturbances on both sides. In our dynamic model, we have focused on the infant, but, as with our other models, we simplify and leave out much. Our model at the next level of complex infant emotions will have to be a truly interactional and transactional one. How are parents influenced by individual differences in infant biobehavioral shifts? What difference do these individual differences in biobehavioral shifts make in the caretaking environment, and how, in turn, does the infant make use of this influence? If emotional expressions are the language of the baby, how does any baby receive emotional messages from the parent? What developmental course does emotional language reception have, and how is affective reciprocity organized? (see Stern 1974). Social signaling must be studied and modeled both in the short run in sequences of "microinteractions" and in the long run in longitudinal studies as it involves interactions between individuals within the larger sphere of developing family life.

In summary, unlike researchers of yesterday, oriented to S–R and drive discharge models, today's investigators have a view of the human infant that has organized complexity as a central concern. This view is influenced by data from multiple disciplines and includes the infant as fundamentally active, socially interactive, and a creative force in its own development. This chapter has reviewed three organizational models of infant emotional development, one representing two biobehavioral shifts in development, one representing social signaling, and one representing a dynamic flow of emotional states. An assumption embedded in these models is that infant emotional expressions have an adaptive role in facilitating survival and social development. This assumption seems in harmony with our research and clinical experience, our theoretical concern for human complexity, and our evolutionary dialogues engendered by the Bielefeld conference.

REFERENCES

Abelson, R. P., & V. Sermat. 1962. Multidimensional scaling of facial expressions. *Journal of Experimental Psychology* 63:546–554.

Ainsworth, M. 1967. *Infancy in Uganda.* Johns Hopkins Press, Baltimore.

Ainsworth, M., & B. Wittig. 1969. Attachment and exploratory behavior of one-year-olds in a strange situation. *In:* B. M. Foss (ed.), *Determinants of infant behavior.* Wiley, New York.

Andrew, R. J. 1964. The displays of the primates. *In:* J. Buettner-Janusch (ed.), *Evolutionary and genetics: biology of primates,* vol. 2. Academic Press, New York.

Arnold, M. G. 1970. Perennial problems in the field of emotion. *In:* M. B. Arnold (ed.), *Feelings and emotion,* the Loyola Symposium. Academic Press, New York, pp. 169–185.

Barlow, G. W. 1977. Modal action patterns. *In:* T. A. Sebeok (ed.), *How animals communicate,* Indiana University Press, Bloomington, pp. 98–134.

Bayley, N. 1969. *Bayley scales of infant development.* Psychological Corporation, New York.

Bergman, T., M. J. Haith, & L. Mann. 1971. Development of eye contact and facial scanning in infants. Paper presented at the Society for Research in Child Development Convention, Minneapolis, April.

Bergstrom, R. M. 1969. Electrical parameters of the brain during ontogeny. *In:* R. J. Robinson (ed.), *Brain and early behavior.* Academic Press, New York, pp. 15–41.

Bernstein, S., & W. A. Mason. 1962. The effects of age and stimulus condition on the emotional response of rhesus monkeys: responses to complex stimuli. *Journal of Genetic Psychology* 101:279–298.

Bowlby, J. 1969. *Attachment and loss,* vol. 1., *Attachment.* Basic Books, New York.

Brazelton, T. B. 1962. Crying in infancy. *Pediatrics* 29:579–588.

Brazelton, T. B., B. Koslowski, & M. Main. 1974. The origins of reciprocity: *In:* M. Lewis & L. Rosenblum (eds.), *The effect of the infant on its caregiver,* vol. 1. Wiley-Interscience, New York, pp. 49–76.

Bridges, K. M. B. 1933. Emotional development in early infancy. *Child Development* 3:324–341.

Campos, J. J., R. Emde, T. Gaensbauer, J. Sorce, & C. Henderson. 1975. Cardiac behavioral interrelations in the reactions of infants to strangers. *Developmental Psychology* 11:589–601.

Charlesworth, W. R., & M. A. Kreutzer. 1973. Facial expressions of infants and children. *In:* P. Ekman (ed.), *Darwin and facial expression: a century of research in review.* Academic Press, New York, pp. 91–168.

Chevalier-Skolnikoff, S. 1973. Facial expression of emotion in nonhuman primates. *In:* P. Ekman (ed.), *Darwin and facial expression: a century of research in review.* Academic Press, New York, pp. 11–89.

Collard, R. 1967. Fear of strangers and play behavior in kittens with varied social experience. *Child Development* 38:877–899.

Darwin, C. 1872. *Expression of emotion in man and animals.* John Murray, London.

de Chateau, P., & B. Wiberg. 1977a. Long-term effect on mother–infant behavior of extra contact during the first hour post partum. 1. *Acta Paediatrica Scandinavica* 66:137–143.

1977b. Long-term effect on mother–infant behavior of extra contact during the first hour post partum. 2. *Acta Paediatrica Scandinavica* 66:145–151.

Dittrichova, J., & V. Lapackova. 1964. Development of the waking state in young infants. *Child Development* 35:365–370.

1969. Development of sleep in infancy. *In:* R. J. Robinson (ed.), *Brain and early behavior.* Academic Press, London and New York, pp. 193–204.

Ekman, P. 1971. Universals and cultural differences in facial expressions of emotions. *In:* J. K. Cole (ed.), *Nebraska Symposium on Motivation.* University of Nebraska Press, Lincoln.

Ekman, P. 1973. *Darwin and facial expression: a century of research in review.* Academic Press, New York and London.

Ekman, P., & W. Friesen. 1975. *Unmasking the face.* Prentice-Hall, Englewood Cliffs, New Jersey.

Ekman, P., W. V. Friesen, & P. Ellsworth. 1972. *Emotion in the human face.* Pergamon Press, New York.

Ellingson, R. J. 1960. Cortical electrical responses to visual stimulation in the human infant. *Electroencephalography in Clinical Neurophysiology* 12:663–677.

Elmer, E., & G. Gregg. 1967. Developmental characteristics of abused children. *Pediatrics* 40:596–602.

Emde, R. N. 1978. Toward a psychoanalytic theory of affect. 1. The organizational model and its propositions. *In:* S. Greenspan & G. Pollock (eds.), *Psychoanalysis and development, current perspectives.* U.S. Government Printing Office, Washington, D. C.

Emde, R. N., & C. Brown. 1978. Adaptation to the birth of a Down's syndrome infant: grieving and maternal attachment. *Journal of the American Academy of Child Psychiatry* 17:299–323.

Emde, R. N., J. Campos, J. Reich, & T. Gaensbauer. 1978a. Infant smiling at five and nine months: analysis of heartrate and movement. *Infant Behavior and Development* 1:26–35.

Emde, R. N., T. J. Gaensbauer, & R. J. Harmon. 1976. Emotional expression in infancy: a biobehavioral study. *Psychological Issues, a Monograph Series,* vol. 10, no. 37. International Universities Press, New York.

Emde, R. N., & R. J. Harmon. 1972. Endogenous and exogenous smiling systems in early infancy. *Journal of the American Academy of Child Psychiatry* 11:177–200.

Emde, R. N., D. H. Kligman, J. H. Reich, & T. Wade. 1978b. Emotional expression in infancy. 1. Initial studies of social signaling and an emergent model. *In:* M. Lewis & L. Rosenblum (eds.), *The development of affect.* Plenum, New York.

Emde, R. N., & K. L. Koenig. 1969a. Neonatal smiling and rapid eye movement states. *Journal of Child Psychiatry* 8:57–67.

1969b. Neonatal smiling, frowning, and rapid eye movement states. 2. Sleep-cycle study. *Journal of the American Academy of Child Psychiatry* 8:637–656.

Emde, R. N., R. D. McCartney, & R. J. Harmon. 1971. Neonatal smiling in REM states. 4. Premature study. *Child Development* 42:1657–1661.

Emde, R. N., & D. R. Metcalf. 1970. An electroencephalographic study of behavioral rapid eye movement states in the human newborn. *Journal of Nervous and Mental Disease* 150:376–386.

Engen, R., N. Levy, & H. Schlosberg. 1958. The dimension analysis of a new series of facial expressions. *Journal of Experimental Child Psychology* 55:454–458.

Freedman, D. G., J. A. King, & O. Elliot. 1961. Critical period in the social development of dogs. *Science* 133:1016–1017.

Freud, S. 1911. Formulations on the two principles of mental functioning. *Standard edition,* vol. 12. Hogarth Press, London, 1958, pp. 218–226.

1915. *Instincts and their vicissitudes: standard edition,* vol. 14. Hogarth Press, London, 1968, pp. 111–140.

Friedrich, W. N., & J. A. Boriskin. 1976. The role of the child in child abuse: a review of the literature. *American Journal of Orthopsychiatry* 45:580–590.

Frijda, N. 1970. Emotion and recognition of emotion. *In:* M. B. Arnold (ed.), *Feelings and emotions.* Academic Press, New York.

Frijda, N., & E. Philipszoon. 1963. Dimensions of recognition of expression. *Journal of Abnormal and Social Psychology* 66:45–51.

Gaensbauer, T. In press. Regulation of emotional expression in infants from two contrasting caretaking environments. *Journal of the American Academy of Child Psychiatry.*

Gaensbauer, T. J., D. Mrazek, & R. N. Emde. 1979. Patterning of emotional response in a modified "strange situation" paradigm. *Infant Behavior and Development* 2:163–178.

Gaensbauer, T. J., and D. Mrazek. In press. Differences in the patterning of affective expression in infants. *Journal of the American Academy of Child Psychiatry.*

Gaensbauer, T. J., & K. Sands. 1979. Distorted affective communications in abused/neglected infants and their potential impact on caretakers. *Journal of the American Academy of Child Psychiatry* 18:236–250.

Gesell, A. L., & C. Amatruda. 1945. *The embryology of behavior: the beginnings of the human mind.* Harper, New York.

Gil, D. 1970. *Violence against children.* Harvard University Press, Cambridge, Massachusetts.

Gladstone, W. H. 1962. A multidimensional study of facial expression of emotion. *Australian Journal of Psychology* 14:19–100.

Green, A., R. Gaines, & A. Sandgrun. 1974. Child abuse: pathological syndrome of family interaction. *American Journal of Psychiatry* 131:882–886.

Haith, M. 1976. Visual competence in early infancy. *In:* H. Held, H. Leibowitz, & H. L. Teuber (eds.), *Handbook of sensory physiology,* vol. 8. Springer-Verlag, New York.

Hamburg, D. A. 1963. Expression of the emotions in man. *In:* P. H. Knapp (ed.), International Universities Press, New York, pp. 300–315.

Hamburg, D. A., et al. 1958. Classification and rating of emotional experiences. *Archives of Neurology and Psychiatry* 79:415–426.

Hebb, D. O. 1946. On the nature of fear. *Psychological Review* 53:259–276.

Hess, E. H. 1959. Two conditions limiting the critical age for imprinting. *Journal of Comparative and Physiological Psychology* 52:515–518.

Hetzer, H., & K. Wolf. 1928. Baby tests. *Zeitschrift für Psychologie* 107:62–104.

Izard, C. 1971. *The face of emotion.* Meredith, New York.

1972. *Patterns of emotion.* Academic Press, New York.

1977. *Human emotions.* Plenum, New York.

Kagan, J. 1970a. Attention and psychological change in the young child. *Science* 170:826–832.

1970b. The distribution of attention in infancy. *In:* D. H. Hamburg (ed.), *Perception and its disorders.* Williams & Wilkins, Baltimore. Research publication, Association for Research in Nervous and Mental Disease, vol. 48, pp. 214–237.

1977. A longitudinal study of development from infancy to age ten. Society for Research in Child Development Symposium, New Orleans, March.

Kaufman, I. C., & L. A. Rosenblum. 1967. The reaction to separation in infant monkeys: anaclitic depression and conservation withdrawal. *Psychosomatic Medicine* 29:648–675.

King, D. L. 1966. A review and interpretation of some aspects of the infant–mother relationship in mammals and birds. *Psychological Bulletin* 65:143–155.

Klaus, M. H., R. Jerauld, N. C. Kreger, W. McApline, M. Steffa, & J. H. Kennell. 1972. Maternal attachment, importance of the first postpartum days. *New England Journal of Medicine* 286:460–463.

Klaus, M. H., & J. H. Kennell. 1976. *Maternal-infant bonding.* Mosby, St. Louis, pp. 1–257.

Klein, M., & L. Stern. 1971. Low birthweight and the battered child syndrome. *American Journal of Diseases in Children* 122:15–18.

Lindsley, D. 1951. Emotion. *In:* S. S. Stevens (ed.), *Handbook of experimental psychology.* Wiley, New York.

Lynch, M. 1976. Risk factors in the child: a study of abused children and their siblings. *In:* H. P. Martin (ed.), *The abused child.* Ballinger, Cambridge, Massachusetts.

Malmo, R. B. 1959. A neurophysiological dimension. *Psychological Review* 66:367–386.

Mandler, G. 1975. *Mind and emotion.* Wiley, New York and London.

Mauer, D., & P. Salapatek. 1976. Developmental changes in the scanning of faces by young infants. *Child Development* 47:523–527.

McCall, R. B. 1977. Stages in mental development during the first two years. Society for Research in Child Development Symposium, New Orleans, March.

Milowe, I. D., & R. S. Lourie. 1964. The child's role in the battered child syndrome. *Journal of Pediatrics* 65:1079–1081.

Myers, R. E. 1976. Cortical localization of emotion control. Invited lecture. American Psychological Association, Washington, D.C., September.

Olds, M., & J. Olds. 1963. Approach–avoidance analysis of rat diencephalon. *Journal of Comparative Neurology* 120:259–295.

Osgood, C. 1966. Dimensionality of the semantic space for communication via facial expression. *Scandinavian Journal of Psychology* 7:1–30.

Oster, H., & P. Ekman. 1977. Facial behavior in child development. *In:* A. Collins (ed.), *Minnesota symposia on child psychology,* vol. 2. Crowell, New York.

Paine, R. S. 1965. The contribution of developmental neurology to child psychiatry. *Journal of the American Academy of Child Psychiatry* 4:353–386.

Parke, R. D., & C. W. Collmer. 1975. Child abuse: an interdisciplinary analysis. *Review of Child Development Research* 5:509–590.

Parmelee, A., & R. Michaelis. 1971. Neurological examination of the newborn. *In:* J. Hellmuth (ed.), *The exceptional infant, studies in abnormalities,* vol. 2. Brunner/Mazel, New York, pp. 3–23.

Parmelee, A., W. Wenner, Y. Akiyama, M. Schultz, & E. Stern. 1967. Sleep states in premature infants. *Developmental Medicine and Child Neurology* 9:70–77.

Parmelee, A., W. H. Wenner, & H. R. Schulz. 1964. Infant sleep patterns from birth to 16 weeks of age. *Journal of Pediatrics* 65:576–582.

Peiper, A. 1963. Cerebral function in infancy and childhood. *In:* J. Wortis (ed.), *The international behavioral sciences series.* Consultants Bureau, New York.

Piaget, J. 1936. *The origins of intelligence in children,* 2nd ed. International Universities Press, New York, 1952.

Platt, J. R. 1966. *The step to man.* Wiley, New York.

Rangell, L. 1967. Psychoanalysis, affects and the "human core": on the relationship of psychoanalysis to the behavioral sciences. *Psychoanalytic Quarterly* 36:172–202.

Robson, K. S. 1967. The role of eye-to-eye contact in maternal–infant attachment. *Journal of Child Psychology and Psychiatry* 8:13–25.

Ryle, G. 1949. *The concept of mind.* London, Hutchinson; New York, Barnes & Noble, 1950.

Sackett, G. 1966. Monkeys reared in isolation with pictures as visual input: evidence for innate releasing mechanism. *Science* 154:1468–1473.

Salapatek, P. 1969. The visual investigation of geometric patterns by the one- and two-month old infant. Paper presented at meetings of the American Association for the Advancement of Science, Boston.

Sameroff, A. J., & M. Chandler. 1976. Reproductive risk and the continuum of caretaking casualty. *In:* F. D. Horowitz (ed.), *Review of child development research,* vol. 4. University of Chicago Press, Chicago, pp. 187–244.

Scarr, S., & P. Salapatek. 1970. Patterns of fear development during infancy. *Merrill-Palmer Quarterly* 16:53–90.

Schachter, S., & J. E. Singer. 1962. Cognitive, social and physiological determinants of emotional state. *Psychological Review* 69:379–399.

Scott, J. P. 1963. The process of primary socialization in canine and human infants. *Monograph Society for Research in Child Development* 28:1–47.

Shaheen, E., D. Alexander, M. Truskowsky, & G. Borbero. 1968. Failure to thrive – a retrospective profile. *Clinical Pediatrics* 7:255–261.

Shepard, R. 1962a. The analysis of proximities: multidimensional scaling with an unknown distance function. 1. *Psychometrika* 27:125–140.

1962b. The analysis of proximities: multidimensional scaling with an unknown distance function. 2. *Psychometrika* 27:219–246.

1974. Representation of structure in similarity data: problems and prospects. *Psychometrika* 39:373–421.

Spencer, H. 1890. *The principles of psychology.* Appleton, New York.

Spitz, R. 1965. *The first year of life – normal and deviant object relations.* International Universities Press, New York.

Spitz, R., & M. Wolf. 1946. The smiling response. *Genetic Psychology Monographs* 34:57–125.

Sroufe, A. 1977. Emotional expression in infancy. Unpublished manuscript.

1979. Emotional development. *In:* J. Osofsky (ed.), *Handbook of infant development.* Wiley, New York.

Stechler, G., & G. Carpenter. Theoretical considerations. *Exceptional Infant, Normal Infant* 1:165–189.

Stern, D. N. 1974. The goal of structure of mother–infant play. *Journal of the American Academy of Child Psychiatry* 13:401–421.

Tennes, K., R. N. Emde, A. J. Kisley, & D. R. Metcalf. 1972. The stimulus barrier in early infancy: an exploration of some formulations of John Benjamin. *In:* R. R. Holt & E. Peterfreund (eds.), *Psychoanalysis and contemporary science,* vol. 1. Macmillan, New York, pp. 206–234.

Thomas, A., S. Chess, & H. Birch. 1968. *Temperament and behavior disorders in children.* New York University Press, New York.

Tomkins, S. S. 1962. *Affect, imagery, consciousness: the positive affects.* Springer, New York.

1963. *Affect, imagery, consciousness: the negative affects.* Springer, New York.

van Hooff, J. A. R. A. M. 1962. Facial expressions in higher primates. *Symposium of the Zoological Society of London* 8:97–125.

Woodworth, R. S., & H. S. Schlosberg. 1954. *Experimental psychology.* Holt, New York.

Wundt. W. 1896. Grundriss der Psychologie. (C. H. Judd, trans.). As quoted in C. Izard, 1971, *The face of emotion.* Meredith, New York.

23

AGGRESSION IN YOUNG ORGANISMS: WHY DOES IT OCCUR DESPITE AVERSIVE STIMULATION?

TORE BJERKE

The aim of this chapter is to review some of the better-known hypotheses about the early development of agonistic behavior in young organisms. These hypotheses will be assessed in light of recent data from naturalistic observations of young children and from the study of nonhuman primates. In particular, the early development of sex differences and peer interactions will be discussed. Emphasis will be on individuals and dyads.

BEHAVIORAL SEX DIFFERENCES IN YOUNG ORGANISMS

Research and models in child psychology

At 2 years of age, children are able to identify the two sexes, and 6 months later most children seem to be aware of cultural sex typing of clothing and household articles (Thompson 1975). In several Western cultures, 5-year-olds are aware that men are expected to be more aggressive than women, and that women are supposed to be gentle and affectionate (Best et al. 1977). It is not surprising, then, to find that among older children, boys are more aggressive than girls. However, sex differences in physical aggression are clearly present at the age of 3. Some studies showing these differences have also included 2-year-olds (for references and discussion, see Block 1976; Feshbach 1970; Maccoby & Jacklin 1974; Terman & Tyler 1954).

Our own studies (Bjerke 1976) include still younger children; we have, in fact, observed 39 infants (6 to 18 months) and 76 young children (18 to 36 months) in day-care centers in Norway. We have divided observed conflicts into three types. First, a child may take something from other children, but without aggressive acts (the victim does not protest, or protests only by crying). Second, if the aggressor or the victim is not immediately successful in securing the object, one of them may use aggressive acts to increase the likelihood of taking (or holding); that is, there may be aggressive conflicts over objects. Third, a child may kick, hit, push, or bite other children spontaneously; that is, without apparent signs of object conflicts, it may initiate aggressive acts.

We found that as early as 6 to 8 months, boys showed more aggressive behavior than girls, starting more purely aggressive actions (actions not involving conflict over object possession) and being more often responsible for the escalation of such conflicts over objects. Among children between 18 and 36 months, boys not only started most aggressive conflicts but also took more objects. (At 6 to 18 months no sex differences had appeared in the frequency of taking objects.)

Can we find data relevant to sex differences even earlier? Korner (1973) suggested that newborn girls tend to discharge energy more frequently via the facial musculature, in particular the mouth region, whereas newborn boys tend to do so via vigorous body activity. Moss (1967) found a tendency for 3-week-old girls to become quiet without maternal intervention more often than boys. He also speculated that girls may be better equipped to withstand adverse conditions because they show less irritability than boys. However, another investigation by Moss (1974) did not reveal any sex differences, and a reasonable interpretation is that even at this early age, stereotyped sex role attitudes may have influenced the parents to treat the two sexes differently. Adult behavior toward a child does appear to depend upon their assumption of its sex (e.g., Rubin et al. 1974; Will et al. 1976). Lewis and Weinraub (1974) suggested that male infants, in contrast to female infants, are discouraged from using proximal forms of behavior.

The fact that sex differences surface very early in life, that they are found in most human cultures for which evidence is available, and that they occur in most mammalian species (where they have been found related to sex hormones) indicates the existence of a biological foundation. This does not mean, of course, that aggression is completely unlearned or that sex differences are natural. Diverse mediating processes may be involved, and behavioral sex differences probably develop through a variety of processes, of which imitation, identification, and external sanctions are the most important. In addition, acquisition of knowledge of sex stereotypes relatively early enables the child to socialize itself in the specified directions.

The most popular hypotheses about the possibility that differential treatment of the two sexes may create the observed sex differences are the following (after Maccoby & Jacklin 1974):

1 Parents treat children so as to shape them toward the behavior deemed appropriate for their sex. For example, boys would be rewarded for being aggressive, girls for being compliant.
2 Because of genetically determined early behavioral differences, the two sexes stimulate their parents differently, thereby eliciting different treatment from them. In addition, the same parental behavior may produce different effects in boys than in girls because of genetically determined sex differences.
3 The behavior of the parents is based upon what they think a child of a given sex should be. For instance, parents may try to inhibit aggression in boys because they believe that boys are naturally more aggressive than girls, or they may accept higher levels of aggression in boys for the same reason.
4 The parent's behavior depends upon whether the child is of the same sex as himself.

The sex differences in aggressive behavior cannot easily be explained by hypotheses stressing that boys more often than girls are encouraged and rewarded for behaving aggressively. The masculine ideals are, of course, powerful at a later stage. But earlier in development, observations both in the home (Lambert et al. 1971; Minton et al. 1971) and in the nursery school (Cherry 1975; Etaugh et al. 1975; Fagot & Patterson 1969; Serbin et al. 1973) indicate that boys are more likely than girls to be reprimanded for aggressive and destructive acts. These studies also indicate that nursery school teachers tend to punish boys' aggression more often. Among parents, some studies using indirect observations indicate a cross-sex effect concerning reactions toward children. Mothers seem to be more acceptant of angry behavior toward themselves from boys than from girls, whereas fathers seem to react in the opposite manner (e.g., Lambert et al. 1971; Rothbart & Maccoby 1966).

Observations indicate that boys receive more physical punishment and other negative sanctions than girls (Minton et al. 1971; Serbin et al. 1973). Boys more often ignore the teacher's requests, and this ignoring often leads to escalating steps of commands and interventions. Girls, on the other hand, may obey the first commands more frequently than boys do, a hypothesis that receives some support from studies in nursery schools (e.g., Serbin et al. 1973). In addition, the aggressive reactions of boys may be, or adults may perceive them to be, more dangerous and intense compared with the aggressive reactions of girls. Consequently, adults may strengthen their interventions with boys from the beginning.

At this point, the possible effects of aversive stimulation should be considered, and the question of why boys show more aggressive behavior despite it must be raised. Although it was earlier believed that adults encouraged and rewarded aggression in boys, it now seems more accurate to say that young boys receive more aversive stimulation consequent upon aggressive acts than girls do. This state of affairs leads to a consideration of the role of negative reinforcement.

The process of negative reinforcement implies that an operant response that results in reduction of an aversive stimulation will become strengthened. Boys could early and more easily learn to counteract aversive stimulation by initiating escalating steps of violent acts. Nevertheless, boys will continue to receive more aversive stimulation than girls, because the reduction of aversive stimulation by means of violent acts occurs well after the escalating process has begun. (However, if boys receive more punishment, reprimand, and direction in response to aggressive acts than girls, they also receive more attention, and this may be conceived of as a positive reinforcement. We will consider this point again later.)

It remains to be explained why boys receive more aversive stimulation. It seems likely that the sex-trait stereotypes of adults support the expectation that boys will be more aggressive; thus adults may react with more aversive stimulation to their behavior. But in addition, genetic and hormonal factors may cause boys to behave a little more vigorously than girls, in turn eliciting more aversive stimulation from adults. Recent trends in the study of nonhuman primates and peer relations will be examined next in order to evaluate this hypothesis.

Studies of nonhuman primates

In most studies of nonhuman primate species, males have been found to be more aggressive than females (Holloway 1974). In addition, male rhesus infants engage in rough-and-tumble play more than do females (Goy 1966; Harlow & Harlow 1965) and they generally spend more time in independent exploration. By an early age, females begin to prefer less intense activities than do males. Similar tendencies have been found in langurs, vervets, bonnet macaques, and baboons, among others (Baldwin & Baldwin 1977). For example, Owens (1975) reported that in free-living baboons (*Papio anubis*), males are more likely than females to take part in active rough-and-tumble play (i.e., they show more wrestling, mock biting, and sparring). Males are also more active during approach–withdrawal play.

It is interesting to note that the behavioral sex differences observed (more aggression, and possibly more independence and peer orientation in young males) and the differential treatment by parents (more punishment and more discouragement of proximal behavior in young males) are congruent not only with the widespread sex stereotypes but also with what we know about the effects of sex hormones. For instance, in the rhesus monkey the average quantity of testosterone is higher in the male than in the female fetus from day 59 (earliest day sampled) to day 163 of gestation. Androgen levels drop sharply soon after birth and remain low until about 3 to 4 years of age (Resko 1975). Sexual dimorphism with respect to rough-and-tumble play and aggression consequently seem not to depend upon blood levels of testosterone. Instead it has been suggested that the prenatal influence of testosterone affects the organization of brain structures mediating the behavior in question. It has been shown that female rhesus fetuses treated with testosterone propionate from 39 to 70 or 39 to 105 days gestational age develop into pseudohermaphrodites, showing more rough-and-tumble play and threats than do untreated females. Although it should be kept in mind that it is difficult postnatally to separate endocrine from experiential factors, the evidence is convincing that sex hormones may influence prenatal neurological organization.

The hypothesis that, at the proximate level, sex hormones produce sex differences in behavior has been popular. The androgens (of which testosterone seems to be the most potent agent) are responsible for the secondary sex characteristics in the male. They are also critical for the prenatal differentiation of the male urogenital system. And, as mentioned earlier, one effect of fetal testosterone treatment on genetic female rhesus fetuses is behavioral masculinization (Goy 1966). However, Rose et al. (1972) showed that dominant male rhesus monkeys introduced into a well-established group of males soon suffered defeats. After 2 hours, the experimental animals were removed and tested. The plasma testosterone level had dropped markedly from the baseline level. Some effects were apparent 9 weeks after this experience. Social and environmental effects such as a loss in status may therefore regulate testosterone secretion. The interaction between social and endocrine events is not well understood, but the existing preliminary findings do not support a simplistic (environmental or genetic/hormonal) explanation of how behavioral sex differences develop. As mentioned earlier, circulating androgens do not seem to be important during the first years of life; thus the significance of this finding for the early development of agonistic behavior is unclear.

There is some evidence for the assertion that both hormones and differential parental treatment shape the behavior of the infants in the same direction. Adult females seem to punish and reject male infants more than female infants, which are more often restricted and protected (Mitchell & Brandt 1970; Vessey 1971; Ransom & Rowell 1972). It is not clear whether female or male infants behave differently toward their mothers and the mothers respond to these differences, or whether the mothers' differential treatment is a response to other cues they receive from the infants by touch, vision, or smell. But differential maternal treatment could result in increased independence, exploration, and play in male infants.

The parallel to the development of aggression in human children is evident, but more studies are needed. The sex differences reported above are not found in all studies (e.g., Young & Bramblett 1977). In addition, some interesting studies (Oswald & Erwin 1976; Sackett et al. 1975) have shown that within groups of adult female pigtail monkeys, physical aggression increases when the control male is removed, and this increase does not seem to be a temporary phenomenon. The potential for aggression in adult females may therefore be greater than is usually stated.

Closely associated with general differential treatment of the sexes is the relation between weaning practices and later aggressiveness in the infant. A good deal of aggressive interaction is found during later stages of the weaning process, the quantity and quality of which depend upon the sex of infant, species, temperament, and the mother's dominance status, among other things (e.g., Poirier 1972). Weaning tactics have been described for a number of species of primates (Clark 1977) and have been shown to have intense, brief effects. The common langur mother may bite her infant during weaning, and the infant may strike and scream at its mother (Poirier 1972). The chimpanzee infant suckles for approximately 5 years, though mild rejection is already observed in the infant's second year of life.Thus the process is long-lasting but does not involve much aggressive behavior (Clark 1977). Unfortunately, for want of detailed longitudinal data, the relation between these early frustrations and later aggressiveness remains unclear.

The reinforcing effects of novelty and arousal may be important in shaping exploratory responses and play (Baldwin & Baldwin 1977). Additional hypotheses are needed, however, to explain the behavioral sex differences. Sackett (1972) concluded that important biological differences exist in infancy that may reflect differential requirements by males and females for early life stimulation. One of these differences may be androgen exposure. Androgens may not only act directly on the brain mechanisms facilitating attack but may also affect attentional mechanisms (Archer 1976). This possibility should be related to the hypothesis that males of many species may have a higher stimulation threshold, which in turn could account for their vulnerability in isolation and their more vigorous activity tendencies. Some researchers have found that isolate animals can often repeat aggressive attacks even though this results in painful experiences (Melzack & Scott 1957; Sackett 1972). Deprivation in infancy can also result in repetitive responses to nonpreferred and nonsocial noxious stimuli (Lichstein & Sackett 1971). Sackett (1970) has presented the hypothesis that isolate monkeys have not developed the ability to inhibit existing high-probability responses, the result of which produce the observed tolerance anomaly. In contrast, socially reared monkeys learn to inhibit these responses.

An alternative but not incompatible interpretation is offered by Rosenblum

(1974). He observed that stimulation that elicits interest and approach in young males may provoke wariness in young females. From that finding, Rosenblum speculated that during the first year of life, males have a higher threshold for withdrawal-provoking stimulation than females. Thus again we could reason that at low levels of stimulation, males would suffer more deprivation effects than females. (Relatedly, in the human species, studies indicate a lower touch threshold for girls, and a greater tolerance for pain in adult men. Few studies have been conducted, however, and the results are controversial; see Maccoby & Jacklin 1974.)

Responses to aversive stimulation and mechanisms of negative reinforcement have not been studied in detail among nonhuman primates. But, as shown both in the study of social isolation and in the study of gender development, effects of punishment, rejection, and other types of aversive consequences are of central importance. Young males behave more vigorously than young females and seem to receive more aversive treatment. If it is confirmed that there are sex differences in sensory and activity thresholds (e.g., in mechanisms regulating approach and withdrawal), it seems even more likely that the proposed hypothesis of sex differences in learning by negative reinforcement is important. We may note, however, that the studies of species differences in aggression among primates in effects of deprivation (Sackett et al. 1976), effects of separation (Rosenblum 1971), and in play and general social development (Seay & Gottfried 1975) suggest a word of caution concerning generalization across species.

PEER INTERACTION

The research on peer influences on children's behavior is extensive (Hartup 1970). Here only a few hypotheses concerning peer reinforcement will be evaluated. We proceed from the assumption that the hypothesized importance of male responsiveness to aversive stimulation should also be evident in peer relations.

Although aggressive behavior can be manipulated in the laboratory, and aggressive behavior in natural settings may be influenced by the laboratory experience (e.g., Walters & Brown 1963), it would be a sounder strategy to identify the actual reinforcement provided by the peers in the normal life of children. This was attempted by Patterson et al. (1967) in Oregon, whose points of departure were the following hypotheses:

1 Positive reinforcers are provided for instrumental assertive–aggressive behaviors in the nursery school. Given that an aggressor shows a particular aggressive response toward a victim, and the victim emits a positive reinforcer, it is predicted that the aggressor in the next instance uses the same response toward the same victim rather than other responses toward other children.
2 Aversive consequences, such as counterattack by the victim or intervention by the teacher, will temporarily suppress the aggressive response. In the next episode, an aggressor having been exposed to an aversive consequence will select a new victim, a new response, or both a different response and a different victim.

The results showed that during five different observational periods in two nursery schools (children's mean age 40.7 months at the beginning of the study), aggressive behaviors were positively reinforced by peers 75 to 97% of the time. Positive reinforcement here meant that the victim was passive, cried, or showed defensive postures. When the victim told the teacher, recovered property, retaliated, or when the teacher intervened, it was tabulated as a negative outcome. The more specific hypotheses above were confirmed. These results have been said to show how peer reinforcement may maintain or increase aggressive behavior (Hartup 1970).

Our own observations, however, give the opposite results. Our study of children between 6 and 36 months in six Norwegian day-care centers reveals that the majority of the conflicts have a negative outcome for the aggressor. Using the definitions provided by Patterson (Patterson et al. 1967), we found that in 60% of the conflicts, the aggressor experienced a negative consequence, and in 24% of the conflicts he or she experienced a positive consequence. In the rest of the conflicts, the outcome could not be determined according to the definitions. The percentage of positive consequence was higher among infants (6 to 8 months, 32.6%) probably because the youngest infants did not always protest when toys were taken.

We speculated that these grouped data could conceal important subgroup differences. For example, highly aggressive children could more often be rewarded than less aggressive children. But our analysis showed that the 10 most aggressive children received positive consequences in 20% and negative consequences in 61.7% of the conflicts they started. In our Norwegian study, the higher frequency of negative outcome for the aggressor was due in part to the high rate of teacher intervention (about 50%). In the two Oregon nursery schools studied by Patterson, on the other hand, teacher intervention was relatively infrequent. The low rate of teacher intervention in his studies would seem, however, a marked departure from the more common pattern. Jersild and Markey (1935) found that teachers intervened in 32% of conflicts; Appell (1942) found intervention frequencies from 22 to 58%; and in a recent study in England, Smith and Green (1975) showed that in 15 nursery schools the average intervention frequency was 40% (variation 17 to 78%).

We find that even when teachers do not intervene, the aggressors do not obtain more positive than negative consequences, due to the effectiveness of the victim's counterattacks. In our study 85% of these counterattacks gave a positive consequence for the victim. If positive consequences should prove to have a maintaining or facilitating effect on later aggression in young children, the effect on children who are often victimized should be strongest.

In our sample of infants and young children, boys started significantly more conflicts than did girls. In addition, boys seemed to select boys as victims more often than girls, whereas girls selected girls as victims more often than boys. One could speculate that girls did not select boys as victims as often as they selected girls because they were punished for doing so. Our analysis shows in fact that girls in the majority of cases received negative consequences when provoking boys. But this interpretation did not hold for boys, because they received the majority of their negative consequences when they provoked other boys; still they continued to attack boys.

The hypothesis mentioned earlier is relevant here. Due to more acquired aggression–anxiety, a lower pain threshold, and so on, girls may be more capable than boys of inhibiting inappropriate, unsuccessful, or pain-producing acts. Concerning young boys, the hypothesis of negative reinforcement might be of some value. Here the negative reinforcement (Hilgard & Bower 1966) hypothesis implies that boys more frequently than girls learn to use aggressive behavior in order to avoid aversive stimulation, which has most frequently been associated with other boys. Our data show, for instance, that when boys initiate purely aggressive actions, the victim is another boy in 65% of the cases. Girls' initiations of purely aggressive actions affect boys and girls equally.

An explanation in terms of negative reinforcement also receives some support from Patterson's more recent work with deviant boys. First, it should be emphasized that Patterson (Patterson et al. 1967) "mistakenly assumed that any consequence which increased the probability of recurrence of a response was probably a positive reinforcer" (Patterson 1973:13). Later Patterson (1973) found that aversive events are facilitatory stimuli for aggression. When a child was presented with what was perceived as an aversive stimulus, he might present an aversive response in return. This interchange could continue until one member of the dyad withdrew his aversive stimulus, which meant a reinforcement for the acts of the other member. The following observations in our investigation point to the importance of this process. First, two-thirds of the escalation of aggressive conflicts over objects occurred because of the victim's responses; second, victims quickly learned to retaliate; and third, the frequency of both conflicts over objects and purely aggressive actions increased during the first 3 years of life. Lambert (1974) has reported that the child who engages in a great deal of aggression that has apparently not been instigated by others receives many injuries at other times.

DISCUSSION

Consequences of aggressive acts

The origins and early development of agonistic behavior have not been studied in detail; thus no definite conclusion can be drawn. There are severe weaknesses, however, in the supposition that positive reinforcement is the main mechanism through which early aggressive responses develop. The explanatory power of hypotheses based upon schedules of positive reinforcement is obviously weakened because almost any pattern of consequences has been shown to accompany the continued use of aggressive behavior. In one study, children were shown to receive 85% rewards for aggressive acts (Patterson et al. 1967). In another study, aggression was more difficult to extinguish if the children had received 50% rewards and 50% punishments (older children; Deur & Parke 1970). And in our study (Bjerke 1976), they have been shown to receive only about 25% rewards and 60% negative consequences. The hypothesis of positive reinforcement may be more useful in the study of older children.

In this chapter I have argued for the importance of aversive events as facilitatory stimuli for aggression. But we clearly need more studies of how consequences influence the strength of the preceding behavior. After all, the apparent effects of the aversive reinforcement pattern may simply be concealing the more significant effects of general attention as a maintaining factor. Brown and Elliott (1965) found a reduction in the number of aggressive acts when teachers tried to ignore them. But the hypothesis proposed by Patterson et al. (1967) implies that, however the teachers behaved, the children should nonetheless have reinforced each other, and the level of aggression should thus have been maintained. Possibly the low frequency of teacher intervention in Patterson et al.'s study accounts for the apparent power of positive reinforcement in their study. The results obtained by Brown & Elliott (1965) may in fact point to the importance of attention as an aggression-maintaining factor. But we encounter severe methodological difficulties when we try to evaluate the behavior-maintaining effects of general attention.

Theoretical implications

Like most complex human behavior, aggression must be under the control of many different motivational variables. The one-sided defense of theories should be replaced by attempts to reveal the various influencing factors, recognizing that their mutual importance may change during the transformations of aggressive behavior. For example, it has been stated that self-injurious behavior is maintained by negative reinforcement. A second hypothesis states that it is maintained by positive social reinforcement. A third states that it provides sensory stimulation. A fourth emphasizes aberrant physiological processes. And a fifth implies that the function of self-injury is guilt reduction (for references and discussion, see Carr 1977). Although my interpretation of the data in this area favors the negative reinforcement hypothesis, some reports indicate that other factors may account for some aspects of the induction and maintenance of the behavior. For example head banging in a child may provide sensory stimulation, but then parents may contribute to its maintenance by attending to it or by removing aversive stimulation.

Similarly, even though children may have to learn how to maintain instrumental aggression, instinctive mechanisms may contribute to the induction of aggressive behavior. Here the various forms of constraints on learning that are demonstrated in ethological research must be considered. In all young organisms, phylogenetic adaptation defines the framework within which learning can operate. Even Bandura, a relatively strict social learning theorist, admits that genetic influences are important when he writes, "Biological structure obviously sets limits on the types of aggressive responses that can be successfully perfected, and genetic endowment influences the rate at which learning progresses" (Bandura 1973:44). Skinner (1974) also asserted that in situations where aggressive behavior has survival value, the reactions may be instinctive.

Comparative research in aggression: value and limitations

To date we have gained substantially from comparing man to animals. In this chapter, for example, the relations between aversive stimulation and aggression have been illuminated in animal as well as human research. At the same time, animal research has taught us the factors that qualify the factors producing aggression. It has been shown, for example, that infliction of pain produces aggressive reactions in many species (O'Kelley & Steckle 1939; Ulrich & Azrin 1962). This is not a completely automatic or reflexive reaction, however, because situational factors, early experience, and the intensity of pain, among other things, influence the outcome. The transition from food reinforcement to extinction has also been shown to result in aggression in some species (Azrin et al. 1966). The occurrence of this phenomenon also depends upon situational and ecological conditions, that is, animals do not always fight when resources become limited.

However, even in animal research much necessary knowledge is lacking. We do not yet have longitudinal data that can enable us to understand the developmental processes underlying aggressive reactions. From primate research we know, of course, that extreme variations in rearing conditions and ecology affect behavioral development, but we know little about the immediate and short-term regulators of behavior. It is surprising, for example, that imitation and experimental manipulation of consequences of aggressive acts have not yet been examined. Further, the interaction between hormones and environmental events has yet to be fully illuminated. Finally, with reference to my own topic of interest, primates should be suitable subjects for studies of reactions to aversive stimulation, and sex differences in sensitivity and tolerance should be examined carefully.

However, we should perhaps not be too optimistic about the value of comparative models in the study of aggression among older subjects. Basically, this statement rests upon our knowledge of human cognitive abilities. The internalization of rules and norms plays an important role in human socialization, and in consequence aspects of early cognitive development must clearly influence conflict behavior. It can be observed, for example, that 2-year-old children repeatedly run into conflicts when adults tell them to alternate in performing a popular exercise. It is often difficult to tell whether the children do not want to wait for their turn, are not able to wait, or simply do not understand the implications of the rule. Insight into the cognitive processes involved would have both theoretical and practical importance. It would also benefit studies of moral development in general. Further, because the context within which most early aggressive responses occur is characterized by conflicts about objects, children's perception and cognitive processing of objects and rules should also be related to their conflict behavior. As Wanda Bronson has stated (1974), in the early years the loss of objects increasingly becomes experienced as a personal affront. Here is an important area of research, where not only object permanence but also early feelings of ownership must be connected to both offensive and defensive reactions.

In addition, by at least 3 to 5 years of age, children become aware of adult sex-trait stereotypes, which they learn through contact with adults and through mass media. This kind of knowledge, expressed in verbal and moral norms, is available to only a limited degree to other primate species. Finally, man's verbal and cognitive structuring allows him to maintain his aggressiveness and hostility beyond the existing social situation.

The above warnings pertain to the dangers inherent in drawing conclusions too easily about the similarity between aggression in animals and older children. Comparative research could nonetheless provide models and information about the facilitatory stimuli for aggression and about the process of negative reinforcement if the study of dyadic interchanges were stressed. As argued above, previous investigations of sex differences and of peer relations indicate that this might be a promising direction.

SUMMARY

Previous research has demonstrated that boys show more physical aggression than girls. In this chapter, data are presented indicating that this sex difference is present in 1-year-old children. It is unlikely that this sex difference develops because boys receive more rewards when behaving aggressively. In fact, recent research indicates that boys receive more negative sanctions than girls. Data are presented showing that in groups of children, aversive consequences are provided for aggressive acts.

It is hypothesized that sex-trait stereotypes cause adults to expose boys to more aversive stimuli, because they expect that this treatment will reduce the natural aggressiveness of boys. However, this aversive stimulation is often withdrawn or reduced when boys behave in an aggressive manner. This withdrawal strengthens the aggressive acts (negative reinforcement). In addition, genetic and hormonal factors may be responsible for more vigorous behavior and higher tolerance thresholds in boys. These characteristics would facilitate learning by negative reinforcement in boys.

Punishment, rejection, and other kinds of aversive stimulation are also of central importance in studies of nonhuman primates. It is suggested that researchers in this area should intensify the study of the short-term regulators of dyadic behavior in order to illuminate processes such as negative reinforcement and possible sex differences in sensitivity and tolerance thresholds.

REFERENCES

Appell, M. H. 1943. Aggressive behavior in nursery school children and adult procedures in dealing with such behavior. *Journal of Experimental Education* 11:185–199.

Archer, J. 1976. The organization of aggression and fear in vertebrates. *In:* P. P. G. Bateson & P. H. Klopfer (eds.), *Perspectives in ethology,* vol. 2. Plenum, New York and London.

Azrin, N. H., R. R. Hutchinson, & D. F. Hake. 1966. Extinction-induced aggression. *Journal of the Experimental Analysis of Behavior* 9:191–204.

Baldwin, J. D., & J. I. Baldwin. 1977. Play and exploration. *In:* S. Chevalier-Skolnikoff & F. E. Poirier (eds.), *Primate bio-social development.* Garland Press, New York.

Bandura, A. 1973. *Aggression.* Prentice-Hall, Englewood Cliffs, New Jersey.

Best, D. L., J. E. Williams, J. M. Cloud, S. W. Davis, L. S. Robertson, J. R. Edwards, H. Giles, & J. Fowles. 1977. Development of sex-trait stereotypes among young children in the United States, England, and Ireland. *Child Development* 48:1375–1384.

Bjerke, T. 1976. Sma barn i fri lek. Institute of Psychology, University of Trondheim.

Block, J. H. 1976. Issues, problems, and pitfalls in assessing sex differences: a critical review of The Psychology of Sex Differences. *Merrill-Palmer Quarterly* 22:283–308.

Bronson, W. C. 1974. Mother–toddler interaction: a perspective on studying the development of competence. *Merrill-Palmer Quarterly* 20:275–301.

Brown, P., & R. Elliott. 1965. Control of aggression in a nursery school class. *Journal of Experimental Child Psychology* 2:103–107.

Carr, E. G. 1977. The motivation of self-injurious behavior: a review of some hypotheses. *Psychological Bulletin* 84:800–820.

Cherry, L. 1975. The preschool teacher–child dyad: sex differences in verbal interactions. *Child Development* 46:532–535.

Clark, C. B. 1977. A preliminary report on weaning among chimpanzees of the Gombe National Park, Tanzania. *In:* S. Chevalier-Skolnikoff & F. E. Poirier (eds.), *Primate bio-social development: biological, social and ecological determinants,* Garland Press, New York, pp. 235–260.

Deur, J. L., & R. D. Parke. 1970. Effects on inconsistent punishment on aggression in children. *Developmental Psychology* 2:403–411.

Etaugh, C., G. Collins, & A. Gerson. 1975. Reinforcement of sex-typed behaviors of two-year old children in a nursery school setting. *Developmental Psychology* 11:255.

Fagot, B. I., & G. R. Patterson. 1969. An in vivo analysis of reinforcing contingencies for sex-role behavior in the preschool child. *Developmental Psychology* 1:563–568.

Fawl, C. L. 1963. Disturbances experienced by children in their natural habitats. *In:* R. G. Barker (ed.), The *stream of behavior.* Appleton, New York, pp. 99–126.

Feshbach, S. 1970. Aggression. *In:* P. H. Mussen (ed.), *Carmichael's manual of child psychology,* vol. 2. Wiley, New York.

Goy, R. W. 1966. Role of androgens in the establishment and regulation of behavioral sex differences in mammals. *Journal of Animal Science* (suppl.) 25:21–35.

Harlow, H. F., & M. K. Harlow. 1965. The affectional systems. *In:* A. M. Schrier, H. F. Harlow, & F. Stollnitz (eds.), *Behavior of nonhuman primates,* vol. 2. Academic Press, New York, pp. 287–334.

Hartup, W. W. 1970. Peer interaction and social organization. *In:* P. H. Mussen (ed.), *Carmichael's manual of child psychology,* vol. 2. Wiley, New York, pp. 457–558.

Hilgard, E. R., & G. H. Bower. 1966. *Theories of learning.* Appleton, New York.

Holloway, R. L. (ed.). 1974. *Primate aggression, territoriality, and xenophobia.* Academic Press, New York.

Jersild, A. T., & F. V. Markey. 1935. Conflicts between preschool children. *Child Development Monographs,* whole no. 21.

Korner, A. F. 1973. Sex differences in newborns with special reference to differences in the organization of oral behavior. *Journal of Child Psychology and Psychiatry* 14:19–29.

Lambert, W. E. 1974. Promise and problems of cross-cultural exploration of children's aggressive strategies. *In:* J. DeWit & W. W. Hartup (eds.), *Determinants and origins of aggressive behavior.*

Lambert, W. E., A. Yackley, & R. N. Hein. 1971. Child training values of English Canadian and French Canadian parents. *Canadian Journal of Behavioral Science* 3:217–236.

Lewis, M., & M. Weinraub. 1974. Sex of parent × sex of child: socio-emotional development. *In:* R. C. Friedman, R. M. Richard, & R. L. Vande Wiele (eds.), *Sex differences in behavior,* Wiley, New York.

Lichstein, L., & G. P. Sackett. 1971. Reactions by differentially raised rhesus monkeys to noxious stimulation. *Developmental Psychobiology* 4:339–352.

Maccoby, E. E., & C. N. Jacklin. 1974. *The psychology of sex differences.* Stanford University Press, Stanford, California.

Melzack, R., & T. H. Scott. 1957. The effects of early experience on the response to pain. *Journal of Comparative and Physiological Psychology* 50:155–161.

Minton, C., J. Kagan, & J. A. Levine. 1971. Maternal control and obedience in the two-year old. *Child Development* 42:1873–1894.

Mitchell, G., & E. M. Brandt. 1970. Behavioral differences related to experiences of the mother and sex of infant in the rhesus monkey. *Developmental Psychology* 3:149.

Moss, H. A. 1967. Sex, age and state as determinants of mother–infant interaction. *Merrill-Palmer Quarterly* 13:19–36.

1974. Early sex differences and mother–infant interaction. *In:* R. C. Friedman, R. M. Richard, & R. L. Vande Wiele (eds.), *Sex differences in behavior.* Wiley, New York, pp. 149–163.

O'Kelley, L. W., & L. C. Steckle. 1939. A note on long enduring emotional responses in the rat. *Journal of Psychology* 8:125–131.

Oswald, E., & J. Erwin. 1976. Control of intragroup aggression by male pigtail monkeys (*Macaca nemestrina*). *Nature* 262:686–688.

Owens, N. W. 1975. Social play behavior in free-living baboons (*Papio anubis*). *Animal Behaviour* 23:387–408.

Patterson, G. R. 1973. Changes in status of family members as controlling stimuli: a basis for describing treatment process. *In:* L. Hamerlynck, L. Handy, & E. J. Mash (eds.), *Behavior change.* Research Press, Champaign, Illinois, pp. 169–191.

Patterson, G. R., R. A. Littman, & W. Bricker. 1967. Assertive behavior in children: a step toward a theory of aggression. *Monographs in Social Research and Child Development* 32:1–43.

Poirier, F. 1972. *Primate socialization.* Random House, New York.

Ransom, R. W., & T. E. Rowell. 1972. Early social developmental of feral baboons. *In:* F. Poirier (ed.), *Primate socialization.* Random House, New York, pp. 195–244.

Resko, J. 1975. Fetal hormones and their effect on the differentiation of the central nervous system in primates. *Federation Proceedings* 34:1650–1655.

Rose, R. M., T. P. Gordon, & I. S. Bernstein. 1972. Plasma testosterone levels in the male rhesus: influences of sexual and social stimuli. *Nature* 238:366.

Rosenblum, L. A. 1971. Infant attachment in monkeys. *In:* H. R. Schaffer (ed.), *The origins of human social relations.* Academic Press, New York.

1974. Sex differences in mother–infant attachment in monkeys. *In:* R. C. Friedman, R. M. Richard, & R. L. Vande Wiele (eds.), *Sex differences in behavior.* Wiley, New York.

Rothbart, M. K., & E. E. Maccoby. 1966. Parent's differential reactions to sons and daughters. *Journal of Personality and Social Psychology* 4:237–243.

Rubin, J. Z., F. J. Provenzano, & Z. Luria. 1974. The eye of the beholder: parent's views on sex of newborns. *American Journal of Orthopsychiatry* 44:512–519.

Sackett, G. P. 1970. Innate mechanisms, rearing conditions, and a theory of early experience effects in primates. *In:* M. R. Jones (ed.), *Miami symposium on prediction of behavior: early experience.* University of Miami Press, Coral Gables, Florida.

1972. Isolation rearing in monkeys: diffuse and specific effects on later behavior. *In:* R. Chauvin (ed.), *Ethology and human behavior.* Colloques Internationales du CNRS, Paris, pp. 61–110.

Sackett, G. P., R. A. Holm, G. C. Ruppenthal, & E. E. Fahrenbruch. 1976. The effects of total social isolation rearing on behavior of rhesus and pigtail macaques. *In: Advances in Behavioral Biology* 17:115–131.

Sackett, G. P., M. Oswald, & J. Erwin. 1975. Aggression among captive female pigtail monkeys in all-female and harem groups. *Journal of Biological Psychology* 17:17–20.

Seay, B., & N. W. Gottfried. 1975. A phylogenetic perspective for social behavior in primates. *Journal of General Psychology* 92:5–17.

Serbin, L. A., K. D. O'Leary, R. N. Kent, & I. J. Tonick. 1973. A comparison of teacher response to the preacademic and problem behavior of boys and girls. *Child Development* 44:796–804.

Skinner, B. F. 1974. *About behaviorism.* Knopf, New York.

Smith, P. K., & M. Green. 1975. Aggressive behavior in English nurseries and play groups: sex differences and response of adults. *Child Development* 46:211–214.

Terman, L. M., & L. E. Tyler. 1954. Psychological sex differences. *In:* L. Carmichael (ed.), *Manual of child psychology.* Wiley, New York, pp. 1064–1114.

Thompson, S. K. 1975. Gender labels and early sex role development. *Child Development* 46:339–347.

Ulrich, R., & N. H. Azrin. 1962. Reflexive fighting in response to aversive stimulation. *Journal of the Experimental Analysis of Behavior* 5:511–520.

Vessey, S. H. 1971. Free-ranging rhesus monkeys: behavioral effects of removal, separation and reintroduction of group members. *Behaviour* 40:216–227.

Walters, R. H., & M. Brown. 1963. Studies of reinforcement of aggression. 3: Transfer of responses to an interpersonal situation. *Child Development* 34:563–571.

Will, J. A., P. A. Self, & N. Datan. 1976. Maternal behavior and perceived sex of infant. *American Journal of Orthopsychiatry* 46:135–139.

Young, G. H. & C. A. Bramblett. 1977. Gender and environment as determinants of behavior in infant common baboons (*Papio cynocephalus*). *Archives of Sexual Behavior* 6:365–385.

24

SOCIAL INTERACTION WITH OBJECTS: A PERSPECTIVE ON HUMAN INFANCY

GLYN M. COLLIS

The prototypical paradigm of reciprocal communication includes two individuals, each emitting signals while responding to signals from the other. In animal communication systems, it seems that most classes of information exchange have to do primarily with behavioral readinesses and organismic states of the individuals themselves, and with the social relationship between them. Smith (1977) lists a number of classes of messages of this type. Among these are individual and sexual identity, reproductive status, and group membership; the animals' attentiveness, readiness to associate or interact socially; and the likelihood of attack, escape, copulation, locomotion, indecisive behavior, and so on. Not uncommonly, though, signals have some kind of orientational component. There is, thus, the possibility that interaction need not be tied solely to phenomena within and between the two individuals in the prototypical dyad. One can conceive of the dyadic interaction as being related to objects, loci, and events that are not part of the dyad itself. This is a theme that can be traced right through to the use of linguistic reference and deixis in *Homo sapiens* and, following von Glasersfeld (1977), beyond the reasonable limits of Hockett's displacement design feature (Hockett & Altmann 1968) to the completely abstract symbolicity that is possible with human languages.

The main object of this chapter is to examine early manifestations of interaction relating to objects and loci in human infancy and their implications for development. First, though, it is instructive to consider, briefly and selectively, something of what is known about the social behavior of animals in this respect. This is helpful in providing a broad perspective. It becomes apparent that rather simple effects, which one might feel uncomfortable labeling *communication,* nevertheless can have important implications for the nature and structure of human interpersonal interaction, especially in its early forms.

A COMPARATIVE PERSPECTIVE

How, by social means, could one individual induce another to attend to a particular object or locus? The concept of *local enhancement,* which Thorpe (1956) defined generally as direction of the animal's attention to a particular object or place in the environment, is relevant here. However, Thorpe's examples refer to the attraction of attention to a locus by virtue of the source animal's presence there and to the recipient following the source animal. It seems useful to distinguish such instances of the attraction of attention from mechanisms for the direction of attention toward a locus away from the source animal. This is similar to the this/that, here/there, and similar distinctions of linguistic deixis (Clark 1978).

Attraction to an object or locus is probably widespread in the context of food finding. Vocal and other displays in the presence of food may facilitate the process even if food sharing cannot reasonably be considered as either the prime meaning or the main function of the display (Marler 1967). In such a context, displays are attractive with reference to individuals who are relatively distant from the one who has located the source. However, when the other individuals are in relatively close proximity, if any attention guidance remains to be done, it should probably be interpreted as directing: Avian displays that incorporate pointing at food with the bill are obvious examples (Williams et al. 1968). In nest site demonstration displays there may be a pointing component at the end of the display sequence, most of which functions by attraction via leading (Smith 1977). Following responses to leading displays can be considered as the result of attraction to a mobile source, although such interactions are often complex, with a two-way exchange of information between leader and follower. Clear illustrations are to be seen in the "tandem running" and similar displays of ants (Möglich et al. 1974) and in leadership toward objects by chimpanzees (Menzel & Halperin 1975).

The direction mechanism, when attention is directed away from the source animal toward a distal locus, includes the most sophisticated developments of our theme. At its simplest, though, an individual in receipt of a signal from the source animal could merely be induced to search. As an example, alarm displays commonly elicit a general scanning of the environment by recipients, thereby increasing the probability that an object of instrinsic interest, for instance a predator, will be detected (Hall 1960). Potentially at least, additional information regarding the source of alarm could facilitate the recognition process, but convincing examples are hard to find. There are a few cases, however, in which different types of alarm calls are known to elicit different types of scanning procedures. One of the nicest examples comes from the arctic ground squirrel, in which a chatter call, given in response to ground predators, alerts other individuals, who cease what they are doing and assume an upright posture. In contrast, a whistling call, which is typically given in response to aerial predators, induces other individuals to freeze, with one eye cocked to the sky (Melchior 1971).

The simplest procedure for detecting directional information per se might be to extrapolate the direction of an individual's locomotion relative to an object. In practice, it could be very difficult to rule out the induction of searching and/or following. In the case of fleeing from a source of danger, in principle the direction of flight could indicate the likely whereabouts of the predator or other source. In practice, flight paths are often erratic, perhaps to prevent the predator from using directional information to its advantage (Curio 1976). The extrapolation of movement toward objects, food items for instance, may also be effective: Van Lawick-Goodall's (1971) description of coordinated movements of chimpanzees toward baboon prey suggests one example, although clearly, other cues were available (see Teleki 1973).

Undoubtedly, the static orientation of an animal or part of its anatomy provides a potent source of directional information. A special case of this type of phenomenon occurs when the prototypical dyad is part of a larger group. Then, when one member of the dyad displays to another animal, orientational features of the display may indicate to whom it is directed (Simmons & Weidmann 1972). In fact, there are many cases in which animals maneuver and orient themselves prior to display: This is seen particularly clearly in the social courtship of ducks (Weidmann & Darley 1971). Probably the majority of visual displays have an orientational component although in most cases it is unclear whether this information is used by bystanders. Altmann (1967), however, seems fairly confident about the efficacy of orientational address cues among primates. The likelihood that individuals monitor attentional relationships between other individuals, rather than just dyadic relationships of which they are a part, has important consequences for any theory of relationships that is based on attention structure (Chance 1967). A social structure in which each individual appreciates relationships between pairs of other individuals will, in all likelihood, be qualitatively different from a social structure in which individuals appreciate only those relationships into which they enter directly.

Two pinnacles of achievement with communication related to spatially remote objects are well known. First, there are the social bees, in particular, the much-studied honeybee (von Frisch 1967; Gould 1975). The dance performance of honeybees provides a useful focus for a conceptual issue that has implications for most of the patterns of interaction being discussed here. Smith (1977) argues forcefully that the message of the dance concerns the fact that the performing bee is likely to fly or has just flown a certain distance in a particular direction. Similarly, the dance's meaning has to do with the likelihood that a recipient bee will fly there too. Insofar as the dance could be said to have a referent, this would be the behavior of the performing bee. Smith thus avoids conceiving of the dance as denoting distance or direction (cf. Altmann 1967). Only in the unlikely case that a display bears a consistent relation to an external event, but no such relation to the behavior of the displaying animal, would Smith be prepared to accept that event as a referent of the display.

It might seem that Smith was reinforcing an unnecessary conceptual discontinuity between communication by animals and by men (or between verbal and nonverbal communication) by refusing to treat this kind of phenomenon in the same terms as linguistic reference. Yet changing views on the nature of linguistic reference reduce the gap. Bruner (1977, 1978), following Harrison (1972), argues convincingly that reference is not so much concerned with the narrowly semantic issue of the linkages of signs with objects, loci, or relations but rather with the pragmatic role of indicating which of the limited number of possible objects, loci, or relations are relevant for the current task that the interacting individuals have in common. Here is a conceptual framework well suited to the study of both human and animal communication.

At the second pinnacle are the primates, with the great apes and man particularly prominent. Menzel's work on chimpanzees shows how subtle communication about objects can be, even in the absence of a man-made language (Menzel 1971; Menzel & Halperin 1975). And the gulf between the performances of apes and the human use of language, whether quantitative or qualitative, is clearly immense. Yet it is important to recognize the possibility that simple processes play an important role in human social interaction. Many species get along rather well socially by making use of simple systems of signs and signals. The possession of a sophisticated cognitive apparatus, which is correlated with a greater concern for objects other than food, predators, or other animals, does not mean that simple cues go unused. It is likely that close analogues of all the mechanisms of object-related interaction outlined above are to be found in the natural history of *Homo sapiens.*

All this is particularly relevant to human infancy for two reasons. First, more sophisticated communicative mechanisms are absent or poorly developed at this time, but the infant still has to get along in an intrinsically social world. Second, in accordance with current ideas about the social context from which cognitive skills of communicative importance somehow emerge (Schaffer 1979), it is likely that linguistic reference and deixis are developmentally rooted in simple manifestations of object-related interaction in early life (Bruner 1977, 1978; Clark 1978).

HUMAN INFANCY

In the first couple of years of life, the human infant will develop an impressive array of skills for handling the world about him. Quite a lot is known about the development of infants' relations with inanimate things in terms of, for example, attention (Kagan & Lewis 1965) and sensorimotor abilities (Bower 1974; Piaget 1952, 1954). Paralleling this, in the social domain, interest has been directed toward infants' reactions to presumed social stimuli with a traditional emphasis on faces (see Vine 1970) and a more recent focus on voices and speech (Condon 1977; Eimas 1975; Morse 1974). Similarly, a lot is known about the output of social signals such as smiling and crying (see Schaffer 1971), gaze (Robson 1967) and, more recently in particular, other means of emotional expression (Oster & Ekman in press; Sroufe & Waters 1976).

Until recently, however, relatively little attention has been paid to the relationship between the actions of infants directed toward the inanimate world of objects and the social world of persons except, perhaps, in terms of a widespread assumption that the child's actions in the two domains are the same. Thus the attainment of object permanence is thought to be related to the attainment of person permanence necessary for attachment (Schaffer 1963), and any difference in the time of appearance of the two phenomena was assumed to result from experiential differences (Bell 1970; Jackson et al. 1978; Piaget 1954). In a similar vein, Sugarman-Bell (1978) has pointed out the analogy between the instrumental coordination of objects and the combining of person-directed and object-directed motions into a single communicative act. However, the evidence suggests (Millar 1976) that infants may fail instrumentally to learn the connection between an action and a contingent event when one of these is intrinsically social and the other nonsocial, even though they can cope with social–social and nonsocial–nonsocial paradigms.

There remains, though, the issue of whether differences such as these are qualitative or ones of degree. To highlight the issue, it is worth examining in some detail one view of early development that is unusual in favoring the existence of distinctive modes of psychological functioning in the social and nonsocial domains.

A view of early development

In a series of papers, Trevarthen (1977a, 1977b, 1978, 1979, in press; Trevarthen & Hubley 1978) has outlined a theoretical account of development in the first year or so of life, paying particular attention to the relationships between infants' activities in the social and nonsocial domains. The discrimination of persons and objects, a capacity believed by Trevarthen (1978) to be present in some degree from birth, has a key rôle in this account.

The nonlearned or rapidly learned recognition of stimuli such as voices or faces is thought to play only a relatively minor role in the discrimination of people and objects, as does the recognition of external events as social when they are contingent on self-produced movement (Watson 1972). More important is the nature of movement produced by animate as opposed to inanimate beings. Inanimate movement "runs down" and, although it may oscillate in simple ways, it lacks the often rhythmic, surging velocity changes of animate movement (Trevarthen 1978). But Trevarthen goes beyond a simple stimulus evaluation model. Sensitivity to the movements of other persons is thought to be linked with processes for the generation of motor output in a manner reminiscent of motor or analysis-by-synthesis theories of speech perception (Liberman et al. 1967; Stevens & House 1972). Movements produced by persons are believed to be detected as such by virtue of their matching, in some sense, an image of a movement that the infant could produce (Trevarthen 1978). Many social acts seem already to be in the infant's repertoire, albeit in a rudimentary form: Detailed descriptive analyses (Trevarthen 1977a) show a similarity in the form and timing of movements produced by infants and expressive movements exhibited by adults. Among these are recognizable facial expressions (Oster & Eckman in press); movements of the mouth that, on the grounds of their similarity to articulatory movements (bearing in mind the absence of teeth in babies), Trevarthen calls *prespeech;* and movements of the hands like rudimentary gesticulation (Trevarthen 1977a). Though prefunctional, such movements are thought to be direct embryonic precursors of later fully functional articulatory and gestural movements.

Recent findings on the imitation by very young infants of actions involving body parts that they cannot see (Meltzoff & Moore 1977), a process that must involve a mapping of percepts on internal representations of bodily movement, gives further support to an account of the detection of animate movement based on some kind of matching with processes involved with generating motor output (Trevarthen 1978b). It is significant that the acts imitated in early infancy are those that are already in the infant's repertoire.

Turning to the course of development, Trevarthen (1977b) characterizes four phases during the first year in terms of the infant's relationship with objects and persons. First, there is the neonatal period. Although behaviorally adapted in various ways for maternal care, the infant's sociability, as well as its interest in things inanimate, is latent. Patterned movements similar in form to those that will later play a role in interaction with objects and persons can be observed in neonates during periods of quiet alertness, especially just after birth, and during light sleep. Movements of the eyes may be precisely coordinated in conjugate saccades with amplitude and timing similar to those of adults. Most other coordinations are more rudimentary and prefunctional. Nonetheless, it is possible to recognize fragments of the motor patterns of prehension (prereaching), such as wrist orientation and adjustment of finger position to the size of an object (Bower 1974). Grasp and pull-in movements can be elicited soon after birth even though visual guidance of these movements will not appear until later (Trevarthen 1978).

In the social domain, facial expressions are readily recognizable in the neonate (Oster & Eckman in press), as are rudiments of gestures. Just as prereaching is poorly integrated with the perception of objects, so these earliest social acts are poorly integrated with the perception of persons. Even so, the first signs of social perception soon appear, as manifest in the imitation of mouth and hand movements that can be seen toward the end of the first month (Meltzoff & Moore 1977).

Toward the end of the second month, the infant enters the second phase, a period of rich embryonic communication referred to as *primary intersubjectivity* (Trevarthen 1979). Gaze behavior becomes better organized, with a much improved capacity for focused visual attention, scanning, and tracking. The development of well-aimed looking at the face of other persons is especially important socially, in terms of its impact on the mother (Wolff 1963). Prespeech movements may be orientated toward an interacting partner, and posturings of the head, trunk, and limbs seem to be systematically related to particular facial expressions, as are gesticulationlike hand movements. Thus a degree of organization is apparent among the different elements of communicative acts. Two-month-olds respond to avoidance or unresponsiveness by adults with facial expressions and bodily movements suggesting anxiety or distress. Thus although it is asymmetrical, communication in an adult–infant dyad is reciprocal, with both partners producing signals and responding to those of the other. The signals are of a nature indicating their source in a person rather than an object – indicating *subjectivity* in Trevarthen's terminology. *Intersubjectivity* refers to the coupling of two subjectivities in reciprocal and shared control of the ongoing interaction.

Significantly, the intrinsically social developments of primary intersubjectivity occur at a time when early indications of interaction with nonsocial objects, via rudimentary reaching, seem to disappear (Bower 1974). Trevarthen (1978a, in press) ascribes this apparent disappearance to maturational changes in mechanisms for controlling the proximal limb segments (upper arm and shoulders). The increased muscular power in this area, which is at first subject to rather poor control, often disrupts the total reaching movement, which is thus not recognized for what it is unless the total act is exceptionally slow and gentle.

With the development of cerebral control of the proximal motor system, the reappearance of reaching in a fully functional form is thought to be connected with the breakup of primary intersubjectivity and the onset of the third of Trevarthen's phases, the *epoch of games,* covering the period from about 4 to 8 months (Trevarthen 1977b). Other authors too have noted the impact on the infant's social relations of its newly found interest in and competence at interacting with objects (Collis 1977; Stern 1977). There is a marked cooling in the infant's interest in persons, reflected in a decline in its willingness to engage in en face, reputedly more so with the primary attachment figure than with other familiar adults (Trevarthen 1977a). During this period, interested adults often have to make use of the child's interest in objects as a vehicle for satisfactory interaction. This interest can be manipulated, with care, by manipulating objects in characteristic gamelike sequences that are widespread among mother–infant couples.

The infant also seems eager to exercise its prehensile skills in reaching for and touching the mother's hands and face, leading to "games of the person" (Trevarthen & Hubley 1978). The infant's burgeoning attentional skills are also exploited in games in which the mother moves parts of her body for visual effect, especially in looming toward the baby and away again. But the infant's delighted responses to these games still give the impression that the social element is secondary to an interest in bodily parts for their own sake. As the infant becomes able to differentiate between various bodily parts, games become ritualized around particular maternal signals. The infant's own bodily parts are drawn in too, with its imitation of the mother's hand and face movements in a seemingly more discretionary and less automatic manner than the early imitation of manual and facial actions.

Later during this phase, object games and games of the person are combined in various ways. Trevarthen and Hubley (1978) describe how, at about 7 months, an infant was engrossed in shaking a toy in the pattern of a classic secondary circular reaction when the mother moved her head and vocalized in synchrony with the baby's actions with the toy, whereupon the infant's interest switched from the noise of the toy to the actions of the mother. Then the mother repeatedly zoomed the toy in to tickle the baby's stomach. Thus the mother's responses to the baby's actions with the toy began to substitute for the reactions of the toy, and the toy became an appendage of the mother in a looming game.

From these kinds of games emerge patterns of interaction with a sharing of interest in objects in friendly and, above all, active and mutual cooperative play between mother and infant. Patterns of true cooperation characterize the fourth of Trevarthen's phases, *secondary intersubjectivity,* beginning about the ninth month. The infant's newfound readiness for cooperative play is well exemplified by the willing giving of objects and the burgeoning of give-and-take games that contrast markedly to its earlier dropping of received objects and refusal to give. Thus objects can now be used for essentially social purposes. And similarly, persons can be used for ends primarily involved with the physical world: Well-integrated acts such as the pointing gesture, having all the appearance of communication meaning, are now used for requests and comments about things (cf. Bates et al. 1975). Above all, such communicative acts are often visibly addressed, in some way, to the recipient.

Trevarthen recognized that his description of the changes in the organization of behavior in the first year of life is not very different from more orthodox accounts (Trevarthen & Hubley 1978). Perhaps the major point of divergence is his insistence that neonatal behavior consists not of reflexes (even in the liberal Piagetian use of the term) but of incomplete rudiments of endogenously organized motor patterns. This is the basis for his frequent emphasis on early intentionality. But because he uses the infant's interaction with objects and persons as a basis, Trevarthen's descriptive scheme provides a useful background against which to consider social attraction and the direction of attention to objects in infancy.

In contrast to its descriptive basis, Trevarthen's interpretation of behavior and development in the first year is provocatively unorthodox. In particular, there is the contention that, from birth, infants have different modes of operation for interaction with persons and inanimate objects; these are termed the *communicative* and *praxic modes,* respectively (an additional *reflective mode* is also posited). The balance between these modes is thought to determine the main phases of development, and thus the way that actions with persons and objects are interrelated, during the first year. The onset of secondary intersubjectivity results from the achievement of free interaction between praxic and communicative modes of action. Trevarthen claims that the full subtlety of meaningful and rule-bound communication, which it is now widely agreed does arise at this time even though language proper has yet to appear, could not be learned or taught through the medium of mechanisms such as Piagetian accommodation and assimilation, and could not be founded on thought processes primarily suited to action on the physical world.

Attraction and direction of attention

In our kind of society, toys or other objects are provided for the amusement of infants and, from time to time, adults take steps to stimulate or check a baby's interest in such things. Piaget's well-known little experiments with his own children are remarkable for their systematic interpretation, not for the fact that a parent should do such things.

There is little hope of directing the very young baby's attention except in the most general sense of facilitating states of alertness so that, through general scanning of the environment within the limits of its focusing abilities, the infant may come to fixate salient loci. In addition, the infant may be transported around or physically moved so that it is orientated in a particular direction.

The young infant's attention may be attracted to objects by various simple means. One strategy is to bring the toy or other object into the infant's visual field. Suitable movement and possibly sound would be useful supplementary cues and, once the infant was able to localize sounds, making noises with an object would be effective beyond the visual field. An alternative strategy would be to lead the infant's visual regard by carefully moving something that holds its attention toward the target object. This might be another object or a manual cue such as finger snapping, which mothers also use prior to trying to direct the gaze of fairly young infants to a distal object with the pointing gesture (Murphy & Messer 1977). Once the infant is mobile, he can be shown things by locomotory leading (Hay 1977).

Figure 24.1. Changes in a mother's body position as she moves to maintain a profile view of her infant's face.

The infant can do very little to attract another person's attention to an object until it exhibits prehension. And, of course, the possibilities are vastly expanded once the infant becomes mobile. Almost any action on an object by a child has great potential for attracting a mother's attention to that object by virtue of the prominence, in the caretaking role, of strategies for carefully monitoring the child. In terms of visual regard, for instance, mothers are extraordinarily attentive to their children, looking at them for about 80% of the time in a laboratory playroom setting (Schaffer et al. 1977). Such data can only be illustrative, of course, as maternal visual attention is reduced somewhat in more representative settings. The fact is that there is a dearth of information on this point; in contrast to recognizing the importance of the infant's visual regard for its mother, the mother's watchfulness over the child has largely been neglected empirically.

The potency of maternal monitoring can be seen in other ways. For instance, the body movements of mothers seated with young children on their knees are dominated by lateral shifts from one side of the infant to the other as the infant's head turns to the left and right (Fig. 24.1). These shifts can be understood in terms of maneuvers to optimize the mother's view of the infant's face (Collis 1978a, 1978b). Interestingly, in observations of mothers and infants playing together at stacking blocks on a table top, this postural shifting was quite evident in mothers of 11-month-olds but not in mothers of 24-month-olds. This age-related difference was correlated with an increase in the amount of time that the mothers of the older group looked at the children's hands and what they were doing. The interpretation was that, at this age and with this task, the hands of the children were a more potent source of information about the state of the ongoing interaction, and hence it was more worthwhile to monitor them than in the younger children, where monitoring the face was of most use (Collis 1978a).

The potency of maternal monitoring means that, effectively, an infant can direct an adult's attention to distal objects in a large number of ways. Merely looking in a particular direction is often sufficient for a mother to respond. This was clearly seen in a study of the gaze patterns of mothers and infants in a relatively unstructured laboratory setting (Collis & Schaffer 1975). Close examination of video recordings showed that, at times when the mother and infant were looking at a set of toys, the chances were that they were both looking at the same toy. It is clearly important to distinguish this pattern of gaze coordination from *mutual gaze,* which is normally understood to refer to simultaneous interpersonal gaze. We therefore coined the term *visual co-orientation* for the state of simultaneously looking at the same locus outside the dyad. A great deal has been written about mutual gaze (Argyle & Cook 1976) but this second, arguably more important, gaze pattern has received scant attention.

Careful examination of gaze patterns in this study revealed that, most commonly, visual co-orientation was established by the mother following the infant's line of regard rather than vice versa (Collis & Schaffer 1975). This is not to say that the infant could not follow their mother's line of visual regard, although there are no observational data on this point. The question has, however, been tackled experimentally by Lempers (1976), Lempers, Flavell, and Flavell (1977), and Scaife and Bruner (1975). The ability may not develop until the second half year of life. Lempers (1976) found that although only 5 out of 12 9-month-olds responded correctly according to a fairly strict criterion, none looked at the wrong member of a pair of toys in the test situation (see also the discussion in Collis 1977). Interestingly, Harlow (1963) mentioned that young monkeys would follow their mother's visual regard to objects outside the cage.

For convenience, we speak of the following of gaze or visual regard but, in fact, what little evidence there is suggests that the eyes themselves need not necessarily be important as cues. In our laboratory setting, mothers were no more likely to follow an infant's look at a toy if they had a good view of the baby's face than if they did not; if anything, the opposite was true (Collis 1978b). On the other hand, if, when it looked at an object, the infant's body (pelvis and lower torso) was oriented away from that object so that the infant had to twist around more than usual, then the mother was especially likely to follow the line of its visual regard.

In their experiments Lempers et al. (1977) found that half of a sample of 18-month-olds did not succeed in a visual following task when the experimenter's eyes, but not his face, were directed at the target toy. The experimenter's eyes were closed to conceal from the subject the actual movement of the eyes toward the target toy. But Lempers (1976), by allowing the subject to see the movement of the experimenter's eyes, made the task possible for 1-year-olds even in the absence of facial orientation cues. In summary, a number of cues are probably sufficient, especially those from the movement of the head and eyes.

There is one means of expression that has a special role in communication about and via objects, namely the pointing gesture. At first, mothers will use this gesture mainly to indicate proximal objects, if necessary, after having transported the infant to the object or vice versa. In many cases, the index finger will actually touch the object, and hence the gesture clearly operates in the attracting mode. This kind of pointing does not vanish as the child becomes more competent at responding (Murphy 1978); in fact, its use is widespread, in suitable contexts, in interaction between adults.

Pointing to distal loci is generally a more complex affair. Elements of the visual leading behavior that mothers use to attract the attention of young infants are still to be found when mothers point for 9-month-olds but less so with 14-month-olds (Murphy & Messer 1977). In addition to the already mentioned auditory cues from finger clicking, Murphy and Messer describe how mothers use a variety of tactile cues such as tapping the child's hands, face or body, and also visual cues such as wiggling the pointing forefinger in various ways. In other respects too the point is not a simple motor act confined to the forelimb. For one thing, the mother's gaze is finely coordinated with the gesture. Typically, at the first sign of pointing, a mother will look at the target toy, whereas about 1 second later, very predictably she will look at the child presumably to monitor its response. Furthermore, there are verbal accompaniments. It is most unlikely that a mother will be silent while pointing: Only 5 of over 400 maternal points were unaccompanied by maternal speech, with toy labeling and interrogative constructions particularly prominent. Regular patterns such as these led Murphy and Messer to talk of a *pointing gestalt* so as to emphasize the complex amalgam of acts in several modalities.

Turning to the infant's responsiveness, the ability visually to follow a point is certainly not an all-or-none affair. Murphy and Messer's results show that some spatial arrangements of toy, infant, and pointing limb could be coped with more easily than others. Points across the baby's face could be followed by 14-month-olds but not by 9-month-olds, whereas points away from the baby's face (Fig. 24.2) were followed by both age groups. Lempers's (1976) results confirm that the failure by 9-month-olds to follow some kinds of point depends on distance and spatial arrangements.

On the other side of the coin, there is the use of the pointing gesture by infants. In the distal pointing situation (Murphy & Messer 1977), only 3 out of 12 9-month-olds were observed to point, as opposed to 8 out of 12 14-month-olds. These points, along with some reachinglike gestures, were generally accompanied by looking at the target toy but seldom at the mother. Much the same increase in incidents between 9 and 14 months was found for proximal pointing in a picture book reading situation (Murphy 1978), but here the addition of two extra age groups, 20-month-olds and 24-month-olds, revealed a much more interesting developmental trend. At these ages there was a marked tendency for the children to combine successive points into a "pointing string" in which the withdrawal of the index finger from one part of a picture was also the initial movement of the next point. As Murphy describes it, seemingly the younger child pointed to a picture of a cat that was thus "done," whereas the older child understood that the cat had ears, eyes, whiskers, tail, and so on and, at the same time, was able to label verbally what it saw. In fact it

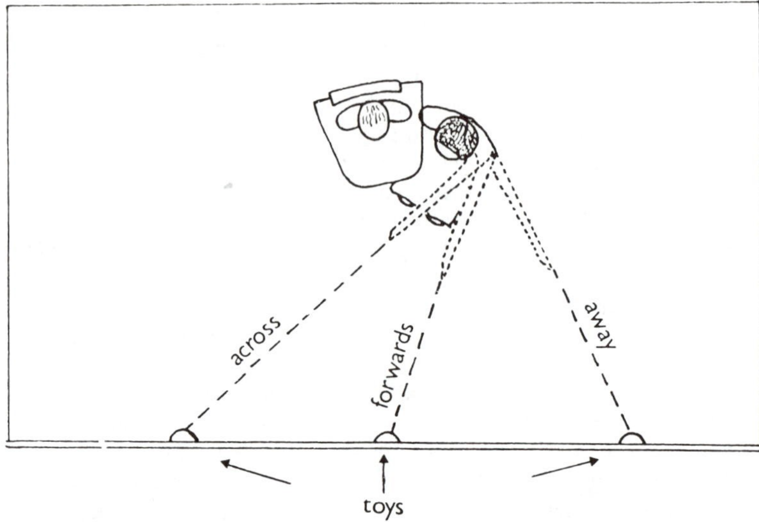

Figure 24.2. Three spatial layouts of an infant, a pointing limb, and a target object create points with varying degrees of difficulty for the infant. (From Murphy & Messer 1977)

was possible to demonstrate that the 20- and 24-month-olds were likely to use the verbal category *naming* (= labeling) more when they were pointing than at other times during the observation session.

The mothers were also particularly likely to label things while the infants were pointing. When the mothers themselves pointed, though, they also used other types of verbal categories in association with the gesture. Naming was prominent when they pointed for 9- and 14-month-olds. With the older children, however, *wh-* questions, in which information is requested rather than given, began to play an important role in this context. Interestingly, other types of interrogative constructions, such as those formally requiring a yes–no kind of answer and tag questions, were not used in the context of pointing. Not surprisingly, though, with infants of all ages, mothers consistently tended to accompany their points with utterances containing "look" or "see" (Murphy 1978; cf. Ninio & Bruner 1978).

Pointing is not the only context in which maternal speech is closely integrated with patterns of shared interest in objects. In the simplest case, that of visual co-orientation, the naming of a toy by the mother was found to be reliably associated with her following the line of visual regard of her 10-month-old infant (Collis 1977, 1978b). Thus the visual following and toy naming seem to be part of the same action complex. In contrast, interrogative constructions seem not to be associated with visual following (Collis 1977).

Messer (1978a) has examined the fine timing integration of mothers' verbal references to toys with toy manipulation. He measured the degree of congruency between the identity of the toy held and the verbal reference to it.

For instance, kappa coefficients of agreement between the toy held and toy labeling with an appropriate common noun ranged from 0.68 to 0.89 depending on the age of the child and whether the mother or child was handling the toy. Even with less specific forms of reference, namely the use of pronouns and indirect reference, verbal–nonverbal congruency was of the same order. In the terminology of information statistics, it was possible to say that knowing which toy was being manipulated reduced the uncertainty about the identity of the toy being referenced by 57 to 89%. It was also possible to demonstrate marked associations between the nature of the manipulative act and the likelihood of a verbal reference from the mother: Actions that seemed to have a special role in bringing an object into the center of physical play were accompanied by words that assured its place as the focus of the discourse.

Implications

Mothers' verbal comments to infants about objects of interest indicate the importance, in early social interaction, of mechanisms to attract and direct attention, with a resulting shared interest in objects. Consonant with the monitoring role of caregiver, for much of the time mothers are content to follow the child's choice of object around which to build an interaction. Mothers can and do attract and direct infants' attention to objects of their own choice, but even so, this is often to elaborate on a theme established by the child, just as, later on, much of a mother's speech imitates and elaborates on the child's utterances (Brown & Bellugi 1964). Murphy and Messer (1977) showed that mothers even tended to point to objects that their infants were looking at and, according to Schaffer and Crook (1980), in two-thirds of the episodes in which mothers of 2-year-olds urged their children to perform actions on toys, the child was already attending to the toy in question. It is of considerable significance that, at this level of analysis, mothers tend to leave to the children the tactical decisions about which object to focus on. The mothers' role in guiding the course of social interaction tends to be more strategic.

The close integration of maternal speech with moments of shared interest in objects by infant and caregiver must surely be important for the beginnings of a simple nominative lexicon. Nouns would seem to provide a relatively easy place to start in the task of cracking the linguistic code and, indeed, nouns dominate the young child's vocabulary (Nelson 1973). Messer (1978b) has investigated some aspects of the information potentially available in maternal speech that could allow nouns to be picked out from the rest of the utterance in which they are embedded. Nouns are often the final word of an utterance and frequently occur at the point of maximum acoustic amplitude. Interestingly, the loudness effect was particularly pronounced when a new toy was introduced, by verbal or nonverbal means, into the stream of the interaction.

Nominal terms are relatively simple ways to encode interest in objects. Deictic terms such as *this, that, here,* and *there* are a little more complex in that the identity of the object indicated is encoded in terms of its spatial relationship with the speaker rather than the properties of the object itself. And with a change of speaker, the same object may be referred to by a different deictic term depending on the relative proximity of the object to speaker and listener. This is the same contrast that forms the basis of the attraction–direction distinction, with the same rather fuzzy boundary. Such contrasts are established slowly, and for a long time there is heavy reliance on nonverbal cues that we have seen to operate in the early months (Clark 1978).

There is more than lexical development to connect the acquisition of language with early manifestations of social interaction via objects. Following Macnamara (1972) the belief is widespread that language skills are founded on cognitive and communicative skills that are in use before the start of language proper (Bates et al. 1975; Bruner 1977, 1978; Halliday 1975). Bates (1976) boldly asserts that the first propositional transactions take place via the exchange of physical objects or the indicating of visible events. Bruner (1978) spells out in more detail some of the formal similarities of shared action on objects and the language process. Almost any human action can be well described in terms of the nature of the act, agent, object, recipient, place and time, and so on. This is closely analogous to the categories of case grammar such as verb, subject, object, indirect object, locative, and tense marker. And interactional routines, such as give-and-take games with objects, exhibit the properties of role reversal, turn taking, and the differentiation of agent and recipient. If Bruner is right in seeing deep significance in these similarities between shared action with objects and shared action with words, then, as Bruner himself emphasizes, the whole enterprise of language is based on procedures for detecting which objects are dominating the interest of one's companions and indicating which objects are most relevant to the social interaction of the moment.

SUMMARY

Even among nonhuman species, communication involves more than just the participating individuals and their behavior. Information about objects and loci in the environment is also conveyed. Basic to this kind of social process is the indication and detection of interest in objects and places via the attraction of attention to a locus relatively near the source animal and the direction of attention to a more distal locus.

Human infancy is characterized by a series of striking changes in the infant's interactions with objects and persons and the interrelationships between these interactions. Detailed analyses of mother–infant interaction indicate the importance of mechanisms for the attraction and direction of attention in the management of shared interest in objects. The sharing of interest in objects has an important role in early social life, particularly in relation to joint action. Maternal speech is closely integrated with shared attention and joint action with objects, and such interactional phenomena provide useful cues for the acquisition of language.

ACKNOWLEDGMENTS

Charles Crook, David Messer, Stuart Millar, Cathy Murphy, and Rudolph Schaffer all provided essential support for the emergence of the ideas presented here. Only the author is responsible for the shortcomings of the final form. I am most grateful to Rudolph Schaffer for his encouragement and for providing the opportunity and facilities to carry out this work, which was supported in part by the Social Science Research Council (U.K.).

REFERENCES

Altmann, S. A. 1967. The structure of primate social communication. *In:* S. A. Altmann (ed.), *Social communication among primates.* Chicago University Press, Chicago, pp. 325–362.

Argyle, M., & M. Cook. 1976. *Gaze and mutual gaze.* Cambridge University Press, Cambridge.

Bates, E. 1976. *Language and context: the acquisition of pragmatics.* Academic Press, New York.

Bates, E., L. Camaioni, & V. Volterra. 1975. The acquisition of performatives prior to speech. *Merrill-Palmer Quarterly* 21:205–226.

Bell, S. M. 1970. The development of the concept of the object as related to infant–mother attachment. *Child Development* 41:291–311.

Bower, T. G. R. 1974. *Development in infancy.* Freeman, San Francisco.

Brown, R., & U. Bellugi. 1964. Three processes in the child's acquisition of syntax. *In:* E. Lenneberg (ed.), *New directions in the study of language.* M.I.T. Press, Cambridge, Massachusetts, pp. 131–161.

Bruner, J. S. 1977. Early social interaction and language acquisition. *In:* H. R. Schaffer (ed.), *Studies in mother–infant interaction.* Academic Press, London, pp. 271–289.

1978. Learning how to do things with words. *In:* J. S. Bruner & A. Garton (eds.), *Human growth and development.* Oxford University Press, Oxford, pp. 62–84.

Chance, M. R. A. 1967. Attention structure as the basis of primate rank orders. *Man* 2:503–518.

Clark, E. V. 1978. From gesture to word: on the natural history of deixis in language acquisition. *In:* J. S. Bruner & A. Garton (eds.), *Human growth and development.* Oxford University Press, Oxford, pp. 84–120.

Collis, G. M. 1977. Visual co-orientation and maternal speech. *In:* H. R. Schaffer (ed.), *Studies in mother–infant interaction.* Academic Press, London, pp. 355–375.

1978a. Describing the structure of social interaction in infancy. *In:* M. Bullowa (ed.), *Before speech: the beginnings of interpersonal communication.* Cambridge University Press, Cambridge, pp. 111–130.

1978b. Body movements and some relations with gaze and vocal behaviour in mother–infant interaction. Unpublished paper.

Collis, G. M., & H. R. Schaffer. 1975. Synchronization of visual attention in mother–infant pairs. *Journal of Child Psychology and Psychiatry* 16:315–320.

Condon, W. S. 1977. A primary phase in the organisation of infant responding behaviour. *In:* H. R. Schaffer (ed.), *Studies in mother–infant interaction.* Academic Press, London, pp. 153–176.

Curio, E. 1976. *The ethology of predation.* Springer-Verlag, Berlin.

Eimas, P. D. 1975. Speech perception in early infancy. *In:* L. B. Cohen & P. Salapatek (eds.), *Infant perception: from sensation to cognition,* vol 2. Academic Press, New York, pp. 193–231.

Frisch, K. von. 1967. *The dance language and orientation of bees.* Harvard University Press, Cambridge, Massachusetts.

Glasersfeld, E. von 1977. Linguistic communication: theory and definition. *In:* D. M. Rumbaugh (ed.), *Language learning by a chimpanzee: the Lana project.* Academic Press, New York, pp. 55–71.

Gould, J. L. 1975. Honey bee recruitment: the dance-language controversy. *Science* 189:685–693.

Hall, K. R. L. 1960. Social vigilance behaviour of the chacma baboon *Papio ursinus. Behaviour* 16:26–294.

Halliday, M. A. K. 1975. *Learning how to mean: explorations in the development of language.* Arnold, London.

Harlow, H. F. 1963. The maternal affectional system. *In:* B. M. Foss (ed.), *Determinants of infant behaviour,* vol. 2. Methuen, London, pp. 3–29.

Harrison, B. 1972. *Meaning and structure.* Harper, New York.

Hay, D. F. 1977. Following their companions as a form of exploration for human infants. *Child Development* 48:1624–1632.

Hockett, C. F., & S. A. Altmann. 1968. A note on design features. *In:* T. A. Sebeok (ed.), *Animal communication.* Indiana University Press, Bloomington, pp. 61–72.

Jackson, E., J. J. Campos, & K. W. Fisher. 1978. The question of decalage between object permanence and person permanence. *Developmental Psychology* 14:1–10.

Kagan, J., & M. Lewis. 1965. Studies of attention in the human infant. *Merrill-Palmer Quarterly* 11:95–127.

Lawick-Goodall, J. van. 1971. *In the shadow of man.* Collins, London.

Lempers, J. D. 1976. Production of pointing, comprehension of pointing and understanding of looking behavior in young children. Unpublished Ph.D. thesis, University of Minnesota, Minneapolis.

Lempers, J. D., E. R. Flavell, & J. H. Flavell. 1977. The development in very young children of tacit knowledge concerning visual perception. *Genetic Psychology Monographs* 95:3–53.

Liberman, A. M., F. S. Cooper, D. P. Shankweiler, & M. Studdert-Kennedy. 1967. Perception of the speech code. *Psychological Review* 74:431–461.

Macnamara, J. 1972. Cognitive basis of language learning in infants. *Psychological Review* 79:1–13.

Marler, P. R. 1967. Animal communication signals. *Science* 157:769–774.

Melchior, H. R. 1971. Characteristics of arctic ground squirrel alarm calls. *Oecologica* 7:184–190.

Meltzoff, A. N., & M. K. Moore. 1977. Imitation of facial and manual gestures by human neonates. *Science* 198:75–78.

Menzel, E. W. 1971. Communication about the environment in a group of young chimpanzees. *Folia Primatologica* 15:220–232.

Menzel, E. W., & S. Halperin. 1975. Purposive behavior as a basis for objective communication between chimpanzees. *Science* 189:652–654.

Messer, D. J. 1978a. The integration of mothers' referential speech with joint play. *Child Development* 49:781–787.

1978b. Mother–child interaction and the use of referential speech. Unpublished Ph.D. thesis, University of Strathclyde, Glasgow.

Millar, W. S. 1976. Operant acquisition of social behaviors in infancy: basic problems and constraints. *In:* H. W. Reese (ed.), *Advances in child development and behavior,* vol. 11. Academic Press, New York, pp. 107–140.

Möglich, M., U. Maschwitz, & B. Hölldobler. 1974. Tandem calling: a new kind of signal in ant communication. *Science* 186:1046–1047.

Morse, P. A. 1974. Infant speech perception: a preliminary model and review of the literature. *In:* R. L. Shiefelbusch & L. L. Lloyd (eds.), *Language perspectives – acquisition, retardation and intervention.* Macmillan, London, pp. 19–53.

Murphy, C. M. 1978. Pointing in the context of a shared activity. *Child Development* 49:371–380.

Murphy, C. M., & D. J. Messer. 1977. Mothers, infants and pointing: a study of a gesture. *In:* H. R. Schaffer (ed.), *Studies in mother–infant interaction.* Academic Press, London, pp. 325–354.

Nelson, K. 1973. Structure and strategy in learning to talk. *Monographs of the Society for Research in Child Development* 38 (serial no. 149).

Ninio, A., & J. Bruner. 1978. The achievement and antecedents of labelling. *Journal of Child Language* 5:1–15.

Oster, H., & P. Ekman. In press. Facial behavior in child development. *In:* A. Collins (ed.), *Minnesota symposia on child psychology,* vol. 11. Crowell, New York.

Piaget, J. 1952. *The origin of intelligence in the child.* Basic Books, New York.

1954. *The construction of reality in the child.* Basic Books, New York.

Robson, K. S. 1967. The role of eye to eye contact in maternal–infant attachment. *Journal of Child Psychology and Psychiatry* 8:13–25.

Scaife, M., & J. S. Brunner. 1975. The capacity for joint visual attention in the infant. *Nature* 253:265–266.

Schaffer, H. R. 1963. Some issues for research in the study of attachment behaviour. *In:* B. M. Foss (ed.), *Determinants of infant behaviour,* vol. 2. Methuen, London, pp. 179–196.

1971. *The growth of sociability.* Penguin Books, Harmondsworth.

1979. Acquiring the concept of the dialogue. *In:* M. Bornstein & W. Kessen (eds.), *Psychological development from infancy: image and intention.* Erlbaum, Hillsdale, New Jersey.

Schaffer, H. R., G. M. Collis, & G. Parsons. 1977. Vocal interchange and visual regard in verbal and pre-verbal children. *In:* H. R. Schaffer (ed.), *Studies in mother–infant interaction.* Academic Press, London, pp. 291–324.

Schaffer, H. R., & C. K. Crook. 1978. The role of the mother in early social development. *In:* H. McGurk (ed.), *Issues in childhood social development.* Methuen, London, pp. 55–78.

1980. Child compliance and maternal control techniques. *Developmental Psychology* 16:54–61.

Simmons, K. E. L., & U. Weidmann. 1972. Directional bias as a component of social behaviour with special reference to the mallard, *Anas platyrhynchos. Journal of Zoology* 170:49–62.

Smith, W. J. 1977. *The behavior of communicating.* Harvard University Press, Cambridge, Massachusetts.

Sroufe, L. A., & E. Waters. 1976. The ontogenesis of smiling and laughter: a perspective on the organization of development in infancy. *Psychological Review* 83:173–189.

Stern, D. 1977. *The first relationship: infant and mother.* Fontana/Open Books, London.

Stevens, K. N., & A. S. House. 1972. Speech perception. *In:* J. Tobias (ed.), *Foundations of modern auditory theory,* vol. 2. Academic Press, New York, pp. 3–62.

Sugarman-Bell, S. 1978. Some organizational aspects of pre-verbal communication. *In:* I. Markova (ed.), *Language and the social context.* Wiley, Chichester, pp. 49–66.

Teleki, G. 1973. *Predatory behavior among wild chimpanzees.* Bucknell University Press, Lewisburg, Pennsylvania.

Thorpe, W. H. 1956. *Learning and instinct in animals.* Methuen, London.

Trevarthen, C. 1977a. Descriptive analyses of infant communicative behaviour. *In:* H. R. Schaffer (ed.), *Studies in mother-infant interaction.* Academic Press, London, pp. 227–270.

1977b. Instincts for human understanding and for cultural co-operation: their development in infancy. Paper presented at the Werner-Reimer-Stiftung Symposium on Human Ethology, Bad-Homburg, October.

1978. Modes of perceiving and modes of acting. *In:* H. L. Pick & E. Saltzman (eds.), *Modes of perceiving and processing information.* Erlbaum, Hillsdale, New Jersey, pp. 99–135.

1979. Communication and co-operation in early infancy: a description of primary intersubjectivity. *In:* M. Bullowa (ed.), *Before speech: the beginnings of interpersonal communication.* Cambridge University Press, London, pp. 321–347.

In press. Basic patterns of psychogenetic change in infancy. *In:* H. Nathan (ed.), Proceedings of the Organization for Economic Co-operation and Development. Conference on Dips in Learning, Paris.

Trevarthen, C., & P. Hubley. 1978. Secondary intersubjectivity: confidence, confiding and acts of meaning in the first year. *In:* A. Lock (ed.), *Action, gesture and symbol: the emergence of language.* Academic Press, London, pp. 183–229.

Vine, I. 1970. The role of facial-visual signalling in early social development. *In:* M. von Cranach & I. Vine (eds.), *Social communication and movement.* Academic Press, London, pp. 195–298.

Watson, J. S. 1972. Smiling, cooing, and "the game." *Merrill-Palmer Quarterly* 18:323–339.

Weidmann, U., & J. A. Darley. 1971. The role of the female in the social display of mallards. *Animal Behaviour* 19:287–298.

Williams, H. W., A. W. Stokes, & J. C. Wallen. 1968. The food call and display of the bobwhite quail (*Colinus virginianus*) *Auk* 85:464–476.

Wolff, P. H. 1963. Observations on the early development of smiling. *In:* B. M. Foss (ed.), *Determinants of infant behaviour,* vol. 2. Methuen, London, pp. 113–134.

25

TRAITS, BEHAVIORAL SYSTEMS, AND RELATIONSHIPS: THREE MODELS OF INFANT-ADULT ATTACHMENT

EVERETT WATERS

Psychodynamic, social learning, and ethological approaches to infant behavior have each yielded important descriptive insights concerning infant–adult attachment. In many respects these insights appear to be complementary. But because of competition and conflict among theoretical systems, integration of descriptive insights has been difficult to achieve.

The pace at which new attachment research appears seems to have slackened. Recent critiques have suggested that everything implied by the notion of a bond between infant and adult can be captured by studying patterns of interactive behavior, without invoking the concept of attachment (Rosenthal 1973). Weinraub et al. (1977) have even wondered whether an attachment construct has any value at all from a logical and scientific point of view.

The goal of this chapter is to step outside the arena of cross-theoretical controversy and to examine models rather than theories of infant–adult attachment. My premise is that difficulties and discouragement have arisen in part because we have failed to look beyond differences of theoretical orientation to examine the models and types of constructs that we use in developing attachment theory and designing research. My primary concern is that the failure to consider various modes of model building has not only made communication across theoretical systems and research paradigms difficult, it has also significantly restricted our descriptive approach to the infant–adult tie.

The basic data from which much of attachment theory and research proceed can be summarized very briefly. Attachment implies that an infant is able to distinguish a presumed attachment figure from other adults; it implies that the infant is aware of the attachment figure's existence even when she or he is not within sight (i.e., object permanence); and it implies that contact with the attachment figure is in some sense or at least in some circumstances preferred to contact with other adults. Behaviorally, the early signs of attachment involve following and greeting behavior, separation protest, and the tendency to use the attachment figure as a base from which to explore. By age 1 year, most home-reared infants are quite sensitive to their surroundings. They explore more actively in their mother's presence than in her absence, especially in unfamiliar environments. Most 1-year-olds are more comfortable with unfamiliar adults when an attachment figure is present. Although 1-year-olds clearly show both interest and affiliative behavior toward strangers, bids for physical contact and for comfort are preferentially displayed toward attachment figures. When 1-year-olds are separated from an attachment figure in an unfamiliar setting, exploratory behavior typically gives way to search and/or protest. Even when this behavior diminishes, exploratory behavior is typically limited until the attachment figure returns. Upon reunion, most 1-year-olds seek proximity and/or contact and eventually return to play. Protest during brief separations declines after age 3. Systematic studies of the organization and development of these behavior patterns are reviewed by Ainsworth (1973a) and by Ainsworth et al. (1978).

The first type of attachment model reviewed here is the trait model. On examination it appears that theorists of diverse persuasions have implicitly conceptualized attachment in terms usually applied to the analysis of personality traits. In research from many perspectives, attachment has often been operationalized in terms of a small number of behavioral indices (e.g., touching, looking, vocalizing, approaching). These indices are usually assumed to be correlated, and their use suggests that "intensity" is the major dimension along which attachment relationships would develop and differ. When this implicit trait model is made explicit, it is not widely accepted within any of the major developmental perspectives. Everyone seems to have had something more involved in mind. Trait models have certain inherent weaknesses, particularly their inability to deal with the context sensitivity and environmental responsiveness of infant behavior. Nonetheless, with some revision of the conventional trait model, trait-type models or descriptions can be of use in the design of specific studies and may find a place in attachment theory.

Behavioral systems models explicitly take into account the organization, context sensitivity, and environmental responsiveness of attachment behavior. Behavioral systems models tend to involve a normative point of view and focus on behavioral detail. Although they can incorporate trait-type variables to some extent, they are not easily applied to studies of individual relationships.

Models of relationships focus less on behavioral detail than on the global organization and functioning of behavior between two individuals across time. Although relationships differ one from another and although these differences can perhaps be expressed using global trait-type descriptions, relationship models explicitly emphasize that the object of study is the dyad. A relationship is not an attribute of either partner.

None of these models is necessarily or exclusively the tool of a particular theoretical perspective. Even within a given theoretical framework, an exhaustive description of infant–adult attachment would require attention to both behavioral detail and behavioral/interactive trends. Both the consistency and the environmental responsiveness of attachment deserve attention. And both the individual's contributions to interaction and the dyad's history of interactions have important implications for a developmental theory of attachment. Thus the models reviewed below are not alternatives but facets of descriptive analysis. If considering complementary models can help broaden the descriptive base within competing theoretical perspectives, then perhaps as a result the prospects for communication and integration across paradigms can be improved.

ATTACHMENT AS A TRAIT CONSTRUCT

What is a trait?

The study of trait constructs has long been the dominant paradigm in personality research. It entails both a theory of trait-type constructs and a model for the measurement of individual differences. According to the classic view of personality, traits are causal constructs. They are the prime determinants of behavior and are the basis for behavioral consistency across situations and across time.

In addition to a theory of trait constructs as major determinants of behavior, the trait paradigm involves a measurement model that assumes that (1) there is a single true score for each individual on each quantitative trait dimension and (2) there is a linear relationship between a person's true score on a trait dimension and his score on response measures (behavior, self-report, etc.) that index the trait in question. The model has generally involved the prediction that rank orders of individuals across situations are stable with respect to indices of a given trait, and by and large the paradigm has been associated with correlational studies of individual differences rather than experimental studies of groups and treatments.

In practice, trait constructs are operationally defined and validated by construction of reliable measures and by evaluating both the convergence of measures of the same construct and the independence of measures of theoretically unrelated constructs (e.g., Campbell & Fiske 1959).

Recently critics from within the field of personality research have taken exception to the notion of traits as underlying causes of behavior (Wiggins 1974) and, in the face of situationalist critiques of the entire individual differences tradition (e.g., Mischel 1968, 1973), they have suggested modifications of the classic view to take into account the environmental responsiveness of behavior that has been such a problem for the trait approach (Endler & Magnusson 1976).

In defense of traits, Wiggins (1974) argues that trait attributions can be appropriate characterizations of an action ("John clung to her affectionately") when they specify that an action belongs to a class of actions that are likely to lead to a particular social outcome. They can also be appropriate characterizations of persons when they are used as categorical summaries of a person's behavior to date ("So far, *affectionate* is the right word to summarize the general trend of John's behavior"). At the same time, Wiggins argues convincingly that trait language does not appropriately refer to (1) primary qualities of particular behaviors, (2) evaluative responses of the observer, (3) intentions of the actor, (4) tendencies of the actor, (5) conditions antecedent to the act, or (6) consequences of the act. In addition, he argues that, contrary to the classic view, traits are inappropriate as causal constructs. Traits are lost causes, patterns of consistency that require rather than provide explanations. As outlined below, these inappropriate uses of trait language correspond closely to the ways in which implicit trait models have typically been employed in attachment theory and research. Endler and Magnusson (1976) have provided a detailed comparison of trait and nontrait models in personality research. They have suggested that models that assess both individuals and situations and that focus upon the interaction of traits and situations offer promising alternatives to the classic trait approach. Both Wiggins's suggestions for more thoughtful use of trait constructs and Endler and Magnusson's suggestions for more elaborate models within the personality paradigm are highly relevant to the existing attachment literature.

Research on attachment as a trait construct

Coates et al. (1972a:218) have observed that "underlying (most recent attachment research) is the tacit assumption that the measures chosen are indices of a unitary trait (i.e., attachment). It is assumed, although seldom explicitly, that different measures such as staying close to the mother and crying following separation are closely correlated. Such interrelations are presumed to hold across time within particular subject samples, and also across samples and stimulus situations."

Procedurally, most research on infant–adult ties has been confined to the study of a relatively small class of individual behaviors in an even smaller set of laboratory settings. Unfortunately, the same measures and procedures are often used in research undertaken from trait (e.g., social learning) and nontrait (ethological) attachment models. This has been particularly true of the widely used Ainsworth and Wittig (1969) Strange Situation. This standardized laboratory procedure involves eight brief (3-minute) episodes and provides opportunities to observe a variety of the 12- to 24-month-old infant's responses to the stress of a new environment and of separation from an attachment figure. As outlined in Table 25.1, mother (or father) and infant are introduced into a room containing toys for the infant and chairs for the mother and another adult. After 3 minutes an unfamiliar adult enters, sits quietly, and eventually engages the infant in play. The mother is signaled to leave; after 3 minutes she returns and the stranger leaves quietly. After 3 minutes more, the separation–reunion sequence is repeated. The procedure was initially developed as an adjunct to an intensive longitudinal study of infant–mother interaction at home and was structured to allow observation of the infant in increasingly (mildly) stressful circumstances (new room, new person, separated but not alone, separated and alone).

The hypotheses by Ainsworth's group were not derived from trait formulations but from Bowlby's (1969) ethological theory. In addition, three distinct types of measurement were developed for analysis of the data: (1) frequency counts and time samples of particular behaviors (touch, look, approach, etc.), (2) scales to assess broad categories of behavior (proximity and interaction avoiding, contact resisting, distance interaction), and (3) a classification system designed to assess the infant's ability to use the adult as a secure base from which to explore and as a source of security when distressed (secure versus insecure or anxious attachment).

Unfortunately, as a matter of convenience, the Strange Situation has become *the* attachment situation in most recent research and has served as a substitute for rather than an adjunct to field observation. Even more unfortunately, most

Table 25.1. *Summary of Strange Situation procedure*

Episode	Persons present	Time	Events and procedures
1	M, B	Variable (approx. 1 minute)	M and B are introduced into S/S room by E. If necessary, M interests B in toys before being seated. M does not initiate interaction but is responsive to bids from B
2	M, B	3 minutes	M remains seated and is responsive to bids for interaction but does not initiate
3	M, B, S	3 minutes	S enters and is seated; sits silently for 1 minute; talks to M for 1 minute; engages B in interaction and/or toy play for 1 minute
4	B, S	3 minutes (less if B extremely distressed)	M leaves room, S allows B to play alone but remains responsive to interactive bids. If B is crying, S offers contact and tries to comfort. If B refuses or resists, S does not persist. Terminate episode after 1 minute hard crying or on M's request
5	M, B	3 minutes	M calls B from outside door and steps inside, pausing at doorway to greet B and to reach and offer contact. If necessary, B is held and comforted then reinterested in toys; otherwise, M is seated and remains responsive to bids from B but does not initiate
6	B	3 minutes (less if B extremely distressed)	M leaves room; B remains alone. Terminate episode if 1 minute hard crying ensues or on M's request
7	B, S	3 minutes (less if B extremely distressed)	S returns and is seated. If B is crying or begins to cry without pause, S offers contact and tries to comfort. If B cannot be comforted and crying continues (or on M's request), terminate episode
8	M, B	3 minutes	M calls B from outside door and steps inside, pausing at doorway to greet B and to reach and offer contact. If necessary, B is held and comforted and then reinterested in toys; otherwise M is seated and remains responsive to bids from B but does not initiate if B is content in toy play

M, mother; B, baby; S, stranger.
Source: Waters (1978).

of the research outside of Ainsworth's group has focused on the method of counting discrete behaviors. Because much of this research tacitly adopted a trait orientation, emphasis was placed on the quantity of behavioral output as an index of the strength of the infant–adult bond.

Several major studies of infants ranging from 10 months to 3 years of age have examined the correlations of looking, touching, approaching, crying, and other presumed attachment behaviors both within a single laboratory session and across intervals of 4 months and longer (Coates et al. 1972a, 1972b; Maccoby & Feldman 1972). In addition, the same researchers have reported on the intercorrelations among these behaviors at various ages. Similar data from extended home observations during the first year of life have been reported by Ainsworth et al. (1972) and by Stayton et al. (1973). Although the results of these studies are complicated and numerous, Coates et al. aptly summarize much of the data:

> Significant correlations were found at all ages among visual regard, touching, proximity to the mother, and among crying and three measures of orientation to the locus of her disappearance. Crying was correlated significantly with touching and proximity to the mother... There was some variation in the magnitude and patterning of the correlations as a function of age and the social situation (before or after separation). The results provide some support for the hypothesis that the patterning of infant social behavior is sufficiently extensive to warrant use of the attachment concept. [Coates et al. 1972a:218]

The results of correlational analyses of discrete behaviors across repeated laboratory sessions are equally complex. In general, however, they have been interpreted in terms of traitlike consistency and/or substantive developmental change, and have generally led to a similar conclusion regarding the value of an attachment concept. Unfortunately these conclusions have not often been tested by relating discrete behaviors in the laboratory to behavior in other settings. Thus the notion that some infants are more strongly attached than others and the notion that attachment to parents wanes after the second year of life have rested primarily upon these data.

A recent critique

Masters and Wellman (1974) have used these same data in an influential critical assessment of the attachment construct. Based on the critical perspective employed by Mischel (1968), the critique is important not only for its analysis of the attachment research but also for the sweeping implications drawn by its authors concerning individual differences strategies in general. In brief, Masters and Wellman ask three questions of the data: (1) are scores on individual attachment behaviors stable within and across laboratory sessions? (2) are the behaviors scored strongly intercorrelated, as measures of the same construct should be? (3) are the behaviors used to measure attachment independent of nonattachment variables such as temperament or cognitive level?

Stability. The stability of four discrete behaviors scored in the Coates et al. (1972b) study was assessed by correlating scores for each behavior across the first, second, and last 3 minutes of a 10-minute nonseparation segment of their modified Strange Situation at age 14 months. Overall, only 5 of 16 correlations were significant in the two samples studied at that age. When data on the entire 10-minute nonseparation period were correlated with data from a 3-minute preseparation period the next day, only one of the four correlations was significant in both samples. Thus the rank order of subjects was not stable with respect to most of the discrete behaviors over even the shortest intervals.

The analyses of temporal stability in discrete behaviors over longer time periods (Coates et al. 1972b; Maccoby & Feldman 1972) yielded similar results, and a brief summary will suffice. The stability of visual regard, vocalization, touching the mother, and proximity seeking across segments of the same laboratory session at 10, 14, and 18 months in the Coates et al. data yielded only 30 significant correlations out of a possible 64. With a single day intervening between laboratory sessions at each age, only 3 of 12 correlations were significant. Over the periods 10 to 14 months and 14 to 18 months only 6 of 16 correlations were significant. Maccoby and Feldman (1972) report stability correlations for proximity seeking, looking, vocalizing, smiling, and crying in a modified Strange Situation from ages 2 to 2.5, 2.5 to 3, and 2 to 3 years. Overall, only 9 of 24 were significant, and of these 3 were less than 0.40. Thus Masters and Wellman (1974:223) conclude that "little stability of attachment behaviors was found if the intervening time was three minutes, one day, three months, four months, or longer."

Intercorrelations among attachment behaviors. Coates et al. (1972a) presented intercorrelations among discrete behaviors within preseparation and nonseparation segments by age. Overall, 25 of 48 correlations were significant. Many of these were the obvious correlations between seeking proximity to the mother and touching her (median $r = 0.83$). Maccoby and Feldman (1972) presented similar data by age and situation, and overall 20 of 60 correlations among attachment behaviors were significant. Thus the data do not strongly support the notion that the behaviors scored consistently assess the same attachment construct.

Independence of nonattachment measures. Masters and Wellman (1974) found few data from which to assess the extent to which discrete attachment behaviors are independent of theoretically irrelevant variables (e.g., temperament, intelligence quotient, social class). In view of the low stability and low levels of intercorrelation reviewed above, however, this would not seem to be a decisive issue.

In summary, Masters and Wellman extended their remarks about the unreliability of the data reviewed to include an assessment of the attachment construct that underlies much of the correlational research on discrete attachment behaviors. They concluded (1974:288) that "the correlational analysis of human infant attachment behaviors does not provide support for the concept of attachment as a psychological trait or as a central motive state. The stability and functional equivalence of theoretically relevant behaviors required by such conceptualizations is not found in the empirical data." As a procedural alternative to the analysis of individual differences, they suggest greater attention to normative data, especially to data reflecting the proportion of subjects whose behavior is affected in the same way (increase, decrease, no change) by various situational factors.

An evaluation

The Masters and Wellman critique is noteworthy for the approach to construct validation that it brings to the study of infant–adult ties. In addition, their review is useful in rendering the implicit trait model underlying so much attachment research more explicit. At the same time, its negative conclusions have discouraged interest in the attachment construct. After more than five years, their review has stimulated little theoretical progress and little methodological innovation, and it has foreclosed consideration of alternative nontrait, nonsituationalist models. This seems premature because many of the "negative indications" discovered by Masters and Wellman, and indeed many of their conclusions (insofar as they concern primarily discrete behaviors), have been noted in previous literature. Others are assimilable within alternative models of the infant–adult tie without the negative implications for an attachment construct implied by Masters and Wellman. For example, Bowlby (1969) has emphasized that behaviors serving the same function need not be positively correlated and may even be mutually exclusive (e.g., flight and freezing or approach and distance interaction). In addition, Baerends (1972) has provided excellent illustrations of the complex influence that time intervals and other aspects of method can have on correlations among behaviors. The same behaviors (e.g., preening and nest building) can be negatively correlated (mutually exclusive) in short intervals, uncorrelated in intermediate intervals (preening serving many functions), and positively correlated (both correlated with reproductive state) over longer intervals. Thus Masters and Wellman's critique itself deserves a critical evaluation, in part because nontrait models may yet be consistent with the data they review and in part because the data may at least warrant narrower conclusions than they offer.

Finally, Masters and Wellman's critique deserves critical evaluation if only because of the logic by which it proceeds from the data to its conclusions. As Cronbach and Meehl (1955) pointed out years ago, negative results in construct validation research are not readily interpretable. They could indicate that the measures employed have not measured the construct well; or they could mean that the experimental design failed to test (or poorly represented) the hypotheses derived from the theory in question; or they could indicate that the body of theory surrounding the construct is incorrect. Only the last possibility is seriously entertained in Masters and Wellman's critique.

Many of the shortcomings in the data reviewed by Masters and Wellman could, they concede, be remedied by the use of larger samples. Nonetheless, a critical review of the time-sampling procedures employed in most Strange Situation research reveals a problem that is a priori more crucial for the interpretation of negative evidence than is the overwhelming number of the nonsignificant correlations cited by Masters and Wellman.

In discussing their results on the stability of attachment behaviors, which they admittedly do not find overwhelming, Coates et al. (1972b) wondered whether the evidence would have been stronger if they had used longer sampling intervals. Indeed, inspection of the reported means and standard deviations for their samples of discrete behaviors reveals that most of the behaviors occurred at relatively low rates (many less than 1.5 per minute). In addition to the possible effect of range restriction on the expression of individual differences, it seems likely that 3- and 4-minute observations are too brief to provide reliable samples of individual differences. If so, this would have clear implications for the interpretation of negative results.

The most elementary fact of time-sampling methodology is that samples of a behavior must accurately estimate the parameters of the population from which they are taken (in this case, one subject's behavior) in order to be useful. In all behavior sampling techniques, the adequacy of a behavior sample is determined by the interplay of sampling interval durations, by the number of times and frequency with which intervals are sampled, and by the duration of each occurrence of the behavior, its rate of occurrence, and temporal patterning (see Altmann 1974). Where the criterion behavior is as rare as each of the discrete behaviors sampled in the Coates et al. nonseparation segments, a large number of observation intervals are necessary to obtain reliable estimates of individual scores. Samples of two, three, or five instances of a behavior easily show fluctuations of 20 to 200% on the basis of differences in behavior that should be trivial for the hypotheses under consideration. Is a child who looks at its mother once today and twice tomorrow twice as strongly attached in only a day's time?

One approach to this issue is afforded by the classical psychometric theory of test reliability (Nunnally 1967). If we consider each sampling interval (5–, 10–, 15–, etc.) to be an item scored pass/fail (i.e., the behavior occurs or does not) and consider the entire sample (usually 3 to 4 minutes) a test of so many items, we can easily compute an index of the dependability of individual scores (Cronbach's alpha). Because a major assumption of time-sampling methods is that the behavior is equally likely to occur in any sampling interval, we can make use of the simplifying assumption that each of our items has the same mean (difficulty level).

I have recently reported this analysis (Waters 1978) for data on looking, vocalizing, smiling, gesturing, approaching, and touching, using Strange Situation data comparable to those of Coates et al. and Maccoby and Feldman. The sample consisted of 30 infants at 12 and 18 months of age. For behavior toward the mother, median alphas were 0.46, 0.61, 0.51, and 0.57 for preseparation and reunion episodes of 6 and 7 minutes at both 12 and 18 months. Spearman-Brown estimates of alpha for the more typical 3- and 4-minute episodes are substantially lower (0.30, 0.45, 0.39, and 0.43, respectively). Behavior toward the stranger in preseparation episodes and separation episodes yielded similar low levels of reliability. These impose severe upper limits on how strongly each of the variables can correlate with itself across time or with other variables.

Spearman-Brown estimates of the length of time sample necessary to yield an alpha of 0.9 (maximum value is 1.0) were particularly telling as to the adequacy of typical assessments of individual differences in discrete attachment behaviors. The estimates for all but the most high-frequency behaviors (e.g., holding on to the mother during reunion) ranged from 20 to over 2,000 minutes (median = 74, 34, 60, and 70 minutes for preseparation and reunion behavior to the mother at 12 and 18 months, respectively). These results suggest that the interpretation of low reliability, stability, and convergent validity of discrete attachment behaviors should focus on measurement failure and need not reflect upon the attachment construct at all in the present case. The assessment procedures employed in the research reviewed by Masters and Wellman seem to have been inadequate for reliable assessments of individual differences.

In the report cited above (Waters 1978), assessments based on Ainsworth's broader behavior scales and classification procedures yielded striking stability across the period from 12 to 18 months. In a subsequent study (Waters et al. 1979), similar assessments at age 15 months were strongly related to social competence in the preschool playgroup at age 3.5 years and were shown to be independent of cognitive level.

At present, hypotheses concerning traitlike consistency among discrete behaviors appear neither to have been demonstrated, nor disproved, nor even fairly tested. Moreover, the importance of stable individual differences in attachment behavior at other levels of analysis remains largely unexplored. Alternatives to trait models are presented below, and although they do not entail a role for traits as causal constructs, they point to important roles for the study of behavioral individuality. But even when trait attributions are used in the manner proposed by Wiggins (1974), they clearly cannot support a comprehensive view of infant–adult ties on their own. We need to look into the behavioral systems that organize attachment behavior during interaction in order to understand what it is that an individual brings to social situations. We also need to highlight the sense in which infant–adult ties are relationships rather than properties of individuals.

ATTACHMENT AS A BEHAVIORAL SYSTEM

A relatively recent approach to the problem of organization and continuity in the context of flexible and changing behavior patterns is the analysis of systems underlying the structure of behavior (e.g., Miller et al. 1960; Baerends 1972; Bertalanffy 1969; Bischof 1975). The study of behavioral systems attempts to describe the mechanisms that organize behavior and contribute both stability and flexibility to social behavior. It is an effort to specify one aspect of the individual's contribution to interactive phenomena that are dyadic (if not even more complex) in nature. From a behavioral systems perspective, every individual brings an internal structural basis for coordinating and regulating behavioral and affective responses to any interactive situation. One great advantage of behavioral systems models over modified S–R and other linear models is their ability to take into account the effects of contextual variables that manifestly affect most social behavior. This is an important characteristic because the argument for situationalism in the study of behavior (Mischel 1968; 1973) depends upon the assumption that there are no models of behavioral consistency that can accomplish this. The development of models that can meet the situationalist challenge is one alternative to adopting situationalism by default rather than on its merits.

Characteristics of behavioral systems

The simplest model for a behavioral system is a thermostat, an apparatus for regulating the behavior of a heating plant. The basic elements of a self-regulating system are a *receptor,* which accepts some type of environmental input (e.g., temperature data); a *center,* which in some way reacts to the input; and an *effector,* which on a signal from the center generates some response to the environmental input (e.g., switch burner off). The output of the control system is monitored by a *feedback loop* to the receptor, which thereby apprises the system of the effects of its response (e.g., "It's cooling off now"). Continuous monitoring of the environment and reference to some standard (set point or set goal) makes self-regulation possible. More complex systems can, of course, be imagined.

Models of this kind have found wide applicability in research on animal behavior, as alternatives to teleological explanations and untenable drive models of motivated and apparently purposive behavior. Behavioral systems capture both the stability and the context sensitivity of behavior. At the same time, they are easily integrated into developmental models. This is because, in their more elaborate forms, behavioral systems share the following characteristics:

1 *Structure.* In contrast to unitary drives, behavioral systems have components. These include sensors, effectors, and comparators.
2 *Interreference.* The components of a behavioral system receive input not only about the environment but about the status of other components within the system. Insofar as this input influences the action of a given component, one component of a behavioral system can be part of the environment of other components. This is a major feature contributing to the ability of behavioral systems to take situational or contextual information into account in responding to a stimulus. It affords the opportunity to make a response conditional upon contextual variables and plays an important role in the development and organization of adaptive behavior.
3 *Selectivity.* Behavioral systems do not respond to every type of environmental stimulus or even to the entire range of stimuli from a single source. This is due in part to and is reflected in species-characteristic constraints and biases in learning abilities.
4 *Calibration.* The goal of a behavioral system is specified by the values of internal parameters to which various inputs are compared. Homeostats have fixed values for these parameters. More complex designs may adjust the parameters in real time by reference to information about either internal or external events or states, as these bear upon the system's status relative to its environment.
5 *Integrity.* The components of a behavioral system are organized such that the system acts as a whole. That is, a response to a stimulus is not the interaction of several components' responses; it is the single (perhaps complex) response selected after all relevant inputs from components are compiled. A

behavioral system may often generate behavioral outputs that compete with the output of another system, but a given system is not conceived of as competing with itself to produce a response.

6 *Need for support.* The behaviors initiated, modulated, or terminated by the effector components of a behavioral system are not properly part of the system. They belong to the animal's repertoire of action skills. Any action skill may at various times serve more than one behavioral system. In addition, a behavioral system may require input from the operation of relevant action skills during development in order to become properly organized and calibrated.

7 *Development.* Behavioral systems are not necessarily operative or even assembled at birth.

8 *Adaptation.* The developmental blueprint for a given behavioral system reflects a species's long experience with an average expectable environment. In that context the system can provide relevant and adaptive response to environmental inputs. In other contexts, as a consequence of either developmental deviations or the type of inputs received, the system may not provide adaptive responses.

It may well be objected that models of this complexity violate the principle of parsimony. But it is important to remember that the principle of parsimony applies to the explanation of a phenomenon, not to its definition. Modified S–R models and causal trait models are parsimonious explanations of infant–adult ties only when we define these relationships in terms narrow enough to fit such models. Suppose instead that we first describe the behavioral basis of infant–adult ties in their own right and then search for parsimonious explanations. That is, suppose we allow that infant–adult ties exist in some substantive sense and that defining them to suit our models will not make them so. Suddenly modified S–R and causal trait models appear inadequate or become complexly ad hoc and cumbersome. The elegance and simplicity of behavioral systems models are most apparent when the behavioral complexity and context sensitivity of infant–adult ties are recognized and understood in detail.

Ethological/control-systems theory

From a behavioral systems point of view, the hallmark of the infant–adult bond is a balance between attachment and exploratory behavior that has as its predictable outcome the maintenance of a certain access or degree of proximity to the mother. This is typically seen by the end of the first year of life. The control system that is said to organize this behavior regulates the infant's exploratory behavior, signaling and approach behavior, and contact-maintaining behavior by reference to an internal characteristic that Bowlby refers to as a *set goal.* A set goal is not a goal object but a degree of access or proximity to the adult that is maintained by periodic activation of increased rates of attachment (proximity-promoting) behavior. By specifying a number of internal and environmental inputs that can influence the calibration of the set goal, the model encompasses the observations that (1) infants seem to desire closer proximity or more contact when they are ill, tired, or frightened, (2) certain situations seem prepotent stimuli to proximity seeking (e.g., darkness, unfamiliar settings, mother's absence), and (3) infants actively explore away from adults in coordination with proximity seeking rather than despite or at the expense of it.

Despite its originality and the contribution it has made in only a few years' time, Bowlby's theory has been subject to several pointed criticisms from within the psychoanalytic tradition in which he was trained. Most of the criticism concerns violations of cherished psychoanalytic concepts and dogma. Engel (1971), however, has added a number of incisive observations from the point of view of general systems theory to his reservations about Bowlby's interpretation of psychoanalytic theory. He points out, for example, that Bowlby's model is primarily a homeostatic mechanism designed to account for the infant's tendency to maintain a degree of proximity to adults. The mechanism is closed with respect to what Bertalanffy (1969) calls *exchange of matter with the environment*. That is, although set goals may be modified from time to time, the mechanism itself remains unchanged. Concepts of growth, development, differentiation, and accommodation are not as easily related to Bowlby's model as they might be to more elaborate models.

In addition, Engel observes that although a number of internal inputs (feelings) are allowed to modify the set goal in Bowlby's model, external events related to infant–mother distance are the major stimuli to action. When the set goal of the attachment behavioral system is viewed as a degree of proximity to an adult, it is difficult to explain the infant's tendency to be more readily upset by repetitions of separation–reunion experiences. Moreover, the effectiveness of alternatives to proximity (e.g., distal interactions such as showing, looking, vocalizing) is difficult to understand when the set goal is so defined. It also seems fair to suggest that if the evolution of an attachment behavioral system reflects nothing more than the advantages of proximity to adults, then this goal could be more economically accomplished by the evolution of a tendency to cling unremittingly than the evolution of a complex system to organize the balance between attachment and exploratory behavior. Finally, Bowlby's control system model does not seem to point the way toward integration of attachment behavior with control system formulations of other behavior patterns such as wariness, fear, play, and exploration.

Toward an ethological–organizational view of infant–adult ties

Ainsworth et al. (1978) have recently collected a large body of data relevant to Bowlby's theory. In the course of an extensive longitudinal ethological study of infant and caretaker behavior at home and in the laboratory, Ainsworth has both elaborated Bowlby's formulation and added descriptive insights of her own. Her work, along with a recent extension of Bowlby's control system model by Bischof (1975) and a recent review by Sroufe and Waters (1977a, 1977b), points the way toward an integrative view of infant–adult ties in terms of the organization of affect, cognition, and behavior in the structure of behavioral systems.

Ainsworth's major conceptual and descriptive contributions to an ethological–organizational view of infant–adult ties lie in her development of two related concepts, the *attachment–exploration balance* and the *secure base phenomenon.* In Bowlby's (1969) control system model, the set goal guiding the infant's attachment behavior was maintenance of a certain degree of proximity to an adult. Although this has the advantage of accounting for the goal-corrected aspect of the infant's behavior, it suggests unfortunate analogies with the imprinting phenomena observed in precocial birds and mammals. That is, it is essentially a unidirectional model. It defines interinfant–adult distance in terms of the physical distance of the infant from the adult and thus overlooks complex aspects of the infant's active interest in the environment.

Ainsworth has reformulated the unidirectional model in terms of a bidirectional model of the attachment–exploration balance. A major function of the attachment behavioral system is to mediate the infant's excursions into the environment and to shift the balance of behavior from exploration to proximity seeking in response to various contingencies. Notably, Ainsworth points out that infants not only return to attachment figures in response to external stimuli but also reliably approach, signal, or make contact as part of an ongoing monitoring of the adult's availability. The emphasis upon the attachment–exploration balance as the basic unit of analysis in observing the infant–adult tie is an important descriptive insight that has not been matched by modified S–R or causal trait analyses. Because the attachment–exploration balance is best observed during extended observations of a variety of behaviors in a variety of contexts, emphasis on this aspect of the infant–adult tie highlights the importance of coordinating laboratory observation with ethological studies of the infant and adult on their own territories. It also points to one possible disadvantage of equating a constructlike attachment with one or a few behaviors without first evaluating patterning and functional equivalences that may be evident only in naturalistic settings and over a period of time.

The *secure base phenomenon* refers to the observation, mentioned above, that an infant often approaches an attachment figure spontaneously or seeks contact for affection as often as for comfort or safety. Within Ainsworth's formulation, the set goal of the attachment behavioral system is not the congruence of interpersonal distance with an internal criterion but rather the congruence of the infant's appraisal of a variety of internal and external inputs with a criterion of *felt security.* Affect is a major component of our experience in adult–adult ties, and the infant's distress and despair during separation and its happy greetings upon reunion suggest that affect is part of its experience as well. But in Bowlby's control system model, information (discrepancy) rather than affect is the primary influence on behavior. There is no evaluation of the meaning of a real world–set goal discrepancy. Loevinger (1976) has pointed out that the inability to explain the evaluative influences on behavior is one of the consistent failures of cognitive models of behavior and development. We are still unable to explain the origin of affect in infant–adult ties, but a first step is to recognize that affect and evaluative appraisals are major inputs into the attachment behavioral system. Recognition of the role of affect in the organization of attachment behavior has important implications for assessment that are described below.

Bischof (1975) has presented an elaborate general systems formulation of the attachment–exploration balance and has incorporated the notion of felt

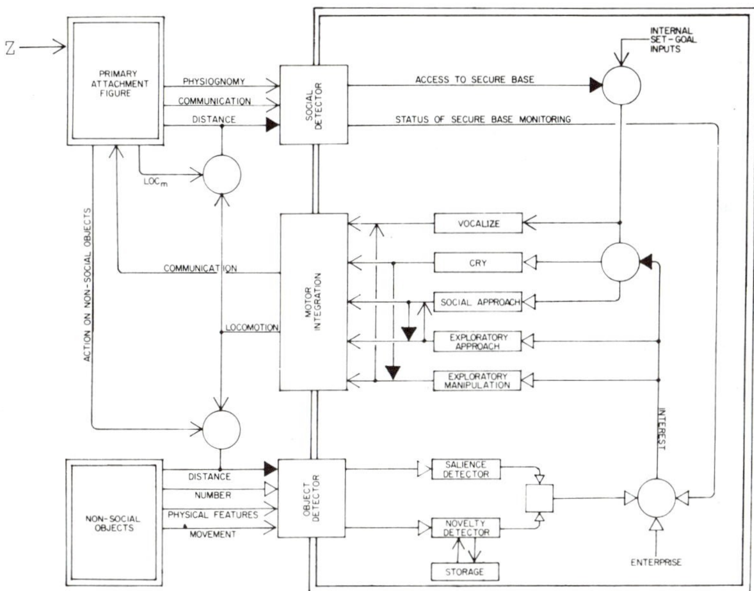

Figure 25.1. Simplified model of attachment and exploratory systems.

security into his model. And although he sees it as only a second step toward conceptualizing behavior in systems terms, it is an elegant integration of current theories of attachment, fear, and exploration. The model also suggests interesting possibilities for incorporating individual differences such as dependency and enterprise as codeterminants of the action of behavioral systems. In Figure 25.1 I have proposed a simplified and modified extension of Bischof's model of attachment and exploratory systems and their interactions. I have retained Bischof's notation and although the model may seem complex at first glance, it is in fact much simpler than an infant. A closer approximation to a complete model would certainly be vastly more involved. Nonetheless the model proposed here can convey the sense of a behavioral systems approach to the attachment construct; it can help summarize the observations and predictions upon which an ethological–organizational attachment theory rests; and in emphasizing the context sensitivity and environmental responsiveness of attachment behavior, it can vividly illustrate the limitations of simple trait models.

The symbols used in the model are as follows. Organisms and objects (e.g., primary attachment figure, nonsocial objects, infant) are enclosed by double lines. The larger system represents the infant, and only its internal systems are presented. Blocks indicate systems or subsystems within the infant system. These may involve either sensory processing or motor programming. Variables within the infant system are indicated by arrows. The orientation of the arrowheads indicates the direction of causation: Arrows pointing toward blocks (inputs) act on arrows leading from the same blocks (output variables).

Arrows originating in open space (e.g., internal set goal inputs) are influences not fully specified by the model but worthy of note. Arrows branch when a variable acts on more than one block. Open triangular arrowheads indicate that a variable is positively correlated with the output variables it influences. Solid triangular arrowheads indicate that a variable is negatively correlated with the output variables it influences. Two-line arrowheads indicate influences that can be either positive or negative and are not specified by the model. Small open circles represent an operation resembling addition (inputs are added or subtracted to determine influence on output). Small squares represent an operation resembling multiplication (if either input is zero, the value of output is zero). Note that only a few of the features of the primary attachment figure and of nonsocial objects that can influence the infant are indicated by arrows between these systems. The many external factors that can influence the primary attachment figure are represented by the single arrow, Z. Finally, within the infant system, arrows indicating motor outputs (more precisely, outputs to action skills) are connected by arrows simply to reflect a few of the operations accomplished during motor integration and that limit the value of single behaviors as indices of attachment.

The major differences between the present model and Bischof's involve the elimination of a complex array of motivational constructs and drives from the infant system, definition of causal arrows in terms more directly tied to attachment theory than to motivational theories, and specification of motor output interactions. In brief, the model specifies that the infant's attachment behaviors are complexly influenced in a coordinated manner by features of the social and nonsocial environment and by the structure of the attachment behavioral system. Within the infant system, exploratory behavior is influenced by characteristics of nonsocial objects, by an individual differences variable reflecting the consequences of past behavior (enterprise), and by the status of the secure base monitor (essentially a function of time away from the adult and/or change in the location or behavior of the adult). Similarly, proximity-seeking behavior is influenced by the accessibility of the primary attachment figure, by internal set goal inputs such as infant state, recent events in the environment, and perhaps by selected individual differences. In addition, proximity-seeking behavior is influenced by the degree of competing interest elicited by salient and novel objects in the environment.

In contrast to trait models that equate all instances of similar behaviors, the model distinguishes two types of locomotion, social approach and exploratory approach. The latter can be directed toward nonsocial objects, unfamiliar social objects, and even attachment figures, especially during play and interaction that involves sharing objects. Thus approach per se is not invariably an index of attachment, and approach to objects has different implications than approach to conspecifics. The model also specifies that related modes of motor response can be viewed as alternatives and that they need not be expected to show strong positive correlations, as required by trait models.

A much more complex model would be required to capture the actual complexity of the attachment–exploration balance, much less the variety of behavior in interactive play between infant and adult. The model proposed here at least has the advantage of pointing to the types of data needed for extensions of this approach. In addition, it defines the attachment–exploration phenomenon in a complexity that is closer to the behavioral details and at the same time apparently beyond the scope of the trait constructs that have dominated attachment theory for so long.

The attachment–exploration balance is so characteristic of the infant–adult relationship that Ainsworth (1973b; Ainsworth et al. 1978; Stayton et al. 1973) has suggested that clear evidence of this kind of organization in the infant's behavior in a variety of situations is the best criterion for the existence of an attachment to an adult in infancy. It is important to note that using this criterion the Strange Situation procedure is not an adequate technique for determining the onset of attachment. Indeed, Ainsworth has never used it for this purpose or for the purpose of assessing the strength of attachment relationships. The Strange Situation provides opportunities to observe a variety of behaviors that, if they can be validated against concurrent observations of the attachment–exploration balance in the field, can be used to assess individual differences in the adaptive functioning of the attachment behavioral system. This, of course, involves the complex problem of developing an appropriate measurement model and the elaboration of attachment theory along lines necessary to support this model. Progress in the assessment of attachment relationships through the use of behavior categories as an alternative to individual discrete behaviors and through the use of profile analyses and classification schemes has recently been summarized by Ainsworth et al. (1978).

Attachment as an ethological–organizational construct: redefinition and implications

Attachment and the meaning of behavior. A wide variety of behaviors support the development of the attachment relationship or mediate proximity seeking and contact maintenance after attachments have formed. These have been labeled *attachment behaviors* because they have the predictable outcome of promoting infant–adult proximity and interaction. This use of the term is consistent with Wiggins's (1974) suggestion that such labels should refer to likely social outcomes of a behavior rather than to some quality of the act itself. Unfortunately, the term *attachment behavior* has most often been interpreted in the latter sense. That is, because the behavior is identified with the attachment construct, it becomes an index of attachment when measurements are required (e.g., Coates et al. 1972a, 1972b; Feldman & Ingham 1975; Masters & Wellman 1974). Although this is entirely consistent with trait models discussed above, it is quite different from the meaning of attachment behavior within an ethological–organizational perspective.

A behavior is an attachment behavior by virtue of, and only insofar as, it is employed in the service of the attachment behavioral system. Most of the individual behavioral signs of the secure base phenomenon are independently present in the infant's behavior prior to the onset of attachment. Eventually these behaviors become integrated with the attachment behavioral system (or they do not) on the basis of experience (Ainsworth 1973b). And, as discussed above, any behavioral skill can serve more than one behavioral system. Sucking and proximity seeking are two clear examples. Bowlby (1969) identified nutritive sucking and nonnutritive sucking as behaviors that promote infant–adult proximity and contact; and yet sucking is also used extensively in exploration throughout infancy. Although it supports the infant's interest in the outside world, it is surely not an index of relationships formed with inanimate objects; nor does its absence in a father's arms mean that he will not become an attachment figure. Similarly, approach behaviors often serve the attachment behavioral system in the operation of the attachment–exploration balance. As such, they are often heightened by threats to the infant (separation, strangers, injury). Approach behaviors also serve the infant's active interest in exploring new environments. Infants often use adults as instruments of their exploratory goals: They find a new toy and carry it to an adult, not because they need proximity but because they need help. In other cases, an infant will approach an unfamiliar adult in what is clearly an exploratory approach rather than a sign of attachment. These approaches often include offering a toy and rarely end in physical contact; they are often followed by a full or partial retreat to an attachment figure, with continued visual regard of the unfamiliar adult. Exploratory approaches of this kind are influenced by the same variables as exploratory behavior toward toys. That is, they are clearly related to the exploratory side of the attachment–exploration balance and do not indicate attachment to an unfamiliar adult.

Cohen (1974) has suggested that because attachment relationships are focused or specific to one or a few figures, the best criterion for validating a behavior as an index of attachment would be differentiality toward presumed attachment figures. In her view, an attachment behavior should be shown more often toward a presumed attachment figure than toward a stranger. Unfortunately, because most behaviors that serve the attachment system can serve other functions as well, it seems possible to design situations in which any of them will be exhibited more often toward nonattachment figures. Needless to say, they remain attachment behaviors under the conditions and in the sense described above.

Whenever attachment relevance is viewed as a quality of a behavior, contextual influences are necessarily ignored. This problem is solved within an ethological–organizational approach by considering the structure and function of the attachment behavioral system when we interpret the meaning of behavior. In addition, we consistently consider the behavioral context in which behavior occurs whenever we attempt to define behavior categories. The importance of this is evident from Tracy et al.'s (1976) demonstration that approach behavior is strikingly differential toward attachment figures when an infant is distressed and when the behavior is defined as approach ending with a bid to be picked up. Approaches mediated by toys are either not shown differentially or are shown more often to nonattachment figures in nonstress free choice situations.

Main's research on active avoidance of the mother upon reunion (Chap. 26) provides excellent examples of the role of context within the ethological–organizational approach. When an infant is distressed by separation and yet refuses to look at or aborts a full approach toward its mother, the attachment behavioral system is clearly not operating in the service of the usual set goal. Under other circumstances, however, an infant's refusal to abandon a toy or an infant's change of direction from the mother to a nearby toy seems to indicate that the infant is comfortably using the mother as a secure base from which to explore. The attachment behavioral system is working as usual. Observers can readily make these distinctions, though the scoring of avoidance does require training.

Maccoby and Feldman (1972) and Feldman and Ingham (1975) have scored avoidance operationally in terms of looking away from the mother, without consideration of context, and have failed to find consistency across time or the kind of correlates reported in Ainsworth et al. (1978). Avoidance is dismissed as "distraction" or preoccupation with toys. Nonetheless, Sroufe and Waters (1977a) have provided a degree of discrimination between distraction and active avoidance of attachment figures through the use of concurrent heartrate recordings. When avoidance is scored, some infants have failed to show characteristic heart rate deceleration in response to objects visually fixated during play. Close behavioral observation suggests that avoidant infants are in fact often looking through or past the objects of their apparent attention, and manipulation of the objects (if any) is often repetitive and stereotyped. This clearly gives the impression of displacement activity, which is Ainsworth's and Main's interpretation of active avoidance upon reunion. In addition, in a study of 50 infants, Waters (1978) reported that avoidance scores were clearly much more stable from age 12 to age 18 months ($r = 0.62$) than scores based on the number of times an infant looked at its mother ($r = 0.22$).

The point here is that within the ethological-organizational approach, the same meaning is not attributed to every instance of phenotypically similar behaviors. The meaning of behavior is acknowledged to be a function of context, including behavioral context. In addition, it is recognized that behaviors can be grouped into meaningful categories on the basis of criteria other than phenotypic similarity. Categories may consist of behaviors that have similar eliciting or terminating conditions, predictable outcomes, developmental histories, correlates, and so on, regardless of whether the behaviors also serve a variety of functions. Any behavior category is a construct and requires validation.

The meaning of attachment. From an ethological–organizational point of view, an infant is attached to an adult when its behavior toward the adult is organized in a manner characteristic of control by the attachment behavioral system. That is, the emergence of the attachment–exploration balance and the secure base phenomenon is the criterion for the presence of an infant–adult bond. To be attached to an adult means that the adult can play a specific role vis-à-vis the operation of the attachment behavioral system. This requires that the infant be able to discriminate the adult from other adults, that he have acquired some expectations as to the adult's behavior in various situations, that infant and adult acquire a repertoire of reciprocal signals and behaviors to mediate interaction, that the infant have some internal mechanism for coordinating behavior toward the adult, and that this mechanism be attuned or sensitive to (calibrated for) features of the adult and the typical environment.

Attachment is a product of learning, to be sure, but of a more complex learning experience than the accretion of so many discrete behaviors.

Masters and Wellman (1974), Gewirtz (1972b), and Cairns (1972) have objected to formulations in which the attachment is an entity residing within the infant. Rosenthal (1973) and Weinraub et al. (1977) have also objected to the idea of a structural basis for attachments. Rather than allow that there is an individual contribution to the dyadic phenomenon labeled *attachment,* they suggest that the attachment exists entirely within the interaction between infant and adult. According to the ethological–organizational point of view, however, there is a structural basis for attachment and it does reside within each individual. But it is not the attachment per se, and it does not completely define a relationship. What resides within the infant is the attachment behavioral system that mediates attachment behavior and a store of experience built up during interaction with the adult in question. Attachment figures are defined as those with respect to whom the attachment behavioral system can function.

It could be objected that conceding an individual contribution to the development and maintenance of attachments does not necessarily entail constructs such as the attachment behavioral system. Perhaps an individual brings nothing more than the familiar repertoire of social/cognitive problem-solving and role-playing skills to interpersonal encounters. That is, the individual contribution might not be as specific to attachment as the behavioral system concept implies. In this regard, it is worth noting that there are individuals who are unable to form attachments (McCord & McCord 1964; Rutter 1972). There is no evidence that a comprehensive explanation of this phenomenon (psychopathy) or of the *affectionless character syndrome* can be made by reference to specific cognitive deficits. Rutter (1972) has reviewed the literature on maternal deprivation and concluded that it is most clearly associated with *bond privation,* the failure to form bonds early in life. From an ethological–organizational point of view, this suggests that the attachment behavioral system is never fully established in these cases. The organization of behavior but not the content of the behavioral repertoire would thus be deficient. This hypothesis is consistent with the clinical picture in such individuals, and thus the hypothesis of an attachment-specific individual contribution to interpersonal ties finds some support here.

Strength of attachment. When attachment is thought of as a unitary drive or causal trait and operationalized in terms of the amount of attachment behavior shown, the major dimension of individual differences becomes the strength of the attachment. The more attachment behavior, the stronger the bond.

When we study infants of an age at which attachment relationships are first developing (7 to 10 months), it seems reasonable to suggest that the more often aspects of the attachment–exploration balance are seen, the more confident we can be that an attachment behavioral system is in operation. Later (12 to 24 months), when all normal home-reared infants can be assumed to have formed attachments to at least one or a few adults, neither the operating characteristics of the behavioral system nor the qualities of the relationship with an attachment figure can be described by the amount of behavior seen. Analogies are easy to think of: The more often a man goes to the bank, the more confident we are that he has some money in an account. But we cannot infer from the frequency of his visits how much money he has or what he plans to do with it or even that he manages his finances well.

From an ethological–organizational point of view, the strength of an attachment bond could perhaps refer to the resistance of the bond to dissolution. How much time and experience would be necessary for an attachment figure to become a neutral input to the attachment behavioral system under all circumstances? For adults this can often take years, if it is accomplished even then. And it clearly is not correlated with either the amount of interactive behavior that typified the relationship before the separation or the degree of protest or distress after separation. Strength of attachment is a concept more akin to the notion of penetrance of relationships, discussed below, than to any operating characteristic of a behavioral system. Although the term *strength of attachment* does mean something, it does not correspond to the dimensions of individual differences that are usually of interest in developmental research. Moreover, it does not seem to be a concept amenable to ethical developmental research.

Development. Operationalizing attachment in terms of one or a few criterion behaviors (usually separation protest and/or following) has led to the conclusion that attachments emerge fully formed toward the end of the first year of life (Coates et al. 1972a; Shaffer & Emerson 1964). Attachment is said to be present when the indices of strength are greater than zero. This view certainly does not leave much for the developmentalist to do, beyond observing the frequency with which discrete behaviors arise during the second year of life and then decline.

The view that attachment relationships emerge fully formed and then change only in intensity is not consistent with the view that attachment is based on the operation of a behavioral system. Behavioral systems develop; they have to be put together, and they change across time. Stayton et al. (1973) have reported a developmental progression in infant responses to separation that seems to reflect the development of a behavioral system rather than the emergence of a unitary drive or a fully formed behavioral trait. Their observations of routine separations at home (mother moves from room to room or leaves the house briefly) indicate that the infant's earliest responses to separation involve only positive greeting of the adult on reunion (early in the second quarter of the first year). Separation protest was seen late in the second quarter, followed by some instances of continued crying and mixed greetings on reunion early in the third quarter of the first year. Following in response to separation emerged late in the third quarter of the first year. From a behavioral systems point of view, these observations are much more interesting for what they tell us about the organization and control of behavior than they are for what the data on individual behaviors might tell us about the onset of strength of an infant–adult tie.

Finally, from a developmental point of view, the concept of strength of attachment has the disadvantage of implying that beyond the second year of life, attachments must either weaken or become a developmental liability. Emphasis on the secure base phenomenon, however, suggests that flexibility rather than dependency is the hallmark of the typical infant–adult tie during the end of the first year and into the second year of life. Attachment is not normally the antithesis of interest in the environment. Thus it seems important to work toward a conceptualization in which infant–adult and later adult–adult ties can be viewed as assets in the development of competence rather than as liabilities.

ATTACHMENT AS A RELATIONSHIP

Both trait constructs and behavioral systems models refer to individual contributions to interactive social situations. Neither explicitly refers to the history of interaction that characterizes each infant–adult dyad. Indeed neither explicitly analyzes attachment as a dyadic phenomenon with a history or affords a means of describing differences in the attachment relationship either across time or across dyads. Thus the concept of a relationship seems indispensable to any definition of the child's tie to an adult (or an adult's tie to a child). It captures the breadth of interactions that constitute interpersonal experience, and it provides descriptive insights into qualitative differences that are not encompassed by the notion of the strength of a tie. The analysis of relationships also has the advantage of placing the infant–adult tie and its constituent interactions in a broader temporal framework than trait attributions have in the past. Relationships develop and change in time, and yet retain a quality that Hinde and Stevenson-Hinde (1976) call *dynamic stability*. The issue of stability or continuity within change is a central one in developmental theory, and it seems that detailed behavioral description, analyses of behavioral systems, and judicious use of trait attributions can each play important roles in efforts to face the issue.

The feasibility of characterizing relationships, and the advantages of doing so where feasible, have been demonstrated in several ethological studies of infant responses to separation and reunion. Hinde and Spencer-Booth (1971, 1971a) have demonstrated that the distress shown by infant rhesus macaques after reunion with their mothers is related to certain aspects of the infant–mother relationship prior to separation. In particular, measures of how often the infant's attempts to gain contact with the mother were rejected, and measures of the infant's active role in maintaining mutual proximity to the mother when they were not in contact, were related to the infant's ability to be comforted by contact. Ainsworth et al. (1971) have demonstrated similar phenomena in human 1-year-olds. And indeed, a wide range of studies within the ethological perspective point to the generalization that the quality of relationships rather than the quantity or intensity of interaction is the better predictor of the development of social competence (see Ainsworth et al. 1978 for reviews).

Hinde (1975, 1976; Hinde & Stevenson-Hinde 1976) has recently outlined a view of the relationship between social interaction and social relationships. Both the theory and its application provide descriptive insights that would not have been possible within the quantitative trait paradigm. At the same time, they offer new opportunities for the assessment of dimensions of infant–adult ties that, with appropriate measurement models, may reveal greater consistency than has been apparent in studies of discrete behaviors. They also suggest new possibilities for the descriptive use of trait attributions in developmental theory.

Describing relationships

A relationship involves a series of interactions (Hinde 1976). One reason that modified S–R models cannot capture qualities often attributed to relationships arises from this fact. The determinants of interactive behavior between individuals who have a long history of interaction do not necessarily lie within a given interaction. They often lie in the (relatively) remote past.

To describe relationships, it is necessary to describe both the content and quality of interactions that occur within the relationship.

> It is necessary to describe what A did to B (and B to A). They may for instance be talking or fighting or kissing. In addition we must specify how they are doing it – are they talking in an animated or dispassionate fashion? What are they talking about? Are they fighting savagely? Kissing passionately, tenderly, or dutifully? In more general terms, to what extent are they involved in what they are doing? To what extent are the different aspects of their behavior consistent with each other? . . . We may refer to such properties of interactions as *qualities,* without of course any implication that they cannot be subjected to quantitative treatment. *In human interactions such qualities can be as or more important than what the interactants actually did together.*
>
> [Hinde 1976:3]

In addition to the content and qualities of interactions, it is also necessary to describe how the interactions are patterned, their absolute frequencies, relative frequencies, when they occur with respect to each other, and how they affect each other. Ultimately, we make an abstraction in characterizing a relationship from observations of interaction. The contrast to the cumulative discrete behavior approach lies in taking the meaning of behavior into account, that is, in paying attention to the behavioral context of behavior, in realizing that all instances of a behavior are not equivalent. This is contextualism as opposed to situationalism.

Dimensions of relationships

In addition to the methodological and measurement problems discussed above, trait theories of attachment have consistently narrowed our view of the range of individual differences in infant–adult relationships. Overemphasis on the strength of infant–adult ties will not be corrected by improving methodology and measurement techniques. We need to develop a broader conceptual framework in which to define the attachment construct.

Hinde (1976) has suggested a number of dimensions along which relationships can be said to differ: (1) content of component interactions; (2) diversity of interactions; (3) reciprocity versus complementarity; (4) qualities of component interactions; (5) relative frequency and patterning of interactions; (6) multidimensional qualities (e.g., "warmth," "rejectingness"); and (7) levels of perspective. There are undoubtedly more that could be added to the list. But a brief outline of the relevance of these dimensions to the description of infant–adult relationships will demonstrate the sense in which we often narrow our perspective when we define the attachment construct to fit a point of view (be it social learning theory, strict operationalism, quantitative trait theory, or a preference for a particular methodology).

Content of interactions. The quality of any relationship may depend on the presence or prominence of certain types of interactions. Infant–mother attachment relationships certainly entail many different kinds of interactions that are never observed in the laboratory or that cannot be captured in terms of discrete behavioral acts (e.g., categories of interactive behavior such as play, affection, punishment). We can use the content of interactions to distinguish among types of relationships (e.g., friendship versus love), as well as to distinguish between different relationships of the same type. For example, we are more likely to describe a relationship as harmonious if there is a predominance of positive affect in interaction and if interactions are initiated and concluded without conflict rather than if negative affect and conflict predominate. Brief observations are not well suited to these types of data, nor are observations in only one or a few contexts or occasions.

Diversity of interactions. Some infant–mother relationships are largely characterized by routine caretaking, whereas others appear to have more breadth, a wider range of interactive patterns. Some mothers may see their interactions with their infants in terms of a few types of interaction, whereas others view the same behaviors in more highly differentiated terms. One feels trapped; another finds it anything but routine. All relationships change in the diversity of interactions across time, a fact not reflected in the analyses of Strange Situation behavior. Hinde (1976:5–6) discusses several reasons for the diversification of interactive behaviors within a relationship.

Reciprocity versus complementarity. Infant–adult interactions are dyadic affairs. That is, they are better viewed in terms of the role each partner plays in the behavior of the other than in terms of the behavior of each taken alone (Cappella 1981; Hartup & Lempers 1972; Hinde & White 1974; contributors to Lewis & Rosenblum 1974). When both participants in an interaction show similar behavior patterns, the interaction is said to be reciprocal in nature. When the interaction is carried out by the meshing of different repertoires of behavior, the relationship is said to be complementary. Infant–adult interactions are, by nature, complementary in the beginning. But dyads differ in the extent to which complementarity is developed. Insofar as a mother allows and facilitates her infant's participation in interaction, she is laying the foundation for the later development of reciprocity, in what Bowlby (1969) calls a *goal-corrected partnership.* Ainsworth has spoken of this aspect of interaction in terms of the mother's cooperation versus interference with the infant's ongoing behavior (Ainsworth et al. 1971, 1977). Hinde proposes that complementarity and reciprocity in interactions and the extent to which interaction is codetermined or unilaterally dictated are important determinants of both stability and change in relationships.

Qualities of interactions. One important quality of interactions within relationships is the extent to which the behavior of one partner is coordinated with or meshes with the behavior of the other. Ainsworth has discussed maternal sensitivity to infant signals in just those terms (Ainsworth et al. 1971). Sensitivity involves (1) perceiving the signal, (2) correctly interpreting it, (3) selecting an appropriate response, and (4) delivering the response in a timely (or contingent) fashion. A given maternal behavior in response to a signal may be timely and appropriate, or it may be inappropriate or too delayed for the infant to notice the contingency. Sensitivity or contingent responsiveness may be characteristic of a wide variety of interactions or limited to one or a few domains (e.g., play but not feeding or other caretaking situations). There are, of course, many more qualities of infant–mother interactions that could be mentioned. Because the rewards obtained in a relationship may depend not only on what the participants do together but also on how they do it, Hinde suggests that qualities of interactions may be of crucial importance for the stability of relationships.

Relative frequency and patterning of interactions. We are not always interested only in the absolute frequency of different behaviors or types of interaction. For example, the relative rather than absolute frequency of maternal behaviors is the key characterizing interactions as responsive or unresponsive. In addition, certain emergent qualities of interactions (e.g., consistency) are not characteristic of any one interaction but only of the patterning of interactions across time.

Multidimensional qualities. Many qualities of interactions cannot be identified with the presence/absence or intensity of a given behavior, but depend instead upon the concurrence of a number of characteristics. Many everyday judgments about relationships turn out to depend on such multidimensional observations. For example, Hinde (1976) suggests that we are most likely to describe a relationship as an affectionate relationship (or bond) if:

1 It involves a diversity of interactions
2 It is of long duration
3 Both partners act to regain proximity when separated from one another
4 The behavior of each is organized in relation to the ongoing behavior of the other
5 The presence of the partner alleviates distress due to strange objects or situations
6 Actions conducive to the welfare of the other are likely to be repeated

Not all of these characteristics imply bonding or attachment, nor is each always present in such relationships. This characterization points, among other things, to the weakness of unidimensional characterizations of relationships (as in strength) and to the inherent weakness of simple operational definitions of multidimensional phenomena. It also makes clear that such qualities will be hard to assess from brief observations of a few behaviors in only a few contexts on only a few occasions.

Levels of perspective. Relationships differ in the level of cognitive complexity with which either or both partners view themselves, each other, the relationship, and so on. They also differ in terms of the congruence of perspectives within a relationship. Infant–adult relationships are strikingly asymmetrical in this respect. In addition, some adults are more realistic than others in their view of what they or their behavior means to an infant. As mentioned above, a major goal of the analysis of infant–adult interaction is to analyze the behavior involved in terms of the level at which it has an impact upon the infant or adult. It is worth repeating that it is not enough to "call them as we see them." In the study of infant–adult ties, attention to levels of perspective implies careful attention to developmental level, probably more attention than we see in comparisons of 12-month-old and 3-year-old behavior in the Strange Situation. Do such comparisons tell us more about the nature of the parent–child tie at different ages or about children's perceptions of the Strange Situation?

Prospects for the study of relationships

The view of relationships sketched here affords opportunities that have not been seized upon in previous attachment research. First, it offers a level of analysis and a unit of analysis that complements both the trait and the behavioral systems approaches. Whereas the trait and behavioral systems models emphasize the individual and his contribution to interaction, the relationship perspective emphasizes the dyad as the basic unit of analysis and focuses on the interactions to which the individual contributes. In this regard, recent suggestions that we shift from emphasis on individuals to emphasis on interactions (e.g., Weinraub et al. 1977) seem as limiting as the imbalances they propose to correct. The coordination of individual and dyadic levels of analysis seems to offer more and can play an important role in expanding our descriptive approach to attachment phenomena and their adaptive significance.

So far, the dimensions of relationships outlined above represent only an early conceptual analysis. The approach is continuing to evolve, and at some point conceptual dimensions will have to be operationalized in terms of measures. In developing means of measuring dimensions of relationships, we would do well to learn from our experience with trait constructs in earlier attachment research. We should recognize the power of the individual-differences measurement models developed within the trait paradigm and take advantage of them in the assessment of dyadic relationships. We should also take advantage of the approaches to reliability and validity developed within that tradition. At the same time, the relationship between measurement models and the construct being measured needs to be kept more explicit than in the past. Relationships can be assessed in terms of dimensions without assuming that these dimensions are causal influences on the behavior of the individuals involved and without assuming that relationships are not responsive to environmental influences. But these are tempting modes of thinking after so much practice. Wiggins's (1974) and Endler and Magnusson's (1976) papers are well worth rereading with the problem of assessing relationships in mind.

Finally, the study of relationships seems to offer new and concrete prospects for interdisciplinary analyses of attachment phenomena. The prospects for fresh input from sociological, anthropological, and social psychological research and theory seem particularly inviting because these approaches have been kept at arm's length by our overemphasis on the individual as the unit of analysis. In brief, the consideration of models of the attachment construct offers fertile ground for cross-paradigm communication and promises at least to broaden our descriptive view of attachment phenomena. It is hoped that the effort will foster more constructive communication across theoretical orientations as well.

SUMMARY

Cross-paradigm communication in the study of infant–adult ties has long proven difficult. The problem appears to lie in part in the failure to look beyond theoretical (psychoanalytic, social learning, ethological) orientations in order to examine models of the attachment construct. Most attachment research has implicitly involved a causal trait model of the construct. This has led to emphasis on intensity or strength of attachment bonds as the major dimension along which relationships develop and differ.

Trait models generally imply that (1) trait dimensions (e.g., dependency) are the major determinants of behavior, (2) individuals' scores on trait dimensions are related to response measures in a simple linear manner, and (3) individual differences on trait dimensions are stable over time and situations. In more recent formulations, trait language is used only to summarize consistency in behavior, not to explain behavior. In addition, recent approaches have moved toward recognition of the environmental responsiveness of individual differences.

The most influential critiques of the attachment construct are in fact critiques of the classical trait concept and have limited empirical or conceptual implication for the study of attachment from other perspectives. A behavioral systems approach to infant–adult ties emphasizes the mechanisms that organize attachment behavior and coordinate it with exploratory behavior. This model can help analyze the individual's contribution to social interaction and present a much more complex descriptive picture of attachment phenomena than is often reflected in laboratory-based attachment research of the past.

Models of relationships emphasize the infant–adult dyad as a unit of analysis and suggest dimensions along which relationships differ. The analysis of relationships complements the study of behavioral systems, and both suggest roles for the study of individual differences variables. It is to be hoped that consideration of models of the attachment construct will facilitate broader descriptive research and constructive communication across paradigms in the study of this important aspect of behavioral development.

ACKNOWLEDGMENTS

The author wishes to thank those who read and commented on previous versions of this chapter, especially Mary Ainsworth, Gordon Bronson, Wanda Bronson, Jack

Block, Jeanne Block, Stanley Coren, Robert Hinde, Mary Main, Alan Sroufe, Brian Vaughn, and Jerry Wiggins.

REFERENCES

Ainsworth, M. 1973a. The development of infant–mother attachment. *In:* B. Caldwell & H. Ricciuti (eds.), *Review of child development research,* vol. 3. University of Chicago Press, Chicago.

1973b. Infant development and infant–mother interaction among Ganda and American families. Paper presented at the Wenner-Gren Conference on Cultural and Social Influences in Infancy and Early Childhood, Burg Wartenstein.

Ainsworth, M., S. Bell, & D. Stayton. 1971. Individual differences in strange-situation behaviour of one-year-olds. *In:* H. R. Schaffer (ed.), *The origins of human social relations.* Academic Press, London.

1972. Individual differences in the development of some attachment behaviors. *Merrill-Palmer Quarterly* 18:123–143.

Ainsworth, M., M. Blehar, E. Waters, & S. Wall. 1978. *Patterns of attachment.* Erlbaum, Hillsdale, New Jersey.

Ainsworth, M., & B. Wittig. 1969. Attachment and exploratory behavior of one-year-olds in a strange situation. *In:* B. Foss (ed.), *Determinants of infant behavior,* vol. 4. Barnes & Noble, New York.

Altmann, J. 1974. Observational study of behavior: sampling methods. *Behaviour* 49:227–267.

Baerends, G. P. 1972. A model of the functional organization of incubation behaviour. *In:* G. P. Baerends & R. H. Drent (eds.), *The herring gull and its egg. Behaviour Supplement* 17:261–310.

Bertalanffy, L. von. 1969. *General systems theory.* Braziller, New York.

Bischof, N. 1975. A systems approach towards the functional connections of fear and attachment. *Child Development* 46:801–817.

Bowlby, J. 1969. *Attachment and loss,* vol. 1, *Attachment.* Basic Books, New York.

Bronson, G. 1972. Infants' reactions to unfamiliar persons and novel objects. *Monographs of the Society for Research in Child Development:* 37, serial no. 148.

Burghardt, G. 1973. Instinct and innate behavior: toward an ethological psychology. *In:* J. Nevin & G. Reynolds (eds.), *The study of behavior: learning, motivation, emotion, and instinct.* Scott, Foresman, Glenview, Illinois.

Cairns, R. 1972. Attachment and dependency: a psychobiological and social learning synthesis. *In:* J. Gerwitz (ed.), *Attachment and dependency.* Winston, Washington.

Campbell, D., & D. Fiske. 1959. Convergent and discriminant validation by the multitrait-multimethod matrix. *Psychological Bulletin* 56:81–105.

Capella, J. 1981. Mutual influence in expressive behavior: adult–adult and infant–adult dyadic interaction. *Psychological Bulletin* 89:101–132.

Coates, B., E. Anderson, & W. Hartup. 1972a. Interrelations among attachment behaviors of infants. *Developmental Psychology* 6:218–230.

1972b. The stability of attachment behavior in the human infant. *Developmental Psychology* 6:231–237.

Cohen, L. 1974. The operational definition of human attachment. *Psychological Bulletin* 81:207–217.

Cronbach, L., & P. Meehl. 1955. Construct validity in psychological tests. *Psychological Bulletin* 52:281–302.

Endler, N., & D. Magnusson. 1976. Toward an interactional psychology of personality. *Psychological Bulletin* 83:956–974.

Engel, G. 1971. Attachment behaviour, object relations and the dynamic–economic points of view: critical review of Bowlby's Attachment and Loss. *International Journal of Psychoanalysis* 52:183–196.

Feldman, S., & M. Ingham. 1975. Attachment behavior: a validation study in two age groups. *Child Development* 46:319–330.

Gewirtz, J. 1972a. Attachment, dependence, and a distinction in terms of stimulus control. *In:* J. Gewirtz (ed.), *Attachment and dependency.* Winston, Washington.

1972b. On the selection and use of attachment and dependent indices. *In:* J. Gewirtz (ed.), *Attachment and dependency.* Winston, Washington.

Hartup, W., & J. Lempers. 1972. A problem in lifespan development: the interactional analysis of family attachments. *In:* K. Schaie & P. Baltes (eds.), *Life-span developmental psychology,* vol. 3. Academic Press, New York.

Hinde, R. 1970. *Animal behavior: a synthesis of ethology and comparative psychology,* 2nd ed. McGraw-Hill, New York.

1974. *Biological bases of human social behavior.* McGraw-Hill, New York.

1975. Mothers' and infants' roles: distinguishing the questions to be asked. In CIBA Foundation Symposium 33. Associated Scientific Publishers, New York.

1976. On describing relationships. *Journal of Child Psychology and Psychiatry* 17:1–19.

Hinde, R., & Y. Spencer-Booth. 1971. Effects of brief separations from mother on rhesus monkeys. *Science* 173:111–118.

1971a. Towards an understanding of individual differences in rhesus infant–mother interactions. *Animal Behaviour* 19:165–173.

Hinde, R., & J. Stevenson (eds.).1973. *Constraints on learning.* Academic Press, New York.

Hinde, R., & J. Stevenson-Hinde. 1976. Towards understanding relationships: dynamic stability. *In:* P. P. G. Bateson & R. Hinde (eds.), *Growing points in ethology.* Cambridge University Press, London.

Hinde, R., & L. White. 1974. The dynamics of relationship: rhesus monkey ventroventral contact. *Journal of Comparative and Physiological Psychology* 86:8–23.

Kuhn, T. 1962. *The structure of scientific revolutions.* University of Chicago Press, Chicago.

Lewis, M., & L. Rosenblum (eds.).1974. *The effect of the infant on its caregiver.* Wiley, New York.

Lieberman, A. 1977. Preschoolers' competence with a peer: influence of attachment and social experience. *Child Development* 48:1277–1287.

Loevinger, J. 1976. *Ego development.* Jossey-Bass, San Francisco.

Maccoby, E., & S. Feldman. 1972. Mother-attachment and stranger-reactions in the third year of life. *Monographs of the Society for Research in Child Development* 37.

Main, M., S. Londerville, & L. Townsend. 1979. Compliance and aggression in toddlerhood: precursers and correlates. Unpublished manuscript. University of California, Berkeley.

Marler, P., & W. Hamilton. 1966. *Mechanisms of animal behavior.* Wiley, New York.

Masters, J., & H. Wellman. 1974. Human infant attachment: a procedural critique. *Psychological Bulletin* 81:218–237.

Matas, L., R. Arend, & L. Sroufe. 1978. Continuity of adaptation in the second year: the relationships between quality of attachment and later competence. *Child Development* 49:547–556.

McCord, W., & J. McCord. 1964. *The psychopath: an essay on the criminal mind.* Van Nostrand, New York.

Miller, G., E. Galanter, & K. Primbram. 1960. *Plans and the structure of behavior.* Holt, New York.

Mischel, W. 1968. *Personality assessment.* Wiley, New York.

1973. Toward a cognitive social learning reconceptualization of personality. *Psychological Review* 80:252–283.

Nunnally, J. 1967. *Psychometric theory.* McGraw-Hill, New York.

Rosenthal, M. 1973. Attachment and mother–infant interaction: some research impasses and a suggested change of orientation. *Journal of Child Psychology and Psychiatry and Allied Disciplines* 14:201–207.

Rutter, M. 1972. *Maternal deprivation: reassessed.* Penguin Books, Baltimore.

Schaffer, H., & P. Emerson. 1964. Patterns of response to physical contact early in human development. *Journal of Child Psychology and Psychiatry* 5:1–13.

Sroufe, L. 1979. The ontogenesis of emotions. *In:* J. Osofsky (ed.), *Handbook of infant development.* Wiley, New York.

Sroufe, L., & E. Waters. 1976. The ontogenesis of smiling and laughter: a perspective on the organization in infancy. *Psychological Review* 88:173–189.

1977a. Heartrate as a convergent measure in clinical and developmental research. *Merrill-Palmer Quarterly* 23:3–27.

1977b. Attachment as an organizational construct. *Child Development* 48:1184–1199.

Sroufe, L., E. Waters, & L. Matas. 1974. Contextual determinants of infant affective response. *In:* M. Lewis & L. Rosenblum (eds.), *The origins of fear.* Wiley, New York.

Stayton, D., M. Ainsworth, & M. Main. 1973. The development of separation behavior in the first year of life: protest, following, and greeting. *Developmental Psychology* 9:213–225.

Tracy, R., M. Lamb, & M. Ainsworth. 1976. Infant approach behavior as related to attachment. *Child Development* 47:571–578.

Waters, E. 1978. The reliability and stability of individual differences in infant–mother attachment. *Child Development* 49:483–494.

Waters, E., J. Wippman, & L. Sroufe. 1979. Attachment, positive affect and competence in the peergroup: Two studies in construct validation. *Child Development* 50:821–829.

Weinraub, M., J. Brooks, & M. Lewis. 1977. The social network: a reconsideration of the concept of attachment. *Human Development* 20:31–47.

Wiggins, J. 1974. In defense of traits. Unpublished manuscript. University of British Columbia, Vancouver.

26

AVOIDANCE IN THE SERVICE OF ATTACHMENT: A WORKING PAPER

MARY MAIN

The present chapter has three principal aims. The first is to describe a pattern of social behavior that is surprisingly prevalent in human infants reunited with their attachment figures. This is the active visual, physical, and communicative avoidance of the mother that appears following stressful major separations (probably for most human infants) and sometimes following even very brief separations (for infants previously experiencing threat and physical rejection by the mother). Understanding the appearance of this behavior in this circumstance is critical to an ethological understanding of human infant social behavior, because it is precisely antithetical to the behavioral expectations that biologically oriented attachment theory (Bowlby 1969, 1973) and recent functional interpretations of infant–parent relationships (Trivers 1974) provide. In this circumstance, according to these theories, only an exaggeration of distress, angry behavior, and physical approach to the attachment figure are expected.

Although visual and physical avoidance of prospective social partners appears in nonhuman as well as human infant and adult animals (e.g., Chance 1962; Erwin et al. 1971; Tinbergen 1959; Tinbergen & Moynihan 1952; van Iersal & Bol 1958), it is not treated as a major category of behavior in any of the animal behavior texts that I know of, nor in any psychology text that I know of, and it certainly is not recognized as such in studies of human infants. Nonetheless, I believe it is a major category of social behavior.

The second aim of this chapter is to review empirical studies of the correlates of this behavior pattern as it appears in human infants. Thus, in the second section of the chapter, I shall show that the human infant's response to separation and reunion relates to both parental and infant behavior observed in other circumstances. The response to reunion with the attachment figure seems to reflect important aspects of the history of the relationship. At the same time, the reunion response is highly predictive of the infant's social and emotional behavior in other situations. Infants who strongly avoid the mother and show no anger following separation are, for example, likely to attack or threaten to attack her in (presumably) stress-free settings.

The final aim of this chapter is to consider alternative explanations of the behavior pattern. Work conducted to date suggests that we are ready to rule out some otherwise rather obvious explanations (e.g., failure to have become attached to the parent, random failure to show attachment to the parent, constitutionally controlled temperamental differences). In this section, I shall also consider what I see as viable beginning explanations of ontogeny and immediate causation. These explanations, in turn, suggest one or several possible biological functions for a behavior that must otherwise be seen as incompatible with survival.

These proximate and ultimate explanations must be seen as speculative, however. The greater part of the work of understanding lies ahead.

SOCIAL AVOIDANCE BEHAVIOR: A BRIEF DESCRIPTION

Attachment behavior

This chapter is intended chiefly to discuss the appearance of avoidance of attachment figures in circumstances in which it is not expected – following major separations, in association with rejection by the mother, and in response to friendly overtures or even to physical contact with the mother. Before embarking on a study of a pattern deviant from expectation, however, it may be well to describe the norm from which the pattern departs (Medawar 1967). This leads to a brief description of what is actually expected in such circumstances and the reason that it is expected. What is expected in such situations is attachment behavior.

Attachment behavior is defined as any behavior that has the predictable outcome of increasing or maintaining proximity between one person and another (Bowlby 1969). Thus signaling to the attachment figure (crying, calling), approaching the attachment figure (creeping, reaching, running), and clinging to the attachment figure may all be considered attachment behaviors in the right context. The context in which such behaviors can best be regarded as attachment behaviors is, of course, any context in which the attachment behavioral system may be reasonably presumed activated: Toddlers creep toward toddlers to snatch toys, but in this context this approach is not considered attachment behavior (see Chap. 25 for a discussion of this issue).

Within an established attachment relationship, forms of angry behavior may also be presumed to serve the function of increasing proximity (Bowlby 1969; see also Trivers 1974). Thus, an infant's tantrum may persuade the mother either to approach herself or to permit approach by the infant; in turn, a mother's angry behavior often brings the infant toward her. Anger may serve a similar proximity-promoting function in well-established adult attachment relationships.

When may we expect to see attachment behavior, and what is its function? Bowlby (1969, 1973) has developed an ethological theory of attachment that rests upon two related sets of observations. One consists of the fact that both human and nonhuman primate infants show a strong and even violent concern with maintenance of proximity to attachment figures. In the case of human infants living in protected environments, this concern can appear irrational. The other consists of the fact that, for most nonhuman primate infants – and presumably for human infants in the environment of evolutionary adaptedness

– survival is almost entirely dependent upon maintenance of proximity to the attachment figure. The infant separated from its attachment figures has usually lost food, water, warmth, shelter, and protection from predators.

Bowlby has developed a theory of the evolutionary origins of the *attachment behavioral system* in primate infants, including humans. It is presumed that under all but extremely abnormal rearing conditions, this system will develop and insure the maintenance of proximity to protective figures. Thus, the system is presumed to have a strong genetic base (to be genetically canalized), although learning is involved in its development at every point. It is presumed, therefore, that almost all human infants will (1) develop preferences for some persons over others on the basis of social interaction; (2) express these preferences clearly once object permanence is achieved; (3) respond negatively, even angrily, to threats of separation while seeking increased proximity and even contact with the attachment figure in this case and (4) in the case of any threats from the environment. Thus, threats of separation from the mother, acts of physical rejection by the mother, and alarming conditions in the environment are presumed to activate the system at particularly high intensities.

In fact, most infants observed in U.S. samples do respond to these changes in circumstances as predicted by Bowlby (see Ainsworth et al. 1978 for a summary of observed responses to brief separations, strangers, and strange environments).

Avoidance of prospective social partners

The social avoidance that is the topic of this chapter is, in fact, limited in degree and somewhat difficult to describe in kind. It refers to movements directed away from a prospective social partner, for example, to gaze aversion, movements away of the head or upper body, turning the back, and moving out of contact or immediate proximity. It also refers to failure to respond to communicative acts of the social partner and even to apparent lack of recognition of a familiar partner. Grouping these behaviors together as might casual observers, we could say that these are behaviors that seem to maintain or increase the physical or communicative distance – or even the level of involvement – between partners. But such a definition rests on casual observation only; some of these behaviors could be *acts* of communication, and in this case this definition is not satisfactory.

The word *avoidance* is clearly not ideal for such a set of behaviors. It has the advantage of descriptive neutrality, but unfortunately, it immediately brings to mind the extreme behavior pattern of flight rather than the limited social avoidance here described. Limited movements that block vision have been termed *cut-off* behaviors by Chance (1962), but I do not choose this term for general use because it refers primarily to acts of visual avoidance and is highly interpretive. (It refers, in fact, to a specific presumed function of the behavior.)

Consideration of the varying ethological interpretations of social avoidance behavior is left to the final section on causation. However, the reader interested in obtaining a broad overview of the literature concerning facial and visual avoidance in animals and man is referred to excellent reviews of facial–visual communication available in Vine (1970, 1973). He is also referred to a study of human gaze interactions (Argyle & Cook 1976).

Avoidance in human infants: variations in degree and in appearance. What does avoidance look like as it occurs in human infants interacting with adult social partners? In a work concerned with human children, Tinbergen and Tinbergen (1973) discuss a most subtle form of avoidance behavior (which they describe as "the mildest form of rejecting behavior"). This consists of:

> a certain expression of the eyes, which is very difficult to describe but which (as we know for instance from novels) is known to many people. It is often described as an "empty" or "blank" expression, also as "letting the mental shutters down" – it is a vague, expressionless look, often aimed slightly *past* the adult's eyes . . . This initial response of the child is, *if the observer keeps looking at it,* followed by partial or complete closing of the eyes. This can be, but is not always, very slow; sometimes so slow that one has the impression that "the eyelids have a very long way to go." When closing the eyes is total, the eyelids look completely smoothed out – not even slightly creased, pressed, or "screwed up," as eyes look when closed on other occasions except in sleep. [Tinbergen 1973:179–180]

The Tinbergens refer here to young children responding to strangers. However, I have now filmed about 400 reunions between infants (12 to 20 months) and parents in a laboratory setting. In this situation, parents call the infant from outside the door, open the door, greet the infant, and make clear that an approach is welcome. In half the episodes, the parent is instructed to pick up the infant and hold it. In some infants filmed in my laboratory, the blank expression and eye closing described by the Tinbergens is the first response to reunion with the parent.

Gaze aversion is another, perhaps slightly less subtle, form of avoidance. This too is not infrequently the first response to reunion with the parent. But how can looking away from someone be distinguished from looking at something else? Waters et al. (1975) used repeated review of videotapes to distinguish the two behaviors. When gaze truly shifted from one object (a person) to another (perhaps an object), an infant often blinked in transition. In the case of gaze aversion, blinks rarely occurred in the transition. To me, this suggests a shift in attention in one case, but not in the other. Waters et al. emphasized (as do the Tinbergens) a peculiarly smooth closing movement of the eyelids accompanying real gaze aversion.

My (as yet unsystematized) impression is that infants viewing the parent from a distance cannot maintain simple gaze aversion for long. Either (often) the infant again looks toward and perhaps greets the parent; or it turns fully about and moves away; or it searches in a rather disorganized way for something to do with its hands. Often it seizes upon a nearby inanimate object. The search for something to do (seize, touch, handle) is striking.

A close repeated viewing of films of the apparent exploratory behavior that occurs immediately on reunion reveals that the inanimate object generally has far from the infant's full attention. The infant may, for example, rather frantically turn toward a table leg and finger it (but with eyes fixed blankly on the wall ahead). Or, in a clumsily decisive move, it may suddenly drop a toy into a box but then (staring straight ahead) close the box on its hand. The general impression is, again, that the infant could not succeed in maintaining its avoidance of the parent without the aid of the object seized.

Studies using telemetry equipment to monitor the infant's heartbeat on reunion support the view that attention to objects at such moments is not complete. Exploration (attention) is normally accompanied by heartrate deceleration, but exploration on reunion fails to show the normal decelerating pattern (Sroufe & Waters 1977). However, after a few moments (if the parent does not insist on attracting attention), exploration seems to recover its normal pattern. The infant who has avoided its parent in this manner may continue to orient itself carefully with its back to the parent for a longer time. In other cases, it may (despite the parent's silence) rise and finally approach the parent.

Some infants respond to reunion with the parent with alternating movements of approach and avoidance. Thus, I have seen a number of infants start for the parent and, without looking up into the parent's face, veer immediately aside and continue to move away at least a short distance. This behavior has a strange appearance. The change from approach to avoidance does not seem related to any changes in the environment, but only to the infant's having reached a certain proximity to the parent. It is my impression that this is usually about a 90-cm distance. Often I cannot see indications of a decision to continue; instead, the change from approach to avoidance is smooth, unhesitating, and hence almost mechanical.

Finally, we may consider the way in which an infant may avoid the parent when the parent attempts physical contact or even simply a friendly verbal or visual overture. Infants who have strongly avoided the parent on reunion but have, nonetheless, been picked up generally make clear their desire to be put down in a subtle manner. Thus, rather than struggling in the parent's arms or protesting vocally, such infants subtly bend toward the floor or indicate a wish for an object. If the parent holds such an infant and tries to gaze at or address it, the infant may seemingly attempt to distract the parent's attention by pointing to an object at some distance (cf. Chap. 24). Freed and set on the floor, the infant occupies itself with an object. Strongly avoidant infants such as these may appear deaf and blind if the parent later attempts to attract attention from a distance.

This has been a summary of informal observations only. In the following section, the reader will see how the behavior is scaled and assessed more formally. This section, it is hoped, has given some overview of the essentials of and variations in the behavior pattern.

REVIEW OF EMPIRICAL STUDIES

Avoidance of attachment figure following major separations

Avoidance of a parent following separations of brief (minutes) duration has been noted only recently; Ainsworth and Bell made their first formal observations of this behavior pattern in 1970. Avoidance of the parent following major separations has, however, long been noted by clinical investigators. The following is a brief review of studies of response to major separations in children between 1 and 3 years of age. By *major* is meant a separation lasting from just over a week to several months.

The first observation of avoidance of an attachment figure I know of was made by Darwin (1877:292). He noted that his 2-year-old son kept his eyes "slightly averted from mine" – for the first time – following his father's absence of 10 days from home.

In 1944, Burlingham and Freud observed avoidance of an attachment figure in a 2-year-old in care in their war nursery. This child was passionately attached to his nurse, who married and consequently left the nursery. He was described as "completely lost and desperate" after her departure, and yet he "refused to look at her when she visited him a fortnight later. He turned his head to the other side when she spoke to him, but stared at the door, which had closed behind her, after she had left the room. In the evening he sat up and said: 'My very own Mary-Ann! But I don't like her'" (1944:63).

Further studies of responses to major separations have been summarized by Bowlby (1973). Children undergoing major separations from parents in environments in which no substitute parental figure is made available (a consistent nurse, etc.) show increasing distress and anger in the separation environment. Over the period of separation and in the separation environment, angry behavior is shown increasingly toward objects, adults, and other children without apparent provocation (e.g., Heinecke & Westheimer 1965).

In general, if the parent visits early in the separation, angry behavior (as well as anxious attachment behavior and distress) is readily exhibited. But if the separation lasts long enough, the parent is typically met instead with avoidance.

These changes in reunion behavior are generally preceded by changes in behavior in the separation environment, and Robertson and Bowlby (1952) have described the child as going through stages of *protest, despair,* and *detachment.* In the stages of protest and despair, the child's concern is centered increasingly despairingly on the absent parent. The child takes little or no interest in the (multiple) attendants,[1] and if the parent visits, the child shows both angry behavior and attachment. Left longer in the separation environment, the child begins to settle in or adapt to it, taking some interest in both the attendants and the toys available. It is in this stage, when reorganization of behavior in terms of the new environment has been achieved, that the child responds to visits or reunion with avoidance. Bowlby and Robertson describe this as the stage of *detachment.*

A controlled observational study of children undergoing major separations (3 to 20 weeks) was conducted by Heinecke and Westheimer (1965). Stable substitute caregivers (assigned to a particular child) were not available. All children had been observed prior to the separation: All were in good health, and several had previously enjoyed secure and harmonious relations with their mothers. Heinecke and Westheimer observed the moment of reunion for each child and mother: "At the time of reunion, all the separated children were unable to respond affectionately to the mother. In order of frequency, this took the following forms: physical avoidance, remaining present but not responding with affection, and apparent lack of recognition" (1965:280). Some children turned their face or back to the mother. The reactions described were seen in relation to the mother and rarely to the father. Lack of recognition seemed not to reflect a failure of memory; rather, it seemed to occur with reference to the person to whom the child was most strongly attached; the child would "fail" to know the mother, yet greet the father with warmth and familiarity (as seen in Freud & Burlingham 1944). In fact, in the Heinecke and Westheimer report, nine of the children responded with affection to the father.

This initial detached response to reunion with the primary attachment figure generally lasts only a few hours or days. Rather than being replaced by either a gradual renewal of the relationship or a return to previous harmonious interaction patterns, it is typically replaced with a disturbance of a specific nature. This consists of an anxious and clinging concern with the whereabouts of the attachment figure and sudden and unprovoked (unpredictable or inexplicable) bouts of hostility and negativism (Heinecke & Westheimer 1965; Robertson & Robertson 1971). This disturbance wanes gradually.

Heinecke and Westheimer proposed that the initial avoidant response to reunion could best be understood as serving a defensive function, permitting the child to maintain control over an anger (and probably distress) that has grown too intense to otherwise permit continued behavioral organization. Because anger is one of the emotions the strongly avoidant child does not exhibit on reunion, this must remain as inference. In the Heinecke and Westheimer report it is, however, based upon a strong correlation between avoidance of the mother on reunion and angry behavior observed in other settings.

Classifications of relationships on the basis of response to brief separations in the laboratory setting: the Ainsworth system

My own studies over the past 3 years have been concerned almost exclusively with the appearance of avoidance in normal infants who have never experienced major separations. Some have been seen as they are reunited with the parent at the end of a day in day-care centers. Most have been seen in the Ainsworth Strange Situation. Each infant observed is assigned a score for the degree to which it avoids the parent upon reunion.

In order for the reader to understand my studies of correlates of avoidance, it is necessary first to present the laboratory procedure utilized (the Ainsworth Strange Situation) and a classification system that permits most infants observed in this situation to be categorized as secure or insecure (insecure-ambivalent or insecure-avoidant) in relation to the mother.

The Ainsworth Strange Situation. The Ainsworth Strange Situation is an established laboratory procedure developed by Ainsworth and Wittig (1969) and used by them to highlight the operation of the *attachment behavioral system* (Bowlby 1969) in normal infants 1 year of age. The situation is designed to elicit exploratory behavior in the early episodes and then, through a series of mildly stressful events, to shift the infant's attention to the maintenance of proximity and contact with the mother.

Infant and mother are introduced to a comfortable laboratory room filled with toys. A stranger enters the room; the mother leaves the infant in the company of the stranger; the mother returns; the mother leaves the infant alone; the stranger returns; the mother returns once more for the second and final reunion episode. Each of the seven episodes lasts 3 minutes unless the infant is more than mildly distressed: Separation episodes are often curtailed by the experimenter, and in my own studies at Berkeley, episodes in which the infant is distressed are reduced to 30 seconds. The situation is described in somewhat greater detail in Chapter 25.

The critical systems of analysis devised by Ainsworth for infant Strange Situation behavior focus upon negative behavior (avoidance and angry resistance) observed in relation to the mother during the two reunion episodes when mother and infant are alone with each other. Most other investigators to date have focused upon frequency counts of the occurrence of attachment and affiliative behaviors in this situation. However, for both statistical (Waters 1978; Chap. 25) and theoretical (Main 1977a) reasons, behaviors of this kind observed in this situation are unstable, uncorrelated, and uninformative (see Masters & Wellman 1974 for an apt critique of these studies).

Ainsworth et al. (1971, 1978) have devised a classification system for infant–parent relationships that permits categorizing of most (not all) infants seen with the parent in the Strange Situation. Infants are classified in three major categories as *secure, ambivalent,* or *avoidant* in relation to the parent. Classifications are based upon infant rather than parental behavior in the Strange Situation, and behavior in reunion episodes is emphasized. As this system was devised using a sample of infant–mother dyads and has to date been used largely with mothers, I shall generally refer to mothers in what follows. My own recent work has shown, however, that the classifications may be used just as readily to describe the behavior of infants with their fathers (Main & Weston 1981).

Infants are classified as secure in relation to the mother when they actively seek proximity and contact following separation, and when these behaviors appear unmixed with strong anger or avoidance. In the preseparation episodes, securely attached infants may examine the toys and explore the strange environment. They may or may not be distressed upon separation, but if they are, the mother's return readily comforts them and enables them to return either to an engagement in play or to pleasant interaction with the mother. At the same time, infants classified as secure (as opposed to avoidant) often show some anger in the Strange Situation. The behavior takes the form of angry crying upon separation, greeting the mother with an outraged cry on reunion, and irritatedly batting away toys if she tries to entertain them rather than to hold them. Angry behavior in all these forms can, of course, be seen as proximity-promoting behavior (see Bowlby 1973).

Infants classified as either ambivalent or avoidant are regarded as insecure in relation to the mother by Ainsworth et al. Infants are classified as ambivalent when they both seek proximity and contact upon reunion, yet resist it, and seem to find little security in the mother's return or presence. Infants classified as ambivalent are often distressed even before the first separation and fearful of the stranger. They are extremely distressed on separation. Proximity seeking may be relatively weak rather than active. In general, these infants seem immature, and their response to the Strange Situation seems regressive and exaggerated.

Infants classified as secure and ambivalent may both show some degree of avoidance in one or even both reunion episodes of the Strange Situation. In fact, although most infants seek proximity and contact with the parent following separation, analyses of videotaped reunions in my laboratory show that a majority of infants (about 80%) show at least brief gaze aversion or blankness immediately upon reunion.

Infants showing strong avoidance of the mother in both reunion episodes are generally classified as avoidant and exhibit a syndrome of associated behaviors. Infants classified as avoidant actively avoid and ignore the mother on reunion, even when she seeks their attention. Picked up, they indicate (in an emotionless way) a desire to be put down, often by pointing to a toy or other object as though to distract the mother's attention. They are often markedly more friendly to the stranger than to the mother (which, of course, makes their treatment of the mother all the more pointed). Throughout the Strange Situation they generally attend to the toys or the rest of the inanimate environment. Unlike other infants, they show virtually no distress, no fear and, most important, no anger.

Interjudge agreement on the classification is very high (Ainsworth et al. 1978; Main et al. 1979; Matas et al. 1978). The distribution of categories varies surprisingly little for seven white middle-class samples seen throughout the United States. One-half to two-thirds of infants are judged secure; one-fifth to one-third avoidant; and a small minority ambivalent. No relationship has been found to the number of siblings, sex, or birth order (Ainsworth et al. 1978; Connell 1976). I should perhaps note that in my own studies I have found approximately 10% of infants (about 16 out of 160) unclassifiable within the Ainsworth system (Main & Weston 1981). This is not surprising, given that the system was devised by Ainsworth to represent the behavior of only 23 dyads.

Studies of white middle-class dyads conducted by three independent sets of investigators (Connell 1976; Main & Weston 1981; Waters 1978) have shown high stability in classification between successive sessions. Waters had independent judges classify infants seen with the mother at the two time periods; 48 out of 50 infants first seen at 12 months remained in their original classification at 18 months. Main and Weston found classifications for fathers as well as for mothers stable from 12 to 20 months.

Note, however, that stability of classification is found only when infants are seen in successive Strange Situations separated by a long interval. Ainsworth et al. (1978) conducted repeated Strange Situations with infants 50 and 52 weeks of age. Although scores for avoidance were stable across the sample (i.e., order was preserved), avoidance on the whole diminished significantly and was replaced by distress and proximity seeking. Clearly this second laboratory separation experience following so soon upon the first was highly stressful. Some infants in the sample cried immediately on finding themselves returning to the same environment. Not one infant classified as avoidant in the first Strange Situation could be clearly classified as avoidant in the second.

Strange Situation classifications related to behavior in other settings. Classifications of infant–mother relationships made in the Strange Situation have been found to be strongly related to both maternal and infant behavior observed in other settings. Ainsworth et al. have published a series of studies showing a strong relationship between the behavior of the infant and mother observed throughout the first year of life and infant Strange Situation security classifications. In recent years, several other independent samples have been collected by other investigators. These samples have employed the Strange Situation at 12 or 18 months but have compared the classifications to relatively brief (usually videotaped) sessions of observation.

Mothers of infants who have been or will be judged secure in the Strange Situation are distinguished for their sensitivity to the signals and communications of the infant (see a series of studies summarized in Ainsworth et al. 1978) and for their supportive presence as they observe their infants engage in problem solving (Matas et al. 1978). In the first quarter of the first year of life, they are found to hold their infants more tenderly and carefully than mothers of infants who will be judged insecure; and at 21 months they show far less anger toward them (Main et al. 1979). Sylvia Bell (reported in Ainsworth et al., op. cit.) has observed a sample of 33 black welfare mothers and infants. In her sample, mothers of secure infants were also judged more affectively positive and more responsive than mothers of insecure infants.

Secure infants differ from insecure infants. They are, for example, more cooperative than insecure infants when observed with both their mother and with other persons (Londerville & Main 1981; Matas et al. 1978; Stayton et al. 1971). In both black and white samples, secure infants show more positive affect; and they are more enthusiastic and persistent in tool using at 24 months (Matas et al. 1978).

Main and Weston (1981) have seen infants in the Strange Situation with each parent, the mother at 12 months and the father at 18 months or the reverse. The joint classification (e.g., secure with mother, avoidant with father) is then used to predict behavior in a situation in which a third person attempts for some time to make friends with the 1-year-old. Infants secure with both parents easily engage in the new relationship; infants secure with neither show little or no interest in this person; and infants secure with just one parent fall in between.

Differences between secure and insecure infants last well beyond infancy. Very recent studies show that they appear not only when infants are observed with adults but with peers as well. Waters et al. (1979) examined videotapes made of an abbreviated Strange Situation test (one separation only) conducted at 15 months by Wanda Bronson at Berkeley. The children were judged secure or insecure in relation to the mother in this situation. The same children were observed again by Bronson et al. at 3.5 years in the nursery school setting. Children classified as secure with the mother at 15 months were found more competent with peers at 3.5 years; in addition, they significantly exceeded the children classified as insecure in ego strength and effectance. Over 2 years after the abbreviated Strange Situation, the securely attached infants were, for example, more sought by other children, less withdrawn, more sympathetic to the distress of peers, more self-directed, more curious, and more likely to be leaders.

In a different study conducted in Minnesota (Gove et al. 1979), children judged secure in the Strange Situation at 18 months have been found more "ego-resilient" (more able to adapt resourcefully to changing personal and environmental circumstances; see Block & Block 1979) in kindergarten. This greater resiliency was shown both in a battery of experimental situations devised by Block and Block (frustration tasks, problem-solving tasks, etc.) and independently in descriptions provided by their kindergarten teachers.

Avoidance of attachment figures, following brief separations

The studies reviewed below are studies of whole samples, that is, they include children classified as secure, avoidant, ambivalent, and unclassifiable. As noted earlier, children receiving high scores for avoidance are generally classified as avoidant, but children in other classifications may show low to moderate avoidance.

The avoidance scoring system: reliability, stability, and field-to-laboratory validation. Ainsworth has developed an *interactive scoring system* that scores infants (from one to seven points) on the degree to which they show avoidance of the mother. The system is unusual in that (1) differences in adult as well as child behavior are taken into account and (2) it is presumed that several different kinds and/or combinations of behaviors can serve the same goal and indicate activation of similar intensities. Each scale point is identified by several alternative behavior patterns.

The highest score on the scale is given to the baby who fails to greet its mother upon her return and then pays little or no attention to her for an extended period despite her efforts to attract its attention. Moderate scores are given to brief but clear-cut avoidance (the baby may begin to approach, but then turn away and ignore the mother for a while) or persistent low-keyed withdrawal (the baby may greet the mother casually and then return to play with toys in a manner suggestive of most babies in the preseparation episodes). Low scores are given to very brief delays in responding to the mother's return or brief instances of mild avoidance such as gaze aversion.

Avoidance can be scored on the Ainsworth scale with very high interrater reliability (e.g., Ainsworth et al. 1978). Means on the seven-point scale for white middle-class samples seen throughout the United States vary little.

In four independent investigations (conducted in Baltimore, Minneapolis, and Bowling Green, Ohio) avoidance scores have been shown to be stable. Over a 2-week period, r (26) = 0.66 (Ainsworth et al. 1978); over a 6-month period, r (50) = 0.62 (Waters 1978; see also Connell 1976); and over an 8-month period in a sample of mothers and fathers seen at 12 and again at 20 months, r (30) = 0.59 (Main & Weston 1981).

These studies show the viability of the Ainsworth scoring system for laboratory observations, but an important further question is whether the behavior observed in the laboratory represents anything that occurs in the field. For this reason, I undertook a study of day-care infants (12 to 24 months). Each was observed in three completely uncontrolled reunions with the parent in the day-care setting and then observed with the same parent in the Ainsworth Strange Situation. The Ainsworth scoring system was easy to apply to the uncontrolled field setting. A person who had no knowledge of behavior in the day-care setting scored Strange Situation behavior. The center reunion avoidances were highly correlated with the two reunion episodes from the Strange Situation. Finally, means for the day-care setting and for the laboratory were virtually identical (Blanchard & Main 1979).

What follows is largely a review of my own studies. In four of these studies, I compare behavior on reunion with the parent in the day-care center or in the laboratory to behavior of the parent or infant in other settings. In each, persons coding or rating behavior observed outside of the Strange Situation have been blind to Strange Situation behavior. All studies have been concerned with medically normal, white middle-class infants, and scores for avoidance are determined for each infant in these samples. These studies consist of:

1 A sample of 38 infant–mother dyads observed in Baltimore in a videotaped play setting and a Bayley Developmental testing session at 21 months, 9 months after the Strange Situation. This sample is described more fully in Main (1977b) and Main et al. (1979).
2 The 23 mother–infant dyads observed by Ainsworth (also in Baltimore) throughout the first year of life. Each was observed for a total of 60 hours in the home situation and again in the Strange Situation at 12 months. Ainsworth has made the full record available for study.
3 The sample of 21 infants seen in day-care centers in Berkeley and previously described (Blanchard & Main 1979).
4 A sample of 60 infants seen with the mother and father, in the Strange Situation and in other laboratory sessions, in Berkeley (Main & Weston 1979).
5 A sample of 10 battered and 10 control children seen in day-care centers in the San Francisco Bay Area. This study did not employ the Strange Situation. However, avoidance of caregivers and peers who made friendly overtures was examined.

Infant characteristics associated with avoidance of the mother in the Strange Situation. Here we consider seven correlates of avoidance of the mother, observed largely in the samples described above.

1 *Avoidance of the mother in the Strange Situation is negatively related to angry behavior toward her (angry crying, hitting, batting away toys, open petulance) observed in the Strange Situation itself.*
2 *However, avoidance of the mother in the Strange Situation is strongly positively related to angry behavior toward her seen in other (stress-free) settings. Often it appears out of context.*

Using my Baltimore sample, I found that avoidance of the mother at 12 months was related to the following behaviors at 21 months: number of (largely unprovoked) attacks and threats of attack upon the mother; number of episodes of nonexploratory hitting and banging of toys; the mother's report that the child was troublesome; active disobedience in response to maternal commands; and scores for tantrum behavior assigned by the Bayley examiner.

These results led to an examination of home behavior between 9 and 12 months in the Ainsworth records. A coding of every episode of angry behavior was undertaken. No relation was found between the number of anger episodes and avoidance of the mother in the Strange Situation. However, there was a strong relation between the number of episodes in which the infant physically attacked or threatened to attack the mother in the home and avoidance on reunion in the Strange Situation. There was also a strong relation between avoidance in the Strange Situation and the number of inexplicable anger episodes in the home situation, that is, the number of well-described episodes for which the coder could find no apparent stimulus. These were often, but not necessarily, related to attacks upon the mother: Thus the observer might report, "The baby is creeping across the floor, smiling. Suddenly he veers toward his mother, strikes her legs, and creeps away."

In an ongoing analysis of the new Berkeley sample of infants and parents, we find an extremely strong relationship ($p < 0.0001$) between active disobedience of the father's commands and prohibitions in a play session and avoidance of the father in the Strange Situation.

3 *Avoidance of the mother is related to difficulties in other social relationships, that is, with persons other than the mother. Often other persons making friendly overtures are actively avoided.*

Blanchard and Main (1979) observed infants in the day-care setting (1 hour) and assigned scores for "social-emotional adjustment" to each infant. This was found significantly negatively related to avoidance of the parent (mother or father) on reunion in the day-care setting. In addition, in another in-progress study of data from the same sample, avoidance of the parent on reunion in the day-care setting was found positively associated with attacks and threats of attacks on caregivers and with avoidance of caregivers as they made friendly overtures.

In the videotaped play session of the Baltimore study, an adult "playmate" entered the playroom to invite the toddlers to engage in a game of ball. Infants who had strongly avoided their mothers tended not to approach the playmate as she greeted them. Those few who did so approached in a peculiar manner – abortively, or only after turning and spinning away, or (in one case) turning a full circle with hands cupped to the ears. A microanalysis of the interactive behavior of the most avoidant infant in the sample showed that she approached the playmate to the rear, or by turning about and backstepping.

Scores given for avoidance of the mother at 12 months were positively related to a simple count of instances of gaze aversion and physical avoidance of the playmate. Not surprisingly, given the foregoing, avoidance of the mother was also related negatively to the tendency to interact playfully with a test examiner in a separate session (Main 1973).

Finally, in an analysis of the new Berkeley sample, Main and Weston (1981) report a strong negative relationship between avoidance of the mother and the apparent readiness to establish relationships with adults attempting to make friends with the infant in a separate setting.

4 *Despite the fact that avoidance of the parent is related to avoidance of (or difficulties with) other adults making friendly overtures, there is no relationship between a given infant's avoidance of its mother and its father.*

This finding has been documented in the Main and Weston study of 60 infants seen with the mother and father (one parent at 12 months, one at 18 months) in

Berkeley. Whereas stability of avoidance of a given parent between 12 and 20 months is high, there is no relationship between scores for avoidance assigned to the infant when it is seen separately with the two parents (r (60) = 0.09).

5 *Avoidance is related to restrictions in affective responsiveness.*

Matas et al. (1978) report significantly less "positive affect" and "enthusiasm" in avoidant as compared to secure infants at 24 months. Gove et al. (1979) report that infants described at 18 months as avoidant are described as overcontrolled by their kindergarten teachers 3 years later.

In the Baltimore study, I found avoidance at 12 months negatively related to the number of instances of smiling or laughing about toys (my only affective measure). Work in preparation using the Berkeley sample indicates a strong negative relation between avoidance of the mother and emotional expressiveness.

6 *Avoidance is related to indices of conflict or disturbance – to odd behaviors and to stereotypies.*

In the Baltimore study, I noted the occurrence of some odd behaviors in strongly avoidant infants. I therefore asked an assistant to provide a tally of such behaviors in the videotaped (hour-long) play observation. This count included stereotypies, hand flapping, echoing of the mother's speech, inexplicable fears (as of small changes in the laboratory room between the time of the Bayley test and the play session), and striking instances of inappropriate behavior. This simple count of odd behaviors was significantly positively related to avoidance.

In the Ainsworth study, four of the six avoidant infants between 9 and 12 months of age showed odd behaviors, behaviors shown by hardly any other members of the sample. One baby stared and appeared to be "in a trance" at times, almost "autistic." Another avoidant baby was described as rocking repeatedly; he had odd vocalizations; his face was "devoid of affect," and he seemed "attached to objects and the environment more than people" – as did another avoidant baby. Clearly here – as, very broadly, in the Strange Situation – there is some symptomatic link to the cardinal attributes of autism.

In the current Berkeley study, we are looking for signs of disturbance (conflict-behaviors such as those listed above) in infants in a situation designed to elicit in sequence apprehension, positive affect, interest in another person, and empathy. Examining behavior at only 12 months, we find signs of disturbance in 75% of the infants classified as avoidant of both parents, but in only a few of those classified as secure with both (8%) or just one (15%) of the parents.

7 *There is no evidence that avoidance is associated either with advances or with deficits in cognitive or other functioning.*

As noted earlier, Waters et al. (1980) were unable to find differences between avoidant and secure infants at birth. I have failed to find a significant correlation between avoidance and the Bayley Mental Development scores or between avoidance and attention span, intensity of interest in objects, or instances of symbolic play at 21 months of age. Similar results (comparing avoidant with secure infants) have been reported by other investigators (Connell 1976; Matas et al. 1978; Waters et al. 1979).

Maternal characteristics associated with avoidance of the mother in the Strange Situation. For theoretical reasons (see Main 1977a), I expected that infant avoidance would be associated with maternal anger and with maternal aversion to physical contact or rejection of contact with the infant. Review of videotapes revealed, in addition, a third associate. (Data concerning the fathers' behavior in relationship to avoidance of the father is being collected but has yet to be analyzed.)

1 *Avoidance of the mother is associated with the mother's apparent aversion to physical contact with the infant.*

This supposition was first affirmed by an exhaustive review of the Ainsworth records for the entire first year of life. Mothers' apparent aversion to physical contact with the infant (as shown both through statements made to the observer - "I have always hated physical contact" - and through behavior toward the infant) was rated for the first 3 months of life. The mother's aversion to contact was very strongly related to avoidance of the mother at the end of the first year. The infant's early cuddliness, however, had no relation to avoidance. (Waters et al. 1980 have also failed to find a correspondence between differences in neonatal cuddliness and later avoidance.)

The mother's attitude toward contact was stable over the first year. Aversion to contact in the first 3 months (rated as above) was highly related to (coded instances of) rejection of the infant's initiations of contact in the fourth quarter [$r(23) = 0.71$]. Coded instances of the mother's rejection of contact in the home during the fourth quarter - "Don't touch me!" - were also highly related [$r(23) = 0.76$] to avoidance of the mother in the Strange Situation.

The mother's apparent aversion to physical contact with her infant has also been assessed using videotaped play sessions in both Baltimore (Main et al. 1979) and Berkeley (in preparation). In each sample, there is a strong ($r > 0.60$) relationship to avoidance of the mother in the Strange Situation.

2 *Avoidance of the mother is associated with angry and threatening behavior by the mother.*

A close examination of the videotapes from my Baltimore sample showed strong differences in maternal anger despite the presence of the camera. Mothers of mother-avoidant infants mocked their infants or spoke sarcastically to or about them; some stared them down. One expressed irritation when the infant spilled imaginary tea. Ratings showed a strong association between avoidance and maternal anger in this sample.

George and Main (1979) suggested that, because of the above associations between avoidance and maternal anger, the infants of abusing mothers should show a pattern of behavior similar to that of infants who strongly avoid the mother. In a partial confirmation of this prediction, they found that battered children observed interacting with peers and caregivers in day-care settings behaved (relative to matched controls) like infants who strongly avoid the mother on reunion in normal samples.Thus, they found battered infants more avoidant of peers and caregivers in response to friendly overtures, more likely to assault and threaten to assault them, and more likely to show unpredictable aggressive behavior toward caregivers.

In studies dealing directly with the response of abused children to reunion with the mother in the laboratory (Gaensbauer et al. 1981) or in the day-care setting (Lewis & Schaeffer 1979), abused children to date have been found typically avoidant.

Using the Berkeley sample of normal white middle-class dyads, Main and Weston (1979) observed occasional rough handling of the infant during transport or during disciplinary interventions in a playroom setting. In this brief (18-minute) observation, 45% of the mothers whose infants were classified as avoidant of the mother on reunion handled the infant roughly on occasion. Only 8% of infants judged secure were handled roughly.

3 *Avoidance of the mother is associated with restriction of the mother's affect expression.*

While undertaking the above analyses of the videotapes collected in Baltimore, it became clear to me that mothers of strongly avoidant infants were restricted in emotional expression. This was not confined to a failure to express pleasure: Some mothers showed no change of expression when physically attacked by their infants. In most cases, this restriction in affect expression appeared as detachment or stiffness rather than as bland unresponsiveness. Actual ratings for maternal inexpressiveness confirmed this association (the study is partially reported in Main et al. 1979).

Because this association had not been predicted, it seemed possible that it was a chance association particular to my Baltimore study. I therefore studied the entire year of the Ainsworth narrative data. The mother's inexpressiveness was again strongly related to infant avoidance.

Finally, this variable has also been assessed in the Berkeley sample. Once more, maternal inexpressiveness in a play setting has been found associated with infant avoidance in the Strange Situation. In addition, the father's inexpressiveness is highly associated with infant avoidance.

EXPLANATIONS THAT LIKELY CAN BE ELIMINATED

I hope that the review of the correlates of avoidance of attachment figures presented above has convinced the reader that the behavior is worthy of further study. This section begins with a review of some explanations of avoidance that are frequently offered and that I believe can be eliminated (at least as necessary conditions for the appearance of the behavior). Some of these explanations will seem most unlikely to the reader who is now familiar with the correlates of avoidance.

1 *The avoidant infant has simply failed to develop an attachment to the parent.*

Because infants who strongly avoid the parent show little or no attachment behavior in the reunion episodes of the Strange Situation, some investigators (e.g., Clarke-Stewart 1978) have simply considered them as yet nonattached to the parent. But in fact, whenever the case has been examined, infants who strongly avoid the parent on reunion (following brief or major separations) are those who are attached to the parent. This can be seen from the studies of responses to major separations reviewed at the beginning of this chapter. Not only were the avoidant children attached before the separation, but strong (anxious) attachment and angry behavior generally emerged on reunion a few hours or days after the initial period of cool indifference. In addition, Ainsworth's initial Strange Situation study of infant–mother dyads followed a full year's observation of the same infants and mothers in the home situation (Ainsworth et al. 1978). All of the infants classified as avoidant had developed an attachment to the mother several months before the Strange Situation. Three of the infants showing the strongest avoidance of the mother in the Strange Situation cried on even very brief separations from her in the home environment.

2 *The avoidant infant is attached but is simply not distressed by the Strange Situation.*

This argument rests chiefly on the observation that most infants classified as avoidant cry little or not at all in the Strange Situation. In this interpretation, avoidance is seen not merely in conjunction with lack of distress but as its consequence. For several reasons, this does not seem a compelling argument.

First, avoidance is a highly active response. An infant merely undisturbed by a brief separation from the parent generally greets the parent and returns to play; this is the case for most infants observed in the home environment. An infant who is merely not distressed has no reason to actively move away from, or seem deaf to, the parent who pursues or addresses it. Second, lack of overt distress is not a necessary prelude to avoidance. Some (few) infants both cry on separation and strongly avoid on reunion. Third, avoidance is selective: Why should a merely undistressed infant approach or even cling to a stranger but actively avoid and ignore its mother? Finally, heartrate acceleration (over a base rate established for an individual) is taken as an index of arousal/distress by many investigators. Sroufe and Waters (1977) report that heartrate acceleration upon separation from the mother is as great for avoidant as for secure (overtly distressed) infants in the Strange Situation. Thus the fact that the infant does not cry upon separation cannot be taken as a sign of indifference or lack of distress on every level. (In this context, it is interesting to note that some infants who have shown an impassive indifference throughout the Strange Situation break down in distress and anger immediately on being taken from the laboratory building.)

3 *The avoidant infant has an inherently greater interest in exploration.*

Infants who strongly avoid the parent on reunion often show a sudden preoccupation with a toy or other object at the moment of reunion. I have already reviewed the data showing that both heartrate indices and detailed behavioral observation indicate that the infant's sudden preoccupation with a toy at the moment of reunion is not a matter of the usual exploratory attention.

It is, of course, a fact that avoidant infants explore the toys throughout much of the Strange Situation, and that before and after the first moments of reunion their exploration does have a normal appearance. The question raised is whether this is an interest in exploration that appears in other situations and carries over into the Strange Situation, or whether (as I think likely) it is an interest that arises because of the circumstances. Analysis of behavior observed in other settings gives no indication that avoidant infants have a generally greater interest in exploration. Indeed, in a free play setting, avoidant infants have (albeit insignificantly) shorter attention spans in play with toys and less apparent interest in them than do secure infants (Main 1973).

4 *The avoidant infant is different constitutionally (temperamental avoidance).*

In the literature reviewed earlier, I showed that infants classified as avoidant of the mother on reunion differed from infants classified as secure both before and for several years after the Strange Situation. In addition, because the classifications were found stable over an 8-month period, the question of simple stability of temperament arises.

Three studies I am aware of are pertinent to this issue. All lead to the conclusion that what is being classified in the Strange Situation is not an individual with an unchanging temperament but rather a relationship that is formed between individuals and consequently is subject to change.

First, as noted earlier, Main and Weston (1981) found no relationship between classifications or avoidance scores when a given infant was seen with the two parents, although classifications and avoidance with a given parent were stable. This is a most unlikely finding if a temperamental avoidance factor were operative. Second, a study of children from lower-class families in Strange Situations with the mother at 12 and again at 18 months showed much lower stability of classification than is found in middle-class samples. The shifts in classification corresponded, however, to shifts in "life-stress" experienced by the mother (Vaughn et al. 1979). A lessening of the mother's life-stress between 12 and 18 months was accompanied by a shift in the infant's classification toward security, and vice versa. The third study bears directly on the question of early differences in behavior. A large sample of infants was seen from the first days of life, beginning with several Brazelton neonatal assessments (Waters et al. 1980). In addition to assessing some of the standard reflexes, the Brazelton test assesses alertness, social responsivity, and the ease with which the newborn infant can be comforted. The same infants were seen in the Strange Situation with the mother at 12 months. The investigators found no significant differences in the newborn period between infants later found avoidant and infants later found secure with the mother – but infants classified as insecure-ambivalent differed significantly from others even as newborns.

5 *The infant avoids the parent on reunion because of a reinforcement history (the parent has rewarded avoidance).*

According to some theories of learning (Hulse et al. 1975), almost every kind of voluntary behavior can be considered a *free operant,* and every operant can be conditioned to appear in certain circumstances providing its appearance in those circumstances has historically been *reinforced* (rewarded). A theory of the operant conditioning of attachment behavior to times and persons has already been offered (Gewirtz 1972).

It would seem at first glance that an operant conditioning analysis could readily be extended to avoidance. Thus differences in avoidance on reunion would be attributed to differing reinforcement histories. Infants who avoid a given parent on reunion would be presumed to have been reinforced for avoidance by that parent (perhaps by increased attention, by physical contact, or even by decreased attention) in the home situation. This explanation is compatible with the stability of avoidance to a given parent (stability of parental reinforcement for the behavior pattern) and with the fact that there is no relationship between avoidance of the mother and the father (there is no reason why both parents would reinforce avoidance). Differing reinforcement histories could account for differing degrees of avoidance.

This theory relating home behavior to Strange Situation behavior cannot be confirmed or disconfirmed without extensive home observation. However, studies of response to major separations show that operant conditioning cannot serve as a necessary condition for the appearance of avoidance. This is because avoidance in response to minor separations varies widely across dyads: Following the operant conditioning explanation, reinforcement for avoidance across dyads must then also vary widely. During major separations, there is no opportunity for parents to change a reinforcement history. The operant conditioning theory must then predict variations across dyads in the appearance of avoidance on reunion with the parent, even following major separations.

This prediction is, of course, incorrect: Virtually all infants left long enough in stressful circumstances avoid the parent on reunion. Because reinforcement histories must have varied for the many infants seen after a major separation, operant conditioning alone cannot explain the universal appearance of avoidance. (Anecdotally, I refer to two case histories. Darwin [1877] claimed to have seen avoidance in his son for the first time after a major separation. Robertson and Robertson [film] report that parents reunited with their 17-month-old son after a stressful major separation also saw avoidance for the first time.)

6 *The infant avoids the parent on reunion because of peculiarities in parental greeting behavior, that is, parental behavior has immediate situational control over avoidance.*

This explanation supposes that avoidance is not dependent upon a history of interactions, a relationship, or a major separation; rather, something the parent does at the moment of reunion causes the infant's avoidance. This form of behavior would presumably have the power to cause avoidance in any infant of any history. However, this explanation is not incompatible with suggestions that avoidant infants do have a special history, that is, that the mother is rejecting of contact and emotionally inexpressive in the home situation. What is peculiar to this view is the supposition that if any of these characteristics present in other situations are important to avoidance, they must also be present at the moment of reunion and have at that moment the power to cause avoidance.

This explanation is not unreasonable. It could best be dealt with by close-up videotapes of parental behavior and expression and by experimenting with changes in the behavior of the parent (or a stranger) as the infant is greeted. It does seem possible that parents of avoidant infants may be somewhat less facially expressive than others in greeting their infants in the Strange Situation (as well as being generally less expressive in other settings), and this may have some immediate control over avoidance. (Inexpressiveness of the parent is of special interest because Tronick et al. report that even 1-month-old infants will actively avoid a suddenly inexpressive mother; see Tronick et al. 1978.)

Yet, reasoning by inference, I find the situational explanation unlikely to account completely for the immediate appearance of avoidance on reunion. First, we know that avoidance appears in virtually all infants who have undergone major separations from the parent. It seems unlikely to me that all parents would behave identically on reunion, all becoming, for example, suddenly inexpressive. Robertson and Robertson filmed the reunion between an infant and its mother after 10 days of stressful separation. The film shows that the mother greeted the child warmly and certainly with emotional expression. Yet she was strongly avoided (Robertson & Robertson film).

Second, I am currently conducting a close review of my own videotapes, focusing on the moment just preceding reunion with the parent, when the parent twice calls the child's name from outside the door (before opening it and pausing to greet the infant). In several cases examined to date, infants who will avoid the parent on reunion show a peculiar change in posture and/or expression at the sound of the parent's voice, one not seen in infants who will seek proximity. This consists of a slight hunching of the shoulders (suggestive of a submissive or crouching posture) or a tense movement accompanied by a slightly apprehensive and confused expression. This peculiar response leads me to conclude that the behavior of the avoidant infant has something to do with the infant's memory of the parent or of its interactions with the parent, that is, with the historical and not merely the immediate. Thus the infant who will avoid, as opposed to the infant who will seek proximity, sometimes crouches slightly in preparation for the return of the parent.

SOME EXPLANATIONS THAT ARE LEFT OPEN

The final section is speculative. Its organization is as follows. I begin with a review of the problems presented by the phenomena. Then, I review some ethological analyses of social avoidance (gaze aversion, headflagging, cut-off) in nonhuman animals observed in conflict situations. These are interesting in connection with our human case both for the immediate causes proposed and for the functions connected to those causes. Finally, I return to avoidance of the attachment figure, integrating the work of ethologists with my own and that of others to arrive at some explanations of the phenomena that have yet to be discarded.

Visual avoidance: Tinbergen's four problems

According to Tinbergen (1963), four problems must be solved regarding each pattern of specific behavior we seek to understand. The problems presented by the phenomena of avoidance are organized into problems concerning the ontogeny and immediate causes of the behavior (the proximate causes) and problems of phylogeny and survival function (the ultimate causes). Thus, each behavior pattern an individual animal exhibits is seen as having a history of development within the individual and a reason for appearing at some moments rather than others. In addition, some behavior patterns also have roots in the evolutionary history of the animal's species, that is, some have a species-specific genetic base, having evolved as a solution to particular problems of survival.

The ontogeny of avoidance. The question of ontogeny may be framed as follows: What in this individual's experience made it likely to show the behavior pattern of interest? My studies of dyadic behavior show that avoidance of the mother following brief separation is associated with maternal aversion to physical contact and proximity, anger, and inexpressiveness. At the behavioral level, this set of associated behaviors can be summarized as maternal rejection.[2]

In considering the ontogeny of avoidance, our first problem is to discover why, to the degree that a human infant has been rejected by its mother, it responds to reunion after brief separations with avoidance. Our second problem is to explain why avoidance also appears in infants who have not experienced rejection but simply stressful major separations from the mother (separations in which no substitute caregiving figure is always available). This latter case makes it clear that avoidance can appear merely as a function of a mental reorganization of the child–mother relationship in the thoughts and feelings of the child, rather than in conjunction with an interaction pattern. Any coherent theory of avoidance must tie these highly divergent origins together.

Its immediate causation. Because infants do not avoid the mother under all conditions, an explanation of avoidance is incomplete unless it explains why avoidance occurs at one moment rather than another. Even if the experience of rejection or of major separation is important to the ontogeny of avoidance in an individual, rejection does not explain why that individual avoids at only some moments.

The moment chosen for avoidance is in fact one of the most intriguing aspects of the pattern. For example, in the case of rejected infants, we might expect avoidance to occur at a moment of what ethologists call *thwarting* – at the moment, for example, when the mother rejects approach and contact. In fact, rejected infants avoid the mother at the moment when she greets them, holds out her arms, and makes clear her availability.

Rejected infants show an avoidant pattern in the Strange Situation, but elsewhere they behave differently: For two reasons their avoidance in the stress situation is not expected. First, distress and anger are expected in all infants in response to separations in the strange environment. Second, as noted earlier, although infants classified as avoidant show virtually no anger or distress in the Strange Situation, in the home and in play settings they are the ones most likely to show angry behavior toward the mother, and many show distress at even the most minimal separations. Thus the infants who respond to the Strange Situation with affectless avoidance are violating expectations based both on theory and on observations.

Finally, we must explain the fact that avoidance greatly decreases (and is combined with distress and proximity seeking) when a second laboratory strange situation is conducted very shortly after a first Strange Situation (see "Strange Situation classifications related to behavior in other settings"). Thus, our questions regarding immediate causation are as follows:

What aspects of the experience of major separation lead to the gradual appearance of avoidance on reunion? What aspects of the Strange Situation procedure lead to the appearance of affectless avoidance in infants who logically would be expected to respond with the greatest distress and the greatest anger? Under the stress of separation in an unfamiliar setting, does avoidance occur as an alternative to distress and anger? Why does avoidance decrease or disappear in Strange Situations conducted in close succession?

Questions of phylogeny. The question of phylogeny of a behavior pattern refers to how it developed as new species evolved from a common ancestry. The nonhuman primates are our closest relatives, and in general their social behavior resembles our own. But here too avoidance presents a problem.

Many experimental studies of rhesus infant–mother separation have been conducted by experimenters alert to the human separation data (specifically, to the stages of protest, despair, and detachment–avoidance described originally by Robertson & Bowlby 1952). Although there are anecdotal reports of avoidance of the attachment figure on reunion in individual monkeys (e.g., Bertrand 1969), with one exception (Abrams 1970) infant primate avoidance of the mother on reunion has yet to be demonstrated experimentally (e.g., see Kaplan 1970; Lewis et al. 1976; Rosenblum & Kaufman 1968; Spencer-Booth & Hinde 1967). Immediately upon reunion after major separations, rhesus offspring seek proximity and cling to the mother; and in the weeks following major separation, time spent "on" mother (and tantrums) shows an increase over preseparation levels. Moreover, in exact opposition to the human case examined in this chapter, the more frequently a rhesus infant has been rejected by its mother prior to separation, the more attachment behavior it exhibits on reunion (Hinde & Spencer-Booth 1971).

The ethological–evolutionary theory of attachment behavior is based in large part on similarities in the development of attachment behavior and in the circumstances activating it in human and nonhuman primates. But whereas intense attachment behavior is characteristic of nonhuman primate infants after major separations,[3] human infants typically show avoidance. How can an antithetical pattern of behavior have developed in such closely related species? And given the arguments for the adaptive nature of attachment behavior and the pressures leading to attachment, how can those showing an antithetical pattern have survived?

The question of adaptive (biological) function. Many behaviors in an animal's repertoire appear only through the action of proximate mechanisms. Though such behaviors may be lawfully related to personal experience and appear in the great majority of individuals, they have no direct relation to species history, that is, they have not evolved through natural selection. Others, such as attachment, have evolved because they solve one or many survival problems. These behaviors are said to have a specific adaptive (biological) function.

Could avoidance in response to major separations (and to minor separations combined with rejection) have a biological function? This question has not previously been considered because only increased attachment behavior has been predicted and seen to have selective advantages. Readers are already familiar with arguments for the biological function of attachment behavior based upon ethological–evolutionary attachment theory. They may be interested to learn, however, that the sociobiologist Robert Trivers also predicts only increased attachment and proximity-promoting behavior in response to separation and/or rejection. The bases on which his predictions are made differ, however, from what I conceive of as the bases of attachment theory. Whereas attachment theorists see mother and infant as engaged in a common enterprise of infant protection, growth, and gradual independence (Bowlby 1969), Trivers sees parent and infant as involved from the first in conflict.

In his 1974 paper entitled "Parent–offspring conflict," Trivers argues that because parent and infant are perfectly related to themselves but only half related to one another, disagreement will inevitably occur over the extent to which the parent should invest energy and attention in the infant. At the beginning of the infant's life, the parent willingly protects and nourishes it, because the infant contains half the parent's genes and its own reproductive success will increase the parent's fitness (the proportion of the parent's genes that will appear in future generations). However, at some point in the development of the relationship, the parent will consider the offspring viable and independent: At that point, the parent would best begin improving its fitness by attention to its other relatives (for example, to younger offspring). But until the cost to the infant is more than it is worth genetically, the infant should quarrel and demand more parental investment. (This would not occur until, say, the infant's demand for the parent's investment reduced the likelihood of reproductive success of more than two of its siblings.)

What means can an offspring use to deal with a parent who would reject, desert, or wean it? "An offspring cannot fling its mother to the ground at will and nurse" (Trivers 1974:257). Rather, an offspring will use psychological tactics, such as mimicry and deception. What tactics will be chosen? Trivers suggests that the offspring can take advantage of selective forces that have acted on its parent to make the parent respond more positively to signals of younger and more helpless offspring. "This suggests that at any stage of ontogeny in which the offspring is in conflict with its parents, one appropriate tactic may be to revert to the gestures and actions of an earlier stage in order to induce the investment that would then have been forthcoming. Psychologists have long recognized such a tendency in humans and have given it the name of regression" (Trivers 1974:257). Trivers suggests, in other words, that a rejected offspring will use the tactics of infants whom Ainsworth classifies as insecure-ambivalent.

Trivers finds support for this prediction regarding infant strategy in the data presented by Hinde and Spencer-Booth (1971) concerning increased "time on mother" following separation. "These data are consistent with the assumption that the infant has been selected to interpret its mother's disappearance as an event whose recurrence the infant can help to prevent by devoting more of its energies to staying close to its mother" (Trivers 1974:258). It is also supported by the still greater increase in attachment behavior on reunion found by Hinde and Spencer-Booth in association with maternal rejection: "The offspring should assume that a rejecting mother who temporarily disappears needs more offspring surveillance and intervention than does a nonrejecting mother who temporarily disappears" (Trivers 1974:258). In both cases, increased offspring intervention means increased pursuit, clinging, distress, and anger.

The survival advantage of attachment behavior and angry behavior after major separation is, then, so accepted that it is difficult to even begin to ask questions regarding a possible adaptive function for a behavior pattern that is antithetical. Of course, one strong possibility is that avoidance has no biological function and no association with maternal rejection other than what is ancillary to proximate mechanisms.

In this case, avoidance would be a pattern that is neutral in terms of survival value. However, in a recent review intended to summarize the ethological-evolutionary approach to attachment, there is a far stronger statement (Rajecki et al. 1978): "[Human] infants whose attachments are insecure will behave somewhat maladaptively within their environment . . . and would be less likely to survive in the long run." Here avoidance is seen not as biologically neutral but as biologically maladaptive.

Visual avoidance in nonhuman animals: ethological interpretations

Visual avoidance has been studied extensively in birds (particularly gulls and terns) in ethological investigations conducted in the 1950s and early 1960s (e.g., Chance 1962; Cullen 1957; Moynihan 1955; Tinbergen & Moynihan 1952). It has also been observed in encounters between mammals (e.g., Grant & MacKintosh 1963) including primates (Altmann 1962; Williams 1968). It has been observed most often in agonistic encounters, but these include courtship situations (in which tendencies to flee, attack, and approach are competing or alternating), as well as situations involving simple questions of submission and dominance. Visual avoidance is often interpreted as indicative of submission or appeasement to a dominant animal (Altmann 1962 describes a careful not-staring that characterizes the subordinate rhesus), although occasionally it is also interpreted as defiance (Williams 1968). But why does avoidance appear in these situations?

As I understand the work of ethologists, visual avoidance is generally seen as enabling an animal to maintain proximity to a partner or prospective partner in conflict situations. It is seen as serving proximity through the effect it has either upon the behavior of the partner (a signal function) or the behavior of the performing animal. These effects are not necessarily incompatible.

Another suggestion is that, because it permits a predominant mood to wane, avoidance permits the performer to maintain flexibility (organization) of behavior. This is a separate notion from avoidance in the service of proximity, though again it is not incompatible.

Avoidance in the service of proximity: the signal function. Tinbergen (Tinbergen & Moynihan 1952) suggests an intriguing and peculiar signal function for avoidance. Whereas most communicative movements reveal some particular intention, mood, or state, Tinbergen suggests that avoidance paradoxically serves the signal function of concealment. Thus, in an original analysis of movements of avoidance ("head-flagging") that occur in the black-headed gull, he proposes that the pattern removes the effects that sight of the threatening brown face would have upon the partner simply by removing the brown face from view. Thus, head-flagging seems "to have the function of nullifying the effect of threatening gestures and structures. Whatever the origins of such appeasing movements may have been, ritualization seems to have followed the opposite course from that which it usually does. In such cases conspicuous structures are concealed rather than displayed" (1952:22).

In a later paper, Tinbergen (1959) observes that "facing away" occurs in other than courtship situations. Eider ducks lift their chins when they are frightened but for some reason (e.g., either a sexual tie to a male partner or a parental tie to the brood) do not want to move. Kittiwake chicks attacked by their siblings face away if they do not want to move (Cullen 1957). And in the black-headed gull, facing away is observed not only in courtship situations but also in (hostile) male–male encounters.

Thus facing away is connected with flight and with approach in hostile as well as sexual situations. Tinbergen again emphasizes its signal function (its effect on the partner) – its appearance in situations in which it is desirable for an animal to maintain proximity. Facing away seems to inhibit both flight and attack in the partner, and to do this by bringing about the disappearance of some of the stimuli that release withdrawal and aggression.

Avoidance in the service of proximity: the effects upon prospective reactions in the individual. In a well-known paper written in 1962, M. R. A. Chance draws upon essentially the same kinds of data as Tinbergen, although he reviews some new and extensive analyses of agonistic male–male encounters in the rat. But whereas Tinbergen sees avoidant movements as inhibiting the release of aggression and flight in the prospective social partner, Chance (1962) suggests that the same movements have the same ultimate effect upon aggressive and flight tendencies (which would interfere with the maintenance of proximity) in the performing animal itself. This is because the sight of another animal almost always arouses tendencies to flee and to attack. *Cut-off* acts and postures are likely to appear whenever an animal faces a "threatening social partner," and they permit a waning of aggressive and flight tendencies.

Thus Chance too suggests that avoidance serves proximity, but through its consequences for the behavior of the performer. An especially appealing feature of his model is that visual avoidance can be seen as paradoxically reducing the likelihood of flight (as well as aggressive acts) in the performer.

Avoidance in the service of maintaining flexibility in behavior. Avoidance in the service of proximity is certainly the dominant theme in the functional analyses presented. But Chance (1962) suggests still another advantage for the performer, one not necessarily connected to proximity per se. In many circumstances, cut-off of awareness may serve to introduce a greater flexibility in behavior than would continuing sensory input from the partner, and "flexibility of behavior is what the subordinate rat needs to maintain in the face of tendencies which make its behavior rigid" (1962:72). Thus, cut-off permits a predominant mood to wane so as to permit a change in behavior if this is appropriate. When the sight of a partner has the power to elicit strongly compelling tendencies of any kind, then visual avoidance helps the animal to maintain voluntary control over its own behavior patterns.

Avoidance of the attachment figure on reunion: ethological interpretations

The ethologists concerned with visual avoidance have suggested immediate causes (e.g., the mere sight of a threatening prospective social partner, or else the flight and aggressive tendencies to which the sight of the partner gives rise); phylogenetic causes (the gradual ritualization of a gesture that nullifies the effects of a previously ritualized threatening pattern); and biological functions (maintenance of proximity and perhaps of continued flexibility in behavior patterns). Ontogeny has not been separately considered in the work reviewed above, largely because the concern is with the evolution of the behavior.

Here I consider how we might apply each of these ethological conceptualizations of visual avoidance to human infants responding to reunion with the attachment figure. Although I shall shortly consider whether this pattern may be evolved to serve specific functions for human infants, the reader can at present safely read *consequences* where I refer to *function*. Thus, the probable consequences of a behavior, or its predictable outcomes, may be psychologically or socially advantageous for an individual without having evolved for the sake of that advantage. To psychologists and others, the consequences are still of interest.

Our problems are, again, (1) to find an immediate cause that leads to the appearance of avoidance together with the disappearance of distress and angry behavior following separations – one that can also account for its relative disappearance in a quickly succeeding Strange Situation; (2) to find an ontogenetic cause that leads to the appearance of avoidance following brief separations for rejected infants – one that can also account for the appearance of avoidance after stressful major separations for all infants; and (3) to determine whether any of the probable consequences of avoidance under these conditions could be more advantageous for the individual than the exhibition of increased attachment behaviors.

Can avoidance of the attachment figure on reunion be seen as either a care-eliciting signal or an appeasement signal that simply inhibits withdrawal and aggression in the partner? If avoidance acts as a signal in the service of proximity, it may conceivably have a positively care-eliciting effect upon the mother, drawing her to approach and contact the infant who is avoiding her. On the other hand, it may simply remove something like threatening gestures from her sight and thus enable the infant to maintain whatever proximity is possible.

Let us consider first the proposition that avoidance is positively care-eliciting

("I am turning just a little away, and ignoring our relationship just a bit, but please do come and get me"). To some extent, this proposition could be tested experimentally. Thus, we might ask how different mothers respond, both by verbal reports and by physiological indices, to infants who in various ways approach and avoid them. Of course, in such experiments we would have to be careful to ascertain whether the mother reported herself drawn by, rather than simply not repulsed by, the avoidant infant.

Consider next the more conservative proposition that avoidance simply inhibits aggression and/or withdrawal in the partner. For several reasons, this interpretation has an intriguing relationship to our data. To date I have referred to the mothers of infants classified as avoidant in the Strange Situation as more rejecting than other mothers. In many ways, however, it would be more pleasing simply to refer to them as more likely to consider the infant an intrusion – and thus as more frequently and firmly signaling their dominance. Thus, the mother's aversion to contact and proximity with her infant could be reinterpreted as forbidding its intrusion into her space, and her anger could be seen as a threat that occurs when her space or her status relative to the infant are violated. A paper by Tronick et al. has drawn my attention to the possibility that even the mother's inexpressiveness (in his work, the *still-face*) could be conceived as a signal establishing her dominance (Tronick et al., op. cit.).

In this case, the infant's avoidance could be considered a kind of appeasement signal made in direct response to the mother's signals of dominance. Avoidance would then be expected whenever a mother in such a mood approached her infant. Avoidance in this circumstance would be a gesture of appeasement that permitted the infant to maintain whatever proximity was possible.

Note, however, that if avoidance is simply an immediate response to the immediate approach of a relatively dominant mother, then there is no necessary relation between the appearance of avoidance and the experience of separation in the Strange Situation. To test this matter, we could have mothers remain within a room but move away, turn, call, and hold out their arms. If the conceptualization of avoidance as a signal of appeasement elicited solely by the behavior of the mother is correct, the infants of dominant–rejecting mothers should avoid them as strongly in these circumstances as when the mother's call and greeting are preceded by a separation.

The above formulation of avoidance as an appeasement signal unfortunately fails to predict the established differing likelihoods of avoidance in conjunction with differing situations. Thus, it fails to predict differing likelihoods of avoidance depending upon differing internal states of the infant. But I believe we can reformulate avoidance as an appeasement signal to provide a more convincing tie to our rejected-infant data and to the fact that even for such infants avoidance probably does not appear in all mother-approach situations. This requires that we consider avoidance as a deception – one more necessary in some circumstances and with some attachment figures than with others.

I do not think it too loose a translation of Tinbergen's (1959) formulation to regard the appeasement signal as a kind of deception, removing from the partner's sight or knowledge a threatening gesture or intention. But in what kind of situation and with what kind of mother is such a deception most necessary? We have already said that the Strange Situation expectably arouses distress and angry behavior, and that infants who avoid are infants in whom such behaviors are most expected. If we now consider avoidance as concealment of such tendencies, we can see an elegant fit to our data. Thus, concealment of distress, anger, and approach tendencies would be most needed (1) with mothers who are demonstrably averse to approach and emotion, and (2) in situations in which the maintenance of proximity is most necessary. Note that we are still considering the effect upon the partner here rather than the effect upon the performing individual. But we are presuming that to predict the appearance of the signal, we need to know something of what is going on inside the infant as well as the imminent behavior of the partner. The infant is concealing strongly aroused tendencies of a sort that are most likely to threaten a particular kind of partner.

Commentary: Avoidance must have some effect upon the partner, though whether the effect is predictable is yet to be determined. Unfortunately, the effect upon the partner has yet to be studied, because for dyads seen within the Strange Situation, real data are not available. This is because the infant acts with presumed freedom, but the behavior of the parent is constrained experimentally.

The signal function interpretation of avoidance has attractive aspects. However, in light of the demands made for a coherent theory, it has several limitations. First, the behavior of strongly avoidant infants simply does not suggest that their avoidance is intended to draw the parent to them - at least, not in any simple physical sense that would fit with an ethological-evolutionary attachment theory interpretation. Thus, if the avoidant infant were merely attempting to elicit approach and care from the mother, we would expect that having avoided her and attracted her to it, the infant would cling or at least, in a satisfied way, accept her physical contact. It hardly fits with the care-eliciting interpretation that the strongly avoidant infant who is pursued and embraced insists in an affectless way on being put down by the parent. (At the psychological level, one might claim that this further avoidance represents a still greater attempt to gain more proximity and attention. Ethologically speaking, however, it is not the care-eliciting behavior of choice if the dyad is out on the moors and the wolves are howling. On the moors, physical contact should be satisfactory.)

Second, the proposal that avoidance is a special kind of signal used with special kinds of mothers does not permit us to link the data for home-reared, dominated/rejected infants with the data on major separations. If we take avoidance as an appeasement signal in response to a dominant mother, we are unable to predict avoidance in undominated infants following major separations. This is because it is unreasonable to suppose that all mothers would suddenly become dominant and averse to physical contact following major separations. To save the theory, we might propose that over a long separation the mother becomes a virtual stranger, and for that reason becomes fear-inspiring in the eyes of her infant. This, however, does not fit with the fact that the mother but not the father is avoided.

If avoidance as an appeasement signal for special use with dominant/rejecting mothers does not satisfy our demand for one theory to account for two ontogenies, then we might try conceiving of it as the most extreme proximity-seeking strategy available. Here we would conceive of it as the signal to be given when the infant is stressed beyond the point at which it exhibits or even can exhibit distress and approach behavior. This would enable us to fit together our two ontogenies, for we could then say that avoidance appears in the most distressed infants in the Strange Situation because they are the most distressed. And for the same reason, it appears in all infants following long and stressful separations.

In this view, of course, the most powerful thing any infant could do to attract its mother would be to threaten to terminate the relationship (a suggestion originally made to me by Eibl-Eibesfeldt). But this view does not fit with the fact that avoidance diminishes in home-reared infants subjected to a second quickly succeeding Strange Situation. And we are still faced with the problem that behavioral observations show the avoidant infant signaling to be put down directly after it has theoretically signaled to be contacted.[4]

Can avoidance be seen as functioning primarily to reduce the infant's own tendencies to exhibit behaviors that would interfere with maintenance of proximity to the partner? In this cut-off view of avoidance, proximity is maintained by avoidance because blocking the sight of the mother reduces the likelihood that the infant will (1) flee from her or (2) show angry behavior toward her.

At the descriptive level, this view is obviously not at all incompatible with avoidance as deception of the partner regarding the arousal of certain behavioral tendencies. However, there are two important differences. First, in contrast to the deception-of-the-rejecting-mother view, we are not permitted to see avoidance as intended to block approach as well as flight or aggressive tendencies. Approach behavior, in contrast to aggressive behavior or flight, would not interfere at all with the infant's maintenance of proximity to its mother.

Second, in the avoidance-as-deception view, we merely conceived of the infant as using avoidance to hide from the mother the arousal of certain tendencies. This led to difficulties in terms of the observed negative response to contact with the mother after the supposed signal for contact. The cut-off view does differ from avoidance as a signal to the partner in that avoidance is seen as necessary to the infant in maintaining control over flight or aggressive tendencies. In this alternative view, we need not be disturbed by the fact that the avoidant infant signals in an affectless fashion to be put down by its mother. Like the sight of the mother, contact with her may be conceived of as momentarily endangering its ability to control tendencies toward flight or aggression.

How does this proposal fit with our data? The reader now acclimated to the notion of the relatively threatening mother might well suppose that flight is the tendency that the infant reduces through visual and other forms of avoidance on reunion. But this supposition fits badly with our need to explain avoidance in response to major separation as well as to rejection. An increase in fear of the mother over periods of major separation is most unlikely.

The proposal fares better, however, if we presume that the infant is avoiding a display of extremely angry behavior. If we suppose that avoidance is more likely the more angry the infant is, we have the advantage of being able to predict avoidance as occurring at the same moment for every infant (a moment of extreme anger when maintenance of proximity is extremely necessary). Moreover, because during periods of major separation angry behavior observably increases, and because rejected infants are expected to experience the greatest anger upon even brief separations, we can use this single account to predict avoidance on reunion with the attachment figure for either of our two ontogenies. Note that this account also has the advantage of not requiring that the home-reared rejected infant continually avoid the mother (which I doubt it does), but rather that it avoid her when it most needs her and is most angry.

The proposal that avoidance appears as an alternative to angry behavior could be tested in many fashions. We could, for example, examine films of Strange Situation behavior to look for extremely subtle facial signals of anger in the avoidant infant. We could also attempt to induce anger toward the mother in secure infants just prior to the Strange Situation. And we could test the signal function of avoidance as against its cut-off function by various exotic means. These include seeing whether intelligent 2-year-olds avoid their blind but rejecting parents or, alternatively, by looking for avoidance in blind infants.

Commentary: How can this theory deal with the fact that avoidance is replaced by strong proximity seeking when stress increases still more greatly? This would indeed cause some embarrassment to the theory if we presumed that an increase in anger is the only thing that leads to an increase in avoidance.

In fact, of course, this theory presumes that a proximity-maintaining mechanism is active, for it is that very mechanism that is presumed to lead to selection of avoidance as an alternative to angry behavior. In extreme situations, attachment (proximity seeking) could simply override anger and hence override avoidance. Thus, because the danger that cut-off presumably guards against is simply exhibition of angry behavior, a display of proximity-seeking behavior is not a difficulty.[5] On the other hand, if avoidance and presumably anger is overwhelmed by attachment behavior in this second Strange Situation, why is it not also overwhelmed by attachment behavior following presumably still more stressful major separations? Thus, the very "out" provided for the theory traps it. However, there are also other problems.

Main (1977b) proposed that avoidance of the attachment figure is primarily an alternative to angry behavior and that its chief function is to maintain proximity to the attachment figure. This view fits with many facts and may indeed explain many cases of avoidance of the attachment figure in stress situations. However, in my present view, this concept was taken too insistently.

First, in the cut-off theory of avoidance, cut-off permits a waning of the proximity-interfering tendencies aroused by the sight of the partner. This does suggest that angry behavior should disappear under stress in favor of avoidance, a suggestion that fits with the facts as stated. But in fact, infants who strongly avoid the attachment figure not only fail to exhibit angry behavior but distress and other forms of proximity-promoting behavior as well. If avoidance functions only to reduce the likelihood of angry behavior upon reunion, why do we not see periods of avoidance followed by periods of distress in the Strange Situation episodes? The suggestion that avoidance appears as an alternative to distress and proximity seeking as well as to anger has already been made by Heinecke and Westheimer (1965) and by Ainsworth and Bell (1970).

Second, avoidance could occur as an alternative to angry behavior not in order to promote proximity but simply because at some point extreme anger and distress grow psychologically intolerable for the individual (a view put forth by Bowlby, e.g., 1960).

In general, the answer to the question of whether avoidance serves proximity seems to me to be left open. It may, and if it does we have a pleasing example of a conditional strategy, an example of avoidance in the service of attachment (see Bateson 1976). Experiments to test this hypothesis in home-reared infants, however, have yet to be conducted. In every Strange Situation study conducted to date, the infants observed were essentially trapped within the environment. It would be simple to design studies in which the infant has alternatives. Rejected infants might then leave the mother.

Can avoidance be seen as permitting maintenance of flexibility and organization in behavior? If I follow Chance correctly, a secondary advantage of visually avoiding a threatening partner is consequent maintenance of flexibility in behavior patterns. An animal that reduces its attention to a partner that has an unwelcome power over its behavior has more freedom to choose among succeeding behavior patterns than one that does not. Here, in my view, we are no longer necessarily concerned with a proximity-promoting advantage to cut-off, that is, a social advantage for the performer. Rather, we have moved to retention of control, organization, and flexibility[6] as advantages – advantages that on the whole I would call psychological.

This third theory of avoidance differs from all others in that avoidance can be seen as an alternative to approach behavior of every kind. The traditional cut-off theory of avoidance logically excluded the possibility that avoidance functions to reduce the likelihood of approach. Avoidance-as-signal allowed for a reduced likelihood of approach, but this was supposedly important only insofar as it ultimately increased the likelihood of proximity. If, however, the function of cut-off is to permit continued control and flexibility in behavior, then we may expect it to occur whenever the sight of the mother would threaten an infant with loss of control, flexibility, and organization. If approach to or by the mother threatens organization, then cut-off could occasionally be used to maintain distance. We could, in short, be seeing real avoidance.

If we are now to present a theory of avoidance as avoidance of behavioral disorganization, we must define what is meant by the latter term. Behavior can be called *disorganized* when it vacillates between opposites without reference to changes in the environment, or when it appears repeatedly in an environment that does not call for it. Disorganized behavior appears in infants reunited with their mothers while still in the stages of protest or despair (Robertson & Bowlby 1952) and in the ambivalent infants in the Strange Situation. Infants in both of these situations pay little or no attention to toys or other objects. Their whole attention seems distressingly focused upon the parent, whether present or absent. The parent's leavetaking has led to violent distress, but for these infants her return does little to alleviate it. Moreover, held by the mother, the infant clings, then angrily pushes away, then clings, then pushes away, and then clings again. All of this vacillation may be accompanied by unpredictable cries of distress. These changes in the infant's behavior cannot be connected by observers to any preceding changes in the mother. It is as though contact with the mother in itself arouses anger and then withdrawal, and withdrawal leads again to contact, which leads again to anger and withdrawal – a sequence that seems entirely dependent on the alternation of competing systems within the infant. This is highly distressed and disorganized behavior, and it is distressing to witness.

If we propose now that avoidant infants are attempting to avoid behavioral disorganization, can we fit the theory to our problem of two ontogenies and to the several problems involved in immediate causation? Let us consider first the problems of ontogeny and immediate causation in rejected infants.

Elsewhere (Main 1977b) I have argued that when an attached infant is subjected to threats from an attachment figure who simultaneously rejects physical contact, it is placed in a theoretically irresolvable and indeed self-perpetuating conflict situation. This is because threats of any kind, stemming from any source, arouse tendencies to withdraw from the source of the threat and to approach the mother. If (as is the case with mothers of avoidant infants) the mother is not only threatening but forbids approach and contact, the conflict is not resolvable. The mere fact that approach is forbidden when it is most necessary should still further activate the attachment behavioral system. It should also activate angry behavior, but approach is still not possible, and this should still further activate the system. Thus, on a theoretical level, a kind of positive feedback loop develops. Angry behavior and conflict behavior should be expected. Indeed, we should in general expect to see the behavior of Ainsworth's ambivalent infants.

Other conflict theories have certainly been formulated to account for the development of disorganization in behavior, for example, the double-bind theory of schizophrenia originated by Bateson. They describe, however, a conflict that is less self-perpetuating and far less innately disorganizing than the conflict that here purportedly faces the attached, threatened, and physically rejected infant. Thus in the double-bind theory of schizophrenia the child must deal with two opposing signals from the mother. The mother may, for example, verbally request her child to approach her while forbidding it to approach nonverbally. The child might withdraw in response to her nonverbal behavior, approach in response to her call, and find itself at a standstill. However, in this conceptualization, withdrawal would not automatically and in itself lead to approach; that is, what is described is not a self-perpetuating system. Two external and opposing signals are all that keep the child in conflict.

In the case of the rejected attached infant, however, only one signal from the mother is required to place the child in conflict. Withdrawal tendencies arise in response to her threat signal and lead automatically to approach tendencies; the connection between these opposing tendencies is internal to the attached infant and has no reference to the environment. Because approach is known to be forbidden, the attachment behavioral system is still further activated, but approach remains forbidden. Vacillation among approach, avoidance, and angry behavior may be expected.

There is no solution to this problem so long as the infant focuses its attention upon the attachment figure. The only solution is a shift in attention.

We have now developed a theory of ontogeny for avoidance in rejected infants. Avoidance is seen as a necessary shift in attention away from the attachment figure – a shift away from a theoretically irresolvable conflict involving the mother. One immediate-cause requirement is that the behavior not be exhibited continually. This theory can meet that requirement because the conflict need not be experienced continually. The mother does not threaten the infant or block its approach constantly. And in comfortable situations, attachment behavior is not aroused by the environment. According to this theory, avoidance should occur whenever the attachment behavioral system is highly activated – at least, at such moments the infant should make an effort toward avoidance, because it is then that behavioral disorganization threatens. This should certainly lead to avoidance of the mother in situations such as the Strange Situation. The only possible solution at such moments is, again, a shift in attention away from everything concerned with the mother.

The theories of avoidance described previously have predicted only avoidance of the mother on her reappearance in the Strange Situation. But if avoidance is conceived of as necessitated by a threat of disorganization contingent upon attention to the attachment figure, we can explain not only avoidance of the mother but also the suppression of distress during separation; the unusual attention to objects throughout the situation; and the seemingly desperate search for an object of attention at the moment of reunion. What is being deactivated in this account is the entire attachment behavioral system (see Bowlby 1980 for an essentially identical proposal). Here angry behavior may fail to appear not because it would interfere with proximity but because it is ultimately proximity-promoting.

Using this theory of avoidance, a very similar account can be given for behavior observed during major separations. Concern with the whereabouts of the attachment figure grows extreme; it is met with frustration; this leads to angry behavior; and continued frustration leads to still stronger activation of the system. Eventually attention must be shifted away from the attachment figure, toward some other stable caregiving figure if possible (Hansen 1977; Robertson & Robertson 1971), and if not, then toward the inanimate environment. Over a long enough period of separation, distress disappears and the child appears adapted to the new environment. But this adaptation is bought at the price of a shift of attention away from the mother. Again we would predict avoidance of the attachment figure on reunion.

This final theory seems satisfactorily to provide a similar account for our two divergent ontogenies. It deals with the fact that the child who avoids in the Strange Situation does not always avoid, for the shift of attention of which avoidance is a part is only an urgent necessity in the face of strong activation of the attachment behavioral system. Because this shift of attention is in fact only an attempt to reorganize or to maintain organization, we should also not be surprised that it disappears in rapidly succeeding Strange Situations. (On the other hand, if the theory is to hold, we would expect disorganized behavior in the avoidant infants in the second Strange Situation. Because secure infants are organized in their behavior, a simple shift to the secure pattern of behavior would act as disconfirmation of this theory.)

The theory of avoidance as preservation of organization also has other advantages. First, of the three major theories presented to date, it deals most straightforwardly with the fact that the avoidant infant signals to be put down as soon as it is picked up by the mother. Second, unlike either of the other theories, it provides a single account for differences between avoidant and other children observed in the separation environment. Theories of avoidance as a signal to a partner can hardly prescribe particular patterns of behavior in the absence of all partners. And the theory of avoidance as cut-off of angry behavior is designed to predict only shifts of attention contingent upon the appearance of the partner. It is not equipped to deal with the effects of what are effectively *thoughts* of the absent partner.

It is only when we conceive of avoidance as part of a more general strategy of shifting attention from the attachment figure that we are able to predict that infants who will strongly avoid will first have maintained an organized attention to the inanimate environment during the period of separation. (A specific prediction can be made on the basis of this part of the theory. Rejected infants should show less avoidance on reunion in the Strange Situation if the mother interacts with them constantly during the preceding episode. This is because they are then given less opportunity to establish a shift in attention.)

Commentary: This final theory of avoidance fits pleasingly with direct descriptions of phenomena observed in the Strange Situation. Most babies who avoid the mother in the Strange Situation have a rigidly organized appearance on separation, and on reappearance of the mother they search desperately for something to attend to. Their search for continued self-organization is certainly more obvious than any immediately rising anger tendencies.

Though this interpretation fits with the surface phenomena, it is not a surface interpretation. The behavior is still seen as an alternative to attachment behavior and angry behavior, and as a conditional rather than a preferred (or indifferent) strategy. Although the avoidant infant may manage to avoid a conflict that is disorganizing and would otherwise have the power to capture its whole attention, it is avoiding precisely because of the power held by the attachment figure. At the same time, it has not lost interest in gaining access to *an* attachment figure and may cling to a stranger if one is available. Battered infants avoid the abusive parent but sometimes cry at the leavetaking of the stranger in the Strange Situation. Hansen (1977) suggests that it is in part the capacity for avoidance that leaves open the possibility of actively searching for a new attachment relation.

If this theory is correct, then avoidance is a shift in attention that certain circumstances render especially necessary. The shift in attention is not, however, conceived of as simple and complete, as when we move from artwork to artwork or from person to person at a party. The human infant is normally emotionally and behaviorally organized around an attachment figure (Sroufe & Waters 1978). This is apparent not only in observations of infants responding to separations but also in the organization of exploration and play and the response to strangers in relation to accessibility to the attachment figure. It is also evident in the search for alternative figures that takes place during major separations (Robertson & Robertson 1971).

Thus a shift in attention away from a primary attachment figure means a blotting out or negation of the person who has been and normally would continue to be the central object of all attention. It is possible that this cannot be accomplished once and for all, and that we need here a concept of antiattention or negative attention. Thus in the separation environment, behavior is best conceived of not only as being reorganized without the parent but as being actively reorganized away from the parent. This theory would predict an active avoidance of all reminders of the mother during separation.

The reader who has come this far will think this section well titled. Three explanations of avoidance have been offered, each in part competing with the others and in part compatible. Although I have presented these explanations in what I presently see as an increasing order of likelihood, not one specific question can be settled without further observation and experiment. All explanations are truly left open. Yet I think that we have made some progress.

I began this chapter with the observation that avoidant behavior on reunion was not expected by any theory that described the simple workings of an attachment mechanism,[7] nor was it predicted by Trivers in his (1974) paper on parent–infant conflict. In a broad sense, the behavior at that point was not regarded as expectable because it seemed entirely disadvantageous. In this section on explanations that are left open, we have been able to consider many consequences that could conceivably also confer some biological advantages. The behavior seems at least less lethal than it did formerly. In addition, two of the alternative explanations suggest that avoidance serves attachment.

Let us now reconsider the problem of phylogeny presented earlier, the fact that nonhuman primates characteristically cling following major separations and cling all the more when rejected prior to separation, whereas human infants behave very differently. Admittedly we are dignifying this issue by calling it a problem in phylogeny, because a real study in phylogeny would trace the development of differences in a similar pattern. Still, can any of the explanations that are left open provide leads for explaining these differences?

One possibility is aligned with both the signal and cut-off functions of avoidance. Facial signaling may be less important in monkeys than in birds and man, and, to the extent that it is, we would expect the monkey to show less avoidance on reunion. If facial signaling is less important to monkeys, then the sight of a partner would not be so threatening, nor would the partner's refusal to look be so reducing of threat or so attractive.

Another possiblity is, of course, that monkey mothers never behave like human mothers, or that they are never successful in keeping a young infant at a distance as well as threatening it. Some monkey mothers do abuse their infants, however, and they must come as close to this pattern as is possible for primates. Would separations of such dyads yield avoidance?

Another explanation of the difference rests on the notion of avoidance as a search for control when disorganization threatens. In this view, the power to shift attention through avoidance can always be overwhelmed through stress. Separation of primate mother–infant dyads is always stressful. Might they avoid if separations were made less stressful or if the infant was kept calmer during the separation period? When an infant (e.g., marmoset) monkey has two primary attachment figures, so that the separation from one is not extremely stressful, might we see avoidance of the other? Would avoidance be more likely to appear following separation from the mother in langur infants who, when multiply reared, are visibly less desperate?

Finally, we must consider an obvious fact of ecology. Avoidance may be lethal for monkeys, but human infants have led a relatively protected existence for a very long time. This means, first, that broad variations in behavior patterns may develop and simply not be selected against. In addition, it seems possible that where the human infant is concerned, maintenance of proximity specifically to the mother is not as critical as it is with the rhesus. The group as well as the mother may be prepared to be solicitous (Hansen 1977). This does not mean that the infant will not continue to seek a primary attachment figure, but a relentless return to a dead or rejecting mother will hardly enhance survival so much as the capacity to transfer attachments (ibid). (Still, the notion of a capacity for attachment transfer must not be taken lightly. If we were not a species that tended to organize our behavior around a primary attachment figure in infancy, the transfer could be accomplished as easily as any other sort of shift in attention. Given the power of the attachment figure over the behavior of the infant, however, transfer to a new figure may be accomplished only at the price of an active negation of attention to the former figure – that is, at the price of an avoidance that is both physical and emotional and that in certain ways must resemble what psychologists call *defense*.)

The advantages of avoidance given above also enable us to reconsider the question of biological function. In an environment in which a shift in attention from a particular attachment relationship is not necessarily lethal, maintenance of behavioral organization and the freedom to find new attachment relationships may certainly be considered an advantage, or at least a consequence that diminishes an otherwise lethal effect.

One most interesting possible consequence of avoidance of the attachment figure is a paradoxical maintenance of proximity. It is only this advantage that I can imagine as having a special evolved mechanism with a biological function identical to its socially advantageous consequence. Here we would conceive of approach behavior, distress, angry behavior, and other displays of emotion as the primary and preferred infant strategy for maintaining proximity under normal conditions (mother accepting). But we could conceive of avoidance and suppression of emotion as a conditional strategy for maintaining proximity under conditions of maternal rejection.

This conception has the advantage of allowing us to imagine the infant as actively responding to maternal rejection, that is, as responding to increase its fitness when acts of maternal rejection threaten it. This is certainly more pleasing than imagining, as do Rajecki et al. (loc cit.), that a rejected infant acts in such a way as to lessen still further its already reduced chances of surviving. Their conceptualization of the rejected infant as responding by behaving in maladaptive ways seems to rest on an assumption (held until recently; see Williams 1966) that the infant is primarily equipped to deal with vicissitudes arising in the environment. The task of dealing with environmental changes is then seen as having a simple solution for an infant – that of maintaining proximity to a mother who has always in phylogenetic history been accepting. Thus rejection is seen as new, anomalous, and maladaptive, and avoidance as a maladaptive response that is permitted only in our present protected environment.

Recent work in sociobiology, however, brings several of these assumptions into question. Maynard Smith (1976) has proposed that what an individual does depends very much on what other individuals are doing; this analysis can be applied with special clarity to ritualized behaviors of the kind appearing in conflict situations (Maynard Smith 1978). Thus animals are presumed equipped to deal with vicissitudes in interpersonal relationships as well as to establish and maintain simple relationships and to respond to shifts in the environment.

This conceptualization bears an elegant relationship to the concept of the infant as from the first having different interests than its parents (Trivers 1974), for in that case conditional strategies for dealing with differing kinds of parental behavior seem likely. When in addition we consider the related fact that primate infants regularly experience rejection in the form of a weaning conflict, the development of an infant strategy for dealing with parental rejection seems a definite likelihood.

Trivers has, of course, considered this problem and has proposed that the infant deals with rejection by the attachment figure by regressive exaggeration of attachment needs or mimicry of the behavior of a younger infant. But the theories of avoidance developed in this chapter permit us to imagine that an infant might also manage to maintain proximity to the attachment figure through a more dignified and less disorganizing strategy of deception. Thus in the interests of maintaining proximity to the mother and simultaneously avoiding behavioral disorganization, the infant may hide its own needs, wishes, or behavioral tendencies from its mother (as in the signal function of avoidance) or even (as in the cut-off function) from itself.[8]

SUMMARY

This chapter has been concerned with avoidance of the attachment figure on reunion, which occurs in virtually all human infants following major separations, and following even brief separations for human infants who have been rejected by the person with whom they are reunited. The chapter refers to a number of studies of normal, home-reared infants seen with their mother or father in a brief laboratory Strange Situation. Scores are assigned to infants for the extent to which they exhibit avoidance of the attachment figure on reunion (looking away, turning away, or ignoring the attachment figure altogether). Infant avoidance of the mother is highly related to the mother's aversion to physical contact with the infant, her anger toward the infant, and her restriction of expressiveness as observed in other situations. Infants who strongly avoid the parent on reunion differ from other infants in that they show virtually no distress or anger in the laboratory Strange Situation. However, scores for avoidance of the mother in the Strange Situation are highly correlated with angry behavior toward her in other settings, that is, when infant and mother are seen in the home or in play settings. The behavior is stable when infants are seen in successive Strange Situations with a given parent, but there is no correlation between avoidance of the mother and of the father. A number of very simple but common explanations of avoidance are ruled out.

On the basis of simple interpretations of the workings of an attachment mechanism, avoidance of the attachment figure on reunion is not expected. Both attachment theory and recent functional interpretations of infant behavior in sociobiology predict only increased attachment behavior and angry behavior in response either to separation or to maternal rejection. The problems regarding the appearance of avoidance of the attachment figure are reformulated as specific questions regarding its ontogeny, immediate causation, phylogeny, and biological function. Ethologists have interpreted the occurrence of visual avoidance in nonhuman animals as a signal that either maintains or increases proximity between partners; and/or as a shift in attention that reduces the likelihood that the performing animal will flee from the partner or attack it; and/or as a behavior that simply permits maintenance of behavioral flexibility for the performing animal. Each of these explanations is examined in turn with the aim of discovering whether it can help to provide a coherent theory of ontogeny and immediate causation for avoidance of the attachment figure in human infants.

NOTES

1 The fact that no single stable caregiving figure is available during this period may be crucial to the appearance of the syndrome. Robertson and Robertson (1971) kept several infants in their home during major separations. Distress, anger, and anxiety were evident, but the infants did not avoid the mother on reunion.

2 I should like to emphasize that this is a literal summary of this set of highly intercorrelated behaviors; as the etymological root of the word *rejection* implies, the infant is "turned back or away from" the mother. This does not mean that she rejects its physical care or its psychological being, that she does not want it, or that she will not send it to college.

3 Abrams (1970) reported detachment from the mother in one-third of a sample of very young (8-week-old) infants separated from the mother for 2 days. It is not clear, however, that the behavior pattern was identical to the limited social avoidance here described. The infants reportedly ran away from the mother on reunion.

4 This invalidation depends on the supposition that there really is increased stress in the quickly succeeding Strange Situation. There is certainly strong support for this supposition, because virtually all infants seen in the second Strange Situation showed greater distress and proximity seeking, and some cried on simply seeing the unhappily familiar "strange" environment. One could argue that the avoidant infant contrasts to the secure infant in that it is actually more relaxed and less in need of avoidance in the second situation. But for many reasons that the reader can discover, this is too esoteric an interpretation.

5 Note again (see "Strange Situation classifications related to behavior in other settings") that infants who avoided in the first Strange Situation avoided somewhat, though to a lesser degree, in the second held soon afterward. To my knowledge, there was no accompanying increase in displays of anger.

6 Chance (1962) is concerned with the risk of inflexibility, but behavior is not

disorganized simply because it is inflexible, and I depart from Chance somewhat here in my concern with loss of organization. An animal can engage in flight in a manner that is inflexible in the sense that for a few moments attention to the environment is reduced, voluntary control is lost, and the pattern is maintained without continued reference to the environment. Behavior of this kind is inflexible, but it is not disorganized.

7 This is not to say that avoidance of the attachment figure was not observed by Bowlby and by Ainsworth (Robertson & Bowlby 1952; Ainsworth & Bell 1970). They were, of course, two of the first observers, and they did not fail to develop accounts for the appearance of avoidance (presented earlier). These accounts, however, stepped outside the bounds of the theory of attachment. It is simple propositions regarding what the attachment behavioral system will do following separation and rejection that are brought into question by the phenomenon of avoidance.

8 The reader familiar with theories of defensive process will have been alert to analogies to defensive process from the first description of avoidance of the attachment figure given in this chapter. Thus, even as it is observed within the Strange Situation, avoidance has a prototypical resemblance to defense. Although the three explanations of avoidance fail to provide a complete explanation for the phenomenon, it is startling that each bears some resemblance to the theory (e.g., Freud 1969) of defense. The theory of avoidance as an avoidance of disorganization, one that involves a shift in attention so active that it may be termed a *negative* attention, and that arises under stress but may also disappear under still greater stress is highly analogous to established theories of the origins and mechanisms of defense. (See Freud 1969 for descriptions of defensive process and what is avoided through it.) The other interpretations of avoidance given here – as a signal intended to conceal an intention (avoidance as deception) or as a reaction to one's own prospective reactions (avoidance as self-deception) bear still more intriguing connections to theories of defense.

The perhaps necessary connection between deception and self-deception has been discussed in passing by Trivers (1976). The philosopher H. Fingarette has eloquently discussed the connections between the concept of self-deception and the concept of psychological defense (Fingarette 1969).

ACKNOWLEDGMENTS

The empirical work reported here was supported by grants from the Department of Health, Education and Welfare under the Bio-Medical Sciences Support program; by the Institute for Human Development, Berkeley; and by the William T. Grant Foundation. The first version of this chapter was read at Bielefeld, and to its critics I owe many debts of gratitude: John Crook, Steve Glickman, Esther Goody, Herb Leiderman, Everett Waters, and John and Marilyn Watson. I learned that I needed to rethink several aspects of my former theory of avoidance through discussions with Klaus Grossmann and through participation in research conducted with Karin Grossmann in their laboratory. I am also indebted to discussions with John Bowlby, Irenans Eibl-Eibesfeldt, Robert Hinde and Joan Stevenson-Hinde, Jürg Lamprecht, Jay Rosenblatt, Niko Tinbergen, and Donna Weston. Donna Weston helped at every stage in the preparation of this chapter.

REFERENCES

Abrams, P. S. 1970. age and the effects of separation on mother and infant rhesus monkeys (*Macaca mulatta*). Unpublished Ph.D. dissertation, University of California, Davis.

Ainsworth, M. D. S., & S. M. Bell. 1970. Attachment, exploration, and separation: illustrated by the behavior of one-year-olds in a strange situation. *Child Development* 41:49–67.

Ainsworth, M. D. S., S. M. Bell, & D. Stayton. 1971. Individual differences in strange situation behavior in one-year-olds. *In:* H. Schaffer (ed.), *The origins of human social relations.* Academic Press, London.

Ainsworth, M. D. S., M. C. Blehar, E. Waters, & S. Wall. 1978. *Patterns of attachment.* Erlbaum, Hillsdale, New Jersey.

Ainsworth, M. D. S., & B. A. Wittig. 1969. Attachment and exploratory behavior of one-year-olds in a strange situation. *In:* B. M. Foss (ed.), *Determinants of infant behavior,* vol. 4. Methuen, London.

Altmann, S. A. 1962. A field study of the sociobiology of Rhesus monkeys (*Macaca mulatta*). *Annals of the New York Academy of Sciences* 102:338–435.

Argyle, M., & M. Cook. 1976. *Gaze and mutual gaze.* Cambridge University Press, London.

Bateson, P. P. G. 1976. Rules and reciprocity in behavioral development. *In:* P. P. G. Bateson & R. A. Hinde (eds.), *Growing points in ethology.* Cambridge University Press, Cambridge.

Bertrand, M. 1969. *The behavioral repertoire of the stumptail macaque.* Karger, Basel and New York.

Blanchard, M., & M. Main. 1979. Avoidance of the attachment figure and social-emotional adjustment in day-care infants. *Developmental Psychology* 15:445–446.

Block, J. H., & J. Block. 1979. The role of ego control and ego resiliency in the organization of behavior. *In:* W. A. Collins (ed.), *Minnesota symposia on child psychology,* vol. 13. Erlbaum, New York.

Bowlby, J. 1960. Separation anxiety. *International Journal of Psychoanalysis* 41:89–113.

1969. *Attachment and loss,* vol. 1, *Attachment.* Basic Books, New York.

1973. *Attachment and loss,* vol. 2, *Separation: anxiety and anger.* Basic Books, New York.

1980. *Attachment and loss,* vol. 3, *Loss.* Basic Books, New York.

Burlingham, D., & A. Freud. 1944. *Infants without families.* Allen & Unwin, London.

Chance, M. R. A. 1962. An interpretation of some agonistic postures: the role of "cut-off" acts and postures. *Symposium of the Zoological Society of London* 8:71–89.

Clarke-Stewart, A. K. 1978. And daddy makes three: the father's impact on mother and young child. *Child Development* 49:466–478.

Connell, D. 1976. Individual differences in attachment related to habituation to a redundant stimulus. Unpublished Ph.D. dissertation, Syracuse University, Syracuse, New York.

Cullen, E. 1957. Adaptations in the kittiwake to cliff nesting. *Ibis* 90:71–87.

Darwin, C. 1877. A biographical sketch of an infant. *Mind* 2:285–294.

Erwin, J., J. Mobaldi, & G. Mitchell. 1971. Separation of rhesus monkey juveniles of the same sex. *Journal of Abnormal Psychology* 78:134–139.

Fingarette, H. 1969. *Self-deception.* Routledge & Kegan Paul, London.

Freud, S. 1969. *An outline of psychoanalysis* (trans. J. Strachey). Norton, New York.

Gaensbauer, T. J., R. J. Harmon, & D. Mrazek. 1981. Affective behavior patterns in abused and/or neglected infants. *In:* N. Frude (ed.), *Psychological approaches to child abuse.* Rowman and Littlefield, Totowa, New Jersey.

George, C., & M. Main. 1979. Social interactions of young abused children: approach, avoidance, and aggression. *Child Development* 50:306–318.

Gewirtz, J. L. 1972. Attachment, dependence, and a distinction in terms of stimulus control. *In:* J. L. Gewirtz (ed.), *Attachment and dependency.* Winston, Washington, D.C.

Gove, F., R. Arend, & L. A. Sroufe. 1979. Competence in preschool and kindergarten predicted from infancy. Unpublished manuscript, University of Minnesota, Minneapolis.

Grant, E. C, & J. H. MacKintosh. 1963. A comparison of the social postures of some common laboratory rodents. *Behaviour* 21:246–259.

Hansen, J. 1977. Multiple attachment figures: monotropy and the function of subsidiary attachments. Unpublished manuscript, University of California, Berkeley.

Heinicke, C., & J. Westheimer. 1965. *Brief separations.* International Universities Press, New York.

Hinde, R. A., & Y. Spencer-Booth. 1971. Effects on brief separation from mother on rhesus monkeys. *Science* 173:111–118.

Hulse, S. H., J. Deese, & H. Egeth. 1975. *The psychology of learning.* McGraw-Hill, New York.

Kaplan, J. 1970. The effects of separation and reunion on the behavior of mother and infant squirrel monkeys. *Developmental Psychobiology* 3:43–52.

Lewis, J. K., W. T. McKinney, Jr., L. D. Young, & G. Kraemer. 1976. Mother–infant separation in rhesus monkeys as a model of human depression. *Archives of General Psychiatry* 33:699–705.

Lewis, M., & S. Schaeffer. 1979. Peer behavior and mother–infant interaction in maltreated children. *In:* M. Lewis & L. Rosenblum (eds.), *The uncommon child: the genesis of behavior,* vol. 3. Plenum, New York.

Londerville, S., & M. Main. 1981. Security of attachment, compliance and maternal training methods in the second year of life. *Developmental Psychology,* in press.

Main, M. 1973. Exploration, play and level of cognitive functioning as related to child–mother attachment. Unpublished Ph.D. dissertation. Johns Hopkins University, Baltimore.

1977a. Attachment behaviors fail as childhood social indicators. Paper given at the biennial meeting of the Society for Research in Child Development, New Orleans, March.

1977b. Analysis of a peculiar form of reunion behavior seen in some day-care children: its history and sequelae in children who are home-reared. *In:* R. Webb (ed.), *Social development in childhood: daycare programs and research.* Johns Hopkins University Press, Baltimore.

Main, M., L. Tomasini, & W. Tolan. 1979. Differences among mothers of infants judged to differ in security. *Developmental Psychology* 15:472–473.

Main, M., & L. Townsend. 1981. *Infant Behavior and Development.* In press.

Main, M., & D. R. Weston. 1981. The quality of the toddler's relationship to mother and to father: related to conflict behavior and the readiness to establish new relationships. *Child Development.* In press.

Masters, J., & H. Wellman. 1974. Human infant attachment: a procedural critique. *Psychological Bulletin* 81:218–237.

Matas, L., R. Arend, & L. A. Sroufe. 1978. Continuity of adaptation in the second year: the relationship between quality of attachment and later competence. *Child Development* 49:547–556.

Maynard Smith, J. 1976. Evolution and the theory of games. *American Scientist* 64:41–45.

1978. The evolution of behavior. *In: Scientific American* (ed.), *Evolution: a Scientific American book*. Freeman, San Francisco, pp. 92–101.

Medawar, P. B. 1967. *The art of the soluble*. Methuen, London.

Moynihan, J. 1955. Some aspects of reproductive behavior in the black-headed gull and related species. *Behaviour* (Suppl.) 4:1–201.

Rajecki, D. W., M. E. Lamb, & P. Obmascher. 1978. Toward a general theory of infantile attachment: a comparative review of aspects of the social bond. *Behavioral and Brain Sciences* 3:417–464.

Robertson, J., & J. Bowlby. 1952. Responses of young children to separation from their mothers. *Courrier du Centre International de l'Enfrance* 2:131–142.

Robertson, J., & J. Robertson. 1971. Young children in brief separations. *Psychoanalytic Study of the Child* 26:264–315.

Young children in brief separation. Film series. Tavistock Institute of Human Relations, London.

Rosenblum, L. A., & I. C. Kaufman. 1968. Variation in infant development and response to maternal loss in monkeys. *American Journal of Orthopsychiatry* 38:418–426.

Spencer-Booth, Y., & R. A. Hinde. 1967. Effects of six days' separation from mother on 18- to 32-week old rhesus monkeys. *Animal Behaviour* 10:174–181.

Sroufe, L. A., & E. Waters. 1977. Heartrate as a convergent measure in clinical and developmental research. *Merrill-Palmer Quarterly* 23:3–28.

1978. Attachment as an organizational construct. *Child Development* 48:1184–1199.

Stayton, D. J., R. Hogan & M. D. S. Ainsworth. 1971. Infant obedience and maternal behavior: the origins of socialization reconsidered. *Child Development* 42:1057–1069.

Tinbergen, N. 1959. Einige Gedanke über Beschwichtigungsgebaerden. *Zeitschrift für Tierpsychologie* 16:651–655. (Trans. in N. Tinbergen, *The animal in its world*, vol. 2. Harvard University Press, Cambridge, Massachusetts, 1973.)

1963. On aims and methods of psychology. *Zeitschrift für Tierpsychologie* 20:410–433.

Tinbergen, N., & M. Moynihan. 1952. Head flagging in the black-headed gull: its function and origin. *British Birds* 45:19–22.

Tinbergen, N., & N. Tinbergen. 1973. Early childhood autism: a hypothesis. *In:* N. Tinbergen (ed.), *The animal in its world*, vol. 2. Harvard University Press, Cambridge, Massâchusetts, pp. 175–199.

Trivers, R. L. 1974. Parent–offspring conflict. *American Zoologist* 14:249–264.

1976. Foreward. *In:* R. Dawkins, *The selfish gene*. Oxford University Press, New York.

Tronick, E., H. Als, L. Adamson, S. Wise, & T. B. Brazelton. 1978. The infant's response to entrapment between contradictory messages in face-to-face interaction. *Journal of the American Academy of Child Psychiatry* 17:1–13.

van Iersel, J. J., & A. C. Bol. 1958. Preening of two species: a study on displacement activities. *Behaviour* 13:1–88.

Vaughn, B., B. Egeland, L. A. Sroufe, & E. Waters. 1979. Individual differences in infant–mother attachment at twelve and eighteen months: stability and change in infant–mother attachment in families under stress. *Child Development* 50:971–975.

Vine, I. 1970. Communication by facial-visual signals. *In:* J. Crook (ed.), *Social behavior in birds and mammals: essays in the social ethology of animal and man.* Academic Press, London.

1973. The role of facial-visual signalling in early social development. *In:* M. von Cranach & I. Vine (eds.), *Social communication and movement.* Academic Press, New York.

Waters, E. 1978. The reliability and stability of individual differences in infant–mother attachment. *Child Development* 49:483–494.

Waters, E., L. Matas, & L. A. Sroufe. 1975. Infants' reactions to an approaching stranger: description, validation and functional significance of wariness. *Child Development* 46:348–356.

Waters, E., B. Vaughn, & B. Egeland. 1980a. Individual differences in infant–mother attachment relationships at age one: antecedents in neonatal behavior in an urban economically disadvantaged sample. *Child Development* 51:208–216.

Waters, E., J. Wippman, & L. A. Sroufe. 1979. Attachment, positive affect and competence in the peer group: two studies in construct validation. *Child Development* 50:821–829.

Williams, G. C. 1966. *Adaptation and natural selection.* Princeton University Press, Princeton, New Jersey.

Williams, L. 1968. *Man and monkey.* Lippincott, New York.

27

PARENT-INFANT ATTACHMENT RELATIONSHIPS IN BIELEFELD: A RESEARCH NOTE

KLAUS GROSSMANN and
KARIN GROSSMANN

The concept of attachment is a very good focus for interdisciplinary work. Its framework is compatible with those of comparative and of behavioral biology. At the same time, it offers significant psychological insights into human ontogenesis – insights that are in agreement with a large body of observations made by researchers as well as clinicians. It is perhaps the developmental concept best suited to integrate the diverse investigations of researchers in disciplines such as pediatrics, psychiatry, behavioral biology, and psychology (Grossmann 1978).

The biological orientation of the attachment concept demands, however, a consideration of the whole situation in which a child develops. Researchers who adopt attachment theory must simultaneously adopt a rather balanced exploratory position: They cannot rely exclusively on a hypothetical-deductive (positivistic) strategy of defining variables too early and in the absence of a species-relevant concept; at the same time, they must avoid too early definition of what is species-relevant. Our in-progress studies of parents and infants in Bielefeld have brought to light a difference in perspective on attachment relationships that warrants further examination.

In the past 2 years, we have undertaken a study of Bielefeld infants and parents modeled in part on the Ainsworth study conducted in Baltimore (Ainsworth et al. 1978). Each infant in our sample of 49 is visited several times in the home and is also seen twice in the laboratory in the Ainsworth Strange Situation. This situation involves two brief separations from the parent in the strange laboratory environment (see Waters 1978 and Chaps. 25 and 26 for a more thorough description of the procedures for the Strange Situation). Ainsworth (Ainsworth et al. 1978) has devised a system for assessing parent-infant relationships based upon the infant's behavior in the Strange Situation. Attachment behavior is expected to occur whenever an infant "appraises himself as in danger," and separation from the attachment figure in a strange environment should signal danger.

Dependent largely upon their response to reunion with the parent, infants are classified as *secure, insecure-ambivalent,* or *insecure-avoidant* in their attachment to the mother. Infants are classified as secure in their attachment relationships when separation activates the attachment behavioral system, so that the infant actively seeks proximity and contact on reunion and then readily returns to play and exploration. Infants are classified as insecure when they either actively avoid and ignore the parent on reunion or exhibit an angry ambivalence and inability to be comforted. Ambivalent infants show high distress, anger, and fearfulness throughout the Strange Situation. Avoidant infants do not cry when separated from the parent, and they tend to explore toys throughout the Strange Situation. If picked up by the parent on reunion, they indicate a wish to be put down, and if the parent seeks interaction they ignore and avoid him or her. They do not show anger toward the parent in the Strange Situation. The behavior of a very small minority of infants is such that they cannot be classified in the Ainsworth system (Main & Weston 1981).

Within the last decade, at least eight samples of white middle-class infants and mothers have been seen and classified in U.S. laboratories (in California, Maryland, Minnesota, New York, and Ohio) in the Strange Situation. In addition, a sample of infants and mothers has been seen in Italy. In all of these samples a majority – generally about two-thirds – of the infants have been classified as secure in relation to the mother. From one-fifth to just over one-quarter of the infants in each sample have been judged insecure-avoidant, and the remainder have been judged insecure-ambivalent or unclassifiable. (Main and Weston 1981 report almost identical proportions in a sample of 66 father–infant pairs seen to date in Berkeley.) Whereas classifications with a given parent are stable over as long a time period as eight months, classifications with the two parents are independent (ibid.). This suggests that the Strange Situation assesses particular infant–adult relationships rather than individual infant temperament.

This is not the place to summarize ethologically oriented attachment theory, which has been reviewed in detail elsewhere (Ainsworth 1969, 1973; Bowlby 1969, 1973). However, because ethologically oriented attachment theorists see the attachment as an enduring affective bond that protects and guides the infant, they naturally tend to interpret the secure pattern of infant behavior as the species-adaptive pattern; empirical findings relating Strange Situation behavior to behavior in other settings seem to support this notion, at least in U.S. samples.

In Bielefeld we have seen 49 infants with their mothers in the Strange Situation at 12 months and, at 18 months, 46 of these same children with their fathers. (These ages were chosen because they are the standard ages used in U.S. samples.) The Strange Situation behavior of our Bielefeld sample was videotaped, and a researcher trained in the Ainsworth laboratory, together with her assistant, obtained high interjudge agreement with our own assistants regarding classifications. The various infant–parent behavior patterns were very similar to those seen in the United States and therefore could be classified using the Ainsworth system. No more of the Bielefeld infants were judged unclassifiable then are so judged in U.S. samples. As in the sample studied by Main and Weston (1981), classifications with the two parents were independent.

The proportion of Bielefeld infants judged insecurely attached to their mothers was approximately twice that in U.S. samples, that is, a majority (two-thirds) of the Bielefeld infants were judged insecure in their attachment. The proportion of children judged insecure-ambivalent in relation to the mother and the proportion who could not be classified was the same as in U.S. samples. The sample difference occurs because of the very high proportion of Bielefeld infants classified as avoidant of the parent. Whereas in the United States the proportions of avoidant infants vary from 17 to 30% of those sampled, in our German sample 49% of the children were classified as avoidant. Almost identical proportions of the various classifications occurred when the children were seen with the father, that is, 54% of our 18-month-olds were judged avoidant of the father.

Studies of parent–infant interaction outside of the Strange Situation (summarized in Ainsworth et al. 1978) have shown that infants whose Strange Situation behavior leads to the classification "secure with mother" have experienced in their first year of life sensitive, responsive mothering; at the same time, they have been from an early period easy and responsive infants. Infants in both groups classified as "insecure with mother" have experienced insensitive and unresponsive mothering and have been less easy and less responsive. The infants judged securely attached to their mothers in the Strange Situation also differ from other infants in that they seem able to use the mother as a secure base for exploration and play in both the home and strange environments. Finally, infants judged secure with mother in the Strange Situation are found more compliant and cooperative with the mother and other persons in other settings (Stayton et al. 1971; Matas et al. 1978; Londerville and Main 1981).

Main has conducted extensive analyses of the behavior of mothers and infants outside of the Strange Situation (Main 1977; Main et al. 1979; Chap. 26). Using three independent samples, she has found mothers of infants judged avoidant in the Strange Situation distinguished by physical rejection of proximity and contact with the infant, low affective responsiveness, and anger. Seen outside of the Strange Situation, infants judged avoidant differ from others in exhibiting sudden bouts of aggressive behavior, in their lack of affect expression, and in their tendency to avoid persons attempting to establish new relationships. In addition, they tend actively to disobey parental commands and prohibitions.

For the Bielefeld samples, home visits conducted during the first year of life provide us with some comparable information regarding the kind of mothering these infants received. Perhaps we can understand the high proportion of infants judged avoidant of the parent in Bielefeld in light of some observable pressure on German children to become self-reliant and independent as early as the first year of life. There have been reports on the primacy of obedience in evaluating children's behavior in Germany (e.g., Kemmler & Heckhausen 1959) as well as on wide differences between scores of German and U.S. mothers on Shoben's Parent Attitude Survey, indicating higher controlling attitudes of the German mothers (Rapp 1961). There is also the likelihood that in German families the notion of obedience is still somewhat biased toward a concept of discipline and not, as with the obedient children in the Ainsworth Baltimore sample (Stayton et al. 1971), toward a concept of compliance.

In our own work we use the terms *gehorchen* and *einwilligen* for the two kinds of obedience. To our knowledge, this distinction has not been made before. In the case of *einwilligen* (compliance), the child obeys directions because they have become part of a secure relationship. The child's compliance in this case implies an easy cooperation between the child and its mother or father on the basis of a well-developed, intimate, and mainly preverbal communication. In the case of *gehorchen* (discipline), directions are not necessarily part of the pattern of a secure and intimate relationship. Rather, by being associated with negative consequences (threat, punishment, etc.), the disciplinary directions may create a stress on the relationship – at least temporarily. It may be, then, that our Bielefeld parents behave to some degree as Main describes mothers of avoidant infants in the United States; that is, to produce self-reliant and obedient infants, they may limit affective communication and reject infant bids for proximity. Perhaps the parent, rather than behaving as an intimate of the child, puts himself or herself at a distance like a teacher in the interests of *gehorchen.*

A related observation seems to support this hypothesis. We have noted many German 18-month-olds approaching their fathers in the Strange Situation with their eyes lowered to the floor and some insignificant object in their hand. Some human ethologists consider a glance-avoiding approach with an object as a strategy for testing a strange person's reaction before making any social commitment (Eibl-Eibesfeld 1970; Stanjek 1978). We are presently attempting a careful analysis of this kind of giving behavior and why it occurs with the familiar father in the Bielefeld children.

Are a majority of Bielefeld children really insecure in their attachment to their mother or father?[1] If we are to pursue this question, or even to compare German and U.S. infants, we must turn to correlates of behavior seen outside of the Strange Situation. We must discover whether – compared to the mothers of our secure infants – the mothers of our avoidant infants have the same characteristics that distinguish mothers of avoidant versus secure infants in Baltimore (Ainsworth et al. 1978) and in Berkeley (Chap. 26). Similar comparisons must be made between characteristics of avoidant and secure infants in our sample. We are currently collecting data that should permit us to answer these questions.

Even if we do find our avoidant infants more aggressive than our secure infants and more avoidant of persons who attempt to establish relationships with them, we still will not know whether they are insecure in any absolute sense. To answer this question, we are undertaking fine-grained videotape analysis. We will use this means to discover whether our avoidant infants show insecurity or even anxiety in posture or facial expression (following Argyle 1975; Emde et al. 1978; Oster & Ekman 1978).

Our study of infants in Bielefeld has revealed, in sum, a troubling and yet intriguing behavioral difference. If two-thirds of the U.S. infants seen in the Strange Situation show a behavior pattern toward either parent that is classified as securely attached, but two-thirds of the Bielefeld infants have to be classified by the same criteria as insecurely attached, which pattern should be considered species-adaptive? Even if the analyses to be undertaken do indicate insecurity in the avoidant children, the differences may constitute either an alternative pathway or simply a matter of differing timing in development. It may be that a somewhat different strategy of child rearing in Bielefeld leads to a temporary disturbance of relationship patterns. If so, it seems likely to be remedied as the Bielefeld children gradually develop their own efficient ways of relating their activities to the wider world, with or without the support of persons to whom they are closely attached. On the other hand, attachment theory implies a logical possibility of a somewhat reduced security in interpersonal relations (Bowlby 1973). Without empirical data the implications of our present findings cannot be formulated.

NOTE

1 As a final note, we wish to add that only a minority of Bielefeld children are avoidant of both their parents. The majority of children who could be classified were found secure with one of the two parents. Main and Weston (1981) are using a joint classification system for their examination of a large sample of children in Berkeley, California. They report little social or emotional difficulty for children so long as the child (seen in successive Strange Situations) is found secure with one of the two parents.

ACKNOWLEDGMENTS

I wish to thank Donna Weston for coming from Berkeley to Regensburg to establish reliability in the videotape analyses and to help us interpret the German children's behavior patterns. Franz Huber and Ulrike Wartner provided excellent analyses of the 12- and 18-month-olds' behavior, and Ursula Stolberg provided minute descriptions of the 18-month-olds' giving behavior toward their fathers.

We thank Stiftung Volkswagenwerk for their support for the study of Bielefeld infants and parents.

REFERENCES

Ainsworth, M. D. S. 1969. Object relations, dependency and attachment: a theoretical review of the infant–mother relationship. *Child Development* 40:966–1025.

1973. The development of infant–mother attachment. *In:* B. Caldwell & H. N. Riccuti (eds.), *Review of child development research,* vol. 3. University of Chicago Press, Chicago.

Ainsworth, M. D. S., M. C. Blehar, E. Waters, & S. Wall. 1978. Patterns of attachment: a psychological study of the strange situation. Erlbaum, Hillsdale, New Jersey.

Argyle, M. 1975. *Bodily communication.* Methuen, London.

Blanchard, M., & M. Main. 1979. Avoidance of the attachment figure and social-emotional adjustment in daycare infants. *Developmental Psychology* 15:445–446.

Bowlby, J. 1969. *Attachment and loss,* vol. 1, *Attachment.* Hogarth Press, London.

1973. *Attachment and loss,* vol. 2, *Separation: anxiety and anger.* Hogarth Press, London.

Eibl-Eibesfeld, I. 1970. *Liebe und Hass.* Piper, Munich.

Emde, R. N., D. H. Kligman, I. H. Reich, & T. A. Wade. 1978. Emotional expression in infancy. 1. Initial studies of social signaling and an emergent model. *In:* M. Lewis & L. A. Rosenblum (eds.), *The development of affect.* Plenum, New York.

George C., & M. Main. Social interactions of young abused children: approach, avoidance and aggression. *Child Development* 30:306–318.

Grossman, K. E. 1978. Emotionale and soziale Entwicklung im Kleinkindalter. *In:* H. Rauh (ed.), *Jahrbuch fur Entwicklungspsychologie.* Klett-Cotta, Stuttgart.

Kemmler, L., & H. Heckhausen. 1959. Mütteransichten über Erziehungsfragen. *Psychologische Rundschau* 10:82–93.

Londerville, S., & Main, M. 1981. Security of attachment, compliance and maternal training methods in the second year of life. *Developmental Psychology* 17:3:289–99.

Main, M. 1977a. Sicherheit und Wissen. *In:* K. N. E. Grossmann (ed.), *Entwicklung der Lernfähigkeit in der sozialen Umwelt.* Kindler Verlag, Munich.

1977b. Analysis of a peculiar form of reunion behavior seen in some day-care children: its history and sequelae in children who are home-reared. *In:* R. Webb (ed.), *Social development in childhood: daycare programs and research.* Johns Hopkins University Press, Baltimore.

Main, M., L. Tomasini, & W. Tolan. 1979. Differences among mothers of infants judged to differ in security. *Developmental Psychology* 15:472–473.

Main, M., & D. Weston. 1981. The quality of the toddler's relationship to mother and to father: related to conflict behavior and the readiness for forming new relationships. *Child Development,* in press.

Matas, L., R. Arend, & L. A. Sroufe. 1978. Continuity of adaptation in the second year: the relationship between quality of attachment and later competence. *Child Development* 49:547–556.

Oster, H., & P. Ekman. 1978. Facial behavior in child development. *In:* A. Collins (ed.), *Minnesota symposia on child psychology,* vol. 2. Erlbaum, Hillsdale, New Jersey.

Rapp, D. W. 1961. Childrearing attitudes of mothers in Germany and the United States. *Child Development* 32:669–678.

Stanjek, K. 1978. Das Ueberreichen von Gaben: Function und Entwicklung in den ersten Lebensjahren. *Zeitschrift für Entwicklungspsychologie und Pädagogische Psychologie* 10:103–113.

Stayton, D. J., R. Hogan, & M. D. S. Ainsworth. 1971. Infant obedience and maternal behavior: the origins of socialization reconsidered. *Child Development* 42:1057–1069.

Waters, E. 1978. The reliability and stability of individual differences in infant–mother attachment. *Child Development* 49:483–494.

28

ADULT MALE–INFANT RELATIONSHIPS: HUMAN AND NONHUMAN PRIMATE EVIDENCE

ROSS D. PARKE and STEPHEN J. SUOMI

The role that males play in the caretaking and socialization of the young has received only limited attention. In contrast to the female–child relationship, particularly the mother–infant relationship, of which we have many rich descriptions, the male–child relationship has been neglected. This chapter outlines some of the reasons and highlights recent evidence that is rapidly revising our views of the male's role in infancy and childhood in both human and nonhuman primate groups.

SOME REASONS FOR OUR NEGLECT OF THE MALE–CHILD RELATIONSHIP

Detailed study of the male role in the caretaking of infants has been limited for a variety of reasons. At the human level, cultural norms prescribing a limited role for males in interaction with infants and children have dampened enthusiasm for research in this area. However, close examination of the cross-cultural evidence indicates that males are not assigned a secondary role in all cultures. There is a number of notable exceptions in which males and females play a more equal role in the care of young children. For example, among the Trobrianders of Melanesia or the Ilocos of the Philippines, mother and father share more equally in the care and feeding of infants and children. In recent years, modern industrialized countries in both Europe and North America have been extensively reevaluating the male role in infant and child care. These shifts serve as a reminder that human social behavior is affected by broad historical developments; changes in technology, economics, and medicine can produce marked alterations in our sex role definitions.

At the animal level, research on infant caretaking has likewise greatly emphasized maternal behaviors to the virtual exclusion of any consideration of possible roles for adult males. In part, this disproportionate emphasis may reflect that for many group-living mammals, including most of the advanced nonhuman primates, promiscuity rather than permanent pair bonding characterizes heterosexual behavior. Thus, it is often very difficult to identify an infant's father among the males in the group, whereas the identity of the mother is usually obvious. Moreover, although there is considerable species variability in the relative incidence of adult male–infant interactions, relatively low levels of such interactions characterize those species that have been popular subjects in both laboratory and field research.

An unfortunate result has been that a few pioneering studies that examined male caretaking in these species were given undue weight and led prematurely to the conclusion that male involvement with the young was limited for all primates. Typically cited are the field studies by DeVore (1963), who found that male baboons take little interest in infants. Few instances of either play or affectionate physical contact were observed. Limited laboratory evidence supported a similar view. For example, in a study by Harlow et al. (Chamove et al. 1967), 20- to 40-day-old infants were introduced to male–female pairs of preadolescent monkeys. The males and females played clearly different roles: Females were 4 times as likely as males to express nurturant behavior to an infant, whereas males were 10 times as hostile as females. In short, early evidence from nonhuman primates indicated that males are less interested and involved in the care and nurturance of infants than are females. As this chapter will document, this early evidence was very incomplete: It is now established that there are indeed wide species differences in levels of male involvement (Hrdy 1976; Mitchell 1969; Redican 1976).

The presumed effect of hormones on caretaking behavior has also limited our attention to the male–child relationship. Hormonal changes associated with pregnancy and parturition are thought to prime the female to engage in caretaking. Impressive support for this view comes from the work of Rosenblatt et al. (Rosenblatt & Siegel 1975), who have shown that as pregnancy proceeds, responsiveness of the female to young rat pups increases. Investigations that suggest that hormonal levels (estradiol) increase as labor approaches (Shaikh 1971), as well as experimental studies showing that virgin female rats treated with female hormones show maternal behavior more rapidly than nontreated control females (Lott & Rosenblatt 1969), have given further support to the hypothesis. However, the assumption that parenting behavior – even in rats – is solely under hormonal control is too simplistic. As Rosenblatt (1970) has demonstrated, maternal behavior is under the control of two systems: a short-term hormonal system surrounding parturition that controls maternal behavior in the prepartum and postpartum periods, and a second social cueing system that predominates in the postpartum period and relies on the presence of the infant as a necessary condition to maintain maternal behavior. This model is consistent with a recent conclusion based on a review of parenting behavior of subhuman mammals:

> The hormones associated with pregnancy, childbirth, and lactation are not necessary for the appearance of parental behavior. With sufficient exposure to newborns, virgin females and males will show parental behavior – although the behavior is not so readily aroused as it is in a female that has been hormonally primed.
>
> [Maccoby & Jacklin 1974:219]

The same argument can be extended to the human level, where cultural and social factors probably play a very important role in determining paternal – including parental – behavior. In fact, recent attempts to demonstrate that human mothers are hormonally primed and sensitized to their infants immediately after birth (Klaus & Kennell 1976) have yielded only equivocal results (Pannabecker & Emde 1977). The role that hormones may play in parenting behavior is not in question; what is questioned is the assumed tyranny of hormonal control and the assumption that hormonal changes are necessary for the appearance of parental behavior. A closer examination of the social and environmental factors that may control parenting behavior - in males as well as females - is required.

On the other hand, closer examination of a genetic factor - kinship - has resulted from the recently rising interest in sociobiological theory and interpretation. A basic premise of the theory is that activities that enhance the chances for an organism's genes to be represented in future generations are genetically selected for; such activites can include preferential behavior toward kin and/or destructive behavior toward nonkin (Dawkins 1976; Wilson 1975). Because this premise applies equally to male and female members of the species, sociobiologists have recently devoted considerable effort to the identification of possible differences in adult male behavior directed toward blood-related versus nonrelated infants (e.g., Hrdy 1976, 1977; Trivers 1972).

A final reason for the revived interest in the male role is our expanded view of the important ingredients of parenting for the promotion of adequate social and emotional development in offspring. The stage was set for an emergence of interest in the male role by the general decline of secondary drive theory (Hinde 1960; White 1959). Specifically, Harlow's (1958) classic demonstration that the feeding situation was not the critical context for early social development, combined with the emerging evidence that social and sensory stimulatory activities, such as play and exploration, were important determinants of development of both humans and animals (Bekoff 1972; Berlyne 1969; Rheingold 1956; Welker 1971), led to a heightened interest in the role of the male as a potentially important interactive partner. Males, of course, are just as capable of providing these important ingredients for early development as females. These shifts legitimized the active investigation of the adult male's role in the development of the young. In the past few years, such investigation has disclosed considerable involvement with infants by adult males at both the human and nonhuman primate levels.

ADULT MALE–OFFSPRING INVOLVEMENT

Human evidence

Adult human males vary considerably in both the quantity and quality of their involvement with infants and children. Males play a complementary and distinctive role rather than one that is a mere duplicate of the female parent's. Although play emerges as a predominant activity for the adult male, it will be argued that males are capable of assuming a caretaking role if this type of behavior is required. Indeed, plasticity in behavior appears to be highly characteristic of the human male's infant-directed activities in general.

Male involvement appears to begin very early in life, as a series of observational studies by Parke et al. have recently demonstrated. In one study (1972), they observed the behavior of middle-class fathers in the family triad of mother, father, and infant. Observation sessions lasted 10 minutes and occurred during the first 3 days after delivery. The following behaviors were noted for each parent: holds, changes position, looks, smiles, vocalizes, touches, kisses, explores, imitates, feeds, hands over to other parent. The results indicated that fathers were just as involved as mothers and that mothers and fathers did not differ on the majority of measures. In fact, fathers tended to hold the infant and to rock it in their arms more than mothers. In short, in a context in which participation was voluntary, fathers were just as involved as mothers in interacting with their infants.

In a later study, a group of lower-class fathers were observed in two contexts: (1) alone with their infant and (2) in the presence of the mother (Parke & O'Leary 1976). This study permitted a much more stringent test of father–infant involvement and wider generalization of the previous findings. As in the earlier study, the father was a very interested and active participant. In fact, in the family triad, the father was more likely to hold the infant and visually attend to it than the mother. Nor was the mother's presence necessary for the father's active involvement; the father was an equally active interactor in both settings – alone and with the mother. Fathers in our studies were just as nurturant as mothers, as indexed by their levels of looking, touching, vocalizing, and kissing. There was only a single nurturant behavior – smiling – in which the mother surpassed the father in both studies.

Fathers, like mothers, adjust their behavior to accommodate to the infant. Fathers speak slower, use shorter phrases, and repeat themselves more when talking to infants than to adults. Presumably, these modifications in speech help to elicit and maintain infant attention to the speaker. The adaptive significance of these speech adjustments may stem from the fact that the infant may learn to recognize the characteristics of its caretakers more quickly as a result (Phillips & Parke 1979).

Although there is considerable cultural variability in the role distribution of males and females, in our present society fathers do appear to play a less active role in caretaking than mothers. In the Parke and O'Leary (1976) study, in which all infants were bottle-fed, fathers fed significantly less than mothers when they were alone with the baby. Additional support for this mother–father difference comes from another study of father–newborn interaction that involved a detailed examination of early parent–infant interaction in a feeding context (Parke & Sawin 1979). Comparisons of the frequencies and durations of specific caretaking activities of mothers and fathers alone with their infants in a feeding context indicate that mothers spend more time feeding the infant and in related caretaking activities, such as wiping the baby's face, than do fathers. These findings suggest that parental role allocation begins in the earliest days of life.

Many of the features that are evident in father–infant interactions in the newborn period characterize the interaction patterns in later infancy as well. The early differences between mother and father in terms of caretaking are evident in later home observations. Fathers spend less time feeding and caretaking than mothers in the first year of infancy (Kotelchuck 1976). However, the lesser degree of father involvement in feeding does not imply that fathers are less competent than mothers to care for the newborn infant. Competence can be measured in a variety of ways; one approach is to measure the parents' sensitivity to infant cues in the feeding context. Success in caretaking, to a large degree, is dependent on the parents' ability to correctly interpret the infant's behavior so that their own behavior can be regulated to achieve some interaction goal. To illustrate, in the feeding context, the aim of the parent is to facilitate infant feeding; the infant, in turn, by a variety of behaviors such as sucking or coughing, provides the parent with feedback on the effectiveness or ineffectiveness of his or her current behavior in maintaining this process.

In this context, one approach to the competence issue is to examine the degree to which the caretaker modifies his or her behavior in response to infant cues. Parke and Sawin (1975) found that the father's sensitivity to an auditory distress signal while feeding - sneeze, spit-up, cough - was as marked as the mother's. Using a conditional probability analysis, they demonstrated that fathers, like mothers, adjusted their behavior by momentarily ceasing feeding, looking more closely to check on the infant, and vocalizing to it. The only difference involved the greater cautiousness of the fathers, who were more likely than mothers to inhibit their touching in the presence of this signal. The implication of this analysis is clear: In spite of the fact that they spent less time overall, fathers were as sensitive as mothers to infant cues and as responsive to them in feeding. Finally, the amount of milk consumed by the infants with their mothers and fathers was very similar (36 versus 34 gm for mothers and fathers, respectively). In short, fathers and mothers were not only similar in sensitivity but were equally successful in feeding the infant based on the amount of milk consumed. Invoking a competence/performance distinction, we argue that fathers may not necessarily be frequent contributors to infant feeding, but when called upon they have the competence to execute this task effectively.

Moreover, fathers in the Parke and Sawin (1975) study were just as responsive as mothers to other infant cues, such as vocalizations. Mothers and fathers both increased their rate of positive vocalizations following an infant vocal sound; in addition, both parents touched the infant and looked at it more closely after it vocalized. However, mothers and fathers differed in the behaviors they showed in response to this type of infant elicitor: Upon vocalization, fathers were more likely than mothers to increase their vocalization rate. Mothers, on the other hand, were more likely to react to infant vocalization with touching than fathers. Possibly, these fathers were more cautious than mothers in their use of tactile stimulation during feeding due to concern about disrupting infant feeding behavior. These data indicate that fathers and mothers both react to the newborn infant's cues in a contingent and functional manner even though they differ in their specific response patterns. The interaction patterns in the newborn period are reciprocal; although our focus in the Parke and Sawin (1975) study was on the role of infant cues as elicitors of parent behavior, in a later study (Parke & Sawin 1980) it was shown that parent vocalizations can modify newborn infant behavior, such as infant vocalizations. Interaction between fathers and infants - even in the newborn period - is clearly bidirectional; both parents and infant regulate each other's behavior in the course of interaction.

Recent laboratory studies of the reactions of mothers and fathers to infant smiles and cries have confirmed our general findings. Mothers and fathers did not differ on measures of psychophysiological responsiveness or reported moods in response to infant cries or smiles (Frodi et al. 1978). Both were responsive to these contrasting infant signals, which suggests that fathers as well as mothers are sensitive to infant cues – a skill that is extremely important for adequate parenting.

Nonhuman primate evidence

How well do the nonhuman primate data correspond to the human findings on male involvement? There is no simple answer to this question, primarily because there is enormous variability in male involvement among different primate species, across different settings for the same species and, in some documented cases, across conspecific males in the same social group. The degree of correspondence thus depends in large part on the particular data set examined. Nevertheless, there are some striking parallels between human data and findings from at least some nonhuman primate studies.

The degree and quality of male involvement range from species in which males actually surpass females in the amount of caretaking to species in which the most prominent infant-directed male behavior is infanticide, at least for some males under certain social conditions. Apart from these extremes, most primate males do not show a high degree of involvement in the care of infants. Two excellent reviews of the literature on adult male involvement across different primate species have been published by Redican (1976) and Hrdy (1976), so a comprehensive species-by-species review will not be presented here.

In general, the degree of male involvement appears to be related to characteristics of the modal social structure for each species. For example, very high levels of male caretaking have been found for virtually all species in which adult males and females typically form monogamous relationships for prolonged periods, and the involvement appears greatest in those species for which the monogamous pairing usually lasts for life and for which nonextended families (i.e., containing fewer than three generations of kin) represent the modal social grouping for the species. Such species include some relatively primitive marmosets and tamarins (Ingram 1978; Stevenson 1978) and the relatively advanced gibbons and siamangs (Chivers 1971, 1972; Fox 1974). At the other extreme are species in which adult males almost never interact with infants; in these species the adult males voluntarily remain isolated from female conspecifics except during the breeding season (which is usually very brief). Such males usually live either in all-male groups (e.g., squirrel monkeys) or as hermits (e.g., orangutans).

Near this lower extreme of male involvement are many of the species whose members live in multimale, multifemale groups, such as some baboons, macaques, and chimpanzees. Adult males of these species typically interact very infrequently with infants, especially during the infants' first few weeks of life. However, not all species of baboons and macaques are characterized by relatively low levels of adult male involvement with infants (just as they do not all live in multimale, multifemale groups). Redican (1976) has hypothesized that the degree of adult male involvement depends on the degree of maternal restrictiveness: When maternal restrictiveness is high, male involvement is low, and vice versa. Although the correlation is not perfect across these species, it is high enough to serve as a reminder that male involvement cannot be understood independently of the activities of other members in the infant's social network. Second, it underlines the important role that current conditions may play in eliciting paternal parenting behavior. Let us briefly consider the evidence in support of Redican's hypothesis.

In rhesus and pigtail macaques the extent of maternal restrictiveness is high, and male involvement – as observed in the wild – is generally low. For example, rhesus macaques observed in the wild can be characterized as "generally indifferent, somewhat sensitive to approach and contact, occasionally aggressive and rarely affiliative" (Redican 1976:356). Southwick et al. (1965) reported only three incidents of male adult–infant play in over 700 hours of observation, and Lindburg (1971) saw only two play instances in over 900 hours of field observation. Although Taylor et al. (1978) reported slightly higher levels among Nepalese rhesus monkey males, interactions with infants still constituted less than 1% of these males' total social activities. In contrast, the level of involvement of males in the care of infants by Barbary macaques is the highest among the macaques, and the level of maternal restrictiveness is the lowest. According to observations by Deag and Crook (1971), Barbary male macaques hold, groom, carry, and protect infants, as well as yearlings and 2-year-olds. Among the Japanese macaques (Itani 1959), a group that also shows a high degree of male care, the majority of the male interactions are with 1- and 2-year-olds and rarely with neonates. Male care appears to occur mainly when mothers are preoccupied with neonates and thus do not restrict their older offspring – a finding that provides further support for Redican's hypothesis.

Additional evidence in support of this line of reasoning comes from studies in which the mother's level of involvement with the infant has been either experimentally or accidentally decreased. In one study (Spencer-Booth & Hinde 1967), when several rhesus monkey mothers were removed from a group, there was an increase in male–infant interaction. Similarly, Bucher (1970) found that rhesus monkey males actively groomed, carried, and played with infants when the mothers' caretaking behavior was impaired by surgical procedures. Thus, some males do show a more active role in interacting with their infants when the female investment decreases.

In most nonhuman primate species, the nature of adult male–infant interactions differs considerably from that of mother–infant interactions. Probably the most noticeable difference (other than nursing) is the almost total absence of sustained ventral contact with and/or cradling of infants by adult males; in marked contrast, most species of monkey mothers spend most of their sleeping and waking hours in intimate ventral contact with their infant during its initial weeks of life. Even among species for which the level of male–infant interaction equals or exceeds that of mother–infant interaction, ventral contact between adult males and infants is relatively infrequent and often quite clumsy. Although males of several marmoset and tamarin species typically carry their infants throughout most of the day (with the mothers taking over only during nursing periods), they usually carry the infants on their backs rather than on their ventrums, whereas most mother–infant contact is ventral–ventral. Macaque males seldom try to cradle their infants, and when they do, they are usually inept, for example, holding the infant upside down.

In sum, adult males of many primate species do show involvement with infants if the situational demands are present. However, they generally avoid ventral–ventral contact, one of the most characteristic patterns of maternal behavior in the majority of primate species. Male behavior toward infants differs from that of females in other respects as well. One behavior pattern – social play – is particularly characteristic of much of the adult male's involvement with infants. Subsequent sections will focus on father–infant play in human and nonhuman primates. First, however, we will examine the degree of plasticity in the manner and amount of adult male involvement with infants.

PLASTICITY IN ADULT MALE–INFANT RELATIONSHIPS

Primate evidence

A number of recent laboratory studies have investigated the plasticity of male involvement with infants by experimental modification of the male's opportunity for involvement. These studies have demonstrated that the level of male involvement is not fixed or preprogrammed. They underline the openness or fluidity of the male–infant relationship and underscore dramatically the important role of experiential factors in modifying male behavior. The studies do not undermine the utility of a genetic preprogrammed model but do serve as an important reminder of the possibility of modifying genetic trajectories by experience. Finally, they illustrate the importance of the competence/performance distinction stressed in our earlier discussion of the human data. Males of at least some animal species are clearly capable of considerable paternal behavior – even though they do not typically display parenting patterns in their natural habitat.

Mitchell (1969; Mitchell & Brandt 1972) and his colleagues, notably Redican (1975, 1976, 1978), have been among the first to investigate the modifiability of male rhesus monkey behavior in terms of interactions with infants. As noted above, male rhesus monkeys who are observed under free-ranging conditions rarely exhibit either interest in or direct care of infants. Laboratory studies often yield a similar picture.

The Mitchell and Redican studies clearly challenge this view of the male rhesus monkey's limited capacity for infant care. Based on observations of four pairs of mature male and infant rhesus monkeys over a 7-month period, these investigators found that male rhesus monkeys are certainly capable of engaging in nurturant behavior when given the opportunity in the laboratory. However, there were differences between adult males and females. Mothers were generally higher in contact, and both mothers and infants initiated contact as often as they ended it. In contrast, adult males consistently broke contact more often than they established it, and the converse was true for their infants. In contrast to mothers, males rarely restrained or retrieved infants, but they actively protected them by directly attacking the source of danger and/or coming between it and the infants. Adult males, however, were observed to groom to the same extent as females.

To measure the effects of rearing infants with adult males on infant attachment behaviors, the infants were separated for 2 days at 7 months. The level of distress vocalization to separation from females and adult males was similar. During separation, both groups of infants showed decreases in solitary play and exploration but increases in self-directed behaviors. "In general the results of the longitudinal and separation studies ... indicate a significant potential for both adult males to form attachments with infants and for infants to form attachments to adult males" (Redican 1976:359). This evidence is highly consistent with the human findings, namely, that adult males are capable of forming attachments to their offspring, and infants, in turn, can develop social attachments to their fathers as well as to their mothers.

Further evidence of the plasticity of male rhesus involvement with infants comes from Suomi's recent (1977) studies of lab-established nuclear family groups, each composed of a father, mother, and infant rhesus monkey. Behaviors exhibited by the adult males were recorded over a 37-month period. Results indicated that males were less active and more stable in their behavioral levels than their female mates or offspring. Nevertheless the adult males directed over 60% of their total social intitiates toward offspring and other infants, which accounted for almost one-third of the total frequency of all adult male behavior. Clearly, this degree of involvement greatly exceeds the meager levels of adult male–infant interaction typically reported in field studies of rhesus monkeys.

Similar plasticity in adult male–infant interactions has been demonstrated for orangutans. Adult male orangutans living in Sumatra are primarily solitary in nature, and ordinarily they do not come into contact with immatures except during brief periods of consort with adult females and their previous offspring (Rodman 1973). However, MacKinnon (1974) did observe a feral-living adult male essentially adopt a young juvenile. In addition, Zucker et al. (1978) studied the behavior of a 19-year-old adult male orangutan living in a zoo compound that also contained two females and a 4-year-old. Ten distinct infant-directed behavior patterns were exhibited by the adult male; the majority of such activity was generally characterized as playful rough-and-tumble in quality, in contrast to the form of most adult female–infant interactions observed by the authors.

A final point about plasticity in primate adult male–infant interactions concerns the magnitude of individual differences among males living in the same social unit: Such differences tend to be enormous, and the contributing factors are inconsistent across different social units. For example, Hendy-Neely and Rhine (1977) found that in one captive group of stumptail macaques the most dominant adult male showed the smallest amount of involvement with infants among all adult males, whereas in a second stumptail group the most dominant male showed the greatest involvement. Brandt et al. (1970) and Estrada and Sandoval (1977) found that younger adult stumptail males interacted with infants more than did older adult males, but Gouzoules (1975) and Hendy-Neely and Rhine (1977) reported exactly the opposite finding, with older adult males displaying the higher levels.

These varying results underline the notion that the adult male's caretaking capabilities are highly flexible and that its actual involvement with infants may well reflect idiosyncratic characteristics of its position within its particular social group. Indeed, we have recently obtained firm evidence that a given male's involvement with infants can change substantially from year to year, particularly if its social status within the group has changed (Suomi & O'Neill 1979). The relevant data concern the beta male in a small laboratory-born group of rhesus monkeys living in a large outdoor enclosure in rural Wisconsin. During the first year in which infants were born into the group, this male avoided virtually all interactions with them. The next year, however, he improved his social standing somewhat, and correspondingly his involvement with the infants increased to the point where he now has the highest interaction levels with all infants in the group, except for the mothers. It is little wonder that there has been such inconsistency in the macaque literature on the relationship of dominance status to the degree of involvement with infants (e.g., Mitchell & Brandt 1972).

In summary, adult males in these and other advanced primate species appear to display considerable plasticity at the species level and substantial flexibility at the individual subject level in their involvement with infants. Even in species in which male involvement in caretaking is usually minimal, at least some adult males are capable of a fairly wide repertoire of generally positive and nonaggressive infant-directed behaviors, and under certain circumstances in which infants are present, these behavior patterns are often displayed. These findings support the hypothesis that primate adult male behavior toward infants is quite flexible and can be adjusted to deal effectively with a variety of circumstances that require increased participation in the infant's social network. Thus, the adult males appear to possess considerable capability for infant caretaking, even though it ordinarily need not be exercised in a feral environment. Our own data (Suomi 1976, 1979a) suggest that such flexibility is not shared nearly as much by macaque mothers, that is, their maternal behaviors show far less variability across different physical and social settings than do the caretaking activities of adult males.

Plasticity of human father–infant involvement

Our review of the nonhuman primate evidence clearly indicates a high degree of plasticity in male adult–infant involvement. Support for similar plasticity in response to experiential and social situational demands is evident at the human level as well. Evidence from naturally occurring modifications in maternal availability as well as recent experimental investigations aimed at modifying father–infant involvement are available.

One important determinant of father–child involvement is maternal employment – a condition that decreases maternal availability for child care. Recent studies of maternal employment (Hoffman 1977; Hoffman & Nye 1974) indicate that in households where women work outside the home, fathers participate more actively in child care.

> This fact has significance for sex differences in several ways. First, it is itself a diminution of sex differences. In the working mother family, the pattern of the father as breadwinner and the mother as the exclusive performer of certain household tasks and parent functions is weakened. Second, the models of sex roles that the parents present for the child are less stereotypically traditional and consequently the child's concept of what males and females are is less differentiated. [Hoffman 1977:653]

In support of this finding, daughters of working mothers saw women as more competent and effective, whereas sons saw men as warmer and more expressive than did the sons of nonworking mothers. The general finding that paternal involvement varies with maternal availability is consistent with evidence from nonhuman primates (Redican 1976), as discussed above.

Recent experimental evidence confirms the importance of situational and experimental factors in modifying the level of male–infant involvement. Lind (1974) demonstrated that Swedish fathers who were given the opportunity to learn and practice basic caretaking skills during the postpartum hospital period were more involved in the home in caring for their infant at 3 months and in household tasks. Similarly, in the United States, Parke et al. (1979b) recently showed fathers a videotape that demonstrated play techniques and caretaking skills during the early postpartum hospital period. In contrast to control fathers who saw no film, the experimental fathers were more likely to diaper and feed their infant sons (although not their daughters) at home 3 months after the intervention. Finally, Zelazo et al. (1977) have successfully modified the levels of father–child interaction with 1-year-old infants. Together, the investigations indicate the plasticity of the father–infant relationship and the potential value of utilizing experimental techniques to establish more firmly cause–effect relationships in this area.

PLAY: A SPECIAL CONTEXT FOR ADULT MALE–INFANT INTERACTIONS

Thus far we have demonstrated that adult male–infant interactions tend to complement those between the infant and its mother. In both human and nonhuman primates the mother's role includes certain unique contributions to the infant's range of social stimulation. But mothers alone do not ordinarily provide their infants with all the social stimulation they need, at least in terms of quality if not quantity. Such stimulation must come from others in the infant's social network, and in most human societies and for most nonhuman primate species, such others include adult males. It appears that across the various primate species the stimulation most consistently provided by adult males is social play.

Nonhuman primate data

As we discussed earlier, there is considerable variability across different primate species in adult male interactions with infants. In some species adult males are, in fact, the primary caretakers, whereas in other species any interaction between an adult male and an infant is rare. Yet, among all those primate species in which interactions between adult males and infants do occur, play behavior always accounts for a substantial proportion. Indeed, in those species for which male–infant interactions are generally low, social play is usually the most frequent nonaggressive behavior pattern shown by these males toward infants. For example, Zucker et al. (1978:382) reported that "it seems appropriate to characterize the vast majority of adult male-juvenile interactions as *playful*" in their description of male–infant interactions among a group of zoo-dwelling orangutans. Taylor et al. (1978) found that approximately 60% of feral Nepalese rhesus monkey male–infant interactions involve social play, and Suomi (1977, 1979a) found almost exactly the same play percentage in his nuclear family-living rhesus males and infants, who in this artificial laboratory environment showed much higher overall interaction levels with infants than have been reported in field studies. Redican (1978) likewise found a high incidence of play between his adult male rhesus subjects and their infant cagemates. Among species for which adult male caretaking of infants is more substantial, the proportion of male–infant interactions that involve social play is generally lower than for the above-described species, but the overall frequency of play is at least as high. Furthermore, as infants of these species grow older and the amount of adult male (and female) caretaking drops, the incidence of play with the adult males actually increases. Such a trend regarding adult male–infant play has been reported in stumptail macaques (Estrada & Sandoval 1977), Japanese macaques (Itani 1959), Barbary macaques (Deag & Crook 1971), and marmosets (Kleiman 1980; Stevenson 1978), among others. Clearly, play represents an important component of adult male–infant interactions, regardless of whether the interactions are frequent or relatively rare.

In contrast, play is not particularly characteristic of interactions between mothers and infants. In fact, by human standards, most primate mothers play surprisingly little with their infants. Among these species, social play between mother and child is about as rare as is ventral contact between the infant and a conspecific adult male (e.g., Golopol & Suomi 1980; Suomi 1979a). Moreover, the little play that does occur between an adult female and her infant is apt to be far less contact-oriented than is typical of adult male–infant play.

Infants, of course, play with other individuals in their social group besides adult males. In fact, in virtually all primate species, infants play more with peers and siblings than they do with adult males. Nevertheless, the significance of play for adult male–infant interactions should not be overlooked. In most primate species, social play by adult males with adolescents or adults of either sex does not occur very often. Thus, virtually all of an adult male's play activity is directed toward infants and young juveniles. As we shall see later in the chapter, in many species this adult male play tends to be directed primarily toward specific infants, rather than being randomly distributed among all immatures in the adult male's social group.

Play between human fathers and infants

Just as in nonhuman primates, human fathers perform a special role – as play partner. Human fathers spend a greater percentage of their interaction time in play activities than mothers (Kotelchuck 1976; Pedersen & Robson 1969). In another study, Lamb (1976) observed interactions among the mother, father, and infant in their homes at 7 to 8 months and again at 12 to 13 months. Lamb reported marked differences in the reasons that fathers and mothers pick up infants: Fathers were more likely to hold the babies during play, whereas mothers were far more likely to hold them for caretaking purposes.

Not only do fathers devote more time to play than mothers, but the style of play during father–infant and mother–infant interaction differs. In a recent study, Yogman et al. (1977) compared mothers, fathers, and strangers in their interactions with infants in a face-to-face play context. Five infants were studied for 2 minutes of interaction with their mother, father, and a stranger from 2 weeks to 6 months in a lab arrangement whereby infant and adult faced each other with instructions to play without using toys and without removing the infant from the seat. Adult–infant interaction patterns were scored using videotaped records and a variety of microbehavioral analyses. Adults differed in their play with infants, as indicated by differences in vocalization and touching patterns. Mothers vocalized with soft, repetitive, imitative burst-pauses, talking more often than fathers, who did so significantly more often than strangers. Fathers, however, touched their infants with rhythmic tapping patterns more often than either mothers or strangers.

Stylistic differences in mother–father play are not restricted to young infants, as revealed by a recent laboratory study of parental play patterns with 8-month-old infants. In contrast to mothers, fathers played more physical games, such as bouncing and throwing the infant in the air (Power & Parke 1981). Recent naturalistic observations indicate similar differences in mother and father play styles. In the Lamb (1977a) study described above, fathers observed in their homes engaged in more physical (i.e., rough-and-tumble) and unusual play activities than mothers. Similar findings emerged from home observations of the infants at 15, 18, 21, and 24 months of age (Lamb 1977b). Again, fathers played more physical games and shared more parallel play with their infants. Mothers, in contrast, engaged in more conventional play activities (e.g., peek-a-boo, pat-a-cake), stimulus toy play (in which a toy was jiggled or operated to stimulate the child directly), and reading than fathers. Similar differences in the style of play patterns were found by Clarke-Stewart (1978) in a study of 15- to 30-month-old infants and their parents.

Not only do fathers and mothers differ in their play patterns, but infants also react differently to mother and father play. Lamb (1977a), in his study of 8- to 13-month-old infants, found that the infants' response to play with their fathers was significantly more positive than play with their mothers. Consistent with Lamb's observations is Clarke-Stewart's (1978) finding that 20-month-old children were significantly more responsive to play initiated by the father than by the mother. At 2.5 years of age, children were more cooperative, close, involved, excited, and interested in play with their fathers. Over two-thirds of the children chose to play with their fathers first in a choice situation and displayed a stronger preference for him as a playmate. The early emergence of fathers as play partners, in short, is reciprocated by the infants in the first 2 years of life.

Although caution is necessary in drawing firm conclusions, the human and primate data on male–infant play patterns appear to show some general parallels. At both the animal and human levels, adult male–infant interaction often consists of play, and adult male play is more intense, physical, and reciprocal than adult female play. Possibly, it is in part through these early playful interactions that the young of the species learn to display and modulate aggressive behaviors.

SEX OF INFANT AS A DETERMINANT OF FATHER–INFANT INTERACTION

Human evidence

One of the most consistent determinants of human parental expectations, perceptions, and organizers of behavior is the infant's sex. There are marked and relatively consistent differences in parental and maternal reactions to male and female infants. In general, adult males appear to be more involved with male offspring.

Differential treatment of male and female children starts as early as the newborn period. Parke and O'Leary (1976), in their hospital-based observational study, found that fathers touched first-born newborn boys more than either later-born boys or girls of either ordinal position. Fathers vocalized more to first-born boys than first-born girls, whereas they vocalized equally to later-born infants irrespective of their sex. Clearly there may be some basis to the claim that fathers really do prefer boys - especially first-born boys.

Nor are the differences in father behavior with male and female infants restricted to the newborn period. Parke and Sawin (1980) observed parent-infant interaction in a structured bottle-feeding and toy play situation during the newborn period in the hospital and again at 3 weeks and 3 months in the home. Fathers looked at their sons more than their daughters and checked on them more frequently by looking more closely at them. Fathers provided more visual and tactile stimulation for their sons, whereas mothers played a complementary role by providing more stimulation for their daughters. During the play sessions, fathers presented the toy and touched their sons more than their daughters. Mothers, on the other hand, more frequently stimulated their daughters with the toy than their sons and touched girls more than boys. During feeding, the same cross-sex effect was evident: Fathers made more frequent attempts to stimulate their sons' feeding by moving the bottle than they did for their daughters; mothers showed the opposite pattern. These findings indicate that parents stimulate their same-sex infant more than the opposite-sex infant; fathers and mothers play complementary roles with their male and female infants.

A similar pattern of father–son involvement is evident in unstructured home observational studies as well. Rebelsky and Hanks (1971), for example, noted that fathers decreased their vocalizations across the first 3 months of life to female infants more than to male infants. Similarly, Rendina and Dickerscheid (1976) reported that fathers spent more time attending to male than female infants and tended to play more with boys than girls. A more provocative finding concerns the differential involvement of fathers with temperamentally difficult male and female infants. Using Carey's Infant Temperament Scale, these investigators reported that fathers were involved in social activities with temperamentally difficult boys (14.6%) more than difficult girls (4%). In short, fathers apparently are willing to persist with difficult male infants more than with troublesome female infants. Consistent with these findings is Kotelchuck's (1976) finding that fathers report playing about half an hour per day longer with their first-born sons than their first-born daughters. Although Lamb (1977a) found no sex-of-parent–sex-of-infant relationships in his home observations at 8 and 13 months, he did find differences in father and mother treatments of their sons and daughters in his study of 15- to 24-month-old infants in their homes (1977b). Fathers vocalized more to their sons than mothers did; in fact, fathers were twice as active in interacting with their sons as with their daughters, although both parents vocalized to their daughters equally.

These recent observational studies suggest that fathers play a more intrusive and paramount role in the sex-typing process (Johnson 1963); fathers discriminate more than mothers in their treatment of male and female infants. In addition, boys are treated more discriminatively by their fathers than girls, which is consistent with other studies indicating that pressures toward sex-role adoption are stronger and occur at an earlier age for sons than daughters (Lansky 1967).

Sex of infant as a determinant of adult male–infant interactions in nonhuman primates

Some of the studies of adult male–infant interactions in nonhuman primates have directly examined possible differences in adult male behavior toward male versus female infants. In most cases, the results are surprisingly similar to the human data: Adult males of several species appear to be more interested and interactive with male than with female infants. Among stumptail macaques, for example, when males routinely engage in active infant caretaking, this enhanced attractiveness of male infants is expressed primarily in higher levels of touching and manipulating the male infants' genitalia (Bertrand 1969; Estrada & Sandoval 1977). On the other hand, among species in which adult males engage in few if any caretaking activities, differences in interaction with different-sexed infants are more likely to appear in the context of play and aggressive behavior. For example, Breuggeman (1973) found that rhesus monkey adult males living in the Cayo Santiago free-ranging colony played more frequently with male than with female infants.

In the early Wisconsin studies of nuclear family triads, similar sex preferences were found (Suomi 1972; Suomi et al. 1973): Fathers played with male infants more frequently than female infants. Some interesting complexities emerge from the more recent (1977) Suomi study of nuclear family interactions. In contrast to earlier studies, adult males did not differ in levels of play intitiatives toward male versus female offspring through the first 16 months, after which more play was directed toward daughters than sons. Similarly, male and female offspring did not differ in levels of play initiation directed toward fathers through the first 18 months, after which daughters had higher levels than sons. However, adult males played considerably more with nonoffspring male than nonoffspring female infants after 4 months. Adult males played equally with sons and other males after the first year, whereas male infants did not differentiate significantly between their own fathers and other adult males in levels of play at any age. Female infants showed high discriminability and high levels of play with their own fathers, but never with other adult males.

Additional evidence of greater adult male involvement with male infants comes from Redican's (1975) long-term laboratory study of male–infant interaction in wild-born rhesus monkeys. In adult male–infant pairs, sex differences in contact were more pronounced than in adult female–infant pairs. Male adults had more extensive contact with male infants. "Mothers tended to play with female infants whereas adult males did so with male infants. In general mothers interacted more positively with female infants and adult males with male infants" (Redican 1976:358–59).

Suomi (1979a) and Golopol (1977) have also made some direct comparisons between rhesus monkey adult males and adult females on the magnitude of differential treatment of male versus female infants. Clearly, adult females do not treat male and female offspring equally; several previous studies (e.g., Hansen 1966; Hinde & Spencer-Booth 1967; White & Hinde 1975) have reported that male infants are retrieved more often, as well as rejected more often, by their mothers; this finding perhaps reflects the fact that male infants are generally more active and tend to create more caretaking problems for their mothers than do female infants. Indeed, rhesus monkey mothers of borderline competence are far more likely to neglect and/or abuse male offspring than female offspring (Ruppenthal et al. 1976; Suomi 1978). Nevertheless, our recent comparisons show that the sex differences in treatment of infants by adult female rhesus monkeys are much smaller than the differences in treatment of male and female infants by adult males. Moreover, as the infants grow older, the sex differences in their interactions with adult males tend to increase, whereas with mothers and other adult females they tend to decrease, at least until adolescence (Suomi 1979a). Thus, the rhesus monkey evidence suggests that the sex of the infant is, if anything, a more powerful variable in adult male–infant interactions than it is in adult female–infant interactions, including mothers. In this respect, the findings clearly parallel the relevant human data.

FATHER–INFANT INTERACTION AND ITS EFFECTS ON THE INFANT

Human data

Although it has been established that fathers are involved with their infants, do infants reciprocate their fathers' investment? Both laboratory studies and home observational studies indicate that infants react positively to both mothers and fathers, but the quality of father–infant interactions is an important determinant of the infant's social responsiveness.

Recent evidence indicates that infants can discriminate among mothers, fathers, and strangers at a relatively early age. In a recent study, five infants ranging in age from 2 weeks to 6 months were observed interacting at weekly intervals with either the mother, father, or a stranger (Yogman et al. 1977). Based on a microanalysis of 2 minutes of playful communication between the adults and the infant, reliable differences in infant behavior were observed as early as 2 months of age. Using frowning as a measure, Yogman et al. demonstrated that infants display less frowning to either the mother (5.3%) or father (7.8%) than to a stranger (28.2%). After 2 months, they found that infants frown differentially to the mother (2.2%) than to the father (7.7%) as well as to a stranger (30.4%). Infant smiles, vocalization, and limb movements also discriminated between mothers and fathers versus strangers.

It is interesting not only to determine that infants can discriminate among different social agents but also to explore their preferences for different social agents. Theoretically, it seems appropriate to evaluate the assumptions underlying the Bowlby–Ainsworth attachment theory (Ainsworth 1973; Bowlby 1969) that most infants are attached to mothers earlier than fathers and that most prefer their mothers to their fathers. Both laboratory (Kotelchuck 1976) and home-based studies (Lamb 1977a) have indicated that infants in the first year of life show no consistent preference for either parent, and "there is no evidence to support the popular presumption that infants of this age (8–13 months) should prefer – indeed be uniquely attached to – their mothers" (Lamb 1977a:179).

The degree of infant social responsiveness, however, does vary with the amount and type of father involvement, whether social behavior is assessed in the laboratory or in the home (see Parke 1979b for a review). Positive relationships between overall proximity to the father for 1-year-old infants in the laboratory and paternal caretaking in the home have been found (Kotelchuck 1976). Similarly, Pedersen and Robson (1969), in their study of 8- to 9-month-old infants, found that father involvement in routine caretaking, emotional investment in the infant, and the stimulation level of play were positively related to the male infant's attachment to his father, as assessed by the age of onset and intensity of greeting behavior directed to the father.

Infant cognitive development is affected by the quality of father–infant interaction. In their study of 5- to 6-month-old infants, Pedersen et al. (1977) found that Bayley mental test scores were positively correlated with the amount of father contact. In a more detailed examination of the components of father–infant interaction in a sample of 16- to 22-month-old infants, Clarke-Stewart (1978) discovered that the fathers' social physical play best predicted boys' cognitive development, whereas the quality of the fathers' verbal interaction was a better predictor for female infants' cognitive status.

In summary, many of the same trends that have been discovered in studies with older children are evident in these investigations of younger infants. Fathers do play an influential role in their infants' cognitive and social development – from a very early age. The task remains to detail the mechanisms through which this influence is mediated, what cognitive capacities and social abilities are most affected by fathers, and at what ages these effects occur. In order to do this, it is important to consider these influences within a family context, as such influences rarely operate in a social vacuum.

Nonhuman primate data

Studies assessing the effects of interactions with adult males on infant development in nonhuman primates are relatively few; most studies of adult male–infant interactions have merely described characteristics of the interactions themselves. However, some relevant rhesus monkey data have been recently collected at Wisconsin (most of these data have not yet been published). First, it is clear that nuclear-family-reared rhesus monkey infants are quite capable of distinguishing fathers (or familiar adult males) not only from mothers and peers but also from unfamiliar adult males as early as 2 to 4 months of age. From that point on, they become increasingly selective in their behaviors toward each class of adult monkeys (Suomi 1979a). Also, rhesus monkeys reared in the presence of adult males develop much stronger preferences for such males relative to the preferences displayed by socially naive infants. Suomi et al. (1973) reported that nuclear-family-reared infants preferred their fathers to other adult males by at least as wide a margin as they preferred their mothers to other adult females; in tests comparing preference for mothers versus fathers, these infants displayed only a slight preference (i.e., 55% to 45%) for their mothers, despite the fact that they typically interacted with their mothers six times as much as they did with their fathers. These preference data are striking in comparison with findings that socially naive rhesus infants of comparable age display overwhelming preferences (e.g., 95% to 5%) for adult females over adult males. The suggestion is that adult males can be exceedingly salient sources of stimulation for infants, even though the actual physical interactions may not be particularly frequent in number.

More direct evidence of the salience of adult male–infant interactions for rhesus monkey infants comes from examination of the relationships between infant initiation levels and adult male response patterns toward those initiations. Suomi (1977) and Golopol (1977) have both found that infants tend to be especially sensitive to the responses of adult males: Behaviors directed toward a specific adult male that are reciprocated increase rapidly in their rate of occurrence, whereas those initiations that are ignored or rejected quickly disappear from the infant's behavioral repertoire toward that adult male. Comparably strong relationships between levels of infant initiations and response patterns from mothers, siblings, or peers have not been disclosed. In other words, it appears that infants alter their own activities as a function of an adult male's reactions more than they do for interactions with others in their social networks.

Finally, we have some preliminary data suggesting that infants reared in social groups containing adult males display more pronounced sex differences in behavior earlier than do infants reared in groups that have no adult males but are otherwise comparable. In addition, there is limited evidence suggesting that infants reared in groups with adult males display less severe reactions to subsequent social stress (e.g., repeated separations from peer groups at adolescence) than do individuals reared in groups without adult males. If these findings continue to hold up in light of data currently being collected, they will represent findings that essentially parallel the documented effects of fatherless rearing for human children (e.g., Hetherington & Deur 1971). However, we still know very little about the actual mechanisms underlying these effects, and additional work is clearly needed in this area if such mechanisms are to be adequately understood.

FUTURE TRENDS

A number of future directions for research on adult male–infant interactions appear to be worthwhile. First, it is important to move beyond the male–child dyad and in both human and animal studies to recognize that much of male influence is probably mediated though other family members. For example, the male's relationship with other members of the troop may alter the manner in which other socializing agents may treat the infant. In other words, males can have indirect as well as direct effects on their offspring. To cite one recent example, Suomi (1977) argued that adult rhesus monkey males in his nuclear family studies may influence infants by regulating differentially the spatial location of male and female infants. By positive reactions to the approaches of male infants (either offspring or nonoffspring) and hostile reactions to the initiations of female infants, especially nonoffspring, adult males may encourage male infants to leave their mothers' living cage while encouraging female infants to stay close to their mothers. Possibly:

> adult males in feral troops can significantly influence the social world of each infant by designating these social spaces within the troop which it can occupy... Thus adult males in feral troops may have considerable indirect influence on the social development of infants in their living group, even if their actual interactions with the infants are relatively infrequent. [Suomi 1977:1268]

Examples at the human level can illustrate this issue as well. Pedersen and his colleagues have underlined the importance of studying the family triad by illustrating the impact of the husband–wife relationship on the parent–infant interaction process. Pedersen (1975) assessed the influence of the husband–wife relationship on the mother–infant interaction in a feeding context. The quality of the mother–infant relationship was rated in connection with two time-sampling home observations when the infants were 4 weeks old. Of particular interest was *feeding competence,* which referred to the appropriateness of the mother in managing feeding: "Mothers rated high are able to pace the feeding well, intersperse feeding and burping without disrupting the baby and seem sensitive to the baby's needs for either stimulation of feeding or brief rest periods during the course of feedings" (p. 4). In addition, the husband–wife relationship was assessed through an interview; finally, neonatal assessments (Brazelton) were available. Pedersen summarized his results as follows:

> The husband–wife relationship was linked to the mother–infant unit. When the father was more supportive of the mother, that is, evaluated her maternal skills more positively, she was more effective in feeding the baby. Then again, maybe competent mothers elicit more positive evaluations from their husbands. The reverse holds for marital discord. High tension and conflict in the marriage were associated with more inept feeding on the part of the mother. [Pedersen 1975:6]

The picture is even more complex, however, as indicated by the observation that the status and well-being of the infant, as assessed by alertness and motor maturity, were also related to the marital relationship. With an alert baby, the father evaluated the mother more positively; with a motorically mature baby, there appeared to be less tension and conflict in the marriage. In Pedersen's view, "a good baby and a good marriage go together" (1975:7).

The importance of these findings is clear: In order to understand the male–offspring relationship, the total set of relationships among members of the family and/or other social network needs to be assessed. Only in this way will the complex nature of such influences be understood. (For a detailed discussion of this issue, see Hinde 1976; Hinde & Herrmann 1977; Parke et al. 1979a; Suomi 1979a).

A variety of other issues merit attention in future studies. Much more research is required to document adequately the developmental changes that occur in male–offspring relationships at both the human and nonhuman primate levels. Particularly useful will be studies of the impact of changes in offspring motoric and social capabilities on male–offspring interactions. These studies will require the simultaneous assessment of infant competencies – outside the interaction context as well as in male–offspring interaction. Recent studies of the effects of changes in infant locomotor abilities on mother–infant interaction can serve as a useful guide (Gustafson 1977; Hinde & Spencer-Booth 1971); these experiments demonstrate quite clearly the controlling role of infant behaviors and skills in modifying adult behavior (Bell & Harper 1977).

As Parke has recently noted elsewhere:

> Perhaps the most urgent conceptual problem that faces researchers and theoreticians in the area of early social development is how to adequately represent the changing nature of social-interaction patterns. It is no longer adequate simply either to describe differences over time or to search for simple continuities between one time point and another. Rather, an approach that recognizes that the behavioral patterns that characterize the individual at any point in time are constantly undergoing revision and reorganization is required. Similarly, the interaction patterns that characterize the mother–infant, father–infant, and mother–father dyad, as well as the nuclear family triad, are susceptible to shifts in organization across time. [Parke 1979a:582]

In our pursuit of these questions, it is clear that no single methodological strategy is sufficient. At both the animal and the human levels, both field and laboratory-based studies are necessary to test the limits of the plasticity of the male–offspring relationship and to understand more fully the role of ecological variables in the development and modification of this type of social relationship (Parke 1979b). In addition, multiple levels of analysis, ranging from the microanalytic to the more macroanalytic, such as global ratings, need to be considered (Cairns & Green 1979; Rosenblum 1978; Suomi 1979b; Waters 1978).

SUMMARY AND CONCLUSIONS

A recent upsurge of interest in the traditionally neglected question of father–infant interactions has resulted in some substantial changes in how we view the role of the adult male in both human and nonhuman primate societies. Although it is evident that there is enormous cultural and species variability in what this role encompasses, it is also clear that adult males can serve functions far beyond those of a substitute or surrogate mother. Instead, adult males tend to complement rather than duplicate maternal roles.

With respect to the variability of adult male involvement in infant care across cultures and/or species described above, it appears that situational factors may be at least as important as any genetically determined behavioral predispositions. The repertoires of adult male behavior toward infants appear to be highly flexible and generally quite sensitive to the demands of the immediate social setting. Perhaps the strongest evidence regarding the plasticity of male care comes from studies in which individual males from primate species notoriously low on a scale of male interest in offspring are forced to live with infants who lack adequate female caretakers; under such circumstances, these adult males typically display considerable competence in rearing the infants.

Despite the variability across primate species in adult male involvement with infants described above, the apparent similarity between the human data and available nonhuman primate findings concerning characteristics of adult male-infant interactions is striking. Primate adult males are much more likely to play with infants than are the infants' mothers. Adult males tend to become more involved with infants as the infants grow older, whereas mother–infant interactions typically decline as the infant matures. Adult males appear to be more responsive to sex differences between infants than are adult females, and these differences tend to increase over time. Finally, it is clear that both human and nonhuman primate infants can develop strong and distinct relationships with specific adult males, even though the frequency of actual physical interactions involved in these relationships may be far lower than between the infant and mothers, siblings, or peers.

Yet many unanswered questions remain regarding adult male–infant interactions in human and nonhuman primates. To date, most of the work has been largely descriptive rather than explanatory in nature. Much remains to be learned about mechanisms underlying the adult male's involvement with infants and about the factors responsible for species, cultural, and individual differences in male care. Moreover, our views regarding the long-term significance of adult male–infant interactions or the possible effects of disruptions in the development of adult male–infant relationships are currently based more on speculation than on solid empirical data. We know that such relationships are probably quite important, but the specifics of how, when, and why remain for future research.

ACKNOWLEDGMENTS

Preparation of this chapter and the research reported here were supported by the following grants: NICHD Training Grant, HD–00244, Office of Child Development Grant, OHD 90-C-900, and the NICHD Program Project Grant, HD–05951. Some of the nonhuman primate research described in this chapter was supported by USPHS Grant # MH–11894 from the National Institute of Mental Health, by the Grant Foundation, and by funds provided by the University of Wisconsin Graduate School Research Committee. Thanks are extended to Brenda Congdon for her preparation of the manuscript.

REFERENCES

Ainsworth, M. D. 1973. The development of infant–mother attachment. *In:* B. M. Caldwell & H. N. Ricciuiti (eds.), *Review of child development research,* vol. 3. University of Chicago Press, Chicago.

Bekoff, M. 1972. The development of social interaction, play, and metacommunication in mammals: an ethological perspective. *Quarterly Review of Biology* 47: 412–434.

Bell, R. Q., & L. Harper. 1977. *Child effects on adults.* Erlbaum, Hillsdale, New Jersey.

Berlyne, D. E. 1969. Laughter, humor, and play. *In:* G. L. Lindzey & E. Aronson (eds.), *Handbook of social psychology.* Addison-Wesley, Reading, Massachusetts.

Bertrand, M. 1969. *The behavioral repertoire of the stumptail macaque. Bibliotheca Primatologica,* no. 11. Karger, Basel.

Bowlby, J. 1969. *Attachment and loss,* vol. 1, *Attachment.* Basic Books, New York.

Brandt, E. M., R. Irons, & G. D. Mitchell. 1970. Paternalistic behavior in four species of macaques. *Brain, Behavior, and Evolution* 3:415–420.

Breuggeman, J. A. 1973. Parental care in a group of free-ranging rhesus monkeys (*Macaca mulatta*). *Folia Primatologica* 20:178–210.

Bucher, K. L. 1970. Temporal lobe neocortex and maternal behavior in rhesus monkeys. Unpublished Ph.D dissertation, Johns Hopkins University, Baltimore.

Cairns, R. B., & J. A. Green. 1979. How to assess personality and social patterns: observations or ratings? *In:* R. B. Cairns (ed.), *The analysis of social interactions.* Erlbaum, Hillsdale, New Jersey.

Chamove, A., H. F. Harlow, & G. D. Mitchell. 1967. Sex differences in the infant-directed behavior of preadolescent rhesus monkeys. *Child Development* 38:329–335.

Chivers, D. J. 1971. Spatial relations within the Siamang group. *In: Proceedings of the third international congress of primatology,* vol. 3. Karger, Basel, pp. 14–21.

1972. The Siamang and the gibbon in the Malay peninsula. *Gibbon and Siamang* 1:103–135.

Clarke-Stewart, A. 1978. And daddy makes three: the father's impact on mother and young child. *Child Development* 49:466–478.

Dawkins, R. 1976. *The selfish gene.* Oxford University Press, Oxford.

Deag, J. M., & J. H. Crook. 1971. Social behavior and agonistic buffering in the wild Barbary macaque (*Macaca sylvanus*). *Folia Primatologica* 15:183–200.

DeVore, I. 1963. Mother–infant relations in free-ranging baboons. *In:* H. L. Rheingold (ed.), *Maternal behavior in mammals.* Wiley, New York.

Estrada, A., & J. M. Sandoval. 1977. Social relations in a free-ranging troop of stumptail macaques (*Macaca arctoides*): Male-care behaviour 1. *Primates* 18:793-813.

Fox, G. J. 1974. Peripheralization behavior in a captive Siamang family. *American Journal of Physical Anthropology* 41:479–489.

Frodi, A. M., M. E. Lamb, L. A. Leavitt, & W. L. Donovan. 1978. Fathers' and mothers' responses to infant smiles and cries. *Infant Behavior and Development* 1:187–198.

Golopol, L. A. 1977. Social behavior patterns in rhesus monkeys: a multigroup comparison of four rearing conditions. Unpublished senior honors thesis, University of Wisconsin-Madison.

Gouzoules, H. 1975. Maternal rank and early social interactions of infant stumptail macaques, *Macaca arctoides. Primates* 16:405–418.

Gustafson, G. E. 1977. A longitudinal study of infants' interactions with their mothers: some contributions of locomotor and social development. Unpublished master's thesis, University of North Carolina, Chapel Hill.

Hansen, E. W. 1966. The development of maternal and infant behavior in the rhesus monkey. *Behaviour* 27:107–149.

Harlow, H. F. 1958. The nature of love. *American Psychologist* 13:673–685.

Hendy-Neely, H., & R. J. Rhine. 1977. Social development of stumptail macaques (*Macaca arctoides*): momentary touching and other interactions with adult males during the infant's first 60 days of life. *Primates* 18:589–600.

Hetherington, E. M., & J. L. Deur. 1971. The effect of father absence on child development. *Young Children* 26:233–248.

Hinde, R. A. 1960. Energy models of motivation. *Symposium for the Society of Experimental Biology,* no. 14, *Models and Analogues in Biology,* pp. 119–213.

1976. On describing relationships. *Journal of Child Psychology and Psychiatry* 17:1–19.

Hinde, R. A., & J. Herrmann. 1977. Frequencies, durations, derived measures and their correlations in studying dyadic and triadic relationships. *In:* H. R. Shaffer (ed.), *Studies in mother–infant interaction.* Academic Press, New York.

Hinde, R. A., & Y. Spencer-Booth. 1967. The behaviour of socially living rhesus monkeys in their first two and one-half years. *Animal Behaviour* 15:169–196.

1971. Effects of brief separation from mother on rhesus monkeys. *Science* 173:111–118.

Hoffman, L. W. 1977. Changes in family roles, socialization and sex differences. *American Psychologist* 32:644–658.

Hoffman, L. W., & F. I. Nye. 1974. *Working mothers.* Jossey-Bass, San Francisco.

Hrdy, S. B. 1976. Care and exploitation of nonhuman primate infants by conspecifics other than the mother. *In:* J. Rosenblatt, R. Hinde, E. Shaw, & C. Beer (eds.), *Advances in the study of behavior,* vol. 6. Academic Press, New York.

1977. *The langurs of Abu.* Harvard University Press, Cambridge, Massachusetts.

Ingram, J. C. 1978. Social interactions within marmoset family groups. *In:* D. Chivers & J. Herbert (eds.), *Recent advances in primatology,* vol. 1. Academic Press, New York.

Itani, J. 1959. Paternal care in the wild Japanese monkey, *Macaca fuscata. Primates* 2: 61–93. Reprinted in English in C. Southwick (ed.), *Primate social behavior.* Van Nostrand, Princeton, New Jersey, 1963.

Johnson, M. M. 1963. Sex role learning in the nuclear family. *Child Development* 34:315–333.

Klaus, M. H., & J. H. Kennell. 1976. *Parent–infant bonding.* Mosby, St. Louis.

Kleiman, D. G. 1980. Sex differences in the reproductive and social inhibition of young adult lion tamarin, *Leontopithecus rosalia. In: Proceedings of the Seventh International Congress of Primatology.* In press.

Kotelchuck, M. 1976. The infant's relationship to the father: experimental evidence. *In:* M. E. Lamb (ed.), *The role of the father in child development.* Wiley, New York.

Lamb, M. E. 1976. Interactions between eight-month-old children and their fathers and mothers. *In:* M. E. Lamb (ed.), *The role of the father in child development.* Wiley, New York.

1977a. Father–infant and mother–infant interaction in the first year of life. *Child Development* 48:167–181.

1977b. The development of mother–infant and father–infant attachments in the second year of life. *Developmental Psychology* 13:639–649.

Lansky, L. M. 1967. The family structure also affects the model: sex role attitudes in parents of preschool children. *Merrill-Palmer Quarterly* 13:139–150.

Lind, J. 1974. Observations after delivery of communications between mother–infant–father. Paper presented at the International Congress of Pediatrics, Buenos Aires.

Lindburg, D. G. 1971. The rhesus monkey in North India: an ecological and behavioral study. *In:* L. A. Rosenblum (ed.), *Primate behavior,* vol. 2. Academic Press, New York.

Lott, D., & J. Rosenblatt. 1969. *In:* B. M. Foss (ed.), *Determinants of infant behaviour,* vol. 4. Methuen, London.

Maccoby, E. E., & C. N. Jacklin. 1974. *The psychology of sex differences.* Stanford University Press, Stanford, California.

MacKinnon, J. 1974. The behaviour and ecology of wild orangutans (*Pongo pygmaeus*). *Animal Behaviour* 22:3–74.

Mitchell, G. D. 1969. Paternalistic behavior in primates. *Psychological Bulletin* 71:399–417.

Mitchell, G. D., & E. M. Brandt. 1972. Paternal behavior in primates. *In:* F. Poirier (ed.), *Primate socialization.* Random House, New York.

Pannabecker, B. J., & R. Emde. 1977. The effect of extended contact on father–newborn interaction. Paper presented at the Western Society for Research in Nursing, Denver, Colorado, May.

Parke, R. D. 1979a. Interactional designs. *In:* R. B. Cairns (ed.), *Social interaction: methods, analysis and illustration.* Erlbaum, Hillsdale, New Jersey.

Parke, R. D. 1979b. Perspectives on father–infant interaction. *In:* J. Osofsky (ed.), *The handbook of infant development.* Wiley, New York.

Parke, R. D., S. Hymel, T. G. Power, & B. R. Tinsley. 1980. Fathers and risk: a hospital based model of intervention. *In:* D. B. Sawin, R. C. Hawkins, L. O. Walker, & J. H. Penticuff (eds.), *Psychosocial risks in infant–environment transactions.* Bruner/Mazel, New York.

Parke, R. D., & S. E. O'Leary. 1976. Father–mother–infant interaction in the newborn period: some findings, some observations and some unresolved issues. *In:* K. Riegel & J. Meacham (eds.), *The developing individual in a changing world,* vol. 2, *Social and environmental issues.* Mouton, The Hague.

Parke, R. D., S. E. O'Leary, & S. West. 1972. Mother–father–newborn interaction: effects of maternal medication, labor and sex of infant. *Proceedings of the American Psychological Association,* pp. 85–86.

Parke, R. D., T. G. Power, & J. Gottman. 1979b. Conceptualizing and quantifying influence patterns in the family triad. *In:* M. E. Lamb, S. J. Suomi, & G. R. Stephenson (eds.), *Social interaction analysis: methodological issues.* University of Wisconsin Press, Madison.

Parker, R. D., & D. B. Sawin. 1975. Infant characteristics and behavior as elicitors of maternal and paternal responsibility in the newborn period. Paper presented at the biennial meeting of the Society for Research in Child Development, Denver, April.

1980. The family in early infancy: social interactional and attitudinal analyses. *In:* F. Pedersen (ed.), *The father–infant relationship: observational studies in a family context.* Praeger, New York.

Pedersen, F. A. 1975. Mother, father and infant as an interactive system. Paper presented at the Annual Convention of the American Psychological Association, Chicago, September.

Pedersen, F. A., & K. S. Robson. 1969. Father participation in infancy. *American Journal of Orthopsychiatry* 39:466–472.

Pedersen, F. A., J. Rubinstein, & L. J. Yarrow. 1979. Infant development in father-absent families. *Journal of Genetic Psychology* 135:51–61.

Phillips, D. M., & R. D. Parke. Parental speech to prelinguistic infants. In preparation.

Power, T. G., & Parke, R. D. 1981. Play as a context for early learning: lab and home analyses. *In:* I. E. Sigel and L. M. Laosa (eds.), *The family as a learning environment.* Plenum, New York.

Rebelsky, F., & C. Hanks. 1971. Fathers' verbal interaction with infants in the first three months of life. *Child Development* 42:63–68.

Redican, W. K. 1975. A longitudinal study of behavioral interactions between adult male and infant rhesus monkeys (*Macaca mulatta*). Unpublished Ph.D. dissertation, University of California, Davis.

1976. Adult male–infant interactions in nonhuman primates. *In:* M. E. Lamb (ed.), *The role of the father in child development.* Wiley, New York.

1978. Adult-male relations in captive rhesus monkeys. *In:* D. Chivers & J. Herbert (eds.), *Recent advances in primatology,* vol. 1. Academic Press, New York.

Rendina, I., & J. D. Dickerscheid. 1976. Father involvement with first-born infants. *Family Coordinator* 25:373–379.

Rheingold, H. L. 1956. The modification of social responsiveness in institutional babies. *Monographs of the Society for Research in Child Development* 21:63.

Rodman, P. S. 1973. Population composition and adaptive organization among orangutans of the Kutai reserve. *In:* R. Michael & J. Crook (eds.), *Comparative ecology and behavior of primates.* Academic Press, London.

Rosenblatt, J. S. 1970. The development of maternal responsiveness in the rat. *American Journal of Orthopsychiatry* 39:36–56.

Rosenblatt, J. S., & H. I. Siegel. 1975. Hysterectomy-induced maternal behavior during pregnancy in the rat. *Journal of Comparative and Physiological Psychology* 89:685–700.

Rosenblum, L. A. 1978. The creation of a behavioral taxonomy. *In:* G. P. Sackett (ed.), *Observing behavior,* vol. 2. University Park Press, Baltimore.

Ruppenthal, G. C., G. L. Arling, H. F. Harlow, G. P. Sackett, & S. J. Suomi. 1976. A ten-year perspective on motherless-mother monkey behavior. *Journal of Abnormal Psychology* 85:341–349.

Shaikh, A. A. 1971. Estrone and estradiol levels in the ovarian venous blood from rats during the estrous cycle and pregnancy. *Biological Reproduction* 5:297–307.

Southwick, C. H., M. A. Beg, & M. R. Siddiqui. 1965. Rhesus monkeys in North India. *In:* I. DeVore (ed.), *Primate behavior.* Holt, New York.

Spencer-Booth, Y., & R. A. Hinde. 1967. The effects of separating rhesus monkey infants from their mothers for six days. *Journal of Child Psychology and Psychiatry* 7:179–197.

Stevenson, M. F. 1978. The ontogeny of playful behaviour in family groups of the common marmoset. *In:* D. Chivers & J. Herbert (eds.), *Recent advances in primatology,* vol. 1. Academic Press, New York.

Suomi, S. J. 1972. Social development of rhesus monkeys reared in an enriched laboratory environment. *Proceedings of the 20th International Congress of Psychology,* University of Tokyo Press, Tokyo.

1976. Mechanisms underlying social development: a reexamination of mother–infant interactions in monkeys. *In:* A. Pick (ed.), *Minnesota symposium on child psychology,* vol. 10. University of Minnesota Press, Minneapolis.

1977. Adult male–infant interactions among monkeys living in nuclear families. *Child Development* 48:1255–1270.

1978. Maternal behavior by socially-incompetent monkeys: neglect and abuse of offspring. *Journal of Pediatric Psychology* 3:28–34.

1979a. Differential development of various social relationships by rhesus monkey infants. *In:* M. Lewis & L. A. Rosenblum (eds.), *The child and its family.* Plenum, New York.

1979b. Levels of analysis for interactive data collected on monkeys living in complex social groups. *In:* M. E. Lamb, S. J. Suomi, & G. R. Stephenson (eds.), *Social interaction analysis: methodological issues.* University of Wisconsin Press, Madison.

Suomi, S. J., C. D. Eisele, S. A. Grady, & R. L. Tripp. 1973. Social preferences of monkeys reared in an enriched laboratory environment. *Child Development* 44:451–460.

Suomi, S. J., & P. O'Neill. Social relationships among a captive group of monkeys living in rural Wisconsin. In preparation.

Taylor, H., J. Teas, T. Richie, C. Southwick, & R. Shrestha. 1978. Social interactions between adult male and infant rhesus monkeys in Nepal. *Primates* 19:343–351.

Trivers, R. L. 1972. Parental investment and sexual selection. *In:* B. Campbell (ed.), *Sexual selection and the descent of man, 1871–1971.* Aldine, Chicago.

Waters, E. 1978. The reliability and stability of individual differences in infant–mother attachment. *Child Development* 49:483–494.

Welker, W. I. 1971. Ontogeny of play and exploratory behaviors: a definition of problems and a search for new conceptual relations. *In:* H. Moltz (ed.), *The ontogeny of vertebrate behavior.* Academic Press, New York.

White, L. E. 1959. Motivation reconsidered: the concept of competence. *Psychological Review* 66:297–333.

White, L. E., & R. A. Hinde. 1975. Some factors influencing mother–infant relations in rhesus monkeys. *Animal Behavior* 23:527–542.

Wilson, E. O. 1975. *Sociobiology: the new synthesis.* Harvard University Press, Cambridge, Massachusetts.

Yogman, M. J., S. Dixon, E. Tronick. H. Als, & T. B. Brazelton. 1977. The goals and structure of face-to-face interaction between infants and their fathers. Paper presented at the biennial meeting of the Society for Research in Child Development, New Orleans, March.

Zelazo, P. R., M. Kotelchuck, L. Barker, & J. David. 1977. Fathers and sons: an experimental facilitation of attachment behaviors. Paper presented at the biennial meeting of the Society for Research in Child Development, New Orleans, March.

Zucker, E. L., G. D. Mitchell, & T. Maple. 1978. Adult male–offspring play interactions within a captive group of orangutans (*Pongo pygmaeus*). *Primates* 19:379–384.

AUTHOR INDEX

SUBJECT INDEX